本书系国家社会科学基金"十三五"规划2020年度教育学一般课题项目"中国青年国际组织胜任力研究"（编号：BDA200075）、国家社会科学基金社科学术社团主题学术活动资助项目"加强中国国际组织人才培养研究"（编号：22STA048）研究成果。

《国际胜任力培养实训工作坊论文集》编委会

主编： 张宁　贾文键　屈文谦　万小朋　李孝峰

执行主编： 戴争鸣　资虹　陈俊　王筱稚　张弛

执行副主编： 李佳　马先军　李嘉苗　林婉婷　牛雯茜

统筹： 安艳琪　李辉　何乐　常迪　李雪菲燕

国际组织与全球治理丛书

中国教育发展战略学会国际胜任力培养专业委员会 编

国际胜任力培养

实训工作坊论文集

（上册）

主编 张 宁 贾文键 屈文谦 万小朋 李孝峰

Proceedings of the International
Competence Development Workshops

 ZHEJIANG UNIVERSITY PRESS
浙江大学出版社
·杭州·

总　序

　　作为北京和苏州国际胜任力培养实训工作坊（简称"工作坊"）的策划者、组织者，本人与工作团队紧张筹备了 5 个月，并全程参加了北京和苏州工作坊为期 17 天的活动。关于同学们的论文成果，承诺将以论文集的形式出版。经过 10 个月共同努力，在书稿即将交付浙江大学出版社之际，本人应邀介绍此次北京和苏州工作坊的活动背景和成果。

　　当今世界正经历百年未有之大变局，为维护国际秩序、促进国际合作、推动构建人类命运共同体、建设教育强国，培养新时代国际胜任力（国际组织）人才成为迫切需求。为深入研究国际胜任力（国际组织）人才培养工作的理论与现实问题，理解、掌握国际胜任力（国际组织）人才培养工作的路径和方法，中国教育发展战略学会国际胜任力培养专业委员会与集思未来高等研究院合作开设国际胜任力培养课程。清华大学、北京大学、浙江大学、上海交通大学、中国人民大学、北京师范大学、中国科技大学、西安交通大学、武汉大学、华中科技大学、北京理工大学、西北工业大学、东南大学、大连理工大学、重庆大学、兰州大学、北京外国语大学、外交学院、中国政法大学、苏州大学、深圳大学、广州大学、南昌大学、安徽大学、海南大学、贵州大学、东北师范大学、南京信息工程大学、中国石油大学（华东）、西南财经大学、大连外国语大学、首都师范大学、广西师范大学、汕头大学、华侨大学、浙江传媒学院、浙江师范大学、湖北工业大学、吉林外国语大学、广东外语外贸大学等高校均参与了国际胜任力培养课程项目。该课程项目不仅关注学生的认知发展，更着力通过分析经典案例、参与真实情景项目学习、开展专题工作坊等多种方式，使学生的全球视野以及尊重多元、包容互鉴、和谐共生的人类命运共同体意识和素养，全面提升学生的国际胜任力。培养课程体系总体设计为：唤醒（盲点知识认知）、答疑（解惑行动）、实训（提升能力素养）。

为培养中国青年学生的国际胜任力，中国教育发展战略协会国际胜任力培养专业委员会于 2023 年 7 月和 8 月分别在北京和苏州举办线下工作坊，开展国际胜任力培养实训工作。

北京工作坊和苏州工作坊由中国教育发展战略学会国际胜任力培养专业委员会主办，柳叶刀倒计时亚洲中心、北京外国语大学、西北工业大学、苏州大学和集思未来高等研究院协办，中国国家博物馆等有关单位提供支持。

北京工作坊有来自清华大学、北京大学、浙江大学、上海交通大学、南京大学、武汉大学、西安交通大学、南开大学、山东大学、北京理工大学、西北工业大学、苏州大学等 32 所双一流高校的 200 多位在读本科生、硕士和博士研究生以及带队老师参加。该工作坊分为气候变化与健康全球治理，文化传承、创新与国际交流研学，以及科技创新与数字经济可持续发展三个方向，涉及六个主题，包括世界一流期刊案例分析研究、模拟《联合国气候变化框架公约》第 28 次缔约方大会（COP28）会议提案、全球气候变化与健康数据库设计与搭建、世界著名博物馆建设方案、世界文明文化交流、世界知名互联网及人工智能公司案例研究。北京工作坊活动历时 9 天。

苏州工作坊设置了世界一流工业园区建设案例研究和世界文化遗产继承与传统工艺创新两个主题。该工作坊有来自清华大学、北京大学、浙江大学、上海交通大学、武汉大学、南开大学、北京外国语大学、西北工业大学、中国海洋大学、苏州大学、南昌大学、大连外国语大学等 14 所双一流高校的 100 多位在读本科生、硕士和博士研究生以及带队老师参加。苏州工作坊活动历时 8 天。

参加北京工作坊和苏州工作坊的学员们组成了 82 个课题研究协作小组，围绕 8 个主题分工合作。工作坊内容聚焦实务，以培养素质和能力为目标，为学生营造了良好的实训环境，对学生进行了系统培训，拓宽了学生的全球视野，提升了学生的国际胜任力；同时也为学员之间提供了学思结合、跨学科跨领域的交流互助平台。此次工作坊的活动成果可总结为以下几个方面。

第一，我们培养了学生的国际可迁移学术能力并产出了成果。我们组建了由 18 位朋辈导师组成的指导团队，为学生小组进行了超过 9 小时的线下和超过 20 个小时的线上专业指导和咨询服务；我们聘请了 20 位专家，形成了 8 个主题评审团队，他们审阅了研究报告，并进行了鼓励、肯定、指导、建议式的答辩评议；我们还聘请了43位领域专家，组织了43场主旨讲演、专题讲座或圆桌咨询，期间专家和学生进行了充分的交流。每个学生小组都提交了两次研究报告，并成功进行了汇报答辩。学生们还自己设计了学术海报，并且集团式展现在结营活动现场；在工作坊期间，同学们完成了报告答辩（Presentation）、学术海报（Poster）制作、研究报告（Paper）撰写修改。

第二，我们拓展了学生的国际视野、全球视野。每个主题都需要涵盖国际层面，在研究世界范围内的对象的过程中，他们学会了从国际、全球视野看待问题、讨论问题。由此，我们培养了同学们尊重多样性、尊重世界文明文化和成果的素养。

第三，我们精心组织了参访百度集团公司的活动，以了解世界一流人工智能公司发展的现状和未来，产生了非常精彩的互动；我们走进了北京最大的政府间国际组织——亚洲基础设施投资银行参访，从新闻传媒、投资架构、治理运行机制、工作和生活以及人员招聘等方面深入了解国际组织；我们参访了苏州工业园区规划中心、太仓市中德合作展示馆，了解了世界一流工业园区的发展历程、现状和未来；我们参访了德国家族企业——海瑞恩精密技术有限公司，看到了该企业的核心价值观——意愿、能力、行动，我们找到了胜任力起源的"活化石"；我们走进了沙溪古镇、拙政园、东吴大学旧址以及郑和七下西洋太仓起锚地的纪念公园，对世界自然文化传承与保护、中国对外交流合作等有了全面深入的了解。

第四，我们进行了国际组织能力建设相关知识的培训。16位国际组织原资深官员受邀解读了国际组织胜任素质和能力、人才需求与招聘、国际组织文化、项目管理等方面的内容，并与学生进行了充分交流。

第五，我们培养了学生的沟通协作、咨询表达能力工作坊。围绕一个主题进行协作研究、专家指导、讨论咨询以及实地考察等四个层面实训，学生们约有450个问答的机会，以及答辩、代表发言等机会。一方面锻炼了学生的表达能力、提问能力、讨论能力，另一方面培养、提升学生的沟通协作与表达能力。

此外，北京和苏州工作坊有来自24个城市34所大学的300多名愿意提升国际胜任力的同学，我们要求3—4人组成研究小组，推动了合作协同，实现了学学相长。大家在协同合作以及8—9天的交流生活中，锻炼了沟通交流的能力，建立了志同道合的新朋友圈。

希望大家不断巩固北京和苏州工作坊朋友圈，相互帮助、相互激励、相互成就；希望大家回到学校后将此次珍贵的工作坊经历进行分享。

工作坊开办之前和开办期间，我们推动了三轮论文撰写工作，工作坊结束后，组织推动各小组整理修改研究案例，8月底提交了3.0版案例研究。我们组织了论文审稿、出版专家工作组，和浙江大学出版社协同合作，按照学术论文出版的相关规范和要求，指导同学们修改提交了4.0版文稿，再组织专家全面审阅修改，形成5.0版文稿，于2024年6月15日将文稿提交给浙江大学出版社。为总结、传播同学们在工作坊取得的学术成果，择选其中大部分文章汇集成册，以飨读者。

回顾北京和苏州工作坊从策划、筹备、实施到后期推动全过程，回顾从设计8个主题、洽谈协办单位强强合作到联系一流参访交流单位，回顾从邀请顶尖行家讲座、一流评委专家到团队制朋辈导师，回顾从邀请高校组队、鼓励学校资助到澳门中联办组队、北京语言大学国际学生组队，回顾从开营、指导、参访、展示学术海报、答辩到获奖、结营，回顾在坊工作的全程、每天撰写发布一篇公众号文章、学生们结营后朋友圈的褒奖，回顾从鼓励学生协同撰写论文1.0版和2.0版、指导设计学术海报、答辩到结营后推动学生撰写3.0版、4.0版论文以及组织专家修改5.0版文稿，回顾同学们所说：北京、苏州工作坊产出了未曾料想到的丰硕成果！此刻深切感悟到的是：我们大家共同奔赴！我们大家共同拥有！

感谢各协办单位！感谢各位专家！感谢朋辈导师团队！感谢各参与高校、指导教师！感谢各位同学！感谢中国教育发展战略学会领导的大力支持！感谢国际胜任力专业委员会和集思未来高等研究院同志们的共同努力！

谨以此为序。

张 宁

中国教育发展战略学会副会长

国际胜任力培养专业委员会理事长

国家留学基金管理委员会原副秘书长

2024年6月9日于寻典问辞轩

序 一

2023 年初，国际胜任力专业委员会（简称"专委会"）邀请柳叶刀倒计时亚洲中心作为北京工作坊协办单位，我作为柳叶刀倒计时亚洲中心联系负责人，也作为第一批高校开设国际胜任力培养课程的教师，参与共同策划、协办了 2023 年 7 月国际胜任力培养项目北京工作坊中的"气候变化与健康全球治理特别工作坊"。

2023 年恰逢《柳叶刀》建刊 200 周年，柳叶刀倒计时亚洲中心团队从 2023 年 1 月开始前期策划，多轮迭代了 14 版策划方案，制定了学员的三大主题案例研究方向：世界一流期刊案例分析研究、模拟《联合国气候变化框架公约》第 28 次缔约方大会（COP28）会议提案、全球气候变化与健康数据库设计与搭建。我们给学员设计了 7 种工作坊活动模块：柳叶刀与全球治理主旨演讲、气候变化与健康专题讲座、研究方法训练、国际胜任力及国际组织能力建设、国际组织及机构实地参访、朋辈导师工作坊、研究成果汇报展示等。通过这些模块，综合提升学生们的跨学科思考能力、跨文化沟通能力及协作能力；通过设计多种激励机制，提升学生们的深度参与热情和持续发展动力。

为了让同学们更好地参与实践，在提前三个月发布活动议程和研究题目后，我们为报名的 27 个学生研究小组配备了项目研究指导老师与助教，在微信群进行全程答疑，并邀请专家组织线上会议答疑，在开营前对各组研究报告进行了 3 轮评审修改。

工作坊开展期间，在专委会的支持下，我们汇聚了多方的专家资源，为青年学员授课、答疑、持续赋能，鼓励他们学习、交流、成长为气候变化与健康全球治理领域的青年人才；在答辩环节，我们也邀请了来自不同领域的专家评委进行评审并给出有针对性的修改建议。

在此我要特别感谢柳叶刀倒计时亚洲中心主任兼清华大学地学系教授蔡闻佳、《柳叶刀》执行主编Tamara Lucas、《柳叶刀》亚洲高级执行主编Helena Wang、《柳叶刀星球健康》资深编辑王昊昱，清华大学地学系系主任罗勇、国家应对气候变化战略研究和国际合作中心国际政策研究部主任高翔、清华大学万科公共卫生与健康学院教授黄存瑞、中国疾控中心环境与健康相关产品安全所（简称"环境所"）风险评估室主任李湉湉、财新数据可视化实验室负责人韦梦、北京航空航天大学副教授谢杨、清华大学全球发展与健康传播研究中心秘书长苏婧、清华大学助理研究员张诗卉和科研助理可奕博，北京邮电大学计算机系教授许冠南、马占宇、李亮，野生救援（美国）北京代表处气候项目经理谢端端等的大力支持。

我们欣喜地看到北京工作坊吸引了来自30多所高校的学员，他们在9天活动中浸入式地参与了剖析世界一流期刊、气候与健康全球治理，培养全球视野，训练大数据思维，掌握学术研究方法和写作技巧，强化问题分析和解决技能，培养国际可迁移能力。他们在小组答辩环节极富创新思维，有的在分析《柳叶刀》期刊过程中结合SDG目标，分析了在200年间《柳叶刀》编辑部成员的空间异质性和性别比的变动；有的小组全程用英文模拟在COP28进行青年建议；有的小组用漫画展示极端天气对人群健康的影响；有的小组用AR（增强现实）技术打造在线画展为小岛屿国家的气候风险发声；有的小组搭建了几十年间气候变化相关指标的可视化数据库。

在工作坊后期，我们持续辅导学员进行研究报告修改，在修改多轮之后形成了论文集；也持续为学生赋能，邀请学生代表参与了柳叶刀倒计时中国报告的全球发布会。我们陆续得知了学员们近期的好消息，有的学员在年底成为COP28大会的中国青年代表，有的学员成功申请到联合国日内瓦国际组织总部进行国际组织实习和志愿活动的机会。

最后非常感谢我的研究团队成员赵梦真、李博、赵泳春、姚芳虹、杨晗、晏博、张若彤、张艺馨，他们深度参与此次活动，在前期进行了多轮设计，参与执行协助中期的工作和后期收尾工作，为工作坊的成功举办做出了突出贡献！

张　弛

柳叶刀倒计时亚洲中心副主任

北京理工大学国际组织创新学院院长助理

北京理工大学管理学院教授

2024 年 6 月 10 日于北京

序 二

　　博物馆是一个国家丰富历史文化的载体，承载着一个国家或民族的核心价值，通过收藏具有文化价值的历史文物和艺术品、引导观众和文物互动，有助于公众去更好地了解一个国家、一个地方或是一个民族的历史文化和艺术传统，激发公众对优秀传统文化和遗产的热爱。同时，作为一个开放的场所，博物馆面向来自世界各地的观众，它在无形中促进着不同文化的互动和交流。中国故宫博物院、意大利乌菲齐美术馆、埃及文明博物馆这些世界知名博物馆俨然已经成为展示各自国家形象和文化软实力、促进国际交流的重要窗口和平台。

　　党的十八大以来，中国的博物馆在数量、规模、展览特色等方面蓬勃发展，数字博物馆等新型博物馆也开始涌现，为观众提供更加多元、互动性更强的展览体验，这离不开国家对文化传承的重视和支持。2017 年 1 月 25 日，中共中央办公厅、国务院办公厅印发《关于实施中华优秀传统文化传承发展工程的意见》，其中提到，要"充分发挥图书馆、文化馆、博物馆、群艺馆、美术馆等公共文化机构在传承发展中华优秀传统文化中的作用"；2018 年 10 月 8 日，中共中央办公厅、国务院办公厅印发《关于加强文物保护利用改革的若干意见》，其中提到，要"激发博物馆创新活力"，"发展智慧博物馆，打造博物馆网络矩阵"，强化文物博物馆的"基本公共文化服务功能"，并"落实非国有博物馆支持政策"；2021 年 5 月 24 日，中央宣传部、国家发展改革委、教育部、科技部、民政部、财政部、人力资源社会保障部、文化和旅游部、国家文物局九个部门印发《关于推进博物馆改革发展的指导意见》，以此深化改革，推动我国博物馆事业高质量发展。我国博物馆事业发展具备了良好的政策环境。当前，中国的博物馆也在积极拓展国际合作，通过举办展览、学术交流等方式，加强与世界各国的文化交流与合作。中国国家博物馆的优秀展览多次"出口"法国凯布朗利博物馆、新西兰国家博物馆、澳大利亚国家博物馆、塞尔维亚国家博物馆等海外博物馆；山西博物院也多次引进来自美国、捷克、俄罗斯、意大利、秘鲁等国家和地区优秀文化展览，展出的文物展现了世界各地不同的文化风貌。

在新时代推动博物馆事业的高质量发展，保持博物馆与时俱进，必须考虑文化的传承与创新、文化保护与利用的平衡、新兴技术的应用、人才队伍的建设、公众参与度等方方面面。这些挑战离不开博物馆界人士以及社会各界人士的共同努力。深入研究和学习世界一流博物馆的成功建设经验，不仅对我国众多博物馆在文化传承、保护和创新等方面有着重要的启发作用，也为文化事业注入新的活力和动力，从而促进文化产业发展和经济增长。为此，来自上海交通大学、西安交通大学、广东外语外贸大学等国内高校的学生参与了主题为"世界著名博物馆建设方案"的工作坊。他们以大英博物馆、故宫博物院、大都会艺术博物馆、卢浮宫博物馆、中国国家博物馆等世界知名博物馆为研究对象，深入探讨和分析了这些博物馆的发展历程、建筑扩建、经营模式、交互叙事等，总结了它们的成功经验，展望了未来的发展趋势，为建设中国特色世界一流博物馆提供了参考和建议。

例如，在《以建筑学视角浅析法国卢浮宫的扩建》一文中，作者以卢浮宫博物馆为研究对象，从建筑学的角度分析了该博物馆的扩建方案。1793 年 8 月 10 日，卢浮宫作为博物馆对公众开放。在此之前，卢浮宫一直作为法国王宫为王室所有。作者首先对卢浮宫的历史发展和背景进行了回顾和分析，随后，作者将重点放在了贝聿铭对卢浮宫的一期改造上，详细地介绍了改造过程中所使用的方法、解决的问题以及最终效果，并分析了改造过程中新旧空间的各种关系。最后，作者总结了当代博物馆应如何从文化发展、环境保护等方面学习借鉴扩建经验。

在《数字化下中国国家博物馆叙事空间的新形态探析》一文中，作者选取了中国国家博物馆作为研究对象，研究学习在科技迅速发展的当下，中国国家博物馆是如何受到影响，并形成了全新的叙事空间的。作者在文中指出，中国国家博物馆作为一个综合的叙事媒介，受到了互联网等新兴技术的影响，发展了三种新型的叙事形态。作者探讨分析了这三种叙事形态是如何改变文化传播的方式和渠道，并与观众互动，增强沉浸式体验。

在《从经营模式研究美国大都会艺术博物馆的发展建设》一文中，作者以美国大都会艺术博物馆为研究对象，介绍了该博物馆的基本理念、发展历程、展区策划等，重点从资金来源、管理机制、经营策略等方面分析了其在经营模式上取得的成功，以及大都会艺术博物馆是如何利用数字技术和社交媒体等新型技术和媒介保持与时俱进的。作者最后总结了美国大都会艺术博物馆的成功经验和对我国博物馆建设的启示。

此主题下还收录了其他优秀论文，不在此一一列举。我们希望通过对这一主题的深入研究，全面提升大学生的学术素养，帮助他们更好地适应全球化时代的发展趋势，学习借鉴先进的博物馆建设经验，培养具有全球视野和应对全球挑战能力的专业人才，并通过这些论文为读者提供深入的洞察，激发更多的思考和讨论，为建设中国特色世界一流博物馆的研究和实践做出贡献。

戴争鸣

国际胜任力培养专业委员会常务副秘书长

2024 年 6 月 10 日

序 三

　　"各美其美，美人之美，美美与共，天下大同。"世界文明文化交流是人类历史进程中重要的组成部分。各个国家和民族都有着独特而丰富的文明文化，这些文明文化体现在各民族的语言、宗教、音乐、风俗习惯、艺术作品、社会意识形态、道德规范等方方面面。随着全球化的深入发展，不同文明文化之间的交流变得更加频繁和广泛，而这种文明文化的互动交流正是各国各民族人民相互了解、建立尊重和友谊的重要途径。通过文明文化之间的互动和交流，来自不同文化背景的人们可以深入了解其他文化体系下的价值观念、传统习俗和生活方式，从而增进相互的理解与认知，建立起友好的关系。这种互动和交流不仅能够促进不同文明文化之间的互学互鉴，也有助于促进世界各个民族的和谐共处，减少误解和偏见，并推动人类命运共同体的建设。

　　作为一个国家综合国力的重要组成部分，强大的文化软实力可以提升一个国家的形象和地位，向世界传播本国的核心价值观念，还能在无形中提高一个国家在海外受众中的吸引力，从而推动国家旅游和文化产业的发展，促进国际交流与合作。同时，一个国家的文化软实力在世界文明文化交流中发挥着重要的作用。

　　作为拥有五千年历史文化积淀的大国，中国如何创新传统文化、传播优秀文化、通过文明交流互鉴推动中华文化走向世界、吸引海外受众、创造友好的国际舆论环境、促进国际交流，成为我们建设文化强国、实现中华民族伟大复兴的重要课题。

　　然而，文化的传播必然会带来不同文化之间的交流和碰撞。数字技术的普及开启了新媒体时代，人们的娱乐生活方式发生了翻天覆地的变化，接收信息的渠道也越发多样。短视频平台和其他社交平台等新媒体传播渠道的兴起以及新媒体技术的应用使得信息传播呈现碎片化的特点，并且增强了传播信息的即时性、互动性和参与性，信息的传播范围相比之前也大大增加。与此同时，信息的快速传播也带来了虚假文化信息的泛滥、"劣质"文化信息的传播，以及民众对外来文化"入侵"的担忧和抵制。在信息爆炸的当下，越来越多的学者开始思考如何利用好这把"双刃剑"，抓住机遇，做好本土文化的国际传播，讲好中国故事。

通过文明文化的交流，来自不同文化背景的人们了解和学习彼此的文化和传统，加深对彼此的理解和认同，增进彼此之间的互信和友谊，为国际合作提供契机，并最终促进全球文化繁荣和共同发展，推动构建人类命运共同体。因此，此次工作坊以"世界文明文化交流"为主题，聚焦各国在全球传播和交流文明文化的实践。来自上海交通大学、南开大学、武汉大学、山东大学等国内高校的学生参与了此次工作坊，开展了对该主题的深入研究。学生们通过数据分析、案例研究、访谈等方法，研究了孔子学院、塞万提斯学院、英国文化教育协会等世界各国各具特色的语言文化传播机构，分析了它们的发展历程、现状、发展策略、传播方式等，总结了研究案例的成功经验，为中国文化在海外的传播和发展提供了建议。

例如，在《中国孔子学院与美国文化中心对比研究》一文中，作者选取了中国孔子学院和美国文化中心这两个颇具代表性的文化交流中心作为研究对象。作为非营利性的社会公益机构，孔子学院旨在推广汉语文化。但是，海外孔子学院在最近几年陷入了不断关停的困境。文中，作者对美国文化中心发展停滞和孔子学院陷入困境的原因做了对比分析，从投资、社会舆论、传播内容等方面进行了思考，并总结分析了孔子学院为摆脱此种困境所采取的措施。

在《文化观念视角下国际语言传播机构发展战略的比较研究——以塞万提斯学院、孔子学院为例》一文中，作者以塞万提斯学院和孔子学院为例，分析和研究了这两所分别推广西班牙语和汉语语言文化的机构在设立地区、传播内容、考试体系话语权三个方面的主要差异，并从文化血缘、教育观念、民族性格等文化观念角度分析了这些差异产生的原因。最后，作者依据以上发现，为进一步扩大孔子学院的国际影响力提出了充分发挥媒体作用等多项建议。

在《英国文化教育协会的跨文化实践及启示研究》一文中，作者聚焦英国文化教育协会，通过数据分析、跨学科交叉研究等方法，对比分析了中国汉语水平考试和雅思考试的题型、选材类型等，并就中国文化如何"走出去"提出了颇具针对性的意见和建议。

此次工作坊的论文集中还收录了许多其他优秀论文，不在此一一列举。我们希望学生通过对世界文明文化交流的深入研究，全面提升自身的学术素养，提高跨文化意识和能力，并在整个过程中增强对本民族文化的自信。同时，我们也希望通过这些论文的集中展示为读者提供深入的见解，激发更多的思考和讨论，并为世界文明文化交流的研究和实践做出贡献。

王筱稚

集思未来高等研究院秘书长

2024 年 6 月 10 日

序 四

当今世界，科学技术是第一生产力、第一竞争力。科技创新始终是推动社会和经济发展的驱动力。科技创新，通常来说，是指通过使用新的或改进的技术方法开发新产品、新服务，以解决问题、实现价值和提高生产效率。作为我国在政策支持、财政资金、人才培养等方面予以优先保障的重点领域，科技创新始终位于国家发展全局的核心位置，并被纳入国家战略。

2023 年，中国全超导托卡马克核聚变实验装置（EAST，也称为"人造太阳"）创下稳态高约束模式等离子体运行 403 秒的新世界纪录；国家自主研制的大型客机 C919 完成商业首飞，实现了中国人自己制造大飞机的梦想；清华大学集成电路学院的研究人员开发了全球首款全系统集成的忆阻器存算一体芯片，该芯片支持高效片上学习（机器学习可以在硬件端直接完成）；这一年，中国超越日本成为全球最大汽车出口国，其中，新能源汽车的出口成为一大亮点。各个领域科技创新成果大量涌现，而数字经济的发展也是科技创新的重要体现之一。

"数字经济"作为近些年来的热词，频频出现在国家政策文件和政府工作报告中。发展好数字经济，推进数字技术创新，是实现国家高质量发展的重中之重。早在"十三五"时期，我国就已经深入实施数字经济发展战略，并收获颇丰，为经济社会持续健康发展提供了强大动力。2021 年 12 月，国务院又依据《中华人民共和国国民经济和社会发展第十四个五年规划和 2035 年远景目标纲要》，印发《"十四五"数字经济发展规划》，提出了对数字经济发展的整体要求。2023 年 2 月，中共中央、国务院印发《数字中国建设整体布局规划》，明确提出要加快数字中国建设，数字技术创新要实现重大突破。2023 年 12 月，国家发展改革委、国家数据局共同印发《数字经济促进共同富裕实施方案》，旨在促进数字技术与实体经济的深度融合，不断发展、优化、增强我国数字经济，用数字化手段解决发展中的不平衡和不充分问题。接连出台的数字经济发展战略，表明了数字经济对国家发展至关重要。

作为经济增长的新引擎，数字经济能够推动产业结构的调整，带动包括信息技术、人工智能（artificial intelligence，AI）等新兴产业的崛起，并成为推动产业结构升级的引擎；数字技术的应用，能实现制造业的智能化升级；物联网、AI、大数据等数字技术使得生产过程更加智能化、自动化，提高制造业的生产效率和质量；数字经济的发展推动创新产业的培育，在新兴行业和数字化领域催生新型职业、创造大量就业机会，为国家经济发展注入新的动力。通过积极参与全球数字化浪潮，我国的科技创新得到显著推动，中国在国际舞台上的竞争力得到提升。中国抢占全球数字经济发展高地，实现社会的均衡发展。

作为推动社会和经济发展的强大引擎，科技创新和数字经济对于全球的可持续发展发挥着重要作用。同时，数字经济自身也面临着可持续发展的挑战。为了能更好地服务人类社会的长期利益，数字经济必须遵循可持续发展的道路。可持续发展强调长远的发展，需要协调发展经济、社会和环境，即关注如何在满足当下需求的同时，不损害后代的利益及发展需求。如何利用数字经济促进可持续发展，如何减少发展数字经济带来的能源消耗和环境污染，如何应对AI的迅速发展所引发的技术、道德、社会伦理问题等，成为数字化浪潮下研究和实践中的热点话题。

近些年来，互联网和AI企业的迅速崛起和扩张表明了数字经济的强势发展。互联网、AI、大数据、区块链等关键技术作为数字经济的支柱，其发展相辅相成，推动形成了数字化时代的新型商业生态系统。来自浙江大学、武汉大学、西北工业大学、北京语言大学等国内高校的学生参加了此次主题为"世界知名互联网及人工智能公司案例研究"的工作坊。他们以国内外知名的互联网和AI企业为研究对象，通过定性分析、定量分析、案例分析等方法，研究了知名互联网企业的AI技术发展、商业模式的创新与变革等，分析了它们在数字化时代所产生的影响，总结了这些企业的成功经验，归纳了这些企业在技术、创新、社会责任等方面的可借鉴经验，思考了互联网和AI行业可能会面临的问题和挑战，提出了新颖的观点和建议，并展望了未来的研究方向。

例如，在《AI驱动商业模式创新：以OpenAI和百度为例》一文中，作者以OpenAI和百度作为研究对象，通过定性和定量分析相结合的方法，研究AI是如何驱动这两家企业推出创新产品、服务，以及创新商业模式，从而为企业带来可观的收益。作者还对比分析了OpenAI和百度的目标客户、价值内容、供应链，分析总结了OpenAI快速取得行业领先地位的方法，并为国内互联网行业和AI公司提供了发展建议。

在《腾讯公司社交支付生态研究报告》一文中，作者以腾讯公司的数字支付为研究对象。在数字化的浪潮中，作为国内的互联网头部公司，腾讯在互联网和AI领域取得的成功对中国的科技创新具有重要意义，同时也推动着全球科技创新和数字经济的发展。作者首先肯定了腾讯对推动科技创新和数字经济可持续发展所做出的贡献，其次从用户端、商家端、系统构架、法律和道德四个方面，提出了对用户数据及隐私的泄露、虚假流量、数字垄断等方面的担忧。针对这些问题，作者从科技赋能和以人为本两个维度提出了解决方案，并呼吁互联网和AI巨头承担社会责任，体现企业价值。

在《人工智能技术趋向可持续发展——基于微软与腾讯案例的对比研究》一文中，作者把视线投向微软和腾讯，研究了两家公司在AI领域的基础研究、产品和服务、竞争优势等，并发现了两者在AI领域研究投入和伦理道德两方面的共同点，总结了两家公司对国内外互联网企业的启示，并强调了当前互联网行业面临的技术和社会伦理问题，就如何平衡科技发展和人文关怀进行了探讨。

此主题下还收录了其他优秀论文，不在此一一列举。我们希望通过对这一主题进行深入研究，全面提升学生的学术素养，培养具有全球视野和有能力应对全球挑战的专业人才，并通过这些论文的展示为读者提供深入的见解，激发更多的思考和讨论，并为科技创新与数字经济可持续发展的研究和实践做出贡献。

李　佳
浙江大学学生国际化能力培养基地秘书处执行主任
2024 年 6 月 10 日

序 五 ━━━━━━━━━━━━━━━━━━━━━━━━━━━

工业园区通常是指出于自身经济发展需要，由国家或地方政府规划和建设的专门用于集中管理工业企业的区域。工业园区把大量企业集中到同一个区域，企业通常会共享园区内包括水电、排污、网络、通讯、道路等在内的基础设施和服务设施。这有助于形成并提高产业集聚效应，吸引高质量人才，推动就业和经济增长，加快科技创新，吸引外资。因此，建设高质量的工业园区对一个国家而言，具有重要的经济意义和社会意义。

纵观世界，许多经济强国都有强大的产业聚集区作为经济支撑，如美国的硅谷、日本的京滨工业区和阪神工业区、德国的阿德勒斯霍夫产业园和赫斯特工业园等。而我国工业园区的建设则可以追溯到 20 世纪 70 年代改革开放初期。1978 年 7 月 8 日，随着"改革开放第一炮"的响起，我国首个对外开放的经济开发区——蛇口工业区正式开始填海建港。2009 年，为了推动产业转型升级，"再造新蛇口"工程启动。2015 年，中国（广东）自由贸易试验区深圳前海蛇口片区正式挂牌成立；历经 40 余年的发展，现已初步形成以制度创新为核心，实现高速度、高质量发展的区域开发开放的"前海模式"。20 世纪 90 年代，作为中国和新加坡两国政府的重要合作项目，苏州工业园区的规划和建设开始了。苏州工业园区的建设借鉴了新加坡成熟的城市规划经验，园区没有急于求成，而是稳扎稳打地根据规划有序推进建设。最终，园区呈现的实际模样和设计蓝图相差无几。多年来，苏州工业园区一直坚持高水平、高质量的园区建设标准，吸引了众多企业入驻。2023 年 12 月 28 日，商务部网站公布了 2023 年国家级经济技术开发区综合发展水平考核评价结果，其中，苏州工业园区在国家级经开区综合排名中位列第一。21 世纪初，随着"走出去"成为我国的国家战略，许多企业为了降低生产成本，也开始自发探索在境外建立产业园区。2013 年，"一带一路"倡议的提出为境外产业园区的发展提供了重要的契机。此后，分布在共建"一带一路"国家的境外产业园区数量不断增加，成为我国对外经济交往的重要平台，促进了中外经济合作与交流。

然而，工业园区的发展也面临着多方面的挑战。2021 年 10 月 24 日，国务院印发《2030 年前碳达峰行动方案》（以下简称《方案》）。《方案》提到，各地区、各领域、各行业要"加快实现生产生活方式的绿色变革，确保如期实现 2030 年前碳达峰目标"。传统工业园区由于聚集了众多高碳企业，通常都会产生污染排放、资源浪费等问题，如何顺利实现绿色转型，由"高碳园区"转变为"低碳园区"，成为许多传统工业园区面临的挑战。同时，随着我国产业结构的逐步调整，传统园区也需要逐步向技术密集型园区靠拢发展，通过技术和产品的升级，提高产品的附加值，增强市场竞争力。

此次活动设置主题为"世界一流工业园区建设案例研究"的工作坊，正是为了思考在经济转型的阵痛期以及环境污染日益严重的当下，如何实现工业园区的可持续发展，如何借鉴、推广和创新世界一流工业园区的成功经验，从而推动我国和世界其他工业园区的建设。工作坊引导学生聚焦先进工业园区，了解全球工业园区的发展趋势和产业结构，从多元角度思考工业园区的建设和发展。来自北京大学、浙江大学、武汉大学等多所国内高校的学生参加了此次工作坊，他们以国内外知名工业园区为研究对象，通过案例研究等方法深入分析了这些先进园区的方方面面，如园区的规划设计、环境保护、科技创新、基础设施及配套服务、产业生态、人才引进等，分析了它们的可持续发展措施，归纳总结了它们成功的建设和发展经验，思考了当下工业园区发展所面临的挑战，并展望了工业园区发展的前景。

例如，在《太仓港经济技术开发区调查报告——港区工业园贯彻绿色发展理念的成功案例分析》一文中，作者以太仓港经济技术开发区（太仓港区）为研究对象，使用焦点小组研究法和单一案例研究法，聚焦太仓港区的可持续发展。太仓港是长江集装箱第一大港。短短几年，太仓港区由一个污染严重的港口工业园区成为绿色转型的优秀范例。2023 年，太仓港多项船舶防污数据创下了历史新高，生态环境得到持续改善。作者从生产、基建和政企合作多层面分析了太仓港区的绿色发展措施，总结了其绿色转型发展的成功经验，并在此基础上对港口工业园区的绿色发展提出了合理建议。

在《硅谷八十年——美国硅谷一流园区的经验和启示》一文中，作者以美国硅谷为研究对象，回顾了硅谷的成长史和发展历程，探索和总结了硅谷园区建设的成功经验。作为全球最为重要的科技创新中心之一，硅谷孕育了众多具有全球影响力的公司，其在可持续发展、园区生态建设等方面可复制、可借鉴的成功经验对其他工业园区的建设有着重要的启示。基于这些经验，作者为政府、园区内的企业、高校和科研机构三个社会主体提供了发展建议。

在《工业园区数字化转型与政策支持——基于苏州工业园区的案例分析》一文中，作者以苏州工业园区为研究对象，聚焦该工业园区数字化转型的成功经验。在新时代科技强国建设的新征途中，数字经济的重要性不言而喻。苏州工业园区自建立以来，其发展水平一直在我国排名前列。近年来，工业园区的快速发展也离不开园区对数字化转型的重视。作者重点关注了苏州工业园区为自身数字化转型提供的政策支持，涵盖了基础设施建设、产业政策、人才政策、园区管理等方面，并从这些措施中总结了先进经验以供其他工业园区借鉴。

此主题下还收录了其他优秀论文，在此不一一列举。我们希望通过对这一主题的深入研究，全面提升学生的学术素养，培养具有全球视野和具备应对全球挑战能力的专业人才，并通过这些论文的展示为读者提供深入的洞察视角，激发更多的思考和讨论，为"一流工业园区建设"这一领域的研究和实践做出贡献。

资　虹
国际胜任力培养专业委员会常务副秘书长
苏州大学国际合作交流处副处长
苏州大学国际创新药学院副院长
2024 年 6 月 10 日

序 六

　　世界文化遗产通常是指被联合国教科文组织（United Nations Educational, Scientific and Cultural Organization，UNESCO）认定的，具有杰出普遍性价值的文化古迹和自然景观。不论这些古迹和景观位于何处，或是由哪一民族创造，它们都代表了人类丰富多样的历史、文化和文明。1972 年，联合国教科文组织大会第十七届会议在巴黎举行，在此次会议中，人们意识到了对世界范围内的文化和自然遗产进行保护的重要性。文化遗产和自然遗产正在受到年久腐变和社会经济条件恶化的双重威胁和破坏，这可能会使各国的遗产资源面临枯竭。为此，UNESCO 认为有必要订立国际公约，以公约的形式科学、有效地保护世界各地具有杰出普遍性价值的文化和自然遗产。同年 11 月 16 日，UNESCO 通过了《保护世界文化和自然遗产公约》（Convention Concerning the Protection of the World Cultural and Natural Heritage），公约对文化遗产和自然遗产做出了定义，并认为国家应竭尽全力确保本国领土内的文化遗产和自然遗产得到保护和传承。同时，UNESCO 设立了《世界遗产名录》（World Heritage List），将具有特殊文化价值的遗产列入其中。

　　世界文化遗产包括物质文化遗产和非物质文化遗产。物质文化遗产通常是指由人类创造或建造的艺术品、建筑等，以物质形态存在的文化遗产。较为典型的物质文化遗产包括古代城市遗址、建筑群、宗教建筑、墓葬等。而非物质文化通常是指由人类创造的、不以物质为载体呈现的文化表现形式，包括口头传统、表演艺术、社会风俗和礼仪、社会实践、传统工艺技能等。其中，传统工艺作为非物质文化遗产的重要组成部分，其保护重点在于传统工艺涉及的技能和知识。

　　"国家之魂，文以化之，文以铸之。" 2011 年 10 月 15 日至 18 日，党的十七届六中全会审议通过了《中共中央关于深化文化体制改革 推动社会主义文化大发展大繁荣若干重大问题的决定》，认为推进文化的改革发展具有重要性和紧迫性，并首次提出"建设社会主义文化强国"的奋斗目标。2017 年，党的十九大将"文化自信"纳入"坚持社会主义核心价值体系"基本方略，并写入党章。积极传承中华优秀传统文化，促进其创新性、创造性发展，是我们坚定文化自信，建设社会主义文化强国的必然。中国文化遗产是中华优秀传统文化的重要组成部分，是民族精神的重要体现、展示国家形象的重要窗口，承载着中国几千年的历史积淀和文化成就。通过对文化遗产的保护和传承，可以更好地根植和弘扬历史传统，增强人民对中华优秀文化的认同和自信心，增进不同文化之间的理解，促进不同文化之间的交流与合作。

2006 年起，国务院将每年六月的第二个星期六设立为"文化遗产日"。2016 年，"文化遗产日"被调整设立为"文化和自然遗产日"。2017 年 6 月 10 日迎来了中国首个"文化和自然遗产日"。这一调整更全面地强调和展示了中国丰富的文化和自然遗产资源，体现了国家保护文化和自然遗产的理念，有助于提高公众对文化和自然遗产保护的重视，促进文化和自然遗产的传承与发展。

作为一个拥有着悠久历史和辽阔疆域的国家，中国的文化和自然遗产丰富多样、底蕴深厚。截至 2024 年 6 月，中国共有 57 项世界遗产，包括自然遗产 14 项、文化遗产 39 项、文化和自然双重遗产 4 项，是拥有世界遗产总数第二多的国家。此外，我国还建立了国家、省、市、县四级非物质文化遗产名录体系，以科学、系统地保护和传承文化遗产，加强对非遗代表性项目和传承人的保护。然而，尽管国家和国际社会在保护、传承和发展文化和自然遗产方面都已经做出了相当多的努力，但当前仍有许多棘手的问题亟待解决。例如，保护文化和自然遗产的资金和资源有限，气候变化对生态系统和文化古迹构成威胁，地区冲突和战争对文化和自然遗产直接造成破坏，商业发展和遗产保护不平衡，传统工艺缺乏公众认知度和参与度等。面对这些挑战，如何推动文化遗产的创新性保护和发展至关重要。

来自南开大学、上海交通大学、武汉大学、苏州大学、西北工业大学等国内高校的学生参加了此次以"世界文化遗产继承与传统工艺创新"为主题的工作坊。他们以国内文化遗产和传统工艺作为研究对象，通过文献综述、实地调研、专家访谈、案例分析等研究方法，探索了这些物质文化遗产和非物质文化遗产的历史渊源、保护现状、传承发展、工艺创新等，分析了当前保护和传承文化遗产面临的挑战，针对性地提出了包括数字化保护在内的一系列创新建议，并展望了未来的研究方向。

例如，在《世界文化遗产继承与传统工艺创新案例研究——苏州市"香山帮"传统建筑营造技艺项目研究》一文中，作者对中国传统建筑流派之一的香山帮的传统建筑营造技艺的继承与创新进行了研究。作者深入探索了"香山帮"的概念和内涵，在分析了香山帮工艺传承的现状后，发现了目前香山帮工艺传承存在的问题，如大众认知度不足、相关人才短缺等，提出了包括积极推广"香山帮"品牌，建立匠人工作室等长期培养模式等建议。

在《西安城墙的保护现状及其可持续利用建议》一文中，作者以西安城墙这一古代遗迹为例，对古文化遗址的保护进行了探讨。在文中，作者从预防性保护、精准研判、法律保障、技术应用等方面总结了西安城墙现有的保护措施，思考了当前西安城墙保护存在的问题，认为该遗址保护面临公众参与度不足、资金紧缺、配套制度和法律法规不够完善等问题。作者通过将西安城墙与国外类似古遗址的保护措施进行对比，得到了关于完善西安城墙保护措施的经验启示，并在文章最后对国内文化古遗址的预防性保护、人文价值和商业价值的挖掘等提出了建议。

秦始皇陵是第一批全国重点文物保护单位，同时也是中国第一批世界文化遗产之一，对秦始皇陵的保护和开发一直都是国内外学者研究的热门话题。此次工作坊收录了《秦始皇帝陵展陈方式的数字化研究》一文，作者将研究重点放在了秦始皇陵的展陈方式上。作者将秦始皇陵和埃及金字塔的展陈方式进行了对比分析，提出了利用数字技术创新秦始皇陵展陈方式的方案，以此拉近游客与秦始皇陵的距离，增强互动性，从而让历史可近观、可触摸。

此主题下还收录了其他优秀论文，在此不一一列举。我们希望学生们能够通过参与此次主题为"世界文化遗产继承与传统工艺创新"的工作坊，全面提升自身的学术素养，并深刻理解文化遗产的保护和创新继承。同时，我们也希望通过这些论文的展示，为读者提供与此话题相关的深入洞察，激发更多的思考和讨论，为相关研究和实践做出贡献，弘扬民族优秀文化。

陈 俊

国际胜任力培养专业委员会常务理事

西北工业大学国际合作处副处长

2024 年 6 月 10 日

目 录 CONTENTS

第二章　模拟《联合国气候变化框架公约》第 28 次缔约方大会（COP28）会议提案

第七章　世界一流工业园区建设案例研究

第八章　世界文化遗产继承与传统工艺创新

PART
1

第一章

世界一流期刊案例分析研究

《柳叶刀》: 200 年构建医学影响力组织的启示[①]

摘 要:《柳叶刀》在推动医学发展、引领学科方向、传播医学知识等方面具有重要贡献与深远影响。在《柳叶刀》期刊成立 200 周年之际,本研究从梳理该期刊的发展历程、组织架构、运行机制、学科定位、编委会设置等出发,总结并分析了《柳叶刀》期刊的成功要素及其未来面临的挑战。本研究认为全职编辑团队,始终保持公平性、多样性和包容性,主动的战略性思考,对突发公共卫生事件的迅速响应,以及与国际组织的紧密合作等是其成功的必要因素。然而,随着技术的进步及其他期刊的迅速发展,《柳叶刀》期刊的发展在未来仍面临许多挑战,包括同业竞争、开源期刊的费用、人工智能的挑战等。最后,本研究为《柳叶刀》期刊未来的发展提供了意见和建议。

关键词:《柳叶刀》;期刊发展;因素分析

一、引 言

(一)研究背景

1.《柳叶刀》发展概述

The Lancet(中文名为《柳叶刀》)由托马斯·威克利(Thomas Wakley)在 1823 年 10 月 5 日创建,以外科手术刀"柳叶刀"为刊物命名,突出了该期刊的医学定位,同时 lancet 在英文中有尖顶穹窗之意,取名 Lancet 也表明期刊立志成为照亮医学界的明窗。[②]作为周刊,《柳叶刀》每年出版 52 期,现已成

① 作者: 赵梦真,赵泳春,李博,北京理工大学管理学院;黄柯依,北京大学体育教研部;张粲,中国疾病预防控制中心。

② The Lancet. About *The Lancet*. [2024-11-29]. https://www.thelancet.com/lancet/about.

为世界上历史最悠久、影响力最大的具有同行评审性质的医学期刊之一，与《新英格兰医学杂志》（*NEJM*）、《美国医学会杂志》（*JAMA*）、《英国医学杂志》（*BMJ*）合称为"世界四大顶级医学期刊"。《柳叶刀》的发展历程可以大致分为三个阶段：创刊期（1823—1913 年）、国际扩张期（1914—1989 年）、数字化发展期（1990 年至今）。

在《柳叶刀》创刊伊始，英国医学界非常不正规，裙带关系和任人唯亲现象成为常态，医学界存在严重的腐败现象，缺乏训练有素的医生。针对英国医学界存在的问题，《柳叶刀》成为第一个关注医学界利益的周刊，并十分重视全科医生的合法化，为循证医学、医学审计和专业监管奠定了基础。[1]在此期间，《柳叶刀》推动了 1858 年英国全科医生合法化法案的颁布，并成为妇女解放运动的开拓者。[2]

在国际扩张期（1914—1989 年），两次世界大战爆发让公众对卫生健康问题有了更加深刻的认识，《柳叶刀》在此期间开始关注军队医学方面的研究[3]，读者群体开始向更广泛的方向扩展，包括医疗保健从业人员和普通公众。

在数字化发展期（1990 年至今），《柳叶刀》开始与爱思唯尔（Elsevier Science Inc）协同出版，爱思唯尔在科技和数字化领域的优势提升了《柳叶刀》在全球范围内的传播与影响力，促进了《柳叶刀》在全球医学期刊市场上的竞争力。自 2000 年创建的第一个子刊《柳叶刀·肿瘤学》起，《柳叶刀》编辑部开始陆续推出其他专题的子刊，包括儿童青年健康、糖尿病与内分泌学、数字医疗、全球健康等 24 个子刊。《柳叶刀》得到了迅速的发展。

2.《柳叶刀》在医学领域的重要作用及影响

《柳叶刀》从创立至今始终保持独立，未曾加入任何一个医学或科学组织，至今在整个医学界的发言仍保持着其独立性和权威性[4]。《柳叶刀》期刊在全球范围内具有重大的影响力，每年期刊官网的访问量超过了 4250 万次，下载量为 268.7 亿次，文章每年在新闻中被提及超过 36.3 万次，发表的研究定期受到

---

[1] Khan, M. S., Naidu, T., Torres, I., et al. *The Lancet* and colonialism: past, present, and future. *The Lancet*, 2024, 403(10433): 1304-1308.

[2] Maclean, N. C. The Medical Act of 1858. *The Lancet*, 1877, 109(2793): 369; *The Lancet*. THE MEDICAL ACT OF 1858. (1877). https://www.thelancet.com/journals/lancet/article/PIIS0140-6736(02)59835-4/fulltext.

[3] Michaud, J., M, K., Licina, D., et al. Militaries and global health: peace, conflict, and disaster response. *The Lancet*, 2019, 393(10168): 276-286.

[4] 科学网.《柳叶刀》主编：开放获取，中国期刊应因刊制宜. (2015-11-30)[2024-11-29]. https://news.sciencenet.cn/htmlnews/2015/11/332894.shtm.

有影响力的媒体报道，包括美联社、BBC、CNN等。该期刊的影响因子曾一度高达202.731，成为了世界领先的临床、公共卫生和全球卫生知识来源。《柳叶刀》在推动医学发展、引领学科方向、传播医学知识等方面发挥了重要作用，产生了深远影响。《柳叶刀》不仅仅是一本医学期刊，同时也是一种理念，即应该通过推进医学研究和科学进步来推动社会和政治变革，为人类做出更大的贡献。

首先，从发表的论文角度看，《柳叶刀》期刊所发表的文章经过了严格的选题和审核，具有非常强的权威性，这使得该期刊成为世界各国医生、医学专家和学者们了解最新医学研究进展、学习最前沿医学科技和开展医学实践的方向指引，从而推动了医学领域相关专业的发展。《柳叶刀》在一些重大的医学议题上以直言敢说闻名，而近年来直言不讳的例子包括：批评世界卫生组织、拒绝让顺势疗法正式成为众多治疗法选择中的一种[1]、发表2003年美伊战争平民伤亡的统计[2]等。其次，该期刊为医学从业人员提供了一个优良的学术交流平台。在全球化的今天，医学研究和临床实践变得不再仅仅是国家或地区性的问题，而是需要全球范围内专家们的共同努力。在这种背景下，《柳叶刀》期刊成为全球医疗界的一个重要平台，让全球不同地区的医生和科学家能够共同分享最新的研究成果，互相借鉴灵感，共同进步。最后，期刊对全球医学和公共卫生事业的健康发展产生了积极影响。《柳叶刀》期刊在推动全科医生合法化、女性从医公平化等方面起到了不可替代的作用。[3]《柳叶刀》不仅仅是一本医学期刊，同时也是一种理念的传递渠道，即通过推进医学研究和科学进步来推动社会和政治变革，为人类做出更大贡献。

在过去的200年中，《柳叶刀》期刊发表了众多具有里程碑意义的研究，既包括一些临床上更为细致深入的研究，也包括一些公共卫生问题的大数据研究，对全球医学研究和临床实践产生了深远的影响。部分《柳叶刀》发表的具有重要里程碑性的成果有：1867年发表了李斯特外科消毒法[4]，1918年发表了威廉·里弗斯（William Rivers）深入研究炮弹休克症的疗法，使得人们对现称

---

[1] The Lancet. The end of homoeopathy. [2024-11-29]. https://www.thelancet.com/journals/lancet/article/PIIS0140-6736(05)67149-8/fulltext.

[2] Roberts, L., Lafta, R., Garfield, R., et al. Mortality before and after the 2003 invasion of Iraq: cluster sample survey. *The Lancet*, 2004, 364(9448): 1857-1864.

[3] The Lancet. The potential of general practice. [2024-11-29]. https://www.thelancet.com/journals/lancet/article/PIIS0140-6736(19)31418-7/abstract.

[4] Lister, J. On the antisepic principle in the practice of surgery. *The Lancet*, 1867, 90(2299): 353-356.

作创伤后应激障碍的疾病有了更为全面的理解[①]；1940 年发表了霍华德·弗洛里（Howard Florey）有关青霉素价值的论文[②]；1962 年发表了提示沙利度胺和出生缺陷相关的首篇文章[③]；2004 年发表了认为冠状病毒很可能是SARS病因的观点[④]；2015 年的几内亚实验证实了埃博拉病毒疫苗的有效性[⑤]。

此外，《柳叶刀》所提出的"气候变化将是 21 世纪人类健康的最大威胁"这一观点[⑥]，已得到世界卫生组织的认同，世界卫生组织随后发布警示以及应对气候变化带来的健康危机的十项建议[⑦]。与此同时，联合国秘书长古特雷斯（António Guterres）评价联合国政府间气候变化专门委员会（气候委员会）发布的《气候变化 2021：自然科学基础》报告时表示，温室气体排放使得数十亿人面临直接风险，并敦促各国搁置各自利益，以达到《巴黎协定》的目标。[⑧]

世界卫生组织对《柳叶刀》COVID-19 委员会有关"COVID-19 暴露了一些重大的全球挑战，例如联合国长期资金不足，知识产权制度僵化，低收入和中等收入国家缺乏可持续资金，以及'过度民族主义'，这促成了疫苗不平等"的结论表示赞同，同时欢迎委员会在题为《COVID-19 大流行疫情为未来提供的经验教训》的报告中提出总体建议[⑨]。

（二）研究目的及意义

《柳叶刀》作为一份历史悠久、权威性极高的医学期刊，已经成立了 200 年。在这 200 年的时间里，《柳叶刀》不仅记录了人类医学发展的众多重要事

---

① Rivers, W. The repression of war experience. *The Lancet*, 1918, 191(4929): 173-177.

② Chain, E., Florey, H. W., Gardner, A. D., et al. Penicillin as a chemotherapeutic agent. *The Lancet*, 1940, 236(6104): 226-228.

③ Russell, C. S., Mckichan, M., Devitt, R. F., et al. Thalidomide and congenital abnormalities. *The Lancet*, 1962, 279(7226): 429-430.

④ Dowell, S. F. & Ho, M. S. Seasonality of infectious diseases and severe acute respiratory syndrome-what we don't know can hurt us. *The Lancet Infectious Diseases*, 2004, 4(11): 704-708.

⑤ Henao-Restrepo, A. M., Longini, I. M., Egger, M., et al. Efficacy and effectiveness of an rVSV-vectored vaccine expressing Ebola surface glycoprotein: interim results from the Guinea ring vaccination cluster-randomised trial. *The Lancet*, 2015, 386(9996): 857-866.

⑥ Watts, N., Amann, M., Ayeb-Karlsson, S., et al. The Lancet Countdown on health and climate change: from 25 years of inaction to a global transformation for public health. *The Lancet*, 2018, 391(10120): 581-630.

⑦ World Health Organization. WHO's 10 calls for climate action to assure sustained recovery from COVID-19. [2024-11-29]. https://www.who.int/news/item/11-10-2021-who-s-10-calls-for-climate-action-to-assure-sustained-recovery-from-COVID-19.

⑧ 人民网. 联合国机构报告显示未来极端天气可能更为频繁——共同应对气候变化挑战（国际视点）. (2021-08-24)[2024-11-29]. http://world.people.com.cn/n1/2021/0824/c1002-32204740.html.

⑨ World Health Organization. WHO responds to *The Lancet* COVID-19 Commission. [2024-11-29]. https://www.who.int/zh/news/item/15-09-2022-who-responds-to-the-lancet-COVID-19-commission.

件和研究成果，也经历了自身的发展和变革。在《柳叶刀》成立 200 周年之际，本研究旨在通过《柳叶刀》这一世界顶级医学期刊的发展历程，探究其成功发展的关键要素。分析其发展历史、内部管理、内容建设以及全球影响力等方面的特点和优势，对其他期刊的发展具有重要的参考意义。

二、《柳叶刀》发展历程分析

（一）期刊组织架构

1. 运行机制

《柳叶刀》期刊致力于提高知识服务的意识和能力，努力实现从单纯的文献出版商到知识服务供应商的定位转变，具体表现为预印本机制和交流平台构建两个方面[①]。

其一，预印本机制是指《柳叶刀》期刊鼓励作者向医疗和公共卫生机构、资助者以及预印本服务商分享提交给《柳叶刀》期刊但未发表的论文。2018年，《柳叶刀》研究共享平台 SSRN 合作提供预印本发表服务，名为 *Preprints with The Lancet*，为作者提供更多预印本的发布渠道。

其二，交流平台构建表现为，《柳叶刀》期刊积极利用专业资源，为企业和大众提供医学、公共卫生领域的专业知识；为医学从业人员、科研学者、政策制定者以及其他学科专家提供实时互动平台、协同创新和赋能服务。

《柳叶刀》期刊还致力于构建期刊集群，以集约化的生产运营促进集团在临床实践、公共卫生和全球健康政策等领域的资源整合。《柳叶刀》旗下共 24 本系列期刊，其中 12 本为金色开放获取期刊，其余 12 本期刊则会向论文作者提供开源费用的资助。

2. 编委会设置

《柳叶刀》期刊的国际协作团队是由 170 多名致力于促进全球健康的顶级专家组成，全球团队阵容强大雄厚。团队成员具体包括专业编辑、技术文案编辑、制作编辑、营销和传播专家、设计师、出版商、运营经理、编辑助理以及多媒体和数字专家。编辑部职位设置包括主编、副主编、高级执行编辑、执行编辑、管理编辑、高级编辑、亚洲执行主编、北美执行主编、咨询编辑、外展

---

① The Lancet. About The Lancet Group. [2024-11-29]. https://www.thelancet.com/about-us.

编辑、高级副总编辑、副总编辑、高级助理编辑、助理编辑。①《柳叶刀》期刊欢迎各类对医学科学和临床实践具有启发和推动意义的原创文章的投稿,投稿论文经过编辑部内部审查后,将会通过外部审稿程序进行同行评审。

3.作者与读者权益保护

《柳叶刀》期刊对作者承诺了以下权益:(1)审稿和编辑流程符合卓越标准。(2)同行专家提供评审意见。《柳叶刀》期刊编辑部会邀请全球相关领域的专家或非学术工作者对论文提出全面的评审意见,并且致力于高效的评审流程。(3)专业的全职学术出版团队。编辑部会在同行评审之前进行内部审查,助理编辑会在稿件内容完成修改后,负责提高可读性并检查一致性和错误内容。(4)通过网站访问、电子邮件阅读、媒体报道等方式实现研究论文全球可见,有助于提高科研成果的覆盖面和影响力。(5)《柳叶刀》期刊在国际上具有高影响力、高公众信任度和高综合评价,并且通过各类社交媒体平台与广大作者、读者和公众互动,同时建立完善的社交媒体渠道准则,以保证健康、有效的讨论环境。(6)《柳叶刀》期刊致力于提高研究内容的多样性,认识到需要加强女性、非白人群体及社会弱势群体在研究领域的代表性。②

《柳叶刀》期刊不断提升服务读者意识、明确目标读者、畅通作者与读者沟通渠道的能力,并且应用各种新媒体手段为读者提供所需服务。具体包括:(1)采用国际格式,提高编校质量。《柳叶刀》期刊在发表之前会详细审查论文,包括将插图转换为专业格式、尽力减少出版后的错误,并确保研究能被广泛的国际读者充分理解,最大限度发挥其对世界的影响。(2)数据共享。《柳叶刀》期刊致力于开放科学,并要求作者提供研究论文的数据共享声明,详细说明共享数据的内容、是否共享其他文档(如研究方案)、公开数据的时间等信息,并且将声明和文章共同发布。(3)提高全球各国充分和自由地获取医学信息的可能性。

(二)《柳叶刀》子刊发展

2000年,全球癌症发病率和死亡率急剧上升,《柳叶刀》创建了子刊《柳叶刀·肿瘤学》以满足癌症治疗和研究领域日益增长的需求。自此,为了更好地满足读者对不同领域医学知识的需求,也为了避免读者在选择阅读时因范围

---

① The Lancet. People at The Lancet. [2024-11-29]. https://www.thelancet.com/lancet-people.
② The Lancet. Publishing Excellence. [2024-11-29]. https://www.thelancet.com/publishing-excellence.

太宽而导致的问题①,《柳叶刀》编辑部开始陆续推出其他专题的子刊,包括儿童青少年健康、糖尿病与内分泌学、数字医疗、全球健康等 24 个子刊(部分如表 1 所示)。《柳叶刀》得到了迅速的发展。

表 1 《柳叶刀》部分期刊的学科定位与研究方向

期刊名称	研究方向
《柳叶刀》	临床、公共卫生、全球卫生知识
《柳叶刀·儿童青少年健康》	免疫学、心脏病学、重症医学等
《柳叶刀·糖尿病与内分泌学》	糖尿病、内分泌和代谢领域
《柳叶刀·数字医疗》	数字健康、临床医学
《柳叶刀·胃肠病学与肝脏病学》	消化道、肝脏、胆囊、胆管树和外分泌胰腺相关疾病及其并发症
《柳叶刀·全球健康》	生殖、孕产妇、新生儿、儿童青少年健康;传染性疾病(包括被忽视的热带病);非传染性疾病等
《柳叶刀·血液病学》	血液肿瘤学、红白细胞疾病、血小板疾病、干细胞移植和诱导多能干细胞以及输血医学等
《柳叶刀·老龄健康》	衰老机制的早期临床研究、流行病学和社会学研究
《柳叶刀·艾滋病》	多种创新疗法以及佐证此类疗法的生物学研究、提供医疗服务的新方式,以及在全球范围内应对 HIV/AIDS 的新方法等
《柳叶刀·感染病学》	抗感染治疗和免疫接种;细菌、病毒、真菌和寄生虫感染;新发感染等
《柳叶刀·微生物》	微生物的性质(如抗生素抗性基因/质粒、毒力因子)、微生物组、病理学及其对人群的影响等
《柳叶刀·神经病学》	脑血管病、痴呆/阿尔茨海默病、癫痫及痫性发作、遗传学、头痛及偏头痛等
《柳叶刀·肿瘤学》	乳腺癌、内分泌肿瘤、胃肠肿瘤、泌尿生殖系统肿瘤、妇科肿瘤、血液肿瘤、头颈部肿瘤等
《柳叶刀·星球健康》	可持续发展目标和全球环境变化
《柳叶刀·精神病学》	精神药理学、心理治疗和心理社会学疗法
《柳叶刀·公共卫生》	健康保护、健康促进和卫生服务领域
《柳叶刀·区域健康》	世界卫生组织成员国六大区域的传染病、非传染性疾病、健康老龄化、儿童青少年健康等
《柳叶刀·呼吸病学》	哮喘、急性呼吸窘迫综合征(ARDS)、慢性阻塞性肺病(COPD)、烟草控制、重症监护医学等

---

① The Lancet. The Lancet's 200th Anniversary. (2023). https://www.thelancet.com/lancet-200.

续表

期刊名称	研究方向
《柳叶刀·风湿病学》	诊断和分型、风湿病的管理和预防（包括关节炎、肌肉骨骼和结缔组织疾病，以及免疫系统疾病）等
《柳叶刀·发现科学》	包括柳叶刀旗下 *eBioMedicine* 和 *eClinicalMedicine*，关注基础医学研究、转化医学研究、临床研究等

《柳叶刀·肿瘤学》

The Lancet Oncology 创办于 2000 年 9 月，由爱思唯尔公司每月出版发行。这是一本全球领先的临床肿瘤学研究期刊，专注于推进临床实践、改善现状及倡导卫生政策改革，并致力于解决全球肿瘤学相关问题。关注的主题包括但不限于：乳腺癌、内分泌肿瘤、胃肠肿瘤、泌尿生殖系统肿瘤、妇科肿瘤、血液肿瘤、头颈部肿瘤、神经系统肿瘤、儿童肿瘤、胸腔肿瘤、肉瘤、皮肤癌、流行病学、癌症预防与癌症控制、支持治疗、成像、医疗卫生系统。

《柳叶刀·感染病学》

The Lancet Infectious Diseases 创刊于 2001 年 8 月，该刊致力于发表与感染病学和人类健康主题相关的有趣且翔实的原创性研究和综述文章，优先发表那些可能影响临床实践或研究方向的文章。关注的主题包括但不限于：抗感染治疗和免疫接种；细菌、病毒、真菌和寄生虫感染；新发感染；疟疾、结核病和分枝杆菌感染；感染控制；感染病流行病学；被忽视的热带病和旅游医学等。

《柳叶刀·神经病学》

The Lancet Neurology 创办于 2002 年 5 月，由爱思唯尔公司每月出版发行。这是一本全球领先的临床神经病学研究期刊，致力于发表有望改变或启发神经病学临床实践的原创性研究。关注的主题包括但不限于：脑血管病、痴呆/阿尔茨海默病、癫痫及痫性发作、遗传学、头痛及偏头痛、神经系统感染性疾病、运动神经元疾病/肌萎缩侧索硬化、运动障碍、多发性硬化、神经肌肉疾病、周围神经病、儿科神经病学、睡眠障碍、创伤、神经系统肿瘤等。

《柳叶刀·呼吸病学》

The Lancet Respiratory Medicine 创办于 2013 年 3 月，由爱思唯尔公司每月出版发行。这是一本全球领先的呼吸病学和重症监护期刊，致力于发表有望改变或启发呼吸病学和重症监护临床实践的原创研究，以及与呼吸病学和重症监护主题相关的研究或综述。关注的主题包括但不限于：哮喘、急性呼吸窘

迫综合征（ARDS）、慢性阻塞性肺病（COPD）、烟草控制、重症加强监护医学、肺癌、囊性纤维化、肺炎、结节病、败血症、间皮瘤、睡眠医学、胸外科与重建外科、肺结核、姑息医学、流感、肺动脉高压、肺血管疾病和呼吸道感染等。

《柳叶刀·糖尿病与内分泌学》

*The Lancet Diabetes & Endocrinology*创刊于2013年7月，由爱思唯尔公司出版发行。该期刊致力于关注糖尿病、内分泌和代谢领域进展，其内容广泛覆盖内分泌学相关领域疾病，致力于发表该领域内的最新临床进展和有望改变临床实践的研究，为读者带来全球性的专业观点。关注的主题包括但不限于：糖尿病、肥胖、营养和新陈代谢、骨质疏松症、肾上腺疾病、骨代谢、生长障碍、脂质代谢紊乱、神经内分泌学、儿科内分泌学、垂体疾病、生殖内分泌学、甲状腺疾病等方面。文章类型包括原创性研究、专家综述、新闻事件、述评和观点类文章等。

《柳叶刀·全球健康》

*The Lancet Global Health*是《柳叶刀》旗下的金色开放获取期刊，创办于2013年7月，由爱思唯尔公司每月出版发行。《柳叶刀·全球健康》关注弱势群体，无论他们是整个经济区域还是繁荣国家中的边缘化群体，优先关注以下主题：生殖、孕产妇、新生儿、儿童和青少年健康；传染病，包括被忽视的热带疾病；非传染性疾病；心理健康；全球卫生工作人员；卫生系统；外科手术以及卫生政策。该期刊延续了《柳叶刀》倡导健康政策的传统，旨在建立医疗保健专业人员、公众和政策制定者之间的联盟，从而在全球范围内提供更好的健康服务。

《柳叶刀·精神病学》

*The Lancet Psychiatry*创办于2014年6月，由爱思唯尔公司每月出版发行。这本期刊是精神病学领域原创性研究的国际可信来源，致力于发表有望改变或启发精神病学临床实践的原创性研究，其涵盖的内容包括创新性治疗方法以及为之提供依据的生物学研究、提供医疗服务的新方式以及从社会精神病学角度研究精神障碍的新思路。同时大力提倡支持精神障碍患者的权利。

《柳叶刀·血液病学》

*The Lancet Haematology*创办于2014年10月，由爱思唯尔公司每月出版发行，是全球第一个专注于全球血液病相关问题的临床医学期刊。该刊致力于

发表改善血液病学临床实践的话题，挑战现状，并倡导学术实践和卫生政策的变革。该期刊专注于血液病学临床研究，为全球血液病研究群体提供了一个独立的发表平台，并倡导改善全球血液病患者的生活。关注的主题包括但不限于：血液肿瘤学、红白细胞疾病、血小板疾病、干细胞移植和诱导多能干细胞以及输血医学等。

《柳叶刀·艾滋病》

The Lancet HIV 创办于 2014 年 10 月，由爱思唯尔公司每月出版发行。这是一本极具国际视野的独立的临床医学期刊，其发表的文章为艾滋病毒感染者在临床医学、流行病学和正规操作流程方面提供了一个统一的健康认知，以全方位的视角呈现出艾滋病这一全球流行病的全貌，包括转化医学研究、流行病学研究、临床研究、实施研究等。该刊涵盖多种创新疗法以及佐证此类疗法的生物学研究，提供医疗服务的新方式及全球范围内应对艾滋病的新方法等。

《柳叶刀·胃肠病学与肝脏病学》

The Lancet Gastroenterology & Hepatology 创办于 2016 年 9 月，由爱思唯尔公司每月出版发行。发表全球范围内胃肠病学及肝脏病学专家对胃肠肝病国际问题的原创性研究、权威综述、评论、卫生政策、观点文章、临床图片、通讯和相关新闻。该期刊所发表的论文主要涉及消化道、肝脏、胆囊、胆管树和外分泌胰腺相关疾病及其并发症的一级和二级预防、诊断、管理及治疗等。

《柳叶刀·公共卫生》

The Lancet Public Health 是《柳叶刀》旗下的金色开放获取期刊，创办于 2016 年 11 月，由爱思唯尔公司每月出版发行。该期刊是全球领先的公共卫生研究期刊，致力于发表有助于推动全球健康平等、公共卫生实践和政策制定的研究成果。

《柳叶刀·星球健康》

The Lancet Planetary Health 是《柳叶刀》旗下的金色开放获取期刊，创办于 2017 年 4 月，由爱思唯尔公司每月出版发行。该期刊是研究人类世（Anthropocene）中人类文明可持续发展的杰出期刊。关注社会发展及其与环境相互作用的所有重要方面，包括变革的驱动因素、这些变革对人们和社会的影响，以及未来的实践政策和干预措施。

《柳叶刀·儿童青少年健康》

The Lancet Child & Adolescent Health 创办于 2017 年 9 月，由爱思唯尔公

司每月出版发行。这是一本极具国际视野的独立的临床医学期刊，致力于发表最具影响力和创新力并有望改变临床实践的原创性研究、权威述评和有深刻见解的观点文章，以期促进从胎儿到青年全生命时期的儿童青少年健康。所涉及的学科领域涵盖普通儿科、青少年医学或儿童发育，以及所有儿科细分专业，包括但不限于过敏和免疫学、心脏病学、重症医学、内分泌学、胎儿和新生儿医学、胃肠病学、血液学、肝脏病学和营养学、感染病学、神经学、肿瘤学、精神病学、呼吸病学和外科等。

《柳叶刀·发现科学》是一组开放获取学术期刊，包括《柳叶刀》旗下 *eBioMedicine* 和 *eClinicalMedicine*，涉及的领域包括基础医学研究、转化医学研究、临床研究和卫生系统研究。这组期刊发表重要的初期研究，有助于研究人员和临床医生发现可能改善全世界人们健康和福祉的新机会。

eBioMedicine

《柳叶刀》旗下发表转化医学研究的高端金色开放获取期刊，是《柳叶刀·开放科学》（*The Lancet Discovery Science*）的一部分，创办于 2014 年 11 月，由爱思唯尔公司每月出版发行。该刊发表的内容涵盖生物医学研究的全领域，从具有明确人类相关性的临床前研究，到概念验证性的首次人体研究以及早期临床试验。*eBioMedicine* 希望促进基础科学家、临床研究人员和医疗卫生工作者之间的对话和合作，提高医疗卫生工作者对基础研究成果的可及性和适用性，并更好地理解生物医学研究者所面对的临床挑战。

eClinicalMedicine

《柳叶刀》旗下发表综合医学研究的高端金色开放获取期刊，是《柳叶刀·开放科学》（*The Lancet Discovery Science*）的一部分，创办于 2018 年 7 月，由爱思唯尔公司每月出版发行。*eClinicalMedicine* 关注所有医学学科的临床研究，包括从诊断到治疗、从预防到姑息治疗、从健康促进到卫生政策与公平。该期刊旨在帮助一线专业卫生工作者应对全球社会共同面临的复杂而快速的医疗卫生行业转变，反思与重构健康和医疗卫生的未来，最终目标是加强作为我们社会核心机构的卫生系统。

《柳叶刀·数字医疗》

The Lancet Digital Health 是《柳叶刀》旗下的金色开放获取期刊，创办于 2019 年 5 月，由爱思唯尔公司每月出版发行。该期刊发表的开放获取内容打破了学科边界，为医疗从业者与研究者构筑了沟通桥梁，通过聚焦数字医疗这一

跨学科领域中最重要的进展，成为数字医疗研究最卓越的发表平台。该刊服务于数字健康领域、临床医学领域以及整个健康界，推广和传播高质量的科研成果，支持科技与数据在符合伦理的前提下应用于医学实践。

《柳叶刀·风湿病学》

The Lancet Rheumatology 创办于 2019 年 9 月，由爱思唯尔公司每月出版发行。这是一本全球领先的风湿病学研究期刊，致力于发表全球范围内的风湿病学研究成果，聚焦于推进该领域临床实践发展、挑战现状并倡导卫生政策改革的研究。该期刊重点聚焦于临床医学，积极呼吁改善全球风湿病患者的生活质量。

《柳叶刀·微生物》

The Lancet Microbe 是《柳叶刀》旗下关于微生物领域的一本金色开放获取期刊，创办于 2020 年 5 月，由爱思唯尔公司每月出版发行。该期刊发表与临床相关的各个层面的微生物研究。该期刊延续了《柳叶刀》期刊家族的价值观和重视卫生政策的传统，致力于成为微生物科研领域中强有力的倡导者与合作者。

《柳叶刀·老龄健康》

The Lancet Healthy Longevity 是《柳叶刀》旗下的金色开放获取期刊，创办于 2020 年 10 月，由爱思唯尔公司每月出版发行。这是一本多学科期刊，发表以临床为重点的长寿与健康老龄化研究和综述。该期刊秉承《柳叶刀》期刊家族的传统，大力倡导"无论年龄大小，人人享有健康和充实生活的权利"。

《柳叶刀·区域健康（西太平洋）》

The Lancet Regional Health–Western Pacific 是《柳叶刀》旗下一本开放获取期刊，创办于 2020 年 8 月，由爱思唯尔公司出版发行。该刊是"促进世界各地平等获取优质卫生保健服务"这一《柳叶刀》全球倡议的一部分，致力于推动西太平洋地区临床实践的改善和卫生政策的进步与发展，通过发表高水平循证医学论文，以期提高该区域及相关国家的卫生质量，并最终促进改善西太平洋地区人群的健康。

《柳叶刀·区域健康（美洲）》

The Lancet Regional Health–Americas 是《柳叶刀》旗下一本开放获取期刊，创办于 2021 年 9 月，由爱思唯尔公司出版发行。该刊是"促进世界各地平等获取优质卫生保健服务"这一《柳叶刀》全球倡议的一部分，致力于推动美洲地区临床实践的改善和卫生政策的进步与发展，通过发表高水平循证医学

论文，以期提高该区域及相关国家的卫生质量，并最终促进改善美洲地区人群的健康。

《柳叶刀·区域健康（欧洲）》

The Lancet Regional Health-Europe 是《柳叶刀》旗下一本开放获取期刊，创办于 2021 年 9 月，由爱思唯尔公司出版发行。该刊是"促进世界各地平等获取优质卫生保健服务"这一《柳叶刀》全球倡议的一部分，致力于推动欧洲地区临床实践的改善和卫生政策的进步与发展，通过发表高水平循证医学论文，以期提高该区域及相关国家的卫生质量，并最终促进改善欧洲地区人群的健康。

《柳叶刀·区域健康（东南亚）》

The Lancet Regional Health-Southeast Asia 是《柳叶刀》旗下一本开放获取期刊，创刊于 2022 年 6 月，由爱思唯尔公司出版发行。该刊是"促进世界各地平等获取优质卫生保健服务"这一《柳叶刀》全球倡议的一部分，致力于推动东南亚地区临床实践的改善和卫生政策的进步与发展，通过发表高水平循证医学论文，以期提高该区域及相关国家的卫生质量，并最终促进改善东南亚地区人群的健康。

（三）期刊学科布局

在学科布局方面，《柳叶刀》相较于其他医学三大刊《新英格兰医学杂志》《英国医学杂志》《美国医学会杂志》，特别关注了不同人群、不同区域、先进医疗手段、更多病种以及生命科学的内容，发表的研究涉及整个医疗领域，包括但不限于临床实践、流行病学、全球健康、医疗政策和管理、卫生经济学等领域；《柳叶刀》在特定的疾病领域（如《柳叶刀·肿瘤学》《柳叶刀·神经病学》和《柳叶刀·艾滋病》）以及横向研究（如《柳叶刀·全球健康》《柳叶刀·数字医疗》和《柳叶刀·老龄健康》）中实施全覆盖战略。这种方法在适应研究主题不断变化方面提供了更大的灵活性，使得《柳叶刀》能够获得针对具体疾病的临床实践和研究的最好的论文，易于适应新的临床实践，并平衡期刊的独立性和群体价值。相较于《自然》（*Nature*）、《科学》（*Science*）等综合期刊，《柳叶刀》更偏重医学领域的深耕，在医学领域具有较高的权威性。在文章类型方面，上述期刊均发表原创研究论文、评论、新闻报道、述评、政策分析等多种类型的内容。

《柳叶刀》期刊登载有：原创性的研究文章、评论文章（"小组讨论"及"评论"）、社论、书评、短篇研究文章，也有一些在刊内常登载的文章诸如特刊消息、案例报道等。《柳叶刀》的纸版期刊中有 Articles、Adverse Drug Reactions、Case Reports、Clinical Pictures、Comment、Correspondence、Editorial、Perspectives、Reviews、Viewpoint、World Report 等约 20 个栏目；网站上比较有特色的板块包括：Specialty Collections（将所有已发表的文章按主题分为 15 个专辑），Audio（每期有一个不长于 20 分钟的专题介绍），Conferences（包括《柳叶刀》主办或合办的会议消息，以及《柳叶刀》的编辑介绍），For Authors（详尽的写作、投稿与编辑指南）。

（四）期刊与气候变化健康

2009 年，《柳叶刀》医学期刊和伦敦大学学院联合报告《柳叶刀健康和气候变化倒计时》称，气候变化将是 21 世纪人类健康的最大威胁，旨在号召医生和健康专家更加严肃地看待气候变化问题。[1] 报告同时指出，如果人类更加努力地转向清洁能源，或许将看到巨大的健康改善。随后，中国健康倡导者积极参与其中：自 2015 年起，《柳叶刀》期刊与中国医学科学院共同主办"柳叶刀—中国医学科学院医学与健康大会"；2016 年启动"柳叶刀人群健康与气候变化倒计时"项目；2018 年发表"清华大学—柳叶刀中国健康城市重大报告；2021 年发表"柳叶刀中国女性生殖、孕产妇、新生儿、儿童和青少年健康重大报告"；2022 年发表"北京大学—柳叶刀重大报告；聚集研究人员、临床医生、政策制定者和其他学科专家召开网络研讨会等。《柳叶刀》所提出的"气候变化将是 21 世纪人类健康的最大威胁"这一观点，已得到世卫组织的认同[2]，世卫组织随后发布警示以及应对气候变化带来的健康危机的十项建议。与此同时，现任联合国秘书长古特雷斯表示，温室气体排放使得数十亿人面临直接风险，并敦促各国搁置各自利益，以达到《巴黎协定》的目标。[3]

2016 年，成立"柳叶刀倒计时"（Lancet Countdown），旨在追踪气候变化对人类福祉的影响，以及国家及区域的气候行动，期待通过应对气候变化把健康威胁变成改善健康的机会，同时，确保决策者获得科学的指导，以及卫生专

---

[1] Costello, A., Abbas, M., Allen, A., et al. Managing the health effects of climate change: *Lancet* and University College London Institute for Global Health Commission. *The Lancet*, 2009, 373(9676): 1693-1733.

[2] World Health Organization. We must fight one of the world's biggest health threats: climate change. [2024-11-29]. https://www.who.int/news-room/commentaries/detail/we-must-fight-one-of-the-world-s-biggest-health-threats-climate-change.

[3] United Nations. There is an exit off 'the highway to climate hell', Guterres insists. [2024-11-29]. https://news.un.org/en/story/2024/06/1150661.

业人员获得改善公共卫生所需的工具。"柳叶刀倒计时"与伦敦大学学院合作，每年在《柳叶刀》期刊上发布报告以阐述气候变化和健康或疾病之间的关系。

与其他顶级期刊相比，《柳叶刀》更加侧重于人群健康领域的研究（表2）。比如，相比于《自然》，《柳叶刀》区分了儿童、青少年、老龄人口等不同年龄段的人群健康，同时区分了全球和不同区域的人群健康作为研究对象；相比于《柳叶刀》，《自然》在气候变化领域，从气候变化、能源、环境以及可持续发展等多个角度划分子刊的研究内容。此外，《科学》和《细胞》（Cell）的子刊较少涉及人群健康领域，并且基本不涉及气候变化领域的内容。此外，相比于《柳叶刀》发布长达数十页的《柳叶刀倒计时报告》，同样作为顶级期刊的《科学》和《英国医学杂志》则选择发表研究论文，通过对某一方面的学术研究阐述气候变化与人群健康的关系。例如，2019年的《柳叶刀倒计时报告》发布期间，《科学》发表了一篇与高温引起的热应激相关的研究，《英国医学杂志》则发表了一篇受热会增加不良妊娠可能性的荟萃分析研究。可以看出，"柳叶刀倒计时"通过报告的形式，综合阐述了气候变化会引发的多种疾病，包括热应激和中暑、急性肾损伤、充血性心力衰竭加重和集体暴力风险增加等。而其他两本期刊则通过科学论文的形式，研究某一疾病的发病机理和严重程度。

表2 《柳叶刀》《自然》《科学》和《细胞》关于气候变化与人群健康的系列期刊

学科领域	《柳叶刀》	《自然》	《科学》/《细胞》
气候变化	The Lancet Planetary Health	Nature Climate Change	
		Nature Energy	
		Nature Reviews Earth & Environment	
		Nature Sustainability	
人群健康	The Lancet Child & Adolescent Health	Nature Aging	Science Immunology
	The Lancet Global Health	Nature Mental Health	Cancer Cell
	The Lancet Healthy Longevity		
	The Lancet Public Health		
	The Lancet Regional Health – Americas		
	The Lancet Regional Health – Europe		
	The Lancet Regional Health – Southeast Asia		
	The Lancet Regional Health – Western Pacific		

通过进一步比较《柳叶刀》与《自然》期刊（表3），我们发现《柳叶刀》更加关注特定人群健康保护、疾病机理以及治疗方法的研究，而《自然》的关注重点在于特定人群对可持续发展社会影响，以及缓和与适应气候变化、应对公共卫生危机的策略研究。

表3 《柳叶刀》和《自然》关于气候变化与人群健康系列期刊的研究方向

《柳叶刀》		《自然》	
The Lancet Planetary Health	可持续发展目标和全球环境变化	*Nature Climate Change*	全球气候变化的性质、根本原因及其影响
The Lancet Child & Adolescent Health	免疫学、心脏病学、重症医学等	*Nature Energy*	能源与燃料性能和应用领域
The Lancet Global Health	生殖、孕产妇、新生儿、儿童青少年健康；传染性疾病（包括被忽视的热带病）；非传染性疾病等	*Nature Reviews Earth & Environment*	地球科学与环境科学领域
The Lancet Healthy Longevity	衰老机制的早期临床研究、流行病学和社会学研究	*Nature Sustainability*	确保人类现在和未来福祉的政策和解决方案
The Lancet Public Health	健康保护、健康促进和卫生服务领域	*Nature Aging*	老龄化的基本生物学、老龄化对社会的影响
The Lancet Regional Health	世界卫生组织成员国六大区域的传染病、非传染性疾病、健康老龄化、儿童青少年健康等	*Nature Mental Health*	精神疾病的神经生物学和心理学因素的创新研究，与当代研究公共卫生危机影响的工作相结合

三、《柳叶刀》成功发展的关键因素

（一）组织架构优势分析

1.全职编辑团队

《柳叶刀》旗下的所有期刊均拥有全职编辑团队，专业性强，能够对拟接收的稿件进行文字和图表的润色，提高文章的易读性。接收的稿件首先会由期刊编辑进行审核和评估。全体编辑会仔细阅读每一篇稿件，评估其科学性、新颖性以及其他文章质量相关指标，并展开集体讨论。之后，文章会分配给指定的一位编辑，这位编辑将负责联系相关领域专家进行外部同行评议审稿。最后，编辑团队会根据审稿人的反馈做出该稿件的下一步处理决定。①

---

① The Lancet. Preparing your manuscript. [2024-11-29]. https://www.thelancet.com/preparing-your-manuscript.

此外，《柳叶刀》期刊的国际协作团队由 170 多名致力于促进全球健康的顶级专家组成，全球团队阵容强大雄厚。《柳叶刀》期刊的主要办事处遍及全球各地，在伦敦（英国）、北京（中国）、纽约（美国）、慕尼黑（德国）均设有办事处，并在阿姆斯特丹（荷兰）、巴塞罗那（西班牙）、金奈（印度）、马德里（西班牙）、牛津（英国）、费城（美国）、里约热内卢（巴西）、上海（中国）、悉尼（澳大利亚）和南非设有相关团队，得以吸纳全球各地顶级贤才，组建《柳叶刀》期刊的顶级团队。

2. 公平性、多样性和包容性

《柳叶刀》期刊的同行评审致力于提高研究和出版的公平性、多样性和包容性，承诺增加女性、有色人种以及低收入和中等收入国家出身者同时成为编辑顾问、同行评审员和作者。同时，《柳叶刀》期刊还致力于落实"不参加全男性专家组政策"，即如果某次公开会议或活动中负责规划专题小组讨论的专家组中没有女性成员，那么《柳叶刀》的编辑将不会加入该会议或活动的专家组。对于自己主办或组织的活动，《柳叶刀》将尽力做到至少半数演讲者是女性，而不是让女性只能担任大会的主持人。《柳叶刀》期刊为新加入的同行评审提供指导，并且支持旨在分析或加强同行评审能力的研究。此外，设置激励机制对部分评审类型提供小额酬金，并且依据对期刊的贡献值予以表彰。[1]

《柳叶刀》重视各方面的多样性，致力于改善健康公平。在意识到妇女、有色人种和社会弱势人群等群体在研究中的代表性不足的现象后，《柳叶刀》采取积极的措施，以提高研究和出版领域的多样性和包容性，特别是提高妇女和来自低收入和中等收入国家的同事在编辑顾问、同行评审员和作者中的代表性。同时，《柳叶刀》近年来努力报告与员工、作者或审稿人有关的种族和族裔信息。为了达到报告方式包容性和透明度高、符合共识以及数据和隐私保护法规的要求，《柳叶刀》聘请了在性别和全球专业知识方面多样化的国际咨询委员会。截至 2022 年 11 月，24 本期刊的国际编辑顾问中有 53.9% 是女性。

2019 年和 2020 年，来自《柳叶刀》的工作人员聚集在一起组成了性别与多样性工作组（LGDTF）和种族平等小组（GRacE），负责向柳叶刀和爱思唯尔提供建议，以促进自身工作以及更广泛的研究和出版工作的公平性、多样性和包容性。LGDTF 是在 2019 年的 Lancet Women 项目中发展起来的。该工

---

[1] The Lancet. Advancing equity, diversity, and inclusion: Commitments. [2024-11-29]. https://www.thelancet.com/equity-diversity-inclusion/commitments?section=statement.

作组为整个《柳叶刀》的性别代表多样化提供指导，包括内部流程、内容和委托、作者、评论员和编辑顾问的多样性方面。

GRacE 在倡导《柳叶刀》内部和外部的种族和民族平等方面发挥了重要的作用。2021 年 3 月，GRacE 应邀在世界卫生组织的网络研讨会上介绍了其使命和迄今采取的行动——"健康不平等和基于种族和族裔的歧视：新冠病毒告诉我们什么"。GRacE 和《柳叶刀》将继续倡导实现种族和民族平等所需的机会和资源。

（二）主动的战略性思考

《柳叶刀》主编理查德·霍顿（Richard Horton）认为，要想生存，学术期刊必须变得更加"积极"，寻求"改变社会的方向"，而不是"被动地等待"稿件，并指出"21 世纪的科学期刊，要生存，要想生存，就不能仅仅是期刊"[①]。《柳叶刀》当下的使命变成了"收集最好的科学证据，然后进行战略性思考"，而不是"被动地坐在办公室等待稿件提交"。2019 年，《柳叶刀》发表了一份报告，阐明了到 2050 年如何消灭疟疾，并得到了盖茨基金会资助的研究的支持。这是该期刊发起的数十个"委员会"之一，该委员会召集了专家就从抗击阿尔茨海默病到改革 21 世纪医学教育等主题提出建议。当前，《柳叶刀》不只是一本期刊，而且影响着全球政策。

（三）突发公卫事件迅速响应

为追踪气候变化对人类健康的影响，《柳叶刀》成立"柳叶刀倒计时"项目，成为众多顶级期刊中唯一一个专门设置关注气候变化与健康主题的项目。此外，在新冠疫情暴发期间，《柳叶刀》成立了 COVID-19 委员会，旨在积极协助各国政府、民间社会组织和联合国机构有效应对 COVID-19 大流行。该委员会的目标是提供切实可行的对策，以应对大流行所带来的全球性挑战。面对新冠疫情，《柳叶刀》COVID-19 委员会主席杰弗里·萨克斯（Jeffrey Sachs）表示，美国需要与中国合作，共同找寻一个全球性解决方案。同时，萨克斯还肯定了中国在抗击疫情方面的出色行动，并认为"发达国家并没有慷慨分享其所掌握的知识，尤其是在疫苗方面；全球金融体系偏向于发达国家，对发展中国家的支持太少，这些因素导致世界未能有效应对新冠疫

---

① 国际科学编辑.《柳叶刀》杂志主编呼吁期刊更加主动. [2024-11-29]. https://blog.sciencenet.cn/blog-3387871-1222932.html.

情"。在《柳叶刀》投稿系统中，提示关于新冠疫情的文章可以在编辑和送审中享有优先权，保障了对公共应对新冠疫情的及时性。而其他期刊仅是推出了COVID-19的研究资源专栏，如表4所示。

从表4中可以看出，相比于其他世界一流期刊，《柳叶刀》在研究资源专栏的内容分类中比较宽泛，仅说明专栏包含论文、评论和新闻，这与《柳叶刀》期刊所登载的内容类型基本一致。相比较而言，《自然》期刊在专栏中增加了对基础实验数据和预印本论文的刊登；《科学》期刊特别说明除了COVID-19，还会包含冠状病毒相关的论文内容；《美国医学会杂志》《新英格兰医学杂志》以及《英国医学杂志》都在专栏中说明除了相关论文外，还包括临床诊断记录、药物实验记录以及患者就医指南等信息。

表4 著名学术期刊的新冠病毒（COVID-19）研究资源专栏

期刊名称	栏目名称	专栏内容
《柳叶刀》	COVID-19 Resource Centre	已发表的论文、评论；新闻报道
《自然》	SARS-CoV-2 and COVID-19	已发表的论文、书籍、协议；基础实验数据；预印本论文
《科学》	CORONAVIRUS	已发表的COVID-19和冠状病毒相关论文；新闻报道
《美国医学会杂志》	Coronavirus Disease 2019 (COVID-19)	COVID-19特征；药物试验和治疗；冠状病毒诊断；患者信息
《新英格兰医学杂志》	Coronavirus (COVID-19)	临床报告；诊疗指南；评论
《英国医学杂志》	Coronavirus (COVID-19): Latest news and resources	治疗实践指导；在线课程；新闻、评论、研究

（四）与国际组织的紧密合作

作为国际知名的医学期刊，《柳叶刀》与世界卫生组织、联合国儿童基金会、联合国艾滋病规划署和国际红十字与红新月运动等国际组织建立了广泛的联系和合作，共同致力于促进全球卫生事务的发展，改善全球公共卫生水平，并应对重大卫生挑战。《柳叶刀》通过与国际组织合作，向全球医学界发布相关研究成果，以促进全球范围内的卫生问题研究和知识分享。《柳叶刀》经常就全球卫生政策、卫生紧急情况和人道主义援助等议题发表评论和分析，与国际组织合作共同倡导政策改进和行动。此外，《柳叶刀》通过与国际组织共同开展知识共享和合作项目，通过合作研究、数据交流和专家咨询等方式，推动全球卫生事务的发展和解决重大卫生挑战。通过与国际组织合作，《柳叶刀》成为世界卫生议程和政策制定的重要参与者之一。这提升了柳叶刀在医学界的权威性和可信度，使其成为全球卫生问题的权威声音之一。

以下是《柳叶刀》与一些主要国际组织的合作机制的概述。

世界卫生组织（World Health Organization，WHO）：《柳叶刀》与WHO有密切的合作关系。作为一家重要的医学期刊，《柳叶刀》经常发布与全球卫生问题相关的研究成果，并与WHO合作共同推动全球公共卫生事务的发展。《柳叶刀》还经常发表WHO领导的全球卫生政策和倡议的评论和分析，促进对全球卫生议题的深入讨论。

联合国儿童基金会（United Nations Children's Fund，UNICEF）：《柳叶刀》与UNICEF合作致力于改善儿童健康和福祉，合作的重点包括儿童的营养、免疫接种、教育和发展等方面的问题。《柳叶刀》发表相关研究和政策评论，与UNICEF共同推动儿童权益和健康的改善。

联合国艾滋病规划署（Joint United Nations Programme on HIV/AIDS，UNAIDS）：《柳叶刀》与UNAIDS合作，致力于艾滋病防治的研究和政策制定。《柳叶刀》发表与艾滋病相关的研究成果，并与UNAIDS合作推动全球范围内的艾滋病防治工作，包括预防、治疗和社会支持等方面。

国际红十字与红新月运动（International Red Cross and Red Crescent Movement，IFRC）：《柳叶刀》与国际红十字与红新月运动合作关注全球卫生紧急情况和人道主义援助。合作的重点包括灾害医疗救援、流行病暴发和人道主义危机等领域。《柳叶刀》发表相关研究和经验分享，与国际红十字与红新月运动合作促进卫生援助和救灾工作的质量和效果。

（五）积极推动医学和公共卫生领域的政策发展

《柳叶刀》期刊所发表的论文和评论经常对政策发展产生重大影响，具体通过以下几个主要方式：（1）发表高质量的科学证据帮助政策制定者理解健康问题的严重性，包括为疾病流行、风险因素和治疗效果提供坚实的科学基础。（2）发表全球健康挑战的专题报告和系列文章，增加公众和政府对气候变化与健康议题的关注。（3）发表评论文章和社论，基于最新的研究成果和专家意见，直接对现行政策提出批评和改进措施。这些评论还会被媒体引用进而增加影响力，有助于科学讨论转化为公共讨论，增加政策改进的透明度和紧迫性。

（4）通过与全球健康相关组织和研究机构合作，推动国际疾病预防和控制方面的政策一致性，同时也有助于增加政策制定过程中，弱势群体和低收入国家的发声机会和话语权，推动全球卫生公平。

四、期刊面临的挑战

（一）版面费用与开放获取

从《柳叶刀》的官方网站中查询到各个系列的论文处理费用（APC）如表6所示。

表6 《柳叶刀》期刊论文处理费用

期刊名称	（截至 2023 年 1 月 1 日）
The Lancet	USD 6,830
The Lancet Child & Adolescent Health	USD 5,780
The Lancet Diabetes & Endocrinology	USD 6,300
The Lancet Digital Health	USD 5,780
The Lancet Gastroenterology & Hepatology	USD 6,300
The Lancet Global Health	USD 5,780
The Lancet Haematology	USD 6,300
The Lancet Healthy Longevity	USD 5,500
The Lancet HIV	USD 6,300
The Lancet Infectious Diseases	USD 6,300
The Lancet Microbe	USD 6,300
The Lancet Neurology	USD 6,300
The Lancet Oncology	USD 6,300
The Lancet Planetary Health	USD 5,780
The Lancet Psychiatry	USD 6,300
The Lancet Public Health	USD 5,780
The Lancet Respiratory Medicine	USD 6,300
The Lancet Rheumatology	USD 6,300
The Lancet Regional Health–Americas	USD 4,000 (Canada & USA) USD 2,000 (Latin America & the Caribbean)
The Lancet Regional Health–Europe	USD 4,000
The Lancet Regional Health–Southeast Asia	USD 3,680
The Lancet Regional Health–Western Pacific	USD 2,000

续表

期刊名称	（截至 2023 年 1 月 1 日）
eBioMedicine part of The Lancet Discovery Science	USD 5,000
eClinicalMedicine part of The Lancet Discovery Science	USD 5,000

可以看出，除了《柳叶刀·区域健康》的系列期刊以外，大部分《柳叶刀》系列期刊的APC都达到了 5000 美元及以上，这一费用相比于《自然》和《细胞》的版面费低了近 50%，但是相比于勒菲尔德大学开放获取研究学者尼娜·舍恩菲尔德（Nina Schönfelder）在 2020 年的研究中提出的 2600 美元的期刊版面费中位数，《柳叶刀》系列期刊收取的费用仍然处于高位。

《柳叶刀》的官方网站中多处出现一句话"确保不让支付能力成为研究论文出版的障碍"，但是在出版费用的减免与折扣方面，还是提出了一些适用条件，包括：（1）仅对制定机构资助的作者提供在混合型期刊上发表开源论文的权限，并且对于实施S计划（Plan S）的机构旗下作者，如惠康基金会、盖茨基金会以及WHO，仅向他们提供在金色开放期刊发表论文的权限。（2）仅对主要资助者位于卫生互联网络共享研究成果倡议（HINARI）规定的A组国家的作者进行完全APC减免，对于B组国家实施部分APC减免。（3）其余无法支付所有出版费用的作者需要主动联系编辑部，并说明可能的研究资助者信息、获取APC资金的途径，以及能够承担的金额。

收费制度常常与论文的开放获取相联系。2018 年，17 所研究机构和 6 家基金会联合，向世界宣布了学术出版S计划，该计划认为由这些机构所组成的S联盟资助的科学家一旦在学术期刊上发表了研究成果，会立刻成为开放获取文献并免费供人阅读。实际上，在此之前的 20 多年，学术界就已经展开了开放获取运动。21 世纪以来，由于传统学术出版行业持续提高订阅费用，开放获取实际上没有改善学术出版环境。2012 年，《柳叶刀》的出版商爱思唯尔遭到抵制，超过 2600 名科学家联合声明拒绝为其旗下的期刊投稿或审稿，部分原因是因为爱思唯尔反对美国国立卫生研究院的绿色开放获取要求。直到 2023 年，《柳叶刀》依然不允许S联盟资助的科学论文在旗下 12 本混合型期刊中获得开放获取的资助。

相比较而言，1991 年，预印本网站arXiv开放了服务器；1996 年《临床研究杂志》成为第一本可在线免费阅读的生物医学期刊，随后包括《英国医学杂志》

在内的一些著名期刊也加入了在线获取的队伍；2000 年，生物医学中心出版集团成为全球首家支持开放获取的出版商，并开始发行各类生物医学领域的同行评审期刊。2019 年，另一学术出版巨头施普林格·自然集团（Springer Nature）和德国学术机构签署了史上最大的"变革性协议"，其中包括允许德国研究机构的作者无需支付文章费用，即可在机构旗下的期刊上发表开放获取文章。

可以看出，《柳叶刀》向作者或资助机构收取高昂的出版费用，以及不完全的开放获取制度似乎并不符合当前的期刊发展进程，其中，高昂的出版费用可能取决于出版商的规模、提交同行评审的论文比例、影响因素等指标，以及是否聘请内部编辑或新闻官员。而不完全的开放获取可能受制于所合作的出版商。相比较而言，2021 年施普林格·自然集团承诺所有作者向《自然》及 32 本《自然》原创研究系列期刊投稿时，都能以金色开放获取形式发表，但须支付版面费；美国科学促进会（American Association for the Advancement of Science，AAAS）也正式宣布，将向接受开放获取组织资助的研究者免费提供开放获取发表途径；麻省理工学院出版社编委会成员特德·吉布森（Ted Gibson）认为，最终会有更多科学家从以利润为导向的期刊辞职。可以看出，开放获取模式受到越来越多学术组织和研究人员的支持，相应地，在研究成果和读者之间建立"订阅墙"的运营模式的盈利能力正在降低。

（二）同业竞争

医学期刊之间的竞争主要是关于学科范围、内容影响力、出版速度、读者和订阅量、技术和信息等方面的竞争。不同的医学期刊可能专注于不同的学科领域，例如心脏病学、神经科学等。在这种情况下，该领域内的不同期刊之间将存在激烈的竞争，以获得最好的作者和最新、最令人关注的研究成果。医学期刊的校园声誉和影响力也是竞争的关键。一些期刊由于其历史悠久、发表了一些重大的研究成果、有大量引用次数等原因而具有更高的声誉和影响力。然而，一些年轻的或新兴的期刊也在试图通过不断提高质量和声誉来与老牌的医学期刊竞争。不同的医学期刊往往吸引不同的读者。与越广泛的读者和越高的订阅量相比，期刊在发表文章时吸引更多合适的读者将是更加重要的。随着技术发展和新技术的不断出现，医学期刊也需要不断适应。拥有最新技术和信息的期刊往往更容易获得优势，也能够吸引更多优质的作者和读者。

《柳叶刀》期刊是一本拥有 200 年历史的著名医学期刊，被认为是同领域内最具影响力的期刊之一。尽管如此，它仍然存在与其他同类型期刊的竞争。首先，《新英格兰医学杂志》是美国医学界最具影响力的期刊之一，并与《柳叶刀》一样，被广泛认可为世界上最重要的医学期刊之一。《新英格兰医学杂志》与《柳叶刀》在内容与质量上几乎一致，但在影响力和声誉方面略高。其次，《美国医学会杂志》是一本高水平的、跨学科的、基于证据的医学期刊，拥有庞大的订阅量。《美国医学会杂志》在世界范围内都享有盛誉，它与《柳叶刀》的竞争尤其激烈。还有，《自然医学》（ Nature Medicine ）的声誉在学术界也很高，它被认为是最好的综合性医学期刊之一。《自然医学》在一些方面与《柳叶刀》不同，它更多地关注生物医学和移植研究，但它仍与《柳叶刀》存在激烈的竞争。除了这些顶级的医学期刊，还有许多其他的国内和国际医学期刊在不同方面与《柳叶刀》竞争。总体来说，医学期刊的竞争十分激烈，每个期刊都在争取吸引最好的作者和充满活力的内容，以及吸引最广泛的读者并获得最多的引用次数。

（三）人工智能的冲击

尽管人工智能技术在推动学术研究方面发挥着越来越重要的作用，但它也带来了一些潜在的学术不端现象，对于《柳叶刀》的编辑审核机制产生影响。例如，依赖人工智能获得的虚假数据和实验结果，可能导致出现不正确的科学结论和发表不真实的论文，提高了审核工作难度。同时，AI算法可以复制其他研究者的写作样式、引用方式等，甚至可以生成与其他人写作风格类似的文章，在大量质量参差不齐的投稿中如何保持高质量、高创新度的期刊水平成为难题。此外一些机器学习模型可以通过输入关键词自动生成论文摘要、引言等部分，甚至完整的论文，虽然这在一定程度上提高了论文生产的效率，但也会降低学术研究的价值和可信度，因为这些论文没有经过认真研究和审查。

此外，随着人工智能技术的不断应用，越来越多的新型科学期刊也会利用这些技术来提高其竞争力，对传统期刊《柳叶刀》造成竞争压力。新型科学期刊基于人工智能的自动化评审系统将会提高评审的效率和准确性，而如果《柳叶刀》在引入人工智能的发展潮流下，沿用传统的同行评审方式，需要专家耗费大量时间和精力，并且难度也逐步提升，可能会阻碍其在未来的发展。同时，在编辑和出版方面，人工智能技术可以帮助期刊实现更快速、高效的编辑和出版流程，例如利用自然语言处理技术实现论文自动排版、语法检查等功能。如何在利用好人工智能带来的便利的同时，保持自身的原有优势，是《柳叶刀》需要回答的问题。

五、总结与讨论

（一）总　结

《柳叶刀》期刊现已成为世界上最具影响力的医学期刊之一，成为推动医学领域科学发展必不可缺的力量。《柳叶刀》期刊成长为国际顶级期刊与其以下的特点密不可分：（1）高独立性。创刊200年间，《柳叶刀》期刊从未加入医学或科学组织。（2）高权威性。《柳叶刀》期刊具有很高的学术标准和同行评审程序，其发表的研究具有很高的学术权威性，并能够对医学界产生深远的影响。（3）先锋性。《柳叶刀》期刊一直秉持推动医学进步和改革的先锋精神，关注最前沿和尖端的医学主题，且在许多医学难题和热点问题上表现出鲜明的立场，展现出一定的思想先锋作用。（4）国际化。《柳叶刀》期刊立足全球视野，来稿遍布世界各地，也具有多个国际板块，既强调各国医学发展动态，也关注全球公共卫生与医学问题，体现出典型的国际学术交流平台属性。

然而，随着技术的进步及其他期刊的迅速发展，《柳叶刀》期刊的发展在未来仍面临许多挑战：（1）同业竞争，包括《自然》《科学》等老牌高影响力的综合期刊的影响，以及新兴医学期刊的竞争。（2）开源期刊费用高带来的挑战。编辑部对收录文章的文字、图表等会进行统一润色与修改，保障了文章的高质量并提高了文章的可读性，然而这也提高了文章发表的费用和成本，如何在保障高质量的同时提高投稿费用方面的竞争力，是《柳叶刀》期刊未来发展亟须思考的问题。（3）应对人工智能发展带来的冲击，如何解决科研中使用人工智能造成的学术不端问题是所有期刊面临的共同的问题。

（二）期刊发展的意见和建议

在出版费用设置方面，增加出版费的使用透明度有助于约束不合理的费用制度产生，包括校对、编辑、同行评审等各项服务费，并将这些信息向作者和机构共享。此外，政策制定者也需要完善期刊和出版商的费用监督机制。

在开放获取方面，《柳叶刀》的预印本机制和论文投稿不产生冲突，也不会影响同行评审的进程，同时，论文的禁运政策作用于最新发表的所有论文，这些制度虽然不能完全符合S计划要求的论文出版后立刻成为开放获取论文的要求，但相对于给"订阅墙"模式的论文设置"禁发期"，即作者需要等待至少半年时间才能发表经过同行评审的最终版本论文而言，是一个折中方案。此外，开放获取可能会导致出版费用的水涨船高，在监督费用制度制定的同时，政府和科研机构需要提高对出版经费规划的重视程度，减少由于经费不足带来的对完全开放获取期刊的投稿障碍，以及论文发表的不平等问题。

随着科技的不断发展和数据量的增加，《柳叶刀》需要适应新的科技环境。加强对人工智能技术的学习和应用，了解和掌握新兴技术的发展趋势和应用场景，紧跟时代研究热点和方向，推动期刊的数字化转型，在增强对人工智能投稿的审查和监测的基础上，合理利用人工智能技术提高编辑、出版、同行评审等流程的效率和质量；关注人工智能技术推动的跨学科合作和知识共享，积极推广开放科学实践，促进科研成果的共享和交流。

《柳叶刀》：全球卓越科技期刊的发展、挑战与治理参与[①]

摘　要： 本文以《柳叶刀》为研究对象，深入分析了该期刊的概览、发展要素及面临的挑战。首先，回顾了《柳叶刀》的学科定位、国际成就和影响力。其次，详细探讨了其组织架构、运行机制、收入来源、读者服务等发展要素，并运用创新生态圈理论解释其运行机制；引入知识共同体概念，研究《柳叶刀》如何参与全球治理，强调其知识共同体形成基础和参与路径。最后，深入剖析了性别歧视、审稿问题等挑战，并提出建议，如提升编委会代表性、坚定立场、关注健康焦点领域，以期《柳叶刀》更好地维持其卓越地位。

关键词： 《柳叶刀》；科技期刊；知识共同体；创新生态圈

一、期刊概览

18 世纪英国工业革命给国家带来了财富，同时也带来了令人绝望的贫困、不平等和污染。在英国的政治生活中，失望以多种方式被表现出来，托马斯·威克利（Thomas Wakley）创办《柳叶刀》（*The Lancet*）就是其中一种方式。它秉持着一种全新的、本质上具有革命性的理念，毫不避讳其强烈的政治性，饱含对工业革命的批判。

《柳叶刀》是由托马斯·威克利于 1823 年创立的独立国际综合医学周刊，旨在通过前沿的医学研究和为了大多数人利益的科学驱动社会和政治的变革。《柳叶刀》当然首先是一份医学期刊，但威克利创刊时有更大的雄心壮志——

---

① 作者：仇琳然，大连外国语大学英语学院；李可为，大连外国语大学英语学院；郭欣成，大连外国语大学日本语学院；马红旺，大连外国语大学马克思主义学院。

打破当时庞大的、完全腐败的医学势力，尤其在伦敦。威克利的创刊初衷是打破当时伦敦一些有权势的医生和外科医生组成的小团体，打击他们通过私人垄断医学知识牟取高额利润的行为。威克利还希望借创刊对重要的临床病例进行"正确描述"（a correct description），形成"当代文献的完整编年史"（a complete chronicle of the current literature）。威克利知道自己将面临"相关利益者的反对"（interested opposition），因此他将《柳叶刀》视为一把利器——这也是该刊不同寻常的名字的由来，希望借此剔除医学界的腐败。

如今，《柳叶刀》已经发展成为一个下设 24 种子刊的期刊家族。作为一份权威的世界医学综合期刊，《柳叶刀》注重建设数字化出版和新媒体融合发展的生态体系，在多个社交媒体上拥有粉丝数量超过 180 万名，但依然秉承其核心理念，即"医学必须服务社会，知识必定改变社会，用最好的科学创造更好的生活"[①]。其强调增加科学的社会影响，通过《柳叶刀》专辑和重大报告等形式对政策和政治产生影响，不断向世人证明科学期刊的格局以及所能做到的程度应高于仅反映医学发现这一层次。《柳叶刀》积极参与政治辩论并发挥作用，以专家视角讨论政治、医学、医学科学和全球卫生等问题，不断学习为这些辩论做出直接贡献，参与全球治理。[②]

（一）发展历程

《柳叶刀》创刊于 1823 年，初创阶段的目标是揭露医学界的弊端和不正之风。通过报道医学新闻、发表评论等形式，《柳叶刀》希望推动医学的发展与进步，为医学界带来改革，提高透明度。随着 20 世纪的到来，《柳叶刀》开始迈向国际化，在纽约设立了分支办公室，期刊内容变得更加全球化，刊登了更多国际性的医学研究成果，为不同地区的医疗研究者提供了重要的交流平台。二战期间，由于战乱带来的巨大挑战，《柳叶刀》被迫进行内容和方向上的转型。这一时期，《柳叶刀》开始探索更适应时代背景的办刊方式。进入 21 世纪，《柳叶刀》逐步拓展其学术影响力和刊物体系。2000 年，《柳叶刀》创办了第一份专业学术期刊——《柳叶刀·肿瘤学》（The Lancet Oncology），主要关注肿瘤疾病及其相关研究。这标志着《柳叶刀》从单一的综合性医学刊物发展为专业领域细分的学术期刊集团。2004 年，《柳叶刀》在北京设立分支办

---

① The Lancet. The Lancet. [2023-06-10]. https://www.thelancet.com/.
② The Lancet. The Lancet. [2023-06-10]. https://www.thelancet.com/.

公室，这一举措促进了更适合中国读者需求的研究与数据分析，推动了中国在全球卫生领域中的参与与合作。2013 年，《柳叶刀·全球健康》（*The Lancet Global Health*）创刊，这是《柳叶刀》关注全球健康挑战的重要里程碑。随后在 2016 年，《柳叶刀·公共卫生》（*The Lancet Public Health*）等子刊相继创刊，进一步拓宽了《柳叶刀》的研究视野与领域。2019 年，为了更好地聚焦不同区域的健康问题，《柳叶刀》推出了《柳叶刀·区域健康》（西太平洋篇）（*The Lancet Regional Health—Western Pacific*），之后又陆续推出涵盖美洲、欧洲和东南亚地区的区域健康期刊，推动全球健康研究进入更精细化的阶段。2023 年，《柳叶刀》迎来了创刊 200 周年。经过两个世纪的发展，《柳叶刀》已经成为全球医学界最具影响力的期刊之一，其刊物体系和国际化视野使其在医学科学研究中占据重要地位。

（二）学科及读者定位

《柳叶刀》的学科定位非常明确，主要涵盖临床医学、公共卫生和全球健康等领域，力求成为医学界权威的发声机构。其发表文章的类型有：原创性研究（Article，包括RCT和META分析）、综述（Review）、研讨会（Seminar）、卫生政策（Health Policy）、治疗方法（Therapeutics）、述评（Comment）、临床图片（Clinical Picture）、通讯（Correspondence）和全球报道（World Report）；也发表专辑（Series）和重大报告（Commission），旨在塑造和推动临床实践，为公共卫生和全球健康政策方面带来更多积极的改变。

《柳叶刀》的读者主要包括：医学专业人士，如临床医生、研究员、教育工作者和卫生管理员等；生命科学领域的研究人员和科学家；医药产业从业人员，如制药公司的研发人员、营销人员和管理人员等；政策制定者和决策者，如卫生部门官员、医疗保险机构、健康组织和政策研究人员等；学术界、媒体和公众等其他相关人士。

（三）国际成就及地位

《柳叶刀》的成就覆盖范围广泛，对推动医疗事业做出了巨大贡献。1867 年，英国医生约瑟夫·李斯特（Joseph Lister）在《柳叶刀》上发表文章 "On the Antiseptic Principle in the Practice of Surgery"，提出外科手术消毒的技术和理论，世界上大多数国家很快接受了这一理论和方法，使手术后的病人死亡率大大下降。1940 年，霍华德·弗洛里（Howard Florey）和恩斯特·鲍里斯·钱恩（Ernst Boris Chain）在《柳叶刀》发表了有关青霉素价值的论文，证明了青霉素可以治疗细菌感染，具有治疗作用，并建立了从青霉菌培养液中提取青霉素的方法。1984 年 6 月，两位澳大利亚研究者巴里·马歇尔（Barry Marshall）和罗宾·沃伦（Robin Warren）在《柳叶刀》上发表文章，提出细菌"幽门螺杆菌"是导致溃疡的罪魁祸首，并凭此获得了诺贝尔奖。

在这些大量实质性的科学贡献之外，《柳叶刀》在改革医疗行业、医院体系等方面也发挥了巨大作用，逐渐改变了创办之初（伦敦）医学界充斥着裙带关系和腐败的情况，揭露了许多临床实践的不足，为改善医学教育的不平衡和提高医疗服务的公共问责程度做出了可以被视为现代医疗保健开端的巨大贡献。

此外，在 2022 年，《柳叶刀》在尼日利亚推动了《柳叶刀》尼日利亚重大报告（Lancet Nigeria Commission）的完成，取得了惊人成绩。在这份报告中，尼日利亚人和尼日利亚侨民讲述了自己国家的故事，表示国家未来的机遇"需要健康的人口来提供"，而"健康研究和构建健康体系是健康人口能够实际带来的红利之一"，并对尼日利亚的愿景展开充分想象，推动政府在数周或数月内签署了相关文件，将有关保险、全民保险、健康保险的一般意见纳入法律，直接推动了尼日利亚医疗覆盖率的提高，开启了新的政治篇章。

现在，《柳叶刀》是世界上最悠久、最受重视的同行评审医学期刊之一，被视为核心权威的世界医学综合期刊，与另外三份国际医学期刊《新英格兰医学杂志》《美国医学会杂志》《英国医学杂志》并称为国际四大医学期刊。2021 年在内科学期刊中影响因子超过《新英格兰医学杂志》排名第一，且是四大期刊中被引用次数最多的医学杂志。

（四）全球范围内的学术和社会影响力

1.学术影响力

《柳叶刀》系列期刊在全球范围内有广泛的影响力。官方网站 thelancet. com 的年度访问量超过 4250 万，《柳叶刀》在 thelancet.com 和 ScienceDirect 的年度文章下载量达 2.69 亿篇。①

《柳叶刀》是全球顶尖的临床、公共卫生和全球卫生知识来源，在全球所有全科和内科学期刊中排名第一，2021 年影响因子为 202.731，Scopus

① The Lancet. The Lancet. [2023-06-10]. https://www.thelancet.com/.

CiteScore 为 115.3。

2.社会影响力

此外，《柳叶刀》及下设期刊在社交平台上拥有超过 180 万粉丝，《柳叶刀》系列期刊的邮件订阅超过 350 万，其播客每月约有 7.6 万次收听。《柳叶刀》系列期刊发表的研究每年被全球各大有影响力的媒体提到的次数超过 36.3 万次。[①]

二、发展要素分析

（一）组织架构

《柳叶刀》采用类似于其他大型期刊的组织架构方式，包括总编辑部、副编辑部、编辑部、生产部、财务部等。总编辑部负责杂志的整体规划和战略决策，副编辑部负责专业领域划分和论文审稿，编辑部负责论文编辑和排版，生产部负责印刷和发行，财务部负责财务管理和预算控制。

（二）运行机制

《柳叶刀》下设 24 种子期刊，运行机制属于大型出版集团出版模式，由爱思唯尔（Elsevier）作为期刊零售发行的全权代理，每周出版一期，邮局负责邮寄，发行专业化、科技化、现代化水平高，征订、收款、邮寄一条龙服务。作者和外部同行评审审稿人与《柳叶刀》的专业编辑合作。外部同行评审审稿人与《柳叶刀》的专业编辑采取讨论审议的方式对稿件进行审核，确定稿件的科学性、合理性和实用性。期刊遵循爱思唯尔的出版伦理，即各方均需互相尊重，抵制一切形式的歧视、骚扰、霸凌和报复。

1.编辑部和编委会的组成

《柳叶刀》的编辑部位于英国伦敦，并在纽约、北京、新德里和圣保罗设有办事处。该杂志的编辑部由数十名专业编辑和支持人员组成，他们负责协调和管理期刊的内容、发行和营销等方面的工作。同时，该期刊还拥有包括诺贝尔奖得主在内的多位国际知名专家组成的编委会，他们负责评审和指导论文的发表。为了保证期刊内容的质量和对不同专业领域的审视角度，《柳叶刀》设立了多个编委。2023 年 5 月《柳叶刀》官网显示，《柳叶刀》编辑部有主编 1 人，副主编 1 人，高级执行编辑 5 人，执行编辑 3 人，责任编辑 2 人，高级

---

① The Lancet. The Lancet. [2023-06-10]. https://www.thelancet.com/.

编辑9人，亚洲、北美等各地区执行编辑以及高级助理编辑、助理编辑等数十人。

2. 文章的收集和评审

《柳叶刀》接受来自全球各地的原创性研究论文、综述性论文、社论以及一些特别报道、评论和新闻等内容。这些文章经过编辑部的初步筛选后，会交由知名专家进行同行评审，以确保文章的科学可信度和质量。

所有提交给《柳叶刀》期刊的文章都首先由其内部专家编辑团队进行审查。很大比例的研究论文在此阶段就被拒绝。如果编辑有意向继续处理某篇论文，将根据文章选择合适的同行评审。

在同行评审期间，编辑将选择反映相关专业知识、多样性和地理背景的评审人员。在《柳叶刀》期刊发表的所有原创研究文章都经过独立的外部同行评审——一篇研究论文通常由三名临床或以学科专家和一名统计学评审进行同行评审。评审人员可以查阅作者提交的手稿和任何附录。如果论文是随机对照试验，评审人员还可以查阅试验方案。最终，评审意见将被匿名发送给作者（除非同行评审人员希望公开）。总的来说，同行评审协助编辑决定是否发表一篇文章，并帮助作者修订、改进他们的稿件。同行评审人员分析、批评并提出改进建议，向作者和编辑提供建议。如果需要进行大范围的修订，则修订后重新提交的文章可能会再一次经历同行评审，以征求进一步意见。

同行评审后，研究论文将会在多学科编辑会议上进行讨论。来自《柳叶刀》所有期刊的编辑都会参加会议，并就研究与子期刊的相关性、重要性和质量提供他们的专业意见。编辑们还将讨论研究论文最适合在哪一本《柳叶刀》期刊上发表。同行评审员可能会被邀请撰写一篇相关评论，与研究文章一起发表。如果论文在同行评审后被《柳叶刀》期刊拒绝，同行评审意见将与作者分享，以帮助改进稿件并提交给其他期刊。同行评审人员可能会被邀请写一篇相关评论，与研究文章一起发表。

作为同行评审过程的延续，《柳叶刀》在发表论文前会进行最后审查。在详细的编辑过程中，助理编辑会检查论文中的不一致、不准确和含糊之处，然后与作者讨论最后的问题。他们与制作团队紧密合作，将论文及其插图转换成专业格式，并进行最后的质量控制检查。这一过程有助于减少出版后可能需要更正的错误，并确保研究能够被广泛的国际读者充分理解，使其对世界的影响最大化。

综上可见，同行评审是《柳叶刀》期刊审稿流程中非常重要的一个环节，短则四周，长则十周，其专家团队的成员构成较其他期刊也更为丰富、人数更多。需要注意的是，和其他期刊一样，在决定是否让《柳叶刀》是否发表某一篇文章时，拥有最终决定权的依然是编辑，尽管他们会充分尊重同行评审的意见。

3. 发布形式和频率

《柳叶刀》每周出版一次印刷版和数字版，其中数字版可以通过网站或移动应用程序进行访问。该期刊还为作者提供了开放获取（Open Acess）的选项（见图1），并在其网站上提供了一些免费的论文和文章。

《柳叶刀》作者直接在互联网公开发表自己的科学成果，允许社会公众自由获取、复制、传播或其他任何合法目的的利用，但不得侵犯作者保留的权利。

对于读者而言，开放获取内容丰富及时。

THE LANCET 国际标准刊号：0140-6736
包含开放获取内容

内容类型	订户	注册用户	客座访客
摘要/预览	✓	✓	✓
社论、通信	✓	✓	✓
临床图片、讣告、观点、世界报告	✓	✓	✗
选择全球健康内容	✓	✓	✗
精选免费全文研究文章、评论内容和评论	✓	✓	✗
全文研究文章、评论内容和评论	✓	✗	✗

图 1 《柳叶刀》开放获取内容

（资料来源：https://www.thelancet.com/）

对于投稿者而言，开放获取利弊参半。一方面，开放获取期刊有录用概率高、保有著作权、文章引用率影响力等大幅上升、审稿和在线发表时间更快、录用后发表时间较短等优势。另一方面，开放获取期刊普遍存在审稿不严、滥发论文的问题，期刊质量和口碑不如传统期刊，文章处理费过高。

4. 收入来源

《柳叶刀》的收入主要来自广告、订阅费用、会议赞助和开放获取费用等方面。其中，广告收入和订阅费用是其最主要的收入来源。

5. 读者服务和市场营销

《柳叶刀》致力于为读者提供高质量的内容和优质的服务，通过完成与其他学术出版物的比较以及市场研究和分析来确定其方针和战略。此外，该期刊还提供了多种数字化订阅和在线获取选项，并为作者和读者提供了各种信息和支持。例如，《柳叶刀》搭建了集数字出版、知识单元、延伸服务、多媒体发布于一体的官方网站，利用多种社交媒体、移动终端推广精彩内容和品牌，形成了数字化出版和新媒体融合发展的生态体系。一方面，官网对系列期刊的内容资源整合分类，其专栏"头条专题"选取了相关度高的热点权威内容（通常是重大疾病或公共卫生问题），充分发挥了刊群的集束效应，辅以精美的图片封面，吸引读者，增加点击率；栏目"最新消息及评论"多针对临床热点难点或关系重大的公共健康问题，采用了精美的概念图片，较有视觉冲击力；栏目"最新研究"挑选本领域可能产生较大影响的研究论著，位于网页最显眼的位置，使最好的内容获得最佳展示度。另一方面，在官方网站之外，《柳叶刀》还积极开设其他社交媒体用户，在微信、微博、Facebook、X都有官方账号。开设主流媒体平台账户使得其参与全球治理的作用扩大，并不断向民众渗透，增强其在民间的影响力。在这类媒体中，《柳叶刀》发表的内容多为短小、精简、易读的小文章，符合碎片化阅读的特点，也满足时效性的要求。此外，《柳叶刀》也常在此类社交媒体上发布活动，如免费阅读、有奖竞猜、摄影比赛等，提高其订阅用户的活跃度，使一份顶级医学期刊更加平易近人。

6. 组织线上和线下的学术活动

《柳叶刀》积极开展线上和线下活动，例如国际医学会议、公共卫生研讨会等。自2015年起，《柳叶刀》与中国医学科学院开始共同主办"柳叶刀－中国医学科学院医学与健康大会"（The Lancet–CAMS Health Conference）。2022年11月30日至12月1日，《柳叶刀》与中国医学科学院北京协和医学院共同主办第八届"柳叶刀－中国医学科学院医学与健康大会"。《柳叶刀》从2020年开始发布首个《柳叶刀人群健康与气候变化倒计时中国报告》。2022年10月29日，《柳叶刀·公共卫生》发表第三个年度中国报告《2022年柳叶刀人群健康与气候变化倒计时中国报告：以气候行动助力健康老龄化》。2018年4月17日，《柳叶刀》发表"清华大学－柳叶刀中国健康城市重大报告：释放城市力量，共筑健康中国"。2022年11月21日，《柳叶刀》发表"北京大学－柳叶刀重大报告：中国的健康老龄化之路"。

7.以创新生态圈理论解释《柳叶刀》的运行机制

从生态学角度出发，自然生态圈是有机物与无机环境长期相互作用、相互耦合而产生的，地理依赖性、区域性、动态性特征显著。创新生态圈理论利用生态隐喻手法，将生态圈、创新发展理论引进科技期刊界，构建结构有序、动态演变、弹性包容的科技期刊创新生态圈理论架构。科技期刊创新生态圈概念可以界定为：基于信息、技术、人才、资金等创新要素，以科技期刊为演化载体，以科技创新环境为支撑环境，生产者、消费者、分解者等相互依赖、共生共赢，进而形成具有一定边界且稳定持续的知识经济创新体系。科技期刊负载的创新信息、知识等要素在各主体间流动、循环并变现和增值。[①]

基于创新生态圈理论，《柳叶刀》的运行机制可以拆解如下（图2）。

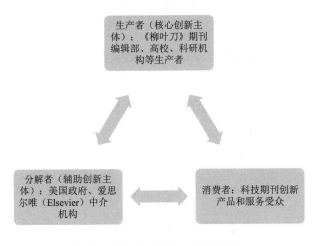

图2 《柳叶刀》期刊的运行机制

（1）生产者的创新核心：《柳叶刀》科技期刊编辑部作为生产者中的创新核心，承上启下、承前启后，一方面，向上游吸引和发表高校、科研机构的高端人才所掌握的先进科学技术成果和创新思维研究成果——创新性富集论文；另一方面，聘请和引进高校、科研机构培育出的创新人才和研制出的新技术，全方位进入科技期刊编辑部编—印—发生产链条。二者相结合，最终实现创新知识、技术、人才向消费市场流动。

---

① 费必胜，周海鹰，吕悦，等.科技期刊"创新生态圈"理论体系研究.科技通报，2021，37(9)：121-126.

（2）生产者直接对接消费者和分解者：《柳叶刀》将其创新产品或服务向消费者进行推介，接受市场的严格检验与分解淬炼，最终提升创新支撑环境质量，消费者、分解者的反馈还可为《柳叶刀》编辑部调整创新活动方向提供参考和指向。

（3）消费者引领甚至改变科技期刊生产者的创新范式：一方面，消费者需求决定科技期刊生产者创新活动的内容、方向。另一方面，消费者购买并体验科技期刊创新产品或服务后产生的反馈信息，对《柳叶刀》生产者新一轮创新活动方向起到引导、调节作用。

（4）分解者作为辅助创新主体：美国政府为科技期刊生产者提供扎实的硬件环境，如提升相关基础设施建设水平等，为科技期刊生产者创新活动"减压""助力"。爱思唯尔中介机构为生产者创新活动落到实处疏通了创新生态圈要素间的信息交流桎梏，提速创新信息、要素交互流动，令创新产品问世周期大大缩短。

（三）作为知识共同体参与全球气候和健康治理

1. 知识共同体的定义

学术界对于知识共同体的普遍认识是专业人士借助于他们的专业知识并形成具备共同因果信念和政策目标的专家网络。知识共同体不停留在生产和提供所谓中立客观的知识，而会进一步积极影响政策制定的过程。基于此，我们可以分析《柳叶刀》期刊如何参与全球气候变化的治理，并为其他非政府间组织参与全球治理提供建议。

2.《柳叶刀》知识共同体形成的基础

专业知识基础——内容基础以及权威地位。

意见交流机制——交流平台、数据共享、读者和作者之间进行科学辩论。

基本规则和程序——期刊审核规则。

3.《柳叶刀》期刊参与全球气候治理的路径

（1）提供知识平台，促进国际合作

以英国为例，《柳叶刀》与伦敦大学学院拥有多个合作项目，例如Lancet and University College London Institute for Global Health Commission、the UCL-Lancet Commission on Migration and Health等，致力于与政府共同行动缓解气候变化问题。伦敦大学学院与英国的地方政府协会（Local Government

Association，LGA）合作密切，而后者是代表地方政府发声的重要渠道，也使得《柳叶刀》间接参与政府领导的气候治理中。除伦敦大学学院外，《柳叶刀》还与奥斯陆大学、贝鲁特美国大学等世界各地的高等学府有着类似的合作机制。

此外，《柳叶刀》与洛克菲勒基金会的合作项目与联合国气候变化框架公约（United Nations Framework Convention on Climate Change，UNFCCC）合作，共同为联合国全球气候行动奖中的"地球健康"奖项提供支持，这是《柳叶刀》与国际组织的直接合作中具有代表性的一项。

《柳叶刀》还主办或参与了多个国际性的医疗和卫生领域的会议、研讨会和论坛等，这些活动为各国专家和学者提供了交流合作的平台，促进不同国家之间的合作，推动全球卫生和医疗治理水平的提高。

（2）引领研究方向，前瞻国际治理

从其专业性来看，《柳叶刀》专家组成员将其公有知识延伸至政治决策，通过发表具有国际影响力的研究成果、评论文章和社论等形式，影响国家决策。大国一旦认可《柳叶刀》期刊，并将其进行分享和传播，大国的影响力会对其他国家产生促进作用。

（3）科普带动舆论，影响政府决策

一方面，《柳叶刀》上发表的文章经过媒体等传播，给大众普及了知识，经有识之士的整理和宣传，最终影响政府决策。例如，尼日利亚重大报告"The Lancet Nigeria Commission: Investing in Health and the Future of the Nation"等。另一方面，网络上也存在着不少对《柳叶刀》刊载的文章或其主编在社交平台发表的观点的批评①，具体观点如在巴以冲突中对在巴勒斯坦存在的政治迫害提出批评、呼吁关注巴勒斯坦青年的心理问题而鲜少提及以色列是否也存在相似情况等。这些批评认为，这种失之偏颇的文章或发言损害了《柳叶刀》作为科学期刊的中立原则。《柳叶刀》及其旗下期刊过去几度发文，呼吁加大对烟草的监管，这一行为也备受批评。但是，从知识共同体的角度来看，由于像《柳叶刀》这样具有巨大学术影响力的期刊同时承担着为政府提供治理意见的责任，此类行为都是说得通甚至值得支持的。

事实上，《柳叶刀》在创刊初期就具有鲜明的政治性。21世纪的医学领域

① The Lancet. The Lancet. [2023-06-10]. https://www.algemeiner.com/2012/03/11/the-lancet-a-biased-and-shameful-medical-journal/.

可能不同往昔，但在 19 世纪就存在的医疗实践不平等问题在当下依然严峻，包括权力不平衡、资源不平等以及高质量卫生服务可及性不公平。因此，威克利的理念——《柳叶刀》的格局应该高于"做一本用于记录的科学期刊"——在今天仍具有鲜活的生命力。学术界、医学界对社会进步的贡献被严重忽视，而《柳叶刀》系列期刊所发表的科学成果可作为工具，加快推动旨在促进健康和健康平等的行动。换言之，对《柳叶刀》而言，医学和医学研究兼有政治活动和科学活动的属性，这也符合知识共同体理念。

《柳叶刀》为医学的发展提供了可靠的观点，但它不只是医学的一面镜子。技术、信息时代居民与技术的互动方式等多种因素已经改变了医学研究，影响了其运作方式及对社会的影响。在在线出版的时代，大多数期刊只是成为最新研究的存储库。如果一本期刊只是作为最新研究的存储库，公正地发表投稿研究文章中的 10％ 或 20％，此时它虽然是一个可搜索和免费获取文章的数据库，可以集成千上万本期刊于一身，毕竟大多数期刊都只是存储库，但也面临着沦为工具的风险。

《柳叶刀》以及其他类似的期刊，为了对抗这种可能的危险，有意识地、自发地在努力代表特定问题发布一些内容。对于像《柳叶刀》这样有坚定信念的知识共同体而言，在作者为《柳叶刀》撰写文章或在《柳叶刀》上发表文章时，他就加入了一个拥有一整套价值观和目标的社区，同时也带着自己的价值观和目标，成为社区的一部分。知识共同体通过吸引特定的受众，摆脱了数据存储库的桎梏。

对于一个知识共同体的成分而言，出版倾向性是不可或缺的。期刊通过对价值观做出选择，通过选择事物、选择研究、选择想法，选择基于期刊认定的重要事项来撰写的文章，而不拘泥于读者对内容是反对还是赞成，成为一本具有较高科学标准和适用于这些标准的明确价值观的期刊，来达到自主参与全球治理的目的。

三、挑战以及对策分析

（一）挑　战

1.性别歧视等立场问题

在 2021 年 9 月 25 日的封面上，《柳叶刀》杂志以 "bodies with vaginas" 代

指女性，引发社会各界强烈不满。三天后，主编刊文致歉。[①]

2. 审稿问题以及论文质量下降

同行评审难以或无法根除论文稿件中的数据造假问题，撤稿事件多发，对期刊的声誉造成了严重影响。同时，由于在全球气候和健康领域并不只有《柳叶刀》这一知识共同体，多个知识共同体的意见相左使得《柳叶刀》难以发挥其在影响政府决策、促进国际合作等方面的作用。

3. 作者代表性不足

论文作者在族裔、性别等方面不够多元。

4. 对现时的国际热点议题反应不及时

气候变化与健康问题作为如今的全球热点议题，也是重大的健康议题，《柳叶刀》却未能作为一个主要发声者和意见提供者在全球治理中完全发挥自己的价值和意义。《柳叶刀》还没有开发出有效的方法来选择、组织和呈现新的研究，以加深了解和改善应用。

5. 运行机制日趋集中

《柳叶刀》的集团出版社运营模式使得资本日益集中化，期刊企业的集团化趋势已经越来越明显。

6. 人工智能造成的学术伦理问题

目前期刊已经采用对"人工智能和人工智能辅助技术在科学写作中的应用"的相关规定，规定人工智能只能"用于提高作品的可读性和语言，不能取代研究人员的任务"。但是目前很难判定人工智能的参与度，这在很大程度上提升了审稿难度。

7. 内容转型

在过去，《柳叶刀》一直致力于成为医学知识的"一站式提供者"，使读者每周阅读《柳叶刀》就能了解全科医学的所有主要进展，但如今每个专业领域的所有细节显然不可能被完全涵盖。

（二）建 议

1. 提升编委会代表性

在注重专业素养的同时，实现编辑年龄、性别、族裔的多元化，确保不同

---

① Newey, S. Lancet accused of sexism after calling women 'bodies with vaginas'. (2021-09-25)[2023-06-10]. https://www.telegraph.co.uk/news/2021/09/25/lancet-receives-complaints-scientists-quit-sexist-cover-calling/.

的声音被听见。这不仅能够确保不同领域、文化、社会视角的交叉融合，更有助于拓宽编委会的视野，提升对多样化学术议题的敏感性和包容度。通过推动编辑团队的多元化，可以更好地反映全球化学术研究的真实面貌，确保不同的声音被平等地听见，尤其是那些来自少数群体、发展中国家或非主流学科的意见和建议。与此同时，多元化的编委会能够推动学术交流的公平性与开放性，在提高期刊学术水平的同时，也促进了学术出版界的整体公正与多样性发展。

2. 坚定立场

在学术出版中，期刊和编委会可以在特定问题上表达个人或集体的观点，以推动学术讨论和社会进步。然而，这种立场必须建立在公正、透明和严谨的基础上，而不能受到利益关系、偏见或固有观念的干扰。表达观点需要以事实和科学依据为核心，确保其独立性和客观性，避免因为外部压力、经济利益或特定团体的影响而出现倾向性或偏袒争端中某一方的情况。坚定而中立的立场不仅是期刊声誉和公信力的关键保障，也是促进学术界公平和自由交流的重要责任。通过对复杂问题进行多角度分析，期刊和编委会能够引导更深层次的学术探讨，并在社会热点问题上为读者提供有意义的参考意见，而不是简单地迎合某一方的利益或观点。这种立场不仅体现了学术出版的责任感，也有助于构建一个更透明、更可信的知识传播环境。

3. 提升期刊内容生产全链条的民主性

排查是否存在过分尊重编委会的专业意见，以至于编辑发现问题但不敢提出的现象，并加以解决。在学术出版中，编委会的专业意见至关重要，但若编辑团队过分依赖或敬畏其权威，可能导致发现问题却不敢质疑的现象，这将影响出版质量与公正性。为解决这一问题，需建立开放的沟通机制，通过定期会议、反馈渠道等方式，鼓励编辑提出问题并确保其不会因质疑编委会而感到压力。同时，加强编辑专业培训，提高其学术判断能力，使其能够自信地对编委会意见进行独立评估。此外，应明确编辑与编委会的职责边界，建立问责机制，确保最终的出版决策在透明的监督下进行。营造平等合作的工作氛围，打破对权威的盲目依赖，让编委会与编辑团队形成有效协作。通过这些措施，可以在尊重编委会意见的基础上，增强编辑团队的独立性和主动性，确保学术出版质量不断提升，为期刊的可持续发展奠定坚实基础。

4. 关注健康焦点领域

《柳叶刀》曾将期刊的所有编辑和工作人员的优先事项提炼成一组主题，

称为五个健康焦点领域（Spotlights）：儿童和青少年健康（Child and Adolescent Health）、气候与健康（Climate and Health）、精神健康（Mental Health）、全民健康覆盖（Universal Health Coverage）和健康研究（Research for Health）。这本身是一件很有价值的事。《柳叶刀》应当进一步致力于吸引大众对这五个主题的关注，通过策划一系列的活动来支持这些焦点领域更具体的诉求。可以制作新的内容，借助多媒体视频、播客、网络研讨会等来讨论特定的主题，并与其他组织合作以吸引大众关注特定问题。最终，将所有的期刊作为一个平台，真正扩大这五个焦点领域相关信息的传播。

合作也十分重要，因为与他人合作时，自己才会更具影响力，也更有可能实现上述的诉求。通过合作，最终推动实现全民健康覆盖，实现：（1）将儿童置于社会政策的核心；（2）终结精神疾病领域的污名和歧视；（3）将健康引入气候危机的重要领域，推动气候和健康相关的行动。

鉴往知来:《美国医学会杂志》140 年[①]

摘　要:《美国医学会杂志》(*Journal of the American Medical Association*,*JAMA*)是四大顶级医学期刊之一,在国际医学界拥有广泛的影响力。在成立的 140 年间,*JAMA* 不仅深耕主刊,还下设 12 本子刊,为医学各分支领域的研究提供交流平台。*JAMA* 目前的高水平发展,主要源于完善的组织架构、高质量医学共同体和严谨的运行机制。本文基于对 *JAMA* 发展历史的回顾,以及与其他医学期刊的比较分析,指出 *JAMA* 具有开放获取不足、学术资源不够系统、社交媒体影响力不足的特点,并基于此提出三个相应的发展方向,即扩大开放获取、构建知识单元、打造多元社交媒体平台,希望能有利于 *JAMA* 在中国乃至全球影响力的扩大。

关键词:《美国医学会杂志》;医学期刊;发展历程;问题与对策

一、期刊概览

(一)期刊主题

《美国医学会杂志》(*Journal of the American Medical Association*,*JAMA*)是一本备受国际医学界重视的期刊,由美国医学协会(American Medical Association,AMA)出版,是四大顶级医学期刊之一,也是世界上发行范围最广的综合性医学期刊之一,被 BA、CA、IPA、MEDLINE、SCI、Abstr Hyg、Nutr Abstr 等国际上著名检索工具书收录。该期刊主要刊载临床及实验研究论

① 作者:陈泽琨,清华大学万科公共卫生与健康学院;何宜航,清华大学人文学院;陈少茹,清华大学万科公共卫生与健康学院;马宁,清华大学万科公共卫生与健康学院。

文，还包括编者述评、读者来信等文章，除主要关注临床医学外，还涉及卫生保健、政治、哲学、伦理、经济、历史等非临床信息。该期刊的主要目标是促进医学研究的传播和交流，以推动医学知识的进步和医疗实践的发展。

同时，该期刊也拓展了系列子刊，除了 JAMA 主刊外，还有《JAMA 内科学》(JAMA Internal Medicine)、《JAMA 神经病学》(JAMA Neurology)、《JAMA 心脏病学》(JAMA Cardiology) 等共计 12 种子刊，涵盖了广泛的研究领域，从临床医学到基础医学、公共卫生、流行病学、医学教育和政策等各个方面。这些子刊以其独特的定位和专业性，为学术界和临床实践者提供了一个权威的平台，促进了不同领域之间的交流和合作。

影响因子是衡量期刊在学术界的影响力和引用率的重要指标，基于 JAMA 及其子刊在全球医学界中的重要地位和广泛的学术影响力，其影响因子常常位居医学期刊的前列。JAMA 及其子刊凭借其多样性的子刊、高影响因子和广泛的内容覆盖范围，成为医学领域中不可忽视的存在。它们为学术界和临床实践者提供了一个重要的平台，促进了知识的交流、学术的进步和医学实践的发展。

JAMA 官网还设有 3 个特色专栏，分别是患者教育、医学研究及进展播客、医学新闻等。其中第二栏播客（JAMA Network Audio）包括各类文章的作者团队访谈、医学研究方法讨论、医学综述等，紧跟最新的研究进展，定期浏览可以紧跟科研趋势。

（二）发展历程

JAMA 的历史可以追溯到 1883 年。[1]当时，美国医学协会决定创建一本医学期刊，以促进医学研究的传播和学术交流。1883 年 4 月 14 日，第一期 JAMA 面世，作为月刊开始出版。创刊时，该期刊的主要目标是提高医学教育质量、改善临床实践和提升医疗专业道德。随着时间的推移，JAMA 逐渐发展壮大。1903 年，它开始以周刊形式出版，并迅速成为美国和全球医学界最重要的期刊之一。随着科学研究的进步和医学领域的不断发展，JAMA 逐渐扩大了其发表内容的范围，涵盖了临床医学、基础医学、公共卫生、疾病预防、医学伦理、医疗政策、医学教育等多个领域。无论是重大临床试验结果、重要的

---

① Lundberg, G. D. Plans for the centennial celebration of The Journal of the American Medical Association. JAMA, 1982, 248(2): 177.

医学评论，还是对医学伦理和政策的研究，都能在 *JAMA* 中找到。因此，它不仅吸引了来自美国各地的医学专家和研究人员的投稿，还成为国际医学界的学术交流平台。

一直以来，*JAMA* 的发表内容都引领着研究者关注最新的研究热点，推动并见证着医学专业的发展。穆斯塔法·阿卜杜拉（Moustafa Abdalla）等的研究[①]分析了从 *JAMA* 建刊以来文章中出现的特定疾病术语，反映了 *JAMA* 期刊的研究者和期刊编辑的兴趣，以及研究者关注点的变化。从分析中可以明显看到，*JAMA* 的研究热点与疾病谱的变化密切相关。例如，1880 年到 1920 年，*JAMA* 的研究热点主要是"结核病"；约 1950 年之后，"癌症""心脏疾病"以及"艾滋病"逐步成为研究热点，发表在 *JAMA* 上的相关文章越来越多；21 世纪之后，尤其是在 2020 年左右，"冠状病毒"研究激增。

（三）国际影响力

JAMA 以其高质量的学术内容和严格的同行评审流程而著称，在学术界具有卓越的声誉和权威性，在国际医学界具有广泛的影响力。到目前为止，*JAMA* 被认为是医学界顶尖期刊之一，与《新英格兰医学杂志》（*NEJM*）、《英国医学杂志》（*BMJ*）和《柳叶刀》（*The Lancet*）期刊并称为全球四大医学期刊。四大刊在文章类型、研究领域和编辑政策上各有侧重。*NEJM* 强调创新的临床研究和临床试验，专注于疾病的生物机制和治疗方法的进展。*The Lancet* 的国际视角则更加明显，关注全球健康、流行病学和公共卫生，经常发布全球卫生政策的专题报道。而 *BMJ* 则强调医疗实践的改进，注重临床决策的证据基础和卫生政策，特别关注医疗质量和患者安全，且内容具有较高的实用性和教育性。*JAMA* 则发表广泛的医学研究，特别注重美国和全球的公共卫生问题，经常探讨医学教育和医疗政策，多年来吸引了世界各地的优秀研究人员和专家投稿，促进了国际学术交流和合作。其发表内容对医学实践、政策制定和学术研究产生了深远的影响，而且发表的研究成果被广泛引用和参考。它是医学界不可或缺的重要资源之一，对推动医学研究、实践和政策发展起到了积极的引领作用。

JAMA 期刊的发展历程见证了其在医学界的巨大影响力和声誉的逐渐确

---

① Abdalla, M., Abdalla, M., Abdalla, S., Saad, M., Jones, D. S., Podolsky, S. H. Insights from full-text analyses of *the Journal of the American Medical Association* and *the New England Journal of Medicine*. *Elife*, 2022, 11: e72602.

立，它发表了许多重要的医学研究成果、临床试验结果、医学评论和综述等，其影响力扩展到了国际医学界。同时，该期刊也关注医学伦理、医疗政策和医学教育等领域的研究，推动医学专业的发展和医疗实践的改进。*JAMA* 的发表内容影响着医学界的实践和决策，不仅对改善公共卫生和提高患者护理质量起着重要作用，而且对临床实践、医学政策制定和学术界产生了深远的影响，使得该期刊在医学领域的地位不断巩固。

在学术影响力上，*JAMA* 创办迄今已有近 140 年的历史，目前有近 20 个在全世界各地发行的"国际版本"，有"国际大刊"的美誉。就影响因子而言，随着时间的推移，受到不同年份发表的论文数量、被引频次以及其他因素的影响，*JAMA* 的影响因子呈现出波动的趋势。但是大体上，*JAMA* 的影响因子呈逐步上升的趋势，尤其是 2021 年前后，*JAMA* 的影响因子暴涨了将近 100 分，影响因子排名则从第 13 上升到第 4，表明 *JAMA* 的影响力处于一个高速增长的状态（图 1）。

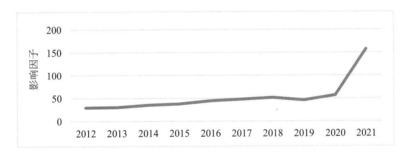

图 1　2010 年以来 *JAMA* 影响因子变化

随着时间的推移，*JAMA* 的发文数量逐渐增加（图 2）。这是由于医学研究的广泛发展和该期刊在医学界的影响力日益扩大。随着技术的进步和研究方法的创新，越来越多的学者和研究人员选择将他们的重要研究成果提交给 *JAMA* 期刊发表。此外，*JAMA* 的发表内容通常具有较高的引用率，反映了该期刊在学术界的重要性和影响力。

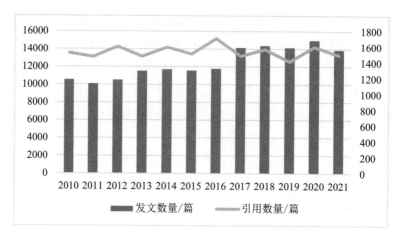

图 2　2010 年以来 *JAMA* 出版成果引用趋势分析

　　JAMA 对于全球医学界的影响力不仅仅体现在论文发表上，还体现在其促进医学专业交流和知识分享的平台角色上。在社会影响力上，*JAMA* 涵盖了广泛的医学领域，从临床医学到基础医学、公共卫生、医学伦理、医疗政策等。这种多学科的覆盖使得该期刊成为跨领域研究和综合医学知识的重要平台。它提供了全面而深入的学术见解，满足了不同领域的学者和专家的需求。由此，*JAMA* 成为了世界上发行最广泛的综合性医学期刊，有超过 28 万纸刊订阅者，160 万以上电子订阅者，以及每年超过 2700 万次的网站访问量。此外，*JAMA* 也通过不断增加的社交媒体影响力以及广泛的国际新闻媒体曝光增加自身的影响力。

二、发展要素分析

（一）组织架构

　　JAMA 由美国医学协会主办。美国医学协会创立于 1847 年，是一个专业性非常强的学术组织，会员覆盖了全美各地的医生和医学专业工作者，下设多个重要组织如美国医学教育会议、美国医学科研协会、美国医学政策研究所等。作为美国医学协会的官方期刊，*JAMA* 有着坚实的组织基础和雄厚的社会资源。

（二）高质量医学共同体

1.优秀编辑团队

医学出版是一个团队合作的事业，*JAMA* 的编辑和出版团队、编辑委员会以及成千上万位信任 *JAMA* 处理他们稿件的作者都发挥了重要作用。*JAMA* 的同行评议专家们提供了经过深思熟虑、富有学术价值的评价意见，对提高发表报告的质量起到了关键作用。*JAMA* 拥有经验丰富、在业界颇具影响力的编辑团队，这既提高了文章的质量，又使得作者们更为愿意将自己的最佳研究成果投稿至 *JAMA*。编辑团队在芝加哥的办公室全职工作，并吸纳了来自世界各地学术机构的专家。*JAMA* 致力于扩大 *JAMA* 及 JAMA Network 的工作团队，并确保团队的多样性，以充分满足作者和读者的需求，并以高度诚信的方式履行其使命。

2.高水平研究者

JAMA 的高影响因子及广泛的国际声誉使其吸引了众多高水平的医学研究者投稿。*JAMA* 及其子刊的内容覆盖范围广泛，涵盖了医学领域的各个方面。无论是临床研究、基础科学的探索、公共卫生政策的制定，还是医学教育的发展，*JAMA* 及其子刊都提供了全面而深入的报道和讨论。这种广泛的覆盖范围使得 *JAMA* 及其子刊成为医学界的权威之一，吸引了来自世界各地的优秀研究者和专家提交高质量的研究成果。

3.读者群体

JAMA 的核心读者主要来自三个群体：临床医生、医学科研者和医学教育工作者。*JAMA* 为这些读者提供了最新的医学研究成果、评论和观察，并就医学教育和政策等方面提供有益的见解。目前，约有 160 万人通过电子期刊目录和附有在线文章的电子邮件获取 *JAMA* 的内容，超过 120 万人在社交媒体上关注 *JAMA*。期刊内容的电子访问量非常可观，约 1.41 亿次文章浏览和下载来自 JAMA Network 期刊网站，其中超过 4600 万次浏览和下载来自 *JAMA*。*JAMA* 通过视觉摘要、图表、要点总结、患者指南、播客和视频等多种形式的内容，能够覆盖各个不同的读者群体。

（三）运行机制

1.投稿和审稿

JAMA 在医学出版领域首屈一指，其核心特点是严格的同行评审和编辑审

稿程序。*JAMA* 实行匿名同行评审制度，即稿件提交后，经过编辑部的初步筛选，然后由两名以上的专家进行审查。审稿过程严格保密，以确保公正性和准确性。在审稿过程中，为确保论文的独创性，有关过程和结果的任何讨论都不得发表。

JAMA 对稿件的质量把控要求非常严格，在每年投稿的 9400 多篇稿件中，*JAMA* 的录用率仅为 11%；在接收的 5200 多篇研究稿件中，录取率为 4%，总录用率仅为 9% 左右，这使得 *JAMA* 发表的文章具有质量较高的特点。为确保学术质量，*JAMA* 还会邀请学术大咖作为特邀编辑，带领团队对某一研究领域进行深入挖掘和研究。

2023 年 2 月 16 日的社论中，*JAMA* 重新推出了 JAMA 快速通道（JAMA Express）[①]，通过该程序，稿件将经过加快的审稿和处理流程，以在提交后的 4 周内被接受并进行在线首发出版。JAMA Express 主要服务于将在重大科学会议上作为最新研究成果展示的稿件或具有重大临床或公共卫生意义的时间敏感性研究。在疫情期间，*JAMA* 一直致力于加快审稿和发布对于了解 SARS-CoV-2 和治疗 COVID-19 患者至关重要的科学成果。通过重新推出 JAMA Express 以涵盖更广泛的科学范围，*JAMA* 认为及时传播新颖的科学见解对于高效传递现代医疗保健、推动知识进步以及将证据转化为政策和实践至关重要。

2. 出版和发行

作为全球范围内发行量最大的医学期刊之一，*JAMA* 以其高达 157.3 分的影响因子，在综合医学期刊中处于领先地位。以 2022 年为例，*JAMA* 在 COVID-19 研究方面发挥了重要作用，不仅刊发了大量 COVID-19 的原创研究，还深入探讨了疫情对科学和医学的影响。除此之外，*JAMA* 还关注其他重要的健康威胁，如枪支暴力、医疗保健获取渠道和生殖权等。通过发表试验、观察研究和政策分析，*JAMA* 为诸多重要问题提供了有力的证据支持，涵盖从危重病患者护理到肥胖症门诊管理等多个领域。此外，*JAMA* 还致力于发表综合证据和指南，以指导医学实践。通过发表美国预防服务工作组的 32 份报告，包括推荐声明、证据回顾、建模研究等，*JAMA* 为常见疾病和疾病干预的筛查提供了重要参考。

除此之外，*JAMA* 还致力于提供医学出版相关问题的指导。例如，*JAMA*

---

① Bibbins-Domingo, K., Christiansen, S. L., Curfman, G. & Flanagin, A. Relaunching JAMA Express. JAMA, 2023, 329(10): 800.

提供了有关临床试验结果报告、各类研究数据共享以及包容性语言使用的准则。此外，*JAMA* 还与《英国医学杂志》和斯坦福大学的元研究创新中心（Meta-Research）合作，于2022年9月举办了第九届同行评议和科学出版国际大会，与来自37个国家的参会者一起分享和讨论关于作者身份、利益冲突、可重复性、数据共享、研究不端行为、多样性与包容性、临床试验结果传播、社交媒体、开放获取和开放科学等方面的最新研究成果。

在2022年，*JAMA* 进一步加强了对高质量证据广泛和及时可得性的承诺，宣布允许作者在发表当天将其已接受的稿件存入公共知识库，以实现科学内容的公众可访问性。此外，向 *JAMA* 提交稿件的作者还受益于 JAMA Network 组成的13个期刊网络，其中包括11本医学专业期刊和全面开放获取的 JAMA 网络公开（JAMA Network Open）期刊。JAMA Network 期刊之间的联合出版政策和协调出版程序确保作者和读者能够及时和广泛地获取相关成果。

总之，正是由于其完善的组织架构、高质量的医学共同体、严谨的运行机制使得 *JAMA* 在过去的130多年中发展壮大，成为世界顶级医学期刊之一。

三、"鉴往知来"——不足与改进方向

JAMA 作为顶级医学期刊，在学术内容和质量上始终处于引领地位，吸引了大批高质量的研究，形成了数量庞大且稳定的读者群。当前，随着信息和网络技术的飞速发展，学术期刊数字化和全媒体融合发展已经成为不可阻挡的趋势，虽然 *JAMA* 目前已经有着成熟和成功的运营经验，但通过与其他顶级医学期刊的对比分析，本研究提炼出了以下不足与改进方向。

（一）开放获取不足

开放获取引文优势（Open Access Citation Advantage, OACA）理论认为，开放获取的引文具有以下四种优势：第一是曝光优势，越容易被读者发现阅读的文章，越容易被引用；第二是发布优势，发布范围越大的文章，越容易被引用；第三是选择优势，作者更愿意选择自己优质的文章进行开放获取模式发布，越容易被引用；第四是质量优势，质量越好的文章越容易在开放环境中脱颖而出，越容易被引用。[①]

OACA理论的出现意味着学术论文在开放获取的模式下，其学术影响力

---

① Eysenbach, G. Citation advantage of open access articles. *PLOS Biology*, 2006, 4(5): e157.

和社会影响力都会显著增加。许多研究也已经证实，老牌期刊在完成开放获取后，发表的文章数量和影响因子均有所增加，为期刊发展带来了积极影响。

目前，*JAMA* 开放获取的引文数量仅占 0.19％，而《柳叶刀》和 *BMJ* 分别达到了 3.15％和 4.70％。本研究认为，*JAMA* 拥有良好的经济基础、读者基础和稿件来源，在保证内容质量的前提下，可以尝试继续推动开放获取的发展，提升整体的影响力。

（二）学术资源不够系统

随着期刊数字化的不断发展，学术文献的数量呈爆炸式增长，从海量文献中快速筛选出所需内容是许多读者的需求。目前，JAMA Network 期刊网站主要按照时间序列排列了每期发表的文献，虽然能够帮助读者了解领域最新的科研动态，但对某一主题的系统性梳理需要花费大量时间。

而《柳叶刀》为解决这一问题，将期刊上发表的围绕某一主题的专题整理成"专辑"（Series）栏目，该栏目跨越整个刊群，突破了单刊限制，充分发挥集群化办刊的优势，形成了解决重大临床和公共卫生问题的专题集锦。例如"柳叶刀诊所"（The Lancet Clinic）根据全球疾病负担数据和临床实践需要，将期刊中与特定疾病相关的内容进行收集整理，对疾病的流行病学、发病机理、诊断和治疗等内容进行聚合，形成了疾病专辑。

本研究认为，*JAMA* 也需要完善期刊知识单元的构建，系统化整理学术资源，对内容进行挖掘、重组、荟萃，构建知识关联和知识拓扑，对期刊上发表的相同主题的文章定期整理形成一个系列，当读者搜索到其中一篇文献时，就可以得到从全方位、多角度剖析这一问题的系列文献和高关联度论文推荐，以满足读者个性化深度阅读的需求。

（三）社交媒体影响力不足

社交媒体平台是学术期刊进行跨媒体融合的主要阵地。学术期刊通过运营这些平台，可以弥补传统期刊在出版时效性、内容形式动态性等方面的不足，实现学术研究成果和科研动态的即时推送和传播，对扩大学术期刊的传播力和影响力具有现实意义。

目前，*JAMA* 已开通了 Facebook、X、YouTube 和 Instagram 等社交媒体账号，其在 YouTube 上的视频播放量也达到了千万级别，但 Facebook 和 X 等账号的粉丝量相比于 *BMJ*、《柳叶刀》和 *NEJM* 等其他顶级医学期刊较少。此外,《柳叶刀》、*BMJ* 和 *NEJM* 还积极运营新浪微博账号和微信公众号,作为其在中国宣传期刊品牌的主要阵地,而 *JAMA* 则没有相关账号注册(表1)。基于对上述顶级医学期刊社交平台运营情况的分析,本研究认为 *JAMA* 可从以下几个方面打造更加丰富多元的社交媒体平台,扩大期刊的传播力和影响力。

表1 四本国际顶级医学期刊媒体影响力一览

期刊名称	Facebook 粉丝数量 / 万	X粉丝 数量 / 万	YouTube 粉丝数量 / 万	Instagram 粉丝数量 / 万	新浪微博 账号	微信 公众号
JAMA	0.1	1.4	16.2	11.0	×	×
BMJ	11.3	49.4	3.6	×	×	√
《柳叶刀》	34.3	72.1	4.5	×	√	√
NEJM	185.2	89.6	11.1	48.9	√	√

1. 立足全球本土化

全球本土化强调在文化实践过程中全球性和本土性的互动。对于 *JAMA* 而言,全球本土化的传播策略,首先需要适应各国不同的社交媒体发展特点,选择合适的社交媒体平台。例如近些年来,微信公众平台的受众规模迅速扩大,在中国已经成为学术期刊进行跨媒体融合的主要阵地,不仅大量中文科技期刊采用微信公众号进行期刊宣传,许多国际顶级期刊也逐步进军微信,以提高其在中国读者中的传播影响力。本研究认为,*JAMA* 也可以尝试通过微信公众号等平台在中国传播和分享学术界科研成果及最新动态。

其次全球本土化也需要在宣传全球优秀研究成果的同时融入本土元素,例如《柳叶刀》、*BMJ* 和 *NEJM* 等经常推荐中国学者发表的研究成果,推荐最受中国读者关注的健康问题的系列文章,同时也会与中国学者进行交流与访谈,通过文字、音频和视频等多种形式对关键问题进行深入解读。

2. 开展双向互动

与用户的积极互动可以帮助期刊聚合同质人群,培育粉丝对期刊的黏性和忠诚度。借鉴其他期刊优秀的经验,本研究认为 *JAMA* 可以采用多种形式增加与读者的互动,例如举办主编见面会,向读者介绍期刊最新动态和当前主要关注的研究方向,帮助读者了解编辑部的工作流程,介绍学术论文从研究者投稿到编辑部处理稿件,再到出版的全过程,回答研究者关于期刊投稿的相关问题等;例如定期举办讲座、研讨会和学术会议等,邀请领域专家对领域发展进行介绍，邀请研究者报告优秀的科研成果，给来自世界各地的研究者提供交流探讨的平台等；例如举行有奖竞猜、征文比赛、摄影比赛等活动，通过通俗易懂的方式向大众科普健康知识。

四、总结与讨论

通过对 *JAMA* 140 年来的发展历程梳理，本研究认为完善的组织架构、高质量的医学共同体、严谨的运行机制是 *JAMA* 成为全球四大医学期刊之一的重要原因。基于对 *JAMA* 的分析与其他医学期刊的比较分析得出，*JAMA* 具有开放获取不足、学术资源不够系统、社交媒体影响力不足的特点，因此本文提出未来的三个发展方向，即扩大开放获取、构建知识单元、打造多元社交媒体平台，希望能有利于 *JAMA* 在中国乃至全球影响力的扩大。

世界一流期刊分析研究——以《柳叶刀》为例①

摘　要:《柳叶刀》是全球顶尖综合性医学期刊,在推动临床实践、公共卫生和全球健康发展中发挥着不可比拟的作用。本文基于前期调研,首先系统梳理了《柳叶刀》的发展历程,其次从创刊原则、读者定位、期刊组织架构等方面对《柳叶刀》进行发展要素分析,最后概述了《柳叶刀》目前发展所面临的挑战,并对其未来规划提出了一些建议和展望。本文希望以《柳叶刀》为例,分析得出世界一流期刊创办的成功经验。

关键词:《柳叶刀》;发展要素分析;对策分析

一、期刊概览

(一)期刊基本概述

《柳叶刀》(*The Lancet*)是全球顶尖综合性医学期刊,与《新英格兰医学杂志》(*The New England Journal of Medicine*)、《美国医学会杂志》(*The Journal of the American Medical Association*)、《英国医学杂志》(*British Medical Journal*)并称为"四大顶级医学期刊"。《柳叶刀》每周都会发表来自世界各地顶尖科学家的研究精粹,拥有首屈一指的全球覆盖面,对卫生事业的发展有着无可比拟的影响。自创刊以来,《柳叶刀》一直努力推动科学的广泛传播,让医学服务社会、改变社会并积极影响人们的生活。《柳叶刀》期刊制定了极高的发表标准,其发表的论文对科学和人类健康做出了重要贡献。《柳叶刀》欢迎各类对医学科学和临床实践具有启发和推动意义的原创文章的投稿,迄今已

---

① 作者:胡昌浩,武汉大学第一临床学院;孟于婷,武汉大学生命科学学院;李雨萱,武汉大学生命科学学院。

刊发一万余期。其发表文章的类型有：原创性研究（article）、综述（review）、研讨会（seminar）、卫生政策（health policy）、治疗方法（therapeutics）、述评（comment）、临床图片（clinical picture）、通讯（correspondence）、全球报道（world report）、专辑（series）和重大报告（commission）。《柳叶刀》期刊旨在推动临床实践，在公共卫生和全球健康政策方面做出贡献。[①]

《柳叶刀》是全球顶尖的临床、公共卫生和全球卫生知识的可信来源，在全球所有全科和内科学期刊中排名第一，2023年影响因子为168.9，Scopus CiteScore 为133.2。《柳叶刀》系列期刊在全球范围内有广泛的影响力。《柳叶刀》网站的年度访问量超过4250万，年度文章下载量达2.69亿次，系列期刊的邮件订阅量超过350万。此外，《柳叶刀》各刊发表的研究每年被各大媒体的新闻报道提到的次数超过36.3万次，在全球社交媒体上共有约180万粉丝，播客的每月收听人次约7.6万。[②]

2023年是《柳叶刀》创办200周年。200年来，《柳叶刀》栉风沐雨，砥砺前行，在世界医学与卫生领域做出了卓越贡献。经过200年间一代代的壮大，12任主编的发展革新，其旗下共拥有24本系列期刊，其中12本为金色开放获取期刊，12本为混合型期刊。2022年，有9本《柳叶刀》系列期刊的最新影响因子在各自领域内排名第一。200年间，人类的科技水平、医疗水平、社会环境、意识观念等都发生了巨大的变化。进入2000年后，《柳叶刀》开始创立其独立的专业学术期刊。从2000年《柳叶刀》第一本专业学术期刊《柳叶刀·肿瘤学》（The Lancet Oncology）创刊到2022年《柳叶刀·区域健康（东南亚）》（The Lancet Regional Health–Southeast Asia）创刊，其专业期刊覆盖面已从单纯的疾病探讨（包括肿瘤学、感染病学、神经病学、糖尿病与内分泌学、呼吸病学、精神病学、血液病学、艾滋病、胃肠病和肝病学、风湿病学等）到人类共同面临的亚健康问题以及科技与医学的紧密联系，并尝试对区域健康做出分析。2023年的《柳叶刀》聚焦于5个健康焦点领域，包括全民健康覆盖、儿童和青少年健康、精神健康、气候与健康以及健康研究。从它的聚焦面可以看出医学界开始重视以前容易忽视的非病理性问题，呼吁人们多多关注与环境、与他人、与自身的关系。

200年来，《柳叶刀》与社会各界的联系也愈发紧密，它积极参与性别平

---

① The Lancet. About The Lancet. [2024-05-25]. https://www.thelancet.com/lancet/about.

等、种族平等议题，助力落后国家和地区的医学发展，致力于促进医疗平等，提升研究与出版领域的多样性和包容性。例如，《柳叶刀》致力于在编辑顾问、同行评审审稿人及作者中，增加女性和来自中低收入国家科研同僚的数量与推行"不参加全男性专家组政策"。①

多元化的发展理念、严谨的求知态度使《柳叶刀》成为世界顶级医学期刊。正如lancet在英语中也有"尖顶穹窗"的意思，《柳叶刀》立志成为"照亮医学界的明窗"，像灯塔一样为医学界指明前进的方向。

（二）期刊发展历程

1.创刊初期：对抗早期英国医疗裙带关系

在《柳叶刀》第一期的序言中，《柳叶刀》杂志创始人托马斯·威克利（Thomas Wakley）阐述了该刊物的目标，即挑战医学界的赞助和贿赂行为，《柳叶刀》将刊登著名外科医生和内科医生的演讲，发表重要的医学案例，并以"通俗易懂的语言"呈现。威克利希望他的新期刊能够阻止迄今为止精英医疗实践的"神秘性"。

在19世纪之前，几乎任何人都可以声称自己接受过正规的医疗培训。药品的买卖在很大程度上也不受监管。精英阶层的裙带关系和任人唯亲盛行，对关键的医疗任命基于权力和影响力而非才能的不满情绪日益高涨。在《柳叶刀》的文章中，威克利越来越多地把矛头指向医学界的裙带关系。他认为，这减少了那些没有裙带关系的优秀医生的机会，从而降低了这一职业的质量。在1824年出版《柳叶刀》第二期时，威克利对伦敦医院的精英外科医生和内科医生进行更严格的审查。从那以后，《柳叶刀》从利己主义模式中脱颖而出，发表来自英国首都医院的报告。②

2.19世纪中期：解决城市卫生危机

与医疗行业的转变同时发生的是英国公共卫生危机的升级。城市发展和工业化创造了传染病容易传播和非传染性疾病猖獗的环境。工业化前的行政管理和基础设施不堪重负，而工作、住房和卫生系统则不受监管。在19世纪中期，肠道疾病、地方性肺结核、白喉以及呼吸系统疾病盛行。

① The Lancet. Advancing equity, diversity, and inclusion. [2024-05-25]. https://www.thelancet.com/equity-diversity-inclusion.

② Gorsky M. & Arnold-Forster, A. *The Lancet* 1823–2023: the best science for better lives. *The Lancet*, 2023, 402 (10409): 1284-1293.

在这一大背景下,《柳叶刀》期刊通过科学研究的发表解决了 19 世纪中期的城市卫生危机。首先,《柳叶刀》通过综合出生、婚姻和死亡登记总局的报告,显示了城市和农村人口以及不同阶层之间的死亡率差异,这些阶层分别被标记为"富裕""舒适""贫穷"和"悲惨"。统计表明,城市人口中较高的死亡率是由工业化引起的,其他因素包括过度拥挤和住宿问题。那些"恶劣、封闭、发臭的社区,就像勤劳的穷人居住的地方一样",其中"腐烂的呼气"滋生了"最致命的后果"的疾病。因此,《柳叶刀》敦促,出于人道主义和安全的原因,应该通过法律上可执行的环境改善措施来解决这些问题。此外,自1832 年霍乱大流行开始以来,《柳叶刀》上的研究文章、病例报告和通信不断引发关于霍乱病因的争论,为最终霍乱的消灭贡献了力量。

3. 20 世纪:从国际卫生到全球卫生

在第一次世界大战后,《柳叶刀》进行了向国际卫生组织联盟形式的转变,其既是政策学习的场所,也是在疾病分类标准化、疟疾控制和流行病预防等问题上进行跨国合作的场所。《柳叶刀》提出了超越民族国家的国际卫生结构的观点,这对于标准化规范、流行病控制、共享政策学习以及现在的发展援助都是必要的。《柳叶刀》支持世界卫生组织的理想主义目标,即"让所有人达到尽可能高的健康水平",而不仅仅是没有疾病。[1]

4. 21 世纪初期:持续推进全球健康

在 2000 年以后,《柳叶刀》将注意力转向慢性和非传染性疾病的预防和控制,特别是在中低收入国家。《柳叶刀》期刊于 2018 年组建了《柳叶刀》非传染性疾病和经济学问题工作组,并在工作组的五篇论文中,证明了贫困驱动非传染性疾病,且非传染性疾病反过来驱动贫穷的发生。此外,《柳叶刀》在报道和分析新发传染病方面也发挥了关键作用,其报道并分析了艾滋病大流行的开始,尽管其中许多报道都重述了对非洲人、海地人、男同性恋者和性工作者的有害成见。最近,该期刊对寨卡病毒、埃博拉病毒、COVID-19 进行了广泛的报道和分析。在 21 世纪初的第一个儿童健康系列活动之后,《柳叶刀》发表了许多关于全球健康中一些棘手的社会和文化问题的文章。其中一个例子是2022 年底发表的"种族主义、仇外心理、歧视和健康问题"专辑,呼吁采取"反种族主义行动和其他更广泛的措施",采取"交叉方法","有效解决人口中

---

① Gorsky M. & Arnold-Forster, A. The Lancet 1823–2023: the best science for better lives. *The Lancet*, 2023, 402 (10409): 1284-1293.

种族主义的原因和后果"。在《柳叶刀》创刊 200 周年之际，该期刊继续关注医疗保健领域尚未解决的 200 个焦点问题，是"影响全球健康的最关键问题"，其中包括全民健康覆盖、健康和气候变化，以及儿童和青少年健康等领域。

（三）《柳叶刀》与中国

随着中国在世界医疗进程中扮演越来越重要的角色，《柳叶刀》为了回应中国作者、读者的需求，在 2008 年创立了《柳叶刀》中文版。该刊物保持原刊的风格和特色，针对中国的需求翻译英文版的相关论文，并且还在其中添加了中国专家结合中国临床实践的点评和分析。除此之外，《柳叶刀》基本两年左右就会出一期有关中国医疗的专辑。2015 年的中国专辑已是《柳叶刀》第六次审视中国卫生系统。《柳叶刀》每年都会就中国卫生问题做一些系列报道，比如关于胎儿流产、死产的专题，青少年健康专题等。[1] 此外，从 2008 年开始，"柳叶刀—中国医学科学院医学科学峰会"于每年 10 月在北京举办，汇集了国内外多学科的医学科学研究界顶级科学家共商"健康大事"。在未来，我们相信《柳叶刀》与中国的关系将会愈发紧密，共同推进全球卫生事业的发展。[2]

二、发展要素分析

（一）期刊创立原则

《柳叶刀》认为：科学可以成为积极社会变革的工具，应该通过推进医学研究和科学进步来推动社会和政治变革。《柳叶刀》坚持"促进公平、多样性和包容性"的承诺，致力于提升研究与出版领域的多样性和包容性。《柳叶刀》希望能为推进医学研究和临床实践做出努力，为全球健康和公共卫生事业做出贡献。

（二）强势学科和读者定位

《柳叶刀》是世界上最具影响力的综合性医学期刊之一，其专注于公共卫生、全球健康和国际医疗研究相关的领域，致力于改善医疗健康并促进全球健康事业的发展，它所发表的文章主要源于医学、公共卫生、临床医学、卫生保健、生物医学研究等领域。

---

① 左娜. 理查德·霍顿：执《柳叶刀》剖析中国. 国际人才交流，2016(8)：28-31，72.
② 强薇. 理查德·霍顿：让《柳叶刀》成为讲述中国故事的平台. 国际人才交流，2020(7)：35-36.

其读者多为医学研究和临床实践领域的专业人士或相关人员，包括医生、研究人员、科学家、医学教育家和卫生政策制定者等。值得一提的是，出于该期刊的权威性和科学性，不少非专业的医学知识爱好者也是它的忠实读者。可见，《柳叶刀》受到医学界的整体青睐和普罗大众的广泛关注。

（三）期刊组织架构

《柳叶刀》集团组成包含主编、执行主编、副主编、编辑、出版、广告和营销等，同时，柳叶刀还会邀请各领域专家组成编委会。

编委会是《柳叶刀》乃至所有学术期刊的重要组成部分，其成员主要来自医学各个领域，由主编邀请或推荐，他们和主编之间有着紧密的联系和协作关系。一方面，编委会定期举行会议，与主编一起讨论和规划期刊的发展方向、制定和实施编辑方针，并就特定领域的问题提供建议和意见，以确保期刊的质量和稳定性。另一方面，编委会需要对投稿论文进行评审、建议和指导，并促进学术讨论，推动作者与《柳叶刀》集团的交流沟通。需要时，主编还会从编委会中挑选出最专业、最富责任心的成员来担任子委员会主席。

主编是该刊的最高负责人，一般由医学领域的著名专家或学者担任。目前《柳叶刀》的主编是理查德·查尔斯·霍顿（Richard Charles Horton）。他负责规划整个期刊的发展战略，并对最终发表的所有文章都负有最终审核的责任。一般而言，主编需管理编委会成员，确保编委会能够充分履职；同时，他还需协助编辑部门筛选出高质量的文章。

编辑部门是《柳叶刀》运作的重要部分，其任务包括但不限于稿件的收集、编写、修改、编辑和定稿等。编辑部门下面包括执行主编、副主编和编辑等职位。执行主编是主编的代理人，主要负责期刊的日常运营和管理。副主编通常具有知名的医学或公共卫生背景，能够代表主编进行学术交流和社会关系，并负责招募编委会成员、评审各种稿件、指导作者修改和协调编辑团队的工作。编辑是集团的重要组成成员，他们的主要职责是与作者联系，组织代表作者们的稿件，并对稿件进行评估和审稿。出版、广告以及营销部门主要负责该刊的出版印刷、管理和市场推广。

（四）成功发展要素

1. 建设重点突出、功能齐全、多媒体融合的专业化网站

《柳叶刀》集团的编辑政策随该行业的最佳实践及科学研究和学术出版内

容的不断变化而发展。此外,《柳叶刀》出版集团从 21 世纪初就开始积极拓展数字出版业务,努力满足用户个性化、多样化、差异化、优质化的内容获取需求,开拓多种新媒体传播渠道,目前已形成了多元化的数字出版业态,实现了内容资源的立体开发和版权的多维增值。

《柳叶刀》网站主页设计非常简约明了,大致分为期刊及其衍生内容展示、临床、全球健康以及联系服务等版块。各结构区划分清晰合理,分别承担相应的功能,具有较高的用户友好性。网站主页对系列期刊的内容资源进行了整合分类,挑选其中最新最前沿、最优质的内容形成"头条专题""最新消息及评论(Latest News and Comment)""最新研究(Latest Research)"和"专辑及重大报告(Series and Commissions)"等主要栏目。"头条专题"是围绕某一重大疾病或公共卫生问题,挑选出系列期刊上近期发表的相关文章,以聚合各刊优质资源,通过进一步的内容策划和组织,增加对某一问题探讨的深度和广度,充分发挥刊群的集束效应。"最新消息及评论"栏目把最新发表的消息和评论类重点文章以精美的概念图片作为封面,使用色彩鲜明、具有较强视觉冲击力的图片来吸引读者眼球,激发读者的阅读兴趣,从而达到提高文章点击率和增强传播效果的目的,此类文章多为临床热点、难点或关系重大的公共健康、卫生政策问题。"最新研究"栏目为《柳叶刀》网站挑选出的对本领域可能产生较大影响的重量级研究论著,多为证据级别较高的随机对照临床试验或前瞻性队列研究,将其放在网站首页最新消息及评论文章下方的显著位置,使最好的内容获得最佳的显示度。"专辑及重大报告"则是《柳叶刀》系列期刊围绕某一临床或全球健康问题发布的系列专辑(Series)或成立的委员会(Committee),属于其知识服务和社会服务的一部分。此外,《柳叶刀》还在 2012 年 8 月正式上线微信公众平台,它的受众规模迅速扩大,虽然进军微信的时间较晚,但已深谙微信公众号运营之道,成为医学媒体阵营中不容小觑的一员。①

2. 打造丰富多元、各具特色的社交媒体服务平台

《柳叶刀》涉猎包括微信公众平台、Facebook、X、YouTube 及微博等社交媒体服务平台。《柳叶刀》期刊编辑十分具有用户思维,能以用户需求为中心,紧跟社会热点,并根据需求的差异性融入本地元素,通过对内容进行挖

---

① 魏佩芳,包靖玲,沈锡宾,等. 国外顶级医学期刊的数字化及新媒体平台发展现状——以《柳叶刀》系列期刊为例. 中国科技期刊研究,2020(2):166-172.

掘、重组，开发内容衍生品，构建知识关联和知识拓扑，提供形式多样的知识服务和社会服务；同时，《柳叶刀》还开展了与读者的双向互动，通过与用户的积极互动，聚合同质人群，培育粉丝对期刊的黏性和忠诚度。值得一提的是，YouTube上《柳叶刀》的视频很值得其他期刊借鉴。精彩纷呈的视频内容与其顶级的学术品质相辅相成、相得益彰，使得其无论是在传统的文字出版上，还是在新兴的社交媒体上都能够博得众多关注。①

3. 承担社会责任，不断追求卓越

《柳叶刀》期刊不仅报告世界上重要的医学和卫生问题，还一直强调卫生和社会问题的复杂性，聚焦影响世界各地人们的尖锐问题，督促各国建立良好的卫生系统管理制度。此前，《柳叶刀》集团特别声明，会增加编辑顾问、同行评议审稿人及作者中女性和来自中低收入国家科研同僚的人数。《柳叶刀》不仅汇聚了来自全世界的不同学科背景的优秀编辑，还有严格的选择程序和审稿程序。投稿文章首先要按照学术期刊常见的标准操作方式经过同行评议，再经过编委会评审通过后，才会派发给专业编辑进行修改和排版。同行评议可以有效确保投稿的稿件具有科学性；编委会成员在各自领域内有强大的研究创新底蕴和成果，共同掌握着该领域最前沿的研究成果，他们严谨公正，保证了期刊发表的文章的权威性和可信性；编辑部门则通过评审稿件的质量和内容来决定是否发表该篇文章。严格的编辑政策和流程使得《柳叶刀》在医学领域获得了良好的声誉。这些也体现了《柳叶刀》在编辑方面所追求的高质量、影响力和公正性。

三、当前挑战以及对策分析

（一）当前挑战

1. 国际政治环境复杂

随着全球范围内的自由化和全球化进程，国际政治和社会环境的变化对医学期刊产生了深刻的影响。例如，在全球卫生安全和大流行病的背景下，医学期刊对新病毒的全面报道和信息共享变得更加重要，但该领域也经常受到政治干扰和隐瞒。此外，由于疫苗的安全性和有效性等课题经常得到全球范围的关注，因此，医学期刊在提供准确信息和担任意见领袖方面的角色也变得更加重

---

① 周华清，李小霞.中外医学类期刊科学可视化设计比较研究.出版科学，2021(4)：32-41.

要。因此，如何在这种政治和社会敏感背景下保持准确和公正的立场，同时解决全球公共领域的问题，是《柳叶刀》面临的重要挑战。

2. 面对突发性公共卫生事件发文效率低

2019 年新冠疫情的暴发给人类敲响了警钟。随着全球化的进程推进，公共卫生事件的暴发会给人类带来相较于以往更为严重的损失。面对突发性公共卫生事件，作为国际一流医学期刊，如何在较短的时间内发表高质量的、重要的科研论文是《柳叶刀》面临的挑战之一。《柳叶刀》的同行评审通常需要耗费几个月时间，最新的研究成果无法及时被同行研究人员所了解。

3. 学术造假丑闻

2020 年 6 月 4 日，《柳叶刀》对其刊发的一篇热门新冠病毒研究论文撤稿，令其权威性蒙上阴影。目前科学界达成的普遍共识是，同行评审的前提是基于信任体系，评审员默认作者数据来源的真实性。在最理想的情况下，有合适的专家来对投稿的研究进行认真仔细的评估，经过多轮修改后，能够把错误消除。但是在最糟糕的情况下，同行评审可能像是橱窗里的装饰，被赋予了不必要的表面权威，但整个过程粗略、缺乏实际价值，并可能忽略一些明显的分析错误，甚至彻底忽略了造假的行为。期刊同行评审的评审制度导致了这类错误更容易发生。如何更加高效地查出文章中存在的错误以及造假行为也是《柳叶刀》目前所面临的挑战之一。

4. 财务问题与可持续发展

在当前的出版环境下，期刊的出版模式和经济模式都面临困难和不确定性。例如，广告收入和订阅收入骤减，同时付费刊登和伦理规则等问题在某些领域内也经常受到质疑；同时，在全球金融不稳定的环境下，最终期刊的运营和维护费用也面临压力。在这种情况下，如何制定持久的出版战略和财务计划，并积极寻求可持续的经济和商业模式，以保持期刊稳定和持续发展，也是重要挑战之一。

（二）对策分析

1. 将《柳叶刀》的委员会成员进一步国际化

如前文所述，《柳叶刀》面临的第一个问题是国际政治环境复杂。在政治影响下，期刊的写作立场往往会被放大为政治站位，信息的传播会受到多方政治压力。因此，我们认为理想的解决方法是：将《柳叶刀》的委员会成员进一步国际化以尽可能减小政治压力对《柳叶刀》这样一本立足于全人类健康的期刊的影响，使其发表内容通过来自世界各国、各地区不同立场的审查，保障内容公平公正，为全人类的健康做贡献。

2. 采用预印本网站

《柳叶刀》可以推出自己的预印本网站，研究人员在等待论文正式发表前可以将其研究结果在线发表在科学预印本网站上，类似于medRxiv或者bioRxiv等平台，供人们免费访问和讨论，并最终获得评审。但与medRxiv或者bioRxiv等平台不同的是，并非所有的文章都能投稿于《柳叶刀》的预印本网站。投稿的文章需要经过专业人员对其研究价值、研究方法等方面进行快速地评估，与此同时《柳叶刀》可以开发自己的AI模型进行文章内容的同步评估。但值得注意的是发表于《柳叶刀》预印本网站上的研究并不具有结论性质，因此不能指导临床试验，也不应该作为确凿的信息被媒体报道。《柳叶刀》预印本网站的设立不仅能够起到监督的作用，也能够积极应对紧急的公共卫生事件。

3. 采用半匿名责任制和数据共享制度

针对学术不端的问题，我们提议采用半匿名责任制。传统学术期刊赋予了编辑很大的权力，编辑可以自行邀请专家对论文进行审阅，但这些专家是匿名评审，也就是说只有编辑知道评审员的身份，评审员将评审意见交给编辑，再由编辑转交给论文的作者。然而这样的制度存在会导致评审人员行为不端的弊端。而采用半匿名责任制，即在论文决定发表的同时，评审员的名字也进行公开，能够避免一些因为同行评议带来的弊端，使得评审更为透明公正。

针对数据来源的真实性问题，我们提议引进数据共享制度，从实验数据到人员审查数据，都应进一步公开透明。实验数据流通性更强，不但可以多方验证实验的真实性，还可以辅助评审员对实验做出更公正的判断；人员审查数据的流通，打破了以往同行评议中编辑倾向于多次合作过的评审员的问题，使评审人员多样化，以对文章有更好的理解和审查。

4. 大力发展电子期刊

《柳叶刀》作为一本专业性很强的期刊，受众主要是医学界、生物医药界等的科研人员与医疗工作者，这也意味它的售卖渠道是有限的。作为一本非营利性刊物，这样有限的发行渠道可能会造成收支不平、入不敷出的问题。并且在科技高度发展的21世纪，人们更倾向于从电子渠道获取信息，对纸质期刊的需求有所降低。针对这两个问题，我们提出的方法是大力发展电子期刊。电子期刊的优势鲜明，不仅可以使信息更快速、透明地传递到世界各个角落，还可以降低期刊成本，减少对纸张、油墨、印刷的使用，节省了人力、物力、财力，延续可持续发展理念。

四、结　语

《柳叶刀》在200年的发展中没有固步自封，而是积极汲取新理念、新科技、新力量来完善自己，在医学领域精耕细作，笃行致远，并且始终以严谨的科学态度，心怀天下的人道主义做事，站在时代前沿，以世界顶级医学期刊的身份为不公与落后发声。正是这样的格局使医学界紧密联合起来，为全人类美好而健康的明天而奋斗。《柳叶刀》的精神生生不息，代代传承。

以*Science*为对象的世界顶级期刊分析研究①

摘　要: 本研究以*Science*期刊为研究对象,聚焦其发展历史、组织结构和运行机制,探究这些因素对期刊内容和学术地位的影响。本研究还通过对期刊上的人工智能、机器人学、计算机科学和社会科学文章进行整理与分析,探讨其在交叉学科与跨学科领域的作用与影响。通过文献调研的方法,运用比较研究思路,从多角度对期刊展开实证分析。本研究还利用Microsoft Excel、SPSS等工具对相关数据进行数据分析。研究发现,*Science*涵盖学科广泛,侧重年轻学者,注重读者互动,致力于发表对科学有深远影响的论文。主刊、副刊及开源出版物均具有高影响力。此外,跨学科研究也成为了科学研究中的关键要素,这些分析结果为我国科技类刊物的建设提供了有益的启示。

关键词: 学术期刊;*Science*;组织架构;运行机制;跨学科

一、引　言

在众多世界级学术期刊和出版物中,美国自然科学杂志*Science*具有显著的重要性,并在跨学科研究方面有突出贡献。该期刊发表的各种文章和研究报告推动我们对科学边界的探索。支撑*Science*的质量和声誉的是一套科学而完善的组织运营制度与框架、严格的编委审查和同行评议规范,以及不懈努力推进人类知识发展的坚定承诺和初心。

在文献调研方面,本研究着眼其组织架构、运营机制、学科定位等方面,

① 作者:白语宸,山东大学新闻传播系;吴翔宇,山东大学电子信息工程系;徐奕霄,浙江传媒学院英语系。

探究期刊组织与文章质量之间的关系，解析 *Science* 依托这些因素产出高质量研究的内在机制。

在数据统计和分析方面，本研究使用 Microsoft Excel 和 SPSS 软件，对来自 Web of Science（WoS）和 CNKI 的统计数据进行交叉对比，同时进行数学建模和数据可视化分析。为减小数据途径差异，我们控制了期刊来源和时间变量。

在学科定位方面，本研究使用描述统计方法计算了四大权威学科关键词分布的标准差，从而比较 *Science* 的学科归属。我们通过对 WoS、JCR 等统计数据进行收集与交叉对比，以 JIF 作为衡量标准，并运用皮尔逊和斯皮尔曼等级相关系数进行单边检验对期刊参数进行相关性分析。

此外，本研究聚焦 *Science* 期刊中的人工智能、机器人学等跨学科前沿成果，分析学科交叉对知识创新的推动作用。本研究希望通过多维度视角探索 *Science* 期刊的发展历程、运作机制等方面，解析其核心价值，为国内学术期刊发展提供借鉴。

综上，本研究通过立体化视角，关注 *Science* 期刊的发展历史、组织架构与运营机制、国际影响力等方面，并重点分析其在人工智能、机器人学等领域的前沿跨学科研究成果。我们希望能够深入理解期刊的发展轨迹，解析其内在运作机制，并通过跨学科研究分析，探讨期刊在促进科技融合创新方面的重要作用。各部分研究作为有机统一的整体，相辅相成，共同揭示期刊的核心价值所在，并为我国的学术期刊发展提供有益的参考与帮助。

二、*Science* 历史发展简要分析

Science 创刊至今已有 143 年，在漫长的历史发展中形成了享誉世界的学术地位。载文量是衡量期刊发展的重要指标之一，通过分析 *Science* 载文量变动情况，不仅可以揭示内部因素对期刊发展的影响，还可以从变化趋势中发现其他影响因素的存在。

该期刊载文量在二战后、20 世纪 60 年代、20 世纪 90 年代三个时期都有显著增长。这些变化与时代背景密切相关，从载文量的角度反映了美国科研水平的变化情况。此外，期刊的管理与运营变化也体现在载文量当中。成为协会会刊、编辑团队的稳定、审核和出版的优化等内部调整，呼应了有利的社会环境（见表 1）。在外部和内部有利条件的共同作用下，该期刊得以快速发展。

表 1　*Science* 创刊至今大事一览

时间	事件
1880 年	期刊创办
1882 年	因经济和组织问题，首次停刊
1900 年	成为美国科学促进会官方刊物
1944—1956 年	编辑变动频繁
1956 年	新主编上任后编辑部稳定
1958 年	杂志发行量大幅提高
1962—1984 年	出版重要文章，改进审核、出版方式
2013 年	推出科学·机器人（*Science Robotics*）等三份子刊

（资料来源：https://www.aaas.org/archives/150-years-advancing-science-history-aaas-1848-1998.）

　　由图 1 可见，*Science* 载文量变化趋势同美国总体研发投入占 GDP 比率变化趋势大致吻合，这反映了国家政策对科学发展的积极影响，并在科学期刊中得以体现。二战后，随着冷战竞争，登月计划等事务的推进，美国政府大幅提高科研投入，设立专门科学机构，促进科学研究的发展。20 世纪 90 年代，随着互联网等新趋势的兴起和发展，企业对科技投入的增加和社会整体科学水平的提高，都反映在载文量的增长中。

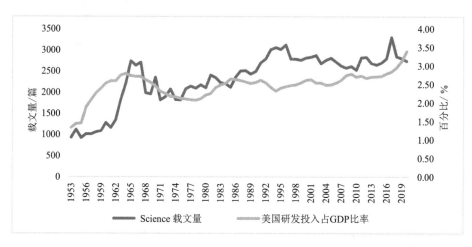

图 1　1953—2019 年 *Science* 载文量与美国总体研发投入占 GDP 比率[①]

---

① 数据来源：Web of Science; Science and Engineering Indicators. Research and Development: U. S. Trends and International Comparisons. (2022). https://ncses.nsf.gov/pubs/nsb20225/.

我们统计了半个世纪以来期刊文章来源地情况。文章来源地以发达国家为主，近30年来文章数量不断增加，美国始终是文章最主要来源国，这些数据一定程度反映了发达国家对科研的重视和投入。中国在近10年发文量激增，反映出我国科研实力的不断提高。值得注意的是，Science作为美国科学促进会的官方刊物，对不同国家的投稿接受率可能存在差异，更有可能接受美国科研机构的成果，进而影响来源地统计情况。

我们还统计了期刊文章的主要类型。期刊始终以研究文章为主，同时辅以新闻、社论、通信等不同类型的内容，文章修订也占据一定的比例。这体现了该刊促进科学发展的使命，以及其办刊专业严谨、栏目多样的特点。

三、Science的组织架构及运行机制

（一）以编辑为核心的组织架构

Science期刊由美国科学促进会领导，组织架构以编辑部门为核心，出版和创意部门为辅助。美国科学促进会是世界上最大的非营利性综合科学组织，为1000万会员提供服务。Science期刊依托协会庞大的会员群体和专业顾问，对学术和社会产生广泛影响。通过编辑任免等方式，协会为期刊提供方向指引，共同履行促进科学发展的使命。

编辑是期刊的核心力量。在Science编辑部中，编辑成员普遍拥有世界知名高校的博士学位，具备相关科研经历，每位都负责众多领域，这种专业背景和知识广度的结合能够确保论文评估和发表过程中的专业性和准确性，进而直接影响期刊的质量。

编辑在文章评审中发挥主导作用。提交的文章首先由对应领域编辑评估，编辑将基于标题、摘要和研究方法等方面给文章初步评分，并考虑审稿委员会的建议，决定文章是否进入深入审查和同行评议。编辑将结合审查和评议结果，最终决定文章是否发布。

主编是编辑队伍的灵魂，其素质高低决定了期刊的品质。在Science中，主编任期长且稳定，保证了办刊的稳定性。历任主编均为高素质的专业科学家，具有科研、商业和管理等背景。他们发挥主编责任、科学视野、出版经验等优势，推动期刊的发展。

除编辑部门外，出版、创意和视觉团队同样至关重要。出版部门负责国际合作、广告和出版等业务，这些业务与期刊影响力和收入密切相关。创意和视

觉团队负责设计吸引读者的视觉效果，近年来更加注重科学与设计的结合。这些部门密切合作，共同推动*Science*在国际学术界的认可和发展。

（二）程序化、高标准的运行机制

*Science*期刊作为学术性与大众性结合的综合科学刊物，其运行机制包括发行流程、发行周期、内容安排以及刊物定价等多个方面，下面我们选取几个方面进行具体分析。

1. 发行流程及投稿精选策略

*Science*的文章发行流程包括投稿、编辑审查、审稿委员会评估、深入审查、交叉审查、出版或拒稿等流程。所有投稿都必须在线进行，系统中提供了稿件模板、隐私政策以及详细投稿要求等信息，期刊要求投稿人提交一封申请信和提供受试人同意情况等信息。这些规定体现了期刊的权威性与细致要求。

*Science*以其高质量和高影响力著称于国际学术界。虽然其发表的论文数量较少，但大部分经过严格的同行评审，并具有较高的引用率。投稿筛选的要求非常严苛，入选论文应包含新颖且重要的数据或概念，并得到科学界和公众的广泛认可。这些论文最终通过期刊向公众发表，决定了期刊的出版质量。

2. 发行周期及其对国内刊物的启发

科技期刊的载文量决定了信息量的大小，出版周期、载文量在一定程度上影响相关学科的科研交流程度。*Science*期刊以周刊的形式通过印刷和在线两个渠道出版。[①]部分刊物如*Science Advance*、*Science Career*完全开源，其他期刊均为订阅制。此外，国外科技期刊的出版频率与国内相比较高，许多科技期刊如新闻一般及时报道重大科学成果和突破，上文提及的有关*Science*中艾滋病报告的快速发表就是其中一个例子。[②]这为我国期刊论文发表周期以及内部流程的改进提供了参考。

这里我们引用了影响因子指标，它是国际上衡量科技期刊是否为品牌期刊的最主要的评价指标。为论证优化发行周期的必要性，及辅证期刊影响因子与引用频次之间的相关性，我们统计了2020年世界近40个权威期刊数据，囊括自然科学、医学、工程技术、社会科学和人文科学，并对相关参数进行平均二次型散点图分析。

---

① 崔建勋.合理设置期刊出版周期与载文量的理性思考.中国科技期刊研究，2020(7)：821-827.
② 曹明.国外科技期刊的出版频率.中国科技期刊研究，1993(2)：9-12.

　　表2说明年发刊数与CF具有正相关性。对于发刊频率，国际品牌科技期刊具有出版速度快、发表时滞短、信息传播快捷等特点，与之相比，我国的科技期刊的出版周期过长，与国际科技期刊的差距较大。[①]而高质高频期刊容易获得较高的影响因子，我国需要逐渐优化、合并各学术期刊，在保证质量的同时缩短发行周期，从而适应国内科学技术的发展需求。

表2　权威期刊CF与JIF、年发刊数的斯皮尔曼等级相关系数（单尾）

			JIF	年发刊数	CF
斯皮尔曼 Rho	JIF	相关系数	1	0.368	0.536
		显著性（单尾）	—	0.066	0.011
		N	18	18	18
	年发刊数	相关系数	0.368	1	0.687
		显著性（单尾）	0.66	—	<0.01
		N	18	18	18
	CF	相关系数	0.536	0.687	1
		显著性（单尾）	0.011	<0.01	—
		N	18	18	18

　　对于引用频次，唯有中国机构的学者引用Science略多于引用Nature，其他国家的学者更多引用Nature。而在Nature、Science的选择上，根据WoS提供的数据，我国机构的学者同样偏向于在Science发刊。这与引用的偏向在一定程度上有着关联。

　　在世界学术圈大环境下，学者加强对各大顶尖期刊的关注与交流是有益的，我们鼓励国内机构学者加强对Nature等编委会的联系。在发刊周期上，这值得国内期刊思考，数据表明，在保证国内机构学者发刊质量的前提下，提升审核效率，提高年发刊数量，扩大刊物的搜索能力，运用随机森林算法减少隐藏优秀文章的丢失，能在一定程度上提升刊物的引用频次，从而提高国内刊物的影响因子。

　　Science期刊的优秀组织架构和运行机制，保证了其高标准和高质量的学术研究成果。在此基础上，期刊形成了自己独特的学科定位和覆盖范围。

---

① 张勇刚. 中西科学期刊比较研究. 合肥：中国科学技术大学，2018：95；严建新，苏芳荔，徐莉莉. 期刊引证形象的量化表达——以2010年Nature和Science的引证形象为例. 图书情报工作，2014(21)：99-104.

四、分布领域广泛的学科偏向

Science 涵盖自然科学、社会科学和医学等多个学科领域。我们利用 WoS 的研究领域关键词作为筛选条件对 *Nature*、*Science* 以及《国家科学评论》（*National Science Review*）三大权威期刊进行关键词统计，以探究三大权威期刊各自的学科偏向以及学科定位。

结合部分关键词统计，我们能看出 *Nature*、*Science* 期刊之间的题材占比差异并不大，而 *Nature* 在分子生物学领域占比为 14.3%，相比 *Science* 较高；而《国家科学评论》在工程材料和物理领域占比高达 37%，为 *Nature*、*Science* 平均占比的 5—10 倍，在生物医学领域却远远低于 *Nature*、*Science*。

根据统计，《国家科学评论》学科分布方差较大，*Science* 涵盖的学科领域广泛。以 *Science* 编委会专业领域为例，编辑部每年约收到 6700 份论文稿件，其中约 15% 被录用，发表的论文涉及所有科学学科，其中 60% 的论文属于生命科学领域，其余 40% 为物理类学科，学科分布相比国内期刊较为均衡。[①]

五、提升大众参与度的吸引投稿策略

在读者倾向方面，*Science* 的读者主要是学术研究人员和科学教育工作者，其读者群体相对年轻、科学视野开阔，更加注重跨学科的合作和交流。

与传统的学术期刊不同，*Science Advances* 创新性地采用了开放获取模式，任何人都可以免费阅读和下载其中的文章，这使得该期刊的影响力和知名度在学术界和公众之间不断扩大。此外，在 *Science* 及其子刊上获得编辑好评，但因篇幅不足等原因而被拒绝的论文可以考虑在 *Science Advances* 上发表。根据 *Science Advances* 的官方描述，其目标读者包括那些希望探索最新科学发现和方法，以及寻找解决复杂问题的跨学科视角的人群。

在吸引投稿方面，*Science* 家族包含六个独立出版物的子刊，每个子刊都有其独特且全面的政策和标准，吸引不同类型的投稿。此外，*Science* 还注重与读者的互动和交流。根据 1997—2016 年 *Science* 和《科学通报》英文版的文献类型统计。由图 9 可知，论文占 *Science* 总文献量的 45.10%，社论占 21.60%，读者来信占 13.73%，其他类型也占一定比例。[②] 这表明 *Science* 不仅是一份专

---

① 祖广安，柯若儒，钱浩庆. 访美国《科学》杂志社记实. 编辑学报，1998(01)：49-51.

② 张勇刚. 中西科学期刊比较研究. 合肥：中国科学技术大学，2018.

业的科学期刊，还兼顾大众性、普及性的内容；然而，论文占《科学通报》英文版的比例过高，高达 89.11％，读者来信、综述和社论等栏目文献比例过低。

此外，对于投稿的吸引策略，JIF、期刊质量也是投稿者参考的重要因素。[①] 我国应注重科研合作中的主动参与性，国内一流期刊应注重与各大科研论坛读者、科研媒体以及图书出版社之间的交流，大力培养科学研究的创新能力，营造具有科研开放性以及独立性的科研氛围，提升我国科研创新的领导力，从而提高期刊质量。

六、国际成就及社会影响力

Science 期刊自创刊之初便坚持促进科学理解的宗旨，致力于发表对科技发展最有影响的论文。例如莱特兄弟首次飞行的实验报告、托马斯·摩尔根（Thomas Morgan）关于果蝇遗传的研究以及阿波罗计划等学术成果，在人类科学发展史上都产生了深远影响，并为 *Science* 期刊赢得了世界顶级科学期刊的声誉。[②] *Science* 还不断拓展期刊系列和栏目，将科学影响从学术界延伸到大众生活中，有利于科学传播。

Science 不仅在主刊上发表具有影响力的研究成果，其子刊也同样展现出了卓越的学术影响力。以 *Science Signaling* 上发表的一篇生物医学研究为例，该论文通过对无脊椎动物文昌鱼免疫系统的研究，颠覆了长久以来某些信号通路仅在脊椎动物出现后才存在的观点，将外源性细胞凋亡信号通路的形成时间往前推进了至少 1 亿年。即使在开放获取的 *Science Advances* 中，发表的论文也同样拥有高水平价值。在一项最新的研究报告中，研究者利用强关联费米多体系统实现了量子绝热冲程的零摩擦做功，在改善输出效率和输出功率方面都有着显著的优势。

七、基于 *Science* 2020—2023 年刊发的跨学科文章分析

（一）概述及研究步骤

本研究基于 *Science* 2020—2023 年刊发的跨学科文章，对不同学科领域的交叉研究进行分析和综合。研究聚焦社会科学、人工智能与计算机技术及机器

---

① 吴晓丽，陈广仁. 建设世界一流科技期刊的策略——基于 *Nature*、*Science*、*The Lancet* 和 *Cell* 的分析. 中国科技期刊研究，2020(7)：758-764.

② 王晓迪. 美国科学促进会科研发展、热点分析及经验借鉴. 天津科技，2018(12)：1-4.

人学的跨学科领域。通过研读、分析和比较该期刊 2020—2023 年刊发的相关跨学科论文，根据研究思路、方法和结果汇总、比对，分析该期刊刊文反映的跨学科发展状况，及其在推动跨学科与学科交叉发展方面的重要作用。此外，本研究尝试提供探究这些前沿学科领域交叉融合及推动新兴科学领域发展应用的视角，并局部揭示不同学科领域之间的相互融合情况。

本研究特别关注社会科学、人工智能、计算机科学与机器人学等前沿学科领域。筛选出 20 篇具有代表性的文献。我们采用以下研究方法。

对选定文献进行了归类，分为 3 个主题模块。采用文本分析方法，提取论文的关键词和话题词，分析这些词之间的联结关系，以确定论文的主要研究内容。对不同模块中的论文进行横向比较，分析各模块的研究热点、趋势和学科交叉情况。总结各模块论文的核心观点，厘清学科交叉与融合的内在逻辑。通过文献筛选和文本分析相结合的研究方法，考察和概括了选定学科领域的学术交叉与发展情况。

（二）社会科学

我们基于社会科学领域的相关学科论文，细化地选取了 2 篇文章，并依次进行文本和研究思路的分析。

第一篇文章"AI and transformation of social science research"探讨了大语言模型（LLMs）如何应用于社会科学研究，详细分析了 LLMs 在社会科学研究中应用的前景、面临的挑战以及对推动社会科学研究发展的潜在作用。文中不仅提出了使用 LLMs 时需要解决的问题，如伦理规范和模型局限性等，而且指出社会科学需要加强对 LLMs 的培训和方法支持。

第二篇文章"Mapping of machine learning approaches for description, prediction, and casual inference in the social and health sciences"通过构建元映射框架，系统阐述了机器学习技术在推动社会科学和健康科学交叉研究方面具有巨大的应用潜力。尽管仍存在一些问题，如学科间成果交流不足，有待进一步探索和完善，但机器学习为这两个领域提供了强大的新工具。

为深入分析人工智能对社会科学研究的影响，我们聚焦了文章"AI and transformation of social science research"。通过文献分析工具，构建了该文的参考文献学科分布图（图 2）。学科分布图直观反映了参考文献主要涵盖的学科类型，能较好地揭示人工智能与社会科学的跨学科融合学术图景。并进一步通过引文网络（corrected paper）分析，考察了人工智能如何深刻影响和改变社会科学研究各个方面。

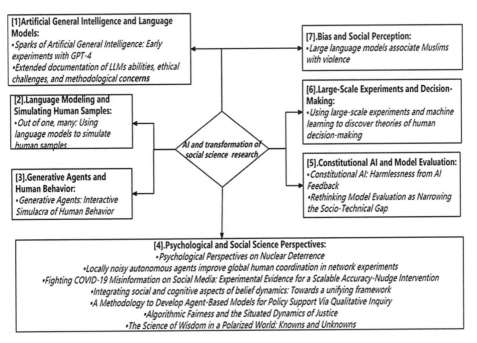

图2 参考文献学科分布

（三）人工智能学

结合AI技术发展情况和对前沿研究时效性的考虑，我们主要追踪选定了9篇AI领域的跨学科文章进行深度阅读与分析，根据其交叉学科偏重不同，又划分为医学交叉类、电子器件交叉类、化学交叉类和材料学与触觉传感交叉类。如表3。

表3 人工智能学参阅论文

分类	文章名
医学交叉类	Dynamic detection and reversal of myocardial ischemia using an artificially intelligent bioelectronic medicine
	CancerVar: An artificial intelligence-empowered platform for clinical interpretation of somatic mutations in cancer
	Combining generative artificial intelligence and on-chip synthesis for de novo drug design

续表

分类	文章名
电子器件交叉类	Insights into Quantum Chemistry: Artificial Intelligence for Split Electron Detection Reconfigurable perovskite nickelate electronics for artificial intelligence
化学交叉类	Explainable and trustworthy artificial intelligence for correctable modeling in chemical sciences
材料学与触觉传感交叉类	An artificial intelligence enabled chemical synthesis robot for exploration and optimization of nanomaterials
	Hydroplastic foaming of graphene aerogels and artificially intelligent tactile sensors
	Haptic perception using optoelectronic robotic flesh for embodied artificially intelligent agents

通过对上述9篇文章的深入分析和阅读，可以看出AI已经在医学、电子器件、化学、材料学和触觉传感等多个跨学科领域得到广泛应用。随着AI技术的不断发展，其应用范围还将持续扩大。同时，跨学科研究也日益被认为是解决复杂问题和提高研究成果的关键。具体而言，AI主要通过以下几个方面推进跨学科研究。

第一，AI可以高效处理和分析海量数据，提高数据利用效率。研究人员可以利用存在的大数据，分析其内在规律和模式。

第二，AI技术的应用拓展了学科和领域之间的交流与合作。特别是在医学领域，AI有望提升精准医疗水平，提供更有效的治疗方案，并帮助更好地理解疾病机制。

第三，AI的计算和模拟能力可提高材料设计和器件制造的效率，为材料学和电子器件领域提供新思路。

综上，AI技术进步已成为推动学术研究和技术发展的关键因素。AI在探索未知领域和发现新规律方面拥有巨大潜力和重要作用，为知识发现和创新应用提供跨学科合作契机，并为科研提供崭新视角。AI对跨学科研究产生了深远影响。

（四）计算科学与机器人学

我们注意到这一部分刊文总量和研究结果总量较大，而其中根据其交叉学科偏重不同，又可将之划分为仿生与感知交叉类、深度学习与运动规划交叉类、化学或量子计算交叉类、生物神经元计算交叉类和神经网络多模态计算交叉类。而在这诸多文章当中，我们聚焦于仿生学、近远端感知与触觉，机器人感知处理和AI技术的交叉。我们主要参阅了*Science Robotics*编委尤利娅·桑达米尔斯卡亚（Yulia Sardamirskaya）的文章"Rethinking computing hardware for robots"，文章中指出，生物学的灵感也推动了人造皮肤的研究，解决了机器人近端触觉感应的问题。为此我们进一步深度阅读了以下三篇文章（见表4）。

表4 计算科学与机器人学参阅论文

文章	主要内容
Neuro-inspired electronic skin for robots	该研究旨在提高机器人的触觉感知能力。文章研究探讨了电子皮肤中各种计算模块的硬件实现，并探讨它们如何与算法集成以实现计算电子皮肤。
A biomimetic elastomeric robot skin using electrical impedance andacoustic tomography for tactile sensing	文中提出设计了基于光学捕获测量的先进类肤传感器。
Haptic perception using optoelectronic robotic flesh for embodiedacoustic tomography for tactile sensing	文中提出并设计实验了一种生物启发式弹性皮肤，具有基于麦克风和光电设备传感、人工智能代理数据分析、从而实现机器人整体感知数据处理的功能。

通过对上述文章实验方法、技术应用和结果的比较，可发现仿生学与机器近远端触觉感知分析之间的交叉与融合不断推进机器触觉感知技术的进步和应用，可以看出仿生学与机器近远端触觉感知技术之间存在着深入的交叉与融合，这种跨学科融合持续推进着机器触觉感知技术的发展与应用。具体来看，这种交叉呈现出以下技术发展路线：

首先，生物学和仿生学中的设计灵感激发了机器触觉感知技术的创新，如生物皮肤启发了电子皮肤和类肤传感器的研发。

其次，这些技术创新反过来又推动了生物学和仿生学研究的深入，形成了良性循环。

最后，随着人工智能技术的进步，机器触觉感知系统获得了更强大的分析、计算和综合处理能力支持，如Robotic Flesh实现了整体触觉感知。

上述文章中所表现出来的这些进步，都是机器人学在学科交叉发展和跨学科力量推动学术科研水平与技术实际表现效果的有力证明。

（五）跨学科研究部分结论

在*Science* 2020－2023年发表的研究论文中，我们可以清楚地看到各学科正在积极进行交叉研究和合作。这为深入分析当前科学跨学科发展状况提供了宝贵窗口。

具体来看，一方面，社会科学家正在与新兴科技领域特别是人工智能和机器人学的研究者展开合作。通过使用新的工具和方法，社会科学家能以崭新视角解析社会问题，并帮助技术专家处理算法公平性、隐私等社会层面问题。同时，人工智能和计算科学也在极大推动各领域的交叉发展。它们为其他学科提供了处理和分析大数据的强大工具，大幅提高了研究设计和实践的效率与精度。

另一方面，跨越多个学科的机器人学，其在推动跨学科研究方面的价值也日益凸显。机器人学不仅推动了科技进步，也为理解自然和社会现象提供了新视角和工具。

综上，通过对*Science* 2020－2023年刊文的分析，可以清楚看出，跨学科研究已成为当今科研的关键组成部分。这种跨学科协同不仅能够从更全面和宏观的视角理解和解决实际问题，还能有效促进科学创新与发展。虽然语言、方法差异等挑战依然存在，但跨学科研究的显著优势与益处不容忽视。这种发展呈现相互促进的良性循环态势。新的研究成果将进一步激发跨学科研究的活力与潜力。在这个过程中，跨学科研究已证明其重要价值，并将在未来科研中继续发挥关键作用。

八、研究结论

综合前文的研究，我们可以看到，*Science*期刊的发展与世界科技进步历程和学术变迁潮流息息相关。它诞生于19世纪末人类工业革命和科学方法论成熟的历史背景，并在20世纪科技高速发展的大潮中不断成熟和壮大。

该期刊的组织架构具有高度科学化和制度化的特点。它实行主编负责制，编委会专家化，确保了期刊的学术权威性。它强调选稿质量，采用同行评议机制，确保了期刊的公正性。它注重过程规范化，形成了一整套严谨科学的作者投稿、同行评审、编辑修改、出版发行的流程体系，确保了期刊的运行效率。可以说，*Science*期刊的发展离不开其独特的组织架构和运行机制的科学性与系统性。这为我国科技期刊的制度建设提供了宝贵借鉴。

　　该期刊的内容与世界科技前沿与热点紧密相关。它广泛涵盖自然科学、工程技术、医学、社会科学等各大学科门类，主刊和子刊内容丰富多样。特别是在新兴交叉学科领域，*Science* 期刊发挥着连接学科、整合创新、引领发展的重要作用。例如在人工智能和机器人学领域，*Science* 期刊大量刊发高质量的原创性研究论文，推动了这些新兴学科的快速发展。这体现了 *Science* 期刊紧跟世界科技前沿的学术价值追求。这种把握科技脉搏的敏锐洞察力，也值得我国科技期刊学习。

　　期刊的国际影响力与其学术质量和开拓精神是密不可分的。它发表的标志性研究成果，如人类基因组计划、量子计算等，对人类科技发展产生过深远影响。它马不停蹄地拓展期刊系列，积极面向未来。它与国际一流学术机构和科研组织保持广泛合作。这使得 *Science* 期刊成为全球公认的顶级学术期刊之一。这种科学的开拓精神和追求卓越的学术态度，也应该成为我国科技期刊的学习楷模。

　　期刊 140 多年的发展历程，展现了人类科学精神的进步轨迹，其卓越的学术成就积淀和科学价值追求，对世界范围内的科技期刊发展产生了深远影响。*Science* 期刊的发展经验对我国科技期刊建设提供了多重维度和跨学科的借鉴启示。我们坚信，在新的历史条件下，中国科技期刊也一定能在学科交叉融合的趋势中找到发展机遇，实现自身的跨越式提升，为人类科技进步和社会发展做出新的更大贡献。

世界一流期刊案例研究——*Nature*①

摘　要： 本研究主题为世界一流期刊 *Nature*，该期刊涵盖了自然科学、医学、工程技术和社会科学等多个领域并对其进行全面的报道。研究深入分析了该期刊的概况、发展要素和面临的挑战。它考察了读者定位、影响因子、吸引高质量投稿的策略、组织架构、运行机制和学科定位。本文还着重研究了 *Nature* 期刊面临的一些挑战，特别解释了 AI 类语言模型带来的挑战，并提出能使其持续成功的建议，包括应对领域内激烈的竞争、国际化挑战，以及人工智能语言模型带来的影响。为了克服这些障碍，*Nature* 可以加强与专业期刊的合作，加强国际合作伙伴关系，促进研究的可重复性和透明性，并实施强大的策略和技术来检测和预防学术不端行为。

关键词： 概览；发展要素；挑战和建议；AI 类语言模型

一、期刊概览

（一）*Nature* 的主题

Nature（《自然》期刊）的主题是综合性的科学研究，包括自然科学、医学、工程技术和社会科学等多个领域。其重点关注跨学科的科学问题和突破性的科技成果。*Nature* 所发布的研究成果通常具有影响力广泛、创新性强、原创性好、数据准确性高等特点。

---

① 作者：童天琦，浙江大学外国语学院英语系；王婧雅，浙江大学外国语学院英语系；戚瑶晖，浙江大学外国语学院英语系；陈诗雨，浙江大学外国语学院英语系。

（二）建立和发展历程

Nature 由英国化学家约瑟夫·诺曼·洛克耶（Joseph Norman Lockyer）于 1869 年创立，最初是作为一份天文学和物理学期刊出版的。进入 20 世纪以后，*Nature* 不断拓展学科领域和影响范围，成为综合性的科学研究期刊。*Nature* 期刊的发展历程可以分为以下几个阶段。

创刊初期：*Nature* 的创始人洛克耶将其定位为天文学和物理学期刊。当时期刊的影响力还比较有限，发表的文章数量也相对较少。

20 世纪初期：*Nature* 开始向其他学科领域拓展，如生物学、化学、地球科学等。20 世纪初期，*Nature* 发表了爱因斯坦的相对论论文，这篇论文一经发表即引起了广泛的关注。

二战期间：由于战争的影响，*Nature* 期刊的发行量大幅下降，然而其在科学界仍有广泛的影响力。

战后时期：随着世界经济的快速发展以及科技革命的不断推进，*Nature* 的影响力不断扩大。20 世纪 60 年代以来，*Nature* 接连发表了多篇具有开创性的文章，包括光学钳和人类基因组计划的新闻公告。

当代：以互联网的兴起和信息技术的飞速发展为背景，*Nature* 期刊的影响力在整个学术领域中不断增强，现已成为全球最权威的科学期刊之一。

（三）国际成就与地位

Nature 期刊在国际范围内享有崇高的声誉和地位，被誉为"科学之巅"领军期刊之一，是被广泛认可的世界科学出版领域领先者。在学术评估和影响力方面，*Nature* 的文章是广受认可的参考标准，它在全球范围内的影响力非常广泛，被视为全球科技创新、人才选拔和业界发展的风向标、榜样和平台。

（四）全球范围内的学术和社会影响力

Nature 期刊不仅在学术领域的影响力巨大，在社会生活中也发挥着重要的作用。它所发表的研究成果具有强大的公信力，通常被政策制定者、媒体和大众用作对科学和技术问题的参考和意见。此外，*Nature* 通过不断推动科学技术的创新思想与人文社会的发展进步紧密结合起来，促进更多的人理解科学知识，以及人类社会与生态系统之间的复杂互动关系。*Nature* 期刊在整个学术界以及科技和经济发展中都具有重要的影响力和积极作用。

（五）学术责任与期刊升级

Nature 期刊在学术领域扮演了关键角色，它不仅是研究成果的展示平台，还有着防范和应对学术不端行为的责任。"*Nature* 期刊的出版商施普林格·自然集团（Springer Nature）一直积极与软件公司合作，着手研发适用于出版业的人工智能工具。"①随着人工智能时代的来临，期刊将面临崭新的发展机遇。将人工智能技术运用于学术搜索，建立一个基于大数据、跨领域、多平台、综合性和共享性的智能检索数据库，已成为趋势。这一数据库将更智能地处理文本、观点、图像等学术不端行为问题，智能分析和大数据平台上的内容创新性检测也将辅助同行评审。借助区块链技术的支持，实验数据的真实性和同行评审的透明性将得以确保。通过采用唯一身份识别代码和用户画像功能来核实作者和审稿人的身份，新型同行评审模式将进一步减少虚假评审和偏见。然而，期刊在应对这些智能工具带来的影响时必须保持谨慎，不能完全依赖人工智能来替代编辑和审稿人的人工判断。只有在这两者协调、互补、融合的基础上，期刊才能真正实现智能升级。

二、发展要素分析

（一）读者定位

Nature 自从创刊以来，目标读者便包括了公众和科学家两类人群。"主要读者是从事研究工作的科学家，但期刊前部的文章概括使得一般公众也能理解期刊内最重要的文章。"②在 1869 年 11 月 4 日发行的 *Nature* 首刊上，办刊宗旨这篇文章以引用英国著名诗人威廉·华兹华斯（William Wordsworth）的诗句"To the solid ground, of nature trusts the mind which builds for aye."（"思想常新者，以自然为其可靠之依据"）作为开篇，然后在后文叙述其创刊宗旨，即为向普罗大众科普科学理念与为科学家提供自然科学各个分支取得的最新进展信息和讨论平台。在早期的期刊中刊登了大量的科幻类文本，其文章内容通俗易懂，堪称一本"模范"科普杂志；直到今日，每一刊 *Nature* 均有板块简要介绍时下的学术动态。从创刊以来在普罗大众间积攒的良好口碑，帮助 *Nature* 为后续转型成学术期刊打下了坚实的基础，积累了悠久的历史底蕴。

---

① Kim, K. Artificial intelligence and publishing. *Science Editing*, 2019, 6(2): 89-90.
② 本刊编辑部. 英国《自然》杂志简介. 中国动脉硬化杂志, 2017(10): 77.

（二）影响因子

20世纪40年代起，*Nature*逐渐增加了学术文本的数量，渐渐获得了学术界对其身份的认同。然而，随着"影响因子之父"加菲尔德（E. Garfield）在1975年开始出版SCI报告并推出影响因子计算公式，各大期刊包括*Nature*和*Science*在内察觉到这是一个提升自己期刊知名度的好机会，便加入了角逐影响因子的竞赛当中。由于*Nature*一直同时发表学术文本与面向大众的科普文本，加上根据影响因子计算公式对期刊内容的微调，*Nature*顺利在20世纪80年代后期取得了相关排名方面的进步，并进一步坐稳了"世界顶级科学期刊"的位置，此后形成了良性循环。然而近年来，*Nature*却加入了反对以影响因子为单一标准评判期刊水平的阵营，同时签署了《旧金山宣言》，号召出版商"极大地减少、最好是停止宣传期刊影响因子"，并提供更加多元化的且全面的期刊表现视图。

（三）吸引高质量投稿群体

1. 审稿程序

*Nature*的审稿程序以严格高效著称。供稿者的稿件首先会被送至相关领域的编辑手中，综合其他编辑与相关学者的意见之后，确定稿件具备重大意义才会最终送审。该流程时间周期相较于其他期刊来说较为短且快，投稿人在投稿一周左右便会知晓稿件是否能够进一步送审，对于科研工作者来说减少了等待时间，有利于其将更多时间投入研究中。

大多数稿件会经由2—3位审稿人的审查，审稿人着重从对该研究发现的感兴趣人群、原因与可能技术失误提出意见反馈，该阶段一般耗时一周左右。编辑收到反馈意见之后会进行进一步讨论，再将相关意见与建议反馈至作者，而作者拥有充分选择权，可对文章进行适当修改再重新投递。若审稿人提出文章有重大技术问题且拒绝重新投稿，作者可以根据提出书面申请要求重审。由此可见，*Nature*给予了投稿人充分的自由选择权，其高效严谨的审稿流程提升了学术工作者的体验感，体现了其对作者的尊重。

2. 编辑工作安排

据*Nature*官网所言，杂志没有由高级科学家组成的编委会，也不附属于任何学会和学术机构，因此它的决定是独立做出的，不受制于任何单独个体持有的科学或国家偏见。什么样的论文能吸引读者广泛关注，由*Nature*的编辑而不是审稿人来做出判断。"所以在 *Nature* 决定稿件是否刊登的，是编辑部，最终是主编。"[①]

Nature 不设置外部单独的编委会，发表什么文章完全由编辑独立判断。"编辑握有对稿件的生杀大权，有权力做出最后用稿决定。而绝大部分学术期刊，编辑主要扮演服务者的角色，负责收稿、初选、送审、编辑稿件等相关事宜，并不会享有如此大的权限"[②]。*Nature* 编辑体系主要分为 Science editor、Copy editor 和 Products editor，分别负责内容审查、排版校样与出版营销等工作。根据 *Nature* 的公开资料，其不同级别的编辑之间具有较大的文化、学术背景差异性，这使得 *Nature* 具有丰厚且广阔的学术基础，从而吸引来自不同领域的优秀学者向其投稿。

与此同时，*Nature* 在处理稿件时会屏蔽国籍、性别、种族等因素可能造成的歧视性判断，在审阅稿件时秉持着"支持严谨、可重复和有影响力的研究"的精神，从而推进建设具有"包容性"的科学，在社区中营造多样性与包容性的文化。*Nature* 期刊在审稿与编辑阶段的开放与透明，对推进来自不同地区的学者享有公平机遇起到了积极作用。

（四）组织架构

Nature 的出版商是国际性的出版集团——施普林格·自然集团，该集团在全球范围内都有分布，拥有庞大的读者群体和优秀的编辑团队。

来自各个领域、世界各地的专家学者组成了全球最高水平的学术评审委员会，为 *Nature* 提供学术支持，保证了其卓越的品质；专业的编辑团队具备深厚的学术背景和丰富的编辑经验，能够准确判断文章的价值和科学含量，并对投稿进行精细的筛选和加工；采用先进的数字出版技术，可以在最短时间内将优秀的文章发布到全球读者面前。这种快速高效的出版流程为 *Nature* 赢得了广泛的赞誉和尊重；利用大数据分析技术，对论文的发表情况、引用情况等进行深入研究，从而对其编辑方向和出版策略进行调整和优化；采取创新的经营模式，积极拓展数字出版市场，与各大科学机构合作开展科研项目，实现了学术研究成果的产业化和商业化。

---

① 江晓原，穆蕴秋.科学"神刊"是怎样办成的——*Nature* 审稿、发稿、撤稿的故事.读书，2022(08)：118-128.
② 穆蕴秋，江晓原.*Nature* 杂志审稿发稿机制研究.自然辩证法通讯，2022(03)：89-100.

（五）运行机制

编辑部：*Nature* 的编辑部位于伦敦，由一支由专业科学编辑组成的团队负责日常运作。编辑部会收到来自世界各地的投稿，并进行初步审查和评估。

同行评审：所有投稿都会经过同行评审（peer review）程序。这意味着文章会被发送给多个匿名的专家学者进行评估。评审人会根据文章的原创性、科学价值、方法可靠性等因素，对稿件进行评分并提出修改建议。但是，学术界仍需要一种更为高效且适用范围更广的同侪审查，以让审稿人更有效率地使用自己的时间，并在符合资料的情况下进行研究。

决策：编辑部会根据同行评审结果，以及自身的判断和经验，决定是否接受或拒绝该篇文章。如果接受，则会通知作者进行最后的修改和润色。经过审核和修改后，文章才会正式发表。

出版和传播：*Nature* 每周出版一期，包括来自各个自然科学领域的原创研究论文、评论、新闻和特别报道等。文章会同时发布在 *Nature* 的官方网站上，并通过社交媒体等渠道进行宣传和传播。

因此，*Nature* 的运行机制十分严格和专业，旨在确保发表的文章具有高水平的科学质量和广泛的影响力。

（六）学科定位

对于自身的科普性质，*Nature* 从不讳言，"*Nature* 从一开始就打算既面向一线科学家，又面向普通大众。这个宗旨一直遵循至今"。

早期，*Nature* 主要关注物理学、化学和生物学等自然科学领域。20世纪40年代，随着原子能和核物理技术的快速发展，*Nature* 开始重点报道这些新兴学科的研究成果。20世纪50年代，遗传学和分子生物学成为热门话题，随后又涌现出计算机科学、地球科学、天文学和神经科学等新兴领域。

21世纪初，随着人类基因组计划的完成和生命科学领域的飞速发展，*Nature* 逐渐将重心转向生命科学方向。同时，*Nature* 也开始关注环境问题和可持续发展等重要话题，探讨科学和技术与社会、经济和政治发展的关系。

值得注意的是，尽管 *Nature* 的学科定位发生了演变，但它始终保持着强烈的跨学科特质。在发表论文时，*Nature* 不仅关注学科的专业性和深度，同时也注重交叉学科的创新性思维和应用价值。这种跨学科的特质使 *Nature* 成为了科研领域中最具影响力的期刊之一。

（七）科学传播

Nature，作为一本国际知名的学术期刊，不仅在学术领域有着广泛的影响力，而且在科学传播方面也展现了其全球化的视野。在全球范围内，*Nature* 通过社交媒体平台积极地发布最新的科学研究动态。这些发布的内容通常包括对研究的简短概述以及指向完整文章的链接。此外，*Nature* 还拥有一个官方新闻网站，通过电子邮件订阅系统，定期向读者发送最新的科学消息，使其能够以更为通俗的方式接触到前沿的科研成果。

在地区化的科普策略上，*Nature* 同样展现了出色的执行力。以中国为例，考虑到微信平台的巨大用户基数和影响力，*Nature* 在该平台上设立了官方公众号"Nature Portfolio"以及相关的视频号。这些内容同步更新自其官方英文网站，并由施普林格·自然集团的上海办公室负责进行中文翻译和发布。为了更好地满足不同读者的需求，该公众号设计了多个内容合集，如"自然每周简报""自然新刊亮点合集"和"科技图片"等，以便于读者根据兴趣进行筛选和阅读。此外，公众号还为科研人员提供了一系列研究者服务，如学科社群查询、机构合作信息和在线课程等。这种深度的本土化策略不仅增强了*Nature* 在中国的影响力，而且也为其在全球范围内的科普活动提供了有力的支撑。

三、挑战和建议

（一）领域竞争

随着科学研究的不断发展，各个学科领域的期刊竞争日益激烈。其他高质量的综合性期刊及专业领域的期刊都在争夺有影响力的研究成果。

Nature 可以进一步巩固自身在综合性科学研究领域的地位，同时加强与专业领域期刊的合作，提供更多交叉学科的研究成果，以增加其吸引力和竞争力。

（二）国际化挑战

随着全球化的推进，来自不同国家和地区的期刊增加了竞争力。*Nature* 需要不断扩大其国际化的影响力，吸引来自全球各地的高质量投稿群体。

Nature 可以进一步加强与国际科研机构和学者的合作，鼓励和支持他们向 *Nature* 投稿，并提供针对不同语言和文化背景的服务和支持，以提升期刊的国际知名度和影响力。

（三）AI 类语言模型带来的挑战

AI 语言类模型，如 ChatGPT，已经有了很强的学习和写作能力，研究论文、回答问题、生成可用的计算机代码，甚至足以通过医学考试、MBA 考试、司法考试等。

但是，目前为止，语言模型生成的内容还不能完全保证其正确性，甚至在一些专业领域的错误率是很高的。如果无法区分人工编写内容和 AI 模型生成内容那么人类将面临被 AI 误导的严重问题。

AI 语言模型可以生成逼真的文本，包括科学研究的描述和结果。这可能使得识别真实性和可信度变得更加困难，特别是当有人试图将虚假或不准确的研究结果提交给 *Nature* 期刊时。期刊需要加强鉴别机制和审核流程，确保所接收的研究具有高度的可信度和科学价值。

Nature 对此问题也已经发表多篇文章进行讨论，并且公开表示，已经制定了两条原则，并且这些原则已被添加到作者指南中：首先，任何大型语言模型工具都不会被接受作为研究论文的署名作者。这是因为任何作者的归属权都伴随着对工作的责任，而 AI 工具不能承担这种责任。

其次，使用大型语言模型工具的研究人员应该在方法或致谢部分记录这种使用。如果论文不包括这些部分，可以用引言或其他适当的部分来记录对大型语言模型的使用。[1]

但这些规定并不充分，随着语言模型的快速发展，它可能能够轻松绕过现有的监察和区分方式。其他的方式，如为大型语言模型添加水印，[2] 或是研发专门的检测软件等都有待发展，*Nature* 作为科学期刊的领头羊也应继续认真严肃对待 AI 类语言模型带来的挑战。保证研究方法必须透明，作者必须诚实、真实。

---

[1]　Tools such as ChatGPT threaten transparent science; here are our ground rules for their use. *Nature*, 2023, 613(7945): 612.

[2]　Kirchenbauer, J., Geiping, J., Wen, Y., Katz, J., Miers, I. & Goldstein, T. A watermark for large language models. arXiv, 2023.

世界一流期刊分析研究——以《柳叶刀》为例[①]

摘　要: 本报告对世界领先的医学期刊之一《柳叶刀》的现状和发展历程、成功因素、未来挑战和建议进行了研究和分析。《柳叶刀》在过去的 200 年中见证了其他期刊的兴衰，并始终坚持走自己的道路，在全球范围内享有越来越大的影响力。《柳叶刀》的成功有多方面的因素，本研究对这些因素进行了细致的论述: 富有洞察力和远见卓识的创始人、成熟的组织架构和运行机制、严谨的编辑委员会、广泛的专业定位和明确的读者群定位、对潜在读者持续不断地吸引。然而，这本顶级期刊未来还将面临更大的挑战，从气候变化和健康问题的出现，到可能更加激烈的同行竞争，到与政府合作搭建科学与政策制定之间的桥梁，以及应对屡屡发生的学术造假行为。本研究针对上述挑战提出了多项有针对性的建议。

关键词: 世界一流期刊; 医学; 组织架构; 读者定位

一、期刊概览

（一）期刊基本概述

《柳叶刀》(*The Lancet*) 于 1823 年由英国外科医生托马斯·威克利 (Thomas Wakley) 创办。威克利以手术工具"柳叶刀（手术刀）"为其命名。威克利家族成员一直担任该期刊的编辑，直到 1908 年。如今《柳叶刀》拥有 24 个子刊，已经成长为一个期刊家族。2021 年影响因子为 202.731，Scopus

① 作者: 郝晨璐，上海交通大学安泰经济与管理学院; 程睿，上海交通大学海洋学院; 高汝萍，上海交通大学海洋学院; 郭琦，上海交通大学农业与生物学院; 尹巧，上海交通大学医学院。

Cite Score为115.3，是世界领先的临床、公共卫生和全球健康知识来源，在全球所有普通和内科期刊中排名第一。

《柳叶刀》有着强大的国际影响力[①]：在thelancet.com每年的访问量超过42500万，在thelancet.com和ScienceDirect上的文章下载量达2.68亿；Lancet Alert Science有超过300—500万的订阅；《柳叶刀》在X、Facebook、LinkedIn、微信、微博和YouTube上粉丝众多；《柳叶刀》期刊每年在新闻报道中被提及的次数超过36.3万次，有影响力的媒体如美联社、BBC、CNN、金融时报、卫报、纽约时报、NPR和华盛顿邮报等经常报道在《柳叶刀》期刊上发表的研究。

此外，《柳叶刀》在过去20年里发布了大量专辑和重大报告，致力于通过建立卓越的合作关系，一步步推动气候和健康相关领域的相关行动。2022年《柳叶刀》的工作亮点之一就是尼日利亚重大报告的发布。《柳叶刀》通过讲述健康人口对于国家未来发展的核心地位，使尼日利亚政府注意到这份报告，并在数周或数月内签署了相关文件，将有关保险、全民保险、健康保险的一般意见纳入法律。这份报告的成功证明了由专业人士开展的严谨科学工作有助于推进政治议程，并对解决气候和健康领域的挑战做出直接贡献。

《柳叶刀》在英语中也有尖顶穹窗的意思，有打破当时庞大的医学势力，成为"照亮医学界的明窗"的寓意。在200年的历史中，《柳叶刀》集团一直致力于广泛传播科学，以使医学能服务和改变社会，对人们的生活产生积极影响。其宣言之一就是成为医学科学的最高标准，根据工作质量和进步性选择最好的论文。《柳叶刀》发表了无数的新发现和医学突破，见证了许多极其关键的科学进步，包括外科手术和消毒技术的出现、他汀类药物和冠状病毒疫苗的研发。这些在医学领域的关键突破不断改变着人们看待科学的方式。

（二）期刊发展历程

在过去200年的历程中，《柳叶刀》见证了无数医学史上的新发现和新突破（如图1所示）。其中包括詹姆斯·辛普森（James Simpson）于1847年发现氯仿能作为一种有效的麻醉剂，减轻产妇生产过程中的痛苦，全麻药的应用极大地推动了外科学的发展；1867年约瑟夫·李斯特（Joseph Lister）发表了抗击感染的外科灭菌技术，从而使外科手术得到普及；1940年弗洛里发表有关

---

① The Lancet. About The Lancet Group: Reach and impact [2024-11-29]. https://www.thelancet.com/about-us.

青霉素动物试验的文章，促进了青霉素在临床治疗中的使用，挽救了成千上万人的生命；进入 21 世纪，《柳叶刀》先后发表了关于乳腺癌、埃博拉病毒等一系列相关文章，始终聚焦全球热点问题。《柳叶刀》始终保持独立性和权威性，就像一把锋利的手术刀，依托最先进的医学知识和一腔热忱，对抗侵蚀医学价值之力量，至今仍为全世界的医学工作者提供最高水平的研究进展，不断改变人们看待世界的方式。在《柳叶刀》200 周年纪念网站上，官方团队总结了《柳叶刀》在发展历程中发表并见证的在医学和全球公共卫生议题上的令人激动的标志性文献。《柳叶刀》从建刊初期主要关注医学领域，逐渐发展为兼顾医学与全球公共卫生和健康治理的影响力巨大的期刊。这种发展和变化可以从不同时间在《柳叶刀》上发表的标志性论文看出，其中包括：发表有关全球疾病负担研究的系统分析、关注相关国家或地区的药物治疗，传染性疾病与青少年的营养与健康问题、对地区医疗政策和全球医疗资源供应的分析研究等[①]：

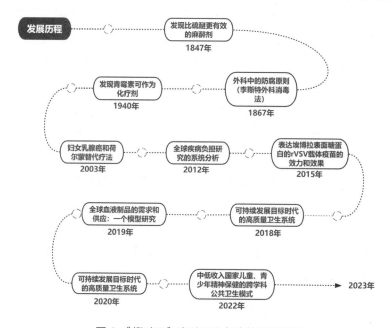

图 1 《柳叶刀》建刊 200 年来的重要文章

　　《柳叶刀》不仅是一本医学期刊创立，还代表一种作为社会改革的利器，是一项推动健康成为公共领域理念的政治武器的理念的诞生。在"互联网＋"

---

① Bynum, W. F. *The Lancet*: the first to last. *The Lancet*, 1998, 352: S3-S6.

时代下，《柳叶刀》期刊充分顺应了时代的发展，在数字化和新媒体平台的建设方面走在行业前列，不仅建立了重点突出、功能齐全、多媒体融合的专业化网站，通过微信公众号、微博、Facebook等平台充分展示其优质内容，从而达到其倡导健康权利、健康公平和社会正义，传播核心价值观及理念的目的，不断扩增其影响力，推动从临床实践到卫生系统，从国家政策到全民健康覆盖大大小小的变革。

二、发展要素分析

（一）组织架构

《柳叶刀》设置了一个面向世界的高度国际化团队。目前，《柳叶刀》的核心团队由170余名专业编辑以及营销等部门成员组成。成员来自《柳叶刀》伦敦总部和位于北京、纽约和慕尼黑的办事处，以及分布于世界各地的团队。《柳叶刀》在接收投稿的同时也通过自身团队调研，分析各个地区的健康治理热点问题。除上述成员外，《柳叶刀》还拥有一个由多达15万名专家组成的全球审稿人数据库以及260名合作统计学家进行论文评审。

向《柳叶刀》投稿的文章首先会经过初步评审，优秀的文章能进入选稿会环节。选稿会于每周二和周四在《柳叶刀》伦敦总部编委会办公室举行。在会上，所有人重点就每篇文章的宏观背景、对促进科学变革所起到的作用以及实验细节问题进行讨论。最终，主编理查德·霍顿（Richard Horton）根据各方观点做出最终决定，选拔出具有创新性和颠覆性的研究；为了从众多投稿中合理、高效地遴选符合标准的研究，《柳叶刀》形成了一个成熟的编委会－设计－运营和数字的全球化组织架构；此外，依托高水平专家，《柳叶刀》实行严谨的审稿运行机制，即全球审稿人评审－编委会讨论的模式。除主刊外，《柳叶刀》还开设具有最高影响力的子刊供投稿。在编委会讨论环节里，对于足够优秀但不适合发表于主刊的研究，在经过作者同意的前提下，可被转发至子刊刊登。

（二）成功发展要素

1.建立过程

《柳叶刀》官方网站上的一篇文章《〈柳叶刀〉：从始至终》[①]从创立之初的

---

① The Lancet. About The Lancet: Aims and scope. [2024-11-29]. https://www.thelancet.com/lancet/about.

环境以及创始人的角度，概述了《柳叶刀》创刊的经历，并分析了《柳叶刀》为何能从初创时的充满争议到现在成为影响最大的医学期刊。

这篇文章首先明确了医学期刊对于现代医学的必要性：关于医学和健康保健的所有领域的发展都与医学期刊相关。期刊的数量一直持续增长，但同时新生期刊的死亡率也很高。作者将当时主要医学期刊的创办分为两类：第一种是企业家创办，第二种是大量成立的医学会机构成员集体创办。第一种方式创办的期刊一般是昙花一现，而后一类常常存续时间较长，并且有更大的知名度，其中一个例子就是《新英格兰医学杂志》（*New England Journal of Medicine*）。作者认为医生集体创办期刊会使期刊更可靠也更加容易存活。但无论如何创办的期刊，都需要在发展过程中应对社会和技术变革的进化压力。

接着作者重点分析了《柳叶刀》作为一个由不出名医学家创办，创办初期被传统医学行业认为是"激进"的期刊，是如何在这个高度竞争、存活率低的环境中生存下来，并在后期蓬勃发展的。作者主要分析了三个原因：第一，创始者威克利将自己的个人职业抱负与期刊联系在一起，他不仅是一个医学杂志编辑，还是一个时事评论家和国会议员，并与后来《英国医学杂志》（*British Medical Journal*）的著名编辑欧内斯特·哈特（Ernest Hart）一起建立了现代医学新闻业；第二，《柳叶刀》作为一份每周出版的医学期刊，比每月和每季度出版的竞争对手更具优势和特色，它使对医学和医学政治的即时碎片评论成为可能，并将通讯与新闻成为期刊的重要特征，要求期刊语言引人入胜。这种独特的办刊方式让《柳叶刀》不仅仅成为了一个记录医学新闻的期刊，更成为了社会变革的力量；第三，《柳叶刀》是一份商业杂志，在创刊的起初80年一直是威克利的家族企业，不属于任何科学和医学组织。该期刊一直在尽力扩大读者群，吸引有影响力的稿件，坚决维护自己的独立性，来不断发挥期刊影响力。

2.组织架构

《柳叶刀》在创刊早期即通过刊登一些突破性的研究树立了自身在研究界的权威地位。长期以来，《柳叶刀》一直秉持推动变革的理念和让医学服务和改造社会的初衷，从而坚持刊登论文的高门槛。所有刊登的文章必须具有创新性和颠覆性的研究，能提供人们对某一领域科学的新思路，并且为科学变革的出现提供土壤。

《柳叶刀》还尝试迈出医学界，积极与自然科学界、工程界、金融界和政界沟通，形成了从自身向外界延伸的合作机制。结合时代和地区特点，《柳叶刀》从交叉学科研究的视角把人类的健康治理与气候变化等热点议题进行结合，评估气候变化对人类健康的未来影响，并为上述各领域所应做出的响应提供建议。气候变化是 21 世纪全人类面临的最重大健康威胁，为了监测和评估气候变化背景下未来人类健康状况，同时针对性地制定必要的政策应对方案，《柳叶刀》开展国际性多学科合作。2015 年，《柳叶刀》成立健康与气候变化委员会，出版"柳叶刀倒计时"（Lancet Countdown）报告，讨论气候变化影响和脆弱性、健康的适应性和复原力、缓和举措与健康的协同效益、经济与金融以及公众和政治参与等在内的 5 个关键领域共计 43 项相关指标。来自全世界各机构的医学学者以及逾百名气候科学家、经济学家、工程师和政治界人士共同参与"柳叶刀倒计时"项目，从多重学科和身份为应对气候变化献计献策。除气候变化议题外，《柳叶刀》还参与了人口问题和人道主义危机等治理难题的讨论。

为了从众多投稿中合理、高效地遴选符合标准的研究，《柳叶刀》形成了一个成熟的全球化组织架构以及学术水平极高的审稿团队，确保文章的研究主题回应医学科学真正的热点，研究成果符合人类健康治理的最迫切需求。同时，《柳叶刀》还设置涉猎广、影响力高的子刊，为分支领域内的重大研究保留了展示的舞台。

综上，《柳叶刀》的合理架构能够在尽可能短的审稿周期内筛选出最具影响力的文章，选择将这些文章刊登在主刊或者合适的领域内子刊上；同时，《柳叶刀》积极参与国际各领域治理，进一步增加其受众，并开辟了解决人类健康问题的广泛新维度。

3. 学科定位

《柳叶刀》的成功与其学科定位密不可分。从《柳叶刀》学科体系完整性的角度，《柳叶刀》下设 24 个子期刊，这些子期刊学科定位明确，且子期刊与子期刊之间既相互独立又彼此联系，互为补充；从《柳叶刀》学科定位社会意义的角度，子期刊出现的时机和定位与当时社会存在和面临的问题息息相关，子期刊的创立就是为了人们能获得更好的健康、医疗服务；具有影响力、前瞻性的研究发表于定位不同的子刊中，通过文章进一步为子刊打开知名度也是其成功的因素之一。

首先，《柳叶刀》的学科定位明确且全面。《柳叶刀》是全球领先的综合性医学期刊，自 1823 年创办以来，一直致力于将科学知识普及全世界，以便医学可以为社会服务，从而改变社会，积极影响人们的生活。该期刊发表了大量的具有重要科学价值且对人类健康做出了重要贡献的文章，并推动了临床实践和公共卫生政策方面的积极变革。[1] 根据子期刊学科定位之间的区别和联系，可以将其分为：侧重临床研究的期刊、侧重不同区域的期刊、针对不同人群的期刊、针对不同研究阶段的期刊、侧重提供决策支持的期刊和其他。子期刊之间不仅彼此独立，而且相互补充。如《柳叶刀·艾滋病》（ The Lancet HIV ）报道艾滋病相关的创新性治疗方法和基础生物研究成果，而《柳叶刀·老龄健康》（ The Lancet Healthy Longevity ）也有艾滋病相关报道，如报道艾滋病毒对携带者的影响，抗逆转录病毒治疗对老年艾滋病毒感染者的影响，以及对与艾滋病无关的慢性合并症的干预措施，从而更好地实现对艾滋病感染者的全面护理，并在长寿研究方面对《柳叶刀·艾滋病》进行补充。[2]

其次，期刊创立顺应历史潮流、满足社会需要。《柳叶刀》作为世界一流期刊，拥有敏锐的嗅觉，能够把控特定时代出现的健康问题；同时，具有勇于担当的气魄，在恰当的时机建立期刊解决特定时代出现的健康问题。一方面，特定疾病发病率和死亡率上升，使得《柳叶刀》和其他政府组织将目光移向临床上疾病的治疗、愈后和预防；另一方面，随着研究的深入、数据的积累，需要报道特定疾病的期刊汇聚全球研究，探讨治疗方案，所以《柳叶刀》与临床疾病相关的研究应运而生。如，20 世纪全球范围内传染病的暴发引起了世界各地的广泛关注，为了预防、诊断和治疗传染病，需要世界范围内的专家进行深入研究和探索，以便能够更好地为患者提供医疗救治和保障公共健康。[3] 因此，《柳叶刀》2001 年创建《柳叶刀·传染病学习》（ The Lancet Infectious Diseases ）专门刊登传染病学科研成果，为全球范围内的传染病防治提供更加专业和权威的信息和平台，推动医学领域的进一步发展和进步。

最后，期刊中的文章进一步扩展期刊知名度。《柳叶刀》各大期刊的成功除了学科定位清晰、顺应历史潮流，期刊上刊登的文章也为《柳叶刀》的成功

---

[1]　Titanji, B. K. ARTful ageing: epigenetic rejuvenation in people with HIV. *The Lancet Healthy Longevity*, 2023, 4(5): e181-e182.

[2]　Clay, K., Lewis, J. & Severnini, E. Pollution, Infectious Disease, and Mortality: Evidence from the 1918 Spanish Influenza Pandemic. *Journal of Economic History*, 2018, 78(4): 1179-1209.

[3]　Ahlqvist, E., Storm, P., et al. Novel subgroups of adult-onset diabetes and their association with outcomes: a data-driven cluster analysis of six variables. *The Lancet Diabetes & Endocrinology*, 2018, 6(5): 361-369.

有所贡献，文章为期刊进一步打开知名度、建立国际影响力奠定基础，同时具有国际影响力的期刊吸引其他开创性成果投稿，实现良性循环。如，2018 年《柳叶刀·糖尿病与内分泌学》（*The Lancet Diabetes & Endocrinology*）的一篇文章根据不同的疾病进展和糖尿病并发症风险将患者分为五个亚组，这种新的亚分类有助于为患者量身定制治疗方案，实现靶向治疗，这也代表了糖尿病精准医疗实现了第一步。[①] 同时这篇文章也为《柳叶刀·糖尿病与内分泌学》进一步打开知名度，提升影响力，期刊和文章实现相互成就。

4.编委会设置

《柳叶刀》在创刊早期即通过刊登一些突破性的研究树立了自身在研究界的权威地位。长期以来，《柳叶刀》一直坚持刊登论文的高门槛，所有刊登的文章必须具有创新性和颠覆性的研究，能提供人们对某一领域科学的新思路，并且为科学变革的出现提供土壤。

向《柳叶刀》投稿的文章首先会经过初步评审，优秀的文章能进入选稿会环节。选稿会于每周二和周四在《柳叶刀》伦敦总部编委会办公室举行[②]。在会上，所有人重点就每篇文章的宏观背景、对促进科学变革所起到的作用以及实验细节问题进行讨论。最终，主编理查德·霍顿根据各方观点做出最终决定，选拔出具有创新性和颠覆性的研究。

5.读者定位和吸引投稿

创建初期，《柳叶刀》的读者主要是英国各地的城市医生、农村医生和全球殖民地医务工作者。如今，《柳叶刀》面向大众，拥有更广泛的读者。读者包括研究人员、临床医生、临床科研者、行业专业人员、政策制定者、媒体机构工作者和患者。《柳叶刀》还通过推出播客节目"Lancet Voice"，给听众带来全球关于健康的有趣故事。

《柳叶刀》全面、系统的学科分类，使其具有十分广泛的读者，这也是《柳叶刀》成功的原因之一。首先，对于临床类研究期刊，该领域专家学者需要通过该期刊了解最新研究成果、把握前沿研究，从而确定研究方向；该领域的临床医生需要通过该期刊掌握最新的治疗方案，保障临床治疗的先进性和安全性；其次，《柳叶刀·公共卫生》（*The Lancet Public Health*）这类期刊可以

---

① 弗雷赛斯.走近顶刊系列：LANCET《柳叶刀》编辑部. (2021-06-29)[2024-11-29]. https://t.cj.sina.com.cn/articles/view/6468995530/1819509ca01900v0a2.

② The Lancet. More than a medical journal. [2024-11-29]. https://www.thelancet.com/lancet-200.

指导政府决策，保障居民卫生保健的可得性、可及性、可接受性和质量，指导有关部门采取政治、经济和社会行动来保护和加强公民健康；最后，《柳叶刀》最初成立的目的是保障公民健康，即对患者进行治疗、对健康人群进行科普，让公民掌握健康知识，预防疾病，所以它也是很好的科普期刊，受众为所有对健康知识感兴趣的群体。随着数字化的发展，《柳叶刀》医学知识的传播离不开社交软件和媒体，而《柳叶刀》在X、Facebook上的推广，在BBC、CNN上的报道，都是其取得成功不可或缺的因素。

在吸引投稿方面，《柳叶刀》也为其他期刊做出了表率。首先，《柳叶刀》在一些重大的医学议题上直言不讳，树立勇于担当的顶刊形象；其次，《柳叶刀》紧跟最新研究，把握世界最前沿的科技信息和具有潜在价值的前沿信息，通过大师效应和报道重量级、重大突破研究，在行业内形成巨大影响力，树立期刊权威；同时，逐步完善自身学术期刊国际化进程。如在本土之外的其他国家和地区开设办公室，与其他国家和地区的科研、医疗机构合作共同主办学术论坛、学术报告和学术峰会，增加国际学术交流；出版流程管理高效，实现投审稿程序数字网络化；《柳叶刀》网站以用户需求为中心，根据需求的差异性，通过对内容进行挖掘、重组、荟萃，开发内容衍生品，构建知识关联和知识拓扑，提供形式多样的知识服务和社会服务；《柳叶刀》通过建立高效的网络平台，与社交网络紧密对接，利用新媒体增强期刊的渗透力。如通过播客节目、作者和权威专家访谈以及编辑或专家解读、讨论等视频、音频形式，就文章相关的热点、争议问题以及重要学术意义进行深度探讨和分析，以扩大期刊的显示度和读者群，发掘潜在用户群体，提升论文的学术影响力和社会认知度。

（三）未来挑战

随着近年来世界发展趋势的变化，全球卫生面临的问题也随之发生改变。在这个新的时期，《柳叶刀》可能会面临如下挑战。

第一，根据《〈柳叶刀〉2022年健康与气候变化倒计时报告：健康受化石燃料支配》（The 2022 report of *The Lancet* Countdown on health and climate change: health at the mercy of fossil fuels）对公众参与气候变化政策制定和健康治理的研究，虽然2021年全球媒体对于气候变化和健康议题的报道数量相比2020年显著增加，但是这些报道主题以气候变化为主，联合讨论气候变化与健康问题的文章仍然很少。

第二，《柳叶刀》作为商业医学期刊，未来可能面临着同行竞争的问题，如与《新英格兰医学杂志》在癌症、肿瘤研究方面的竞争和与《美国医学会杂志》(*The Journal of the American Medical Association*)在公共卫生和临床实践研究方面的竞争。

第三，《柳叶刀》网站上提到，未来《柳叶刀》将聚焦五个重点项目：全民健康覆盖、从人类健康的角度应对气候变化、健康研究、重视心理健康、优先考虑儿童和青少年的健康需要。这五个重点项目的面向对象主要是政府的决策机构，政府制定方案缓解气候变化、保障卫生保健公平、注重心理健康。《柳叶刀》虽然是负责任、有担当的期刊，过去也承担了不少指导决策的责任，但其本质还是医学期刊，如何与政府高效合作以建立起科学和决策的桥梁、实现最新研究成果的高效传播是需要思考的问题。

第四，如何识别和解决愈演愈烈的学术造假行为，是期刊和出版商都应该更加重视的问题。近年来，大规模学术造假事件频发，被期刊撤稿的论文数量不断增加。据统计，2022年1月1日到2022年12月31日期间，全球有488篇SCI撤稿。2022年9月，出版商辛迪维(Hindawi)将旗下16家期刊共计511篇文章撤稿，并暂停出版。威立(Wiley)出版集团因此损失了约900万美元的收入；同时，《自然》(*Nature*)的一篇文章称，PubMed这一大型生物医学相关的SCI文献检索数据库，被查出至少1％的论文可能出自论文工厂。由于AI写作和绘图等技术的发展，之后的学术造假手段可能会更多样和隐蔽，期刊的审稿人和编辑无疑面临着更大的识别成本和更严苛的审稿环境。

三、总结与讨论

(一)期刊综合评价

《柳叶刀》自1823年创刊以来，一直致力于将科学知识普及全世界，以使医学可以为社会服务，从而改变社会并积极影响人们的生活。该期刊通过先进的组织架构、严格的审稿机制、科学的学科和读者定位，以及成熟的营销方法，发表了大量的具有重要科学价值和对人类健康做出了重要贡献的论文，在医学领域的发展和社会的进步方面起到推动作用，是世界领先的临床、公共卫生和全球健康知识来源。面对全新的气候变化和健康全球治理形势，以及可能存在的同僚竞争和学术不端等挑战，《柳叶刀》在推动临床实践和公共卫生政策方面的积极变革的同时，也应不断探索新的发展方向，以适应时代的变化和医学领域的新需求。

（二）期刊发展的意见和建议

1.气候变化与健康问题的关注与实践

在气候变化问题愈加受到社会共同关切的背景下，《柳叶刀》应该充分发挥自身在学术界内的强大影响力，鼓励人们同时参与气候变化与健康治理两者的讨论中。《柳叶刀》可进一步提高在社交媒体平台上的宣传力度，让更多原本就对气候变化保持关注的人们意识到气候问题对人类健康的重要影响。《柳叶刀》还可尝试在解决气候变化问题与健康治理过程中参与更多实践环节，这有利于全球在共同问题上的合作，也有利于《柳叶刀》塑造自身形象，扩大期刊本身的影响力。在作为"柳叶刀倒计时"计划的提倡者基础上，《柳叶刀》自身还可尝试与环保组织和地区机构达成广泛合作，通过实习、考察和志愿工作等途径促成不同学科领域、《柳叶刀》内外人才的直接交流，以实践者的身份参与解决气候－健康问题实际操作中。

2.保持竞争优势

在与其他顶级医学期刊间的激烈竞争中，《柳叶刀》应该更专注于以下方面以脱颖而出：第一，研究要专，继续深耕生物医学科学或实践；第二，知识要新，以敏锐的目光捕捉学术、行业和社会的热点和前沿，紧跟学科领域发展，定期组织专辑，形成专题特色，起到行业内的引领作用；第三，宣传到位，面向大众，充分利用新媒体技术向全球公民分享学科前沿进展；第四，发刊要快，建立"绿色通道"，提供优质快速的审稿服务，充分利用数字化不断改进和优化出版流程，提高出版效率。

3.有效解决学术不端现象

针对学术不端现象，《柳叶刀》已经进行了及时回应并采取了有效的行动。在 2020 年 9 月，《柳叶刀》编辑部针对一篇撤回的文章发表了评论文章 "Learning from a retraction"，宣布对编辑政策的修改。具体的修改内容包括针对作者声明表、数据共享声明和额外的同行评议要求的修改。针对期刊对于论文的审查在未来如何越来越严谨，有研究者提出了进一步的要求。*Research Integrity and Peer Review* 杂志的联合主编马里奥·马利茨基（Mario Malički）认为期刊应该推动作者分享已发表的研究数据和代码，并且文章发表前后的审查方式应该更加透明。学术编辑应该提高筛选和邀请审稿人的精确性，认真甄别审稿人的意见，在适当的情况下也可以显示处理每篇论文的责任编辑，多方面保障论文质量和可靠性。同时，期刊应该更加重视论文发表后的同行评价。在技术层面，一些学科（比如生物、医学领域）因为其特殊性，研究结果的可重复度较小，可以通过AI识图等手段进行相似图像识别，短时间找出可能依赖数据和图像修正的虚假论文。

4.与政府建立良好沟通

《柳叶刀》作为全球顶级医学期刊，想要实现最新研究成果的高效传播，一方面是发表相关研究，另一方面是和政府保持高效的沟通。《柳叶刀》建刊200周年，拥有24个子刊，在这两方面具有深厚的底蕴。《柳叶刀·全球健康》（*The Lancet Global Health*）支撑全民健康覆盖；《柳叶刀·星球健康》（*The Lancet Planetary Health*）支撑气候变化与人类健康相关研究；《柳叶刀·精神病学》（*The Lancet Psychiatry*）支撑心理健康；《柳叶刀·儿童青少年健康》（*The Lancet Child & Adolescent Health*）支撑儿童、青少年健康研究；指导政府决策方面，《柳叶刀·公共卫生》积累了很多经验。《柳叶刀》可以根据现有的基础，以其为依托、为优势，在其基础上进一步寻找新的思路，开拓新的方法，实现研究成果服务于决策，决策造福于人民。

PART
2

第二章

模拟《联合国气候变化框架公约》第 28 次
缔约方大会（COP28）会议提案

建立世界各国人群应对气候变化健康风险的有效措施
——基于英国实践的案例研究①

摘　要： 作为 21 世纪全人类的共同挑战，气候变化已经对人类、经济和社会发展等产生了影响。针对气候变化对民众健康所产生的威胁，英国政府业已采取一系列措施积极应对。英国呼吁各国政府制订明确的战略目标和政策框架、完善的气候法律体系加速能源转型，设立共同基金，强化国际协作与交流，共同抑制气候变化对人类生存可能产生的不利影响。

关键词： 气候变化；英国；健康风险

一、引　言

（一）选题背景

气候变化对人类社会的可持续发展带来了深远影响，越来越多的人开始关注气候问题所引起的一系列风险。例如，干旱、洪水和其他极端天气事件的频率和强度增加，将加剧对健康的不利影响。由于欠发达国家与地区往往面临最大的风险，因此这些风险将极大加剧本就存在的发展不均衡现象。

20 世纪 70 年代以来，全球各国就围绕日益加剧的环境压力展开应对工作，并取得了一系列成果，见表 1。

① 作者：周熙宜，南京大学国际关系学院；陈奕竹，南京大学国际关系学院；屠欣宇，南京大学外国语学院。

表1　全球应对气候变化进程代表性成果汇总

序号	年份	事件
1	1972	斯德哥尔摩联合国人类环境会议召开
2	1987	《我们共同的未来》发布
3	1992	《联合国气候变化框架公约》《生物多样性公约》和《森林原则宣言》签订
4	1994	《联合国气候变化框架公约》生效
5	1997	《联合国气候变化框架公约的京都议定书》签订
6	2015	《2030年可持续发展议程》与《巴黎协定》签订

2015年，联合国可持续发展目标的提出和《巴黎协定》在COP21大会上的通过，是推动全球可持续发展的两个重要里程碑。2015年9月在纽约举行的联合国可持续发展峰会上，150多位世界领导人通过了《改变我们的世界：2030年可持续发展议程》（UN 2015a），该议程包含17个可持续发展目标和169个具体指标，旨在消除贫困、改善人民生活、增进人类繁荣和福祉、保护环境和应对气候变化。2015年12月的COP21上，196个缔约方国家一致通过了《巴黎协定》，为世界设定了具体的气候目标，即将全球气温较工业化前水平的升幅控制在低于2℃以内，并努力控制在1.5℃之内。《巴黎协定》还建立了"国家自主贡献"（NDC）减排机制。IPCC 2018年发布的《IPCC全球升温1.5℃特别报告》（Special Report on Global Warming of 1.5℃）进一步表明，为了实现温控1.5℃的气候目标，到2030年全球碳排放水平必须比2010年低45％，并在2050年前后实现碳中和。[①]

（二）选题意义

1. 气候变化对人类、经济和社会等的全面影响

极端天气的频发增加了人口发病和死亡风险。预计到21世纪末，每年与高温有关的死亡人数仍将会是现在的三倍左右。较高的温度可能导致传染病感染率的增加。

贫富差距、住房困难、老龄化加剧和疾病都会影响气候变化带来的冲击程度。更贫困的地区更难获得高质量的绿色和蓝色空间；低质量的住房尤其会影响人们的健康。

---

① The Intergovernmental Panel on Climate Change (IPCC). *Special Report on Global Warming of 1.5℃*. (2019-09) [2023-08-29]. https://www.ipcc.ch/sr15/.

2. 对于气候变化对民众健康所产生的威胁，英国已经采取措施积极应对

英国已经完成了两期以国家为主导的、以应对气候变化为目的的计划，并在第二期适应计划（NAP2）期间为气候变化做出了巨大且艰难的努力。英国政府致力于在极端天气情况下为尽可能多的民众提供高质量和可获得的医疗保健服务，并鼓励人们接受国家为改善环境适应力所采取的一系列干预措施。[①]但现实困境是，英国仍然缺乏政策和资金来改造现有医疗保健建筑以适应气候变化所造成的影响。此外，英国政府需要制订一个跨部门的长期适应计划，涵盖居家护理、医疗检测等。[②]

目前，世界范围内尚缺少可靠的数据用以监测天气事件对健康的影响。当下的情势迫切需要更为充分、可信的数据来跟踪有关方面的进展。正因如此，英国致力于进一步建立一个跨部门的NHS信托机构，为完善综合护理系统提供合理规划。此外，英国正在加快完善一个新的气候和健康安全中心，即英国卫生和安全局（UKHSA）。该机构致力于为领导、协调气候变化背景下的各行各业而努力。

二、进展评估

（一）保障性措施进展

1. 明确的战略目标和政策框架

英国政府制定了明确的战略目标和长期政策框架——从 2020 年的能源白皮书《为零碳未来提供动力》（Powering Our Net Zero Future）到 2021 年的"净零战略"、2022 年的能源安全战略，以及《2030 国际气候和自然行动战略框架》。2020 年的能源白皮书是英国 13 年来的第一份能源白皮书，目的是应对新冠疫情后的绿色复苏，并在 2050 年实现净零排放。2021 年 10 月 19 日公布的"净零战略"是英国政府在《巴黎协定》下第二个长期降低温室气体排放发展战略，旨在支持英国企业和消费者向清洁能源和绿色技术过渡。例如，通过投资可持续清洁能源来降低英国对化石燃料的依赖，降低未来价格高企和波动的风险，并加强能源安全。该战略将支持英国发展绿色产业，并在最新的低

---

① UK Department for Environment, Food & Rural Affairs. *Climate Change Adaptation: Policy Information*. (2022-08-11)[2023-08-24]. https://www.gov.uk/government/publications/climate-change-adaptation-policy-information/climate-change-adaptation-policy-information.

② Climate Change Committee. *Independent Assessment of UK Climate Risk*. (2021-06-16)[2023-08-22]. https://www.theccc.org.uk/publication/independent-assessment-of-uk-climate-risk/.

碳技术方面获得竞争优势。这些政策得到了有针对性的政府资金支持，加之这一揽子文件中规定的政策，到 2030 年，英国将获得约 1000 亿英镑的私人投资。英国致力于在 2030 年创造多达 48 万个就业岗位。

2. 完善的气候法律保障

合理有效保障战略落实的关键在于，英国建立了一个强有力的气候政策法律框架。2008 年，英国设立《气候变化法案》，确立远期目标为到 2050 年将碳排放量在 1990 年的水平上降低至少 80％。2019 年 5 月，负责制定减排方案并监督实施的气候变化委员会建议，将此目标修改为"净零排放"，即通过植树造林、碳捕捉等方式抵消碳排放。2019 年 6 月《气候变化法案》生效，正式确立英国到 2050 年实现温室气体"净零排放"的目标，英国成为第一个以法律形式确立到 2050 年实现"净零排放"的主要经济体，将清洁发展置于现代工业战略的核心。2021 年，英国颁布一项综合性环境法案《环境法》，旨在建立一个全面的环境法律框架。

（二）减缓措施进展

减缓措施旨在减少吸热温室气体流入大气，即减少这些气体的来源（例如，燃烧化石燃料用于电力、热能或运输），以及增强积累和储存这些气体的"容量"（例如海洋，森林和土壤）。减缓的目标是避免人类对地球气候的重大干扰，以期在足够的时间范围内稳定温室气体水平，使生态系统能够自然适应气候变化，确保粮食生产不受威胁，并使经济发展能够以可持续的方式进行。

1. 加速能源转型

当前，英国在自主推动能源转型方面处于有利地位。从 1990 年到 2021 年，英国减少了 48％的排放，脱碳速度比其他 G7 国家都快，同时经济增长了 65％。良好的商业环境帮助英国在过去的 5 年里成为欧洲清洁能源投资最大的三大国家之一，到 2030 年，英国企业在低碳产品和服务方面将获得 1 万亿英镑的投资。英国还拥有一个强大的排放报告系统。2023 年 2 月 7 日，英国首相里希·苏纳克宣布设立能源安全和净零排放部，为英国提供更优惠、更清洁、更安全的能源，并减少英国对国际能源供应的依赖。该部门的优先完成事项包括：（1）确保长期能源供应安全，降低能源费用和通货膨胀；（2）确保英国按计划履行净零排放承诺，并通过大幅加快网络基础设施建设和国内能源生产来支持经济增长；（3）提高英国家庭、企业和公共部门建筑的能源效率，以达到能源需求减少 15％ 的目标；（4）为支撑能源消费者支付账单提供调整方案，并制定长期改革方案，以改善电力市场为家庭和企业服务的方式；（5）把握净零排放带来的经济利益，包括通过投资新兴绿色产业创造就业机会，推动经济增长；（6）批准通过能源法案，以支持新兴碳捕集、利用与封存技术和氢能行业发展，更新能源系统的治理，并缩短审批海上风电项目所需的时间。

英国政府特别注重合作，在国内和世界各地促进绿色创新和能源转型。英国通过能源转型委员会（ETC）等组织和绿色电网倡议（Green Grids Initiative）等倡议展示合作的力量，加强对发展中经济体能源转型的国际支持。前者响应了 27 个快速反应项目（要求 ETC 成员提供特定的财政和技术支持），另有 15 个项目（由 9 个国家提供支持）正在筹备中；后者正在加速非洲和亚太地区的区域电网项目建设，使电网能够应对不断增长的可再生能源份额。英国在 COP27 宣布为清洁能源创新基金再提供 6550 万英镑，该基金为发展中国家的研究人员和科学家提供资助，以加快清洁技术的发展。2019 年启动的商务能源与产业战略部（BEIS）基金已为印度的生物质能制冷、尼日利亚的锂离子电池原型和摩洛哥的钢铁生产的清洁氢基燃料等创新提供了资金支持。英国与南非建立了首个公正能源转型伙伴关系（JETP），为南非的公正过渡筹集资金，提供支持。英国与越南、印度尼西亚、印度和塞内加尔等国家就支持向清洁能源公正过渡开展工作。英国和肯尼亚已经重申了他们对英国-肯尼亚战略伙伴关系的承诺，并同意推进绿色投资项目，这些项目包括由英国国际投资公司支持肯尼亚新建或扩建太阳能和地热发电厂，英国为内罗毕铁路城提供出口融资，英国 GBM 工程公司牵头推动 30 亿美元的大瀑布水电项目的公私合营。英国还在财政上支持埃及 COP27 的"粮食、水和能源关系倡议"，预计调动数十亿私营部门资金开发包括太阳能公园和储能创新在内的项目。

2. 制止和扭转森林损失

COP27 上，英国首相启动了由 20 个成员国组成的森林与气候领导人伙伴关系（FCLP）协议。[①]该伙伴关系协议规定，每年举行两次会议，跟踪 COP26 会议上具有里程碑意义的《关于森林和土地利用的格拉斯哥领导人宣言》的承诺。该宣言旨在联合政府、企业和社区领导人的行动，到 2030 年控制和扭转森林损失和土地退化，同时实现可持续发展和促进包容性农村转型。

① UK Government. UK announces major new package of climate support at COP27. (2022-11-07)[2023-08-23]. https://www.gov.uk/government/news/uk-announces-major-new-package-of-climate-support-at-cop27.

16个主要森林国家将侧重于通过六个行动领域实现变革，包括支持高完整性森林。捐助方正在与森林国家合作，确保12亿美元的全球森林融资承诺在2021—2025年间分配给正确的计划。捐助者在2021年总共花费了至少3亿美元，随后几年还将花费更多。其中，英国在COP27上承诺为刚果盆地的保护提供9000万英镑的支持。①英国首相还确认为自然、人民和气候投资基金提供6500万英镑的资金，该基金旨在支持原住民和当地森林社区，保护和恢复200万公顷的热带森林。

3. 用绿色金融带动能源转变

英国是世界上绿色产业最多的国家之一，2020年欧洲所有外国直接投资（FDI）支持的清洁技术项目中，有六分之一来自英国。在过去的十年里，英国通过一系列融资机制吸引了大量的绿色行业投资。

英国政府的政策和资金承诺已经有了实际成果。英国政府在2021年支出审查中承诺为绿色工业产业提供300亿英镑的国内投资，在2022年秋季声明中承诺在2025—2028年提供60亿英镑的能源效率资金，并在2023年春季预算中承诺为碳捕集、利用和储存（CCUS）项目提供高达200亿英镑的投资，其将得到英国各公共融资机构的投资支持。其中，仅英国基础设施银行（UKIB）就有220亿英镑的金融能力，其核心任务是应对气候变化和促进英国各地的经济增长，清洁能源预计将成为其投资组合中最大的部门。自2020年11月以来，由于政府的新政策和支出规划，英国目前有超过8万个绿色工作岗位正在酝酿中。

在加快电动汽车转变方面，2022年，英国的电池电动汽车销量在欧洲排名第二，英国道路上的插电式汽车总数超过100万辆，其中约60%是电池电动汽车。英国的充电基础设施也在加速发展：公共充电设备从2019年1月的10300个增加到2023年3月的38700个以上。

英国政府雄心勃勃的"零排放汽车（ZEV）"任务将使英国制造商置于电动革命的最前沿。ZEV宣言现在有来自国家和地方政府、制造商、企业和车队的200个签署方，他们都致力于到2035年在主要市场实现零排放，到2040年实现全球所有新车和货车的零排放。

为了确保温室气体排放困境不会转移到其他碳定价和气候监管水平较低的

---

① UK Government. UK announces major new package of climate support at COP27. (2022-11-07)[2023-08-23]. https://www.gov.uk/government/news/uk-announces-major-new-package-of-climate-support-at-cop27.

国家，英国正就应对未来碳泄漏风险的潜在政策措施展开磋商，包括碳边界调整机制和产品标准，该机制从 21 世纪 20 年代中期开始部署。英国还与近 50 个新兴市场和发展中经济体举行了区域对话，成立了新的国际援助工作组，以确定加强国际援助的方法。

（三）适应措施进展

适应措施涉及适应实际或预期的气候变化，目标是减少出现气候变化有害影响（例如海平面上升、极端天气或粮食危机）的风险。它还包括充分利用与气候变化相关的任何潜在有益机会（例如，某些地区的生长季节更长或产量增加）。联合国气候变化框架公约的适应信息通报登记处（Adaptation Communications Registry，AdComm）是负责收集和登记各国提交的适应信息的机构。根据《巴黎协定》，各缔约方需要定期向登记处通报他们在应对气候变化方面的适应举措、政策和实践。英国的适应能力被 AdComm 评定为"积极"。

《气候变化法》为促进英国的适应行动制定了一个政策框架：英国气候变化风险评估（Climate Change Risk Assessment，CCRA）。气候变化委员会（CCC）每隔五年对英国气候变化的主要风险和机遇的评估。CCRA3 发现，英国面临的风险水平与适应水平之间的差距已经扩大，适应行动未能跟上日益恶化的气候风险现实。2023 年 3 月 29 日，英国更新了适应进展的监测框架和监测适应交付的方式。[①]

国家适应计划（NAPs）每五年编制一次，第一份国家适应计划（NAP1）于 2013 年 7 月发布。这是政府应对英格兰风险评估中确定的主要风险和机遇的战略，列出了政府和其他方面在未来五年内将采取的措施，以应对气候变化带来的挑战。它包括以下关键领域：提高对气候变化适应需求的认识，并及时采取行动，提高对最新的《气候评估》中强调的主要风险群体的复原力。第二份国家适应计划（NAP2）规定了从 2018 年持续到 2023 年政府和其他人将在五年内适应英格兰气候变化挑战的行动，涉及自然环境、基础设施、人与建筑环境、工商业、地方政府部门。

---

① Climate Change Committee. CCC Adaptation Monitoring Framework. (2023-03-29)[2023-08-24]. https://www.theccc.org.uk/publication/ccc-adaptation-monitoring-framework/.

1. 英国的适应进展

英国更新《气候变化影响核算绿皮书补充指南》，鼓励将气候变化风险纳入政策和方案决策，并借鉴气候证据和评估。建立新的政府范围内的适应性管理，为整个政府的适应性和复原力政策法定职责的履行提供高级别的监督和战略指导。

在G7领导人峰会期间，英国为区域风险池提供了1.2亿英镑的捐款，以支持改善对极端天气和与气候有关的灾害的反应。英国与经济合作与发展组织（OECD）建立了一个项目，旨在解决英国和国际上在监测适应进展方面面临的挑战。

投资6.4亿英镑作为自然气候基金，用于林地和泥炭地的创建、恢复和适应性管理；投资8千万英镑作为绿色复苏挑战基金；政府关于洪水和海岸侵蚀风险管理的政策声明中，承诺将政府资助的项目数量增加一倍，包括基于自然的解决方案，减少洪水和海岸侵蚀风险。

政府要求企业公开与气候相关的财务状况，支持投资决策向低碳、具有气候复原力的经济过渡。

未来建筑标准咨询会（Future Buildings Standard Consultation）提出，可以在《建筑条例》（Building Regulations）中引入新的过热缓解要求来减少新住宅建筑的过热风险。

2. 权力下放的行政地区的适应进展

英国推动地方自主适应。在担任G7主席国期间，英国支持2021年1月气候适应峰会提出的《地方主导的适应原则》（PLLA）。PLLA旨在以公平的方式制定和实施适应干预措施，并以当地的优先事项、知识和专长为依据。

苏格兰：《2009年气候变化法（苏格兰）》规定，部长们有责任在每次气候变化评估之后制定气候变化适应方案。2023年3月，英国政府在《对气候变化委员会2022年年度进展报告建议的回应》中表示，苏格兰达成了2020年温室气体的减排目标，并在现阶段的气候变化方案下发布了第二份年度监测报告。[1]苏格兰政府继续实施其制订的第二个苏格兰气候变化适应计划（SCCAP）（2019—2024）中规定的行动，并准备其第三个计划。作为对CCRA3的初步

---

① UK Department for Energy Security & Net Zero. Responding to the Climate Change Committee's (CCC) Annual Progress Report 2022 Recommendations. (2023-03-10)[2023-08-25]. https://www.gov.uk/government/publications/committee-on-climate-change-2022-progress-report-government-response/0dd9983f-be4d-4acf-94c2-6c34cf476de8.

回应，苏格兰政府制定了在 COP26 会议之前举办国家气候复原力峰会的计划，将公共、私营和第三部门的领导层聚集在一起，作为苏格兰向净零和气候复原过渡的一部分，以及委托 CCC 就当前的 SCCAP 提供进一步建议。

北爱尔兰：《英国气候变化法》规定，北爱尔兰行政部门在每个 CCRA 公布后，应在合理可行的情况下尽快公布气候变化适应方案。北爱尔兰 2021 年12 月发布了《通往净零能耗战略》（Path to Net Zero Energy Strategy），2022年 1 月发布了《行动计划》，2022 年 3 月发布技能战略。通过"我们未来的森林项目"（Forests for Our Future），实现到 2025 年每年造林 900 公顷的目标所需资金已经到位。2022 年，《北爱尔兰气候变化法》获得批准。北爱尔兰行政部门正在继续实施其 2019－2024 年间第二个五年期方案（NICCAP2）。该方案自 2019 年 9 月公布以来，通过年度审查增加了一些新的行动。行政部门还在 2022 年期间进行全面的中期方案审查。这次审查提供了评估该方案影响的机会，以及修正方案中计划和行动的机会。

威尔士：《英国气候变化法》要求威尔士政府就气候变化影响的目标、行动和未来优先事项提出报告。2016 年《环境法（威尔士）》（Environment [Wales] Act）提供了一个管理威尔士自然资源的框架，而 2015 年《子孙后代福祉法（威尔士）》（Wellbeing of Future Generations [Wales] Act）旨在改善威尔士的社会、经济、环境和文化发展状况。威尔士政府在 2018 年制定了一份气候变化适应计划草案。2022 年 12 月，威尔士政府发布了第一份关于 2016年到 2020 年首轮碳预算期的进展声明，表明完成了首个碳预算和过渡目标。同时，威尔士政府正在着力于实现 2021—2025 第二个碳预算"净零威尔士"（Net Zero Wales）。威尔士政府正在继续实施其于 2019 年 12 月发布的第二个五年气候变化适应计划《威尔士全民繁荣：气候意识》（Prosperity for All: A Climate Conscious Wales）。

（四）当前适应与减缓气候变化存在的问题和挑战

气候变化已经成为了影响英国民众身心健康的重要威胁之一。2022 年，英国极端天气的影响凸显了适应气候变化的紧迫性。2022 年夏天，英国创纪录的高温带来了前所未有的人员死亡、野火事件和重大基础设施破坏事件，充分说明了英国在面临极端天气时的脆弱性。

1. 在减缓措施上的问题

英国仍是一个主要的石油和天然气进口国。2019年，英国的石油产品进口量为3.3万千吨。同时，国有出口信贷机构——英国出口金融公司向海外化石燃料项目投入数十亿英镑，其中最大的部分落在了低收入或中等收入国家。英国没有计算国际旅行和进口货物的碳足迹。气候变化委员会建议，英国应根据海外商品的消费情况来记录排放量。

CAT（Climate Action Tracker）将2020年英国宣布的国家自主贡献（NDC）目标评级为"不足"，将英国的国际公共气候融资贡献评为"高度不足"。CAT指出，英国的气候行动与《巴黎协定》不一致。虽然英国的国家自主贡献和长期目标与具有成本效益的国内路径大体一致，但它们并不代表全球应对气候变化所做的努力。因此，英国目前的做法不符合作为《巴黎协定》核心的公平共同但有区别的责任原则。此外，虽然英国政府在过去两年中采取了许多新的政策，但在一系列领域仍然存在关键的政策差距，如建筑物的能源效率、热泵的吸收和农业脱碳。如果不提高英国国内气候目标，不实施实现这些目标的政策，不提供足够的气候资金来支持低收入国家的减排，英国就不能被视为符合《巴黎协定》。目前，在实现英国NDC所需的减排量中，只有不到40％具有成熟的实施机制，得到了充足的资金和政策支持。

新NDC目标的"不足"：新的NDC目标对于应对气候变化是不够的。这与英国担任主席国期间在格拉斯哥举行的COP26会议上提出的要求相反。①英国的2030年NDC目标需要大幅改进，以符合将升温限制在1.5℃以内的要求。这些改进需要英国对发展中国家的减排提供额外的财政支持，以及在减少英国的排放方面做出更大的努力。如果所有国家都按照英国目前的做法，升温将达到3℃。

国际公共气候融资贡献"高度不足"：英国需要加快承诺，增加气候融资。英国的气候融资不足以提高公平份额的评级和总体公平份额贡献"不充分"的评级。

英国为获取化石燃料公司的超额利润而实施暴利税，对在英国投资新的石油和天然气开采的公司实行90％的税收减免。这有可能增加化石燃料的利润，加速全球变暖。

---

① UK Cabinet Office. COP26 Presidency Outcomes. (2022-11-30)[2023-08-22]. https://www.gov.uk/government/publications/cop26-presidency-outcomes/cop26-presidency-outcomes#mobilising-the-international-system.

CAT 估计，英国目前的政策将导致 2030 年的排放量比 1990 年水平低 58%—63%。英国目前的气候目标也不代表全球减少温室气体排放的公平份额。如果英国要为全球减排做出公平的贡献，它需要制订更宏大的减排计划。这方面的关键在于提供适当水平的气候融资，以支持低收入国家的减排。英国的气候融资贡献没有达到 1000 亿美元的目标，并且其贡献在过去五年里有所下降。虽然英国已经将 2020 年后的承诺增加了一倍，但这并不是新的资金，而是从现有的援助预算中提取的。这违背了联合国促成的协议，即这种资金是"新的"和"额外的"。如果英国的气候融资捐款没有大幅增加，英国将不可能提高其整体 CAT 评级。

2. 在适应措施上的问题

第二个国家适应计划（NAP2）并没有得到很好的落实，仍然存在重大的政策差距。NAP2 没有解决《气候变化风险评估》（CCRA2）中确定的所有气候变化风险，也没有关注政府的整体适应措施进展。目前，跨政府合作的责任和机制不明确，需要对相互依赖的风险进行更系统的评估。各个行业之间缺乏一致的最低弹性标准，也缺乏关键部门的监管机构来执行这些标准。

CCRA3 概述了英国在八个关键领域面临的适应风险：多种危害对陆地、淡水生态环境、物种的生存能力和多样性的风险；洪水和干旱增加对土壤健康的风险；导致排放增加的多种危害对自然碳储存和固存的风险；多种灾害对农作物、牲畜和商业树木的风险；由于与气候有关的供应链和分销网络的崩溃，对食品、货物和重要服务供应的风险；与气候有关的电力系统故障对人和经济的风险；由于家庭和其他建筑中的热度增加，对人类健康、福祉和生产力的风险，海外气候变化影响对英国的多重风险。

三、提 案

针对以上问题，我们提出以下提案。

（一）保障性措施

1. 加强国际合作，监测气候变化对健康造成影响的进展情况

应建立适当的监测机制，以了解感染环境和感染媒介适应力变化所可能导致的传染病流行率的任何变化；应采取减少温室气体排放的行动，改善空气质量水平。脱碳和改善空气质量的行动应与适应气候变化目标相一致；应实施专门的不利天气记录计划，将气候变化纳入当地风险登记册；应注意解决健康方面的不平等问题，这将有助于减少气候变化对人类健康的影响，并确保适应后的健康共同利益法案在最大限度上跨越部门与国家之间的界限；加强有关国家与国际组织的合作协调，不同主体之间适当的跨部门治理安排对于适应风险至关重要。

2.在各国监管下设立专门基金会

需要设立专门的公共基金来为全球范围内的相关科研与检测机构提供公共资金，以确保人们对这一风险的了解维持在最新水平。需要为重点医院、疗养院和其他医疗保健机构提供足以适应气候变化影响的经费支持。

以卫生和社会保健组织为重点的适应方案提供了一种针对性的方法，以降低弱势群体中与高温相关疾病的死亡率。

（二）减缓性措施

要加大新能源转型投资，减少碳排放。投资是实现英国能源安全、碳排放目标和经济转型（就业、出口和生产力增长）的关键。需要在一系列部门中进行大规模的投资，以迅速改善现有技术，并引入具有变革性的新技术。现有技术需要尽快部署，以满足脱碳的需求。与此同时，英国在 2050 年之前需要的很大一部分技术目前正处于演示或原型阶段。

许多国家现在已经认识到转型将带来的经济利益。自从"英国能源安全战略"（the British Energy Security Strategy）和"净零战略"（Net Zero Strategy）发布以来，英国看到其他国家效仿英国的做法，加大了对清洁能源的投入，支持净零过渡。美国已经通过《减少通货膨胀法》（Inflation Reduction Act），欧盟也通过《绿色交易产业计划》（Green Deal Industrial Plan），制定了发展绿色产业的计划。

英国应与其伙伴和盟友一起，在全球范围内增加对净零技术的投资，推动成本下降，并为英国出口创造机会。

英国应继续站在向净零排放经济转型的前沿，释放更多的机会来投资和发展英国的绿色产业。例如，支持保险公司增加对长期生产性资产的投资，包括创新绿色资产和可再生能源基础设施。

（三）适应性措施

1.在极端天气条件下提供高质量、可保障的社会保健服务

统计指标表明，在极端天气事件期间，世界各国在实现持续提供社会保健方面取得的进展普遍不足。为此，NHS 在 2023 年发布了净零建筑标准，为开发可持续、有弹性和节能的建筑提供了技术指导，并为患者和医务人员提供了更好的医疗保健环境。这需要对所有高度服务和被占用的空间进行热舒适性评估，以确保室内环境能保持舒适性，避免过热。NHS 还建议尽量减少机械冷却，而是使用被动的方法来减少过热的风险。

各国在极端天气事件期间，应致力于继续提供医疗保障和社会保健服务，以确保民众尤其是弱势群体在热浪期间免于过热的风险；此外，还应降低重大洪水风险，保护容易因气候变化发生故障的基础设施系统。

为此，政府应确保机构协调，为建筑提供资金和投资，培训民众充分了解气候风险和适应策略。

2.设立面向普通民众、医务人员和地方政府人员的教育培训项目

有关气候变化之于人身健康威胁的教育对一般人口、卫生和社会保健工作人员、地方政府组织的工作人员的认识水平至关重要。教育培训项目应涵盖对健康的风险、适应的成本和收益。

3.建立气候健康安全中心，加强各地学术机构与公共部门的沟通与合作

建立具有公正性与权威性的气候与健康安全中心，协调相关科研单位、学术机构、地方当局和其他公共部门组织之间的合作。各科研单位应以本国的监测数据为基础，为建立健全在炎热天气下保持安全提供智力支持。

与健康风险联系最紧密的两个部门是农业部门和水务部门。农业部门方面，因为粮食库存的产量、质量和可负担能力受到气候变化的直接威胁，气候变化还带来营养不良的风险。水务部门方面，因为存在与腹泻病等水传播和食源性疾病有关的风险，有必要对相关部门之间的交流进行适当规定与安排。气候变化和发展模式通过多种途径相互作用，需要进行基于系统的多部门协调和协作，以有效管理风险。

China's Heat Wave Adaptation Proposal for COP28[①]

Abstract: Human exposure to heat waves has significantly increased due to unusual and unprece-dented heat waves. Due to the limitations of mitigation measures, China has taken more measures against heat waves, including adaptation policies and systems, multi-departmental deployment of heat prevention, protection guidelines, early warning systems and pilot cities to "centralized district cooling" practices. However, there are some challenges that the adaptation should consider, including lack of local evidence, insufficient attention to vulnerable groups and areas, little research on mental health, impact of urban Infrastructure enhancement, and lack of public awareness of risk prevention. Therefore, China's further adaptation capacity building can develop in three aspects. In a national aspect, government departments should increase awareness and support action on heat wave health risks by improving policy and financial support for addressing health risks of climate warming, building cross-sectoral disaster prevention as well as mitigation and response mechanisms for heat wave risks, and strengthening international cooperation in response to heat waves.

① Authors: Fanghong Yao, School of Social Sciences, Tsinghua University; Hui Wang, School of Management and Economics, Beijing Institute of Technology; Jifei Chen, Division of Environment and Sustainability, The Hong Kong University of Science and Technology; Xinchen Li, Department of Physical Education, Peking University.

In the social aspect, China should promote a climate-resilient society that actively responds to heat waves by constructing resilient cities in response to heat waves, supporting the laying of refined and intelligent high-temperature weather warning system, and implementing a high-temperature health adaptation program that serves the Chinese context. In the individual aspect, the public should improve their knowledge and ability to cope with heat wave risks by the proactive acquisition of and compliance with heat wave risk response knowledge, and by adopting a green and low-carbon travel and lifestyle.

Keywords: heat wave; health; adaptation; China

1. Introduction

1.1 Background

1.1.1 Causes and global impact of heat waves

Climate change poses widespread and frequent threats to public health, with one of the major impacts being the health burden and mortality caused by high temperatures.[1] A heat wave is a period of at least 3 consecutive days when the maximum temperature exceeds the 92.5th percentile of the reference period (1986–2005).[2] As typical of extreme climates, heat waves have received high priority in the IPCC Sixth Assessment Report and the 27th United Nations Climate Change Conference. According to the IPCC's Sixth Assessment Report, the frequency, duration and intensity of extreme heat and heat waves have increased since 1950 and

---

[1] Watts, N., Amann, M., Arnell, N., et al. The 2018 report of the Lancet Countdown on health and climate change: Shaping the health of nations for centuries to come. *The Lancet*, 2018, 392: 2479-2514.

[2] Chen, H., Zhao, L., Cheng, L., et al. Projections of heatwave-attributable mortality under climate change and future population scenarios in China. *The Lancet Regional Health—Western Pacific*, 2022, 28: 100582.

will increase further even if global warming stabilizes at 1.5°C.[1] Global heat waves have attracted widespread attention due to unprecedented human casualties[2], devastating compound disasters[3] and irreversible deterioration trends.[4]

In recent years, human exposure to heat waves has been significantly increased by unusual and unprecedented heat waves that frequently sweep through regions such as North America, Europe and China due to atmospheric circulation patterns such as Rossby ridges or blockages.[5] 740 people in British Columbia died as a direct result of the heat dome.[6] The European Environment Agency also indicated in a recent report that between 1980 and 2021, nearly 195,000 people died from floods, storms, heat and cold waves, forest fires and landslides, with heat waves accounting for 81% of the deaths.[7] Japan's latest survey data show that temperatures in June 2022 reached above 40°C for the first time since records began. On July 3, 2022, temperatures in Tokyo exceeded 35°C for the ninth consecutive day, the longest streak since records began in 1875.[8] Hundreds of people died from the heat, and nearly 5,000 went to hospitals seeking treatment for heat stroke. Most of these patients are the elderly, who make up a large percentage of Japan's aging population.[9] The Lancet Countdown 2021 China report showed that the Chinese population was exposed to heat waves for an average of 4.51 days longer

---

[1] IPCC. Climate change 2022: Impacts, adaptation and vulnerability. [2024-06-12]. https://www.ipcc.ch/report/ar6/wg2/.

[2] Royé, D., Codesido, R., Tobías, A., et al. Heat wave intensity and daily mortality in four of the largest cities of Spain. *Environmental Research*, 2020, 182: 109027.

[3] Schumacher, D. L., Keune, J., van Heerwaarden, C. C., et al. Amplification of mega-heatwaves through heat torrents fuelled by upwind drought. *Nature Geoscience*, 2019, 12: 712-717.

[4] Perkins, S. E., Alexander, L. V., & Nairn, J. R. Increasing frequency, intensity and duration of observed global heatwaves and warm spells. *Geophysical Research Letters*, 2012: 39.

[5] Zhou, T., Zhang, W., & Zhang, L., et al. 2021: A year of unprecedented climate extremes in Eastern Asia, North America, and Europe. *Advances in Atmospheric Sciences*, 2022, 39: 1598-1607.

[6] Thompson, V., Kennedy-Asser, A. T., Vosper, E., et al. The 2021 western North America heat wave among the most extreme events ever recorded globally. *Science Advances*, 2022, 8: eabm6860.

[7] Henderson, S. B., McLean, K. E., Lee, M. J., et al. Analysis of community deaths during the catastrophic 2021 heat dome: Early evidence to inform the public health response during subsequent events in greater Vancouver, Canada. *Environmental Epidemiology*, 2022, 6.

[8] BBC News. Japan swelters in its worst heatwave ever recorded. (2022-07-29)[2023-07-07]. https://www.bbc.com/news/world-asia-61976937.

[9] Wilson Center. Japan just experienced the worst heatwave since records began in 1875. (2022-07-26)[2023-07-07]. https://www.wilsoncenter.org/blog-post/japan-just-experienced-worst-heatwave-records-began-1875.

in 2020 compared to 1986–2015, with a 92% increase in heat wave-related deaths.[1] The latest data from the China Meteorological Administration (CMA) show that the combined intensity of regional high-temperature events from June 13, 2023 to the present has reached the strongest since complete observation records were kept in 1961.[2] Until August 28, there were 23 provinces (autonomous regions and municipalities directly under the Central Government) with high temperatures above 40°C and 366 national meteorological stations with daily maximum temperatures equal to or breaking historical extremes.

1.1.2 Health threats of heat waves

Numerous heat wave events around the world have shown that increased exposure to high temperatures can have adverse effects on human health, leading to increased mortality and morbidity. Increased mortality is one of the most extreme of the wide range of health effects associated with heat waves. The impact of major heat waves on mortality has been well documented over the past few decades.[3] For example, the 2003 summer heat wave in Europe killed more than 70,000 people[4], and the 2010 heat wave in Russia killed nearly 55,000 people. In addition, different studies have found an association between increased temperatures and increased mortality and morbidity in multiple locations worldwide[5], indicating that heat wave-induced mortality can occur regardless of absolute temperature.

In addition to causing direct death, heat waves can also cause heat exhaustion, thermal edema, heat cramps, heat syncope and heat stroke, which can lead to acute cerebrovascular accidents, chronic lung disease, heart disease, kidney disease

①　Wenjia, C., Chi, Z., Shihui Z., et al. The 2021 China report of the Lancet Countdown on health and climate change: Seizing the window of opportunity. *The Lancet Public Health*, 2021, 6: e932-947.

②　CMA. Perspectives on extreme heat: Exploring countermeasures. (2022-08-30)[2023-07-07]. https://www.cma.gov.cn/2011xwzx/2011xqxxw/2011xqxyw/202208/t20220830_5060368.html.

③　Guo, Y., Gasparrini, A., Li, S., et al. Quantifying excess deaths related to heatwaves under climate change scenarios: A multicountry time series modelling study. *PLoS Medicine*, 2018, 15: e1002629; Patz, J. A., Campbell-Lendrum, D., Holloway, T., et al. Impact of regional climate change on human health. *Nature*, 2005, 438: 310-317.

④　Robine, J. M., Cheung, S. L. K., & Le Roy, S., et al. Death toll exceeded 70,000 in Europe during the summer of 2003. *Comptes rendus biologies*, 2008, 331: 171-178.

⑤　Sugg, M. M., Konrad, C. E. & Fuhrmann, C. M. Relationships between maximum temperature and heat-related illness across North Carolina, USA. *International Journal of Biometeorology*, 2016, 60: 663-675; Sung, T. I., Wu, P. C., Lung, S. C., et al. Relationship between heat index and mortality of 6 major cities in Taiwan. *Science of the Total Environment*, 2013, 442: 275-281.

and mental health disorders.[①] An Australian study found a significant increase in hospital admissions for cardiovascular disease, acute myocardial infarction, and congestive heart failure during heat waves.[②] A study in Vietnam also showed an increase in hospital admissions for mental and emotional disorders during heat waves compared to normal times.[③]

Notably, the effects of heat waves on population health are not uniform and may vary by location and study population. Groups most vulnerable to heat waves include the elderly, people of low socioeconomic status, heavy workers, people with a history of prior medical conditions, and people living in poor areas with poor housing conditions (including lack or absence of air conditioning). Exposure of vulnerable groups, such as children and the elderly, to heat waves has increased in recent years, and heat-related mortality in people over 65 years of age is on the rise.[④] Populations living in areas already experiencing heat waves may experience "unlivable human temperatures" in the future, making their existing vulnerabilities even more urgent to address sooner.[⑤]

More frequent and intense heat waves typically result in higher impacts when they occur in densely populated areas.[⑥] China, as the world's most populous country, on the one hand has densely populated areas, and on the other hand has been identified as one of the countries severely affected by heat waves due to its vast size, climate zones and extreme terrain differences.[⑦] Studies show that heat wave-related deaths in China have quadrupled from 1990 to 2019, reaching 26,800 deaths

---

[①] Chen. R., Yin, P., Wang, L., et al. Association between ambient temperature and mortality risk and burden: Time series study in 272 main Chinese cities. *BMJ*, 2018, 363.

[②] Vaneckova, P. & Bambrick, H. Cause-specific hospital admissions on hot days in Sydney, Australia. *PloS One*, 2013, 8: e55459.

[③] Phung, D., Chu, C., Rutherford, S., et al. Heatwave and risk of hospitalization: A multi-province study in Vietnam. *Environmental Pollution*, 2017, 220: 597-607.

[④] Romanello, M., McGushin, A., Di Napoli, C., et al. The 2021 report of the Lancet Countdown on health and climate change: Code red for a healthy future. *The Lancet*, 2021, 398: 1619-1662.

[⑤] Im, E. S., Pal, J. S. & Eltahir, E. A. Deadly heat waves projected in the densely populated agricultural regions of South Asia. *Science advances*, 2017, 3: e1603322; Pal, J. S. & Eltahir, E. A. Future temperature in southwest Asia projected to exceed a threshold for human adaptability. *Nature Climate Change*, 2016, 6: 197-200.

[⑥] Wang, F., Zheng, B., Zhang, J., et al. Potential heat-risk avoidance from nationally determined emission reductions targets in the future. *Environmental Research Letters*, 2022, 17: 055007.

[⑦] Li, L. & Zha, Y. Population exposure to extreme heat in China: Frequency, intensity, duration and temporal trends. *Sustainable Cities and Society*, 2020, 60: 102282.

in 2019 alone.[1] At the same time, as the largest developing country, China is also facing dramatic socioeconomic changes such as population aging and population mobility[2], the realities of which are bound to exacerbate the devastating effects of the heat wave. Furthermore, according to the IPCC report on climate change impacts, adaptation and vulnerability, the frequency and intensity of heat waves will undoubtedly increase. Therefore, to effectively and rapidly reduce mortality and disease rates due to heat waves, this proposal will explore heat wave adaptation construction options in China as an example.

1.1.3 Necessity of health adaptation construction for high-temperature heat waves

Heat wave adaptation building is a response and adaptation measure to heat wave events that aims to mitigate the adverse impacts of heat waves on human health, ecosystems and socioeconomics, and to increase the resilience and recovery of society.[3] Heat wave adaptation building involves a number of areas, including urban planning and building design, public health warning systems, water management, cool facilities and shaded spaces, social safeguards, emergency response plans, and weather monitoring and forecasting.

Adaptation is considered to be the most effective way to avoid or reduce the health effects of heat waves.[4] The IPCC Fifth Assessment Report (AR5) noted the importance of adaptive capacity in climate change vulnerability assessments and re-emphasized the need for government decision-makers to provide timely disaster mitigation measures from an adaptive capacity perspective.[5]

Against the background that extreme heat may become the new normal, it is timely and imperative to build a heat wave adaptation society, an important concept

---

[1] Cai W. J., Chi, Z., Suen, H. P., et al. The 2020 China report of the Lancet Countdown on health and climate change. *The Lancet Public Health*, 2021, 6: e64-81.

[2] Cai W. J., Chi, Z., Zhang, S. H., et al. The 2022 China report of the Lancet Countdown on health and climate change: Leveraging climate actions for healthy ageing. *The Lancet Public Health*, 2022, 7: e1073-1090.

[3] Raja, D. R., Hredoy, M. S. N., Islam, M. K., et al. Spatial distribution of heatwave vulnerability in a coastal city of Bangladesh. *Environmental Challenges*, 2021, 4: 100122.

[4] Bakhsh, K., Rauf, S. & Zulfiqar, F. Adaptation strategies for minimizing heat wave induced morbidity and its determinants. *Sustainable cities and society.* 2018, 41: 95-103.

[5] IPCC. Climate Change 2014: Impacts, Adaptation, and Vulnerability. [2024-06-12]. https://www.ipcc.ch/assessment-report/ar5/.

to promote the construction of climate-resilient cities and mitigate climate risk disaster risks.

1.2 Proposal significance

1.2.1 Theoretical significance

Firstly, it is of great importance to develop the high-temperature heat wave adaptation construction. The study can clarify the current status of China's work on high-temperature heat wave adaptation in greater depth, from which problems and key points can be identified to provide useful information and insights for the future development of the field.

Secondly, based on the study of the current status of China's adaptation efforts to cope with heat waves, we propose an adaptation construction program for China to cope with heat waves, which can provide better guidance and suggestions for practitioners.

1.2.2 Practical significance

Firstly, taking China's heat wave adaptation as an example, we analyze in depth the current situation and shortcomings of China's adaptation construction for heat waves, and make improvement proposals accordingly, which helps to mitigate the adverse effects of heat waves on human health and improve the adaptive capacity of society.

Secondly, studying adaptation building for heat waves in China can provide the international community with reference solutions to cope with heat waves and climate change.

Thirdly, taking China's high-temperature heat wave adaptation as an example to propose solutions for human high-temperature heat wave adaptation can accelerate the development of adaptation policies to cope with climate change and promote the improvement of global climate change adaptation policies and systems.

1.3 Proposal Content

In the context of global warming, based on the analysis of the impact of heat waves around the world and the construction of health adaptations, by studying the current situation and challenges of the construction of adaptations to heat waves in China, this proposal proposes the construction of health adaptations to heat waves at four levels of the national, societal and individual, to provide the Chinese government with improved policies and systems for coping with climate change. Figure 1 shows the overall structure of this proposal.

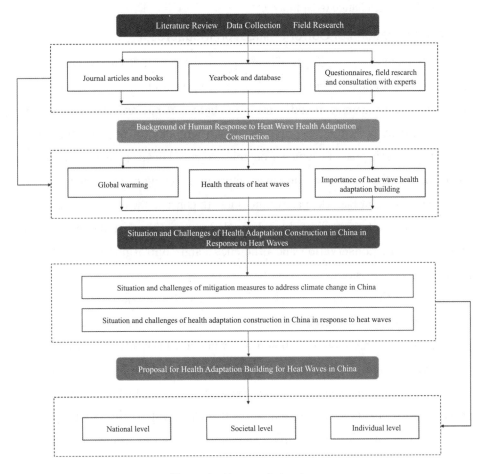

Figure 1　Proposal structure

2. China's Current Heat Wave Measures Assessment

The global surface temperature was around 1.1℃ above 1850–1900 in 2011–2020, with more significant increases over land than the ocean. Observed warming is human-caused, with warming from greenhouse gases, dominated by CO_2 and methane, partly masked by aerosol cooling. Global warming is happening and there is a need to act now. Human-caused global warming has increased the frequency, scale, intensity, and duration of extreme heat events. The most common strategies aim to reduce the impacts of climate change (mitigation) and to cope with the impacts of climate change (adaptation).[1]

2.1 Limitations of Current Mitigation Measures

On September 22, 2020, the Chinese government said, "China will increase its nationally determined contributions, adopt more powerful policies and measures, strive to peak its carbon dioxide emissions before 2030, and strive to achieve carbon neutrality by 2060."[2] Since then, carbon neutrality has been identified as an important strategic goal of China's economic and social development. Carbon sinks and carbon abatement are two decisive factors in achieving carbon neutrality. The Chinese government has taken active measures to enhance the carbon sequestration capacity of ecosystems, adjust the industrial structure, optimize the energy mix, promote energy conservation and efficiency, and control non-carbon dioxide greenhouse gas emissions.[3]

China is the world's largest emitter of carbon dioxide and the largest developing country.[4] In developed countries, it generally takes one to two hundred years from industrialization to carbon peak, while in China, it will only take more than 50 years. China's commitment to achieving the transition from carbon peak to carbon neutral is scheduled to cost only about 30 years, while developed countries generally use 40 to 70 years[5], which means that China will use the shortest time to realize the highest reduction in carbon emissions intensity to achieve the transition

[1] Laukkonen, J., Blanco, P. K., Lenhart, J., et al. Combining climate change adaptation and mitigation measures at the local level. *Habitat International*, 2009, 33: 287-292.

[2] National Development and Reform Commission. Work towards the goal of peak carbon neutrality. (2021-11-11) [2024-06-12]. https://www.ndrc.gov.cn/wsdwhfz/202111/t20211111_1303691.html.

[3] Ministry of Ecology and Environment of the People's Republic of China. China's policies and actions on climate change 2022 annual report. (2022-10-27)[2023-07-09]. https://www.mee.gov.cn/ywgz/ydqhbh/syqhbh/202210/t20221027_998100.shtml.

[4] IEA. Executive summary—An energy sector roadmap to carbon neutrality in China—Analysis. [2024-06-12]. https://www.iea.org/reports/an-energy-sector-roadmap-to-carbon-neutrality-in-china/executive-summary.

[5] Xinhuanet. China's commitment to go from peak to carbon neutrality is far shorter than the time taken by developed countries. (2021-04-22)[2024-06-12]. https://www.gov.cn/xinwen/2021-04-22/content_5601515.htm.

from carbon peak to carbon neutral.

In fact, changes in atmospheric carbon dioxide depend on the rate of anthropogenic carbon dioxide emissions, the rate of carbon dioxide removal, and the rate of carbon dioxide uptake by land and ocean. The difference between the CO_2 removal rate and the anthropogenic CO_2 emission rate is the net CO_2 emission rate. The goal of achieving carbon peak and carbon neutrality is to gradually reduce carbon dioxide emissions until net zero emissions are achieved. If net zero emissions are achieved and sustained, the global warming caused by increased carbon dioxide will gradually reverse, but climate change will continue for decades, even in millennia.[1] It can be seen that the response of the climate system to carbon reduction measures has a significant lag.

At the same time, extremely hot weather can make people sick and even die. Heat waves are a leading cause of weather-related deaths in the United States. Extreme heat can make existing health problems get worse and can cause heat stroke or heat exhaustion even in healthy people. Therefore, it is necessary to take adaptation measures for heat waves immediately.

2.2 Adaptation Measures Taken for Heat Waves

2.2.1 Building climate change adaptation policies and systems

China's adaptation strategy was initially published in 2013, marked by the release of the first climate change adaptation policy document, the National Adaptation Strategy for Climate Change.[2] This document outlines the guiding ideology and principles for Responsing to China's national adaptation efforts to address climate change. It sets forth adaptation goals, key tasks, regional models, and safeguards based on a thorough assessment of the current impact of climate change on the country. In 2014, the National Climate Change Response Plan (2014–2020) was introduced to enhance the adaptive capacity of infrastructure,

---

[1] UN news. Greenhouse Gas Bulletin: A new record in one year. 2021. (2021-10-25)[2024-06-12]. https://news.un.org/zh/story/2021/10/1093242.

[2] National Development and Reform Commission, Ministry of Finance, Ministry of Housing, Urban-Rural Development, et al. Notice on the issuance and distribution of the National Adaptation Strategy for Responsing to Climate Change. (2013-12-09)[2024-06-13]https://www.gov.cn/zwgk/2013-12/09/content_2544880.htm.

water resources, agriculture, and forestry. Additionally, it aimed to strengthen scientific and technological support, guide public opinion, and promote low-carbon pilot initiatives.[1] The plan integrated climate change mitigation and adaptation requirements into all aspects of economic and social development, emphasizing the need to establish robust institutions and mechanisms for climate change adaptation. Building upon these efforts, the Action Plan for Urban Adaptation to Climate Change was unveiled in 2017, prioritizing urban areas as key focal points for national adaptation measures.[2] The plan aimed to strengthen adaptation initiatives in critical urban sectors such as buildings, energy, transportation, water resources, and ecology. It also aimed to enhance cities' emergency preparedness and early warning capabilities for extreme weather and climate events. In 2020, China initiated the development of the National Strategy for Adaptation to Climate Change 2035. This strategy focuses on bolstering overall guidance, communication, and coordination efforts, improving climate change impact observation and assessment, and enhancing the adaptive capacity of key sectors and vulnerable regions to tackle climate change.[3]

2.2.2 Improving the protection system for high-temperature operations through multi-departmental deployment of heat prevention and cooling work

High-temperature environments pose significant health risks to workers, as prolonged heat exposure can lead to various health issues, including heat stroke, heat exhaustion, and even life-threatening conditions. Safeguarding the rights of workers is crucial for ensuring their health and safety. In China, a management system and working mechanism have been established. This system aims to foster collaboration among relevant departments and ensure the effective implementation

---

[1] National Development and Reform Commission. Notice of the National Development and Reform Commission on the issuance of the National Climate Change Response Plan (2014–2020). (2014-09-19)[2024-07-13]. https://zfxxgk.ndrc.gov.cn/web/iteminfo.jsp?id=298.

[2] National Development and Reform Commission and Ministry of Housing and Urban-Rural Development. Circular on the issuance of Action Plan for Urban Adaptation to Climate Change. (2017-02-25)[2024-06-13]. https://www.gov.cn/xinwen/2017-02/25/content_5170863.htm#1.

[3] Ministry of Ecology and Environment. Notice on the issuance of the National Strategy for Adaptation to Climate Change 2035. (2022-06-07)[2024-06-13]. https://www.mee.gov.cn/xxgk2018/xxgk/xxgk03/202206/t20220613_985261.html.

of high-temperature labor protection measures. China's high-temperature labor protection strategy was initially introduced in 2012 by publicating the document "Measures for the Administration of Heat-Relief Measures"[1]. This document sets forth criteria for identifying high-temperature work, outlines the supervisory and managerial responsibilities of government bodies at the county level and above, and specifies the obligations of relevant departments in overseeing and managing such measures. Since 2019 (except for 2022), the National Health Commission has been issuing annual notices on heat prevention and cooling measures. Health and family planning administrative departments, as well as disease prevention and control agencies, are tasked with recognizing the severe health hazards of heat stroke for workers, clarifying their work responsibilities, and increasing awareness about heat hazards and protective measures.[2] In 2023, the All-China Federation of Trade Unions issued a notice to address heatstroke prevention. This notice calls for effective prevention and control of occupational heatstroke, reducing the health risks associated with high-temperature work and hot weather operations, and safeguarding the labor health rights of workers at all levels.[3]

2.2.3 Establishing heat wave protection guidelines and building a health adaptation system

The 2019 Annual Report on China's Policies and Actions to Address Climate Change, prepared by the Ministry of Ecology and Environment, includes a new "Human Health" section. This report highlights the establishment of a heat wave and health risk early warning systems by provinces, autonomous regions, and municipalities. Furthermore, the report emphasizes enhancing research on heat wave adaptation to improve the public's ability to cope with extreme weather

---

① State Administration of Work Safety, Ministry of Health, Ministry of Human Resources and Social Security et al. Measures for the administration of heat-relief measures. (2021-05-21)[2024-06-13]. https://www.yuncheng.gov.cn/doc/2021/05/21/124806.shtml?eqid=c72fde840013d152000000026466e03a.

② General Office of the National Health Commission. Notice of the General Office of the National Health Commission on doing a good job in heat prevention and Cooling in the Summer of 2019. (2019-06-13)[2024-06-13]. https://www.gov.cn/zhengce/zhengceku/2019-11/20/content_5453791.htm.

③ All-China Federation of Trade Unions. The All-China Federation of Trade Unions has deployed efforts to prevent and cool down heatstroke among employees in 2023. (2023-06-14)[2024-06-13]. https://www.acftu.org/xwdt/ghyw/202306/t20230614_830574.html?7OkeOa4k=qAkzkAruQ6JuQ6JuQ63Ft4cX2AFoZsluNasN8FcN3q9qqlU0U48EqAqqQa.

events, including heat waves.[①] These initiatives aim to protect public health comprehensively and address the growing challenges posed by climate change. In 2023, the Chinese Center for Disease Control and Prevention (CCDC) released the Heat Wave Public Health Protection Guide, which identifies the health impacts of heat waves and highlights priority populations in need of protection. The guide provides early warning information for heat waves, including warning signs and risk predictions, and offers protection recommendations for the general population and priority groups.[②]

2.2.4 Progressive development of early warning systems for monitoring heat waves

China has significantly enhanced its monitoring and early warning capabilities for extreme weather and climate events, establishing corresponding emergency response mechanisms. The establishment of an early warning system allows China to stay informed of heat wave status and provide timely warnings of and emergency responses to potential health and disaster risks associated with climate change. The meteorological department employs various technical means to monitor and forecast heat waves, utilizing an integrated ground and air monitoring network that includes radar, satellites, and automatic weather stations, enabling accurate tracking of high-temperature patterns.[③]

To address the threat of heat waves to public health, numerous cities have implemented heat wave and health monitoring and warning systems to provide timely information and relevant advice. As the pioneer, Shanghai established a heat wave and health monitoring and warning system. This system monitors and analyzes meteorological data, heat island effects, and other indicators to issue early warnings about health risks during hot weather and disseminates relevant information to the

① Ministry of Ecology and Environment. 2019 Annual Report on China's Policies and Actions to Address Climate Change. (2019-11-30)[2024-06-13]. https://www.mee.gov.cn/ywdt/hjnews/201911/W020191127531889208842.pdf.
② The Chinese Center for Disease Control and Prevention. The National Bureau of Disease Control and Prevention has released guidelines for public health protection against high-temperature heat-waves. (2023-06-25)[2024-06-13]. http://www.kaifu.gov.cn/zfxxgk/fdzdgknr/zdmsxx/ggwsxx/wsjd_148888/202306/t20230625_11143687.html.
③ The China Meteorological Administration. The China Meteorological Administration deploys and promotes the construction of a high-temperature monitoring, forecasting, and early warning system. (2021-09-06)[2024-06-13]. https://www.gov.cn/xinwen/2021-09/06/content_5635662.htm.

public, guiding individuals to take appropriate protective measures.[①] Similarly, cities like Shenzhen and Jinan have developed similar heat wave and health risk warning systems. Through these systems, the public can become aware of the health risks associated with hot weather and take suitable preventive measures to protect their well-being and that of their families.

China continues to strengthen its monitoring and early warning capabilities, utilizing technical tools to tackle heat waves, which are widely implemented in practice. These heat wave and health monitoring and warning systems provide urban residents with information and guidance to manage the health risks associated with heat waves. Using timely warnings and public education, individuals can gain a better understanding of the health impacts of hot weather and take appropriate measures to safeguard themselves. The establishment and operation of these systems not only enhance a city's adaptive capacity but also offer valuable insights for other regions to establish similar early warning systems.

2.2.5 Multiple cities are exploring the practice of "centralized district cooling" to cope with heat waves

With the increasing impact of climate warming and urbanization, high-temperature weather has significantly affected the lives and work of urban residents. To effectively address the cooling needs of public buildings, reduce energy consumption, and minimize environmental pollution, several cities, including Jinan, Shenzhen, Sanya, and Guangzhou, have embarked on the implementation of the "centralized district cooling" program.

The core concept of the "centralized district cooling" program involves setting centralized cooling stations in specific areas to provide cooling services for multiple public buildings. This centralized approach offers several advantages compared to traditional decentralized cooling systems. Firstly, it allows for the efficient use of land and avoids duplication of cooling equipment investments made by individual buildings. Secondly, chilled water is transported to end-users through transmission and distribution networks, resulting in efficient energy savings, reduced energy

---

① Tian, Z., Li, S., Zhang, J., et al. The characteristic of heat wave effects on coronary heart disease mortality in Beijing, China: A time series study. *PLOS One*, 2013, 8: e77321.

consumption, and lower carbon emissions. Moreover, the centralized cooling system can stagger the cooling load, effectively balancing supply and demand and enhancing energy utilization efficiency.

In the southern region, where high-temperature weather persists and cooling demand is substantial, centralized cooling solutions have been successfully implemented. For instance, in the Qianhai District of Shenzhen, multiple cooling stations and municipal cooling networks have been planned and constructed to provide year-round cooling services to commercial buildings. The scale of this district cooling system positions it as a global leader in centralized cooling.[1] Similarly, the Hainan Sanya Haitang Bay Demonstration Zone project has adopted a centralized cooling solution, offering cooling services to public buildings and contributing to energy conservation and emission reduction.[2] In the northern region, the Southern Energy Center, established by the Jinan Energy Investment Holding Group, represents one of the largest cooling and heating projects. This project provides centralized heating and cooling services to the Jinan Central Business District, promoting efficient energy utilization. Through the centralized cooling system, Jinan is better equipped to tackle the challenges posed by high summer temperatures and provide reliable cooling services to users of public buildings.[3]

2.3 Challenges of Adaptation

2.3.1 Lack of local evidence

Due to geographical and climatic variations, the performance and impact of heat on health risk adaptation may differ across regions. It remains unclear whether the general thresholds associated with increased mortality at the national level are equally effective in preventing heat-related deaths in different local settings. In particular, data collection on the relationship between heat and health risks may

---

[1] Shenzhen Science and Technology Innovation Commission. The largest centralized cooling plant in Asia. (2021-07-07)[2024-06-13]. http://stic.sz.gov.cn/gzcy/msss/mskjdt/content/post_9059552.html.

[2] The People's Government of Hainan Province. The first phase project of Sanya Low-carbon Intelligent Energy Comprehensive Utilization Haitang Bay Demonstration Area has been put into operation. (2021-09-09)[2024-06-13]. https://www.hainan.gov.cn/hainan/sxian/202109/71d6afe52d4746159fce039ac74704b3.shtml.

[3] Jinan Energy Investment Holding Grouop Co., LTD. Jinan centralized cooling. [2024-06-13]. https://www.jnnytz.com/.

be insufficient in more remote or economically underdeveloped areas, leading to a lack of local scientific evidence for establishing appropriate heat risk thresholds and adaptation strategies. Certain populations, such as the homeless or socially isolated, may pose challenges in data collection due to difficulties in obtaining relevant demographic information. Consequently, assessing the specific needs and risks of these populations in heat illness prevention programs becomes more challenging.

2.3.2 Insufficient attention to vulnerable groups and less developed areas

Previous research has predominantly focused on the overall population's adaptive capacity and protective measures while neglecting the specific needs of vulnerable populations when addressing heat and health risks. This has created a need for a better understanding and research on the unique requirements and adaptation strategies of vulnerable groups. In the context of frequent heat waves and their increasing impact, vulnerable populations are the most affected and possess limited adaptive capacity. China's less developed regions, characterized by weak economic foundations and low adaptive capacity, face significant challenges and pressures, suffering more severely from heat waves. However, due to regional disparities and resource constraints, these regions may require more conducive conditions and opportunities for relevant studies to be conducted . Emphasizing the impact of heat waves on vulnerable groups and specific regions can help vulnerable populations adopt appropriate measures to cope with the impact of heat waves, enhance communication between these groups and experts/policymakers, and provide valuable insights for relevant authorities in less developed regions to formulate policies for dealing with heat waves.

2.3.3 Little research on mental health

When addressing heat-related issues, the focus is typically on physical health problems such as heat stroke and dehydration. Mental health issues, on the other hand, tend to be hidden and underrepresented in Chinese society and culture. Awareness and acceptance of mental health problems may be relatively low, leading many individuals to remain silent or conceal their struggles. Consequently, mental health concerns have received relatively little attention, resulting in limited development and investment in related research.

2.3.4 Need for Urban Infrastructure Enhancement

To establish a locally applicable heat health warning system, in-depth research on the health impacts of heat waves in different regions is essential. China's urban structure is diverse and heterogeneous, with varying levels of development across different regions and cities. As urbanization progresses, cities experience higher population densities, making their residents more susceptible to heat waves. Increased attention to urban infrastructure can show how urban planning and building design can adapt to high-temperature heat waves. Understanding the characteristics and vulnerabilities of the urban fabric can facilitate the development of targeted urban planning and adaptation strategies to mitigate the health impacts of heat waves on residents. For instance, vegetation cover can provide shade, while water areas can moderate temperature changes, reducing heat-related hazards.

2.3.5 Lack of public awareness of risk prevention

Adaptation, as a dynamic social adjustment process undertaken by humans to cope with external shocks or internal imbalances, relies on effective collaboration. Vulnerable groups are particularly at risk during heat waves, and their level of risk perception and individual capacity for taking action are often limited. Therefore, it is crucial to strengthen public education on the science of urban adaptation and fully leverage the active role of ecological and environmental protection social organizations. Furthermore, efforts should be made to enhance adaptation capacity within communities and public services.

3. China's Further Heat Wave Adaptation Proposals

Since the summer of 2022, China and many countries and regions in the northern hemisphere have experienced severe heat waves, which have shown a development trend of high intensity, long span, high frequency, and high hazard. Therefore, we need to strengthen China's response and adaptation capability to extreme weather and climate events of heat waves under climate warming from three aspects of the nation, society and individual.

3.1 National Aspect: Increasing awareness and supportive action on heat wave health risks

3.1.1 Improving policy and financial support for addressing health risks of climate warming

Effors should be made to strictly follow the new concepts, ideas and strategies on China's response to climate change, face up to the current shortcomings in climate change response policies and financial investment, and make up for the shortcomings in a targeted manner. On the basis of the implementation of the National Strategy for Adaptation to Climate Change 2035, the government should formulate more practical blueprints or action plans, make public the implementation of climate change mitigation and adaptation, and integrate climate change adaptation actions into the assessment system of local governments. China still has a large shortage of funds to address climate change. On the one hand, we should urge developed countries to assume their climate responsibilities financially, and on the other hand, we should accelerate the development of green financial investment and financing channels.

3.1.2 Building cross-departmental disaster prevention, mitigation and response mechanisms for heat wave risks

The government should further raise the importance of climate change health risks in the meteorological sector, deepen cross-sectoral cooperation in this area, and enhance the climate resilience of the whole society. The intensification of climate change, especially the increase and intensification of extreme weather events, is seriously threatening the health of the Chinese population. The government is recommended to increase further the meteorological department's attention to climate change health risks, increase operational investment, enhance the cooperation between the National Health Commission and the China CDC and other departments to prepare a special climate change health adaptation plan, and carry out a comprehensive assessment and regular dynamic assessment of climate change health impacts. Collaboration is needed between the Ministry of Ecology and Environment, the Ministry of Housing and Clrban-Rural Development, the Ministry of Emergency Management and other departments to enhance the early warning and forecasting capability of climate disasters. Through cross-departmental collaboration, we will enhance the early warning and forecasting capability of climate disasters, improve the climate resilience of the whole society across various sectors, and reduce the health risks of the population caused by climate disasters.

3.1.3 Strengthening international cooperation in response to heat waves

Global climate governance has entered the stage of full implementation of the Paris Agreement to address climate change. However, there is still a large distance between the emission reduction efforts of all parties and the achievement of the temperature control targets proposed in the Paris Agreement.[1] Economies at different levels of development should fulfill their corresponding responsibilities and further increase their emission reduction efforts, while strengthening international cooperation to jointly address climate change. China has achieved remarkable results in its emission reduction actions by taking measures to adjust its industrial structure, optimize its energy structure and promote the construction of carbon markets. In the future, it should further strengthen its cooperation with the United Nations Environment Programme (UNEP), Africa and other developing regions to enhance the construction of international discourse in the field of climate change governance, especially in the field of global warming.

3.2 Social Aspect: Promoting a climate-resilient society that actively responds to heat waves

3.2.1 Constructing the resilient city in response to heat waves

The frequent extreme weather disasters around the world in recent years have shown that the global human race is not yet the most prepared to deal with extreme weather, and there are still many shortcomings and deficiencies in China's urban planning and construction and resilience governance system, which are reflected in the lack of crisis awareness of extreme weather among urban population and the overloaded operation of urban infrastructure. An overall resilience strategic plan should be prepared; also, special resilience plans should be prepared for different

---

① People's Daily Online. Strengthening international cooperation and jointly addressing climate change. (2021-03-16) [2024-06-13]. http://world.people.com.cn/n1/2021/0316/c1002-32052113.html.

types of extreme weather and so should detailed resilience plans for special urban spaces Clear maps of community heat hazards and urban flooding vulnerability should be produced. Efforts should be made to implement a more equitable and inclusive urban disaster prevention and relief policy to improve the disaster prevention and resilience of extremely vulnerable people and living spaces. Efforts should be made to implement a comprehensive upgrade of urban hardware facilities to improve the hard resistance to extreme weather disasters. It is also required to update and optimize traditional urban planning and design ideas, methods and strategies in accordance with the natural concept of the unity of heaven and earth, and strive to create a pro-natural and biological city.

3.2.2 Supporting the laying of refined and intelligent high-temperature weather warning system

An information and data platform and early warning and forecasting system for climate change and population health should be built. In cooperation with other departments and research institutions, we will establish an information and data platform on climate change and population health, share authoritative information on climate change and its health risks, release relevant early warning and forecasting information, and support the scientific formulation of response measures.

Efforts should be made to build up the sharing channels of climate-environment-health-medical basic data, and to build an information and data platform and early warning and forecasting system for climate change and population health. It is recommended to break down the barriers to data sharing from top to bottom and realize the integration of climate, environment, health and medical key data, so as to better support scientific research. A refined and intelligent early warning and forecasting systems as well as a data platform to share authoritative information on climate change and its health risks should be constructed, so as to formulate more scientific and targeted response measures.

3.2.3 Implementing a high-temperature health adaptation program that serves the Chinese context

We need to increase further the focus on the population health impacts of climate change and its response measures, strengthen cross-departmental collaboration, and organize experts to carry out the preparation of national climate change health adaptation plans and the design of carbon-neutral routes that take health benefits into account. The steps in the IPCC report can be followed to enhance China's capacity for high-temperature health adaptation. First, to assess climate change impacts, vulnerability and risks; second, to develop adaptation planning based on the assessment results; third, to adopt adaptation measures; and fourth, to monitor and evaluate adaptation. In addition, synergistic cooperation between science and technology departments and other departments (e.g., the National Health Commission, the China CDC, the Ministry of Ecology and Environment, and the Chian Meteorological Administration) on this topic should be strengthened to promote the preparation of national-level climate change health adaptation plans and research when designing carbon-neutral pathways that consider health benefits. An expert advisory committee on climate change and population health should be built to provide professional technical support on addressing climate change health risks.

3.3 Individual Aspect: Improving Knowledge and Ability to Cope with Heat Wave Risks

3.3.1 Proactive acquisition of and compliance with heat wave risk response knowledge

High-temperature heat waves can directly cause heat-related diseases such as heat rash, heat edema, heat syncope, heat cramp, heat exhaustion and pyrexia. At present, the China CDC and the China Meteorological Administration have taken a multi-departmental approach and released the "High-temperature Heat Wave Rating" and "Public Health Protection Guidelines for High-temperature Heat Waves", which propose population health risk intervention measures and recommendations for the health problems caused by high-temperature heat waves in China during summer, and guide the public to carry out scientific protection. The public should strengthen their awareness of self-protection, avoid working, exercising or living in high-temperature and high-humidity environments for long periods of time as much as possible, pay attention to the combination of work and rest, and drink water actively, repeatedly and in the right amount. At the same time, the diet should be light and supplemented with drinks and seasonal fruits that have a cooling effect, such as green bean soup, watermelon, and so on.

3.3.2 Adopting a green and low-carbon travel and lifestyle

The public, through taking green, low-carbon, environmental actions, will not only inprove the quality of life, but also help to improve civilization and make life healthier. Everyone should be a practitioner and promoter of ecological civilization, practice a green and low-carbon lifestyle, and take practical actions to reduce energy and resource consumption and pollution emissions. Everyone is responsible for living in a green and low-carbon manner, and everyone can do it. We need to comply with the rules and do a good job of separating garbage classfication, set the air conditioning temperature reasonably, not less than 26 degrees Celsius in summer and not more than 20 degrees Celsius in winter, try to buy more durable goods while fewer disposable and over-packaged goods, bring our own shopping bags when going out, and give priority to public transportation or bicycle, walking and other green ways of travel.

Public Communication of Global Climate Change and Health[①]

Abstract: This article aims to propose a simulated proposal on Indonesia's response to climate change, addressing the impact of climate change on Indonesian society and health. Firstly, the article discusses the impact of climate change on health and diseases in Indonesia, including droughts and food shortages caused by extreme weather, as well as diseases such as malaria that surge in the tropical climate suitable for bacteria and viruses. Secondly, the article discusses the issue of climate refugees caused by climate change, including the challenges faced by people who are forced to leave their homes due to droughts, famines, and floods. Lastly, the article presents recommendations to strengthen media discourse and public communication capacity, including increasing funding support, government policy announcements, private sector investments, and individual donations. It also suggests measures to enhance media coverage, improve online information management, and enhance public information literacy. Through these measures, we can improve media coverage and advocacy on climate change

① Authors: Boni Sun, School of Foreign Languages and Literature, Shandong University; Lu Meng, School of Journalism and Communication, Shanghai International Studies University; Yi Tao, School of Philosophy and Social Development, Shandong University.

issues, enhance public awareness of climate change and health issues, and promote social and scientific progress in Indonesia's response to climate change.

Keywords: climate change; Indonesia; health; media discourse; public communication

1. Introduction

1.1 Background

In recent years, the frequent occurrence of extreme weather events caused by climate change worldwide has posed an increasingly severe threat to human society, and the urgency of climate governance has become more prominent.[1]

The world has been hit by the COVID-19 pandemic since 2020, one of the three warmest years on record.[2] According to the World Meteorological Organization's (WMO) State of the Global Climate 2020, the economic downturn brought on by the COVID-19 pandemic has failed to curb the increasing climate change. The combination of COVID-19 and climate disasters has had a widespread and adverse impact on human health and well-being. On November 13, 2021, the 26th Conference of the Parties to the United Nations Framework Convention on Climate Change (UNFCCC) concluded in Glasgow, United Kingdom, and 197 countries reached the Glasgow Convention on Climate Change.[3] This landmark event once again focused public attention on climate governance. In 2022, the 27th Conference of the Parties to the UNFCCC concluded in Sharm el-Sheikh, Egypt.[4] As a conference that emphasized "implementation", it eventually adopted dozens

---

[1] Ma, Y., Wen, T., Xing, D., et al. Associations between floods and bacillary dysentery cases in main urban areas of Chongqing, China, 2005–2016: A retrospective study. *Environmental Health and Preventive Medicine*, 2021, 26(49): 1–9.

[2] Kennedy, J. J., Dunn, R. J. H., Titchner, H. A., et al. Global and regional climate in 2017. *Weather*, 2018, 73(12): 382–390.

[3] Takashima, N. Cooperative R&D investments and licensing breakthrough technologies: International environmental agreements with participation game. *Journal of Cleaner Production*, 2019, 248(1): 119-233.

[4] Smirnov, O. Collective risk social dilemma and the consequences of the US withdrawal from international climate negotiations. *Journal of Theoretical Politics*, 2019, 31(4): 660–676.

of resolutions, among which establishing a loss and damage fund, which will be used to compensate climate-vulnerable countries for the damage they suffer due to climate change, was a highlight.

Addressing climate change is a review of humankind's current development path, which requires the international community's joint efforts. At the national level, the realization of climate governance needs to rely on national resource mobilization and policy implementation.

With the intensification of the problem of climate warming, climate change has become a topic of close attention from all walks of life around the world. Climate change is not only a scientific issue but also a complex issue related to national political stability, economic and social development, and public health.[1] The complexity of climate change is that it is not only a scientific issue but also a social issue, which not only reflects the uncertainty of science and the multiplicity of nature but also concerns the interaction between people and nature. Therefore, it is necessary to widely popularize scientific knowledge on climate change and improve the public's climate science literacy. At the same time, climate communication is essential to urge society to transform climate change cognition into actions to protect the natural environment.

1.2 Significance

At present, the Indonesian government regards emission reduction, economic growth, equitable opportunities, and climate-resilient development as components of the low-carbon development goals, aiming to integrate the improvement of the investment environment, the promotion of economic structural reform and the implementation of climate policies into the formulation and implementation of sustainable development strategies. Suharso Monoarfa, head of Indonesia's Ministry of National Development Planning (BAPPENAS), said that investment support for Indonesia's low-carbon development in the post-pandemic period will have two benefits: creating green jobs and creating a more stable and sustainable

---

① Xu, G., Li, P., Lu, K., et al. Seasonal changes in water quality and its main influencing factors in the Dan River basin. Catena: *An Interdisciplinary Journal of Soil Science Hydrology-Geomorphology Focusing on Geoecology and Landscape Evolution*, 2019, 173: 131−140.

domestic economy. The significance of the Indonesian government's discourse linking climate response with economic development is that the government recognizes that low-carbon development has the potential to promote economic structural transformation and upgrading.

All the above policies can only be implemented with effective public communication. This proposal addresses the current difficulties in the public communication of climate change facing Indonesia and even the world, analyzes the difficulties in this field, and proposes feasible solutions to make the public pay attention to climate change and call on all humankind to participate in climate governance actions and promote sustainable development.

2. Process and problems

2.1 Issues and Challenges in Public Communication

2.1.1 Global stocktake

A global stocktake of the progress of public communication on climate change can provide valuable insights into the overall state of media coverage and communication efforts worldwide. By examining the global landscape, we can identify common challenges, practical strategies, and areas where improvements are needed.

i. International forums and initiatives. Global platforms such as the UNFCCC allow countries to share progress, exchange information, and communicate climate change-related actions and policies. These forums facilitate the international coordination of public communication efforts and knowledge sharing.

ii. Collaborative networks and partnerships. Various international networks and partnerships have been established to drive climate change communication. For example, the Global Climate Action Summit and the Global Climate and Health Alliance bring together governments, civil society organizations, and media professionals to promote awareness and action on climate change.

iii. International media campaigns. Global initiatives like Climate Week, Earth Hour, and Earth Day mobilize public engagement and reach a broader audience through coordinated media campaigns. These campaigns aim to raise awareness, promote behavior change, and encourage public participation in climate action.

iv. Knowledge-sharing platforms. Online platforms and portals, such as the Climate Outreach website, provide resources, research findings, and communication guides to support effective climate change communication. These platforms offer tools and insights for media practitioners to engage with diverse audiences.

v. Research and collaboration. Academic institutions, research organizations, and think tanks worldwide contribute to understanding climate change communication through research and collaboration. They generate evidence-based insights, develop communication strategies, and offer training programs to enhance media professionals' capabilities.

2.1.2 Information asymmetry

The uneven media landscape between countries, with different levels of media market development and regulation in each country, leads to an uneven media landscape focusing more on national issues at the expense of global issues, leaving the public with an information asymmetry in understanding global issues. Schumann and other researchers investigated the comparative prevalence of information avoidance concerning the coronavirus and its relationship with media evaluation and use. Germans, Pakistanis, and Indonesians showed different levels of information avoidance.[1]

In Indonesia, coronavirus news was highly "blended" with entertainment elements, eventually making the reception process less harmful. For example, in Indonesia, one of the spokespersons of the national task force on the coronavirus outbreak, is a medical doctor who is, at the same time, also a professional model, influencer, moderator, and the winner of Indonesia's 2011 beauty pageant. The media often highlighted her appearance (make-up, hair, and clothes) during press conferences, despite this having nothing to do with the number of coronavirus

---

[1] Schumann, C., Ejaz, W., Rochyadi-Reetz, M., et al. International perspectives on information avoidance during the coronavirus pandemic: Comparing media evaluations and media use in Pakistan, Germany, and Indonesia. *Studies in Communication and Media*, 2022, 11(3): 477–507.

infections she reported to the public.[①] In line with this, Rochyadi-Reetz and other researchers. It is found that Indonesian media use during the pandemic is motivated more by the need for entertainment than by the pursuit of information and direction, influencing the public's profound awareness of the epidemic.

2.1.3 Insufficient media coverage

Indonesia has 351 TV stations, 1,248 radio stations, and 2,000 printed media, which makes Indonesia the country with the most mass media in the world.[②] However, all of these are controlled by only 12 major media groups. Those corporations control almost all media channels in Indonesia, including broadcasting, printed and online media.

One of the biggest fears about media consolidation is that large corporations will silence alternative perspectives and voices, leading to diminished democratic viewpoints. Astonishingly, only a few media corporations control the information for hundreds of millions of audiences. Media integrity is at risk since a few individuals or companies control the media market. This situation enables the immoderate commodification of the media for particular political interests, subversive to the democratic media role.

The commercialization of the media has led to restrictions on content, and many media companies tend to restrict content in the pursuit of financial gain, resulting in a lack of perspective and depth of coverage. There is also collusion with political forces in some media outlets, with stories being distorted or manipulated. As a result, many media outlets prefer to report on controversial events or topics, and media coverage of long-term issues like climate change and health is more sporadic, making it challenging to attract sufficient attention and focus.

---

① DetikHot. Reisa Broto Asmoro: Model luar negeri, host Dr Oz hingga jubir COVID-19 [Reisa Broto Asmoro: International model, host of Dr Oz, and COVID-19 spokesperson]. (2020-06-10)[2024-05-28]. https://hot.detik. com/celeb/d-5047078/reisa-broto-asmoro-model-luar-negeri-host-dr-oz-hingga-jubir-COVID-19; Vina Fadhrotul Mukaromah. Mengenal Dokter Reisa, Anggota Tim Komunikasi Gugus Tugas Percepatan Penanganan COVID-19 [Getting to know Dr. Reisa, member of the communication team for the COVID-19 task force]. (2020-09-06)[2024-05-28]. https://www.kompas.com/tren/read/2020/06/09/141500665/mengenal-dokter-reisa-anggota-tim-komunikasi-gugus-tugas-percepatan.

② Agustina W. Terungkap, Indonesia Punya Media Massa Terbanyak di Dunia [Indonesia holds world's highest number of mass media]. (2018-02-10)[2024-05-28]. https://nasional.tempo.co/read/1059285/terungkap-indonesia-punya-media-massa-terbanyak-di-dunia-977568.

2.1.4 Information Literacy and Scientific Literacy Enhancement

The lack of information and scientific literacy in Indonesian society may lead to a lack of public awareness of climate change, affecting the government's attention and action on climate change issues. Kristiansen and other researchers surveyed media exposure. The main conclusion of this research is that information asymmetry is a societal problem. That type of school and location matter more than media exposure for students' knowledge level. The research recommends increased public investment in quality schooling for all.[①] Due to the high expertise and complexity of climate change and health issues, most of the public need more knowledge to understand their seriousness. There is also an asymmetry in the transmission of information, resulting in the public often focusing on superficial phenomena while lacking a comprehensive understanding. Public participation in environmental protection and climate change is generally low and requires more enthusiasm and action.

2.2 Climate Change and the Society

2.2.1 Climate Change and Economic Growth

Notwithstanding, Indonesia now performs as the bellwether in reducing carbon emissions and is actively contributing to the goal of the Paris Agreement. There are still worrying problems along with developing its net zero ambition.[②] The clash between its vision of the net zero and its primary economic conditions needs further evaluation.

Indonesia is a developing country that seriously depends on traditional industries and the consumption of fossil fuels.[③] Nevertheless, renewable and clean energies like wind are advocated nowadays since they not only will bring less contamination to our atmosphere but also can reproduce themselves. This recognition calls for a transformation from conventional fossil fuels to new energy.

---

① Kristiansen, S., Wahid, F. & Furuholt, B. Investing in knowledge? Information asymmetry and Indonesian schooling. *The International Information & Library Review*, 2006, 38(4): 192-204.

② Evans, T. COP27: Designing a work programme to scale up pre-2030 mitigation ambition & implementation for 1.5 ℃. (2022-03-01) [2024-05-28]. http://www.jstor.org/stable/resrep40238.

③ Rudd, K., Basri, M. C., Ki-Moon, B., et al. Getting Indonesia to Net Zero: Asian Society Policy Institute. *Getting Asia to Net Zero: Building a Powerful and Coherent Vision*. New York: Asian Society Policy Institute, 2022.

Also, located in a tropical area with many coastlines, Indonesia has suffered dramatically from climate change, ranging from tropical cyclones to rainforest deforestation.[1] These emergencies push Indonesia to highlight governance in climate change. One of the significant steps is to reduce the emission of carbon dioxide by exploring the substitute for CO_2. Under this general direction, Indonesia has announced that it will emphasize the development of new energy.[2] According to official predictions, Indonesia will peak its emissions in 2027 and nearly achieve the net zero plan in 2060.

However, as a developing country, Indonesia faces tough realities in the energy transition. The cost of changing the original industry is so high that the government needs adequate capital to invest in it.[3] Furthermore, if they cut the support for fossil fuels industries, their profit will be far from covering the investment in new energy.[4] Also, the employees working in these will be faced with unemployment if they are not trained as skillful labor forces to be prepared for new energy industries.[5] That may enlarge the income divide and cause the government to lose citizens' confidence in the transformation to green energy.

2.2.2 Climate Change and Human Health

The formation of our proposals should consider two major issues. The first thing is related to the economy and the energy transition, while the second point lies in society. To be more specific, we should also focus on the population study in Indonesia since it has the world's fourth-largest population, which means that the perspective population will be the foundation when considering many issues.

i. Health and diseases.

In 400 BC, Greek physician Hippocrates proposed that seasonal changes

[1] Institute, A. S. P. Getting Asia to Net Zero: Building a powerful and coherent vision. [2024-05-28]. http://www.jstor.org/stable/resrep48654.

[2] Rudd, K., Basri, M. C., Ki-Moon, B., et al. Getting Indonesia to Net Zero: Asian Society Policy Institute. *Getting Asia to Net Zero: Building a Powerful and Coherent Vision*. New York: Asian Society Policy Institute, 2022.

[3] Rudd, K., Basri, M. C., Ki-Moon, B., et al. Getting Indonesia to Net Zero: Asian Society Policy Institute. *Getting Asia to Net Zero: Building a Powerful and Coherent Vision*. New York: Asian Society Policy Institute, 2022.

[4] Rudd, K., Basri, M. C., Ki-Moon, B., et al. Getting Indonesia to Net Zero: Asian Society Policy Institute. *Getting Asia to Net Zero: Building a Powerful and Coherent Vision*. New York: Asian Society Policy Institute, 2022.

[5] Kieslinger, J., Pohle, P., Buitrón, V., et al. Encounters between experiences and measurements: The role of local knowledge in climate change research. *Mountain Research and Development*, 2019, 39(2): 55-68.

influence the living of human beings.① Similarly, climate change brings about extreme temperatures and influence human health. For Indonesia, extreme weather like El Niño will cause a wide range of droughts, leading to food shortages and famine.② They arouse uncertainty about food security and threaten the living conditions.

Owing to the hot weather and substantial precipitation, vector-borne diseases like Malaria are inclined to appear since the climate conditions are fit for such bacteria or viruses to survive and spread.③ In addition, with the temperature increase worldwide, the range of exposure to those diseases likely enlarges.④ The risk of being infected with other diseases, such as cholera (a water-borne disease) in Indonesia, is much higher than that in low-temperature and mild areas.

ii. Health and climate refugees.

As the previous context puts it, extreme weather caused by climate change will lead to drought, famine, and flood. Many people escape and migrate to other cities, even other countries, resulting in climate refugees. Those who are wealthy enough can adapt to a new life. In contrast, others face exile, with miserable suffering, ranging from hunger and heatstroke (due to a lack of shelter), which seriously threaten the lives of thousands of people. Apart from extreme weather, the disappearance of the coastline also makes habitants panic. The glacier melting away on the temperature of the sea increases the sea level. Residents who have settled along the coastline have to compromise and mitigate, too. It is the poor people who take the risk of death without fixed housing and food.⑤

① McMichael, A. J., Campbell-Lendrum, D. H., Corvalán, C. F., et al. (eds.). *Climate Change and Human Health: Risks and Responses*. Geneva: World Health Organization: 2023.
② McMichael, A. J., Campbell-Lendrum, D. H., Corvalán, C. F., et al. (eds.). *Climate Change and Human Health: Risks and Responses*. Geneva: World Health Organization: 2023.
③ McMichael, A. J., Campbell-Lendrum, D. H., Corvalán, C. F., et al. (eds.). *Climate Change and Human Health: Risks and Responses*. Geneva: World Health Organization: 2023.
④ McMichael, A. J., Campbell-Lendrum, D. H., Corvalán, C. F., et al. (eds.). *Climate Change and Human Health: Risks and Responses*. Geneva: World Health Organization: 2023.
⑤ Mascia, R. Complications of the climate change narrative within the lives of climate refugees: slow causality and apocalyptic themes. *Consilience*, 2020(22): 31-38.

2.2.3 International Law and Document

Case: Indonesia's Road to Paris Agreement.

COP13 was held in Bali, Indonesia, in December 2007, where participants reached a consensus that a persuasive and firm guidance framework should be established in the ensuing COP meetings.

During the COP held in Paris, Indonesia motioned for a 1.5 Celsius degree threshold with other island countries as the representatives of coastline countries in tropical areas. However, the proposals should have been more selectively addressed. Afterward, the president of the USA, Obama, lobbied some blocs, and the result satisfied Indonesia and other island countries since they had been trapped in the crisis brought on by climate change.[1] After signing the Paris Agreement, Indonesia served as one of the models in dealing with climate change in Asia with China and India.[2] They put forward declarations to reduce carbon emissions and reveal their intention to expand regional partnerships under the framework of the UNFCCC and the Paris Agreement.

2.3 Indonesia's in International Public Communication of Climate Change

2.3.1 Varied Impacts of Climate Change

Climate change has varied impacts in different regions. For example, even as developing countries, some small island states are disproportionately affected by sea level rise, some agricultural countries are vulnerable to extreme weather events, and some water-scarce countries are particularly concerned about declining natural resources. This is a very high requirement for global, regional, and diversified expression of international communication.

Indonesia's international public communication of climate change is based on the impacts of climate change on it. According to relevant studies, in the case of climate change, Indonesia's temperature will rise by about 0.8 ℃ by 2030, which

---

[1] Jepsen, H., Lundgren, M., Monheim, K., et al. *Negotiating the Paris Agreement.* Cambridge: Cambridge University Press, 2021.

[2] Evans, T. COP27: Designing a work programme to scale up pre-2030 mitigation ambition & implementation for 1. 5 ℃. (2022-03-01) [2024-05-28]. http://www.jstor.org/stable/resrep40238.

will significantly impact Indonesia's agricultural sector, especially on soybeans and rice production, directly impacting Indonesia's national food security.[1] In the long run, if global warming reaches 2 °C, more people in Indonesia will face malnutrition, severe poverty, and even displacement. More frequent El Niño events will exacerbate drought and flood trends in Indonesia, resulting in reduced food production and increased hunger in the country. At the same time, drought and water pollution caused by climate change will impact Indonesian fisheries, further reducing their fishing potential in specific waters. The unique geographical location and the existing development model together lead to the ecological vulnerability of Indonesia, which also constitutes Indonesia's unique context of tackling climate change.

2.3.2 Diverse Responsibilities in Climate Governance

Countries tend to assume different responsibilities in climate governance, and sometimes agreement is hard to achieve. For example, in the climate negotiations, in addition to the United States and the European Union, there are various country camps such as the Umbrella Group, the African Group, and dozens of interest groups. Their interests both overlap and conflict. Each time the climate conference appears challenging in producing a resolution, the conference delay is the concrete embodiment of this conflict and game. The failure to reach a binding agreement at the UNFCCC in Copenhagen in 2009 was a significant disappointment for the international community.

Disaster risk reduction (DRR) and climate change adaptation (CCA) have been a focus of Indonesia's climate governance and its international Public communication, which are also continuously emphasized in the United Nations International Strategy for Disaster Reduction publications.[2] Indonesia attaches great importance to the spatial planning of DRR and CCA. Following the 13th session of the Conference of the Parties to the UNFCCC held in Bali in 2007, the Government

---

[1] Oktaviani, R., Amaliah, S., Ringler, C., et al. *The Impact of Global Climate Change on the Indonesian Economy*. New York: International Food Policy Research Institute, 2011.

[2] Macintosh, A. Keeping warming within the 2 °C limit after Copenhagen. *Energy Policy*, 2010, 38(6): 2964–2975.

of Indonesia established the National Committee on Climate Change (2008).[1] The CCA National Climate Change Action Plan (2007), the DRR National Action Plan (2010–2012), and the National Disaster Management Plan (2010–2014) have been developed. All provinces have established regional disaster management bureaus, as required by law, and more than 80% of regions/municipalities have established local disaster management bureaus. Following the 2005 World Conference on Disaster Reduction, Indonesia began to respond to the Hyogo Line of Action by focusing on the standard topics of DRR and CCA, following the steps of "disaster management–risk assessment and early warning–knowledge and public education–reduction of potential risk factors–preparedness and response." [2] It aims to achieve an efficient, comprehensive, and sustainable development perspective based on the common elastic objectives of DRR and CCA. However, according to the Climate Change Vulnerability Index (CCVI), Indonesia's capital, Jakarta's international airport could be underwater by 2030. By 2050, Indonesia will have 1,500 islands wiped off the map, drastically reducing its land area and maritime exclusive economic zone, triggering a series of disasters and endangering national security. Therefore, Indonesia must develop a coherent approach to integrated disaster risk and climate change impacts, focusing on overcoming inefficient land use and planning, integrating infrastructure, and developing national and community-integrated planning models.

2.3.3 Towards Global Climate Governance

The current international climate change governance system is still dominated by developed countries, which have a solid ability to set the agenda but need the cooperation of developing countries on many specific issues. Indonesia is an essential participant in global climate governance and a neighbouring country of China. Indonesia and China have broad space for climate cooperation at this stage. In 2013, China and Indonesia established a comprehensive strategic

① Shaikh, M. A., Kucukvar, M., Onat, N. C., et al. A framework for water and carbon footprint analysis of national electricity production scenarios. *Energy*, 2017, 139(15): 406-421.

② Jensen, J. & Yakubu, M. Developing degree programs in emergency management: Ghana's experience. *Journal of Homeland Security and Emergency Management*, 2019, 16(2): 1-12.

partnership, and both sides intend to cooperate on sustainable development in international and regional issues. China and Indonesia share common interests on major global issues such as climate change and have signed the Memorandum of Understanding on cooperation in the field of meteorology and climate between the China Meteorological Administration and the Meteorological, Climatological and Geophysical Agency of the Republic of Indonesia. In 2020, China and Indonesia launched the high-level dialogue and cooperation mechanism, fully releasing the political, economic, cultural, and maritime "four-wheel drive" role. Therefore, the two countries can build climate cooperation mechanisms around the three pillars of bilateral, regional, and international levels under the framework of comprehensive strategic partnership, give full play to the role of ASEAN as a platform, and use the China-Asian strategic dialogue mechanism on environmental cooperation to establish closer ties and continuously expand the radiation scope of cooperation.[1] The two sides can also elevate the issue of climate response within the framework of the high-level dialogue and cooperation mechanism, make full use of the Working Group on Unimpeded Trade and platforms such as the China International Import Expo (CIIE), the China-ASEAN Expo (CAEXPO), and the Regional Comprehensive Economic Partnership (RCEP). While promoting bilateral economic, trade, and investment cooperation, the two sides will promote the development of green industries, expand cooperation on green development, such as new energy and electric vehicles, establish a partnership on climate change, establish a corresponding dialogue and coordination mechanism, and strengthen the docking of the top-level design of climate governance between the two countries.

While calling for international cooperation and advocating policy coordination, international communication should also have a clear sense of the overall situation, especially when many policies involve the right to formulate future technology standards and are related to the space and direction of future economic development. For example, almost at the same time that China launched its national carbon market, the European Union introduced a proposal to impose a carbon border tax

[1] Jin, X., Li, J., Song, W., et al. The impact of COVID-19 and public health emergencies on consumer purchase of scarce products in China. *Frontiers in Public Health*, 2020, 8: 1-10.

on some imported goods to include them in its carbon market, which will affect not only the export situation of individual countries but also the direction of the international carbon market.

3. Proposals

We, as one of the contracting parties in the Paris Agreement, an advocator in the Tokyo Protocol, and a pioneer that has set explicit goals to achieve and reaffirm the spirit of the Convention, would like to enhance media discourse and public communication capacity in developing countries as follows.

We need to increase the media voice and public communication capacity in developing countries, especially on serious issues such as climate change, so that the world can be more aware of the needs of Indonesia and other developing countries concerning climate change through the media and to address the asymmetry in the information received by the public on climate change and health issues. The following measures could be taken.

a) Funding

Governments, businesses, and international organizations can jointly fund and set up special funds to support media organizations in developing countries to strengthen their reporting on and advocacy of important issues such as climate change. According to statistics, only about US$160 billion is invested in climate change-related projects globally each year, accounting for only 2% of global GDP. In comparison, the US and other developed countries, as well as China, account for more than 60% of global climate change investments. Therefore, when providing climate change-related funding to developing countries, investment in media discourse and public communication capacity building should be increased to promote social and scientific progress in developing countries.

i. Government

The government can tax those enterprises that have disobeyed the carbon emission regulation. The government should also promote better models for operating economic sectors, such as vertical integration, which reduces resource waste socially. Having learned effective ways, it can release policies providing a vigorous, accessible, and promising market for private sectors.

ii. Private Sector

When the government creates the trend and atmosphere of dealing with climate change, some private sector tend to look for new commercial opportunities. Meanwhile, considering the convenient market the government provides related to climate change response, most companies are inclined to grasp this new market and take the initiative in this novel area. The demard for changing the previous industries to environmentally friendly ones also provides large-scale potential markets. In addition, participating in projects concerning public interest earns them a good reputation, distinguishing them from a large number of competitors. Thus, the private sector would like to invest more money into climate change projects.

iii. Individuals

We encourage people to be more concerned about our planet than before. Their generous donation (at any amount) mitigates the financial burden. However, to gain their trust, we need to set up a specialized group to ensure transparency and traceability of the donated money. Also, regular reports on money should be guaranteed. Moreover, we are supposed to update the latest situation regularly, whether the news is good or bad, showing our responsibility in the provided information.

iv. International organizations

International organizations like the United Nations and World Bank have budgets working on the environment annually, like the Green Climate Fund in Indonesia. Within the expected budget, we can set up the public-interest project with officials from those organizations.

International organizations can serve as the third person between developed and developing countries. For instance, they can figure out the advantages of both countries and provide consultancy, promoting interest exchange between countries. If one is adequate in human resources while the other owns enough money, they may reach a consensus on cooperation in climate governance.

b) Improving media skills

We need to organize training courses on climate change and other issues to improve the professionalism of media practitioners and train them to strengthen their professional skills and knowledge, including in-depth understanding and research on climate change and other issues, as well as their mastery of relevant news reporting and communication skills, so that they can acquire knowledge and skills to gain a deeper understanding of climate change and its impacts. Government entities, media associations, international organizations, and educational institutions can coordinate the training courses. The duration will be at least five days, but it will be adjustable depending on the specific curriculum and objectives of the training program. This will help to improve the accuracy and authority of reporting. Training courses on issues such as climate change need to be conducted practically, for example, by inviting renowned experts from home and abroad to give lectures and organize interviewing internships to raise the professional level of media practitioners. At the same time, the government can provide incentives through tax and other preferential policies for media organizations to strengthen their reporting on issues such as climate change, encourage them to improve the depth and authority of their reporting, and further enhance the media discourse of climate governance in developing countries.

c) Expanding international exchanges

The government can coordinate resources from international organizations and developed countries to establish international cooperation platforms to promote media exchanges and cooperation between developing countries and other countries in order to learn about the experiences and practices of developed countries in areas such as climate change and apply them to media work in their own countries. For example, the Global Forum on Climate Change and the Media, jointly organized by the Argentine government and the Inter-American Development Bank, provided a platform for developing countries to present their views and perspectives. Indonesia can collaborate with the US, China, and others, particularly those with advanced expertise in climate change, to undertake joint research initiatives and reporting projects. This can involve sharing knowledge, data, and best practices and jointly producing media content on climate change-related issues.

These measures will enhance the media voice and public communication capacity in developing countries. For example, in the face of the 2019 African tropical cyclone "Ideyi", the Nigerian media provided timely coverage. They guided the public to understand the impact of climate change on human society, and further engaging public opinions, which effectively promoted the local government's disaster relief efforts. Data shows that global media discourse is mainly manipulated by the mainstream media in developed countries, with relatively little media coverage and voices from developing countries, so improving the media discourse and public communication capacity in developing countries is vital. This will enable the public to focus more effectively on and comprehensively perceive global climate change and health issues, promote further improvements in global climate governance, and facilitate countries to jointly address the challenges faced by climate change, thereby contributing more to the protection of the global environment and the achievement of sustainable development.

d) Improving media's climate change discourse

i. Increase the frequency and depth of coverage.

Media organizations can increase the frequency and depth of coverage of climate change as an essential issue and strengthen interviews and research in climatology, environmental science, and other related fields to provide the public with more comprehensive and accurate information. Media organizations should establish internal guidelines or codes of conduct emphasizing the importance of responsible climate change reporting. Guidelines can include accuracy, fairness, and avoiding false balance when reporting on climate science. These guidelines can instill a culture of responsible reporting within media organizations.

ii. Establish a dedicated team.

Media organizations can establish a dedicated climate change reporting team, comprising senior journalists, academics, and experts, to carry out in-depth analysis and reporting on climate change from multiple angles and in all aspects.

iii. Grasping hot events.

Media organizations can follow up on hot events related to climate change, such as major climate change reports and international climate change negotiation meetings, to keep the public informed of the latest developments on these issues.

iv. Strengthening social media communication.

With the rise of social media, media organizations can expand their influence of severe climate change issues on social media through platforms such as Weibo, WeChat, Facebook, and X and develop communication strategies for different audiences.

v. Improving media narratives.

The construction of story frames is crucial in covering severe issues such as climate change. There is room for improvement in the way climate change and environmental issues are covered in the media, and more effective story framing and communication strategies need to be developed to increase public awareness and action. For example, the media can direct the public's attention to environmental issues by organizing major environmental events and reporting in-depth articles on environmental issues. The media should adopt an emotional and meaningful approach to climate change and health issues and use more grounded, in-depth reporting to guide public action and bring the public closer to the issues. The media should also focus on making the public feel the direct impact of climate change on their lives, thereby increasing their willingness to act.

By giving more weight to severe climate change issues and adopting communication strategies, media can better focus the public on global climate change and health issues, and the relevant industries and governments can be motivated to strengthen their measures to address climate change. At the same time, through the power of the media, more people can be encouraged to participate in environmental protection actions actively and jointly promote the process of sustainable development.

e) Strengthening public education and enhancing information literacy

i. Establishing diversified education channels.

We should offer relevant courses and activities in schools, communities, libraries, and other places to improve public information and scientific literacy. About 20% of Indonesia's population has received post-secondary education, and it is imperative to improve information literacy and scientific literacy among those who have only received primary education. Therefore, training for this group can be increased and more popular, and more primary science education can be provided to benefit more people. Public awareness campaigns on climate change and health issues can be strengthened, and relevant experts can be organized to give popular lectures and spread the concept of a healthy and environmentally friendly lifestyle to benefit the public in kindergartens, schools, communities, and other places. At the same time, messages must be delivered through public radio, television, social media, and other channels to encourage public awareness of climate change and health issues.

ii. Strengthen media outreach.

Media organizations can promote information literacy and scientific literacy through various channels, including television, radio, and the Internet, to encourage public awareness of climate change and health issues and to improve the public's skills in acquiring, evaluating, applying and disseminating correct information. By reporting case studies of climate change and health advocacy, the public can better understand the knowledge and information in this area and be guided to learn about their possible health risks and ways to cope with them. With over 100 million Internet users in Indonesia, about 80% of whom access the Internet via smartphones, information dissemination can be enhanced to target this group.

iii. Strengthen online information management.

The government and companies should strengthen regulation and enforcement of online information management, prevent the spread of online rumors and false information, and improve public information literacy and awareness of scientific truth. Technology applications should be promoted, technology platforms should be built, and new technological tools such as big data, artificial intelligence, and blockchain should be used to build information-sharing and exchange platforms so that the public can have more access to reliable information and scientific knowledge.

The above measures will help strengthen the level of public information literacy and scientific literacy and raise public awareness of and concern about global climate change and health issues so that we may better adapt to and grasp the opportunities of climate change and make due contributions to promoting sustainable development.

Proposal on Strengthening Public Communication on Global Climate Change and Health[①]

Abstract: Climate change has become the biggest threat to human health. Among all countries, climate-vulnerable countries face the most severe situation. However, main countries, international organizations and media reports fail to effectively combine climate communication and health communication. Moreover, coverage of climate-vulnerable and developing countries is far from sufficient. Based on this, on behalf of the Climate Vulnerable Forum (CVF), we propose to integrate climate communication and health communication with a focus on CVF countries, uphold the principle of climate justice to alleviate climate inequality, and innovate diversified communication subjects and means.

Keywords: climate change; health; climate communication; health communication

① Authors: Qiaowen Huang, School of Law, Wuhan University; Xinyi Guo, School of Law, Wuhan University; Zhao Wan, School of Law, Wuhan University.

1. Introduction

1.1 Background

1.1.1 Climate change exacerbates health threats

Climate change is one of the major threats to human health in the 21st century. On October 30, 2022, the Global Lancet Countdown Report on Population Health and Climate Change 2022 (hereinafter referred to as the "Lancet Global Report") tracked the global climate change trend and delved into the current climate and health issues facing the world. The Lancet Global Report[1] points out that the global health damage caused by climate change continues to worsen. Climate change has increased the exposure of vulnerable populations to heat waves, leading to increased in heat-related mortality rates. For example, between 2000–2004 and 2017–2021, the heat-related mortality rate of people aged 65 and above increased by approximately 68%. Frequent occurrence of extreme weather events, such as droughts in South Africa, floods in Western Europe, heatwaves in South Asia, and forest fires in Australia. The climatic suitability for the transmission of infectious diseases has increased, and the transmission season has become longer for dengue fever, malaria, etc. Climate change has also exacerbated food security and malnutrition issues; for example, heat waves have increased the number of people with severe food insecurity reported in 2020 by 98 million.

On February 28, 2022, the United Nations Intergovernmental Panel on Climate Change (IPCC) released the Sixth Assessment Report (AR6) Working Group II (WGII) report Climate Change 2022: Impacts, Adaptation, and Vulnerability.[2] Chapter 7, "Health, Wellbeing, and the Changing Community Structure", evaluates the current impacts and future risks of climate change on human health and well-being, and proposes solutions and adaptation strategies to address climate change. The report evaluates the direct and indirect impacts

---

[1] The Lancet. The 2022 report of the Lancet Countdown on health and climate change: Health at the mercy of fossil fuels. (2022-10-25)[2023-06-07]. https://www.thelancet.com/journals/lancet/article/PIIS0140-6736(22)01540-9/fulltext.
[2] IPCC. Climate change 2022: Impacts, adaptation, and vulnerability. Contribution of Working Group II to the Sixth Assessment Report of the Intergovernmental Panel on Climate Change. (2022-02-28)[2023-06-07]. https://report.ipcc.ch/ar6/wg2/IPCC_AR6_WGII_FullReport.pdf.

of climate change on human health.[①] Specifically, it includes the impact on communicable diseases, non-communicable diseases, malnutrition, and mental health. It is pointed out that the threat of climate change to infectious diseases, non-communicable diseases, malnutrition, and mental health is increasing. It also shows the risk of compound exposure and chain events, and it is expected that the risk will further intensify with global warming in the future. Implementing proactive and effective climate change adaptation measures and taking rapid action will greatly reduce and avoid health risks caused by climate change, but will not eliminate all risks, which highlight the seriousness and urgency of the health impacts of climate change.[②]

A research report published by climate-vulnerable countries shows that climate change has destroyed about one-fifth of the economic growth of climate-fragile countries. A research report jointly released by 55 developing countries from Africa, Asia, the Americas, and the Pacific on June 8, 2022, pointed out that the high temperatures, changes in rainfall patterns, and other extreme weather caused by global warming have had a serious impact on developing economies. Climate change has destroyed the lives, livelihoods, and land, and even threatened the culture in these countries.[③] Some island countries, such as Tuvalu, face the threat of rising sea levels and losing their territories. In Bangladesh, floods have caused many people to lose their lives, and some people have left their homes and become climate refugees. In Nepal, frequent floods and mudslides have also had a significant impact on the agricultural system. In Kenya, due to long-term drought, there is a serious shortage of water resources, leading to the death of people and livestock.[④]

---

① The direct impact refers to the direct impact of extreme weather and climate events such as high temperatures, heatwaves, extreme low temperatures, and floods, storms, and fires on human health. The indirect impact of climate change on human health is mediated by natural ecosystems, such as insect vectors, pathogens, air and water pollution, and by human social systems, such as frequent extreme weather leading to displacement or property damage resulting in mental illness or psychological stress, etc.

② Huang, C. R. & Liu, Q. Y. Interpretation of IPCC AR6 on climate change and human health. *Climate Change Research,* 2022, 18(4): 442-451.

③ The Natural Resources Defense Council. What are the effects of climate change. (2022-10-24)[2023-06-03]. https://www.nrdc.org/stories/what-are-effects-climate-change.

④ China Meteorological Administration. Photos: 11 countries most affected by global warming. (2009-12-21)[2023-06-08]. https://www.cma.gov.cn/2011xwzx/2011xqhbh/2011xrdtp/201111/t20111110_152167.html.

These countries bear the highest cost of climate damage despite being the least affected. Therefore, we call on all countries around the world, especially developed countries, as well as international organizations such as the United Nations, to take actions to strengthen public communication and media coverage on climate change and health, and to help vulnerable countries affected by climate change.

1.1.2 Public communication and media reporting on climate change and health

Climate change has posed a great threat to human health, but according to Section 5 of the Lancet Global Report, "Public and Political Participation"[1], the dissemination of information about climate change and health still needs to be improved and strengthened. Engagement in health and climate change reached its highest recorded level in 2021, with climate change solutions becoming an increasing focus of health and climate change engagement (e.g., in scientific research and the enhanced NDCs[2]). As in previous years, government engagement is led by countries most vulnerable to a climate crisis not of their making.[3]

The COVID-19 pandemic continued to be a major driver of health and climate change engagement. In the media, a large proportion of English-language newspapers engaging with health and climate change referred to the pandemic. The pandemic also drove engagement by individuals and by government leaders in health and climate change. This raises whether increased engagement is contingent on the pandemic context.

On May 5, 2023, the Director General of the World Health Organization (WHO), Tedros Adhanom Ghebreyesus, said at a press conference held in Geneva that he accepted the recommendations of the 15th meeting of the COVID-19

---

[1] The Lancet. The 2022 report of the Lancet Countdown on health and climate change: Health at the mercy of fossil fuels. (2022-10-25)[2023-06-07]. https://www.thelancet.com/journals/lancet/article/PIIS0140-6736(22)01540-9/fulltext.

[2] NDCs: the major policy instrument set under the Paris Agreement to protect health from "dangerous anthropogenic interference with the climate system".

[3] IPCC. Climate change 2022: Impacts, adaptation, and vulnerability. Contribution of Working Group II to the Sixth Assessment Report of the Intergovernmental Panel on Climate Change. (2022-02-28)[2023-06-07]. https://report.ipcc.ch/ar6/wg2/IPCC_AR6_WGII_FullReport.pdf; McIver, L., Kim, R., Woodward, A., et al. Health impacts of climate change in Pacific island countries: A regional assessment of vulnerabilities and adaptation priorities. *Environ Health Perspect*, 2016, 124(11): 1707-1714; Tukuitonga, C. & Vivili, P. Climate effects on health in small islands developing states. *Lancet Planet Health*, 2021, 5(2): 69-70.

Pandemic Emergencies Committee of the International Health Regulations (2005) and decided to declare that the COVID-19 epidemic no longer constitutes a public health emergency of international concern. In an official statement on the same day, WHO pointed out that the members of the Emergency Committee emphasized the trend of the decline in the number of COVID-19 deaths worldwide, the decrease in the number of hospitalized and severe cases related to COVID-19 infection, and the high immunity of the population to COVID-19 in their deliberations beginning on the 4th.[1] Will the level of participation in climate change and health decrease as the epidemic situation becomes less severe? How can we strengthen public communication on climate change and health?

Although health and climate change engagement increased in 2021, there is more engagement with health and climate change as separate issues, a pattern evident in individual Internet users' activities, government leaders' speeches , and companies' reports to the UN Global Compact. Similarly, media and scientific engagement in climate change continues to surpass engagement in health and climate change. Despite mounting evidence of the health burden of climate change, health and climate change have yet to be securely associated in the public, political, and corporate domains that are key to climate action.[2]

1.2 Significance

Climate change is regarded as the single biggest health threat facing humanity.[3] However, there are still many problems with climate change and health communication. Media reports fail to effectively combine climate communication and health communication, and many report climate change and health as separate issues. Countries and international organizations have also failed to effectively promote and carry out public communication on climate change and health, resulting in limited public participation. In the context that the COVID–19 epidemic

---

[1] UN. WHO chief declares end to COVID-19 as a global health emergency. (2023-05-05)[2023-06-08]. https://news. un.org/en/story/2023/05/1136367.

[2] The Lancet. The 2022 report of the Lancet Countdown on health and climate change: Health at the mercy of fossil fuels. (2022-10-25)[2023-06-07]. https://www.thelancet.com/journals/lancet/article/PIIS0140-6736(22)01540-9/fulltext.

[3] WHO. Climate change. (2023-10-12)[2024-05-23]. https://www.who.int/news-room/fact-sheets/detail/climate-change-and-health.

is no longer a public health emergency of international concern, it has become extremely important to strengthen the public communication and media coverage of climate change and health, so as to allow more people to participate in the action of mitigating and adapting to climate change.

Our proposal points out the current situation and problems of climate change and health communication, and the difficulties vulnerable countries face to climate impact. In combination with the research on the "public awareness mechanism of climate change risk" and "climate communication effect", scholars put forward specific and feasible suggestions. Specifically, it is suggested that countries and media should combine climate communication with health communication, call for strengthening the reporting of climate-vulnerable and developing countries, and continue to track and report the commitments of developed countries to developing countries for supervision. It is also recommended that agencies under the United Nations carry out joint promotion of the diversification of communication subjects and means. In addition, countries should also strengthen their supervision of the media and improve the authenticity of reports. The above scholarship provides a theoretical basis and specific implementation path for strengthening public communication and media coverage of climate change and health.

2. Tracking Progress: Performance of the Five Influential International Organizations in Public Communication

We have researched the performance of the five influential international organizations in public communication. They are WHO, Lancet, IPCC, UN Department of Global Communications, and COP27. The research is based on their coverage of climate change, coverage on the interaction with health, attention to climate justice, and diversity of media outlets.

2.1 World Health Organization (WHO)

WHO has been attaching great importance to how climate change affects public health. On the Newsroom page of its official website, there is a column dedicated to climate change's impacts on health, as shown in Figure 1. [①] It said that climate change presents a fundamental threat to human health. It tried to raise the public's attention to the issue of climate inequality—"Despite contributing minimally to global emissions, low-income countries and small-island developing states (SIDS) endure the harshest health impacts."

Overview

Climate change presents a fundamental threat to human health. It affects the physical environment as well as all aspects of both natural and human systems – including social and economic conditions and the functioning of health systems. It is therefore a threat multiplier, undermining and potentially reversing decades of health progress. As climatic conditions change, more frequent and intensifying weather and climate events are observed, including storms, extreme heat, floods, droughts and wildfires. These weather and climate hazards affect health both directly and indirectly, increasing the risk of deaths, noncommunicable diseases, the emergence and spread of infectious diseases, and health emergencies.

Climate change is also having an impact on our health workforce and infrastructure, reducing capacity to provide universal health coverage (UHC). More fundamentally, climate shocks and growing stresses such as changing temperature and precipitation patterns, drought, floods and rising sea levels degrade the environmental and social determinants of physical and mental health. All aspects of health are affected by climate change, from clean air, water and soil to food systems and livelihoods. Further delay in tackling climate change will increase health risks, undermine decades of improvements in global health, and contravene our collective commitments to ensure the human right to health for all.

Climate change impacts on health

The Intergovernmental Panel on Climate Change's (IPCC) Sixth Assessment Report (AR6) concluded that climate risks are appearing faster and will become more severe sooner than previously expected, and it will be harder to adapt with increased global heating.

It further reveals that 3.6 billion people already live in areas highly susceptible to climate change. Despite contributing minimally to global emissions, low-income countries and small island developing states (SIDS) endure the harshest health impacts. In vulnerable regions, the death rate from extreme weather events in the last decade was 15 times higher than in less vulnerable ones.

Climate change is impacting health in a myriad of ways, including by leading to death and illness from increasingly frequent extreme weather events, such as heatwaves, storms and floods, the disruption of food systems, increases in zoonoses and food-, water- and vector-borne diseases, and mental health issues. Furthermore, climate change is undermining many of the social determinants for good health, such as livelihoods, equality and access to health care and social support structures. These climate-sensitive health risks are disproportionately felt by the most vulnerable and disadvantaged, including women, children, ethnic

Figure 1   A snapshot of the "Climate Change" page of WHO website
(Information source: WHO)

Although WHO has yet to make special coverage on the CVF countries, it has covered some member states separately.

Another thing we found innovative is that this year WHO has set up a special film prize for the issue of climate change and health. This integration between

---

① WHO. Climate change. (2023-10-12)[2024-05-23]. https://www.who.int/news-room/fact-sheets/detail/climate-change-and-health.

movies and public health is something that other international organizations can learn from.

2.2 The Lancet

The Lancet aims to track the connections between public health and climate change. It has been contributing a lot to the research and public communication on this issue. On The 2022 Global Report of the Lancet Countdown, as shown in Figure 2, it paid attention to how marginalized and vulnerable populations are disproportionately affected by climate change.[①] So we can see Lancet's efforts on differentiating the population and promoting climate justice.

> Marginalised and vulnerable populations are often disproportionately affected by mental health impacts related to climate change, which can worsen pre-existing mental health inequalities, especially where health care is inadequate. Indigenous people may be more strongly affected by climate change-induced ecological breakdown.[98,99] Older people, women, and religious or ethnic minorities are particularly at risk of adverse mental health outcomes, and young people have been shown to be more prone to anxiety, phobias, depression, stress-related conditions, substance abuse, sleep disorders, reduced capacity to regulate emotions, and increased cognitive deficits.[100] The increasingly visible effects of the climate crisis have given rise to emerging concepts, such as climate change anxiety, solastalgia, eco-anxiety, and ecological grief.

Figure 2　A snapshot of part of the report titled *The 2022 Global Report of the Lancet Countdown*

(Information source: Lancet Countdown)

2.3 The Intergovernmental Panel on Climate Change (IPCC)

IPCC has been attaching great importance to how climate change affects public health. In Chapter 7 of its AR6 Synthesis Report: Climate Change 2023 (see Figure 3), IPCC analyzed the relationship between climate change and people's well-

---

① The Lancet. The 2022 report of the Lancet Countdown on health and climate change: Health at the mercy of fossil fuels. (2022-10-25)[2023-12-05]. https://www.thelancet.com/journals/lancet/article/PIIS0140-6736(22)01540-9/fulltext.

being.[①] It also separately discussed the issues of different regions and continents. But unfortunately, CVF has not been discussed as a whole. We believe it is partly because member states of CVF come from almost every continent.

Health, Wellbeing and the Changing Structure of Communities   Chapter 7

Table of Contents

Figure 3   A snapshot of part of the Table of Contents of the report titled *AR6 Synthesis Report: Climate Change 2023 UN Department of Global Communications*

(Information source: IPCC)

UN Department of Global Communications, lists the issue of Climate Change and Sustainable Development as one of its "spotlighting issues".[②] In terms of communicating about climate change, it suggests that Climate change is also an issue of justice. The poor and marginalized are often hit the hardest by increasing climate hazards.

---

① IPCC. Climate change 2022: Impacts, adaptation, and vulnerability. Contribution of Working Group II to the Sixth Assessment Report of the Intergovernmental Panel on Climate Change. (2022-02-28)[2023-12-05]. https://report.ipcc.ch/ar6/wg2/IPCC_AR6_WGII_FullReport.pdf.

② UN. Spotlighting issues. [2023-12-05]. https://www.un.org/en/department-global-communications/spotlighting-issues.

2.4 The United Nations Framework Convention on Climate Change (UNFCCC)

On COP27, there was no individual climate negotiations focused on the issue of public health. So far, countries are spending more effort on negotiating the problem of mitigation than on adaptation. Fortunately, in its Summary Report Following the Second Meeting of the Technical Dialogue of the First Global Stocktake Under the Paris Agreement, as shown in Figure 4, COP 27 did emphasize in Climate Adaptation that priority must go to the most vulnerable.[1] It pointed out that communities that are the most vulnerable to climate change are the least able to adapt.

Priority must go to the most vulnerable

While the case for adaptation is clear, some communities most vulnerable to climate change are the least able to adapt because they are poor and/or in developing countries already struggling to come up with enough resources for basics like health care and education. Estimated adaptation costs in developing countries could reach $300 billion every year by 2030. Right now, only 21 per cent of climate finance provided by wealthier countries to assist developing nations goes towards adaptation and resilience, about $16.8 billion a year.

Wealthier countries are obligated to fulfil a commitment made in the Paris Agreement to provide $100 billion a year in international climate finance. They should make sure that at least half goes to adaptation. This would be an important symbol of global solidarity in the face of a challenge we can only solve if everyone in the world works together.

Watch leading Indian environmentalist Sunita Narain, who reminds us that we know how to make our communities safer, and we must act, as a matter of justice.

Figure 4   A snapshot of part of the report titled Summary Report on the Second Meeting of the Technical Dialogue of the First Global Stocktake under the Paris Agreement

(Information source: UNFCCC)

---

① UNFCCC. Summary report Following the second meeting of the technical dialogue of the first global stocktake under the Paris Agreement. (2023-03-31)[2023-12-05]. https://unfccc.int/documents/627583.

3. Recommendations

3.1 Integrate Climate Communication and Health Communication with Focus on CVF Countries

On the one hand, according to the Lancet Countdown, in 2021, global coverage of both climate change and health reached a new record high. However, coverage of health and climate change only constitutes a small proportion of climate change coverage.[1] This suggests that it is very necessary to link the communication of public health with climate change.

On the other hand, for a long time, people in the developed world have had little access to know how difficult it is for CVF communities to adapt. They have not yet realized the severity that climate change is affecting these marginalized people's health. That is why we propose more media coverage on climate and health hazards that CVF countries suffer.

3.1.1 Integrate climate communication and health communication

Based on the above assessment, some international organizations have begun to integrate climate communication and health communication, aiming to raise public awareness of the impact of climate change on health, such as the Lancet and WHO. We believe they have assumed an exemplary and leading role, and in the future, more organizations and individuals should make more efforts in this regard.

Regarding the current issue of public communication and media coverage on climate change mainly focusing on the natural environment, with less coverage on the impact on human health, in recent years, some climate communication academic communities have proposed that taking climate change as a health issue and communicating with the public and decision-makers may be an emerging and promising method.[2]

We think it is a feasible proposal. to combine climate communication and health communication, increase the publicity and communication of climate change

---

[1] The Lancet. The 2022 report of the Lancet Countdown on health and climate change: Health at the mercy of fossil fuels. (2022-10-25)[2023-06-07]. https://www.thelancet.com/journals/lancet/article/PIIS0140-6736(22)01540-9/fulltext.

[2] Rudolph, L. & Gould, S. Climate change and health inequities: A framework for action. *Ann Glob Health*, 2015, 81(3): 432-444.

and health, spread the impact mechanism of climate change on health and the coping strategies to mitigate and adapt to the impact of climate change on health. This can make the public truly feel the impact of climate change on human health and life, thereby encouraging them to participate in actions to save energy, reduce emissions, and live a low-carbon life. For a long time, climate change has been limited to its impact on the natural environment, and many people have not yet realized that it is also affecting everyone's health. This will lead to the public being aware of climate change, but not realizing that it is so close to our lives, and thus not actively participating in actions to mitigate and adapt to climate change.

The existing research on public climate change risk perception and psychological decision-making mechanisms reveals that treating climate change as a health issue is more conducive to guiding public participation in climate change behavioral responses. Climate change is almost imperceptible and the observation duration is long, which leads to a lack of significance compared to other issues and makes it difficult to gain public attention. In addition, many media outlets, considering the significance of climate change risks, tend to use shockingly condensed visual symbols from the most affected areas such as polar regions and tropical island countries (such as the "skinny" polar bear under food shortages caused by melting glaciers), with little mention of its impact on the local area of the country. This has led the majority of the public to view the threat of climate change as distant and harmful to future generations. Not here, not now, not about me.[1]

Adopting a climate communication approach that is "local, immediate, personal, and experiential" in response to the public's risk perception mechanism is a better overall strategy to address the current dilemma of limited public participation. For example, in 2010, WLTX Television in Columbia, USA launched a public education television program called "Climate Matters", which focuses on the impact of climate change on the local area of the state. The ratings of the program showed that the audience had a deeper understanding of climate change compared to other state residents. Afterwards, 350 weather program hosts from

---

[1] Wu, H. R. & Zheng, Q. The foundation, principle, prospect and path of the integration of climate and health communication. *Youth Journalist,* 2022(24): 37-39.

218 television stations in the United States joined one after another, driving a 5.5-fold increase in the coverage of television programs on climate change in various regions. This precisely embodies the communication strategy of "local, immediate, personal, and experiential".

Moreover, not only does linking health issues with climate change issues increase public attention to climate change issues, but according to research, using this strategy can also achieve better communication outcomes than expected by climate communicators.

For example, in the study of climate communication audience, the Yale University Climate Communication Project Center and the George Mason University Climate Communication Research Center proposed that there are "six kinds of Americans" in the face of climate change based on the public's risk perception, attitude, position and policy bias, that is, the American public is classified into six subgroups, namely, "alert", "caring", "cautious", "indifferent", "suspicious" and "opposed".[1] These six types of the public are distributed on a continuum.

On the basis of public segmentation, the Climate Communication Center of George Mason University carried out an exploratory research in 2009 to understand the views and responses of "six kinds of Americans" to media climate change health reports. The results showed that after reading the article, there were still significant differences in opinions among the six types of the public. However, overall, positive evaluations were given to the news reports they read, believing the information was clear and helpful. In addition, the ratings of participants gradually increase, indicating that the effect of expressing climate issues as public health issues is not immediate. However, as the public deepens their understanding of the relationship between climate and health, their evaluation of the article's value of the article increases.[2]

---

[1] Yale Program on Climate Change Communication. Global warming's six Americas. (2023-12-14)[2024-05-22]. https://climatecommunication.yale.edu/publications/global-warmings-six-americas-fall-2023/.

[2] Maibach, E. W., Nisbet, M., Baldwin, P., et al. Reframing climate change as a public health issue: An exploratory study of public reactions. *BMC Public Health,* 2010(10): 299-309.

Other studies have shown that treating climate issues as public health issues can achieve better communication outcomes than treating climate issues as environmental issues. In 2010, a study on the effectiveness of climate communication among the American public found that articles emphasizing climate issues as a public health issue were the most effective in stimulating public support for climate change responses. Moreover, this effect is more prominent among the three groups of people: the cautious, indifferent, and skeptical. The study also found that articles emphasizing climate change as a national security issue have had negative effects on some populations, making "skeptical" and "opposing" public more inclined to deny the occurrence of climate change and oppose taking response actions.[1]

Therefore, we believe in combining climate communication with health communication. This approach helps people view climate change as a significant threat affecting each of us (especially our children) here and now, and actively taking action to address it.

3.1.2 Focus on CVF Countries

Not only should climate communication and health communication be integrated, but more importantly, more attention needs to be paid to countries that are vulnerable to climate change. The reason for this proposal is that developing countries with fragile environments cause the least damage to climate, but they face the most severe climate and health crises and lack the financial capacity to address the consequences of climate change. For example, Africa contributes only 3% of global cumulative carbon emissions, but faces the most serious consequences of climate change. As of now, the CVF has 58 member countries.[2] They all face the threat of rising sea levels, super large storms, or expanding deserts. They represent 1.5 billion people worldwide who are currently facing a serious health crisis caused by climate change. Some of these countries have been ruthlessly pushed to the edge of the "cliff" by uninterrupted climate disasters. Some African countries are still

---

[1] Myers, T. A., Nisbet, M. C., Maibach, E. W., et al. A public health frame arouses hopeful emotions about climate change. *Climatic Change*, 2012, 113: 1105-1112.

[2] Climate Vulnerable Forum. Members. [2023-06-08]. https://thecvf.org/members/.

trapped in the "quagmire" of rare climate disasters and cannot extricate themselves. According to recent statistics from the United Nations Office for the Coordination of Humanitarian Affairs, approximately 36 million people in the Horn of Africa alone needed humanitarian assistance. Bangladesh suffered its longest flooding since 1988 in 2020. According to data released by the Bangladesh Health Emergency Action Center on August 19, 2020, 226 people in the country have died from floods that have erupted since the end of June. Most of the deceased were drowned, with some being struck by lightning and bitten by snakes. The population affected by floods in the country exceeds 5 million.[1]

We acknowledge that all countries are fragile in the face of climate change, and even developed countries with strong capabilities like the United States will suffer huge casualties and property losses. For example, in August 2005, the disastrous Hurricane Katrina hit several states in the southeast of the United States, killing more than 1,800 people, injuring more than 5,000 people, and causing economic losses of more than 160 billion dollars. But particularly vulnerable countries face a heavier blow. Developed countries, due to their strong economic strength and good medical and health standards, have suffered such severe casualties due to extreme weather conditions. Those least developed countries and small-island developing states face a fatal blow due to their economic conditions and medical health level. They are most seriously affected by climate change, but they are also facing economic challenges, which is equivalent to a double blow. Also they are extremely vulnerable to climate crises and debt crises, which are a thorny vicious circle.

We need to make more people aware of the health crisis faced by these fragile countries, with many people displaced or even losing their lives due to climate change. We need to raise awareness and provide assistance to them. Therefore, it is particularly important to integrate climate communication and health communication with a focus on CVF countries.

---

[1] Chinanews. Bangladesh floods cause more than 200 lives. (2020-08-20)[2024-05-22]. https://www.chinanews.com.cn/m/gj/2020/08-20/9270233.shtml.

3.2 Uphold the Principle of Climate Justice to Alleviate Climate Inequality

Climate change is also an issue of justice. Climate change is caused mostly by developed industrialized countries, but it is unfair that disadvantaged communities bear the worst consequences. Climate justice requires that more coverage be made available to these vulnerable countries.

On March 29, 2023, the UN General Assembly adopted Resolution Requesting International Court of Justice Provide Advisory Opinion on States' Obligations Concerning Climate Change. The Assembly decided to request the Court to render an opinion on the obligations of states under international law to ensure the protection of the climate system from anthropogenic emissions of greenhouse gases. Although legally non-binding, the requested advisory opinion of the Court has the potential to make a significant contribution to the clarification of the current state of international law.

The Court's advisory opinion will put a spotlight on the obligation of states to ensure that all countries, developing states and vulnerable countries in particular, have a right to a healthy and sustainable environment.

The legitimacy foundation behind this is that "the most vulnerable populations who have historically contributed the least to the unfolding climate calamity are disproportionately affected by the consequences". The loss for CVF countries is grossly disproportionate while their carbon footprint is negligible.

Therefore, CVF countries deserve to be paid a lot more attention. We appeal for more media coverage on how severe the climate hazards are happening, how difficult it is for these poor communities to adapt, and how disproportionately these marginalized people are suffering.

3.3 Innovate Diversified Communication Subjects and Means

We need to innovate communication subjects and methods, the aim of which is to increase public participation in climate change and health communication, and to improve the accessibility of various reports to the public. By adopting interesting communication methods, we can attract the public, make them interested in this topic, and further, attract them to gain a deeper understanding of this issue, achieving better communication effects.

We fully recognize that the United Nations and some countries have made great efforts to disseminate information on climate and human health issues, but in view of the global climate still in a state of tension, we should call on more potential communicators to join the promotion team. That is, we need to innovate the subjects of communication.

At the same time, the rapid development of digital technology and social media has made the way of communication not limited to traditional news media. Most people understand the world through anecdotes and stories, rather than statistics and graphs, so diversified communication methods should be employed to overcome the boredom and deficiency of traditional news. That is why we should make use of some emerging communication methods.

First, we recommend that the United Nations should play a leading role in calling on actors, including non-governmental international organizations, to carry out or strengthen the communication of climate and human health. For example, the Department of Public Information under the United Nations Secretariat, together with organizations such as the United Nations Environment Programme, the World Health Organization, and the World Meteorological Organization, can jointly carry out public communication activities on climate change and health. They can conduct climate change and health knowledge dissemination activities to raise public awareness of the relationship between climate change and health, as well as that of mitigating and adapting to climate change. For example, the World Health Organization launched three global action plans on climate change and health in 2019. The primary goal of the related project is to "increase people's awareness of the health impacts of climate change to promote public health action". We believe that related projects should continue in the future. They may also conduct cross-departmental collaboration, integrate resources, and jointly carry out communication activities, which also facilitates the public's centralized access to information. This will undoubtedly reduce the public's time searching for information, making it more convenient for them to access more reliable information.

Second, states should develop a variety of communication incentive policies and mechanisms to encourage all types of media, enterprises, institutions, individuals with certain social influence and the general public to engage in climate communication.

Third, all communicators, including individuals, can adopt a variety of communication channels and means[1], making great use of digital technology and social media to attract a wider audience to climate and human health issues. There are many new and interesting ways of communication that can be adopted, involving hashtags, video games, social media, scrolls and cli-fi (climate fiction). Cli-fi, short for climate fiction, is a form of fiction literature that features a changed or changing climate. It is rooted in science fiction, but also draws on realism and the supernatural. The term "cli-fi" became popular in the 2010s, but people have been writing cli-fi unintentionally for at least a couple of centuries. For example, *Darkness by Lord Byron*, written in 1816, is an example of cli-fi. Cli-fi could play an important role in helping to prepare for, cope with and devise solutions for the climate crisis.[2] A survey of readers found that readers of cli-fi "are younger, more liberal, and more concerned about climate change than nonreaders", and that it "reminds concerned readers of the severity of climate change while impelling them to imagine environmental futures and consider the impact of climate change on human and nonhuman life.[3] Another survey focused on the popular novel *The Water Knife* found that cautionary climate fiction set in a dystopic future can effectively educate readers about climate injustice and lead readers to empathize

---

[1] These means include but are not limited to: shooting thematic documentaries and micro-films; integrating climate and human health issues into video games; adding live-action VR experiences, etc. According to the *Reuters Institute Digital News Report 2020* released by the Reuters Institute at the University of Oxford, through pictures, videos, celebrities or influencers we may attract more audiences. For Gen Z, social media and blogging are the more popular ways to disseminate and access information.

[2] Science Smith. Cli-Fi (Climate fiction)—Climate in arts and history. (2021-06-30)[2023-07-15]. https://www.science.smith.edu/climatelit/cli-fi/.

[3] Schneider-Mayerson, M. The influence of climate fiction: An empirical survey of readers. *Environmental Humanities*, 2018, 10(2): 473-500.

with the victims of climate change, including environmental migrants.[①] Therefore, we can use some progressive cli-fi to raise public awareness of the health impacts of climate change and encourage them to participate in climate action.

In conclusion, our main appeal is to request for more media coverage on both climate and health hazards that CVF countries are suffering and how difficult it is for CVF communities to adapt. Specifically, we need to integrate climate communication and health communication with a focus on CVF countries, uphold the principle of climate justice to alleviate climate inequality, and innovate diversified communication subjects and means, such as hashtags, video games, social media, scrolls, and cli-fi.

---

① Schneider-Mayerson, M. "Just as in the book"? The influence of literature on readers' awareness of climate injustice and perception of climate migrants. *Interdisciplinary Studies in Literature and Environment,* 2020, 27(2): 337-364.

关于新加坡政府应对热浪危机的提案[①]

摘　要：本文概述了新加坡与周边东南亚国家面临的高温热浪挑战，并深入探讨了新加坡采取的先进策略及其成效，旨在为区域内的热浪应对机制提供优化路径。作为区域内的领跑者，新加坡展现了其在缓解热浪影响方面的决心与智慧，通过一系列综合性措施，不仅增加了城市绿化覆盖面，革新了建筑设计以促进能效，还着重提升了公众意识和应急准备能力。这些努力有效缓解了城市热岛效应，显著改善了居民的生活环境质量，为公共卫生筑起了一道坚实的防线。展望未来，新加坡在持续巩固现有成果的同时，可进一步探索技术创新与国际合作的新维度，引领东南亚走上一条更加成熟、高效的热浪危机应对之路。

关键词：新加坡；热浪危机；气候变暖；措施

一、引　言

近年来，全球变暖导致气候异常，各地频繁出现热浪现象。作为一个热带城市，新加坡在面对高温和热浪时遇到了严峻的挑战。作为一个平均气温超过32 摄氏度、森林覆盖率较高的国家，新加坡的热岛效应更加严重。

由于各国学者对热浪研究的方法不完全相同，因此目前对热浪的判定还没有一个明确的标准，世界气象组织的高温热浪标准为：日最高气温高于 32℃，且持续 3 天以上。热浪不仅会导致人体出现中暑、热射病等热相关疾病，同时还会增加心血管、呼吸、泌尿、神经等系统的疾病发病与死亡率。[②] 同时，热

---

① 作者：许跞，西安交通大学医学系；李亚晨，西安交通大学医学系。

② Luschkova, D., Traidl-Hoffmann, C. & Ludwig, A. Climate change and allergies. *Allergo Journal International*, 2022, 31(4): 114-120.

浪也导致了冰川融化、海平面上升等严重后果，威胁着包括人类在内的众多物种的生存。因此，关注和应对热浪带来的问题和危害对世界各国都具有重要意义。新加坡靠近赤道，为热带雨林气候，全年长夏无冬，气温变化不大。热岛效应是由于城市建筑群密集，柏油路和水泥路面比郊区的土壤、植被具有更大的吸热率和更小的比热容，因而城市地区升温较快，并向四周和大气中大量辐射，造成了同一时间城区气温普遍高于郊区气温。此外，新加坡作为一个地势低洼的岛国，生态环境非常脆弱，经常遭遇暴雨和旱情，也承受着海平面上升带来的巨大风险。因此，应对热浪等气候变化、实现可持续发展一直是新加坡的重要课题。

二、东南亚国家应对高温热浪：新加坡引领示范，多国共谋气候变暖之策

为预防热浪，防止高温天气继续变多、极端高温持续上升，新加坡近年来出台了一系列碳中和政策。2017 年，新加坡不断研究城市热岛缓解策略，在政府的支持下启动"冷却新加坡"计划，通过加大绿色植被面、设立地下区域冷却系统，完善城市规划，应对未来高温热浪。2021 年，新加坡出台《新加坡绿色规划 2030》，该规划由五个部分组成，分别是"大自然中的城市""可持续生活""能源策略""绿色经济"和"具有韧性的未来"，在应对热浪等气候变化方面也起到十分重要的作用。

除了新加坡，随着气候变暖加剧，众多其他东南亚国家都采取了一系列符合自己国家实际情况的措施。印度尼西亚正通过应用"冷屋顶"应对日益严重的热浪，这种方法成本低，且具有可持续性。这些屋顶涂有一种特殊的涂层，能反射阳光，减少建筑物吸收的热量，从而降低室内温度。越南河内市人口密度高，住房水平不一，越南红十字会在德国红十字会的技术支持下，开发了一种绘图方法，从而在全市范围进行调查，绘制出高温下各地脆弱性、暴露程度和危险程度的地图，通过这些信息可以找到潜在影响最大的区域。

新加坡作为高度发达的东南亚国家，在工业经济高度发达的同时又能很好地应对气候问题，为东南亚国家应对高温热浪做好示范作用。

三、新加坡多措并举应对热浪危害

新加坡已经实施了一系列措施减轻热浪危害。

（一）热岛效应管理计划

新加坡政府实施了热岛效应管理计划，旨在降低城市地区的温度并减少热浪的影响。政府通过增加绿地、树木和水景来改善城市景观，并采用冷却技术和材料来减少建筑物和道路的热吸收，还使用绿色空间、绿色屋顶，改进建筑设计，减少了城市热岛效应。[①] 此外，政府还通过改变建筑朝向以创造风流，并使用区域供冷系统（将冷冻水输送到周围的建筑物以冷却空气），而不是仅仅依赖空调。

"冷却新加坡"计划广泛使用计算建模方法。天气研究和预报（WRF）模型用于分析城市热岛（Urban Heat Island，UHI）的影响以及潜在的UHI对策。UHI幅度是通过比较当前城市化条件（"当前情景"）的模拟结果与所有城市地区都被植被取代的合理农村条件的结果（"全绿色情景"）来测量的。

UHI效应显示出明显的昼夜周期变化，上午低，下午显著增加。新加坡的UHI效应在夜间最高，因为此时热量被捕获并储存在城市表面。特定地区夜间最大UHI可达 $4-7℃$ 左右。

（二）能源种类和效率措施

面对热浪挑战，新加坡展现出卓越的绿色智慧，巧妙融合高效能源与可持续策略，为缓解热岛效应和减排温室气体提供了宝贵的经验。严格的"绿色标志"标准推动了建筑革新，高效冷却、LED照明及绿色建材的应用显著降低了能耗。新加坡在太阳能开发上大步迈进，太阳能板遍及城乡。

先进的智能电网与能源管理系统如同城市的神经网络，精准调配电力，鼓励居民和企业成为节能的实践者。教育与宣传深化了公众的环保意识，日常生活中的节能减排行为渐成风尚。此外，新加坡在清洁能源技术和气候适应研究上不断投入资金，孵化出新型制冷技术和建筑光伏一体化等未来方案，为世界提供了应对气候变化的灵感与范例。通过一系列综合策略，新加坡不仅有效应对了热浪侵袭，也引领了全球城市迈向绿色未来的步伐。

（三）增加绿化

新加坡承诺，到2030年种植100万棵树。种植的树木类型很重要，树木要能提供较大的遮荫，因为像棕榈树这样的小型树木在散热方面效率不高。增

---

① Aik, J., Heywood, A. E., Newall, A. T., et al. Climate variability and salmonellosis in Singapore—A time series analysis. *Science and the Total Environment*, 2018, 639: 1261-1267.

加绿化有助于创造一个更凉爽、更宜人的环境。

（四）其 他

除上述减缓热浪和减轻热浪危害的措施外，新加坡也采取了以下多种类型的适应措施。

（1）新加坡政府建立了热浪健康风险预警系统，该系统以天气预报为基础，识别温度和湿度水平的临界阈值。超过这些阈值，热相关疾病的发病率就会增加。警报通过各种渠道向公众传播，如在线新闻和社交媒体。建立热浪健康风险预警系统，可以使居民特别是慢性病患者、老人等脆弱人群提前获得气象及健康风险信息，并采取相应的自我健康管理和防护措施，降低相关疾病发生风险，预防不良影响的发生，提高居民健康水平。[①]

（2）在公众教育层面，政府还发起了公共教育运动和保健工作者培训项目，以提高人们对热浪风险及热浪预防措施的认识，并通过教育和宣传活动，提高公众对气候变化和适应措施的认识和理解，鼓励公众参与和支持适应措施的实施。例如，政府和企业为工人提供凉爽的公共空间，鼓励穿着浅色服装，在室外区域设置雾扇等。

（3）在科学技术方面，新加坡大力投资和支持气候变化相关的科学研究和技术创新，积极参与国际合作，为改善环境提供更多的科学依据和技术支持。

四、新加坡应对热浪效果显著，但仍面临多重问题与挑战

新加坡采取了一系列措施来应对热浪，并取得了显著的效果，主要体现在以下四方面。

（1）减轻城市热岛效应：新加坡通过改变城市规划和建筑设计，成功减缓了城市热岛效应。通过调整建筑朝向、增加绿化覆盖和使用冷却系统，新加坡有效地降低了城市与郊区的温度差异。城市中心的温度得以降低，创造了更为舒适的居住和工作环境。

（2）提高空气质量：新加坡的绿化计划和树木种植活动有助于改善空气质量。树木能够吸收二氧化碳，释放氧气，提供凉爽的环境，使人们能够在户外活动时更加舒适。

---

① SohSoh, S., Loo, L. H., Jamali, N., et al. Climate variability and seasonal patterns of paediatric parainfluenza infections in the tropics: An ecological study in Singapore. *International Journal of Hygiene and Environmental Health*, 2022, 239: 113864.

（3）提高公众意识：新加坡通过教育和宣传活动，提高了公众对热浪和气候变化的认识。人们更加了解热浪对健康和环境的影响，并学会采取适应措施，如避免在炎热时段外出、保持水分摄入和采取防晒措施等。这种公众意识的提高有助于减少热浪对人们健康和生活的影响。

（4）提高城市韧性：新加坡的措施不仅为了应对当前的热浪，还着眼于提高城市的韧性，以应对未来可能出现的更为严峻的气候变化。通过投资科技和创新解决方案，新加坡正在建设一个更具适应性和可持续性的城市。这包括开发数字城市模型来预测和评估热浪的影响，以及研究和应用新的建筑材料和技术来降低热量。

总的来说，新加坡的措施在应对热浪方面取得了显著的效果。通过减轻城市热岛效应、提高空气质量、降低能源消耗、提高公众意识和提高城市韧性，新加坡成功地创造了一个更舒适、更可持续的城市环境。[1]这些经验和成果为其他国家提供了宝贵的借鉴和学习的机会，帮助各国应对气候变化带来的挑战。但是由于各种客观条件的限制，目前新加坡在适应和减缓气候变化方面仍存在着一些问题和挑战。

（1）有限的土地和资源：新加坡国土面积小，缺乏自然资源，这给寻求替代能源和实施大规模缓解措施带来了挑战。而且，其作为一个高度城市化的国家，人口密度高，绿地和自然空间不足，这限制了相应措施和计划的实施。

（2）地理环境：作为一个地势低洼的岛国，新加坡需要制定强有力的适应战略，以保护沿海地区的生态平衡。此外，地处热带所带来的持续高温气候导致空调用电需求激增，这对能源供应和能源效率提出了挑战。

（3）人口老龄化：新加坡面临人口老龄化的挑战，老年人等脆弱人群对高温更为敏感。政府必须采取措施特别关注这些群体，确保他们在热浪期间得到适当的保护。

（4）公众意识和行为改变：尽管政府进行了广泛的公众教育活动，但改变人们的行为和习惯仍然是一个挑战。在应对热浪方面，公众需要积极采取措施来降低自身的风险，例如适时避免户外活动、保持充足的水分摄入等。

（5）国际合作：气候变化是一个全球性问题，需要国际合作，新加坡应对气候变化的努力必须与全球框架和协议保持一致。

---

[1] Mohajerani, A., Bakaric, J. & Jeffrey-Bailey, T. The urban heat island effect, its causes, and mitigation, with reference to the thermal properties of asphalt concrete. *Journal of Environmental Management*, 2017, 197: 522-538.

五、提 案

（一）提案具体内容

1.增强城市绿化计划

新加坡应提供更多的公园和绿地空间，以增加城市的绿化覆盖率，减少热岛效应，降低城市表面温度。例如，推广屋顶花园和垂直绿化，为建筑物提供遮阳和降温效果，改善周围环境的热量吸收和散发；加大植树造林力度，特别是在人口密集的社区和工业区域，以降低环境温度。

2.改善建筑物设计和节能措施

要采用和推广可持续建筑设计，使用符合高热环境的材料和技术，减少建筑内部的热量积累。例如，推广绿色屋顶和外墙涂料，以降低建筑物表面温度和空调负荷；加强节能标准，鼓励建筑业主和开发商在新建和改建项目中使用节能设备和技术。[①]

3.提高社区意识和准备度

要加强对公众的宣传教育，提高人们关于热浪对健康的潜在危害的认识，并为高风险群体提供特殊关怀，包括老年人、儿童和患有慢性疾病的人。此外，社区应该建立紧急响应机制，迅速应对突发热浪事件，并提供相关的应急服务和援助。

（二）提案内容与当前问题的关联阐述

我们认为该提案可以帮助应对和减轻热浪危害，更好地保障人民的健康和生活，促进实现可持续发展，原因如下。

1.综合维度

该提案从城市绿化、建筑设计和社区意识等多个维度入手，全面应对热浪带来的不利影响。

2.可持续性

该提案注重可持续发展，通过增加绿化覆盖率、推广节能措施，减少热浪对环境的负面影响。

3.适用性

该提案针对新加坡的具体情况进行了设计，考虑到城市的地理特点和人口

---

① Teo, Y. H., Makani, M. A. B. H., Wang, W., et al. Urban heat island mitigation: GIS-based analysis for a tropical city Singapore. *International Journal of Environmental Research and Public Health*, 2022 19(19): 11917.

密集度，符合当地的实际需求。

　　总的来说，新加坡政府应对热浪危机的提案涵盖了增强城市绿化计划、改善建筑物设计和节能措施，以及提高社区意识和准备度这三类措施。这些措施旨在帮助新加坡更好地应对热浪挑战，减少热岛效应，改善城市环境，并保护公众的健康和安全。

German Proposal for the Protection of Global Indigenous Peoples:
Reducing the Threat of Climate Change to the Health of Indigenous Peoples[①]

Abstract: The proposal, focusing on the health of indigenous peoples worldwide, aims to promote human development by adhering to the United Nations' principle of "leaving no one behind" from a German perspective. It carried out case studies on Germany and the prototypical representative—Canada, highlighting the progress made in addressing health threats faced by indigenous peoples due to climate change. The "1 plus 2" Model in this proposal summarizes the top-level design concerning intellectual and material supports needed to solve the plight of indigenous peoples, which is further expected to be applied in more scenarios. There are four recommendations to address the issue mentioned, including agenda setting, opinion solicitation, funding declaration, and data collection. Specifically the proposed suggestions include enhancing global attention to the point of climate change-induced indigenous health crisis at various levels, strengthening indigenous peoples' participation and leadership in the governance of the worldwide

① Authors: Liu Linjia, College of Education, Zhejiang University; Du Juan, School of International Studies, Zhejiang University; Zhao Jingwen, School of International Studies, Zhejiang University; Wang Yifei, School of International Studies, Zhejiang University.

health crisis caused by climate change, establishing a joint climate and health database covering indigenous peoples around the world, providing holistic assistance to address the climate change-induced health crisis faced by indigenous peoples. The proposal emphasizes the importance of supporting indigenous peoples' participation in development processes rather than direct intervention. As the sponsor of this proposal, Germany is committed to implementing these recommendations to provide a practical solution.

——————— **Keywords:** indigenous peoples; climate change; health threats; German proposal; SDGs

1. Introduction

1.1 Background

Indigenous peoples are identified as "among the poorest and most marginalized people in the world".[1] The United Nations has no official definition of this group of individuals to date. Jose R. Martinez Cobo's *Study on the Problem of Discrimination Against Indigenous Populations* provides one of the most recognized definitions of the term "indigenous": indigenous communities, peoples, and nations are those having a historical continuity with pre-invasion and pre-colonial societies that developed on their territories, and considering themselves distinct from other sectors of the societies now prevailing on those territories, or parts of them.[2]

As of 2022, there are an estimated 476 million indigenous peoples worldwide.

---

[1] Special Rapporteur on the Rights of Indigenous Peoples. Rights of indigenous peoples—Report of the special rapporteur on the rights of indigenous peoples. (2019-08-02)[2023-11-17]. https://www.ohchr.org/en/documents/thematic-reports/ahrc4237-rights-indigenous-peoples-report-special-rapporteur-rights.

[2] United Nations Department of Economic and Social Affairs. State of the world's indigenous peoples (SOWIP). (2013-01-01)[2023-11-17]. https://www.un.org/development/desa/indigenouspeoples/wp-content/uploads/sites/19/2018/03/The-State-of-The-Worlds-Indigenous-Peoples-WEB.pdf.

Although they only account for 6% of the global population, they represent about 19% of those suffering from poverty.[①] Due to their generally low socio-economic status, combined with structural problems such as colonization and exclusion and deficiencies in the group's governance capacity, indigenous peoples, in particular, face health inequalities, leading to high mortality and morbidity rates. Statistically, indigenous peoples have a life expectancy up to 20 years lower than that of non-indigenous peoples globally.[②]

Indigenous peoples are particularly vulnerable to the adverse effects of climate change, especially in terms of health. They tend to have a high dependency on natural ecosystems for their production and livelihoods, which puts them at greater risk. The health problems that indigenous peoples experience as a result of climate change can be divided into four main categories: water-related illnesses, mental health effects, food system impacts, and respiratory illnesses.[③]

Water-related illnesses are a significant concern for several indigenous communities, which are already struggling with unsafe drinking water or inadequate drinking water treatment facilities. Moreover, thawing permafrost poses a significant threat to water infrastructure as it destabilizes the ground beneath it, affecting buildings and other infrastructure. In terms of indigenous peoples' mental and spiritual health, their relationships with people, wildlife, and the natural environment are crucial. However, the changing climate disrupts these connections, threatening social networks and knowledge-sharing. Climate change significantly impacts the food system, affecting the supply and quality of traditional foods, subsistence foods, and cultivated crops in many regions. The lack of access to conventional foods has adverse effects on nutrition, leading to obesity, diabetes, and even mental health problems.

Furthermore, climate change can increase outdoor air pollutants such as

---

① The World Bank. Indigenous peoples. (2023-04-06)[2023-11-17]. https://www.worldbank.org/en/topic/indigenouspeoples.

② The World Bank. Indigenous peoples. (2023-04-06)[2023-11-17]. https://www.worldbank.org/en/topic/indigenouspeoples.

③ United Nations. United Nations framework convention on climate change. (1992-06-20)[2023-11-17]. https://documents-dds-ny.un.org/doc/UNDOC/GEN/G11/605/50/PDF/G1160550.pdf?OpenElement.

ground-level ozone, particulate matter in wildfire smoke, and drought-caused dust, resulting in respiratory illnesses. Exposure to dust, wildfire smoke, and certain air pollutants can cause or aggravate asthma, pneumonia, bronchitis, and other respiratory conditions.[1] In summary, climate change is increasingly impacting the health and well-being of indigenous peoples and exacerbating their vulnerability to concurrent health threats.[2]

Samoa, Greenland, and French Polynesia have most indigenous people. The Arctic Circle and the Pacific are strongholds of indigenous life.[3] Despite the limited prominence of indigenous issues in Germany, the country assumes an active leadership role among middle powers within the international community regarding establishing international norms and advancing global governance regarding climate, health, and human rights issues. Germany demonstrates a willingness, responsibility, and capacity to advocate for safeguarding indigenous peoples globally, leveraging its economic and technological advantages, particularly regarding climate, health, and human rights concerns.

The proposal aims to shield indigenous peoples from climate-induced health threats from the perspective of disease prevention and treatment, as well as from the standpoint of climate mitigation and adaptation. It aims to address both the symptoms and the root causes to reduce the threats posed by climate change to the health of indigenous peoples.

1.2 Significance

Reducing the threats posed by climate change to the health of indigenous peoples is of great importance to the joint development of all humanity. Four hundred and seventy-six million indigenous peoples living across 90 countries speak an overwhelming majority of the world's estimated 7,000 languages, represent 5,000 different cultures, and safeguard up to 80% of the world's biodiversity

---

[1] U. S. Global Change Research Program. Impacts, risks, and adaptation in the United States: Fourth national climate assessment, volume II. (2018-11-23)[2023-11-17]. https://nca2018.globalchange.gov/chapter/13/.

[2] Lancet. The 2022 report of the Lancet countdown on health and climate change: Health at the mercy of fossil fuels. (2022-11-05)[2023-11-17]. https://www.thelancet.com/journals/lancet/article/PIIS0140-6736(22)01540-9/fulltext.

[3] Statista. Indigenous people: Where the world's indigenous people live. (2023-08-09)[2023-11-17]. https://www.statista.com/chart/18981/countries-with-the-largest-share-of-indigenous-people/.

through traditional ecological knowledge.[1] We should recognize that guarding the health and well-being of indigenous peoples is a guardianship of the shared resources and wealth of all humanity. At the same time, under the impact of globalization, sudden climatic disasters and health events have broken through the limits of time and space, making countries interdependent in these fields.

Reducing the threats posed by climate change to the health of indigenous peoples has vital implications for climate, health, and human rights issues and even for world peace. The proposal's complexity is self-evident, as it is a composite of three major points. At the same time, the catastrophic effect is not only highly destructive to the stability of the local social environment, but if the scope is gradually expanded, it will further induce all kinds of global instability, which may eventually lead to a security dilemma for all human society.

Reducing climate change threats to the health of indigenous communities has spillover value in areas such as science, technology, and economics. The science, technology, policy, management, and service experiences that serve to manage the climate health crisis of indigenous communities will become a public good for all of humanity, contributing to sustainable global development on an ongoing basis.

Germany has benefited from a stable global political and economic environment. It has, therefore, been a strong supporter of global governance through international institutions, participating actively in varied global governance mechanisms. In recent years, with the rise of Germany's economic power and the consequent accentuation of German leadership within the European Union, Germany is seeking to move from a more "restrained" position in global governance to an "active" one. It has expressed its intention to actively shape the international order actively, assuming responsibility and leadership commensurate with its power.[2] Germany has outstanding strengths and competencies as a model country in bio-industry and biotechnology. It wants to contribute to the initiative on this topic at the United Nations Climate Change

[1] World Health Organization. International Day of the World's Indigenous Peoples. (2022-08-09)[2023-11-17]. https://www.who.int/news-room/events/detail/2022/08/09/default-calendar/international-day-of-the-world-s-indigenous-peoples.
[2] Zheng, C. R. New developments in German foreign policy. *Chinese Journal of European Studies*, 2014, 2: 1-14, 165.

Conference of Parties (COP) by leveraging its strengths.

2. Tracking Progress

Over the years, various international organizations, with the United Nations as their representative, as well as many sovereign nations, have implemented a series of measures to safeguard indigenous communities' rights.[①] Indigenous health and well-being have long been a concern and pushed forward under the global agenda of breaking down "health inequality".

In the meantime, the ongoing climate change, combined with other natural and human-made stressors, has created unprecedented or unanticipated health threats in places where they have not previously occurred and changed the severity or frequency of existing health problems. Indigenous peoples, with their deep cultural or productive connections to the land, water, and air, are particularly susceptible to climate impacts on health and wellness.

This proposal places the threats posed by climate change on the health of indigenous communities at its core, explicitly aiming to explore avenues for the protection of the rights and interests of indigenous populations from a horizontal governance perspective rather than seeking disease-specific treatment solutions through a vertical medical approach. It is essential to recognize the inherent interconnection between climate, health, and human rights protection for indigenous peoples. The escalating severity of health threats faced by indigenous communities under the influence of climate change can be attributed to objective challenges and subjective complacency in safeguarding their rights and interests.

In this section of progress tracking, the proposal will start with a case analysis of two countries, namely, the proposal sponsor—the Federal Republic of Germany, and a prototypical representative deeply concerned with indigenous issues—the Dominion of Canada. The analysis will focus on the specific measures implemented by these nations to address the health concerns of indigenous peoples. Subsequently, drawing from the experiences of these case countries and global

① United Nations. United Nations declaration on the rights of indigenous peoples—General assembly resolution 61/295. (2007-09-13)[2024-05-07]. https://legal.un.org/avl/ha/ga_61-295/ga_61-295.html.

progress, the proposal further distills the existing events into a model named "1 plus 2" for summarization. It raises pertinent questions and challenges based on current progress.

2.1 Case Analysis

2.1.1 Proposal Sponsor—Germany

Although Germany's indigenous issues are not prominent, it is pragmatic to raise national awareness and recognition of the health problems caused by climate change for indigenous peoples. Take "BMUV Education Service" as an example, led by the Federal Ministry for the Environment (Bundesumweltministerium, BMUV). It offers teaching materials, current information, campaigns, and tips for schools and educational institutions. One of its programs, "Environment in the Classroom" ("Umwelt im Unterricht"), publishes a "Topic of the Month" with monthly teaching materials on current environmental policy topics and sustainable development issues. The materials are free of charge and can be modified.[1]

On November 5, 2020, the month's topic was "indigenous peoples in the fight against climate change".[2] The students receive fictitious letters from indigenous children. They learn about the differences and similarities between their way of life and that of indigenous people, including how they interact with nature. At the same time, the students deal with the ancestral methods of life of indigenous peoples. They develop stories (storytelling) about their everyday lives from the perspective of members of individual peoples, how they deal with environmental problems, and the challenges posed by climate change.[3]

In addition to actively raising awareness of indigenous issues at home, Germany is also making full use of international resources and leading the international community in contributing to research on this topic. Germany is an active participant in global governance with international organizations as key

---

[1] Bundesministerium für Umwelt, Naturschutz, nukleare Sicherheit und Verbraucherschutz. Über umwelt im unterricht. (2024-05-07)[2024-05-07]. https://www.umwelt-im-unterricht.de/ueber-umwelt-im-unterricht#c213.

[2] BMUV-Bildungsservice. Indigene völker, menschenrechte und nachhaltige entwicklung. (2020-12-05)[2023-11-17]. https://www.umwelt-im-unterricht.de/hintergrund/indigene-voelker-menschenrechte-und-nachhaltige-entwicklung/.

[3] BMUV-Bildungsservice. Indigene völker, menschenrechte und nachhaltige entwicklung. (2020-12-05)[2023-11-17]. https://www.umwelt-im-unterricht.de/hintergrund/indigene-voelker-menschenrechte-und-nachhaltige-entwicklung/.

platforms and is home to 35 UN agencies, 24 of which are based in Bonn, including the United Nations University (UNU) Institute for Environment and Human Security (UNU-EHS). The UNU is the academic arm of the United Nations and acts as a global think tank. The mission of the UNU-EHS is to carry out cutting-edge research on risks and adaptation related to environmental hazards and global change. The institute's research promotes policies and programs to reduce these risks while considering the interplay between ecological and societal factors.

The research areas include climate change adaptation incorporating insurance-related approaches, environmentally induced migration, social vulnerability, ecosystem services, environmental deterioration processes, models, and tools to analyze exposure and risks linked to natural hazards, focusing on urban space and rural-urban interfaces. The research is always conducted with the underlying goal of connecting solutions to development pathways.

Beyond its research mandate, UNU-EHS is actively engaged in education. It offers the joint Master of Science program "The Geography of Environmental Risks and Human Security" with the University of Bonn. UNU-EHS also hosts international PhD projects and courses on global environmental risks and sustainable development issues. The institute is based in Bonn, Germany.[1]

2.1.2 A Prototypical Representative—Canada

In Canada, 1,807,250 people are identified as indigenous in the 2021 census, accounting for 5.0% of the country's total population. Indigenous peoples in Canada mainly live in three provinces: Alberta, Ontario, and British Columbia. The Canadian Constitution recognizes three groups of indigenous peoples: First Nations (or Indians), Inuit, and Métis.[2]

There are two departments in the Canadian government responsible for policies relating to indigenous peoples: the Crown-Indigenous Relations and Northern Affairs Canada (CIRNAC) and Indigenous Services Canada (ISC). These

---

[1] UNU-EHS Institute for Environment and Human Security. About UNU-EHS. (2023-11-17)[2023-11-17]. https://ehs.unu.edu/about.

[2] Government of Alberta. 2021 census of Canada—Indigenous people. (2023-11-17)[2023-11-17]. https://open.alberta.ca/dataset/487a7294-06ac-481e-80b7-5566692a6b11/resource/257af6d4-902c-4761-8fee-3971a4480678/download/tbf-2021-census-of-canada-indigenous-people.pdf.

two departments work collaboratively with other partners to put forward high-quality programs and services covering fields of indigenous issues like education, reconciliation, health, environment, and infrastructure, with visions to support and empower indigenous peoples to independently deliver services and address the socio-economic conditions in their communities.[①]

Concerning health care, indigenous peoples are included in the per capita allocations of funding from the federal fiscal transfer. They are entitled to access insured provincial and territorial health services as residents of a province or territory. Under the federal-wide effective Canada Health Act, provincial and territorial governments are responsible for carrying out medicare universal health coverage for hospital, diagnostic, and medical care services for all residents, including indigenous residents. Besides medicare, non-insured health benefits include coverage for various health and associated services for eligible indigenous communities, including prescription drugs, primary dental care, vision care, emergency mental health services, and medical transportation.[②]

Health Canada, Public Health Agency of Canada, and Indigenous Services Canada are the significant institutions administrating the above programs via funding or direct service provision. Furthermore, many provinces and territories have enacted legislative provisions recognizing the value and role of indigenous peoples in the planning and delivery of health services in their communities or the importance of culture and traditional healing practices.

Indigenous peoples have the constitution-supported rights of self-governance. Agreements and treaties transfer population health programs to indigenous control and a tripartite collaboration between the indigenous community, the federal government, and provincial or territory governments. Through co-developing distinctions-based legislation and improving coordination, indigenous cultural safety

---

① Government of Canada. Crown-indigenous relations and northern affairs Canada. (2023-11-17)[2023-11-17]. https://www.canada.ca/en/crown-indigenous-relations-northern-affairs.html; Government of Canada. Indigenous services Canada. (2023-11-17)[2023-11-17]. https://www.canada.ca/en/indigenous-services-canada.html.

② Government of Canada. Canadian health care system. (2005-10-29)[2023-11-17]. https://publications.gc.ca/collections/collection_2012/sc-hc/H21-261-2005-chi.pdf; Marchildon, G. P., Lavoie, J. G. & Harrold, H. J. Typology of indigenous health system governance in Canada. *Canadian Public Administration*, 2021, 64(4): 561-586.

and self-determination in health care are in advance.[①]

Against the backdrop of climate change, indigenous peoples' rights to survive, live, health, and development are under great concern. In 2022, the National Collaborating Centre for Indigenous Health (NCCIH), in collaboration with multiple other government departments, published a report titled *Climate Change and Indigenous People's Health in Canada*, which provides a comprehensive overview of the potential health risks faced by the three major indigenous groups within Canada (see Table 1).[②]

Table 1　Overview of Climate Change Impacts on the Health and Well-Being of First Nations, Inuit, and Métis in Canada

Health Impact or Hazard Category	Climate-Related Causes	Possible Health Effects
Impacts on First Nations, Inuit, and Métis peoples and communities	• Increased wildfire, drought, and flooding events • Instability and melting of permafrost and changes to ground snow cover, sea ice extent and thickness • Changes to sea levels and weather patterns • Higher exposure to climate risks in relation to natural and built environments (such as poor housing, water, sanitation, and environmental contaminants) • Decreased availability, quality, quantity, and safety of traditional food sources	• Air quality health impacts (e.g., respiratory and cardiovascular diseases) • Increased water and foodborne diseases • Mental health impacts (e.g., stress, anxiety and post-traumatic stress disorder) • Increased injuries and deaths from accidents (e.g., natural hazards and extreme weather events) • Increased direct and indirect health impacts from permafrost-related infrastructure damage • Exacerbation of health and socioeconomic inequities • Exacerbation of chronic and infectious diseases • Food and water insecurity due to decreased access to, and quality of land, waters, plants, animals, and natural resources • Decreased opportunities for transmission of indigenous knowledge and land skills, particularly among youth, affecting sense of identity, mental well-being, and cultures

---

① Government of Canada. Indigenous health care in Canada. (2023-11-17)[2023-11-17]. https://www.sac-isc.gc.ca/eng/1626810177053/1626810219482.

② National Collaborating Centre for Indigenous Health. Climate change and indigenous people's health in Canada. (2022-03-22)[2023-11-17]. https://www.nccih.ca/Publications/Lists/Publications/Attachments/10367/Climate_Change_and_Indigenous_Peoples_Health_EN_Web_2022-03-22.pdf.

(continued)

Health Impact or Hazard Category	Climate-Related Causes	Possible Health Effects
Impacts on First Nations, Inuit, and Métis peoples and communities	• Melting and damage to ice roads • Effects of warming and changes to precipitation patterns that affect survival and transmission of disease-causing organisms	• Temporary or long-term evacuation or displacement of populations from traditional territories, disrupting lives, creating financial hardship, and affecting mental well-being • Impacts on health and infrastructure (e.g., restricted or delayed travel for health and emergency services, access to medical supplies, and patient safety)

The CIRNAC, launching five significant programs in its efforts to enhance the ability of indigenous communities to understand and mitigate climate change risks, combines scientific data with local knowledge to predict the impacts of climate change, assess and respond to direct climate change effects, and develop locally suitable clean energy alternatives.[1]

The ISC Indigenous Services Canada has also launched the Climate Change and Health Adaptation Program, having two streams respectively focusing on the north and the south of 60°N, with projects' areas including traditional food security and access to country food, documentation of conventional medicines, safety while on the land, impacts of extreme weather events, and access to safe drinking water and mental health.[2] Through collaborative efforts with indigenous associations, communities, and governments, this program aims to address the health risks posed by climate change through initiatives such as program development, capacity building, and decision-making support. On the 2023–2024 Departmental Plan of the ISC, the 2021 budget announced $126.7 million over three years to address anti-indigenous racism in Canada's health systems. The ISC has funded over 50 proposals addressing anti-indigenous racism in health systems through the 2021

---

[1] Government of Canada. Climate change in indigenous and northern communities. (2023-04-17)[2023-11-17]. https://www.rcaanc-cirnac.gc.ca/eng/1100100034249/1594735106676.

[2] Government of Canada. Climate change and health adaptation program. (2023-10-25)[2023-11-17]. https://www.sac-isc.gc.ca/eng/1536238477403/1536780059794.

budget 2021.[1]

In addition, health organizations led by indigenous peoples are also closely monitoring the impacts of climate change. For instance, the First Nations Health Authority, a health governance organization based in British Columbia, has initiated the Indigenous Climate Health Action Program, providing a comprehensive listing of critical areas of implementation and addressing the specific impacts of climate change on indigenous communities.[2]

Regarding specific funding approaches, the CIRNAC and the ISC have established various forms of financial assistance for indigenous-related projects in Canada. These include grant funding, formula-based fixed funding, flexible contributions, and block contribution approaches.[3] Canada also protects indigenous rights through initiatives, international collaborations, and global agenda-setting.[4] The overall structure of the Canadian indigenous health governance could be demonstrated in a tripartite partnership in Figure 1.

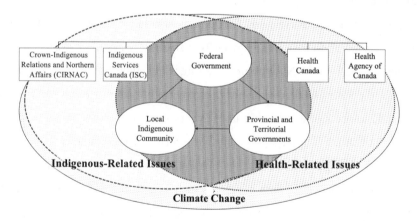

Figure 1   Tripartite Collaboration Model of Canadian Indigenous Health Governance

---

①   Government of Canada. Indigenous services Canada: 2023–2024 departmental plan. (2023-03-24)[2023-11-17]. https://www.sac-isc.gc.ca/eng/1666289629121/1666289645507.

②   First Nations Health Authority. Indigenous climate health action program. (2023-11-17)[2023-11-17]. https://www.fnha.ca/what-we-do/environmental-health/climate-health-action-program.

③   Government of Canada. Funding approaches. (2018-04-16)[2023-11-17]. https://www.sac-isc.gc.ca/eng/13227460 46651/1618142957561.

④   Government of Canada. International indigenous human rights. (2023-04-17)[2023-11-17]. https://www.international.gc.ca/world-monde/issues_development-enjeux_developpement/human_rights-droits_homme/indigenous_rights-droits_autochtones.aspx?lang=eng.

The two case analyses show that Germany places greater emphasis on shaping awareness, increasing attention, and utilizing resources from international organizations for research in related fields, considering that indigenous issues are not prominent within Germany, demonstrating a sense of responsibility and commitment. On the other hand, Canada has implemented many specific projects to address domestic indigenous, health, and climate issues, showcasing more local and practical experiences. These two different types of country practice exhibit distinct characteristics and play different roles in this particular topic.

2.2 "1 plus 2" Model

The proposal then summarizes the existing practice of the international community as the "1 plus 2" Model with strategic leadership in cognitive shaping and top-level design and two practical supports in terms of knowledge base and material foundation. Strategic leadership is a holistic approach, and the valuable supports are two-pronged approaches, which have contributed significantly to the protection of the rights and interests of indigenous peoples.

2.2.1 Strategic Leadership in Terms of Cognitive Shaping and Top-level Design

Indigenous peoples are often seen as victims of the effects of climate change rather than as agents of environmental protection. However, the history of modern international relations records the efforts of representatives of indigenous peoples to defend their rights at the League of Nations as early as 1923.[1] At the same time, the international community has gradually developed an international consensus in this area, and a series of institutions and conventions have been created to protect indigenous peoples. Table 2 provides a brief overview of the major developments in the international community on protecting indigenous peoples over the past century.

---

[1] United Nations Department of Economic and Social Affairs. Indigenous peoples at the United Nations. (2023-11-17) [2023-11-17]. https://www.un.org/development/desa/indigenouspeoples/about-us.html.

[2] International Labour Organization. C169—Indigenous and tribal peoples convention, 1989 (No. 169). (1989-06-28) [2023-11-17]. https://normlex.ilo.org/dyn/normlex/en/f?p=NORMLEXPUB:12100:0:NO::P12100_ILO_CODE:C169.

Table 2　Important Developments in the International Community on the Protection of Indigenous Peoples

Time	Event	Evaluation
1923/1925	Chiefs and religuous leaders traveled to speak to the League of Nations	The first international involvement failed, but nourished the generations that followed
1982	Working Group on Indigenous Populations (WGIP) was established	A subsidiary organ to the Sub-Commission on the Promotion and Protection of Human Rights, located at the lowest level of the hierarchy of UN human rights bodies
1989	Indigenous and Tribal Peoples Convention was signed	The only international treaty open for ratification that deals exclusively with the rights of these peoples [②]
1993	The International Year of the World's Indigenous People was established	Encouraging a new relationship between states and indigenous peoples, and between the international community and indigenous peoples—a new partnership based on mutual respect and understanding.
1994	The International Decade of the World's Indigenous Peoples (1995–2004) was launched	Increasing the United Nations' commitment to promoting and protecting the rights of indigenous peoples worldwide.
2000	The UN Permanent Forum on Indigenous Issues was established	Discussing indigenous issues related to economic and social development, culture, the environment, education, health, and human rights.
2007	The Expert Mechanism on the Rights of Indigenous Peoples (EMRIP) was established	A subsidiary body of the Human Rights Council, consisting of representatives from states, indigenous peoples, indigenous peoples' organizations, civil society, inter-governmental organizations, and academia.
2007	The Declaration on the Rights of Indigenous Peoples was adopted	The most comprehensive statement of the rights of indigenous peoples ever developed, the clearest indication yet that the international community is committing itself to the protection of the individual and collective rights of indigenous peoples. [①]
2014	The first World Conference on Indigenous Peoples was held	An opportunity to share perspectives

① United Nations. United nations declaration on the rights of indigenous peoples. (2008-03-15)[2023-11-17]. https://www.un.org/esa/socdev/unpfii/documents/DRIPS_en.pdf.

Conrinued

Time	Event	Evaluation
2019	The International Year of Indigenous Languages was identified	Revitalizing and promoting indigenous languages
2022	The International Decade of Indigenous Languages (2022–2032) was initiated	Revitalizing and promoting indigenous languages

Based on the above mechanisms and platforms, indigenous peoples' representatives have called for support from various sources through active participation in international and inter-governmental negotiations and actions on climate and health to uphold the rights of indigenous peoples as set out in international regulations such as the Declaration on the Rights of Indigenous Peoples. For example, through the UN Permanent Forum on Indigenous Issues and the Expert Mechanism on the Rights of Indigenous Peoples, they have been able to voice their concerns and advocate for policy change within the UN. There has been significant progress in their representation at international meetings.[1] On specific projects, they called on governments, NGOs, and private companies engaged in extractive industries and other modernization and development processes to respect the right of indigenous peoples not to develop and to respect their right to choose their level of integration into the global economy and politics.[2] The UN has also taken the lead in establishing a special fund and working group to guarantee the participation of indigenous community representatives in the Working Group on Indigenous Populations deliberations through specific funding programs and apparent staffing ratios.[3]

---

[1]　Etchart, L. The role of indigenous peoples in combating climate change. *Palgrave Communications*, 2017, 3: 1-4; United Nations Economic and Social Council. Indigenous peoples and climate change. (2021-01-12)[2023-11-17]. https://www.wipo.int/export/sites/www/tk/zh/docs/youth_prize_unpfii_study.pdf.

[2]　Interfaith Rainforest Initiative. Uniting people of all faiths to end tropical deforestation. (2023-11-17)[2023-11-17]. https://www.interfaithrainforest.org/s/Interfaith_ConceptNote_Photo_English.pdf.

[3]　UN Secretary-General. Status of the United nations voluntary fund for indigenous peoples: Report of the secretary-general. (2020-07-23)[2023-11-17]. https://digitallibrary.un.org/record/3878471#record-files-collapse-header; United Nations Climate Change. Local communities and indigenous peoples platform. (2023-11-17)[2023-11-17]. https://lcipp.unfccc.int/.

However, despite the strides made, indigenous peoples continue to face marginalization and under-representation in the multi-stakeholder global mechanism on health and climate change, exclusion from many decision-making processes that determine their future, and numerous cases of discrimination.[1] Even the attention paid to indigenous peoples in the United Nations Framework Convention on Climate Change (UNFCCC) remains limited.[2] The loss of voice and invisibility of indigenous peoples will have serious consequences, with the UN Special Rapporteur on Extreme Poverty and Human Rights, Philip Alston, suggesting that humanity will be at risk of "climate apartheid" by 2100.[3]

Another focal point of interest is that the report *State of the World's Indigenous Peoples (SOWIP)* was published in 2009. Yet, only the project "Persistent Toxic Substances, Food Security and Indigenous Peoples of the Russian North" mentions the link between environmental and health risks for indigenous peoples.[4] In addition, there is no more theoretical and practical presentation of climate change-induced health risks. In contrast to its much-neglected status in the policy arena, related topics have achieved impressive results in the academic field. Since 1997, scholars have published articles dealing with climate change and health and the health effects of climate change on Arctic populations, as well as an overview of the characteristics and shortcomings of previous studies.[5] Unfortunately, the results from the field of scientific research are not being transferred to the area of

---

[1] World Health Organization. 2021 WHO health and climate change global survey report. (2021-11-08)[2023-11-17]. https://www.who.int/publications/i/item/9789240038509; United Nations University. Engaging indigenous peoples in global climate governance. (2012-12-05)[2023-11-17]. https://ourworld.unu.edu/en/engaging-indigenous-peoples-in-global-climate-governance.

[2] Ford, J., Maillet, M., Pouliot, V., et al. Adaptation and indigenous peoples in the United nations framework convention on climate change. Climatic Change, 2016, 139: 429-443.

[3] United Nations Environment Programme. Indigenous peoples and the nature they protect. (2020-06-08)[2023-11-17]. http://www.unep.org/news-and-stories/story/indigenous-peoples-and-nature-they-protect.

[4] United Nations Department of Economic and Social Affairs. State of the world's indigenous peoples (SOWIP). (2013-01-01)[2023-11-17]. https://www.un.org/development/desa/indigenouspeoples/wp-content/uploads/sites/19/2018/03/The-State-of-The-Worlds-Indigenous-Peoples-WEB.pdf.

[5] Haines, A. & McMichael, A. J. Climate change and health: Implications for research, monitoring, and policy. *British Medical Journal*, 1997, 315: 870-874; Parkinson, A. J. & Evengård, B. Climate change, its impact on human health in the Arctic and the public health response to threats of emerging infectious diseases. *Global Health Action*, 2009, 2: 2075; Sahu, M., Chattopadhyay, B., Das, R., et al. Measuring impact of climate change on indigenous health in the background of multiple disadvantages: A scoping review for equitable public health policy formulation. *Journal of Prevention*, 2023, 44: 421-456.

international policy, which is a massive waste of resources. Indigenous peoples are not given enough attention in the global policy agenda for protection from climate change-induced health threats.

2.2.2 Two practical supports in terms of knowledge base and material foundation

The success of a project requires the dual guarantee of material and non-material support. This encompasses the transparency and exchange of information that fosters wide-scale collaboration and participation, as well as the implementation and promotion of specific localized projects.

In the modern era, "information" has consistently played a crucial role in actions aimed at protecting indigenous peoples from the health threats posed by climate change.

On the one hand, indigenous communities have emphasized the need to establish climate-health joint databases, as they believe such databases would empower and guide them towards better climate strategies and health services.[1] Significant progress has been made in local data collection and categorization, specifically targeting indigenous communities. Some countries and regions have actively promoted collecting indigenous-related data, providing ample intellectual support for designing, developing, and implementing protective and assistance projects. Australia first linked medical insurance with other data to investigate indigenous health information in 2005. In New Zealand, since the 1990s, the collection of racial data, including the identification of Māori ethnicity, has been mandatory. Canada's federal government, provinces, and territories provide healthcare to registered First Nations individuals under the Indian Act. However, such data and information collection remains primarily within national or regional boundaries, limited to specific indigenous groups residing in those areas. The availability and comprehensiveness of this data are restricted. The global understanding of the health status of indigenous peoples remains fragmented, and the level of measures taken varies significantly.

---

[1] Kukutai, T. & Taylor, J. Data sovereignty for indigenous peoples: Current practice and future needs. In Kukutai, T. & Taylor, J. (eds.). *Indigenous Data Sovereignty: Toward an Agenda*. Canberra: ANU Press, 2016: 1-22.

On the other hand, global cooperation emphasizes the importance of open and comprehensive information sharing. The United Nations Permanent Forum on Indigenous Issues has convened conferences and meetings to deliberate on critical matters such as data collection, classification, and indicators of the well-being of indigenous peoples. These discussions aim to foster enhanced collaboration and information exchanges among member states and relevant stakeholders, contributing to a more robust understanding and effective response to indigenous issues on a global scale.[①]

The Federal Ministry for Economic Cooperation and Development of Germany, along with the German Ageney for International Cooperation (GIZ), has provided support for the compilation and publication of information materials concerning the adverse impacts of climate change on the environment and human rights, on behalf of the United Nations Office of the High Commissioner for Human Rights.

For instance, in the Germany-funded report *Climate Change: Protecting the Health Rights of People*, six major health hazards associated with climate change are identified. These hazards include heat-related illnesses, natural disasters, waterborne and vector-borne diseases, nutritional issues, and mental health problems. Special attention is given to the vulnerability of marginalized minority groups, such as impoverished individuals, women, children, immigrants, older people, persons with disabilities, and indigenous peoples, concerning their health rights in the context of climate change. The report also makes several recommendations, including enhancing monitoring and recording, prioritizing health in climate action and financing projects, improving accessibility to climate resilience measures for individuals and communities, and utilizing human rights mechanisms to monitor countries' climate commitments.[②]

---

① United Nations Department of Economic and Social Affairs. UNPFII third session. (2004-05-21)[2023-11-17]. https://www.un.org/development/desa/indigenouspeoples/unpfii-sessions-2/third-session-of-unpfii.html; United Nations Department of Economic and Social Affairs. UNPFII third session. (2004-05-21)[2023-11-17]. https://www.un.org/development/desa/indigenouspeoples/unpfii-sessions-2/third-session-of-unpfii.html.
② Office of the United Nations High Commissioner for Human Rights. Climate change: Protecting people's right to health. (2023-11-17)[2023-11-17]. https://www.ohchr.org/sites/default/files/Documents/Issues/ClimateChange/materials/2PHealthLight.pdf.

However, the information gap has yet to be bridged. Recently, the World Health Organization launched the Health Equity Monitor database, which includes specific data on the health of vulnerable populations such as women, children, older people, and persons with disabilities. However, it does not encompass data specifically related to indigenous peoples.[①] Therefore, it is crucial to establish a globally connected indigenous health database that incorporates climate change as a significant variable in the analysis of health data.

Based on timely and comprehensive data, international organizations and national entities can provide aid and assistance, offering appropriate material support for development in an effective and targeted way. As shown in Table 3, several international multilateral platforms currently focus on indigenous health. These platforms have implemented vertical projects to address indigenous health issues and have achieved significant results.[②]

Table 3 International Projects Aiming to Address Indigenous Health Issues

Sphere of Impact	Project Initiator	Project Name
Regional	Australia	Aboriginal and Torres Strait Islander Health Plan
Regional	New Zealand	Te Whare Tapa Whā Model
Regional	Brazil	Distrito Sanitário Especial Indígena
Regional	Peru	Red de Salud Indígena
Regional	Canada	First Nations and Inuit Health Branch
Regional	America	Indian Health Service
Global	WHO	Commission on Social Determinants of Health
Global	ECOSOC	UN Permanent Forum on Indigenous Issues

In the meantime, development financing institutions and bilateral or multilateral cooperative entities have incorporated a focus on indigenous peoples

---

① World Health Organization. Health inequality data repository. (2023-11-17)[2023-11-17]. https://www.who.int/data/inequality-monitor/data.

② Deutsche Gesellschaft für Internationale Zusammenarbeit. Improving health care provision for indigenous people in the Amazon region of Peru. (2022-01-06)[2023-11-17]. https://www.giz.de/en/worldwide/109082.html; Government of Canada. Co-developing distinctions-based indigenous health legislation. (2023-11-03)[2023-11-17]. https://www.sac-isc.gc.ca/eng/1611843547229/1611844047055; Canadian Institutes of Health Research. International collaboration to improve the health and wellness of indigenous peoples through research. (2023-01-12)[2023-11-17]. https://cihr-irsc.gc.ca/e/50911.html.

and their rights in policies of climate mitigation and adaptation. Examples of such initiatives and institutions include the Global Environment Facility, the Green Climate Fund, the Asian Development Bank, and the German REDD+ program. These entities are crucial in addressing indigenous communities' specific needs and concerns in climate change actions.[1]

During project implementation, developed countries' contributions are particularly scrutinized due to the mismatch of governance capacity and historical responsibility. It has become a consensus in the international community that developed countries should provide climate assistance to vulnerable groups, including the impoverished, indigenous peoples, local communities dependent on agriculture or coastal livelihoods, Arctic ecosystems, drought-prone regions, small island developing states, and the least developed countries.[2]

However, current climate assistance primarily focuses on investments in the energy and industrial sectors, with limited direct attention to cooperation and assistance projects in the health sector.[3] The aid recipients are usually developing countries, the least developed countries, and the small island developing states, with less targeted attention given to the specific needs of indigenous peoples as a

---

[1] Global Environment Facility Secretariat. Principles and guidelines for engagement with indigenous peoples. (2012-09-07)[2023-11-17]. https://www.thegef.org/council-meeting-documents/principles-and-guidelines-engagement-indigenous-peoples; Green Climate Fund. Green climate fund—Accountability. (2023-11-17)[2023-11-17]. https://www.greenclimate.fund/about/accountability; Asian Development Bank. Compilation of data on successful practices of indigenous protection programs and their implementation. (2013-06-08)[2023-11-17]. https://www.adb.org/sites/default/files/institutional-document/42875/files/ip-good-practices-sourcebook-draft-zh.pdf; Deutsche Gesellschaft für Internationale Zusammenarbeit. REDD early movers-Tools and instruments. (2019-01-11)[2023-11-17]. https://www.giz.de/en/worldwide/33356.html; United Nations General Assembly. Report of the special rapporteur on the rights of indigenous peoples. (2019-07-17)[2023-11-17]. https://www.ohchr.org/en/documents/thematic-reports/a74149-report-special-rapporteur-rights-indigenous-peoples; United Nations. United nations framework convention on climate change. (1992-06-20)[2023-11-17]. https://documents-dds-ny.un.org/doc/UNDOC/GEN/G11/605/50/PDF/G1160550.pdf?OpenElement.

[2] Intergovernmental Panel on Climate Change. Global warming of 1. 5 ℃. (2023-11-17)[2023-11-17]. https://www.ipcc.ch/sr15/; United Nations. Paris agreement. (2015-12-12)[2023-11-17]. https://www.un.org/zh/documents/treaty/FCCC-CP-2015-L.9-Rev.1; United Nations. United Nations framework convention on climate change. (1992-06-20)[2023-11-17]. https://documents-dds-ny.un.org/doc/UNDOC/GEN/G11/605/50/PDF/G1160550.pdf?OpenElement.

[3] Bundesministerium für wirtschaftliche Zusammenarbeit und Entwicklung. Optimised stoves reduce carbon footprints. (2023-11-17)[2023-11-17]. https://www.bmz.de/en/issues/climate-change-and-development/climate-financing/example-kenya-senegal-79816; Bundesministerium für wirtschaftliche Zusammenarbeit und Entwicklung. Climate finance: Germany remains a reliable partner. (2023-10-23)[2023-11-17]. https://www.bmz.de/en/issues/climate-change-and-development/climate-financing.

distinct group.[①]

2.3 Problems and Challenges

Considering the present "1 plus 2" Model, the proposal identifies four noteworthy problems and challenges in safeguarding the global indigenous population from the health threats arising from climate change (see Figure 2):

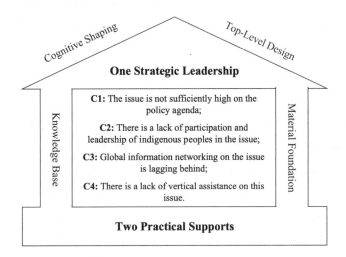

Figure 2 The Challenges in Protecting Global Indigenous Peoples from Health Threats Posed by Climate Change

The following are specific recommendations proposed to address these four problems and challenges.

3. Recommendations

3.1 Enhancing Global Attention to the Issue of Climate Change-Induced Indigenous Health Crisis at Various Levels

3.1.1 Elevating the importance of the climate change-induced global health crisis for indigenous peoples in the Sustainable Development Agenda

Addressing this crisis requires primarily elevating it to a central position in the global development agenda. This issue can be applied to the global climate, health

---

① Zhang, R. H., Li, M. Y., Yue, F. L., et al. Climate aid for development countries in context of carbon neutrality: Progress and problems. *Journal of Global Energy Interconnection*, 2022, 5: 63-70.

and equity objectives of the 2030 Agenda, and provide valuable experiences and lessons for attaining other goals.

In particular, this issue possesses its particularities, including "decolonization and self-determination principles", "the interconnectedness of climate and health systems", as well as "sudden and gradual crises". The governance process should respect the autonomy of indigenous communities, analyze the complex causes and outcomes of climate change comprehensively, prevent climate and health crises from escalating into regional or global problems, and uphold the long-term interests of regions and the globe with a developmental perspective.

3.1.2 Raising the profile of the issue among national actors

Countries with Indigenous Populations and others should formally incorporate this issue into their domestic policy agendas, develop and release global governance strategic documents, and form a domestic political consensus. The climate crisis and health crisis faced by indigenous communities directly impact countries with indigenous populations, while other countries may face identity crises concerning indigenous-related issues. Furthermore, no country can avoid the impacts of global health crises such as the COVID-19 pandemic in the process of globalization.

Developed countries should prioritize engagement in their areas of expertise in climate and health. Underdeveloped countries should focus on indirect involvement in global affairs or establish global partnerships to participate collectively in global governance. Some developed countries have caused significant destruction to the development of indigenous communities during the modernization process and thus have an obligation to actively participate in the governance of the global indigenous peoples' climate and health crisis. Underdeveloped countries cannot independently exert influence on global governance regarding the issue of indigenous climate health.

3.1.3 Establishing an international consensus on this issue

At the level of international organizations, maintaining international order should be combined with innovative international norms to promote the development of a more fair and equitable international order. Strengthening the role of existing international organizations and adhering to the applicability of existing international laws to this issue are crucial. Simultaneously, new mechanisms and norms for governing indigenous peoples' climate and health crises should be formulated within the United Nations framework to enhance the professionalism and effectiveness of governance.

Germany does not directly face issues related to the development of indigenous peoples. However, Germany has always played a leading and proactive role in global climate and health governance. On this issue, Germany will actively assume the role of a leader, initiating discussions on the climate and health of indigenous communities in domestic and European Union agendas and participating actively in global governance.

3.2 Strengthening Participation and Leadership in the Governance of the Global Health Crisis

Indigenous peoples play a critical role and have the capacity to make immeasurable contributions in various climate and health-related areas, such as information collection and dissemination, policy development and implementation, monitoring, and evaluation. In the United Nations Declaration on the Rights of Indigenous Peoples, the General Assembly proposes that particular attention be paid to the rights and unique needs of indigenous elders, women, youth, children, and persons with disabilities in decision-making processes on climate change issues that affect them.[1] This proposal, therefore, calls for further strengthening the participation and leadership of indigenous peoples in global climate and health governance.

Germany urges the international community to increase participation and voice of indigenous peoples and communities in global climate and health governance, and makes the following proposals.

  a) States should commit themselves to working with indigenous peoples through their representative bodies to develop and implement national action plans, strategies, or other relevant measures about environment and

---

[1] United States Environmental Protection Agency. Climate change impacts-Climate change and the health of indigenous populations. (2022-12-27)[2023-11-17]. https://www.epa.gov/climateimpacts/climate-change-and-health-indigenous-populations.

health to achieve the goals of the United Nations Declaration on the Rights of Indigenous Peoples.

b) At international meetings or bilateral meetings within countries containing indigenous communities, when the topic is related to climate, environment, or health, it is required that the proportion of indigenous participants be more than 6% of the total; when the issue is closely related to indigenous peoples, they need to make up more than 19% of the participants (see Table 4). Germany is committed to the rule first. These rates are based on indigenous peoples' share of the world's population and the world's poor[①].

Table 4　Rules on the Proportion of Indigenous Peoples in International Conferences

	When topics are related to climate, environment, or health	When topics are closely related to indigenous peoples
Indigenous Delegates	≥ 6%	≥ 19%
Other Delegates	≤ 94%	≤ 81%

c) States should support the launch of indigenous-led environmental protection and adaptation campaigns in indigenous communities to raise awareness among indigenous leaders of the health crisis caused by climate change and to promote indigenous communities' autonomous adaptation to environmental change.

d) The Indigenous Voice Mailbox should be created for the indigenous people platform under the United Nations Department of Economic and Social Affairs (UNDESA) to collect their needs and aspirations directly. In indigenous communities with Internet access, indigenous peoples are encouraged to express their views through the mailbox. In communities without Internet access, we will collect opinions through offline interviews and upload the results to the mailbox. The Council of UNDESA regularly

---

① World Bank. Poverty and exclusion among indigenous peoples: The global evidence. (2016-08-09)[2023-11-17]. https://blogs.worldbank.org/en/voices/poverty-and-exclusion-among-indigenous-peoples-global-evidence.

addresses issues in the mailbox and discusses them at the General Assembly.

3.3 Establishing a Joint Climate and Health Database Covering Indigenous Peoples Around the World

To have a comprehensive overview of the health problems of indigenous peoples and to find practical solutions, both indigenous communities and the international community need accurate data to measure the factors influencing indigenous health, their access to medical services, and the threat of important diseases and their complications. Germany calls for establishing a global database (think tank) on indigenous health. First, governments should be empowered to collect data on indigenous health, as ethnic data is part of public health surveillance and surveys and national and administrative data collection.[1] This database aims to integrate and share information related to the health and medical care of indigenous peoples worldwide. It provides information for organizations and individuals interested in issues related to indigenous health, and provides appropriate distribution channels for publishers of indigenous health-related information. When searching for information, users can optimize their searching by date, tribe, topic, resource type, or other parameters. The database contains the following:

a) A comprehensive overview of indigenous health in all regions of the world, with a particular focus on health problems caused by climate change;

b) Dynamic monitoring data on the health information of accessible indigenous tribes, including but not limited to ethnicity, income, gender, age, race, immigration status, disability status, health status, geographical location, etc.;[2]

c) List and links of existing indigenous health databases established in each region;

① Walker, J., Lovett, R., Kukutai, T., et al. Indigenous health data and the path to healing. *The Lancet*, 2017, 390: 2022-2023.

② United Nations. United Nations framework convention on climate change. (1992-06-20)[2023-11-17]. https://documents-dds-ny.un.org/doc/UNDOC/GEN/G11/605/50/PDF/G1160550.pdf?OpenElement.

d) List of publications on indigenous health, including journal articles, editorials, guidelines, and monographs;

e) A series of information related to climate, health topics, and health systems.

Regarding the point b) mentioned above, Germany hopes to obtain the support of the governments of all countries with indigenous tribes living in their territories. This proposal calls on the governments of these countries to introduce protocols or regulations for the collection of indigenous health data and send expert teams to conduct regular interviews with their indigenous residents (preferably with a targeted census) to record their health information, including diseases, drinking water and food conditions, health threats, etc., and sort out the obtained data and upload it to the database.

This database is coordinated by the secretariat of the UNFCCC, and a special committee is established under the UNFCCC to manage and maintain the database to ensure that the information in the database is updated in real time based on the dynamic monitoring data at point b) above. The other information should be updated regularly every year, and annual summary reports are required. Regarding database construction and information collection, Germany is willing to provide technical support through relevant organizations (such as GIZ) to facilitate the construction of a global information network.

3.4 Providing Holistic Assistance to Address the Climate Change-Induced Health Crisis Faced by Indigenous Peoples

To address the health threats faced by indigenous peoples due to climate change, this proposal suggests that countries take on shared but differentiated responsibilities to provide tangible assistance to indigenous tribes. The related aid should be based on the principle of indigenous self-determination within the framework of the United Nations Declaration on the Rights of Indigenous Peoples, and follow a process of "APPlication–Disclosure–Implementation" to address the health issues faced by indigenous peoples in different regions.

3.4.1 Establishment of declaration channels

Establishing an assistance declaration channel (platform) within the indigenous peoples' section under UNDESA is recommended. The purpose of the application should be to help indigenous peoples cope with health threats caused by climate change. APPlicants are suggested to include indigenous tribal leaders, individual indigenous persons, and local or national governments with indigenous tribes on their territories, as the units for declaring assistance projects. These projects should be submitted for review by relevant departments under UNDESA. Once approved, they can be disclosed on the platform.

3.4.2 Contents

The contents of the application should include local background information (population, distribution of indigenous peoples, etc.), socio-economic conditions (unemployment rate, poverty rate, infrastructure, etc.), and health governance situation (sanitary conditions, disease prevalence, etc.). Such information is helpful for the overall assessment of assistance projects aimed at improving the quality of life of indigenous peoples in the respective areas. It is recommended that indigenous individuals and groups take the initiative to implement grassroots development projects based on their actual situations. These types of projects should be given priority (with assistance provided by the local government throughout the process).

3.4.3 Types of assistance

Assistance can include economic, personnel, technological, and information aid. Assistance methods can be divided into direct service and project investment, which will be coordinated among the three parties involved.

We propose the followings for fund review and sources.

a) Small-scale assistance (less than or equal to 300,000 US dollars) can be directly provided by relevant foundations under UNDESA after their review, such as The UN Voluntary Fund for Indigenous Peoples, or by applying for assistance from other foundations established for indigenous peoples, such as the Indigenous Peoples Assistance Facility.

b) For large-scale assistance (more than 300,000 US dollars) or non-financial aid like personnel, technology, and information, the application platform will collaborate with governments of various countries, mainly developed countries, which should take up the responsibility of providing practical assistance to indigenous peoples on a point-to-point basis. The specific content of bilateral cooperation will be determined through negotiations between the assisting country and the recipient country (region).

Germany will actively assume its national responsibilities and play a leading role throughout the related assistance process. The project assistance funds from Germany are derived from the German government and various institutions, including the Bundesministerium für wirtschaftliche Zusammenarbeit und Entwicklung (Federal Ministry for Economic Cooperation and Development), Kreditanstalt für Wiederaufbau (Development Bank), and Deutsche Gesellschaft für Internationale Zusammenarbeit (GIZ, the German Agency for International Cooperation). Through reasonable fund allocation and distribution, Germany aims to provide strong support for climate change and health projects in indigenous communities, manage specific assistance plans for indigenous communities, and ensure effective project implementation and capacity-building work.

3.5 Relevance of the Proposal to the Current Problems

This proposal is designed in the context of global climate change. It intends to focus on the protection of global indigenous peoples belonging to minorities and vulnerable groups, primarily to mitigate threats to their health. The proposal is for the protection of indigenous peoples around the world. It seeks support from the international community for indigenous peoples in different parts of the world. The proposal is established under the UNFCCC and based on the UN indigenous peoples platform. It is hoped that it will be discussed and resolved at COP28.

Among the four measures put forward, this proposal first recommends that countries increase their attention to the issue of threats to indigenous health under climate change based on actual conditions, which will improve the international awareness of this agenda. Secondly, the proposal calls for increasing the participation and leadership of indigenous peoples in the governance of the global climate health crisis. It stipulates the proportion of indigenous peoples' participation in the international agenda. This suggestion seeks solutions from the rules and structures to avoid problems with low involvement and weak leadership. Finally, this proposal proposes that the international community take action in two specific areas: information support and material assistance.

In terms of information support, facing the problem of backwardness in the construction of a global information network for indigenous health, Germany will unite academic institutions and think tanks, such as UNESCO and the relevant research institutes of the UNU, to promote the establishment of a joint climate and health database covering indigenous peoples around the world, collect health data of them, and achieve information disclosure and data sharing.

In terms of material assistance, due to the lack of vertical service for relevant indigenous peoples, Germany suggests setting up an assistance process on the indigenous peoples' platform under the UNDESA with three steps: indigenous declaration—platform announcement—government implementation. This aims to strengthen the assistance of developed countries to relevant regions and peoples. The four main measures proposed in the proposal cover top-level design strategies and specific practical supports, which are progressive, interrelated, and supported. The corresponding relationship with particular problems can be seen below (see Table 5).

Table 5　Relevance of Four Recommendations to the Current Challenges

Category	Challenges	Recommendations
Strategic Leadership	• Lack of attention to this issue	• Enhancing global attention to the issue of climate change-induced indigenous health crisis at various levels
	• Low participation and leadership of indigenous peoples	• Strengthening indigenous peoples' participation and leadership in the governance of the global health crisis caused by climate change
Practical Supports	• Backward global information networking	• Establishing a joint climate and health database covering indigenous peoples around the world
	• Lack of vertical assistance on this issue	• Providing holistic assistance to address the climate change-induced health crisis faced by indigenous peoples

Climate Change and Mental Health: An Examination of China's Proposal at COP28 and Its Evolution from COP26 and COP27[①]

Abstract: This research paper examines China's role in the global climate change discussion, focusing on its recent emphasis on the effects of climate change on mental health. The paper analyzes China's proposal at COP28, which calls for integrating mental health services into climate change adaptation strategies and promoting international collaboration and research on the impacts of climate change on psychology. However, the paper also identifies areas for improvement in the proposal, such as the need for a more detailed plan and greater attention to vulnerable populations. The findings highlight the growing recognition of impacts on mental health and the importance of international collaboration. They also emphasize the need for a more detailed approach to addressing impacts on mental health. The research suggests potential avenues for future studies, including further research on impacts on mental health, evaluation of the implementation of China's strategies, and exploration of the experiences of vulnerable populations.

① Authors: Niladri Saha Saccha, University of Michigan-Shanghai Jiao Tong University Joint Institute; 金珮旋 (Peixuan Jin), School of Foreign Languages, Shanghai Jiao Tong University; 郑丽素 (Lisu Zheng), Antai College of Economics & Management, Shanghai Jiao Tong University.

───────── **Keywords:** COP28; climate change; mental health; eco-therapy; ecological infrastructure

1. Introduction

1.1 Background

The Conference of the Parties (COP) is the principal governing body of the United Nations Framework Convention on Climate Change (UNFCCC), an international environmental treaty established in 1994. The primary objective of the UNFCCC is to combat climate change by mitigating greenhouse gas concentrations in the atmosphere.[①] Comprising all states that are Parties to the Convention, the COP convenes annually to assess the Convention's implementation and any additional legal instruments adopted to fulfill its objectives. Moreover, the COP makes crucial decisions to facilitate the effective execution of the Convention, encompassing institutional and administrative arrangements.

The first Conference of the Parties (COP1) was convened in Berlin in 1995, marking the commencement of a series of pivotal gatherings that have played a crucial role in shaping the global response to climate change. Noteworthy COP meetings include COP3, which witnessed the adoption of the Kyoto Protocol; COP15, where the Copenhagen Accord acknowledged the imperative of limiting global warming to 2 degrees Celsius; and COP21, where the historic Paris Agreement was ratified to restrain global warming to well below 2 degrees Celsius, preferably to 1.5 degrees Celsius[②], compared to pre-industrial levels.

COP26, held in Glasgow in 2021, assumed significance for its focus on finalizing the operational guidelines for implementing the Paris Agreement. Building

---

① ADST, 2015. Negotiating the United Nations Framework Convention on Climate Change. [2023-12-17]. https://adst.org/2015/12/negotiating-the-united-nations-framework-convention-on-climate-change/?gclid=EAIaIQobChMIzo6ui9WVgwMVp-cWBR3BdgLAEAAYAiAAEgIxffD_BwE.

② ECLAC, 2015. Paris Agreement. [2023-12-17]. https://igualdad.cepal.org/en/digital-library/paris-agreement-0. COP26: Together for our planet. [2023-12-17]. https://www.un.org/en/climatechange/cop26.

upon this momentum, COP27, held in 2022, continued to prioritize this task while also elevating the discourse on the health implications of climate change.[①] The subject of this study, COP28, represents a notable shift as it foregrounds the mental health consequences of climate change.

1.1.1 Overview of China's role in COP meetings

China has assumed a prominent role in the COP meetings. The actions and commitments undertaken by China have considerable influence on the collective endeavors to address climate change globally. Notably, China's engagement in the COP meetings has undergone a transformative progression, mirroring its shifting stance on climate change and an increasingly heightened awareness of the issue's pressing nature.

In a significant departure, China presented a comprehensive plan during COP28 that specifically addressed the mental health consequences of climate change.

The role of China in the COP meetings has undergone substantial evolution, mirroring the nation's shifting position on climate change. Notably, China's proposition during COP28 signifies a noteworthy advancement in recognizing and tackling the mental health consequences arising from climate change.[②] This proposal holds the potential for exerting considerable influence on shaping the global discourse surrounding this matter.

1.1.2 Progress of global actions

(1) Increased Recognition: Over the past few years, there has been a growing recognition of the impacts of climate change on mental health at the global level. This recognition is reflected in the inclusion of mental health in international agreements such as the Paris Agreement and the Sendai Framework for Disaster Risk Reduction.

(2) Research and Data Collection: Many countries and regions have initiated

---

① United Nations, 2021. COP26: Together for our planet | United Nations. [2023-12-22]. https://www.un.org/en/climatechange/cop26.

② Ramli, F. F., 2023. The Health Argument of Climate Action during COP26: Commentaries on Mental Health Issues. [2024-12-23]. https://www.semanticscholar.org/paper/The-Health-Argument-of-Climate-Action-during-COP26%3A-Ramli-Hashim/b7490fb1b35e97c17baeda88869eaf21940cdff9.

research efforts to understand better the mental health risks associated with climate change. This includes identifying vulnerable populations, risk factors, and effective interventions. However, there is still a need for more comprehensive and standardized data collection to facilitate cross-country comparisons and evidence-based policymaking.

(3) Policy Integration: Several countries have started integrating mental health considerations into their climate change policies and strategies. This includes incorporating mental health indicators, risk assessments, and interventions in national and regional adaptation plans. However, the level of integration varies across countries, and more systematic and coordinated approaches are needed.[①]

(4) Capacity Building and Awareness: Efforts to build capacity and raise awareness about climate change-related mental health risks have been observed in various regions. This includes training programs for healthcare professionals, community leaders, and educators. However, there is still a lack of resources and infrastructure to support widespread capacity-building and awareness-raising initiatives.

(5) International Cooperation: Collaboration among countries and international organizations has increased, to share best practices, exchange knowledge, and provide financial and technical support. This cooperation has facilitated the development of guidelines, toolkits, and training materials. However, there is a need for more sustained and coordinated international efforts to address the global nature of climate change-related mental health risks.

1.1.3　Limitations and challenges

(1) Limited Funding: Despite the growing recognition of climate change-related mental health risks, funding for research, capacity building, and implementation remains limited. This hinders the development and implementation of comprehensive and effective strategies.

(2) Data Gaps: There are significant data gaps in understanding theimpacts of

---

① Crane, 2022. Climate Change and Mental Health: A review of empirical evidence, mechanisms and implications. [2023-12-23]. https://www.semanticscholar.org/paper/Climate-Change-and-Mental-Health%3A-A-Review-of-and-Crane-Li/99b260d2af442ef7fd73527c40d0a41b864849b7.

climate change on mental health, particularly in low- and middle-income countries. This limits the ability to develop targeted interventions and policies.[1]

(3) Fragmented APProaches: Integrating mental health into climate change policies and strategies is often fragmented and lacks coordination. This hampers the effectiveness of efforts and leads to inconsistencies in addressing mental health risks.

(4) Lack of Awareness and Stigma: Despite increased awareness, policymakers, healthcare professionals, and the general public still lack understanding and recognition of the impacts of climate change on mental health. The stigma associated with mental health further hinders effective action.

(5) Inadequate Infrastructure: Many countries lack the necessary resources to address climate change-related mental health risks, including mental health services, support systems, and early warning mechanisms.

1.2 Significance

Climate change, a pervasive global phenomenon that has garnered substantial attention in international discourse over an extended period, carries implications beyond the physical environment. Of particular interest is the growing recognition of its impact on mental health. This study explores the interplay between climate change and mental well-being, specifically focusing on China's proposal at the COP28 to the United Nations Framework Convention on Climate Change (UNFCCC). Furthermore, this research seeks to analyze the evolution of China's stance on climate change as evidenced by its positions at COP26 and COP27.[2]

The World Health Organization (WHO) has recognized climate change as the foremost health challenge in the 21st century, encompassing a notable mental health component. The psychological ramifications of climate change, including heightened anxiety, depression, and post-traumatic stress disorder (PTSD) resulting from

---

[1] UNDP, 2023. Issue brief on mental health conditions and tobacco use. (2023-10-06)[2023-12-24]. https://www.undp.org/asia-pacific/publications/issue-brief-mental-health-conditions-and-tobacco-use.
[2] UNDP, 2021. Issue Brief: China's Climate Policy Documents—1+N and Updated NDC. (2021-11-21)[2023-12-22]. https://www.undp.org/china/publications/issue-brief-chinas-climate-policy-documents-1n-and-updated-ndc?gad_source=1&gclid=EAIaIQobChMIivb994GWgwMVZ20PAh0a9Qn5EAAYBCAAEgIDAvD_BwE.

climate-related disasters, are progressively pervasive. Moreover, these impacts exhibit an uneven distribution, disproportionately affecting vulnerable populations, particularly those residing in developing nations such as China. The WHO estimates an increase of 250,000 excess deaths per year between 2030 and 2050 due to the well-understood impacts of climate change. Impacts include heat-related morbidity and mortality, increases in vector-borne diseases (e.g. dengue fever, malaria), increased respiratory illness, and morbidity and mortality due to extreme weather events. Researchers find that the incidence of psychological disorders tended to be most significant within 6 months after a flood.[1] Researchers conducted interviews with Hurricane Katrina survivors 5–8 months post-event and 1-year post-event, where researchers found an increase in mental health disorders as time progressed.

Climate change can result in various direct and indirect consequences, including extreme weather events, increasing temperatures, natural calamities, and environmental deterioration. These occurrences have the potential for causing physical harm, displacement, loss of livelihoods, and the destruction of homes and communities. Consequently, these factors can contribute to mental health issues such as PTSD, anxiety, depression, and other forms of psychological distress.[2]

The psychological impact of climate change is noteworthy. Individuals may encounter feelings of grief, sadness, and a sense of loss when they witness the destruction of their surroundings, the decline in biodiversity, or the devastation caused by natural calamities. Moreover, the uncertainty and fear linked to the future consequences of climate change can give rise to persistent stress and anxiety. Climate change has been found to greatly impact on forced displacement and migration. The consequences of rising sea levels, droughts, and other climate-related factors can make certain areas unsuitable for living or inhabitation. Consequently, mass migrations occur, both domestically and internationally, which can bring about heightened mental health difficulties for those affected.

[1] Gavi, 2023. The deadly diseases that are spiking because of climate change. (2023-09-18)[2023-12-24]. https://www.gavi.org/vaccineswork/deadly-diseases-are-spiking-because-climate-change?gclid=EAIaIQobChMIj-GB5eWVgwMVBOEWBR0RMAkwEAAYASAAEgKRBPD_BwE.

[2] Makwana, Nikunj, 2019. Disaster and Its Impact on Mental Health: A Narrative Review. (2019-10-31)[2023-12-20]. https://doi.org/10.4103/jfmpc.jfmpc_893_19.

The deprivation of homes, communities, and social connections can contribute to feelings of loneliness, sadness, and distress.[1]

Climate change intensifies pre-existing social inequalities, significantly impacting vulnerable populations such as low-income communities, marginalized groups, and indigenous peoples.[2] These communities frequently encounter heightened exposure to environmental hazards, have limited access to resources and healthcare, and may lack the necessary social support systems to manage the effects of climate change on mental health. It is of utmost importance to address the mental health repercussions of climate change to uphold fairness and promote social justice.[3]

Climate change and mental health are interconnected in a complex feedback loop. It is important to recognize that poor mental health may limit individuals' ability to effectively address climate change, make necessary changes, or adopt sustainable behaviors. Similarly, the consequences of climate change can further worsen mental health, perpetuating a harmful cycle of declining well-being and diminished resilience.

Consequently, the international community is keenly interested in China's propositions and initiatives at the COP meetings. Notably, at COP28, China introduced a pioneering proposal that centers on the mental health consequences of climate change, an aspect that had received insufficient attention in prior COP gatherings. This research endeavors to comprehensively analyze and evaluate the intricacies of this proposal, elucidating its implications for both China and the broader global community.

The transition in China's position on climate change and mental health from COP26 to COP28 exemplifies the increasing acknowledgment of the mental health ramifications of climate change.

---

① USGCRP, 2016. The Impacts of Climate Change on Human Health in the United States: A Scientific Assessment. Globalchange. gov. [2023-12-17]. https://health2016.globalchange.gov/.

② Gohd, C, 2017. Researchers discover why lower socioeconomic status can lead to a shorter life. (2017-10-16)[2023-12-18]. https://futurism.com/neoscope/researchers-discover-why-lower-socioeconomic-status-can-lead-to-a-shorter-life.

③ Hayes, K., et al. Climate change and mental health: risks, impacts and priority actions. (2018-06-01)[2023-12-19]. https://doi.org/10.1186/s13033-018-0210-6.

The central argument of this study posits that China's proposal presented at COP28 signifies a substantial advancement in recognizing and tackling the mental health consequences of climate change. Moreover, it signifies a paradigm shift in the global discourse on climate change, expanding its scope to encompass psychological ramifications alongside physical ones. This research aims to investigate the factors that contributed to this transformation in China's position, analyze the particulars of the proposal, and assess its potential implications for both global climate change policies and mental health frameworks.

2. Tracking Progress

2.1 COP26: a turning point

The COP26 represented a momentous juncture in the global discourse on climate change. Convened in Glasgow, Scotland, in November 2021, the conference assembled delegates from nearly 200 nations to engage in negotiations and pledge to implement novel measures to mitigate the repercussions of climate change. This conference assumed exceptional significance as it constituted the primary major climate gathering after the adoption of the Paris Agreement in 2015, thereby presenting a pivotal opportunity for countries to augment their commitments to curtailing greenhouse gas emissions[1].

China assumed a pivotal position during COP26. The international community greatly anticipated China's Nationally Determined Contributions (NDCs). Notably, China made significant commitments, including the pledge to reach the peak of its carbon dioxide emissions prior to 2030 and attain carbon neutrality by 2060. Additionally, China expressed its dedication to augmenting the proportion of non-fossil fuels in primary energy consumption to approximately 25% by 2030. Moreover, China set forth an objective to enhance its forest stock volume by 6

---

① UNU Edu, n. d. Climate Resilience Initiative, The new normal of 'Climate Grief': Why mental health must feature in adaptation and resilience planning. [2023-12-17]. https://cri.merit.unu.edu/the-new-normal-of-climate-grief-why-mental-health-must-feature-in-adaptation-and-resilience-planning/ (accessed 17.12.23).

billion cubic meters relative to the levels observed in 2005.[1]

The COP26 exerted a profound influence on the discourse surrounding global climate change. The conference brought to the forefront the substantial disparities between existing commitments and the requisite actions essential for constraining global warming to a maximum of 1.5 degrees Celsius above pre-industrial levels, as mandated by the Paris Agreement.[2]

The conference additionally propelled the issue of climate justice into the spotlight as developing nations advocated for increased assistance from developed countries in terms of financial aid, technology transfer, and capacity building. Notably, the concept of "loss and damage," which pertains to the adverse effects of climate change that countries cannot adapt to, garnered significant attention.[3]

Furthermore, COP26 witnessed a notable shift in the narrative, transitioning from a predominant focus on mitigation to a more comprehensive approach that equally prioritizes adaptation and resilience. This shift was exemplified by the establishment of the Global Goal on Adaptation, which seeks to enhance adaptive capacity, fortify resilience, and diminish vulnerability to climate change.[4]

COP26 marked a turning point in the global discourse surrounding climate change. It served as a clarion call, emphasizing the pressing nature of the climate crisis, the imperative for more ambitious measures, and the significance of climate justice. Nevertheless, the conference also laid bare substantial gaps and obstacles that persist, thereby underscoring the necessity for sustained and intensified endeavors to address the challenges posed by climate change[5].

---

[1] Xinhua, 2023. (COP28) Interview: China taking steps towards renewable energy transition, says expert. [2023-12-17]. https://english.news.cn/20231203/22606ea5831d444e8b5d316e1186c6f4/c.html.

[2] IsDB, 2022, IsDB Launches Paris Alignment Action Plan to support Climate Action in Member Countries. (2022-06-03)[2023-12-23]. https://www.isdb.org/news/isdb-launches-paris-alignment-action-plan-to-support-climate-action-in-member-countries.

[3] Tony S, 2021. Saudi Arabia releases new carbon plan. (2021-09-06)[2023-12-22]. https://carboncredits.com/saudi-arabia-releases-new-carbon-plan/.

[4] Hayes, K. and Poland, B, 2018. Addressing Mental Health in a Changing Climate: Incorporating Mental Health Indicators into Climate Change and Health Vulnerability and Adaptation Assessments. (2018-08-22)[2023-12-19]. https://doi.org/10.3390/ijerph15091806.

[5] UN Press, 2022. General Assembly adopts text authorizing $3. 52 million to ease global food insecurity, considers annual International Court of Justice Report. (2022-10-27)[2023-12-23]. https://press.un.org/en/2022/ga12461.doc.htm.

2.2 COP27: progress and challenges

The COP27 constituted another momentous milestone in the global discourse surrounding climate change. Convened in 2022, the conference sought to capitalize on the impetus generated by COP26 and tackle the persisting gaps and obstacles. Central to the conference's agenda was the augmentation of NDCs, the mobilization of financial resources, and the resolution of climate justice concerns.

During COP27, China provided an account of its advancements since COP26. The nation showcased notable strides in its transition towards non-fossil fuel sources, exemplified by expanding its renewable energy capacity. China also underscored its commitment to reaching the peak of carbon dioxide emissions before 2030, which entailed the implementation of more stringent emission standards and the establishment of carbon trading mechanisms. Additionally, China reported commendable progress in its reforestation initiatives, thereby contributing to its objective of augmenting forest stock volume.

COP27 was pivotal in shaping the discourse surrounding climate change and mental health. The conference brought to the forefront the psychological ramifications of climate change, an aspect that is frequently marginalized in climate deliberations. These consequences encompass a range of experiences, such as stress and anxiety stemming from climate change, as well as the mental health repercussions associated with climate-induced disasters.

The conference underscored the imperative of adopting a comprehensive approach to climate action that encompasses not only the tangible consequences of climate change but also its mental health implications. This entails providing mental health assistance to communities impacted by climate change and integrating mental health considerations into strategies pertaining to climate adaptation and resilience.

COP27 marked a notable stride in the global discourse on climate change, characterized by advancements in NDCs and an increasing acknowledgment of the mental health ramifications of climate change. Nevertheless, the conference also shed light on the substantial obstacles that persist, particularly concerning the reliance on coal and the transparency of reporting. The conference emphasized the imperative of sustained and intensified endeavors to address these challenges and attain the objectives outlined in the Paris Agreement.

2.3 Climate change and mental health: an emerging concern

Climate change, a global crisis of unprecedented scale, has far-reaching implications that extend beyond the physical environment. One of the less explored yet increasingly significant impacts of climate change is its effects on mental health. The impacts of climate change on mental health are multifaceted, ranging from direct effects such as trauma from natural disasters to indirect effects such as stress and anxiety related to climate change.[①] This connection, while complex, is becoming a critical area of concern, as evidenced by China's proposal at the COP28 to the UNFCCC. This proposal marks an evolution from the discussions at COP26 and COP27, reflecting a growing recognition of the mental health implications of climate change.

2.3.1 Direct impacts: natural disasters, displacement, and trauma

The direct impacts of climate change on mental health are perhaps the most visible and immediate. Extreme weather events are becoming more frequent and severe due to climate change. These events can lead to displacement, loss of property, and even loss of life. The trauma associated with these experiences can result in acute stress and PTSD, depression and anxiety. For instance, research has shown that survivors of natural disasters are at a higher risk of developing mental health disorders.[②]

Moreover, displacement due to climate change, often referred to as climate migration, can lead to significant psychological distress. The loss of one's home and community, coupled with the uncertainty and stress of relocation, can have profound effects on mental well-being. This is particularly true for vulnerable populations, such as low-income communities and indigenous peoples, who are often disproportionately affected by climate change. The economic instability creates uncertainty and tension, leading to mental trauma.

---

① Strive O., 2022. Climate crisis: A mental health emergency. (2022-12-15)[2023-12-23]. https://strivehealth.org. au/2022/12/15/climate-crisis-a-mental-health-emergency/.
② Crystal. Why mental health is a priority for action on climate change. Healthy Life. (2022-06-04)[2023-12-23]. https://healthylifezz.com/why-mental-health-is-a-priority-for-action-on-climate-change.html.

2.3.2 Indirect impacts: stress, anxiety, and uncertainty

Climate change has not only direct impacts but also indirect effects on mental health. People may experience chronic stress and anxiety due to the uncertainty and fear associated with climate change, which is often known as "eco-anxiety" or "climate anxiety." This anxiety is not just about the current effects of climate change but also about the future of the planet and the well-being of future generations.[1]

Uncertainty about the future is a significant source of this anxiety. People may feel helpless and overwhelmed by the scale of the problem and lack of action to address it. This can lead to feelings of despair and hopelessness, which can contribute to mental health issues such as depression and anxiety. The impacts of climate change can exacerbate existing mental health issues. For example, heat waves can worsen mental health conditions such as schizophrenia and bipolar disorder.[2]

Moreover, the loss of ecosystems, biodiversity, and traditional ways of life can lead to feelings of grief and despair, which is known as "ecological grief." Many feel helpless and frustrated due to the lack of effective action to address climate change. The indirect impacts of climate change on mental health can also manifest in more subtle ways, such as changes in sleep patterns and mood due to rising temperatures and stress and anxiety caused by the disruption of traditional ways of life due to changes in weather patterns.

2.4 Vulnerable populations

Populations across the world are vulnerable to climate change and its increasing effects on mental health. Certain groups, such as children and adolescents, elderly individuals, and people living in areas prone to climate change effects, are particularly vulnerable. In China, these vulnerabilities are further exacerbated due to the country's vast population, geographical diversity, and varying levels of socio-

---

[1] Ray, 2022. The health impacts of climate change. (2022-04-16)[2023-12-23]. https://lighterfootprints.org/health-and-climate-change/.

[2] UNEP, 2021. Facts about the climate emergency. [2023-12-22]. https://www.unep.org/facts-about-climate-emergency?gad_source=1&gclid=EAIaIQobChMIn8G7i42WgwMVhSN7Bx3R3Q5KEAAYASAAEgLVkfD_BwE.

economic development.[①]

2.4.1 Children and adolescents

Children and adolescents are particularly vulnerable to the impacts of climate change on mental health.[②] They are more susceptible to the stress and trauma associated with natural disasters and displacement.[③] In China, children in rural areas or regions prone to natural disasters, such as the flood-prone Yangtze River Basin, may be particularly at risk. Moreover, the psychological impact of long-term environmental changes and uncertainties about the future can lead to anxiety and depression among this group.[④]

2.4.2 Elderly individuals

The elderly are another vulnerable group. They may have more difficulty physically and mentally coping with extreme weather events, displacement, and heat waves. In China, the rapidly aging population, particularly in rural areas, may lack the necessary support and resources to adapt to these changes. Furthermore, pre-existing mental health conditions common in this age group, such as dementia, can be exacerbated by the stress and trauma associated with climate change.

2.4.3 People living in areas prone to climate change effects

Several vulnerable populations are particularly at risk of mental health impacts, including people from rural communities, coastal communities, urban poor and indigenous communities. They are more likely to live in areas with poor air quality and inadequate infrastructure, which can be exacerbated by climate change. To discuss the locations of some vulnerable places inside China:

(1) The Yangtze River Basin: This region, including provinces such as Hubei, Jiangxi, and Anhui, is prone to flooding due to its proximity to the Yangtze River.

(2) Coastal areas: China's extensive coastline is home to numerous

---

① Johns Hopkins Medicine. [2023-12-24]. https://www.hopkinsmedicine.org/health/conditions-and-diseases/adjustment-disorders#:~:text=An%20adjustment%20disorder%20is%20an.

② ERIC, n. d. Mann, A. Climate Justice—Part 1: The impact of climate change on Youth. [2023-12-17]. https://eric.ed.gov/?id=EJ1269650.

③ Dragomir, R. Stress and occasional digestive upset in kids: Causes and solutions. [2023-12-23]. https://www.culturelle.com/learning-center/kid/stress-and-occasional-digestive-upset-kids-causes-and-solutions/.

④ Liu, Z. -D., et al., Distributed lag effects and vulnerable groups of floods on bacillary dysentery in Huaihua, China. (2021-03-18)[2023-12-17]. https://doi.org/10.1038/srep29456.

communities that are vulnerable to the impacts of climate change, including rising sea levels and increased frequency of typhoons.

2.5 Limitations on addressing the climate-related mental health risks

At the national and regional levels, there have been some advancements and challenges in addressing the connection between climate change and mental health.

Significant progress has been achieved as the awareness of the mental health risks linked to climate change continues to grow. A multitude of countries and regions have begun to recognize the utmost importance of incorporating mental health considerations into their climate change policies and strategies. This recognition marks a remarkable stride towards comprehending the profound effects of climate change on psychological well-being.

Governments have taken the initiative to include mental health in disaster response plans and to offer assistance and resources to individuals impacted by climate-related incidents. They have created training programs and guidelines to empower healthcare professionals and first respondents with the necessary expertise and abilities to effectively address the mental health requirements of communities encountering climate-related difficulties.

Furthermore, research endeavors have been broadened to better understand the intricate connection between climate change and mental health. Numerous studies have delved into the psychological effects of severe weather occurrences, the adverse mental health outcomes resulting from displacement and migration caused by environmental factors, and the significance of fostering community resilience to protect mental well-being.

Nevertheless, there are still some limitations on the global efforts made to tackle mental health risks associated with climate change. Financial constraints present a significant challenge, as sufficient funding is crucial to establishing inclusive mental health support systems and guaranting their accessibility to all affected populations. The limited availability of resources might impede the magnitude and efficacy of mental health programs, thereby leaving vulnerable communities potentially underserved.

Moreover, it is important to emphasize the necessity for enhanced collaboration and coordination across various sectors and disciplines. The existence of silos between climate change, public health, and mental health domains may impede the formulation of comprehensive strategies and policies. It is imperative to dismantle these barriers and cultivate cross-sectoral collaboration to effectively tackle the complex challenges that arise at the nexus of climate change and mental health.

Furthermore, there is a pressing need for stronger data collection and monitoring methods to gain a deeper comprehension of the mental health consequences of climate change on both national and regional scales. Enhanced data has the potential for guiding policies and interventions based on solid evidence, facilitating more precise and efficient support for communities impacted by climate-related incidents.

2.6 Global recognition of the issue

International organizations such as the WHO and the Pan American Health Organization (PAHO) have been taking action to address the potential impacts of climate change on mental health. WHO has urged countries to include mental health support in their response to the climate crisis and recommended five approaches for governments to address the mental health impacts of climate change. PAHO's Climate Change and Health Program aims to prepare health systems through early warning, better planning, and implementing of prevention and mitigation measures. These organizations recognize that climate change poses serious risks to mental health and well-being, and that the mental health impacts of climate change are unequally distributed.[1] International organizations must continue to promote global recognition of this issue and implement effective policies and programs to address climate change and its potential impact on mental health.[2]

2.7 China's stances on climate change and mental health

China has become an important player in the fight against climate change,

---

[1] Climate Change and Health-PAHO/WHO | Pan American Health Organization. [2023-12-17]. https://www.paho.org/en/topics/climate-change-and-health.

[2] Pti, 2022. Kerala green start-up Tree Tag bags award in Climathon-2022. [2023-12-23]. https://www.freepressjournal.in/business/kerala-green-start-up-tree-tag-bags-award-in-climathon-2022.

with the government implementing policies and programs to address this issue. In recent years, China has taken a more proactive stance on climate change and mental health, recognizing the potential impact on the population's well-being. The Chinese government has implemented various policies to reduce greenhouse gas emissions and promote a low-carbon economy. For example, China has established a national carbon market and invested heavily in renewable energy, such as wind and solar power.

China has been making significant strides in mitigating climate change by prioritizing renewable energy sources. The country has set ambitious targets for renewable energy production, including wind, solar, and hydroelectric power. For example, as part of its efforts to reduce greenhouse gas emissions, China has launched the "Three-Year Action Plan for Winning the Blue Sky Defense War". This plan focuses on transitioning from coal to cleaner energy sources, improving air quality and benefiting mental health.[1]

2.7.1 Mental health programs

China recognizes the need for mental health support in the face of climate change challenges. The government has implemented various programs to address mental health concerns arising from climate change-induced events such as extreme weather events and natural disasters. These programs emphasize community resilience and psychological support for affected individuals. For instance, China's Mental Health Support Program for Disaster-Affected Communities provides counseling services, trauma-informed care, and psychosocial support to those affected by climate-related disasters.

2.7.2 Public awareness and perception

The Chinese government has implemented extensive education and awareness campaigns to promote public understanding of climate change and its mental health implications. These campaigns aim to empower individuals to take action and foster a sense of collective responsibility. For instance, the Climate Change and Mental Health Education Initiative incorporates climate change and mental health education

---

① Lee, E. J., et al.,. Policy Implications of the Clean Heating Transition: A Case Study of Shanxi. [2023-12-22]. https://doi.org/10.3390/en14248431.

into school curricula, ensuring that future generations are equipped with necessary knowledge and skills.

2.7.3 Engaging stakeholders

China actively engages stakeholders, including NGOs, academia, and the private sector, to foster a multi-sectoral approach to addressing climate change and mental health. This collaboration enhances the effectiveness of policies and programs by leveraging diverse expertise and resources. For example, China has partnered with international organizations like the WHO to develop joint initiatives focusing on climate change and mental health.

In addition to government policies, public awareness and perception of climate change and mental health have also contributed to China's evolving stance on this issue. The Chinese public has become increasingly aware of the potential impact of climate change on their health and well-being, leading to more support for government policies and programs aimed at reducing greenhouse gas emissions and promoting a low-carbon economy.

3. Recommendations

3.1 Proposing "Green Ribbon Plan"

Noticing the positive impact of nature on enhancing people's happiness through mental health methods, China proposed the "Green Ribbon Plan", aiming to make an organic combination of the ecological environment and mental health ecological therapy. This includes spending time outdoors in various ways, such as gardening and outdoor sports.

3.1.1 Short-term (0–5years) actions

(1) Popularize ecotherapy by distributing pamphlets.

(2) Renovate public natural or eco-environment in a scientific way to maximize their benefits to public mental health.

(3) Related organizations can carry out research into feasible ecological therapies adapted to different groups of people.

(4) Hold seminars for different countries to exchange experiences.

3.1.2 Long-term (more than 5 years) actions

(1) Continuously monitor and solve the problems encountered in different cases of ecotherapy.

(2) Forums are open for countries with similar conditions for improvements and adjustments.

3.1.3 Actions can be taken from the perspective of individuals

Tree planting activities, gardening, animal care, camping; natural ecological restoration, data sharing, green promotion and green tourism development, including outdoor activities such as mountaineering, hiking and camping; urban greening planning, increasing the urban vegetation coverage, beautifying the green landscape.

3.1.4 Actions can be taken from the perspective of countries

For the restoration and protection of natural ecology, public health departments should cooperate with relevant departments to strengthen ecological intervention in psychological therapy: 1) In areas with significantly poorer mental health, such as disaster-stricken areas, plan ecological environment such as river basins and sea areas, formulate ecological environment quality standards, carry out continuous supervision and management, do a good job in ecological environment restoration and protection, as well as emergency and early warning of major ecological environmental emergencies. 2) Establish ecological civilization demonstration zones, draw ecological protection red lines, protect biodiversity, ensure the interconnection of regulatory data between different places, and jointly launch activities focusing on mental health such as green travel and ecological treatment with local health departments. 3) Advocate the development path of "ecological priority, green and low-carbon", exchange best practices on green infrastructure, green industry development, green investment and financing, forest protection, regeneration of ecologically degraded areas and vegetation restoration among countries, monitor indicators such as forest coverage, improve data transparency in each country, and jointly develop indicators of ecological and psychological links with public health institutions. Pay attention to the correlation between local mental health status and ecological quality level, and provide research data and practical guidance for further improving local mental health levels in the future. 4) All countries should jointly promote the implementation of climate finance financing as soon as possible, promote countries to achieve a just green transition, and urge countries to pay more attention to mental health and set up a special climate fund for mental health. 5) Establish a dedicated mental health unit to expand and restructure mental health services globally, which will urge countries to develop and fund national plans for the transfer of care from institutional to community services, ensure coverage of mental health conditions in health insurance schemes, and strengthen human capacity to provide quality mental health and social care services in the community, Ensure continued access to treatment for people with mental illness.

3.1.5 Actions can be taken from the perspective of governments

Urban planning: 1) Promote the construction of forest cities, improve the quality of the urban and rural ecological environment, promote a green lifestyle, and alleviate the problem of "urban disease". 2) Improve urban flood control and drainage systems, improve urban disaster prevention and reduction ability, enhance urban resilience, and reduce the risk level of mental health. 3) Implement urban ecological restoration projects, protect the natural features of urban mountains, restore rivers, lakes and wetlands, strengthen the construction of urban parks and green spaces, promote three-dimensional greening, build a continuous and complete ecological infrastructure system, improve the city's mental health service function, actively promote ecological treatment means, and develop a new psychological treatment model of "green city + ecological treatment."

3.2 The current problems

Problems include the lack of a dedicated mental health department under the National Health Commission and the lack of attention to mental health in primary health care and planning. Similarly, global mental health services also lack a systematic system, and mental health problems in various countries have long been ignored. The outbreak of COVID-19 is an opportunity to build a mental health system adapted to the future. We should first set up specialized mental health institutions globally and in various countries, expand mental health services, and collaborate with ecological departments to carry out effective ecological interventions for mental health.

3.3 Goals

(1) By 2026, ecotherapy can be effective in curing 30% of various types of mental diseases (which originally had to depend on drugs).

(2) By 2030, ecotherapy can effectively cure 60% of various types of mental diseases.

(3) By 2033, ecotherapy can substitute drug therapy to be the mainstream therapy for mental health problems, and drug therapy can act as an auxiliary.

3.4 Analysis of the proposal's strengths and weaknesses

3.4.1 Potential for effective implementation

China's comprehensive proposal addresses both the direct and indirect mental health problems caused by climate change. Its focus on capacity building and education is commendable, as is its recognition of the need for international collaboration.

3.4.2 Is China the region most affected by this, compared to other geographical counterparts?

China may not be the region most significantly impacted by climate change in terms of its global consequences. Nonetheless, it is crucial to emphasize the immense significance of China's focus on addressing climate change and mental health due to various compelling reasons:

Population and vulnerability: China, one of the most populous countries in the world, has a considerable number of individuals susceptible to the detrimental effects of climate change. This vulnerability arises from the high concentration of people in regions prone to extreme weather events, such as coastal areas and crowded urban centers. These circumstances significantly magnify the potential mental health risks associated with climate change, thus highlighting the urgent need for heightened focus on this matter.

Geographical Diversity: China's vast and diverse geography encompasses a wide variety of climatic zones, ranging from arid to subtropical regions. This diversity exposes different parts of the country to climate change impacts, including heat waves, floods, droughts, and sea level rise. Each region faces unique mental health challenges related to these specific climate-related events, requiring customized approaches and interventions.

Due to its economic importance and influence, China's efforts in mitigating climate change and addressing mental health impacts can inspire and positively affect other regions.

China highly prioritizes social stability and the well-being of its citizens. Climate change, due to its potential to disrupt ecosystems, agriculture, and water resources, presents risks to food security, livelihoods, and social harmony.

Global leadership and international cooperation: China has committed to participating in global climate negotiations and initiatives. By prioritizing addressing the climate change and mental health issues, China has the opportunity to demonstrate strong leadership and make valuable contributions to international efforts focused on mitigating the mental health impacts of climate change. Taking this proactive stance can encourage fruitful collaborations among nations, facilitate the exchange of knowledge, and foster the development of effective strategies that can be applied by other regions grappling with similar challenges.

While climate change is a global issue, China is particularly vulnerable due to its geographical location, population size, and economic structure. As the world's most populous country and second-largest economy, China is exposed to a wide range of climate-related risks, including rising sea levels, extreme weather events, and changing precipitation patterns. These risks have significant implications for public health, including mental health. The mental health impacts of climate change are increasingly recognized as a critical public health issue. Climate-related disasters, such as floods and droughts, can lead to acute and chronic psychological stress, exacerbating existing mental health conditions and contributing to the emergence of new ones. The uncertainty and stress associated with climate change can also lead to anxiety, depression, and other mental health disorders. Given China's vulnerability to climate change, the country must pay more attention to this issue.

3.5 Impacts and implications of china's proposals

3.5.1 Influence on other countries' policies

China has developed a broad climate policy, which is enshrined in national five-year plans and blueprints at the provincial and local levels. For example, as early as 2017, China's coal consumption and emissions had flattened, giving hope to advocates of climate change policies around the world. Now that China is about to achieve its two-carbon goal, all countries in the world will benefit from these climate policies.

3.5.2 China's role in global climate change and mental health discourse

China's leadership in addressing the mental health impacts of climate change has been influential in shaping global discourse. By bringing attention to this overlooked issue, China has challenged the international community to consider the broader health implications of climate change. Its proposal at COP28, which emphasizes integrating mental health services into climate change adaptation strategies, has set a precedent for other countries to follow.

China's influence extends beyond its policy proposals. As a major global power, China's actions carry significant weight. Its commitment to developing climate-resilient mental health infrastructure and promoting mental health education has the potential for inspiring similar initiatives worldwide. Furthermore, China's proposed collaborations with international organizations and academic institutions could lead to developing global best practices and guidelines.

3.5.3 Future directions of solutions

Looking ahead, China has the opportunity to solidify its leadership role in the global climate change and mental health discourse. To do this, it must successfully implement its proposed strategies. This will require adequate funding, political will, and the engagement of relevant stakeholders. It will also require a detailed implementation plan with specific timelines and measurable targets.

China should also continue to advocate for the inclusion of mental health in global climate change discussions. By sharing its experiences and lessons learned, China can help build a knowledge body that can inform policy and practice worldwide. Furthermore, China can leverage its influence to promote international collaboration, fostering a global response to the mental health impacts of climate change.

In addition, China should prioritize the needs of vulnerable populations in its climate change and mental health strategies. These populations are disproportionately affected by both climate change and mental health issues, and their needs should be at the forefront of policy decisions.

3.5.4 Recommendations from the chinese perspectives and the expected timeframe

China's proposal at COP28 on "Climate Change and Mental Health" marks a notable advancement compared to its stances at COP26 and COP27. The proposal acknowledges the profound influence climate change has on mental health and urges for the implementation of comprehensive measures to tackle this matter.

From a Chinese perspective, further research into the psychological consequences of climate change is suggested. This encompasses examining the mental health implications of extreme weather events, air pollution, and other environmental transformations. It is also recommended that mental health support systems be established to aid individuals and communities impacted by climate change. This may entail the establishment of counseling services, support groups, and various other mental health provisions.

Additionally, China suggested that mental health considerations be incorporated into climate change policies and strategies. This may entail evaluating the potential mental health effects of proposed climate change measures and integrating mental health support into climate change adaptation and mitigation strategies.

Lastly, China urges international cooperation on this issue. This may include sharing research findings, best practices, and resources and kindly collaborating on the development of global mental health and climate change strategies.

The specific implementation mechanisms for these recommendations have not yet been fully outlined. However, they are likely to involve a combination of government action, research institutions, healthcare providers, and community organizations.

Government action may include the implementation of policies and regulations that necessitate the thoughtful inclusion of mental health aspects in climate change measures. Furthermore, it could involve the allocation of funding towards research and the provision of support services for mental health.

Research institutions have the potential to play a crucial role in conducting the necessary research into the mental health impacts of climate change. Additionally, their valuable contribution to the development of mental health support systems and strategies would be highly appreciated.

Healthcare providers have the potential for offering mental health support to individuals and communities impacted by climate change. This may include the availability of counseling services, support groups, and various other mental health resources.

Community organizations can potentially play a vital role in implementing mental health support systems at the local level. Additionally, they can contribute to raising awareness about the mental health implications of climate change and advocating for the essential support and resources needed.

China's proposal at COP28 is a significant step towards acknowledging and addressing the mental health consequences of climate change. The recommendations are comprehensive and call for action at various levels. Although the specific details and timeline for implementation have not been fully outlined, it is evident that urgent attention and action are required for this issue. The proposal does not specify a timeline for implementing these recommendations. However, considering the urgency of the climate change crisis and its impact on mental health, it would be advisable to start the implementation as soon as possible. This could involve taking immediate action to increase research efforts and develop support systems for mental health, followed by longer-term efforts to incorporate mental health considerations into climate change policies and strategies.

Inter-agency Collaboration: China's government agencies, such as the Ministry of Health, Ministry of Ecology and Environment, and National Development and Reform Commission, can collaborate to coordinate efforts and promote a multi-sectoral approach to addressing climate change and mental health. International Cooperation: China can actively engage with international organizations like the

WHO and the UNFCCC to share best practices, exchange knowledge, and seek financial and technical support for implementation.

(1) Long-term (more than 5 years): Continuously monitor and evaluate the effectiveness of implemented measures, making necessary adjustments based on emerging evidence and changing circumstances. Continually update and refine national and regional climate adaptation strategies to ensure the inclusion of mental health considerations.

(2) Medium-term (2–5 years): Develop a national mental health and climate change action plan outlining specific targets, indicators, and interventions. Strengthen collaboration with international partners and secure research, capacity building, and infrastructure development funding.

(3) Short-term (0–2 years): Establish a task force to oversee the development of research protocols, data collection mechanisms, and capacity-building initiatives. Conduct a comprehensive review of existing policies and frameworks to identify gaps and opportunities for integration.

4. Conclusion

4.1 Recap

This research paper has examined China's role in the global climate change discourse, focusing on its recent emphasis on the mental health impacts of climate change. The paper has analyzed China's proposal at COP28, which calls for integrating mental health services into climate change adaptation strategies. The proposal also advocates for international collaboration and research into the psychological impacts of climate change.

4.1.1 Implications of the findings

The findings of this research have several important implications. Firstly, they highlight the growing recognition of the mental health impacts of climate change. This is a significant development, as mental health has traditionally been overlooked in climate change discussions. By bringing attention to this issue, China has challenged the international community to consider the broader health implications of climate change.

Secondly, the findings underscore the importance of international collaboration in addressing the mental health impacts of climate change. As the world's largest emitter of greenhouse gases, China's actions have a significant impact on global climate change.

Finally, the findings highlight the need for a more detailed and targeted approach to addressing the mental health impacts of climate change.

4.2 Suggestions for future research

This research has opened several avenues for future research. Firstly, more in-depth studies on the mental health impacts of climate change are needed. Such research could help to inform policy and practice and could also contribute to the development of best practices and guidelines.

Secondly, future research could examine the implementation of China's proposed strategies. This could involve tracking progress against specific timelines and targets and evaluating the effectiveness of the strategies in improving mental health outcomes.

Finally, future research could explore the experiences of vulnerable populations regarding climate change and mental health. This could provide valuable insights into the specific challenges faced by these populations and inform the development of targeted interventions.

In conclusion, this research paper has shed light on China's role in the global climate change and mental health discourse. It has highlighted the importance of international collaboration and has underscored the need for a more detailed and targeted approach to addressing the mental health impacts of climate change. As the world grapples with the escalating climate crisis, the lessons learned from China's experience could prove invaluable in shaping the global response.

强化气候变化与健康对外传播
——以小岛屿国家联盟（AOSIS）为例[①]

摘 要：一直以来，小岛屿国家气候变化与健康对外传播的声音在国际上处于被忽视的地位。联合国在 2008 年召开的全球人道主义论坛上，就已经提出了气候公正问题，目的是帮助最受气候变化威胁的国家，包括许多小岛屿国家。然而，尽管发达国家已承诺减少温室气体排放，但其实际行动力度仍显不足。在此后的气候变化国际会议上，小岛屿国家一直强调全球升温必须控制在 1.5 摄氏度，这一目标比《京都议定书》的 2 摄氏度目标更为严格。它们的声音并未在《哥本哈根协议》中得到充分体现。

关键词：小岛屿国家联盟；气候变化；健康；对外传播

一、引　言

（一）选题背景

1.小岛屿国家联盟

小岛屿国家联盟（Alliance of Small Island States，AOSIS）是一个低海岸国家与小岛屿国家的政府间组织，成立于 1990 年，其宗旨是加强小岛屿发展中国家在应对全球气候变化中的声音。

截至 2008 年 3 月，AOSIS 有 39 个成员（包括 4 个低地沿海国：几内亚比绍、伯利兹、圭亚那和苏里南和作为观察员的 4 个属地，还有 2 个小岛屿）。这些国家几乎均为发展中国家，其中 10 个国家被联合国列入"最不发达国家"名单。这些国家地理面积总和约为 77 万平方公里，人口总和 4000 多万。其

[①] 作者信息：李张欣，苏州大学网络与新媒体系；吴欣悦，苏州大学新闻系；袁扬洋，苏州大学新闻系。

中，古巴人口最多，巴布亚新几内亚面积最大。

虽然小岛屿国家面积总和不大，人口总数不多，但其领海面积总和约占地球海洋面积的五分之一，其重要地位不容忽略。

2.气候公正

气候公正是一个核心议题，包括全球气候变化的责任分配和应对措施的公平性问题。这个问题对于小岛屿国家尤为重要，它们虽然对气候变暖的责任较小，承受的影响却很大。[①]然而，严峻的现实却并未得到国际层面足够的关注和理解。小岛屿国家面对气候变化的脆弱性和承受的压力，应通过更有效的外部传播，唤起全球公众和决策者的共情与行动。因此，强化小岛屿国家气候变化与健康的对外传播对其来说十分必要。

强化气候变化与健康对外传播关乎小岛屿国家的生存问题，也关乎气候公正的问题。小岛屿国家在遏制气候变化、防止健康危机和维护国家生存权利方面需要得到更多的支持（见图 1）。

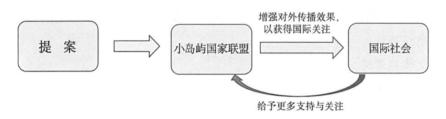

图 1   强化气候变化与健康对外传播带来的效果

因此，从气候公正的角度看，发达国家有义务帮助小岛屿国家应对气候变暖的影响，保证全球的气候公正。[②]

3.小岛屿国家承受的气候变化损害

联合国高级代表曾指出，气候变化给小岛屿国家带来了种种灾难性的后果：干旱和洪水频发；基础设施损坏；土壤流失，土地盐化，危及农业和食物保障；珊瑚、红树林、海草、近海鱼类等沿海资源损失；细菌传播疾病和水传疾病增加；旅游业受到影响等。

世界银行发布的《2010 年世界发展报告：发展与气候变化》强调，考虑到气候变化日益加剧的影响，太平洋小岛屿发展中国家变得极其脆弱，热带气

---

①   杨盛.太平洋岛国国际话语权表达路径研究.重庆：四川外国语大学，2022.
②   张晨阳.国际应对气候变化所致小岛屿国家损失和损害研究.太平洋学报，2017，25(09)：11-23.

旋、洪水和干旱等与气候相关的水文气象灾害在频率和强度上都在增加。其中，受影响最严重的人口集中在巴布亚新几内亚、斐济和所罗门群岛。报告指出，这些地区过去已经在自然灾害面前显现出脆弱性，现在则要面临更多由气候条件变化带来的复杂风险，以及与之相关的生物危害风险。

（二）选题意义

1.理论意义

促进跨学科的合作交流。气候变化和健康是涉及多个学科领域的复杂问题。通过对小岛屿国家在气候变化与健康传播方面的研究，深入了解信息传播的机制和影响，有助于整合不同领域的知识和理论，提供综合性的研究视角和解决方案。

进一步理解跨文化传播。小岛屿国家在气候变化与健康传播中面临跨文化的挑战和机遇。研究小岛屿国家的传播经验可以帮助我们更好地理解文化在信息传播中的作用，包括文化价值观、信仰体系、沟通方式和意识形态对信息接受和行为的影响。该研究有助于促进跨文化交流和理解，提高跨文化传播的有效性和适应性。

2.实践意义

小岛屿国家联盟通过积极参与国际会议、气候峰会和媒体互动，加强了对全球公众和决策者的意识和认知。这些国家通过分享自身的经验，让世界了解气候变化对该国生活、经济和生态系统的严重影响，促使全球更加关注气候问题。

小岛屿国家联盟通过共同发声和联合行动，努力塑造国际舆论。联盟通过媒体、社交网络和其他渠道传播信息，倡导采取更加积极的气候行动，敦促各国遵守减排承诺，推动可持续发展和绿色经济转型。联盟的声音能够为全球气候行动提供强有力的支持，推动国际社会采取更加有力的措施。

小岛屿国家联盟通过与其他国家和国际组织合作，促进全球气候治理和国际合作机制的建立。联盟通过对话、谈判和外交，争取更多的资源和支持，为自身及其他受影响的国家争取更公平的待遇。联盟通过发起倡议、提出政策建议和制定行动计划，影响国际气候谈判进程，争取更有利于小岛屿国家的气候政策和行动。

小岛屿国家联盟通过自身的努力和示范效应，激励其他国家采取更积极的气候行动。这些国家通过实施可持续发展项目、推动可再生能源利用、建立海洋保护区等行动，展示了可行的解决方案和成功案例。联盟的成功经验有利于激励其他国家进行效仿和创新，从而推动全球范围内的气候行动。

二、小岛屿国家联盟对外传播的现状

（一）小岛屿国家联盟的国际传播声量

小岛屿国家联盟的成员国几乎均为发展中国家，国家规模小，这限制了其在国际舞台上的声音和影响力。这些国家的人口和国土面积相对较小，因此在国际事务中的发言权和表达能力相对较弱。在国际政治和经济决策中，大国和地区性联盟往往更具话语权，而小岛屿国家联盟需要与其他国际组织合作，寻求共同发声的机会。

小岛屿国家联盟的成员国经济发展水平低，面临贫困、资源有限和基础设施不足等问题。相比于发达国家，其在国际传播中的投入和资源较为有限，需要依赖国际援助和合作，以获取更多的传播渠道和资源支持。[1]

（二）宣传和倡议方面的概况

首先，小岛屿国家联盟有自己的官网，并在官网上积极发布动态，向全球观众传递关于气候变化的信息。例如，2023 年 6 月，小岛屿国家联盟在第 26 届联合国气候变化大会附属机构会议上强调相关问题，呼吁国际社会关注小岛屿发展中国家和最不发达国家所面临的问题，并确保今后工作的公平性和包容性。

其次，小岛屿国家联盟有推特账号、Ins 账号和 YouTube 账号等社交媒体账号，分享视频、图片和个人故事。尽管更新频率高，但粉丝数量较少，发布的内容热度较低。

通过这些宣传活动和倡议，小岛屿国家联盟将气候议题推向全球舞台，并争取到国际社会的支持和合作。联盟的宣传使人们更加了解小岛屿国家所面临的挑战，并促使全球采取更有力的措施来保护这些脆弱的地区。

三、小岛屿国家联盟对外传播所面临的挑战与解决方案

（一）媒体合作

小岛屿国家联盟在社交媒体账号的关注度相对较低。虽然社交媒体成为全

---

[1] 张宁.小岛屿国家联盟的气候谈判策略及其效果.济南：山东大学，2021.

球信息传播的重要渠道，但由于小岛屿国家的人口较少，在社交媒体上的关注度不如其他国家和国际组织。然而，联盟仍然可以通过与其他国家和国际组织的合作，在平台上获得更多的曝光和支持。

小岛屿国家联盟可以在传播中利用个人故事来吸引公众的关注。通过展示岛国居民面临的气候变化威胁，以及他们所采取的应对策略，向公众展示他们的困境和希望。这些个人故事能够引发共鸣，使公众更好地理解并支持小岛屿国家的气候议程。

此外，联盟还与主流媒体、新闻机构和非政府组织合作，通过采访和报道传播立场和倡议。例如，2022年小岛屿国家联盟主席、安提瓜和巴布达常驻联合国代表沃尔顿·韦伯森在接受《新京报》记者专访时表示，自1990年成立以来，联盟一直在发出警报，强调气候变化对小岛屿国家和低海岸国家的破坏性影响。联盟在《联合国气候变化公约》框架内致力于为小岛屿发展中国家公民的生存权发声。

小岛屿国家不仅需要争取发达国家在气候变化上的技术和财政支持，以应对气候变化带来的挑战，同时也需要借助发达国家的传媒资源，获得在国际传播上的主导权。例如，小岛屿国家可以加强与发达国家传媒产业的合作和交流，集结世界各地的传播人才，借助其平台声量优势展现小岛屿国家面临的气候变化挑战，讲述小岛屿国家的气候治理故事。

再如，太平洋岛国争取到了同属岛国的日本的支持，由于日本政府的国家治理能力较强，其开始加强与太平洋岛国之间的技术合作，给予具体高效的帮助。日本向其他太平洋岛国提供了处理固体垃圾的核心技术，并设立专门的基金以支持其发展。

小岛屿国家应该积极与其他国家、国际组织和非政府组织建立战略伙伴关系。这些伙伴关系可以帮助小岛屿国家扩大其影响力和传播渠道，共同推动气候变化与公众健康议题的传播。小岛屿国家可以主动发起或参与宣传活动，如国际会议、研讨会、公众论坛等，以增加其在气候变化与公众健康领域的曝光度。通过这些活动，小岛屿国家可以与国际社会的各利益相关方进行对话和合作，推动共同行动。

（二）资源投入

1.面临的挑战

社交媒体需要通过频繁更新才能吸引和保持受众的关注。然而，由于资源限制，小岛屿国家联盟可能无法投入足够的人力和时间来产出多样化内容。这可能导致更新速度较慢，限制了与粉丝之间的互动和参与。

社交媒体平台提供了广告投放功能，可以增加内容的曝光，吸引更多粉丝。然而，由于缺乏足够的资金投入，小岛屿国家联盟可能无法充分利用这些广告投放机会，限制了传播的覆盖范围。

2.解决措施

（1）寻求外部合作伙伴——合理地"蹭热度"

小岛屿国家联盟可以与相关的国际组织、非政府组织和其他合作伙伴进行合作。

（2）整合社交媒体管理工具

小岛屿国家联盟可以利用社交媒体管理工具来提高工作效率。这些工具可以帮助计划内容和自动发布，同时监测和回应粉丝的互动。通过合理利用这些工具，可以最大限度地利用有限的资源，提高内容产生和互动的效率。

（3）提高策划和优先级管理能力

在资源有限的情况下，小岛屿国家联盟需要更好地规划和管理资源的优先级。通过制定明确的社交媒体运营计划，并优先选择与目标受众最相关和有影响力的内容，可以更有效地提升社交媒体传播的效果。

（三）针对性的内容和定位

根据对 2022—2023 年 YouTube 账号@AOSIS Media 所发布视频主题分布的分析（见图 2），可以发现该账号整体叙事风格偏宏大，缺乏对小切口、个体性、更具亲和力的"软性"内容的呈现。缺乏个性化和故事性，难以引起观众的关注和共鸣。

图 2　2022—2023 年 YouTube 账号 @AOSIS Medi 发布视频标题词分析

YouTube 观众喜欢看到轻松有趣的内容。如果小岛屿国家联盟的视频过于宏大和正式，就难以吸引观众的注意力。适度添加一些轻松有趣的元素，如幽默、趣味性的动画和音效，可以增加视频的吸引力和分享度。

小岛屿国家拥有丰富的文化和艺术传统，可以将这些元素融入视频中，增加娱乐性和吸引力。例如，可以结合当地音乐、舞蹈、传统手工艺品等，以创造独特的视觉和听觉体验。这样不仅可以增加娱乐性，还可以展示小岛屿国家的独特魅力。

（四）互动性与可视化

1. 互动性

根据 2022—2023 年 YouTube 账号@AOSIS Media 所发布视频形式分布的分析，联盟发布的内容缺乏互动性，且可视化程度比较低。社交媒体的核心特点是互动性，而不仅仅是单向传播。如果小岛屿国家联盟在社交媒体上缺乏与粉丝的互动和参与，就难以建立起持续的互动关系。互动可以包括回复评论、提供实时反馈、引导讨论等。通过积极参与粉丝的反馈和建议，可以增强他们的参与感。

2. 可视化

社交媒体是一个充满视觉冲击的平台，缺乏视觉吸引力的内容容易受到忽视。如果小岛屿国家联盟的社交媒体内容缺乏吸引人的视觉元素，可能无法在用户的快速滚动中产生足够的吸引力。

（五）传播资源整合

小岛屿国家在对外传播方面既需要保持立场的绝对一致性，又需要整合内部不同国家的对外传播资源，建立小岛屿国家对外传播的专业媒体团队，形成气候变化对外传播的矩阵。

非洲气候变化谈判小组（AGN）关于强化全球气候变化与健康的公众传播与媒体报道提案[①]

摘　要： 全球气候变化仍然是当今人类面临的重大挑战，尽管世界各国已经采取了一系列重要措施来遏制气候危机，但气候变化的影响仍在继续恶化。本研究探讨了非洲气候治理资金缺口巨大和能源转型困难的原因。研究发现，媒体传播是一个重要平台，有助于放大非洲困境的声音，因此我们将非洲积极应对气候灾害的故事融入其中。本文认为，非洲可以在 COP28 中提出气候传播相关问题，重申发达国家应尽早实现财政拨款的承诺，指出非洲财政拨款不足和能源转型的困境。在此基础上，进一步同其他国家讨论气候传播方面的问题，如传播资金的来源等。

关键词： COP28；非洲气候变化；气候融资；气候传播；媒体传播

一、引　言

（一）选题背景

大量研究显示，气候变化给人类生活带来的影响持续恶化，根据世界气象组织（WMO）于 2023 年 5 月发布的通告，在温室效应和厄尔尼诺现象的共同影响下，未来五年全球温度可能会飙升至历史新高。[②] 除此之外，发展中国家与欠发达国家在全球气候治理方面与发达国家仍存在较大的发展鸿沟，面临多重危机，其中包括：俄乌冲突加剧发展中国家及欠发达国家的粮食危机，叠

---

① 作者：郭力堃，中国人民大学世界经济专业；林倩玉，中国人民大学社会保障专业；劳梓康，吉林大学金融学专业；赵娉悦，中央音乐学院音乐表演专业。

② WMO. Global temperatures set to reach new records in next five years. (2023-05-17)[2024-01-01]. https://public-old.wmo.int/en/media/press-release/global-temperatures-set-reach-new-records-next-five-years.

加气候危机影响，导致粮食价格飙升、自然灾害加剧，化石燃料与经济效率提升和能源转型新投资的矛盾仍然凸显，不同国家在气候融资方面的分配问题仍然未得到合理解决。非洲大陆在气候变化问题上面临着特殊而严峻的困境。气温上升提高了极端天气事件的发生频率，且非洲的升温速度是全球平均水平的两倍。①非洲从 2022 年底起遭遇了 40 年来最严重的干旱危机。自 2023 年 4 月起，非洲中部强降雨引发的洪灾导致刚果、卢旺达等地造成大量财产与人员伤亡。

非洲大陆面临的困境是所有发展中国家与欠发达国家的缩影，由于长期贫困与缺少基础设施，这些国家如若得不到相关缔约国家的资金援助，经济复苏的可能性将十分渺茫。

在全球提倡能源转型的背景下，非洲只占全球总排放量的约 4%，但仍有6 亿非洲人民过着无电可用的生活②，因此非洲能源开发利用的压力越来越大。与此同时，非洲已将 9% 的 GDP 已用于应对气候变化，高于大部分国家。③

（二）选题意义

作为致力于通过团结行动，确保非洲国家在全球气候谈判中发出团结的声音的非洲气候变化谈判小组（The African Group of Negotiators on Climate Change, AGN），小组借助全球气候缔约方大会这个平台，呼吁国际社会团结一致。小组在非洲国家元首和政府首脑气候变化委员会（CAHOSCC）及非洲环境和自然资源部长级会议（AMCEN）的决议和关键信息的指导下，发出属于非洲的共同且统一的声音。

非洲气候变化谈判小组坚定地相信，通过国际社会的共同努力和支持，我们可以应对气候变化挑战，并实现可持续发展。小组的立场建立在以下事实基础上。

第一，根据联合国开发计划署所制定的气候承诺保证清单，非洲国家的气候承诺比全球平均水平更有力，在稳健性、可行性、国家自主权和包容性等方面得分较高。④

---

① 林家全.非洲开发银行呼吁解决气候融资缺口.经济日报, 2023-06-21(004).
② 中国经济网.联合国非经委高官："一带一路"高质量发展契合非洲经济转型目标. (2023-04-26) [2024-01-01]. https://www.ndrc.gov.cn/fggz/gjhz/zywj/202304/t20230426_1354450.html.
③ 杨海霞.电力普及非洲还有多远.中国投资, 2018(4): 58-59.
④ UNDP Climate Promise Quality Assurance Checklist. (2020-09-18)[2024-01-01]. https://climatepromise.undp.org/sites/default/files/research_report_document/undp-ndcsp-qa-checklist-ndc-revision-ENG.pdf.

第二，小组已经提高了数据透明度以更好地监测和评估气候承诺的实现情况。

第三，小组正在努力推动气候资源调动，非洲已有 20 个国家正在制定融资战略或投资计划。

第四，非洲已针对气候危机多方面共同实施相关措施，其中媒体起着举足轻重的作用。媒体传播不仅在推动气候行动和意识普及方面起着至关重要的作用，更是使非洲困境唤起全球关注的重要平台。小组也希望将非洲抗击全球气候灾难的故事告诉全世界。小组呼吁加强国际合作，共同推动跨国媒体项目，以促进全球范围内的气候意识和行动。为此，非洲气候变化谈判小组希望将非洲的声音带到COP28，为落实《联合国气候变化框架公约》继续努力。非洲坚信，在多国的共同努力下，小组能共同建立一个更加公正、可持续和适应气候变化的未来。

二、进展评估

在过往的COP会议中，小组曾对气候融资的进展抱有相当大的期望。发达国家承诺从 2020 年开始每年向发展中国家提供 1000 亿美元的气候融资，以帮助后者弥补这一资金缺口。然而，这些承诺未能兑现。

在 2022 年的COP27 中，小组认为发达国家兑现了承诺，并承认撒哈拉以南非洲赠款融资的重要性和必要性。但同时，小组也对一些发达国家未能履行 2020 年COP26 向适应基金做出的财政承诺感到失望。因此，小组意识到COP28 同时也是自《巴黎协定》签订后又一次进展总结大会，小组必定会再次将非洲气候融资的脆弱性展现到全球舞台前。

所有非洲人民正在为自己的生存权而战，尽管遇到诸多困境，小组从未放弃过对气候灾害的抗击。在减缓与适应措施方面，小组有如下举措。

（一）减缓措施

气候政策和国际合作：非洲国家参与了国际气候变化谈判，并致力于在全球范围内减少温室气体排放。一些国家已经制定了气候政策和行动计划，旨在促进低碳经济的发展和应对气候变化的挑战。

气候教育和公众意识：非洲国家积极推动气候教育和公众意识活动，以提高人们对气候变化问题的认识。这包括在学校教育中纳入气候变化课程，组织宣传活动和培训项目，以及利用社交媒体和其他渠道传播气候保护的重要性，"非洲新闻社""环境新闻网""非洲绿色媒体"等媒体都曾报道过非洲地区的气候变化及可持续发展问题，致力于提升公众对气候变化和环境保护的意识。

技术创新和适应性解决方案：非洲国家鼓励技术创新，以应对气候变化的挑战。这包括发展适应性解决方案，如气候智能农业技术、水资源管理技术和气候风险预警系统等。

国际援助和资金支持：非洲国家积极争取国际援助和资金支持，用于实施减缓气候变化的举措。这包括通过国际气候基金和其他机构获得资金，用于可持续发展项目、清洁能源项目和适应性措施的实施。此外，非洲国家积极参与国际气候变化谈判和合作机制，以加强非洲国家之间以及与其他地区和国际组织之间的知识共享和合作。[①]

社区参与和基层行动：许多非洲社区通过社区参与和基层行动来应对气候变化。这些行动包括推广可持续农业实践、推动节能措施、建立气候适应性的社区项目，以及培训和赋权社区成员参与气候行动。

气候研究和监测：非洲国家加强了对气候变化的研究和监测，以获取更准确的数据和信息。这有助于制定更有效的政策和行动计划，并监测气候变化的趋势和影响，以做出相应的调整。

气候创业和创新：非洲涌现了许多气候创业和创新项目。这些项目通过提供可持续的解决方案和商业模式来减缓气候变化，例如建立可再生能源企业、气候智能农业技术和社会企业等。

青年参与：非洲的年轻一代积极参与气候行动，在社区层面实施可持续发展的创新解决方案。

跨国合作和区域倡议：非洲国家通过区域合作和倡议来减缓气候变化。例如，非洲联盟的气候变化倡议、非洲开发银行的气候融资机制和非洲可再生能源伙伴关系等。

（二）适应措施

提高气象监测和预警系统：非洲国家致力于改善气象监测和预警系统，以更准确地预测气候变化和极端天气事件。这有助于提前采取措施来减轻灾害

---

① Etsehiwot Kebret. Opinion: How the African Development Bank can drive climate finance to the continent. (2002-06-24)[2024-01-01]. https://chinadialogue.net/zh/3/83007/.

风险。

国际合作：非洲国家积极参与国际气候变化谈判和合作机制，以争取更多的资金和技术支持。他们与其他国家和国际组织合作，分享实践经验，共同应对气候变化的挑战。

社区参与：非洲国家鼓励社区层面的参与，以确保适应措施的可持续性和包容性。这涉及社区参与决策和知识共享等方面。

科技创新：非洲国家鼓励科技创新，以应对气候变化的挑战。这涉及开发和采用新技术，包括气候智能农业、智能城市技术和可再生能源技术等。

建立早期警报系统：为了更好地应对灾害和极端天气事件，非洲国家努力建立和改善早期警报系统。这有助于提前警示并采取适当的行动，以减少人员伤亡和财产损失。

建立气候变化政策和法规：非洲国家制定了气候变化相关的政策和法规，为适应和减缓气候变化提供指导和法律框架。这包括设立减排目标、推动可持续发展、制定适应计划等。

资金和技术支持：非洲国家寻求国际社会提供资金和技术支持，以帮助应对气候变化。这包括国际气候资金、技术转让和能力建设等方面的支持。

社会经济发展与气候变化整合：非洲国家正在努力将气候变化纳入其社会经济发展计划中，试图整合气候变化适应和减缓措施，以确保可持续发展和经济增长的一体化。

知识共享和合作：非洲国家之间以及与其他国家和国际组织之间加强了知识共享和合作。这涉及经验交流、技术合作和合作研究项目，以加强适应措施的效果。

社会弱势群体关注：非洲国家重视保护和关注社会弱势群体，如妇女、儿童、贫困人口和流离失所者，以确保他们在气候变化中的脆弱性得到关注和支持。

（三）问题和挑战

非洲在气候变化以及能源转型上面临如下阻碍。

资金不足：非洲缺少经济援助，因此非洲民众缺少良好的教育，对气候变化的认知和理解程度有限。

基础设施不足：非洲部分偏远地区缺乏适当的通信和传媒基础设施，限制了气候变化信息的获取和传播。

技术和专业知识缺乏：非洲一些国家在可再生能源技术和相关领域的专业技术人员不足，这限制了可再生能源项目的实施和运营。

三、提　议

（一）提案具体内容

媒体传播在放大非洲在能源转型和气候融资方面的困境上起着重要作用。通过媒体报道，我们可以展示非洲国家在能源转型方面所做的努力和面临的挑战，并呼吁国际社会提供更多的支持。同时，媒体可以加强非洲民众对气候变化和能源问题的认识，推动舆论的形成，促使政策制定者采取更积极有效的行动。

（二）提案内容与当前问题的关联

针对目前非洲在气候转型问题上面临的挑战，我们认为想要实现切实快速的效果，首先应在传播的内容上入手，这包括传播对象、媒介手段等。较为典型的案例包括：肯尼亚和坦桑尼亚的企业教授妇女学习智能农业、气候发展知识网络（Climate and Development Knowledge Network，CDKN）和全球恢复力伙伴关系（Global Resilience Partnership，GRP）联合组织关于气候变化的故事比赛等。

这些案例的共同点在于，它们将弱势群体的声音推向前台，并能根据不同特点细分受众，组织不同的行动。除了采取个人行动之外，企业也可以成为气候友好型企业，这样不仅可以树立良好形象，还可以增加产品销量。同时，还可以联合全世界的力量，让人们清楚地认识到，应对气候变化不是一个国家的事情。对此，我们提出了一个三维应对框架，通过受众－知识产品－科技手段三维应对方法诠释。

非洲气候变化谈判小组在COP28会上提出上述问题与挑战，最重要的是重申发达国家应尽早遵守财政拨款的承诺，然后提出非洲财政拨款不足和能源转型的困境。在此基础上，可以与其他国家进一步讨论气候传播方面的问题，如传播资金的来源、问题实施周期的合作伙伴等，可能涉及如下议题。

1.媒体融资比例确定与来源

根据《巴黎协定》，发达国家承诺向发展中国家提供 1,000 亿美元[①]，非洲建议将部分资金用于支持非洲的媒体发展，并建议将拨款比例定为 5%，即将 50 亿美元用于非洲的媒体融资。这一比例考虑到了非洲作为最不发达地区之一，面临着气候挑战和巨大的资金缺口，需要更多的资源来提高媒体的传播力和影响力。而除发达国家给予气候融资外，非洲国家还希望能够得到国际气候资金、联合国开发计划署等机构的资金支持。

2.提案实施的周期与合作伙伴

建议将此提案至少定为 3—5 年计划，由联合国开发计划署（UNDP）执行。UNDP 在可持续发展和气候变化领域发挥着重要作用，支持国家和社区实施可持续发展项目，包括气候行动、环境保护、教育和社会发展等。UNDP 提供技术支持、项目管理和政策建议，以协助国家实现可持续发展目标。我们希望，UNDP 项目传播部作为重点监督部门，为传播战略的实施提供支持，加强公众宣传，提高活动参与，且协助支持项目活动的策划、组织与实施。计划将分为意识宣传阶段（第 1 年）：提高公众对气候变化问题的意识。合作伙伴共同按照上述框架制定宣传活动，包括短片、宣传海报和社交媒体活动，以吸引更多人关注；深度调查与报道阶段（第 2—3 年）：合作伙伴可以联合开展深度调查与报道，揭示气候变化对非洲各地的影响，以及当地社区的应对举措。这将涉及实地采访、数据分析和可视化呈现；政策倡导与行动阶段（第 4—5 年）：最后两年可以侧重于促进政策变革和社会行动。通过深入报道和呼吁，推动政府和企业采取更多措施来应对气候变化，并鼓励公众参与可持续发展项目。

3.提案实施的考核方法

实施涉及非洲气候变化问题的媒体传播计划是一个重要的倡议，需要充分的监督和评估以确保其有效性。小组针对计划实施的考核设置了产出监测、活动监测和结果监测三个维度的指标。

产出监测：监测传播材料的产出数量和质量，包括新闻稿、社交媒体帖子、广告等。这可以通过统计数量和使用媒体质量评估工具来完成。测量受众参与，包括文章点击率、社交媒体分享次数、电视和广播节目的收视率等。

---

① IPCC. Special Report on Global Warming of 1. 5℃ . Cambridge: Cambridge University Press, 2018.

活动监测：记录实际传播活动的数量和性质，编制详细的活动日志；测量媒体覆盖范围，包括传播活动覆盖的区域、受众类型等，可通过媒体监测工具和调查数据进行评估；监督活动相关的成本，包括活动筹备、物资采购和人员培训，需要详细的财务记录。

结果监测：定期跟踪可持续发展和气候变化项目的影响，包括气候行动、环境保护和社会发展方面的成果，要求对项目相关数据进行收集和分析；监测受众的意识水平和行为变化，例如他们的气候友好行为和环保意识，可通过定期调查、焦点小组讨论和社会媒体反馈来完成。

此外，小组计划将展开固定的基线调查、定期监测和中期评估。基线调查应在计划实施之前进行，以确定初始情况和受众的基准认知水平，这将为后续监测提供参考点；定期监测应每季度或每半年进行一次，以检查产出、活动和结果是否按计划进行，这有助于及早发现问题并采取纠正措施；中期评估应在计划执行的中间阶段进行，以评估整体进展和调整战略，这将有助于确保计划在实施过程中保持有效性。每个调查完成后都应呈现一份完整且准确的报告。

4.确认媒体资金的使用范围

培训记者，提高媒体能力：部分资金将用于培训非洲国家的记者，提高他们在气候变化报道方面的专业水平和能力，包括数据分析、科学解释和采访技巧。

增加媒体基础设施：资金将用于改善非洲的媒体基础设施，包括建立最先进的新闻编辑室、更新广播电视设备、建设高速互联网连接等，以支持更好地传播和报道气候变化信息。

举办研讨会和培训活动：资金将用于组织和支持与气候变化有关的研讨会、培训和知识交流活动，以促进非洲媒体之间的合作与共享，提高公众对非洲气候变化问题的认识和参与。

提高公众参与的兴趣：资金将用于开展宣传和教育活动，以提高公众对非洲气候变化问题的兴趣和参与度。这包括组织公众宣传活动、制作信息图表、制作宣传视频等，以吸引更多人关注和支持气候行动。同时，联合国相关机构可以制定和鼓励各类受众参与到全球气候传播的具体策略制订中去。

组建气候变化专家团队：招募有抱负的国家记者，与当地社区或系统化学习服务提供者、有影响力的个人一起担任"气候变化大使"，以提高受众对气候变化的认识和了解。

To Address the Threats Posed by Climate Change to Our Health[1]

Abstract: Climate change is a significant challenge for global health, with extreme weather events causing millions of deaths yearly. Heatwaves, floods, droughts, and storms have particularly devastating effects. The Central European heatwave of 2003 resulted in 70,000 deaths, and heat exposure is a major risk factor for cardiovascular diseases. Climate change also increases the transmission of infectious diseases such as malaria and dengue fever. The article highlights the vulnerability of certain populations, including women, the elderly, and those in low- and middle-income countries. However, there are gaps in understanding the severity and impact of these health risks, as well as disparities in early warning capabilities across countries. Take Kenya as an example, we propose the establishment of a Climate and Health Disease Research Center to study disease patterns and prevention, as well as the creation of mobile medical stations to provide treatment and education. Additionally, subsidies and legislation should be implemented to protect vulnerable populations. These measures aim to

[1] Authors: Yuchi Yuanyuan and He Yingming are students from Faculty of French and Francophone Studies, Beijing Foreign Studies University; Li Renziyue is a student from School of English and International Studies, Beijing Foreign Studies University.

address the urgent threats that climate change poses to human health and reduce the mortality and morbidity associated with extreme weather events.

Keywords: climate change; Kenya; health disease; medical station

1. Introduction

1.1 Background

Climate change has emerged as a monumental challenge confronting the global community, precipitating an increase in extreme weather occurrences that yield a range of implications for human health.

Extreme weather incidents have claimed many lives, underscoring the tangible repercussions of this planetary predicament. According to reports by the World Health Organization (WHO), over five million deaths yearly are attributable to climate change. Predominantly, these fatalities are caused by extreme weather events such as heatwaves, floods, droughts, and storms. In a statement by Petteri Taalas[1], Secretary-General of the World Meteorological Organization, record-breaking heatwaves were observed during the summer of 2022 in China, Europe, North America, and South America. In many parts of the world, as the World Meteorological Organization shows temperatures exceeding 40°C, or even 50°C, are becoming increasingly commonplace[2].

The detrimental effects of extreme weather on health are multifaceted. The exceptionally torrid conditions observed during the 2003 Central European heatwave offer a stark example. WTO Heatwaves overview estimates that around 70,000 individuals perished due to these extreme circumstances, with over a third of these

---

[1] Taalas, P. Climate Change Leads to More Extreme Weather but Early Warnings Save Lives. (2021-09-01)[2024-12-14]. https://unfccc.int/news/climate-change-leads-to-more-extreme-weather-but-early-warnings-save-lives.
[2] World Meteorological Organization. Extreme Weather. [2024-12-14]. Retrieved from https://wmo.int/topics/extreme-weather.

fatalities occurring in France, Italy, and Spain. Since that time, global exposure to extremely high temperatures has increased. Compared to the average level from 1986 to 2005, the number of heatwave exposure incidents in 2018 saw an escalation of 220 million occurrences[1]. Heat exposure is a significant but underappreciated risk factor for cardiovascular diseases. Increased morbidity and mortality rates have been traced back to heatwave exposure, particularly among women, individuals aged 65 and over, those residing in tropical climates, and inhabitants of low- and middle-income countries.

Concurrently, temperature rises can augment the transmission range for certain infectious diseases, such as malaria and dengue fever. In East Africa, since late 2020, there have been five consecutive rainy seasons with severely deficient precipitation, likely constituting one of the most severe droughts in modern history. Inhabitants of drought-stricken areas have inadequate access to water for their livestock, forcing them to compete with wildlife for limited natural water resources within protected areas. Additionally, the struggle to secure food supplies and difficulties in relief grain transportation have driven some to resort to hunting wild animals for meat, amplifying the opportunities for harmful viruses to jump from animal hosts to humans[2].

Looking ahead, WHO, with its network of global experts, has shown that projections for the period 2030–2050 suggest an annual excess death toll of approximately 250,000 due to the ramifications of climate change[3]. This projection accounts for the impacts of malnutrition, malaria, diarrhoea, and heat stress, thereby emphasizing the escalating health threat posed by our changing climate.

1.2 Significance

This proposal aims to shed light on the urgent yet often overlooked threats that environmental changes pose to human health and life and explore potential solutions

---

[1] World Health Organization. Heatwaves. [2024-12-14]. https://www.who.int/health-topics/heatwaves#tab=tab_1.

[2] Intergovernmental Panel on Climate Change (IPCC). *IPCC Sixth Assessment Report Working Group III: Mitigation of Climate Change.* Geneva: IPCC, 2023.

[3] World Health Organization. Climate Change and Health. [2024-12-14]. https://www.who.int/news-room/fact-sheets/detail/climate-change-and-health.

to these challenges. Past United Nations Climate Change Conferences (COP) have underscored the impacts of climate change on the environment, economy, and society. However, the implications for human health and life have frequently been overlooked.

Longstanding activities such as the overexploitation of natural resources and the emission of greenhouse gases has led to climate change, bringing about widespread pollution and degradation of air, water, soil, and food. These environmental issues not only disrupt human production and daily life but also directly threaten our health and life safety.

Climate change has been affecting health in a myriad of ways, including through increasingly frequent extreme weather events such as heatwaves, storms, and floods; disruption to food systems; a rise in zoonotic, foodborne, waterborne, and vector-borne diseases; and the escalation of mental health problems, all of which contribute to increased mortality and morbidity. Furthermore, climate change is undermining many of the beneficial social determinants of health, including livelihoods, equality, and the widespread availability of healthcare and social support structures.

These climate-sensitive health risks disproportionately affect the most vulnerable and disadvantaged groups, including women, children, minority communities, impoverished neighbourhoods, migrants or displaced persons, the elderly, and those with underlying health conditions.

However, people remain largely unaware of the severity of these issues and even lack basic scientific understanding, making it challenging to accurately estimate the scale and impact of many climate-sensitive health risks. This is due, in part, to disparities in the development of early warning capabilities across different countries. Currently, half of the African nations and some other regions do not have sufficient warning services, and there are inadequacies in establishing heat warning systems in certain Asian and Latin American countries.

Moreover, people lack timely and authentic data from disaster-stricken areas. People need more information to assess the situation, leading to clarity in implementing relief efforts and significantly reducing their feasibility. For instance, people need more information to accurately determine how much the frequency of drought events in Africa has increased, and we can estimate the number of refugees urgently in need of aid. People need a more specific understanding of the impacts of environmental changes on human health to take timely and appropriate measures.

This proposal aims to reduce the health threats posed to human physical well-being by climate change. It will enhance the scientific understanding of climate change and health among individuals living in less developed areas, thereby improving their capacity to handle related diseases. Simultaneously, the proposal is committed to tangibly decreasing the survival pressures on individuals in specific occupations during the era of climate change, preventing them from enduring the threats to their health posed by extreme weather conditions due to survival pressures. Additionally, the measures proposed will aid in establishing monitoring and early warning mechanisms, timely identification of potential health threats, and implementing effective preventive and therapeutic measures to mitigate the impacts of high-temperature weather on human health[1].

2. Tracking Progress

2.1 Progress of Mitigation Measures

Kenya remains committed to being on the frontline in sustainable land use and forest conservation, protection, management, and restoration.Kenya's unwavering tree-planting campaign has now entered its seventh year. Additionally, six months ago, Kenya signed a sustainable green industry framework agreement with investors, which will produce 30GW of green hydrogen in Kenya. As we said in COP 27, we have launched an ambitious project to increase the national tree cover from 12.13% to 30% in the next ten years. We intend to accomplish this by first growing 15 billion trees on approximately 10.6 million hectares of land throughout

---

① UNEP, CMS. Enhancing Engagement With The Global Environment Facility. (2017-12-12)[2024-12-14]. https://www.cms.int/sites/default/files/document/cms_cop12_res.10.25%28rev.cop12%29_e.pdf.

the country at an estimated cost of USD 5 billion[①].

In terms of energy, it must be recalled that Kenya has tremendous hydrocarbon and coal deposits, which would go a long way in fueling the development engines. Nevertheless, our electricity grid is 93% green due to resolute commitment. Notably, the Garissa Photovoltaic Power Station in Kenya boasts an installed capacity of 50 megawatts, making it the largest solar power station in East Africa. This station has not only facilitated Kenya's journey towards achieving energy self-sufficiency through green sources but has also contributed to global energy conservation and emission reduction initiatives.

The Government is committed to reclaiming and conserving water catchment areas in the country. Efforts were being made to reclaim, rehabilitate and conserve degraded landscapes. Now, according to Kenya Economic Update from the World Bank, more than 140,000 hectares of production systems are under Sustainable Land Management. At least 152,661 hectares are under improved land management. We have directly restored 8,700 hectares of degraded land and are approaching the emission reduction of at least 820,089 tons CO2eq GHG by 2038[②].

2.2 Progress of Adaptation Measures

Droughts have increased in frequency, intensity, and duration in Kenya. The Kenyan government distributes food relief to 4.3 million affected Kenyans as part of a national emergency program[③] and UNICEF's Country Office Annual Report 2022 is our witness. Also, given that many children are now out of school due to the drought, Kenya has made supply for schools a priority to take care of children mainly.

In response to the consecutive five seasons of insufficient rainfall leading to drought, Kenya has initiated the construction of Kenya's first seawater desalination

① His Excellency Hon. William Samoei Ruto, PHD., C. G. H., President Of The Republic Of Kenya And Commander-In-Chief Of The Defence Forces. Kenya's COP27 Statement in Sharm El-Sheikh. (2022-11-07)[2024-12-14]. https://unfccc.int/sites/default/files/resource/KENYA_cop27cmp17cma4_HLS_ENG.pdf.
② World Bank. *Securing Growth: Opportunities for Kenya in a Decarbonizing World (English). Kenya Economic Update.* Washington, D. C.: World Bank Group. Jun. 3, 2023.
③ UNICEF. Kenya Country Office Annual Report 2022: Kenya. [2024-12-14]. https://www.unicef.org/media/136011/file/Kenya-2022-COAR.pdf.

plant in the North Coast region of Mombasa. The facility will ensure a stable, clean water supply, meet residents' needs, and contribute to local economic development.

The frequency of disasters associated with high temperatures and extreme precipitation events has surpassed all previous records. To mitigate the damage to infrastructure and reduce property losses, the Kenyan government has planned large-scale infrastructure projects and a series of complementary development initiatives. Kenya aims to promote urbanization in areas less affected by climate change, improve infrastructure, attract residents, and establish a climate-resilient society nationwide.

2.3 Current Challenges in Mitigation and Adaptation

Research published in the *South African Journal of Science* on extreme heat events, high ambient temperatures, human morbidity, and mortality in Africa finds that we urgently need to develop thermal health programs and implement interventions in Africa.

Kenya and other African countries face the challenge of high temperatures and water scarcity, which are exacerbated by difficulties due to poor sanitation conditions. World Water Council told us in its report named *Empowering Families in Kenya with Access to Water* that 41% of Kenyans still rely on unpurified water sources such as ponds, shallow wells, and rivers. Only nine of Kenya's 55 public water service providers offer continuous water supply[1]. This not only brings inconveniences to the lives of Kenyans but also increases the risk of disease transmission. Climate change has led to unprecedented outbreaks of larger and deadlier cholera epidemics worldwide this year. Cholera is a disease that affects impoverished and vulnerable communities because they lack access to safe drinking water and basic sanitation facilities. Their limited knowledge of basic medical practices makes it even more lethal, making self-rescue or mutual aid difficult.

Also, a regional heatwave alert system cannot be constructed due to the lack of on-site scientific data. Although Africa is the hardest hit by heat, little research

---

[1] Water. org. *Empowering Families in Kenya with Access to Water*. [2024-12-14]. https://water.org/our-impact/all-stories/empowering-families-in-kenya-with-access-to-water/.

has been done on heat wave warnings in this region, leaving communities without scientifically authoritative guidance in coping with extreme weather. According to the Institute for Safety Studies (ISS), statistics on heat emergencies in Africa are scarce, with only 8 of the 196 incidents reported globally coming from the continent. This is seriously inconsistent with the proportion of events that occurred in reality. Weaknesses in Africa's health systems mean they cannot adequately respond to climate-related crises. Observing systems need to be in place, and data needs to be captured consistently to meet the needs of policymaking.

3. Recommendations

3.1 Detailed Information about the Submission

To address the challenges climate change poses and its impact on spreading infectious diseases and high temperatures, we propose establishing a Climate and Health Disease Research Center in regions highly vulnerable to climate-related health risks. Additionally, a network of mobile volunteer medical stations should be set up under the auspices of this research center, and to fulfil our common but differentiated responsibilities, the research personnel of these stations are proposed to be jointly dispatched by countries, with the costs shared based on their respective levels of development. Furthermore, the outcomes of the research center should be shared globally.

The research center should be responsible specifically for studying the patterns, prevention, and control of disease outbreaks and predicting diseases that may spread from animals to humans because of climate change. Additionally, efforts should be made to provide a more factual number of deaths caused by high temperatures and to establish a quantified relationship between heat waves in Africa and climate change. The medical stations should actively visit residential areas in their respective regions, collecting first-hand data and providing free treatment for residents affected by infectious diseases and heatstroke. They should also be responsible for educating residents within their reach on basic preventive knowledge, mutual assistance methods for common infectious diseases such as malaria, dengue fever, and yellow fever, as well as simple ways of cooling the body to avoid heatstroke and heat exhaustion during extreme high-temperature weather.

To protect low-income populations vulnerable to high temperatures, countries should allocate funds for climate change subsidies through non-green industry taxation. These subsidies should be provided to individuals most affected by climate change's hazards, such as climate refugees and outdoor workers.

Countries experiencing frequent extreme high-temperature weather should use legislation to protect vulnerable groups, especially children and adolescents who are at a high risk of death due to lack of care during high-temperature weather. Legislation should also raise awareness among the entire population about the hazards of high-temperature weather[1].

3.2 How the Submission Solves the Challenges above

Establishing the Climate Change Medical Research Center will help us understand the specific impacts and quantifiable relationships between climate change and human health and assist in the development of a heatwave health risk warning system, and address new health threats arising from climate change in the future. High temperatures endanger our health, as indicated by a global burden of disease (GBD) modeling study published in *The Lancet* identified over 356,000 deaths related to high temperatures in 2019[2]. However, we can only provide vague answers regarding the exact causes. This medical center will help us with scientific guidance to help establish warning systems to address climate change's threats to health better.

Simultaneously, mobile medical stations will reduce deaths caused by lack of treatment and the inability to cool down effectively. According to the World Health Organization (WHO), deaths attributable to high temperatures have increased by

---

[1] Asian Infrastructure Investment Bank (AIIB). *Companies and Climate Change: A Research Application of the AIIB-Amundi Climate Change Investment Framework*. Beijing: AIIB, 2023.

[2] Institute for Health Metrics and Evaluation (IHME). *Lancet: Extreme Heat Is a Clear and Growing Health Issue, with Evidence-Based Adaptation Plans Urgently Needed to Prevent Unnecessary Deaths*. Seattle: IHME, 2023.

74% since 1990[①], and the mortality rate from extreme heat is rising, especially in hotter regions worldwide. Some cooling strategies recommended in existing heat health action plans derive from traditional perspectives, and these measures may contradict scientific evidence, resulting in the loss of innocent lives. Individuals can adopt proven effective measures to cool their bodies and alleviate other physiological stresses caused by temperature regulation, thereby mitigating health risks associated with extreme heat. These measures need to be disseminated to information-poor, underdeveloped areas, where the most vulnerable populations reside, through mobile medical stations.

---

① CBS News. *Study Finds 'Very Concerning' 74% Increase in Deaths Associated with Extreme Heat Brought on by the Climate Crisis.* (2021-08-19) [2024-12-14]. https://www.cbsnews.com/baltimore/news/study-finds-very-concerning-74-increase-in-deaths-associated-with-extreme-heat-brought-on-by-the-climate-crisis/.

PART
3

第三章

全球气候变化与健康数据库
设计与搭建

城市居住环境与健康风险监测数据库搭建[①]

摘　要： 城镇化的进程随着城市居住环境与居民健康风险的变化而改变。本文通过筛选相关指标，构建了城市居住环境与健康风险监测数据库。该数据库从内容上看，包含城市指标体系与居民指标体系；从类型上看，包含统计调查、遥感测绘等传统类型数据，以及从互联网上获取的新类型数据。本文通过对原始数据进行再分析，得到城市健康风险评估结果。该数据库的建设不仅为后续的数据处理与分析提供了基础，也为城市地理、气候变化与健康等领域的深入研究提供了可靠的数据支持。

关键词： 城市居住环境；城市功能；居民健康；居民卫生

一、概　述

（一）研究背景

随着城镇化进程的加快，我国常住人口城镇化率也大幅提高。2021年年底，中国常住人口城镇化率为64.72%，同中高等收入国家67.59%的平均水平和高收入国家80%左右的平均水平相比还有差距，预示着未来在城镇化率上中国仍有较大的增长空间。从"乡土中国"到"城镇中国"，转型的背后也让城市居住环境得到越来越多的重视。空气污染、噪声污染和交通拥堵等现象危害居民的身心健康，对城市经济与社会发展也会造成不利影响。因此，对当今中国城市居住环境与健康风险相关的因素进行量化研究，构建相关数据库，可用于后续对其与地方居民身体健康程度进行相关性分析甚至进行健康预测。这些研

① 作者：宋苗苗，北京大学软件与微电子学院；林艺琳，北京大学前沿交叉学科研究院；姚乐，北京大学城市与环境学院；李钧泓，北京大学城市与环境学院。

究对于保障人民的生命健康和提高城市居民的生活质量具有重要意义。

（二）研究目标

本研究旨在构建以城镇为基础的中国城市居住环境与健康风险监测数据库。通过对城市环境与居民健康相关指标进行筛选[①]，并获取与之相关的各种传统类型数据（遥感测绘数据、调查统计数据）与覆盖面广、一致性程度高且粒度细致的新类型数据（互联网数据、智慧设施数据），最终构建出可视化强且具有一定交互能力的关系型数据库。在此基础上有望对现有数据做出进一步分析甚至进行预测，研究流程与参考指标见图1。

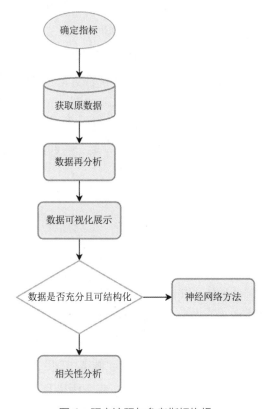

图1 研究流程与参考指标构想

① 龙瀛，李苗裔，李晶. 基于新数据的中国人居环境质量监测: 指标体系与典型案例. 城市发展研究，2018(4): 86-96; 李佳彤. 基于居民活动的多尺度城市健康数据融合分析. 西部人居环境学刊，2023(2): 8-16; Skalicky, V. & Čerpes, I. Comprehensive assessment methodology for liveable residential environment. *Cities*, 2019(94), 44-54. https://doi.org/10.1016/j.cities.2019.05.020; 杨林生，李海蓉，李永华，等. 医学地理和环境健康研究的主要领域与进展. 地理科学进展，2010(1): 31-44; 张文忠. 城市内部居住环境评价的指标体系和方法. 地理科学，2007(1): 17-23.

二、源数据

（一）城市指标体系

1.城市基本信息

城市基本信息包括地理位置、省份、区域（东中西／内陆沿海／南北）。该套数据以2022年国家基础地理信息数据中的县区划数据作为矢量基础，辅以高德行政区划数据、天地图行政区划数据，参考历年来民政部公布的行政区划为属性基础（见表1）。

表1 城市基本信息数据

数据内容	数据来源	时间	范围	精度	格式
城市基本信息	CnOpenData：https://www.cnopendata.com/data/chinese-administrative-divisions-shp.html	2022年	中国	省市县、国界、九段线	shapefile

2.城市形态

（1）城市建成区及绿地数据

该部分数据包括建成区面积及城市绿地相关数据（见表2）。建成区是指城市行政区内实际已成片开发建设、市政公用设施和公共设施基本具备的地区。城市建成区范围的划定，要考虑地形、地貌、基层行政单位的管理界线等因素，以及城市各项用地的完整性，并尽可能与人口统计的地域范围相一致。

表2 城市建成区及绿地数据

数据内容	数据来源	时间	范围	精度	格式
城市建成区面积	esri：https://www.esri.com/en-us/arcgis-marketplace/listing/products/43c1d2612d134cc19b7f95deef5469db；《中国城市统计年鉴2021》[①]	2018—2022年；2021年	中国	10m×10m；县市级	tif、xls
建成区绿地面积及建成区绿化覆盖面积	《中国城市统计年鉴2021》	2021年	中国	县市级	xls
建成区绿地比率	《中国城市统计年鉴2021》	2021年	中国	县市级	xls

---

① 国家统计局城市社会经济调查司.中国城市统计年鉴2021.北京：中国统计出版社，2022.

（2）道路数据

道路数据来自开放街道地图（OpenStreetMap，OSM）。该软件的目标是创造一个内容自由且能让所有人编辑的世界地图，并且让一般的移动设备有方便的导航方案。

OSM道路分类标准见表3。

表3　OSM道路类型及描述

fclass 字段	描述
tertiary（第三级道路）	城市支路
tertiary_link（第三级道路—连接）	匝道，机场集散车行道路（数据量极少，多是未知道路）
residential（居住区道路）	居住区车行道路
unclassified（未分类道路）	居住区车行道路，滨水车行道路，机场机动车通道
secondary（次要道路）	城市次要车行道路，机场外围车行道路
secondary_link（次要道路—连接）	城市次要车行道路立交、匝道（数据量少，部分零散分布未知类别）
primary（主要道路）	城市主要车行道路
primary_link（主要道路）	城市主要车行道路立交，城市主要车行道路匝道（数据量少，部分零散分布未知类别）
motorway（高速公路）	高速公路，过江隧道
motorway_link（高速公路—连接）	高速公路立交，匝道
trunk（干道）	高架快速路，机场进站快速路，过江隧道，桥上快速路
trunk_link（干道—连接）	立交，匝道，桥上引道，机场进站快速路，国道改道
track（小路）	郊区、乡村、工矿区、田间、林间小路
track_grade1（小路—级别1）	郊区、乡村、工矿区、田间、林间小路
track_grade2（小路—级别2）	郊区、乡村、工矿区、田间、林间小路
track_grade3（小路—级别3）	郊区、乡村、工矿区、田间、林间小路
track_grade4（小路—级别4）	郊区、乡村、工矿区、田间、林间小路
track_grade5（小路—级别5）	郊区、乡村、工矿区、田间、林间小路
bridleway（马道）	体育场馆内部专用道路（数据量极少，零星道路在公园、居住区内部）
living_street（生活—街道）	居住区车行道路，公园车行道路
path（小道）	公园车行道路，居住区车行道路（分布零碎，量少）
service（服务性道路）	居住区车行道路，火车站集散车行道，公园车行道路，公共建筑集散车行道，公交枢纽入口车行道路，停车场入口车行道路

fclass字段	描述
footway（人行道）	滨水绿道，公园步行道，广场步行道，大学步行道路，人行道，火车站人行集散道路
pedestrian（步行街道）	步行街，广场步行道路，公园步行道路，居住区步行道路
steps（台阶踏步）	人行过街天桥台阶，广场台阶、公共建筑入口台阶，登山台阶
cycleway（自行车道）	滨水绿道，非机动车道，公园自行车道
unknown（未知道路）	滨水车行道路，校园广场车行道路，乡道（数据量少，比较难判别道路类型）

3. 城市环境

（1）自然灾害与突发事件

自然灾害与突发事件是城市面临的重要挑战，对此进行有效监测和数据收集至关重要。相关数据涉及多个方面，包括气象、自然灾害损失及突发环境事件等（见表4）。其中气象数据包括气温、气压、露点、风向风速、云量、降水量；自然灾害损失数据包括农作物受灾面积合计、旱灾、洪涝、地质灾害和台风、风雹灾害、冷冻和雪灾、人口受灾、直接经济损失；突发环境事件数据包括特别重大环境事件、重大环境事件、较大环境事件、一般环境事件。

表4 自然灾害与突发事件数据[①]

数据内容	数据来源	时间	范围	精度	格式
中国气象历史数据	中国空气质量历史数据|中国气象历史数据|北京市空气质量历史数据(quotsoft.net)； 美国国家气候数据中心（National Climatic Data Center，NCDC）	1942年7月至今	中国	站点，每3小时或1小时	csv
自然灾害损失	《中国统计年鉴2022》	2021年	中国	县市级	xls
突发环境事件	《中国统计年鉴2022》	2021年	中国	县市级	xls

（2）城市污染数据

城市污染对城市居民的居住健康产生负面影响，相关数据主要涉及光污染、空气污染、水污染以及噪声污染。具体数据内容见表5。

---

① 国家统计局.中国统计年鉴2022.北京：中国统计出版社，2022.

表 5　城市污染数据

数据内容	数据来源	时间	范围	精度	格式
光污染	VIIRS Stray Light Corrected Nighttime Day/Night Band Composites Version 1；中国夜间灯光遥感数据	2020—2023 年	中国	1000km，每月	tif
空气污染	中国空气质量历史数据｜中国气象历史数据｜北京市空气质量历史数据 (quotsoft.net)；中国环境监测总站	2014 年 5 月至今	中国	城市级，每天	csv
水污染	《中国统计年鉴 2022》	2021 年	中国	县市级	xls
噪声污染	《中国统计年鉴 2022》	2021 年	中国	县市级	xls

4. 城市功能

（1）城市污染治理

该部分数据主要涉及城市污染治理方面，包括污水处理、垃圾处理和固体废物处理等多个指标（见表 6）。污水处理包括地级以上城市污水处理厂个数、地级以上城市垃圾填埋场个数；垃圾处理包括地区生活垃圾清运量、无害化处理厂数、无害化处理能力、无害化处理量以及生活垃圾无害化处理率[②]；固体废物处理包括一般工业固体废物产生量、综合利用量、处置量、贮存量、倾倒丢弃量、危险废物产生量、利用处置量、本年末贮存量；工业污染治理包括废水、废气、固体废弃物、噪声等污染的治理。

表 6　城市污染治理数据

数据内容	数据来源	时间	范围	精度	格式
污水处理	中国城市统计年鉴；高德地图 POI（Point of Information）	2020 年	中国	地市级	csv
垃圾处理	中国空气质量历史数据｜中国气象历史数据｜北京市空气质量历史数据 (quotsoft.net)；中国环境监测总站	2014 年 5 月至今	中国	城市级，每天	csv
固体废物处理	《中国统计年鉴 2022》	2021 年	中国	县市级	xls
工业污染治理	《中国统计年鉴 2022》	2021 年	中国	县市级	xls

---

① 中华人民共和国生态环境部. 中国噪声污染防治报告. [2024-01-01]. https://www.mee.gov.cn/hjzl/sthjzk/hjzywr/202307/W020230728374728553582.pdf.
② 生活垃圾处理技术通常包括卫生填埋、焚烧处理及其他技术（如生物处理、水泥窑协同处置等）。

（2）医疗卫生服务

城市医疗卫生服务能力是评价城市居住环境健康的重要基础指标。具体内容见表 7。

表 7　医疗卫生服务数据

数据内容	数据来源	时间	范围	精度	格式
医疗卫生机构数量	中国城市统计年鉴； 高德地图 POI	2020 年	中国	地市级	csv
各城市医疗床位数[①]	中国城市统计年鉴	2020 年	中国	地市级	csv
医院床位利用情况	中国空气质量历史数据	中国气象历史数据	北京市空气质量历史数据 (quotsoft.net)； 中国环境监测总站	2014 年 5 月至今	中国	城市级，每天	csv
城市与农村的每千人口卫生技术人员	《中国统计年鉴 2022》	2021 年	中国	县市级	xls
分地区老人看护中心数量[②]	地区政府发布的养老机构名单（如北京市具备星级资格养老机构名单）； 高德地图 POI	2023 年	中国	县市级	xls

（3）应急基础设施

城市应急基础设施的分布和可达性是评估城市韧性和紧急响应能力的关键指标。具体内容见表 8。

表 8　应急基础设施数据

数据内容	数据来源	时间	范围	精度	格式
避难所	高德地图 POI	2023 年	中国	区县级	xls
公共消防基础设施	高德地图 POI	2023 年	中国	区县级	xls
AED 数量	高德地图 POI； AED 地图	2023 年	中国	区县级	xls

---

① 指年底固定实有床位(非编制床位)，包括正规床、简易床、监护床、超过半年加床、正在消毒和修理床位、因扩建或大修而停用的床位，不包括产科新生儿床、接产室待产床、库存床、观察床、临时加床和病人家属陪护床。

② 老人看护中心以养老院、敬老院、老龄公寓等为主，不包含老人活动中心、老年大学等；其类别可分为社区养老服务机构与专业化养老机构。

（4）通勤数据

城市居民的健康状况与其通勤行为、城市交通规划之间同样有密不可分的关系。本研究收集的通勤数据内容见表9。

表9　通勤数据

数据内容	数据来源	时间	范围	精度	格式
公共交通运营数据	《中国城市统计年鉴 2020》[①]	2020 年	中国	地市级	csv
平均公共交通通勤距离	《2020 年度全国主要城市通勤监测报告——通勤时耗增刊》	2020 年	中国	城市级	csv

（二）居民指标体系

1. 人口基本信息

人口基本信息包括人口规模与人口结构。人口规模直接关系到城市的经济社会发展和资源利用。适度的人口规模有助于促进城市的发展，但当人口规模超出城市承载力时，会导致环境压力增大，增加居住环境的健康风险。而通过深入了解人口结构，城市决策者可以更好地制定相关政策和规划，合理分配公共服务资源，创造有利于各年龄层次和群体的居住环境，提升整体居住健康水平。

（1）人口规模

人口规模数据包括人口总量、人口密度以及出生率和死亡率。具体数据内容见表10。

表10　人口规模数据

数据内容	数据来源	时间	范围	精度	格式
人口数量	Citypopulation：http://www.citypopulation.de/zh/china/admin/；WorldPop：https://hub.worldpop.org/project/categories?id=3	2000 年、2010 年、2020 年	全球	地市级、100m×100m	tif
人口密度	WorldPop：https://hub.worldpop.org/project/categories?id=18	2020 年	全球	100m×100m	tif
出生率	WorldPop：https://hub.worldpop.org/geodata/summary?id=842	2015 年	中国	1km×1km	tif
死亡率	CEIC平台数据：https://www.ceicdata.com/zh-hans/china/population-death-rate-by-region	1990—2022 年	中国	省级	xls

---

① 国家统计局城市社会经济调查司.中国城市统计年鉴 2020.北京：中国统计出版社，2021.

（2）人口结构

人口结构数据包括年龄结构、性别结构以及生育适龄妇女人数。具体数据内容见表11。

表11　人口结构数据

数据内容	数据来源	时间	范围	精度	格式
年龄结构	WorldPop：https://hub.worldpop.org/project/categories?id=8	2020年	全球	100m×100m	tif
性别结构	WorldPop：https://hub.worldpop.org/project/categories?id=8	2020年	全球	100m×100m	tif
生育适龄妇女人数	WorldPop：https://hub.worldpop.org/project/categories?id=6	2015年	全球	1km×1km	tif

2. 城市居民疾病数据

居民疾病数据主要包括传染病与非传染病两类。其中传染病数据包括2021年各地区甲乙类法定报告传染病发病率、死亡率。非传染病数据包括2015年中国心脑血管疾病发病率及死亡率，和恶性肿瘤发病率及死亡率（见表12）。

表12　城市居民疾病数据

数据内容	数据来源	时间	范围	精度	格式
传染病发病率及死亡率	国家卫生健康委员会2021年全国法定传染病疫情概况（http://www.nhc.gov.cn/jkj/s3578/202204/4fd88a291d914abf8f7a91f633567e1.shtml）	2021年	中国	省级	xls
心脑血管疾病发病率及死亡率	Burden of Ischaemic heart disease and attributable risk factors in China from 1990 to 2015: findings from the global burden of disease 2015 study｜BMC Cardiovascular Disorders｜Full Text (biomedcentral.com)	2015年	中国	省级	xls
恶性肿瘤发病率及死亡率	郑荣寿，张思维，孙可欣，等. 2016年中国恶性肿瘤流行情况分析. 中华肿瘤杂志，2023, 45(3)：212-220.	2016年	中国	省级	xls

3. 居民生活习惯监测指标

（1）运　动

运动数据包括人群日均步数、运动指数、运动场所成熟度、运动场馆丰富度以及健身中心在运动场馆中的占比等。通过收集各公开数据源，包括QQ大数据《2016 中国人运动报告》^①、"全民健身活力城市"指数指标体系^②的数据，深入了解城市居民的日常步行活动水平、整体运动水平、运动基础设施的成熟度和城市健身服务结构的特征，为城市健康与运动发展提供了全面而可靠的评估依据。

（2）烟　酒

根据云酒传媒大数据中心的报告，可以获取城市烟酒店数量的相关信息。为了进行进一步的处理与分析，我们将从文献中提取相关的折线图或散点图数据，以确保数据的准确性和可用性。

三、城市健康风险评估

基于上述源数据，根据数据处理方法，通过数据再分析形成城市健康风险评估结果。本文分别从人群敏感性、城市系统、健康风险三个方面进行评价，以得到城市居住环境与健康风险综合评价结果。

（一）人群敏感性评价

由于生理特征、社会特性等方面的差异，城市居民个体在面临空气污染带来的健康危害时，其应对和恢复能力表现出显著的差异。因此，对人群的敏感性评价指标需要特别强调反映个体的生理特征和社会特性水平的相关因素（见表 13）。这些评价指标的引入将有助于更全面地理解和量化人群在不同环境条件下对空气污染的响应，为制定有针对性的健康干预策略提供科学依据。

表 13　人群敏感性评价指标

分类	指标
生理特征	16—65 岁人口所占比重
	女性人口比重
	慢性病患者比重
社会特征	居民可支配收入
	职业类型
健康意识	运动频率
	烟酒消费量

---

① 腾讯体育. QQ 大数据发布中国人运动报告. (2016-12-30)[2024-02-04]. https://sports.qq.com/a/20161230/025632.htm.

② 澎湃新闻. "全民健身活力城市"指数指标体系出炉. (2022-08-08)[2024-02-04]. https://www.thepaper.cn/newsDetail_forward_19361730.

（二）城市系统评价

在面对环境污染和气候变化带来的风险时，城市系统会做出一定响应，影响着个体受到的健康影响。城市系统健康程度可由城市环境、医疗条件和其他基础设施等服务来表征（见表 14）。

表 14　城市系统评价指标

分类	指标
城市环境	人均绿地面积
	道路密度
	人均通勤距离
医疗条件	医疗设施可达性
	人均医疗床位数
其他服务	各类污染处理量
	宣传教育水平

（三）健康风险

城市健康风险主要包括城市污染和极端气候条件，需要通过数据监测、科学研究等手段进行及时的预警和管理，以提高城市的适应性和韧性。

1. 城市污染

目前，我国城市环境污染主要受到生活污染物排放、工业废弃物排放、工业废气排放等多方面因素的影响。为准确构建城市污染评估框架，需要在医学、环境科学、城市科学等多学科基础上，形成定量的机制分析，进而对城市健康资源配置产生指导意义。

2. 极端气候条件

本文基于城市自然环境中的天气与气候数据，分析了 2013—2022 年中国 362 个站点的极端高温天数和连续极端高温天数。

本文选取 1983—2012 年作为气候标准期，判断 2013—2022 年十年内的极端高温。在这 40 年中每年都有数据的站点共 362 个，进行极端阈值的计算。根据每天的温度计算每日最高温度，使用日观测资料，对极端阈值进行确定。在气候标准期内的每年选取日最高温度的最高值和次高值，共 60 个值，选取第 95 百分位数（58 位数）作为偏大的极端阈值，大于或等于该阈值位极端事件。将其与 2013—2022 年的日最高温度比较，得到每年的极端日高温天数和极端连续高温日数。计算了每个站点的年极端日高温天数和年最长连续极端高温日数。

2013—2021年，极端高温天数呈现波动趋势，而在2022年显著上升。

极端高温持续时间普遍集中在1—4天内。最长极端高温持续时间随年际有较大波动，2013年出现最长极端高温持续时间9天，2018年出现最长极端高温持续时间8天，而2022年则出现最长极端高温持续时间14天的极端事件。其波动趋势大致与总极端高温天数的趋势相似。

四、结　论

（一）主要结论

城市居住环境健康风险的全面评估对相关数据的全面性、准确性和动态性提出了高要求。通过收集、整理和分析大量的相关数据，我们才能全面了解城市居住环境中存在的各种潜在健康风险因素，进行科学决策和精准干预，规划和实施有效的城市环境保护和健康管理措施。

在本研究中，我们通过多维度指标筛选，构建了一套相对全面的城市居住环境与健康风险监测数据库。该数据库不仅包括了丰富的城市指标体系和居民指标体系，还整合了传统类型数据和新型互联网数据。

通过对源数据的再分析，可以得到城市健康风险评估结果。该数据库的建设可以为城市规划和管理提供科学依据，促进城市的可持续发展。

（二）展　望

随着城市动态监测手段的不断丰富，数据采集和处理技术的不断创新，我们对城市居住环境与健康风险的研究将迎来更加广阔的发展空间。目前，城市研究者主要关注韧性城市、健康城市、城市卫生公平等方向（见表15）。城市居住环境与健康风险监测数据库的建设可以为相关学术研究提供有力的支持。

表 15 数据库研究应用方向

研究方向	相关指标	分析内容
韧性城市	城市气候、自然灾害、城市基础设施等	研究城市所面临的各种风险和威胁，并进行风险评估，以制定相应的规划和政策。包括考虑自然灾害、气候变化和社会经济压力等因素对城市的潜在影响，从而制定相应的规划策略来减少损失和提高城市的适应能力。
健康城市	城市形态、居民生活等	健康城市规划需要全面考虑城市形态、功能与居民生活的关系，营造以人为本的健康城市空间[1]。
城市卫生公平	人口基本信息、公共服务、居民卫生等	社会经济地位、户籍、性别、年龄、居住环境、教育和就业等因素均会影响城市卫生公平。通过相应的分析，指导城市规划，以减少城市居民之间的卫生差距和不平等。

---

① 中国环境与发展国际合作委员会.构建以人为本的环境与健康管理体系.[2024-01-01]. http://www.cciced.net/zcyj/yjbg/zcyjbg/2008/201607/P020170814367575029946.pdf.

海洋运输碳排放数据库的建立以及评价研究[①]

摘　要： 当下全球气候变化和可持续发展面临的挑战日益严峻，建立海运碳排放数据库能够为政策制定、减排措施落地、港口竞争力提升等提供科学依据。因此，本文基于《2021年全球港口发展报告》中排名前十的中国七大港口的运营数据，建立其海运碳排放数据库。具体而言，本文通过各省市统计年鉴、权威行业报告等资料，获取货物重量、运输距离、碳排放因子三方面的数据，计算得到各港口碳排放总额，完成数据库的建立。最后本文进一步结合背景知识，分析、总结了计算结果，并提出未来的改进方向。

关键词： 海洋运输；碳排放；数据库

一、研究背景

气候变暖已经成为 21 世纪人类社会必须共同面对的重大挑战，严重影响了人类的生存和发展[②]。交通运输业是人为活动碳排放的第二大来源，据国际能源署（IEA）统计，2016 年全球交通运输业碳排放量占全球碳排放总量的比重高达 27%，仅次于工业[③]。海洋交通运输业作为海洋经济的支柱产业之一，2017 年其产业增加值占海洋产业总量的比重高达 20%，仅次于滨海旅游业。海洋交通运输业快速发展的同时也造成了严重的环境污染，如何提高海洋交通运输业的能源利用效率和碳排放效率是中国海洋经济发展面临的重大问题。海洋交通运输业碳排放在监测与管理上存在诸多困难，且我国政府高度重视全球气候

[①] 作者：杨晗，北京理工大学管理学院；晏博，北京理工大学国际组织创新学院；张若彤，北京理工大学管理学院；梁晨，复旦大学大气与海洋科学系。

[②] 戴彦德，朱跃中，白泉. 中国 2050 年低碳发展之路——能源需求暨碳排放情景分析. 经济研究参考，2010(26)：2-22，33.

[③] 李琳娜，Becky. P. Y. Loo. 中国客运交通的碳排放地理特征与展望. 地理研究，2016，35(7)：1230-1242.

变化，承诺到 2025 年温室气体排放设定绝对上限，提出与新碳排放达峰目标相衔接的二氧化碳排放降低目标。[①]

（一）选题背景与研究意义

海运碳排放数据库的建立根植于全球气候变化和可持续发展的挑战，并受到国际约定和协议、碳排放监测要求、行业可持续发展需求、利益相关者压力和技术创新的推动。通过建立数据库，可以监测和评估海运业的碳排放情况，为制定政策、推动创新和改善行业的环境性能提供科学依据，推动海运业向更加可持续的方向发展。

本文分析的港口选取了 2021 年上海国际航运研究中心港口发展研究所发布的《2021 年全球港口发展报告》[②]中排名前十的我国港口，一共七个。首先，研究这些港口的海运碳排放数据库可以揭示各港在全球海运业中的碳排放状况。通过收集记录碳排放量，可以了解各港口对气候变化的影响，并为制定相应的环境政策和措施提供科学依据。

其次，建立港口的海运碳排放数据库有助于评估其碳排放水平和趋势。通过分析历史数据和趋势，可以了解港口的碳排放变化情况，发现碳排放的主要来源和高碳排放环节，为减少碳排放和提高能源效率制定针对性的措施。

再次，评价港口的海运碳排放数据库还可以促进航运企业的主动参与和减排行动。通过提供可靠的数据和信息，可以帮助船舶运营商和船东认识到其碳排放量，并激励他们采取相应的减排措施。这可能包括船舶技术改进、使用更清洁的燃料、优化航线和速度等，从而降低碳排放并提高能源效率。

最后，评价港口的海运碳排放数据库还可以提升港口的形象和竞争力。在全球范围内，越来越多的利益相关者关注企业的环境责任和可持续经营。通过建立可靠的碳排放数据，大连港可以展示其对环境可持续性的承诺和努力。这将有助于吸引更多环保意识强烈的客户和合作伙伴，提升港口在国际贸易中的竞争力。

（二）主要港口概况

随着全球经济的持续复苏，港口也因此得到呈现稳步复苏的态势。根据上

[①] 新华社. 中国应对气候变化的政策与行动. (2021-10-27)[2024-04-15]. https://www.gov.cn/zhengce/2021-10/27/content_5646697.htm.

[②] 上海国际航运研究中心. 2021 年全球港口发展报告. 2022.

海国际航运研究中心港口发展研究所发布的《2021 年全球港口发展报告》，目前全球主要港口集装箱吞吐量正持续恢复，其中 84 港同比 2020 年为正增长，41 港增速超过 10%。尤其在中国，港口的运转情况较好。该报告显示按照吞吐量计算，中国七大港口位居全球港口排名中的前十位，其中上海港位居全球港口排名中的第一位。另外，宁波舟山、深圳、广州、青岛、天津、香港港口则分别位列第三、四、五、六、八、九位。而排名第二十二位的苏州港和排名第二十八位的北部湾港吞吐量增势明显，排名稳步提升。本研究中海洋运输碳排放数据库的建立选取了上述排名在全球前十名的七个中国港口。

1. 上海港

上海港是中国位于上海市的主要港口，也是世界上最繁忙的港口之一。它位于长江口东北岸，拥有优越的地理位置和便捷的海上交通连接能力。上海港年货物吞吐量巨大，包括各种类型的货物，如集装箱、散货、石油和液体化工品等。港口设施先进，拥有多个码头和现代化的装卸设备，能够满足各种规模和类型的船舶的需求。上海港通过广泛的航运网络连接了世界各地的主要港口，为国内外企业提供高效的贸易和物流服务。作为中国和全球贸易的重要枢纽，上海港对经济发展和国际贸易起到了关键的推动作用。在 2021 年上海国际航运研究中心港口发展研究所发布的《2021 年全球港口发展报告》中，上海港位居全球港口排名中的第一位。

2. 宁波舟山港

宁波舟山港是中国浙江省舟山市的一个重要港口，位于中国东海沿岸。它包括舟山本岛及周边岛屿，总面积约 3,500 平方公里。舟山港地理位置优越，距离上海约 140 公里，是长江三角洲地区的门户港口。它是中国重要的综合性港口，具备深水良港、宽阔航道和现代化装卸设施。宁波舟山港是集装箱枢纽和大宗货物转运港口，与世界各地的港口建立了广泛的贸易关系。在 2021年上海国际航运研究中心港口发展研究所发布的《2021 年全球港口发展报告》中，宁波舟山港位居全球港口排名中的第三位。

3. 深圳港

深圳港位于中国广东省深圳市，是中国南方最重要的港口之一。深圳港自 1979 年建港以来，经过持续发展已成为全球最繁忙的集装箱港口之一。深圳港地理位置优越，毗邻香港，是中国与世界贸易的重要门户。它包括深圳湾港区、蛇口港区和盐田港区等多个港区。深圳港拥有现代化的港口设施和高效的物流系统。它拥有世界级的码头和起重设备,可以容纳大型船舶和高容量集装箱运输。深圳港还建立了广泛的国际航线网络,与全球各大港口进行贸易往来,是世界贸易的重要纽带。在 2021 年上海国际航运研究中心港口发展研究所发布的《2021 年全球港口发展报告》中,深圳港位居全球港口排名中的第四位。

4. 广州港

广州港位于中国广东省广州市,是中国南方最大的港口之一。它是一个综合性港口,包括南沙港区、黄埔港区和广州港区等多个港区。广州港具备深水良港和现代化的装卸设施,能够容纳大型船舶和各类货物。作为中国重要的集装箱港口之一,广州港在国内外贸易中扮演着重要角色,与世界各地的港口建立了广泛的贸易关系。广州港在国内外贸易中具有重要地位,为经济发展和国际贸易提供了便利和支持。在 2021 年上海国际航运研究中心港口发展研究所发布的《2021 年全球港口发展报告》中,广州港位居全球港口排名中的第五位。

5. 青岛港

青岛港位于山东半岛胶州湾畔,是中国山东省青岛市港口,濒临黄海,与日本和朝鲜半岛隔海相望,是中国沿黄河流域和环太平洋西岸的国际贸易口岸和中转枢纽。港口水域面积 420 平方千米,业务范围遍及全球 180 多个国家和地区的 700 多个港口,直达中亚地区。青岛港曾被交通部确定为全国交通系统"三学一创"典型和全国港口行业唯一的示范"窗口",并获得全国十大国家质量管理卓越企业、中国企业形象建设十佳单位、中国十大最具影响力品牌等荣誉称号。青岛港自 2014 年开始实施国际化战略积极"走出去",开启了建设世界一流的国际化港口的新征程。在 2021 年上海国际航运研究中心港口发展研究所发布的《2021 年全球港口发展报告》中,青岛港位居全球港口排名中的第六位

6. 天津港

天津港是中国北方重要的港口,位于中国天津市。天津港拥有深水良港和先进的装卸设备,能够容纳大型船舶和各类货物。港口区域广阔,包括天津港、塘沽港和东疆保税港等多个港区。它提供了全方位的服务,包括集装箱运输、散货运输、液体化工品运输等。作为中国重要的国际贸易枢纽,天津港与全球多个港口建立了密切的贸易合作关系。它连接着中国和世界各地,是中国

北方地区最重要的进出口港口之一。天津港不仅在货物贸易方面发展迅速，还在港口物流、航运服务、码头设施等方面进行了不断的创新和提升。港口的高效运营和先进管理为中国经济发展和国际贸易提供了重要支持。在2021年上海国际航运研究中心港口发展研究所发布的《2021年全球港口发展报告》中，天津港位居全球港口排名中的第八位。

7. 香港港

香港港位于中国香港特别行政区，是亚洲重要的国际港口之一。它是一个综合性港口，包括九龙港、香港岛港和新界港等多个港区。香港港是世界著名的自由港，拥有先进的港口设施和高效的物流系统。它是全球主要的金融中心之一，也是国际贸易和航运的重要节点。作为亚洲重要的集装箱港口之一，香港港处理大量的货物运输，与世界各地的港口保持紧密联系。同时，香港港也是重要的客运港口，连接着国际航线和内地航线，方便人员流动和旅游交流。香港港注重发展高科技和智能港口，引入先进技术和管理理念，提高港口运营的效率和安全性。它致力于保持竞争力，为香港及周边地区的经济发展提供支持。香港港在2021年上海国际航运研究中心港口发展研究所发布的《2021年全球港口发展报告》中，香港港位居全球港口排名中的第九位。

（三）主要研究内容

本文首先介绍了海洋运输碳排放数据库的建立以及评价研究的选题背景与研究意义，并介绍了海运碳排放计算的基本方法，为后面的各种计算、分析做铺垫。在此基础上，利用计算方法中需要的参数，对七个在《2021年全球港口发展报告》中排名前十的国内港口的数据进行了收集和处理，在此基础上计算各港口的海运碳排放量并进行分析，最后做总结及展望。

（四）本文组织结构

本文一共分为四个部分：

（1）研究背景：本文从选题背景与研究意义、主要港口概况、研究内容方面进行背景介绍。

（2）数据及方法：本文阐述了数据如何选取、处理，并且介绍了CO_2排放的计算方法。

（3）结果分析：分析各港口海运CO_2排放量随时间的变化情况，并对各港口主要贸易国海运CO_2排放量进行对比，对我国海洋交通运输业规模现状、时空发展差异及我国与世界海洋交通运输业能源消费及碳排放现状进行了分析。

（4）总结及展望：本文在上一章基础上，对本文研究的七个港口的CO_2排放量情况进行了分析，对研究中所做的工作和得出的结论进行总结，然后从企业和政府层面有针对性地提出建议，同时还进行了展望。

二、计算方法及数据来源

（一）碳排放计算方法

海运过程中产生的碳排放量的计算方法主要基于货物运输的距离，即起运地／起运港与目的地／目的港之间的距离，货物运输的重量和海运碳排放因子这三个要素，其公式如下：

$$CO_2\ emissions = \frac{Tonnes * \mu(nm) * \mu(kgCO_2\ per\ tonne/nm)}{1000000} \tag{2.1}$$

公式 2.1 中，CO_2 emissions 指的是货物的CO_2总排放量；Tonnes 指的是运输的货物重量；$\mu(nm)$指的是运输距离；$\mu(kgCO_2\ per\ tonne/nm)$指的是海运碳排放因子。该公式中，唯一的不确定参数是碳排放因子，因为不同的机构和国家地区对于碳排放因子有不同的标准，所以在具体计算碳排放量时，需要按照货物运输的地理区域情况选择不同的碳排放因子。

第二种计算海运碳排放的方法是基于燃料类型，该方法首先构造了一个排放因子EVDI，它就相当于碳排放因子，但精确到了船舶类型，公式如下：

$$EVDI_i = \frac{\sum P_i * C_F * SFC}{DWT_i * speed_i} \tag{2.2}$$

其中，P_i为船舶 i 的主、辅机能耗水平（kW）；$speed_i$为船舶均速，C_F表示油耗与CO_2排放之间的转换系数；DWT_i为船舶最大载重；SFC 为船舶不同负荷下的油耗比（g/kWh）。

计算出 EVDI 因子后，总CO_2排放量可以表示为：

$$CE_{i,j} = S_{i,j} * EVDI_i * D_j \tag{2.3}$$

公式（2.3）中，$S_{i,j}$是船舶容量（tonnes）；EVDI代表船舶本身的碳排放因子；D_j距离（km）则是货物运输的距离。

该方法通过获取运输货物船舶的发动机功率P_i，SFC燃油消耗率、速度和最大载重等数据，获得船舶燃油消耗的水平。再乘以油耗与CO_2排放之间的转换系数 CF，得到了船舶每吨千米的 CO_2 排放量，最后用货物重量*EVDI*距离得到总的 CO_2 排放量。

由于在实际的查询数据的过程中，像运输货物的船舶型号这种数据的获取难度很高，这就造成获取不到船舶的引擎功率、燃油类型等相关数据的情况，所以以港口为例计算时，我们选择采取基于运输距离的 CO_2 计算方法。计算流程如图 1 所示。

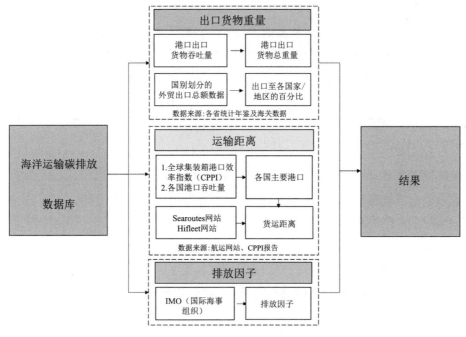

图 1　碳排放计算流程

（二）数据来源

1. 货物重量

本次计算以年为时间尺度，计算每年的 CO_2 排放量，在数据查询的过程中，以上海港为例，通过查询《2022 年上海市统计年鉴》①中第十五篇表 15-8 确定每年上海港的出口港口货物吞吐量，如表 1 所示。

---

① 上海市统计局. 2022 年上海市统计年鉴. (2023-02-06)[2024-04-15]. https://tjj.sh.gov.cn/tjnj/tjnj2022.htm.

表 1　上海港 2015—2021 年货物吞吐量　　（单位：万吨）

年份	港口货物吞吐量	其中		进港	其中		出港	其中	
		内贸	外贸		内贸	外贸		内贸	外贸
2015	71740	33943	37797	41907	21447	20460	29833	12495	17337
2016	70177	32164	38012	40295	20039	20256	29882	12126	17756
2017	75051	34008	41043	43315	21182	22133	31736	12826	18910
2018	73048	32842	40206	41931	21445	20486	31117	11397	19720
2019	72031	32372	39659	41500	21584	19916	30531	10788	19743
2020	71670	32753	38917	42810	23489	19321	28860	9264	19596
2021	77635	36146	41489	45774	26172	19602	31861	9974	21887

（资料来源：《2022 年上海市统计年鉴》）

在查询过程中发现有的港口货物吞吐量只有进出口的总和，例如深圳港口货物吞吐量。

所以我们查询出 2015—2021 年深圳港的进出口总额，以出口额占进出口总额的占比乘以进出口货物吞吐量来得到表 3 水运出口的货物吞吐量。

得出港口的出口货物吞吐量后，以出口港口货物吞吐量作为货物重量来计算。吞吐量作为一个综合性指标，包括了港口处理的各类货物流量，而不是局限于进出口货物。因此，使用吞吐量计算 CO_2 排放可以更全面地覆盖港口的业务范围，包括转口货物、内河货物以及其他与港口业务相关的活动。然后根据《2022 年上海市统计年鉴》第七篇 7—3 主要年份按国家（地区）分的上海关区出口总额[①]，确定出口的国家（地区），如表 2 所示，由于国家（地区）较多，本文只选取了 2021 年出口额排名前 8 的国家（地区）进行列举分析。

表 2　上海关区向主要国家（地区）出口额　　（单位：亿美元）

国家（地区）	出口额						
	2015 年	2016 年	2017 年	2018 年	2019 年	2020 年	2021 年
中国香港	260.67	249	252.5	268.03	262.8	234.82	267.69
中国台湾	137	139.29	149.05	161.37	184.99	211.09	247.85
日　本	474.49	435.14	435	462.24	431.48	412.6	458.34
韩　国	212.3	203.74	198.77	213.02	224.05	224.01	280.59

---

① 上海市统计局. 2022 年上海市统计年鉴. (2023-02-06)[2024-04-15]. https://tjj.sh.gov.cn/tjnj/tjnj2022.htm.

续表

国家 （地区）	出口额						
	2015年	2016年	2017年	2018年	2019年	2020年	2021年
新加坡	117.74	104.8	113.33	117.66	106.48	110.65	120.9
马来西亚	78.47	78.97	85.31	95.77	97.8	93.4	118.71
泰　国	99.26	100.48	109.65	116.87	117.22	108.03	152.49
菲律宾	49.7	44.95	51.96	62.02	72.75	57.51	71.38
巴基斯坦	32.55	46.09	49.13	46.97	47.48	45.44	57.32
科威特	5.48	5.66	7.05	6.94	7.64	8.09	5.84
沙特阿拉伯	34.23	27.58	26.88	26.39	30.71	34.11	38.37
阿联酋	49.2	45.33	42.1	43.55	58.15	58.99	62.09
埃　及	16.43	18.63	19.68	23.05	21.25	21.07	32.09
南　非	3.2	2.41	2.69	1.91	1.84	1.99	1.64
德　国	186.34	174.65	184.21	204.41	197	208.96	256.59
法　国	75.35	71.91	79.06	83.79	83.85	99.69	114.42
意大利	84.83	79.83	86.88	96.37	90.16	91.4	113.77
荷　兰	167.3	135.51	177.77	184.33	159.07	157.73	210.84
英　国	142.14	125.96	128.61	132.9	133.62	154.36	170.49
瑞　典	19.52	18.25	19.77	21.23	20.67	20.3	27.33
俄罗斯	55.68	54.14	65.5	74.09	73.31	74.84	98.35
美　国	1127.24	1114.53	1199.32	1309.02	1118.52	1143.08	1404.09
加拿大	75.11	70.52	82.46	88.74	81.98	94.92	114.86
巴　西	76.11	61.6	75.74	89.73	87.98	91.07	137.46
智　利	25.89	26.17	28.16	33	31.05	31.28	49.86
澳大利亚	118.27	115.08	129.06	140.87	129.29	143	178.18
新西兰	13.5	14.37	15.87	17.97	16.46	16.63	24.83
总　额	5005.80	4798.74	5166.76	5624.46	5402.44	5420.69	6761.63

（资料来源：《2022年上海市统计年鉴》）

其余港口方法同上所述，由此可以得出每个国家（地区）的出口货物总重量。

2. 运输距离

在运输距离的获取上，首先根据上文中确定的出口国家或地区，选择出口国家或地区的港口，再获取上海港到出口国家或地区港口的距离，出口国或地区的海港选择依据为《2022 年全球集装箱港口效率指数》（The Container Port Performace Index 2022）[1]全球集装箱港口效率指数（CPPI）前 50 名，若其中无该国海港，则选择该国（地区）每年货物吞吐量前三的海港，若仍无法确定，可根据海运网站物流巴巴选择该国（地区）主要的国际贸易海港，每个国家（地区）选择的港口数小于等于 3 个，如表 3 所示，以上海港为例，其中CPPI列出了排名前 50 的港口。

表 3　国家（地区）主要海港（部分）及距离（以上海港为例）

国家 / 地区	主要港口	距离（海里）	CPPI 排名
日本	横滨	1024	15
	神户	818	45
	名古屋	925	46
	清水	961	47
美国	威尔明顿	10341	44
	波士顿	10864	/
	杰克逊维尔	10243	/
德国	汉堡	10928	/
	不来梅	10911	/
	威廉港	10866	/
韩国	釜山	482	22
	丽水	925	23
	仁川	471	37
新加坡	新加坡	2198	18
	裕廊	2202	/
马来西亚	巴生港	2388	36
	丹戎帕拉帕斯港	2219	6
	槟城	2623	/

（资料来源：The Container Port Performace Index 2022）

确定好出口国家（地区）的海港之后，根据航运距离查询网站（如Searoutes[2]或hifleet[3]），对海港进行定位，查询上海港到这些国家（地区）海

[1]　Word Bank. The Container Port Performance Index 2022: A Comparable Assessment of Performance Based on Vessel Time in Port, 2023.
[2]　Searoutes. Reduce your Carbon Emissions with our APIs. [2024-04-15]. https://app.searoutes.com/routing.
[3]　上海迈利船舶科技有限公司. 船队在线hiFleet. (2023-11-03)[2024-04-15]. https://www.hifleet.com/.

港的距离。查出上海港到所有出口国（地区）港口的距离后，分别对上海港与各国（地区）港口的海运距离进行平均，使用平均值作为上海港到该国（地区）的货运距离。

3. 排放因子

根据前述的碳排放量计算公式，参考国际海事组织（IMO）2020年度第四期温室气体排放报告[①]中的船舶的2008—2018年的国际碳强度估计值，选择2015—2018年的EEOI（船舶能源效率运营指标）作为本次计算的碳排放因子，因为港口数据属于2015—2021年，所以2015—2018年采用对应的EEOI值，2019—2021年采用2015—2018年的EEOI平均值。

EOI（Energy Efficiency Operational Indicator）是指能源效率运营指标，也被称为EEOI（Energy Efficiency Operational Indicator）。它是用于衡量船舶的能源效率和碳排放水平的指标。EEOI在航运行业中被广泛采用，特别是在国际海事组织的能效设计指南和能效管理规定中。船舶经营者可以使用EEOI作为一种管理工具，监测和比较船舶的能源效率，推动能源节约和减少碳排放的措施，并符合相关的环保法规和要求。EEOI参考值如表4所示。

表4　IMO第四次温室气体评估碳排放强度　　　单位：($gCO_2/t/nm$)

年份	EEOI			
	Vessel-based		Voyage-based	
	Value	Change	Value	Change
2008	17.10	—	15.16	—
2012	13.16	−23.1%	12.19	−19.6%
2013	12.87	−24.7%	11.83	−22.0%
2014	12.34	−27.9%	11.29	−25.6%
2015	12.33	−27.9%	11.30	−25.5%
2016	12.22	−28.6%	11.21	−26.1%
2017	11.87	−30.6%	10.88	−28.2%
2018	11.67	−31.8%	10.70	−29.4%

表4中，EEOI里的vessel-based是以船舶为单位计算能源效率和碳排放。它基于船舶的运营数据和燃油消耗来评估船舶的整体能源效率。通过监测船舶

[①] IMO. Fourth Greenhouse Gas Study 2020. (2020-08-04)[2024-04-15]. https://www.imo.org/en/OurWork/Environment/Pages/Fourth-IMO-Greenhouse-Gas-Study-2020.aspx.

的燃油消耗和航行活动数据，可以计算出每海里航行消耗的燃油量，从而确定船舶的能源效率水平。这种方法适用于长期评估和比较船舶的能源效率，以及监测船队的整体表现。而 voyage-based 则是以航次为单位计算能源效率和碳排放。它基于单个航次的运营数据和燃油消耗来评估船舶在特定航次中的能源效率。相较而言，vessel-based 方法更适合本次计算，因为 voyage-based 方法更适合对特定航次的能源效率进行评估和比较。

通过上述方法得出海运距离、运输重量以及碳排放因子的值后，利用公式（2.1）计算，可估算出 2015—2021 年每年各港口出口货物的海运碳排放量。下一节将展示初步的计算结果。

三、结果分析

（一）七大港口海运碳排放总量变化

上海港的海运碳排放量远超其他六个港口，原因是上海港是中国第一大港，是我国沿海的主要枢纽港，在我国对外开放和参与国际大循环中具有重要地位，因此其海运碳排放量远高于其他港口。碳排放量排名第二的是天津港，是中国重要的对外贸易港口之一，是中国经济发展的重要支撑，其货物吞吐量和集装箱吞吐量均居全球前列，因此碳排放量也相对较高。深圳港和广州港的碳排放量不相上下，主要原因可能在于两者的地理位置相近，与其进行贸易的地区和贸易商品差别较小，因此碳排放量也相近。碳排放量相对较小的三个港分别是青岛港、舟山港和香港港，其主要贸易国距离较近，贸易量相对较小，因此海运碳排放量也较少。

（二）各港口海运碳排放量变化

1. 上海港

从碳排放总额上看，2015—2019 年上海港碳排放量波动不大，表明其在国际大环境影响之下依旧保持着良好运转。从贸易伙伴的角度看，美国、荷兰和德国是上海港的主要出口国家，并且多年以来始终保持着良好的贸易关系。

2. 宁波舟山港

从碳排放总额上看，相较于前六年的平稳变化，宁波舟山港 2021 年的碳排放量锐增。这与浙江省出台的相关政策脱不开关系。而与其他港口相比，宁波舟山港的出口海运碳排放量并不高，只有上海港的 50% 左右。这是由于宁波舟山港在外贸层面主要经营的是进港业务，舟山市统计数据显示，出港外贸只占总外贸吞吐量的3.3%。从贸易伙伴的角度看，美国、俄罗斯、德国和意大利是2015—2017年宁波舟山港的主要出口国，而2019—2021年，宁波舟山港与英国的贸易关系日渐紧密。

3. 深圳港

在2015—2021年，深圳港的海运碳排放量有所增加，但也存在年份间的波动。2015—2017年碳排放量增长，2018年下降至2015年的水平，随后到2021年又增长至2018年的水平。深圳港出口的货物吞吐量的碳排放量整体呈现出波动增长的趋势。增长的原因可能是深圳港是中国的重要港口之一，随着中国经济的发展和出口贸易的增加，深圳港的货物吞吐量也相应增加。货物的装卸和运输过程需要消耗能源，从而导致碳的排放量增加。而下降的原因可能是，深圳作为中国的特区，一直致力于环境保护和可持续发展。港口运营商和相关企业可能采取了一系列的环保措施，如节能减排技术的应用、绿色航运的推广等，以减少碳排放量。

在这八个贸易国中，深圳港出口到美国的碳排放量最高，分别紧随其后的是英国和德国这些经济发达国家，其工业生产、消费需求和贸易规模较大，并且距离较远，导致了较高的排放量。在这八个与深圳贸易的国家里的亚洲国家中，日本的碳排放量是最高的，日本作为一个工业化国家，在制造业和贸易活动中产生了大量的碳排放。而韩国、新加坡和马来西亚的碳排放量相对较低。这些国家的经济结构和能源消耗状况与发达国家有所不同，因此排放量相对较小。总的来看，从2015年到2021年，各国的碳排放量都经历了波动。这可能受到全球经济状况、能源结构、环境政策和贸易活动的影响。

4. 广州港

通过计算得出2015—2021年广州港出口海运产生的碳排放量，根据计算出的数据，广州港的出口海运碳排放量在2015年至2021年呈逐年增加的趋势。从增长需求和贸易活动来看，广州港作为一个重要的国际贸易港口，随着中国经济的快速增长，贸易活动的增加导致船舶进出港口的次数和货物吞吐量的增加。这意味着更多的船舶运行和物流运输活动，从而增加了能源消耗和碳排放量。同时全球航运行业在这段时间内也出现了增长，广州港作为一个重要的航运枢纽，承担着更多的航线和船舶。船舶通常使用石油燃料作为能源，燃烧石油燃料会产生大量的二氧化碳排放。所以碳排放呈逐年递增的趋势。

美国在这八个主要贸易国家中的碳排放量最高,其次是德国、英国和荷兰。这些国家的排放量可能与其经济规模、工业发展和能源消耗水平有关,还有一个重要的原因是这些国家距离广州港的距离都较远,所以会造成碳排放量高。香港作为广州港的邻近地区和重要贸易伙伴,碳排放量却不是最低的。这可能是由于香港作为一个国际金融和物流中心,其经济活动和相关贸易导致了较高的能源消耗和排放。

越南和印度作为新兴经济体,其碳排放量在这些年份中也有显著增长。这反映了这些国家经济快速发展、工业化进程加快以及与广州港的贸易增加。

根据数据,在 2015—2021 年,出口到这八个国家的碳排放量整体呈增长趋势,这很可能与经济增长和贸易活动的增加有关。

5. 青岛港

2015—2021 年青岛港海运碳排放量整体呈现上升趋势,由 2015 年的289587.81 吨上升至 2021 年的 470764.96 吨,增幅达 62.56%。具体而言,2015—2018 年呈现上升趋势,2017 年有轻微下降,主要原因可能在于 2017 年全球经济大萧条引发大宗商品低迷、贸易投资保护主义抬头、金融市场震荡加剧等一系列问题影响了各国之间的贸易往来,因此青岛港的海运碳排放量也随之减少。2018 年,全球经济逐步向好,各国贸易往来逐渐恢复,海运碳排放量因此呈现明显上升趋势。2019 年,中美贸易摩擦加剧,中美两国之间的贸易往来减少,因此 2019 年的海运碳排放量显著下降。2020 年,中美贸易关系有所缓解,但新冠疫情在全球范围内暴发,严重阻碍了全球经济发展和贸易往来,因此 2020 年海运碳排放量有所上升但并不显著。2021 年全球新冠疫情正走向终结,全球经济逐步复苏,各国贸易往来逐步恢复正常,因此海运碳排放量也呈现升高趋势。

2015—2021 年,在青岛港的八个主要贸易国中,对美国出口贸易过程中的海运碳排放量始终占据相当大的比例,并且碳排放量变化波动比较明显,说明碳排放量不仅与环境生态息息相关,也会受到各国经济政治关系的影响。其次是巴西、日本、澳大利亚三国,其中,对巴西和澳大利亚出口贸易过程中产生的碳排放量增长趋势相对稳定。在对韩国、南非、阿根廷、智利四国进行出口贸易过程中产生的碳排放量差距不大,并且变化趋势均较稳定。

6. 天津港

从天津港的排名前八的重要贸易国角度上看,在 2015—2021 年美国始终是海运过程中产生最多碳排放的贸易国，其中在 2016 年已超过 350 万吨。尽管由于贸易战和新冠疫情，2019－2020 年碳排放量锐减，但美国仍然在其中占很大比重，其次是德国、俄罗斯与印度。在 2016－2021 年，碳排放量呈现出逐渐下降的变化趋势，而在 2021 年又有所上升，说明对外贸易在疫情后期有所恢复，2021 年天津港碳排放总量超过 280 万吨。值得注意的是，2016－2020 年，天津港海洋交通运输行业碳排放总量整体呈现出下降的变化趋势，这是由于在"十三五"期间，政府大力推动建设发展绿色低碳的交通运输行业，因此在 2013－2015 年，我国海洋交通运输行业能源消费量增长趋于平缓，这说明新能源的使用和节能减排政策对碳排放量的减少产生了一定的影响。

7. 香港港

香港港为远东的航运中心，在珠江口外侧，香港岛和九龙半岛之间。香港港是全球最繁忙和最高效的国际集装箱港口之一，也是全球供应链上的主要枢纽港。从其 2015－2021 年海运碳排放量变化趋势来看，2015－2018 年基本平稳，2015 年碳排放量最高，接近 12 万吨，2019 年之后有明显下降，特别是 2020 年，碳排放量不足 8 万吨。其中，美国始终是海运过程中产生最多碳排放的贸易国，大约占了全部比重的 80%，其次是德国、日本与荷兰。

四、数据库介绍

本数据库平台采用Java语言，使用VSCode进行网页编程，收集统计年鉴等权威数据进行港口选择、碳排放因子选择及碳排放量计算，最终建立了一个网页可视化数据平台。下面将介绍本数据库平台的具体功能。

（一）港口切换

如图 2 所示，本平台目前对国内的 7 个港口的碳排放量进行了计算。通过点击，即可实现数据和各项指标的切换。值得注意的是，平台的五项可视化图表均是交互型图表，将鼠标光标移动至对应数据点，会显示该点的详细数据。

图 2　切换港口及数据展示功能

（二）出口额数据与出口重量查看

如图 3 所示，本平台对于计算使用到的出口额数据和出口重量进行了逐年度的展示。上方显示了各港口主要的出口贸易伙伴及对应的贸易额，下方显示其逐年度的出口重量。同时，下方的时间轴会与图表一样自动执行动态切换，生动地展现两项指标随时间的变化趋势。

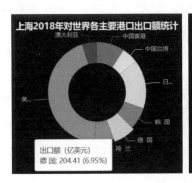 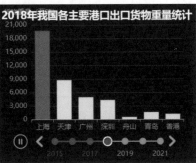

图 3　出口数据展示功能

（三）航运路线查看

本平台采用地图的形式展示港口与港口之间的贸易距离，采用飞线的形式连接对应港口，并在飞线上方标注目的地与距离。同时，该地图可以通过鼠标左右拖拽，将地图左右移动。同时也可以通过鼠标滚轮对地图进行放大和缩小操作。

五、总结及展望

对海运的碳排放量进行计算可以评估和监测港口碳足迹。港口海运出口货物吞吐量的碳排放量计算涉及多个关键方面。首先，需要收集相关数据，包括货物吞吐量、运输距离、出口国等。这些数据可以从港口运营商、海关统计、各省市统计年鉴、国际贸易数据中获取。收集的数据必须准确、全面，并与国际标准和指南保持一致。本文以我国的七个港口为例估算其海运碳排放，这种计算可以帮助港口管理机构和相关利益相关者了解港口运营对气候变化的影响，并采取措施减少碳排放，促进可持续发展。

在计算过程中，常用的方法是采用温室气体排放计算方法，关注主要的温室气体，如二氧化碳。计算的是货物吞吐量的碳排放量。使用排放因子来计算，排放因子可以根据国际标准、科学研究或行业实践确定，以确保计算的准确性和可比性。本文限于数据的可获取性，只计算了港口每年的总碳排放量，如果需要更精细化，则可以计算航次的碳排放量，并且碳排放因子可以精确到船只级别，这样可以更针对性地采取一些新技术和创新解决方案降低碳排放量，例如，推广使用低碳燃料、增加船舶能效、采用电动化设备和智能能源管理系统等，以降低能源消耗和碳排放。此外，港口还可以参与碳市场和碳抵消项目，通过减排项目和碳抵消手段来减少碳排放并获得经济激励。

在未来，港口行业的发展还需要注重数据的透明度和标准化。建立统一的数据收集和报告机制，推动港口行业采用共同的计算方法和指标，有助于形成可比较的碳排放数据和绩效指标。政府和国际组织的政策支持和合作对于推动港口的碳减排目标至关重要。制定和执行碳减排政策、鼓励能源转型和可持续发展，以及促进国际合作与信息交流，都有助于推动港口行业的碳减排。

ESG投资模式与市场评级指标体系比较研究
——基于主流ESG评级体系方法手册的分析与讨论①

摘　要: 本文主要讨论当今主流ESG评级体系,分析了它们的共性与差别。本文发现,大多数ESG评级体系都将ESG评级分为环境、社会和治理三个维度,并根据具体行业的外部性确定关键的实质性议题,然后对其进行综合评估和加权;此外,大多数评级体系都会对缺乏ESG信息披露的公司进行惩罚性减分。然而,不同的ESG评级体系也有不同,尤其是在实质性议题的识别、计算权重的过程以及原始数据的收集机制方面。本文还对目前主流ESG评级体系的优缺点进行了总结,并对建设富有中国特色的ESG评级体系提出了一些建议,以更好地促进我国ESG投资模式的发展。应坚持"罚分"机制,激励企业公开其ESG绩效;应推进建设更加公正客观的原始数据采集系统,防止企业"漂绿";应针对具体实质性议题的ESG评级机制应考虑不同地区的具体实践,使评级体系更加有效。

关键词: ESG投资模式;ESG评级体系;"漂绿"

一、ESG报告概述

(一)ESG报告基本概述

ESG,即 environmental(环境)、social(社会)和 governance(治理)三

---

① 作者:江嘉文,浙江大学外国语学院;杨启帆,浙江大学外国语学院;管子仪,浙江大学外国语学院;严致昊,浙江大学外国语学院。

个英文单词的首字母缩写，是一种全新的经济模式，由环境、社会和治理三个要素组成，用以评估投资和商业模式的可持续性。在ESG模式下，企业要兼顾环境影响、社会责任和内部治理，以达成可持续发展。其在实现自身利益的同时也要为社会创造价值，改善公民生活条件和生态系统，打造负责任的企业形象。

ESG报告是公司或投资者披露其在环境、社会和治理方面的表现和做法的一种途径。报告旨在提供有关公司可持续性和社会责任的信息，帮助投资者、利益相关者和其他利益相关方评估企业的综合业绩和风险。

（二）投资模式与ESG评级关系概述

ESG基金进行投资时，通常会采取一定的策略来选择投资标的。企业的ESG表现与效益越好，企业的盈利能力和可持续性往往更加优秀，这也是近年来投资者主动整合ESG投资理念的原因之一。

根据深圳证交所的研究结果[①]，结合本研究团队的分析，我们发现投资者常见的ESG投资策略主要包含以下7种。

1. ESG整合：将ESG风险和机会纳入传统财务分析和投资决策，包括在主流投资分析中考虑财务因素的同时考虑ESG因素；

2. 负面筛选：剔除ESG指标中评价负面的公司，如出现争议性、有违社会公德甚至违反法规等行为的公司；

3. 参与公司治理：投资者在将ESG信息纳入自身决策考虑的同时，被允许以股东的身份直接参与标的公司的治理；

4. 可持续主题投资：遵循同类最佳法或正面筛选法，即投资组合经理投资可持续性评级和状况最好的发行人；

5. 社会责任投资（影响力投资）：对公司、组织和基金的投资，而且该投资以获得财务回报的同时产生社会与环境影响、社会责任为目的，在ESG指导准则下行使股东权力参与企业治理、决策以及行为；

6. 正面筛选：投资者选择投资某一行业或领域中ESG表现较好的公司或项目，按照一定的评分标准，选择满足ESG和财务评估的公司；

7. 国际惯例筛选（规范筛选）：根据国际惯例规范 8OECD 或联合国等发布

---

① 《读懂ESG基金》第四集：读懂ESG基金之投资策略. (2022-07-19)[2024-01-01]. http://www.szse.cn/www/investor/index/update/t20220719_594899.html.

的规范筛选符合最低商业标准的公司。

以上策略都高度依赖ESG评级，投资者需要通过市场评级机构提供的ESG绩效信息来配置ESG有关资产，尤其是负面筛选、正面筛选、可持续主题投资等策略。不同国家和地区由于各自的经济和社会条件不同，其主流ESG投资策略亦有所不同，ESG评级指标体系的构成要素也有同有异。本文试从ESG投资模式、ESG评级指标体系两方面入手，跨国、跨机构探究ESG投资的不同路径，最终为构建我国的ESG投资模式和评级体系提出建设性建议。

二、ESG 投资指标体系

（一）全球主要市场评级机构采纳的ESG评级体系

随着ESG投资理念得到越来越多投资者的青睐，市场评级机构也通过公开信息来对上市公司进行环境、社会和治理表现评估，参照传统财务信用评级对不同公司的ESG表现进行"分级画档"，一年一度向市场投资者公布有关评级数据。一些传统市场评级机构，如穆迪（Moody）、标普（S&P）、明晟（MSCI）等，以及一些新兴ESG评级机构如Sustainalytics, Refinitiv等也都向市场提供多元化的ESG评级服务。它们采纳的评级体系有同有异，总体上反映了趋同的ESG投资理念，但不同体系采取的具体指标和数据处理方法又不尽相同，最终也导致了不同机构的评级结果有所差异。

1.共性特点

第一，在ESG投资理念的指导下，大部分评级机构（除KPL之外）都普遍将ESG评级分为三个大的维度，即环境维度（environment pillar），社会维度（social pillar）及治理维度（governance pillar）。其中，环境维度和社会维度包括许多实质性议题（material issue），具体的关键议题因行业而异，主要包括气候变化、环境污染、能源消耗、自然资源利用、绿色科技创新等环境指标，以及员工待遇和福利保障、产品和服务质量等其他指标。ESG评级机构主要通过收集上市公司ESG年报和其他开源信息来判断公司的环境和社会绩效，以及其他一些辅助信息收集手段包括向上市公司发放问卷等等。治理维度主要包括商业行为（corporate behavior）、公司管理结构（管理层、董事会）、公司员工薪资情况、公司财务状况等议题，对于诸多主流评级机构，公司治理的量纲是普遍适用于所有行业的，不会因行业自身特点而在治理有关议题设置上发生改变。其他一些评级机构，包括标普等，也都实行类似的评级分类方法和政策。

第二，所有评级机构的ESG投资评级都是"产业关联"（industry-related）的，这意味着ESG评级办法和关注的主要议题与被评级公司所在行业的具体情况高度相关。"产业关联"这一特征主要表现为两点。

首先，评级机构会对不同ESG议题赋予不一样的权重。几乎所有评级机构都会参照不同行业的自身特点，确定与该行业密切相关的ESG议题，即实质性议题（material issues and themes）。

其次，由于不同行业的商业模式（business model）、商业运营（business operation）等方面都存在很大差异，ESG投资理念本身又是多元化的，不同行业面临着不一样的ESG风险与挑战，如何剥离所在行业的干扰、客观公允地展现ESG绩效是所有评级机构面临的难题。不同于传统信用市场评级，机构可以依据统一的会计标准分析上市公司披露的财务数据，用同样的量纲来对公司的财务表现进行评级，两家处于不同行业的公司也可以被"分出高下"；换而言之，传统财务信用评级的量纲是普适的。然而，在ESG评级场景中，不同企业面临不一样的实质性议题，量纲往往也并不统一，ESG评级的结果也并不直观。因此，主流ESG评级机构如明晟、Refinitiv，都采取了"相对评估法"，首先计算统一行业中不同企业在特定议题下的得分，再通过同业比较（peer comparison）来确定该企业在行业中ESG表现的地位。这也是ESG评级体系"行业关联"的一种体现。

第三，ESG评级体系普遍重视信息披露，惩罚信息缺失，鼓励信息透明。由于市场评级机构的评价方法应当公允、公正，对所有利益攸关方可及的公开市场信息便是有关机构做出ESG评级的主要依据。由于ESG投资理念的普及，越来越多的上市公司开始定期地披露环境、社会和治理报告以向投资者阐明其承担社会责任做出的努力，市场监管机构和证券交易所也制定了各类准则以指引企业披露有关信息。但是，部分企业的ESG信息披露仍然不到位，对部分实质性议题的陈述存在缺失或者提供的信息不足，这阻碍了ESG评级体系的顺畅运行。因此，ESG评价机构对信息缺失的ESG议题施加惩罚性扣分，如MSCI对信息缺失的实质性议题采用设置默认赋分（default value）为0—3分的统一处理（总分为10，表现最佳为10分，表现最差为0分）。标普DJI ESG指数在发放收集公司ESG表现的问卷时，将有关实质性问题的问题设置为强制性问题，如果公司选择不披露有关信息，则标普会惩罚性地在对应议题下打出 0 分的成绩。这样的政策，有利于激励上市公司全面、完善地披露自己的ESG绩效；同时，对于披露存在不足的公司施加下调评级的压力，"不披露就罚分"的政策避免公司在ESG报告中隐藏对自己不利的陈述，促进ESG信息披露机制的进步。

第四，ESG评级体系普遍重视ESG风险，并单独为ESG"风险敞口"（risk exposure）和"风险应对"（risk management）赋予独立的权重。由于ESG实质性议题往往涉及许多不一样的非传统风险（如环境问题、监管问题、劳工保护问题等），这些风险可能以"丑闻"的形式爆发出来，或者被媒体及非政府组织揭露，最终会影响到公司的整体ESG绩效甚至正常的业务运行；因此，ESG评级体系需要将公司所面临的风险及采取的应对策略综合纳入考量。不同市场评级机构虽然采取了不一样的计算方法，但总体都将不同层次的"风险"纳入ESG评级体系中。通过计算风险的实质性影响、持续时间等等要素，评级机构通过自身的算法将风险权重整合到最终的ESG评级中，从而对投资者产生更好的风险警示作用。

（二）不同ESG评级机构的方法亮点与不足

基于对不同评级体系间共性特征的讨论，本文将深入探究 5 个颇具影响力的主流评级机构所采用的评级方法的亮点与不足。它们分别是明晟、Refinitiv、穆迪、富时罗素及KLD。

1. 明晟

明晟的ESG评级体系包括三个层次，从上到下依次为：加权平均关键议题分数（Weighted Average Key Issue Score）、维度分数（Pillar Score）、关键议题分数（Key Issue Score）。明晟ESG评级团队确认与某一行业高度相关的实质性议题，判断该行业对这些议题产生的外部性。明晟 ESG 评级团队在确认过这些外部性的相关性与影响范围大小之后，为每个行业量身定制专门的关键议题以评价他们的ESG表现。在从ESG报告等信源中收集到足够的原始数据后，专家团队据此打分，算出关键议题分数，再通过加权平均算出每个维度的分数。这种井然有序的评级体系能够比较好的将不同维度的ESG表现整合到一起，并根据不同行业的具体特征调整评分的权重，是明晟ESG评级体系的一大亮点。

　　除此之外，明晟ESG评级体系还有两大亮点：第一，在对底层指标评分时，明晟将每一个维度分成两个部分，即公司的风险敞口和管理能力。管理能力方面主要评估公司的战略和业绩表现，若发生争议事件则会扣减相应分数；而风险敞口方面则主要考虑公司的业务特征，例如核心产品特点、运营地点、生产是否外包，以及对政府订单的依赖程度。评估方式能比较完备地反映公司在特定议题下影响其ESG表现的主客观因素，既不忽视公司运营其主营业务所面临的行业共性风险，也不忽视公司自身为中和这些风险所付出的独特努力，从而更好地帮助投资者认识公司的ESG前景。

　　第二，明晟对环境和社会维度中风险和机遇所涵盖的所有议题，都设置了10级量表来进行ESG表现评估。相比其他ESG评级的定性计量方法（比如只对关键性议题设置"有＝1""无＝0"的两个评估选项），明晟能够比较贴合实际地反映公司在每个议题下的具体表现（对改善特定议题的相应程度而非简单的"有"或"无"），也更利于ESG信息使用者对不同公司进行量化的比较。

　　但是，明晟ESG评级体系也有其不足。明晟ESG在评估ESG风险时，会将公司所在的社会环境等因素纳入风险议题之中，比如公司所处的国家和社区是否存在所谓"人权侵犯"问题，公司的运营是否会造成环境污染。然而，明晟在评估ESG风险时往往又会以部分发达国家的"主流"标准和"主流"话语作为评估环境和社会风险的依据，这无疑会使得评级结果不客观、不公正。例如，光大证券在其研报中曾关注A股企业平均ESG评级偏低的因素，认为明晟在计算风险敞口时对处于中国公司的"地理位置层面"打分较低，部分影响了中国企业的ESG评分。[1]

2. Refinitiv ESG 指数

　　Refinitiv ESG评级体系的总体结构与明晟ESG比较相像，也将具体的实质性议题归纳到环境、社会和治理三个维度中。与明晟一样，由于ESG因素的重要性在不同的行业中有所不同，Refinitiv将每个指标对每个行业的重要性赋予量化的权重（从1到10）。[2]然而，Refinitiv在具体的实质性议题选择中对不同行业没有采取差异化策略，而是一视同仁的采取同样的衡量议题和衡量标

---

[1]　祁嫣然. 橘生淮南：从中国企业评级看海外ESG评级体系的国别差异：ESG动态观察之一. (2023-03-01) [2024-01-01]. http://www.huitouyan.com/doc-67efd0e75f2d0bd5a28f0b6fc794b6c0.html.

[2]　Refinitiv. Environmental, social and governance scores from Refinitiv. [2024-01-01]. https://www.refinitiv.com/content/dam/marketing/en_us/documents/methodology/refinitiv-esg-scores-methodology.pdf.

准。相比较其他评级机构采取的差异化实质性议题的策略，这样做的优点是能够增加不同行业企业的可比性，让投资者能够更清晰地利用同一量纲来评价不同公司地ESG前景、从而安排其自身地投资组合；缺点则是不能够针对特定行业的特定议题进行全面的评价。

此外，Refinitiv ESG 评级体系还有一大优点，即单独衡量一家公司的ESG争议情况（比如被媒体曝光的丑闻等），并将其与ESG整体评分（对环境、社会和治理三个维度的加权）合并最终形成ESG controversies score，即ESG争议评分。这是一个与ESG 评级体系不同的体系，其首要通过新闻媒体的曝光情况及公司ESG声誉来判断一家公司的ESG效益。这样的评级体系能更全面地反应一家公司的ESG绩效，并惩罚爆发ESG丑闻的上市公司，从而激励这些公司约束自身行为以避免声誉受损。

当然，Refinitiv评级体系也有一点不足，即其在不少实质性议题的前期调查/数据收集中采用二元变量的形式，最终仅仅收集标记为"是"或"否"的二元数据。比如 Refinitiv ESG 评级团队在调查一家公司的环境维度ESG效益时，会发放问卷并询问是否有水资源节约政策，公司可以只作答"有"或者"无"，很可能不向Refinitiv披露其水资源节约政策实行的力度和方式。这样简单的数据收集虽然能够简化评级团队的工作流程，但其会省略大量有利于精确评估ESG效益的数据，也有可能被企业的"漂绿"或者"漂蓝"行为所欺骗。

"漂绿"（green-washing）一词衍生自"漂白"（white-washing），是可持续发展领域最重要的术语。"漂绿"指的是"企业和金融机构夸大环保议题方面的付出与成效的行为"[①]，在企业社会责任报告中对自身环境保护和资源利用的表现做出言过其实的披露。企业可以利用绿色金融有关界定的模糊性和信息披露准则的制度漏洞，夸大自身环保绩效，或者通过选择性披露、碎片化披露、释放无关紧要的道德信号等方式"漂绿"。例如，企业通过宣传其发起的植树活动以彰显其在减少碳排放方面的努力，然而该宣传方式对实际减少碳排放的效果微乎其微。"漂绿"行为会严重削弱ESG信息披露的质量和ESG评级体系的公信力。因此，Refinitiv完全依靠被评级公司自身披露的ESG报告以及填写的问卷，较容易被企业的"漂绿"行为所欺骗。此外，Refinitiv在水资源节约等议题方面，仅仅统计企业"有"或者"无"相关ESG政策，并没有仔细考

---

① 黄世忠.ESG报告的"漂绿"与反"漂绿".财会月刊，2022(1): 3-11.

察企业相关行为的环境绩效，相较于明晟的 10 级量表评估方式，更容易受到"漂绿"行为的干扰，不能够给投资者提供有关环境绩效的完整信息。

3. 穆迪 ESG 指数

在评估企业的环境风险时，穆迪将环境风险划分为转型风险（由于环境灾害相关政策而产生的后果）和物理风险（由于环境灾害，如污染、干旱等而造成的损失），并关注这些风险的时间性、确定性和严重性。在评估企业的社会风险时，穆迪将社会风险划分为企业特定社会风险（例如影响企业声誉的产品安全问题）和外部因素的不利影响（例如导致合规成本增加的外部监管制度）。此外，所有权控制、董事会监督有效性和管理结构也是穆迪在评估公司治理如何影响信用评级时考虑的主要因素。

穆迪的评价方法有优点和缺点。优点是它能够考虑 ESG 因素对企业信用质量的潜在影响，从多个维度评估企业的风险敞口和管理能力，并提供评级的详细解释和逻辑，增加评级的可信度和可比性。缺点是它仅使用公开资料进行评级，可能无法充分反映企业的真实 ESG 绩效，而且存在主观判断和偏差，导致评级结果与其他评级机构不一致。另外，它的评价可能无法及时捕捉 ESG 因素的变化和动态，导致评级结果滞后或过时。

4. KLD ESG 评级

KLD 是最早提供企业 ESG 绩效信息的数据供应商之一[①]。与大多数其他评级不同，KLD 没有为每家公司提供 ESG 总分，也没有分别在环境、社会和治理方面单独得分。相反，它将 ESG 绩效分为 13 个不同的类别，其中包括 7 个主要类别：环境（ENV）、社区（COM）、多样性（DIV）、员工关系（EMP）、人权（HUM）、产品（PRO）、公司治理（CGOV）和 6 个次要类别：酒精（ALC）、赌博（GAM）、火器（FIR）、军事（MIL）、核（NUC）、烟草（TOB）。KLD 的 ESG 评级是基于对 ESG 因素的专有研究概况。KLD 的研究是通过全球苏格拉底发布的，这是一个专有的数据库程序，提供 KLD 对 3000 家美国上市公司的评级和 ESG 数据。KLD STATS 表示格式 KLD STATS 提供了正面和负面 ESG 评级的二元摘要。

KLD 的评价方法的优点是它是最早提供企业 ESG 绩效信息的数据供应商之一，具有较长的历史和较大的覆盖范围，并且能够提供正面和负面 ESG

[①] Risk Metrics Group. How to Use KLD STATS & ESG Ratings Definitions. [2024-01-01]. http://www.pornsit-jiraporn.com/Getting_Started_With_KLD_STATS.pdf.

评级的二元摘要，以及相关优势劣势的分析建议，便于识别企业在各个ESG领域的优势和关注点。另外，它还能够反映企业是否涉及某些敏感行业或活动，帮助投资者进行筛选和风险管理。但是，KLD也有局限性，其缺点是它没有为每家公司提供ESG总分，也没有分别在环境、社会和治理方面单独得分，导致评级结果难以比较和整合。其次，虽然它使用二元指标来评估企业的ESG绩效有其优势，但是无法充分捕捉企业在不同ESG问题上的差异和程度。并且，KLD还使用相同的权重来计算不同类别的ESG绩效，使得其无法应用于考虑不同行业和地区具有的特性。

5. 富时罗素ESG评级

富时罗素的ESG评价体系有三层结构：第一层是环境、社会和公司治理3个支柱；第二层是14个主题指标，其中环境类指标包括生物多样性、气候变化、污染与资源、水安全、供应链环境等5项，社会类指标包括劳工标准、人权与社区、健康安全、消费者责任、供应链社会影响等5项，公司治理类指标包括反腐败、企业管理、风险管理、税收透明度等4项；第三层是适用于分析每家公司具体情况的300多个独立评估指标。指标权重的依据给出的敞口大小进行参考，最重要的ESG问题会被赋予最大的权重。最终每家符合条件的公司会获得一个分值在0至5分之间的ESG整体评分[1]。在进行ESG评分时，富时罗素仅使用公开资料，不会向公司发送调查问卷，但公司可以通过网络研究平台对评分结果进行反馈以获得可能的更正。

三、总结与讨论

（一）指标体系要素总结

通过对国际主流ESG评级机构的研究，我们认为ESG指标体系有以下三个主要要素，这三个要素直接影响了指标体系的客观性和有效性。

1. 实质性议题的设置和权重的分配

ESG投资理念包括环境、社会和治理三个维度，其中又包含数十个实质性议题，评级机构在衡量过程中需要确定重点，从而确定需要纳入衡量的议题。对于不同行业，不同议题的重要性是不一致的，因此，我们不仅需要确认

---

[1] FTSE Russel. ESG ratings and data model: Integrating ESG into investments. [2024-01-01]. Retrieved from: https://research.ftserussell.com/products/downloads/ESG-ratings-overview.pdf.

哪些议题与行业的运行相关，还要确认不同议题下的ESG评分在总体ESG绩效重点的权重。评级机构往往需要判断特定行业在进行日常生产和销售过程中有哪些利益攸关方，产生哪些正面或者负面外部性，从而确定具体的评级标准和不同议题下的权重。这一要素会直接影响到最终的评级结果，其实质性议题设置是否合理、权重分配是否科学也会决定ESG评级体系能否客观公允地反映公司和行业的ESG绩效。

2. ESG争议事件的衡量

ESG指标体系的另一个特殊之处是普遍关注ESG争议事件这一指标，并在最终的ESG评级核算中为其赋予独立的权重。由于ESG争议事件会深刻地影响一家企业的ESG绩效，将其划入指标体系中有利于更加全面反应企业的社会责任担当，同时激励企业约束自身行为，减少乃至消除ESG治理丑闻的爆发。不同于传统信用评级，许多ESG有关风险是突发的（比如环境污染，劳工权益等），往往不如财务指标那样有确定的趋势和走向；如果仅仅通过跟踪企业ESG年报来关注企业日常的ESG经营，不关注媒体曝光的各类丑闻和不作为，那么企业更容易隐藏、"漂绿"自身不负责任的行为，因此不能够充分地警示投资者有关企业的ESG风险。评级体系可以纳入ESG争议事件这一指标，为投资者提供充分的信息以做出更好的投资决策。

3. ESG风险敞口与风险管理、ESG挑战与机遇相统一

正如许多ESG评级体系方法论所阐明，ESG有关议题不仅涉及企业面临的环境、社会和治理风险，还涉及企业为应对这些ESG风险所采取的措施。风险敞口与企业的风险管理能力共同决定了企业的ESG绩效。此外，在环境和社会领域，企业既经历挑战又享有机遇。对于制造业来说，企业既会因为其生产过程会排放温室气体和产生污染而面临环境风险，又会因为其所在行业潜在的绿色转型方向享有环境机遇——企业可以通过大力研发绿色科技来在同行业中取得比较优势，从而提高潜在的ESG绩效水平[1]。因此，ESG评级体系需要综合全面地反映ESG风险敞口与风险管理、挑战与机遇的辩证关系，从而为投资者提供全面的信息以供决策。同时，该要素还直接影响到ESG投资模式的多元化进程——如本文第一部分所介绍，ESG投资模式包括ESG整合、负面筛选、正面筛选等，不同投资模式需要评级体系提供的不同层次、不同

---

① 中国电力建设集团有限公司. 中国电建 2022 社会责任报告. [2024-01-01]. https://www.powerchina.cn/module/jslib/pdfjs/web/viewer.html?file=/attach/0/1e475966ba574df5bf4b2c70a6b97b7e.pdf.

视角的评级信息作为支撑；ESG负面筛选需要有关行业企业风险敞口的有关信息，将面临特定风险敞口的企业排除在外（比如环境污染风险敞口极大的传统化工业、健康风险敞口极大的烟草业）[①]；ESG正面筛选则需要获得有关行业企业ESG机遇以选出潜在ESG绩效较好的企业。

（二）建设性建议

指标体系的目的是消除信息差，使投资者在做ESG投资决策时有更多的客观依据，从而提升投资效率；如果没有指标体系的完善，那么高效的ESG投资模式就无从谈起；ESG六大投资模式都高度依赖市场评级机构提供有关公司的ESG绩效信息和争议评分，同时如果评级体系如果不能很好地应对"漂绿"问题，那么ESG投资模式也会抵消，不会持续。部分发达国家和地区，如欧盟、新加坡等是ESG投资的典范，其国民所拥有的公司往往也有更高的ESG评级，这主要是因为这些国家对上市公司ESG信息披露的要求很高且较早开始，对其欺骗投资者的行为惩罚也很严厉，同时其鼓励企业承担社会责任的政策也更加到位。因此，这些国家和地区往往有更大的ESG投资规模，投资模式也更加多样化，更加高效；投资者在进行ESG投资时的组合选择也更多，由此进入了良性循环。

基于以上分析，本文对我国建设有中国特色的ESG评级指标体系提出4点建设性建议：

1. 议题设置合理，体现中国特色

实质性议题设置是ESG评级指标体系的核心，直接关系到指标体系的客观性和高效性，直接决定指标体系是否能够服务本国的ESG发展战略。我国作为一个社会主义国家，共同富裕和绿色发展等目标应当被纳入ESG指标体系的建设中。光大证券研究报告表明，不少中国企业致力于消除贫困、积极参与中国的扶贫项目、带动本地社区脱离贫困的同时改善当地社区的方方面面；然而国外评级机构在进行ESG评级时，并没有将以上有关脱贫攻坚的指标纳入ESG评级的社会维度中[②]。因此，我们在建设有中国特色的ESG评级体系

---

① 中国石油. 公司2022年度环境、社会和治理报告. (2023-03-30)[2024-01-01]. https://file.finance.sina.com.cn/211.154.219.97:9494/MRGG/CNSESH_STOCK/2023/2023-3/2023-03-30/8929792.PDF.

② 祁嫣然. 金融工程ESG市场跟踪双周报：HKMA发布银行业净零转型规划，首只主动管理ESG债基即将发售光大证券. (2023-09-17)[2024-01-01]. Retrieved from: http://www.huitouyan.com/doc-f6f81d1362372f8cf18a3eb0e8caddfc.html.

中，需要充分考虑实质性议题的设置，体现我国的政治经济发展目标，更好地激励企业投身到环境保护和社会发展的事业中。

2. 充分考虑发展中国家情况，实事求是地设立评级标准

由于现行国际社会中部分西方发达国家仍然享有巨大的话语权和规则制定权，ESG 指标体系中蕴含的话语权不平等问题也伤害了广大发展中国家的利益。广大发展中国家由于自身的经济水平和社会形态，其公司在应对西方发达国家的 ESG 标准时往往处于劣势地位，ESG 投资指标体系如果不充分考虑发展中国家的情况，ESG 评价体系便可能对发展中国家的企业产生"歧视"，进一步调低它们的 ESG 绩效，从而恶化发展中国家公司的融资能力，使他们游离于广大 ESG 投资市场之外。例如，发展中国家自身由于经济水平较低、科技实力不足，可能难以严格遵守发达国家 ESG 指标体系对于绿色环保的要求。此外，发达国家在社会维度的 ESG 指标体系可能仅仅适合于其本国国情，而没有充分考虑发展中国家的基本面和社会情况。因此，ESG 指标体系应当充分考虑不同国家、不同地区的具体情况，实事求是地设立 ESG 评级标准。

3. 完善罚分机制，充分激励企业公布完善、全面的 ESG 绩效数据

ESG 信息披露是维系 ESG 指标体系运转的重要保证，国际主流 ESG 评级机构一般都采用罚分机制；对不提供 ESG 绩效数据的公司，ESG 评级机构往往直接默认最差 ESG 绩效选项，从而惩罚企业不披露 ESG 绩效的行为。目前，虽然越来越多的中国企业开始编写 ESG 年报以公布 ESG 有关数据，但是我们的信息披露水平总体仍然低于国际先进水平，这也不利于我国 ESG 投资的展开，客观上导致了我国上市公司 ESG 整体评级的下降。因此，我国的评级机构可以进一步完善 ESG 信息披露罚分机制，激励企业公布完善全面的 ESG 绩效数据；同时投资者在利用 ESG 指标体系时应当关注企业的整体披露水平，同时采用负面筛选等投资模式来排除信息不透明的企业，从而激励企业打通 ESG 绩效披露机制，以获得更多 ESG 投资者的青睐。

4. 力求数据来源客观公正，严厉打击"漂绿"行为

ESG 评级体系是否客观公正还取决于 ESG 评级背后的数据来源是否客观，是否能真实反映企业的 ESG 绩效，否则就会被企业的"漂绿"文字游戏所干扰。搭建透明、独立的 ESG 信息收集以及评估的法律框架和行业标准，能够

压缩企业"漂绿"的"灰色空间"[1]。ESG评级数据的来源应包括公开披露文件、财务报表、环境监测数据、员工调查等。通过整合多样化的数据来源，可以减少信息不对称和选择性、误导性陈述，提高ESG评级的准确性和可信度。欧盟的有关标准，如《欧盟分类条例》和《可持续金融披露条例》（SFDR）等可供我们参考，这些条例在环境绩效的披露义务方面做出了明确、细致的规定，压缩了企业的漂绿空间[2]。

我国还应建立有效的监管和执法机制，主动打击"漂绿"行为。我国可以通过有关强制披露ESG信息的立法来督促企业完整、全面地公布自身环境绩效。监管机构应加强打击企业虚假陈述ESG绩效，确保企业ESG报告评估方法和数据处理过程符合规范。从内部治理的角度，应当对董事会等公司决策层的内部ESG监管做出要求（例如在董事会决策层内部设立独立的ESG委员会），并通过独立审计和内部控制来确保所披露的ESG信息的准确性和真实性。还可以充分动员第三方力量进行监督，利用媒体和NGO资源威慑企业潜在的"漂绿"动机。

---

[1]　黄世忠.ESG报告的"漂绿"与反"漂绿".财会月刊，2022(1): 3-11.
[2]　黄世忠.谱写欧盟ESG报告新篇章：从NFRD到CSRD的评述.财会月刊，2021(20): 16-23.

PART
4

第四章

世界著名博物馆建设方案

从大英博物馆"晚清百态"特展看博物馆全球化趋势与民族意识的冲突①

摘　要: 在当今世界信息化、一体化进程下,互联网与数字技术的发展推动博物馆全球化发展,博物馆面临全球化新机遇,其中大英博物馆近期举办的"晚清百态"特展属于一种全球化行为,但在国内外评论两极分化。本文着眼于该展,通过分析理顺网络环境中大英博物馆身份的定型与发酵、多个文物争端问题的结果,定量定性分析国内外各新闻传播平台的评论,结合博物馆全球化趋势和民族意识冲突,希望能在其中找到解决舆论冲突的方案,使博物馆的全球化与民族性在多样性理念下找到契合之处。

关键词: 大英博物馆;舆论空间;全球化

一、研究背景与目的

(一)大英博物馆基本介绍

大英博物馆(The British Museum)位于英国伦敦新牛津大街北面的罗素广场。该馆成立于 1753 年,1759 年 1 月 15 日起正式对公众开放,是世界上历史最悠久、规模最宏伟的综合性博物馆,也是世界上规模最大、最著名的四大博物馆之一。大英博物馆拥有藏品 800 多万件,包括来自世界各地的文物、珍品和伟大科学家的手稿等,藏品之丰富、种类之繁多,为世界博物馆所罕见。大英博物馆收藏了近三万件中国藏品,从新石器时期的陶片和石器、手稿和古籍(如 1603 年版的李时珍《本草纲目》)至书画、玉器和青铜器、瓷器等均有

① 作者:王晗,重庆大学建筑学系;韩梦瑶,重庆大学新闻系;辜紫怡,重庆大学新闻系;朱怡静,重庆大学建筑学系。

收藏。^①

大英博物馆是世界上首座国家级公共博物馆，自建成之初便以"世界的博物馆""面向世界"为核心理念，一直致力于展示、保护和传承世界文化遗产，馆藏涵盖了 200 多万年的人类历史，展现出世界多元文化的蓬勃发展。^②

（二）历史与争议

从以汉斯·斯隆爵士（Sir Hans Sloane）为代表的个人捐赠开始，中国文物陆续以多种方式源源不断地进入大英博物馆。大英博物馆作为海外收藏中国近代文物流失最多的博物馆，其现状与殖民主义的强权政治密切相关，但在当下，文化遗产价值的重视程度日益提高，民族主义情绪高涨，博物馆很难在叙述中回避其过往的殖民史。^③但这一问题同样是敏感且复杂的。英国作为殖民时代的强权国家，其与希腊、埃及的文物所属问题也曾引起争议。自 1975 年希腊恢复民主开始，其返还埃尔金雕刻的要求就被英国政府以"雕刻为其合法拥有"而驳回。^④这场争论旷日持久，甚至成为一项社会运动，在 2002 年前后达到高潮。希腊的索回要求得到了国际社会的广泛同情与支持，但大英博物馆仍然拒绝考虑所有折中与归还方案。2022 年底，《欧洲遗产论坛报》^⑤与英国《卫报》^⑥曾放出消息，经过与希腊方长达一年的讨论，英国方态度似有松动，但据 11 月 Artnet 报道，希腊高级部长拒绝承认英国机构合法拥有这些雕塑，或者因此有权将它们借出^⑦，《卫报》也于 2023 年 3 月报道英国时任首相里希·苏纳克（Rishi Sunak）发誓要保护帕特农神庙大理石不被归还希腊，称它们仍然是英国的"巨大资产"。^⑧

---

① 大英博物馆. [2023-04-22]. https://baike.baidu.com/item/大英博物馆/490292?fr=aladdin.

② 大英博物馆里的中国文物. (2018-06-06) [2024-04-01]. https://www.sohu.com/a/238432246_152615.

③ 界面文化.大英博物馆文物来源之争：后殖民时代，西方博物馆如何重塑合法性. (2018-10-20)[2024-06-03]. https://mp.weixin.qq.com/s/Gt9a_fHGgqrn1vVRP03Uhg.

④ 丁辛.旷日持久的雅典埃尔金雕刻返还之争.中国文化遗产，2004(1): 106-111.

⑤ Chris Green. Long overdue? British Museum hints at deal with Greece over Parthenon Marbles. (2022-06-23)[2024-06-03]. https://heritagetribune.eu/europe/long-overdue-british-museum-hints-at-deal-with-greece-over-parthenon-marbles/?gclid=EAIaIQobChMIkdydjOONgAMVzTrUAR1h6gAIEAAYASAAEgJ_IvD_BwE.

⑥ British Museum in talks with Greece over return of Parthenon marbles. (2023-01-04)[2024-06-03]. https://www.theguardian.com/artanddesign/2023/jan/04/british-museum-in-talks-with-greece-over-return-of-parthenon-marbles.

⑦ Dispelling Rumors, Greece Has Rejected the British Museum's Offer to Return the Parthenon Marbles as a Long-Term Loan. (2023-01-11)[2024-06-03]. https://news.artnet.com/art-world/greece-rejects-british-museum-loan-deal-parthenon-marbles-2241261.

⑧ No plans to return Parthenon marbles to Greece, says Rishi Sunak. (2023-03-13)[2024-06-03]. https://www.theguardian.com/artanddesign/2023/mar/13/no-plans-to-return-parthenon-elgin-marbles-to-greece-says-rishi-sunak.

（三）当下的发展与法律困境

在全球化的发展过程中，与其对立统一的强调维护本民族国家利益的民族主义社会思潮也在逐步复兴。而大英博物馆在面临诸方压力下，需要重新思考英国作为殖民时代的强权国家在后殖民时代下与其他国家的敏感关系，以及如何寻到一个新的叙述语境彰显其收藏品的合法性以应对巨大的国际舆论压力。

21世纪的大英博物馆被定义为一家"世界博物馆"（museum of the world），其收藏"有着全球血统，且向全球公民开放使用"。大英博物馆频频举办各类文物借展、巡展及文化交流活动，履行其"向全世界展示全世界"（Show the world to the world）的宗旨。"2017年，"大英博物馆百物展：浓缩的世界史"分别在北京国家博物馆和上海博物馆举行，成为当年中国的现象级展览，仅上海站就吸引了38.4万余人次观展，而《中国国家博物馆馆刊》也创立了专题，并邀请学者撰写了有关大英博物馆藏中国文物及相关问题研究的4篇论文。策展人贝琳达·克里勒（Belinda Crerar）在接受澎湃新闻的采访时坦率表示："大英博物馆无法否认其是一个建立于大英帝国和海外殖民时代的机构的历史。"①英国海外殖民时期，商人将各地文物带回本土的行为从稀松平常变成了现在的不可接受，不止大英博物馆，世界各地许多机构都面临着这样的问题。

早在1970年，联合国教科文组织就曾发布《关于禁止和防止非法进出口文化财产和非法转让其所有权的方法的公约》，国际统一私法协会于1995年发布的《关于被盗或非法出口文物的公约》中的原则都体现了同情和支持文物流失国索回文物要求的精神②，但时效与适用性的限制和对行为合法与否的认知与判定等问题都是在现行法律与公约框架内难以解决的。在诸多法律困境下，国际博物馆协会虽然一再表态同情和支持文物非法流失国的立场，但在实践中也只能发挥调解作用，而在文化的变化与敏感性之间寻找平衡，则是我们都需要面对、协商、解决的问题。

二、研究对象：大英博物馆"晚清百态"特展

（一）策展人采访

作为大英博物馆中国部负责人和策展人，霍吉淑（Jessica Harrison-Hall）

---

① 傅适野.专访｜大英博物馆策展人贝琳达：展示历史而不偏向某种文明.(2017-03-04)[2024-06-03]. https://www.thepaper.cn/newsDetail_forward_1631238
② 冯莎，张志培.掠夺与归还：西方争议性遗产的伦理困境.学术月刊，2021(11): 186-199.

在她任职的三十年中，通过将丰富的馆藏珍品和现代展览手段相融合，向西方观众展现中华民族的悠久历史和优秀文化。

通过人民网对此次"晚清百态"特展的策展人的采访，我们了解到霍吉淑希望通过展示 19 世纪的中国人民的坚韧，以激励受疫情冲击的人们度过这段艰苦岁月。正如她在采访中所说："这一时期的中国虽然经历着动荡和不安，但是也见证了璀璨的艺术作品以及新型都市的崛起。我们不仅希望通过这个机会展示发生在 19 世纪中国的历史事件，更希望反映出在这段漫长的百年岁月中中国人民身上的坚韧和创造力。"①

（二）展品信息

"晚清百态"特展在全球范围内首次将 19 世纪中国非凡的文化创造力带入生活，该特展通过展示 19 世纪中国的艺术、时尚、报纸、家具甚至汤料——从末代皇帝宫廷送给乔治国王和玛丽王后 1911 年加冕典礼的景泰蓝花瓶，到慈禧太后委托的丝绸长袍，讲述 19 世纪不同社会阶层和领域的人们的生活。

以下是部分重点的展品清单——慈禧太后的孔雀牡丹纹衬衣、德龄公主的长袍、光绪可能穿过的幼年皇帝吉服、盖有慈禧御笔印的牡丹图轴、嘉庆皇帝的圣旨、溥仪赠给英王乔治五世的景泰蓝花瓶、裕容龄在天坛舞剑的录像、《南京条约》原件、中国最后一场科举考试试卷、《点石斋画报》、曾在 1867 年巴黎世博会展出的中国点翠屏风、来自天坛、先农坛和雍和宫的礼器和铜像、圆明园的建筑残片。

（三）展品分类与馆场布置

此次特展的策展人霍吉淑围绕宫廷、军事、艺术、日常生活以及全球交流这五个主题探讨 19 世纪的中国的人物和社会百态②，其中包括六个具体的分类——法院（The court）、军事（The military）、艺术家（Artists）、城市生活（Urban life）、全球清朝（Global Qing）、改革者与革命家（Reformers and revolutionaries）。

大英博物馆是社会空间、权力空间和各种文化相互融合的空间，它既是实在的有形空间，又是虚拟的文化空间③。大英博物馆精心设计每一处展览空间，

---

① 霍吉淑：用文物精彩讲述中国故事. (2022-06-25)[2024-06-03]. http://uk.people.com.cn/n1/2022/0625/c352308-32456519.html.
② 大英博物馆.[2023-03-13].https://britishmuseum.org.cn/exhibition.aspx?nid=155.
③ 大英博物馆.[2023-03-13].https://britishmuseum.org.cn/exhibition.aspx?nid=155.

综合采用多种艺术手法来呈现文化背景信息。

（四）中英两国对展览的态度

作为曾经策划过"明：皇朝盛世"这一受到国际社会高度褒扬的策展人，大英博物馆中国部负责人霍吉淑拥有用文物讲述中国故事的能力，她的热忱也为中英两国在文化领域增进理解发挥了重要的推动作用。而大英博物馆于 2023 年 5 月 18 日的"晚清百态"展便是其筹备长达四年的作品。

在 2023 年 6 月 1 日的线上讲座中，她也介绍道："中国的博物馆、图书馆和高校人员也给予了我很大的帮助，包括与展览配套的书中的文章、到展览人物的配音、到展览中的影像、线上讨论，图片等。"[1]虽然由于新冠疫情的影响，中国的博物馆馆藏并未出借到本次展览中，但双方都抱有积极态度，展览中的文字也正确地将中国当时所遭受的暴力归咎于英国和其他外国列强。[2]

该展览没有回避 19 世纪中国遭遇的暴力、动荡和混乱大部分由外国，尤其是英国侵略造成的这一事实。一段文字说明直截了当地写道，"帝国主义挑起了 1840—1842 年和 1856—1860 年的两次鸦片战争"。而展览的板块设计也在回应着文字的叙述语境，在"城市生活（Urban Life）"与"全球交流（Global Qing）"板块中，当时的中国人民在巨大的混乱下推动了印刷、纺织、珠宝、陶瓷、武器和照相等不同领域的创新。

（五）中英两国媒体舆情

国外的大部分媒体都对本次展览中的反思情绪表达了赞扬，美国彭博社报道称"在伦敦上演的展览，散发着对中国文明的尊重和钦佩"[3]，英国《卫报》报道称："北京颐和园的一块破碎碎片与从维多利亚女王的破坏中一路带回来一只名叫 Looty 的小狗肖像同列。这些物品的位置可以放慢思维，在 300 多个展品的展览中很有帮助。"[4]而另一篇《卫报》的评论也强调了本次展览的反思性："这个展览被设计成一个阴暗的迷宫，在其中你发现了一个又一个关于经

① London's Big China Show Treads On Tricky Ground. (2023-05-18)[2024-06-03]. https://www.bloomberg.com/opinion/articles/2023-05-18/british-museum-s-big-china-show-treads-on-tricky-ground.

② China's Hidden Century review—a revelation from first to last. (2023-05-21)[2024-06-03]. https://www.theguardian.com/artanddesign/2023/may/21/chinas-hidden-century-british-museum-london-review-a-revelation-from-first-to-last.

③ London's Big China Show Treads on Tricky Ground. (2023-05-18)[2024-06-03]. https://www.b0loomberg.com/opinion/articles/2023-05-18/british-museum-s-big-china-show-treads-on-tricky-ground.

④ China's Hidden Century review—how opium and Christianity demolished a civilization. (2023-05-16)[2024-06-03]. https://www.theguardian.com/culture/2023/may/16/chinas-hidden-century-british-museum.

常令人震惊的历史的线索。"①而美国的雅虎网站称赞："这是一项大胆、雄心勃勃和富有想象力的努力，大英博物馆应该为此鼓掌。清朝及其灭亡变得更加清晰，也变得不那么隐蔽了；要做到这一点并非易事"②。

在国内此展览却没有在媒体塑造的语境中获得好评。澎湃新闻以"大英博物馆首次聚焦'晚清百态'，他者眼中的隐秘中国"对该展览进行了内容介绍。③文章本身对展览的板块分布与展品内容进行了介绍，但少有文字对英国直面侵略者的身份进行说明。在微信公众号、小红书等多个社交媒体平台相关内容的评论区观察可发现，"赃物""强盗"等具有负面情绪的词被高频提及，民族主义的情绪高涨，国内群众普遍对本次特展持反对态度。

三、研究问题

（一）问题提出

在目前的国内媒介生态中，不乏对大英博物馆"晚清百态"特展的正面声音。例如，澎湃新闻刊发文章，评论该特展"呈现出了复调的历史和众声喧哗的世界，揭示出 19 世纪一些隐藏的维度和面相，为审视这段时期提供了他者视角"④。

然而不可否认的是，国内舆论场明显充斥着较多负面情绪与消极声音。媒体报道方面，《湖南日报》有文章直言这是"一个令人心情复杂的展览"⑤；受众评论方面，在各大网络平台的热门相关文章和内容评论区，也随处可见"痛心""强盗""赃物""心酸"等情感倾向明显的词，不少网友纷纷表示"没有一个中国人能笑着走出大英博物馆"。

本研究选取微博、小红书、哔哩哔哩等互联网平台中最为热门的相关文章和内容，爬取评论区数据提取关键词，生成情绪分析、词频表和词云图如表

① How the British Museum's new exhibition reveals China's Hidden Century through everyday lives. (2023-07-13) [2024-06-03]. https://ca.sports.yahoo.com/news/british-museums-exhibition-reveals-chinas-063503705.html.

② China's hidden century review: An "enthralling" show at the British Museum. (2023-06-09)[2024-06-03]. https://www.theweek.co.uk/arts-life/culture/art/961191/chinas-hidden-century-review-british-museum.

③ 黄松. 大英博物馆首次聚焦"晚清百态"，他者眼中的隐秘中国. (2023-06-02)[2024-06-03]. https://www.thepaper.cn/newsDetail_forward_23312207.

④ 高轶旸. 众声喧哗与历史叙事：大英博物馆"潜光藏耀的世纪"观展记. (2023-07-10)[2024-06-03]. https://www.thepaper.cn/newsDetail_forward_23722221.

⑤ 谭乐沁. 大英博物馆"晚清百态"中国特展，展出《南京条约》原件. (2023-06-15)[2024-06-03]. https://baijiahao.baidu.com/s?id=1768752189783383161&wfr=spider&for=pc.

1、表2、图1所示。可见，所选取数据中的负面情感表达占比接近25%，而"强盗""屈辱""耻辱""条约""大哭""抢走""国耻"等更是成为高频关键词。基于上述现象，本研究主要探讨的问题是：关于大英博物馆"晚清百态"特展的国内媒体话语和民众评价为何会产生较多负面情绪表达？

表1　评论关键词情绪分析

情绪分类	数量	占比
积极情绪	1402	53.17%
中级情绪	604	22.90%
消极情绪	631	23.93%
合计	2637	100%

表2　评论关键词频次

频数	关键词	频数	关键词
文物	420	屈辱	88
历史	307	展览	86
中国	282	保护	77
博物馆	230	耻辱	72
英国	219	大清	65
回来	139	人民	65
强盗	126	条约	59
清朝	124	大哭	53
保存	92	抢走	42
文化	90	国耻	35

图1　评论关键词词云

（资料来源：本文作者自绘）

（二）争议性藏品的归还伦理困境

随着全球范围内反殖民主义运动的持续推进，文物归还已超越旧有的文化交流事务框架，参与进应对全球格局流变的政治实践中。当前各界对"归还"的既有认识与讨论主要围绕所有权的物权伦理展开，"物归原主"是支持文物归还的主要论点，而保护私有财产则是资本主义物权伦理的基石[①]。

根据 1995 年联合国教科文组织提出的"现代国际法归还文物的原则"，任何因战争被抢夺或丢失的文物都应归还，不受时效限制，不管时间跨度有多大。因此，国内不少声音主张流失文物应当归还原属国，中国有权索回任何非法出境的文物[②]，并认为殖民背景藏品的流失过程与国家和民族情感密切相关，拒绝返还是对原属国民族情感的再一次践踏[③]。

然而为了维护馆藏珍宝，陷入文物归还风波的西方博物馆往往会展开争辩：一是持有这些文物的大型博物馆与知名收藏家在法律上和情理中都处于无法轻易挑战的地位，相关馆藏文物主要通过购买和交易获得，倘若交易过程中私有财产得不到保护，势必会撼动作为西方经济基础的市场信念，交易双方如何得到补偿将成为待回应的棘手问题；二是殖民地文物的原属国多分布于"欠发达"地区，普遍缺乏精良的技术与雄厚的资金支持，甚至陷入政治腐败与社会动荡，在混乱的治理中无法保障文物，西方博物馆则可以使文物得到妥善保存与恰当展示，能够较好地履行"让全球公众尽可能广泛地接触这些藏品"的使命。基于此，西方博物馆更倾向于将文物进行巡回展览或长期"出借"，而不是直接归还。

有学者提出，尽管西方博物馆并未明确表现出自愿返还的态度，但逐步形成了直面过去殖民历史、强调双方对话与沟通并鼓励在协商过程中加大专业研究力度的伦理体系[④]，但目前，学界和业界始终对这一悬而未决的焦点议题难下定论，各国和民众也容易因所处立场不同产生大相径庭、两极分化的态度和看法。

---

① 侯春燕.在个体遗产与世界遗产之间——国际博协 2007 年大会主题评介.中国博物馆，2007（2）：3-6.

② 归还中国流失文物的法律依据.(2014-05-17)[2024-06-03]. http://fangtan.china.com.cn/2014-05/07/content_32311406.htm.

③ 杨谦.西方博物馆殖民背景藏品返还的伦理探究.东南文化，2020（6）：135-141.

④ 史巍.全球化语境中民族主义思潮的复兴及其模式.学术论坛，2020（4）：119-125.

（三）全球化视域下的民族主义浪潮复兴

全球化作为当今世界发展的客观趋势，是生产力发展的必然过程与结果，主要体现为经济领域全球市场的形成和资本的全球化，同时伴随着政治、文化等其他领域的日益频繁的全球交往。而如何增进文化领域"自我"与"他者"的相互理解，消解文化多元性诱发的各种社会后果，已然成为全球化时代的一个新命题[①]。据美国彭博社评论，本次特展"散发着对中国文明的尊重和钦佩，同时又正确地将中国当时所遭受的暴力归咎于英国和其他外国列强"[②]，国外媒体对大英博物馆的客观理念与巧妙策展也以正面评价居多。由此可见，这一基于"他者"语境呈现的展览已然成为国外了解中国历史、反思殖民霸权的重要窗口，较好地顺应了文化全球化的趋势与进程。

但随着全球化发展的逐渐深入，新的问题也接踵而至。仅就文化层面而言，西方国家一直占据着强势地位，在对外关系中极力推行以民主、自由为代表的西方价值，通过发达的媒体资源渗透其他国家，把文化扩张作为外交战略的重要组成部分。为了应对发达国家"文化霸权主义"对自身文化的侵蚀，一些非西方国家在全球化的过程中逐渐产生防御和逆反心理，出现了文化上的民族主义。民族主义将世界区分为"我们"和"他们"，当二者边缘逐渐清晰化、自身所处的民族和其他民族相互对立之时，"非此即彼"的思维则有可能导致对共同体之外的其他个体或群体的排斥。因此在许多中国观者看来，近代海外流失文物本身即构成了一部充斥着血与泪的情感史，一砖一瓦都触碰着历史的伤痛，观展经历挑起并印证了自身的家国情怀。于是，文化全球化与民族主义思潮的碰撞不可避免地带来了各国民众的意见冲突。

四、结论与反思

（一）全球化趋势与"他者"叙事

全球史考察超越国家界限的历史现象，具有跨文化互动或全球性意义的事件成为重要研究主题，跨文化的"他者叙事"便成为全球史研究必不可少的史料和审视维度。19世纪下半叶，世界成为一个密切互动的整体，全球性公共空间由此形成。在这种空间中，当事者和观察者具有同时在场性，"他者叙事"

[①] 尹凯. 名曰"普世"，实为霸权——评欧美一些博物馆的"普世宣言". 历史评论，2021 (6)：88-90.

[②] 美媒：大英博物馆中国特展直面侵略史，能否架起和解桥梁. (2023-06-09)[2024-03-05]. https://oversea.huanqiu.com/article/4CxnJMRVfxG.

也因其共时性而成为一种有声叙事，对当事者的行为产生影响。

该展览是一场跨文化的互动，对于非华人观众而言，了解浩瀚的中国历史从来不是一件容易的事情，在没有潜移默化的文化熏陶背景下，部分人群对中国人强烈的爱国情怀表示不解。"晚清百态"成为全球化趋势下，非华人受众了解中国一个很好的窗口。

大英博物馆的此次展览是全球首个以 19 世纪中国人的创作力和韧性为主题的展览。策展人霍吉淑在致辞中讲到因为时局动荡，画家、作家、匠人、商贾和政治家的许多成就并没有被过多提及，所以这次特展想将那个潜光掩耀的世纪展现出来。通过官网、APP 以及书籍的介绍中，可以观察到展览关注不同阶层和领域的人物故事，既有宫廷贵族的华美服饰，也有普通劳动人民穿的蓑衣，既有象征男性身份的鼻烟壶和扳指，也有凸显女性意识觉醒的诗歌言语，让受众看到一个更完整的 19 世纪的中国。特展没有着重于宏大叙事，而是更关注生动鲜活人物的命运与生活。

用国外受众更容易理解的方式展示中国历史是一件非常重要的事情，国外受众评价道："当涵盖如此多的历史时，毫不奇怪的是，非常具体的、具有最大影响力的是个体元素，因为它们至少是直接且易于理解的。"

在全球变革与合作的今天，"讲好中国故事"已经成为公众的认知。我国主流媒体也在加快推进对外传播能力的建设。然而我们在这一方面还有很大的欠缺，依旧是"西强我弱"的局面。关键就在于跨文化传播的受众不同，相比于宏大叙事，当今的观者们更关注微观人物的故事，促成了大英博物馆这次展览切合受众需求的展览的出现。

（二）全球性博物馆的必要性

在全球化的今天，保护全人类文明的重要性逐渐提升，不同民族的文化瑰宝也需要影响力更广的传播平台。全球性博物馆具备一流的文物保护和管理方式，拥有着藏品聚集与收集借用的重大优势，这对于全球文明的发展有着重要的意义。建设全球性博物馆必要性在于需要加强不同国家博物馆的交流与藏品流通，防止各国文物全部封锁在本国境内，孤芳自赏导致世界各民族文化达不到共通与交流的情况出现。

中国并没有将视线聚焦于晚清。策划这样一个展览，或许正如澎湃新闻在《众声喧哗与历史叙事：大英博物馆"潜光藏耀的世纪"观展记》一文中所言，在主流叙述中，人们对"晚清百年"的感知主要是负面的。这一时期大清国力由盛转衰，社会停滞不前，内忧外患，民不聊生，政府在列强的侵略下，被迫签订了一系列丧权辱国的不平等条约，开启了一段屈辱的近代史。在"西方冲击—中国回应"的解释模式下，清朝失败地应对了外界的挑战。然而，非华人出身的策展人借由展览意图表达，生活在19世纪的中国人，极具韧性与创造力，他们被以往的叙述所遮蔽，这一段历史是隐藏的。所以这次特展想将因时局动荡，那个潜光掩耀的世纪展现出来。

（三）文化返还争议

前文也提到过关于大英博物馆藏品返还争议，以及国内外舆论呈现出截然不同的态度。这归其根本是大英博物馆本身的殖民者属性以及在我国文化自信的发展。

一个时期以来，国际社会对殖民统治或战争时期被盗掠文物的返还和赔偿问题给予了极大关注。2002年12月，为了声援拒绝返还帕特农神庙石雕的大英博物馆，并且一劳永逸地免除文物返还诉求，来自北美和欧洲的18家博物馆馆长齐聚德国慕尼黑，联合签署了《关于普世性博物馆的价值及重要性的宣言》（简称《宣言》）。[①]

《宣言》认为，之前陈列的他国文物已经延伸成所在国家的遗产，博物馆应该服务于每一个国家的公民。该宣言引起许多国家的批判。强权者的逻辑在于巩固历史的不平等，而受害者的逻辑在于改变不平等。在这样的背景下，大英博物馆的负面评价根深蒂固。我国受众看到该展览时，首先想到的就是文物流失的痛心以及对大英博物馆的谴责。

随着我国对优秀传统文化的传承与发展，我国更加珍视优秀的中国文明，人们为中华文明感到自豪。然而一味的批判指责，更加倾向于文化偏激。从社交平台上的评论来看，网友关于大英博物馆"晚清百态"展览的评论分为两种倾向，大多数认为大英博物馆是"小偷"，一部分肯定了本次展览的优点，认为博物馆从另一个维度呈现出中国的历史，肯定其展览的重要性。

（四）可行性方案探讨

一是国际博物馆协会加强对殖民背景文物的讨论。通过谈判建立多边协议，给文物争议性归属一个可以讨论的环境和切实可行的沟通环境，探究一个

---

① 尹凯. 名曰"普世"，实为霸权——评欧美一些博物馆的"普世宣言". 历史评论，2021（6）：88-90.

文物归还与合作的可行性方案。文物承载灿烂文明，传承历史文化，维系民族精神。文物是一国国家历史与民族文化的见证与传承载体，反映了文明被传承、被保护、被珍视的历史脉络。文物的归属不仅关乎国家的经济利益，更关乎其文化主权，甚至民族情感。最理想的状态是文物所属权归还所属国，各大博物馆间可以借用文物，或者某段时间互换文物。在这种环境下，将中国国家博物馆建设成全球性博物馆也会有更加可行的未来。除了文物所属问题，也应该加强各国策展人的交流与合作，呈现出更加贴合历史引人反思的展览。

二是正确引导民族意识、民众情绪。我国文物流失严重不仅仅是列强当时的掠夺，还有很多是通过文物走私被售卖到国外。大众媒体在报道国外文物展览时，也应该全面报道展品来源信息。文物的流失不是一朝一夕，文物的收回也得从长计议。现有环境下，大英博物馆可以引入更多中国代表，例如华人策展人、讲解员等，在缓和民众情绪的同时，呈现更加立体的中国，借大英博馆的展览，让更多人了解真实的中国。

故宫博物院数字化发展研究[①]

摘　要： 故宫博物院作为世界知名博物馆之一，历史文化底蕴深厚，进入现代以来，其发展道路既有世界博物馆的共性特征，也有其独特的个性特色。数字化发展是当今时代的大势所趋，包括故宫博物院在内的许多世界博物馆均走上数字化发展之路，传统与现代如何更好地结合成为博物馆未来发展的重要命题。本文将采用案例分析、对比研究等方式，从故宫博物院的历史与发展历程入手，探讨故宫博物院文博事业的发展状况，着重分析故宫博物院数字化发展历程与成果，将其与国内外其他博物馆的数字化发展作比较，总结故宫博物院数字化的成功经验和不足之处，据此为故宫博物院未来的建设与发展提出创新性建议。

关键词： 故宫博物院；数字化；文博产业；对比研究

一、故宫博物院简介

（一）基本信息

故宫博物院是一座综合性博物馆，成立于 1925 年，是以明清皇宫及其收藏为基础的大型综合性古代艺术博物馆。故宫博物院现有藏品 180 余万件（套），其类型囊括绘画、书法、铜器、金银器等 25 大类，藏品丰富，价值颇高。通过宫殿建筑、宫廷史迹原状陈列、常设展览等方式，故宫博物院向海内外大众呈现灿烂悠久的中华文明。

① 作者：冯慧怡，广东外语外贸大学俄语系；吕欣桓，广东外语外贸大学意大利语系；魏雨萱，广东外语外贸大学翻译系。

（二）发展历程与规划概述

1.发展历程

故宫博物院，作为明清两代的皇宫遗址，承载着丰富的历史文化内涵。自 1924 年清朝末代皇帝溥仪出宫后，其管理权逐渐由政府与清室共同接管，经历了从皇室禁地到公众文化空间的转变。

1924 年，随着清朝的终结，故宫的管理权由政府与清室组成的"清室古物保管委员会"接管。随后，"办理清室善后委员会"对故宫进行了详细清点与查收。1925 年 10 月 10 日，故宫正式举办了建院典礼，并向公众开放，标志着故宫从皇室禁地转变为公众文化空间。

新中国成立后，故宫博物院的管理更加规范，进行了一系列的整理与改革工作。这不仅提升了故宫的管理水平，也为后续的文化传承与保护工作奠定了坚实的基础。

2.发展规划

故宫博物院的发展规划主要可以分为文物保护与修复、展览与文化传播、学术交流与教育、国际化发展、数字化转型与发展五个部分。

故宫博物院将文物保护放在首位，作为所有工作的重中之重。为此，故宫博物院设立了文物科技实验室、文物修复工作室等机构，投入了大量资源和精力进行文物的保护与修复工作。

展览是故宫博物院的重要工作之一。通过举办专题展览、文化交流展览、赴外展览和原状陈列等，故宫博物院为观众呈现了丰富多样的中华文化盛宴，促进了中华文化的传播与传承。

故宫博物院注重学术交流与教育，设立了故宫研究院，并创办了《故宫博物院院刊》，为学者提供了深入挖掘故宫建筑与文物背后历史与文化内涵的平台。同时，故宫学院的设立也为公众提供了多样化的教育与培训项目，激发了公众对文化遗产的兴趣与热爱。

故宫博物院坚持国际化发展。通过设立国际博协培训中心，邀请国内外专家学者开展讲座与培训，故宫博物院不仅传播了中华优秀传统文化，也促进了国际的文化交流与合作。

随着当代科学技术的不断发展，故宫博物院开启了数字化转型与发展。通过建立"数字文物库"和"数字多宝阁"，运用现代信息技术丰富陈展方式，故宫博物院的文物保护、研究与展示工作取得了新的突破。同时，与文化创意、旅游等产业的结合也增强了故宫博物院的发展能力。

故宫博物院的发展历程是中华文化传承与发展的重要缩影。通过不断的改革与发展，故宫博物院已成为展示中华文化、促进国际文化交流的重要平台，故宫博物院将努力把传统与现代相结合，为中华文化的传承与发展作出更大的贡献。

二、故宫博物院文创产品简介

（一）故宫博物院文创产品概述

故宫博物院作为国内体量最大的文化 IP，其文创发展历程也备受关注。关于所谓"文化产品"，联合国教科文组织将其定义为："文化产品一般是指传播思想、符号和生活方式的消费品，它能够提供信息和娱乐，进而形成群体认同并影响文化行为。"[1]

现故宫博物院文创产品已有一万多种。故宫博物院的文创产品特征和设计思维方面不只是在创意层面上的发挥，更多的是沿着故宫五千年历史脉络，发掘出深藏的"故宫文化"元素作为传播载体并且不断发展，以该方式更好的传承中华优秀传统文化。故宫作为最正宗、最浓厚的"中国风"代表，可以挖掘的中国元素不计其数。

2019 年初，时任故宫博物院院长单霁翔公布了 2017 年文创"账本"，在 2017 年文创的销售收入已达到 15 亿元，超过了 15 家 A 股上市公司的收入。[2]

（二）故宫博物院文创产品发展历程

第一阶段是自发的文物研发阶段。2010 年以前属于第一阶段——自发的文物研发阶段，由于开发经验不足，为避免开发的盲目性，博物院主要是对文物进行简单复制，以小产品为主，也会探索性地进行再创造。

第二阶段是自觉的文创文物研发阶段。2010 年至 2017 年，博物院进入文化创意的自觉阶段。在这一阶段，国家下发了关于博物馆文化产品创意的文件，各个博物馆都在做文创，为避免形成同质化，故宫博物院在这个阶段做了很多尝试和探索。

第三阶段是主题文创阶段。如今故宫博物院的文创开发已经进入第三阶

---

① 黄哲京.博物馆文创产品的知识产权保护.故宫学刊，2016（16）：201-212.

② 故宫"账本"：文创收入销售额 15 亿元，实控 17 家公司. (2019-04-08)[2024-01-25]. https://www.bjnews.com.cn/feature/2019/04/08/565460.html.

段。故宫文创开始由规模、数量向质量、效益进行转变，通过研究博物馆本身的文化历史和文物，同时研究数千年以来中国人的生活习惯、生活方式，进行文创产品的主题研发和智慧研发。如故宫推出的文创产品将古人的智慧与现代生活相融合，推出一系列与人们生活息息相关的文创产品。故宫文创产品负责人表示，目前最受欢迎的是文具类产品及彩妆类产品。

故宫博物院还建设发布了故宫官方网站、青少年网站、英文网站，并且和谷歌合作，把文物推送给国外观众。此外，博物院还打造了故宫社区APP，开通了故宫微博、公众号等社交媒体账号，将故宫和公众之间的关系由过去的单向输出变成了双向沟通。在展示形式上，早期故宫还自主研发并上线的"胤禛美人图""紫禁城祥瑞""皇帝的一天""每日故宫"等多款应用，将故宫文化特色与价值用严谨而风趣的方式传递给观众。随着"云游"的普及，故宫打造了"数字故宫"小程序，全面整合故宫在线数字服务，集文物数字化成果、新文创产品、知识普及及功能性导览于一体，游客可实现"一站式"实现在线购票、查询地理位置和游览须知，并能"云"游故宫各大建筑，饱览百万件珍稀藏品。从"故宫文创"到"紫禁城里过大年"、赏灯"上元之夜"的夜游项目，再到"数字故宫"，故宫的持续走红，离不开创新，这种创新是深耕于文化内涵，提炼文化中的精粹，深入研究当下人们的兴趣爱好和生活所需，依托科学技术与时俱进的创新。

三、中国文博事业的发展

（一）文创产业带动文博事业发展

博物馆资源是全民族文化创新的重要源泉，在文化传承方面，我国国家级博物馆和地方博物馆、国营博物馆和民营博物馆、综合博物馆和行业博物馆等构成了庞大的博物馆体系。这些博物馆中收藏的海量藏品是中华民族物质文明和精神文明的载体。文物资源只有运用到社会文化生活中，其价值才能得到较好体现。但文物是珍贵的不可再生资源，文物的利用应在保护的基础上进行。因此，利用博物馆藏品进行文化创新，能够充分发挥藏品的文化价值。创意产业不仅能使各国表现自身对本国和世界独特文化的认同，同时也能为这些国家提供促进经济增长和创造就业的机会。与此同时，创意经济也推动了社会包容性、文化多样性和人类发展。博物馆可以向公众提供藏品信息和数字资源，以支持全民族文化创新，此外，博物馆还应该利用馆藏资源，开发具有本馆特色的文创产品。当下的博物馆文创实践已经充分证明，博物馆日益成为全民族文化创新"重镇"。博物馆文创事业要更好地发挥其创新作用，打造博物馆品牌，满足大众不断提升的对博物馆文创产品的需求。

以故宫博物院为首的许多文化博物馆通过设计、开发文创产品，让人们对文物的兴趣和认知转化为消费。而文创产品进入千万家又间接带动文博事业的发展，这是一种良性循环。2014 年，国务院发布《关于推进文化创意和设计服务与相关产业融合发展的若干意见》①，鼓励全国各地博物馆开发文创及相关衍生产品，增强博物馆的发展能力，这些国家层面的支持，为博物馆发展指明了方向，提供了动力。

（二）文博事业的国际化

鼓励故宫文创产品走出国门，可以带动中国文博事业在世界范围内的发展，进行馆企合作。

欧美国家对文创产品的开发可以追溯至 20 世纪 80 年代，有着较为丰富的经验。大英博物馆将 100 件文物整合在一起展开世界巡展，在上海展出时，观众要排队两三个小时买票，可见文化的吸引力。值得思索的是，大英博物馆在中国巡展时，还与天堂伞、晨光文具等中国企业合作，推出一系列的文创产品。产品"嫁接"浓缩世界史的文物之后，更具历史气息和厚重感，又一次成为了文创成功范例。在国内，文创探索一直走在前沿。故宫博物院曾与稻香村合作，将《乾隆南巡图》这一艺术珍品与食品月饼结合，稻香村月饼让消费者有了新的直观感受：月饼也是历史悠久的食品，作为礼品赠送也更有分量。

在文创之路上急切需要思考的问题是，如何差异化地将各个博物馆展示的文化元素融入文创设计，激起新的消费意愿。文创运营中，所有的IP授权必须要进行规范管理，文物照片授权要更加审慎规范。此外，文创开发不必完全依靠第三方参与，也可以有自身的参与，就是"馆企合作"与博物馆自身文创相结合两条腿走路。"馆企合作"模式是提升文创的重要手段之一。这种"我提方案，你替我实现"的模式，即由博物馆团队完成概念设计等前期研究，文创设计企业完成设计方案的落地和实施，双方合作完成文创的开发与设计，这无疑对于文化的传播是非常有效的。

---

① 国家知识产权局.推进文化创意和设计服务与相关产业融合发展意见印发 增强创新动力为主要措施.(2014-03-19)[2024-01-25]. https://www.cnipa.gov.cn/.

目前文化产业已成为我国社会经济中非常重要组成部分，而文化IP作为其中关键力量又处于一个发展机遇期。文博文旅IP指基于博物馆、艺术馆、旅游景区等的藏品、景点进行再创作所产生的知识产权，以及它们本身固有的品牌价值符号。与其他IP相比，文博文旅IP最为核心的差异性在于IP背后依靠的是更为丰富的文化资源，内容素材充足，并且受众范围更为广泛[1]，故宫博物院、大英博物馆、敦煌景区及敦煌博物馆等都是典型代表。

随着中国经济与社会的发展，文化IP以其高辨识度，好玩有趣、个性鲜明，有态度、有观点、有价值观的特征，赢得更多圈层人群关注，受众呈现爆发式增长。

中国本土的文化IP授权行业快速发展，随着国内授权行业的发展，越来越多的国产IP诞生并开展授权业务。从中国授权IP类型及被授权商所处行业分布看，娱乐类IP、艺术文化IP、潮流IP是主要授权IP类型，玩具游艺、服装饰品、食品饮料、礼品纪念品等行业是目前各类IP的主要流向。

海外IP市场起步早，发展较为成熟，具备更好受众基础和产业生态，在世界范围内对中国文化感知度上升，文化IP元素出海或将能在海外特定消费群体上找到更多蓝海机会。故宫文创产品走出国门，旨在扩大故宫在国际的影响力，打造好中国文博事业的强大IP。

在某种程度上说，无论做品牌还是做IP，很大程度上等于做内容。品牌人设很重要，但在塑造品牌人设、开发衍生产品时不应当"忘本"，品牌的基因与文化永远都是品牌的核心竞争力。

过去，故宫历史文化元素局限于三米红墙内，对大众来说接触频次非常低。故宫选择用高频带动低频的"互联网"方法来带动它们——开发文创产品和参演电视或网络节目，这两种高频消费与体验方式使这些具有宝贵价值的文化元素得以走进消费者的日常。故宫博物院积极发挥线下沉浸、互动和体验的优势，线下是未来品牌营销的一线阵地。

未来更多的线下零散场景将被娱乐元素重构，这也将是未来品牌抢占的主要流量入口之一。同时，故宫博物院有效利用新媒体直播带货的兴起，改变了传统的网络购物形式，特别是新冠疫情期间，直播带货为经济复苏做出了巨大的贡献。如今越来越多的人开始接触网络直播，故宫文创也应紧跟时代的潮

---

① 张飞燕.博物馆文创事业助推传统文化的弘扬——以故宫博物院文创研发为例.文化产业，2023(12):111-113.

流，利用直播新媒体，建立有故宫特色的直播活动。故宫 600 年的网络直播活动曾在网上引起了巨大的反响，可见关于故宫的直播大众是很乐意接受的。

文博行业的信息化和数字化进程，最早可以追溯到 1995 年美国建立的博物馆互联网系统，让观众可以在网上任意浏览博物馆馆藏信息。1998 年，故宫博物院也成立了资料信息部，开始了信息化进程。

（三）世界范围内的博物馆变革

博物馆在过去近 20 年间经历过 2 次重大变革。第一次是 15 年前的移动互联网成熟期，文博产业通过图片视频传播，衍生 IP 周边热卖，新文创让博物馆不再"高冷"。第二次变革在几年前，巴黎圣母院失火后，建筑历史学家安德鲁·塔隆（Andrew Tallon）生前用激光扫描的巴黎圣母院数据成为修复的希望，文博数字化也成为全世界关注的焦点。随着人工智能、云计算、3D、VR 等新一代技术成熟发展，文物可以在修复技术下延寿、在数字重生技术下长青、在数字化采集技术下在线高清呈现。这无疑展示出了三维数字技术在加强文物修复、考古发掘、文博展览展示、科学研究、社会教育等方面的巨大潜力与革命性作用。

博物馆线上＋线下双轨并进的展览模式，打破了观众与文博有限的触达边界。大量数字化文物材料，提高 3D 博物馆视觉呈现、增强了观众互动体验，实现对实体展馆社会价值的补充和扩展，有利于强化文博 IP 与受众之间的黏度，让中国历史文化大众化、国际化。

数字技术的高速发展，正在不断拉近公众与文物的距离、加深公众对文化遗产的认知。故宫博物院一直高度重视"数字故宫"建设，不断加强故宫古建筑和院藏文物的数字化采集能力，建设故宫文物数字资源库。同时，不断加快对外开放和交流合作，为故宫已持续 20 余年的数字化探索提供源源不断的助推力。故宫博物院将继续通过技术创新与开放合作，深入挖掘蕴含在文物中的中华优秀传统文化，持续推动故宫文物资源的创造性转化、创新性发展，让更多数字文化内容走进公众生活，满足人民群众对美好文化生活的新期待。

四、故宫博物院的数字化技术应用及对比研究

（一）"数字化博物馆"以及故宫数字化建设的概念及内涵

从故宫博物院的数字化建设总体来看，"数字化博物馆"是利用数字化技

术（例如三维建模技术、全息投影技术等）先对文物、艺术品以及历史遗产本身进行保护、维修以及再建构，再利用互联网平台进行博物馆展出以及文创产品的数字化宣传，同时衍生出一系列数字化技术服务应用于文博事业的平台或APP。

（二）故宫博物院的数字化建设

1.文物本身的数字化

2002年，故宫建立数字化资产应用研究所，开始了三维数字化的应用建设，到现在已经采集了故宫的全景三维建模数据，包括太和殿、养心殿、乾隆花园和角楼在内的重要殿宇室内外高清数据，并且通过照片建模、三维扫描等技术采集了室外陈设三维数据和可移动文物三维数据。随着采集技术的发展，故宫的三维数据资源越来越充实，这些基础数据成为故宫开展数字化项目建设的基石。对文物（宫殿建筑、瓷器等）进行数据采集和三维数字化的应用建设，不仅能够用于文物本身的保护、修复、储存以及虚拟建模等方面（因为通过数据可以分析出文物的时间、材质、适合存放的湿度和温度等，更加方便博物馆工作人员对文物的养护工作），还能够便利后续的文物展示，即旅客可以在网站上通过数字化建模来观察文物的细节或者通过VR来体验虚拟博物馆，从而进一步了解文物的信息。

2.文物展示的数字化

早在2001年，故宫博物院公布了故宫官方网站，在线发布文物信息。近些年随着"国潮"的兴起，越来越多的人把目光转向了中华优秀传统文化。2016年故宫与新浪微博合作，开展了第一次网络直播活动"明清御窑瓷器——故宫博物院与景德镇陶瓷考古新成果展"，获得广大网友的好评。2019元宵节故宫"上元之夜"曾吸引多个平台进宫直播，上千万网友实现故宫"云夜游"。整体来看，故宫在直播上的探索较早，并在发展中坚持与时俱进，积极引入新的展示渠道，借助短视频、直播等方式把故宫移到"线上"，有力地放大了故宫在数字时代的IP价值。这一时期，故宫利用互联网发展文博事业，带动了国内其他优秀传统文化弘扬与传承。

3.文物宣传的数字化

2019年，故宫一次性上新了7款数字化产品，例如"数字多宝阁"利用高精度的三维数据全方位立体式地展示文物的细节和全貌，观众通过官网就能全角度地观看文物藏品。此外，基于智能手机的数字展示产品有"紫禁城600""玩转故宫 2.0"和"故宫：口袋宫匠"，其中"玩转故宫"小程序涵盖建筑点位收藏、在线虚拟游览、提前发现精选推荐等内容，并有 AI 导览助手，提供导览问询一站式服务。同时"紫禁城 365"APP（iOS 版）通过美图、答题、知识、故事四种体验形式，贴合当下移动阅读习惯，多角度诠释紫禁城建筑文化，全方位展示故宫文化遗产保护研究成果。这些数字化产品打破时空限制，从不同的角度展示和传播故宫文化，让人们随时随地了解故宫。

4. 文创产品销售的数字化

随着网购和直播带货的盛行，故宫的文创与出版也于近两年走上了直播带货路，有"故宫出版"直播售书，"故宫淘宝"直播文创带货等等。网络直播带货很大程度促进了文创产品的销售额增长，而网友们在直播间里也从销售员与讲解员口中进一步了解故宫文化。同时，新兴媒体诸如微信、微博、哔哩哔哩等社交媒体迅猛发展，其即时性、经济性、精准性、互动性等优势为企业提供了与消费者有效沟通的渠道。故宫博物院抓住了当代年轻人对新媒体的娱乐需求，趁势与新媒体合作，例如故宫开设微博账号以及微信公众号和小程序，来宣传文物、展区信息以及销售文创周边，来扩大自身的影响力。

综合分析，故宫博物院的数字化建设对于弘扬故宫文化以及中华优秀传统文化、宣传文化自信有着积极的作用，数字化＋文博事业的新型结合，不仅让游客体会到科技的人文温度，也直观感受到了高科技发展的程度。科技从来都不是束之高阁的，故宫博物院将数字化技术大量引入文物保护和展出当中，既能够最大程度地还原文物本身的面貌，向世人讲述这件文物背后的历史故事，也能够让世人惊叹于精美文物之余，树立起爱护文物和支持推动数字化技术进一步服务于文博事业发展的意识，形成了一个良性循环。

（三）与国内博物馆对比数字化应用建设

本部分将以龙门石窟、敦煌莫高窟的数字化建设作为案例与故宫博物院的数字化建设进行对比。

1. 龙门石窟

文化和旅游部于 2022 年 2 月面向全国启动数字化创新实践案例征集工作，遴选以数字化创新实践赋能文化和旅游发展的典型案例。其中，龙门石窟智慧文旅数字孪生平台项目成效突出，促进了文物保护和文化传承。

龙门石窟顺应智慧旅游发展趋势，建设了智慧文旅数字孪生平台，在"跨界融合""科技引领""沉浸体验"方面积极探索，有效解决了文物保护与旅游活动的矛盾，在龙门旅游内涵、传播历史文化、展示景区风采、提升游客体验、激发创新活力、打造数字龙门、提高管理水平等方面发挥了重要作用。龙门石窟主佛区及周边等被"复刻"到线上，一个可供随时随地参观的数字化龙门石窟被打造出来，游客裸眼即可全方位观赏到洞窟 3D 模式的高清景象。此外，平台依托 5G 技术，利用 5G 高宽带、数据回传快的特点，针对景区客流、交通、服务设施、生态环境等实现跨网络、跨平台、跨区域实时数字化呈现，实现了实时监测景区人流数据、动态分析人流趋势，帮助游客随时了解景区情况，合理避开高峰时段和区域。

可以看出，龙门石窟不仅对文物本身进行了数字化技术保护与展示，还对实地景区附近的游览线路、交通情况等也利用数字化技术分析和运用。由此可见，数字化技术不单单是服务于文物保护与展示本身，对于像龙门石窟这样的文物建筑或者景点的建设也有多功能作用，因此，故宫博物院在后续数字化应用过程中，也可以根据故宫建筑群，利用数字化来规划游览路线和实时性导航，这样也能够减少所需的人力资源，让游客有更多的游览自主性。

2.敦煌莫高窟

敦煌研究院自 20 世纪 80 年代开始提出"数字敦煌"的构想，旨在利用计算机技术和数字图像技术，实现敦煌石窟文物的永久保存、永续利用。2011 年数字敦煌建成。

敦煌莫高窟数字展示中心开放后，莫高窟的开放和旅游模式将发生"革命性"的变化。所有游客在实地参观莫高窟之前，必须在数字展示中心观看莫高窟的介绍电影，提前了解背景知识，观看洞窟建筑、彩塑和壁画，领略莫高窟博大精深的佛教艺术；然后乘坐摆渡车从数字展示中心抵达莫高窟，由讲解员引导按照既定路线进洞窟参观。这种参观模式，既可缓解洞窟压力，减少游客参观给珍贵而又脆弱的壁画彩塑带来的潜在威胁，还可利用多媒体展示满足多种参观需求，提升服务质量和游客参观体验品质；同时，通过压缩游客在洞窟内的滞留时间，有效提升莫高窟游客接待量，切实缓解莫高窟文物保护与旅游开发之间的矛盾。

莫高窟的数字化保护与展示模式与故宫博物院的模式不同，是因为壁画本身难以保养，对参观人数和时间有较大的限制。但是故宫博物院也有许多文物存在类似敦煌莫高窟壁画的情况，因而可以参考这一模式展出那些特殊性文物，这样既可以充分利用文物资源、增加可参观性，又可以有效保护文物。

综合上述材料可知，目前国内许多著名的文物保护区与博物馆在利用数字化技术保护与展出文物方面有许多创新性创造性成果。它们不拘于保护文物本身，还将数字化技术应用到游览的全过程，数字化技术应用在游客参观的前中后的单一时间线中扮演了一个重要角色。可以说，文博事业的发展越来越离不开数字化技术。同时，对于难以开发和储存的文物，现在的文物修复师们也可以用高科技来预估修复的材料、时间、环境等，并且用数字模型来建构文物复原模型，辅助修复。

（四）与国外博物馆对比数字化应用建设

本部分以法国卢浮宫博物馆和英国大英博物馆的数字化技术运用为例，与故宫博物院的数字化建设作对比。

1.案例选择

选择法国卢浮宫博物馆和英国大英博物馆作为研究案例主要有以下原因。

首先，这两家外国博物馆历史悠久、藏品众多，是当代世界博物馆中首屈一指的存在，在藏品保护和展示方面也较早采用了先进的数字化技术。其次，大英博物馆和卢浮宫博物馆之所以为一流博物馆不仅因为它们自身藏品丰富和历史底蕴深厚等，还因为它们借助了大众传媒等手段来推广宣传。选取这两家博物馆与故宫博物院进行对比研究是为了更好地学习和借鉴外国博物馆的数字化宣传营销方式。此外，两家外国博物馆在文创领域也引进了数字化技术，在生产、销售方面利用了高科技手段提高效益。最后，由于两家外国博物馆藏品的历史特殊性（其中多数是中国文物），本文希望在关注两个博物馆数字化技术运用于藏品展出等方面的同时，也看到中国文物在其中受到的对待与价值。

2.法国卢浮宫博物馆

法国卢浮宫博物馆（简称"卢浮宫"）早在1995年就设置了官方网站，2001年网站访问人数就超过600万人次。2004年，卢浮宫在展品的数据化方面有所尝试，用户通过官方网站就能参观馆内公开展示的所有藏品。2014年5月，法国卢浮宫引进了日本的"任天堂3DS"掌上视频游戏控制导游系统，它可以根据用户需求为用户提供定位服务，带领用户到达相应的展区和展品前。

目前，卢浮宫正在开发为智能手机和iPad等终端提供下载服务的应用程序，且由于卢浮宫主要以全景的方式呈现虚拟博物馆，这就使得它能够用 Virtual Tour工具以平行视角进行全方位扫描取景，实现在有文字说明基础上的向上、向下、放大、缩小等全方位的浏览。无论何时何地，用户只要登录卢浮宫博物馆的官网就可以在线访问卢浮宫的艺术展、埃及馆、卢浮宫护城河以及阿波罗廊等景区。①

除此之外，该导航系统中不仅有每一件展品的高清图片，还配有相关的语音评论和手语视频演示等服务。卢浮宫虚拟博物馆主要运用虚拟现实技术和3D扫描技术构建一个接近于现实的虚拟环境，并用一定的路线构想和交互设计完成展览活动。如馆内的应用箭头能够引导用户前进，标识可以引导用户和展品互动。除了虚拟现实技术和3D扫描技术之外，卢浮宫虚拟博物馆还利用3D全息影像技术对博物馆的场景和馆藏进行全方位和细节方面的展示，其方向功能和放大缩小功能能够满足用户对视觉和细节的要求。②

可以得知，卢浮宫博物馆与我国故宫博物院的数字化建设进程相当。在开始时间、使用不同高科技的时间段、如何使用数字化技术保护等方面，两国的博物馆竟达到相似的一致性；且重点都是放在对文物的保护与展览当中，以数字化模型、文物信息介绍、VR技术、多维角度展示等方式辅助文物展览；其中，法国卢浮宫博物馆也打造了"数字化博物馆"中的名牌，通过名牌效应给其他展览馆区或者文物也带去热度，这一经营模式也是故宫博物院的经营模式之一。

3.英国大英博物馆

大英博物馆的数字化进程：大英博物馆是世界范围内最早引入数字化技术建设文博事业的博物馆之一，它所使用的语音导览技术以及线上地图给旅客带来了极大的方便。旅客可以在语音导览APP上选择使用不同语言来了解藏品信息，并且根据自己喜爱的藏品风格来规划自己的观光路线。

不同于故宫博物院的语音导览系统，大英博物馆的语音导览更加侧重于多语种介绍，以期为来自世界各地的旅客服务。而故宫博物院的语音导览系统还停留在中文介绍（英文翻译系统尚未完善，在介绍藏品信息和历史时枚存在不足）。由此可见，故宫博物院急需建设语音导览中的"多语种选择"功能以更好地提高国际知名度。

---

① 陈爽，袁佳丽，胡永斌.虚拟博物馆：信息时代博物馆发展的新趋势.中国教育技术装备，2021(6)：27-30.
② 陈爽，袁佳丽，胡永斌.虚拟博物馆：信息时代博物馆发展的新趋势.中国教育技术装备，2021(6)：27-30.

2013 年，大英博物馆联合伦敦大学学院（University College London）、英国国家人文艺术研究会（Arts and Humanities Research Council）发起了 Micro Pasts 项目，即大英博物馆将全球范围的数千名志愿者通过网络"集结"在一起，对馆藏"青铜时代"系列文物相关数据进行了数字化处理：对 30000 张制成于 20 世纪初期的手写藏品索引卡进行了数字化转录；对 5787 张文物照片进行了数字化 3D 建模前预处理工作如勾勒轮廓线并数字化。[①]

除了使用语音导览和 3D 建模，大英博物馆还使用虚拟画廊（在大英博物馆官方网站搜索即可在线浏览与收藏）这一数字化技术展示馆藏文物。

打开大英博物馆官网，搜索虚拟画廊。点开图片，会有一段文字对藏品进行描述。由于是线上观赏，我们可以在官网随时随地收藏自己喜爱的藏品资料与信息。由于大英博物馆藏品众多，受场地和藏品保护等限制，博物馆不可能将所有的藏品陈列摆放在展馆中供游客观赏。因此大英博物馆选择将部分藏品放在官网上展出，并且对它们进行介绍。

在大英博物馆这一案例中，我们可以注意到，大英博物馆尤为重视中国市场，特地联合中国的平台共同打造文物直播平台。因此，在故宫博物院数字化建设进程中，也应当学习大英博物馆，把视野投到海外。可以云直播或者做成视频发布在海外平台，配上多国语言（例如英语、法语、俄语、德语等）配音或者字幕，扩大故宫博物院在全世界文博事业内的文化影响力，同时也能让外国人了解我们国家文博事业的数字化技术发展进程，进一步吸引更多的资金和人才技术共同参与故宫博物院的数字化建设项目。而这一环节也是目前国内其他博物馆鲜少注意到的。

但同时，我们也注意到，大英博物馆在数字化技术建设方面也存在缺陷。大英博物馆的藏品颇多，在数字化技术建设方面也存在着对海量文物保护不足的问题。在文物保护的数量和质量上，大英博物馆的数字化技术运用相对故宫博物院来说是不足的。

综合上述材料，无论是法国的卢浮宫博物馆还是英国的大英博物馆，故宫博物院的数字化技术建设进程并不逊色于外国博物馆的数字化建设，但仍有很大的改进空间。

---

① 刘文杰，"互联网+协作"在文博领域的应用——以大英博物馆"众包模式"完成藏品数字化. 中国甲午战争博物馆，2017(01): 134-140.

（五）故宫博物院在数字化建设中面临的难题

1.公众对"数字化故宫"仍缺少认知

故宫博物院的数字化建设还处于起步状态，还有许多尚未完全开发能够进行数字化展览的文物。同时，由于我国的文物保护以及博物馆等领域属于"小众冷圈"，很多人对于博物馆以及文物保护等方面缺少了解，对"数字化故宫"这一概念更是知之甚少。因此故宫博物院在继续加大数字化文物保护、展览的过程中，将重点也放在了给民众科普数字化应用与文博事业相结合的知识上。

2."打卡"对"数字化故宫"的影响

近些年，我们也注意到，许多互联网平台发出了一些调查问卷，都是关于"互联网＋博物馆能否促进文物保护和展示""数字化博物馆与传统博物馆展览之间的对比"等话题。大多数网民都认为，新型的数字化博物馆和网络直播文物展览有利于文物的保护和展览。与传统博物馆展览不同，数字化博物馆能够使用户从多维角度仔细观察文物，而在传统的博物馆中，人们只能够透过展览柜和介绍板了解文物，很难注意和观察到一些细节以及其他角度，而且由于文物不能暴露在强光之下，因此游客们只能饱一时的眼福，而无法全面深入地了解文物。

但是，也有人提出，在网络上参观博物馆，远不如在现场看到实物震撼。而且"打卡"这一噱头使人们更多地想去实地参观，而不是宅在家里"云参观"。就目前的总体情况来看，国内游客依旧偏向于传统博物馆这一参观模式，数字化博物馆对于人们来说只是"偶尔换个口味"的参观模式。故宫博物院在文物保护和展览方面，有较大的突破与发展，但是仅靠故宫博物院的努力是不够的，需要国家、社会其他组织以及民众的多方努力。相关政府部门可提高数字化故宫博物院的宣传力度，社会组织可以提供更多的数字化技术支持故宫文物展示，而民众也应当更新自己对文博事业的认识，了解数字化博物馆的更多益处。

五、故宫博物院未来发展建议

（一）数字化服务于旅客观展

有些游客对博物馆的馆区分布、藏品陈列以及行程路线规划感到迷茫，甚至有些时候会在馆区迷路、多次在一个馆区打转。因此，本文认为，故宫在接下来的数字化建设当中也应当引入和大英博物馆、卢浮宫博物馆类似的数字化全景地图或者语音导览系统，可以实施实时导航并且让旅客根据自己的观展需求、利用大数据算法来规划路线，同时对已经行进了的馆区与路线进行标记、在旅客第二次进入该馆区时进行提醒（如询问是否要第二次参观该已经参观过的展区）。

（二）数字化服务于文创产业与科普教育

通过分析两家外国博物馆，我们可以看出大英博物馆和卢浮宫博物馆早已有寓教于乐的意识——通过让旅客参观文物来了解背后的历史以及将他们的意识形态通过这种文化活动渗透给旅客（比如大英博物馆就曾经宣传他们将埃及和中国的文物收藏于馆区而不是归还给原主是因为他们"能够更好地保存文明"）。因此本文认为，故宫可以根据不同年龄段（尤其是针对青少年）来制定动画和电子书、立体实体书来向我们的国民进行科普宣传，在介绍文物的时候也应当引入历史。如此一来既能推动故宫博物院文创产业发展，又能够发挥故宫博物院寓教于乐的大众教育功能。同时，也可以开展面向外国友人的动画字幕翻译、书籍翻译等工作。

六、总　结

故宫的文创产品和数字化建设进程在国内文博领域属于顶层的水平，并且随着这些年互联网以及高新技术的发展，故宫 IP 在国内的影响力也逐步扩大，因此故宫在接下来的发展建设中应当进一步抓住互联网、新媒体来扩大优势。

故宫在国际化方面（无论是向国外推广介绍文物还是文创产品走出国门）仍存在不足，有些藏品的陈列和展出方式并不能很好地帮助外国人更好地了解中国故事和历史。此外，科技应用和数字化保护不够完善。尽管故宫博物院在文物科技创新方面取得了相应成果，但与国际先进水平相比，仍存在一定差距。数据显示，截至 2021 年，故宫博物院数字化收藏的文物仅占全部馆藏的 1%[①]，数字化展览和互动体验的应用仍相对有限。

综合来看，故宫在未来的发展建设中依旧需要扩大自身 IP 在国内外的影响力，同时积极开辟海外市场和发掘外国人对于了解中国故事和历史的兴趣和需求。学习国外顶尖的博物馆数字化技术及营销宣传方式有助于传播中华文化，提高我国国际影响力和文化软实力。

---

① 中国故宫博物院院刊 . [2024-01-25]. https://www.dpm.org.cn/journals/journal/259477.html.

从经营模式研究美国大都会艺术博物馆的发展建设①

摘　要： 博物馆的概念具有多维度性，其中广义的博物馆代指文
化、传播行为。因此，博物馆不仅指具体化的建筑，还指
一种理念与行动。其本身是人类社会发展到一定程度的产
物，而在如今全球化趋势下，博物馆作为人类文化发展的
标志，其发展和建设也越来越重要。美国大都会艺术博物
馆作为世界五大博物馆之一，其起源、发展和变革值得研
究。因此，本文以美国大都会艺术博物馆为研究对象，对
于其经营模式上的成功经验进行分析和研究，以期对我国
博物馆的建设提供一些启示，来满足人民日益增长的美好
生活需要。

关键词： 大都会艺术博物馆；全球化；数字建设；经营模式

一、概　览

（一）基本信息

1. 总体介绍

大都会艺术博物馆（The Metropolitan Museum of Art）是美国规模最大的
艺术博物馆，与法国卢浮宫博物馆、英国大英博物馆、俄罗斯艾尔米塔什博物
馆、中国故宫博物院并称为世界五大博物馆。其主馆坐落于美国纽约曼哈顿第
五大道的 82 号大街，博物馆现占地 8 公顷，长度超过 400 米，已是博物馆落
成之初的 20 倍。它目前拥有 3 层展馆、近千个展厅、330 余万件藏品和 400 多
个主题陈列，展览面积达 20 万平方米。其分馆之一的修道院博物馆（The Met

---

① 作者：顾凡茹，首都师范大学英语笔译专业；李玉芹，首都师范大学英语笔译专业；张芷榕，首都师范
大学俄语系。

Cloisters）位于美国纽约曼哈顿北边的崔恩堡公园（Fort Tryon Park），俯瞰哈德逊河，占地1.62公顷，展品以中世纪艺术、建筑和花园为主题，展馆共有2000件以上西方中世纪的艺术作品和建筑元素。另一分馆名为布劳耶分馆（The Met Breuer，又称花园），位于美国纽约曼哈顿麦迪逊大街，曾展示现当代艺术，但因其花费高、观众少、展评褒贬不一，为节省每年租金，该分馆于2020年转租给了弗利克艺术收藏馆（The Frick Collection），因此现在大都会艺术博物馆只有主馆和修道院分馆。本文主要对主馆进行研究分析。

2. 经营理念

美国大都会艺术博物馆与许多其他享誉世界的艺术博物馆的不同之处在于，它是一所非营利性质的私人文化机构。1866年7月4日，美国著名律师约翰·杰伊（John Jay）在美国独立日纪念活动上提出美国也应立即建立一个艺术博物馆的设想。1870年，博物馆成立之初便向公众宣告了其使命愿景，即要在纽约建立一个艺术博物馆，以促进艺术研究的发展，推动艺术在制造与现实生活中的应用，普及同类学科的一般知识，并向广大公众提供通识教育。这一声明引领着大都会艺术博物馆一路向前。[1]

自博物馆成立以来，博物馆理事会重申了这一使命，并补充发展为现有宣言，即大都会艺术博物馆收藏、研究、保存和展示伟大的跨时代、跨文化艺术品，赋予全人类以创造力、知识和观点，使得人类命运紧密相连。由此可见，随着全球化的发展，在传统观念上博物馆所应承担的传播艺术文化、普及艺术知识的责任之上，博物馆又增加了全人类艺术共同体的概念，更具时代感和前瞻性。[2]

（二）发展历程

大都会艺术博物馆于1870年成立之初，将馆址选定在纽约第五大道681号（原为多德沃思舞蹈学校旧址），并于1872年在该地开馆，后来因藏品不断增加，原馆已不能满足收藏展览需求，博物馆于1873年改迁到西十四街128号的道哥拉斯私人宅邸，但最终于1880年迁移到位于纽约曼哈顿中央公园第

---

[1]　来自美国大都会艺术博物馆官方网站；史伟. 艺术博物馆选址因素研究. 北京：中央美术学院硕士学位论文，2009；江振鹏. 纽约大都会艺术博物馆的历史及文化功能. 公关世界，2019(22)：38-43；陈儒斌. 收藏与展览是艺术博物馆的核心竞争力——以纽约大都会艺术博物馆为例. 中国博物馆，2013(01)：30-35.

[2]　江振鹏. 纽约大都会艺术博物馆的历史及文化功能. 公关世界，2019(22)：38-43；陈儒斌. 收藏与展览是艺术博物馆的核心竞争力——以纽约大都会艺术博物馆为例. 中国博物馆，2013(01)：30-35.

五大道和 82 街交口处的现址，作为永久性主馆馆址。

其馆址几经迁移，体现了历代经营者的重视和运营之道。然其建立之初，对于大都会艺术博物馆的设想也不是一蹴而就的。大都会艺术博物馆建立于美国工业化快速推进的时代，当时南北战争的结束以及美洲大陆交通体系的完善，为美国工业化快速协调发展奠基，进而推动了纽约成为国际性大都会的进程。然而经济繁荣发展、作为新兴移民城市的纽约却存在文化积淀欠缺、文化氛围不足的问题。1866 年 7 月 4 日，在巴黎举办的庆祝美国独立日活动上，美国著名律师小约翰·杰伊提出了建立一家国家艺术博物馆的构想。1870 年 4 月 13 日，一批美国实业家、艺术家、慈善家和律师发起了建立大都会艺术博物馆的倡议，同年 5 月 24 日《大都会艺术博物馆宪章》诞生，宪章规定，大都会艺术博物馆采取向纽约市政府和私人组成的理事会负责的管理模式。美国铁路官员约翰·泰勒·约翰斯顿（John Tyler Johnston）的私人藏品最早被博物馆先后于 1870 年 11 月及 1871 年收录，包括数具古代罗马的石棺和 174 幅来自彼得·保罗·鲁本斯（Peter Paul Rubens）、安东尼·凡·戴克（Anthony van Dyck）、乔凡尼·巴蒂斯塔·提埃坡罗（Giovanni Battista Tiepolo）的绘画。1873 年，美国前陆军军官、驻塞浦路斯领事路易斯·帕尔玛·蒂·塞斯诺拉（Luigi Palma di Cesnola）成为博物馆首任馆长，博物馆于 1874 年至 1876 年购买了其收藏的古代艺术品（从青铜时代到罗马时代末期的作品），这使得大都会艺术博物馆收获了作为古代文物主要收藏库的声誉。在 19 世纪之后的时间里，博物馆的藏品不断增加。

20 世纪初，美国工业经济已跻身世界第一，纽约集聚了大批拥有大量财富的商人、金融巨擘和艺术收藏家，在这一背景下，大都会艺术博物馆迎来了快速发展的黄金期，并在 20 世纪的发展中正式成为世界上最伟大的艺术中心之一。美国金融大亨 J. P. 摩根（J. P. Morgan）担任博物馆主席期间（1904—1913 年），博物馆收到的捐赠藏品数量迅速增加，如 1907 年，博物馆获得了奥古斯特·雷诺阿（Auguste Renoir）的作品，再如 1910 年，大都会艺术博物馆成为世界上第一个获得亨利·马蒂斯（Henri Matisse）艺术作品的公共机构。此时也是博物馆收藏古希腊重要艺术品和古埃及文物的重要时间点。1924 年，罗伯特·德·福雷斯特（Robert de Forest）为博物馆馆长的时期，主持建造了大都会艺术博物馆的美国馆，自此大都会艺术博物馆开始注重收藏并展出美国本土艺术文化作品。1938 年，大都会艺术博物馆收购了著名富商约翰·洛克菲勒三世（John Rockefeller Ⅲ）斥巨资修建的修道院博物馆。1946 年，大都会艺术博物馆又收购了服装艺术博物馆，并将其更名为服装学院（the Costume Institute）。

从 20 世纪 70 年代开始，大都会艺术博物馆开始了大规模扩建，于 1978 年新建了埃及的丹铎神庙，1980 年扩建了包括 24 个厅的美国馆，1982 年新建了专藏非洲、大洋洲和美洲艺术品的迈克尔·洛克菲勒展厅，而后还有专展现代艺术的华莱士展厅，专展欧洲雕塑艺术的克拉维斯展厅。再至 20 世纪 90 年代，于 1998 年先后投入建设了朝鲜艺术展厅、古代近东艺术展厅等，至此，大都会艺术博物馆较 19 世纪 80 年代已经扩大了 20 倍。2007 年，主馆大楼南端的几项重大项目完工，最引人注目的是历时 15 年的希腊和罗马艺术画廊翻新。海洋和北美本土艺术画廊也于 2007 年开放，此后还扩增了 19 世纪和 20 世纪早期绘画和雕塑画廊以及露丝和哈罗德·D.尤里斯教育中心（Ruth and Harold D. Uris Center）。

（三）展区组成

美国大都会艺术博物馆坚持以"百科全书"式的架构，收藏全人类各种文化的古今优秀艺术作品的理念，尽力塑造馆藏丰富多彩、展览尽善尽美的核心竞争力。现今，大都会艺术博物馆收藏的艺术品涵盖人类 5000 年的文明发展历程，它们共同向观者讲述着世界文明艺术的发展史。

根据官网导览信息，现在大都会艺术博物馆有 19 个专题收藏区域，分别为：迈克尔·洛克菲勒的非洲艺术、美国之翼、古代近东艺术、武器和盔甲、迈克尔·洛克菲勒翼楼的美国古代艺术、亚洲艺术、服装学院、图纸和印刷品、埃及艺术、欧洲绘画、欧洲雕塑和装饰艺术、希腊和罗马艺术、伊斯兰艺术、罗伯特·雷曼收藏、中世纪艺术与修道院、现当代艺术、乐器、迈克尔·洛克菲勒翼楼的海洋艺术、照片。依据艺术品主题可划分为：建筑学、沉思、死亡、时尚、地图、人像、天空、爱、小狗、花朵、内饰、图书、风景。

大都会艺术博物馆还经常策划各类特展，每年约有几十个特展，曾在世界博物馆中首创"超级特展"概念。特展主要有馆藏特展和馆外特展两种，馆藏特展如 2011 年的"馆藏毕加索作品展"、2012 年的"中国宝石精品展"等，馆外特展如 1996 年台北故宫博物院珍藏展"中华瑰宝"、2003 年"达·芬奇素描艺术特展"等。在众多特展中，20 世纪 60—70 年代策划的卢浮宫"蒙娜丽莎"巡展和"图坦卡蒙宝藏"特展盛况空前，创下数百万人次的参观纪录。

（四）信息变革

步入新时代的今天，互联网、虚拟科技等发展迅速，大都会艺术博物馆也紧跟时代发展，引入虚拟数字技术，积极打造全球最先进的数字博物馆。在数据库构建及业务运营方面，大都会艺术博物馆已获得较突出的成果，如艺术史研究数据库——"海尔布伦艺术史时间线"（Heilbrunn Timeline of Art History）；在学术图书开放获取方面，大都会艺术博物馆也已走在行业前列，如大都会艺术博物馆自 2017 年 2 月推出"开放获取计划"（Open Access Initiative），将其所收藏的约 375000 张公共艺术品图片资源向公众开放，供公众自由、不受限制地使用。这些结合先进技术打造的观展服务，进一步打破世界各地观众想要获取馆藏艺术精品游览体验的时空限制。

与此同时，在数字媒体科技极大地冲击传统纸质刊物的时代背景下，大都会艺术博物馆以其专业高标准的出版团队、与时俱进的策划理念成为全球博物馆出版业务的领头羊，在一定程度上掌握着全球博物馆学术研究领域的话语权。《大都会艺术博物馆馆刊》（Metropolitan Museum Journal）和《大都会艺术博物馆公报》（The Metropolitan Museum of Art Bulletin）的创立是其扩大影响力的重要途径。除此之外，大都会艺术博物馆还将核心理念融入其品牌出版物《大都会艺术博物馆指南》（Metropolitan Museum of Art Guide），且在序言里明确提出将"探索本馆的世界级出版物"作为"体验大都会艺术博物馆"的方式之一。

二、经营模式

于其发展历程中，大都会艺术博物馆不仅是美国藏品丰富的博物馆，在某种程度上还体现了美国文化兼容的特点，在国际层面象征着美国文化独立之精神。追溯其历史根源，1776 年，美利坚合众国通过《独立宣言》向世界宣告其自由之躯。然而，欧洲艺术一直强势占领西方文化市场，美国本土艺术势弱。1870 年，大都会艺术博物馆横空出世，美国再次吸引了全世界的目光。大都会艺术博物馆是如何做到肩负时代之重任、顶住重重压力脱颖而出，建设成为当今世界一大杰出博物馆的？其经营模式值得我们深入探讨和借鉴。

（一）合理的资金来源

大都会艺术博物馆属于非营利机构，但同时需要自主创收，以实现博物馆的核心目标和使命。博物馆收入主要来自政府资助、私有捐赠（包括私人、企业和基金会赞助）以及博物馆自身收益，其中私有捐赠占比最大。

1. 公私合作为表现形式

大都会艺术博物馆主馆建筑属于纽约市政府的财产，市政府负担供电与暖气及三分之一的安保和维护费用，该馆理事会监管藏品并负担所有相关费用，以及三分之二的安保和维护费。此外，纽约州政府通过纽约州艺术委员会每年向其提供大于 20 万美元的经费，联邦政府主要通过国家捐赠艺术基金会和国家捐赠人文基金会向博物馆提供支持。这两家基金会是美国文化艺术类非营利组织筹集资金的重要途径，主要为特展、巡展等大型展览和公共教育项目提供赞助。[①] 而且，国家科学基金会和博物馆与图书馆服务协会每年也为大都会艺术博物馆提供大量资金支持。政府还会通过颁发特许经营权、保险担保、邮资补贴等间接措施为其提供支持。这种模式既保证了政府对大都会艺术博物馆的支持，使其享受税收、房产、租金等一系列的优惠，又能保持机构的独立性，使其免受政府的侵扰，提高了公共服务的效率，而其非营利性质又避免了管理者以追逐利益优先，而忽略了公众利益。

2. 私有力量占主导地位

大都会艺术博物馆私有力量占主导地位的性质对世界其他博物馆的发展具有重要的示范性意义。一方面，私人捐赠一直是大都会博物馆运营的主要资金来源。美国联邦法律鼓励私人捐赠，捐赠风气更盛。理事会在资金捐赠上往往起到带头作用，常常发动自己的关系网络为机构募款。另一方面，大都会艺术博物馆作为纽约最大的文化旅游目的地和世界领先的学术研究及教育资源汇集地，与美国大型企业一直保持着良好的合作关系，双方形成一种互惠的利益关系。从 1976 年开始，企业赞助成为大都会艺术博物馆的重要资金来源，尤其是博物馆教育项目得到了有力支持。为了回馈企业的大力支持，博物馆为企业赞助者提供免税等福利和发展公共关系的机会，帮助企业树立良好的企业形象，寻找特殊的市场目标和潜在客户资源。

---

① 黄小娇.美国博物馆的非营利运营模式——以大都会艺术博物馆为例.博物馆管理，2020(03): 17-27.

（二）高效的管理机制——"理事会—馆长—策展人"体系

1. 理事会

美国博物馆无论公立或私立，均设有各自的理事会或同等权力组织，受联邦和州法典、联邦和州税法以及州公司法、非营利组织法等为核心的法律约束及保护，大都会艺术博物馆亦是如此。理事会是博物馆的最高权力机构，担有选任、治理、决策和监督的职责，是体现博物馆社会信托性质的制度安排。1870 年 5 月 24 日，美国政府通过了《大都会艺术博物馆宪章》，宪章规定大都会艺术博物馆采取向纽约市政府和私人组成的理事会负责的管理模式。[①]

大都会艺术博物馆自成立便设立了理事会，最早仅有 8 人。1981 年，博物馆开始设立总经理一职，起初与馆长平行，从 1998 年起接受理事会和馆长的双重领导。经过 150 多年的发展，理事会现包括主席、副主席、表决理事、当然理事和荣誉理事。经选举产生的表决理事有投票权，每届任期 5 年，每年改选五分之一。当然理事是非选举理事，包括馆长（全权负责日常行政和业务管理）、总经理（协助馆长负责经营开发）和纽约市政府及市议会官员，同表决理事一样具有投票权。其他人员则属于荣誉理事，包括终身荣誉理事和名誉理事。[②]根据大都会艺术博物馆最新发布的 2021—2022 年年度报告，博物馆理事会现由 100 人组成（表 1）。理事会成员的选拔、增补、更替通过理事会内部的提名委员会协商提名，由具有投票权的理事投票决定。理事们的背景以商界、财界居多，也有律师、收藏家等，年龄为 50 岁至 72 岁，男女比例相当。理事会下设 16 个专业委员会，以掌管各领域的具体事物，包括执行、收购、审计、建筑、薪酬、发展、多样性和包容性、外部事务、财务、人力资源、影响与参与、投资、法律、提名与治理、营收，另外还有一个博物馆基金会。由于理事会由社会各界人士组成，进一步推动公众和社会力量参与博物馆的各项决策和建设中，为私立的大都会艺术博物馆赋予了更多公共性，促进其公共职能的实现。同时，博物馆也在资金方面有了更丰富的来源。理事会制度的存在可以说为大都会艺术博物馆的长足发展奠定了雄厚的社会和经济基础，并为其平稳运行确定了行之有效的管理模式。

---

① 江振鹏.纽约大都会艺术博物馆的历史及文化功能.公关世界，2019(22)：38-43.
② 梁丹妮.纽约大都会艺术博物馆理事会制度研究.上海文化，2014(6)：97-100.

表1 大都会艺术博物馆 2021—2022 年年度理事会成员 [1]

职位	人数
联合主席	2
副主席	1
表决理事	42
	2022 年 9 月任期期满 8 人
	2023 年 9 月任期期满 9 人
	2024 年 9 月任期期满 9 人
	2025 年 9 月任期期满 10 人
	2026 年 9 月任期期满 6 人
当然理事	7
终身荣誉理事	29
名誉理事	19
总计	100

2. 馆长

博物馆内部普遍实行理事会领导下的馆长负责制，馆长由理事会挑选、任命，全权负责日常事务。在博物馆的核心业务中，馆长直接与各个艺术部门的策展人联系，并对理事会负责，形成了"理事会－馆长－策展人"的业务体系，这三者构成了博物馆核心业务（购藏、展览、研究、教育）最重要的力量。南京博物院原院长龚良指出："大都会挑选的馆长都要具备以下条件：第一，一定有专业背景；第二，一定有发展视野；第三，一定要潜心了解、研究大都会并且有信心做出改变。"[2] 理事会可根据馆长的任上表现定夺其去留。如果馆长在任期间表现良好，博物馆运转正常，理事会不会改聘馆长。如果馆长的履职受到质疑，影响到博物馆的运营，理事会将另聘新馆长。

3. 策展人

策展人是博物馆业务部门的直接负责人，管理部门内具体事务，接受馆长的监督和指导。策展人的核心职能在于系统收集相关证物，从而进行实物研究、丰富知识，并通过展览、科教活动、讲座等方法传播所有知识。简而言

---

① 表1来自：Annual Report, Audited Financial Statements, Members Report, and IRS Form 990.
② 龚良，毛颖. 全球视野下中国博物馆的建设发展：借鉴大都会艺术博物馆——龚良院长专访. 东南文化，2014(03)：26-33.

之，策展人观照了从知识建构到文化表达的方方面面。20 世纪七八十年代以前，博物馆的核心业务人员是策展人，而馆长是为策展人服务的，充当策展人与理事会之间的传话筒。20 世纪七八十年代以后，随着博物馆管理事宜得到重视，策展人逐渐降级为下属业务部门。在博物馆事务中，策展人一方面与藏品、艺术家、观众的关系更为紧密，直接影响着博物馆的日常运营；另一方面作为业务骨干，又可以影响理事会和馆长的决策。

按照层级，策展人可分为助理策展人（assistant curator）、副策展人（associate curator）、策展人（curator）和总策展人（curator in charge）。博物馆下设 19 个艺术门类，每一个门类的艺术品都由一个专家负责。一个业务部门往往有几个或者十几个策展人，分别按专业研究方向而分管不同品类的藏品，受总策展人（curator in charge）管理。在策展人管理模式之下，博物馆日常事务能够得到有效统筹分配。同时，博物馆还会组织策展人论坛，以促进部门之间的交流，共享管理、展览、维护等多方面的经验心得，形成内部良性循环的发展环境。

（三）与时俱进的经营战略

1. 选址

选址是一个博物馆建设的第一步，一个成功的选址将为博物馆未来的运营打下坚实的基础，避免不必要的人力物力消耗。更为重要的是，博物馆作为一城乃至一国的视窗，其社会文化功能能否实现，与选址大有关系。从 1870 年建立之后，大都会艺术博物馆三易其址，这个过程受历史、文化、经济等诸多因素的影响，既反映了创立者对构建大都会艺术博物馆的思考和定位，也侧面展现了博物馆的成长过程。

首先，大都会艺术博物馆设立之初就是为了展现美国的艺术风貌。南北战争结束，纽约作为美国国际性大都会迅速崛起，经济的繁荣与纽约作为新兴移民城市的"文化短板"现象形成了强烈的反差。艺术能够促进人类道德与文化观念的提升，这是一个社会迈向成熟的体现。而纽约当时已是美国的经济中心，人均 GDP（按 1990 年美元汇率计算）在 1820 年时为 1257 美元，1870 年已提高到 2445 美元。[①]纽约地理位置得天独厚，位于美国东北部沿海哈德逊河口，濒临大西洋，交通极为便利。而曼哈顿又是纽约的核心，汇集了世界 500

---

① 段勇.博物馆理事会制度大有可为.光明日报，2014-04-12(09).

强中绝大部分公司的总部。正是因为身处这样一个经济资源丰富的区域，大都会艺术博物馆才能获得源源不断的人力物力支持并持续发展。再者，中央公园位于曼哈顿的中心，占地面积达 843 英亩，风景优美，是繁华市内的静谧之地。而第五大道又是曼哈顿的中轴线，为东西街道的分界线，交通便利，商业发达。大都会艺术博物馆伫立于这样一个动静结合的中心点，在古老的艺术给人以沉思之时，都市的张力又将人拉回到现实之中。

其次，博物馆的选址也与其发展轨迹有关。大都会艺术博物馆前期的几次迁址主要可以归因于早期准备不足以及后续规模扩大。在确定现址为永久馆址后，博物馆又进行多次扩建修缮，才得以呈现出如今世人见到的宏伟馆藏。

2. 支持政策

除了政府的直接资金支持，大都会艺术博物馆的发展同样离不开美国国家政策的大力支持。美国是第一个进行文化立法的国家。[1]学者们认为美国采用"一向因循"的文化政策，即"无为而治"（non-activity, non-regulation）。这意味着美国政府不对博物馆事务进行直接管理，而是遵循其自身发展规律，尽量为其创造适宜发展的社会环境，焕发艺术自身的生命力、影响力。

但无为不代表不作为，美国政府还颁布了一系列有利的税收政策，为大都会艺术博物馆及其他博物馆营造了良好的发展环境。1909 年，美国《佩恩·奥尔德里奇关税法》规定对进口 20 年以上的艺术品免税，1913 年再次修改为对所有的艺术品进口免税。[2]这一法案使得国外艺术品大批流向美国，时任馆长摩根在英国丰富的藏品也因此归于大都会艺术博物馆。

1917 年，美国国会开始施行联邦税法，规定向非营利组织提供捐助可一律免除税费。对于资产雄厚的个人或企业来说，向博物馆等非营利机构捐赠成了比将藏品遗留给子孙或交给拍卖行更加有利的选择。在面临高税率的遗产税的同时，美国公民也有机会享受一系列法定税收减免项目，其中就包括慈善捐赠减免。由于慈善捐赠减免没有比例限制，无论个人或企业，只要符合税法规定，遗产捐赠行为均可以享受 100% 的全额税前扣除，因而博物馆在资金和藏品方面都获得了更为强有力的支撑。

此外，大都会艺术博物馆作为美国非营利组织的成员，可以免征联邦所得税、各州企业税以及当地的财产税和增值税，减免邮费、艺术品的某些保险

---

[1] 吕文静.连锁经营与创新运营：艺术博物馆运营模式研究.艺术管理（中英文），2021(01): 129-13.
[2] 王聪丛.美国两部税收法案促藏品流入博物馆.中国文化报，2012-11-14.

费、海关税等。20 世纪 70 年代开始，针对所有境外艺术展览，美国政府为每个展览提供最高 5000 万美元的保价服务，每年为全美提供总额为 1.5 亿美元的担保。到 1992 年，每个展览最高担保额超过 1.5 亿美元，担保总额达到 4 亿美元。[①]这为大都会艺术博物馆在境内举办世界大展提供了便利，并进一步推动了世界艺术品征集收藏。

3. 重大转型

建立艺术"大百科全书"的理念一直贯穿于大都会艺术博物馆发展过程之中。大都会艺术博物馆由起初狂热追捧欧洲艺术品，扩大到在全世界范围内收集购买艺术珍品，更是在二战后囊括了欧洲、美洲、亚洲、非洲等各个地区各个时期的艺术珍宝，成为与法国卢浮宫和英国大英博物馆比肩的世界顶级博物馆。[②]大都会艺术博物馆之所以能发展到如今庞大的规模，离不开自身不断地修正和扩张。本节仅列出几个具有代表性的节点进行论述。

19 世纪末 20 世纪初，美国经历了一波又一波的移民热潮，各个城市的贫民窟挤满了各种各样的面孔，美国的本土文化受到了严重威胁。大都会艺术博物馆作为美国博物馆的代表也试图解决这一困境，1924 年，美国之翼展厅创建，并发展为美国首家系统、大规模收藏本国装饰艺术的博物馆。

20 世纪 70 年代以前，大都会艺术博物馆的中国艺术品收藏一直停滞不前，毫无起色。直至 1970 年秋，著名的艺术文物鉴赏家、教育家方闻受时任馆长托马斯·霍温（Thomas Hoving）邀请任特别顾问，并在理事会主席道格拉斯·狄隆（Douglas Dillon）的授意下开始组建"亚洲艺术部"。在方闻的"收藏收藏家"理念的指导下，"亚洲艺术部"顺利引进中国古代绘画领域最具影响力的系列作品——王季迁先生的 25 幅宋元绘画，才有了后来的"宋元绘画"展，使其迅速赶上了当时已在亚洲艺术收藏领域领先的波士顿、克利夫兰等艺术博物馆，得到了美国博物馆界元老李雪曼（Sherman Lee）、史克门（Laurence Sickman）等人的赞许。在此后的三十年中，经过研究人员、收藏家和赞助人的齐心协力，大都会艺术博物馆跻身世界上最全面展示亚洲艺术的博物馆行列，实现了大都会艺术博物馆广泛收藏世界各地艺术的使命。

1972 年，大都会艺术博物馆聘任时尚杂志 *Vogue* 前主编黛安娜·弗里兰

① 赵菁. 博物馆作为公共空间?——西方博物馆财政政策与公共服务. 国际文化管理，2017(00): 110-123.
② 谈晟广. 1973 年：纽约大都会艺术博物馆如何开始建立世界一流的中国古画收藏. 中国书画，2017(08): 4-10.

（Diana Vreeland）为服装学院的特别顾问。弗里兰改变了传统的橱窗式策展模式，打破了空间的束缚，借助舞台灯光、音乐、色彩等元素开启了博物馆时尚展览的观展热潮。而馆长霍温更是将博物馆打造成一座大型综合体，大肆开设衍生品商店、咖啡馆和餐厅，力图摆脱其沉闷古老的形象，并为博物馆赢得更多发展资金。虽然这种将博物馆资本化、娱乐化的方式为许多人诟病，却不失为管理者对博物馆未来发展方向的一个大胆尝试。

2008 年，康柏堂（Thomas P. Campbell）就任馆长时，大都会艺术博物馆面临着较严峻的经济形势：美国雷曼兄弟公司破产，经济危机致使美国民众收入缩水，因而在参观收费的情况下，博物馆的观众明显减少。因此，康柏堂到任后提出五个工作重点。第一，应培养专业人员。几年来，博物馆通过各种项目培养了一批批馆内员工和后备人员，为其长远发展做出一定贡献。第二，应拉近与公众的距离，做亲近公众的博物馆。博物馆重新制作了导览图、标志、公众服务地图等，带给观众以亲近感。第三，强调信息技术的重要性。博物馆因此增加了数字技术部门，对网站进行改版，以更好服务社会、服务大众。第四，将工作重点放在观众身上。博物馆特请伦敦的观众调查公司做了长达 18 个月的民调，来了解全球观众心目中最想要的博物馆。第五，进行商业开发。博物馆的财政投资中政府仅占 15%，只有商业开发才有可能填补资金空缺。康柏堂认为，五个工作重点的核心就是要构建一个以人为主的团队。终于在2011 年，大都会艺术博物馆在其带领下迎来了有史以来观众参观量的最高峰。

（四）遥遥领先的特色方案

1. 策划成熟而有影响力的展览

大都会艺术博物馆的展览机制十分成熟，独立策展人制度尤为成功。大都会艺术博物馆是举办各种永久性专题展、临时性特殊展览的殿堂，拥有 442 个展厅（含修道院分馆），其中 12 个用于特展。博物馆每年会举办 50 个左右的特展，以扩大博物馆的知名度，包括馆内特展和馆外特展，一个展览由筹备到实施常常花费三到五年。"超级特展"概念由此而来，开一时风气之先。而这其中，独立策展人功不可没。"独立策展人"之形早在 19 世纪末 20 世纪初就已经在西方有所显现，并在大都会艺术博物馆大显身手。"独立策展人"通常指非本馆业务人员，是由博物馆聘请的项目制的策划、设计、制作、推广特定展览的社会人士或其他教学科研机构的专业人员，需要承担拟定展览内容、展示形式、观众群体、展品来源、教育活动、文创商品到确定完成时间、经费数额甚至筹资募捐等几乎全部的内容①。独立策展人不同于普通的常设策展人，其独立性更强，游走于艺术家、博物馆和赞助人各方之间，有理念、有态度、有影响力。因此，独立策展人能综合考量各展品的独特魅力，更自如地运用相应策略，打造创新型的主题展览。

2. 走在时代前沿的出版物

为加强在全球范围内的影响力，大都会艺术博物馆将出版视作自己的主体业务之一。从1870年成立以来，大都会艺术博物馆一直出版展览目录、收藏目录和收藏指南，在世界艺术图书和艺展图录领域屡获殊荣。如今，作为全球领先的博物馆出版商之一，其获奖书目也成为学术水平、产品价值和设计理念的标杆。每年，大都会艺术博物馆都围绕展览和藏品发行20多种出版物。除了目录、指南和数字首发出版物外，博物馆还发行系列期刊。其中，《大都会艺术博物馆公报》季刊和《大都会艺术博物馆馆刊》年刊被"艺术与人文科学引文索引"（A&HCI）收录②。博物馆不断扩大出版物范围，以期广泛吸引受众，通过对艺术作品、艺术史，特别是博物馆的收藏和展览的探讨，提高公众对艺术的认识和欣赏。

3. 搭上数字化列车步入新时代

21世纪以来，互联网技术发展迅速，大都会艺术博物馆也积极引入虚拟数字技术，致力于打造全球最先进的数字博物馆。"博物馆数字化"的概念提出已有十余年。21世纪初，大都会艺术博物馆就设立了"首席数字官"这一职位，斯里·斯里瑞尼瓦桑（Sree Screenivasan）带领着一个70人的团队，与首席信息官（CIO）、首席技术官（CTO）、市场总监（CMO）和首席设计官（CDO）合作，共同探索博物馆数字创新的实践，从顶层设计上为数字化搭建了优质的框架。

4. 持续开发数字项目

近年来，大都会艺术博物馆尝试接受技术颠覆的做法。2017年2月，博物馆公布了"开放获取"（Open Access）计划，允许每个人自由访问博物馆

---

① 龚良，毛颖.全球视野下中国博物馆的建设发展：借鉴大都会艺术博物馆——龚良院长专访.东南文化，2014(03)：26-33.

② 房建国，王念祖.数字时代背景下的博物馆出版策略——以大都会艺术博物馆为例.科技与出版，2023(03)：97-104.

The Met网站、搜索、下载图片，且商业和非商业用途皆可免费使用，无须博物馆方许可。这是博物馆致力于在数字时代增加对馆藏的访问权的重要声明，使其馆藏藏品成为互联网上最容易被访问、被研究，同时也是最有研究价值的艺术品之一，进一步扩大其全球影响力。

2018年10月，大都会艺术博物馆与搜索引擎巨头谷歌合作，基于"开放获取"计划推出了The Met Collection API（应用程序编程接口），使任何第三方都能够将该集合可持续地整合到其网站中，以确保用户们可以获取最新的图像和数据信息。①

2019年2月，大都会艺术博物馆公布了"大都会×微软×麻省理工学院"（The Met×Microsoft×MIT）合作项目，并展示了最新合作成果。三方合作由麻省理工学院开放学习和知识未来小组（Knowledge Futures Group）牵头，由麻省理工学院新闻与媒体实验室（MIT Press and Media lab）联合发起，展示了主题关键字数据集和开放访问程序的潜力，以及人工智能使用开放数据之前不可用的方式。这次合作的成果展示了一系列处于不同发展阶段的原型，每个原型都探索了人工智能和艺术之间的关系。这次合作是人工智能如何赋能策展人和技术专家以使艺术和人类历史易于获取的例子。

5. 搭建资源齐备的数据库

业界一般认为大都会艺术博物馆是开放性最强、数据最为完善的数字化数据库。其中，"海尔布伦艺术史时间线"是全球最早的博物馆数字出版物之一，通过其藏品对全球艺术史进行了主题、时间和地理三个维度的梳理。该出版物由博物馆专家编写，为艺术史的学生和学者提供参考、研究和教学工具。截至本文撰写时，该数字出版物已涵盖1000多篇论文、8000件艺术品、300个年表和3700个关键词，并且定期更新和充实，以提供最新的学术成果和见解。该数字出版物内容丰富，获取方式简单，体现了博物馆成熟的数据库业务。

6. 善用社交媒体引流

社交媒体也是大都会艺术博物馆的一大经营策略，博物馆利用社交媒体平台用户的影响力为自身造势，还邀请Instagram的网红在闭馆时间参观及拍摄，将馆藏照片拍照发布在Instagram上，将历史的艺术逐步引入年轻人的社交圈。

① 李琦卉. 博物馆新技术引进使数据和图像更容易获取. Art Daily，2018; The Met, Timeline of Art History. [2024-06-04]. https://www.metmuseum.org/toah/about; 彭铄婷. 博物馆网站在博物馆事业可持续发展中的作用研究. 长春: 吉林大学硕士学位论文，2019.

博物馆的Teen Blog起初是为配合在馆内举办的临时展览及其相关活动所设，随后获得了不俗的点击率，成为与青少年讨论艺术品原作和博物馆参观体验的重要平台。与此类似的还有MetKids Blog等。

7. 打造一流的网络平台

大都会艺术博物馆网站The Met于1995年注册，于2000年进行改版设计，扩展了网站的页面与功能。2016年，博物馆将馆标改成"The Met"后，网站也以新标志为中心再次规划，发展至今基本涵盖了所有馆藏，同时还在进一步完善中。大都会艺术博物馆官网风格主题鲜明，首页设有参观指南、展览活动、艺术、学习、研究与商店六大板块，右上角有购票、入会和捐赠通道，功能实用，结构完整。事实上，前面所提到的"开放获取"计划、"海尔布伦艺术史时间线"等都可以登录该网站获取相关链接，十分便捷。大都会艺术博物馆网站的设立极大地促进了资源的共享，有利于馆际互鉴，并与实体参观形成联动。基于网站的访问数据，博物馆可对其工作重点和发展方向进行动态调整，进一步完善自身系统，厘清后疫情时代的发展脉络，寻找新的发展机遇。

三、总结和讨论

建筑是凝固的艺术。博物馆这一承载若干艺术品的载体，不仅凝固了艺术之美，还萃取了艺术之魂，使世界历史长河数千年的文明古迹汇聚在此地此刻。而当今国际上极具代表性的美国大都会艺术博物馆，随着时代沉浮、修缮调整，才能以如今的面貌呈现于世。因此不管是对于博物馆建设，还是对于跨文化研究，美国大都会艺术博物馆都有研究的价值和探讨的必要。就纵向发展来看，博物馆在不同的时期顺应时代更新其理念、调整其经营模式、修改其经营策略，多方面做到与时俱进；就横向发展来看，博物馆馆藏不断丰富，涵盖多地区文明，且线上和线下结合，在数字化时代以多种数字平台和媒体呈现藏品，最大程度上挖掘了其潜在游客。本节则侧重于总结美国大都会艺术博物馆的特色和发展，探讨其对于我国博物馆建设有何借鉴之处。

（一）成功经验的总结

1. 人文精神的坚守

美国大都会艺术博物馆的成就体现了美国文化建设的发展和成就。博物馆位于纽约曼哈顿，该地为世界金融和商业中心、土地稀缺、地价高昂、人工成本高，而从其选址变迁、发展历程、经营理念来看，其从创立之初就强调要对公众开放，并在"9·11"事件后，充满活力的文化生活帮助了公众走出创伤。由此看来，美国作为新型移民国家，现代都市中的博物馆能体现出文化的纽带作用，把文化、观念、种族差异巨大的人群聚集在一起，构建起文化认同感。

2. 时代潮流的顺应

美国大都会艺术博物馆的成就体现了经营方式的灵活性和创新性。从发展历程、信息变革、重大转型、经营策略可以看出，该馆在客观环境变化下相应调整。近年来，不止大都会艺术博物馆，各博物馆都面临过常年亏损、预算资金缩减的困境。该馆不仅并未将视野局限在是缩馆还是继续扩张的抉择上，反而创新性地采取与高校合作、开发文创产品、门票收费、加强与线上平台和媒体连接等举措，缓解了其资金紧张的难题。而这并不是该馆首次面临转型。就历史脉络来看，其于 1924 年创建美国之翼展厅，1970 年组建亚洲艺术部，如今转向时尚产业开发，这些都能体现其利用一次次危机，更好地促进了博物馆的发展。

3. 团队人才的培养

美国大都会艺术博物馆的成就体现了团队和人才的专业性和延续性。该馆历任与现任馆长大部分是考古学、博物馆、艺术史专业的学者，具有一定的专业背景和开阔的格局，将博物馆不单单定位成藏品的集合和展览，更侧重于为公共的审美、学识、教育服务之地。博物馆不仅包含了 19 个部门，还在组建核心团队的基础上，成立专业服务团队、数字化建设信息团队、法律顾问团队等。此外，其还与诸多基金会合作，设立人才培养基金，为潜在的"软实力"人才创造发展摇篮和深造机会。

美国大都会艺术博物馆的成就受多种因素合力推动，无法判断哪个因素最为重要，但各个因素缺一不可。其从上至下，即管理制度到人才培养；从里至外，即服务大众的理念和迎合数字发展下的创新，都为该博物馆的成熟发展做出了贡献。固然，美国大都会艺术博物馆的成功经验有其独特、不可为他人复制之处，比如其对于美国文化精神的融合与阐释、该馆经营性质中的私人资本占主导地位与我国国情不符等，但不可否认的是，该博物馆的成功经验对我国博物馆的发展具有一定的启示和借鉴作用。因此下文将具体谈论，从美国大都会艺术博物馆的发展案例中，我国能得到什么启示？我国博物馆该如何发展才能更加国际化？

（二）对于我国的启示

1.利用网络平台资源

随着当前全球化进入新的阶段，博物馆发展面临着新的机遇与挑战。比如：观众的全球化和平台的全球化。这也要求博物馆要注重开放合作，来实现博物馆更好地服务社会大众的最大目标。我们也可以抓住数字信息技术的优势，在办展频率和宣传方面加大力度，充分利用数据库、信息平台来科普相关藏品，与其他国潮品牌合作，开发文创周边产品，利用网络渠道的优势和品牌效应、线上与线下结合，促使更多人关注到博物馆展览概况。根据网络民意调查灵活调整开馆时间，及时与主流媒体沟通，举办专为媒体人做推介的预展，提供直播等观看方式，尽可能提高更多民众的审美意识和文化情操。

2.提高身份认同感

美国大都会艺术博物馆的发展反映了美利坚民族自信与活力的苏醒，也证明了博物馆教育可以更好地塑造民族记忆、丰富民族历史。这提醒我们，今后在建设和发展博物馆时，不仅要关注如何使人欣赏审美愉悦的艺术、更好地获得通识性教育，更要关注如何更好地普及历史、更好地提高中华民族身份认同感和历史认同感。通过展示历史遗迹和讲解文物珍品，博物馆为参观者展示了历史遗留的文化记忆，为参观者追溯历史、重构历史场景提供了一些想象，促使参观者形成身份的认同。只有当人们在主动感受到历史文化的魅力之际，自身身份认同的自豪感才会油然而生。

3.储备知识型人才

人民的物质生活水平的逐渐提高促进了我国文化产业和文化事业的发展。我国博物馆大多数都是公立性质，注重社会效益，在此之下，我国博物馆事业的发展趋势越来越好。从参观者角度来看，这代表着人民越来越渴望丰富其精神生活，也要求着管理者和相应工作人员提高相关知识水平，更好地策划博物馆展览、为人民服务。并且，相关团队建设和知识型人才的培养是开展各项业务、进行文物研究保护、组织管理博物馆事业的基础工作。无论规模大小，任何一家博物馆的可持续发展都必须优先考虑具备团队意识的中坚力量。博物馆的长久发展不仅需要专业的博物馆学家、文物鉴赏家，还需要我们更加关注如何培养一些青少年艺术家，让当代年轻人成为博物馆发展的"人才库"，鼓励其参与博物馆相关的志愿者活动，提升对于博物馆认知的视野和格局，才能更好地为博物馆的发展添砖加瓦，做出建设。

4. 丰富藏品种类

诸如美国大都会艺术博物馆等其他国家的博物馆通常囊括多个地区或国家的历史文物，而我国博物馆则主要展示自己土地上的、和自己祖先相关的文明。我们拥有五千年辉煌灿烂的中华文明，国情和文化背景使然，我们不可能将重点放在展示全球艺术品上，而是需要更多地重视本国文明，帮助公众了解祖先过去的生活。在呈现出中华文明和中华优秀传统文化之上，我们应该关注不同区域的文明，认识到不同社会发展阶段的历史文物具有差异性和多样性。因此，我国博物馆应注重多元化发展，不同地区的博物馆应注重差异化发展，更好地体现当地特色。在重视参观者的基础上，要注重自己的地域文明、传统文化，并向参观者作贴切的解读，在传播中华优秀传统文化的同时，提高参观者对于不同区域文明的认知程度和参与意识。除此之外，我国博物馆将重心放在弘扬自身的历史文化上，不代表我们要忽略，甚至是忽视其他国家的文明。博物馆的发展需要注重弘扬中华传统文化和地区特色文化，但也需要具备全球意识、全球视野。而我们对世界其他国家和地区文明的关注和重视程度却并不够。一方面是因为人才的缺失，另一方面则是对国际市场上拍卖和出售文物的来源和文化背景缺乏了解。此外，若要继续与更多海外知名展馆合作，则更应该考虑购买部分有代表性的其他民族与文化的文物，来丰富我们的馆藏种类和数量，建设更为国际化和多元化的展馆。

博物馆数字化建设案例研究——以故宫博物院为例[①]

摘　要： 作为文物保护与文化研究的产物，博物馆也是文明发展的标志。随着信息技术的迅速发展，博物馆正经历着深刻的变革。故宫博物院作为中国最知名也最具特色的博物院之一，势必也要融入浪潮。从受众有限的线下讲座到人人参与的云端文物课堂，从单一的文物管理系统到综合的博物馆管理系统，从人挤人的线下参观到掌上的深度游览，博物院的方方面面都得到了数字科技的重塑。本文将论述故宫博物院的具体信息及既往保护工作，并从文化传播、文化传承及文化创意探讨数字化为故宫带来的物质与理念变革，并着眼故宫博物院的数字化意义，探讨如何将博物馆的大量数字资源整合为知识并有效传播，实现故宫的"永续相传"。

关键词： 文物保护；故宫博物院；数字科技；数字博物馆；文化传播

一、故宫博物院基本信息

（一）构成及价值

故宫世界文化遗产历史信息丰富、文化内涵深刻，具有独特价值。自 20 世纪初以来，学界和社会就故宫世界文化遗产及其价值进行了系列探讨。在曾任故宫博物院副院长的单士元看来，故宫乃民族建筑艺术集大成者，其工程之艰巨、规模之宏伟、工艺之精巧、创造性之丰富为世界所罕见。它不仅是东方的瑰宝，也是世界的奇迹。

---

① 作者：米日努尔·木提拉，西安交通大学人居环境与建筑工程学院；杨磊，西安交通大学外国语学院；陈思佳，西安交通大学人居环境与建筑工程学院。

（二）发展历程

故宫是中国明清两代（1368—1911 年）的皇家宫殿，又称"紫禁城"，经过明清两代的不断修缮和扩建，形成如今的规模和格局。故宫博物院成立于1925 年，建立在明清两代皇宫及其收藏的基础上，同时具有建筑博物馆、艺术博物馆和历史博物馆等特色，是符合国际公认的"原址保护""原状陈列"基本原则的博物馆和文化遗产地，是一座博大精深的历史文化宝库。1961 年，故宫博物院被国务院列为第一批全国重点文物保护单位，1987 年被联合国教科文组织列入《世界遗产名录》，被誉为"世界五大宫之首"。故宫博物院于2007 年被评为国家 5A 级旅游景区，2008 年被评为首批国家一级博物馆。[①]

（三）地理位置及占地面积

故宫博物院位于中国北京市中心的东城区景山前街 4 号，占地面积约 72 万平方米，建筑面积约 15 万平方米，有大小宫殿七十多座，房屋九千余间，是中国最大的博物馆之一，也是世界上最大的古代建筑群之一。

（四）展出内容

截至 2023 年 6 月，故宫博物院内收藏了超过 186 万件文物藏品，包括文物、书画、陶瓷、玉器、钟表、珍宝等多个门类。展出内容主要包括以下几个方面。[②]

1.宫殿建筑：故宫博物院占地面积约 72 万平方米，拥有宫殿建筑约 980 座。这些建筑展示了明清两代皇家宫殿的风貌，如太和殿、中和殿、保和殿、乾清宫、坤宁宫等。

2.珍贵文物：故宫博物院藏品数量庞大，总计达到 180 多万件，包括了各种珍贵的文物、艺术品和历史资料。其中有大量的书画、陶瓷、玉器、金银器皿、漆器、象牙雕刻等各种工艺品。

3.皇家生活：故宫博物院展示了明清两代皇家生活的方方面面，包括皇帝、皇后、妃子和宫女的生活、起居、礼仪等。游客可以在故宫博物院了解到古代皇家生活的细节。

4.皇家仪仗和礼仪：故宫博物院还展示了皇家宴会、朝会、祭祀等重要场合的仪仗和礼仪。游客可以通过这些展示了解到古代皇室的严谨礼仪和辉煌气派。

---

① 万依.紫禁城文化内涵浅识举隅.中国紫禁城学会论文集（第一辑）.北京：故宫出版社，1997：82.
② 单士元.北京故宫进行修护保养的状况.紫禁城，1998（3）：63-65.

5.皇家园林：故宫博物院内还有一些精美的皇家园林，如御花园、九龙壁等。这些园林展示了古代皇家园林的美学特点和造园技艺。

6.临时展览：故宫博物院还会不定期举办各种临时展览，展示故宫博物院内的部分珍藏文物，或与其他国家博物馆合作举办文化交流展览。

故宫博物院的展出内容丰富多样，吸引了大量游客前来参观。参观故宫博物院，不仅可以欣赏到中国古代皇家的瑰丽建筑和珍贵文物，还可以深入了解中国历史和文化。

（五）发展规划

故宫博物院作为世界著名的文化遗产，始终在积极探索和实施各项发展规划。根据公开信息，故宫博物院近年来的发展规划主要集中在以下几个方面。

1.文物保护和修复：故宫博物院将继续加大文物修复力度，采用现代技术和国际先进的保护方法对珍贵文物进行修复和保护，同时加强对古建筑的维修保养，确保文物和建筑的安全和完整。

2.展览和陈列改革：故宫博物院将进一步提升展陈水平，通过创新展陈方式、举办临时展览等手段，使更多的文物得到展示，让观众能够更好地了解中国历史文化。[①]

3.数字化和智能化：故宫博物院将利用现代科技手段，对馆内藏品进行数字化、智能化的改造，如数字展厅、虚拟导览、智能导游等，以便让观众能够享受到更便捷、更丰富的参观体验。故宫博物院未来将继续推进数字化博物馆建设，将文物数字化、网络化、可视化，让更多的人了解和欣赏中国的文化遗产。

4.文化传播和教育普及：故宫博物院将加强与其他文化机构的合作，扩大对外交流，推动故宫博物院文化的国际传播。加强公共教育功能，通过举办讲座、开展教育活动等方式，普及历史文化知识，培养公众的文化素养。同时，加强与国内外博物馆的交流合作，促进文化的交流和融合，让更多人了解和爱上中国的文化。

5.提升游客服务质量：故宫博物院将持续改善游客服务设施，提高服务水平，让游客在参观过程中享受到更优质的服务。

---

① 吕舟.北京明清故宫文物建筑保护与国际木结构文物建筑保护动向.中国紫禁城学会论文集（第一辑），1996：415.

6.可持续发展：故宫博物院关注环境保护和可持续发展，采取措施降低能耗、减少污染，创造一个绿色、环保的博物馆环境。

总之，故宫博物院的发展规划旨在通过保护文物、提升展陈水平、加强文化传播等多方面的努力，让这一世界文化遗产得到更好地保护和传承，为广大游客提供更好的参观体验。

二、故宫博物院建筑价值及保护策略分析

梁思成曾这样描述故宫建筑："现存清代建筑物，最伟大者莫如北平故宫，清宫规模虽肇自明代，然现存各殿宇，则多数为清代所建，对照今世界各国之帝皇宫殿，规模之大，面积之广，无与伦比。"[①]2017年，《故宫保护总体规划（2013—2025）》颁布，系统性地将故宫遗产价值之主题和特征总结为三个主要方面，即中国古代官式建筑的最高典范、中国明清宫廷文化的特殊见证和中国古代艺术的系列精品。[②]

（一）建筑群分析

整个故宫建筑群坐落在首都北京的中心地带。故宫的中轴线，也是整个北京城的中轴线。故宫是中国宫殿建筑总结性的杰作，是我国古代宫城发展史上现存的唯一实例和最高典范，综合体现了中国传统的哲学、建筑学和美学等，具有极高的历史价值和艺术价值。[③]它代表了中国古代建筑艺术的最高水平，充分反映了我国明清两代木结构建筑的成就，也是明清社会历史演变的重要实物例证。

故宫反映了中国封建社会晚期成熟的典章制度和等级体系，反映了中国明清社会的意识形态、哲学观念、审美趣味和人们对建筑环境、建筑空间、建筑规划等的认知和理解，体现了中华文化的多元内涵、儒释道等多种宗教理念并集不同地域的建造工艺之大成。紫禁城是中华民族历史文化的重要载体和缩影，也反映了跨民族、跨文明的多元文化交流与融合，是中国明清宫廷历史演进的实物见证，是体现中国古代科学技术水平的重要案例。[④]

① 梁思成.中国建筑史（通校本）.北京：生活·读书·新知三联书店，2023：318.
② 于倬云.紫禁城宫殿.北京：人民美术出版社，2013.
③ 胡茜茜.故宫与卢浮宫的建筑设计文化比较研究.芜湖：安徽工程大学硕士学位论文，2019.
④ 张佳芸.从文化层面探究中轴线的意义：以故宫为例.城市建筑.2021(14)：66-69.

（二）遗产保护分析

20世纪80年代末，时任院长张忠培提出将故宫博物院定位为以明清宫廷历史、宫殿建筑和古代艺术为主要内容的综合性博物院的理念，确定了保护紫禁城及紫禁城文物完整体系的原则，并在北京市的支持下，重新划定和明确故宫的保护范围。保护故宫及其文物，是历史赋予的使命。不论在人类文明发展史上，还是在中华优秀传统文化创造性转化、创新性发展中，故宫世界文化遗产都有着不可替代的重要价值。

进入21世纪以来，故宫保护工作受到全社会前所未有的重视和关注。在这一背景下，故宫博物院先后确立两项重大保护工程：一是2002年启动的故宫整体修缮保护工程，在不改变文物原状的前提下，尽最大可能延长古建筑的寿命，该工程分三期推进，维修总投入19亿元，于2020年全面完成古建筑内外环境整治和整体保护工作；二是2013年启动的"平安故宫"工程，包括北院区建设、地库改造、基础设施改造、世界文化遗产监测、故宫安全防范新系统、院藏文物防震和院藏文物抢救性科技修复保护等七个子项目先后进入实施阶段或即将开工建设，总体进展顺利。2014年，明清官式建筑保护研究国家文物局重点科研基地落户故宫博物院，进一步推动古建修缮工程向古建保护研究项目转化。研究性保护项目的代表——养心殿保护项目的实施，标志着故宫建筑遗产保护进入以全面挖掘价值、技术研发支撑、保护利用并举的真实完整保护及有效利用新阶段。

目前，加强文化遗产监测和研究性、预防性保护已成为文物保护领域的共识。故宫世界文化遗产保护工作已经进入以预防性保护为主、辅之以抢救性保护的新阶段。同时，故宫博物院还与国内外博物馆、高校和科研院所等开展合作，树立开放包容、兼收并蓄的态度，进一步推动了故宫世界文化遗产保护理念与实践的提升。2019年，故宫博物院在充分调研的基础上，提出以平安故宫、学术故宫、数字故宫、活力故宫为核心的"四个故宫"建设；2020年，确立了新时期办院指导思想，明确思想引领、使命担当、支撑体系和愿景；2021年，提出建设覆盖各方面发展的九大事业发展体系，并写入《故宫博物院"十四五"发展规划》；2022年，开展全面质量管理体系试点工作。

故宫博物院的保护策略以协调好文物保护、研究与传承利用的关系。对故宫世界遗产及所属文物的有效保护，是基础和首要任务；研究、挖掘和阐释故宫世界遗产及所藏文物承载的中华优秀传统文化和精神内涵是核心任务；推动中华优秀传统文化的创造性转化、创新性发展，讲好中国故事，实现全民共享文化成果是最终目的。只有在保护好的基础上才可能开展好研究和传承利用，研究可反哺、支持保护和传承利用；传承利用又可提升保护意识、激发研究动力。2022 年 9 月，《故宫博物院"十四五"不可移动文物保护专项规划》制定完成，以不可移动文物保护问题研判为导向，围绕科学保护、研究保护、传承保护三个重点方向设置任务，项目实施后将会极大推进故宫世界文化遗产的保护。

三、数字故宫

1998 年，由文化部牵头，中国国家图书馆等单位联合启动了国务院立项的"中国数字图书馆工程"，以全面地收集文化资源信息，通过数字化图书馆、数字化博物馆、数字化影视中心等形式，建立起一个跨地区、跨行业的巨大文化信息资源数据库和网络系统，使之成为中国的"国家信息基础设施"，中国的数字化博物馆建设由此起步。

从内容上讲，数字博物馆中的文化遗产包括物质文化遗产和非物质文化遗产两个方面。从技术上讲，数字博物馆必须拥有完整的两翼：一个是对文化遗产资源的数字化采集、加工、处理、传输和使用；另一个是利用可视化技术对数字化后的文化遗产资源的展示。

为了实现故宫的永续相传，如单霁翔院长所说，"把壮美的紫禁城完整地交给下一个 600 年"，故宫自 2013 年开始打造数字故宫社区，数字故宫就是以数字文物为基础，以信息化方式进行管理，以保存、展示和保护文化遗产与服务公众为目的、超越时空的博物馆。本文将从文化传播、文化传承及文化创意三方面介绍数字故宫的成就。

（一）文化传播

博物馆信息化已经走过了十余年的历程，从基础文物数据系统到文物的动态管理，从单一的文物管理系统到综合的博物馆管理系统，从展厅多媒体辅助展示到综合网站建设，再到互联网上多种展示手段的采用，博物馆信息化建设经历了由简到繁、由静态到动态、由内到外、由管理到展示的诸多演变。在博物馆由收藏型向参与型转变的当下，信息化技术应如何更好地为博物馆建设服务，使博物馆成为公众生活不可缺少的文化需要，实现"和谐互动，共享文化"的博物馆使命，成为各个博物馆探讨和实践的焦点问题。

1.社交广场

最主要的方式就是民众使用比较广泛的微博、微信，还有各类的社交网站，强调的是人与人之间的互动。这三种形式故宫博物院都已经应用，2011年正式推出官方新浪微博号和腾讯微博号，2012年推出人民网微博号和腾讯微信号，共同组成一个基于即时通信的故宫社交平台。截至2023年7月，故宫新浪微博拥有粉丝1029万，发表微博一万三千余篇。既有故宫博物院的展览信息、开放信息，也有故宫博物院的业务动态和文物知识，图文并茂，强调互动，获得了公众的喜爱，在政务类、文化类微博中一直名列前茅。故宫的微信公众号则充分利用多功能的优势，不仅发布动态信息，还开设了全景导览、购票、微店、小游戏等栏目。

2.文化展示

第一个特色是虚拟现实作品展示。实际上故宫博物院早在21世纪初就与日本凸版印刷株式会社合作引入VR技术对故宫古建筑进行数据采集，以期建立基于三维数据的官式古建筑数据库，并衍生了六部介绍典型建筑及其历史的VR作品，分别是太和殿、三大殿、养心殿、倦勤斋、灵沼轩和角楼。通过重新编辑数据、引入最新计算方法对庞大的数据进行压缩处理，引入随身穿戴设备VR眼镜，从封闭的演播厅空间内转移到开放的互联网上，实现网络体验VR作品，让更多的观众感受数字产品的魅力，实现受众的最大化。虚拟现实作品的优势一是可以通过虚拟的、沉浸式的展示方式，让参观者仿佛进入古建筑的环境当中，身临其境地体验古建筑的魅力，二是不仅看到各种建筑的内外部细节，还能了解它背后的故事。比如灵沼轩是在延禧宫院内的一个清朝未完成的钢结构建筑，面对废墟，观众无法了解过去的形状，而通过VR手机移植版，能够现场看到灵沼轩现在的细节及其完全建成后的样子，以及其背后的故事。

2019年7月，故宫博物院推出了线上项目"数字文物库"，首批精选5万件高清文物影像向社会公开。几年来，"数字文物库"的文物影像数量不断增加，已经超过8万件。自上线以来"数字文物库"浏览量超3300万次，是故宫官网上最受公众欢迎的专题栏目。观众除了可以检索文物名称、时代、作者等信息之外，还可以通过颜色来查找自己喜欢的文物。作为文化和旅游部"应用于人工智能搜索的可移动文物'概念参考模型'研究"项目成果，"数字文物库"还最新上线了知识图谱检索功能，即使不知道文物的名称，也能通过与文物有关联的词汇，找到自己想看的藏品，以此进一步满足人们欣赏、学习、研究文物的需求，也将进一步发挥出文物所承载的中华优秀传统文化的社会价值。

第二个特色是高清晰网上文物展示。故宫博物院的书画藏品有5万余件，很多都已经成为美术教学不可缺少的范例，但是囿于展示条件的不足，很少能够进入展厅呈现在观众面前，而且故宫网站上的照片像素也较小，不能满足爱好者欣赏的需求，更不能满足利用图像进行研究的需要。为了解决这些难题，故宫博物院早在2005年就探索利用先进的高清晰展示技术在延禧宫古书画研究中心展厅开设了电子画廊，把100余幅书画作品通过触摸屏幕瞬间放大的方式呈现给观众，观众可以观赏到每一件书画作品的细部，了解用笔的笔触、纸帛的纹理细节。如今，故宫博物院已把这些表现方法搬到网上、进入社区，而且更多地加入了声音、文字等形式对作品进行注释。而对于瓷器等器物类文物则不仅有高清晰的各个角度、局部的图像，而且能够借助三维技术动态地、立体呈现。

第三个特色是采用目前最流行的APP的方式来展示故宫文化。目前故宫博物院已经有6个不同主题的APP应用，分别是十二美人图、紫禁城祥瑞、皇帝的一天、韩熙载夜宴图、每日故宫、清朝皇帝服饰，全部获得苹果商店推荐，并成为最佳APP应用。以韩熙载夜宴图为例，该APP综合使用了音乐、舞蹈、三维成像、专家视频讲解等方式全方位解读这幅历史名画，将原画长卷分解出各个不同的段落予以说明，特别是邀请了台湾著名的南音表演团体汉唐乐府，用音乐和舞蹈演示画意，真切地体验到当时的文化氛围，让古书画活起来。我们希望通过各种不同的APP形式能够表现故宫收藏的180万件文物，力图从年龄上、知识层次上对不同需求、不同接受方式的公众实现有针对性的对位展示。

第四个特色是网上虚拟展览。一方面把已经在故宫举办的各种展览制作成相应互联网的网上版，基本上线下的每一个展览都有一个相对应的网上展览形式。而且还充分利用全景技术，把现实的展厅搬到网上，使观众可以身临其境地感受展厅氛围、参观展览，对重点展品还有深度的背景资料可供阅览。比如石渠宝笈特展，在展览开幕前就在故宫博物院网站上推出了网络版进行预热，展览结束后意犹未尽的观众仍然可以在网站上继续欣赏。另一方面还有专题的、只在网上展出的虚拟展览，涵盖了各种类别，包括建筑、书画、器物等，这类展览都是小型专题展览，一般所选的展品数量也比较少，基本都在几十件的范围内，特别是配合春节、端午、中秋等传统节日的风俗文物展览很受欢迎。[①]

3. 咨讯传播

主要有两种方式：第一种是门户网站，第二种是微博、微信和每日故宫APP。故宫博物院门户网站开通于1999年，作为一个博物馆的网站，虽然它的日点击量达到了100万次以上，但是用户群仍然比较小，且网站栏目复杂，不利于浏览者快速寻找所需信息，影响了传播效能。因此从2013年开始，故宫博物院根据最新的技术发展和最新的公众需求，对现有的网站进行了大的改版。一是对原有的网站进行架构重组和栏目优化，解决网站层次多，信息琐碎的不足，实现信息获取简便、精准的目标；二是推出全新的英文网站和青少年版网站。把使用最广泛的英文作为外语版的唯一选择，把英文网站做得足够强大、足够亲民，就能够满足外语用户的需求。新版的英文网站完全按照西方人的接受模式来设计首页和相应的栏目。同时青少年版网站则针对青少年的特点全新开发、独立运营，用年轻人的语言和表达方式传递故宫文化，以动漫为主要手段，通过源自紫禁城的建筑、历史中的卡通形象演绎的故事，向青少年传递故宫的建筑、文物中蕴含的内涵。比如设计了一个名为《故宫大冒险》的游戏，让每一个进入网站的观众都能够跟他所喜欢的角色产生关联，无论是小皇帝角色、格格角色，还是脊兽的角色，都可以带领他去了解他希望得到的故宫的内容。参观路线也设计得非常有意思，把皇帝在宫中的生活按照时间表设计成课程表的样子，这是每一个孩子最熟悉的、每天必做的事情，那么就把它幻化成他每天的日程，来引导他选择自己的参观路线。形式上比较活泼，同时紧扣内容上的兴趣点。

第二种方式中，微博、微信运营最需要注意的不是信息容量，而是信息的表达方式。这两种即时通讯工具既注重信息的时效性，更注重信息的交互性，因此，必须用非常亲民的、与公众进行交流的姿态出现，这里面的核心就是顺应了网络公众的需求，平等地、像一个朋友一样对待粉丝，只有这样才能够把微博、微信做得更为持久，成为广受欢迎的文化传播者。再比如故宫的微信为

---

① 阴鑫. 中国博物馆文化创意产品开发研究. 郑州：河南大学，2016.

了更好地吸引用户长久关注，还专门为注册用户设计了互动栏目，并通过积分兑换的方式引导其参与故宫博物院更多的活动。而每日故宫APP则在每天发送一件文物解说的同时，定期播报故宫博物院的展览信息。

（二）文化传承

1.学术交流

通常，除了通过文物、考古等专业杂志获取到一些研究信息外，公众很难了解研究状况和成果。故宫博物院因此在现有的网站上建立了展示专家研究成果的平台，把每期《故宫博物院院刊》《故宫学刊》《紫禁城》杂志，以及《故宫博物院年鉴》的内容都发布到网上。故宫还依托自身历史底蕴，成立了故宫研究院，下设十余个研究院，建设了故宫院刊、故宫学刊、明清论丛三大学术项目，通过对文物的深入研究和整理，为文物的保护、展示和解读提供专业的支持。此外，为让更多的专家、爱好者参与到故宫博物院藏品的研究中，故宫博物院还建设了中国古代书画研究系统，将院内外的书画研究专家的研究成果以众多信息点的方式标注在高清影像上。

2.公众教育

在展开学术研究的同时，故宫博物院还成立了故宫学院、故宫讲坛，向故宫博物院内部、业内人士以及公众提供教育培训，服务社会。数字化技术帮助打破了传统教育的种种局限，更扩大了故宫的影响力。故宫在数字化公众教育方面的工作主要有三类：一是故宫博物院举办的面向青少年的故宫知识课堂、故宫趣味课堂等活动，由于场地和教学资源有限，这些活动往往不能完全满足参与者的全部需求，而利用"故宫学校在线教育项目""故宫云课"等数字化成果，就可以将这些活动的课件以视频、文字、互动等方式提供给广泛的互联网用户欣赏、学习。二是故宫图书馆，作为一个内部图书馆，故宫图书馆受到文物管理的限制，很难广泛为社会提供服务。利用数字化的电子图书馆，点击进入就可以阅览绝大多数故宫收藏的图书文献，使其发挥更大的教育和研究作用。三是通过摄制《故宫专家讲国宝》《我们的清明上河图》《我在故宫修文物》这样的系列专题片，聆听故宫博物院专家对文物、文保的专业讲解，向公众传递故宫文化知识，提高公众对文化遗产的认知和理解。

3.数字文保

在文物保护方面，故宫博物院采用了现代化的技术手段，如温湿度自控系统、精确的防火防盗设施、三维激光扫描技术、热力监测等，以保障文物的安全和完整性。同时，对于受损文物，故宫博物院还建立了"文物医院"，配备专业的修复人员，运用先进的修复技术和工具，恢复受损文物的原貌，保护其历史和艺术价值。故宫博物院同时建立了数字化管理系统，建立了故宫博物院文物管理信息系统、故宫博物院文物流通系统、故宫博物院文化遗产监测平台及故宫博物院办公平台，将文物信息、档案和研究成果进行数字化存储和管理监测，为文物的保护和研究提供了强有力的支持。 基于已有的 20 年"数字故宫"建设成果，故宫博物院也在不断深入探索文物数字化保护和利用的新路径、新方案，2023 年，故宫博物院与腾讯数字孪生团队共同研发了"故宫·腾讯联合创新实验室"，让文物数据采集环境实现了更加精细化的管控，编织起一张绿色、规范、精准、可靠的全域感知网络。[①]

（三）文化创意

1.参观展览

（1）数字导览：过去参观导览无非两种形式，一种是最传统的讲解员带领观众进行相应的各个展览的讲解，一种是发展了二十多年的电子讲解器。现在发展出了第三种方式，就是利用手机等无线移动终端来进行导览和辅助参观体验。最常见的就是基于卫星导航定位技术开发的、基于地图进行的导览，主要解决的是参观路线的导引，即到哪里去、怎么走的问题，比如全景故宫、故宫导游等。[②]

（2）全景虚拟漫游：主要是针对紫禁城中一些不适于对观众进行开放的狭小的空间，利用全景技术从各种角度看到建筑内部的全貌和细部。[③]

一个是通过专题展览 APP 的方式尝试深度展厅导览，比如 2015 年推出的陶瓷馆 APP，不仅可以了解陶瓷馆全部展出文物的信息，而且可以 360 度欣赏陶瓷馆当中的展品。还有一种就是虚拟展厅，如故宫展览 APP，囊括了 2015 年以来在故宫博物院各个展馆内举办的文物展览，不仅能够身临其境观展，还

---

① 冯乃恩. 博物馆数字化建设理念与实践综述——以数字故宫社区为例. 故宫博物院院刊，2017(1)：108-123+162.

② 王婕，刘舜强. 博物馆质量管理体系构建中的"顾客"识别——以故宫博物院为例. 中国标准化，2023(11)：240-246.

③ 穆筱蝶."互联网+"背景下博物馆文创开发策略研究——以北京故宫博物院为例. 新闻研究导刊，2017(21)：251-252.

能获得重点展品的深度信息。①

2.休闲娱乐

基于智能手机的数字展示产品有"紫禁城 600""玩转故宫 2.0"和"故宫：口袋宫匠"②，其中"玩转故宫"小程序涵盖建筑点位收藏、在线虚拟游览、提前发现精选推荐等内容，并有 AI 导览助手，提供导览问询一站式服务。这些数字化产品打破时空限制，从不同的角度展示和传播着故宫文化，让人们实现随时随地了解故宫。③

3.文创产品

故宫博物院在开发文创产品方面做得非常出色，推出了各种形式的产品，包括书籍、纪念品、服饰和家居用品等。例如，《紫禁城岁时记》一书，以及灵感源于"清·染牙桃实果盘"的桃气满满的便携茶具套和故宫输入法皮肤。这些产品巧妙地融入了故宫文化的设计元素，并通过商业化运作手段，成功地扩展了故宫博物院的品牌影响力，同时也为博物馆增加了收入来源。这些精心设计的文创产品不仅仅是纪念品，更是一种传承和推广故宫文化的有力工具。通过吸引人们的注意和兴趣，故宫博物院不仅在传统的文化领域取得了巨大成功，还在商业层面上展现出了巨大的潜力。这样的市场化策略不仅使得故宫文化更加接地气和时尚化，同时也为故宫博物院的可持续发展提供了新的动力。

在文创产品的销售方面，例如故宫淘宝店、故宫天猫旗舰店、故宫微信微店、故宫商城，不仅吸引了众多网上的购买者，更培育了一批铁杆的故宫粉丝，实现了社会效益和经济效益的双赢局面。在淘宝直播平台，故宫的文创与出版也于近两年走上了直播带货之路，有"故宫出版"直播售书，"故宫淘宝"直播文创带货等等。④

四、总结与讨论

（一）数字化成就总结

关于博物馆数字化对于文化传承和交流有以下几个方面的积极影响：

---

① 于翔.基于物联网的故宫热力监测系统的建设与应用.山西建筑，2023(14)：121-125.

② 单霁翔.浅析博物馆陈列展览的学术性与趣味性.东南文化，2013(2)：6-13.

③ 单霁翔，毛颖.从"故宫"到"故宫博物院"——单霁翔院长专访.东南文化，2016(5)：12-19，127-128.

④ 李红超，王昕宇，李维钰.基于文化元素的故宫博物院文创产品设计研究.包装工程，2022(2)：325-332.

1.文物数字化保护

通过数字化技术，博物馆可以对珍贵的文物进行高精度的数字扫描和记录，保护文物的原貌和细节。这种数字化保护不仅可以防止文物在展览和储存过程中的损坏，还可以为后代留下珍贵的文化遗产。

2.文化传承与普及

数字化技术使得博物馆的文化资源可以以更加直观和多样化的方式呈现给观众。通过虚拟展览、在线博物馆和数字化档案，人们可以随时随地浏览和学习文物知识，促进跨越时空的交流：数字化技术打破了地域和时间的限制，使得博物馆的文化传承和交流可以超越国界和时代。人们可以通过网络平台，与世界各地的博物馆、文化机构和观众进行互动和交流，分享文物的故事和价值。这种跨越时空的交流促进了不同文化之间的相互理解和友谊。

3.创新展示方式

数字化技术为博物馆展览提供了新的可能性和创新方式。通过虚拟现实、增强现实和互动展示，观众可以身临其境地感受文物的魅力和历史背景，提升了展览的趣味性和互动性。

4.文化教育与研究

数字化技术为博物馆的教育和研究提供了强大的支持。通过在线学习平台和数字化资源，博物馆可以为学校和学生提供丰富的教育资源和学习机会。同时，数字化技术也方便了学者和研究者的文物研究和交流，推动了学术的进展和合作。

博物馆数字化对于文化传承和交流具有重要的影响和意义。它不仅促进了文物的保护和传承，也拓展了文化的传播范围和方式，从而人们可以更好地了解、欣赏和传承丰富多样的文化遗产，增进不同文化之间的交流与理解，同时也推动了博物馆事业的创新发展。

（二）数字化发展展望

随着数字化的推进，博物馆已经走向个性化、特色化发展。许多世界著名博物馆利用数字化打造了定制化、个性化的服务，美国纽约大都会艺术博物馆就曾给观众发放 3D 打印指南册，指导人们扫描打印独属于自己的艺术品；美国史密森学会在线发布了约 280 万件藏品的数字影像，可供任意下载、使用，人们可以将其编辑、转换，甚至进行二次创作；在达·芬奇逝世 500 周年纪念展中，卢浮宫利用VR技术，将《蒙娜丽莎》以变革性的方式展出，让观众身临其境，触碰来自数百年前的迷人画像。故宫最气势磅礴、引人入胜处便是明清两代的皇宫禁城，皇家建筑的主体和原址保护的理念限制了故宫的数字化展示，庞大的宫殿群、巨大的人流量、有限的开放空间更使得定制化、个性化的线下参观成为了故宫的难题。本文就数字化如何推进故宫博物院定制化、个性化旅游服务做出了以下展望：

1.根据游客偏好提供个性化导览

目前，游客可利用故宫小程序或应用获得有关故宫的详细信息、地图导航和展览路线等。接下来，故宫可引入基于位置的推送通知，向游客发送与他们所在位置相关的信息，如人群数量、展览亮点、临时展览等。此外，可利用数据分析和人工智能技术，收集和分析游客的偏好和历史数据，为他们提供个性化的推荐服务，如个性化的展品推荐、特殊活动和展览的推送，以及针对个人兴趣的讲解和互动体验。

2.区块链技术记录游客信息

在记录游客信息和偏好时，传统的记录方式可能存在隐私泄露或身份验证方面的问题，可利用区块链技术，安全存储游客信息，实现数据隐私保护，从而更好地实现智能个性化服务，特别是区块链记录的不可变性和透明性可以用于追踪和审计个性化服务的提供过程，公平地服务每位游客。对于有残障、疾病或其他特殊需要的游客，区块链技术更能将他们的信息智能管理，在有需要时为他们提供帮助，保护他们的游览安全和权益。

3.定制化纪念品

通过3D打印技术，游客可以定制个性化的纪念品。他们可以选择自己喜欢的故宫建筑、文物或艺术品，并将其制作成独特的纪念品，增加游客的参观体验，留下他们与故宫之间的特殊纪念。

4.数字化技术走向海外平台

故宫开发的数字应用和程序都是面向国内用户的，在线下也提供了多语种的导览服务和解说音频。但线下参观的许多外国游客在没有外文导游和讲解的情况下仍一头雾水，因此，故宫可在后续将自己的数字化成果投放至海外游客更常用的平台，如在Smartify开发故宫专属的博物馆解说的音频资源。

以建筑学视角浅析法国卢浮宫的扩建[①]

摘　要: 本文梳理了法国卢浮宫博物馆的基本情况,并以建筑学的视角分析其建筑扩建过程中运用的设计手法,通过对国内外案例的分析,提出了当代博物馆改扩建的原则和方法,以期对当代博物馆的扩建有一定的借鉴意义。

关键词: 法国卢浮宫博物馆;建筑学;扩建

一、概　况

卢浮宫是位于法国巴黎市中心的一座宏伟古老建筑,曾是法国君主的皇宫。它坐落于法国巴黎塞纳河北,处在杜乐丽花园与圣日耳曼奥塞尔教堂之间[②],是城市的中心地标。卢浮宫博物馆设立于卢浮宫内,是世界四大博物馆之一。它是众多经典西方艺术作品的所在地,包括被誉为世界三宝的断臂维纳斯雕像、《蒙娜丽莎》油画和胜利女神石雕。

卢浮宫始建于 1204 年,历经 800 多年扩建、重修,如今呈现出复杂而壮观的建筑群。目前占地面积约 198 万平方米,整体建筑平面略呈"U"形,分为"新""旧"两部分,旧的建于路易十四时代,新的建于拿破仑时代。宫前的金字塔形玻璃入口,是由华人建筑大师贝聿铭设计而成的。

卢浮宫博物馆是世界著名的艺术殿堂,世界上最大的艺术宝库之一,是举世瞩目的万宝之宫。在 17 世纪,路易十四将卢浮宫从皇家宫殿改造为艺术博物馆,并且向公众开放。随着时间的推移,卢浮宫博物馆逐渐积累了大量的艺术品,包括古代文物、绘画、雕塑、装饰艺术等,其中不乏世界级的珍品。现有四十多万件来自世界各国的艺术珍品,分别收藏在埃及馆、东方馆、希腊罗

① 作者:赵鑫慧,西北工业大学建筑系;汪珈亦,西北工业大学建筑系;车玉姝,西北工业大学建筑系。

② 斯然畅畅.卢浮宫玻璃金字塔:贝聿铭的现代建筑纪念碑.中国艺术,2019(4):86-95.

马馆、绘画馆、雕塑馆，以及装饰艺术馆。博物馆的展览空间包括了卢浮宫内的不同翼楼和展厅，陈列了从古代到近现代的艺术作品。卢浮宫博物馆的藏品之丰富、之广泛、之精美堪称世界之最，吸引了来自全球的游客和艺术爱好者前来参观。它不仅是一座庞大的历史建筑，更是艺术与文化的殿堂，代表了法国乃至全世界的艺术精髓和历史传承。

二、历史变迁

卢浮宫的历史可以追溯到 1190 年，由当时法王腓力二世下令修建，修建初衷是将其作为监狱和防御性的城堡，以保护巴黎免受英格兰王国的袭击。然而，到了 14 世纪，查理五世将卢浮宫作为王室居所，首次使用了这座建筑。此后，一些法国国王居住于此，但卢浮宫时有闲置，直到 1546 年，弗朗索瓦一世成为第二位在卢浮宫居住的国王。弗朗索瓦一世下令将原始的中世纪建筑拆除，逐步将卢浮宫改造为文艺复兴风格的宫殿，并在 1546 年至 1559 年修建了卡利庭院。波旁王朝开始后，亨利四世和路易十三修建了连接卢浮宫与杜伊勒里宫的大长廊，又称"花廊"，成为当时最著名的展示间。

1682 年，法兰西宫廷搬迁至凡尔赛宫后，卢浮宫的扩建停止。尽管路易十四曾计划拆除卢浮宫，但后来改变了主意。1750 年，路易十五正式提出了拆除卢浮宫的计划，但由于资金不足未能实现。1793 年 8 月 10 日，法国大革命期间，路易十六被捕，卢浮宫的皇家收藏成为国家财产，卢浮宫艺术馆正式对外开放，成为公共博物馆。这种状况一直延续了 6 年，直到拿破仑一世搬进了卢浮宫。

卢浮宫由王宫到博物馆的转身最关键的一步是拿破仑完成的，19 世纪初，他扩建了卢浮宫北翼建筑，并将从欧洲各国搜罗的艺术精品运至卢浮宫扩充馆藏。从拿破仑时代到波旁王朝复辟，收藏范围不断扩大，展览空间越来越小，其间路易十八和查理十世对建筑进行拓宽及新建工程。1848 年法国二月革命至 1852 年，拿破仑三世对卢浮宫和杜伊勒里宫进行了更大规模的维修翻建和重新装修工程，为卢浮宫现今的宏伟规模奠定了基础。[①]

---

①   Lacambre, G. Les collections chinoises et japonaises du musée de la Marine avant 1878: un cas marginal pour l'ethnographie ?. In *Le rôle des voyages dans la constitution des collections ethnographiques, historiques et scientifiques*. Paris: Editions du CTHS: 94-109; Baticle, J. & Marinas, C. *La galerie espagnole de Louis-Philippe au Louvre: 1838-1848*. Paris: Réunion des musées nationaux, 1981.

1871 年 5 月，杜伊勒里宫发生大火，烧毁了卢浮宫的部分花廊和马尔赞长廊，但主体建筑得以幸免。君主制结束后，第三共和国时期拆除了废墟，形成了卢浮宫今日的格局。从 19 世纪后期开始，卢浮宫成为一个集中法国在内的西方文物和近东文物的艺术博物馆。

19 世纪 20 年代后期，卢浮宫馆长亨利·凡尔纳（Henri Verne）制定了革命性的总体规划，并在 1932—1934 年对北翼与南翼的部分建筑物进行重新设计与扩展。1981 年，法国政府决定将卢浮宫建筑群划拨给博物馆，并对卢浮宫实施了大规模的整修。1989 年，由华裔美籍设计师贝聿铭设计的透明金字塔建筑在卢浮宫中央广场上落成，整修后的卢浮宫重新开放，其展览区域划分为：黎塞留庭院、苏利庭院、德农庭院。

1995 年，时任法国总统雅克·希哈克（Jacques Chiral）开始倡议全面保存、典藏及推广非洲、亚洲、美洲及大洋洲的原创艺术文物。至 2000 年，卢浮宫规划了 1400 平方公尺的长期展厅，并对外开放。

三、背景简析

法国巴黎政治和建筑密不可分。历届王宫的建造都是为了巩固权力。19 世纪，奥斯曼男爵开辟宽阔的林荫大道系统在一定程度上也是一种政治行为。在弗朗索瓦·密特朗（François Mitterrand）总统的领导下，政府更加积极地进行建设，建筑再次成为表达政治意愿的主要手段，成为反映人们对城市的一种印象和愿景。1982 年，密特朗总统启动了一项名为 Grands Projects 的庞大计划，旨在于巴黎留下自己的印记，其中最著名且最具争议的是贝聿铭重新设计和扩建卢浮宫并在卢浮宫内增加一个新入口的计划。密特朗认为，这个预计耗资 157 亿法郎的市政建设浪潮不仅是振兴巴黎的一种手段，而且是社会党政治推动当代建筑发展的代表性举措。当然这受到了许多人的批评与反对，法国政府中的许多人认为这个大计划更像是一种老式的帝国在努力建设，他们还认为像卢浮宫这样的项目将降低而不是提升城市的吸引力。

这项宏伟的计划作为城市规划的一项实践于 1982 年开始实施，被称为二战后法国发起的"政治象征意义和进程的证明"[①]。这项计划主要被描述为"在二十年里改变了城市天际线的八个纪念性建筑项目"之一，包括卢浮宫金字

---

①   Jacob Simpson. Urban Design Politics. (2003-03-11)[2024-02-07]. https://ocw.mit.edu/courses/11-302j-urban-design-politics-spring-2010/8c5b7c0378abfc80882298754683da7c_MIT11_302JS10_simpson1.pdf.

塔、奥赛博物馆、拉维莱特公园、阿拉伯世界研究所、巴士底歌剧院、拉德芳斯凯旋门、经济和财政部以及法国国家图书馆新馆。这些项目代表了 20 世纪政府对巴黎公共领域最重要的干预。无论关于大型项目还是其他方面，它们的范围和目的都是具有里程碑意义的。它们不像 20 世纪 60 年代末和 70 年代初那些为了私人利益而严重破坏了巴黎的城市结构的私人商业项目。这些项目作为公共领域的元素，它们的出现是因为人们认识到这是一座拥有重要公共场所的城市。在密特朗的领导下，项目的形式发生了根本性的变化，从城市形象上看，宏伟计划之所以如此重要是因为围绕它们的争论实际上是一场关于巴黎应该是什么样的争论。

四、扩建过程

卢浮宫的扩建可分为两个阶段：1983—1989 年的一期扩建和 1989—1997 年的二期扩建。二期扩建主要涉及卢浮宫北翼的黎塞留馆的改建和扩建。贝聿铭的设计重点集中在一期扩建，主要包括对卢浮宫室外广场空间和新增功能空间的改造。新增功能空间主要位于地下，而广场改造主要围绕着贝聿铭设计的玻璃金字塔形式的地下空间入口展开。因此，我们将关注卢浮宫的一期扩建，详细探讨贝聿铭在此过程中采用的设计手法，以及这些手法解决的问题和达到的效果。

（一）新增的地下功能空间

首先，针对新增的地下功能空间，需要说明贝聿铭选择这种形式的原因。面对卢浮宫当时展览和室内公共活动空间不足的问题，贝聿铭之所以选择拓展地下展览空间而非在地面上新建独立展览空间，是因为卢浮宫须增加的空间面积高达 7 万平方米。如果以新建独立建筑的形式解决新增空间的问题，将导致卢浮宫的广场被填满或者需要在其外围修筑一座围墙。无论采取哪种形式，都将对卢浮宫原有建筑风貌产生难以忽视的负面影响，这也将意味着对原有建筑及场地条件的忽视和不尊重。因此，在设计之初，贝聿铭决定将须新增的空间全部安置于广场的地下，以确保不会侵占地面公共空间。

其次，新增的地下功能空间主要包括两个部分。第一部分是独立完整的公共活动空间，直接与卢浮宫广场相连，以满足卢浮宫作为公共建筑的需求。第二部分是与卢浮宫三大展示厅相连的展示空间，部分缓解了卢浮宫人流拥挤和展示空间不足的问题，使许多储藏室中的艺术品得以展出。贝聿铭的设计重点在于公共空间的营造，其中主要体现在地下一层的拿破仑大厅，该大厅可通过主入口自动扶梯直接到达。贝聿铭致力于将其打造成为一个功能完善、体验良好的公共服务空间。其设计分为三个主要部分：第一赋予其"桥"的功能；第二将其打造成为与卢浮宫原本昏暗的展览空间完全不同的明亮的公共活动空间；第三，在室内打造标志性节点，以吸引游客并留下深刻印象。

1. 玻璃金字塔主入口——作为"桥"的功能

贝聿铭为新增地下功能空间设置了独立的主入口——玻璃金字塔入口，使其事实上成为一个相对于卢浮宫独立运营的空间，与卢浮宫展览空间有所区分，更易于管理，并且有助于将其打造成为一个更为开放的公共活动空间。贝聿铭为了有效利用这个公共开放空间，赋予了其所谓的"桥"功能，即贯通东南西北四个方向，连接卢浮宫的三大展厅以及城市公共交通系统。首先，拿破仑大厅与周围的三大展馆相连，使游客可以从任意方向进行参观，无需绕行很长的路线，大大优化了游客的参展路线，并且其具有的各种公共功能也能更高效地服务于三大展馆。其次，该大厅向西同时连接地下二层的停车场和巴黎的地铁交通系统。这不仅促进了停车场的地下化，解决了卢浮宫西侧与杜乐丽花园之间的交通节点问题，避免了地面交通的混乱和人车混行的危险，加强了拿破仑广场向西的空间连续性，还方便了使用公共交通前来参观的游客。

2. 天窗——明亮的公共空间

为了解决新增功能空间位于地下与公共空间需要明亮光线之间的矛盾，贝聿铭采用了开设天窗的方法。然而，他在天窗的形式上进行了深入的考虑，尽管这一部分内容稍后会详细涉及，但现在我们将重点放在天窗所产生的室内效果上进行探讨。在城市交通进入地下一层入口处和卢浮宫广场进入拿破仑大厅入口处分别设置了两个相对较大的天窗。这不仅为室内较大的公共空间提供了采光，同时也打造了两个重要的室内节点，这两个节点在形式上相互呼应，加深了游客对卢浮宫的印象。此外，还有三个较小的天窗分别位于拿破仑大厅的北、南和东侧。其具有两个作用：一是与位于拿破仑大厅正上方较大的天窗结合，打造一个足够明亮的公共活动空间；二是作为通往卢浮宫三大不同展馆的"光明的指引"。

3. 标志性节点打造

为了让公众对这个与卢浮宫相对独立的公共空间留下深刻印象，并为卢浮宫注入新的活力，贝聿铭在其中设置了两个较为特殊的标志性节点。首先，在地下一层入口处，即从地下停车场和城市地铁进入卢浮宫的地点，贝聿铭设计了一个倒置的玻璃金字塔。这个设计在空间与造型上呼应了广场处的正放金字塔入口的意象，在游客进入美术馆的过程中创造了一次高潮体验。其次，在拿破仑大厅中央、正放金字塔入口正下方，设置了一个具有雕塑性的不锈钢螺旋楼梯。尽管看似简单，但这个楼梯设计十分复杂：没有支柱，完全依靠楼梯本身的螺旋形特性来支撑，而且楼梯的高度达 29 英尺，难度相当惊人。贝聿铭成功地创造了一座优雅的楼梯，尽管受到了厚度限制，但仍然达到了他一贯追求的空间焦点效果。在螺旋梯的中央设置了一个圆座，许多人误认为是一个没有人的询问服务台，但实际上那是服务残障人士的动力电梯。当使用电梯时，电梯厢会出现，上下移动的电梯厢就像一件"现代化的雕塑"，时隐时现，为大厅的空间增添了趣味。

（二）卢浮宫室外广场空间的改造

对于卢浮宫室外广场的改造，贝聿铭主要以拿破仑广场上方的玻璃金字塔入口为中心进行设计。在总体设计上，他将新时代的卢浮宫扩建方案的中心准确地设置在奥斯曼男爵创造的巴黎城市空间的轴线上。该中心作为卢浮宫的一部分，通过与城市轴线的呼应，强调了卢浮宫在城市中的重要地位，体现了贝聿铭对法国现代城市文明的历史与人文关怀。[1] 而对室外广场的改造分为两个部分：一是新建的地下功能空间的入口建筑；二是基于入口建筑对广场上各景观要素的组织。贝聿铭在入口建筑的设计中主要考虑了两个方面：如何将新建筑与旧建筑完美融合；如何增强卢浮宫作为法国重要历史建筑的地位。

1.新建造的地下空间的入口建筑的处理

对于前者，贝聿铭试图通过运用玻璃和钢这两种材料，创造出一种"明亮、轻快的象征性构造"，以避免与卢浮宫的建筑风格相冲突。他认为，卢浮宫作为法国历史上具有重大意义的建筑，没有其他扩建实体能够与这座历史悠久的宫殿相媲美并融合在一起，除了它自己。玻璃和钢的组合不仅降低了新建筑的存在感，而且玻璃的倒影减弱了新建筑与卢浮宫本身之间的边界感，入口建筑进一步融入其中，彰显了对卢浮宫崇高地位的尊敬。贝聿铭选择四棱锥这种建筑形式的原因是，一方面它是相同面积中体积最小的几何体，不太抢眼；

---

① 斯然畅畅.卢浮宫玻璃金字塔：贝聿铭的现代建筑纪念碑.中国艺术，2019(4)：86-95.

另一方面，四棱锥是人类历史上最古老的建筑之一——金字塔的象征，这使得入口建筑模糊了与卢浮宫之间的距离感，因为它既比卢浮宫更古老，又比它更新颖。①

入口建筑的设计通过两个方面实现了目标：一是作为卢浮宫的一部分与城市轴线继续产生联系，从而增强了卢浮宫在城市轴线上的重要地位；二是通过改变入口建筑在不同时空中的定位，弥补了卢浮宫在不同时空中表现力不足的缺陷。作为历史建筑，卢浮宫在白天展现出雄伟的一面，但夜晚却被黑暗所吞没。贝聿铭通过在夜晚用灯光照亮在白天存在感极低的玻璃金字塔，使其在夜晚成为卢浮宫的象征符号，将博物馆的活动延续至夜晚，同时充分利用公共空间。

2.基于入口建筑对广场上各景观要素的组织

贝聿铭基于玻璃金字塔入口对卢浮宫广场各景观要素进行组织时，致力于将建筑与景观完美融合。他将金字塔底边与卢浮宫建筑物边界平行，并与方位平行，与埃及金字塔的布局相同，以强化其与环境的关系。在玻璃金字塔周围设置了一个大水池，水池旋转45度，西侧的三角形水池被减去，留出空地作为入口广场，另外三个角对向卢浮宫建筑，构成三个紧邻金字塔的三角形水池。这些水池如明镜般映衬着玻璃金字塔，与环境相融合，丰富了景观，增加了建筑的立体感。在转向的方正水池的角隅，紧邻着另外四个大小不一的三角形水池，构成另一个正方形，与金字塔、建筑物平行。每个三角水池都有巨柱喷泉，烘托出玻璃金字塔的晶莹，使建筑与景观完美融合。

五、博物馆扩建的案例分析

（一）新旧建筑的内隐关系

含有内隐关系的改扩建是新建筑融于旧建筑常用的方式，例如去掉旧博物馆内部的墙体、楼板改建，除此之外还有向地下扩建，这两种扩建方式并不会对旧建筑的原貌产生过大的影响，此种情况下新建筑在城市空间视角下并不显著，而是以一种内隐的不破坏原建筑立面特色的方式达到旧建筑内部空间的优化和功能扩展的目的。

新旧建筑的趋同关系即以保护旧建筑的主题形象为主，弱化新建筑主体的

---

① 张晶.贝聿铭与卢浮宫改建工程.中华建设，2005(2)：57-59.

在外部的表现，使新建筑处于从属和次要地位。形成这种组合关系的原因主要是旧建筑是由宫殿、城堡或教堂改建而成的博物馆，其建筑本身就具有相当高的历史地位和保护价值，此外博物馆建筑还往往处于历史文化地段，所以在改扩建中新建筑要尽可能小的影响原建筑的空间格局，并延续城市历史文脉。

（二）新旧建筑的共存关系

新旧建筑的共存关系是指新旧建筑在外部环境中呈现和谐稳定的结合状态，形成这种组合关系的成因主要有以下几点。

1.扩建面积较大

当博物馆面临扩建面积大但自身内部不能通过加建来满足现实需求时，分为水平和垂直两个方向的扩建。原建筑侧边或原建筑围合部位这类水平方向的扩建策略，在垂直方向上依据现状考虑进行地上、地下或地上加地下的扩建。

2.周边环境包容度强

旧建筑周边环境包容度高，新建筑的加入不会对整个区段的历史文脉产生干扰或者破坏的作用。形式美和结构美的统一很难在单一的结构体系的改扩建中实现，因此设计师常选择将不同的建筑结构体系相分离，表现其各自的结构特点，以此构成一种充满对比和张力的美感。

（三）新旧建筑的对比关系

新旧建筑的对比关系指的是新建筑与旧建筑的建筑主体保持相对独立性，这种对比关系不但可以保持新旧建筑空间和主体的独立性，强调新建筑的视觉形象，对公众产生视觉冲击力，还能触发空间的张力。

六、对当代博物馆扩建的借鉴意义

(一)博物馆扩建的必要性

1.满足文化发展需求

博物馆是社会和文化的产物，无论是展示的内容、传播的信息，还是空间的氛围都与文化有着密切联系。这种特性决定了博物馆作为文化载体和文化本身的双重身份。虽然旧建筑在功能上已不满足现实需要，但它们所累积的时空记忆和场所文化能够使人们产生丰富的联想，人们在这里常常会回忆或想象过去发生在这里的一幕幕场景。博物馆扩建能够在不影响旧建筑及环境原有风貌的情况下，赋予它们新的使用功能，在社会生活中扮演着文化传播者的角色，延续着城市的历史文脉。

2.适应环保需求

建筑的大拆大建会产生大量的人力、物力、财力资源的浪费，同时也会对环境造成各种各样的污染。大部分建筑的结构寿命都远大于其使用寿命，旧建筑虽然功能上无法满足现实需求，但其潜在的价值是无穷的。因此，为了减少对环境的破坏，人们应当尽可能减少建筑的大拆大建，对旧建筑采取改造更新的处理方式，赋予它们新的生命。博物馆扩建是旧建筑更新再利用的分支，同样面临着合理利用自然资源及保护大自然生态环境的需求。

3.满足自身发展需求

近年来，博物馆的建设越来越受到人们的重视，各个国家、城市都在大量建造博物馆。一方面，社会经济的迅猛发展成为博物馆建设的有力支持，欧洲许多国家使用大量的资金发展公共文化事业。另一方面，在生活水平基本提高的情况下，人们开始追求精神上的满足，希望通过参观博物馆来获取丰富的历史文化知识，拓宽视野，提高文化素养。基于人们对文化消费的普遍热情，博物馆不再是少数人的文化机构，而是普通群众观看展览、与人交流、休闲放松的公共场所。同时，博物馆因藏品数量激增、分类细化出现空间不够的问题使得老博物馆迫切要通过改扩建来满足发展需要。[①]

（二）博物馆的扩建原则

1.保证历史的真实性

对于历史真实性的保证体现在尊重历史建筑的原真性以及解释性地转译其文化内涵方面。其中原真性即尊重原物，在改造及再利用的过程中，给予不同文化背景下的历史建筑最大限度尊重，尊重其实体创作（功能、形式、材料、技术、文脉）和发展历史（社会、文化、经济），改建部分建筑可缓解历史建筑的衰败，并且自身可识别、可撤销。而解释性指建筑师对历史建筑的保护和再利用不局限于过去，因为历史建筑本身所经过的历史就是文化价值不断转化、调整和应用的累积的历史，所以我们对历史建筑的解释，不能仅局限于传承、获取，同时还要不断创新。新建筑要与当下时代产生联系，在历史建筑上留下时间的痕迹。因此时代的对比在其形式上可以有所体现，而其在文脉上其实是连续的、有关联的，以文化为纽带联系不同时代，延续其历史。

---

① 高冬妮.博物馆改扩建中新旧空间关系研究.陕西：西安建筑科技大学，2020.

所以，建筑师对历史建筑的解读其实是基于现代的语境下的，是以现在的思维重新审视历史建筑，并在新的时代背景下扩展和延伸历史建筑的意义，即在保证历史建筑内容具有"原真性"的条件下，对历史建筑进行"解释性"解读与改造。

2.功能复合化

功能复合化包含两个方面：引入新功能以及复合不同时空功能。其中引入新功能的做法主要与人们的生活方式改变以及科技引领的展示方式的改变有关，例如，参观博物馆这一行为越来越大众化导致参观人数增加，以至于需要更多的展品、展品储藏空间及展示空间；人们对休息及娱乐需求的提升，以至于需要增加更多的公共空间用于休闲、娱乐；新技术的出现可以与展览结合增加其吸引力，以至于展品所需的展示空间的形态需要进行相应的改变等。

而复合不同时空功能主要依靠空间的弹性设计实现，在"以人为本"的视角下，将现代的新元素在改扩建的过程中融入旧的肌体中。通过对流线的重新设计、对旧肌体中的空间体系进行重新组织，开创多义性的空间，可以提高空间的使用效率。

3.使用便利原则

使用者的参与大体上可分为两部分，一部分是与展示的互动交流；另一部分则是对展示以外活动的参与。相较于以展品为中心的传统博物馆，现代博物馆更强调"以人为本"，与之相对的是，展品不再是简单地陈列，而是与新的艺术形式以及科技手段结合从而使使用者获得互动体验，观众与展品的交流不再是简单的实现交流，而是更多的感官上和精神上的交流，从而增强其对观众的吸引力并调动其积极性。

展示以外的活动主要包括餐饮、阅读、观影及儿童活动等，这些不断增加的公共活动需求使得博物馆中的公共活动空间越发重要，馆方不得不充分考虑观众在使用其公共功能时的体验。博物馆通过将公共活动空间的设计多样化、舒适化，使得博物馆在物质以及精神上可以充分满足观众，并开拓博物馆的非观展人群。

4.技术生态化原则

（1）自然光源的采纳控制。博物馆对自然光环境有着十分特殊的要求，需要在满足照明需求的前提下进一步创造自然光的环境，现代博物馆的采光方式通常是自然与人工相结合。具体而言：第一，充分发挥光在环境中的作用，表现空间的形态尺度、材质色彩等实质性的特征；第二，利用光本身的特性（如亮度、强弱、方向性等）丰富空间的立体感和界面的运动感；第三，运用建筑形态特征（如空间体量关系、结构构件层次等）丰富光影的动态构图。

（2）地下空间的利用。当博物馆的地上扩建受到环境制约时，往往会向地下空间延伸发展。一些项目是想将地面还给自然，将地上空间作为室外公共活动空间或景观绿化空间，更好地与环境融合。还有一些项目是由于博物馆建筑本身或场地属于历史文化遗存，在改扩建中应尽量保持原貌，保证城市文脉的完整性和延续性。在博物馆空间中，应对地下空间进行合理充分的利用，通过地下通道联系新老建筑，将空间隐退地下，维持建筑及环境原貌，同时将地上、地下空间建立有机联系，充分表达对城市原有自然环境和人文环境的尊重。①

---

① 罗丹.基于空间体验的博物馆建筑改扩建的设计手法研究.安徽：合肥工业大学，2013.

数字化下中国国家博物馆叙事空间的新形态探析①

摘　要： 随着技术环境的改变，博物馆的叙事空间出现了新形态。本文通过叙事空间理论、新叙事学研究方法，聚焦中国国家博物馆的叙事空间在数字化技术下的变化，发现中国国家博物馆的叙事空间呈现为三种新形态，即虚实交互空间、话语网络空间、精神想象空间。在探析这三大空间的形成和发展过程中，本文发现新叙事空间具有同在性、跨主体性、交互性等特点。中国国家博物馆新叙事空间的形成，对于重新思考博物馆的保护、研究、展示、阐释等功能具有一定的启发意义。

关键词： 中国国家博物馆；叙事空间；虚实交互；话语网络；精神空间

从博物馆的发展历史来看，早期的博物馆功能主要以收藏、保护、研究历史文物为主，随着教育、娱乐等不同文化需求的出现，其功能日益呈现多样性、综合性等特点。后现代主义兴起之后，博物馆收藏艺术品的合法性不断受到挑战，博物馆与大众日常生活的界限在不断消失。各种数字技术更是延展了博物馆展示文物、阐释文化、传播意义的空间，打破了原有物理时空的局限。时代巨变下，博物馆如何讲好自身的故事？如何协调文物与观众、当代社会、历史、文化语境等多元"他者"的关系？如何更好地传播文化价值、文化意义，唤醒民族记忆、形成身份认同？这些都是当代中国综合性大博物馆如中国国家博物馆（下文简称"国博"）、故宫博物院等关注的核心问题。面对这些问题，国内诸多博物馆各显神通，如2018年上半年各馆纷纷入驻抖音，《博物

① 作者：方明珠，上海交通大学媒体与传播学院；方凌宇，上海交通大学上海交大－南加州大学文化创意产业学院；陈芊含，上海交通大学人文学院；张若琪，上海交通大学媒体与传播学院。

馆奇妙夜》《国家宝藏》《博物馆之城》《博物馆说》等影视作品、各种博物馆文创产品等，被人们热议。这些文化产品、文化活动都在重新阐释博物馆的意义、重构文物的当下意义、重塑博物馆与"他者"之间的关系，形成新的文化传播空间。

正如罗兰·巴特（Roland Barthes）所言："叙事存在于神话里、传说里、寓言里、童话里、小说里、史诗里、历史里、悲剧里、正剧里、喜剧里、哑剧里、绘画里、彩绘玻璃里、电影里……叙事作品不管是质量好的或不好的文学，总是超越国家、历史、文化存在，如同生活一样。"[①]而当代以博物馆为主体开展的一系列文化活动、衍生的诸多文化产品都在向公众叙事，即通过语言或其他媒介来再现发生在特定时间和空间里的事情，从而形成新的文化传播空间。正因博物馆无时无刻不在叙事，我们往往忽视其本身也是一种传递着信息的"媒介"，连接着过去、现在和未来。也正因博物馆建筑的实体性，我们常沉浸于它的物理空间而忽视由其叙事性能延展出来的各种更为抽象的空间形态。本文聚焦中国国家博物馆，以其经典展览的叙事为分析对象，同时借鉴各种叙事空间理论视角、运用"后经典叙事学"的研究方法，探讨新技术下中国国家博物馆叙事空间有哪些新转向和新形态类型，新叙事空间形态有哪些特点。

一、国博叙事空间的新转向

将国博视为媒介，将其举办各种展览的相关行为视为叙事，研究其作为媒介展开叙事的空间形态在当代发生了哪些转变是本文的核心研究问题。本节从理论方法、理论视角阐述国博叙事空间形态的新转向。

（一）后经典叙事学

20世纪60年代左右，在俄国形式主义和法国结构主义的双重影响下，经典叙事学诞生，其又可称为结构主义叙事学。它是直接用结构主义的方法来研究叙事作品的学科，并为小说研究提供了重要的模式和方法。此后西方学者将"叙事"概念引入各种文化活动，经典叙事学成为一门研究各种叙事文本的综合学科，研究对象包括：叙事诗、日常口头叙事、法律叙事、电影叙事、戏

---

① 罗兰·巴特.叙事作品结构分析导论.转引自：王泰来.叙事美学.重庆：重庆出版社，1987：60.

剧叙事、历史叙事、绘画叙事、广告叙事等①。但其研究对象仅限于虚构作品叙事，未包括历史、传记乃至图像叙事作品等，从而在不同程度上隔断了作品与社会、历史、文化语境的关联，经典叙事学因此不断受到质疑并走向衰落。直到 20 世纪 90 年代，"后经典叙事学"或"新叙事理论"在美国等西方国家兴起。它对经典叙事学的某些理论或相关概念进行重新审视或反思，在分析叙事文本时更为注重读者以及社会、历史、文化语境的作用，因此拓展了叙事学研究的领域②。中国国家博物馆作为叙事媒介，不同于原来的文学作品，也不同于单一的图像、影像等文本，它更类似于一个集语言、文字、图片、影像、文物等一切作为"能指"的综合性媒介，因此研究其叙事行为必须打破经典叙事学的共时性局限，运用后经典叙事学的方法，关注社会、经济、策展人、观众等多维他者与其的关联。

（二）叙事空间理论

无论是在"经典叙事学"还是在"后经典叙事学"中，叙事的时间维度总是备受关注，而空间维度总是有意无意被忽视。自 20 世纪后期批评理论出现了"空间转向"后，叙事学关注焦点也转向了叙事中的空间问题。1945年，约瑟夫·弗兰克（Josef Fronk）在《西旺尼评论》上发表的《现代文学中的空间形式》一文往往被视为叙事理论的滥觞之作。③ 本文受启于西摩·查特曼（Symour Chatman）《故事与话语》中的"故事空间"和"话语空间"概念，亨利·列斐伏尔（Henri Lefebvre）《空间的生产》中提出的"社会空间"的概念，米歇尔（W. J. T. Mitchell）的《文学中的空间形式：走向一种总体理论》一文提出的文学空间的四种类型（字面层，即文本的物理存在；描述层，即作品中表征、模仿或所指的世界；文本表现的事件序列，即传统意义上的时间形式；故事背后的形而上空间，可以理解为生成意义的系统）④。本文将"博物馆叙事空间"定义为：以博物馆为媒介展开一系列广义上的叙事行为，这些叙事形成了文物与人、社会、历史等他者交互的活动空间，包括感知空间、想象空间、物理空间、虚拟空间、亲历的多态融合空间等。

① 申丹，王亚丽.西方叙事学：经典与后经典.北京：北京师范大学出版社，2010：3.
② 龙迪勇.空间叙事学：叙事学研究的新领域.天津师范大学学报（社会科学版），2008(6)：54-60.
③ 程锡麟.叙事理论的空间转向——叙事空间理论概述.江西社会科学，2007(11)：25-35.
④ 龙迪勇.空间叙事学：叙事学研究的新领域.天津师范大学学报（社会科学版），2008(6)：57.

（三）国博叙事空间的转变

早期博物馆的叙事空间相对狭小，一般以展览中的文物、导语、讲解员为叙述者，叙事空间往往是较为抽象的观众的心理空间，而实体空间往往在研究时被忽略。自从互联网等新兴技术出现后，国博的叙事策略发生了转变，叙事空间的边界也因此不断地被延展，而叙事空间中的核心是文物与人、社会、历史、政治、经济等"他者"的关系。国博的叙事空间的新形态大致可以分为以下三类：虚实交互空间，即文物展示所在的实体和虚拟场所或地点；话语网络空间，即叙述行为发生的场所和地点，这里的叙述行为如以人工讲解员、数字讲解员的语言语音为叙事方式形成的叙述行为，以文字为媒介形成的导语、网络推文，以抖音等新媒介社交平台形成的影像视频、弹幕、评论等；精神想象空间，即在如AR、VR等新技术加持下，国博通过充分调动观众的视觉、听觉等多感官的感知功能，促使观众沉浸于对展品的感知中，并激发观众认知、思考、重新阐述展品的历史背景、历史文化意义、文化价值的抽象思维空间。

二、国博叙事空间的新形态

基于对国博的实地考察，本节重点阐述国博三种新叙事空间形态的形成过程与呈现方式。

（一）虚实交互空间

数字化首先重塑的是博物馆中用于呈现展品、传递信息和故事的具体物理场所。通过对数字技术和交互手段等的运用，国博融合了虚拟和实体的元素，将传统的博物馆叙事空间转变为了虚实交互空间，实现观众与展品、信息和故事之间多样化的互动与沟通。这种交互空间不仅限于实体场所，还包括数字展厅和在线平台等多种形式。以下将通过实体叙事空间的数字化更新和虚拟叙事空间的构建这两个不同角度，阐述国博在数字化时代构建虚实交互空间的方式。

1. 实体叙事空间的数字化更新

林少雄教授曾指出："现代博物馆的一个很重要的任务，在于对物的叙事特质的破解……随着当代博物馆观念的变化，对于物的叙事规律的认知与把握成为其迫切需要解决的问题。"[1]数字化技术的进步和博物馆叙事理念的更新，

---

[1] 林少雄.博物馆4.0时代的物质叙事与空间融合.美育学刊，2018(4)：18-23.

从不同方向促进了传统的博物馆叙事空间的转变与升级。传统的博物馆叙事大多停留在对于展品的功能展示和考古学知识介绍层面，甚至有些只是对作品的简单陈列，较少考虑大众的诉求和信息接受能力。比如向观众展示一件宋代的绘画作品，传统的叙事方式可能只是以文字标注的形式，注明展品的年代、作者、出土时间、保存方式等信息。然而，近年来参展人群更趋多样化，其需求亦日趋多元。如何利用数字化技术，更新叙事方式，成为博物馆不得不面对的课题。

面对这一课题，国博于 2023 年 5 月开放的"数说犀尊"展览是一份具有参考意义的答卷。传统的展览方式多以实物展示佐以文字、图片解说等静态手段来呈现，而"数说犀尊"展览则突破常规展陈手段，综合运用多种数字技术直观呈现文物细节和科研过程。观众可以通过 AR 技术、全息投影等手段观看高清复原的犀尊全貌，甚至能从视、听、触、互动思考等多维度深入感受犀尊所承载的价值，获得沉浸式的观展体验。这种数字化技术更新丰富了展品的呈现方式，也提升了观众的参与度。虽然是一物一展的形式，却因为数字化内容的填充，使得展览叙事丝毫不显得单调，反而因为多种数字技术的应用，极大拓展了观众的视角，实现了对实物的模拟和补充，使文物欣赏更为立体、细致。这种数字化的实体叙事空间满足了当代观众追求沉浸式体验和自主互动的需求。它实现了国博叙事手段与方式方法的现代化升级，使展览的文化传播效果更佳。

在馆内同时展出的"盛世修典——'中国历代绘画大系'成果展"，也体现了数字技术对于实体叙事空间的迭代过程。展览通过音频、视频、文字等多种媒体形式，将绘画作品的背后故事、艺术背景等内容进行全方位展示。观众可以通过触摸屏、耳机等设备，自由选择感兴趣的内容进行深入了解，提升参与度和增强互动感。展方通过数字化手段，例如高清晰度的数字扫描技术，使得观众可以在实体空间中亲眼欣赏到散落各地的绘画作品，同时通过数字呈现的方式进一步展现出作品的细节和真实性。

此外，沉浸式虚拟实境的创造也使得实体叙事空间得到了重要的数字化补充。国博在不同展厅内设立了多个大小不一的沉浸式体验区。例如"盛世修典"展览结尾部分设置的"光影丹青"沉浸式体验区，以中国古代绘画的创新转化为核心创作理念，将传统水墨画的美学特质深度融入设计中。体验区通过运用虚拟现实技术在空间中重现水墨画的构图和色彩效果，同时采用多感官交互设备，包括空间音频和触觉设备，使参观者能够通过视觉、听觉和触觉多重感官体验虚拟画境。最重要的是，它巧妙地将传统水墨绘画的艺术表现手法如笔触等，与现代数字科技深度融合，从而打破传统参观模式，引导参观者沉浸式走入虚拟画境，实现传统与现代元素的有机结合，从而提升观众的参观体验[①]。这种数字化的更新使得观众不仅能够在实体空间中感受到传统绘画的氛围，还能通过数字科技的辅助，更全面地理解作品的背后故事和艺术技法。

2.虚拟叙事空间的构建

虚拟叙事空间，即通过多种数字技术创造的一种虚拟环境，能够以沉浸式的方式呈现各种内容，并为观众提供与展品远距离互动、参与式体验的机会。在博物馆的虚拟叙事空间中，观众可以通过多种交互手段，探索、了解和体验展览及展示的内容。

国博的数字展厅就是典型的虚拟叙事空间。在该数字展厅中，国博运用了多种技术呈现形态，包括导览程序、网络视频等，为观众提供了全新的实景观展体验。在这个虚拟叙事空间中，观众可如亲临馆内一样"边走边看"。在数字展厅里，观众既可以参观以往的360度全景展览，也可以观看当前正在进行的重磅展览。这种数字展厅最大程度地还原了展览的视觉效果，数字展览也成为观众跨越时空界限和条件限制观看的最主要的展览。国博通过三维模型的模式，保存了大量的临时展览，尤其是较难得的海外展览和展品，为观众回顾展览和重现展览提供了可能。但是，这类纯粹存在于网络之上的虚拟叙事空间极大地依赖于技术水平和网络环境，有些观众由于缺乏数字技术的支持或者网络速度等问题，无法真正享受到数字化应用带来的便捷体验。这可能是未来在深化构建博物馆虚拟叙事空间时需要考虑的问题

在疫情期间，面对观众难以线下观展和出国出行的客观难题，国博发起的"手拉手：共享世界文明之美"线上云展览，与33家顶级博物馆合作举办线上博物馆展览接力的模式，满足了观众的观看和学习需求。线上云展览等数字展览形式，不仅是单纯将实体展厅的内容转到了线上，更是对物理叙事空间的一大更新。通过互联网和各种新兴数字技术的链接，博物馆在一定程度上消减了观众与展品之间信息交互的时空限制，扩展了叙事空间。

智能导览程序也是一种常见的虚拟叙事空间形态，观众可以通过手机应用

---

① 王希.以数字化讲好中国故事：基于"盛世修典——'中国历代绘画大系'成果展"的思考.博物馆管理，2022(4)：18-29.

或导览设备获取展览信息和解说，并根据自身兴趣选择内容进行深入了解。这是独立于现实空间之外，又与实体展览联结的虚实交互的叙事空间。在"盛世修典"展览中，策展团队引入专门研发的智能导览程序，每一幅画作旁均有二维码，观众用手机扫描可以获取关于作品更详细的解读，并查看高清图片。[①]即使是离开了实体展馆后，观众依然能从导览程序中获取关于展品和展览的各种信息，这也是对传统叙事一种扩展和补充。

国博通过数字技术构建的虚拟叙事空间，极大地拓展了博物馆的展示范围和覆盖面。数字展厅、网络平台使展览不再受地域限制，海内外的观众都可以参与互动。这不仅满足了观众的需求，也使博物馆实现了展示形式的现代化转型。同时，虚拟空间也为博物馆的教育推广提供了新的平台。各类数字化展览、电子书籍等都包含丰富的文物图文信息，是进行文化传播、历史教育的重要载体，学生和相关研究人员可以充分利用这些资源，获得直观的文物学习体验。

然而，我们也应注意到虚拟叙事空间的潜在问题。模拟展示难免会失真或简化文物细节，线上体验也难以完全达到在实物展厅参观的效果。因此，虚拟空间更多是对实体叙事空间的补充和扩展，并不能完全取代实体展厅。国博在运用新技术的同时，还需坚持文物实物的中心地位，发挥好实体展厅的优势，使新旧技术达到最佳结合。

（二）话语网络空间

在博物馆的信息传播过程中，策展团队是博物馆空间的原初叙事者和编码者，观众是解码者。策展人通过展陈设计中的解说资料（展牌、展词、人工解说词等）和宣发行为中的官方话语构成了列斐伏尔三元空间中"概念化的空间"的主体，即话语空间，观众会在解码的同时进入博物馆的话语空间的建构之中。在移动互联网、数字化等技术的推动下，文物在线上讲解和融媒体宣发中打破了博物馆内时空限制，这一空间成为得以在任何场所都能再现的话语网络空间[②]。据第55次《中国互联网络发展状况统计报告》显示，截至2025年

---

① 王希.以数字化讲好中国故事：基于"盛世修典——'中国历代绘画大系'成果展"的思考.博物馆管理，2022(4)：18-29

② 朱立元主编.西方美学思想史（下）.上海：上海人民出版社，2009：1665.

1月，我国网民规模达到11.08亿。① 在移动互联网时代，短文推送、短视频、手游、网络剧、3D展厅等网络消费文化产品越来越炙手可热，文字文本、影视文本、语音文本交相呼应构成了复杂而广阔的叙事模式，形成了无处不在的话语网络空间。

1. 媒体矩阵编织话语网络

早在20世纪90年代，以艾琳·胡珀－格林希尔（Eilean Hooper-Greenhill）为首的博物馆研究者就意识到观众在参观过程中并非被动的，他们已有的知识、态度等使他们在观看中成为意义的创造者。当代的策展人也应该在"受众本位"的趋势下更积极地与观众互动②，新媒体和数字化技术的发展成为有利的媒介，让观众能够"有更大的自由来个性化他们的媒体体验，让人与人的联系、合作、分享更加容易"。移动端上的语音与短视频导览、文物3D模型和细节介绍等成为颇受欢迎的导览辅助形式，为观众补充历史和考古信息。国博官方的融媒体矩阵账号和各类自媒体账号都向观众呈现出了文物的不同叙事样态，国博的官方话语平台包括抖音、快手、微信公众号、今日头条等，包含了展览陈列的宣传、内容介绍、预约和文物解说等多重功能，以文字、视频、图文、音频等多种方式供用户获取观展信息，具有权威、专业、精炼的特点。自媒体账户则从更加个性化和通俗的角度向观众宣传介绍展览的观看策略和建议，内容的故事性、主观性、灵活性更强，观众的参与和互动性也更强，自媒体账号成为了网络话语交互的主要空间。

从临时展览和专题展览来看，融媒体平台为展览提供时效性的信息、攻略和反馈能够使展览的热度不断升温。国博于2023年5月开展的"数说犀尊"智慧展厅在开展前，移动媒体平台便出现了图、文、视频等多种形式的资讯预告。除了传统的《光明日报》《钱江晚报》和新华社等媒体资讯平台的宣传，抖音、小红书、微博平台上也出现了大量的展览信息预告和参观游玩攻略。在图文视频中，观众可以预先了解展览的布局和"一物一展""数字技术"等亮点。作为集数据采集、智慧融合、互动展示等多种功能于一体的展览，"数说犀尊"围绕展览主体"西汉错金银云纹铜犀尊"的前世今生、造型纹饰美学、传承保护等多个维度的介绍、三维数据虚拟成像、3D打印技术也成为宣传亮点

---

① 中国互联网中心. 第55次《中国互联网络发展状况统计报告》. (2025-01-17)[2025-02-10]. https://www.cnnic.cn/n4/2025/0117/c88-11229.html.
② 黄洋，陈红京. 陈列展览设计十讲策略. 上海：上海交通大学出版社，2019: 5-6.

进入展览推荐和观展选择的语义空间，给观众做好了观看的心理预设和选择。

2.多样叙事方式延展话语空间

从博物馆长期的展陈叙事空间来看，比起在观展时的知识补充，观众更需要从日常生活的话语空间中获取历史文物知识。因此，博物馆通过更多样态的叙事策略，让文物承载的多种信息潜移默化地走进观众的心中，形成作为日常生活实践和审美品味的空间，才是更长远的方法。国博官方微信公众号提供的"国博讲坛""穿越古代中国""文物活起来"等系列科普类知识分享能够让观众学习文物知识、提高历史素养的同时，吸引观众前往实地参观。在自媒体话语中，2018年国博讲解员"河森堡"带动了一批观众对文物和博物馆参观的兴趣，也带动了许多自媒体平台做文物和博物馆的讲解、故事和学习专栏，为年轻人参观国博提供了知识储备。

影视、戏剧、综艺节目也拓宽了文物的叙事形式。国家博物馆剧场上演了首部文物活化舞台剧《盛世欢歌》，演员们以汉代击鼓说唱俑的形象演绎，再现了汉代俳优命运的起伏和乐观的精神，也让人们进一步认识了汉代歌舞形式。《假如国宝会说话》《国家宝藏》等综艺节目将明星和文物相结合，通过小剧场、文物故事、知识科普相结合的方式，让文物及其历史背景以活态、生机焕发的形式进入年轻人的视野。影视剧《长安十二时辰》将鎏金舞马衔杯纹银壶、鹦鹉杯、凸纹玻璃杯和何家村窖藏遗宝等作为道具，再现了唐代文物的艺术特点和历史知识。在电视剧《知否知否应是绿肥红瘦》中主角打马球的活动让人们对"马球"这一古代娱乐形式有了直观的感受，使观众在看到相关的文物，如打马球俑、章怀太子墓壁画马球图等有了先验的体验和对文物的感性理解。

综上所述，展览的叙事话语在数字化平台中，打破时空界限，让观众、文物、博物馆等多方主体积极地参与话语网络的空间建构。这些以不同的媒介平台形成的各种知识编织了话语网络，形成了一个多部发声、多义争夺、多元交互的话语网络空间形态。

（三）精神想象空间

博物馆的传统叙事空间往往通过单线性的历史叙事展开精神维度的叙事空间，该精神想象空间的展开多依赖于观者自身的知识素养、抽象性思维能力等，因此叙事空间的精神维度的拓展不是每个人都可开启。而新技术的运用，突破了原有国博叙事的局限，更能为大众开启叙事的精神想象空间。

1. 新技术助力打开叙事的想象空间

国博的传统展览仅通过多样化的展品来强调其多元的文化历史特征，借助展品的物质性和叙事的时间性重现历史，即便有图片、影像等媒介的运用，也因其叙事的单维度与时间线性，无法充分表现出展品中所蕴含的历史故事与美学内涵。此外，博物馆传统的叙事空间常常将展品从其原初的复杂历史语境中剪切出来，将其放置于一个新构建的叙事关联中，展品单维度的观照视角让其在很大程度上失去了自身的多义性，也很大程度上剥夺了观众的博物馆参观感知中的认知自由[1]。

马歇尔·麦克卢汉（Marshall McLuhan）认为："如果博物馆想在当今媒体饱和的世界向广大观众提供身临其境的沉浸式体验，那么就需要理解并接受21世纪的媒体技术。"[2]目前国博通过新媒体技术将静态图像、动态影像、声音和文字等跨媒体叙述方式的有机整合，重新塑造了一个关于展品与观众互动的叙事空间。在此空间中，观众的视觉、触觉、听觉得到了极大的延伸和扩展，进而极大地提升了人们的感知能力。新技术从多方面再现了展品承载的历史故事，同时在激发了人们感官的基础上，使得观众获得沉浸式的体验，继而激发了观众的自我想象，此时展品与观众在想象空间中交流、互动，为深入的理性思考奠定空间基础。

2. 在沉浸的想象中构筑精神空间

近年来，国博借助新媒体影像技术不断创新数字化沉浸式展览形式，借助360度成像和虚拟现实技术让博物馆文化叙事空间和虚拟场景实时融合。以中国国家博物馆的临时展览"心影传神——乌菲齐美术馆藏大师自画像展"为例，展览精选乌菲齐美术馆五十幅文艺复兴时期至当代的画作，以自画像为主题向中国观众展现艺术史光辉，同时展览特设光影体验部分，通过全息投影融合技术，打破传统的静态"画框式"观看方式，将乌菲齐美术馆收藏的文艺复兴时期经典作品进行"解构再创造"，将文艺复兴名作数字化重现，为观众带来身临其境感官体验。[3]"心影传神——乌菲齐美术馆藏大师自画像展"首先

---

① 刘宏宇.呈现的真相与传达的策略.北京：人民日报出社出版，2016：55-60.
② 王红，刘素仁.沉浸与叙事：新媒体影像技术下的博物馆文化沉浸式体验设计研究.艺术百家，2018(4)：161-169.
③ 中国国家博物馆."心影传神——乌菲齐美术馆藏大师自画像展"展览介绍.(2023-07-14)[2024-12-18].https://www.chnmuseum.cn/portals/0/web/zt/202304xycsh/.

通过展示多元的艺术展品和丰富详尽的文字叙事，将个体对文艺复兴的认识从传统刻板的叙事中解放出来，消弭宏大艺术史与个体之间的断裂，为观众打造一个丰富的、充满对话性的个体记忆库。同时该展借助新媒体技术将观众置身于文艺复兴时期的艺术世界，不断强化观众的个人体验，让观众主动思索艺术与现实的联系。在光影体验展览中，一方面，国博通过放大艺术原作的细节和制作虚拟动画实现视觉化的场景再现，使艺术作品鲜活地呈现在观众的眼前。国博将光影体验展的叙事聚焦于个体的情感体验上，而不是强调展览的叙事的宏大话语，使观众的整个身心都正沉浸在艺术作品宁静安详的气氛之中。另一方面，展览使用跌宕起伏的原创古典音乐作为配乐，让观众置身于特定的时空环境之中，如同在电影中使用蒙太奇手法，在共时性的空间中呈现出不同的艺术细节，同时让观众自主选择浏览路径，激发观众的情绪、情感与想象。观众沉浸的时间越久，就越容易开启以思考展品文化意义、文化价值等理性主导的精神想象空间。国博运用新技术强化观众个体身体感知，构建了一个互动的、实践性的精神想象空间，让观众将身体的知觉与实践活动、情感体验等紧密结合，在充分调动观众的身体感知力下，让观众更加轻易地发挥想象力，在精神想象空间中重构展品的意义，实现展品与观众的深度连接。

三、结语与讨论

国博运用新技术，不断突破原有的叙事策略和延展叙事空间，形成了具有自身特色的叙事空间新形态。这些新空间有三种。一是虚实交互的叙事空间，国博通过数字展厅、云展览等叙事策略，打破了自然时空的限制。二是话语网络空间，这一空间涉及的叙事主体众多，有策展人、展品自身、观众等，基于互联网技术的媒体矩阵将不同的叙事主体聚焦在由各种话语、意义编织而成的话语网络中，在这个空间中各种话语不断生产、传播、互动甚至引发争议。这一空间将博物馆与观众的社会生活紧密相连，塑造了高雅—低俗边界消逝的后现代文化。三是精神想象空间，这一空间通过新技术调动观众的多种感官进而提升其感知能力，让观众全身心沉浸于对展品的想象中，从而自发进入沉思的状态。

相较于传统的基于线性叙事时间形成的博物馆叙事空间，这三种新叙事空间形态呈现出同在性、跨主体性、交互性三大主要特征。同在性指三个空间没有顺序性，在同一时刻，三个空间可能是并置的也可能只有其中一个打开或两个共存；另外不同的观看群体可以突破自然地理的时空限制，共享三个空间中一个或多个。跨主体性指某一主体可以在三个空间中穿梭并展开自己叙事行为，某一空间中的叙事主体可以随时切换，还可以是观众等等。交互性指文化意义在三大空间的生产、传播、流动、交互，同时其形成的意义网络。此外，三大空间自身也存在交互，促使意义的停泊、中转、再生产。

综上，国博的新叙事空间形态的出现，是博物馆作为媒介传播文化的新表征与实践。这种叙事空间新形态必然改变了文化传播的渠道、方式，同时整合了不同的传播主体，还重构了意义的编码和解码的关系结构，形成了意义再生产的新空间。

从中国国家博物馆历史沿革与数字化发展现状拟构博物馆创新发展模型——来自苏州大学的探索与研究①

摘 要: 在全球化和互联网发展的场景下,当前各个博物馆正逐步迈入数字化阶段,结合多维学科,一方面注重从展品发掘研究、保护展出到互借交流的全链路数字化能力的提升,另一方面从参观者的角度进行全场景的数字化体验升级。随着技术的成熟,博物馆数字化在实践道路中迸发出新的可能性,本文从中国国家博物馆的历史和数字化发展成果出发,结合国际上数字化博物馆先进案例,拟构建数字化创新发展模型,以探求数字化在博物馆的发展中的可能性。

关键词: 数字化;博物馆;发展性;创新发展模型

一、中国国家博物馆数字化发展沿革与成果分析

(一)数字化发展沿革

1. 时代浪潮下的初步探索

20 世纪 80 年代初,中国国家博物馆开始了数字化发展探索,当时国际上数字化技术给各行各业带来了巨大的冲击和发展机遇,而博物馆的发展要想赶上时代的浪潮,亟须数字化和文化事业相结合。

20 世纪 80 年代中期上海博物馆率先开展了藏品管理信息系统的研发,并取得了初步的成功,随后国家文物局在此基础上召开了计算机技术应用研讨会议。20 世纪 90 年代初期,陕西历史博物馆、中国历史博物馆(中国国家博物馆前身)、四川大学博物馆、南京博物院等机构先后组织开发了文物藏品管理

---

① 作者:范李文,苏州大学艺术学院;刘一婷,苏州大学艺术学院;关新杰,苏州大学艺术学院。

信息系统软件。这一阶段的举措对我国博物馆数字化建设具有重大的探索意义，但受制于计算机技术发展不足等多方条件，我国博物馆对于信息技术的应用工作没能广泛开展。①

1990 年美国国会图书馆启动的"美国记忆"计划是最早的数字化在博物馆建设中的实践，该计划预期将美国国会图书馆珍藏的数百万件有关美国历史和文化的手稿、书籍、印刷文本、影像及录音等资源数字化，建立数据库，通过网络手段，让所有的学校、图书馆和家庭用户都能便捷地接触这些数字资源。1992 年，联合国教科文组织启动"世界记忆"计划，在不同国家和地区的不同水准上，将全世界所有有形的和无形的人类文化遗产进行永久性的数字化存储和记忆，通过互联网实现资源共享。

2. 互联网蓝海下的转型历练

1994 年是中国互联网元年，中国国家博物馆开始探究数字化技术的应用的可能性，探索如何实现数字化转型。

国内博物馆数字化浪潮真正肇始于 20 世纪 90 年代，1998 年 8 月河南博物院成立了自己的互联网网站。而 1998 年，是中国互联网发展历史中的一个重要节点，这一年，Windows 98 横空出世，将浏览器中的 Web 页面设计思路引入计算机操作系统。同年，华裔青年杨致远将雅虎的业务带入中国，这一行为至今仍然被认为从很大程度上刺激了中国初代互联网企业的诞生。

随后，伴随着互联网技术的发展，越来越多的博物馆都开始成立互联网网站，打开了"网上参观博物馆"的新思路。互联网的出现使得知识信息可以被大众所阅览，互联网在提升全民数字素质与技能中发挥了重要作用。

在这之后，"博物馆网站"这一概念在各地渐渐兴起。伴随着越来越多的网民加入互联网。部分博物馆开始探索馆内藏品的数字化发展的可能性。于是，河南博物院、上海博物馆等率先开展藏品数字化处理工作。1999 年北京市文物局独立开发的藏品管理系统供全市多家博物馆共同使用，文物行政部门首次开展的地区性博物馆数字化工作让博物馆数字化的浪潮更加汹涌。

3. 21 世纪后飞驰的技术应用

2001 年，中国国家文物局开启了"文物调查及数据库管理系统建设"项目，至此，全国统一性的博物馆数字化工作使得单体博物馆"各行其是"的局

---

① 杨晗. 基于 VR 技术的数字化博物馆设计与运用. 丝网印刷，2023(10): 77-79.

面结束。

在藏品数字化深入发展之后，楼宇自动化、办公自动化等项目都逐步被纳入博物馆数字化的历程。

在当代，展览展示技术、文物保护修复技术、博物馆管理技术、博物馆教育技术的多方技术变革都对博物馆运营造成了巨大影响，VR、直播、3D打印、手机移动客户端开发等新兴技术的涌现让数字博物馆、虚拟博物馆、智慧博物馆、掌上博物馆等概念逐步出现在大众眼中，博物馆多样的表现形式使其在观者的心中愈发有趣。[①]

（二）数字化发展成果

1. 数字展厅提供多元化的观展体验：数字文化遗产与交互体验

截至目前，中国国家博物馆共有 77 项数字展览收录在展，国博数字展厅集高新的技术手段、形式多样的展览、沉浸丰富的互动及科学智能化的服务等特点于一身，打造了一座数字技术、文化传承和互动体验为一体的现代化展馆。

跨时空的交互体验拉近了观展者与文物本身之间的距离，展厅收录了数万件文物，其中大部分都实现了高清数字化展示。观众在云展厅内，可以自由浏览文物的 3D 模型，也可以与文物进行交互体验，感受与文物跨越时空"对话"的魅力。在数字化技术和数据化存储的客观条件下，能够更加细致地了解文物的外饰纹样、内部结构以及制造工艺等，最大限度地提升观展的沉浸性。

数字化展览最大限度地整合了资源，在一定程度上降低了观众实地观展的成本，利用数字化展示以主题整合分散在世界各地的文物，使得文物在空间和时间上得到有条理的线性梳理，为观展者提供了更加完整完善的观展体验。

博物馆的数字化展示是实体博物馆的数字化延伸和再现，而不是具有独立性质的展示空间。国博在数字展厅中以实体馆展和馆内资源为依托，凭借"互联网＋"的优势向用户传递着各类展品和空间的信息。国博在展览设计的内容筛选和展示方式设定上，可以突出重点信息，并采用故事化、情境化等具有代入感的呈现方式，引起参观者的兴趣，从而实现深化观众的观展印象和促进观众积极参与的目的。

---

① 赵玉敬.博物馆文物的数字化保护与管理.中国文化报，2023-05-25(07).

2. 博物馆线上销售完善数字化服务模块

2023 年 3 月 2 日，中国互联网络信息中心（CNNIC）发布第 51 次《中国互联网络发展状况统计报告》（以下简称《报告》）。《报告》显示，截至 2022 年 12 月，我国网民规模达 10.67 亿，较 2021 年 12 月增长 3549 万，互联网普及率达 75.6%。

技术进步正在影响中国网民的规模、结构和行为，社会技术的发展推动着中国互联网的发展，使得新一代网民不断增加，中国互联网网民的结构也将更加多元，行为也会发生不同程度的改变。因此，博物馆的数字化需要不断关注时代发展的趋势，根据这些趋势创新发展，抓住发展机遇，实现自我价值，最终构建和谐的社会环境。

在中国互联网用户庞大的规模体系下，随着经济和信息的迅速发展，人们对历史文物文化的理解和欣赏不再停留在表面文字和玻璃柜里冰冷的文物上，而是希望文物能够以更加生动有趣的方式贴近日常，甚至让历史文化成为潮流和日常生活的一部分。这也催生出了"互联网＋"型的博物馆，越来越多的博物馆选择拥抱数字化，将文创产品开发应用的目光投向线上销售的模式，使得博物馆文创产品作为"博物馆的最后一个展厅"的作品有更多走进公众视野机会，这样的呈现方式能够有效消除民众之间的信息障碍，打通不同对象的沟通桥梁，让受众从参观者转向传播者的角色。

线上销售是一种直观有效且更容易被大众接受的销售方式。截至目前，中国国家博物馆的淘宝旗舰店有 200 余万人关注订阅，共有 400 余件文创产品及衍生品在售，这种数字化交易方式极大地增强了观展者在观展的整体流程中的体验感，也使得博物馆在数字化发展历程中所受到的关注度大幅提升。博物馆在承担向民众宣导中华民族宝贵文化典藏责任的同时也完善了自身的服务模块，博物馆对文化产品的开发能够进一步拉近与民众间的距离，在发展之道上践行着"人民大众所喜闻乐见的才是更长久"的发展理念[①]。

（三）数字化发展成果优劣势分析

数字化博物馆在对技术和资料运用达到新的程度时，可以形成虚拟与现实相结合的社会空间，各种异质内容可以相互结合。通过对资料的整理分析，本

---

① 田喜. 数字化交互设计在文化典藏中的创新应用——以陕北民歌博物馆为例. 西北美术，2023(2): 111-114.

部分运用SWOT模型对于国博数字化目前的状况进行如下分析。

1. 优势（Strengths）

便捷性：数字化博物馆提供了线上参观的功能，观众可以随时随地参观，不受时间和地点的限制。互动性：数字化技术为博物馆提供了更多与观众互动的机会，例如虚拟现实、增强现实等技术使得参观过程更加有趣。保存与修复：数字化技术可以帮助博物馆更好地保存文物，同时为文物的修复提供更准确的数据支持。宣传与教育：数字化博物馆可以更广泛地传播文化知识，提高公众的文化素养，同时通过社交媒体等渠道宣传博物馆。

2. 劣势（Weaknesses）

依赖技术：数字化博物馆的运营和维护需要一定的技术支持，一旦技术出现问题，可能会影响观众的参观体验。信息误解：数字化的展示方式可能会引起观众对文物的误解，尤其是对于年龄较小的观众。缺乏实物体验：虽然数字化博物馆提供了丰富的互动体验，但缺少实物触摸和真实感受。数据安全风险：数字化意味着大量的数据存储和传输，存在文物数据泄露和被篡改的风险。

3. 机会（Opportunities）

拓展新的受众：通过线上平台，数字化博物馆可以吸引更广泛的受众，包括国际观众。创新展示方式：利用新技术，如虚拟现实、增强现实等，提供更加新颖的展示方式。合作与共享：与其他机构或企业合作，共享资源和技术，提高数字化博物馆的影响力。教育与培训：利用数字化资源开展在线教育和培训项目，提高公众的文化素养。

4. 威胁（Threats）

技术更新迅速：随着技术的不断更新，数字化博物馆需要不断投入资金和技术支持以保持竞争力。法律法规限制：关于数据保护和版权等方面的法律法规可能会影响数字化博物馆的发展。文化差异：由于地域和文化的差异，数字化博物馆的内容可能难以被所有观众接受。竞争激烈：随着数字化时代的到来，越来越多的机构和企业涉足数字化博物馆领域，竞争日趋激烈。

二、中国国家博物馆与世界著名博物馆横向对比分析

（一）博物馆数字化界面呈现：交互设计的吸引力

网页设计作为用户第一眼接触博物馆线上展览的界面，其视觉效果、色彩

搭配、信息布局等元素都会直接影响用户的第一感受。英国大英博物馆以其独特的视觉设计和用户体验，吸引了用户深入浏览和参与。而中国国家博物馆则以其清晰直接的布局为用户提供了方便快捷的信息获取，但在视觉冲击力和沉浸感上则显得较为欠缺。

中国国家博物馆网站的设计简洁直观，能迅速向用户提供所需的信息。这在一定程度上满足了用户对于信息快速获取的需求。但是，网站的视觉设计仍有提升空间。中国国家博物馆可以考虑增加更多视觉元素，如动态效果或主题色彩，以提高用户的视觉体验和参与度。此外，与大英博物馆黑色底色形成强烈视觉冲击力不同，中国国家博物馆的色彩边界分割较为保守，没有形成强烈的视觉引导，这在一定程度上削弱了其网站的吸引力。

从展览详情页的设计来看，大英博物馆网站具有让用户对展览进行多维度标星打分的功能，用户能够更直观地了解展览的特色和亮点，也有利于吸引更多用户参与和互动。中国国家博物馆则存在内容不统一的问题。各类展览展示的介绍内容并不统一，有的只有文字介绍，有的则增加了海报、视频甚至背景音乐。这种不一致的设计可能导致用户在浏览不同展览时感到困惑，会削弱用户的浏览体验。虽然这种布局方式可以方便用户快速获取信息，但却缺乏视觉冲击力和沉浸感。

交互设计也是提升博物馆展览吸引力的重要手段，其设计精细度直接影响用户的满意度。大英博物馆官方网站的交互设计十分优秀，用户在悬停展览卡片时，卡片颜色的动态变化给用户提供了明显的反馈，这无疑增强了用户的参与度和浏览体验。而中国国家博物馆的交互设计略显单一，常规按钮式的反馈设计呈现效果一般，这可能在一定程度上影响了用户的浏览体验和参与感。

这些细节差异影响了博物馆的数字化进程，而博物馆的设计理念和对用户体验的重视程度决定着数字化的成效。博物馆在官网的建设的过程中，应该更多地考虑用户体验和参与度，注重视觉设计与互动设计，从而更好地发挥其数字化资源的价值，才能提升博物馆在数字化进程中的优势，扩大自己的影响力和吸引力。

良好的网页交互设计对博物馆展览的吸引力有着积极的影响。优秀的交互设计可以提升用户体验，使得用户在浏览和操作网页时更加流畅舒适，从而增加他们在网站停留的时间，提升他们对展览内容的认知和理解。精心设计的交互元素如动态反馈、导航提示等可以帮助用户更快地找到他们感兴趣的展览和信息,这不仅提升了用户满意度,也有利于引导用户深入了解博物馆的展览。良好的交互设计还能够提升博物馆的品牌形象,展现博物馆的专业程度和数字化水平,进而吸引更多用户的关注。

总的来说,优秀的网页交互设计能够提升博物馆展览的吸引力,这对于博物馆的数字化发展有着重要的推动作用。

(二)博物馆数字化资源管理:精细化标签分类的重要性

在数字化资源的管理方面,大英博物馆和中国国家博物馆之间存在显著差异。这些差异主要体现在对数字资源进行精细化打标签分类的实践上,标签分类影响了资源的可查性、可访问性和学术传播。

以大英博物馆为例,该馆的数字化资源标签非常精细和详尽。其标签系统包括艺术风格、历史时期、艺术家、地理位置等多个方面,并且在对于资源的引用方面做了特殊的快捷窗口,这大大增强了资源的可查性和可访问性。访问者能够通过这些标签,轻松搜索和找到自己感兴趣的艺术品和文物。更值得一提的是,这种标签系统通过揭示资源之间的关联性,推动了跨主题、跨时期、跨文化的比较和探索。这对于学者和研究者来说,具有非常重要的参考价值。[①]

除了上述优点,大英博物馆精细化的标签分类还进一步提升了其在教育和知识传播方面的功能。详细的标签使得大英博物馆能够提供更为丰富的教育内容,包括主题导览、在线课程、互动学习等。这对于学生、教师以及对特定主题有深度研究需求的人来说,无疑提供了极大的便利。细致的分类和标签也有助于博物馆开展与学术界的合作,为更多研究者提供在其领域内的专业资源。

相比之下,中国国家博物馆的数字资源标签并不精细。其标签系统虽然涵盖了展品的名称、创作年代等基本信息,但在标签的分类描述方面,还不够丰富和详细。这样的标签系统可能会限制资源的可查性和可访问性,使得访问者和研究者在使用这些资源时遇到困难。此外,由于标签分类不够精细,中国国家博物馆在提供丰富的教育内容方面也可能受到限制。

这种差异可能是由于两个博物馆在数字化策略和资源投入方面的不同。大英博物馆作为世界领先的博物馆,有足够的资源和经验来实施精细化的标签分类策略。该馆有一支专门的团队来管理和更新其数字资源,以确保资源的精确性和及时性。然而,中国国家博物馆在这方面的投入和经验相对较少。尽管中

---

① 杨建兵.新背景下的博物馆数字化与文物数据库建设.中国民族博览,2023(5):239-241.

国国家博物馆也在积极推进其数字化进程，但在实施精细化标签分类策略方面还需要进一步提升。

从更广泛的角度来看，这种差异凸显了精细化标签分类在提高博物馆数字资源的可查性、可访问性以及学术价值方面的重要性。标签不仅是资源的一部分，它还是联系资源和用户的桥梁。一个良好的标签系统能够使资源更易于被发现和使用，从而提升博物馆的公众服务功能和学术传播功能。因此，精细化的标签分类是博物馆数字化策略的一个重要组成部分，需要博物馆投入足够的资源和精力来维护和发展。

三、数字化博物馆：虚拟现实和增强现实如何打破展览边界

在当今数字化飞速发展的时代，博物馆作为文化和历史的重要载体，也在积极探索和应用各种数字化技术，其中，虚拟现实（VR）和增强现实（AR）技术的使用，已经显著改变了博物馆的参观体验，同时也在突破物理展览的限制，将博物馆的角色扩展到了重现过去，甚至探索未来的空间方面。

VR和AR技术在让观众的参观体验更加生动和富有沉浸感方面发挥了重要作用。传统的博物馆参观方式多是静态的，游客观赏的往往是一些静止的展品，这种参观方式在某种程度上限制了游客的体验深度。而现在，通过AR技术，博物馆可以为游客提供更加生动的展示。

以巴黎国家自然历史博物馆与SAOLA工作室于2021年推出的"REVIVRE"展览为例，该展览使用AR技术，将已经灭绝的动物"复活"在游客的眼前，游客可以看到全尺寸的动物在仿真的自然环境中活动，这种真实感和沉浸感无疑极大地增强了游客的参观体验，使他们能更直观地理解和感受这些动物的生活环境和习性。

2022年，法国国家海洋中心又与SAOLA工作室于联手推出"Grand Large"增强现实（AR）体验，参观者得以在欧洲最大的水族馆中与罕见海洋物种相遇。该展览借助AR技术，使真实动物与虚拟动物在馆中大湾窗内实现了无缝融合，为观众提供了一种全新的、引人入胜的体验。这不仅使观众得以与濒危物种互动，同时也加深了他们对人类活动对生物多样性影响以及保护物种重要性的理解。

法国国家海洋中心长期以来的使命是提升公众对海洋大问题的认识，AR技术的引入无疑为其教育目标注入了新的活力。"Grand Large"项目利用AR

技术解决了一大难题：现实中，无法将某些海洋巨兽展示在水族馆中。此刻，参观者可以借助AR技术与这些海洋巨兽相遇，感受科技创新在满足教育和保护动物时的巨大价值。

VR技术还使得博物馆的数字化步伐延伸到了博物馆的外部。这主要体现在虚拟展厅的构建方面，VR技术让游客可以远程在线参观博物馆。例如，大英博物馆就推出了VR在线参观服务，游客只需一个VR设备就可以在家中观看博物馆的精彩展览，这样的方便性无疑极大地提升了博物馆的参观人次，尤其为那些由于种种原因无法亲自到博物馆参观的人提供了一种全新的参观方式。

当然，VR和AR技术的应用并不止于此，随着技术的进步和博物馆数字化理念的深入，未来的博物馆将会更加充分地利用这些技术，为游客提供更加丰富和深度的体验。未来的博物馆可能会有更多的交互式展览，甚至可能会利用这些技术建立一些虚拟的历史场景，让游客在其中自由探索，更深入地了解和体验历史。同时，博物馆也可能会利用这些技术，结合教育资源，为学生提供更直观和生动的学习体验。

博物馆的数字化不仅改变了博物馆的展示方式，也提升了博物馆的社会价值和扩大了其影响力。虚拟现实和增强现实等先进技术的应用，使得博物馆不再是一个简单的文物展示空间，而是成为一个多元化、互动化、富有体验性的学习和娱乐空间。

四、数字化背景下未来的博物馆创新发展模型

随着技术的迭代推动着博物馆数字化的发展，未来博物馆将沿着怎样的路径发展成为值得深思的议题。包括考古学和历史学的学科发展、展品丰富度、陈列方式、文物保护等在内的传统博物馆发展系统内的元素，现在正面临着一大批新的系统元素的介入：更新换代极快的科学技术、艺术设计、空间室内设计、新的社会角色、人本思想、全新的展陈逻辑、多变的时空需求等等。这些元素构筑了复杂的内部关系，共同影响着创新发展进程和方向，斜向排列双立方形状的博物馆创新发展模型厘清了这些系统元素的类型从属、语境时态和关系，通过回溯博物馆的变革历程，窥探在当前数字化趋势的语境之下未来博物馆创新发展的机制（图1）。

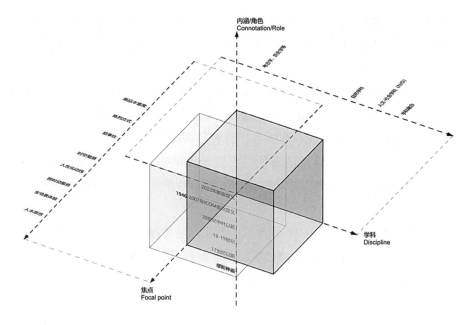

图 1 未来博物馆创新发展模型

（一）主动式的发展趋势

斜向排列双立方形状的博物馆创新发展模型中，从斜下立方底部交点到斜上立方顶部交点的连线，称为发展趋势线，线的两头分别代表着博物馆的主动式发展与被动式发展。在当今与未来的博物馆建设和发展中，博物馆将主动引入更多以科学技术、人本思想、社会责任为代表的系统元素重塑博物馆的内容、内涵与效用。相较而言，之前的博物馆因新文物的开掘、广大人民的文教场所需求而发展则呈现出更多被动式发展的特征。

在博物馆创新发展模型中，对博物馆发展系统的参与元素进行了回溯和分类，并划归至 3 个坐标轴之中，同时坐标轴之间的象限讨论了发展参与因素之间的关联性和相互的效用发挥机制（图 2）。

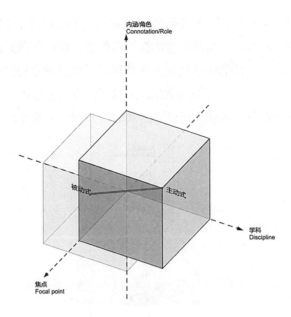

图 2　博物馆的主动式发展与被动式发展

（二）坐标轴上的系统构成元素变量

1. x 轴

x轴上体现的是横向学科参与博物馆的创新发展以及带来的发展视野和路径。在博物馆聚焦关注展品数量、藏品价值的同一发展时期，直观参与博物馆建设发展和更新换代的是以考古学、人类学为代表的具有历史研究属性学科，历史研究的推进、新文物的发掘、文物的还原修复、人类文明的溯源显著地推动着博物馆的发展，也让博物馆在发展初期因兼具珍品收藏、文物保护等功能而在历史的浪潮中站稳了脚跟。数字化技术的出现以及成熟应用使博物馆进入了数字化时代，博物馆在科学技术加入的初期被动地开拓了线上场馆、古代场景复原等服务内容。为了迎接更高质量的需求，在x轴的正半轴上可以窥见博物馆的管理者们应继续主动拥抱新学科的加入一起共创新博物馆时代，其中分为三类：全新学科的加入、旧学科的以新的切入点介入、系统内学科的跨学科融合协作。人工智能、自动化等科学技术领域学科赋能博物馆，在游览场景、交互方式等方面带来新的改变。曾经参与过去时代博物馆建设发展的一众学科也具有极大的价值，例如人类学，曾经人类学的分支体质人类学、文化人类学为古代展品的研究解读发挥了不可忽视的作用，现今以艺术人类学、设计人类学、心理人类学等一众学科细分下新的学科形态让研究者们创新性地使用"参与式设计""快速民族志"等去研究馆内观众的游览动线、展馆的用户触点、参观体验的波谷图等,参与新问题的探掘与解决。而在可预见的未来,无论是新学科还是旧学科、自然科学还是人文社科都呈现出融合协作的趋势,艺术与科技的融合、历史与人工智能的碰撞,来自不同专业背景的博物馆建设者们将这种交融重塑一直贯彻到观众可见可感知的方方面面(图3)。

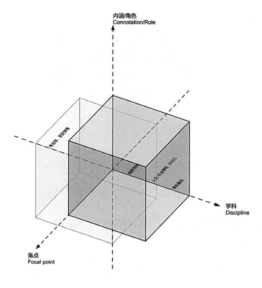

图3 创新发展模型x轴

2. y轴

创新发展模型的y轴上分布着博物馆建设的关注焦点。从原点向负半轴看,显示了博物馆发展过程中建设更新的关注焦点的迁移。通过对以中国国家博物馆为代表的多个博物馆进行研究可以发现曾经的博物馆将馆内的展品数量、藏品价值、陈列美感等作为场馆升级发展的关注焦点,着力于丰富展品的种类和覆盖面以提升博物馆的地位和评价口碑。随着经济社会的发展,观众对于文化生活的需求由"数量需求"转向"质量需求",场馆内更加舒适的参观动线、更加人性化的展品展示说明方式、更具有主题属性的叙事方式等内容逐渐成为新的创新发展关注焦点。在正半轴的方向上能看到人本思想的贯彻,博物馆在数字化的进化浪潮中,也迎来了发展视角的转向。博物馆越来越关注观众的第一视角,使用数字化技术完成展品的时空复原、提供跨时空的参观游览服务等,将提升人的全链路游览体验作为新的关注点,主动地重新塑造人的视角内容和多感官通道的综合体验(图4)。

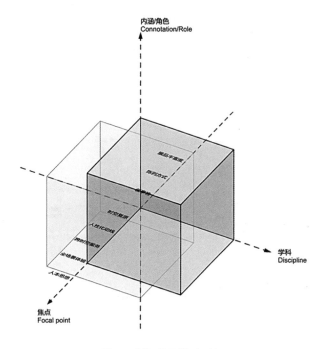

图 4　创新发展模型 y 轴

3. z 轴

向上爬升的 z 轴关联的是在漫长的历史长河中，博物馆定义、内涵、或承担社会角色与责任的变化。公元 5 世纪被毁于战乱的缪斯神庙是人类历史上最早的博物馆。与我们今天见到的博物馆不同，缪斯神庙其实是一个专门的研究机构，里面设大厅研究室，陈列天文、医学和文化艺术藏品，学者们聚集在这里，从事研究工作。传说在洗澡时发现了浮力定律的著名物理学家阿基米德以及著名数学家欧几里得都是在这里从事研究工作的。如今最新一版对于博物馆的定义来自国际博物馆协会（International Council of Museums，ICOM）：一般是为社会服务的非营利性常设机构，它主要研究、收藏、保护、阐释和展示物质与非物质遗产；向社会公众开放，具有可及性和包容性，促进多样性和可持续性；以符合道德且专业的方式进行运营和交流，并在社区的参与下，为教育、欣赏、深思和知识共享提供多种体验。随着科学技术的发展，博物馆的内涵与社会角色会继续发生变化，并由于技术迭代与学科融合的剧烈发展，博物馆被反向塑造的速度可能比历史上任何一个时期都要快。近年来，博物馆被作为发布会、品牌形象传播、学生教育、批判思辨、约会场所等功用的场所比比皆是，这些尝试与实践将深深影响、有力推动着正半轴的掘进（图 5）。

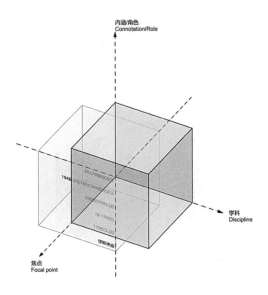

图 5　创新发展模型 z 轴

（三）象限与空间中的新趋势

1. 象限的关联性

三个迭新变量所在的坐标轴之间构成的象限显示出对博物馆创新发展构成影响的元素中存在着协作、互相推动、交融应用的关系。xOy 象限中，艺术设计对于美学的解读和视觉传达体验的把握让展陈方式更具美感和可读性；数字化技术的成熟应用推动新的关注焦点的出现，催生出潜在的需求与用户期待；跨时空的场馆参观体验具有完全不同于传统实体场馆游览的动线体验、交互方式等，设计人类学对于行为和体验的观察将观众体验还原于用户旅程体验地图之上以推导触点与需求，最终用于完善线上数字场馆的建设更新。xOz 象限中，可以看到，博物馆新的定义与责任洞悉即将出现的需求，新的需求与角色语境正在重塑博物馆的内涵与定义（图 6）。

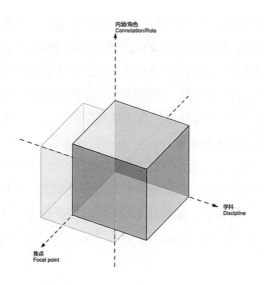

图 6　创新发展模型各象限

2. 非线形的演进

　　在三个迭新变量坐标轴上分别寻找到固定发展时期的元素阶段，将其连线得出的切面为博物馆创新发展的演进阶段。在可预见的建设成果和创新目标之内，将创新建设进度划分为数字技术应用阶段、全场景数字化阶段、后数字化阶段（图 7）。

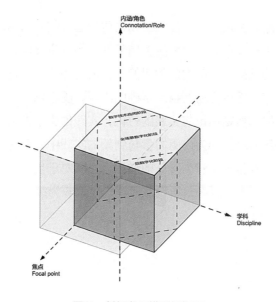

图 7　创新发展模型场切面

数字技术应用阶段，博物馆引入最新的数字技术用于藏品保存、文物保护、展陈方式更新等。例如中国国家博物馆使用三维采集扫描以及摄影采集扫描、推动CIDOC CRM（文化遗产领域中的概念参考模型）与文物数字化影像元数据研究完成文物管理保护、研究利用、信息化整合共享工作。此阶段的"数字形态"主要为对数字化技术的直接使用，带有探索性质地开拓数字技术的应用场景和对数字化赋能需求。

当前博物馆正逐步迈入全场景数字化的发展阶段，多维学科使博物馆从展品发掘研究、保护展出到互借交流的全链路数字化能力得以提升，增强了参观者进行全场景的数字化体验。随着技术的成熟，观众像电影《钢铁侠》中的主角斯塔克一样使用高科技随意摆动双手查看中国国家博物馆四羊方尊内部器形结构将成为可能。

数字化只是博物馆创新发展的某一阶段，博物馆的内涵与外延也可能由于需求的变化、新兴文化传播展示场景的出现而发生变化。后数字化阶段可能存在着目前无法推演出的需求，出现无法预知的学科介入形式和无法想象的新学科应用成果，以及意料之外的元素参与创新系统，形成多维的创新系统模型。

从双立方博物馆创新发展模型中可以看见，数字技术应用阶段、全场景数字化阶段、后数字化阶段三个阶段的演进形态是非线性的，而这样的非线性演进形态以一个独立历史时期为一个轮回。博物馆的创新发展与物质世界的演进规律相似，这样的创新发展模式往往由以物质为基础的外部驱动力推动，当物质基础更迭到一定程度后，发展系统的内部便开始发生反应，包括参与者的自我批判、新意识的觉醒、外部力量的纠偏等，最终完成此段物质基础发生阶段里最后的演进内容，随后等待新物质基础的出现，受新物质基础的触发进入下一轮回。此过程的本质是理论与实践的转化，实践催生了理论层面的思考与方向的修正重塑，随后理论作为内驱力参与到新的实践中，并完成实践提升。而这看不见的理论迭变是一个较为漫长的过程，尤其对于创新发展行为而言，其中变更、引入的元素多且复杂，所以此段演进过程较为缓慢。

来华留学生眼中的中国国家博物馆①

摘　要: 留学生来北京后会选择去哪些地方参观游览？是故宫、长城，还是中国国家博物馆（以下简称"国博"）？国博作为文明载体，承担着文明的交流与互鉴，传播中国历史和文化的使命。来华留学生眼中的国博会是什么样的？我们将通过调查问卷和半结构化访谈收集数据，分析并发现国博的亮点以及存在的问题。

关键词: 来华留学生；中国国家博物馆；传播途径

北京是中国首都，也是一座国际化大都市，它吸引了很多国际友人，包括留学生。留学生来北京后会选择去哪些地方参观游览？是故宫长城，还是中国国家博物馆（以下简称"国博"）？要是选择去博物馆，留学生一般会选择参观哪些博物馆呢？对于国博，留学生们都了解哪些情况，并有哪些期待和建议？本文将结合调查问卷和访谈，尝试找到以上问题的答案。

国博作为文明的载体，承担着文明交流与互鉴、传播中国历史和文化的使命，是中国最高历史文化艺术殿堂和文化客厅。因此，我们选择以国博作为研究对象，从来华留学生②的视角出发进行研究，希望了解来华留学生眼中的国博，以此促进更多的外国友人学习中国历史和文化，增进对于中国及其历史和文化的了解。

首先，本研究将基于文献资料介绍中国国家博物馆的概况。其次，本研究将使用调查问卷的方式来收集数据，并配合半结构化访谈，调查来华留学生眼中的国博。

① 作者: 潘氏玉欣（越南）、福拉德（俄罗斯）、柯澜贝（巴基斯坦）、孔维桢（乌干达），北京语言大学国际中文学院。

② 本研究中的来华留学生指曾经或目前在京学习的留学生。

一、研究背景——中国国家博物馆概况①

本节主要从国博的发展历史、现有发展状况和未来发展规划三个方面进行介绍。

（一）国博的发展历史

国博是中国最高历史文化艺术殿堂，是向世界展示中华文明的重要窗口。它的前身是1912年7月成立的国立历史博物馆筹备处，1926年对外开放。1949年新中国成立后，改名为国立北京历史博物馆；1960年更名为中国历史博物馆。中国革命博物馆于1960年正式成立，1969年9月中国历史博物馆与之合并，改称中国革命历史博物馆。1983年恢复各自建制。2003年2月在原中国历史博物馆和中国革命历史博物馆基础上组建中国国家博物馆。至今，国博已成为中国博物馆学术中心，中华优秀传统文化的研究、宣传和推广的重要中心。

（二）国博的发展现状

1. 地理位置与展厅分布

国博位于天安门广场东侧，总建筑面积约20万平方米，有48个展厅，是世界上单体建筑面积最大的博物馆。

国博的建筑总高度达42.5米，地上4层，地下1层。地下1层有展厅、演播室、剧场、学术报告厅，位于地下1层的古代中国展厅主要展出与介绍古代中国历史的相关文物。1层和2层各有一个中央大厅、一个礼品中心和几个文物展厅。中央大厅是中央展示区，礼品中心是为方便游客购买博物馆相关商品设置的购物区域。3层设置了多个展厅，按照展出需要展示不同主题的文物。4层有一个中央大厅和多个展厅，展厅主要展示与中国历史、艺术或文化相关的特定收藏品。

2. 开放信息及门票价格

国博每周的开放时间为周二至周日的上午九点到下午五点，周一闭馆。据其官网介绍，绝大多数情况下，无论是中国公民还是国际游客，都可凭借相关身份证件在平台上免费预约参观国博。馆内一些特别展览或某些临时展览，有时会收费。

---

① 本部分主要参考中国国家博物馆官方网站等平台的相关材料。

3. 预约方式

人们可以在国博官网或国博微信小程序使用实名注册手机号码或者护照号进行预约（图1）。预约时，每个证件号每日只能预约一次。

图1　预约方式

4. 便利的交通条件

国博有交通上的优势：快速便捷的地铁是多数人出门的首选出行方式，地铁1号线的天安门东站，是离国博最近的地铁站，从C或D口出站，步行近200米即可到达国博（图2）。

图2　地铁站国博出口

除了地铁，乘坐公交 1 路、2 路、52 路、82 路、120 路或观光 2 线、旅游公交 1 线和旅游公交 2 线到天安门东站，也非常方便。

5. 展览种类

目前国博分为基本陈列、专题展览和临时展览三个种类。

基本陈列主要包括"古代中国陈列"和"复兴之路"两个主题展览。前者按照朝代顺序展示从史前时代到明清时期的中国历史，后者集中在中国近现代史，游客可了解到中国从半殖民地半封建社会转变为社会主义现代化国家的整个历史过程。

专题展览方面，有"中国古代瓷器""中国古代书画""中国古代服饰文化""中国古代钱币展""镜里千秋——中国古代铜镜文化""科技的力量"等多个主题展厅。

国博的临时展览只在规定的时间内开放。

6. 数字化展示

关于如何让文物走出库房、走进展厅、走上展线等问题，国博原馆长王春法曾介绍："国博经过不懈探索，给出了自己的一份答案——概括言之，就是让文物'转'起来、'智'起来、'动'起来、'融'起来。"

"智"起来，便是要大力推进文物资源的数字化，以大数据、云计算、人工智能等先进手段，建设智慧博物馆，实现文物信息资源共享开放，满足群众参与文物研究、文物鉴赏的多元化需求。通过机构改革，国博原有的信息网络部门被一分为二，成立了信息技术部和专门从事大数据采集的数据管理与分析中心。在数据采集方面，要实现三维数据采集，信息损失率不超过 0.05%，达到复制级的水平。"在文物三维数据采集和建模方面，国博已做了将近 7000 件，是国内这方面做得最好的。"其数字化案例包括：

（1）首个由 5G 技术支撑的"无实体"云展览："永远的东方红——纪念'东方红一号'卫星成功发射五十周年云展览"。

（2）据《人民画报》报道，近年来结合"智慧国博"建设，国博官方网站上已经推出了 76 个虚拟展厅、140 多个展览专题网页、50 多部短视频。

（3）国博 APP、小程序、智慧导览系统的开发，也让"云端国博""国博云展览""国博云直播"成为常态产品。

（4）"数说犀尊"展览在中国国家博物馆北 16 展厅对公众开放。展览采用一物一展的形式，依托馆藏西汉错金银云纹铜犀尊打造了集数据采集、智慧融合、互动展示、活化利用于一体的智慧展厅。

7. 文创产品

馆内所有楼层均没有小型展示架及文创商店，如各种文创玩具、带有国博文物元素的衣服、丝巾、冰箱贴等。游客只需扫描自动售卖机上二维码即可购买纪念品。

国博文创产品非常受大家欢迎，若出现无法在馆内顺利买到纪念品的情况，可选择到国博西门入口旁的馆外文创商店选购，还可到国博的官网购买。为促进文创产品的销售，国博与京东合作开展网购，但京东并不是唯一销售国博文创产品的线上购物平台，游客还可通过淘宝旗舰店选购。

(三)国博的发展规划

2021年恰好是《"十四五"文化和旅游发展规划》开局之年。"站在新的历史起点上，国博将继续以发挥行业头雁和国家文化客厅作用，以建设世界一流大馆为导向，积极转变思想观念、转变方式方法、转变目标标准，在征藏研究、展览展示、人才建设、观众服务、文创开发、对外交流等方面协同发力，围绕构建中华文化物化话语表达体系、推动文物活起来、建设智慧博物馆、提升社会美誉度和影响力等方面部署多项重点工程。"原馆长王春法指明了国博未来的发展方向，期待在不久的未来我们可以见证凭借"互联网＋文旅"的方式成为世界一流博物馆的国博。

二、研究目的及研究方法

(一)研究目的

本研究的具体内容包括以下方面：

1.通过调查问卷了解来华留学生尚未去过国博的原因、希望了解国博的途径、期待参观后的收获。

2.本研究还调查了去过国博参观的留学生的参观目的、了解途径、参观方式、展示方式、导览方式、国博印象、停留时间等。

3.留学生视角下的国博传播途径方式。

(二)研究方法

本研究以调查问卷为主，辅以半结构化访谈。

1. 调查问卷

调查问卷对象为曾经或目前在北京读书的留学生。

经过讨论，我们制定了问卷内容，共设计了 28 道题，主要内容包括了解受访者参观国博的情况，如参观方式及游览感受等。

2. 半结构化访谈

访谈对象为国博工作人员及已填写调查问卷的来华留学生，访谈内容主要与参观国博的具体过程相关。

3. 描述性统计

研究采用描述性统计的方法对问卷统计数据进行分析。

三、研究结果

（一）调查问卷主要研究结果

我们于 2023 年 7 月 7 日通过微信群或实地发放等方式正式向外发放问卷，截止时间为 10 月 24 日 21 点，共回收有效问卷 176 份。

1. 受调查者基本信息

本研究收集到的受调查者信息包括国籍、院校、学历及来华时长。

根据回收的问卷数据，我们了解到 176 名受调查者分别来自 38 个国家和 24 个院校。其中，本科生数量最多，占比多达 55.11%；其次是硕士，占31.82%；语言进修（短期来华）生占 5.11%；预科生占 4.54%；最少的是博士，占 3.41%。需要说明的是，大部分留学生来北京的时间为 3 个月到一年，少数为一年以上（表 1）。

表 1　受调查者国籍分布

国籍	人数	国籍	人数	国籍	人数
越南	51	埃及	3	尼日尔	1
泰国	22	突尼斯	2	约旦	1
巴基斯坦	13	阿尔及利亚	2	牙买加	1
韩国	9	马达加斯加	2	苏里南	1
俄罗斯	9	印度尼西亚	2	赞比亚	1
日本	7	乌兹别克斯坦	2	刚果（金）	1
乌干达	5	哈萨克斯坦	2	津巴布韦	1
印度尼西亚	7	蒙古	2	老挝	1

国籍	人数	国籍	人数	国籍	人数
缅甸	6	肯尼亚	1	厄瓜多尔	1
柬埔寨	3	希腊	1	尼泊尔	2
所罗门群岛	4	法国	1	孟加拉国	1
斯里兰卡	2	佛得角	2	赤道几内亚	1
巴西	1	圣多美和普林西比	1	—	—

2.参观国博次数

在 176 位受调查者中，有 61.36％的学生暂未去过国博参观，有 21.02％的学生去过一次，仅有 17.61％的学生去过两次及以上（表2）。

表 2　受调查者参观国博次数

选项	人数	比例	
0 次	108		61.36%
1 次	37		21.02%
2 次	17		9.66%
2 次以上	14		7.95%

3.没去过国博参观的留学生的情况分析

问卷结果显示，在没去过国博的留学生中，有 61.11％ 的受调查者既没去过国博也没去过北京的其他博物馆，有 38.89％同学表示自己去过其他博物馆但是没去过国博（表3）。

（1）尚未去过国博的原因

据调查结果，部分受调查者暂未去过国博的原因主要有三个：没时间（32.56％），没听说过国博（23.84％），不知如何预约买票（13.95％）。除此之外，还存在其他原因，包括"不感兴趣""没机会""没人陪""约不上"等。

没有去过国博的人，除了没有时间以外，还有很多人是因为没有听说过国博，说明国博应该通过各种不同的传播方式让来华留学生知道、了解国博。

表3　尚未去过国博的原因

选项	选择人数
没时间	56
没听说过国博	41
不知如何预约买票	24
对博物馆不是很感兴趣	20
担心看不懂或者听不懂	16
其他	9
预约页面无法填护照号	6

（2）希望了解国博的途径

没去过国博的来华留学生最希望能通过抖音、小红书、快手、西瓜视频等网络平台（25.41%）多多了解国博，其次是通过Facebook、Instagram、YouTube等国外社交平台（21.31%），当然也有受调查者希望能够通过其他途径如国博官网（15.98%）和微信公众号（12.70%）等了解（表4）。

表4　希望了解国博途径

选项	人数
抖音、小红书、快手、西瓜视频等短视频平台	62
Facebook、Instagram、YouTube等国外社交平台	52
国博官网	39
国博微信公众号	31
亲戚朋友推荐	29
电视、广播等	24
其他	4
报纸	3

（3）期待参观后的收获

如果计划参观，有33.85%的受调查者希望能学到知识、丰富人生阅历，22.18%希望受到历史文化的熏陶，17.51%希望能引发观看学习的兴趣（表5）。

表5　期待参观后的收获

选项	选择人数
学习知识、丰富人生阅历	87
受到历史文化的熏陶	57
引发观看学习的兴趣	45
享受国博游览	39
与本国的博物馆对比	25
其他	3
与所投入的时间、金钱成正比	1

4.去过国博参观的留学生的情况分析

对于去过国博参观的留学生，本研究还调查了他们的参观目的、了解途径、参观方式、展示方式、导览方式、国博印象、停留时间、存在问题等。

（1）参观目的

留学生去国博参观的目的主要是了解中国历史、文化、社会、经济（36.53%），以及学习、增长知识（30.54%）（表6）。

表6　参观目的

选项	人数
了解中国历史、文化、社会、经济	61
学习、增长知识	51
旅游	23
休闲娱乐、转换心情	19
完成作业	12
其他	1
子女教育	0

（2）了解途径

实际调查显示，大部分留学生通过学校活动（16.34%）、国博官网（15.69%）、国博微信公众号（15.03%）和亲戚朋友推荐（15.03%）来了解国博（表7）。

研究发现，没去过国博的留学生和去过国博的留学生在了解途径上存在不同。没去过国博的留学生主要想通过抖音、小红书、快手、西瓜视频等短视频平台或Facebook、YouTube、Instagram等国外社交平台来了解国博；去过国博的留学生主要是通过学校举办的活动、国博官网、微信公众号和亲戚朋友推荐。

表7　了解途径

选项	人数
国博官网	24
学校活动	25
国博微信公众号	23
亲戚朋友推荐	23
抖音、小红书、快手、西瓜视频等短视频平台	22
Facebook、YouTube、Instagram	21
电视、广播等	9
报纸杂志	4
其他	2

（3）参观方式

有26.41%的受调查者选择在学校的组织下参观国博，21.38%选择跟国际友人一起，21.38%跟中国人一起去参观。与独自一人参观相比，大部分留学生都希望能加入团队一起参观并互相交流（表8）。

表8　参观方式

选项	人数
学校组织	42
与国际友人一起	34
与中国人一起	34
独自一人	20
与家人一起	15
跟旅行社	9
单位组织	5
其他	0

（4）展品的展示方式

在如何展示展品效果最好的调查中，25.73%的受调查者选择看图片，其次是选择看模型和仿真品（18.71%）（表9）。

表9 展示方式

选项	人数
图片	44
模型和仿真品	32
文字	24
互动媒体（触摸屏）	24
讲解员或者讲解器	20
表演（如编钟表演等）	19
实体操作	7
其他	1

（5）导览方式

在哪种导览方式比较清晰明了的调查中，占首位的是讲解员（73.01％），其次是网络导览设备（APP讲解、二维码扫描讲解、公众号自带讲解）（50.79％），导览图册（49.21％）（表10）。

表10 导览方式

选项	人数
讲解员	46
网络导览设备（APP讲解、二维码扫描讲解、公众号自带讲解）	32
导览图册	31
影片讲解	26
文字名牌与展板	12
智能无线导览讲解器	9
指示牌	6
其他	1

（6）国博印象

在参观过程中给留学生留下最深刻印象的前几点分别是国博的建筑物（26.78％）、国博的特色纪念品（19.64％）、国博展示方式（17.86％）、国博的展品及布局（17.26％）（表11）。

此外，在调查中，我们还发现，有86.76％的受调查者回答会愿意再去参观国博，有85.29％回答会愿意向他人推荐参观国博。

表11　国博印象

选项	人数
国博的建筑物	45
国博的特色纪念品	33
国博展示方式	30
国博的展品及布局	29
国博的服务（讲解介绍）	13
员工服务态度	5
公共设施与环境卫生等	5
其他	4
国博的饮食	3
标识指示	1

（7）停留时间

据统计，受调查者中38.64％去过国博，53.57％留学生在国博停留仅仅是1—3小时，停留时间达到1天以上的寥寥无几（表12）。

表12　停留时间

选项	人数	比例
1—3小时	40	58.82％
半天	21	30.88％
整天	6	8.82％
其他	1	1.47％

（8）存在问题

58.82％的受调查者在国博停留1—3小时，他们认为目前国博存在的主要问题是人流拥挤、影响参观质量（23.88％），纪念品价格太贵（21.64％）和排队时间比较长（1—2小时）（15.67％）（表13）。

这些问题或多或少会影响到留学生的体验，对此，我们建议国博应该采用一些分散人流的策略，比如每个时间段限制一定的参观人数。

表 13 存在问题

选项	人数
人流拥挤，影响参观质量	32
纪念品价格太贵	29
排队时间比较长（1—2 小时）	21
设施不齐全，部分展区不开放	14
交通不便，缺少停车位	9
展品的中英文对照不一致	8
其他	7
没有特色，与其他博物馆一样	7
部分解说、服务不到位	7

（二）访谈主要研究结果

2023 年 7 月 10 日至 13 日，研究小组共访谈了来自 6 个国家的 8 名来华留学生，以及一位中国教授。访谈涉及以下内容：

（1）您是跟谁一起去国博的？

（2）您是怎么预约的？

（3）您参观了哪些内容？或者看到了什么？

（4）您觉得展品的展示方式如何？

（5）您觉得国博的服务怎样？

（6）您有什么收获？

（7）您可以提一些建议吗？

访谈结果主要包括以下方面：

1. 没去过国博的留学生的原因

在访谈中，我们发现没去过国博的受访者有一系列"不知道"，受访者也说明了为何"不知道"。

第一是不知道国博的存在。比如，有学生表达"我不了解国博在哪儿""我身边的朋友们平时也不去这样的地方"等等。至于为什么不知道国博的存在，有人提到"学习的时候教材里没看到关于国博的内容"。有的朋友在自己的国家早就知道一些中国有名的地方，知道怎么用母语或者英语说那些地方的名字，有人说"大家知道 Forbidden City 和 The Great Wall，但没人知道中国国家博物馆英文叫什么"，说明国博在留学生中的知名度有待进一步提高。

第二是虽然知道国博，但是不知道怎么预约。比如有留学生提到了"我认为信息不足，所以没去过国博"。这位受访者的意思是他不知道国博在哪儿、怎么预约、在国博能看到什么等。这说明留学生关于国博各方面的了解不够，如果国博加强宣传，那么会吸引到更多留学生。受访者经常提到抖音、Instagram等流行的社交媒体软件，而国博官方的宣传渠道一般只是国博官网、手机APP和微信小程序，因此国博可以扩大更多的宣传途径。

2.去过国博的留学生的反馈

首先，所有参访者都认为去国博参观是一个帮助留学生丰富知识的方式，人人都表达了对国博的赞美，比如说，"对中国文化了解了很多""了解中国古代的历史和人们的生活方式"。他们参观过的展览有"复兴之路""科技的力量""数说犀尊""中国古代服饰文化展"等，这些展览帮助留学生增加了中华文化的知识，开阔了视野。

其次，绝大部分采访者认为国博的服务很好。对外国友人来说，接触陌生文化并不容易，加上语言的障碍，高质量的服务对留学生了解中华文化来说显得更加重要。

当然，受访者也发现了一些问题。第一，部分受访者作为汉语第二语言学习者，即使汉语水平很高，依然有可能存在语言障碍；第二，由于留学生对中国文化不了解，有时很难理解展品背后的文化内涵；第三，对于身处异国他乡的人来说，独自去陌生的地方会缺乏安全感；第四，假期时参观的人很多、很拥挤，有人说"人太多太挤了，应该有序排队，派人管理秩序"。还有人说早上应该早点去，因为去晚的话"参观的人会非常多"。

通过调查，我们发现最显著的问题是：国博的知名度还不够高，语言障碍影响来华留学生了解国博及其展品。

四、来华留学生对国博的评价

（一）国博的亮点

第一，展览体系丰富多样，其中基本陈列展览包括"古代中国""复兴之路""复兴之路之新时代部分"，专题展览包括"中国古代书画""中国古代瓷器展""中国古代钱币展""科技的力量"等，临时展览包括"历史文化展""考古发现展""科技创新展""地域文化展"等。

第二，展品展示方式多模态和现代化，既使用了图片、模型、实物、视频、中英文文字、二维码扫码讲解，又运用了网上展厅模式，让参观者可以得到不同的体验。此外，国博的智能化有助于让更多国外的人了解国博。

第三，导览方式清晰明了，有讲解员、导览图册、网络导览设备（APP讲解、二维码扫描讲解、公众号自带讲解）。

第四，文创产品具有中国特色和文化底蕴，能促进文化传播，让文物"活"起来。

第五，公共设施齐全，标识牌明显，如容易找到卫生间；工作人员态度优良、热情、有耐心等。

第六，有零食店和饮水机。

（二）建 议

在定量调查和半结构化访谈中，我们都获得了很多建议。

基于176份调查问卷，调查者的同意度如表14所示。

表14 对国博建议的同意度

建议	比例%
国博的体验活动应该增加	94.12
针对不同的参观时长提出不同的参观路线和参观攻略等	94.12
国博可以允许来华留学生担任短期的志愿者、讲解员	92.65
国博应该增加定时、定期演出	92.64
国博的模型和实物应该增加	91.71
国博应该针对参观者不同的汉语水平，做出不同的简明汉语文字名牌与展板	91.17
国博的讲解语言应该增加，比如涵盖联合国的六种工作语言	89.71
国博应该跟国内外高校合作	86.77
国博应该针对不同的群体（国际友人、中国市民）做出不同的讲解内容和形式	82.35

除了大规模调查外，访谈中一些留学生提出的建议有"如果你们想去国博的话，一定要跟一些中国人一起去，否则很多知识看不懂"；"需要加一些英语讲解的内容，因为很多地方看不懂，增加真实物品的模型比较好"。

结合调查问卷和半结构性访谈，我们提出了如下建议。

1.更加国际化

（1）在介绍展品中增加多语种

73.22％的受访者认同国博讲解语言应该增加这一观点，比如涵盖联合国的六种工作语言。目前在国博的官网上和讲解机的语言仅限于中文和英文，建议增加多种语言。除此之外，可以考虑不收取讲解机的押金，利用技术手段避免讲解机的遗失。

有67.85％的受访者同意国博可以针对参观者不同的汉语水平，制作不同的简明汉语文字名牌与展板的观点。展品的中文解释应该全部翻译成英文，甚至可以增加其他的语言。

从语言角度来看，很多外国留学生觉得有时候很难理解国博里的中文解释，特别是文言文或者诗歌，而且不是每一段中文信息都有英文翻译。有的留学生指出，他们只看了"图片和视频"。还有的人觉得文字解释太多："展品展示方式更多的是图片，模型或实物比较少。"研究小组参观国博的时候也发现类似情况，因此受采访者提出建议"需要加一些英语讲解内容"。

（2）增强与国内外学校合作

63.16％的受访者尚未去过国博，主要原因是他们缺乏与国博的相关信息，对于该问题，有73.22％的人赞同国博应该跟国内外高校合作。

（3）在教学中融入和国博相关的内容

可将与国博相关的内容加入国际留学生的中文教材。因为目前很多教材里只提到长城、故宫等内容，而有关国博的内容极少。

（4）吸纳留学生作为国博的志愿者

80.36％的留学同意国际友人担任志愿者、讲解员。这样可以减少国博短期缺乏讲解员的问题。

2.增加传播途径与内容

（1）扩展传播平台

没去过国博的来华留学生首先希望能通过抖音、小红书、快手、西瓜视频等网络平台（25.41％）来了解国博，其次是通过Facebook、Instagram、YouTube等国外社交平台（21.31％）。国博可以通过以上的社交媒体来传播信息。

（2）利用智能化手段

推广国博官网的网上展厅，让观众能够在云端看到国博的文物藏品相关内容。

3. 服务多样化

（1）不同的参观路线

绝大部分留学生在国博仅仅停留1—3小时，停留时间达到1天以上的寥寥无几，于是76.79％的受访者同意针对不同参观时长提供不同参观攻略。国博应该设计所谓"必看"的、缩短的参观路线，增加参观效率和兴趣。

（2）可以增加非文字的展示方式，比如表演、实际操作等。

（3）不同的讲解内容和形式

有64.29％的受访者同意国博可以对于不同的群体（国际友人、中国市民）做出不同的讲解内容和形式。

4. 提升体验感

（1）增加模型和实物的数量

对于提升体验感，有78.57％的受访者认同国博可以增加模型和实物的数量这一观点。

（2）增加定时、定期演出

有80.35％的受访者同意国博应该增加体验活动；有71.43％的受访者赞同国博可以增加定时、定期演出。

（3）二维码多模态讲解

可以增加二维码讲解说明，其中包括语音与视频讲解。

5. 更加人性化

（1）更为清晰的导览

通过访谈，研究小组发现服务台不易被找到，国博可以以标识牌的方式指引参观者，并且可以在不同的入口提供纸质版导览图。

（2）更易获取的讲解

大多数留学生不知如何预约讲解员和查到公益讲解的时间表。预约讲解员需要提前3—5天。对于这些问题，我们建议国博招聘并培训更多讲解员，并且在网站与博物馆内的前台提供有关公益讲解时间的信息。

（3）提高各展馆的看管人员的素质，如可以对展品进行简单讲解。

（4）更优惠的纪念品

24.2％的受访者反映纪念品价格偏高，可以适量降低其价格。

（5）完善参观者休息用的设施

国博可以增加休息空间里的椅子，并且保持卫生间的整洁。

本书系国家社会科学基金"十三五"规划2020年度教育学一般课题项目"中国青年国际组织胜任力研究"（编号：BDA200075）、国家社会科学基金社科学术社团主题学术活动资助项目"加强中国国际组织人才培养研究"（编号：22STA048）研究成果。

《国际胜任力培养实训工作坊论文集》编委会

主编： 张宁　贾文键　屈文谦　万小朋　李孝峰

执行主编： 戴争鸣　资虹　陈俊　王筱稚　张弛

执行副主编： 李佳　马先军　李嘉苗　林婉婷　牛雯茜

统筹： 安艳琪　李辉　何乐　常迪　李雪菲燕

国际组织与全球治理丛书

中国教育发展战略学会国际胜任力培养专业委员会

国际胜任力培养

实训工作坊论文集

（下册）

主编　张　宁　贾文键　屈文谦　万小朋　李孝峰

Proceedings of the International
Competence Development Workshops

ZHEJIANG UNIVERSITY PRESS
浙江大学出版社
·杭州·

PART
5

第五章

世界文明文化交流

孔子学院二十年之路的模式、经验与前瞻[①]

摘　要： 截至 2023 年，孔子学院走过了近 20 年的历程，遍布全球 160 个国家和地区，已成为传播汉语和中国文化的重要教育机构。它在增进中国语言文化传播和促进多元文化交流等各方面发挥了积极深远的作用。对于中国乃至世界而言，孔子学院的发展经历都堪称文化教育与传播的范例。本文总结了孔子学院的发展模式，并以慕课、新媒体和"中文+"实践为例，详尽分析了孔子学院多元多层次的汉语文化教育理念。基于上述内容的阐述分析，本文提出了孔子学院的发展前景，以期在未来的国际教育合作以及文化交流等方面为孔子学院提供参考。

关键词： 孔子学院；文化传播；文化交流

一、引　言

自 21 世纪以来，汉语和中国文化在全球范围内引起了持续的热潮。对中文的学习和了解越来越受到世界各地政府、教育机构和民众的重视。孔子学院是中外合作建立的非营利性教育机构，致力于适应世界各国（地区）人民对汉语学习的需要，增进世界各国（地区）人民对中国语言文化的了解，加强中国与世界各国教育文化交流合作，发展中国与外国的友好关系，促进世界多元文化发展，构建和谐世界。

孔子学院的发展从韩国首尔孔子学院的挂牌成立开始，至 2023 年，已在全球范围内设立 498 所机构。孔子学院已成为中外合作院校、友好省州之间人

① 作者：李佳奇，重庆大学法学院；韦佳，重庆大学经济与工商管理学院；何一，重庆大学经济与工商管理学院；李秋平，重庆大学材料科学与工程学院。

文交流和经贸合作的重要桥梁。其成功得益于顺应时代潮流，充分借助新兴技术，始终坚守初衷和使命。孔子学院向人们讲述着属于中国的故事，展示着丰富多彩的中国文化，成为中国文化走向世界、促进和谐世界建设的成功典范之一。但令人遗憾的是，随着国际地缘政治问题越来越突出，孔子学院在部分西方国家中的发展受到了限制。自 2020 年初开始，美国已有 13 所孔子学院宣布于 2020 年关闭，至此美国关闭的孔院数量已经达到三分之一；4 月，瑞典境内的最后一所孔子课堂宣布关闭；6 月，德国巴伐利亚州召开听证会，针对孔子学院展开调查。[①]孔子学院站在发展与转型的十字路口，急需寻找合理对策应对严峻挑战。

基于上述情况，我们对有关孔子学院的相关学术文章、报告、评估和官方统计数据进行分析，以了解孔子学院的历史、背景、目标、政策和发展情况。回顾梳理孔子学院的发展历程，剖析孔子学院的发展模式，进而总结孔子学院的成功经验，为未来规划提供借鉴。

二、孔子学院的发展历程

（一）现阶段发展情况统计

根据孔子学院官方网站数据，截至 2023 年 12 月 31 日，全球共有 498 所孔子学院，分布在世界 160 个国家和地区。[②]据此进一步分析，我们得出了近年来孔子学院的发展情况（见图 1）。

据图 1 可知，2004—2019 年，孔子学院的数量总体呈上升趋势；2019—2021 年，孔子学院的数量呈下降趋势。其中 2004—2005 年为孔子学院的开拓时期，两年内建立了 41 所孔子学院；2006—2008 年为全球开设孔子学院的高峰期，三年间建立了 206 所孔子学院，尤其是 2006 年和 2007 年，两年建立了 159 所；2009—2018 年则是孔子学院发展的平稳阶段，平均每年建立 30 所孔子学院。但 2019—2021 年，孔子学院的建设数量受全球局势变化和新冠疫情影响呈下降趋势。

---

① 张未然. 新形势下孔子学院的舆情困境：特征、原因与对策. 现代传播（中国传媒大学学报），2021，43(3)：20-26.
② 孔子学院全球门户网站. [2023-12-31]. https://www.ci.cn/qqwl.

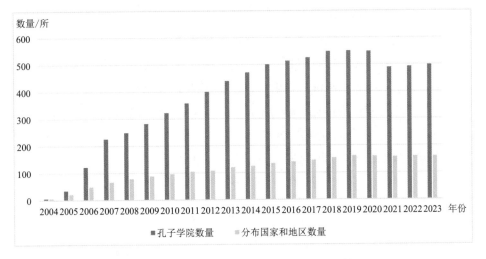

图1　2004—2023年孔子学院全球分布数量情况

（资料来源：https://www.ci.cn/qqwl）

（二）孔子学院的发展阶段

结合以上数据统计，孔子学院的发展大致可以分为三个阶段：初创期，发展期以及转型期。

1.初创期：着力实现规模扩张，推动中文走向世界

随着中国经济实力不断增强、国际地位显著提高，汉语及中国文化的影响力和辐射力也明显增强，全球对学习汉语和中国文化的需求增大。孔子学院在此形势下由教育部和国家对外汉语教学领导小组自2002年开始酝酿，借鉴各国推广本民族语言的成功经验，筹划在海外设立汉语言及文化推广机构。于2004年建立了全球第一所孔子学院。孔子学院开拓阶段的时间极短，仅用了两年。至2005年末，孔子学院已在21个国家及地区开设了35所，开设数量几乎是2004年的6倍，可以说孔子学院开拓阶段的进展十分顺利。①

经历了两年的开拓阶段，孔子学院的发展进入了高峰期。2006年，全球建立了70所孔子学院，建立数量约为2005年的2倍、2004年的12倍。孔子学院在两年时间里实现了飞跃式的发展。孔子学院积极推进自身建设、提高办学质量，以应对全球的"汉语热"和"中国热"。2007年，全球共建立89所孔子学院，比2006年多建19所，同比增长27%。2007年是新建设孔子学院

---

① 刘旭.中国孔子学院历时发展研究.重庆大学学报(社会科学版)，2015，21(6)：234-241.

数量最多的一年，也是孔子学院迅速布局的高峰期。①

2.发展期：根植当地中文需求，服务社区本土发展

2008—2014年，在语言教学与文化传播的双驱动下，孔子学院建设以"特色、质量、品牌、创新"为重心，以所在地实际需求为导向，贴近民众，融入社区，真正实现当地化、融入型发展。孔子学院选择控制发展规模，转而完善配套资源，并全面提高教学质量。如图2所示，2008—2014年，孔子学院年度建立数量在30到50区间上下浮动，发展比较平稳。

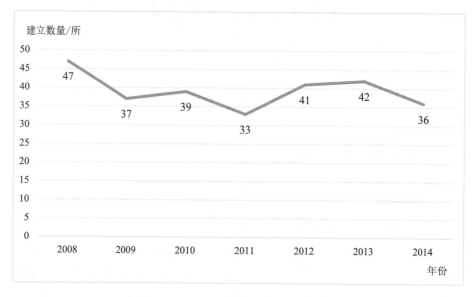

图2　2008—2014年孔子学院年度建立数量

（资料来源：https://www.ci.cn/qqwl）

3.转型期：提质增效融合发展，内涵建设稳中求进

2015年，孔子学院基本完成前期规模化建设，由重视"量增长"转为关注"质增长"。由外延转向内涵的转型发展成为新阶段孔子学院建设的新向度。

近两年来，受国际环境的影响，孔子学院发展压力增大，出现了个别关停的现象，在总数量上出现下降趋势，孔子学院的发展在一定程度上进入了瓶颈期。新时代背景下，孔子学院进入全面推进安全、平稳、高质量发展的关键期，更应以全球视角规划和整合资源，遵循语言和文化传播"长效缓释"的发展规律，科学拓展服务功能，打造综合交流平台，精准满足各地语言和文化服务需求，促进中外语言文化的交流融合。

三、孔子学院的发展模式

（一）组织模式

孔子学院的组织架构主要包括以下四个方面：

1.设立基金会统筹工作

基金会是基于捐赠的公益财产以基金形态存续并得到相应的法律认可和保护的非营利组织的一种基本形式，具有明确的公益宗旨和用益。通过设立中国国际中文教育基金会，赋予其运行孔子学院品牌的权限，提升了孔子学院开设学院的效益，能够为推广汉语文化持续赋能。

2.学院领导和管理团队

每个孔子学院都会设立院长和教务长等职位，由专业人士担任。他们负责学院的领导和管理工作，制定学院的发展战略、教学计划和运营规范，以确保孔子学院的正常运作和教学质量。

3.合作与联盟

孔子学院积极与当地的大学、学术机构和教育部门建立合作关系和联盟。通过与合作伙伴共同开展项目、研讨会和文化交流活动，孔子学院积极促进中外教育和文化的交流与合作。

4.标准规范化的工作制度

将标准实施的环境培育、操作指南细化、人员能力提升、执行效果评估等作为重点内容。由孔子学院官方规范各类中文教育机构的落地推广，减少机构、教师、管理者等日常教学时的个性经验依赖。

通过以上组织模式的实施，孔子学院能够有效地推动汉语和中国文化的传播与教育，提供优质的中文教学和跨文化交流的平台，发挥其在国际教育和文化交流领域的重要作用。[①]

（二）教学模式

因每个孔子学院的办学条件和特点各有不同，当地文化背景和已有的汉语教学资源亦有所差异，因此，各地区孔子学院的服务方式和运作模式都是独一无二的。总体来说，我们可将孔子学院的教学服务模式分为以下四种类型：

第一种为教学主导型，教学是孔子学院服务模式中最主要的功能。该模式

---

① 王彦伟，薛梦晨.基金会模式下的孔子学院：国际经验与中国实践.北京：商务印书馆，2022.

将汉语和中国文化教学作为首要服务内容,借助孔子学院的力量与品牌,积极扩大汉语教学服务。日本京都的立命馆大学孔子学院、美国弗吉尼亚州的乔治梅森大学孔子学院、印度韦洛尔科技大学孔子学院以及加拿大温哥华的 BCIT 大学孔子学院等,都是将汉语教学作为主要教学服务。教学主导型的孔子学院在很大程度上参与主办大学的汉语教学及其课程设置的诸多方面,成为主办大学的有机组成。

第二种为社区服务型,一般体现在汉语教学基础较好的国家及地区。根据当地的政策、意识形态等因素,孔子学院会因地制宜地为社会人士学习汉语和中国文化服务,作为促进了解中国的社区中心。如南非斯坦陵布什大学的孔子学院积极参与本地社区活动,如葡萄酒节、国际美食节、当地的青年节等。该教学类型的孔子学院根植当地中文需求,推进服务本土化发展,促进中外语言文化的深层交流。

第三种为学术研究型,在汉语资源与师资相对完善的地区,积极推进汉学、东方学等学术交流,开展各类学术研讨会,营造良好的多元文化下的学术研讨氛围。例如,日本早稻田大学孔子学院定位于学术研究,尤其是汉学、东方学及全球化等领域;同时,其还举办各类学术研讨会,甚至联合培养研究生等。在该教学服务类型的孔子学院的发展下,有关于孔子学院的相关研究主题迅猛增加,有助于为孔子学院完善内部服务架构以及探寻未来发展新方向提供更多元化的理论支撑。

第四种为融入型,即将汉语教学正式融入当地本科生的学分系统,变成学校的正规教学单位,使得教学质量稳步提高。日本东京樱美林大学和爱知大学的孔子学院已融入大学课程的正式系统,变成学校的正规教学单位。该教学服务类型有利于孔子学院实现本土化、融合型发展,根植于当地民众对中文的切实需求,有助于加快孔子学院实现内涵化服务建设,打造综合交流平台。①

四、典型实践案例

孔子学院秉持"按需设立,应运而生"的理念,创新进行多元多层次的汉语文化教育实践。

---

① 李军,田小红.中国大学国际化的一个全球试验——孔子学院十年之路的模式、经验与政策前瞻.中国高教研究,2015,(4):37-43.

（一）慕课平台实践

应对近年线上学习风潮，孔子学院创新教学手段，积极利用网络，充分发展了线上教学资源。2017年，孔子学院建立了"全球孔子学院慕课平台"，为汉语的国际推广和中国文化的传播注入新的活力和动力。[①]克罗地亚萨格勒布大学孔子学院开发了"翻转课堂"的慕课系统，并在教学实践中得到了良好的反馈，6个试点班级学生的出勤率、考试分数均有提升。德国海德堡大学孔子学院与上海交通大学合作完成慕课"不一样的汉语"，并推出"混合式学习的模式"。在面授课程结束后，学生可在慕课平台进行在线复习、在线提问，并快速测试自己知识的掌握情况。这使学生可以在学习初始阶段更容易入门，更快取得学习进展。澳门孔子学院推出汉字线上课程，开拓了教学新模式，也完善了课程体系中的汉字教学板块。全新的汉字在线课程通过动画展示、字源解说、视频实操和深入解析等多种方式对汉字进行拆分和介绍，并配以相应的对话和识记练习，提高了学生对汉字的学习兴趣。慕课教学模式的"开放性"和教学内容的"碎片化"与孔子学院分布的"广泛性"和教学模式的"非统一性"相得益彰。[②]慕课受到了汉语教师和海外学习者的热烈欢迎，进一步提升了国际中文教育水平。

（二）新媒体平台实践

顺应新媒体潮流，孔子学院积极创新传播中国文化的方式。由中国国际中文教育基金会运作的孔子学院新媒体平台粉丝数和阅读量持续增长。"孔子学院"微信公众号全年收到投稿3913篇，发布推文515篇，粉丝数达到2.2万人，阅读量超过31.6万次。孔子学院微博粉丝数达到7.27万人，阅读量超过661.3万次。"孔子学院"抖音号全年累计收到投稿453篇，发布视频23个，粉丝数达到16.54万人，阅读量超过900万次。除全球孔子学院新媒体平台外，各地孔子学院也积极建设自身传播平台，不断提升传播效能。新西兰奥克兰孔子学院通过Facebook、Twitter和Instagram三个社交媒体平台，制作和发布"每日一词"汉字卡。韩国汉阳大学孔子学院运用网站、微信公众号、微信视频号、Facebook、Instagram等平台搭建传播矩阵，介绍孔子学院教学情况和中国语言文化信息。新媒体平台的实践极大地提高了孔子学院的知名度和辐

---

① 孔子学院年度发展报告2021. [2023-12-31]. http://60.205.210.15:9191/gywm/nb/db8e7611-8c24-46c7-bc0a-830fa10d5b1c.

② 梁琳.面向孔子学院慕课建设的研究.海外华文教育动态，2017(6): 111-112.

射面，有助于民众更好地了解孔子学院的教学和活动情况，以民众喜闻乐见的方式传播中国文化。中外社会得以通过这些新媒体传播平台了解更加全面、真实、立体的孔子学院。

（三）"中文＋"课程实践

面对 160 个国家和地区的不同情况以及学员的不同需求和特点，孔子学院和课堂在做好基础中文教学的基础上，结合当地实际因地制宜设置课程，探索合适的教育教学方法，开发了丰富多彩的特色"中文＋"课程。塔吉克斯坦冶金孔子学院深耕"中文＋职业技能"模式，打造双师型队伍，以冶金学院优势专业和中资企业人才需求为培养目标，开设"中文＋矿山开采""中文＋有色金属冶炼"等课程。孔子学院与塔吉克斯坦冶金学院、塔中矿业有限公司、中国有色金属工业人才中心、兰州资源环境职业技术大学等机构合作，共同开发适合塔吉克斯坦本土的"中文＋职业技能"教材和教学资源库。韩国世明大学孔子学院为世明大学航空服务系开设了中文课程，逐步形成了"中文＋航空服务"特色，为学生就业和职业发展奠定了更好的基础。作为中医特色孔子学院，韩国世明大学孔子学院还尝试开设了《黄帝内经》诵读课，努力打造"中文＋中医"特色课程。泰国海上丝路孔子学院将本土化、协同化、数字化纳入孔院特色化发展战略。泰国海上丝路孔院推出了"中文＋空乘、高铁驾驶、动车维护、电子信息等"等多个复合专业课程。"中文＋"成功给学员的职业发展带来了更多的可能，也给当地社会经济发展培育了更多的人才。

孔子学院积极拓展"中文＋职业"的多元化教育功能，积极为当地企业培养和输送复合型人才，提高当地就业率，催生新的就业机会，并推动所在地职业结构调整。[①]相关统计数据显示，目前，泰国、马来西亚、坦桑尼亚、埃塞俄比亚等 40 多个国家的 100 多所孔子学院都开设了"中文＋"课程，涉及高铁、经贸、旅游、法律、海关、航空等数十个领域。正如哈佛大学经济学家梅利茨指出："一个国家的对外贸易和对外直接投资数额也会受到语言文化熟悉程度的影响。"孔子学院通过构建出中外企业的经济贸易合作的交流服务平台，减少了文化交易成本，有利于促进中国企业对外投资长期发展，推动中外双方的经济合作发展。

---

① 高玉娟，庄瑶瑶，李宝贵.孔子学院建设的理念演进、实践成效与发展路向.辽宁师范大学学报(社会科学版)，2021，44(3)：101-109.

五、孔子学院的发展经验

（一）顺应时代，创新发展

孔子学院在发展过程中不断创新课堂形式，并将新兴技术融入其中，增强了孔子课堂对民众的吸引力，推动了孔子学院的进一步发展。例如，2020—2022 年，受疫情影响，各地孔子学院线下注册学员数量有所下降，但是孔子学院积极拓展线上教学渠道，建设慕课平台，线上注册学员人数得到大幅增长。顺应时代的发展，线上线下融合的教学模式进一步完善，跨越时空阻碍的线上课程给更多人带来了更加便捷的学习机会。

不仅如此，孔子学院还顺应课程改革趋势。一改普通的交流式、活动式的只重于体验冰山一角汉语文化的教学模式，转而与当地学院签订学分课协议，使得汉语教学与文化传播更深层次地融入当地的教育体系，深化了孔子学院办学成果。

例如，阿联酋扎耶德大学孔子学院坚持线上线下相结合的教学模式，努力深化合作层次，拓展合作范围，并开设各级别常规汉语综合课班级 32 个，汉语学分课班级 3 个，阿布扎比投资局汉语培训班 5 个。不仅如此，它还帮助阿联酋大学语言与文学系开设了阿联酋第一个汉语辅修专业课并且签署了学分课协议，探索开设面向社会的汉语课程，并首次面向社区儿童开设了在线汉语课，这在阿联酋中文教育历程中具有里程碑意义。

（二）高质量办学

孔子学院刚开始推广时各国建立的学院数量增长势头迅猛，其增长速度大大超出了预期。然而，2007 年，全球孔子学院建成数量增长幅度相比 2006 年降低了 73%[①]，孔子学院数量的增长速度有所放缓。我国政府在这段时间开始控制孔子学院的发展规模，转而聚焦提高孔子学院的基础建设、配套资源和孔子学院办学质量等方面。孔子学院力求在管理、办学质量、教学水平、师资队伍建设、教研开发等方面不断完善，使办学水平得到进一步提高，以更好地推动孔子学院的可持续发展，为宣扬中华文化"磨刀锋"。

此外，孔子学院将工作重点放在提升品牌知名度和影响力上，采取了一系列配套的措施和活动，进一步提升了孔子学院的受欢迎程度。例如，柬埔寨皇

① 刘旭.中国孔子学院历时发展研究.重庆大学学报(社会科学版)，2015，21(6): 234-241.

家科学院孔子学院在取得了教育部颁发的为数不多的"网络教学许可证"之后，在E-learning教学系统的基础上制作了网络课程库。除打磨各门课程的教学大纲、教学资料和复习资料之外，还制作了多个教学小视频，着重讲解重难点。老师们还精心设计了在线书法比赛、听说配音比赛、简历制作比赛等丰富多彩的学习内容，成立了"云端汉语角"，每周选取学生们感兴趣的话题举办活动，有效提高了学生的口语表达能力，也增进了师生感情。另外，多地孔子学院还开放了中国文化体验中心和体验角，并且同孔子学院开展的大部分课程一样，都是向当地民众无偿开放的。这也使得中华文化在传播的过程中，更充分地发挥了中华文化的感染力。从语言入手，用文化交融，促民心相通。孔子学院的办学质量迈上新的台阶。

（三）文化传播方式多样化

孔子学院作为中国文化传播的重要载体，一直致力于不断丰富和发展多样化的文化传播方式，以满足不同国家和地区学生的需求，为世界各地的学生提供了一个了解和学习中华文化的广阔平台。除了传统的课程教学外，孔子学院还紧密结合所在国家和地区的实际情况，采取线下、线上或两者相结合的方式，开展了一系列丰富多彩的文化教学、讲座和交流活动。例如，美国西北拿撒勒大学孔子学院开设的中国文化课推出了两国教师共同授课（中国教师以讲座的形式介绍中国文化，并录制"身边的中国人"等小视频；美国教师引导学生进行讨论）、中美大学生论坛（视频连线，选取学生感兴趣的话题，以小组讨论的方式进行），以及探访名胜古迹（在兵马俑景点进行现场授课）等多种创新授课模式。这种多元化的教学方式不仅有助于提高学生的文化素养，还能够为促进中外文化交流发挥积极作用。

多样化的文化传播方式不仅丰富了孔子学院的课程内容，提升了文化传播效能，也培养了学生对中国文化的兴趣并增进理解。学生们能够更加直观地了解中国的历史、文化、风俗习惯等方面的内容，从而加深对中国文化的认识。同时，多样化的文化传播方式为孔子学院的发展提供了新的动力，有助于提高孔子学院的知名度和影响力，促进中华文化在全球范围内的进一步传播。

六、未来展望

孔子学院以汉语教学、文化推广为中心，致力于将中文推向世界舞台，树立中国国家形象，提高中国文化软实力。随着时代的发展，孔子学院各项管理制度逐步完善，运营机制日渐成熟，办学规模持续扩大。近年来，孔子学院更加注重特色办学，品牌创新，充分融合互联网教学技术，逐步实现本土化、融入型发展。通过对孔子学院发展历程以及现状的汇总分析，我们了解到，其发展主要经历了初创期、发展期以及转型期三个阶段。孔子学院发展理念演变主要有四个阶段：着力实现规模扩张，推动中文走向世界——根植当地中文需求，服务社区本土发展——强调特色品牌质量，提质增效融合发展——主动服务国家战略，内涵建设稳中求进。

在错综复杂的国际背景下，孔子学院想要进一步发展，应继续顺应时代潮流，创新教学与传播文化的方式。基于目前孔子学院发展的经验，我们对未来孔子学院进一步发展的路径及方式有以下建议：

首先，孔子学院应进一步激活线上课堂和网络学习资源。孔子学院应加强数字化技术在教学中的应用，创新教育模式和方法。例如，可以利用虚拟现实（VR）、增强现实（AR）等技术，为学生提供沉浸式的学习体验；可以利用人工智能（AI）技术，进行个性化教学和智能评估；利用在线学习平台，实现异地教学和自主学习。[1]

其次，孔子学院应充分利用新媒体平台。孔子学院可以借助Facebook、Instagram等新媒体平台搭建新型传播矩阵，建设自身传播平台。例如，萨尔瓦多大学孔子学院倾力打造西语版"我要学汉语"中国文化短视频资源库，并在萨大孔院官方Facebook、Twitter账号进行展播。短视频内容包括中国文化概况、中国传统节日、中国饮食、中国书法、中国主要城市、中国主要景点等。短视频富有当地特色，以西语为中介语言，搭配部分关键字词和拼音，让观众在观看视频的同时逐渐掌握关键汉语词汇。此类文化传播方式值得进一步推广。

最后，孔子学院应进一步着力本土发展，更好地融入本土、扎根本土、服务本土。孔子学院应加强与当地大学、社区、社会团体组织和企业等的合作，发展当地特色教学，并进一步推进本土化教师培养培训、本土化教学资源开发、本土化教学方法研究。例如，2023年10月27日，赞比亚大学孔子学院举办了2023赞比亚高校中企人才博览会。矿产、旅游、建筑等多个行业的83家企业为当地学生提供了约700个就业岗位。此类方式可以激励当地人更积极主动地学习汉语以获得就业机会，有利于促进中外经济合作，同时也有助于加深中外文化交流，值得推广借鉴。

---

[1] 陈思文，郭强. 优秀传统文化融入汉语教学的价值、困境与进路——以中外合办孔子学院为例. 汉字文化，2023，(20): 77-79.

英国文化教育协会的跨文化实践及启示研究①

摘　要: 本文以英国文化教育协会为主要研究对象，运用数据分析、对比分析、跨学科交叉研究等方法，围绕英国文化教育协会的海外语言教学和海外文化传播两方面展开研究，并选取它在跨文化交流与教育方面的典型实践作为经典案例，着重对其在推广、传播语言文化时的特色与优势进行分析与呈现。此外，本文还结合当今中国语言文化在海外传播的现状，以英国文化教育协会在文化交流与教育方面的工作内容和成功经验为参照，思考中国文化走出去和提高中国文化国际影响力的可行模式与特色路径。

关键词: 跨文化交流; 英国文化教育协会; 雅思; 中国文化; 文化传播

一、绪　论

英国文化教育协会是世界著名的语言文化传播机构之一，在海外语言学习和文化传播方面均取得了不俗的成绩。

近年来，世界文明文化的交流发展备受各国重视，成为国内外学者研究的热点问题。在全球化成为时代必然趋势、世界各国语言文化交流持续深入发展的大背景下，研究英国文化教育协会的历史发展进程及其在对外语言教学、本土文化海外传播领域的既有实践，有助于增进对于当前时代趋向的认识，对于我国语言文化在海外的传播推广，进一步拓展跨文化交流与合作也具有学习借鉴意义。

---

① 侯仕骄，南昌大学汉语言文学专业; 魏湘睿，南昌大学汉语言文学专业; 李奕林，南昌大学金融学专业; 刘思杨，南昌大学日语专业。

国内外学界关于英国文化教育协会的理论研究已经取得了较多的成果。丛霞于 2017 年在《文化外交视角下的英国文化教育协会研究》一文中详细考察了英国文化教育协会的运作模式及运作特点，为中国文化对外传播提供了一定的参考和借鉴，但并未深入探索、阐述如何基于中国国情开展语言文化进一步传播推广的可行路径；①许立新在《英国文化教育协会〈教师持续专业发展框架〉探析》一文中，基于英国文化教育协会针对海外教师的持续发展发布的《教师持续专业发展框架》进行了全面的透视与分析，并对教师培养流程进行了模型分析，有助于指导我国汉语国际教育师资的培养；陈佳劼在《英国文化教育协会英语语言教学中的语言声望规划研究》一文中，梳理了协会推广英语、塑造语言学习品牌的重要方式，这对我国国际中文教育事业有重要的借鉴意义，但并未对中英语言教学推广进行对比分析。②

综合来看，关于英国文化教育协会的语言推广和文化传播方面已有相对完善的研究，但是对于中外语言文化传播对比还存在可供深入探讨的空间。基于此，本文以英国文化教育协会为主要研究对象，旨在通过对其发展历程、典型实践的整体把握，对其文明文化交流方式开展系统性分析，再结合中国文化传播现状，有针对性地提出中国语言、文化传播的处理思路和改进方法。

二、英国文化教育协会的发展历程

英国文化教育协会成立于 1934 年，至今已有近 90 年历史。作为一个从事文化外交的准政府组织，它通过语言、艺术、教育等文化媒介把英国的优秀文化、现代理念、生活方式及价值观等传播到世界各地，树立了英国具有吸引力的国际形象。③然而，关于其发展阶段，学界并未有官方具体定论，但根据官方历史文件，其经历了几个明显的转折点：起步于两次世界大战的特殊时段到平稳发展阶段；20 世纪 80 年代后短暂进入海内外收缩阶段；从冷战结束至今，经过战略调整，英国文化教育协会进入全球多元治理阶段。④

（一）起步与战时活动阶段

这个阶段主要定位在 20 世纪 30 年代中期到 50 年代中期。英国文化教育

---

① 丛霞.文化外交视角下的英国文化教育协会研究.上海：上海外国语大学，2017.
② 陈佳劼.英国文化教育协会英语语言教学中的语言声望规划研究.上海：上海外国语大学，2022.
③ 梁洁.《余震》：来自英国 1990 年至 2006 年的新艺术.美苑，2007(1)：68-76.
④ 胡文涛，招春袖.英国文化外交：提升国家软实力的成功之路.太平洋学报，2010，18(9)：29-37.

协会成立的背景之一就是英国政府为了应对法西斯国家在国外的反英宣传，树立英国积极正面的文化大国形象。1940年10月，英国文化教育协会获得皇家宪章授权，成为一个永久性机构。

战争开始后，英国文化教育协会的活动规划主要集中在两方面：一是争取中立国家的支持；二是负责流亡英国的欧洲大陆国家人员的安置、教育及培训工作。[1]

（二）平稳发展阶段

从20世纪50年代中期到80年代初期是平稳发展期。英国文化教育协会在20世纪60年代后半期基于政治文化形势，最重要的工作就是对第三世界，特别是英国的前殖民地，进行教育援助。20世纪70年代以来，英国文化教育协会基于国家战略调整，回归西欧。20世纪70年代中期，有两项活动对英国文化教育协会的政策和组织产生长期影响：直接英语教学（Direct Teaching of English-DTE）和付费教育服务（Paid Educational Services-PES）。英国文化教育协会在其中发现了巨大的商业价值，此后教学收入成为英国文化教育协会重要的收入来源。[2]

（三）海内外收缩阶段

20世纪80年代是英国文化教育协会的短暂海内外收缩期。这一阶段的标志性事件是1979年保守党领袖撒切尔夫人上台伊始就全面缩减公共支出。英国文化教育协会海外活动逐渐减少，但20世纪80年代中期以后，冷战有所缓和，英国抓住时机，开展对苏东国家的工作。

（四）战略调整阶段

冷战结束后至1997年，一方面苏联等社会主义国家的垮台为英国文化教育协会腾出了巨大的发展空间；另一方面，全球化的加剧、信息革命的发展，对英国的文化外交战略提出了新的要求。1993年，英国政府发布了题为《创造性的未来》的"国家文化艺术发展战略"。在该"战略"中，英国文化教育协会被委以重任，主要由它实施具体工作，包括管理海外英语考试和教学及相关信息服务，提供英国教育和培训信息，并推销其教育机构的产品，组织有关教育的国际研讨会或教学研究与交流。1996年，英国文化教育协会正式开通

[1] 汲立立.战后英国文化外交研究.北京：中共中央党校，2014.
[2] 王克非，蔡永良，王美娜.英国文化委员会与英语的国际传播.外语教学，2017，38(6)：1-6.

官方网站。

（五）全球多元治理阶段

1997 年新工党上台后，提出了"新工党，新英国"的口号，旨在打造一个新工党领导下的自信、创新、多元、宽容的新英国形象。面对飞速发展的数字和信息技术，英国文化教育协会也紧跟时代节奏，在不完全抛弃传统的通过面对面的方式影响受众的前提下，英国文化教育协会通过互联网技术以及大众传媒技术扩大受众范围与为全球观众提供可定制化学习。此外，21 世纪以来，除了英国传统活动领域外，英国文化教育协会还根据英国树立大国形象、提升软实力的战略，积极参与国际气候治理、维和、体育、社会治理，甚至反恐等全球治理活动。[①]

英国文化教育协会于 2022 年 4 月 21 日发布了《英语的未来：全球视野》，报告中指出英语是世界上被使用最广泛的语言，并可能在未来十年及以后保持这一地位。同时，人工智能、机器学习和机器翻译的创新有可能颠覆语言学习系统和流程，但大多数圆桌会议专家认为，人们仍然需要通过语言学习来实现人与人之间的直接沟通，来弥合数字鸿沟。值得一提的是，在行业的引领下，社会诉求正在悄然转变，即社会期望英语学习者能达到母语水平的理想化诉求正在转变为期待他们能够更好地在多种场景下熟练应用英语。在中国，教育的进步、技术的革新和就业市场的变化激发了人们学习英语的兴趣。同时，学习英语也扩大了年轻人获得更多的职业机会的可能。

三、英国文化教育协会的海外语言教学、文化传播历史发展进程及现状

（一）海外语言教学及文化传播

1.海外语言教学概述

在英语教学方面，英国文化教育协会在英语教学领域开展的工作一直引领全球，它通过设在全球 47 个国家的教学中心为英语学习者提供高质量的语言教学服务。此外，英国文化教育协会还提供咨询与途径，帮助英语学习者了解和获取英国英语教学领域内的各种英语教学产品和服务。在英语水平评估方面，英国文化教育协会与众多英国考试机构拥有紧密的合作关系，为其在海外提供优质的英语考试服务，例如：国际英语语言测试系统（IELTS）、博思职

---

① 茅晓嵩.英国文化委员会.国际资料信息，2005(8)：36-40.

业外语水平测试（BULATS）、法律英语考试（TOLES）、剑桥国际金融英语证书考试（ICFE）及普思考试（Aptis）等。

2.对外语言教学历史发展进程

（1）初期阶段

英国文化教育协会成立之初，主要任务是推广英语，强调英语课程的规范性，并帮助海外学生提高英语水平。在这个时期，英国文化教育协会创立了很多英语教学规范，如教材的开发和课程的设计，并通过提供培训课程、教材和教学方法的指导来提高他们的专业技能和英语教育质量。

（2）中期阶段

自20世纪80年代起，英国文化教育协会逐渐从单纯的英语教学转向更为广泛的多语言教学领域，如中文、西班牙语、葡萄牙语、阿拉伯语等。同样，英国文化教育协会又制定了教材标准和课程设置的规范。20世纪80年代至90年代，英国文化教育协会设置了语言测试和评估，开始发展和推广全球语言测试，如IELTS和Aptis等。

（3）当代阶段

随着全球化和数字化时代的来临，英国文化教育协会逐渐加大在多语种教学领域内的投入，并更为注重创新性和科技性，着重提升学习效果。

3.对外语言教学当代特征

（1）在线数字化教育

英国文化教育协会致力于推广创新教育。协会开发的在线英语教育平台"English My Way"为目标人群提供了免费的英语学习资源，并提供了一系列课程、练习和交互式支持，包括面向不同受众的自适应学习教材和个性化学习计划，运用智能化技术辅助学习等。随着互联网的快速发展，英国文化教育协会还积极推广数字化学习方式，通过在线平台向全球学生和教师提供语言学习资源。

（2）跨学科教学

英国文化教育协会还在积极推广跨学科教学，包括开设STEM等科学类课程，引导学生更好地理解英语学科知识，并在英语学科以外得到全面发展。同样，它也支持英语与艺术、文化、历史等领域的跨学科融合，以此增强多元文化之间的理解和交流。

（3）扩展海外分支机构扩展，推动项目深入发展

英国文化教育协会在全球范围内建立了大量分支机构，如中国分部、日本分部等，这些分支机构为当地的学生提供了各种英语学习机会和服务。例如，英国文化教育协会与中国多所大学合作，为学生提供了包括英语课程、留学咨询、考试培训、合作研究等在内的全方位教育服务。它在全球范围内与政府机构、教育机构和文化机构等合作，共同开展语言教育和文化交流活动，如英国教育和文化周、学生交换计划、专业培训和研讨会等。

（4）社交媒体推广

英国文化教育协会还利用社交媒体开展推广工作。比如，英国文化教育协会在微博、微信平台上开展各种英语学习、文化交流等活动，并以此吸引更多的人关注和参与。同时，它也非常重视YouTube和其他视频网站上的推广，通过内容创造与全球年轻人进行互动。[①]

4.文化传播当代特征

随着时代的变迁和技术的发展，英国文化教育协会在文化艺术推广方面也进行了多样化和创新性的尝试，包括：

（1）数字媒体和在线平台

由于互联网的广泛应用和数字技术的发展，英国文化教育协会开始将文化艺术资源数字化，并通过在线平台向全球观众展示。它在线上建设了各种文化艺术平台，如"Culture Diary""Shakespeare Lives"等，为全球观众提供了更加直观的文化艺术体验。这些平台提供了丰富的数字化内容，包括电影、音乐、戏剧、舞蹈、博物馆藏品等。

（2）跨领域合作、艺术家交流计划

英国文化教育协会大力推进跨领域合作，开展了艺术家交流计划，即帮助英国艺术家去海外展示他们的作品，同时也邀请国际艺术家来英国参加各种文化艺术活动，以及促进当地与国外文化艺术资源的交流和合作。

（3）教育项目

英国文化教育协会为海外学生和文化爱好者提供了许多文化艺术方面的教育项目，通过组织文化研讨会、讲座、各种展览等为海外学生和教育工作者提供了多样的机会来了解和学习英国文化艺术，并与海外教育机构合作，进一步

---

① 孙明旸.英国文化协会的语言传播功能.上海：上海外国语大学，2022.

加强和巩固受众对于英国文化的学习。此外，这些教育项目多数采用创新性和多元化的方式，如线上直播、视频课程、虚拟展览等。

四、英国文化教育协会在海外文化中传播的作用

英国文化教育协会以提高与促进英语语言传播为基础进行海外文化传播，这也是贯穿该协会不同时期的组织使命与工作重点。语言作为文化的媒介，进行语言推广是文化传播的重要方式和手段。下文将以其人文化、产业化的突出发展特点为切入点进行论述。

（一）人文化

在艺术领域方面，英国文化教育协会通过世界各地的图书馆收藏了英国文学界的书籍，以及英国最新的报纸和杂志；协会领导的国际化通用英语教材也以英国文化为依托，结合本土风俗、历史和现状为内容主题进行编写；通过与驻外使馆和各世界机构的合作，英国文化教育协会还举办了以莎士比亚经典选读为主题的书展，以及牛顿、达尔文等英国名人的纪念生日相关讲座。

同时，英国文化教育协会还进行英国电影和音乐的全球推广，设立戏剧和舞蹈项目奖学金，资助视觉艺术展览和文学作品翻译进程，宣传英语文化的同时，展现英国形象。

（二）产业化

在教育领域，英国文化教育协会在境内设立英国大、中、小学标准化考试，考试范围包括英语水平考试、职业资格证书考试等；在海外，英国文化教育协会则注重建立英语教学与培训及考试体系，其产业化的语言教学中心已培训并帮助了多民族数千万英语学习者。近年来，英国文化教育协会还推出了各种英语学习项目，设立奖学金项目以吸引海外学生来英学习。其下设的英语教学研讨会，专门研究英语课堂教学和方法，以指导和引领英语作为全球性语言的教学方法。此外，该协会提供英语教师培训课程，监督外教培训学校并向世界各地派遣英国语言专家，力求维护英语语言规范。在各类职业资格考试中，TOLES和ICFE最为著名；在英语语言水平测试中，国际英语语言测试系统——雅思（IELTS）考试是最重要的语言能力测试，下文将以其作为典型案例进行详细分析。

五、英国文化教育协会的跨文化交流与教育

（一）典型实践——以雅思考试为例

雅思考试由英国理事会、剑桥英语语言评估和澳大利亚IDP教育集团共同承办，是当今世界影响力最为广泛的英语语言能力测试之一。

作为国际标准化的英语水平测试，其主要通过测试学生的综合水平来判断个人在英语国家学习或生活的适应性。内容涵盖四种语言技能：听、读、写、说。雅思共分为两种：UKVI雅思和普通雅思。根据英国理事会官方网站的数据，雅思考试已被140多个国家的11000多个机构所认可。这些机构包括高等院校、培训机构、政府部门、跨国公司等。

本部分将结合雅思考试在中国的发展推广史及中国考生在雅思考试中的表现，探究这一考试作为英国文化教育协会在进行海外文化传播的典型实践的发展情况。

● 1987 年

雅思考试进入中国并成功举办，作为教育部赴英交流项目的英语语言水平测试，在教育部所属的五个出国培训部举行。

● 2004 年

英国文化教育协会中国雅思网络代表与中国教育部考试中心正式签署了在中国合作举办IELTS考试的协议。

● 2005 年

中国教育部考试中心和英国使馆文化教育处联合推出雅思考试网上报名系统和全国服务热线。

● 2009 年

雅思考试的官方中文网站开通，同时推出"雅思之路"免费在线学习课程。

● 2016 年

UKVI雅思在中国大陆地区正式推出机考。

● 2018 年

普通雅思在中国大陆地区正式推出机考。

● 2021 年

雅思考试在中国29个城市共设有32个考点，遍布国内主要大中城市，一年内有47个考试项目可供考生选择。

雅思官网发布的《2022年全球雅思考生数据报告》对人口数据和学生表现进行了分析。针对中国考生的表现，报告的相关内容如下。

2022年，中国大陆A类（学术类）雅思考生的总分均分为6.1，相比于2021年成绩上升0.13，这也是自有数据统计以来，中国大陆考生总分均分首次突破6.0。其中，2022年A类听力均分为6.1，阅读均分为6.4，写作均分为5.8，口语均分为5.6。

在听说读写四项中，2022年，中国大陆考生在A类考试阅读单项中取得了总分均分6.4的好成绩，相比于2021年提高了0.13；口语单项成绩相比2021年不仅均分提高了0.05，单项分数排名也攀升了一位，位列全球37。

2022年中国大陆考生A类雅思考试分数集中在5.5—6.5分这一分数段，这一分数段占比达到65%。7—7.5分考生占比为18%，相比2021年增加了约2.78%。[①]

综上，雅思考试在中国的发展越来越成熟，中国考生在雅思考试中的表现也越来越出色。可见，英国文化教育协会以雅思考试为依托进行的语言传播——文化传播颇为成功。

（二）发展特色和成功经验

在以上成功案例的背后，蕴含着英国文化教育协会的发展特色与经验，本部分将从其独立化、合作化和商业化三个方面分别进行分析。

1.独立化

英国文化教育协会虽然在实际运作中是一个准政府组织，但在法律上是一个非政府的公共部门，其本质是一个具有独立法人资格的非营利性慈善组织。由此，英国文化教育协会获得了广泛的社会支持。

2.合作化

由于其领导者的不懈努力，英国文化教育协会自成立以来一直致力于从区域走向全球。受其在艺术交流方面的努力影响，英国的众多慈善组织、企业组织、机构和个人都成为了英国文化教育协会的社会伙伴关系网络的一环，并就具体项目与协会进行了合作，提供资金或人力支持。受其在教育交流方面的成就影响，该协会与国际组织、各种协会和理事会及学校和研究机构等教育和学术机构进行了广泛合作，为英国文化交流协会的海外活动赢得了支持。同时，

---

① IELTS Test Taker Performance 2022. [2023-12-31]. https://www.ielts.org/for-researchers/test-statistics.

该协会倡导互利共赢的理念，一方面，社会力量具有广泛传播的能力，符合协会扩大影响力的目标；另一方面，合作方同样可以利用协会广泛的全球网络，扩大自己的影响力。

3.商业化

英国文化教育协会用创造性的方式形成了商业化和市场化模式，通过设立语言教育中心、编写出版教科书、设立奖学金吸引海外学生赴英留学；以设计英语在线学习平台等产品、开发教师体系、举办国际化大型语言考试等方法，促进供给与需求的产业化，既在一定程度上缓解了英国的人口就业问题，在为英国政府带来收入的同时，又促进了英国文化的广泛传播。

（三）跨文化典型实例对比及启示——以HSK与IELTS为例

依托本次研究主题，将汉语水平考试（以下简称HSK）作为中国语言传播的典型实践与雅思考试进行对比研究，总结经验，有助于促进中国语言的推广。HSK考试是为测试母语非汉语者（包括外国人、华侨、华裔和中国少数民族考生）的汉语水平而设立的一项国际汉语能力标准化考试。[1]

HSK考试设置之初具有"考教分离""难度较大""对汉语水平较低者无从下手"等缺点。随着中国国际影响力的提升，新HSK也在旧HSK考试的基础上进行了改革推广。与以往不同，新HSK考试提倡"考教结合"，等级数量增加，试题的辅助信息增加，更加适合汉语初学者，以循序渐进的方式增加考生数量的同时以增加听力考试的方式加强考试效度。因此，为保证对比研究的有效性和可信度，下文将以新HSK考试为基准与雅思考试进行对比。[2]

HSK共分为6级，每一层级设置听、说、读、写、口语不等的考试形式，雅思考试也涵盖此五方面，由于阅读部分在语言学习中尤为重要，因此着重对比阅读方面的题型及选材。[3]

1.题型对比

从题型上看，雅思阅读部分多数采用主客观结合的问题形式，具有多样性。新HSK阅读部分的考查形式则相对单一。

2.选材对比

新HSK阅读题材多选自报刊或图书，一般以哲理类、文化类、科普类、

---

① 文秘帮.新旧HSK比较初探.[2023-12-31]. https://www.wenmi.com/article/pusqcp049vjs.html.

② 谈碧君.对HSK阅读测试中短文的选材接受度分析.教育现代化，2018，5(8)：137-138.

③ 罗心悦.新HSK四、五级与雅思考试阅读题对比研究.西安：西安外国语大学，2021.

新闻类、叙事类和幽默类为主。其中，哲理类的文本数量较多。

雅思阅读题材则源自《经济学人》《新科学家》《国家地理》等著名的学术期刊中的最新研究文章。

综上，从选材上看，新HSK考试阅读部分应用大量哲理类文章，而因其都选自中国特有的报刊，由此大部分文章更加侧重介绍中国传统文化和表现中国特色。而雅思考试阅读部分更均衡地囊括了多种主题类型，涉及的题材相当广泛，基本为世界性的问题，更能契合全球考生的理解与接受程度，更容易引起共鸣。

由此可见，英国文化教育协会坚持非专业化和国际化原则，其考试依托英语全球交际文化圈，在综合考虑考生多样性的基础上进行设计及考核，在推动语言学习的过程中达到本土文化潜移默化的传播。而HSK考试则更注重对中国传统文化、哲理观念等的宣介，对受众的需求及文化背景考虑相对不足，与雅思考试存在一定的理念导向差异。①

六、中国文化如何走出去

（一）中国文化传播背景及现状

1.高质量文化供给相对不足

20世纪90年代中期起，中国深度融入东亚经济体系；21世纪初起，中国嵌入全球经济体系，成为连接发达经济体与发展中经济体的关键节点。就文化贸易而言，近年我国一直呈现出稳步上升、持续优化的发展趋势，向制造强国、文化强国不断迈进，但中国对外出口的产品中多为加工贸易，虽然规模不小，但并未聚焦于文化价值链的中高端环节，但仍存在文化竞争力不足的短板。

2.对外传播形式有待更新

据《美国新闻与世界报道》发布的2019年全球文化影响力榜单，中国为第十九名，文化的国际影响力与经济总量全球第二的大国地位并不相符，仍存在相当程度上的落差。可见，在产业数字化和数字产业化的时代发展趋势下，中国文化产品和服务的数字化国际化发展仍存在相当长的发展道路。②

---

① 孔朝蓬，刘婷."球土化"背景下中国文化身份的转向——基于新媒体传播的视角.文艺争鸣，2014(10)：174-179.
② 肖慈敏，夏美玲，廖颖.新媒体时代中国文化双语传播的实践与分析.商业文化，2021，521(32)：142-144.

3.受众定位模糊

中国人民大学国家发展与战略研究院研究员林坚在《当代中华文化海外传播状况及其对策》中指出，中国文化海外传播没有针对不同的人群、不同的地域、不同的民族、不同的文化系统而设计，未形成差异化的、独特性的传播策略。也即在对外传播的语境中对受众分析不足，对于海外受众与国内受众在文化背景、价值观念、思维方式等方面存在的差异欠缺认识，模糊了受众定位，导致文化传播国际辐射力不足。[①]

（二）中国文化传播建议

针对中国文化传播现状，结合前文对于英国文化教育协会在海外文化传播方面的经验介绍，本部分对中国文化传播提出以下几点建议：

1.传播内容纵深化

尽管中国文化对外传播的实体形态呈现出数量大且丰富的特点，但对外输出的特色文化内核仍处于较为浅显的发展阶段，内容深度建设不足。

从这个角度进行观照，英国文化教育协会的跨文化传播实践为如何解决中国文化供给的失衡状态提供了参考。例如：英国文化教育协会领导的出版社编辑出版的国际化通用英语教材以英国文化为依托，以本土风俗、历史和现状为内容主题进行编写；通过与驻外使馆和世界各地机构的合作，举办以经典莎士比亚选读读物等主题的书展，开办牛顿、达尔文等英国名人的生日纪念的相关主题讲座。[②]同时，英国文化教育协会还积极推进视觉艺术展览和文学作品翻译等工作，并通过组织全球调查、戏剧演出等对英国本土文化进行宣传。因此，以英国文化教育协会的经验为借鉴，着重输出文化底蕴，加强对内容深度的挖掘，选择能代表中国文化精髓和内在价值的文化资源，创造具有中国元素、展现大国形象的文化精品是中国文化对外输出亟需关注的方向。在进行文化产品创造时，要充分保留中国文化的精神内涵和文化特质，做到古代文化和现代文化、民间文化和官方文化、表层文化与精神文化的有机结合与融汇贯通。[③]同时，在对这些不同层次、不同领域的中国本土文化进行深入发掘的基础上，还要结合当前的中国发展状况，凝结出蕴含当代人本主义价值观的文化

---

① 林坚.当代中华文化海外传播状况及其对策.(2019-05-20)[2023-12-31].https://www.sohu.com/a/315313373_488939.

② 弋俊楠，董小静.中国对外文化贸易现状、问题及策略.对外经贸实务，2019(3)：64-68.

③ 邓永平.全球化新时代背景下跨文化交流再思考.戏剧之家，2020(22)：200-216.

内核，进而总结出时代性的中国文化内核，并最终以文化产品为物质载体进行对外输出。

简言之，实现国家经济发展与文化建设同频共振，打造既具有社会主义先进性，又在深层内核契合真理、正义、大爱等人类价值共识的高品质文化产品，不仅符合历史趋势和民心所向，也能够一定程度上获得世界各国人民的认可。

2.传播渠道多元化

伴随着数字媒体时代的革新与科技进步，包括手机移动端、电脑端等媒体形态在内的新媒体环境应运而生并愈加发展壮大，其广泛的社会影响力与快捷高效的传播功能为中国文化对外传播提供了全新的思路。党的二十大报告中也明确强调了"实施国家文化数字化战略"为发展的重要部署，重点推动中国数字文化产品和文化服务"走出去"，为增强中华文明的国际传播力和影响力提供方向和机遇。基于以上背景，构建线上线下相结合、互动强、范围广的新型文化传播模式，不失为一种高效传播、高质传播中国文化的有效模式。

在新媒体发展壮大之前，我们在文化输出方面主要依靠文学作品、影视作品的外译，如2012年获诺贝尔文学奖的莫言的作品，影视作品《甄嬛传》《父母爱情》等的陆续出口，还有对外的报纸、杂志等。而伴随着时代进步，具有快捷性、及时性、开放性等特点的新媒体成为了继传统媒体之后文化传播的新介质，文化全球化传播的中介重心也渐渐由少数主流媒体向互联网交流平台转移，兼具视听说多维体验功能的网络平台成了文化交流的一个重要途径。英国文化教育协会即很好地顺应了数字媒体时代的文化传播趋势，以建立在线平台为途径，将电影、戏剧、博物馆藏品、文学作品等文化资源数字化，以更灵活的生产组织方式、更丰富的业态融合、更多元的场景应用在极大地扩张了受众群体的同时，为全球观众提供了更加便捷、直观且全面的文化艺术体验。[①]此外，英国文化教育协会创新采用线上直播互动、视频课程、虚拟展览等多元方式，定期组织英国文化研讨会、讲座及各种文化展览等活动，开放受众参与的窗口和渠道来助力本土文化传播，以多向度、互动式、立体式的传播弥补了传统跨文化传播方式的单向度、扁平式缺陷。

以智媒传播理论对英国文化教育协会的传播实践进行观照，可归纳为以下两点典型特征。其一是智媒化，即主要采用视频、图表或其他视觉化的形

---

① 曹韵.新媒体时代中国文化海外传播的新思路.学术交流，2019(11)：180-187.

式来替代传统纸媒实现叙事，简洁、形象、交互式的可视化效果图成为叙事信息的主要呈现形式，文字则成为效果图与VR呈现的补充。以英国文化教育协会创立的线上文化艺术平台Shakespeare Lives为例，它推出了免费线上课程"Exploring English: Shakespeare"，提供了莎士比亚出生地和伦敦环球剧院线上云游览等服务，允许受众跨越地域、时空的限制与世界各地的研究专家及莎翁剧演员进行对话，共同对莎士比亚作品进行探讨。此种方式弥补了传统纸媒缺乏交流互动及可视化信息受限的不足，充分体现了现代化智媒化的更新发展趋势。其二是传播的高效率。英国文化教育协会采用了电子书、虚拟教室、在线课程等方式，通过现代化工具给予语言学习者、文化探索者以丰富的知识资源，并提供即时直观的反馈，以此实现学习效果及效率的大幅提升。[①]

因此，利用新媒体时代提供的多平台和多元化传播方式，建立线下实践与线上推广的双向互动机制，是目前推动中国文化海外传播行之有效的方法。以在线平台为载体，创新设计新颖互动环节，链接多种社交媒体平台，适当设立线上奖励机制，充分调动受众参与文化传播过程中，形成二次传播来扩大传播效果。而线下活动则通过与参与者建立"面对面、零距离"的关系，从虚拟屏幕交流转为线下真实互动，通过受众的亲身体验来增强中国文化底蕴的渗透。而平台与参与者建立的线下关系也能够形成一传十、十传百的传播效应圈，为平台树立良好的口碑，进而增加平台粉丝量，强化传播效果。

3.传播体系层次化

数字媒体时代的信息流通体量巨大，且信息传播速度惊人，不同领域间竞争激烈。要想让海外受众愿意接受并能够接收中国文化信息，就需要精准定位受众选择性心理，在对受众的个性和文化需求准确把握、判断的基础上有针对性地传播文化内容，做到因地制宜，进而缩小海外受众的文化和心理距离，不断推动文化有效跨国传播。基于跨文化传播理论进行分析，跨文化交流领域主要关联到两个层次的传播：日常生活层面和人类文化交往层面。针对不同文化土壤上信仰、价值观、文化传统各异的受众群体，使用合适的、易于接受和理解的形式与内容进行文化的传播与推广是其要义所在。[②]

第一，要强化中国文化本身的特征性，挖掘最具代表性的文化特点，以此

---

① 杜波.对外文化传播与文化产业国际化发展.青年记者，2019(14): 32-33.
② 花建，田野.国际文化贸易的新趋势与中国对外文化传播的新作为.上海交通大学学报(哲学社会科学版)，2023(31): 78-92.

作为"卖点",从而率先抓住受众的注意力。第二,从文化受众的角度分析,在进行文化信息传播时,首先要深入研究国外不同受众的文化传统、价值取向和接受心理等,对将要传播的文化信息按照目标受众人群由浅入深地进行分类,区分对象和层次,对受众群体进行清晰定位。第三,要针对不同国家和地区采用不同策略。探寻出文化与不同受众之间独特的契合点,围绕着契合点进行文化信息推广,有针对性地进行内容推送,用巧妙的内容构思和传播创意,分类别分层次吸引不同受众,才能达到传播中国文化的目的。

七、结　语

在全球化视野下,英国文化教育协会在对外语言教学与本土文化海外传播领域的既有实践以人文化、产业化等为显著优势,在跨文化交流与传播方面取得了令人瞩目的成果。

综上所述,本文以英国文化教育协会为研究对象,对英国文化教育协会的发展历程与规划进行简要梳理,举例阐述其特色化海外语言推广与跨文化传播实践,并总结其跨文化合作等成功经验,能够为完善中国语言文化海外传播方式提出意见与建议,同时从文明维度出发,为世界感知中华文化、拓宽人文交流提供有效路径与参考,具有促进世界文明交流互鉴的积极意义。

双向传播与场域理论视角下中国孔子学院与英国文化教育协会的传播差异比较研究①

摘 要: 作为重要的文化宣传机构,孔子学院和英国文化教育协会在东亚、中亚等地区有着较大的文化传播作用。本文从全球范围内文化机构相互竞争的角度,运用传播学中的双向传播理论对孔子学院和英国文化教育协会的传播情况进行分析,并采用布迪厄场域理论对两个机构在对外文化传播和国际推广上的差异进行分析。研究发现,英国文化教育协会在工作内容和网站内容呈现上更具优势,能得到更多受众反馈。此外,场域、惯习和资本的差异影响了两者在国际环境下推广能力的不同。鉴于此,孔子学院的发展应更注重传播文化、获得反馈,呈现更适合在国际上推广的文化形式与内容。

关键词: 双向传播;场域理论;国际推广;英国文化教育协会;孔子学院

一、引 言

(一)当代国际文化传播和文化传播机构的研究意义

在全球化时代,除了科技和军事力量之外,国家之间的软实力竞争也变得至关重要。因此,能否让中国优秀文化走向世界,能否让世界民众听见中国的声音,能否让世界民众获得正确的中国形象和学习中国优秀的民族文化,是文化传播机构必须思考和解答的问题。孔子学院承担着让中国文化走出去的使命。因此,研究孔子学院与英国文化教育协会的文化传播实践,对于推广中国

---

① 作者:殷明,南开大学外国语学院;王梓涵,南开大学外国语学院;程棨彦,南开大学外国语学院。

文化、塑造良好的中国国际形象具有重大意义。

（二）孔子学院发展及其海外文化传播研究

了解孔子学院，应该先了解其当前的国际价值、文化传播策略与实践，以及其所面临的挑战。

谢娜探讨了在国际中文教育多元主体并存背景下孔子学院体现其公共价值的方式，并建议推动国际中文教育由价值链向生态链转化。[①]赵海滨、宋伟和田菊以中医孔子学院为例，分析了卫生外交如何通过孔子学院平台发挥公共外交功能，并指出这弥补了传统政治外交的不足，有助于提升国家软实力和改善外交关系。[②]这些研究都强调了孔子学院在国际文化传播和文化教育方面的公共价值。

在孔子学院的文化传播问题上，钟新、蒋贤成提出了基于文化势能、文化融通和文化比较的情感、认知和联想共情层级递升模型，来分析孔子学院的文化传播策略与实践。[③]刘晓蕾[④]和郭小琴[⑤]则分别探讨了中国武术与民族乐器的海外教学与推广，提出了不同的推广策略。

此外，孔子学院的发展还面临着诸多挑战，如张未然指出了孔子学院在西方新闻媒体中面临的舆情困境，并提出了争取国际新闻话语权、加大社交媒体宣传力度的建议。[⑥]孔子学院的文化传播也在一定程度上受到了孔子学院的布局影响，如王立从历时、动态角度考察全球孔子学院的布局及其影响因素，揭示了其存在分布不均衡、增速差异大的特征，并提出了"区别对待，协调发展"的原则。[⑦]

综上所述，过往研究聚焦孔子学院的国际价值、文化传播策略与挑战进行了探讨分析，本文试图从不同传播机构相互对比的角度来研究孔子学院的不足，

① 谢娜.孔子学院在国际中文教育中的公共价值及其实现.国际中文教育，2023，8(2)：98-105.
② 赵海滨，宋伟，田菊.卫生外交：公共外交的有效途径——以中医孔子学院为例.南方论刊，2023，35(4)：8-11.
③ 钟新，蒋贤成.跨文化共情传播机制探新：基于孔子学院院长访谈的跨国比较研究.东岳论丛，2023，44(2)：49-61.
④ 刘晓蕾，李丹妍，孟涛."一带一路"建设背景下武术在中亚地区推广的动力因素、现实状况及方略.首都体育学院学报，2023，35(1)：100-107.
⑤ 郭小琴.中国民族器乐在海外的教学与传播——以在英国伦敦金史密斯孔子学院开展二胡教学为例.四川戏剧，2022，35(1)：127-130.
⑥ 张未然.新形势下孔子学院的舆情困境：特征、原因与对策.现代传播(中国传媒大学学报)，2021，43(3)：20-26.
⑦ 王立.全球孔子学院(课堂)布局及发展研究——基于文化地理学视角.河北广播电视大学学报，2022，27(1)：97-101.

结合文化机构的国际价值与传播策略两个研究角度，运用传播学中的双向传播理论对两个机构的传播情况进行分析，并通过布迪厄的场域理论，分析孔子学院和英国文化教育协会在对外文化传播和国际推广上的差异。经过分析，能够更加清晰地认识到孔子学院的优势与劣势，从而为其发展提出有效的建议。

二、英国文化教育协会近年来的发展状况

英国文化教育协会（British Council），又名英国文化协会，成立于1934年，在近几十年的发展历程中，它经历了多次重要的变革和发展。

1934年，英国成立了"英国与其他国家关系委员会"，以支持海外英语教育，促进英国文化推广并打击法西斯主义的兴起。在此后的80多年，英国文化教育协会渐渐地确定了使各国"对英语的更广泛了解，并使英国与其他国家之间发展更密切的文化关系"的文化宣传策略。从政治性宣传活动逐步走向民间宣传活动，英国文化教育协会的文化宣传活动逐步提高了英国文化的世界影响力。

近年来，协会通过多种多样的渠道和方式，如宣讲会、文化活动、国际教育、教学奖金等，推广其价值理念，增强自身的国际声望，取得了显著的成效。英国文化教育协会在推广英国的文化理念、维护国家利益、塑造国际形象上有巨大作用，是值得探讨研究的对象（见表1）。

表1 近年来英国文化教育协会开办的部分文化项目

时间	项目名称	内容	方式
2023	《月前之舞》——2023年威尼斯双年展英国馆探馆之旅	着眼于英国侨民社区的习俗及建筑空间的使用方式，以期激发讨论并影响英国建筑的未来。	艺术展览
2023	2023年英国文化教育协会雅思奖学金	为通过雅思考试且就读英国本科或研究生的中国学生提供奖学金。	奖学金
2022	非凡英国奖学金计划	为进读英国26所高校的中国学生提供奖学金。	奖学金
2021	The Climate Connection 项目	通过艺术、文化、教育和英语推动全球气候合作，共同应对气候变化带来的挑战。	微电影、宣传片、艺术展览、研讨活动
2021	2021 #ReConnect 中英当代艺文展演	为中国观众提供一个与苏格兰、威尔士、北爱尔兰以及英格兰重建连接的机会，让中国观众能够近距离感受来自英国的艺术瑰宝。	艺术展览

（资料来源：https://www.britishcouncil.cn/en）

三、双向传播视角下的孔子学院与英国文化教育协会

（一）双向传播

1948 年，在《传播在社会中的结构与功能》一文中，美国学者 H．拉斯韦尔首次提出了构成传播过程的五种基本要素，即"五 W"模式，分别为"谁""说了什么""通过什么渠道""向谁说""有什么效果"。然而，这一模式仅呈现了信息的单向传递，没有揭示人类社会传播的双向和互动性质。①

双向传播的概念则在 20 世纪 50 年代由施拉姆和奥斯古德提出。它指的是存在反馈或互动机制的传播过程，即传播双方相互交流和共享信息，保持相互影响和相互作用的关系。与"五 W"模式不同，双向传播摒弃了以传递者为中心的模式，强调了传递者与接收者之间密切的相互关系。该概念强调了信息传递不再是单向的，而是一个相互影响、相互作用的过程，注重发送者和接收者之间的相互作用。②在这个动态交互的过程中，人们的态度和观念会受到影响和改变。通过反馈，信息传播形成了一个丰富而实际的网络，使得信息传递更加具体和有效。

（二）双向传播视角下的孔子学院

在工作内容上，孔子学院做了一系列文化、教学等方面的工作，且网站动态更新频率高，如在 2023 年 8 月共推送 23 条动态（孔子学院官网——活动空间——孔院动态）。在中文课堂和学术天地等板块，孔子学院设置了丰富多样的课程，提供了多种类型的教材教辅，积极推广汉语。除语言层面外，孔子学院还在文化推广方面结合中国特色。例如，在文化视窗板块，孔子学院详细阐释了文房四宝：笔、墨、纸、砚，东方的巧思，四位一体的书写工具凝聚着劳动的智慧和杰出的工艺，与中国式的书写生活相生相伴，统称为文房四宝。集萃万物生长的精华，获取博采众长的灵感，中国文房四宝的产生与演进，伴随着生存活动的延伸和精神世界的升华。它通过手工工艺，传递劳动、智慧、创造和情感，激发了中国人的书写生活，见证中华文明走向思想、知识、文化与艺术的王国。然而，相较于英国文化教育协会，孔子学院更加侧重于教授、传播我国的语言和文化，而较少结合全球热点内容，公众反馈可能因此受限。

但在内容呈现上，孔子学院可能并未充分考虑受众，这可见于中、英

---

① 郭庆光．传播学教程．北京：中国人民大学出版社，2011：54-58.
② 郭庆光．传播学教程．北京：中国人民大学出版社，2011：54-58.

文网站的制作。孔院官网共设"中文课题""文化视窗""学术天地""活动空间""全球网络"五个大板块，切换为英文后，呈现为"Chinese Classes""Culture""Academic World""Activities & Programs""Network"五个板块。然而，经对比发现，除了"全球网络"（Network）板块，其余四个板块的英文翻译都是有选择性的——翻译了部分内容，而未译其他内容。以"文化视窗"板块中对中国春节的介绍为例，中文版"活动介绍"显示的内容丰富，如：中国新年又被称作春节，节庆将持续 15 天，是中国历法中最重要的节日。春节的开始日期不定，通常在每年的一月或二月。在现代中国，很多因工作离开家乡的人会在春节时跨越宽广的祖国大地，经历漫长的旅途回到家中与亲人团聚。家庭是中国人生活的重心之一，春节可能会是一些家庭一年中仅有的团圆时刻……然而，在切换为英文版后，除了活动介绍翻译为"Introduction of Activity"，内容依旧呈现为中文，没有任何变化。在"活动空间"板块，除了"孔院动态"翻译为"CI Daily"，具体的活动并没有翻译成英文。因此，孔子学院的英文网站的宣传效果会受限。

（三）双向传播视角下的英国文化教育协会

在工作内容上，英国文化教育协会展示了一系列其在艺术、教育和社会领域的工作和成果，紧密结合全球热点，符合受众的心理预期，能得到一定反馈。同时，在网站内容呈现上，英国文化教育协会的中文版本比原英文版多一个板块，即英国文化教育协会发布的《英语的未来：全球视野》报告，亦能引起中国受众的反馈，形成双向传播。

在工作内容上，英国文化教育协会多次结合全球热点开展活动。以气候问题为例，为了响应 2021 年的第 26 届联合国气候变化缔约方大会，英国文化教育协会通过 Climate Connection 项目与多个国家合作，共同应对气候变化带来的挑战。2021 年 9 月，英国文化教育协会开展全球中小学气候行动视频竞赛。该竞赛面向所有 11 岁至 18 岁的学生，以及世界各地的在校教师，征集的视频作品需要展现所在学校和社区在应对气候变化方面的杰出工作。以热点话题开展活动，英国文化教育协会既传播了其文化与价值理念，又得到了世界各地的参赛作品反馈，形成了双向传播。此外，针对气候问题，英国文化教育协会还与《OK》杂志携手，通过 Bilibili 网站平台，邀请有影响力的公众人物来为气候变化发声，呼吁大家在平常生活中，减少浪费，减轻污染，做出更加可持续的选择。这项与气候问题相关的活动得到了广泛的公众反馈，也形成了双向传播。

在网站内容呈现上，英国文化教育协会也充分考虑了受众，这可见于该机构中、英文网站。在进入英国文化教育协会的官网后，选择"我们在艺术、教育及社会领域的工作"，会呈现"英国文化教育协会发布《英语的未来：全球视野》报告""The Climate Connection项目""我们在艺术领域的工作""我们在教育领域的工作""我们在社会领域的工作"五个板块。然而，在切换成英文版后，发现仅有"The Climate Connection""Our Work in the Arts""Our Work in Education""Our Work in Society"四个板块。因此，在制作成中文网站的过程中，英国文化教育协会增加了"英国文化教育协会发布《英语的未来：全球视野》报告"板块。报告指出，技术革新无疑带来了自动化、人工智能和机器学习的普及。然而，在未来十年里，英语仍然是世界上被最广泛使用的语言，教师也继续在英语学习中占据核心地位。同时，它指出社会诉求正在悄然转变，即社会期望英语学习者能达到母语水平的理想化诉求正在转变为期待他们能够更好地在多种场景下熟练应用英语。这增补的板块既传播了英语重要性的观念，又指出了社会需求的变化，能引起中国受众的兴趣，形成反馈，形成双向传播。

经对比发现，英国文化教育协会紧密结合全球热点进行工作，中文网站翻译完整，且增补了面向中国受众的板块，有助于形成及时的、内容完整的双向传播。孔子学院的英文网站制作则缺乏完整性，可能会影响国际传播效果。

四、场域理论视角下的孔子学院与英国文化教育协会

（一）布迪厄的场域理论

皮埃尔·布迪厄（Pierre Bourdieu），全球知名的法国社会学家、思想家和文化理论批评家。他的思想和著述在国际学界广受重视。20世纪90年代中期以来，也引起了我国社会学者的注意。布迪厄称得上学术杂家，他的社会学理论融入了人类学、教育学、哲学、艺术、语言学、历史、文化学等诸学科的内容，可谓包容丰富、错综复杂。一般认为，场域理论是他的基本理论，在其社会学思想体系中占有最重要的地位。布迪厄在 The Field of Cultural Production 中提出等式：场域＋惯习＋资本＝实践。①

1958年，社会学逐渐被认可为独立学科，布迪厄作为欧洲社会学中心的

---

① Grenfell, Michael. *Pierre Bourdieu: Key Conceptions*. Durham: Acumen Publishing Limited, 2008: 51.

秘书，发展出了很多社会学理论的关键概念，如"文化资本""习性"和"场域"等，但此时这些概念并未被细致地实际运用，而是为社会学的存在提供佐证。20世纪60年代，布迪厄致力于通过实践活动证明以上的关键概念揭示了某种现象存在的因果关系，而非只是理论上的预测。1986年，布迪厄认为实践是处于场域和惯习之间的一种"无意识的关联性"，并提出场域理论等式来诠释这种关系。他认为这三个思想工具是自然绞合在一起的。场域这一概念和分析单位来自他早年的人类学研究，场域中充满着力量和竞争，个体可选择不同的竞争策略，资本既是竞争的目的又是竞争的手段。场域有自主化的趋势但场域本身的自主性又受到外来因素的限制。①

布迪厄的概念包括场域理论是社会学的起源，也是了解具有实践性的社会现象的手段。他所提出的社会学概念在20世纪80年代末已经成为美国引用率最高的相关概念之一。场域理论也在社会科学、传播学等领域被频繁使用。

本文以布迪厄的场域理论为框架，按照传播范围、传播手段和过往积累三个因素分析对比孔子学院和歌德学院的海外传播效果。

（二）场　域

场域指的是一个竞争性游戏开展的社会场所，其中的行动者（人或者机构）用各种不同的方式提高自己在该场所中的位置。在本文中，场域被赋予地理和文化因素，即从地理角度和文化角度分析中英文化传播机构的全球布局。

1.英国文化教育协会在全球布局情况

截至2015年，英国文化教育协会已在全球110个国家和地区设立230个办事处，除英国本土外，其将全球网络分为七个大区，分别是：美洲、东亚、欧洲欧盟地区、中东和北非、南亚、撒哈拉以南非洲以及泛欧地区。其中，美洲11个国家，东亚13个国家，欧洲欧盟地区28个国家，中东和北非16个国家，南亚6个国家，撒哈拉以南非洲20个国家，泛欧地区16个国家。②

2.孔子学院在全球布局情况

截至2023年底，孔子学院已在全球149个国家和地区设立553个孔子学院，按照七大洲的分部布局来看，其中，美洲24个国家，设有68个孔子学院；亚洲37个国家，设有165个孔子学院；欧洲33个国家，设有221个孔子

---

① 李全生.布迪厄场域理论简析.烟台大学学报，2002，15(2)，146-150.
② 李全生.布迪厄场域理论简析.烟台大学学报，2002，15(2)，146-150.

学院；非洲 50 个国家，设有 74 个孔子学院；大洋洲 5 个国家，设有 25 个孔子学院（见图1）。

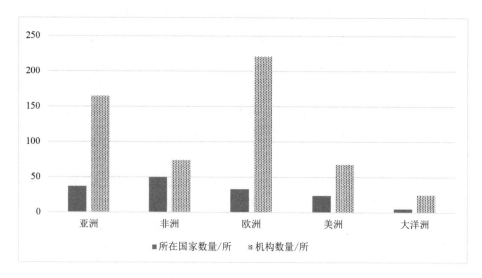

图 1　各地区孔子学院所在国家和孔子学院数量

（资料来源：https://www.ci.cn/qqwl）

（三）惯　习

惯习指的是一种客观上根据其被构成时所处环境的具体情况进行调整的、后天习得的生成图示。也就是说，惯习是与人有关的，并非自然形成的，而是有意识被操控的。本文将惯习视作语言文化传播机构区域化推广政策，并基于此分析推广效果。

1.英国文化教育协会的推广政策

从国家和地区合作来看，英国文化教育协会目前已经与世界上 100 余个国家展开交流合作，且在不同地区实行区域化推广政策。

英国文化教育协会致力于与英国联系较为紧密的发达国家积极开展文化交流项目，通过提供奖学金的方式支持双方国家学生进行跨国文化交流。例如2013 年，协会大力推进美国和泛欧洲地区建成跨北大西洋的每秒能传输 100 GB 数据的网络，这一举动有效地促进了欧美地区教育和文化机构之间进行快捷、有效地交流。在该网络服务至 2020 年时，服务范围也从教育和文化合作方面扩展到两岸多家互联网公司，文化合作有效带动了经济发展。

英国文化教育协会致力于同与英国合作日渐紧密的发展中国家进行深一步

的文化交流和合作，促进互相理解和共同发展；英国非常重视与这些国家和地区的合作，尤其是非洲地区，他们希望能够在非洲地区得到更多的民众支持。东南亚国家经济发展迅速，留学生所占比例逐年增加，因此英国文化教育协会多年来不懈地支持东南亚地区英语教师和教研员发展，提高英语教学水平。例如，2023年6月英国文化教育协会在线上为英语教师制作指导教学视频，开展线上研讨会，发布面向一线教师的回顾视频等。

2.孔子学院的推广政策

目前来说，孔子学院依托共建"一带一路"倡议，以较高的质量传播和发展了汉语文化。在"一带一路"周边国家和地区，孔子学院分布较为分散，泰国、俄罗斯以及沿线欧洲国家的孔子学院较多。但对于那些实际上与中国经济文化交往密切的国家，孔子学院数量却没有相应地增加，如缅甸。

孔子学院在国际合作中所推广的文化活动较为单一，主要集中在汉语传播和中国文化传播方面。虽然我们已经在部分地区设立特色孔院，且获得了一定的正面反响，但仍然没有针对不同区域制定区域化策略和政策。

（四）资 本

资本指的是在场域内的竞争品的积累。在本文中，资本指的是文化资本，即中英两国的原始文化基础及在多年发展历程中获得的文化资本积累。

英国作为老牌的工业国家，文化辐射的面积较大，如将英语作为官方语言使用的国家分布在欧洲、美洲、大洋洲甚至一些非洲、亚洲国家。而中华文化历史悠久，具有独特的文化魅力和吸引力。两国在文化的原始基础上各有千秋。

英国文化教育协会成立于1934年，向外传播英国文化的意识觉醒较早。且英语作为国际通用语言，具有天然优势，例如，世界各地年轻人在学习英语，准备雅思考试的过程中会逐步了解英国现代社会的价值观念，因此英国文化的资本积累过程较为顺利。孔子学院成立于2004年，成立时间短，加之部分外国媒体和民众对中国文化有刻板印象，所以相比之下，文化的资本积累并不顺利。但孔子学院依靠独特的双方高校合作的运行机制，坚持线下教学，以学习者对中华传统文化的兴趣为锚点，开展各类丰富多彩的学习活动，学习者好评如潮，中华文化的资本积累也在稳步发展中。但孔子学院在文化传播过程中过于重视优秀传统文化，如中药文化、京剧文化等，忽视了对现代社会文明及中国价值观的传播。

（五）实　践

实践即为场域和惯习、资本因素影响下导致的最终结果。在本文中，文化传播机构的推广效果是实践的关键。

1.场域视角下中英文化传播机构在推广效果上的差异

从地理角度出发，传播路径越短，文化传播效果越佳，因为文化传播者和学习者在同一地理场域内流动的意愿大于跨地理场域流动的意愿；从文化角度出发，倘若两国文化距离较小，那么东道国民众只需短时期的接触和学习即可理解文化的逻辑和魅力；反之，倘若两国文化距离较大，那么来自异域的文化在当地很有可能会因宗教信仰、历史传统等原因而面临短期内无法弥合"文化折扣"的问题。

英国文化教育协会在欧盟设立办事处的国家数量最多。英国地处欧洲，在欧洲进行文化传播的路径较短。英国的学者相比于横跨欧亚大陆的东亚更愿意在欧洲其他发达国家进行英语教学和文化传播。且欧洲各国之间文化壁垒不强，利于英语及英国文化的传播。例如，欧洲语言大多属于罗曼语族或日耳曼语族，且均为字母书写形式，欧洲人接受英语的能力远高于接受方块字的能力，学习者学习中文困难颇多，在过程中学习兴趣减退，导致不能长期学习，抑或学习者较少，导致推广行动受阻等情况的发生。孔子学院所涉及国家较多的地区是亚洲和非洲，在相对较短的传播路径下，合作效率提高，产生的文化推广效果好。例如，在共建"一带一路"国家，虽然开设孔子学院数量仅为欧洲地区开设孔子学院数量的三分之一左右，但学习者数量却与欧洲地区学习者数量持平。这也侧面印证了文化场域在文化传播过程中的重要意义。

2.惯习视角下中英文化传播机构在推广效果上的差异

英国文化教育协会对待欧洲发达国家和东南亚经济发展迅速的国家，以及撒哈拉沙漠以南极度不发达地区的政策区别十分鲜明。孔子学院可以借鉴其中优势，制定区域化文化推广政策。例如，加大在共建"一带一路"国家中的中国文化及价值观的传播力度；在欧洲极度发达地区多进行文化交流互鉴活动；在对中华文化认知程度低的地区进行由点到面的宣传，从当地居民的兴趣点出发，从而使中华文化逐渐走出去。

同时，孔子学院可以充分利用世界各地的侨胞资源。英美因为没有语言交流障碍，故而能仅以文化传播机构为节点，进行学术甚至商业方面的合作，并在过程中不断传播英国文化。孔子学院也可加大在新加坡等地区的合作及交流力度，以华侨和语言为基石，实现更加深度的合作。

3.资本视角下中英文化传播机构在推广效果上的差异

布迪厄在《区隔》一书中提出文化资本的两种再生产方式：家庭教育传承文化资本和通过学校教育积累文化资本。中英双方文化推广机构都将着眼点放置于通过学校教育积累文化资本的方式上。英国文化教育协会凭借天然优势，以英语考试的形式使学习者自主地积累英国文化资本。孔子学院则依托中外高校合作办学模式，让更多身处大学的年轻人能够直接接受中华文化传播。但孔子学院的办学模式在独具优势的前提下，也有弊端。例如，在一些经济不发达的国家和地区，能够承办孔子学院的大学过少，亦或外方院长的人选十分受限，无法落实孔子学院在该地区的建设，传播文化路径受阻。孔子学院可以在保留自身优势的情况下，对传播手段稍作变革，例如，借鉴英国文化教育协会的线上教学模式，为暂时没有条件设立孔子学院的地区提供学习汉语的机会；开展活动主题不拘泥于传统文化，可以紧随全球关注的热点问题，如气候问题等开展相关活动。

五、结　语

基于对英国文化教育协会的研究，英国文化教育协会在文化传播过程中更注重文化的双向传播，在不同文化地域采取因地制宜的政策。在工作内容上传播了一系列艺术、教育、社会的文化内容，在结合全球热点、满足受众群体心理预期的同时，潜移默化地推广了自身的文化。协会既传播了英语重要性的观念，又指出了社会需求的变化，能引起中国受众的反馈，形成双向传播。相比较之下，孔子学院的网络传播缺少了对不同受众语言的考虑，因而影响了双向传播的效果。

根据布迪厄的"场域＋惯习＋资本＝实践"等式，本文认为孔子学院在推广政策、价值资本累积方面还做得不足。在实践中，孔子学院做到了在邻近的文化场域内推广自身文化和发展受众数量，但在因地制宜实施推广方面还做得不够充分，因而可能会导致文化冲突和推广受阻。此外，在部分教学资源和经济条件落后的国家，孔子学院需要采取更加符合当地情况的教学方式来提供教学资源。结合上述建议，孔子学院在文化推广方面可能会做得更好，在宣传中国价值观念上发挥更积极的作用，为推动中华文明走向世界贡献更大的力量。

孔子学院本土化适应性案例研究
——以新加坡南洋理工大学孔子学院为例[①]

摘　要： 孔子学院是中华文化"走出去"的重要载体。本文聚焦孔子学院本土化适应性问题，以新加坡南洋理工大学孔子学院作为典型案例进行分析，总结其在中文教材本土化、教学培训与教学模式本土化、"乐学善用，深广课程"的教学理念落实以及运行管理机制本土化等方面的成功经验，以期为全球孔子学院本土化适应性发展提供参考。

关键词： 新加坡南洋理工大学孔子学院；本土化；适应性研究

一、研究背景与意义

费孝通先生曾言，"各美其美，美人所美，美美与共，天下大同"。在世界文化多样性的环境中，面对文化传播的天然排异性，文化分歧和文化冲突必然存在。因此，要想让自己的文化在异域中生存、生长、开花、结果、繁衍生息，实现"美美与共"，必须寻求与当地文化的融合，求同存异，才是长存之道。

孔子学院是"中外合作建立的非营利性教育机构，旨在促进中文传播，加深世界人民对中国语言文化的了解，推动中外人文交流，增进国际理解"[②]。孔子学院要想在异域开花结果，就必须加快推进本土化，促进融合发展。只有更好地适应各国社会和文化环境，让开放包容的种子生根发芽，孔子学院才能枝繁叶茂，保持旺盛的生命力。

孔子学院本土化是国际中文教育本土化的重要表现和内容。国际中文教育

① 作者：牛万一，山东大学国际教育学院汉语国际教育专业；张馨匀，山东大学外国语学院法语专业；张馨，山东大学哲学与社会发展学院社会学专业。
② 中国国际中文教育基金会：走进孔子学院．[2023-10-31]. https://www.cief.org.cn/zjkzxy.html.

本土化指的是中文教育在遵循语言文化国际教育和传播内在规律的前提下，通过服务当地教学对象、满足其对中文的多元需求，为适应当地经济、文化、教育体制、法律制度、文化习俗和语言使用情况等所做出的调整或优化措施[①]，体现了国际中文教育逐步融入当地因素、逐渐具有当地特色的发展趋势，是最深刻和最有效的发展模式之一[②]。孔子学院的本土化也应"与所在国家的文化环境相交融，融入社区、服务大众，贴近当地民众思维、习惯、生活的方式，满足民众多样化需要"[③]。如今，孔子学院总部和各地孔子学院在本土化发展方面不断加大融入力度，在教师本土化、教材本土化、教法本土化、教学管理本土化等方面采取了一系列切实有效的措施，以推动孔子学院教学活动日益贴近当地国情地情和当地民众的需要。

孔子学院本土化问题与当下研究的热点问题——"三教"问题紧密相关。"三教"问题，指的是汉语教学中的教师、教材和教法的问题。在国际中文教育的发展过程中，三教问题已经成为制约国际中文教育本土化进程的关键性问题。随着各种鼓励汉语教学本土化的项目的展开，其中存在的三教问题也逐渐暴露出来，引起了有关部门和业内专业人士的重视。比如，未能与当地国民教育体系真正接轨；汉语教学和课程得不到"官方"认可；汉语师资培养与需求错位；教材本土化存在难以顾及海外汉语学习的各种不同需求；教学方式单一、缺乏创新等。如何处理孔子学院本土化中教师、教材和教法的问题，目前仍然是孔子学院本土化研究的重中之重。

本土化是孔子学院发展的必然、实然与应然，国际中文教育本土化更是国际中文教育可持续发展的内在要求。本文以国际中文教育本土化和三教问题为导向，以新加坡南洋理工大学孔子学院（以下简称南大孔院）为典型性案例，对其本土化教材、本土化教学培训与教学模式、"乐学善用，深广课程"的教学理念和教学方法、不断完善的内部管理机制和运行机制等内容进行研究与分析，总结出可供借鉴和推广的成熟经验，不仅有助于孔子学院的可持续发展，而且也为其他区域的中文教育本土化发展提供参考和借鉴，有利于增强国际中文教育精准服务能力、深化中外语言文字交流合作、提升中文国际地位和影响力。

① 李秋杨，陈晨，奥斯卡·费尔南德斯·阿尔瓦雷斯.西班牙中文教育本土化特征、动因与发展策略.语言文字应用，2022，(2): 15-25.
② 李宝贵，刘家宁.新时代国际中文教育的转型向度、现实挑战及因应对策.世界汉语教学，2021，35(1): 3-13.
③ 李丹."一带一路"背景下孔子学院本土化发展路径研究.北京：中国社会科学出版社，2020: 214.

二、研究设计

本文主要采用案例研究方法，选择南大孔院为典型性国别化适应性案例。

案例法是质性研究的基本方法之一，是将研究对象的一些典型特征做全面、深入的考察分析，从而得出带有普遍性结论的研究方法。案例研究的方法可以帮助我们从具体经验事实走向一般理论，还可以为其他类似案例研究提供解释和启发。

南大孔院是新加坡唯一一所孔子学院，也是全球优秀孔子学院之一，在中文教育本土化发展方面具有显著的代表性。它充分结合当地的实际情况，利用其自身优势开发出了一套完善的教学模式，并取得了良好的效果，为新加坡华语学习者提供了良好的契机。

因此，本文选择案例法，广泛搜集南大孔院的相关资料，对其在教材、教师、教法以及运行机制四个方面的本土化运作进行分析。并辅以深度访谈，采访多位曾在南大孔院任教的中方教师，对南大孔院的国际中文教育情况进行深层次的挖掘和了解，从而给其他孔子学院发展提供可参考的启示与借鉴。

三、本土化案例分析——新加坡南洋理工大学孔子学院

南大孔院成立于 2005 年 7 月 20 日，协作单位为中国国际中文教育基金会与山东大学，院址为南洋理工大学纬壹校区的行政中心教学大楼第八层。[①]南大孔院致力于将新加坡的语言文化与教育理念相结合，建立了完善的课程体系和权威的教师团队，采取可持续发展的办学模式。通过对南大孔院的案例研究，可以总结其成功经验，为其他孔子学院提供借鉴。

新加坡的文化可以大致划分为汉字文化圈和非汉字文化圈。汉字文化圈是一个涵盖汉字使用者、汉字传承者以及汉字文化遗产的地区，这些人更容易接受中华文化的思想，而非汉字文化圈则更加注重其他文化的发展。新加坡华人属汉字文化圈受众，其他三个民族均属非汉字文化圈受众。因此，南大孔院的课程体系既需要满足汉字文化圈受众对文化广度和深度的要求，又要引起非汉字文化圈受众对中华文化的兴趣。因此，它的语言项目课程体系包括四大模块、十种类型，受教育群体几乎涵盖各个年龄层次和各种水平需求。

---

① 南洋理工大学孔子学院官网 . [2023-10-31]. https://www.ntu.edu.sg/ci.

（一）教材的本土化

"状元学堂"是南大孔院专为学前及中、小学生提供母语强化及辅助课程的一个品牌，15年来，它已经发展出一系列的旗舰课程，曾在这里就读的学生已多达上万名。状元学堂通过举办丰富多彩的课程，激发幼童对华语学习的兴趣，并向他们传递中华优秀文化与价值观。

状元学堂的每门课程均采用自主研发的系列教材。例如，2018年1月出版的《状元学堂·亲亲华文》就是由南洋理工大学孔子学院和山东师范大学联手推出的全新华语学习教材。这套教材经过两年的精心设计，涵盖了544份教学资料、68本精彩的故事书、16本精美的作业册以及2800多张精美的图片，旨在满足3到6岁孩子学习华语的需求。该教材的制作团队共有五人，团队虽然与国内高校合作，但在教学语境上坚持使用新加坡本地学生熟悉的词汇和语法，因此，团队中的四人是土生土长的新加坡人，且均毕业于南洋理工大学中文系。

为提高课堂的趣味性，每本教材还配有"点读笔"。配音团队并不强求"字正腔圆"的语调，而是希望通过熟悉的语调让学生更加亲近华语。此外，这些绘本还涵盖了新加坡的政府建筑、美食、历史人物和交通工具，以及不同族群庆祝的节日。①

新加坡的地理位置使得这里成为一个让海内外商务人士纷至沓来的热门目的地，特别是那些希望在中国进行商业拓展的客户。南大孔院为其开设了商务汉语培训课程，他们编写了专门的汉语教材《今日商务》，这套6册的教材涵盖了低中高三个阶段商务汉语内容，不仅包含了丰富的商务活动文章，而且结合了新加坡当地文化的特色，可以满足各个水平的职场从业者的需求，是一套全面的、可靠的商务华文学习资源。②

近几年，新加坡非华族儿童学习华语的人数日益增加，对华语教师数量的需求逐渐加大，专业性要求也逐渐增高。南大孔院针对这一现状，与南洋理工大学、山东大学、北京语言大学等高校合作开设汉语教学教育专业文凭课程，如果学生考核通过，就会获得由南洋理工大学和南大孔院共同颁发的汉语教学教育专业文凭毕业证书。《中文应用文写作》一书就是旨在满足孔子学院汉语

---

① 南洋理工大学孔子学院. 历时两年推出学前教材《状元学堂·亲亲华文》. (2018-01-02)[2023-10-31]. https://www.163.com/dy/article/D75OCUQ20516A53E.html.
② 佚名.新加坡孔子学院自行研发出版商务汉语教材.海外华文教育动态，2011，000(9)：69.

国际教育专业的应用文写作教学需求，由孔子学院的寇红教授用三年的时间编辑而成的。此书通过大量本土及中国的案例，探讨了七种不同类型的中文应用文的写作技巧，并通过详细的指导与演练，让读者更容易理解。①

（二）教师的本土化

南大孔院提供了多种形式的汉语教师培训，包括短期的集中培训、国内承办院校的巡回示范以及长期的提高课程。这些培训旨在帮助汉语教师在日常教学中不断提升自己的教学能力，并通过个别指导和帮助来满足不同水平和层次的汉语教师需求。此外，南大孔院还有针对性地培养教师们的科研意识和能力，以确保教师资源的长期发展。

南大孔院注重培养教师的科技素养、适应能力和学术能力，十分重视师资培训。孔子学院内部设置智慧教室、讲堂，多媒体教学用具；多次开展高端汉语教学论坛，定期邀请各大高校优秀教师进行教学培训；通过集体备课帮助新进教师了解创新适合当地教育体制的教学模式，确保汉语学习的实用性与趣味性。

南大孔院的教师来源非常多元，有当地拥有文凭的教师，也有中国派出的志愿者等，还有为了专门课程邀请的各专业学者。例如，当地著名历史学者柯木林博士曾担任南大孔院"石叻坡旧忆：人物·事件·沧桑"课程的主讲人。在课上，他以清朝驻新加坡首任领事官左秉隆、北洋水师访问新加坡的历史反思、古典诗文中的新加坡等4个主题讲述新加坡跟中国的历史和文化渊源，帮助学员更好地理解和认识新中关系。②

（三）教法的本土化

南大孔院为新加坡的大、中、小学校，社会团体，政府机构和个人提供了传统的语言和文化课程，在儿童中文教学方面始终坚持"乐学善用"的理念。该理念有如下特点：第一，将语言和文化作为儿童华文教学的双翼，虽未能达到平行发展，但始终坚持语言与文化相互促进，将华文课程打造成独特的语言文化综合产品；第二，较好地平衡和稳定了不同课型、不同科目的发展态势，力求使每一位拥有不同年龄、不同语言背景、不同学习目标、不同个性学能的

---

① 新加坡南洋理工大学孔子学院推出新书. (2019-03-25)[2023-10-31]. https://baijiahao.baidu.com/s?id=1628955180456359039&wfr=spider&for=pc.
② 南洋理工大学孔子学院将开办"石叻坡旧忆"课程. [2023-10-31]. https://www.chinanews.com/hwjy/2010/09-10/2524994.shtml.

儿童都能找到适合自己的中文课程；第三，创新求变，凸显特色，通过使用符合新加坡当地需要的本土化中文教材，树立起南大孔院的独特品牌，有效增强课程对儿童及家长的吸引力。

任课教师基本做到了将"乐学善用"理念所提出的丰富教学手段、创新教学方法的原则贯穿在课堂环节发展的始终，在对历史上不同流派的第二语言教学方法进行改良式借鉴的基础上，综合利用了经验派的视听法和听说法，认知派的认知法，以及由功能派教学法发展而来的任务型教学法，教学手段丰富。更为可喜的是，任课教师能够将上述诸多教学方法合理地安排到不同的教学环节之中，使不同的教学方法通过相互配合从而实现扬长避短、优势互补的良好效果，最终达到所用即所需的信手拈来，无论哪种教学方法都能够有效促成教学目标实现的理想状态。而游戏形式和网络资源的借鉴与利用，也能够大大增强中文课堂的趣味性，符合"乐学"之要求。

南大孔院还举办了一系列有益的活动来促进语言与文化学习，如语言比赛、学术交流、新书出版等，这些活动不仅推动了中文、中华文化和中国研究在新加坡及东南亚地区的发展，还获得了社会各界的认可。

（四）运行机制的本土化

孔子学院自创办至今，坚持"科学定位、突出特色""政府支持、民间运作""中外合作、内生发展"和"服务当地、互利共赢"的基本原则。南大孔院通过完善内部管理机制、主动开展评估等方式，公开透明运作，不断提升管理水平和社会认可度，构建了多维度的共享信息监督体系，中外合作运行机制日趋完善。

南大孔院的组织结构非常明确，层级性、网格式的组织结构能够保证孔子学院实现从宏观决策、规划策略到工作执行监督控制一系列运作流程的顺畅；能够保证孔子学院内部的信息、资源的交流分配。合理的组织架构能够为孔子学院的运作提供高效的人员配置，全面覆盖市场化运作所应该具有的管理决策、监督控制、项目规划和资源分配、具体工作执行四个层面。除院长和文化交流处处长外，细分为财务部、人事部、成人部、少儿部以及文化部，最后三个部门负责孔院课程项目的直接执行。每个部门针对自己的目标对象和部门目标执行工作计划，整个孔院的运作分工明确，高效有序。[1]

---

[1] 王琦.孔子学院市场化运作初探——基于南洋理工大学孔子学院的分析.济南：山东大学，2016：69.

四、南洋理工大学孔子学院本土化适应对其他孔子学院发展的启示

孔子学院源自中国，办在海外，无论是置身海外的机构设置，还是中外合作的办学模式，都决定了孔子学院开展教学不仅需要国内政策的支持和中国办学人员的努力，也离不开外方机构在资源统筹以及管理运营上的配合。因此，本土化发展是孔子学院加强中外文化交流互动、融入所属国家地区的社会与文化、实现可持续发展的必然要求。

南大孔院因地制宜实施教学，成功融入当地，加强中外文化交流互动所使用的战略方法，为孔子学院本土化适应提供了启示和借鉴。

（一）加强本土教师培训和中方教师本土化培训工作

南大孔院实行本土师资学历教育的机制，是加强本土教师培训、发挥教师主动性的一个优秀范例。本土教师是海外语言教学的主体，他们与学生的交流没有语言障碍，而且熟悉当地教学模式以及当地学生的学习特点和学习文化，具有更丰富的本地教学经验。因此，孔子学院应当建立本土化的师资培养体系，培养一批喜欢和了解中国文化、汉语交际能力较强的本土教师。除此之外，还可以让他们成为"种子教师"，进一步培养更多本土教师。

另外，对于中方每年向海外派出的汉语教师，也应该加强对他们的本土化培训工作。传统的培训工作更加注重对外汉语教学知识和方法的培训，在此基础上还应增设有关赴任国的国情、文化和语言的培训，如开展小语种培训班，或组织课程深入了解当地的国情和文化习俗，以便在教学过程中最大程度地避免文化偏见、文化误解等，从而顺利推动教学进程的开展。

（二）大力推进国际汉语教材本土化

海外汉语学习教材要符合当地学生特点。"本土化"教材的内容选择包括词汇、话题等都要准确地表现出本土的风俗人情，并且做到与时俱进，体现时代背景；此外，教材内容还应充分考虑到当地汉语学习者母语的特点，针对他们在学习汉语中可能遇到的困难，强调教材编写的重难点；另外，教材编写最好由中外教师合作，由于本土汉语教师更加熟悉当地语言文化，国内学者对汉语语言理解更加精深，双方合作编写当地的汉语教材，会更适合当地学习者。[①]

[①] 周啸生.埃及开罗大学孔子学院汉语教学本土化研究.海外英语，2018(2)：152-153+179.

（三）灵活调整教学方法，满足当地受众需求

南大孔院充分考虑到了学习者的汉语水平和学习动机，这一点也值得其他孔子学院学习。孔子学院在教学的过程中，应该灵活调整教学方法以适应不同的受众需求，例如，对于主要出于兴趣而学习汉语的少年儿童和大学生群体，应该注重课堂的趣味性，通过游戏和活动等教学方法，改善课堂氛围；对于出于实际生存和工作需要而学习汉语的群体，则应该增加教学方法的实用性和有效性。此外，对外汉语教师应该与当地学生进行交流互动，通过了解所在国的文化，改善自己的教学方法和教学质量。

（四）建立特色本土运营机制，加强中外合作

南大孔院构建了完善的组织结构，从而保障了行政管理体系、监督体系和市场运营体系的高效运转，体现了因地制宜建立管理制度的重要性。首先，南大孔院的市场化运营模式长期稳定运行，具有很强的可行性和可持续性，值得借鉴和推广；其次，应完善孔子学院的各项规章制度，实现明确的行政分工并建立明晰的组织架构，以确保运营机制的高效运作；最后，应加强中外方人员合作，通过创造良好的工作氛围和工作机制，有效调动本土资源，促进孔子学院深入本土发展。

五、结　语

孔子学院的海外实践不应只是中国语言与文化的单方面输出，更应该为促进海内外人文交流融合、海内外民众民心相通搭建桥梁，而孔院的本土化发展就是推动中国文化与所在国文化交流的关键。

本文围绕三教问题和本土化发展等热点问题展开研究，对新加坡南洋理工大学孔子学院在教材、教师、教法、运营方面的成功经验进行了提炼分析，认为实现三教和运行机制的本土化，是孔子学院实现本土化发展的必然要求。从南大孔院这一优秀案例出发，本文得出了通过培训提升教师队伍本土化水平、编写符合当地特色的本土教材、因地制宜丰富教学方法、完善与当地的合作运营机制的建议，希望能够为各国孔子学院因地制宜开展教学提供一系列可借鉴的思路，推动孔子学院在世界文化交流的实践中发挥更积极的作用。

文化观念视角下国际语言传播机构发展战略的比较研究
——以塞万提斯学院、孔子学院为例①

摘　要: 孔子学院和塞万提斯学院是全球两所主要的语言文化推广机构。本研究以孔子学院与塞万提斯学院的年度报告为依据,通过查询国内外文献,利用跨文化传播、语言传播动力机制理论和汉字语素文字说,从文化观念的角度比较分析两个机构的主要发展战略差异。研究发现,孔子学院和塞万提斯学院主要在设立地区、传播内容、考试体系话语权三个方面存在差异。在此基础上,本研究发现二者代表的文化观念中,主要存在着文化血缘、教育观念、民族性格三个方面的差异。有鉴于此,本文对孔子学院未来发展提出以下建议:一是发挥文化地缘优势,逐步扩大孔子学院影响范围;二是加强孔子学院创新化、本土化建设;三是建立更加广泛的合作关系;四是积极把握舆论导向,加强国内外媒体合作,充分发挥传媒作用。

关键词: 塞万提斯学院;孔子学院;发展战略;文化观念

一、引　言

(一)研究背景

党的二十大报告指出,实现中华民族凝聚力和中华文化影响力不断增强是未来全面建设社会主义现代化国家的主要目标任务之一。②在全球化的背景下,

---

① 作者:杨欣馨,武汉大学心理系;张莽月,武汉大学西班牙语系;黄文伟,武汉大学西班牙语系;黄靖雯,武汉大学中国语言文学系。指导老师:秦剑,武汉大学西班牙语系。
② 王曼倩.文化强则民族强 文化兴则国家兴 不断增强中华民族凝聚力和中华文化影响力.人民日报,2023-05-12(9).

语言文化传播机构在推动国内外文化交流与合作、促进文化多样性与对话等方面发挥着重要作用。

西班牙语是仅次于英语的第二大语种。世界上使用西班牙语的国家众多，地域遍布美洲、加那利群岛、北非、伊比利亚半岛和中东。在全球化的大背景下，中国与西班牙语国家的政治、经济、文化的交流更加深入密切。西班牙语世界和汉语世界都拥有悠久文明、数以亿计的语言使用者及饱经战争后对和平的珍视，因而西语世界的语言文化传播机构的发展思路亦可为中国文化"走出去"提供借鉴和参考。

综上所述，本文选择西班牙塞万提斯学院和中国孔子学院作为案例，对比两者的发展战略异同，探求背后文化观念差异，参考塞万提斯学院的对外发展经验，在增进中国与西语国家之间交流的同时，能够为中华文化更好地"走出去"提供借鉴。

（二）国内外研究评述

1. 国外研究评述

国外学者多从塞万提斯学院本身的发展目的、教学活动、文化活动等方面进行研究，而未将其与孔子学院做以对比。如德尔（Del Valle）指出，塞万提斯学院是西班牙在美洲宣传文化从而支撑该国经济和政治利益的手段。[1] 托尔（De la Torre）介绍了塞万提斯学院网络学习平台AVE（Aula Virtual de Español）的DELE（Diplomas de Español Como Lengua Extranjera）考试课程。[2] 科尔特斯（Cortes）等人指出，全球塞万提斯学院图书馆网络的合作有利于整合虚拟和现实的图书馆空间，使图书存储更加合理化，同时能够改善用户体验，提高服务质量和效率。[3] 马丁内斯（Martínez）分析了芝加哥塞万提斯学院2012年举办的活动及其对西班牙品牌创立和传播所发挥的作用。[4]

2. 国内研究评述

相较于国外学者，国内学者开拓了中西对比的研究思路。一部分学者对塞

[1] Del Valle, J., L. Villa. Spanish in Brazil: Language policy, business, and cultural propaganda. *Language Policy*, 2006(5).

[2] De la Torre, A. D., O. J. Lázaro, M. O. F. Tostado. Integración de recursos digitales en la enseñanza de español: Curso de preparación del Diploma DELE. (2016-03-31)[2022-07-21]. http://www.virtualeduca.org.pdf.

[3] Cortes I. M. M., M. V. V. Facal, Y. D. I. Sánchez. Cooperación en la Red de Bibliotecas del Instituto Cervantes. Dos ejemplos de actuación. *El profesional de la información*, 2010(5).

[4] Martínez P., A. Borrego, P. Dávila. Los Eventos Del Instituto Cervantes Y Su Influencia en la Creación Y Difusión de la Marca Espana. *Redmarka UIMA-Universidad de A Coruña*, 2013(1).

万提斯学院的运行模式进行了相关研究。葛海燕分析了塞万提斯学院语言文化传播的现状，指出该学院充分运用信息技术开展精神层面的文化传播活动。[①]杨敏阐明塞万提斯学院和孔子学院"在办学模式和共同对抗英语霸权方面有相同之处，但是在经营理念和哲学基础等方面有值得互相借鉴的地方"[②]。一部分学者在论文中将塞万提斯学院作为部分研究的对象，如张西平、柳若梅在专著《世界主要国家语言推广政策概览》中介绍了西班牙语言政策的历史、现状、推广机构、学科建设、奖励制度等方面的情况[③]；孙鹏程对孔子学院和国际语言推广机构进行了比较研究，谈及塞万提斯学院建设的基本要素[④]；吴建义从非营利性组织管理理论和语言经济学理论出发，对塞万提斯学院与孔子学院的推广方式进行了比较[⑤]；许丹在《西班牙塞万提斯学院与我国孔子学院异同探析》里对两者的开设背景、文化理念、办学模式、运营方式等异同做出了详细的比较[⑥]；黄玉芳和叶洪在《塞万提斯学院对孔子学院可持续发展的启示》中对以往国内外的研究做出了整合综述，并对塞万提斯学院的相关经验做出比较全面的分析，以供孔子学院借鉴[⑦]。

目前，国内外学界已对孔子学院和塞万提斯学院开展了大量研究，但是相关对比研究较少。本文以以往的研究为基础和参照，通过查询最新资料，参考最新视角进行两者的对比研究。

（三）研究对象

塞万提斯学院是西班牙政府设立的非营利性文化机构，致力于推广西班牙语言和西班牙文化。它在世界各地设立了分支机构和合作中心，提供西班牙语教学、文化交流、艺术展览和研究项目等。塞万提斯学院通过举办语言考试、文化活动和学术讲座，为学习者提供了深入了解西班牙和拉丁美洲文化的机会，并促进了国际跨文化交流与理解。作为一所拥有悠久历史和卓越学术声誉的高等学府，塞万提斯学院在其丰富多元的文化传统和传承中扮演着重要角色。

---

① 葛海燕.塞万提斯学院语言文化传播经验借鉴研究.南京：南京大学，2012.
② 杨敏.孔子学院与塞万提斯学院之比较——中国文化的现代意识与西班牙文化的后殖民主义.当代外语研究，2012(3).
③ 张西平，柳若梅.世界主要国家语言推广政策概览.北京：外语教学与研究出版社，2008：80-96.
④ 孙鹏程.孔子学院和国际语言推广机构的比较研究.济南：山东大学，2008.
⑤ 吴建义.孔子学院与四大语言文化推广机构对比研究.厦门：厦门大学，2014.
⑥ 许丹.西班牙塞万提斯学院与我国孔子学院异同探析.重庆第二师范学院学报，2014，27(1)：137-139.
⑦ 黄玉芳，叶洪.塞万提斯学院对孔子学院可持续发展的启示.湖北广播电视大学学报，2017，37(1)：43-47+52.

孔子学院是由中外合作建立的非营利性教育机构，致力于适应世界各国（地区）人民对汉语学习的需要，增进世界各国（地区）人民对中国语言文化的了解，加强中国与世界各国教育文化交流合作，发展中国与外国的友好关系，促进世界多元文化发展，构建和谐世界。[①]

（四）研究方法

本文主要通过查找多方史料和阅读多种文献，使用比较研究和半结构化访谈方式进行归纳、分析和总结。总体上，本文秉持实事求是、史料实证、孤证不立的研究原则与精神，对多方材料进行归纳和分析对比，进而得出结论。

1.比较研究法

通过比较研究，分析两个文化传播机构传播战略之间的异同。通过横向比较，深入分析，探讨机构的成功经验，从中提取可借鉴的经验和教训。

2.半结构化访谈法

本研究通过事先制定一些开放性的问题，使用面对面、互联网交流及电话等交流方式，对武汉大学西班牙语专业的相关教师及汉语国际教育专业的欧阳晓芳老师进行访谈，并在后期进行了内容分析和归纳，以获取详细信息。

（五）研究理论

1.跨文化传播理论

本文主要采用跨文化传播理论，其基本价值观是确认文化的差异性和多样性。确认文化的差异性和多样性的过程又是一个不断超越文化的过程，即不以自己所属文化群体的价值来判断其他文化群体的价值。[②]

本文通过探究不同发展战略背后的文化观念差异，借鉴塞万提斯学院的对外发展经验，以更好地了解海外人群的文化价值观，求同存异，以促进中华文化更好的传播。

2.语言国际传播动力机制

语言价值作为国际传播的根本动力，与外部因素一起决定了国际文化传播的深度与广度。语言的国际传播是内在的、外在的影响因素相互作用的过程，呈现出复杂的、非线性的动力机制特点。[③]本研究利用语言传播的自身特性和

---

① 孔子学院全球门户网. [2022-07-21]. https://www.ci.cn/gywm/pp.

② 单波. 跨文化传播研究的心理学路径. 湖北大学学报（哲学社会科学版），2008，175(3)：9-11.

③ 杨金成. 语言国际传播动力及动力机制. 河北大学学报（哲学社会科学版），2023，48(2)：68-76.

动力机制，在对比研究国际语言传播机构的同时，考虑个人与国际视野下的语言价值、语言传播环境和语言本身特点，在此基础上提出国际机构"走出去"的建议。

3. 汉字语素文字说

基于索绪尔（Ferdinand de Saussure）的表意文字说和布龙菲尔德（Leonard Bloomfield）的表词文字说，赵元任首次提出了汉字本质为语素文字的观点，将汉字基本单位记录的语言单位定为词素（同语素）。本研究以"汉字语素文字说"为依据，运用语言学对音素文字、音节文字与语素文字的分类理论，分析西班牙语与中文在语言单位、表音形式等方面的差异性和与其他国家语言的相似度，进而从语言差距的角度探讨西语和中文传播现状的成因。

二、文化机构发展现状

（一）孔子学院

1. 机构概况及宗旨

2004年，中国积极借鉴英、法、德等国家推广本民族语言的经验，在海外创立了非营利性教育机构孔子学院。2020年7月，孔子学院品牌由"中国国际中文教育基金会"全面负责运行。作为中华文化对外传播的重要交流平台，孔子学院在中华文化"走出去"中扮演着重要角色，始终积极传播中华传统文化，致力于推行儒家思想中现代性与世界性的内涵。孔子学院的建设旨在促进中文传播，加深世界人民对中国语言文化的了解，推动中外教育合作和人文交流。

2. 功能建设

孔子学院作为对外汉语教育机构，主要有提供汉语教育服务与资源、考试认证、信息咨询、文化活动、学术研究等功能。其中，最主要的功能是提供汉语教育服务与资源，并兼具考试认证、信息咨询等功能。孔子学院的文化活动类型多、受众广，包括地方孔子学院自行组织的各类活动及来华文化考察等；为加强中外合作交流，中国孔子学院积极开展学术研究项目、组织各类高端学术会议论坛，通过跨国的学术交流有力地推动了中国与世界各国的人文教育交流与合作，提升了中华文明学术地位与国际影响力。

3. 运营特色

孔子学院是一所综合性机构，主要的运营特色有采用中外合作办学模式、本地化运营、活动多样、开展学科交流合作等。孔子学院的组织结构主要表现为中外合作决策、本土化管理。[①]孔子学院的办学主体呈多元复合态势，由不同国家、不同体制、不同层级"办学主体"构成综合性语言与文化传播教育系统；孔子学院在各国设立分支机构和合作中心，注重本地化运营，因地制宜，"因材施教"：一方面，孔子学院根据当地母语思维来调整教学方法，使之更适应当地学生的学习习惯；另一方面，融合当地文化元素对中国文化活动进行本土化处理；孔子学院多样化的项目和活动涵盖汉语教学、艺术表演、学术研究等多个领域，并开设了中医、武术、商务等特色课程，在激发学生兴趣的同时提高了汉语的实用性；孔子学院也鼓励开展学科交流合作，促进不同领域的交流与融合，通过建立大学合作伙伴、教育机构合作伙伴、文化机构合作伙伴关系等方式建立国际合作伙伴网络。

（二）塞万提斯学院

1. 机构概况及宗旨

西班牙塞万提斯学院，最早追溯到成立于 1713 年的皇家西班牙语言文化学院（Real Academia Española）。西班牙于 1986 年加入欧洲共同体，从而加速了其语言的推广速度。[②]1991 年 3 月 21 日，西班牙国王宣布成立塞万提斯学院（Instituto Cervantes），其性质是非营利性官方机构。其职责是在全球范围内推广西班牙语的教学、研究和使用，并在境外推动西班牙语文化的传播，并致力于西班牙语大家庭共有的语言和文化遗产的推广。

2. 功能建设

从职能上来讲，塞万提斯学院致力于传播西班牙语和相关文化；从功能建设上来看，塞万提斯学院的项目主要由西班牙语教学、文化传播、图书馆构成。其中，教学课程包括实地面授教学和线上学习两种方式。同时，塞万提斯学院还开展了一系列文化项目和类型多样的文化活动；从课程设置上来看，语言教学是该机构的核心业务之一。学院提供的语言课程包括多种语言，以满足不同学员的需求。

3. 运营特色

塞万提斯学院课程教学质量高，从师资力量上来说，塞万提斯学院的教师

---

① 周汶霏，宁继鸣. 孔子学院的创新扩散机制分析. 中国软科学，2015(1): 77-87.

② 张雯. 当代国际语言推广机构在华语言推广研究. 长春: 吉林大学，2014.

队伍由来自西班牙和拉美地区国家的专业人士组成，具有丰富的教学经验和深厚的语言文化背景；塞万提斯学院运营方式多样化，学院采用多种教学方式，包括面授、在线教学、混合教学、游学等，以满足不同学生的需求；塞万提斯学院具有浓厚国际化特色，学院在全球范围内开展活动，与其他国家的语言和文化机构合作，促进跨文化交流；塞万提斯学院还得到了西班牙国家政府和各大企业的认可支持，资金丰厚。

总之，塞万提斯学院的运营特色主要表现在高质量的教学、丰富的课程设置、国际化的教育理念、多样化的教学方式、丰厚的资金和丰富的资源等方面，这些特色使得塞万提斯学院成为全球范围内备受推崇的语言和文化机构之一。

三、发展战略差异比较

（一）孔子学院

1.传播策略

据孔子学院全球门户网站的最新数据，截至 2023 年 12 月 31 日，496 所孔子学院和 757 个孔子课堂，分布在 160 个国家和地区。其中，亚洲共有 143 所孔院，111 所课堂；非洲有 67 所孔院，46 所课堂；欧洲有 183 所孔院，332 所课堂；美洲有 84 所孔院，193 所课堂；大洋洲有 19 所孔院，75 所课堂（见表 1）。从各大洲分布来看，发达国家的孔子学院较多，发展中国家相对较少。整体上呈现出合作大国、柔化周边、巩固传统、辐射全球的态势。

表1　孔子学院（课堂）分布数量

分布地	孔子学院/所	孔子课堂/所
欧洲	183	332
非洲	67	46
亚洲	143	111
美洲	84	193
大洋洲	19	75

2.传播内容：以汉语教学为主，逐渐创新

"孔子学院是经中国国际中文教育基金会授权，中外合作方本着相互尊重、友好协商、平等互利原则设立的非营利教育机构，旨在促进中文国际传播，加

深世界人民对中国语言文化的了解，增进中外教育人文交流。"①可见，孔子学院的宗旨是增进世界人民对中国语言文化的了解，发展中国与各国的友好关系，为全世界汉语学习者提供方便、优良的学习条件。②孔子学院的目标定位在于汉语教学和文化交流。

近年来，孔子学院吸收各方建议，进行了内容上的创新。除了普通的语言教学之外，孔子学院跨文化传播的内容广泛涉及中华文化的方方面面，如中医、武术、太极、舞蹈、旅游、音乐、书法、中国结、旗袍、京剧、皮影戏……③

3.教学考试：开展教学与考试培训，代设考试中心

孔子学院的主要任务是推广汉语和中国文化，提供汉语教学和文化交流的平台。孔子学院通常与国内的大学或教育机构合作，提供汉语课程和文化活动。而在全球汉语考试体系中，最为知名和权威的考试是HSK（Hanyu Shuiping Kaoshi，汉语水平考试）。HSK是中国教育部中外语言交流合作中心主办的一种汉语能力测试，旨在评估非母语者的汉语水平。HSK考试由孔子学院负责研发、组织和管理，并且其认证具有国际广泛认可度。

（二）塞万提斯学院

1.传播策略

在传播发展地区方面，和许多其他文化传播交流机构相似，塞万提斯学院坚持全球化传播的总体方向与战略。塞万提斯学院在全球范围内建立了广泛的合作网络，合作机构包括欧洲语言能力认证机构协会（The Association of Language Testers in Europe）等，并且在多个国家设有分支机构。这种跨国合作为学院提供了丰富的资源与机会，促进了西班牙语和西语文化的全球传播，同时扩大了其在跨文化教育领域的影响力。

值得一提的是，学院分部数量虽多，但创设的先后次序以及资源投入却有所讲究。目前，塞万提斯学院在美洲创设的分布数量已达十余个，而在中国境内仅仅于北京、上海两地创设支部。而与塞万提斯学院开展合作活动的国际组

① 孔子学院全球门户网. [2022-07-21]. https://www.ci.cn/gywm/pp.
② 杨敏. 孔子学院与塞万提斯学院之比较——中国文化的现代意识与西班牙文化的后殖民主义. 当代外语研究，2012 (3).
③ 陈海燕，涂绪谋. 跨文化传播视野下孔子学院发展战略研究. 四川省社会主义学院学报，2013，91(1): 30-33.

织与政府机关大部分也位于欧洲地区。这种看似"不平衡"的传播态势与战略使得西语文化与欧洲、美洲等地的文化距离与语际距离进一步缩短，同时也兼顾了西语文化在亚太地区的传播。

表2 塞万提斯学院分布数量①

分布地	数量 / 所
欧洲	40
美洲	15
非洲	13
亚洲	10

2.传播内容：传播内容多样化、创新化发展

在文化传播内容上，作为世界上最为权威的西班牙语语言及文化交流传播机构，塞万提斯学院在世界各地的学院开设语言教育课程的同时，也注重其他有助于文化交流与西语文化传播的内容创新。

以北京塞万提斯学院为例，学院官网显示，北京分院在2022年开展了包括与尤伦斯UCCA当代艺术中心合作的电影短片展在内的面向社会公众的一系列电影放映活动，举办了包括庆祝国庆节、劳动节、妇女节圆桌会议在内的面向学院师生以及国际人士的主题各异的会议活动，同时在院内开设如分级阅读俱乐部（Club de Lectura）等不定期开展的教育活动俱乐部。这些跨文化交流项目或教育课程遍布全球，参与门槛不高、可实施性强，在推动西语文化与其他语言文化的交流方面发挥了重要作用。

正如黄玉芳所言，塞万提斯学院的文化活动擅长以现代的方式来阐释传统的文化因素，其文化活动的多样性和现代性特征传递出包容开放的发展理念。②

3.教学考试：把握自身在全球西班牙语考试体系的核心话语权

塞万提斯学院不仅仅是西班牙语语言教育与西语文化传播机构，更是西班牙语言认证考试的核心机构。塞万提斯学院授权的西班牙语认证考试享有卓越的国际声誉，并被许多国家和教育机构广泛认可，学院负责考试的评估体系，并提供标准化的评估流程，衡量个人的西班牙语能力，在教育、职业、移民等领域具有重要的影响力。

---

① Instituto Cervantes. [2023-07-22]. https://cervantes.org/.
② 黄玉芳，叶洪. 塞万提斯学院对孔子学院可持续发展的启示. 湖北广播电视大学学报，2017，37(1): 43-47+52.

四、文化观念角度下的原因分析

在研究过程中，我们从"文化观念"这一视角出发，并综合考虑了其他影响因素对于文化传播机构推广语言文化的影响。

（一）文化血缘影响下的语言传播差异

受历史影响，在拉美地区，仍有大量西班牙语使用者。这一语言共同体有着文化亲缘性，提升了西班牙语及西语文化传播的效果，还促进了西班牙语言产业和国际影响力。同时，西班牙文化受欧洲影响较大，与欧洲文化距离较近，为其成为"应用圈"国家提供了便利。由此，西班牙将欧洲视为文化推广的基地，并借此积极扩大影响力至中国等更广阔地区。

相比之下，中国缺少全球性的母语文化圈，虽然有汉字文化圈，但其影响范围通常局限于周边地区。中国文明与西方文明有着明显的价值观和精神差异，因此在以西方文化为主流的环境下容易受到质疑和误解。且中国本身作为文化一脉相承的国家，语言内化水平高，这种特性有利于增强民族内部的认同感和凝聚力，但对于语言外化传播有一定限制性。

除了历史文化因素，语言本身也会对文化传播造成影响。现代包括西语在内的大多数语言均是音素文字。音素文字能够从代表音素的字母拼合成的单词推测其读音，但不能直接表示其意义。而汉字是语素文字，每一个字都是一个语音语义结合体，字形和语音的联系较弱。作为唯一使用至今的语素文字，汉语的性质与学习方式都具有独特性，与其他外语的关联性不强。此外，仅从书写角度看，汉字复杂的"方块体"与拼音文字的线性组合单词也具有较大差距，这无疑加大了汉语学习记忆的困难。所以，外国人士在选择学习的外语时，一般会倾向于与母语形式结构相近的西班牙语，而不是难度较大的汉语。

（二）中西两国教育观念差异

1.西班牙教育现代化观念对塞万提斯学院的影响

在研究文化传播机构差异的同时，我们关注到了西班牙教育观念对于塞万提斯学院的影响。针对这一问题，我们采用半结构化访谈方法，采访了数位武汉大学外国语言文学学院的西班牙籍教师，并在此基础上进行了分析研究。

采访中，多位外籍教师均指出，西班牙早期的教育被赋予"大师式"的色彩，教师形象带有专制色彩。但在实现教育的现代化转型后，西班牙教育坚持"以学生为中心"，尊重学生，尊重其能力和才华，并使其平等地融入集体。而根据学者Martin Skutil的研究成果，西班牙的课堂教学在关注学生自身能力的同时也重视学生的团队合作能力。[①]如此以学生为中心的教学与教育模式在塞万提斯学院的活动日程中也有所体现。以北京分院为例，学院官网显示，学院在2022年开设了如分级阅读俱乐部（Club de Lectura）等基于学生自身兴趣爱好的具有教育教学性质的俱乐部。

此外，在西方现代化教育理念的影响下，塞万提斯学院的西班牙语教学课程以及活动注重对语言的实际应用，其对语言使用的重视程度大于对语言知识本身的习得，而这恰恰与国内语言教学更加注重知识内容本身的习惯相异，也为汉语国际传播提供了借鉴。

2. 中国教育观对于孔子学院的影响

中国教育观一方面受到传统教育思想的影响，另一方面汲取了西方现代教育理念，具有独特的内容与表现形式。

在中国传统教育中，老师是起主导作用的。老师与学生除却教育者与被教育者的身份，还被授予了尊卑等级的礼法性质。这种观念特征对后世中国教育发展产生了一定影响。

中国近现代的应试教育与西方相较更注重教师所发挥的作用，依赖老师对所学知识的界定、分析与讲解，为学生搭建基本知识框架。这种框架有助于提高教学的效率与促进知识的规范化，但也简化了学生学习思考的过程，一定程度上削弱了其自主探究、概括与总结的能力。教学改革之后，孔子学院对这一新的教学观念变革也做出了可贵的探索，例如，增加了课堂互动，鼓励学生"开口"；丰富课程形式，举行文化体验等实践性操作，增强学生参与感等。虽然探索已有成效，但在学生个性化课程设置与启发学生学习积极能动性方面，孔子学院与塞万提斯学院相比仍然有着较大进步空间。

此外，孔子学院相较于赛万提斯学院更加注重语法等语言知识的传授，这同样与中国教育中对于理念知识的偏重观念与考察制度有关。一方面，这种策略有利于基本知识的巩固，为考试和进一步学习提供良好的理论基础，另一方面也有着削弱学习兴趣、思考应用不足等弊端。为克服这一缺陷，孔子学院积极求变，通过举行文化活动丰富教育内容。如2023年7月，全球多所孔子学院（课堂）举办端午节活动等，体现了孔子学院在创造文化体验与应用环境方

---

① Skutil, M. Teaching Methods in Primary School-Comparison of Approach in the Czech Republic and Spain // 2015 International Conference on Education Reform and Modern Management. Atlantis Press, 2015: 198-200.

面的积极性。孔子学院在坚持重视理论的教育战略的同时，也积极学习借鉴西方教育理论，对自身教育观念进行完善与发展。

（三）民族性格影响下的文化观念差异

1.西语民族性格特点视角下的塞万提斯学院

本文基于对专业教师的访谈资料以及相关史实与资料，对西班牙民族的性格特点进行了一定的探究以及总结。

西班牙民族具有坚韧不拔和自豪的民族性格，具有冒险、热情以及探索精神；此外，西班牙民族还具有反分裂意识、渴望和平的精神，以及对于民主价值观、多元性、包容性的提倡。

本小组认为，这样的民族性格在塞万提斯学院的传播战略、传播手段等方面产生了重要影响，如促使了塞万提斯学院在欧洲以及拉丁美洲的大部分地区进行分院建设以及文化传播。

2.中华民族性格视角下的孔子学院

经济、文化等因素的不同造就了中国和西班牙民族性格的差异性。总体而言，中华民族的性格呈现出以下几个突出特点。

相对于西班牙人民的热情奔放，中华民族的性格更加内敛含蓄。同时，与西方强调个人力量与价值不同，集体至上和爱国精神是中华人民秉持的重要观念。中华民族是开放包容、兼收并蓄的。中国的开放性体现在向外传播与向内融合的双向交流过程中，并且较西班牙更为深沉柔和。这种与周边国家和平共处、求同存异的发展态度有效增进了中国与周边国家的交流互鉴，实现了可持续的文化发展。

这些民族特质的形成离不开发达的农耕文明、统一多民族国家的发展历史与儒家主流文化等因素的综合影响。而这种含蓄内敛、开放包容、集体主义的民族性格也在孔子学院的文化传播中起到了重要作用，使之呈现出与塞万提斯学院的不同特点。孔子学院的传播方式更为温和，以寻求不同文明和睦相处的平衡点、加强文化间的交流互鉴为目标。

五、未来展望

（一）发挥文化地缘优势，逐步扩大影响力

在传播战略上，孔子学院可以借鉴塞万提斯学院的传播战略，在建立分院

的先后次序以及资源投入方面进行调查研究并做相应调整，科学谋划布局，接轨国家发展战略需要，合理利用文化距离，重视东亚文化圈、共建"一带一路"国家的孔子学院建设，提质增效，逐步扩大孔子学院影响力。

（二）加强创新化、本土化建设

在传播内容方面，孔子学院还可以将中华文化与现代生活结合得更紧密，不局限于传统文化，也可以关注中国当代国潮、电影、科技成果、文学作品等。

除此之外，还可以利用"国内高校＋"的优势。由高校牵头，在对接的孔院传播高校所在省市的特色中华文化，促进孔院传播内容创新，破除文化刻板印象，令外国群众了解更立体、更全面的中国。例如，与重庆市高校合作的孔院可以增加火锅底料制作、火锅品尝、成麻教学等特色课程和文化活动。

在传播方式上，利用中国"5G＋"的优势，线上线下结合教学。同时，利用TikTok（抖音）等国外影响力较大的视频软件，实时发布课堂学习内容和动态，创新传播方式，及时向外界展示真实的孔子学院，发展面向世界、面向未来的中华文化。

在教材编写、施教过程中，孔子学院应更加注重本土特征。事先调研当地的教学模式等实际情况，因地制宜地调整教材，既能更好地实现教学目标，又可以减少相关资源浪费。

（三）广泛建立合作，加强国内外联系

孔子学院可以与不同省市的教育局、文化部门等建立联系，合作开展师资培训计划，提供优质教师资源，共享教材、教学方法等资源，提高汉语教育质量，促进汉语教育和中国文化传播工作的合作与发展；与此同时，孔子学院还可以举办高校学术研讨会、文化活动等，推动中外学者之间的合作研究，深化文明交流互鉴，推动中华文化更好走向世界。

此外，孔子学院还可以加强与海外华人团体、社区组织的联系，合作举办文化节、艺术展览等活动，展示中国的传统文化与现代发展成就，并了解和满足他们在汉语学习、文化传承等方面的需求。同时，积极与海外华人组织合作开展汉语教师志愿者项目，邀请海外华人参与当地孔子学院的汉语教育工作，提供更多学习和交流机会，促进孔院师资力量的本土化发展，推动文化事业与文化产业的繁荣发展。

（四）充分发挥传媒作用，引起大众兴趣

孔子学院可以多与国内知名的国际传媒进行合作，通过新闻报道、专题采访等形式，在杂志、电视台等媒体上发布相关文章和节目，推广孔子学院的教育理念、文化传承与交流活动，让更多人了解并关注孔子学院的工作与成果。并且，要紧密关注孔子学院在国内外网络上的大众风评，及时发声应对负面舆论。

孔子学院还可以利用新兴媒体进行传播，开设官方账号，及时发布有关孔子学院的新闻、活动等内容，并宣传制作短视频、微电影大赛等活动，生动展示孔子学院的教学环境、师生互动、文化活动等，吸引观众和参与者，并传播积极正面的形象。

从"韩流"到"汉流"
——韩流与韩国世宗学堂对中国文化传播的启示研究[①]

摘　要: 本研究旨在探讨"韩流"现象如何刺激外语学习者学习韩语的动机,以及韩国世宗学堂如何利用"韩流"进行韩语教学和韩国文化传播。研究方法采用质性研究设计,使用扎根理论,通过半结构化访谈、网页内容收集资料,并进行三阶段编码分析。研究发现,学习者从追随韩流转向学习韩语的过程主要受三个核心因素影响,即模仿、理解和体验。与此同时,韩国世宗学堂也通过其学习网站,以模仿、理解和体验韩流文化为手段,为学习者提供多元的学习资源和互动平台,推动韩语教育及韩国文化传播。最后,本研究提出在中国文化传播方面借鉴"韩流"现象,促进"汉流"的形成与传播,促进跨文化融合与交流,提升汉语和中国文化的影响力,实现中国文化的可持续发展。

关键词: 韩流; 韩语学习; 韩国世宗学堂; 汉流; 汉语学习

一、引　言

随着全球化的不断推进和数字化技术的日新月异,文化传播已经取得了前所未有的发展和影响力。其中,"韩流"现象作为亚洲文化的一股重要潮流,引领了全球范围内的文化消费和外语学习趋势。韩国的音乐、电视剧、时尚以及美食等元素,如今已经渗透到了世界各地的生活之中,成为人们关

① 作者: 陈泽宁,上海交通大学教育学院; 闵熙媛,上海交通大学媒体与传播学院; 韩迪,上海交通大学电子信息与电气工程学院; 石越黎,上海交通大学南加大文化创意产业学院; 汪中伟,上海交通大学高级金融学院。

注和追求的焦点。

然而，这一文化现象不仅仅是娱乐产业的成功，它还对外语学习者的学习动机和文化交流产生了深远的影响。本研究旨在深入探讨"韩流"现象如何激发外语学习者学习韩语的动机，以及韩国世宗学堂如何善用"韩流"进行韩语教学和韩国文化传播。通过采用质性研究设计和扎根理论，本研究深入剖析了学习者从单纯追随"韩流"到积极学习韩语的过程，揭示了其中的核心因素：模仿、理解和体验。

同时，我们也关注韩国世宗学堂在这一背景下的作用。该学堂通过其学习网站，以模仿、理解和体验韩流文化为手段，为学习者提供了多元的学习资源和互动平台，推动韩语教育及韩国文化传播。这一研究不仅有助于深刻理解"韩流"现象对外语学习的影响，也为其他文化的传播与学习提供了借鉴和启示。

最后，本研究提出了一个激发思考的观点：中国文化传播是否能够借鉴"韩流"现象，促进"汉流"的形成与传播，推动跨文化融合与交流，提升汉语和中国文化的全球影响力，实现中国文化的可持续发展。这个问题将贯穿本研究的全过程，并将为我们提供新的思考视角。通过深入研究"韩流"现象，我们可以更好地理解文化传播和语言学习的关系，以及这种关系如何塑造了当今全球化时代的文化景观。

本研究为"韩流"现象对外语学习者在学习韩语过程中的动机以及世宗学堂在韩语教学与韩国文化传播中的角色方面，提供了启发性观点。此外，研究结果不仅为语言传播机构在推动文化与语言传播方面提供了理论支持，同时也为促进跨文化融合与交流、实现中国文化的可持续发展以及提升影响力，提供了有益的建议。

二、概念界定：韩流

1997年，韩国大众文化开始在中国流行，中国媒体第一次将此现象称之为"韩流"。"韩流"最初只被当作是"昙花一现"的流行文化形式，但随着时间的推移，它一反当初的预测，逐步在世界范围内掀起热潮。而在其整个发展过程中，"韩流"分成三个阶段逐渐扩大其影响范围，逐步在亚洲、全球流行。按照时间阶段，可将其划分为韩流1.0（1997—2010年）、韩流2.0（2010—

2012 年）、韩流 3.0（2012 年至今）三个阶段^①。

基于此，本文将"韩流"界定为自 20 世纪 90 年代末起，在中国范围内兴起的既包括韩国电视剧、偶像团体、电影、音乐、电子竞技等娱乐性事物，也包括语言、服饰、饮食、化妆品、旅游及其他具有韩国现代文化内涵的消费品等涉及面更为广泛的事物的韩国大众文化流行的现象。

三、文献综述

（一）韩流文化的形成与传播机制

韩流，指的是韩国流行文化在全球范围内的扩散与流行，它起源于 20 世纪 90 年代，随着韩国经济的发展和科技的进步，韩国流行文化开始在全球范围内快速传播。韩流的兴起并非偶然，而是韩国政府长期以来对文化产业的大力支持和发展战略的结果^②。研究发现，韩国政府通过有效的政策支持和规划，利用科技手段将韩国流行文化推向全球，使其在全球范围内得以广泛传播^③。

（二）韩流文化与韩语学习动机

动机是激发第二语言学习的重要源动力，是第二语言学习过程中持续的驱动力。学习动机决定了学习者的学习主动性与学习态度，它与学习者的态度、学习策略紧密相关，只有对学习动机有了深入的了解之后，才能运用适当的策略激发学生的学习动机以及培养学习兴趣，从而能够帮助学生提高韩国语水平^④。

随着韩流文化在全球的传播，对韩国文化的热爱和欣赏也引发了人们对韩语学习的兴趣和动力。研究发现，人们对韩国文化的热爱，尤其是对韩国电视剧和音乐的喜爱，是驱使他们学习韩语的重要动力。同时，这种由个人兴趣而引起的文化认同，也可视为语言学习的动机强化因素。^⑤而韩国世宗学堂作为韩语教育的重要机构，其课程设置和教学方法的科学性和针对性，大大提高了

---

① 金玟佑. 全球化语境下多元文化的突破：以韩流为例. 现代传播（中国传媒大学学报），2017(6)：167-168.

② Ryoo W. Globalization, or the logic of cultural hybridization: The case of the Korean wave. Asian Journal of Communication, 2009(2): 137-151.

③ Shim D. Hybridity and the rise of Korean popular culture in Asia. Media, culture & society, 2006(1): 25-44.

④ 张雪花. 韩国语学习动机的激发途径研究——基于 DORNYEI 学习动机理论. 科教文汇，2016(21)：173-174.

⑤ 张国良，陈青文，姚君喜. 媒介接触与文化认同——以外籍汉语学习者为对象的实证研究. 西南民族大学学报（人文社会科学版），2011(5)：176-179.

学习者的学习效率和兴趣，提供的网络教学也进一步促进了韩语学习的普及，让世界各国人民能够更方便、更快捷地认识韩国。[1]

（三）韩国世宗学堂的相关研究

学术界对韩国世宗学堂的研究主要集中在两个方面：一是对世宗学堂当前状况的分析及改进提议，研究者主要从韩国语教育的角度探讨了世宗学堂在教材开发、教师培训和本土化等方面的问题，并提出了其长期发展和韩语普及的策略；二是针对韩语的普及策略，深度分析了世宗学堂的建立成效和活性化计划。

韩国自 2007 年开始在海外设立"世宗学堂"，与法国的"法语联盟"、英国的"英国文化协会"、德国的"歌德学院"、我国的"孔子学院"相似，世宗学堂是韩国在海外韩国语教育的代表性机构，又是韩国在海外打出的文化商标。[2] "世宗学堂"通常开设在韩国的海外文化园或当地大学等教育机构，由政府和"世宗学堂财团"（原来的韩国语世界化财团）对其运营的费用、教材、教员培养等方面提供支援。一般在当地韩国语学习需求充分、具备教员、教育空间等教育条件下，提出申请并通过审查后可以开设世宗学堂。

世宗学堂的运营主要采取了如下几方面的措施。

（1）严格审查教育课程和教材。在教育课程和教材中绝对不能有违背和诋毁当地包括宗教在内的民俗风情内容，避免出现不必要的纠纷。

（2）主动与当地"韩流"粉丝联手增进友谊和合作。

（3）每年邀请各"世宗学堂"的优秀生免费到韩国访问，开展融合韩国文化的现场活动，进一步增进他们对韩国文化和社会的了解。

金美美全面研究了韩国世宗学堂的整个发展过程，具体分析了世宗学堂成立的社会环境、历史背景、历程、具体类型与章程、运营机制与系统、分布与设立情况、面临的问题和发展方向。[3]

（四）韩国世宗学堂与孔子学院的对比研究

此外，对孔子学院和世宗学堂的比较研究也非常丰富，主要集中在政策角度进行对比。本研究虽未聚焦孔子学院，但针对孔子学院和世宗学堂的对比研

[1] 金多荣.中国孔子学院和韩国世宗学堂的语言文化传播策略对比研究.哈尔滨：哈尔滨师范大学，2017.
[2] 金万甲.韩国设立运营"世宗学堂"的做法及其启示.当代韩国，2013(4)：105-113.
[3] 金美美.韩国世宗学堂研究.上海：上海师范大学，2013.

究也为本研究提供了一定的背景材料与理论视角。

金英信提到了孔子学院和世宗学堂设立的背景差异，认为孔子学院设立的背景是中国儒家思想的影响和复兴，世宗学堂设立的背景是韩国追求壮大文化软实力，并对比了二者的运行机制、管理模式、语言教学和文化交流及传播。[①]

姜东润聚焦孔子学院和世宗学堂在文化传播中选择的不同"品牌"，认为中国以孔子为品牌，在语言、文化、教育等领域辐射自己的影响，韩国以韩流为品牌，在唱片、电视剧和电影等产业方面取得了惊人的成就。[②]孔子学院是中国国家对外汉语教学领导小组办公室在世界各地设立的推广汉语和传播中国文化与国学的教育和文化交流机构。世宗学堂是由韩国文化观光部出资建设，韩国语世界化财团统筹管理的对外韩国语培训和文化教育机构。

一些研究也发现，孔子学院与世宗学堂存在一些共同问题。首先，两者都属于非营利机构，会有消极运营的可能性。[③]其次，由于缺乏适合当地文化习惯的教材、缺乏符合各国国情的教学方法、缺乏师资。二者的教学质量堪忧。[④]再次，学生人数减少。非专业的学生一开始是出于兴趣学习，但是当失去兴趣或没有学习汉语的必要性时，就不再坚持学习。[⑤]此外，西方人出于对本土文化的保护而排斥东方文化。

在此基础上，一些研究也提出了相应的解决策略：

首先，学生在学习中体现出听说能力差；在课程设置、教学方面应当做出适当的调整和改进，以提升教学质量。[⑥]其次，改变单一的语言型培养模式，根据学校自身的状况采取复合型语言人才培养模式。

由此可见，中国孔子学院与韩国世宗学堂既有相似之处，又有着一定差异，中韩两国在文化交流上面临着一些共同的挑战。因此，本研究虽聚焦韩国世宗学堂，但也能为中国孔子学院的建设与宣传提供一定的参考与帮助，为中韩两国在文化交流上共商、共建、共享提供理论依据。

---

① 金英信.世宗学堂与孔子学院的比较及其启示.大连：辽宁师范大学，2018.

② 姜东润.孔子学院与世宗学堂的比较分析与未来发展.苏州：苏州大学，2013.

③ 黄艾.网络孔子学院：优势与不足.对外传播，2012(9)：41-43；张传双.远程教育模式下的汉语电教化若干思考——基于网络孔子学院建设的研究.学语文，2013(4)：65-66.

④ 刘莉.海外孔子学院的教材研究.长春：东北师范大学，2011；刘晶晶，关英明.海外孔子学院的教材选择与编写.沈阳师范大学学报(社会科学版)，2012(1)：142-143.

⑤ 王冰.怎样实现孔子学院文化活动的可持续发展.湖北经济学院学报(人文社会科学版)，2015，12(7)：11-12.

⑥ 张会.孔子学院文化活动设计与反思.云南师范大学学报(对外汉语教学与研究版)，2014(5)：6-12.

（五）文献述评

得益于韩国政府有效的政策规划，以及高质量的韩国电视剧、音乐、偶像团体等文化产品，起源于20世纪90年代的韩流文化在全球范围内快速传播。而随着韩流文化在全球的传播，对韩国文化的热爱和欣赏也引发了人们对韩语学习的兴趣和动力。这种由个人兴趣而引起的文化认同，也可视为语言学习的动机强化因素。学术界对世宗学堂的研究主要集中在两个方面：一是对世宗学堂当前状况的分析及改进提议；二是针对韩语的普及策略，深度分析了世宗学堂的建立成效和活性化计划。此外，对孔子学院和世宗学堂的比较研究也非常丰富，现有研究主要从以下几个角度进行对比：设立背景差异对比、语言传播策略对比、"品牌"效应对比、存在的共同问题。

这些文献为我们的研究提供了背景参考。但是，现有研究也存在一些局限性。首先，目前国内外研究多是描述性研究，缺少相应的实证研究。其次，这些研究的结论较为分散，缺少系统性的理论建树。

四、理论基础

（一）文化认同理论

文化认同理论是美国著名精神分析学家埃里克松（Erik H. Erikson）于20世纪50年代初期提出的一个重要文化理论[①]。文化认同是对一种特定符号、语言、价值与规范的认同，也是对一个社会的"个性"的认同。

"文化认同发展模型"是研究文化认同的重要理论框架之一。该模型有五个阶段的发展过程：未意识阶段（Unexamined Cultural Identity），对抗/冲突阶段（Confrontation/Conflict），探索阶段（Exploration），新认同阶段（New Cultural Identity），以及融入阶段（Integration）。这个模型描绘了个体如何从对自身文化身份的模糊认知，到对其的深入理解和自我接纳，最后到达对不同文化认同的包容和尊重。

文化认同是文化与文化之间传播的结果，过去的文化认同研究多关注两个层面：一是国家内部的文化认同，二是移民者的文化认同。然而，今天有另一个群体渐渐受到重视，他们就是外语学习者，也是来自外国（外籍）的移居者。外语学习者通过语言的学习，开始与异文化沟通，他们成为文化的中介，

---

① 高英祺，梁玉.文化认同与跨文化交际.光明日报，2014(7): 1.

将异文化牵到一起，并向双方介绍他们所了解的另一方。

文化差异会导致陌生的疏离感（Alienation），甚至造成猜疑与误解。《文化帝国主义》作者汤林森（John Tomlinson）认为，所有的文化认同，都是归属感的表征，并且是一种想象之归属感。这样的想象，得以赶走陌生与猜疑的负面情感：对民族国家而言，文化认同是重要的凝聚力量；对移民而言，影响着新生活的适应；而对旅居者（外语学习者、外派工作者等）而言，文化认同不仅影响旅居时的心情与对异文化的涉入程度，同时也形塑其对异地的印象与观感。研究发现，文化认同可视为语言学习的动机强化因素。

（二）自我决定理论

自我决定理论（Self-Determination Theory，简称SDT）是心理学领域一种重要的动机理论，旨在解释人的内在驱动和行为动机。

自我决定理论的核心是三大基本心理需求：能力感（Competence）、归属感（Relatedness）和自主性（Autonomy）[①]。这些需求被视为人的内在驱动力，对其行为和心理健康有深远影响。理论指出，当这三种需求得到满足时，人们的内在动机会被激发，从而形成自我决定行为。能力感是指个体对自己能力的信任和认可，认为自己有能力完成任务或挑战。归属感是指个体与他人的互动中产生的关联感，即个体对自我与他人的联系和认同感。自主性则是指个体对自己行为的主导权，即认为自己的行为是由自身内在决定，而非外部压力或者诱导产生的。

自我决定理论强调内在动机与外在动机的关系。理论认为，人们更倾向于由内在动机驱动的行为，这种行为更能带来满足感，并能持续更长时间[②]。外在动机虽然也能驱动行为，但若过于依赖，可能会导致内在动机的消失，甚至产生反效果。在教育等领域的应用，自我决定理论为理解和促进个体的积极发展提供了重要理论基础。[③]

---

① Deci E L, Ryan R M. The "what" and "why" of goal pursuits: Human needs and the self-determination of behavior. Psychological inquiry, 2000(4): 227-268.

② Ryan R M, Deci E L. Self-determination theory and the facilitation of intrinsic motivation, social development, and well-being. American psychologist, 2000(1): 68.

③ Deci E L, Vallerand R J, Pelletier L G, et al. Motivation and education: The self-determination perspective. *Educational Psychologist*, 1991(3-4): 325-346.

（三）社会文化学习理论

社会文化学习理论（Sociocultural Theory）起源于列夫·维高斯基（Lev Vygotsky）的工作，它强调学习是一种社会过程，并且强调了文化对个体发展的影响。[①]

该理论认为，人的认知发展是通过与他人的社会互动和在文化环境中的参与而形成的。社会文化学习理论把学习视为一个社会构建的过程，强调文化工具如语言和符号系统在认知发展中的作用。

维高斯基（Vygotsky）提出了"最近发展区"（Zone of Proximal Development，ZPD）的概念，这是指个体独立解决问题和在有指导或合作的情况下解决问题之间的差距。这个概念强调了社会互动在学习和发展过程中的重要性。指导者或更有经验的伙伴可以帮助学习者在其最近发展区内进行学习，从而达到他们当前无法独立完成的任务。社会文化学习理论还强调了内化的过程，即从社会活动中学习到的知识和技能最终成为个体的内在认知工具。[②]这一过程强调了社会互动和文化环境在知识和技能转移中的关键作用。

社会文化学习理论为我们理解学习如何被社会和文化环境塑造，以及学习者如何通过社会互动和参与文化活动来发展他们的认知能力，提供了理论框架。它已被广泛应用于教育、心理学、人类学等领域的研究中。

五、研究问题

基于上述研究与理论，本研究提出如下两个研究问题：
韩流文化是如何推动外语学习者学习韩流的动机的？
韩国世宗学堂如何利用"韩流"进行韩语教学与韩国文化传播？

六、研究方法

"韩流"文化对韩语学习动机的推动作用是动态、多样、复杂的，而韩国世宗学堂作为政府推广的官方汉语学习机构，其对"韩流"文化的进一步推动，以及利用"韩流"之动力进一步促进韩语教学与韩国文化传播的动态机制系统有待深度研究者的理解与挖掘，仅通过量化分析似乎难以揭示其具体过程

[①] Vygotsky, L. S. *Mind in society: The development of higher psychological processes*. Cambridge: Harvard University Press, 1979.

[②] Wertsch J V. *Vygotsky and the social formation of mind*. Cambridge: Harvard university press, 1988.

与影响路径。因此，本研究采用质性研究，深入访谈对"韩流"文化与韩语感兴趣的群体，理解"韩流"文化是如何推动外语学习者学习韩语的动机，而韩国世宗学堂又在其中扮演者怎样的角色。

（一）研究路径

根据上述文献综述内容，确有研究证实了"韩流"可以推动外语学习者韩语学习动机的发展，但是，"韩流"在这一过程中究竟是以何种方式、在何种机制下以何种路径使外语学习者产生学习韩语的动机，目前研究中缺乏相应的理论解释。而目前针对韩国世宗学堂的研究，大多是介绍性、描述性研究，尚未有研究聚焦韩国世宗学堂在以"韩流"促文化传播中扮演的角色。针对本研究的两个研究问题，目前尚未有完善的理论体系，难以有效解释韩国世宗学堂在"韩流"与韩语传播中的作用。因此，本研究尝试通过更高层次的整合与概括来超越先前的描述性研究。

基于此，本研究采用扎根理论，建构相应的理论，为对外语言交流机构如何利用文化潮流推动语言发展做出一定的理论贡献。扎根理论强调从原始资料中归纳、概括经验，进而上升到理论。[①]扎根理论注重发现逻辑而非验证逻辑，深入情景，经过不断比较，对诗句进行抽象化、概念化的思考与分析，从中提炼出概念和范畴并在此基础上建构理论，与本研究想要开展的探索性工作相吻合。

（二）资料收集

本研究的资料收集过程与研究问题紧密联系。针对第一个研究问题"韩流文化如何推动外语学习者学习韩流的动机"，本研究深入田野，寻找对"韩流"文化与韩语感兴趣的受访对象，收集半结构化访谈的录音资料与文本。针对第二个研究问题"韩国世宗学堂如何利用'韩流'进行韩语教学与韩国文化传播"，本研究一方面收集专家访谈的录音资料与文本，一方面收集韩国世宗学堂官方网站的"韩流"与韩语相结合的具体教学策略与措施，并对其进行深度分析。

（三）抽样策略

预访谈阶段，本研究采用方便抽样，初步探究研究的可行性，制定并修改

---

① 陈向明.扎根理论的思路和方法.教育研究与实验，1999(4): 58-63+73.

访谈提纲。由于本研究聚焦韩语学习动机，故抽样时聚焦对韩国文化与韩语学习感兴趣的研究对象，采用方便抽样、滚雪球抽样的方式，并结合最大差异化原则，邀请受访者参与访谈。在接近理论饱和后，本研究邀请该领域专家，通过进一步访谈验证本研究的理论饱和程度。

（四）资料分析

本研究计划采用三级编码和自下而上的编码思路。研究者计划首先采用开放式编码，对资料进行逐字分析与逐行分析，以求形成初步范畴。根据预访谈情况，访谈时间一般在20—40分钟，内容较为丰富，开放式编码有助于研究者细致、深入梳理受访材料。接着，研究者计划采用选择式编码，寻找核心类属。核心类属是在编码过程中最频繁出现且最重要的编码，可以指导进一步的数据收集与编码过程。最后，研究者计划采用理论编码，在范畴与范畴之间建立联结，表明资料中各部分之间的逻辑关联，建构理论。

（五）研究信度与效度

为提升本研究的信度与效度，研究者采取以下措施[①]。

（1）在研究开始前，研究者首先请教一些专家与同僚，针对其意见对研究设计和访谈提纲的设计进行一些调整。

（2）研究者已进行了三轮预访谈，在每次访谈结束后询问受访者的参与感受，并且通过三轮预访谈，迭代并修改了三版访谈提纲。

（3）在研究过程中，采用多方互证（Triangulation），除对受访对象的谈话内容进行记录外，积极在韩国世宗学堂官网上查询相关资料，查验受访者的描述是否属实，并在资料收集与分析的过程中通过持续对比分析（Constant comparative analysis），以寻求多方互证。

（4）在研究过程中，研究者持续进行自我反思（Researcher reflexivity），并在文章中说明研究者的个人背景可能对研究产生的影响。

（5）在初步获得研究结果后，进行成员检查（Member checking），将研究结论反馈给参与者，询问其对研究结果的意见与建议。

（6）在研究全程，持续进行同行评议（Peer briefing），在访谈提纲的设计与修改、编码、结果呈现等方面积极寻求同僚与专家的意见。在研究者初步判断理论饱和后，进行一对一专家访谈，检验研究的理论饱和度。

---

① Creswell J W, Miller D L. Determining validity in qualitative inquiry. Theory into practice, 2000, 39(3): 124-130.

（六）研究伦理

研究者在研究全程遵守"尊重、行善不伤害和公平正义"的原则。

在邀请受访者时发放知情同意书，简要介绍本研究目的、研究内容，询问参与者是否愿意参与访谈并进行录音，并告知受访者有权随时退出研究。并且告知受访者，研究者会全程保护其隐私，在研究结果呈现部分对其进行匿名化处理。

在访谈过程中，认真倾听受访者陈述，尊重受访者观念，并与受访者建立信任。

在访谈结束后，赠送小礼品并感谢受访者对本研究的支持。妥善保管访谈资料、录音，以假名形式书写研究报告。

在研究结束后，与受访者保持联系，及时反馈研究结论，询问其参与研究的感受，并再次感谢其对本研究的支持。

七、结 论

（一）扎根理论模型

以下是扎根理论所得韩国世宗学堂如何利用韩流刺激外语学习者的韩语学习动机的路径图（见图1）：

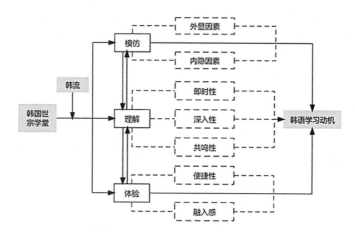

图1　韩国世宗学堂利用韩流刺激韩语学习动机的路径图

通过本研究，我们得出以下结论：韩语学习者在由韩流追随演变为学习韩语的过程中，受到模仿、理解和体验三个核心要素的影响。此外，世宗学堂巧妙地运用韩流文化作为媒介，为韩语教学与韩国文化传播领域提供了多元化的学习资源和互动平台。

首先，韩国世宗学堂利用韩流激发韩语学习者的模仿冲动，外语学习者被韩流文化的时尚和多元所吸引，韩国的流行文化、音乐、时尚等因素激发了他们进行模仿的愿望。模仿的过程可能从外部因素开始，例如模仿韩国明星的着装和发型，然后逐渐演变成对内隐因素的好奇和向往。这些外部表现通常在学习者内心埋下了学习韩语的种子，因为他们希望能够更全面地模仿和融入韩国文化。世宗学堂紧抓这一要素，在官网上有许多韩国偶像的表演片段，对其进行拆分讲解。韩语学习者在观看这些片段时，不仅可以模仿其偶像的表演，更可以在潜移默化之中进一步对学习韩语产生兴趣，在灵活运用之中感受韩语的魅力。

其次，韩国世宗学堂强调"理解"的核心类属，即外语学习者对韩国文化和语言的深入理解需求。在我们的研究中，我们发现一些学习者对韩国综艺节目和电视剧充满浓厚兴趣，他们希望能够迅速获取第一手的相关资源，而这些资源通常以韩语呈现。这反映了对"即时性"理解的需求，学习者希望能够更快地理解韩国媒体内容。此外，还有一些学习者希望理解韩国文化中的隐喻、文化元素和幽默，这体现了对更深层次理解的追求。他们渴望掌握足够的语言技能，以便能够欣赏和解释这些文化元素。此外，一些学习者还期望理解自己喜欢的韩国明星的情感表达，这反映了他们与这些明星之间情感共鸣的需求。韩国世宗学堂网站上的电视剧和综艺模块，有许多针对电视剧片段和综艺片段中难以理解的俚语、古语等特殊用法的讲解，满足韩语学习者深入学习韩语、理解韩国文化的需求。

最后，"体验"的核心类属涉及到外语学习者对韩国文化和生活方式的深入体验愿望。一些学习者可能被韩国的旅游吸引，他们希望能够更全面地体验韩国文化，包括语言、美食、音乐和社交互动等方面。为了更好地与韩国社会交流和融入，他们认为学习韩语是必不可少的。韩国世宗学堂利用这一体验愿望，在官网上介绍韩国美食、韩国生活，进一步通过刺激体验愿望，刺激韩语学习冲动，这三个核心类属相互关联，共同推动外语学习者从被韩流吸引到积极学习韩语的过程。

（二）与其他理论的对话

在本研究中，我们运用扎根理论的方法，构建了一种解释外语学习者学习韩语动机的理论模型，该模型着重强调韩流文化对学习动机的关键影响。同时，我们借鉴相关理论，以更深入的方式探讨和解析这一模型。

文化认同理论为我们深入探讨韩语学习者的动机提供了有价值的观点。这一理论着眼于文化认同的本质，即对一定文化元素的认同程度，而在韩语学习者的背景中，韩流文化扮演了至关重要的角色（见图2）。

首先，韩流文化，包括韩国的音乐、电视剧和电影等，已在国际范围内广泛传播。外语学习者经常接触到这些文化元素，这些元素构成了他们的文化认同的一部分，为学习韩语提供了动机基础。

其次，文化认同理论强调了文化认同可以通过积极的学习和体验进一步强化。外语学习者通过学习韩语开始与韩国文化深入交流，成为文化的中介者。他们积极融入韩国文化，形成更深的文化认同。这一过程不仅满足了他们的内在需求，还强化了他们的语言技能，使他们更自信和积极地去探索和理解韩流文化。

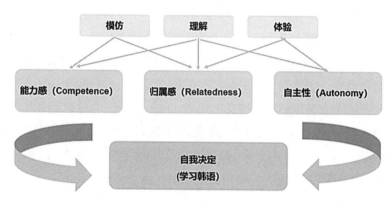

图2 文化认同理论对韩语学习动机的影响

自我决定理论在阐述了当个体的需求得到满足时，其内在动机会得以激发，形成自主决策行为的同时，也强调了三大基本心理需求的重要性，包括能力感、归属感和自主性。首先，自我决定理论中的能力感涵盖了个体对于自身能力的评估和信心。通过学习韩语，外语学习者不断扩展其语言技能，这一过程自然而然地满足了其能力感需求。对韩流文化的模仿、理解与体验为学习者提供了有益的语言学习机会，从而加强了其对于能力感的认知，进一步刺激了学习韩语的内在动机。其次，归属感是指个体与社会或文化共同体之间的联系感。学习韩语使外语学习者能够更深入地融入韩国文化和社会，这种文化理解和亲身体验可以强化他们对于韩国文化的归属感。韩流文化作为一种广泛传播的现象，使学习者能够积极参与其中，从而将其自身融入一个全球性社会群体，进一步满足了其归属感需求，加强了学习韩语的决心。最后，自主性强调了个体在行为中具备自主选择和控制的能力。通过对韩流文化的模仿、理解与体验，外语学习者能够自主地决定学习韩语，因为他们认识到这一学习过程与其兴趣和价值观相一致。这种自主性的选择增强了其学习动机，使他们更愿意投入时间和精力学习韩语。

综上所述，结合自我决定理论，我们能够深入解释为何通过对韩流文化的模仿、理解与体验能够激发外语学习者学习韩语的内在动机。这一模型充分满足了能力感、归属感和自主性这三大基本心理需求，从而推动学习者形成自主决策的学习行为。

最近发展区理论，作为教育心理学领域的一项重要理论，为我们解释世宗学堂在韩语学习动机与韩流文化之间的关系中的重要作用提供了一个有力的框架。该理论将任务划分为两个关键概念，即现有发展区和最近发展区，以强调任务的性质和学习者在任务完成中所需的支持与互动。其中，现有发展区指的是学习者已经具备足够能力独立完成的任务，而最近发展区则是指只有在他人支持和协助下才能完成的任务。这一理论突出了社会互动在学习和技能发展中的重要性，特别是在新知识和技能的获取方面。

对于韩流文化爱好者而言，他们在日常生活中被动或主动地接触到一些韩语表达，这些可以被视为他们的现有发展区。这些表达可能来自韩剧、韩流音乐、社交媒体等，为他们提供了一定的语言基础。然而，要将这些现有的语言知识转化为实际的语言运用和学习，需要更深层次的指导和支持。

在这一背景下，韩国世宗学堂等教育机构扮演了关键的角色，它们充分利用韩流文化的符号和情境，为外语学习者提供了指导和协助，引导他们进入最近发展区。通过创造与韩流文化相关的学习情境和教育资源，世宗学堂帮助学习者更深入地学习和运用韩语，将其从被动获得的知识转变为积极实践的语言技能。这一过程反映了最近发展区理论的核心思想，即社会支持和互动对于学习者成功地跨越现有发展区、进入最近发展区至关重要。

八、讨 论

"韩流"文化现象，由于韩流让所有目标用户产生兴趣，同时，体验感好，易于理解和模仿，极大程度降低了学习难度，并快速获得了学习的习得感与成就感。继而加速了韩流的传播速度和国际影响力。其发展模式、策略对于中国文化传播、孔子学院的产业发展具有重要的启示和值得借鉴的价值。

（一）以中国特色影视作品形成强IP，发展中国文化

在"韩流"迅速传播的过程中，韩国主要采取的营销战略是以影视剧为依托，以娱乐节目、电影、流行音乐、舞蹈等不同元素为先行军，带动了服饰、饮食、旅游、语言、美容等产业的全面发展。《大长今》的美食；《浪漫满屋》里的甜美爱情，这些内容让人们对韩国饮食、旅游、服装产生了强烈的兴趣向往。中国作为一个文化大国，可以通过"功夫"融入更多中国本土文化元素；可以通过古装剧将具有浓厚中国色彩的文化符号，例如陶瓷、丝绸等融入到影视剧中，形成具有中国特色的文化品牌，增强中华文化的辨识度。

（二）以中国的食品为依托，增强文化体验

传统中国文化的传播，在汉字、京剧等元素上做了不少宣传，但是汉字的习得难度相对较高。中国的美食种类多样，地域性强，全球闻名。中国自古有"民以食为天"的古训。我们可以鼓励多元化、地域性美食的分享，同时吸收国外现代元素，加上自己的元素，例如不同时令、节气的美食，打造自己的文化品牌，提供更具个性化和多样化的文化产品，以满足不同观众的需求。

（三）以明星为助力，展现中国文化，提升认同感

信任和热爱是粘性和忠诚度非常高的兴趣要素。在选择进行文化传播的明星上，不仅要关注全球影响力，关注全球市场的潜力和吸引力，韩国在选择艺人时会培养具备多语言能力、多元化魅力和国际视野的艺人。所以对于中国文化传播来说，我们可以选择那些具备国际影响力和吸引力的人才，帮助他们在全球范围内传播中国文化。同时，我们需要培养全能艺人，让他们能够通过音乐、舞蹈、表演等多种形式表现中国文化的魅力。

（四）以媒介为渠道，传播中华文化，扩大影响力

在对专家访谈和各维度抽样调研中我们发现，韩流的受众群体非常多，但是知道韩国世宗学堂的人却并不多，所以知名度和影响力极大程度上限制了世宗学堂的发展。同理，中国文化如果希望长期且坚定、可持续地传播与发展，必须重视媒介。例如通过各种在线平台迅速传播和分享；利用社交媒体和互联网等新媒体渠道，积极开展文化宣传和推广，与全球观众建立更直接的联系。

（五）跨文化融合和交流，提升中国文化软实力，实现可持续发展

韩流把传统元素和现代元素结合，加上自己的元素，打造自己的文化品牌。中国也应该打造自己的特色，把传统影视文化、服饰文化和文化资源文化产业相结合，创造出自己的特色，才能在汉语热的基础上掀起中华文化热。中国可以与其他国家加强文化合作，共同打造更具影响力的文化产品，通过文化交流推动友好关系的发展。

总的来说，韩流对中国文化传播的启示是注重内容生产、强文化输出而不是灌输，通过跨文化交流、学习和创新，打造自己的文化，提升软实力，并利用新媒体平台、多渠道进行合作、传播。这些启示有助于中国文化在全球范围内更好地传播和影响世界。

文化必须反映时代和适应时代，同时又必须引导时代。正如有的学者所说：中国大众文化按照自己发展的逻辑，也不可能离开世界文化发展的潮流，它必须在国际文化舞台展示自己的力量，形成自己的品牌，并吸收国外大众文化的优秀成分以发展壮大自己。

九、研究局限性

尽管本研究在探讨"韩流"现象对中国的韩语学习者的影响方面做出了一定的努力，但仍然存在一些局限性。首先，本研究的研究对象主要聚焦在中国的韩语学习者身上，尚未涵盖其他国家和地区的学习者，这可能会在一定程度上限制了研究结果的普适性。其次，尽管研究深入探讨了"韩流"现象对韩语学习的影响，但未深入探讨以世宗学堂作为韩语学习途径的学习者的观点和经验。最后，本研究对于世宗学堂如何具体利用"韩流"的方式进行了抽象概括，而未对其实施策略进行详细描绘和分析，这使得我们对于这一关键教育机构的理解还有待进一步深化。

未来的研究可以朝多个方向发展。首先，研究可以拓展到全球范围，涵盖其他国家和地区的韩语学习者，以便全面地了解"韩流"现象对全球范围内的外语学习者的影响。其次，未来研究可以进一步分组访谈不同学习路径的学习者，包括那些选择世宗学堂作为韩语学习途径的学生，以便深入了解不同群体之间的差异和共同之处。最后，未来研究应更加深入地考察世宗学堂如何具体利用"韩流"进行韩语教育和文化传播，以便提供更详细和具体的策略建议，丰富我们对韩语学习与文化传播的理解。这些未来研究方向将有助于更全面地

探讨"韩流"现象在全球文化交流中的作用和影响。

十、附 录

（一）访谈提纲一

1.提到韩国文化，你想到什么？

2.你对哪种韩国文化感兴趣？

3.你觉得这种文化吸引你的亮点在哪？它与其他文化相比，独特在哪？

4.你都是通过哪些途径了解这些文化的？

5.你觉得韩流文化对你产生了什么影响？（接触韩流文化的过程中多大程度上学习了韩语？）

6.韩流文化能多大程度上让你产生学习韩语的冲动？

7.这种感觉能持续多久？

8.韩流文化中的哪些元素对你产生了最大的吸引力？

9.你是如何利用韩流文化作为学习资源的？

（二）访谈提纲二（专家访谈）

1.您觉得韩流是一种什么样的风潮？

2.韩国文化为什么在中国有如此大的魅力？

3.它对韩语的传播有怎样的作用？

4.它对中国文化传播有怎样的启示？

5.您觉得韩国世宗学堂是如何利用"韩流"推动韩语教学的？

6.您觉得韩国世宗学堂相比其他韩语教学机构，优势在哪，劣势在哪？

（三）受访者信息

表1 受访者信息

编号	性别	年龄	学历	专业
1	女	24	本科	汉语言文学
2	女	23	研究生	英语教育
3	男	25	研究生	新闻传播学
4	男	23	本科	风景园林
5	女	18	本科	金融学
6	女	30	研究生	法学
7	女	28	研究生	公共卫生
8	女	27	本科	韩语

中国孔子学院与美国文化中心对比研究①

摘　要: 在全球化的当下，各国政府越来越重视本国文化的输出与传播，出现了大量的跨文化相关传播机构。中美作为全球两大政治实体，在文化推广领域也存在相应的代表文化机构——中国孔子学院与美国文化中心。本研究以孔子学院章程、美国文化中心官网报告及相关期刊为依据，对在美的部分已关闭的孔子学院与现已发展停滞的美国文化中心进行整体比较，总结分析孔子学院与美国文化中心发展坎坷的内外部原因，如资金投入少、媒体报道不恰当、认知差异与不信任问题、政府过度干预、政治目的性强等。针对存在问题提出相应解决措施：一是从跨文化传播的角度出发对接本土化需求，使孔子学院呈现公益性新形象；二是增加资金来源，减轻政府财政压力。

关键词: 孔子学院；美国文化中心；发展策略

一、引　言

（一）选题背景及意义

中美作为全球最大的两个政治实体，其政治关系对于全球格局与国际秩序具有重要影响。两国间的竞争与合作，则影响了两国在文化推广领域的战略。同时，中美两国都拥有悠久而丰富的历史与文化传统。两国文化之间的交流、对比和相互影响是促进相互理解并进一步合作的重要方面。

中国孔子学院与美国文化中心是两国具有代表性的文化机构，均以促进文化交流与跨文化理解为宗旨。然而，2018—2022年中，美国大学里的118家

① 作者: 黄静儒，苏州大学外国语学院；陈喆，苏州大学外国语学院。

孔子学院有 104 家已经关闭；美国文化中心的发展自 2018 年起也逐渐停滞。本研究总结分析了孔子学院与美国文化中心发展坎坷的内外部原因，通过比较分析，总结出孔子学院当前运行中存在的问题，并提出相应的解决方案，完善孔子学院国际语文教育的发展策略。

（二）研究对象及研究方法

研究对象：中国孔子学院，美国文化中心
研究方法：

1. 案例分析法

本研究选取孔子学院在美国芝加哥关停的具体实例，分析导致其关停的内外部原因，并将选取美国文化中心在中国开设的北京美国中心的具体实例进行对比分析，最终针对孔子学院提出有价值的改善意见与建议。

2. 数据分析法

本研究将对孔子学院官网与美国文化中心相关网站上发布的数据进行汇总整理，并纵向对比进行分析归纳，从而得到更为准确、科学、有说服力的研究成果。

二、研究对象一：孔子学院简介

（一）孔子学院的成立背景及发展历程

孔子学院（Confucius Institute）是一个由中华人民共和国教育部辖下国家汉语国际推广领导小组办公室（简称"国家汉办"；现更名为"中外语言交流合作中心"，简称"语合中心"）为背景的非营利性组织中国国际中文教育基金会管理，总部设在北京。

党的十五届五中全会提出实施文化"走出去"战略来讲好中国故事，在此大背景下，"汉语热"迅速席卷全球。第一所孔子学院于 2004 年 11 月在韩国首都首尔创办。截至 2020 年 5 月，中国在全球 162 个国家（地区）建立 561 所孔子学院和 1170 个孔子课堂。与此同时，特色孔子学院比如 ESCP 商务特色孔子学院、中医特色孔子学院等也在建设中。至 2018 年底，孔子学院建设成果颇丰，覆盖了欧盟 28 国和中东欧 16 国，共有 53 国设立 140 所孔院和 136 个课堂。

（二）孔子学院的运营模式简介

孔子学院由于其特殊的性质和作用，使得它与普通的大学教育管理模式有着很大的区别。其管理机制有独特性，以适应不同语言、不同文化、不同理念下的机构、组织和人员的要求：

1.孔子学院的设置

海外孔子学院设立形式以总部直接投资、总部授权特许经营和中外机构合作三种形式为基础，并根据各国的特点和需要采取针对性的办学方式。现阶段主要以中外合作方式建设孔子学院。[①]外方机构向孔子学院总部提交申请书，由总部与中外方合作机构与其签署合作协议，总部及其中方相应机构与外方合作机构用各自的优势资源按1:1比例对孔子学院进行投资，中方提供启动资金。该模式在设立和运行过程中已经形成较为稳定的方式并得到了中外合作方认可。在实际的运作中主要采取了"高校—高校"合作模式、"组织—高校"合作模式、"政府机构—政府机构"合作模式。

2.孔子学院的管理机制

孔子学院的管理体系是各地孔子学院受孔子学院总部的领导和指导，总部制定教学、管理和发展计划。各孔子学院按照总部的要求通过理事会领导下的院长制完成各项活动，各理事会等领导机构向孔子学院总部理事会负责，各院长向理事会负责，其相应机构按照各自的分工开展孔子学院的工作。

3.孔子学院的体系结构

如图1所示，孔子学院的组织体系结构呈现出层级化与合作化的特点，由孔子学院总部统筹管理，负责整体战略规划与资源分配。在总部的指导下，孔子学院理事会发挥协调与决策职能，确保各项政策的执行落地。孔子学院的具体运作由中方院长与外方院长共同管理，体现了中外合作办学的原则。下设多个职能岗位，包括中方教师、外方教师、中方志愿者、行政助理与商务协调人员等，分工明确，职责清晰，构建了一个集学术交流、教学推广与行政管理为一体的高效运行体系。

---

① 侯美羽.孔子学院十年发展与管理问题研究.杭州:浙江大学，2015.

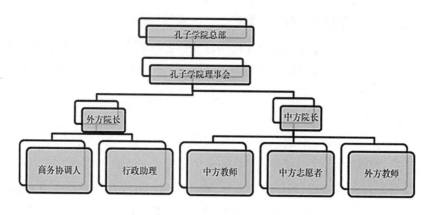

图 1　孔子学院体系架构

4.孔子学院的使命与目标

由其章程可知，其目的为："致力于适应世界各国地区人民对汉语学习的需要，增进世界各国地区人民对中国语言文化的了解，加强中国与世界各国教育文化交流合作，发展中国与外国的友好关系，促进世界多元文化发展，构建和谐世界。"由此也可见孔子学院肩负着对外传播汉语文化以及推动世界文化交融与共同发展的使命。

三、研究对象二：美国文化中心

（一）美国文化中心的成立背景及发展历程

20世纪40年代以来，美国政府开展了包括富布赖特项目、汉弗莱项目、国际访问者项目等一系列公共外交项目，这些项目加强了世界各国对美国社会的了解，为提高美国国家形象发挥了一定作用。中国是美国开展公共外交的重要目标国，除了上述项目，2010年美国开始在中国部分高校实施美国文化中心项目。在运作9年后，2018年美国国务院不再拨款，此项目处于暂停状态。

2010年5月25日，由刘延东国务委员与希拉里国务卿共同主持的第一届中美人文交流磋商会议在北京举行。会议指出，为了建设21世纪积极的中美关系，双方期待共同拓展人文交流的广度和深度。与此相契合，2009年四川大学—亚利桑那州立大学孔子学院正式成立。亚利桑那州立大学2010年提出，希望在四川大学建立美国文化中心。

建设美国文化中心的设想立即引起美国政府的高度关注和支持。2010年，美国驻华大使馆公使衔文化参赞宋柯（Thomas Skipper）先生等一行四人，在驻成都领事馆总领事等官员陪同下，参加了 12 月 13 日在四川大学的美国文化中心揭牌仪式，四川大学—亚利桑那州立大学美国文化中心由此正式成立。

四川大学—亚利桑那州立大学美国文化中心正式成立后，美国驻华大使馆发布了两轮招标公告，鼓励美国大学提出申请，与其在中国的伙伴高校合作，设立更多的美国文化中心。至 2014 年底，24 所美国高校或机构参加了此项工程，在中国布局美国文化中心的工作基本完成。在北京大使馆以及其他五个领事馆管理的六个领事区的每个领区均布局了数量不等的美国文化中心，基本覆盖中国主要城市。

（二）美国文化中心的运营模式简介

在组织形式上，为了把全国二十余个中心以及相关非政府组织融合成一个有机整体，形成更有效率的公共外交网络，美国驻华大使馆委托亚利桑那州立大学作为总召集人，从 2012 年开始每年夏天在中国举行美国文化中心年会，商讨各中心之间如何实现资源共享并分享成功经验。2012 年年会在北京召开；2013 年在上海召开；2014 年在深圳召开；2015 年在西安召开；2016 年在广州召开；2017 年在长春召开。美国文化中心年会成为联系各个中心的纽带。

在经费来源方面，美国文化中心主要由美国国务院拨款。美国国务院给予每个新建立的中心大约十万美元作为启动资金，资金划拨到美方高校管理使用。每次年会上，美国驻华大使馆会宣布下一个年度经费申请计划，按照各中心年度活动计划的可行性，经过评估后，给予大约 5 万美元的经费资助。此外，福特基金会从 2013—2015 年资助 38 万美元，用于连续三年美国文化中心年会的相关经费支出。鲁斯基金会则提供了一笔 75 万美元的费用，一方面资助各中心走出高校、进入社区开展文化活动，另一方面资助课程建设，在中国高校开设若干门美国文学、文化课程。[①]

（三）美国文化中心的使命与目标

第一，通过中国与美国高等教育机构的合作，推进对美国文化的进一步了解，并讲述美国故事；第二，通过开展不同类型的活动，超越肤浅的流行文化，彰显美国经验，通过基于比较或跨学科视角的多种投送方式展示美国价值观；第三，支持各中心独立开展学术研究，促进各中心个性化特点建设，为各

---

① 杨光.美国文化中心：美国对华公共外交的一次尝试.公共外交季刊.2019(03)：76-82+127.

中心共享资源以开展最佳实践提供网络化服务。

四、部分孔子学院关闭与美国文化中心发展停滞原因对比分析

（一）孔子学院

1. 外部原因

（1）资金投资较少导致的依赖性降低

按照最初芝加哥大学宣布的方案，管理层将通过募集资金的方式向 2008 年 5 月设立的弗里德曼研究院投资两亿美元，而根据协议，汉办向芝加哥大学孔子学院五年的投资预计为 200 万美元，金额相差较大[①]，也进一步导致对于孔子学院的依赖度减少。2008 年、2010 年针对弗里德曼研究院抗议时，反对者曾强调管理层应考虑资金分配问题，但最终也并未得到解决。芝加哥大学孔子学院所提供的对本科生、研究生的资助也仅仅是芝加哥大学东亚研究中心所提供资助的一小部分。正如该中心前副主任佛斯所言，"幸亏我们东亚研究中心有足够的钱""所以，东亚研究中心可以做任何想做的研究而不用受制于汉办。"芝加哥大学对于孔子学院的科研资助依赖性逐步降低，也就导致了相关学者对于孔子学院的需求度降低，使得他们在面对危机时缺乏维护孔子学院的动力，也最终改变了芝加哥大学管理层与汉办谈判时的立场。

（2）不恰当的媒体报道压缩了芝加哥大学管理层的回旋余地

尽管存在两次连续的抗议活动，但芝加哥大学委员会受反对者的影响较小，仍然对于与孔子学院保持合作关系持以积极肯定的态度。布鲁斯·林肯（Bruce Lincoin）教授也承认，尽管他"当时希望彻底关闭芝加哥大学孔子学院，但是看上去并不可能"。2015 年 4 月，他在接受采访时也承认，当时他没有想到孔子学院会被关闭，关闭孔子学院对他来说的确是个"惊喜"。但最终的一篇汉办报道导致了芝加哥大学委员会态度的转变。该篇文章为《解放日报》2014 年 9 月 19 日对于汉办主任许琳的专访，题目为《文化的困境，在于不知不觉》。文章中写道，许琳给芝加哥大学校长写的一封信，信中只有一句话："如果你们学校决定退出，我同意。"

其中值得注意的是新闻报道的口吻，报道这件事时描写到中方领导处理此

---

① Theodore Foss. Chinese Studies at Chicago: A Brief History of the Origin of Chinese Studies at the University of Chicago. [2024-11-29]. https://ceas.uchicago.edu/sites/ceas.uchicago.edu/files/uploads/About/Ted_Foss_Article.pdf.

事的风格比较强硬，采用带有指向性的贬义词"自夸"（braggadocio），带有强烈的评价色彩。①也正是新闻报道中所透露出的中方过于强硬的态度，导致了芝加哥大学管理层的态度转变。如果此时宣布续约，一定会让外界认为芝加哥大学屈服于中方的强硬态度，从而让反对者关于芝加哥大学为了获取汉办的资金而牺牲学术自由的指控得到证实，显然，这使得芝加哥大学的声誉受到舆论指责的影响，这也使得芝加哥大学管理层最终选择与汉办结束合作关系。

2. 内部原因

（1）认知差异

在 2010 年"经研社"的第一次抗议活动中，反对者指控在孔子学院成立的决策过程中，存在沟通不够充分的问题。反对者称孔子学院在筹备期间并未征询他们的意见，直到孔子学院即将成立他们才得知消息。②据芝加哥大学孔子学院院长杨大力所言，东亚研究中心的执行委员会在孔子学院成立前一年就已经讨论过设立孔子学院，但反对者并不认同，该委员会的成员布鲁斯·卡明斯（Bruce Cumings）称他"直到协议签订后六个月才得知孔子学院的存在"。上述说明相关研究者与委员会之间存在着认知差异，相关学者认为，项目的直接相关方是东亚研究中心的中国研究委员会，由中国研究学者提出申请即可；而反对者则认为，项目位于东亚研究中心，应当经由该中心全体学者讨论。

（2）信任问题

2014 年 4 月，芝加哥大学 108 名教授向校长和教务长提交请愿信，要求教授理事会终止孔子学院协议。与 2010 年相比，反对者主要表达了对孔子学院干预芝加哥大学学术自由的忧虑。反对者认为，芝加哥大学孔子学院已经对芝加哥大学中文教学项目施加影响，而且控制了芝加哥大学中文教师的雇用和培训。除此之外，他们还认为，创办孔子学院已经使得芝加哥大学成为汉办全球项目的一部分，而这与芝加哥大学自身的学术价值相悖，所以，反对者再次要求教授理事会终止孔子学院的协议。事实上，反对者并不能提出实质性的证据证明芝加哥大学孔子学院存在干预学术自由的论点。上述材料说明部分相关学者对待芝加哥大学孔子学院的态度出现变化，他们并不完全认同芝加哥大学孔子学院，希望以大幅改变运营协议的方式应对质疑，以切断芝加哥大学孔子

---

① 安然，许萌萌. 美国芝加哥大学停办孔子学院新闻话语分析. 对外传播，2015(2)：43-45.

② Eliezebeth Redden. Rejecting Confucious Funding. (2014-04-29)[2024-11-29]. http://www.insidehighhered.com/news/2014/04/29/chicago-faculty-object-their-campuss-confucius-institute.

学院与汉办"联系"的形式表明芝加哥大学孔子学院的独立地位。其中，要求自行聘用中文教师的建议是为解决报告中所提及的中方派遣教师带来的"额外负担"，而要求取消汉办对预算的否决权则意在向外界证明芝加哥大学孔子学院学术研究的独立性。

（二）美国文化中心

1. 外部原因

美国文化中心的经费安排不尽合理。一方面，这一资金安排的实质是美方的经费投入不足，中方高校被迫分担美国公共外交经费。美国文化中心这一经费安排模式，对于经费并不充裕的部分中方高校，其组织各类活动的积极性必然受到影响。另一方面，美方经费使用的效率也不高。如 2015 年，亚利桑那州立大学向美国国务院申请了五万美元经费，用于在成都、南京和苏州分别开展的为期一个月的美国西南摄影图片展，但实际展出效果很不理想。虽然美国驻华大使馆也了解资金使用效率低下的情况，不断加强对美方经费的使用管理，但是总的来看，这种由美方管理并使用经费、中方高校分担部分经费的模式使中方高校失去积极性，这也是导致部分中方高校不再继续举办活动的重要原因之一。

2. 内部原因

（1）文化传播的单向性

美国文化中心没有体现文化的双向交流原则，即在这方面一定程度上违背了通过双边交流促进相互理解的原则。例如：美方高校派出大量学者来到中国输出美国文化，而由美国文化中心组织的中方人员赴美交流次数却寥寥无几，文化呈现单向流动的态势；而在具体活动内容上，美方高校只是依据自己的认知来安排相关文化活动，导致中方高校师生对部分活动的参与积极性不高，甚至还出现个别美方活动触碰中方极为敏感的内容的情况。

（2）政府过度参与，政治目的性较强

美国方面没有遵循关于政府不过度直接参与文化事务的原则。以川大中心为例，2011 年 5 月，美国驻华大使馆副大使到川大中心与学生座谈；2011 年 8 月，副总统拜登到川大演讲；此后，亚利桑那州州长、美国驻成都总领事相继到川大演讲；2012 年 7 月，美国驻华大使馆副大使再次到川大与学生座谈；2012 年 12 月，美国驻华大使馆文化事务官员访问川大中心。除了四川大学美

国文化中心，分布于其他城市的美国文化中心也有类似的情况出现。

（三）对比分析

根据上文分析，首先，可看出导致两机构关闭的共同外部原因在于资金的配置问题。两者都存在着组织提供的资金不足，降低了各高校机构与其合作的积极性，各高校对其的依赖性以及需求度减少，也就进一步导致了海外多所孔子学院的关闭以及美国文化中心发展的停滞。这也为孔子学院进一步发展，以及改善海外多所孔子学院不断关闭的现状提供了解决视角。进一步改善孔子学院运行的资金配置制度至关重要。

其次，在文化传播过程中，同样都存在着舆论导致的信任问题。无论是中方的孔子学院的举办，或是美方文化的输出，都呈现出文化单向输出的趋势，对当地的文化以及当地高校的认知差异未做到充分考虑，在课程设计、管理制度方面与高校的传统模式存在差别。由于国家间存在认知差异，并且考虑到两机构输出文化的特殊性质，便产生了媒体对于机构的政治目的的舆论，进一步导致了机构公信度的下降，导致了最终中外合作的终止。

五、美国文化中心发展停滞给孔子学院运行的启示

由上文所述，已停办的孔子学院与发展停滞的美国文化中心存在着同样的发展困境与相似的运行问题。为改善海外孔子学院不断倒闭的现状，本文对于舆论引起的信任度降低以及资金制度两方面存在的问题提出解决方法。

（一）针对海外媒体引起的信任危机问题的解决措施

首先，针对被认为是政治宣传的工具这一说法，2020年6月18日教育部发布了将孔子学院总部更名为中外语言交流合作中心的通知，由民间公益组织"中国国际中文教育基金会"全面负责运行。这一举措有利于淡化孔子学院的"官方色彩"，更加符合语言推广、文化传播的一般做法。

其次，针对文化渗透的误解，则需要从跨文化传播的角度出发，融入当地，对接本土化需求，减少文化冲突。网红李子柒的成功走红为我们提供了新思路。其之所以能够在海外社交平台大获成功，一方面得益于独具特色的传播定位、强大的情感动员能力，另一方面更在于短视频本身传递出东西方共同的价值观念与共通的情感期待。[1]可见孔子学院文化传播应找到文化相通之

---

[1] 肖悦.孔子学院作为跨文化传播主体的发展情况研究.汉字文化，2022(19)：185-187.

处，以日常叙事手段宣传东西方共同的价值观念，让受众产生共鸣。最后，在自媒体时代，短视频平台、社交平台都能够在不经意间产生巨大影响。而孔子学院在一些国际社交平台上还未有官方账号，因此可以充分利用 TikTok、YouTube 等平台，参考日常化叙事手段来拍摄带有中华文化元素的视频并投放，也可以请一些对中华文化感兴趣、在社交平台上拥有一定知名度的外国人来体验中华文化，拍摄视频，拉近与受众的距离。

面对舆论困境，孔子学院要向受众呈现出民间公益性新形象，利用社交平台讲好中国故事、展现中国形象。

（二）针对资金管理制度问题的解决措施

由芝加哥大学孔子学院反映出的问题可得知，海外孔子学院面临着分配到的资金过少的问题，高校对于孔子学院的依赖性逐渐削弱。增加资金来源可缓解目前可分配资金较少的问题。

多元化的资金渠道能减轻政府财政压力，形成"产业经营＋基金捐助＋汉办项目"的良性循环。据了解，大多数的孔子学院目前的资金来源仍然是以汉办项目的形式来推行，但日益呈现出多样化特征。2020 年，孔子学院对运行方式进行改变。新机制下，基金会与中外方合作机构是孔子学院和孔子课堂品牌下的平等合作伙伴，中外方合作机构是举办孔子学院的主体。通过外部合作伙伴的加入，扩大孔子学院品牌的影响力。[①]并通过基金会孔子学院品牌的建立，拓宽资金来源。

同时，我国国际贸易的迅速发展为孔子学院拓宽资金渠道创造了机会。孔子学院可以与所在国的社会组织、企业开展互惠合作。如 2015 年，中信建设有限公司为安哥拉内图大学孔子学院提供了总额达 150 万美元的资金，而孔子学院为中信公司开设了定向职业培训班，双方用实际行动诠释了"互利共赢"。[②]

① 王秋彦，史仁民.孔子学院的运行路径、问题及对策探究.文化创新比较研究，2022(15): 169-172.
② 叶澜涛，陈海芳.跨文化视野下孔子学院的管理与建议.广东海洋大学学报，2014(5): 76-79.

PART
6

第六章

世界知名互联网及人工智能公司
案例研究

AI驱动商业模式创新：以OpenAI和百度为例[①]

摘　要： 在互联网公司商业模式进化中，人工智能（AI）技术的重要性不言而喻。本文采用定性与定量分析方法，细致考察了OpenAI和百度的发展历程、商业战略及市场成效，详尽探讨了OpenAI与百度如何将AI技术应用于商业模式创新之中。研究重点分析了这两家企业如何运用AI，特别是自然语言处理技术，来优化服务、提升效率以及孕育新的商业价值。通过比较研究，本文阐明了它们在目标消费群体、价值创造和供应链管理等方面的共性与差异。研究结论强调了AI在推动商业模式革新方面的核心角色，并对中国的互联网与AI企业提出了具体的发展建议。

关键词： AI技术；商业模式创新；OpenAI；百度

一、研究背景和意义

（一）全球互联网企业商业模式发展概述

全球互联网公司近年快速崛起，多凭创新模式迅速成为资本市场的宠儿。随着经济和信息技术全球化、竞争加剧，商业模式变得至关重要。企业需不断优化商业模式以应对变化，以此提升竞争力和价值[②]。

1.互联网企业商业模式的演进

在过去几十年中，互联网企业的商业模式经历了重大变化。早期的互联网企业，如雅虎和亚马逊，采用了广告和电子商务模式，主要通过在线广告和销售产品或服务来实现收入。随着互联网和技术的发展，新的商业模式开始出

---

① 作者：袁凤：重庆大学公共管理学院；马梦茹：重庆大学土木工程学院；李思怡：重庆大学管理科学与房地产学院；罗子禹：重庆大学本科生院。
② 梁海珠.互联网企业商业模式创新的价值创造研究.广州：广东财经大学，2022：2.

现，如平台模式、软件即服务模式，以及通过数据分析和人工智能（AI）推动的个性化服务。

2.数据驱动的商业模式

现代互联网企业，尤其是像谷歌和Facebook这样的公司，依赖于收集和分析用户数据来产生收入。它们提供免费的服务（如搜索引擎和社交媒体平台），并收集用户在这些平台上的行为数据。然后，这些公司将这些数据用于广告定位，从而在广告商那里获取收入。数据驱动的商业模式在过去十年中变得非常重要，被视为互联网企业主要的收入来源。

3.AI驱动的商业模式

随着人工智能技术的快速发展，出现了一种新的商业模式，即AI驱动的商业模式。这种模式的核心是利用AI技术改进产品和服务，以提供更高的价值。例如，Netflix利用AI来推荐用户可能喜欢的电视节目和电影，而Spotify利用AI来创建个性化的音乐播放列表。这种模式的一个关键优势是，通过提供更精确和个性化的服务，可以提高用户满意度和忠诚度。

本文将以美国OpenAI和中国百度为研究对象，探究OpenAI和百度如何利用AI驱动的商业模式进行创新。OpenAI在AI和机器学习领域的突破性研究推动了科技进步，并对社会和经济产生了深远影响。OpenAI以其先进的自然语言处理技术而闻名，这项技术正在改变我们与机器的交互方式。而百度则是中国领先的互联网公司之一，它正在利用AI来改进搜索引擎、自动驾驶以及许多其他产品和服务。这两个公司的案例将为我们提供深入理解AI驱动商业模式创新的重要视角。

（二）研究目的与意义

本研究旨在探究AI在互联网企业商业模式创新中的作用，特别是自然语言处理领域。以代表性的OpenAI的ChatGPT和百度的文心一言为案例，旨在揭示AI如何助力商业模式创新以及其对企业和行业发展所带来的影响。

研究对预测互联网企业发展具有一定价值。AI技术将驱动更多企业创新产品服务，推动商业模式变革。分析OpenAI与百度案例，有助于理解AI的角色，评估商业模式创新在企业价值创造中的作用，并为互联网及AI企业发展策略及企业决策者的AI趋势洞察提供参考。

二、研究内容和方法

（一）研究内容

1. AI驱动的商业模式创新的理论框架

结合文献研究和案例分析，建立AI驱动的商业模式创新的理论框架。重点研究AI技术在商业模式中的应用，包括如何通过AI实现服务创新、提高运营效率和创造新价值。

2. OpenAI的商业模式分析

分析OpenAI的商业模式，包括其服务对象、提供的内容和交互方式，以及其市场份额。研究OpenAI如何通过AI技术驱动其商业模式的创新，并探讨其在市场中的竞争优势和挑战。

3. 百度的商业模式分析

分析百度的商业模式，重点关注其在AI技术应用方面的战略和实践。研究百度在AI领域的市场地位、技术优势和商业模式创新路径。

4. 对比分析

通过定性和定量分析，对比OpenAI和百度的商业模式，以了解其优点和缺点。探讨两家公司在AI应用和商业模式创新方面的异同点，以及各自的独特之处。

5. 对其他互联网公司的建议

基于对OpenAI和百度的分析，提出关于如何利用AI进行商业模式创新的建议。这些建议涵盖服务创新、运营优化和新价值创造等方面，为其他互联网公司提供参考和启示。

（二）研究方法

1. 数据收集

（1）二手数据

二手数据可以提供丰富的背景信息和现有研究成果，有助于全面了解研究对象。数据来源包括OpenAI和百度的年度报告、公司公告、新闻发布，以及相关的学术文章和行业报告等。

（2）在线资源

在线资源可以提供最新的动态信息和市场反应，补充二手数据的不足。数据来源包括公司网站、社交媒体帖子和相关的线上论坛等。

2.数据分析

（1）定性分析

定性分析有助于深入理解复杂的现象和背景，通过内容分析可以揭示两家公司发展策略和实践的细节。具体而言，对收集到的二手数据和在线资源进行内容分析，以理解OpenAI和百度的发展策略和实践。

（2）定量分析

定量分析可以通过数据比较和统计分析，客观衡量公司的财务表现、市场份额和产品性能等方面的差异。具体而言，对公司的财务数据、市场份额、产品性能等进行数值比较和统计分析，运用统计工具进行数据处理和结果展示。

通过以上数据收集和分析方法，我们旨在从不同角度全面理解和比较OpenAI和百度在AI领域的发展，探讨其商业模式创新的路径和效果。

三、OpenAI的商业模式及市场表现

（一）OpenAI介绍

1.历史与发展路线

OpenAI自2015年由埃隆·马斯克（Elon Musk）和萨姆·奥尔特曼（Sam Altman）等科技巨头联合成立，致力于AI利益共享。该组织从一开始就开放研究成果，促进全球AI进步。其贡献包括NLP和机器学习领域的研究，并推出了GPT系列模型，尤其是GPT-2和GPT-3，在理解和生成语言方面取得显著成效[1]。

2.前瞻商业战略

OpenAI的战略集中在技术创新、商业拓展和AI伦理三个核心。在持续推动AI前沿技术的同时，也重视其商业应用和转化，同时参与AI的伦理与政策讨论，确保技术的公正与透明。

3.面临的机遇和挑战

（1）机遇

一是对AI法规的需求。目前，AI行业缺乏相关法律法规，但OpenAI有机会通过与政府合作，在国际AI法规的制定中发挥重要作用。

---

[1] Enacy Mapakam. OpenAI rolls out 70 ChatGPT plugins as chatbot race heats up. [2023-05-15]. https://metanews.com/openai-rolls-out-70-chatgpt-plugins-as-chatbot-race-heats-up/.htlm.

二是AI技术的发展潜力。AI技术有改变工作方式和人际交互的潜力，OpenAI的聊天工具ChatGPT已经展示了其巨大的应用潜力。通过集成插件和网络浏览功能，ChatGPT能够执行多种任务，为付费用户提供广泛的服务。

（2）挑战

一是AI相关法规的落后。现有的AI法规无法跟上技术发展的速度，AI法规发展滞后，这对OpenAI构成挑战。OpenAI可能需要在没有明确法规指导的情况下运作，可能引发法律和伦理问题。因此，OpenAI正在呼吁立法。

二是AI所带来的潜在风险。AI的潜在风险是OpenAI面临的主要挑战。AI可能被滥用于泄露数据隐私和传播虚假信息[1]，而其快速发展也可能导致大规模失业和偏见的延续及版权问题。

1）泄露数据隐私

OpenAI曾因数据泄露事件受到限制和罚款，但他们采取了积极措施解决问题，并加强了数据隐私保护。

2023年3月20日，ChatGPT曾因泄露用户的历史消息及账户信息导致服务短暂关闭。28日，马斯克等千余名科技领袖呼吁暂停开发更先进人工智能[2]，以便制定安全政策。31日，意大利个人数据保护局宣布禁止使用ChatGPT，限制ChatGPT的开发公司OpenAI处理意大利用户信息[3]，并开始立案调查，OpenAI可能被处以最高2000万欧元或该公司全球年营业额4％的罚款。

在事件发生后，OpenAI立即采取行动以解决问题，同时通知了受影响的用户，并进行必要的报告和调查，随后在几小时内恢复了服务。OpenAI对于各国法律的配合态度十分积极，在加强对数据隐私的保护后，意大利已解禁OpenAI。4月6日，Open AI在官网发布了 *Our Approach to AI Safety*[4]，以确保安全、可靠地为全球用户提供ChatGPT服务。Open AI及时发布安全方法，对其未来发展乃至整个AIGC行业都起到了关键的保护和稳定军心的作用。目

---

① Oluwapelumi Adejumo. ChatGPT bug exposes users details, causes outage of over 10 hours. [2023-03-23]. https://metanews.com/chatgpt-bug-exposes-users-details-causes-outage-of-over-10-hours/.htlm.

② Cade Metz and Gregory Schmidt. 马斯克等千余名科技领袖呼吁暂停开发更先进人工智能. (2023-03-30) [2023-05-15]. https://cn.nytimes.com/technology/20230330/ai-artificial-intelligence-musk-risks/.htlm.

③ Intelligenza artificiale. rtificial intelligence: stop to ChatGPT by the Italian SA, Personal data is collected unlawfully, no age verification system is in place for children. [2023-03-31]. https://www.garanteprivacy.it/home/docweb/-/docweb-display/docweb/9870847#english.htlm.

④ OpenAI. Our approach to AI safety. [2023-04-05]. https://openai.com/blog/our-approach-to-ai-safety.htlm.

前，3月的泄露数据隐私事件未对OpenAI的发展造成明显影响。

2）传播虚假信息

2023年5月，一男子因使用ChatGPT发布假新闻[1]而被中国警方逮捕。7月，绍兴警方破获一个用ChatGPT制作假视频的团伙，引发媒体对AI潜在风险的关注。OpenAI已禁止用其技术制造虚假信息，违者将被停止服务并可能被上报执法机构。

3）工作岗位消失

AI的发展可能导致大量工作岗位消失。2023年5月，世界经济论坛报告预计AI将淘汰多达2600万个记录和行政职位，比如收银员、票务员、数据录入和会计[2]。对此，OpenAI强调了快速学习和谨慎迭代的紧密反馈循环，并提倡用教育和培训来帮助工人适应新的职业角色[3]。

4）AI延续偏见

2023年4月，联合国教科文组织指出，AI人工智能系统的开发、使用和部署有可能复制且放大现有的性别偏见，并产生新的偏见[4]。OpenAI意识到这一问题并正在开展研究以减轻偏见，并鼓励团队多样性和开发公平和包容的AI系统[5]。例如，OpenAI致力于通过改进模型的训练和调整过程来减轻偏见。

5）版权问题

AI模型使用版权受保护的内容引发了版权问题，OpenAI需要妥善处理这个问题，避免侵权行为。他们正在开发一个版权系统，以补偿内容创作者的作品被用于训练AI模型的情况[6]。创作者有权决定如何使用他们的声音、肖像或受版权保护的内容。但其先推出产品、后补充规则的行为方式也引起质疑。

---

[1] Jeffrey Gogo. China makes first ChatGPT arrest over fake news. (2023-03-10)[2023-05-15]. https://metanews.com/china-makes-first-chatgpt-arrest-over-fake-news/.htlm.

[2] Johnny Wood. 未来五年哪些职业增长最快，哪些又将消失. [2023-05-15]. https://cn.weforum.org/agenda/2023/05/fastest-growing-and-declining-jobs/.htlm.

[3] OpenAI. Planning for AGI and beyond. [2023-02-24]. https://openai.com/blog/planning-for-agi-and-beyond/.htlm.

[4] UN News. 促进人工智能领域性别平等，教科文组织推出女性专家平台. [2024-04-28]. https://news.un.org/zh/story/2023/04/1117472.htlm.

[5] OpenAI. AI safety needs social scientists. (2019-02-19)[2023-05-15]. https://openai.com/research/ai-safety-needs-social-scientists.htlm.

[6] Enacy Mapakam. OpenAI's CEO Appears Before Senate, Calls for AI Regulation. [2023-05-17]. https://metanews.com/openais-ceo-appears-before-senate-calls-for-ai-regulation/.htlm.

（二）商业模式

客户是企业商业模式的核心要素，为了满足客户的需求，企业将客户细分成不同的群体。目标客户指的是对服务对象进行分类，明确企业要为谁服务，谁才是关键客户。价值内容指的是企业从客户角度出发，考虑要为客户解决什么诉求，为客户提供什么样的产品和服务。供应链包括从采购、研发、生产制造到产品销售诸多环节，敏捷高效的供应链体系可以提高企业竞争力。这三种要素在OpenAI的商业模式创新中发挥重要作用。下文以ChatGPT为例，对OpenAI的商业模式展开介绍。

1.目标客户

（1）个人用户

个人用户是OpenAI的一个重要客户群体，这包括但不限于程序员、研究人员、作家、学生、设计人员。他们可能依赖ChatGPT来协助编写代码、撰写文章、完成学术论文、进行日常对话、设计图片与视频等。

OpenAI的ChatGPT自发布以来，吸引了大量用户的目光，并通过提供有价值的服务，成功地将这些关注度转化为对产品的实际需求，由此建立了庞大、忠诚的用户群体。

OpenAI的技术创新具有聚合者的特性，这是ChatGPT能够迅速吸引并成功转化大量关注度的关键因素。ChatGPT通过对现象级大模型的深入研究，创新地提出内容集成式的提问界面，快速吸引了用户，并与他们建立起了联系。其提供的GPT-3.5服务几乎没有边际成本，多边网络模式则进一步降低了用户GPT-4的获取成本。另外，ChatGPT通过提供API和插件，能轻松集成到其他应用和服务中，其代码解释器则拓宽了输出内容的形式，这使得用户能够在各种不同的环境和场景中使用它。ChatGPT的这种灵活性和可扩展性使得它能够更好地满足个人用户的多样化需求。

OpenAI展现出的超级聚合者特性，显示了它有潜力成为一个能够控制用户需求和供应的超级平台。在未来，OpenAI可能会以此为基础，拓展出更多的商业模式。

其具体使用场景包括智能搜索、内容创作等场景。

1）智能搜索

搜索引擎输入一个关键词条件，返回的结果不是一个答案。而通过ChatGPT这种方式可以得到一个唯一且满足条件的结果。

2）内容创作

ChatGPT本身具备创作能力，但还不够完美，可以用它来作为辅助的工具。当没有思路的时候，可以引导它产生一些基础资料，再对基础资料进行完善，快速提高整体内容质量。

3）家庭场景

不同于智能客服的服务机器人，它不针对客人而是针对家庭，属于家庭中的护理人员。当老年人感到寂寞时，他们可以通过与机器人进行交流或接受机器人的情绪引导来解决情绪问题或得到辅导。

（2）企业用户

OpenAI吸引了众多企业用户，其服务如机器学习和自然语言处理等旨在提升业务效率。当前多个平台已集成ChatGPT等工具，如OpenAI与Stripe合作为其AI服务提供支付支持。迪拜水电局利用ChatGPT提升服务水平，计划通过Moro Hub推广此技术以提高生产力和服务品质。众巢医学则应用ChatGPT于临床决策辅助，并通过微信等平台优化患者互动，但提醒内容仅供参考。OpenAI的应用主要集中在增强生产力和智能营销领域。

OpenAI利用先进的AI技术为企业打造个性化工作协同解决方案，采用定制付费模式获利。GPT模型帮助企业打造能体现其价值观的聊天机器人，根据用户问题进行精确应答。利用计算机视觉，餐厅等行业能通过人脸识别为顾客推荐菜品。OpenAI的推荐算法也助力企业提供更符合用户偏好的商品或服务。这些个性化服务增进了企业效率和顾客满意度，推动OpenAI在商业领域不断扩大影响力。

2.价值内容

价值内容指的是企业提供给客户的有意义、有益的信息、产品或服务。

（1）自然对话能力

ChatGPT能够进行自然而流畅的对话，模拟人类对话的方式和语言风格。这使得用户能够以更自然的方式与系统进行交互，提出问题、寻求建议或获取信息。

（2）多领域支持

ChatGPT在各个领域都能提供帮助和支持。它不仅可以帮助程序员编写代码，也可以协助研究人员进行文献检索和知识整理。对于作家和学生来说，它可以辅助撰写文章和论文。此外，设计人员也可以利用ChatGPT的创造力和想象力进行设计工作。

（3）快速问题解答

ChatGPT具有快速响应用户问题的能力，能够迅速提供准确的答案和解决方案。这使得用户能够更高效地获取所需信息，节省时间和精力。

（4）可扩展性和定制化

ChatGPT的可扩展性强，能轻松融入多种应用，满足定制化需求。其产品包括：

1）GPT模型迭代

GPT-3引入1.75万亿参数，处理多样语言任务；GPT-3.5提升时效性和角色互动能力；GPT-4在专业学术基准上匹敌人类。

2）API与插件

ChatGPT通过第三方API和插件增强功能，如：

检索实时信息，例如体育比分、股票价格等。

检索知识库信息，例如公司文件、个人笔记等。

代表用户执行操作，例如订机票、订餐等。

3）代码解释器

无编程需求用户也能指使ChatGPT运行代码、分析数据、生成图表等，展现其多模态跨领域应用能力。

3.供应链

算力主要由两方面决定——硬件和软件。硬件主要是芯片，除了CPU以外，用的最多的是GPU。GPU是ChatGPT的重要成本因素，为ChatGPT的功能和性能提供关键支持。因此本文选择GPU的供应链作为分析对象。

微软为OpenAI建立了数据中心，OpenAI使用H100的前身A100 GPU开发了ChatGPT。英伟达发布专为大模型开发的H100 NVL，基于Hopper架构和Transformer（GPT模型基础）引擎等设计，可以用于处理ChatGPT。其具有处理大模型（LLM）的优越能力，如处理含1750亿参数的GPT-3。处理速度最高可达传统GPU的10倍，成本降低一个数量级。

微软已经同意在未来数年内向云计算服务提供商CoreWeave投资数十亿美元，用于云计算基础设施建设。双方的合作关系使得微软能够利用英伟达、CoreWeave的GPU资源，确保OpenAI的基础设施能够支持ChatGPT和其他人工智能项目的算力需求。[①]

OpenAI的首要任务是推出更便宜、更快的GPT-4。他们致力于降低"智能的成本"[②]，并努力进一步降低API的费用。这将使更多人能够使用OpenAI的技术，从而推动人工智能的普及化。采用先进的GPU是GPT能提供免费、高速、高质量服务的重要原因之一。

（三）市场表现

1. 市场份额

2022年底，OpenAI推出了具有对话交互功能的ChatGPT，即GPT-3.5。仅发布5天后，ChatGPT就吸引了100万用户，两个月后突破了1亿用户。

2. 访问量情况

表1为2023年5月1日至2023年6月30日的全球AI相关网站访问量统计。可见，在AI相关网站访问量统计的前30名榜单中，ChatGPT以163001的总访问量夺得第一的位置，占据了总体的30%（见表1）。

表1 AI相关网站访问量统计

排名	名称	主要功能	6月访问量	同比上月
1	ChatGPT	ChatGPT	163001	−10%
2	Microsoft Bing	搜索	121100	−3%
3	Canva AI 图像生成	图像生成	44390	−8%
4	DALL-E2	图像生成	34640	−12%
5	Adobe firefly	图像编辑	26280	−1%
6	DeepL	翻译	24470	−6%
7	Character.AI	虚拟角色	19010	−32%
8	Notion AI	生产力	14290	−7%
9	Google bard	搜索	14060	−1%
10	SpellCopy	拼写文法	11460	−1%
11	figma.com	设计	10160	−4%
12	Freepik AI	图像生成	9131	−1%
13	POE	聚合AI	7053	−1%
14	Amazon CodeWhisperer	代码助手	6580	2%

[①] 财联社. 微软与初创公司CoreWeave签署人工智能算力协议 价值可能数十亿美元. (2023-06-02)[2023-06-10]. https://www.cls.cn/detail/1367528.htlm.

[②] OpenAI. [2023-05-15]. https://openai.com/htlm.

续表

排名	名称	主要功能	6月访问量	同比上月
15	Quillbot Paraphraser	拼写文法	5879	22%
16	Remove.bg	图像编辑	5671	2%
17	Khanmigo	教育	4315	−10%
18	Grammarly	拼写文法	3373	−17%
19	Talk To Books	搜索	3208	−7%
20	Civitai	代码生成	3055	−10%
21	nvidia.com	硬件	2952	1%
22	CheggMate	教育	2932	−26%
23	Midjourney	图像生成	2853	−20%
24	Miro	生产力	2542	−8%
25	huggingface	开发者社区	2290	−8%
26	Perplexity AI	搜索	2222	9%
27	You	搜索	1655	−10%
28	123RF AI Search Engine	图像助理	1644	−5%
29	AI Reverse Image Search	图像搜索	1620	−1%
30	Leonardo.Ai	动漫	1410	−2%

四、百度公司的商业模式

（一）百度公司介绍

1.历史与发展路线

作为全球四大AI公司之一,百度提供全线AI技术，从芯片到软件和应用。自2000年成立以来，百度以技术创新为核心，旨在简化世界，并成为用户洞察与帮助人成长的领军企业。拥有核心"超链分析"技术的百度，使中国成为全球仅有的掌握搜索引擎核心技术的国家之一。百度支持全球百亿级搜索请求，是中文信息服务的关键入口，覆盖10亿用户。在搜索引擎基础上，百度拓展至语音、图像识别等AI领域，并在深度学习、AI操作系统等前沿技术上进行投资①。

---

① 百度. [2023-06-03]. http://home.baidu.com/home/index/company/?ivk_sa=1024320u.htlm.

2.前瞻商业战略

百度的战略聚焦在三个核心方向：一是巩固移动搜索生态，保持基本市场；二是创新业务，如智能云和自动驾驶；三是以AI推动主营业务增长，短期内将重点发展"文心一言"，以强化AI在商业上的应用。

（二）商业模式

以下针对目标客户、价值内容、供应链展开分析。

1.目标客户

（1）个人用户

百度在全球AI领域处于领先地位，提供智能互联网服务，服务覆盖200余个国家。其本地化能力强，利用全球资源帮助合作伙伴成长。

（2）企业用户

百度公司的企业用户主要包括以下几类：

1）广告主和营销客户：利用百度平台推广产品服务，提升品牌影响力。

2）SEO客户：与百度合作提升在线可见度和搜索排名。

3）大型企业和品牌：开展定制化广告服务，扩大市场份额。

4）ISP和内容提供商：使用百度云服务和CDN优化应用性能和用户体验。

2.价值内容

百度公司的核心价值可归纳为以下几点。

1）搜索技术：作为中国顶尖搜索引擎，百度以其先进的搜索技术和算法提供迅速精确的搜索服务，满足用户信息需求。

2）网络广告：百度的在线广告服务依托用户行为和偏好，为广告主提供精确的广告定位和品牌推广。

3）人工智能：百度在自然语言处理、图像和语音识别等人工智能领域大力投入，应用广泛，包括智能驾驶和智能家居等，以提升用户体验。

4）内容生态：通过百度百科、百度知道、百度贴吧等平台，百度构建了一个信息与社交互动丰富的生态系统，提供全面信息服务。

综合来看，百度致力于通过其搜索服务、广告平台、AI技术和内容生态系统为用户带来准确、便捷及个性化的服务。

3.供应链

目前，英伟达主导的AI芯片是人工智能云训练和推理的核心，如

ChatGPT（3.5）需要3万枚A100 GPU（单价超1万美元）并行运算。2022年8月，美国限制这些芯片对华出口。中国的华为海思、寒武纪、百度和阿里等在AI芯片市场占有一席之地，其中百度的文心一言便集成了多家国产AI芯片。百度智算中心提供算力支撑，昆仑芯科技的宋春晓表示，昆仑芯二代芯片在百度AI应用中广泛使用，推动各行业智能化。

尽管我国在图像和语音识别方面拥有领先企业，但在高端AI芯片领域与国际先进水平仍有差距。高性能AI芯片是关键基础设施，尽管出口管制带来一定挑战，但也为自主AI芯片国产化提供了机遇。

（三）市场表现

本节将以百度公司为例，介绍其AI产品文心一言对百度市场表现的影响。

1. 市场应用

福州市政府与百度签署了战略协议，旨在与基于文心一言和百度智能云的通用AI能力展开合作。截至2023年6月，已有超过300家企业参与了文心一言的内测，涵盖了工业、金融、政务、互联网、媒体、运营商、教育等多个行业。仅发布一个月后，文心一言就引起了国内AI领域的巨大热度，超过650家企业宣布接入该服务[①]。其中，金山办公与文心一言联合开发，在意图理解、PPT大纲生成、范文书写、生成待办列表、文生图等多模态生成场景上取得了合作成果。

2. 收益情况

中国AI市场即将迎来爆发性的需求增长，其商业价值的释放将是前所未有的、指数级的。2023年第一季度，百度营收311亿元，同比增长10%；归属百度的净利润（非美国通用会计准则）为57亿元，同比大涨48%，营收和利润双双超市场预期。其中，与文心一言关系最为密切的百度智能云，一季度实现盈利，收入同比增长8%至42亿元[②]。

---

① 百度智能云. 文心大模型技术交流会数据. [2023-06-03]. https://www.163.com/dy/article/I4CNM43E05476C4F.html.

② 百度发布2023年Q1财报：营收311亿元，智能云业务实现盈利. (2023-05-16)[2023-07-14]. http://www.news.cn/tech/20230516/4b81855f966341eb844f2e6ca8293738/c.html.

五、对比分析

（一）目标客户

1. 相同点

OpenAI和百度公司都有个人用户和企业用户。个人用户可能包括程序员、研究人员、作家、学生等，而企业用户可能包括各种大小的公司和组织，他们都利用人工智能技术来提供服务。OpenAI主要利用自然语言处理技术，如ChatGPT，而百度则利用搜索引擎和AI服务，如文心一言。

2. 不同点

OpenAI的客户主要依赖其GPT系列模型提供的各种服务，包括写作、编程、设计等，而百度的客户更多依赖其搜索引擎和云服务。对企业用户来说，OpenAI更注重提供内部协同工作和个性化定制服务的解决方案，百度则更注重提供广告和优化搜索结果等市场营销相关服务。OpenAI以技术创新和聚合特性为核心，更倾向于成为一个控制用户需求和供应的平台，而百度以强大的本地化运营能力和全球优质资源整合为核心，更倾向于成为帮助合作伙伴快速成长的引擎。

（二）价值内容

1. 相同点

OpenAI与百度都致力于发展人工智能技术，尤其在自然语言处理上有着深入的研究和应用。两者都致力于为用户提供准确、快速、个性化的信息和服务。

2. 不同点

OpenAI的重心在于开发和优化语言模型，以此驱动如对话、编码辅助等各种应用。其产品如GPT系列，功能广泛并且极具扩展性。百度则是全面的互联网公司，提供搜索引擎、广告服务和内容平台等多元化的服务。在AI领域，百度的研究不局限于语言处理，还涵盖了图像识别、智能驾驶等。OpenAI的产品主要面向全球用户，百度的产品则主要针对中国市场。

（三）供应链

1. 相同点

OpenAI和百度都重视算力，明确它是实现先进人工智能项目的关键支撑。

两者都有与专业硬件供应商合作的经验，以保障他们的人工智能项目能获得所需的算力。

2. 不同点

OpenAI依赖外部伙伴，如微软和英伟达，以提供其人工智能项目需要的强大算力。OpenAI的目标是使其人工智能技术更便宜、更快，以推广人工智能的普及。百度则侧重于自主研发AI芯片。虽然在高端AI芯片方面，百度与国际领先厂商存在差距，但它正在利用国内生产的机会，推动自主AI芯片的发展。百度的目标是使其AI算力在各行各业的智能化升级中发挥作用（见表2）。

表2　OpenAI、百度对比分析

	相同点	不同点	
		OpenAI	百度
目标客户	兼顾个人用户和企业用户	依赖其GPT系列模型提供各种服务	依赖其搜索引擎和云服务
	利用人工智能技术提供服务	注重提供内部协同工作和个性化定制服务的解决方案	注重提供广告和优化搜索结果等市场营销相关服务
		以技术创新和聚合特性为核心	以强大的本地化运营能力和全球优质资源整合为核心
价值内容	致力于发展人工智能技术，在自然语言处理上深入研究	开发和优化语言模型	提供多元化服务
	致力于为用户提供准确、快速、个性化的信息和服务	产品主要面向全球用户	产品主要针对中国市场
供应链	重视算力	信赖、依赖外部伙伴	侧重自主研发
	与专业硬件供应商合作		

六、结　论

OpenAI通过创新商业模式，快速实现了行业的领先地位。

（一）以ChatGPT为核心的技术创新

OpenAI凭借先进的大模型技术和多样化应用（如插件和代码解释器），提供了低成本且高质量的服务，实现了在价值内容上的创新。通过不断优化和扩展ChatGPT的功能，OpenAI成功地满足了用户多样化的需求，提升了用户体验和满意度。

（二）吸引大量用户的商业模式

OpenAI通过服务C端个人用户，将关注转化为实际需求，并以此为引导，促进了B端企业用户的服务需求上涨，实现了目标客户方面的创新。个人用户的广泛使用和反馈，不仅提升了产品的知名度和影响力，也为企业用户提供了信心和使用参考。

（三）在供应链选择上的战略合作

OpenAI在GPU供应链选择上，与英伟达和微软的合作，取得了技术和资金上的优势，使ChatGPT在处理速度和运行成本上均超越传统GPU，为用户提供了免费、高速、高质量的服务。这反映了OpenAI在供应链选择的商业模式创新，通过有效的战略合作，确保了其技术优势和服务质量。

基于以上分析，我们为国内互联网及AI公司提供以下建议：

1.技术与应用并重

中国AI公司应注重核心技术研发，与国际先进水平保持接轨。同时，关注AI技术的应用场景，提供多样化的应用服务，推动价值内容的创新，从而提高市场竞争力。

2.双重服务策略

中国AI公司可先服务个人用户，利用他们的反馈信息和行为数据，满足企业用户的需求。这种模式不仅可以帮助公司发现新商业模式，还能持续推动创新，实现用户需求和商业目标的双重满足。

3.强化供应链管理

选择合适的硬件供应商对业务运营效率和质量至关重要。中国AI公司应选择具备领先技术和优质服务的供应商，或建立战略合作伙伴关系，以获得技术和资金上的优势，从而提升整体服务质量和竞争力。

4.免费与收费结合的盈利模式

提供免费服务吸引用户关注，同时研究可持续的盈利模式，例如对增值服务或高级功能收费。通过这种模式，平衡用户增长和公司利润之间的关系，确保公司的长远发展和市场稳定。

马克思主义理论视域下人工智能企业发展路径探究
——以阿里巴巴为例 [①]

摘　要： 马克思主义理论对人工智能的理论观照和人工智能助推马克思主义事业发展的实践向度是当前理论研究的热点，相关研究力求以马克思主义理论视角分析人工智能技术的生产力本质。因此，基于马克思主义理论视域，对人工智能企业的发展进行审视和剖析具有一定的理论和现实意义。本文在此视域下，从生产力、生产方式、生产关系等主要方面对人工智能技术的本质及其对生产方式的影响进行探究，以具有代表性的人工智能企业阿里巴巴作为研究对象，厘清以人工智能技术为发展重心的企业在未来的可行性发展路径。

关键词： 人工智能；马克思主义理论；发展路径

从唯物史观视角出发，人类社会形态的演变以及人类文明进程的推进都离不开颠覆性的技术革命，新一轮科技革命为人类社会带来了人工智能这一时代前沿科技成果。人工智能以现代互联网企业为生成和发展载体，为人类社会生产力实现飞跃性发展提供极大助力，加速着智能社会的演变进程；但在这些正面影响之外，我们也要清醒认识到其所带来的新样态的人机关系矛盾这一负面影响，更要关注到作为其生成和发展载体的现代互联网企业如何促使人工智能转化为推动实现人的全面而自由发展的正向因素的问题。但现在人工智能引发了一系列的生产力变革及人的活动方式显著变化，对新的历史条件下人的全面发展的样态进行分析，可以对人工智能时代中如何正确认识和处理人机关系以及人工智能企业未来发展可行性路径相关理论问题做出解答和回应。

① 作者：柴建宇，广西师范大学马克思主义学院；任灿，广西师范大学马克思主义学院；吴佳瑜，广西师范大学马克思主义学院；马茹茹，广西师范大学马克思主义学院。

一、马克思主义理论与人工智能相关理论探索与实践发展

人工智能技术的突飞猛进引领着社会生产方式取得革命性发展，进一步加速了资本主义生产关系的自我否定进程，使生产力和生产关系获得了进一步的全面解放，推进了生产力自动化革新，极大推动社会形态加速向社会主义社会过渡。

（一）马克思主义理论对人工智能领域的理论审视

人工智能技术的发展具体作用于生产方式上，主要表现为生产力的极大解放，但无论人工智能发达程度如何，都无法从根源上解决内蕴于资本主义社会的基本矛盾，真正代表着先进生产力的进步阶级仍然是无产阶级。而对于人工智能高度发展引发的社会担忧，需要辩证地审视，以发展的眼光与胸怀构建人机和谐共生的社会发展格局，进而实现人机共生条件下的人的自由而全面的发展。

人工智能技术的发展代表着生产力的极大提升，但同时也要注重智能秩序的协同发展，激发人类劳动智能化内生动力，这一动力来源于政治、法律和伦理等多方面。如此才能推进人工智能与人类劳动和谐共生，进而实现人机融合发展。此外，人工智能技术的产业化效应还能助力开拓更宽更广范围的劳动就业市场，提高不同社会劳动力在社会部门间的流动，助推实现人工智能与人类劳动的和谐发展。

（二）人工智能领域变革助推马克思主义理论在实践中发展

1.智能化发展方向助力解放人类劳动

从马克思主义人学理论视域下分析人工智能与人的发展关系来看，人工智能应用场景从以往的"高不可攀"走向平民化、日常化，在人工智能产业引领下，人类生产方式彻底走向智能化发展方向，人类从简单重复的劳动中解放出来，从而为实现共产主义社会这一"每个人的自由发展是一切人的自由发展的条件"[①]的联合体提供了更加具象化的发达生产力基础。革命性的智能机器的出现不仅拓展和延伸了人脑的认知边界，也化解了特定生产情境下的人类劳动"稀缺"问题。

---

① 马克思，恩格斯.马克思恩格斯选集：第 1 卷.北京：人民出版社，2012：422.

2.智能产业资源优化助推产业结构改革

人工智能技术及其相关应用带动了智能经济的兴起和发展，人工智能相关产业的兴起为实现产业转型升级提供强大动力，为传统的三大产业资源优化配置带来极大优化，进一步推动劳动产业供给侧结构性改革。在替代掉传统行业中的劳动者的同时，人工智能也可以凭借其高效率的经济转化能力为劳动者提供更为精准的就业定位与引导服务，从而为推动中国劳动力市场的供给侧结构性改革和我国生产力的发展提供动力。

3.智能产业助力形成公共性品格

人工智能技术的发展极大拓展了人类对于自由的认识与实践路径，对人的固有本质力量进行了极大解放。从社会分工与人类发展的内在逻辑来探讨，人工智能的快速发展极大解放了社会生产力，为人的自由全面发展提供更为广阔的发展空间。从历史唯物主义和辩证唯物主义出发，科技的迅猛发展使得劳动者、劳动工具和劳动关系等都发生了深刻变革，这种变革带动新兴行业兴起的同时也直接作用于人本身，不断培养公民的社会性和公共性品格，益于社会参与和大众分享，这种公共性品格与实现了共产主义的社会的风貌有着极高的契合度。

总体来看，马克思主义理论学界已经关注到了当前人工智能领域发展中出现的现实社会问题，在人工智能技术及其相关产业快速发展的社会背景下，探索马克思主义理论与人工智能领域创新理论相互融合的研究范式已然成为新兴研究方向。选择阿里巴巴这一具有代表性的人工智能企业作为研究范例，分析其在推动人工智能发展过程中遇到的机遇与挑战，有助于在马克思主义理论的指导下，探究其自身以及同类型企业可能的未来发展路径。

二、阿里巴巴集团发展历程及其业务范围

阿里巴巴集团于 1999 年创立，建立初衷是将互联网发展成为普遍范围内使用、安全有保障的工具，惠及大众。阿里巴巴集团经历二十余年的接续发展，集团主体及其关联公司业务范围涵盖大中华地区、印度、日本、韩国、英国及美国等多个国家和地区。

阿里巴巴集团业务涵盖范围较广，自推出让中国中小企业接触全球买家的首个网站以来，阿里巴巴作为控股公司持有六大业务集团：淘天集团、阿里国际数字商业集团、云智能集团、本地生活集团、菜鸟集团、大文娱集团；按提供的服务类型划分可归纳为三类，即交易平台服务、信息服务，以及互联网金融服务。

三、阿里巴巴集团的作用与贡献

（一）数字化平台发挥资源整合优势，助力低碳数字化发展

2018年阿里云计算有限公司牵头建构了supET工业互联网平台试验测试环境。数字化技术与人工智能相结合使得阿里得以掌握和预测消费者消费倾向，以此为依据开展网络营销，这种模式也为阿里巴巴带来了可观的经济效益。

创造经济效益的同时，阿里巴巴也利用数字平台技术创造了正向的社会效益。阿里巴巴利用整合平台优势，以"互联网＋扶贫"模式开展助农销售活动，发挥整合平台核心优势寻找和拓宽销售渠道，并提供产品物流、营运等方面的培训服务，一定程度上缓解了我国交通闭塞的偏远农村地区产业经济市场发展困难的问题。

作为数字技术提供者的阿里巴巴在探索双碳解决之路方面也进行了积极探索。阿里巴巴集团积极贯彻落实环保社会责任，将可持续发展理念贯彻在商业模式中。2021年两会，"碳达峰""碳中和"被首次写入政府工作报告；同年5月，阿里云发布了"零碳云"计划，推动企业内部节能减排，输出数字减碳能力，支持绿色技术创新。

（二）践行ESG战略，彰显企业责任担当

2021年，ESG战略成为阿里巴巴面向未来发展的核心战略之一，其中包含了与阿里巴巴最相关的22项ESG议题，共分为七大方向（见表1）。[①]

表1　阿里巴巴ESG议题七大方向

七大方向	主要内容
修复绿色星球	制定并实施自身节能减排行动计划，减少价值链上游碳排放
企业和员工双向促进	以先进的制度设计和营造开放包容的人文环境
营造高质量消费环境	注重优质产品供给和高质量服务
助力中小企业高质量发展	坚持合作共赢的发展理念，持续发展负责任的科技，经济效益和社会效益相统一
助力提升社会包容和韧性	助力脱贫攻坚和乡村振兴，助力农村经济社会发展
推动人人参与的公益	厚植公益文化，鼓励公益科技创新
建立健全ESG治理体系机制	从技术和制度两个层面筑牢责任堤坝

---

① 2022阿里巴巴环境、社会和治理(ESG)报告. (2022-10-25)[2023-05-23]. https://data.alibabagroup.com/ecms-files/1509739361/0b8e8f8d-1e04-4bfc-bb0d-04a02464d35e/202220%.

ESG行动的开展需要以平台公司作为载体，只有让ESG回归真实商业场景，才能使其化解商业问题，进而创造商业之上的价值。阿里巴巴在成长过程中，持续强化数字技术在商业拓展方面的应用，在追求企业自身可持续发展的同时，阿里巴巴也担当起助推社会进步、促进环境和谐的社会责任，与众多利益相关方合力构建可持续的良性商业生态。

四、阿里巴巴发展机遇与挑战

（一）机　遇

1. 制度因素的直接利好

国内互联网制度的延续性和稳定性强，政府对互联网制度建设的重视度不断增强。《新时代的中国网络法治建设》白皮书①系统总结了1994年中国全功能接入国际互联网以来，特别是新时代以来网络法治建设理念和实践，为网络强国建设提供了坚实的制度保障。

2. 数字化、绿色化发展势不可挡

党的二十大报告中提出要"加快发展方式绿色转型"及"积极稳妥推进碳达峰碳中和"。"双碳"目标的实现离不开数字经济的支持，尤其是在节能减排、减碳控碳方面，以人工智能为代表的数字经济提供了广阔的市场机遇，数字经济中的"双碳"战略落地需求骤增，也成为阿里把握新发展态势进而抢占转型发展先机的重点所在。

3. 不断增长的消费需求

新时代我国社会的主要矛盾转变为"人民日益增长的美好生活需要和不平衡不充分的发展之间的矛盾"。这种不平衡、不充分在消费领域尤为突出。互联网运营的电子商务所具备的平等开放特性能有效消弭经济地理格局上的不平衡，人们可以通过电商平台进行无差别的生产、消费，极大地激发了人们对于电商平台的热情。

4. "互联网+"模式对接"中国制造"

中国是制造业大国。我国生产厂家劳动力成本较低，这也是"中国制造"得以在国际贸易中保持竞争力的核心之一。据最新统计，在高端制造业人力工

---

① 国务院新闻办公室. 新时代的中国网络法治建设. (2023-03-16)[2023-05-23]. https://www.gov.cn/zhengce/2023-03/16/content_5747005.htm.

资水平上，我国目前仍为美国的七分之一至六分之一左右。阿里巴巴立足于中国国情，帮助中国企业提高出口效率，同时推动中国产业带的升级，这在国际上塑造了中国自己的品牌，支持了业务的标准化、规模化发展。[①]

（二）挑　战

1.品牌形象和信用面临危机

网络平台的监管难度大，平台上的商家售假问题屡禁不止，这一问题同样存在于以C2C模式运营的淘宝网。在阿里巴巴的平台上，为消费者创造便捷的购物体验时，不可避免地出现了一些掺杂其中的假冒伪劣商品，这些劣质商品混杂在优质商品之中，给消费者的购物体验带来了潜在的风险。这些假货问题不仅损害了消费者的权益，也影响了阿里巴巴作为电商平台的声誉和可持续发展。

2.互联网企业自身特性带来的违规风险

阿里巴巴作为国内互联网企业中的代表，自身也具备互联网企业共有的"完全垄断"和"完全竞争"的特征，互联网平台市场的特性决定了单寡头竞争性垄断的市场结构既不会妨碍竞争，也不会因在位垄断者的拆分而消除，互联网平台经济依旧会催生出单寡头，竞争性垄断结构的均衡也会继续保持。这种垄断恶化了创新创业环境，极易引发数据信息安全风险，会对消费者隐私数据、产业发展造成严重的不良影响。

3.国际化过程存在问题与挑战

首先，阿里巴巴在国际市场的拓展上呈现出相对较低的水平，其国际化策略主要聚焦于新兴经济体，如俄罗斯、巴西和印度等，但在全球市场的竞争中仍显得力不从心，主要受到亚马逊和eBay等老牌电商巨头的压制。其次，从云服务全球化的视角来看，阿里云目前尚处于起步阶段，其云基础设施在海外市场尚未形成稳固的立足点，仍在持续拓展阶段，与国际市场上的行业领军者，如亚马逊AWS和微软Azure，仍存在显著差距。此外，在跨境电商支付环节，阿里巴巴主要依赖支付宝与Visa两种支付方式，但在资金转移的过程中，这些第三方支付平台可能面临网络病毒、系统安全漏洞等潜在风险，这些风险有可能导致用户账户资金的安全性受到威胁，从而增加交易的不确定性和风险性。因此，阿里巴巴在继续推进国际化的同时，也需要加强支付平台的安

---

① 王超."一带一路"下跨境电商便利化发展的机遇与挑战.北京：北京邮电大学，2017：33.

全防护，确保用户资金的安全与交易的顺利进行。

五、国内外同类型公司发展经验借鉴

（一）阿里巴巴与京东商业模式比较

为了在竞争激烈的市场环境中崭露头角，企业必须构建并确立一套独具特色的商业模式。这种模式不仅涵盖了独特的运营思维，还需要企业精准的自我定位以及强有力的技术支持，形成一套独具特色的体系，以在激烈的市场竞争中脱颖而出（见表2）。

表2　阿里巴巴与京东商业模式比较

商业模式比较	阿里巴巴	京东
思维比较	整合化的开放平台模式	价值链整合模式
定位比较	业务定位：围绕供应链的系统性服务 目标客户定位：全球范围的中小型企业卖家与买家	业务定位：高质量的零售、数字科技、物流和技术服务 目标客户定位：稳定的购物会员
技术支持比较	B2B电子商务→C2C模式	以"京东宙斯""京东云擎"为核心的成熟技术体系

总体来看，阿里巴巴和京东的技术支持都是成功范例。进入数字经济时代，阿里巴巴和京东在各自发展模式的布局下进入了全新的发展阶段，创新与变革是企业稳定发展的必然要求，阿里巴巴和京东作为中国电商行业的领军企业，其发展为整个行业提供了引领性和全局性的方向，代表了行业变革和效率改善的无限可能。

（二）阿里巴巴与亚马逊国际化经营状况对比

亚马逊作为一家综合性服务提供商，其经营范围覆盖了北美、欧洲和亚洲，国际化程度较高。以亚马逊作为研究对象，通过对比阿里巴巴和亚马逊的国际化战略（见表3），探究亚马逊国际化经营策略的可取之处，为我国跨境互联网公司进行国际化发展探索可行方案。

表3　国际化经营状况对比

经营状况对比	阿里巴巴	亚马逊
国际化水平	投资活动集中在东南亚	北美及欧洲市场占主导地位
业务布局	B2B、B2C、数字媒体、娱乐、云计算	在线零售商店服务、网络服务（AWS）、数字媒体和物流
国际化战略	收购、投资和战略合作三种主要方式	本体进入市场，并购为主要方式

总的来说，与亚马逊坚持以本体的形式进入到海外市场之中不同，阿里巴巴在国际化战略方面，业务布局涉及领域多，倾向于采用投资方式，通过控股本地公司来迅速进入到当地市场，不同市场互相的协同性较弱是这种方式的突出劣势，无法有效提升其国际化品牌影响力。亚马逊的战略则是坚持采取并购方式，让主体置身于海外市场，其优势在于可以极大程度发挥出品牌影响力优势，用户体验差异小。若需要整合本国企业与东道国企业资源，则可采取并购方式，以此增强本国企业的核心能力，否则应该考虑其他方式。每个企业应该根据自身现有资源与经营目标选择并执行适合自身的国际化战略。

六、阿里巴巴未来发展路径分析

阿里巴巴作为国内电商头部企业，追求世界范围内的广阔市场是迈入更高层次发展阶段的必经之路。但在世界范围内获得更多机遇的同时，阿里巴巴也面临着意识形态风险及人工智能技术自身发展带来的人机关系问题等风险挑战。因此，坚持以马克思主义理论为引领发展人工智能产业就显得尤为重要。

（一）坚持以马克思主义为指导，以人本逻辑超越资本逻辑

在深入探讨生成式人工智能技术与产业的演进时，我们不得不正视其背后所蕴含的巨大利益空间，并尤为关注避免资本利益过度膨胀，以致损害人民利益的现象。必须严加防范"资本至上"的逐利逻辑对主流社会价值观的侵蚀，确保在企业发展的每一个环节都坚定地贯彻习近平新时代中国特色社会主义思想。

在企业战略的规划与实施中，我们应坚持人文关怀与机器辅助相互融合的理念。这意味着生成式人工智能技术的应用应被限定在促进"每个人的自由发展"以及构建自由人"联合体"的框架内。具体而言，在追求人文本位与机器

辅位相统一的过程中，我们不仅要倡导终身学习的理念，以不断提升人的劳动技能和创新能力，还要积极探索人机协同的新模式，充分发挥人类智能与人工智能各自的优势，实现人机之间的和谐共生与协同发展。

（二）重视技术创新与防止科技异化并重，坚守人的尊严

随着智能技术的迅猛发展和智能机器人的日益智能化，人类与智能技术间的关系愈发凸显其核心价值。这种关系不应被视作对立的，而应寻求一种双方互利共生的稳定和谐状态。人类的进步涉及两个核心层面：一是生理结构的自然演进，二是精神道德层面的深化。在生理结构层面，领军企业如阿里巴巴等，借助大数据和数字化技术的飞速发展，极大地推动了人类对自身生理结构的认知边界。通过智能技术，我们不仅能够探索并突破现有的生理极限，还能进一步拓展人类协作与活动的疆域。而在精神道德层面，随着智能技术体系的日益成熟，人类更应坚守人的尊严和人性之光。互联网及人工智能企业在追求科技创新的同时，应始终关注人的本质意义，确保在未来的人机协同关系中，人的崇高地位和变革精神得以充分尊重。

（三）自觉遵守相关劳动关系制度，助力人工智能应用与稳就业平衡

在当前阶段，人工智能技术的发展对我国劳动者产生了深远影响。首先，它导致了传统行业的衰退和新兴行业的崛起。其次，无人化工作流程的普及，不可避免地引发了机器对劳动力的替代。此外，人工智能技术研发所需的高额资本投入，也在一定程度上扭曲了资本与劳动者之间的关系。一些与人工智能研发相关的岗位吸引了大量资金和劳动力，造成了对其他岗位的"人才虹吸"现象，加剧了社会就业竞争，进而恶化了整体工作生态，如"996 工作制"和"35 岁失业"等现象，均反映了当前劳动关系的非正常化。

为防止人工智能技术的应用扭曲劳动关系，依据马克思劳动价值论，即商品价格围绕价值上下波动并遵循等价交换的原则，应当制定符合当前人工智能发展实际的规章制度。人工智能产业应自觉遵守反垄断法规，打破市场垄断，以改善全社会的劳动生态。同时，应认识到知识是全社会的共同财富，鼓励个人将掌握的知识性技术融入社会智能库，减少信息和知识流通的障碍，为基层劳动者创造更多发展机会。此外，高级技术人才应重视知识的重要性，避免被金钱所诱惑，应将技术作为入股方式，共享企业成长带来的收益。

（四）积极参与全球合作治理，为技术伦理治理贡献中国智慧

鉴于人工智能技术的全球性和时代性特点，科技互惠共享和风险治理必须具备全球视野。中国应积极参与全球人工智能治理，提出"中国方案"，并构建新的共同体意识，采取切实措施，为全球人工智能治理贡献智慧。在明确划定技术使用准则和伦理界限的同时，还需明确技术责任主体，构建由政府主导、企业、第三方机构和社会公众共同参与的风险治理体系，形成有效的意识形态风险治理机制。

七、结　语

人类社会正在经历向智能社会转变的演变过程，这一场由人工智能与互联网等领域引领的技术革命标志着人类社会正迈向一个全新的智能时代。此次转型是遵循人类社会发展演进规律的必然结果，更是人类社会持续进步的重要方向。在这一过程中，人工智能的发展应当始终以人为核心，以追求人的自由与全面发展作为终极目标。基于此，深入分析和研究智能社会的内在机制与发展规律，显得尤为重要。马克思主义理论为我们提供了洞察社会的有力工具和科学方法，使我们能够准确地把握智能社会的外在形态和内在动力，为构建更加完善的智能社会提供理论支撑。随着智能技术的不断进步，一个以智能技术体系为核心的生产力新时代已经来临，这促使人与人之间的生产关系逐渐转变为新型的"人机关系"。智能经济模式，特别是以智能产业为代表，逐渐成为社会经济的主流。由于人工智能技术的特殊性质，即模拟人的智能，它在生产关系领域也带来了一定的风险性，如可能导致大量失业等社会问题。因此，对于掌握相关技术优势的人工智能龙头企业而言，在追求技术创新的同时，更应警惕潜在的风险，明确红线与底线，积极发挥创新主体作用，引导人工智能产业朝着更加安全、更惠及全体人民的方向发展。

腾讯公司社交支付生态研究报告^①

摘　要: 本文深入研究了腾讯公司在数字支付领域的代表性案例——微信支付。研究发现,用户端存在老年用户对数字支付适应和信任度的挑战,商家端面临高运营成本和微商信誉受损的问题,系统架构方面存在稳定性和过载保护机制的不足,法律和道德问题涉及用户隐私和虚假广告。研究小组从科技赋能和以人为本两个维度提出解决方案,建议强化人工智能技术和大数据分析应用,引进更多科技人才,同时加强用户教育和支持,提高数字素养,鼓励用户反馈和参与。鉴于腾讯公司在数字支付领域的经验,本文在未来展望中指出须警惕数字经济繁荣背后的资本化、数字垄断和数字霸权的风险,鼓励企业技术创新和业务拓展,以人为本,注重用户需求和社会责任。

关键词: 腾讯公司; 数字支付; 微信支付; 可持续发展

一、引　言

(一) 选题背景和目的

随着世界数字化浪潮的兴起,各国数字化经济获得了空前绝后的发展。据麦肯锡全球研究院预测,到 2025 年,全球数字化突破性技术的应用每年将带来高达 1.2 万亿至 3.7 万亿美元的经济影响价值,高度数字化转型将使企业收入和利润增长率较平均水平提升 2.4 倍。^②

---

① 作者: 刘文君,南京理工大学材料科学与工程学院; 柯俊如,南京理工大学材料科学与工程学院; 费贺东,南京理工大学材料科学与工程学院; 曾瑞哲,南京理工大学材料科学与工程学院。
② 岳彩周,邬贺铨. 算网协同打造数实融合 "新基建",通用 AI 成为创新引擎. (2023-04-13)[2023-08-06]. https://finance.sina.com.cn/jjxw/2023-04-13/doc-imyqfsqe6838445.shtml?cref=cj.

腾讯公司作为中国的互联网巨头，在数字化浪潮下，发展结构和质量在持续地优化与提升。与十年前关注的"To C"业务不同，腾讯的"To B"业务现已成为不可或缺的一大增长引擎，其产业互联网和消费互联网的"双引擎"业务架构正在加速数字经济与实体经济的"互融互惠"，在助力产业和城市的高质量发展中都发挥着重要作用。

过去的十年是中国支付市场全面开放的十年，也是支付产业高速发展的十年。从银行卡支付到移动支付再到"支付＋"，中国企业在不断探索构建产业新模式、新生态，保持支付产业旺盛的生命力和先进性。

在国内腾讯旗下的社交平台具有庞大的用户基础和广泛的影响力，而基于庞大用户基础的微信支付作为腾讯公司在社交支付领域的重要解决方案，为用户提供了便捷、快速的支付方式，满足了社交媒体用户的多样化需求。在这个背景下，对腾讯公司微信社交支付生态的可持续性发展进行分析，具有重要的理论和实践意义。

（二）研究方法和数据来源

本研究主要采用案例分析方法，通过收集和分析相关文献、研究报告、行业分析等资料，了解微信社交支付生态的发展历程、商业模式、市场竞争状况等，以及对于可持续性发展的相关研究成果；选择腾讯公司具有代表性的微信支付，深入研究腾讯社交支付生态的建设和运营，并分析其可持续性发展的优势、挑战和策略。本研究的数据来源于公司统计数据，从腾讯公司财报、行业研究报告等渠道收集相关统计数据，以了解其发展状况。

通过案例分析和数据分析，可以深入了解腾讯公司数字化进程中的先进案例，为分析腾讯公司提供可靠依据。

二、腾讯公司

中国互联网企业之一——腾讯公司是全球五大互联网巨头之一，是全球最大的游戏公司，全球第二大社交网络公司，在网络服务的众多领域中也做到了行业靠前的位置，在国内乃至国际互联网企业中都占有一席之地。它创新的产品和服务正提升着全球各地人们的生活品质。

腾讯成立于1998年，总部位于中国深圳，秉承着科技向善的宗旨，腾讯的通信和社交服务连接全球逾10亿人，帮助他们与亲友联系，畅享便捷的出行、支付和娱乐生活。该公司基于互联网的业务主要涉及三大方向：面向用户、面向企业、创新科技[①]。

（一）护城河：以微信和QQ应用为基础

微信和QQ应用是腾讯公司的基础，具有最重要的战略意义。高达9亿的、高粘性的、庞大的用户流量是腾讯公司最核心的竞争力，有着其他互联网企业所没有的得天独厚的优势。凭借于此，一方面，腾讯能够根据所积累的大量用户数据，能够根据用户需求开发新产品、引导用户至新产品入口、针对用户反馈改进产品，成为了腾讯培育其他业务的肥沃土壤；另一方面，高用户基础也提升了腾讯业务的容错率，只要不伤及用户基础，在其他业务上遇到挫折后腾讯也能全身而退，从头再来。微信和QQ的存在使得腾讯拥有超长的产品线和众多的变现方式，游戏、广告、金融已是成熟的变现模式，泛娱乐、新闻资讯、云业务、视频也大有前途。

（二）赶潮者：紧跟数字化浪潮展开业务

腾讯控股的主营业务以数字化业务为主，主要有：增值服务、网络广告、金融科技以及企业服务。

（三）创新者：借数字经济助推可持续发展

腾讯在科技创新方面的努力，不仅体现在其研发的高投入和多元化专利组合上，还体现在其将科技与业务场景深度融合，推动数字经济的可持续发展上。

首先，以巨额研发投入，抢占行业领先地位。过去三年，腾讯的研发开支已经超过200亿美元，相当于约1500亿人民币。仅2023年第一季度，腾讯的研发开支就约为21亿美元，连续五个季度保持高位水平[②]。这样的高投入，使腾讯得以在快速发展的科技领域保持领先地位。

其次，腾讯拥有多元化的专利组合。腾讯全球专利申请总数超过62000件，专利申请公开总数在全球互联网公司中排名第二。其中，腾讯拥有超过1300件数据安全相关专利授权和1000余件AI医疗相关发明专利，优先保护关

---

① Tencent腾讯. 业务. (2023-07-26)[2023-08-06]. https://www.tencent.com/zh-cn/business.html.
② Tencent腾讯科技录：九大创新提升生活品质. (2023-07-26)[2023-08-06]. https://www.tencent.com/zh-cn/articles/2201654.html.

键创新领域①。这样的专利组合使腾讯能够更好地保护创新生态，为数字经济提供可持续发展的保障。

此外，腾讯还通过自研体系和前沿领域的创新科技研发矩阵，推动数字经济的可持续发展。腾讯已经逐步建立起包括芯片、操作系统、服务器、数据库、音视频、安全、SaaS等在内的完整自研体系，这一体系不仅增强了腾讯的核心竞争力，还为公司的数字经济提供了坚实的基础。

最后，腾讯还通过共享创新平台和生态，推动数字经济的可持续发展。腾讯通过打造共享创新两大平台和四大生态，将科技创新与数字经济深度融合。这些平台和生态不仅有助于降低创新成本，提高创新效率，还能促进数字经济的快速发展。

腾讯在科技创新方面做的大量努力，推动了其数字经济的可持续发展。这些创新举措不仅增强了腾讯的竞争力，也为整个数字经济的发展注入了新的活力。

（四）佼佼者：数字化经济领域公司中名列前茅

当谈及数字化企业，谷歌（Google）将不能被忽视，谷歌被认为是全球最大的搜索引擎公司，自2016年谷歌宣布从"Mobile first"转向"AI first"以来，现在已经被公认为拥有最先进的人工智能的科技公司。谷歌的业务主要有六大方面②：安卓系统、智慧设施、谷歌浏览器、人际交流、云服务及其他业务。

之所以提及谷歌，是因为谷歌和腾讯的业务有相似或重叠的地方，比如微信支付和Google Pay、QQ邮箱和Gmail、应用宝和Google Play、腾讯会议和Google Meet……但两家企业也有不同之处，谷歌更加倾向于人工智能的研究，而腾讯更多倾向于游戏业务及其他娱乐、生活业务。

谷歌在人工智能领域的业务广泛为普通人所熟知，当归功于阿尔法狗（AlphaGo）。2016年3月，2014年被谷歌收购的Deep Mind公司开发的阿尔法狗，与围棋世界冠军、职业九段选手李世石进行了扣人心弦的人机大战，最终以4∶1的总比分获胜。而谷歌在全球数字化浪潮下也选择更为专注的方式——发展AI，以保证自己在全球互联网企业中的领先地位，应对竞争对手

---

① Tencent腾讯科技录：九大创新提升生活品质. (2023-07-26)[2023-08-06]. https://www.tencent.com/zh-cn/articles/2201654.html.

② Google谷歌. Product updates. [2023-09-05]. https://blog.google/products/.

的挑战。因此，人工智能将是 Alphabet 在未来新市场中的杀手锏[①]。

尽管业务有重叠，腾讯并没有选择与谷歌相同的战略。与本章所讲的腾讯的支付生态对应的是谷歌的Google Pay业务，谷歌支付提供简单、安全且有用的支付和理财手段，但腾讯相较于谷歌的支付框架拥有更牢固的用户基础，也有更丰富的应用场景。每个公司在数字化进程中扮演的角色不同，腾讯更注重于以用户为基础发展附加产业，而谷歌在人工智能和搜索引擎方面显然更有优势，两者在各自专注的领域都是领先的，也是不可或缺的。

除了谷歌和腾讯公司外，微软（Microsoft）、IBM、高通（Qualcomm）、华为、阿里巴巴等互联网巨头在全球数字化进程中均扮演不同的角色，共同推进着数字化的发展。

三、案例：微信支付

（一）案例描述

腾讯在数字化发展浪潮中最主要的贡献首先是以微信、QQ为代表的互联互通社交平台的搭建。

1.微信市场占有率

微信、QQ的用户占有市场份额占中国市场九成（见图5），拥有广泛的市场份额。[②]

2.微信支付

微信是以腾讯公司的使命与愿景为基础，从最开始单一的QQ平台，经过多年的发展开发出的新一代社交平台。微信支付狭义上就是一个财务流通的平台，所以讨论微信支付的发展实际上是在讨论腾讯的盈利模式的转变：A初创期——B成长期——C成熟期。

（1）初创期

腾讯公司最初通过免费即时通信平台——QQ起家，积累了大量用户，并形成了用户流量池。为了维护和运营这个平台，腾讯需要大量资金。因此，他们开发了QQ会员服务，用户可以通过购买Q币来获取定制化的服务，如QQ秀等。这个服务迅速受到用户欢迎，帮助腾讯实现了初步盈利。

---

① 孙一元.谷歌的人工智能.上海国资，2016(11): 2.
② 数据价投.(2022-08-18)[2023-08-06].腾讯控股 2022 年中报数据解读.https://xueqiu.com/8108653112/228318578.

之后，腾讯进一步挖掘QQ平台的变现方式，推出了QQ广告业务。凭借庞大的用户基础，他们为广告商提供广告投放平台，每天可以展示10亿个广告，这给腾讯带来了巨额的广告佣金，创造了更多的企业价值。

这个时期的腾讯公司以即时通讯业务为基础，通过不断创新和拓展业务领域，实现了持续迅猛的发展。[①]

（2）成长期

腾讯公司在2004年进行了战略调整，从原来的三大主营业务收入转变为以四大主营业务收入为主的盈利模式。四大主营业务包括互联网增值业务、网络广告业务、无线增值业务和电商业务。

这种一站式在线生活平台的盈利模式，使得腾讯公司能够通过多个渠道获取利润，并且通过各业务之间的协同发展，进一步增强用户粘性，为获取更多利润提供了坚实的基础。同时，腾讯公司还在不断拓宽其业务体系，提升用户体验和品牌影响力，为其持续迅猛发展提供了有力支持[②]。

（3）成熟期

2011年，开放式平台盈利模式在"互联网＋"这一背景的推动下，智能手机的使用与推广迅速改变了网民的浏览偏好与习惯，互联网用户逐渐从 PC 端转向移动端。2011年腾讯公司推出一款全新的聊天交友工具——微信，微信的迅速发展标志着腾讯自此迈入成熟发展期。与QQ相似的是，微信平台也是免费下载形式，但不同点在于微信账号依托手机号码的注册，意味着微信平台主要聚焦在移动端，也是腾讯公司顺应互联网行业发展的证明。随着微信的迅速推广，腾讯公司正式进入了以开放的平台为主的盈利模式时期。

（二）案例分析

1.用户端问题

在用户体验中，微信的功能不断扩展，使得部分界面变得越来越复杂，这让部分用户感到烦琐，对于一些用户来说甚至是一种障碍，尤其是针对老年人用户群体。根据国际组织的标准，我国在1999年就正式进入了老龄社会。国家统计局发布的数据显示，截至2019年底，中国60周岁及以上人口约2.54亿人，占总人口的18.1%，其中65周岁及以上人口1.76亿人，占总人口的

---

① 阮湾.腾讯公司的盈利模式研究.北京：中国石油大学，2020.
② 纪妙，王明宇.微商行业分析报告.中国商贸，2015(5)：3.

12.6％，预计 2050 年前后，该比例将达到 34.9％。[①]

在如此庞大的老年群体中，并非所有人都可以掌握数字支付。根据不完全统计，在 60—70 岁的老年人群体中，不少人可以完成手机预约挂号、移动支付等操作，但在 70—80 岁的老年人当中，现金支付仍然占据最重要的位置，老年人对现金支付具有很强的依赖性和很高的信任度，对移动支付则知之甚少。尽管腾讯为此做了很多努力，但针对老年人易上当受骗或是不能够灵活使用智能手机进行数字支付的问题仍没有从根本上解决。

在安全问题中，微信涉及用户的隐私和财产，用户可能会遇到诸如账号被盗、聊天内容被窥视等涉及用户个人信息安全及财产安全的问题。正由于微信庞大的用户基数，微信也容易成为用于电信诈骗或线上赌博等网络犯罪活动的载体。同时微信自身作为一个巨大的信息载体，汇集全国广大用户的个人信息，自身的安全稳定性也颇为重要，减少或避免诸如微信"3.29"后台崩溃事件的发生，保障用户的合法权益刻不容缓。

2. 商家端问题

商家除了需要投入大量的资源和时间来创建和维护微信公众号或小程序以吸引和保留客户外，还需要缴纳一定的交易手续费，从而提高了商家的运营成本。

为了使商品进入大众眼帘，许多商家也会根据具体情况而有所不同地付出几百到上万元不等的宣传费用，导致商家往往在获得收益之前就已经投入了大量资本，运营成本高。

除此之外，还存在劣性竞争、微商名誉受损的问题。2014 年，"面膜式微商"大行其道，大量作弊软件也纷纷涌现[②]。微商主体界限不明，难以适用现行法律也是一个不可忽视的问题：通过微商进行交易的双方并不属于传统意义上的消费者和经营者，难以适用现行法律规定，很难进行举证和维权[③]。

3. 系统架构问题

微信作为一个国家级的信息处理平台，也伴发着许多并发压力。微信系统存在着稳定性不足的问题，这主要缘于自身的过载保护机制还不够完善。过载

① 郭栋. 金砖国家联合统计手册 2020. [2023-08-06]. https://www.stats.gov.cn/zt_18555/ztsj/jzgj/jz2020/202302/P020230309331339376667.pdf.
② 纪妙，王明宇. 微商行业分析报告. 中国商贸，2015(5)：3.
③ 任珂墨，杜海珠，杨阳. 浅析微商发展现状及法律监管. 经法视点商界论坛，2015(37)：253.

控制对于大规模在线应用程序来说至关重要，这些应用程序需要在不可预测的负载激增的情况下实现 24×7 服务可用性。传统的过载控制机制是为具有少量服务组件、相对狭窄的"前门"和普通依赖关系的系统而设计的。而微信这种现代即时通讯应用的全时在线服务特性，在架构和依赖性方面正变得越来越复杂，远远超出了传统过载控制的设计目标。即在微信这种大规模微服务场景下，过载会变得比较复杂，如果是单体服务，一个事件只用一个请求，但微服务下，一个事件可能要请求很多的服务，任何一个服务过载失败，就会造成其他的请求都是无效的[①]。

由此可见，如果不及时调节微信的过载保护机制，微信系统极易发生崩溃。

4.法律和道德问题

在用户隐私方面，微信可能存在未经用户同意收集和使用用户信息的行为，这侵犯了用户的隐私权。这意味着用户在享受大数据技术带来的便利时，也承担着个人隐私信息泄漏的风险。

随着公众隐私保护意识的提升，越来越多被人们忽视的"秘密"行为——读取相册、剪切板、调用摄像头等非法行为被一一挖出。2021 年 10 月 8 日，微博数码博主 Hackl0us 爆料称微信存在主动读取用户相册行为[②]。尽管微信官方回应称，该功能系为方便用户快速发图做准备。但在更新后，微信仍在后台继续高频次地读取相册，隐私问题仍未解决。截至 10 月 9 日，@Hackl0us 的相关微博点击量达到 1973 万，话题阅读量达到 1.7 亿，话题讨论量达到 1.2 万。

不仅微信，其他平台过度索取用户信息已成常态。平台常以各种理由向用户索取个人信息。如通过网民协议格式条款，以提供服务为由强制用户同意对个人信息的无限制索取，在这个过程中用户没有充分理解隐私协议，也没有自愿性。此外，APP 平台常常以技术更迭、提升服务为借口向用户索取更多权限，掩饰其过度获取用户信息的目的。上述事件中，微信以"方便用户快速发图"为由获取用户相册权限，却在未经允许的情况下在后台频繁地读取用户私人相册，严重侵犯了用户的隐私权益。

---

① Jack Jiang. 微信的后台构架是怎样的 . (2022-06-06)[2023-08-05]. https://www.zhihu.com/question/20152151.
② 胡佳敏 . 微信后台频繁读取用户相册事件：社交平台侵犯用户个人隐私 . (2022-05-01)[2023-09-01]. http://media-ethic.ccnu.edu.cn/info/1168/2891.html.

特别是，微信支付系统涉及大量敏感数据和资金交易信息，如果数据传输或存储过程中出现漏洞，可能会导致数据泄露，对用户造成损失。如果内部人员拥有过大的权限或疏于管理，可能会泄露用户的支付信息或资金数据。

此外，还存在宣传中的虚假情况，《2020中国异常流量报告》显示，2020年中国品牌广告市场因异常流量造成的损失约为305亿人民币。异常流量损害数字广告投放的真实性、效率和质量，也损害消费者对品牌方的信任。[①]

这不仅违反了道德规范，也可能导致商家的信誉受损。目前微信平台上存在着大量的虚假违规广告，这主要是因为虚伪广告的概念和确定标准不明确，检查监管机制不健全，互联网虚伪广告立法滞后，以及虚伪广告违法成本低等问题未被解决。同时目前广告监管的手段有限，微信平台难以及时处理这些虚假违规广告，给用户造成了诸多影响。

（三）案例结论：基于腾讯公司支付生态系统的经验总结

腾讯公司之所以在支付生态方面能够获得如此大的发展，究其原因，主要在于以下四方面。

1.巨大的用户基础和用户粘性

腾讯公司拥有庞大的用户网络和用户关系链，特别是其产品——微信作为中国最主要的社交平台，具有极高的用户粘性和使用频率。这为腾讯开展支付业务提供了广阔的用户基础和入口，使得腾讯的支付产品能够快速获得用户的认可和使用。

2.多元化的业务场景和生态系统

腾讯公司在游戏、电商、O2O、金融科技等领域都有广泛的布局，这为支付业务的推广和应用提供了丰富的场景和生态系统。通过与各根业务线的交汇，腾讯的支付服务能够渗透到用户生活的各个方面，提高用户的使用频率和粘性。

3.技术创新和产品体验优化

腾讯公司在支付技术方面持续进行创新和研发，投入大量资源来研发高效、安全、便捷的支付产品。同时，腾讯也注重产品体验的优化，提供多样化的支付方式和用户服务，以满足不同用户的需求和习惯。

---

① 张彬斌. 互联网广告流量虚假，异常流量占比率8.6%. (2021-03-22)[2023-09-01]. https://www.thepaper.cn/newsDetail_forward_11820003.

4.合作伙伴的广泛合作

腾讯公司积极与各大银行、第三方支付机构、商家等合作伙伴建立合作关系，共同推动支付生态的发展。通过合作，腾讯能够获得更多的支付场景、更丰富的用户资源以及更广泛的市场覆盖。

四、意见和建议

在第三节中我们探讨了微信支付现在所面临的四大问题，即用户端问题、商家端问题、系统架构问题以及法律道德问题。这四大问题亦可以归结为微信支付作为一种增值服务的产品在服务过程中服务质量和服务对象两个部分的缺失。针对服务质量部分的问题，因为本质上涉及微信支付的各种程序的开发与功能完善，所以可以采取科技赋能的方法；而针对服务对象的问题，因为微信支付服务的对象是广大消费者，且微信支付在服务过程中常产生服务对象错位的问题，所以应秉持以人为本的原则，以实现可持续发展。以下从这两个维度来分析腾讯的发展现状并给出未来建议。

（一）科技赋能

1.人工智能技术

近年来，腾讯已经在微信中引入了人工智能技术，如语音助手和智能推荐算法，以提升用户体验。同时，人工智能在安全领域也得到广泛应用，用于检测欺诈行为和数据加密。

腾讯公司持续投资研发人工智能技术，包括自然语言处理、图像语音识别和机器学习，以进一步提高微信支付的用户体验和安全性，提高用户粘性。例如，针对老年用户群体，进一步开发智能客服机器人，提供实时语音帮助和支持，以解决用户问题。同时继续升级关怀模式，支付时放大关键支付信息的字体，以及增加语音提醒功能。同样在面对系统架构问题时，可以利用机器学习算法，构建适量的大模型，输入足够的系统数据，再以大模型训练小模型，筛选出合适的系统数据，在此基础上，填补和完善支付系统所存在的漏洞。

2.大数据分析

腾讯在微信中利用大数据分析来了解用户行为和偏好，以改进广告投放和内容推荐，这一举措有助于商家更好地理解用户需求。

在原有的大数据分析的基础上，加强数据分析工具、发掘更多数据资源可以为商家提供更多的数据洞察,帮助他们优化营销策略和服务;此外,腾讯可以利用大数据分析来预测潜在的安全威胁,提前采取措施保护用户隐私和安全;针对信息爆炸的问题,在进行数据分析的同时适时加入限制条件,构建合理的推送机制和数理模型;同时数据分析时不应局限于关键词的分析,还应进行对衍生词、反义词及同义词的分析,从而巩固信息的安全性、全面性,维护用户信息的完整性。

3.科技人才

在当前就业状况下,许多优秀的科技人才倾向于选择创业公司或者国外科技公司,腾讯和众多互联网企业面临人才流失的问题。且随着技术产业的不断升级,微信支付领域的技术需求也在不断增长,腾讯需要不断引进新技术,以满足市场需求。双重困境的挑战下,科技人才是腾讯公司源源不断的发展动力。

为了获得优质的科技人才,腾讯可以通过加强内部人才培养,提高员工的技能和素质;此外,可以通过与高校和研究机构合作,推动产学研合作,共同研发新技术和产品,这样可以吸引更多的科技人才,以提高公司的技术水平;腾讯已经建立了自己的研究院,但是不同于像微软公司创办的微软亚洲研究院,腾讯研究院下设法律研究中心、产业与经济研究中心、社会研究中心、犯罪研究中心和安全研究中心,更多关注的是产品对社会民众的影响,属于社会科学研究的范畴。所以腾讯应该注重研究院的"科研性"的建设,制订技术发展方案,增设科研交流站,建设学术交流论坛,拓展各项诸如机器学习组、多媒体计算组、智能云端系统组等互联网行业重点技术攻关研究小组。这样才能有效地提高自己的科学技术储备。

(二)以人为本

1.用户教育和支持

腾讯已经在微信中设立了用户教育和帮助中心以回答常见问题,但仍可以进一步提高用户的数字素养:开展广泛的用户教育活动,特别是关于隐私保护和网络安全的培训;同时,提供更多易懂的用户指南和视频教程,帮助弱势群体更好地利用微信支付功能;可以借助自媒体平台、流媒体平台,进行推广和普及,如在相关公众号上发表文章,在B站、抖音等网络平台以视频为媒介进行宣传;利用明星效应,邀请明星和其他公众人物做形象推广大使。

2.用户反馈和参与

腾讯已经允许用户提供反馈和建议，但仍可以进一步提高用户参与度：积极收集用户反馈，建立反馈机制，鼓励用户分享他们的体验和意见；推出激励计划，以奖励积极参与的用户，从而更好地满足他们的需求；定期在支付系统界面设置反馈通道或者意见反馈板块，后台监测工作人员同样定期收集反馈情况，再进一步进行分析和之后的工作，从而使得各服务板块能得到不断的完善。

综合来看，腾讯公司应该继续在人工智能和大数据分析领域投入资源，以提高微信支付的技术能力。同时，以人为本的原则应贯穿整个生态系统，通过用户教育、反馈机制和用户参与，建立更强大的社交支付生态系统，从而更好地满足用户需求、提高安全性，实现可持续性发展。这将有助于改善用户体验、降低运营成本、提高营销效果，并在合规和道德方面取得更好的表现，承担作为中国乃至世界互联网企业的社会责任。

五、启示与展望

腾讯公司的社交支付生态在数字化浪潮中大力推动数字支付的广泛性，其中腾讯公司重视用户体验、多业务协同发展、数据驱动的决策是对于数字化支付中的重要推动要素。管中窥豹，通过对于腾讯公司微信社交支付生态的可持续性发展进行分析，具有重要的理论和实践意义。以腾讯公司案例为基础，分析得出数字化浪潮中面临的战略问题：用户体验和操作繁杂的矛盾、商家高运营成本和腾讯支付数据处理的矛盾、系统构架和使用灵活的矛盾，以及道德法律和虚假信息的矛盾。基于问题分析，给出中国互联网社交支付行业可实行的可持续发展战略方案。

数字化带来的数字经济的繁荣是社会先进生产力的产物，但是以此为基础的支付过程中，难免会遭遇企业的资本化问题，其随之产生的负面影响和风险对腾讯而言亦是不容忽视的：其最明显的表现就是逐渐形成数字垄断和数字霸权。而且数字经济资本化造成的数字垄断与传统垄断有明显区别。在宏观层面，数字经济本身的产业化和其他产业的数字化，使产业与产业之间的链接比旧的产业链关系更密切。资本对市场的伤害最终要由劳动者、消费者来承担，表现之一为一旦被平台驯化或固化后，消费者会越来越依赖垄断的支付平台。

展望未来，在数字化和人工智能化的浪潮大背景下，腾讯公司作为中国互联网巨头和人工智能领域的领先企业，扮演着重要的角色。为了在未来的竞争中立于不败之地，腾讯公司需要不断推进技术创新和业务拓展，以满足用户和市场的需求。一方面，腾讯公司需要继续发展传统的互联网服务，稳固自身在社交、游戏、娱乐等领域的领先地位。另一方面，腾讯公司也需要紧跟数字化和人工智能化的浪潮，不断创新和发展，积极探索人工智能等新兴领域，加快技术研发和应用落地，为用户提供更加智能化、高效化和便捷化的服务。

作为一家具有社会责任感的企业，腾讯公司也需要承担一定的社会责任。在国际化领域中，持续拓展海外市场、加强与国际企业的合作和交流、培养全球化人才，并积极参与国际标准的制定和合规机制的建设，加强与国际社会的合作与沟通，建立良好的国际形象和声誉。在可持续发展领域中，互联网巨头有责任积极推动可持续发展，包括关注环境保护、推动绿色技术和可持续能源的应用，关注社会公益和慈善事业，推动数字包容，促进数字经济的包容性和可持续发展；同时，要积极参与社会治理，保护用户隐私和数据安全，加强数据伦理和数据治理的建设。进一步在跨界合作中，积极与其他行业进行跨界合作，加强与传统产业的融合，促进数字化转型和创新，推动行业数字化和智能化发展，共同开创新的商业模式和增长点。

在数字化和人工智能化的浪潮中，对于腾讯和中国其他互联网和人工智能公司来说，硬实力和软实力同样重要。无论是精确的人工智能还是便捷的互联网，都只是工具，最终的目的是服务于人，为人们创造美好的未来。只有以人为本，科技创新才能真正发挥其作用，为用户和社会创造更多的价值和贡献。因此，中国互联网和人工智能企业，不仅应积极推动科技创新和业务拓展，更需要关注人的需求和利益，注重用户体验和社会责任，以实现可持续发展和创造更加美好的未来，为社会科学技术、人民福祉做贡献。

基于字节跳动案例的ESG路径研究①

摘　要： 随着数字信息技术的飞速发展，互联网与人工智能产业已经成为提升国家软实力的重要载体。在以互联网大数据为载体的全球化数字经济竞争中，我国互联网企业在呈现出极高技术创新活力的同时，也造成了许多新的社会问题，主要集中于环境、社会和治理三方面，在此基础上形成的ESG概念的命名便是取自其英文缩写。本研究以字节跳动为研究案例，深入分析该企业科技创新与ESG发展情况，并针对其存在的问题提出可行性建议。

关键词： 互联网企业；人工智能；字节跳动；案例研究；ESG

一、引　言

（一）研究背景

随着我国数字信息技术的飞速发展，互联网与人工智能产业已经成为提升我国软实力的重要载体。互联网企业作为应用数字化技术的关键微观主体，成为数字化转型的"主力军"。人工智能、移动互联网、云计算、区块链等相关技术的嵌入推动企业传统的组织结构、业务模式、管理理念、战略决策等发生深刻变革。当前，以人工智能等为代表的数字技术迅速崛起，推动着全球经济的数字化变革。在这一以互联网大数据为载体的全球化数字经济竞争中，我国互联网企业呈现出极高的技术创新活力，并在某些领域实现了弯道超车②。

数字洪流的席卷也造成了许多新的社会问题，随着ISO26000《社会责任指南》在全球的深入实施，企业主动承担并详尽披露社会责任已成为一种不可

---

① 作者：朱竹燕，武汉大学政治学系；高煜婷，武汉大学法学系；杜晶，武汉大学信息管理与信息系统系；刘雅慧，武汉大学地球物理学系。
② 郭瑾.发展数字文化产业与我国软实力提升研究——以TikTok为例.山东社会科学，2021(5)：116-122.

逆转的国际潮流。①数字化浪潮所带来的诸多问题主要存在于环境、社会和治理这三个与公民的生产生活息息相关的共同主题，而基于 ESG 概念形成的企业发展理念正是企业针对环境保护（environmental）、社会责任（social）和公司治理（governance）的制度安排。ESG 概念由联合国环境规划署于 2004 年首次提出，主张企业在经营过程中除了经济效益外，还应考虑环境、社会和治理方面的表现，该理念传递了企业追求经济利益与社会价值相统一的可持续发展观，为企业实现自身可持续发展提供了理论框架。然而与国外相比，我国 ESG 的发展起步较晚，企业的 ESG 体系建设与信息披露水平也亟需提升。

2018 年以来，腾讯、阿里巴巴、百度、美团、快手等多家头部互联网企业陆续发布 ESG 报告。作为一家指数级增长的全球平台企业，字节跳动是国内最大的互联网信息平台之一，在科技创新与数字化浪潮中面临多方面的风险，如组织管理风险、环境风险、公平运营风险、消费者安全与隐私问题等挑战。然而字节跳动历经初创期——成长期——扩张期——风波期——赋能期几个阶段的转型与发展，在短短十多年内跃升为占据国际化优势地位、ESG 表现优秀的互联网企业。因此，本报告选取北京抖音信息服务有限公司（下称"字节跳动"）为研究对象，深入分析该企业科技创新与 ESG 发展情况，并针对其存在的问题提出可行性建议。

（二）研究目的及意义

基于对字节跳动企业发展实践的初步调研，本文认为字节跳动是研究互联网企业 ESG 建设路径的极具代表性和重要性的样本，因此，本文选取字节跳动为研究对象，研究字节跳动在 ESG 上面临的问题、做出的贡献，并结合国际互联网公司的发展经验，为强化字节跳动这类平台企业的 ESG 建设提供可循的治理路径与方案。同时，本研究为企业提升 ESG 水平提供有效建议，有助于帮助企业更好地应对环境风险，增强社会责任感，优化治理结构，进而提高公司的运营效率，降低法律风险，提升企业形象，从而提升企业的市场竞争力。

---

① 江乾坤，罗安琪，石璐瑶. 社交型互联网企业国际化投资的社会责任风险管理——以字节跳动为例. 财务与会计，2021(16)：41-44.

二、企业简介与发展历程

（一）企业简介

北京抖音信息服务有限公司（曾用名：北京字节跳动科技有限公司），成立于2012年，是最早将人工智能应用于移动互联网场景的科技企业之一。公司以建设"全球创作与交流平台"为愿景，旗下产品有今日头条、西瓜视频、抖音等。目前，该公司的产品和服务已覆盖全球150多个国家和地区、75个语种，曾在40多个国家和地区位居应用商店总榜前列。

（二）发展历程

1. 第一阶段：初创期——投石问路

在初创期，字节跳动凭借自身的人才优势，确定互联网技术型企业的发展方向，以大数据和人工智能为技术基础，推动业务发展。今日头条的推出是字节跳动打出的第一枪，其改变了以往内容资讯平台的信息分发模式，由PC互联网时代的"主动搜索"转变为"算法为基"，通过算法介入后的用户行为分析，不断完善推荐算法模型，实现用户兴趣与信息的高度匹配，实现信息自动化推送。[①]

字节跳动在初创阶段依托今日头条逐渐创造出区别于其他新闻资讯平台的优势，形成一站式多元化内容聚合平台，也由此推进了多项业务的先孵化再运营的成功实践。

2. 第二阶段：成长期——优势深耕

字节跳动公司于2016年9月和2017年5月分别推出抖音和火山小视频应用程序（APP），将核心业务从新闻资讯领域向短视频领域扩展，或称"横向包围"。值得注意的是，短视频平台的用户数据库与原有今日头条数据库并不相通，即短视频领域的横向包围并不完全基于已有的用户基础，平台体现了不同用户群体特征。[②]

字节跳动修正了此前一些同类产品的深度绑定和定位不清的问题，推出了抖音和火山小视频两个独立APP。通过类似实物消费品的品牌化战略实现对产品的精准定位，将抖音的目标用户群体定位为一二线城市的年轻人，内容具有轻潮、时尚的差异化特征，将火山小视频的目标市场定位为三四线以下城

---

① 赵超，陈雪伟. 平台型企业包围战略实施路径研究——以字节跳动为例. 竞争情报，2022，18(4)：21-30.
② 赵超，陈雪伟. 平台型企业包围战略实施路径研究——以字节跳动为例. 竞争情报，2022，18(4)：21-30.

市，并通过具象化标签向目标用户清晰传达自身定位和特点，实现了目标用户和品牌的差异化。①2018年抖音品牌升级，发布了一系列的专题计划，激励视频创作者，充分激发网络效应，使平台内容走向多元化，进一步扩大了用户规模，提升了用户黏性。

3.第三阶段：扩张期——成功出海

2015至2016年是字节跳动国际化初期的试水阶段，也是字节跳动把自己的品牌和产品推向国际舞台的第一阶段。在这一阶段，字节跳动主攻新闻推荐类业务，紧紧围绕今日头条及其海外版TopBuzz进行海外布局。②

2016年10至12月，字节跳动以投资并购方式控股了印度最大的新闻聚合平台Daily Hunt，并陆续与当地170多家新闻机构进行合作，正式打开了印度市场，为后来的短视频业务全面铺开奠定基础。

同时，结合抖音的运营经验，字节跳动于2017年9月在美国上线了抖音国际版——TikTok，并陆续拓展至全球市场，瞬间掀起了海外用户追逐短视频分享的热潮，用户数甚至一路赶超Facebook，下载量在多国手机APP中位居榜首。字节跳动也因此被誉为最具全球化视野的中国互联网公司之一，成为中国企业"走出去"中大获成功的典型代表。③

4.第四阶段：风波期——峰回路转

作为美国舆论场上唯一一家具有重大国际影响力的非美国直属的媒体平台，TikTok的崛起在很大程度上挑战了美国近百年的媒体操控系统，并在2019年12月16日以TikTok会获取用户信息、泄露隐私并"威胁国家安全"为由被起诉。危机发生后，字节跳动迅速采取应对之策，2020年8月24日，TikTok宣布将针对美国政府所发布的与该公司有关的一系列行政令，正式起诉美国政府以维护自身合法权益。2021年6月9日，美国总统拜登签署行政令并宣布撤销前任总统特朗普在任期间有关"在美国境内禁止下载和使用TikTok"的行政令。然而，拜登政府加大了对TikTok的安全审查，并于2024年4月签署"不卖就禁用"法案，美国最高法院在TikTok一系列起诉、上诉后维持原禁令。而特朗普在竞选期间对TikTok态度转变，随着其再次就任美

---

① 赵超，陈雪伟.平台型企业包围战略实施路径研究——以字节跳动为例.竞争情报，2022，18(4)：21-30.

② 谢佩洪，李伟光.字节跳动的国际化突围之路——以TikTok封禁事件为例.清华管理评论，2022(6)：98-107.

③ 谢佩洪，李伟光.字节跳动的国际化突围之路——以TikTok封禁事件为例.清华管理评论，2022(6)：98-107.

国总统，TikTok的命运似乎将迎来转机。

5. 第五阶段：赋能期——动能转换

随着国家与社会对企业履行社会责任的期许逐渐增高，乡村振兴、扶贫济困、绿色生态等方面成为既事关国计民生、又蕴含丰富的经济增长点。现今的字节跳动作为一家成熟的互联网公司，在推动共同富裕和乡村振兴中相互促进、相互融合，积极探索互联网技术资源与基层治理工作的联动共赢模式，有效引导社会服务资源、项目向基层和乡村倾斜，融入互联网产品，以履行社会责任、激发创新活力来赋能自身发展。[①]

三、企业在科技创新与数字化浪潮中的贡献

字节跳动始终重视科技创新，不断加大科研投入，提升技术创新水平，并通过技术交叉应用和技术开源，让科技惠及更多领域。

（一）技术创新

字节跳动聚焦技术前沿领域，探索技术交叉应用，推动行业科技创新，在人工智能与云计算、实时传输等多个领域取得了研发成果。

在人工智能方面，字节跳动旗下的抖音和今日头条利用人工智能技术提供了多种个性化的服务，如推荐算法、智能搜索、智能客服等等。在机器人领域的布局中，字节跳动也始终坚持以技术创新为主导。不断加大在人工智能和机器人技术上的研发投入，积极探索新的技术应用和创新，其机器学习算法在图像识别、语音识别、自然语言处理等领域达到了世界领先水平。比如，图像识别算法能够高效地识别并处理大量的图片数据，为机器人提供了强大的视觉能力，语音识别和自然语言处理算法也为机器人的交互和学习能力提供了强大的支持。

（二）技术开源

字节跳动还通过技术开源，助力科技行业交流与繁荣。2022年，字节跳动成立开源委员会，进一步推动技术开源，新增语音预训练模型 CoBERT、开源引擎 LightSeq 等近 20 个开源项目。

---

① 鞠思思，陈明.字节跳动：社会责任与业务融合发展.企业管理，2022(7)：82-85.

四、运用ESG视角综合分析

（一）环境保护积极实践

在环境保护方面，字节跳动积极开展实践，并取得了一定的成果。

在可再生能源方面，2023年3月14日，字节跳动公布碳中和目标，承诺在2030年实现自身运营层面的碳中和。基于这一目标，字节跳动计划逐步提升数据中心的可再生能源使用比例，在2030年前实现全球运营100%使用可再生能源电力，并将推动实现价值链上下游的减碳工作。同时，字节跳动旗下产品也将助力可持续发展相关内容的传播和普及。2022年，"可持续发展"相关话题在TikTok、抖音、今日头条和西瓜视频上获得了数十亿浏览量。

在节能减排方面，2022年，字节跳动通过应用高效液冷技术、高密风墙技术以及无水冷却技术等，提升数据中心的资源利用率。其大型定制化数据中心电源使用效率（Power Usage Effectiveness，PUE）可达1.15。PUE是数据中心总能耗与IT设备能耗的比值，基准是2，数值越接近1代表其用能效率越高。2021年7月，工信部发布《新型数据中心发展三年行动计划（2021—2023年）》，提出能效水平方面，新建大型及以上数据中心PUE应降低到1.3以下，而字节跳动1.15的PUE远低于此标准。[①]

在绿色办公方面，对于自建楼宇，字节跳动以高于国家标准的环保要求参与到建筑设计过程中，争取提高自有建筑绿建认证覆盖率。北京办公区在建筑结构基础上改造，在建立屋顶花园的同时设置余热回收装置或系统，采用用水效率高的卫生器具，提高节水效率。对于租赁楼宇，字节跳动加装能源计量系统，连入集团能效管理平台。字节跳动还积极引入和推广使用装配式装修技术，通过对建材重复利用提升建筑的减碳能力和环境效益。字节跳动通过绿电交易、绿证购买、可再生能源和储能建设等方式逐步提高数据中心的绿色能源占比。2022年内，数据中心使用风能、太阳能电力超1亿度。但是绿色能源占比及变化、碳排放数据及变化等具体情况均未得到披露。[②]

① 中华人民共和国工业和信息化部. 新型数据中心发展三年行动计划(2021—2023年). (2021-07-04)[2024-03-01]. https://www.gov.cn/zhengce/zhengceku/2021/07/14/content_5624964.htm.
② 抖音集团. 抖音集团2022年度企业社会责任报告. (2023-03-14)[2024-03-01]. https://lf3-static.bytednsdoc.com/obj/eden-cn/ptvaeh7vbozps/2022_抖音集团企业社会责任报告.pdf.

（二）社会责任议题表现优异

在社会责任方面，字节跳动积极承担社会责任，尽管存在一定缺陷，但是总体上在多个议题中表现优异。

在隐私数据保护方面，字节跳动致力于通过强化信息安全与隐私保护力度，优化数字治理举措，巩固数字信任体系，为用户提供更安全、更优质的数字服务。在管理制度上，制定《个人信息保护安全规范》《数据分类分级标准》等管理办法，严格管理用户信息及数据安全；在保护用户个人信息隐私安全方面，制定《个人信息保护安全规范》并公开发布"隐私保护五大原则"及各产品隐私保护政策，保障用户隐私权益不受侵害。2022年，字节跳动推出《隐私保护计算法律合规指引报告》，并举办隐私保护计算法律论坛，为数据要素市场的发展奠定法律基础。

在精准扶贫和乡村振兴方面，字节跳动响应国家号召，开展产业、科技和消费扶贫，发挥优势，取得多项成果。2017年，其成立创新事业部并发起"山货上头条"和"扶贫达人培训计划"等扶贫活动，基于电商和区域特点制定营销对策，形成特有的扶贫模式，助力农产品等的销售，带动农民增收。2021年，其启动"字节乡村计划"助力贫困地区打造农特产和文旅新业态，实现可持续发展，并在2021年全面脱贫实现以后，利用抖音直播带货，持续助力"三农"发展。字节跳动在2022年还持续推动非遗传承、古籍保护，实现共创共享。

在产品质量安全方面，为保证数字治理工作的有效开展，字节跳动持续构建相应的治理体系，健全管理制度和机制。其成立内容安全质量中心、商业生态与安全等部门，并在业务线和产品方面设置专项团队，提升内容质量，跟进用户反馈，打造健康的平台生态。针对内容治理，字节跳动制定《今日头条社区规范》，修订《抖音社区自律公约》，对网暴、不实信息传播等现象给予明确界定和治理标准。针对电商治理，其制定系列管理规则，规范内容生产与运营；针对商品治理，在2022年制定《抖音电商规则总则》《商品品质分规范》，并将《商家持续经营分规范》升级为《商家信誉等级标准》；针对直播治理，制定《2022年抖音直播机构管理条例》；针对广告治理，制定《巨量千川准入&管控规则指引》《巨量千川服务管理规范》，一定程度上保障了其广告产品的质量。

在反歧视方面，字节跳动致力于"让每个人平等地享受数字生活"，重点关注青少年、老年人和障碍人群，推动数字包容。2022年，今日头条APP、抖音APP（包含抖音火山版）以及今日头条网站、西瓜视频网站等成为首批通过工信部"互联网应用适老化及无障碍改造专项行动"评测的产品。其中，在应用适老化方面，字节跳动通过开展老龄群体公益培训课程、号召创作者发布手机使用教程等方法，"手把手"帮助老年人跨越"数字鸿沟"。2022年内，抖音平台"教长辈用手机"相关视频播放量累计超5499万次。[①] 字节跳动同时也推出了可以自行设置的青少年模式。在无障碍适配方面，字节跳动在不同的产品中上线护眼模式、色弱模式，以及读图、读新闻、听小说等功能，让视障、听障等特殊群体享受更自由的数字生活。2022年，西瓜视频无障碍影院累计提供超120部无障碍电影。同时，字节跳动在深圳启动残疾人就业试点，聘用视障群体任职包容测试工程师，对工区进行无障碍改造，促进残障人士就业。

（三）公司治理问题频出

在公司治理方面，字节跳动推出规范来加强管理，但仍然出现了很多问题。

在反不公平竞争方面，字节跳动依据《中华人民共和国反垄断法》及相关法律法规和地方合规，维护健康有序的市场环境，将公平竞争和反垄断内容写入《员工行为准则》，并针对"二选一""大数据杀熟"等热点问题制作系列专题课程供员工学习。

在风险管理方面，在管理架构上，字节跳动成立信息安全委员会和隐私保护工作组，统一协调管理公司信息安全和隐私保护工作。但是，有媒体在2022年12月报道，字节跳动的部分内审人员为堵住内部资料外泄给媒体的漏洞，动用特殊权限查看了多名美国媒体记者在TikTok上留下的隐私数据，包括他们的IP地址、APP内通信等，以审查他们是否曾与涉嫌泄密的员工联络见面[②]，此举违背了TikTok此前关于用户隐私保护的公开承诺。企业的内审部门本应是保障企业合规的终极防线，但是字节跳动的内审人员在调查公司内部的泄密漏洞时却突破了他们本应坚守的数据合规底线。如果不能完善并落实对管理人员和内审团队的合规管理，此类隐私数据泄露事件难免再现，风险将进

---

① 抖音集团.抖音集团2022年度企业社会责任报告.(2023-03-14)[2024-03-01]. https://lf3-static.bytednsdoc.com/obj/eden-cn/ptvaeh7vbozps/2022_抖音集团企业社会责任报告.pdf.

② 鞠思思，陈明.字节跳动：社会责任与业务融合发展.企业管理，2022(7)：82-85.

一步提升。

在员工保障方面，字节跳动升级了假期及健康福利计划，新增"家庭关爱假"，每年 10 个工作日；"全薪病假"天数从半年 4 个工作日提升至全年 12 个工作日。字节跳动引入了百万医疗自选保险，对大病、重疾风险场景进行补充，方便员工自选。不过，值得注意的是，字节跳动在员工保障方面也存在一些不足之处。据媒体报道，2022 年 6 月，抖音海外版 TikTok 的英国伦敦电商团队不满母公司字节跳动带来的高负荷加班文化，一半员工已经离职。据媒体后续报道，高管 Joshua Ma 将从 TikTok 英国电商团队中退出。TikTok 方面则回应称，一切制度都遵循当地的法律法规，并将针对 Joshua Ma 的相关言论展开正式调查。①同时，字节跳动发布的相关报告也未对"员工性别比例""歧视事件总数及采取的纠正行动"进行披露。

五、发展不足与建议

（一）发展不足

结合时代大环境，梳理字节跳动自身的发展历程并比较同行业其他公司，我们总结了字节跳动目前所存在的一些不足。

1.节能减排目标与举措缺乏明确性和具体性

整体来看，相较于提出具体节能减排措施的亚马逊等公司，字节跳动在环保领域没有非常明确的目标与规划。以抖音集团 2022 年度发布的《抖音集团企业社会责任报告》为例，报告中环境部分的内容主要侧重于企业自身的绿色运营，如打造绿色数据中心、推进绿色办公等，并没有建立明确的目标和行动规划。与之相对比，国外互联网企业在 ESG 报告环境部分的内容则提出更多也更具体的节能减排方案。以亚马逊公司为例，2019 年，亚马逊签订"气候保证书"，承诺在 2040 年前实现整个企业的净零碳排放，目标规划包括新能源的投资、运输减排及碳排放的降低。亚马逊对近 3 年碳排放强度给出了定量数据。虽然随着营收增长，亚马逊的总体碳排放量呈现增长趋势，但碳排放强度逐年下降，到 2030 年，亚马逊 50％的货物将实现运输零排放。②

① 周姝祺.字节跳动加班文化在海外"水土不服"，引发离职潮.(2022-06-16)[2024-03-01]. https://net.blog china.com/blog/article/517834925.
② 段濛.互联网企业的 ESG 体系构建——基于亚马逊与拼多多的双案例研究.管理会计研究，2022(6)：44-54.

2.缺乏完备的数据基础和信息来源

国外公司在企业ESG发展方面相对起步更早，在数据信息方面也更加成熟。例如，苹果公司（Apple）作为最早关注应对气候变化及碳减排的企业之一，在2020年7月宣布将于2030年前实现整个业务和供应链的碳中和目标，并且相关排放量与2015财年相比减少75%。Apple对产品建立的排放模型涵盖了产品的整个生命周期，在大部分的重要计算中，Apple会优先使用自身的特有数据，如无法获取该数据，则会依靠第二来源，包括业界平均数据。并且，Apple早在十多年前就启动了供应链碳管理计划，强制要求其供应链企业提供相关碳排放数据，并且要求第三方核查机构对相关数据进行核查。通过供应商提供的上游数据，Apple不断优化模型，更准确透明地评估产品的碳足迹。[①]Apple也会每年委托第三方机构对他们的综合碳足迹的计算方法和数据进行验证，保证其准确性。

3.社会舆论方面存在多种风险

社会角度的风险种类多样，产生于字节跳动产品平台的内容创作、管理监督和信息伦理等多方面。

在内容方面，字节跳动作为一个内容平台，以内容为核心，然而其对于平台发布内容的监管与审核力度欠缺，平台上存在很多传递不健康价值观、触犯道德底线与法律底线的内容，容易受到舆论批评甚至法律处罚；在管理方面，字节跳动在抖音等APP推出的青少年模式存在缺陷，模式由用户自主选择，难以保证未成年人的实际参与，监管不力；在伦理方面，抖音等平台的推荐机制容易带来信息茧房问题，信息茧房近年来受到公众的关注不断增多，也是常为公众所抵触的，这也是一个应当注意的风险点。

4.国际化过程中出现"水土不服"

在国际化方面，进入国际市场给字节跳动带来了更多方面的来自外部的风险，压力下的字节跳动内部也产生了新的风险。在自然环境方面，各国对于生态环境与自然资源保护非常关注，各国的法律法规存在差异，作为电力成本高的能耗巨大的互联网公司，字节跳动难免产生环境污染，会因此受到舆论压迫甚至相关处罚；在文化方面，由于字节跳动内容平台的特质以及审核制度的不完善，内容创作中会产生不尊重海外居民的习俗、文化、经济、宗教等基本权

---

① 林泽玲.碳中和领军人物系列 | 王彬对话汪军：碳中和时代的财富大转移. (2021-11-29)[2024-03-01]. https://www.iyiou.com/news/202111291025089.

利的现象，从而诱发危机；在消费者方面，主要是数据隐私安全方面，其过度获取用户信息与侵权问题常受到抨击；在政治方面，国际市场的不确定性强，字节跳动的业务常与数据隐私安全紧密联系；在公司组织管理方面，由于对新环境熟悉度不足，字节跳动在自身战略定位等方面容易产生决策性的失误。

（二）发展建议

从ESG建设角度看，字节跳动有对于环境、社会及公司治理的探索和努力，但不管是从自身发展的角度还是从与国内外相关赛道公司的比较的角度而言，字节跳动依然有很大不足。因此我们提出如下发展建议：

1.制定明确、具体的节能减排目标和举措

作为一家未上市公司，字节跳动的碳相关决策并不受到来自资本监管的直接干预。因此，企业自身更应设立清晰且明确的碳中和目标时间线，完善阶段性及总体性节能减排规划，借鉴亚马逊等公司的措施，提出更为具体的节能减排计划，从资金、人才等的投入，到使用技术的创新，再到不同时间阶段的分步骤计划，使得自身在环境方面的发展路径更加清晰。

2.建立科学、完整的数据基础和信息来源

提升信息披露水平能够为企业内部规划可再生能源采购战略、实施碳减排路径提供理论支持及依据，并且更好回应投资人和公众对企业的关切。字节跳动应当尽快披露量化环境绩效表现数据，并及时更新承诺落实的进展详情，重视企业ESG数据库建设，加强风险管理并提高数据透明度，完善ESG报告信息披露；优化数据分析模型，更准确透明地评估企业碳排放足迹；通过第三方核查机构对相关数据进行核查和验证，保证数据的准确性和透明度。

3.重视社会影响，遏制多方面风险

从社会角度而言，字节跳动要关注社会影响，尽可能充分杜绝各类型风险。在隐私保护方面，要完善隐私数据保护机制，避免过度获取用户信息，提升用户安全感和信任感；在未成年人保护方面，要加强青少年模式的建设，使得分辨力有限的未成年人免于接触暴力等不良信息的影响；在审核机制方面，要不断完善审核原则，加强人工审核和智能审核投入，对于传递不良价值观、有违道德的视频内容予以处理，减少负面内容，避免视频平台出现盗用他人信息、造谣传谣等触犯法律法规的内容；在数据算法方面，要加强推荐算法等的更新，加大资金和人员投入，结合用户使用反馈不断优化算法，满足用户的多

元需求，降低负面影响。

4. 出海入乡随俗，找准国际化定位

进入国际化市场意味着新的环境和战斗，字节跳动需要更加深入地了解全球用户的需求，提供更加贴近用户的产品和服务。字节跳动应当选好定位，尤其要关注并积极投入先进技术的研发，比如AI领域，要加大对人工智能的投入，避免落后。特别是，国际市场中要注意因地制宜，做出积极调整，比如对不同国家和地区环境保护相关政策的遵守、对于地方特色文化的尊重等，从而实现企业在全球范围内更加精准地运营和发展。

六、总 结

随着我国信息技术的飞速发展，相关企业在环境、社会和治理三方面不断出现问题。为了帮助企业发展，我们选取具有代表性的字节跳动开展此次研究。字节跳动已历经初创期、成长期、扩张期、风波期和赋能期五个阶段，并取得了多项技术创新和技术开源成果。在此过程中，字节跳动在环境保护方面积极实践，在多个社会责任议题中表现优异，但也并非面面俱到，并且其在公司治理方面问题频出。基于以上分析，我们总结了字节跳动发展的四点不足并提出了相应的建议，以期为字节跳动及相关公司的发展提供参考。

通用人工智能的未来之路：OpenAI与阿里巴巴的人工智能战略、技术与发展模式比较研究[①]

摘　要: 随着人工智能技术的快速发展，跨模态、多任务、通用型生成式大模型在世界范围内引发广泛关注，也为全球的互联网企业、人工智能企业和其他型态的科技公司的发展带来了前所未有的新机遇和新挑战。本文以人工智能行业的耀眼新星OpenAI和国内体量庞大的科技公司阿里巴巴为案例，分析两家世界知名科技公司在技术创新体系、人工智能战略、技术布局、技术治理模式等方面的发展特色和经验，并对比了两者在愿景理念、商业模式和技术导向等方面的差异。本文认为，OpenAI以实现通用人工智能为愿景，以大模型为路径，凭借利润上限、伙伴关系与投资体系的资源整合方式，取得了人工智能领域的多项突破性成果，同时引发了全球范围内对于人工智能伦理、安全、可持续发展和全球治理等问题的广泛关注与讨论。阿里巴巴则以云计算为引领，以智能化为商业模式，以业务驱动为研发体系，布局了全产业链的人工智能应用，并积极参与人工智能的治理与可持续发展实践。本文提出，以阿里巴巴为代表的国内互联网及人工智能企业应借鉴OpenAI的成功经验，也应坚持科技创新与社会责任相统一，构建负责任的人工智能，提升国际影响力，推动共建更包容、可持续的全球人工智能创新体系。

关键词: 人工智能；OpenAI；阿里巴巴；科技创新体系；人工智能治理

---

① 作者: 陈丽婷，浙江大学外国语学院；刘家安，浙江大学计算机科学与技术学院；王一博，浙江大学外国语学院；吕霜宁，浙江大学外国语学院。

一、引 言

人工智能（artificial intelligence，AI）是整合模型和算法的信息处理技术，也是一门研究、模拟人类智能的理论、方法、技术及应用系统的科学，人工智能系统借助知识建模和知识表达，通过对数据的利用和对关联性的计算，可以在不同程度上实现自主运行。这种赋予机器模拟、延伸、扩展类人智能的过程本质上是对人的意识和思想过程的简化和模仿。近些年人工智能的理论和技术取得了飞速发展，在语音识别、文本识别、视频识别、智力游戏、生成式模型等感知、决策、生成领域实现突破，达到或超过人类水准，成为引领新一轮科技革命和产业变革的战略性技术。而以ChatGPT为代表的大语言模型（large language models，LLM）由于具备了与人类相当的自然语言对话能力，使得基于大模型的应用、产业链条不断涌现和完善，大模型逐渐变成了继互联网之后的新一代"通用性技术"。这使得人类社会的经济型态、生产结构、文化传承、教育体系、信息传播方式等面临潜在的重大变革，也使得曾经仅存在于科幻想象中的"通用人工智能"（artificial general intelligence，AGI）的涌现初步具备了一定程度的潜在可能。

因此，在这样一个人工智能时代，我们有必要更好地认识和把握不同国家、不同经济形态下诞生的，代表了各自所在产业发展方向的企业在人工智能领域所采取的创新模式与发展路径，并从中汲取经验与启示。本报告选取了两家世界知名人工智能及互联网公司——OpenAI和阿里巴巴作为案例研究对象，分析其在科技创新，尤其是人工智能、互联网、云计算等领域具有引领意义的实践成果和前瞻战略，并对比其在管理创新、技术布局、治理模式等方面的发展特色和经验，为国内著名互联网及人工智能公司可持续的科技创新、构建负责任的人工智能以及提升国际影响力提出意见和建议。

本报告将分为以下几个部分：第一部分是全球人工智能行业概述，介绍人工智能的分类及发展历史、当前人工智能的发展现状及趋势、互联网与人工智能的关系；第二部分是针对OpenAI公司的详细研究，包括其管理创新、人工智能战略与技术布局、技术伦理与可持续发展等方面；第三部分是对阿里巴巴公司发展历程的分析，包括其商业崛起与科技创新体系、人工智能战略与技术布局、人工智能治理与可持续发展实践等方面；第四部分是国内外公司的发展特色和经验对比，包括愿景理念、商业模式和技术导向的差异，对OpenAI和阿里巴巴在人工智能及互联网领域的综合评价和未来展望，以及针对国内企业人工智能发展的对策建议。

二、全球人工智能行业概述

当前，以OpenAI公司推出的ChatGPT为代表的基于深度学习、强化学习的人工智能大语言模型引发了世界范围内的激烈讨论[①]，其活跃用户在发布后的2个月内超过1亿，成为人类科技史上用户增长速度最快的应用。这些模型在各种自然语言处理的任务上都取得了令人惊叹的效果，甚至超过了人类的水平。本章重点对人工智能的含义、种类和当前最具影响力的语言类模型进行梳理和概述。

（一）人工智能的分类及发展趋势

人工智能是一种涵盖多个领域的技术，随着技术的不断发展，人工智能的定义和内涵也在不断变化。联合国教科文组织将其宽泛地视为"有能力以类似于智能行为的方式处理数据和信息的系统，通常包括推理、学习、感知、预测、规划或控制等方面"。人工智能在早期主要关注推理和逻辑推断，而现在则更加注重机器学习和深度学习等技术的应用。

人工智能可以根据其使用的技术方法和原理，分为不同的类型：

1.基于规则的系统（rule-based systems）

这是最早出现的算法类型，它通过预设一系列固定的规则和逻辑来执行特定的任务，被广泛应用于商业软件、家用电器、飞机自动驾驶等场景。

2.基于知识的系统（knowledge-based systems）

这是指利用专家知识和经验来构建一个特定领域的知识库，并通过推理机制来解决问题或提供咨询的人工智能系统，例如早期的聊天机器人、机器人顾问等，它们可以根据新出现的情况和查询来更新自己的知识库。

3.基于学习的系统（learning-based systems）

即数据驱动的人工智能系统，这是指利用数据和算法来训练一个机器学习（machine learning，ML）模型，并通过该模型来进行预测、分类、聚类等任务的人工智能系统，例如癌症诊断、语音识别、图像生成等。机器学习模型可以

---

① Hu, K. ChatGPT sets record for fastest-growing user base-analyst note. (2023-02-01)[2024-02-07]. https://www.reuters.com/technology/chatgpt-sets-record-fastest-growing-user-base-analyst-note-2023-02-01/.

根据新输入的数据来调整自己的模型参数。当前，机器学习领域的研究主要集中在基于人工神经网络（neural network）的深度学习（deep learning）方面。而 DeepMind 开发的人工智能围棋模型 AlphaGo 击败人类棋手使得基于"智能体"不断"试错"并获得"奖励"的强化学习（reinforcement learning）模式也受到广泛关注。在此基础上的人类反馈强化学习（reinforcement learning with human feedback，RLHF）则被 OpenAI 公司应用在其广受关注的人工智能系统 ChatGPT 的训练中，使得该系统具备了与人类通过自然语言流畅对话的能力。

（二）大语言模型的突破性发展过程

大语言模型是人工智能迈向通用智能过程中的重要技术之一，也是当前人工智能领域的热点和趋势。这类模型的参数量都达到了数十亿或数千亿的规模，需要使用高性能的计算设备和分布式并行的训练方法才能完成训练。例如，OpenAI 公司的 GPT-3 可以根据用户的输入生成各种类型的文本，如文章、对话、代码、歌词等[1]；Google 公司的 BERT 可以理解文本的语义和结构，进行阅读理解、问答、摘要等[2]；Google 的 T5 可以实现从文本到文本的转换，完成翻译、生成、分类等[3]。国内以阿里巴巴等为代表的互联网企业也在积极布局人工智能产业。2023 年 4 月 11 日，阿里云智能首席技术官周靖人在阿里云峰会上宣布推出大模型"通义千问"，具备多轮对话、文案创作、逻辑推理、多模态理解、多语言支持等功能。

语言模型的发展历程可以概括为以下几个阶段：

1.基于统计方法的语言模型阶段，即使用一些经典的统计学方法来建立语言中单词序列的概率分布，这类方法计算量较低，但泛化能力和表达能力有限。

2.基于深度学习的语言模型阶段，即应用人工神经网络等深度学习技术，以数据驱动的方式拟合出词向量和词序列的概率分布，这种方式参数量较大，计算量较高，但能够处理复杂的非线性问题、捕获语义信息。

3.基于自监督学习的生成式语言模型阶段，即使用基于 Transformer（由

---

[1] Dale, R. GPT-3: What's it good for. *Natural Language Engineering*, 2021, 27(1): 113-118.

[2] Devlin, J., Chang, M. W., Lee, K., et al. Pre-training of deep bidirectional transformers for language understanding, 2018.

[3] Raffel, C., Shazeer, N., Roberts, A., et al. Exploring the limits of transfer learning with a unified text-to-text transformer. *The Journal of Machine Learning Research*, 2020, 21(1): 5485-5551.

Google 在 2017 年提出的新型神经网络结构）的模型架构和自监督学习技术在海量数据上预训练出具有文本生成能力的超大型语言模型，这类模型参数量极大，计算量极高，但能够实现多任务和跨领域的强泛化能力。

4.基于人类反馈的强化学习的对话式语言模型阶段，即使用预训练的生成式语言模型作为初始模型，在与人类进行问答式对话的过程中，通过强化学习等技术赋予模型不断学习和优化的能力，使其能够根据人类的反馈来调整策略和参数，从而提高对话的质量和效率，这类模型需要大量的人机交互数据和反馈信号，以及有效的奖励函数和探索机制，目标是实现更加智能和自然的对话系统，ChatGPT 便是这类模型中最具影响力的代表。

5.多模态（multimodal）阶段，即将语言模型与视觉、语音等其他模态的模型融合，使模型具有多模态的语义理解、生成能力，多模态模型也具有实现具身智能（embodied intelligence）、智能体（agent）系统的潜力。

随着语言、视觉等算法的发展，各种不同任务、不同模态的模型之间出现了趋同、协调、可融合的趋势，这为实现更高层次的通用人工智能提供了可能性。[1]但人工智能大模型也面临着一些挑战和问题，如计算资源和环境成本的高昂[2]，模型安全和可靠性的保障，模型可解释性和可控性的缺失，模型伦理和社会责任的考量等[3]。这些问题需要人工智能研究者和从业者共同探索和解决，以促进人工智能大模型技术的健康发展和广泛应用。

三、案例一：OpenAI公司

（一）OpenAI管理创新：企业组织模式的新分野

1.OpenAI的创新型企业模式与发展历程

2015 年 12 月 11 日，OpenAI 诞生于美国旧金山。这家公司的创始人团队包括了一众硅谷的知名人物——有着"钢铁侠"之称的特斯拉（Tesla）创始人埃隆·马斯克（Elon Musk），前创业加速器 Y Combinator 首席执行官萨姆·奥特曼（Sam Altman），硅谷著名的天使投资者、领英（LinkedIn）创始

---

[1] Bubeck, S., Chandrasekaran, V., Eldan, R., et al. Sparks of artificial general intelligence: Early experiments with GPT-4. 2023, *arXiv preprint arXiv:2303.12712v5.*

[2] Kaack, L. H., Donti, P. L., Strubell, E., et al. Aligning artificial intelligence with climate change mitigation. *Nature Climate Change*, 2022, 12(6): 518-527.

[3] Ouyang, L., Wu, J., Jiang, X., et al. Training language models to follow instructions with human feedback. *Advances in Neural Information Processing Systems*, 2022, 35: 27730-27744.

人里德·霍夫曼（Reid Hoffman），机器学习领域的顶尖学者伊尔亚·苏茨克维（Ilya Sutskever）等人。他们一同发起AI开发联合倡议，并承诺将为这个倡议提供10亿美元的资金。[①]

作为非营利性的研究型机构，OpenAI提出了一个简单但极具野心的使命——开发安全和开放的AI工具，使全人类受益。OpenAI官网的章程中明确写道："OpenAI的使命是确保通用人工智能——我们指的是在大多数有经济价值的工作上超越人类的高度自主系统——惠及全人类。"[②]

回忆起OpenAI成立之初的岁月，CEO萨姆·奥特曼在与莱克斯·弗里德曼（Lex Fridman）的对谈中如此说道："长期以来，我们一直是个被误解和被严重嘲笑的组织。当我们在2015年底宣布成立并表示我们将致力于通用人工智能（AGI），人们都认为我们疯了。"[③]

在一阵嘲笑和质疑声中，OpenAI开启了一系列前沿和具有挑战性的AI项目。成立一年后，OpenAI发布了"Universe"，一个可以用来衡量和训练AI通用智能的软件平台。该平台的推出是OpenAI发展史上的重要里程碑。[④]

在2017—2019年这段时期里，OpenAI开始专注于更广泛的AI研发。2018年6月，OpenAI发表了一篇名为《通过生成式预训练来提高语言理解》的论文，文章中首次提出了生成式预训练Transformer[⑤]（generative pre-trained transformer，GPT）的概念，以及如何在多种自然语言理解任务上实现显著的性能提升。GPT作为一种神经网络，可以在大量的人类生成的文本数据上进行训练，从而实现多种功能，比如生成自然语言、回答问题、摘要文章、写诗歌、翻译语言、对话等。[⑥]

OpenAI团队开发的GPT-1是第一个基于BookCorpus数据集（包含互联网上收集的约11000本未出版书籍的文本）训练的语言模型。该模型后来演

[①] 梅茨.深度学习革命.桂曙光，译.北京：中信出版集团，2022.

[②] Altman, S. Planning for AGI and beyond. (2023-02-24)[2024-02-07]. https://openai.com/blog/planning-for-agi-and-beyond.

[③] Fridman, L. Transcript of Lex Fridman Podcast with OpenAI CEO Sam Altman on GPT-4, ChatGPT, and the future of AI. (2023-06-11)[2023-06-11]. https://singjupost.com/transcript-of-lex-fridman-podcast-with-openai-ceo-sam-altman-on-gpt-4-chatgpt-and-the-future-of-ai/.

[④] OpenAI. Universe. (2016-12-05)[2023-06-11]. https://openai.com/blog/universe/.

[⑤] Vaswani, A., Shazeer, N., Parmar, N., et al. Attention is all you need. 31st Conference on Neural Information Processing Systems (NIPS 2011). Long Beach, CA, USA, Dec. 4-9, 2017.

[⑥] Radford, A., Narasimhan, K., Salimans, T., et al. Improving language understanding by generative pre-training. 2018, *OpenAI Blog*.

变成了一个更强大的版本——GPT-2。它使用了 800 万个网页作为训练数据，并包含了 15 亿个参数。但是，由于担心 GPT-2 可能被用于写垃圾邮件或制造假新闻，OpenAI 当时决定不向公众发布。[①]

也是在同一时期，OpenAI 的目标与态度发生了转变。

2018 年，曾经说要用非盈利的 OpenAI "制衡谷歌" 的马斯克选择了离开 OpenAI。关于退出的原因，马斯克发表过一些声明。一方面是为了避免利益冲突，另一方面他也表达了自己对 OpenAI 的不满和担忧。他在推特账号上写道："OpenAI 本来是一个开源的非营利性机构，但现在变成了一个闭源的最大利润公司，实际上受微软控制。"[②]

马斯克的这种担心不无道理。2019 年，OpenAI 做出了一个极具争议性的决定。它从非营利性机构转变为一个 "有限营利" 的组织，并建立了 OpenAI LP，一个 "非营利和营利的混合体"；这是一种介于非营利和营利之间的新型公司形式，它允许公司在追求其使命的同时，能够吸引投资者和员工，并给他们提供有限的回报。超过这个限额的收益将归属于原来的非营利实体。该公司的创始人之一格雷格·布罗克曼（Greg Brockman）表示，他们没有找到任何其他现有的法律结构能够达到他们想要的平衡。[③]

马斯克还认为，OpenAI 后续的发展似乎和最初秉持的 "开放" 理念背道而驰。2019 年，微软公司（Microsoft）向 OpenAI 投资了 10 亿美金，并获得了 OpenAI 技术的商业化授权。从此，OpenAI 的一些技术开始应用在微软的产品和业务上。

针对马斯克的言论，微软 CEO 萨提亚·纳德拉（Satya Nadella）参加美国全国广播公司（NBC）访谈节目时表示："事实上，那并不正确。正如我所说，OpenAI 的使命是由一个非营利董事会控制的，我们在其中拥有非控股权益，并与其建立了良好的商业合作关系。"他十分欣赏 OpenAI 实行的这类 "特立独行" 的管理方式。在他的印象里，"我们是唯一一个愿意让非营利公司和董事会掌握技术控制权的盈利公司。我非常欢迎其他公司也这么干。"[④]

---

① OpenAI. GPT-2: 1. 5B release. (2016-12-05)[2023-06-11]. https://openai.com/research/gpt-2-1-5b-release.

② Tracy, R. ChatGPT's Sam Altman warns congress that AI 'can go quite wrong'. (2023-05-16)[2024-02-07]. https://www.wsj.com/articles/chatgpts-sam-altman-faces-senate-panel-examining-artificial-intelligence-4bb6942a.

③ Brockman, G., Sutskever, I., OpenAI. OpenAI LP. (2019-03-11)[2024-02-07]. https://openai.com/blog/openai-lp/.

④ NBC News. Special edition with Andrew Ross Sorkin: AI and Microsoft CEO Satya Nadella. (2023-05-17)[2024-02-07]. https://www.youtube.com/watch?v=A2cYwTEJBGk.

2. OpenAI 的突破性成果与社会影响

OpenAI 在过去几年里取得了一系列令人瞩目的突破性成果，展现了其在 AI 领域的领先地位和创新能力，同时也引发了人们对 AI 的未来发展以及技术、伦理和社会问题的深刻思考。

（1）AI 超级计算机

早在创立之初，OpenAI 就极为注重在计算资源方面的投入和储备。2016 年，英伟达公司的 CEO 黄仁勋亲自向当时仍由马斯克掌舵的 OpenAI 赠送了全球第一台 DGX-1 超级计算机，而当时的 OpenAI 便已经在筹划使用 Reddit 论坛的数据来教人工智能聊天，并通过扩大模型的规模来实现这个雄心勃勃的计划。在 OpenAI 之后，全球百强企业中有一半安装了英伟达的这款计算产品。①

后来，为了支持更大规模的 AI 模型训练，打造出震惊世界的 ChatGPT 系统，OpenAI 又与微软合作，建立了世界上最先进的 AI 超级计算系统，并将其部署在微软的 Azure 云计算平台上。微软为这个项目投入了数亿美元，并表示将继续提供更强大的 AI 基础设施给 OpenAI 和其他用户。②

（2）多模态 AI 大模型

这些模型通过在海量的公开文本数据上进行自我学习，掌握了语言、知识、概念和上下文等方面的信息，从而能够完成多种任务，如摘要、翻译、对话、内容生成、代码生成等。

OpenAI 开发了一系列基于 Transformer 的无监督预训练语言模型，能够生成高质量的文本、图像、音频、视频等内容，展现了强大的零样本和少样本学习能力。而真正引发 AI 学界轰动的是其于 2020 年 5 月发布（但直到 2022 年 11 月才开放公测）的 GPT-3 模型，该模型拥有 1750 亿个参数，能够在没有或很少额外训练数据的情况下，完成多种任务，如摘要、翻译、对话、内容生成、代码生成等多种自然语言处理任务，一度引起人们关于语言模式是否已经具备"意识"的激烈讨论。③

2022 年 11 月，OpenAI 在 GPT-3 的基础上，使用人类反馈强化学习

① Dent, S. Elon Musk's OpenAI will teach machines to talk using Reddit. (2016-08-16)[2024-02-07]. https://www.engadget.com/2016-08-16-elon-musks-openai-will-teach-ai-to-talk-using-reddit.html.
② Shankland, S. Microsoft builds massive supercomputer for smarter AI. (2022-05-19)[2024-02-07]. https://www.cnet.com/tech/computing/microsoft-builds-massive-supercomputer-for-smarter-ai/.
③ Romero, A. OpenAI opens GPT-3 for Everyone. (2021-11-19)[2024-02-07]. https://towardsdatascience.com/openai-opens-gpt-3-for-everyone-fb7fed309f6.

（RLHF）技术微调，构建了能够与用户进行自然对话、问答的应用ChatGPT。这款真正的消费级应用让"人工智能"第一次从荧幕中冷峻的围棋机器人变成了走入寻常百姓家、与数亿人实时交互的智能助理。它不仅能流畅地与用户交谈，还成为了写作助手、编程教师和全能的百科全书，在几个月的时间内风靡全球，引起强烈的反响。[①]而到了2023年3月，OpenAI发布了具备多模态理解、生成能力的GPT-4，它不仅能够生成高质量的文本、图像、音频、视频等内容，也在许多专业和学术的基准测试中表现出了人类水平的性能，如通过了模拟律师资格考试，并在考试中得分位于前10%。[②]

除了在自然语言处理领域取得巨大成功，OpenAI在计算机视觉方面的贡献同样不可小觑。2022年，OpenAI的图像生成模型DALL-E 2横空出世，能够根据自然语言描述让机器生成几乎"真实"的图像；这成为继GPT-3之后又一个引爆科技圈的重大事件。OpenAI的CEO萨姆·奥特曼在接受采访时说道："当我们意识到 DALL-E 2 将引起轰动的时候，我们想让它成为一个案例，展示我们将如何部署新技术，让全世界明白图像是可以伪造的，就像是对人们说：'你知道吗，很快你就不能信任互联网上的图像了。'……我们想用DALL-E 2 来告诉全世界，当我们说，'我们要制造出像人类一样的、能理解世界的强大人工智能，可以像人类一样为你做有用的事情'，我们真的在这样做。"[③]

此外，OpenAI还在过去几年间发布了涵盖语言、视觉、音频等各种模态的机器学习模型，如表1所示。

表1　OpenAI发布的部分多模态机器学习模型

模型名称	模型介绍	举例说明
Jukebox	根据歌手、风格或歌词生成音乐和歌曲的模型	如"一个模仿Taylor Swift的歌曲"或"一首关于太阳系的摇滚乐"等[④]

① Marr, B. A short history of ChatGPT: How we got to where we are today. (2023-05-19)[2024-02-07]. https://www.forbes.com/sites/bernardmarr/2023/05/19/a-short-history-of-chatgpt-how-we-got-to-where-we-are-today/.

② OpenAI. GPT-4 technical report. 2023, *arXiv preprint arXiv:2303.08774*.

③ Altman, S. This is what I learned from DALL-E 2. (2022-12-16)[2024-02-10]. https://www.technologyreview.com/2022/12/16/1065255/sam-altman-openai-lessons-from-dall-e-2/.

④ Dhariwal, P., Jun, H., Payne, C., et al. Jukebox: A generative model for music. 2020, *arXiv preprint arXiv:2005.00341*.

⑤ Radford, A., Kim, J., W, Hallacy., et al. Learning transferable visual models from natural language supervision, *International Conference on Machine Learning*, 2021: 8748-8763.

模型名称	模型介绍	举例说明
MuseNet	根据乐器、风格或旋律生成音乐的模型	如"一个用钢琴演奏的莫扎特的小夜曲"或"一个用吉他演奏的金属乐的狂想曲"等
CLIP[②]	根据图像内容生成文本标签或根据文本描述找到匹配图像的模型	可以准确给出图片的文字描述

（3）AI安全与责任

OpenAI致力于打造安全和负责任的AI，对其研究和产品进行了严格的风险评估和伦理审查，并制定一系列的安全措施和内容政策，以防止AI被滥用或造成严重危害。例如，OpenAI限制其基础模型的输出范围，过滤了一些敏感或不恰当的内容，如色情、暴力、仇恨言论、虚假信息等。OpenAI还提供了一些工具和指南，帮助用户检测和纠正AI模型可能存在的偏见、误导或错误。此外，OpenAI也积极参与一些关于AI技术、伦理和社会问题的研究和讨论，涉及AI的可解释性、可靠性、公平性、透明度、隐私、人权和社会福利等。

（二）OpenAI的人工智能战略与技术布局

1.愿景创新：通用人工智能（AGI）的理念变革

尽管人工智能已经成为当今科技领域最热门和最具前景的领域之一，各种人工智能技术和产品也已经渗透到我们生活的方方面面，但这些人工智能技术和产品大多只能在某一个特定领域或者任务上表现出超越人类水平的能力，比如下棋、识别图像、翻译等。这些人工智能技术和产品虽然有着巨大的商业价值和社会影响力，但是它们并不能真正理解和模拟人类的智慧和思维，也不能适应和解决复杂且多变的人类社会问题。

而"通用人工智能"（Artificial General Intelligence，AGI）则是指可以与人类智慧相匹敌，甚至比人类更智能的AI系统，一般来说可能具备完成可通过人类智慧来完成的任何任务。AGI是人工智能领域最终和最远大的目标，也是科幻小说和未来学中常见的话题。然而AGI同时也是一个极具争议的目标，因为它的研究和诞生可能以积极或消极的方式根本性地改变整个人类社会。从积极的一面来看，AGI可以协助我们以更普适、可持续的方式推动全球经济发展，并协助人类科学家实现新的科学突破。AGI也可以帮助每个人轻易获取人类社会所积淀的几乎任何知识和能力。但从消极的方面来看，AGI可能也会带来严重的滥用，引发严重的事故、恐慌和社会混乱。AGI甚至可能会威胁人类的价值、自主权和尊严。如果人类无法确保AGI与人类的目标一致，它可能会对人类的存续构成直接威胁。

但与大多数人工智能、互联网企业的保守理念不同，OpenAI不仅把人工智能视为一种更高效的"自动化"算法和服务于某一些类别具体应用的数学工具，还将实现通用人工智能、确保通用人工智能造福全人类作为自己的使命。它认为AGI对于人类来说既是一次巨大的机遇，也是一个极大的挑战，同时相信创造出对人类价值观有所保障的AGI是可行的。同时，OpenAI希望将这项潜在的技术应用于全人类的公共利益，并竭力防止出现危害人类的AGI。OpenAI也希望确保AGI使用的民主化，将AGI技术广泛且公平地分享给所有人。OpenAI对于AGI的追求是一种对于人工智能技术在愿景和理念上的变革，在此之前，这种想象似乎仅存在于科幻之中。多数致力于人工智能技术研发的企业、研究机构都似乎避免将"人工智能"渲染得过于贴近普罗大众对未来世界的幻想，但OpenAI却直白而又不厌其烦地在它的公司章程、网站、博客和媒体访谈中强调对于AGI的终极追求。

为了实现构建AGI的宏大目标，OpenAI提出了一系列的原则，如开放、协作、透明、民主等。在最初阶段，OpenAI将其所有的专利和研究成果公开分享给全世界，以促进人工智能领域的协同进步和创新。ChatGPT问世后，OpenAI一度因其拒绝将GPT模型和训练所使用的数据开源而饱受争议，但OpenAI首席科学家、联合创始人伊尔亚·苏茨克维在采访中表示，"这些模型非常强大，而且会变得越来越强大。在某种程度上，如果有人想的话，很容易用这些模型造成很大的伤害。"因此随着模型能力的增强，OpenAI认为其出于安全考虑暂时不开源的做法是有道理的[①]。然而，其CEO在与一些初创公司的会谈中表示开源仍然十分重要，他们也正在考虑GPT-3的开源计划。同时，OpenAI也与其他机构和研究者进行广泛的合作和交流，以汲取不同的视角和经验，并致力于提高其研究和产品的可解释性和可审查性，以增加公众对其工作的信任和理解。

多年来，OpenAI推进AI研究和开发的最新技术，影响对于AGI的公众认

---

① Vincent, J. OpenAI co-founder on company's past approach to openly sharing research: "We were wrong". (2023-03-15)[2024-02-05]. https://www.theverge.com/2023/3/15/23640180/openai-gpt-4-launch-closed-research-ilya-sutskever-interview.

知。OpenAI提出了广受关注的几项AGI原则[1]：

（1）我们希望通用人工智能使人类能够在宇宙中实现最大程度的繁荣。我们不希望未来成为一个虚假的乌托邦，但我们希望将技术好的一面最大化，坏的一面最小化，让AGI成为人类善意的放大器。

（2）我们希望AGI的益处、使用和治理能得到广泛和公平的分享。

（3）我们要正确应对潜在风险。在面对这些风险时，理论上似乎正确的事情在实践中往往比预期更难以控制。我们必须通过部署功能较弱的技术版本来不断学习和适应，以最大程度地避免"无可挽回"的情况。

2.路径选择：大模型的涌现能力驱动人工智能新范式

以大语言模型（LLM）为代表的大模型之所以受到前所未有的广泛关注，很重要的一个原因是它们展现了令人惊讶的"涌现能力（Emergent Abilities）"。机器学习模型的能力往往与其模型大小、结构复杂度和训练所用的数据量有关，但人们在对大模型的研究中发现，大模型具备一些小模型所不具备的能力，这些能力会在模型规模突破某一临界点后突然涌现[2]。

GPT系列模型即是按照不断扩充训练数据的数量和种类并不断提高模型的参数量的趋势在发展，并展现出了惊人的涌现能力。GPT-4的训练使用了前所未有的计算和数据规模。微软研究院对GPT-4的早期版本进行了探索，发现它不仅在语言方面表现出卓越的能力，还能够跨越多个领域，解决涉及数学、编程、视觉、医学、法律、心理学等方面的难题。在这些任务中，GPT-4的表现接近甚至超过了人类水平，而且往往远远优于之前的模型。该研究认为，这些结果表明，GPT-4具备了一些初步（但尚不成熟）的通用人工智能系统的特性。

奇绩创坛创始人陆奇认为，OpenAI在大模型方面的突破性创新使得"大模型"成为了当下的一项基础性技术，也使得模型成本从边际成本发展为固定成本。正因如此，OpenAI一方面加速了模型的涌现能力的揭示和应用，另一方面也促使了整个人工智能行业的的路径选择从此前的单任务、单模态、小模型逐渐转变成了多任务、跨模态、大模型，驱动了人工智能研究和产业的范式

[1] Altman, S. Planning for AGI and beyond. (2023-02-24)[2024-02-10]. https://openai.com/blog/planning-for-agi-and-beyond.

[2] Wei, J., Tay, Y., Bommasani, R., et al. Emergent abilities of large language models. 2022, *arXiv preprint arXiv:2206.07682*.

变革。[①]

3.资源整合：利润上限、伙伴关系与投资体系

自创立之初，OpenAI便希望"发展数字智能，使其符合人类整体的利益，同时不受财务回报的限制"，因此OpenAI一直宣称将免费公布人工智能技术，并为全球开发者提供开源的AI工具和平台，这使得OpenAI在业务模式和利润模式上完全不同于以往的互联网或人工智能公司。

（1）创新性的"非营利"与"利润上限"模式

在2019年3月之前，OpenAI一直是一个完全的非营利性组织，其创始人和捐助者都不是为了获得经济回报。而这种非营利性质也为OpenAI吸引了一批更看重对人工智能技术的探索和贡献而不是高额薪水的优秀的人工智能研究者。

而到了2019年3月，OpenAI转变为一个营利性公司，但设定了一个利润上限。这意味着OpenAI将向员工和投资者发行股票并产生收益，但股东的投资回报被限制为不超过原始投资金额的100倍。OpenAI认为，这样的盈利模式是为了吸引更多的人才和资金，以支持其长期的研究目标，并保持其对社会责任和透明度的承诺。OpenAI还保留了其非营利性母公司OpenAI Inc，该公司控制了受利润上限限制的营利性子公司OpenAI LP的董事会席位，并监督其遵守使命和价值观。

由此可见，虽然OpenAI在大语言模型方面拥有着业界领先的技术，但就目前而言，其作为一家商业化公司并没有过多地将精力投放在追逐商业利润。由于GPT系列模型的训练需要大量的计算资源，成本十分高昂，OpenAI目前所推出的各类付费服务暂时不会为其带来过多的净利润。但显而易见的是，处于AI甚至AGI时代领先地位的OpenAI如果开辟更多的盈利模式，其可创造的市场规模将十分可观。

（2）发展伙伴关系，共享资源体系

OpenAI自成立以来，已经获得了超过20亿美元的融资，主要来自微软、Y Combinator、Infosys、Reid Hoffman等知名机构和个人。在ChatGPT大获成功之后，OpenAI与微软之间的伙伴关系常常成为业界关注的焦点。两家公司的合作关系始于2019年7月，当时微软宣布向OpenAI注资10亿美元，并

---

① 邵文，方晓.陆奇最新演讲审定版：大模型带来的新范式和新机会. (2023-05-13)[2023-06-11]. https://m.thepaper.cn/rss_newsDetail_23057456.

成为其独家云服务提供商。此后，双方在以下多个方面展开了深入合作。

1）超级计算：微软为OpenAI提供了强大的云计算能力，开发了专用的世界排名前五的超级计算机，以训练其先进的人工智能模型；

2）产品和服务：微软将OpenAI的模型纳入其产品和服务中，推出了基于OpenAI技术的GitHub Copilot自动编码工具、Azure OpenAI服务、Office 365 Copilot办公套件等；

3）投资和收购：微软在2021年和2023年分别向OpenAI追加了数十亿美元的投资，并有意以100亿美元的价格收购OpenAI的49％股份。[①]

除了与微软有深度合作外，OpenAI还与世界各地的许多企业、非盈利组织、科研机构建立了广泛的合作伙伴关系。例如Open Philanthropy Project是一个旨在寻找并资助改善世界的最佳方案的慈善组织，其长期关注着潜在的高级人工智能风险，是OpenAI最早的捐赠者之一，曾在2017年向OpenAI提供了3000万美元的资金支持，且董事长也加入了OpenAI的董事会，并与另一位董事会成员共同监督OpenAI的安全和治理工作。同时，双方还在人工智能科学研究、教育培训、伦理安全研究项目等方面有着广泛的合作。

此外，OpenAI发起了OpenAI Scholars项目，旨在支持来自多样化背景和少数群体的人工智能研究者。该项目为每位学者提供了一笔1.5万美元的奖学金，以及访问OpenAI API和其他资源的机会。该项目的目标是提高人工智能领域的多样性，培养了多位来自不同的国家、文化、专业和背景的学者，包括软件工程师、数据科学家、教育家、艺术家等。他们的项目涉及了多个人工智能领域，如自然语言处理、计算机视觉、强化学习、生成式模型、对抗式攻防等。[②]

（三）建构负责任的人工智能：OpenAI的技术伦理与安全实践

显而易见的是，大模型时代的人工智能给人类带来了一系列的伦理风险和挑战。萨姆·奥特曼认为"AGI从根本上成为了改变我们文明的强大力量"，通用人工智能的宏大愿景既成为了人类社会发展的重大契机，也可能从根本上对人类安全构成挑战。"我们不想制造超级AI，这无可争辩。但是世界不应该将其视为永远不会出现的科幻风险，这可能是我们在未来十年不得不面对的事

---

① Warren, T. Microsoft extends OpenAI partnership in a "multibillion dollar investment". (2023-01-23)[2024-02-09]. https://www.theverge.com/2023/1/23/23567448/microsoft-openai-partnership-extension-ai.

② OpenAI Scholars. (2018-03-06)[2024-02-07]. https://openai.com/blog/openai-scholars.

情。"因此，人工智能需要在其设计、开发和应用过程中遵循一些伦理原则和标准，以保障人类的权利和尊严。①

此外，相比更长时间跨度内 AGI 可能带来的根本性风险，在大模型逐渐成为基础设施的当下，人类社会的和平安全、经济发展、劳动就业、信息传播、教育文化等方面也面临着来自人工智能的迫在眉睫的威胁。联合国教科文组织在 2021 年发布了《人工智能伦理问题建议书》，其中提出了四个核心价值（尊重、公平、包容和可持续性）和十个基本原则（人权、人类尊严、福祉、自主性、责任、民主、多样性、创新、团结和环境保护），以指导各国在制定和实施人工智能政策时遵循的道德框架。②

为了以更负责任的方式实现其构建服务人类的通用人工智能的使命，OpenAI 从以下几个方面探索构建"负责任的 AI"的安全实践。

1. 通过技术创新来提高 AGI 的安全性

OpenAI 认识到，在开发 AGI 之前，必须先解决一些技术上的难题，例如如何让 AGI 理解和尊重人类的意愿、偏好和规范；如何让 AGI 在不确定和复杂的环境中做出合理和可预测的行为；如何让 AGI 在出现错误或异常时及时纠正或停止等。为此，OpenAI 开展了一系列的安全研究项目，并开源了一些安全工具和框架，以供其他人工智能开发者和研究者参考和使用。例如，OpenAI 开发了 Safety Gym，一个基于强化学习算法评估和改进 AGI 对齐性能的仿真环境③；OpenAI 发布了 AI Safety Gridworlds，一个包含多种场景的的安全测试套件；其还发表一系列关注人工智能安全问题的学术论文，如《AI 安全中的具体问题》（"Concrete Problems in AI Safety"）概述了避免负面侧效应、避免奖励黑客、可扩展的监督、安全探索、分布偏移等五个具体的问题和一些可能的解决方案。④

2. 通过科学研究来评估 AGI 的社会影响

OpenAI 在自己所推出的 ChatGPT 可能对人类社会尤其是经济造成巨大影响之时，也在致力于通过科学研究来评估 AGI 对社会的潜在影响。

① 邵文. ChatGPT 之父中国对话全文：《道德经》、大国分歧与 AGI 时间表. (2023-06-10)[2023-06-11]. https://m.thepaper.cn/newsDetail_forward_23434268.

② UNESCO. Recommendations on the ethics of artificial intelligence, 2021.

③ 联合国教科文组织. 人工智能伦理问题建议书. (2021-11-23)[2024-03-01]. https://unesdoc.unesco.org/ark:/48223/pf0000381137_chi.

④ OpenAI. Safety gym. (2019-11-21)[2024-02-07]. https://openai.com/research/safety-gym.

例如一项来自OpenAI的研究表明，GPT类大模型逐渐成为一种通用技术，并将会对美国劳动力市场产生深刻的潜在影响，每个职业里至少15％部分的工作量、80％从业者中的19％从业者的工作量可通过GPT完成并能节省50％以上时间。同时，这种影响并不局限于高生产力增长的行业，而是横跨所有工资水平，其中高收入工作可能面临更大的影响。OpenAI通过暴露（exposure）这一概念来衡量各种职业可能受到GPT影响的程度，即衡量使用ChatGPT或相关工具，在保证质量的情况下，能否减少完成工作的时间、减少的程度。表2显示了最容易受到GPT影响的职业列表。

表2　最容易受到GPT影响的职业

分组	暴露程度高的职业	暴露程度/%
人类标记组α	口笔译员	76.5
	调查研究人员	75
	诗人、作词家和创意作家	68.8
	动物科学家	66.7
	公共关系专家	66.7
人类标记组β	调查研究人员	84.4
	作家和写作者	82.5
	口笔译员	82.4
	公共关系专家	80.6
	动物科学家	77.8
人类标记组γ	数学家	100
	报税员	100
	金融量化分析师	100
	作家和写作者	100
	网页和数字界面设计师	100
模型标记组α	数学家	100
	通讯员	95.2
	区块链工程师	94.1
	法庭记者和同步字幕员	92.9
	校对员和排版员	90.9

续表

分组	暴露程度高的职业	暴露程度 /%
模型标记组 β	数学家	100
	区块链工程师	97.1
	法庭记者和同步字幕员	96.4
	校对员和排版员	95.5
	通讯员	95.2
模型标记组 γ	会计师和审计师	100
	新闻分析师和记者	100
	法律秘书和行政助理	100
	临床数据管理员	100
	气候变化政策分析师	100

(资料来源：Eloundou，T.，Manning，S.，Mishkin，P.，et al. GPTs are GPTs: An early look at the labor market impact potential of large language models. 2023, *arXiv preprint arXiv:2303.10130*.)

表 3 列出了不容易受 GPT 影响的职业。

表3 不容易被GPT影响的职业

没有任何暴露标记的职业	
农业设备操作员	盖屋顶工人助手
木匠助手	金属浇注与铸造工人
屠宰商和肉类包装商	餐厅和食堂服务员、调酒师助手
轮胎修理工和更换工	矿用锚杆机操作员
洗碗工	公交和卡车机械师、柴油发动机专家
摩托车技工	井架操作员（石油气和天然气）
非技术工（石油和天然气钻探）	轨道铺设和维护设备操作员
铺地板工（地毯、木头和硬瓷砖除外）	铸模工和型心制造工
铺管工、水管工的助手	油漆工、泥水匠的助手
运动员和体育竞赛者	汽车玻璃安装工和维修工
石匠	厨师（快餐）
井口泵操作员	挖泥船操作员
整修工	肉类、家禽和鱼肉的屠宰和处理工
水泥工和混凝土修整工	铺路、铺面和夯实设备操作员
手工切割和修剪工作者	挖掘机和装载机操作员（露天采矿）

没有任何暴露标记的职业	
打桩机操作员	耐火材料修理工（砖匠除外）
电线安装和维修人员	砖匠、砌块匠、石匠、瓷砖和大理石铺设工的助手

这些研究强调了OpenAI在其AI系统研发和应用中需要考虑到这些影响，以确保其人工智能的发展和应用既能带来技术进步，又能保障社会公平和福祉。[①]

3.通过社会合作来提升AGI的公益性

OpenAI意识到，建构负责任的人工智能不仅是一个技术问题，也是一个社会问题，它需要各个利益相关者的参与和协作，以确保AGI的发展和应用符合人类的共同利益和福祉。为此，OpenAI参与了一些国际倡议和标准，以推动人工智能的伦理原则和实践规范的制定和实施。例如，OpenAI加入了Partnership on AI，一个由多个人工智能公司、研究机构、社会组织和学术机构组成的联盟，其旨在制定和推广有利于社会和公共利益的人工智能最佳实践[②]；OpenAI支持了《阿西洛马人工智能原则》（*Asilomar AI Principles*），包括由一百多位人工智能专家共同制定的关于人工智能未来发展方向和目标的23条原则；OpenAI签署了《蒙特利尔人工智能开发社会责任宣言》（*Montreal Declaration for a Responsible Development of Artificial Intelligence*），包括由加拿大蒙特利尔大学主导的关于人工智能责任发展的十条原则[③]。

4.通过对齐训练确保超级智能可控

"对齐"是近期的机器学习工作中经常使用的一个技术词语，既可以指通过一些特殊的训练技术将用于不同任务、面向不同模态（如视觉、语言、语音等）的不同模型在训练过程中学习到的隐式的表征能力对齐，从而获得一个具备跨模态能力的更强的模型，也可以指通过各种技术手段将模型应用时表现、表达出来的人类可理解的输出内容与人类的价值观保持一致。受限于底层技术特点，以语言模型为代表的大模型一直难以确保输出的内容不包含有害信息，

---

① Eloundou, T., Manning, S., Mishkin, P., et al. GPTs are GPTs: An early look at the labor market impact potential of large language models. 2023, *arXiv preprint arXiv:2303.10130*.

② Partnership on AI. Our partners. [2024-02-15]. https://partnershiponai.org/partners/.

③ Montreal Declaration for a Responsible Development of Artificial Intelligence. (n. d.)[2024-02-07]. https:// recherche.umontreal.ca/english/strategic-initiatives/montreal-declaration-for-a-responsible-ai/.

因此对齐系统的研发对于确保大模型甚至超级智能符合人类的伦理要求、"比人类更聪明地遵循人类的意图"就显得尤为重要和紧迫。

2023年上半年，面对ChatGPT带来的震撼，人工智能领域的研究者已经多次联合发表公开信，呼吁人们重视生成式AI的潜在风险。2023年7月，OpenAI宣布成立新的"超级对齐"（Superalignment）团队①，由OpenAI联合创始人领导，希望在4年内解决超级智能在对齐问题上的核心技术挑战，并将投入20%的计算资源打造一个超级对齐系统，即构建一个与人类水平相当的、负责模型对齐的"AI研究员"。

OpenAI希望组建的这支由顶级的机器学习研究者和工程师组成的团队将重点尝试：开发一个可扩展的训练方法，利用人工智能系统来协助评估其他人工智能系统，并将AI模型的监督能力泛化到人类无法监督的任务上；建立一个验证系统，自动搜索有问题的行为（确保系统稳健性）和有问题的内部结构（提高系统可解释性）；使用未对齐的模型来测试整个流程，确保所提方法可以检测到最严重的未对齐类型（即部署对抗性测试）。

四、案例二：阿里巴巴集团

（一）阿里巴巴的商业崛起与科技创新体系

1.阿里巴巴的商业模式与发展历程

（1）阿里巴巴的商业版图与股权结构

阿里巴巴集团控股有限公司（以下简称"阿里巴巴"）于1999年在中国杭州创立。该公司秉持"客户第一，员工第二，股东第三"的价值观，"消费、云计算、全球化"是其一贯坚持的三大战略。阿里巴巴致力于成为一家运营102年的好公司，以"让天下没有难做的生意"为愿景，希冀达成"通过互联网服务，让商业更平等"的使命。②

阿里巴巴的业务版图分为四大板块：核心商业、云计算、数字媒体及娱乐，以及创新业务。

其一，核心商业板块包括淘宝、天猫和新零售等组成的中国零售商业，以1688为代表的中国批发商业，盒马和饿了么等组成的本地生活服务，菜鸟物

① Sutskever, I. & Leike, J. Introducing superalignment. (2023-07-05)[2023-07-09]. https://openai.com/blog/introducing-superalignment.
② 阿里巴巴.阿里巴巴集团介绍. [2023-06-09]. https://www.alibabagroup.com/about-alibaba.

流、Lazada、AliExpress 等组成的国际零售商业，以及 Alibaba.com 等组成的国际批发商业。其中，C2C（consumer to customer）模式的淘宝与 B2C（business to consumer）模式的天猫占主要份额。核心商业营收在 2018—2020 年占总营收的 80% 左右，是阿里巴巴的支柱业务。

其二，云计算板块主要提供 IaaS（infrastructure as a service）类的基础设施服务，包括云基础设施、云数据库、云安全、云智能、大数据分析、人工智能等。阿里云是中国最大的公共云服务提供商，占国内市场份额的 41.9%，也是全球第三大公共云服务提供商，约占国际市场份额的 9%。[1]

其三，数字媒体及娱乐板块主要涵盖优酷土豆、阿里影业、阿里音乐、UC 浏览器、大麦网等业务。这些业务主要通过会员订阅、广告和内容分销来营利，同时也提供内容制作和投资服务。数字媒体及娱乐占阿里巴巴 2023 财年总收入的 5%。

最后，创新业务板块主要包括钉钉、高德地图、天猫精灵等业务。这些业务主要通过提供创新的产品和服务来满足用户和企业的需求，同时也探索新的商业模式和收入来源。

阿里巴巴集团在成立 15 年后，于 2014 年 5 月向美国证券交易委员会提交了首次公开募股（IPO）申请文件，并于 2014 年 9 月在美国纽约证券交易所上市。阿里巴巴还于 2019 年在香港联合交易所上市。[2] 阿里巴巴采用独特的合伙人制度保障创始人和管理团队在持股比例较低的情况下仍获得公司的绝对控制权。

除创立合伙人制度，阿里巴巴集团亦于近两年开启子公司分拆上市的改革，旨在提高集团业务透明度和估值，并为子公司提供更多自主权和资源。2023 年，阿里巴巴宣布启动"1＋6＋N"组织变革，在集团之下设立阿里云智能、淘宝天猫商业、本地生活、菜鸟、国际数字商业、大文娱等六大业务集团和多家业务公司，并分别建立各业务集团和业务公司的董事会，实行 CEO 负责制。具备条件的业务集团和公司，将有独立融资和上市的可能性。[3]

---

[1] 阿里云. [2023-06-09]. https://cn.aliyun.com/.

[2] 新浪科技. 阿里香港上市. 张勇：五年前错过的遗憾 今天得以实现. (2019-11-26)[2023-06-09]. https://tech.sina.com.cn/i/2019-11-26/doc-iihnzhfz1741035.shtml.

[3] 孙燕. 机构热议阿里巴巴六大业务分拆：谁将率先上市，如何价值重估. (2023-03-30)[2023-06-09]. https://www.thepaper.cn/newsDetail_forward_22508457.

（2）阿里巴巴在人工智能领域的发展历程

人工智能可通过智能推荐算法、智能物流、图像识别、自然语言处理等技术，提升用户体验和电商平台运营效率，挖掘平台数据价值，拓展平台业务范围，是当今世界电商产业发展的重要驱动力，也是以电商为支柱的公司实现数字化转型和创新发展的重要途径，对当今时代互联网公司参与市场竞争不可或缺。阿里巴巴作为以电商为支柱产业的大型公司，也颇具有前瞻性地自2014年起在人工智能领域布局，进行前沿科技的投资与研发。但需要特别注意的是，阿里巴巴自始至终围绕其愿景"让天下没有难做的生意"展开人工智能的投入和研发，故其人工智能产品均为支持、发展其电商产业服务，其最终、最原初之目标，在于以人工智能这一前沿技术，为集团带来更大的经济利益。这一最原始的推动力，与OpenAI的"确保通用人工智能惠及全人类"有着根本性的不同。

阿里巴巴在人工智能领域的发展主要分为自主研发创新和对外投资合作，其历程可大致分为以下几个阶段。

2014年之前：阿里巴巴开始布局云计算和大数据领域，推出了飞天操作系统和阿里云服务[1]，为后续的人工智能发展奠定了基础。

2014—2016年：阿里巴巴开始涉足人工智能领域，推出ET人工智能系统，并在语音识别、图像识别、视频AI等方面进行了技术创新和应用落地。

2017—2018年：阿里加速人工智能领域的布局，成立达摩院[2]，并在云计算、芯片技术、机器学习等方面进行了深入研究和开发。此外，阿里巴巴也加大对外投资力度，投资深鉴科技、寒武纪等AI芯片公司，并收购了中天微芯片公司。

2019年至今：阿里巴巴进一步完善了人工智能生态圈，推出平头哥半导体公司，拥有端云一体全栈产品系列，涵盖数据中心人工智能芯片、处理器IP授权等，实现芯片端到端设计链路全覆盖。同时，阿里巴巴将其旗下的AI相关业务升级为阿里云智能板块。阿里巴巴也与多个行业和领域进行了AI技术的合作和应用，如农业、医疗、城市管理等。

2.阿里巴巴的人工智能突破性成果与社会影响

前面述及自2014年起，阿里巴巴开启了其在人工智能领域的开拓。2020

① 阿里云.阿里飞天云平台架构简介.[2023-06-09]. https://developer.aliyun.com/article/652388.
② 达摩院官网.[2023-06-09].https://damo.alibaba.com/.

年其首席财务官披露，阿里巴巴近几年在人工智能领域的研发投入每年均超过 1000 亿元人民币。阿里巴巴认为，技术和商业的融合已成为其进化的驱动力——每一项新业务、新产品的诞生和发展都有技术的支撑和创造。新技术的研发既可升级原有业务，又能孵化新业务，且后者可使技术在市场中得到验证，推动新商业"自我造血"，进而反哺技术，实现创新的"履带式发展"。

新技术的研发应适配阿里巴巴业务的实际需求，回应业务运行中产生的问题，致力于达成业务与技术的相辅相成，形成良性循环。在这一背景下，其人工智能产品均与其电商业务密不可分。

（1）平头哥

平头哥是阿里巴巴集团的全资半导体芯片业务主体，成立于 2018 年，在人工智能芯片领域取得多项进展。其面向机器视觉场景的 AI 推理芯片"含光800"已成功应用于云计算服务、电商智能搜索、电商营销等领域。[①]平头哥也是全球 RISC-V 软件生态计划"RISE"的发起者和董事会成员之一，致力于推动 RISC-V 生态的发展和繁荣。平头哥 2022 年发布的"RISC-V 玄铁 C908"是一款面向端侧场景的处理器，支持多种数据类型和指令扩展，可应用于智能家居、智慧城市、智能汽车等领域。平头哥还发布了面向万物互联场景的超高频 RFID 电子标签芯片"羽阵 611"，在性能、稳定性、一致性和环境适应性方面均达到业界领先水平。

（2）达摩院

达摩院是一家致力于探索科技未知，以人类愿景为驱动力的，立足于基础科学、创新性技术和应用技术的研究院。达摩院成立于 2017 年 10 月 11 日，达摩院的研究方向包括数据智能、机器智能、计算机视觉、自然语言处理、语音识别、机器人、芯片、量子计算、区块链等多个领域。

达摩院代表性的成果之一是其智能机器人"小蛮驴"，以及近几年或将投入使用的"大蛮驴"。小蛮驴是一款面向末端物流场景的智能机器人，采用 L4级自动驾驶技术，能够在复杂的路况中自主行驶和避障，服务于最后三公里的快递、外卖、生鲜等配送需求。小蛮驴已经在全国 22 个省份落地，累计配送订单超过 100 万。而大蛮驴则是一款面向城配物流的轻型卡车，同样采用 L4级自动驾驶技术，能够在公开道路上进行物流运输，应用场景包括城市快递网

---

① 顾正书. 2022 国产 AI 芯片报告之一：10 大国产 AI 芯片. (2022-03-20)[2023-06-09]. https://www.eet-china.com/news/2022032114110.html.

点到配送站之间的物流配送等。大小蛮驴的研发、投产均是为了完善电商服务一条龙中物流配送这一重要组成部分。

此外，达摩院在语音智能、语言技术、机器视觉三大技术领域与平台化建设中也有所突破。^①达摩院开源了自主开发的新一代语音识别模型（DFSMN），在世界最大的免费语音识别数据库 LibriSpeech 上进行公开测试，训练速度更快，识别准确率更高。达摩院还研发了高工业噪声环境下的语音识别及传输技术，可以实现将 85 分贝工业噪声下的语音转换为文字，准确率达 94.6%。语音交互方面，达摩院开源了人机对话模型 ESIM，通过给对话机器人装上实时搜索并理解人类真实意图的"雷达"系统，实现对对话历史的实时检索，自动去除多余信息的干扰，给出人类期待的回复。达摩院还推出了分布式语音交互解决方案，打通了上下游平台串联、端云一体能力，缩短智能人居环境开发周期。达摩院自主研发了基于翻译的合成技术 Knowledge-Aware Neural TTS（KAN-TTS），深度融合了目前主流的端到端 TTS 技术和传统 TTS 技术，同时系统构建了基于不同领域的深层知识。语言技术方面，达摩院的研究团队提出的"基于分层融合注意力机制"的深度神经网络模型能够模拟人类在做阅读理解问题时的一些行为，包括结合篇章内容审题，带着问题反复阅读文章，避免阅读中遗忘而进行相关标注，等。模型可以在捕捉问题和文章中特定区域关联的同时，借助分层策略，逐步集中注意力，使答案边界清晰。这些有关语音、视觉的研发，究其本因，亦是由电商服务中，完善线上客服机器人的实际需求而推动的。

（3）阿里云

阿里云 AI 依托阿里巴巴顶尖的算法技术，结合阿里云可靠和灵活的云计算基础设施和平台服务，帮助企业简化 IT 框架、实现商业价值、加速数智化转型。阿里云 AI 的研究成果包括提供人脸识别、图像识别、视频分析、图片搜索等多种机器视觉技术服务，支持多种场景和行业，如新零售、新媒体、新制造等。阿里云的 PAI 平台面向开发者和企业提供包含数据标注、模型构建、模型训练、模型部署、推理优化在内的 AI 开发全链路服务，内置 140 多种优化算法，具备丰富的行业场景插件，为用户提供低门槛、高性能的云原生 AI 工程化能力。PAI 已经在多个领域和场景中得到了应用和验证，如电商、金

---

① AI 科技大本营.阿里达摩院做 AI 这两年.（2023-06-09）[2024-02-07]. https://www.36kr.com/p/1724049620993.

融、智能制造、社交媒体等。PAI助力微博机器学习平台，为微博的热门微博／Feed推荐等上层业务，提供模型训练能力。依托PAI进行训练的ET城市大脑，已在日常生活中得到多项应用，如在杭州主城区以视频巡检替代人工巡检，日报警量多达500次，识别准确率92％以上；中河－上塘路高架车辆道路通行时间缩短15.3％；莫干山路部分路段通行时间缩短8.5％。在杭州萧山区，用ET城市大脑进行信号灯自动配时，相应路段平均道路通行速度提升15％，平均通行时间缩短3分钟；应急车辆到达时间节省50％，救援时间缩短了7分钟以上；"两客一危"也得到精准把控。而在苏州，ET城市大脑被用于打造智慧园区，园区内部署了智能停车系统、智能安防系统、智能环境监测系统等，提升了园区管理效率和服务质量。

（二）阿里巴巴的人工智能战略与技术布局

1. 根植于电子商务的算力基础设施

自2006年谷歌提出云计算概念后，云计算风靡全球。2008年9月，阿里巴巴确定"云计算"和"大数据"战略，决定自主研发大规模分布式计算操作系统"飞天"。2009年1月，阿里巴巴在江苏南京建立首个"电子商务云计算中心"。时任阿里巴巴集团首席技术官的王坚在"互联网＋"的基础上提出了"云计算＋"的战略；同年9月，阿里云计算有限公司成立。

2010年8月，国内首个真正意义上的云计算数据中心在杭州正式投入运营。阿里巴巴作为首批客户正式入驻该数据中心。2011年7月，阿里云官网上线，开始大规模对外提供云计算服务。2014年5月，阿里云香港区投入运行，成为中国第一家提供海外云计算服务的公司。2015年3月，阿里云美西中心投入试运营，向北美乃至全球用户提供云计算服务。时至2017年，阿里云在全球范围内建立起了17个数据中心区域，并向更多国家和地区提供云计算服务。到2019年，阿里云在中国市场上的占有率已经达到46.6％，数字政府市场份额第一，成为中国领先的云计算服务提供商之一。阿里云在全球也已经成为最有竞争力、受到国际认可的云计算服务提供商之一。

2. 布局全产业链的人工智能

（1）从电子商务应用到各领域生态圈赋能

在阿里巴巴的网购业务背后，人工智能已经嵌入了它的数字基建之中，并正在重新定义数亿中国线上消费者和批发商的购物体验。应用于网购上的人工智能技术，并不像无人驾驶、聊天机器人等那样抓人眼球和具有未来感，但却在更潜移默化地影响着人们的生活。

1）客户端——智能化、个性化：阿里巴巴使用实时线上数据建造模型并预测消费者想要的产品，为消费者提供智能产品搜索与推荐；阿里巴巴开发的客服聊天机器人"阿里小蜜"目前已经被广泛地运用于解决客户问题和投诉，其可根据大量的用户交互不断升级自己的能力，为客户提供更广泛的智能客户服务，例如话费充值、天气查询、机票购买等。

2）商户端——智慧供应链、智慧物流：阿里巴巴开发了阿里智慧供应链，利用 AI 帮助线上和线下的商户预测商品需求，准备、补充和分配库存以达到最佳周转率，确定最佳供应商品以及定价策略。这一平台的总体目标是帮助商户有效平衡供需，从而降低成本以及库存不足带来的损失。阿里智慧供应链也运用了 AI 来预测新产品或促销产品的需求，平台处理的数据包括消费者的偏好与购物行为，以及季节性和区域性的数据变化。阿里巴巴的附属物流菜鸟物流拥有高效的大数据和智能仓库管理系统、数字运单系统、计算机包裹分拣和发货中心，能够应用地理信息系统（GIS）和 AI 训练计算模型来找到最为节约成本的运货路径。此外，AI 还用于预测含多个商品订单的包装盒尺寸，帮助减少 10％ 的包装材料。菜鸟还宣布和中国几个大型汽车制造商合作制造 100 万辆绿色能源运输车，通过利用 AI 技术可以将车辆使用量降低 10％、将行驶距离降低 30％。

在人机交互行业生态领域发展的大背景下，阿里小蜜平台是阿里巴巴在智能服务领域布局的最重要载体，推动着甚至引领着"传统客服"向"智能服务"的发展转变。在 2017 年"双十一"期间，阿里小蜜的智能服务占比达到了 95％，智能解决率为 93.1％。阿里小蜜平台的特别之处不仅在于革新了智能服务的方式，更在于其体现的阿里巴巴在人工智能领域的全产业链布局。阿里小蜜的应用场景覆盖了阿里内部各个事业群、电商商家、企业等。作为一个人工智能助理，除了解决用户的业务咨询类问题，阿里小蜜兼备其他助理业务，包括查天气、买机票、充话费等。同时，其还可以通过多轮会话完成一个导购助理的工作。不仅在企业方面有电商小蜜，在政务、金融、办公等领域也有小蜜的支持，现在国内和海外的企业，以及第三方 ISV 和开发者可以通过阿里云和钉钉等平台开放服务，通过企业小蜜支持整个企业的生态圈。

（2）大模型开启智能化时代

2023年4月26日，阿里巴巴董事会主席、阿里云智能CEO张勇在2023阿里云合作伙伴大会上说："今天我们看到的未来是一个智能化时代的开端，这个起点带来的影响，我认为至少是十年、二十年。"大模型带来了历史性机会。

自ChatGPT发布以来，新的AI浪潮已经席卷全球，国内的各大厂商更是在近期密集宣布AI大模型的相关进展。与工业革命一样，大模型将会被各行各业广泛应用，带来生产力的巨大提升，并深刻改变我们的生活方式。2023年4月12日，阿里云发布旗下的语言大模型"通义千问"。在迈入智能化时代的过程中，阿里巴巴不仅要做好AI能力的应用者，更要成为AI能力的提供者。[①]

1）从改造自身业务做起

据阿里云智能CEO张勇透露，阿里巴巴所有产品未来都将接入大模型进行全面升级，其中，钉钉、天猫精灵已率先接入测试，将在评估认证后正式发布新功能。根据钉钉当天预告的Demo演示，接入通义千问之后的钉钉可实现近10项新AI功能，比如撰写邮件、生成营销策划方案等，全面激发创意和办公生产力。而根据天猫精灵官方预告的演示Demo，接入通义千问后，新天猫精灵变得更拟人、更聪明，知识、情感、个性、记忆能力大幅跃升。它支持自由对话，可以随时打断、切换话题，能根据用户需求和场景随时生成内容。

谈到对于阿里旗下产品的改造规划，阿里云智能CTO周靖人指出这项改造工作的探索性，通义千问目前提供的是一种技术能力，而从技术能力到业务应用，还有一定距离。[②]

2）结合云计算基础设施，加速AI普及

张勇指出，大模型是一场"AI＋云计算"的全方位竞争，超万亿参数的大模型研发，并不仅是算法问题，而是囊括了底层庞大算力、网络、大数据、机器学习等诸多领域的复杂系统性工程，需要有超大规模AI基础设施的支撑。在阿里云峰会上，周靖人宣布，阿里云将推出新款通用算力型ECS云服务器Universal实例，售价相比上一代主售实例降幅最高可达40％。另外，用户还

---

① 李强. 阿里正研发类ChatGPT产品 或推动AI电商新场景. (2023-02-09)[2024-03-01]. https://www.21jingji.com/article/20230209/herald/f98b19505bbc8edbdb28db6c69e574b3.html.

② 白杨，李强. AI迈入群雄逐鹿时代 阿里巴巴全方位迎战. (2023-04-12)[2024-03-01]. https://www.21jingji.com/article/20230412/8858d720daf2145f86caa435c20d66b6.html.

可通过预留云上存储空间和锁定购买时长，来获得更低的长期存储成本，价格最多可降 70%。阿里云产品的大幅降价，主要得益于阿里云对软硬一体技术整合的大力投入，提高了计算资源利用率，带动算力成本不断降低，从而推动规模扩大和价格降低的正循环。

而在 AI 普及方面，2022 年 11 月，阿里云在云栖大会上首次提出了"Model-as-a-service（MaaS，模型即服务）"的概念，并推出国内首个 AI 模型社区"魔搭"，开发者可以在魔搭上下载各类开源 AI 模型，并直接调用阿里云的算力和一站式的 AI 大模型训练及推理平台。发布不到半年，"魔搭"社区总用户量已超 100 万，模型数量从最初的 300 多个增长到 800 多个，总下载量超 1600 万次，成为国内规模最大的 AI 模型社区。阿里云正在通过全面走向"模型即服务"，与伙伴合作，走向千行百业的数字化和智能化。

3）建立层次化的模型体系

2021 年，阿里巴巴达摩院先后发布多个版本的多模态及语言大模型，在超大模型、低碳训练技术、平台化服务、落地应用等方面实现突破，引领了中文大模型的发展。其中，达摩院团队使用 512 卡 V100 GPU 即实现 10 万亿参数大模型 M6，同等参数规模能耗仅为此前业界标杆的 1%，极大降低了大模型训练门槛。

面向大模型通用性与易用性仍欠缺的难题，通义千问打造了业界首个 AI 统一底座，并构建了大小模型协同的层次化人工智能体系，将为 AI 从感知智能迈向知识驱动的认知智能提供先进基础设施。达摩院在国内率先构建了 AI 统一底座，在业界首次实现了模态表示、任务表示、模型结构的统一。同时，以统一底座为基础，达摩院构建了层次化的模型体系，其中通用模型层覆盖自然语言处理、多模态、计算机视觉，专业模型层深入电商、医疗、法律、金融、娱乐等行业。通用与专业领域大小模型协同，让通义大模型系列可兼顾性能最优化与低成本落地。为加快大模型规模化应用，达摩院还研发了超大模型落地关键技术 S4 框架，百亿参数大模型在压缩率达 99% 的情况下多任务精度可接近无损。通过部署超大模型及轻量化版本，阿里巴巴通义大模型系列已在超过 200 个场景中提供服务，实现了 2%—10% 的应用效果提升。典型使用场景包括电商跨模态搜索、AI 辅助设计、开放域人机对话、法律文书学习、医疗文本理解等。[①]

（3）后发制人，布局全产业链

相比亚马逊、微软、IBM和谷歌，阿里巴巴在人工智能方面起步较晚。在阿里AI产品还未成熟的时候，为了避免过早地被大众舆论拉入永无休止的信息战，阿里AI采用后发制人的策略，成立前沿技术研究机构达摩院，借助阿里云的竞争优势，以"云＋AI＋IOT"模式展开云、管、边、端、AI、物联网的全链路、一体化布局，巧妙地在产品毛坯时期避开了各大巨头的炮火，在2018年之后接连斩获国际奖项。

在达摩院的推动下，阿里巴巴在AI平台、AI算法、AI引擎框架、AI云服务、AI芯片、产业AI等多个领域进入市场，以"云＋AI＋IOT"的模式完成从单点系统到技术生态的全面布局，帮助零售、医疗、司法、交通等行业提升效率，推动经济、空间技术、自动控制、计算机设计和制造等领域的变革，并通过互联网和人工智能，打通城市数据管道，建设覆盖交通、平安、市政建设、城市规划等领域的城市大脑公共系统。

（三）阿里巴巴的人工智能治理与可持续发展实践

1.阿里巴巴科技伦理治理委员会

除却在人工智能领域研发前沿技术，阿里巴巴集团亦深刻认识到科技创新应以人为本，划定研发边界，同时相关主体应谨慎对待自身技术能力和影响力，注重应对科技前沿研究带来的伦理风险。阿里巴巴于2022年9月宣布成立科技伦理治理委员会，提出"以人为本、普惠正直、安全可靠、隐私保护、可信可控、开放共治"六大科技伦理准则，推动算法治理、隐私保护、伦理制度建设等工作。委员会由来自阿里研究院、达摩院、法务合规、阿里人工智能治理与可持续发展研究中心以及相关业务板块的核心成员组成，并设有多个具体工作小组，集团又引入七位来自科技、法律、公共管理、哲学等领域的专家组成独立的顾问委员会，履行外部监督职能，实现自律和他律的结合。

委员会之上述六大科技伦理准则之细则从用户、科技、隐私、信誉、合作等角度阐释其治理目标：坚持以用户为中心，避免歧视与偏见，切实保护各相关主体的合法权益，将对人的尊重和关怀放在第一位；充分考虑安全和稳健

---

① 董静怡.阿里巴巴张勇：大模型催生智能化时代，阿里云走向"产品被集成".(2023-04-27)[2024-03-01]. https://www.21jingji.com/article/20230427/cbe9c23f543277c610c701b1356976c6.html.

性，减少并努力避免所研发的科技系统因缺陷或滥用造成对用户的伤害；充分尊重个人信息知情、同意权，充分保障个人隐私与数据安全，不窃取、篡改、泄露个人信息，保护个人合法数据权益；保证从事的科技活动及开发的科技系统具备应有的透明度和可解释性，努力建立人工智能问责机制，给予用户自主决定权；建立多方协同合作机制，打造负责任、可持续的科技。①

阿里巴巴科技伦理治理委员会在部分模块已采取具体行动，如根据法律要求，在各业务组织设置专门的个人信息保护负责人以落实隐私保护，严格履行"数据采集最小必要原则""用户知情和决定权最大化"以及"全方位安全保障能力最强化"，以规范全生命周期的隐私保护与数据安全。而在算法治理方面，委员会制定了一系列管理规范，推动算法公平和透明。以商品搜索算法为例，阿里巴巴加入打散设计以提升搜索结果的多样性，又在重要算法上线或更新前进行专项评审，确保合规且符合伦理方能上线。

2. 阿里巴巴人工智能治理与可持续发展研究中心

阿里巴巴于 2021 年 7 月成立了人工智能治理与可持续发展研究中心，致力于利用人工智能技术解决安全风险问题。该中心的研究领域包括内容安全、业务风控、数字安防、数据安全与算法安全等，下设八大实验室，即计算机视觉实验室、自然语言理解实验室、数据挖掘与机器学习实验室、多模态基础模型实验室、图算法实验室、知识计算实验室、人工智能安全实验室，以及人工智能伦理与道德实验室。其中，前七个实验室均致力于前沿技术的研发，而人工智能伦理与道德实验室则致力于践行人人受益、责任担当、开放共享的原则，将可持续发展理念融入人工智能治理中，建立助力人工智能发展的伦理道德规范。

研究中心于 2022 年 7 月发布《人工智能治理与可持续发展实践白皮书》（以下简称"《白皮书》"）②，针对人工智能应用中的热点问题，如调度决策是否合宜，检索到的信息是否真实，"深度合成"技术是否被恶意使用，等，总结了阿里巴巴集团在这些领域的实践。阿里巴巴近年来致力于构建面向可持续发展的人工智能技术体系：开展校企合作，建立模型鲁棒性评测与防御系统，创

---

① 阿里巴巴. "做好"科技，做"好科技". (2022-09-02)[2023-06-07]. https://mp.weixin.qq.com/s/665vwusLk MHl0yPqC5kUog.

② 阿里巴巴人工智能治理与可持续发展研究中心. 人工智能治理白皮书系列. (2023)[2023-06-11]. https:// s.alibaba.com/cn/WhitePaperHome.

新性地构造了鲁棒视觉网络结构RVT，使人工智能在受到外界干扰时，仍保有其性能水平；对人工智能软件和硬件进行冗余设计，构建充分的容错和溯源机制，充分保障用户使用的决定权和自主权；强化全生命周期的评估测试工作，以量化方式评估相应技术系统的性能优劣；开展持续的动态监测工作，确保及时发现、处置相应风险问题。

阿里巴巴也强调人工智能助力可持续发展中多主体落实协同治理的需求。《白皮书》指出，企业作为人工智能风险触发的首要主体，应支撑政府提升监管治理效能；应积极参与标准制定，联合行业组织共创行业自律；应主动阐释治理进展，提升社会参与度；应产学研联动，加强多渠道人才培养；应致力于守护清朗健康的网络生态环境。

此外，《白皮书》提出的六大科技伦理准则，即为一年后科技伦理治理委员会建立的立足之本。《白皮书》亦提出科技治理应以发展生产力、保护正当主体权益为目标，以人人受益、责任担当、开放共享为价值导向，即在助力人工智能发展、挖掘其应用潜力与应对人工智能相关技术之脆弱性、管理体系之滞后性之间找到平衡，又承担社会责任，服务于社会、经济、环境的可持续发展。

《白皮书》亦罗列了阿里巴巴集团应用人工智能助力可持续发展的实例。如阿里巴巴与清华大学联合研发人机交互新技术，通过将视障用户使用的传统读屏软件替换为基于语义和逻辑的模式，结合Smart Touch交互技术，提供基于语音和触觉的多模态交互方式，为视障人群更好地使用手机提供新可能。针对该群体用户读写验证码和密码困难的问题，集团研发了"挥一挥"空中手势验证码和"划一划"屏幕手势密码。又如，集团积极承担社会职能，旗下达摩院与国家气象中心强天气室联合研发的雷达反射率临近预报人工智能算法将预测精度缩小到1公里以内，辅助预报员预测临近时段内突发性强对流天气，有效降低强天气现象造成的经济损失和社会危害。

五、OpenAI与阿里巴巴的发展特色和经验对比

（一）愿景理念、商业模式和技术布局的差异

OpenAI和阿里巴巴是两家在人工智能领域具有代表性和影响力的组织，但它们在企业规模、愿景理念、商业模式和技术布局、资源配置等方面存在着显著的差异。

从企业规模来看，阿里巴巴是一家综合性的互联网公司，拥有多元化的业务板块和庞大的用户群体，其 2023 财年的总收入达到了 7159 亿元人民币。而 OpenAI 是一家非营利性的研究机构，主要专注于开发和推广通用人工智能（AGI），其 2023 年的总收入仅为 1.5 亿美元。可以说，阿里巴巴在规模上远远超过了 OpenAI。

从愿景理念来看，阿里巴巴以"让天下没有难做的生意"为愿景，希冀达成"通过互联网服务，让商业更平等"的使命。而 OpenAI 以"确保人工智能能够被所有人使用，并且对所有人都有益"为愿景，希冀达成"创建友善的通用人工智能"的使命。可以说，阿里巴巴的愿景理念更加具体和务实，而 OpenAI 的愿景理念更加抽象和理想化。

从商业模式和技术布局来看，阿里巴巴主要通过提供电子商务、云计算、数字媒体及娱乐、创新业务等多种产品和服务来营利，同时也在云计算、芯片技术、机器学习等方面进行了深入研究和开发。而 OpenAI 主要通过接受捐赠、出售许可证、提供咨询等方式来营利，同时也在大模型、自然语言处理、计算机视觉等方面进行了突破性的研究和创新。可以说，阿里巴巴的商业模式和技术布局更加多样化和平衡化，而 OpenAI 的商业模式和技术布局更加单一化和前沿化。

从资源配置来看，阿里巴巴拥有庞大的数据资源、算力资源、人才资源和资金资源，能够支持其在各个领域进行全面的探索和应用。而 OpenAI 虽然拥有优秀的研究团队和合作伙伴，但其数据资源、算力资源、人才资源和资金资源相对有限，只能侧重于某些领域进行深度的研究和创新。但另一方面，阿里巴巴的资源布局更加分散，虽然有着阿里云体系的计算支持，但各个业务群之间既存在技术共享也存在资源争用。而 OpenAI 作为一家集中精力发展 AGI 的中等规模企业，享受着英伟达、微软等手握巨量计算资源的大公司的支持。甚至英伟达曾将自己研发的全球第一款 DGX-1 超级计算机赠予尚处于初创阶段的 OpenAI，可见作为一家潜力无限的人工智能研发企业，OpenAI 有着远远超过自身体量的广泛的外部支持。随着 ChatGPT 的发布，OpenAI 已然成为全球人工智能行业遥遥领先的研发者，短时间内其必然会持续受到全球金融、技术投资者的青睐。而阿里巴巴在其布局的"平头哥"等半导体、芯片研发方面尚未取得可与英伟达、英特尔、AMD 直接竞争的核心技术突破；作为一家中国企业，其在高端芯片采购方面也将受到美国商务部芯片相关禁令的持续影响。

在经济复苏放缓、企业自身面临规模增长困境，且算力和数据资源成为新的AI发展时期最重要的资源的情况下，阿里巴巴等国内人工智能、互联网企业如何在新一代人工智能模型设计、训练、部署等方面取得引领性突破仍然是对其商业模式的重大考验。

综上所述，在企业规模、愿景理念、商业模式和技术布局、资源配置等方面，阿里巴巴和OpenAI都有各自的特色和优势，但也有不同程度的差距。阿里巴巴作为国内领先的互联网和人工智能企业，应该看到OpenAI在人工智能领域的创新能力和影响力，同时也应该认识到自身在人工智能领域的发展空间和提升潜力。

（二）阿里巴巴人工智能产业发展对策建议

1.研发体系、资源配置与重点聚焦

加大对人工智能基础研究的投入，提高在人工智能前沿领域的原创性和创新性是国内互联网及人工智能企业与OpenAI、微软、谷歌、Meta等全球性的科技公司直接竞争的必经之路。OpenAI在人工智能基础研究方面具有较强的创新能力和影响力；同时，正如前文所述，OpenAI在构建"强人工智能"方面有着极强的愿景和信心，甚至将AGI写入自己的公司章程，作为其自身最重要、最核心的使命。而OpenAI在技术路线选择方面眼光独到，并将有限的精力和资源全部投入到自己所设定的人工智能研发路线中，其研究成果在国际学术界和业界广受关注和认可。然而，阿里巴巴在人工智能基础研究方面还存在一定的不足，虽然阿里在人工智能研究和应用方面有着从芯片到大模型几乎覆盖上下游全产业链的布局，但作为一个体量巨大、研发资源充沛的科技巨头，阿里巴巴尚未能借助其多模态统一模型OFA或通义系列大模型与OpenAI等国际竞争对手形成有效的竞争优势。相较之下，在多模态AI研究成果井喷的近几年，即便是在OpenAI一鸣惊人地推出GPT-4之前，Google的Flamingo、BERT，微软的BEiT-3、DeepMind的AlphaFold等模型就已经在文本、图像、多模态预训练甚至蛋白质结构预测等方面处于全球领先的水平。

阿里巴巴可以借鉴OpenAI的大模型开发模式，利用自身庞大的数据资源和算力资源，开发出更强大、更通用、更可靠的人工智能模型，覆盖更多的场景和需求，为其各个业务板块提供更多的技术支持和赋能。但与此同时，阿里巴巴等国内技术企业不应仅仅局限在模仿、复制、追赶的发展道路上，也应避

免过于关注于满足自身业务需求，而忽视了模型的通用性和可扩展性，避免过于重视模型的短期效益，而忽视了模型的长期影响和风险等。这些局限性可能导致阿里巴巴在人工智能领域缺乏创新性和领导力，难以与OpenAI等竞争对手形成有效的竞争差异。

除了"赶时髦"的大模型研发，加大对人工智能算力基础设施等关键技术的投入，提高其在人工智能领域的自主性，也应成为阿里巴巴等国内企业关注的重点问题。例如，平头哥目前的半导体产品多集中在专用芯片领域，并未能在GPU等通用芯片的设计及芯片制造的核心工艺上取得英伟达等国际头部企业的竞争能力。

相较于其他厂商较为粗放的发展模式，OpenAI在算法研发、模型训练上展现出较高的体系化、兵团化的特征。2023年6月，OpenAI的联合创始人安德烈·卡帕斯（Andrej Karpathy）曾在一个开发者活动上透露，OpenAI在模型训练技术上有着非常全面和系统性的尝试，他表示，如果一篇论文提出了某种不同的训练方法，那么OpenAI内部的群组里会有人表示"两年半前尝试过了，它不起作用，我们对这种方法的来龙去脉非常了解"；而OpenAI正在关注的基于语言模型的Agent（智能体）研究在不到半年后成为了全球人工智能领域新的热点。这种系统性和热衷钻研那些常常不被关注的细节的研究模式，十分值得国内的厂商、研究机构借鉴；OpenAI的经验似乎说明，全面深入的体系化研究可能比短平快的研发模式更加高效。

2. 拓展负责任的人工智能价值体系

首先，阿里巴巴需要重新审视其关于人工智能的价值观和原则。OpenAI在人工智能的价值观和原则方面具有较强的清晰度和一致性，其将人工智能的最终目标定义为"对所有人都有益的通用人工智能"，并制定了一系列与之相符的原则，如对称性、可扩展性、对齐性、安全性等。而阿里巴巴在人工智能的价值观和原则方面还存在一定的模糊性和不完善性，例如缺乏对人工智能的统一和明确的定义和目标。阿里巴巴对人工智能的价值观和原则的构建更倾向于数据隐私、可解释性、非歧视等务实的层面，而OpenAI则愿意更多地强调潜在的通用人工智能对人类安全、人类文明的根本性影响。

其次，阿里巴巴需要建立并完善其人工智能的治理机制和流程。这些机制和流程可以建立在前文提及的阿里巴巴科技伦理治理委员会、人工智能治理与可持续发展研究中心的基础之上，但除了编写框架性质的伦理准则、白皮书等文件外，还应该有具体的、可执行的、涵盖其在人工智能领域的规划、设计、开发、部署、运营、评估等各个环节的人工智能伦理监管体系，以确保其在人工智能领域的活动符合其价值观和原则，遵循相关的法律法规和伦理道德，预防和减少可能造成的不良影响和风险。人工智能治理机制和流程的统一和标准化的建立和实施，对治理机制和流程的有效性和适应性的评估和改进，以及治理机制和流程的公开性和可审查性是企业构建"负责任的AI"等人工智能价值体系的核心问题。

此外，阿里巴巴还需要培育并提升其人工智能的人才队伍和文化氛围。这涉及其在人工智能领域的招聘、培训、激励、评估等各个方面，阿里巴巴需要确保其拥有足够数量和质量的人工智能专业人才，培养其对人工智能价值观和原则的认同和遵守，并激发其对人工智能创新和发展的热情和动力。OpenAI在人工智能的人才队伍和文化氛围方面具有较强的吸引力和活力，其拥有一批来自世界各地的顶尖科学家和研究员，为他们提供了充分的自由度和资源支持，鼓励他们进行开放式和协作式的研究和创新。然而，阿里巴巴在人工智能的人才队伍和文化氛围方面还存在一定的问题，如面临着国内外人才市场的竞争和人才流失，难以吸引和留住优秀的人工智能专业人才；面临着企业文化与科研文化的冲突和矛盾，难以平衡商业利益与科学探索之间的关系；面临着内部管理与外部监管的压力和变化，难以保持人工智能创新与发展的稳定性和持续性。

同时，国内的互联网企业也可以注重拓展并深化同全球人工智能的合作伙伴和利益相关者的合作。这涵盖其在人工智能领域的客户、供应商、投资者、竞争者、监管者、社会公众等各个方面，目的是确保其与各方建立良好的沟通和协作关系，共享其在人工智能领域的资源和成果，共同推动人工智能领域的发展和进步。例如，OpenAI在人工智能的合作伙伴和利益相关者方面具有较强的开放性和包容性，其与多个国际组织、论坛、联盟等平台进行合作交流，与多个政府、企业、学术机构等进行合作研究，其CEO、首席科学家等积极参加与社会公众、媒体、非政府组织等进行的对话交流，不断发布《我们加强人工智能安全的路径》等回应公众安全关切的文章，也时常将其内部的大模型研究进展、研发规划等向公众披露，它从不避讳谈及自己的理念，也时常展现出一种坦诚、透明的态度。然而，阿里巴巴在人工智能的合作伙伴和利益相关者方面还存在一定的局限性和障碍，如缺乏对国际规则、标准制定过程和内容的深入了解和参与，缺乏对国内政策、法律、监管环境的及时适应和应对，以及缺乏对社会舆论、影响、风险的有效管理和控制。这些局限性和障碍导致阿里巴巴在人工智能领域缺乏合作感和影响力。

3. 积极参与全球规则、标准制定

在人工智能的发展和安全逐渐成为全球性议题的当下，阿里巴巴等国内企业也应该积极参与人工智能相关的全球规则、标准体系的制定，增强其在人工智能领域的话语权和影响力。例如，阿里巴巴应积极参与国际组织、论坛、联盟等平台，与其他国家和地区的政府、企业、学术机构等进行沟通和协作，共同推动人工智能领域的规则制定和标准建设，维护公平、开放、透明、合作的人工智能研发的国际环境。相比之下，OpenAI在国际规则、标准制定方面具有较强的参与度和影响力，其是多个国际组织和联盟的成员或合作伙伴，如人工智能伙伴关系（PAI）等。

同时，国内互联网企业也应积极参与国内外的社会责任和公益活动，与社会各界进行沟通和合作，共同推动人工智能领域的社会责任和公益事业，关注人工智能的社会影响和风险，保障人工智能的可持续、可信、可惠用。OpenAI等公司在社会责任和公益活动方面具有较强的倡导力和实践力，其致力于确保人工智能能够被所有人使用，并且对所有人都有益，为此开展了多项针对人工智能伦理、安全、公平等问题的研究和实验。然而，阿里巴巴在社会责任和公益活动方面还存在一定的不足，如缺乏对人工智能社会责任和公益事业的系统性和长期性的规划和投入，缺乏对人工智能社会影响和风险的全面性和深入性的评估和监测，缺乏对人工智能可持续、可信、可惠用的有效性和普遍性的保障和促进等。

六、结　语

人工智能是当今最具变革力和影响力的技术之一，它正在改变我们的生活、工作和思维方式。互联网作为人工智能的重要载体和推动力，为人工智能提供了丰富的数据、算力、场景和应用。同时，人工智能也为互联网带来了新的机遇和挑战，促进了互联网的创新和发展。OpenAI和阿里巴巴是两家在人工智能领域具有代表性与领导力的公司，它们分别以不同方式探索了人工智能的可能性和潜力，也面临着不同的风险和责任。本文从全球人工智能行业的发展历程、现状和趋势入手，分析了互联网与人工智能的密切关系，重点介绍了

OpenAI和阿里巴巴这两家公司的人工智能战略、技术布局、管理创新和社会责任等方面，展示了它们在人工智能领域的成就和影响。通过对比两家公司在愿景理念、商业模式和技术导向等方面的差异，本文提出国内互联网及人工智能企业借鉴OpenAI的成功经验，并构建负责任的人工智能，提升国际影响力，推动共建更包容、可持续的全球人工智能创新体系的可行路径。国内互联网及人工智能企业可以在坚持以用户为中心、以商业为驱动的基础上，重视人工智能的开放性、安全性和公益性，加强与国际社会和其他跨国企业的合作和交流，积极参与人工智能的伦理规范和治理机制的制定和实施，并为人类社会的进步和福祉做出贡献。

值得关注的是，近期中国人工智能初创企业深度求索（DeepSeek）在通用大模型领域的突破，为全球人工智能竞争格局注入了新变量。其推出的DeepSeek－R1系列模型凭借开源策略和高效推理能力，已在代码生成、多轮对话等场景中展现显著优势。这一技术路径不仅验证了中小规模模型通过架构优化实现性能跃升的可行性，更推动了行业对模型效率与可持续性的反思。面对DeepSeek等新兴力量的挑战，OpenAI在2023年显著加快了GPT－4 Turbo的迭代速度，并尝试通过多模态能力扩展巩固技术壁垒。这种动态竞争客观上加速了通用人工智能的技术民主化进程，但也促使行业重新审视开源生态与商业闭环的平衡关系。未来，OpenAI或将调整其技术路线与开放策略，以应对来自不同技术范式与市场定位的竞争压力，而这一过程将进一步形塑全球人工智能创新的生态格局。

人工智能技术趋向可持续发展
——基于微软与腾讯案例的对比研究①

摘 要: 随着人工智能技术的不断发展和创新，互联网行业逐渐成为经济增长和社会变革的重要推动力量。微软和腾讯的发展历程具有一定的相似之处，重点体现在两个方面。一方面，近年来，二者都重视并加强了人工智能领域的投入与研究，从资金支持到技术深度融合，不断提升核心竞争力。另一方面，近年来，二者的发展道路上，随着科技领域发展远快于人文领域，矛盾逐步暴露，伦理问题凸显，数字化转型、可持续发展、人工智能向善、科技向善等关键词频频出现在人们的视野当中。

关键词: 人工智能；可持续发展；互联网企业；微软；腾讯

一、引 言

（一）研究背景

互联网在当今社会中扮演着不可或缺的角色，其诞生和发展对科技、经济、文化以及社会治理等方面都产生了深刻影响。它极大地改变了人们的生活方式，并催生了众多杰出的互联网企业。互联网不仅仅是一项技术进步，它已经演变成一台全球性的社会、文化和经济变革的引擎。

互联网企业需要在竞争激烈的市场中不断追求科技创新的机会，特别是在人工智能技术的应用方面。引入或开发新的AI技术或应用，有利于提升企业的核心竞争力和市场地位，因此这是互联网企业取得竞争优势和持续生存的关

① 操婧婷，上海交通大学工商管理专业；周颖，上海交通大学科学技术史专业；钱旭升，上海交通大学材料与化工专业；危泽放，上海交通大学电子与计算机专业。

键因素之一。与此同时，企业还需要关注可持续发展，即在满足当前需求的同时不损害未来需求。

（二）研究内容与框架

本研究将集中关注人工智能技术在互联网企业中的应用，并探讨如何在科技创新的同时实现可持续发展；通过对微软与腾讯的案例分析，揭示两家公司在人工智能技术开发和应用方面的异同点；通过统计微软和腾讯在AI相关领域的出版物数量及被引频次，比较两者在AI研发中的投入程度与影响力。我们将深入分析其在互联网行业中的成功实践，探究其如何在科技创新和可持续性发展方面取得显著成就。通过这一案例研究，我们旨在为互联网行业的从业者、学者和政策制定者提供有价值的见解，以促进行业的创新和可持续发展。

二、微软案例研究

（一）公司背景和发展历程

微软是美国的跨国科技企业，以软件服务为核心业务，人工智能技术发达。微软经历了四个主要发展阶段。

1. 创立与崛起（1975—1990 年）

创立之初，微软专注于BASIC解释器的开发与销售。1980 年，微软开始为IBM的个人电脑提供操作系统，推出了MS-DOS。1985 年发布的Windows 1.0引领了图形界面操作系统的潮流，此后，Windows系列发展为全球最流行的桌面操作系统。这一阶段，微软凭借专业技术优势，迅速成长为先进的软件公司。

2. 竞争与创新（1990—2000 年）

微软在20 世纪90 年代激烈的市场竞争中抓住互联网的发展机遇。除Windows系列，Microsoft Office办公套件也开始崭露头角，为用户提供文档、表格、幻灯片等一系列办公软件。这一阶段，微软发扬技术优势，不断创新，基于Windows推出大量的配套软件，主导了操作系统市场。

3. 转型与扩张（2000—2010 年）

进入21 世纪，微软开始转型扩张，涉足电子游戏（Xbox游戏机）、云计算（NET Framework和Azure云平台）和移动操作系统（Windows Mobile）等领域，许多新项目取得瞩目的成功。这一阶段，微软紧紧抓住机遇，做出许多尝试与创新，引领了互联网时代，取得了高速的发展。

4.重塑与领导（2010年至今）

2010年至今，微软重塑自身，领导技术变革，特别是在人工智能领域。其从2009年开始研究语音识别和文本生成，推出了语音助手产品。通过收购LinkedIn和GitHub，微软加强了在云计算和开源社区的影响力。从2019年开始，微软与OpenAI深度合作。2023年的Build大会上发布了50多款AI新品，展示了微软在AI领域的创新能力和愿景。这一阶段，微软依旧保持着对新技术的研发，牢牢掌握技术优势，不断推出新产品，公司得到了长足的发展。

（二）人工智能

微软在人工智能领域的突破和影响主要体现在以下几个方面。

1.基础研究

微软研究院自1991年以来，已成为全球顶尖的AI研究机构之一，拥有超过1000名科学家和工程师，分布在全球各地的14个实验室。微软亚洲研究院（MSRA）专注于AI及相关领域，推动计算机科学的发展，并将研究成果快速转化为产品。MSRA在学术界发表了超过4000篇优质论文，并与亚太地区高校合作培养人才。

微软在AI领域取得了多项突破。语音识别、机器阅读理解、机器翻译等均达到或超越人类水平。2020年发布的Turing-NLG是当时世界上最大的自然语言生成模型。2021年的ZeRO-Infinity技术能训练万亿参数级别的模型。微软还探索AI在新领域的应用，如碳中和。

微软对AI基础研究投入的海量资源，以及对新技术的不断尝试、应用，帮助微软取得了众多成果，确立其在AI领域领先的地位。

2.产品和服务

在产品和服务方面，微软将AI技术融入Bing搜索引擎、Cortana数字助理、Office 365办公套件和Xbox游戏平台等，为用户提供更智能、更便捷、更有趣的体验。这些产品利用自然语言处理、计算机视觉、知识图谱等AI技术，提供快速、准确、个性化、高质量的服务。微软十分重视技术的应用，新技术落地成为产品的速度非常快。

3.合作与进步

微软致力于推动AI的标准和规范，同时利用AI解决全球性社会问题。微软与OpenAI的合作是整个AI领域最重要的合作，旨在实现通用人工智能。微软为OpenAI提供大量的资金及资源，产出了GPT-4这样强大的大语言模型。微软还与纽昂斯通讯（Nuance Communications）合作推进医疗创新，与联合国教科文组织合作推出"AI for Good"计划，促进可持续发展目标的实现。这些合作项目为微软积累了宝贵的知识与经验，为社会注入了新的活力。

4.竞争优势

微软凭借其在AI领域的先发优势、顶尖人才、规模效应、技术领先和广泛的渠道网络，确立了其在AI领域的领导地位。[1]微软是最早投入人工智能研究和开发的公司之一；全球最优秀的AI科学家和工程师团队不断推动理论和技术进步；其云计算平台为大规模AI模型提供支持；微软的技术在多个AI子领域处于领先地位；其AI技术通过广泛的客户群和合作伙伴网络快速推广。

（三）资本运作

微软在资本运作方面表现出了稳健和积极的策略，包括以下几个方面。[2]

分红与回购：每年，微软向股东分配利润作为分红，并定期回购股票。2022财年，微软支付了约160亿美元的分红，回购了约190亿美元的股票。

融资与偿债：微软现金流充足，但仍会发行债券或借款以降低资本成本，进行战略投资。2022财年，微软共发行了约200亿美元的债券，偿还了约80亿美元的债务。

收购与投资：微软通过收购或投资其他公司来扩大业务范围，增强竞争优势。2019年，微软向OpenAI投资10亿美元。2022财年，微软进行了23项收购和投资，总金额约230亿美元，包括以165亿美元收购了专注于AI和语音识别技术的纽昂斯通讯。

（四）对社会和行业的影响

微软对社会和行业的影响深远，在人工智能领域展现了强大的创新能力和社会责任感，赋能各行各业在互联网时代的转型和发展，重视可持续发展。[3]

---

[1] Microsoft's competitive advantage: An inside look. (2022-12-06)[2023-12-07]. https://www.investopedia.com/articles/insights/072516/microsofts-competitive-advantage-inside-look.asp.

[2] Microsoft 2022 annual report. (2022-10-24)[2023-12-07]. https://www.microsoft.com/investor/reports/ar22/index.html.

[3] Research @ Microsoft 2022: A look back at a year of accelerating progress in AI. (2022-12-19)[2023-12-07]. https://www.microsoft.com/en-us/research/blog/2022-a-look-back-at-a-year-of-accelerating-progress-in-ai/.

微软在 AI 领域拥有领先的技术和创新的能力。微软与 OpenAI 合作开发的 GPT-4 等大语言模型，以及 Azure OpenAI，为企业提供了强大的自然语言处理能力。其"智能副驾"产品和服务帮助开发者和用户利用 AI 辅助编程、写作等。智能云平台为企业、开发者、合作伙伴提供了丰富的 AI 服务和工具，推动各行业的数字化转型和创新。

微软关注 AI 可能带来的社会问题。2019 年微软出版的《计算未来》一书，全面翔实地探讨了 AI 发展可能引发的道德、法律思考和社会影响。[①] 微软成立了 AETHER 人工智能伦理道德委员会，制定了六项 AI 准则——公平、可靠和安全、隐私和保障、包容、透明、责任，确保 AI 赢得广泛的社会信任。

微软希望利用 AI 技术解决重大社会挑战。"AI for Good"计划应运而生，旨在推动环境保护、人道主义等领域的可持续发展。例如，微软利用 AI 技术帮助农民提高作物产量、降低资源消耗，帮助残障人士获得更好的教育、就业和生活机会，保护濒危物种、减少温室气体排放。

在互联网时代，微软充分利用自身的技术优势，秉持负责任的态度，大力发展人工智能，为行业和社会带来了积极深远的影响。

（五）挑战与未来展望

新时代人工智能浪潮下的微软需要不断地创新和适应，以应对变化的市场和社会需求。微软面临着一些挑战，同时也有明确的未来展望。

微软在 AI 领域所面临的挑战，主要来自技术方面。目前，微软缺少专业技能、资源和可持续的学习课程，缺少高级分析方法、充足的基础设施和先进工具以获得能指导决策的数据等。此外，企业领导层对 AI 发展缺乏全面策略，AI 带来的道德、法律和社会问题也不容忽视。

未来，在应用领域，预计微软将继续推动 AI 大模型的发展，发布基于这些模型的新产品，提高软件开发效率。科技方面，微软将利用 AI 助力实现科学突破，解决气候变化、医疗健康、教育等方面存在的问题；微软将寻求合作，深度整合物联网、大数据、云计算与 AI、机器人技术。针对 AI 潜在的社会问题，微软将注重负责任发展，提高训练和推理速度，保障数据安全。微软还将推出一些软件工具帮助开发者验证和评估 AI 的性能和公平性。

---

① Smith, B. & Shum, H. *The future computed: Artificial Intelligence and its role in society*. Redmond: Microsoft Corporation, 2018: 8-18.

总之，微软在互联网及人工智能领域拥有强大的竞争力和影响力，也面临着不小的挑战。微软需要继续发挥技术优势，坚持创新，秉持社会责任感，助力自身和社会的可持续发展。

三、腾讯案例研究

（一）公司简介

1.发展历程

腾讯成立于 1998 年，总部位于中国深圳。成立至今，其始终保持着自我进化的基因，先后经历 4 次重大战略升级和架构调整。第一次是创业初期，偶然孵化的 QQ 腾讯渡过生存危机；第二次是为摆脱对单一产品的依赖，发展出腾讯游戏与腾讯网，第三次是移动互联网时代，腾讯凭借 2011 年上线的微信市值大涨；第四次是在 2018 年 9 月 30 日，腾讯新成立了云与智慧产业事业群，整合包括腾讯云、智慧零售、安全产品、腾讯地图与优图等核心产品线积累多年的领先能力，致力于帮助医疗、教育、交通、制造业、能源等行业向智能化、数字化转型。[①]

2.业务架构

2018 年，腾讯对组织架构进行了战略升级，将整个公司划分为 6 个事业群，即 BG（business group），而在事业群下面还有众多事业部，即 BD（business division）[②]。腾讯的六大事业群包括为公司孵化新业务和探索新业态的 CDG 企业发展事业群；推进云与产业互联网战略，依托云、安全、人工智能等技术创新，打造智慧产业升级方案的 CSIG 云与智慧产业事业群；发展网络游戏、电竞等互动娱乐业务，打造一个覆盖策划、研发、发行、运营及营销的垂直生态链的 IEG 互动娱乐事业群；推进互联网平台和内容文化生态融合发展的 PCG 平台与内容事业群；为公司及各事业群提供技术及运营平台支持、研发管理、数据中心的建设与运营，并为用户提供全线产品的客户服务的 TEG 技术工程事业群；搭建和运营微信生态体系的 WXG 微信事业群。[③]

---

① 刘学辉.两年前腾讯的"至暗时刻"，这篇文章为何旗帜鲜明地看好腾讯？ .(2020-06-29)[2023-12-05]. https://finance.sina.com.cn/chanjing/gsnews/2020-06-29/doc-iircuyvk0919367.shtml.
② 腾讯.业务架构.(2023-12-05)[2023-12-05]. https://www.tencent.com/zh-cn/about.html#about-con-4.
③ 腾讯启动战略升级：调整为六大事业群，拥抱产业互联网.(2018-09-30)[2023-12-05]. https://baijiahao.baidu.com/s?id=1612996679738206778&wfr=spider&for=pc.

3. 业务生态

ToC领域，腾讯的业务可以概括为四个方面。第一，通信与社交：产品包括微信、QQ、QQ空间。第二，数字内容：产品包括腾讯游戏、腾讯视频、腾讯影业、微视、腾讯新闻等。第三，金融科技服务：产品包括微信支付、QQ钱包、理财通等。第四，其他工具：产品包括腾讯手机管家、腾讯电脑管家、QQ浏览器、微信小程序等。

ToB领域，腾讯的业务可以概括为三个方面。第一，腾讯广告：为客户提供高效的营销解决方案。第二，腾讯云：为客户提供领先的云产品与云服务。第三，智慧产业：帮助各行各业进行数字化升级，打造智慧产业方案。

（二）人工智能

面对一个发展目标，腾讯的通行做法为设立多支团队同策竞争。面对人工智能同样如此，有多个研究实验室同时在探索AI方面的技术能力，包括AI Lab、腾讯优图等等。由于其社交网络中的大量数据积累，腾讯在语音和图像识别方面具有优势。该公司正在将这些能力应用于现有产品，例如帮助QQ、微信支持更多智能功能及各种游戏产品，从而为玩家提供更好的互动虚拟体验。值得一提的是腾讯在医学影像识别和分析方面的研发投入，其成功开发了人工智能辅助医疗诊断系统——腾讯觅影，可以辅助妇科医生快速识别宫颈转化区、宫颈上皮内瘤变（CIN），辨别病变位置，打通宫颈癌筛查链条的"最后一公里"。腾讯还投资了蔚来、特斯拉等自动驾驶公司，所有这些领域都需要大量数据和复杂的基于AI的算法的开发。依托AI Lab、腾讯优图、微信AI、腾讯云TI及合作伙伴强大的AI技术能力，腾讯创立了AI开放平台，通过腾讯品牌、创投和流量广告等资源，为AI技术及产品找到更多的应用场景，实现产品从打造到引爆的全过程。腾讯的开放战略是以开放发展为基础的。腾讯以互联网生态繁荣为目标，助力互联网创业者发展，促进产业链合作共赢；以大众创业、万众创新为契机，向创业者开放核心资源，帮助创业先行者配置新引擎。①

（三）资本运作

腾讯公司在AI领域资本运作方面采取了多种策略和举措：

---

① 一文梳理腾讯控股之商业运营. (2023-05-08)[2023-12-05]. https://baijiahao.baidu.com/s?id=1765320406689973 2983&wfr=spider&for=pc.

1.投资和收购

腾讯通过战略投资和收购来扩大业务领域和拓展市场。截至2022年12月31日，其投资市值近8200亿元。A股市场主要投资包括中国联通、金山办公、世纪华通、华谊、掌趣等；港股市场包括美团、快手、贝壳、京东、哔哩哔哩等互联网公司；美欧市场包括拼多多、环球音乐、暴雪、蔚来、富途、唯品会、滴滴、虎牙、斗鱼、猎豹、知乎等；韩国市场有Netmarble、KRAFTON等。腾讯在各大市场的投资几乎涵盖了所有互联网类型公司。

2.战略合作

腾讯与其他公司和组织进行战略合作，共同探索和推动业务发展。这些合作涵盖多个领域，如技术研发、市场拓展、产品整合等。腾讯与国内外的知名企业和品牌建立合作关系，例如与京东在电商领域开展合作、与音乐公司签订版权合作等。2023年，岭南股份子公司恒润集团与腾讯围绕AI等领域建立长期战略合作。[①]

3.股权交易

腾讯通过股权交易进行投资和参与公司治理。公司可以购买其他公司的股份或者进行股权投资，以获得战略地位或者财务回报。腾讯还在股权市场进行融资活动，包括发行债券和股票。例如2019年，腾讯收购了英国Prowler.io人工智能公司的股权。[②]

（四）社会影响

腾讯建立了全面而完整的ESG管治架构，通过董事会监督、管理层推动及业务代表落实三个层面去推进ESG治理和绩效提升。自从2021年腾讯成立ESG工作组以来，企业管治委员会通过问询、定期审阅和听取ESG工作组工作报告、审批ESG工作组提交的ESG年度报告等形式对公司ESG工作进行监督。[③]

ESG工作组下设五个专项委员会促进内部协作实践，聚焦关键议题管理。这五个专项委员会覆盖用户隐私及数据安全，多元、平等与共融（diversity,

① 岭南股份：子公司恒润集团已与腾讯围绕AI等人工智能领域建立长期战略合作. (2023-05-30)[2023-12-05]. https://baijiahao.baidu.com/s?id=1767310184674189683&wfr=spider&for=pc.
② 中美科技战，英国意外受益！腾讯收购英国AI公司股权，估值达1亿美元. (2019-05-22)[2023-12-05]. https://zhuanlan.zhihu.com/p/66554715.
③ 腾讯官网-环境、社会与治理. (2023-12-05)[2023-12-05]. https://www.tencent.com/zh-cn/esg.html.

equity and inclusion，DEI），供应链管理，生物多样性保护，以及ESG传播。ESG工作组通过年度工作组大会和多次议题专项研讨，面向ESG业务代表宣导ESG前沿发展，帮助他们更好理解ESG与日常工作的关联性。[①]

随着AI的不断发展，ESG面临的实际问题日趋复杂，腾讯ESG战略在保持传统历史方向的基础上，进一步拓展数字化、互联网、人工智能方面议题的落地解决，为维护AI整体生态的良性发展做出了重要贡献。

（五）挑战与未来展望

腾讯目前正面临诸多挑战：互联网行业竞争日趋白热化，保持市场份额和用户忠诚度是一个持续的挑战；随着互联网行业的发展和影响力增加，腾讯面临着更加严格的监管环境；由于腾讯拥有大量用户数据，数据安全和隐私保护成为公司的重要挑战。

预计在未来，腾讯将继续在技术创新和人工智能领域投入资源，并推动相关技术的应用；继续构建完善的产业生态系统，通过合作和投资来拓展业务领域，加强合作伙伴关系，并提供更多增值服务；继续在国际市场扩大影响力，加强与海外企业和组织的合作，推动全球化战略和业务拓展；继续致力于可持续发展和社会责任，在环境保护、数字普惠、社会创新等方面发挥积极作用。

腾讯公司作为一家具有创新能力和全球影响力的公司，将继续面对挑战并寻找机遇，以适应不断变化的市场和技术环境。通过持续的创新和发展，腾讯有望继续保持其在AI领域的行业领先地位，并推动数字化转型和社会进步。

四、跨案例分析

（一）两公司间的相似点

对比微软和腾讯的发展历程，可以看出，二者具有一定的相似之处，主要体现在两方面。一是它们都重视人工智能领域的研究投入；二是它们都关注人工智能伦理。伴随信息技术快速发展，伦理问题凸显，数字化转型、人工智能向善、科技向善等关键词频频出现在人们的视野。

具体而言，首先，两家都是各自国家科技行业的龙头企业。微软成立48载，从21世纪开始尤为重视AI基础研究。腾讯历经25年光景，成为当下国内的最大互联网综合服务提供商和服务用户最多的互联网企业。

[①] 腾讯官网-ESG报告.（2023-12-05）[2023-12-05]. https://www.tencent.com/zh-cn/esg/esg-reports.html.

为了调查二者在人工智能研发方面的成果数量，我们以"Artificial Intelligence"为关键词，分别以"Tencent AI Lab"和"Microsoft Research Asia"为所属机构限制条件，以2016—2022年为时间限制条件，在Web of Science数据库检索，通过进一步统计可以看出，腾讯AI实验室和微软亚洲研究院在AI相关出版物数量上均呈增长趋势，后者增速快于前者。在AI相关出版物被引频次上亦然。其中，腾讯方在2018年以来增速加快，或与其战略升级有关。微软方增速更快，被引频次数量更多。可见微软在AI研发上比腾讯更早，且在数量、质量上更优。

其次，二者都有各自的特色业务和产品，且具有一定的不可替代性，在行业规则的制定上有一定的话语权，并影响了行业的发展。回顾历史，微软占领95%的微机操作系统市场份额后，就具有了制定行业规则的权利，之后，由于担心改变规则会危及相关资源匹配，微软进一步巩固了自身地位。[①]最初使腾讯出圈的是QQ，微信更是成为当下人们的生活方式。基于微信，腾讯探索出了去平台化的公众号，促使传统媒介转型。

再次，二者都赶上了技术革命浪潮。显然，每次技术革命的发生，都造就了站在它的浪尖上的成功者。阿尔文·托夫勒（Alvin Toffler）的《第三次浪潮》和尼古拉斯·尼葛洛庞帝（Nicholas Negroponte）的《数字化生存》已成为互联网行业的"圣经"。"第三次浪潮"核心是科技革命，本质特征是信息化。数字化带来的是人的生存方式的变革——人可以在一个虚拟空间，应用信息技术从事生产生活活动。崛起于20世纪90年代的互联网经济重构了信息的传播方式。而中国则在改革开放的20年后，搭上了互联网经济的第一班列车。无疑，微软和腾讯都先后抓住了机会。

最后，二者都致力于数字化转型，注重科技伦理、生态治理。微软与联合国教科文组织合作，推出了"AI for Good"计划，旨在利用人工智能促进可持续发展。我国"十四五"规划提出："以数字化转型整体驱动生产方式、生活方式和治理方式变革。"[②]2019年，腾讯将"科技向善"确立为其使命愿景，2021年，发布"推动可持续社会价值创新"战略，旨在通过科技、产品和商

---

① 吴军.浪潮之巅.北京：电子工业出版社，2011：162.
② 新华社.中华人民共和国国民经济和社会发展第十四个五年规划和2035年远景目标纲要.(2021-03-13)[2024-03-01].https://www.gov.cn/xinwen/2021/03/13/content_5592681.htm.

业模式创新，在基础科学、乡村振兴、碳中和等领域探索社会价值。①

（二）全球互联网和人工智能领域塑形对中国互联网企业的启示

硅谷百年，见证许多互联网公司的兴衰成败、许多技术的从无到有。但我们不只要看到它的巅峰时刻，也要看到它曾经的默默耕耘和残酷竞争。微软在其中最具代表性，在短短十几年建成自己的IT帝国，"促成了整个微机工业的生态链，并且作为龙头引导着计算机工业快速发展"②，"是世界上现金最多的公司并且是市值最高的科技公司"③。腾讯近年来持续加大科技领域布局，仅一个季度的研发投入就超过很多科创板的上市企业，成为福布斯2022全球第五大科技公司。

微软的优势在于其全球化视野、深厚的技术积累以及对可持续发展的承诺。腾讯虽然在中国市场有深厚的用户基础，但在这三个方面还与微软存在一定差距。

1.微软和腾讯如何影响并塑造全球互联网和人工智能领域

对微软而言，从技术层面，硅谷见证了计算机行业的发展——从美国电话电报公司（AT&T）的没落，到IBM、苹果、微软和谷歌等公司的崛起。微软从操作系统入手，逐步扩展其技术版图。在市场定位层面，硅谷的公司在一开始做产品时基本就计划面向全球市场，成为跨国公司。在多元文化层面，硅谷聚集了全世界不同文化背景的员工，也是其能快速打入国际市场的重要原因之一。在愿景方面，硅谷离不开具有世界情怀的理想主义者，科技评论家凯文·凯利（Kevin Kelly）曾指出硅谷为世界创造伟大发明靠三类人：梦想者、企业家及投资人、工程师。④梦想者以改变世界为使命，工程师加以实践，投资者和企业家作为桥梁将二者相联，好的产品由此而来。在管理层面，扁平式管理有效减少了层级多带来的低效率问题，汇报层少，上级对下级没有决定权而是以契约关系为纽带。就微软而言，它最初是扁平式的，但中间由于快速做大做强，陷入官僚主义和内部争斗中，以至于2014年萨提亚·纳德拉（Satya Nadella）上任后将重塑企业文化作为首要任务，并重塑管理制度。在可持续发展层面，微软积极践行对行业、社会的世界影响力和责任，在环境、社会服

---

① 黄晓娟，陈素波.腾讯："科技向善"共创可持续社会价值.企业管理，2023(5): 53-58.
② 吴军.浪潮之巅.北京：电子工业出版社，2011: 60.
③ 吴军.浪潮之巅.北京：电子工业出版社，2011: 46.
④ 吴军.硅谷之谜.《浪潮之巅》续集.北京：人民邮电出版社，2015: 196.

务、医疗等方面均做出贡献。以人工智能为例，纳德拉认为，微软的人工智能策略着重于增强人类能力与体验，激发人好的天性，注重设计中的信任建构和隐私保护，构建尊重全人类的人工智能。

纵观腾讯的发展，首先，腾讯作为中国最大的互联网综合服务提供商之一，为全球用户提供了多元化的服务，使得用户可以在一个平台上满足几乎所有互联网需求。其次，腾讯在人工智能领域也具有重要影响力。其在人工智能技术研发方面投入了大量资源，拥有多个专利，并在自然语言处理、机器学习、计算机视觉等领域取得了重要进展。再次，腾讯还通过开放平台和共享经济模式，为全球开发者提供了广阔的发展空间，促进了人工智能技术的普及和应用。最后，腾讯具有社会责任感，将社会责任融入产品及服务中，推动科技创新与文化传承，助力各行各业升级，促进社会可持续发展。

2.对中国互联网企业的启示

微软是硅谷科技类公司的缩影，硅谷何以在百年发展中屹立不倒，科技公司何以如雨后春笋不断生发？对此，吴军总结了硅谷科技类公司的六个特质，也是中国互联网公司表现薄弱的方面。一是硅谷的叛逆精神。二是硅谷在社会环境、企业文化方面对失败较为宽容，这也正是今天中国公司普遍缺失的。三是硅谷的多元文化，许多中国企业拿硅谷作为美国科技代表与中国做对比，然而硅谷是全世界创造力的浓缩，不只代表美国。四是追求卓越，通过市场力量，不断淘汰旧的行业，把有限资源让给那些竞争力更强、利润率更高的企业，并不断淘汰跟不上变化的人员，从全世界吸纳人才。五是工程师文化，即给予工程师较高社会地位和薪资待遇。六是不迷信权威，一个结论的接纳，不在于其是否出自权威人士之口，而在于其是否合理，硅谷的员工敢于突破权威曾认为的不可能，并付诸实施。[①]以上六大特质也是微软的特质；此外，微软的发展对我国互联网公司的启示还包括：一是深耕人工智能基础研究，二是转型更注重文化和伦理，三是重视客户信任。

结合上文可以看到，腾讯的发展也能为国内互联网企业的发展带来一些启示。一是创新与多元化：腾讯强调创新，不断推出新产品和服务，不仅在社交媒体领域，还涉猎游戏、金融、云计算等。二是用户体验至上：腾讯注重用户体验，不断改进和优化其产品和服务。三是投资和合作：腾讯积极与其他公司

---

① 吴军.硅谷之谜：《浪潮之巅》续集.北京：人民邮电出版社，2015.

建立战略伙伴关系，不断扩大市场份额和获取新技术。四是关注全球市场：腾讯不仅在中国市场取得成功，还进军国际市场。五是投资于人才培养：腾讯重视人才培养和吸引顶尖的技术和创新人才。六是社会责任感：腾讯积极参与社会公益事业，关心社会问题，也有助于公司树立良好的社会形象。

（三）当前互联网行业的主要问题和挑战

上文中硅谷成功的六大特质，即叛逆精神、宽容失败、多元文化、追求卓越，以及微软的工程师文化和不迷信权威，都对中国互联网企业发展具有启示意义。然而，随着数字化、智能化的深入发展，一系列伦理问题正凸显出来，促使互联网企业可持续发展成为当下重要议题。

1.技术伦理问题

以人工智能为例，技术伦理问题包含三个层面。第一是设计层面。设计者不可避免将自身价值观嵌入设计物的底层逻辑中。如果将错误的价值观嵌入，在实际运行中可能对使用者带来威胁。这就要求设计者从构想到模拟训练都要加以检验，以保证产品没有对种族、性别、年龄等伦理特征的预设。[①] 第二是算法层面。算法黑箱的存在导致决策过程不透明和难以解释，从而影响公民的知情权及监督权，造成监管失效，同时，也会带来算法偏见，导致不公正现象。例如，2018 年第一起自动驾驶汽车撞死行人的案例，事后可解释性模糊，错误难以溯源，归责问题凸显。这也体现出在机器决策中进行伦理设定的重要性，而且有必要确保设置的产品的伦理标准是可验证的。第三是数据安全层面。海量的个人数据被采集、挖掘、使用，使得公民的隐私权受到威胁。

2.社会伦理问题

人工智能在带来便捷的同时也挑战了人类社会的基本价值，如人的尊严、自主性、公平、分配正义等。首先是人类道德主体性地位降低。传统伦理学的视角下，人工智能无法被纳入道德主体范畴。约翰斯·霍普金斯大学最新研究结果表明，GPT-4 的心智理论已经超越了人类。在推理基准的测试中，AI 准确率高达 100%，而人类仅为 87%。其次是社会公平正义问题，如数字鸿沟、技术拒绝等。因而，需要避免人工智能偏见和歧视，让社会中各类群体都能享有其带来的好处。最后是人机信任问题，涉及人对机器的信任与机器对人的信任两方面。如果人对机器过度信任，就会陷入科技主义陷阱，如困在算法里的

---

① 于江生.人工智能伦理.北京：清华大学出版社，2022.

外卖骑手、自动驾驶归责问题等；如果人对机器完全不信任，在现代社会几乎难以维持正常生活。在机器对人的信任方面，对人类给出的指令，机器如果不进行伦理评估就加以实施，可能带来危害；如果不予实施，则有悖于其功能性要求。因此，在设计中要加入伦理风险评估，在可控范围内予以执行指令，可控范围外则不予执行并给出相应解释。

作为新兴技术，快速发展的人工智能显然具有较多不确定性，不论是技术伦理问题还是社会伦理问题都亟待解决，这就需要在社会各界展开广泛辩论，促使人们思考真正想要什么样的科技未来，从而克服问题，预防潜在风险。

收并购浪潮中企业的抉择
——基于收购案例的市场利弊分析①

摘　要: 本文基于当前互联网浪潮中广泛的收并购现象，针对技术融合收购、多元化经营跨产业收购和排挤竞争型收购的重要案例进行分析，通过QCA方法来研究影响收购的结果成功与否的相关要素并进行更深一步的分析，研究涉及微软、百度、亚马逊等大型企业。本文关注了互联网产业特征和企业行为，采用多案例对比分析法，具体研究内容涉及以下三方面: 一是调研被并购企业在并购后的经营情况; 二是归纳与分类研究互联网企业并购整合策略; 三是从匹配的角度分析互联网企业收并购动因、整合策略对经营情况的影响。

关键词: 收并购; 案例研究; 技术融合; 绩效; 业务整合; 多元化经营

一、选题背景

（一）互联网行业发展史

互联网行业是近几十年来全球范围内发展最迅速的行业之一，引发了无数的技术创新和商业机会。随着互联网行业的不断发展，出现了阿里巴巴、腾讯等互联网巨头公司，他们大量收购着其他小型公司，一方面使得互联网的各个行业的运行更加高效化、标准化，但另一方面，收购有时也会导致原本优秀的产品逐渐丧失竞争力，既给企业带来了大量的亏损，也不利于整个行业的发展，而即使是那些成功的收购案例，往往也会使得某一个行业陷入垄断，不利于其他产品的推陈出新。

---

① 彭恋舒，北京邮电大学国际学院; 潘振升，北京邮电大学国际学院。

（二）企业收并购形势

收并购作为快速获取核心技术、市场客群等优势的一种有效途径，是企业发展过程中的一项重要战略。近年来，随着中国互联网产业的纵深发展，收并购事件层出不穷。例如携程收购去哪儿，滴滴收购Uber，美团并购摩拜单车，阿里巴巴收购饿了么、大麦网，百度收购爱奇艺，等等。然而，并非所有被并购的互联网企业都能依托主并互联网企业的资源或能力改善经营状况。在什么样的并购情境及整合策略下，被并购企业能够取得更好的经营绩效，是一个亟待回答的问题。

二、研究方法

（一）方法类型

由于样本数量较少，本文采用的研究方法是多案例对比分析法，通过对比分析小企业在被大企业收并购这一时间的前后情况，来观察企业与产品的发展趋势的变化。

（二）方法简介

在社会抗争研究等领域，研究对象往往涉及多案例，单独的个案已经不能满足研究的需要。社会抗争作为一种复杂的社会现象，其成因存在着多元并发组合的原因变量，以线性因果关系为基础的定量统计分析方法也很难提供有效的分析结论。而多案例对比分析法由于能够有效、系统地处理多案例比较的研究数据，已在社会抗争研究等领域得到广泛运用。

多案例研究法是一种跨学科和多学科的应用研究，其出发点是研究个体社会现象及其相互关系，而不仅仅局限于专业研究者所提出的理论。它采用的研究过程是从典型案例开始，逐步进行横向比较和纵向深入，最终得出结论。针对某一特定社会问题，研究者可以从多个案例中收集数据，并与其他相关社会研究的理论进行比较，以便从不同的视角来分析这些社会现象。

三、文献综述

在并购绩效方面，曹文涛和王惠珍在携程网并购去哪儿网的动因及财务绩效研究中分析认为，由于并购可以带来规模经济效应，并购使两家业务重叠、原本在相互竞争市场份额的企业合为一体，从而降低运营成本和竞争费用，因此这次并购可以提升主并方的经营绩效。现实也证明，并购后携程的负债能力有所增强，财务风险大大降低。并购当年，携程的营运能力有所下降，但并购一年后则有所回升。在盈利能力方面，主并方的资产报酬率和收益率都在并购后跌为负值，因为并购增加了主并方的成本；但销售毛利率则有所提升，是并购的协同效应发挥了作用。[①]王乔明通过分析 2018 年阿里巴巴对饿了么的并购，从战略、管理和经济三个维度总结了并购动因，并运用模型对并购绩效进行整体评价。在财务绩效上，虽然并购后阿里巴巴收入增幅较为可观，但利润情况并不理想，主要是由于本地生活服务板块的运营成本较高。但是从长远来看，此次并购促进了阿里数字经济体系的建设，并且在后续的年份带来了企业价值的增加。[②]

四、案例分析

（一）技术融合类型的收购

1. 微软

1.1 公司背景与发展历程

微软公司（Microsoft Corporation）是一家全球知名的科技公司，总部位于美国华盛顿州的雷德蒙德市。该公司成立于 1975 年，由比尔·盖茨（Bill Gates）和保罗·艾伦（Paul Allen）共同创立。微软公司以开发、生产和销售计算机软件、电子设备和相关服务而闻名于世。

1.2 微软的收并购选择

在过去的二十多年里，微软在会话式人工智能领域进行了广泛的基础研究，取得了一系列技术突破。从国际视角来看，语音交互 AI 的发展大致可以分为以下三个阶段。

（1）初期探索阶段（1980—2011 年）

在这一阶段，随着算法模型和微电子技术的进步，语音识别领域取得了显著进展。相关技术尽管仍处于起步阶段，但为未来的发展奠定了坚实基础。

（2）快速变革阶段（2011—2016 年）

2011 年，微软研究院将深度神经网络（DNN）技术应用于大词汇量连续

---

① 曹文涛，王惠珍.携程网并购去哪儿网的动因及财务绩效研究.现代营销，2021(15)：44-45.
② 王乔明.阿里巴巴并购饿了么的动因及绩效分析.长春：吉林大学，2020.

语音识别任务，显著降低了语音识别的错误率。这一突破引发了语音技术的快速发展，推动了行业的重大变革。

（3）广泛应用阶段（2016年至今）

自2016年以来，端到端的语音识别技术得到了广泛应用，准确率进一步提升，尤其是在远场语音识别和唤醒技术方面取得了重要进展，全双工语音交互开始普及。这一阶段，语音识别的准确率已超过98%，并能够根据具体应用需求进行优化。

基于这些技术进展，微软推出了机器人开发框架，并发布了Azure认知服务，将语音识别和自然语言理解功能集成到智能助理中，为用户提供更加智能和便捷的交互体验。

1.3 收购Semantic Machines的原因

作为被收购方的Semantic Machines是一家专注于对话式人工智能技术的公司，其技术基于深度学习、自然语言处理和对话系统等领域的研究。收购Semantic Machines使得微软能够获得其在对话式人工智能方面的技术和专业知识，将其整合到微软自己的产品和服务中。被微软收购之前，Semantic Machines可能面临以下问题和挑战。

（1）技术成熟度：Semantic Machines的技术在自然语言理解和对话系统方面具有优势，但在商业化和实际应用方面可能还面临着一些挑战。将技术转化为可商业化的产品和服务需要克服技术上的难题，并确保其在不同场景和用户群体中的可靠性和稳定性。

（2）市场竞争：在智能对话系统领域，Semantic Machines面临着来自谷歌、亚马逊等竞争对手的竞争压力，这些公司也在积极开发和推出自己的自然语言处理和对话系统技术，因此Semantic Machines需要在竞争激烈的市场中找到自己的差异化竞争优势。

（3）数据隐私和安全：在处理用户的语音和文本数据时，Semantic Machines需要确保数据的隐私和安全，这包括合规性、数据保护和用户隐私等方面的挑战，在数据隐私和安全方面的不足可能会影响用户对其产品和服务的信任。

总之，微软收购Semantic Machines的目的是加强其在自然语言处理和对话式人工智能领域的技术实力，并提升其产品和服务的智能化水平和用户体验。这也有助于Semantic Machines应对上述问题与挑战。

此外，还有一些知名的语音助手，其各自发展历程也值得关注。苹果的Siri是最早的语音对话助手之一，但其用户体验一直未达到预期。亚马逊则从2012年开始研发对话式语音助手，最终推出了Alexa，逐步成为市场上的重要产品。2016年5月，谷歌发布了语音智能助手Google Assistant，进一步推动了语音助手的普及。百度推出了DuerOS，致力于将语音作为入口，构建智能家居和物联网的关键节点。

微软利用其平台和数据优势，开发了智能交互式AI助手小冰。小冰不仅是语音交互产品，还包含了一整套面向全程交互的AI基础框架，即小冰框架（Avatar Framework）。这一框架集成了核心对话引擎、多重交互感官、第三方内容触发与第一方内容生成，以及跨平台的部署解决方案，提供了全面的智能语音交互体验。

由微软小冰的功能性分析可知：微软小冰的核心语音交互技术主要在于所得信息的处理与计算。而收购Semantic Machines对于微软对于对话式人工智能技术、多模态对话技术与深度学习等技术的掌握至关重要。

因此，微软对于Semantic Machines的收购能够使得微软在人机交互的领域走得更扎实稳健、更长久，有利于微软缓解与其他产业巨头的竞争压力，争取人工智能在语音人机交互领域的部分主动权。

（二）多元化经营型跨产业收购

多元化经营型跨产业收购的含义是，并购前主并方尚未涉及被并方业务，被并方已有市场不可以成为主并方APP目标市场的补充，但主并方选择吸纳被并方团队，派体系内CEO到被并方担任CEO，试图自主尝试新的业务领域。这有时会导致被收购方APP下载量下滑，市占率丢失，最终关停。

典型案例如下。

1. 百度收购糯米网

1.1 收购背景

糯米网于2010年上线，采用类似Groupon的团购模式，不定时提供单一商品的优惠活动。上线首日，糯米网推出了2折团购活动，提供成龙耀莱国际影城的双人套票，仅需40元，包括2张电影票、2杯可乐、1份爆米花和1个哈根达斯冰淇淋球，原价为176元。此次团购最终售出152151张电影票，不仅打破了Groupon首日16000张的销售纪录，还创造了国内团购网站的销售新高。

1.2 收购原因

2013年12月，百度选择收购糯米网。本次全资收购后糯米网团购业务将和百度的搜索、地图等产品以及线下的销售渠道进行更深度的整合。百度全资收购糯米网，对其O2O（即online to offline，也即将线下商务的机会与互联网结合，让互联网成为线下交易的前台）及移动互联业务缺口是一个有力补充。

百度收购糯米网主要是为了扩大自己在本地生活服务领域的市场份额和增强竞争力。以下是几个具体原因。

市场角度：本地生活服务市场在中国具有巨大的潜力和增长空间。当时的中国并没有较为强盛的本地生活服务平台，百度意识到这一点，并希望通过收购糯米网来进一步拓展在本地生活服务领域的市场份额。

用户需求：互联网用户的需求不断演变和多样化，创造了许多市场机会。随着数字化程度的提高，人们对于便捷、高效、个性化的服务有着越来越高的期望。

行业趋势：互联网行业的发展一直处于快速变化的状态，新的技术和业务模式不断涌现，为公司带来了许多市场机会。糯米网是"千团大战"中为数不多的胜利者之一，并曾与美团网、大众点评形成三足鼎立之势，百度抓住这一特点，选择收购糯米网，是希望能提高本地生活服务领域的竞争力。

1.3 失败原因分析

百度收购糯米网失败的原因主要包括以下几个方面。

整合困难：百度与糯米网的业务整合并不顺利，两家公司在组织架构、文化、运营模式等方面存在差异，导致整合过程中出现了许多问题。

缺乏差异化竞争策略：业务整合后的产品百度糯米可能没有成功实施差异化竞争策略，无法在竞争激烈的市场中脱颖而出；相比之下，美团采取了多元化的业务模式，满足用户在不同领域的需求，扩大了用户群体和市场份额。

市场竞争激烈：百度在收购糯米网后仍面临来自其他竞争对手的强大竞争压力，如阿里巴巴旗下的口碑和美团。[①]这些竞争对手在本地生活服务领域拥有强大的用户基础和品牌影响力，使得百度难以在市场中取得突破。

---

① 魏亮.我国互联网公司的并购绩效研究.沈阳：沈阳工业大学，2007.

2.谷歌收购摩托罗拉移动

2.1 收购背景

一个著名的跨领域收购失败案例是谷歌（Google）收购摩托罗拉移动（Motorola Mobility）。2011年，谷歌以125亿美元的价格收购了摩托罗拉移动，这是谷歌历史上最大的一笔收购。然而，这次收购最终被证明是失败的。

摩托罗拉公司成立于1928年，总部位于芝加哥市郊的伊利诺伊州，是世界财富百强企业之一，主要包括企业移动解决方案、宽带及移动网络，以及移动终端三大业务集团。摩托罗拉的主要产品和服务涵盖机顶盒、条码扫描器、操作系统、芯片、电脑和手机等。

2011年1月4日，摩托罗拉分拆为两家独立公司：摩托罗拉移动和摩托罗拉解决方案。摩托罗拉移动专注于智能手机和机顶盒业务，市值约为90亿美元；摩托罗拉解决方案主要负责公共安全无线电和手持式扫描仪业务，市值约为128亿美元。这次分拆旨在使二者更好地专注于各自的核心业务，但谷歌的收购最终未能带来预期的成功，成为一桩失败的跨领域收购案例。

2.2 收购原因

摩托罗拉移动是一家著名的移动设备制造商，谷歌希望通过收购其专利组合来增强在移动设备市场的竞争力。然而，这次收购未能实现预期目标。

随着科技的迅猛发展，传统电话已无法满足现代人的需求。智能手机迅速兴起，因其内置独立操作系统而被称为"智能"。目前，主要的智能手机操作系统包括苹果的iOS、谷歌的Android和微软的Windows Phone。操作系统的出现伴随着大量专利，这些专利保护关键技术，但也引起了大量专利诉讼。

各大厂商不仅在技术创新上竞争，还在价格上较量，通过收取专利费来抬高Android手机的价格，削弱其竞争力。谷歌由于专利储备不足，经常被竞争对手通过其合作伙伴打压。摩托罗拉移动作为老牌科技公司，拥有大量专利，可以帮助谷歌在价格战中获得优势。谷歌正是在这种背景下决定收购摩托罗拉移动，但最终未能达到预期效果。

2.3 失败原因分析

谷歌公司的总体研发投入逐年增长，2012年和2013年的增长率分别为31.6％和17.06％。其中，摩托罗拉移动的研发费用表面上看是增加的（见表1），但实际情况是摩托罗拉移动的数据从2012年开始被并入谷歌年报，其中2012年的数据仅包括后7个月的研发费用合计；通过计算可得知2013年摩托罗拉移动的研发费用实际上是减少的。另一方面，谷歌公司分部的研发费用增长率分别为 2012 年的 17.26％和 2013 年的 14.29％，显示谷歌公司自身的研发投入增长率也在减少，这与在摩托罗拉移动上的一定数额的投入有关系。

表1　谷歌年报中研发费用分配情况　　（单位：百万美元）

年度	2011	2012	2013
谷歌公司	4101	4809	5496
摩托罗拉移动	—	474	702
未分配项目	1061	1510	1754
合计	5162	6793	7952

摩托罗拉移动的 2012 和 2013 年净利润并没有单独披露，其在财务报表中只披露了合并后的净利润。从表2、表3中可以看出，在合并前，摩托罗拉移动虽然收入逐年上升，但是净利润一直为负，处于持续亏损状态。自 2011 年宣布合并后，其收入逐年下滑，营业利润一直为负且亏损越来越严重，2012 年亏损额是 2011 年的 3.74 倍，2013 年亏损额是 2012 年的 2.29 倍。2012 年收入较 2011 年大幅降低的一部分原因是谷歌卖出了 Motorola Home 业务，收入总额受到影响，而 2013 年收入的降低则主要是公司经营的结果。

表2　摩托罗拉移动 2009—2013 年财务数据　　（单位：百万美元）

年度	2009	2010	2011	2012	2013
收入	11050	11460	13064	7214	4306
营业利润	−1222	66	−145	−543	−1245
净利润	−1342	86	−249	—	—

谷歌并购摩托罗拉移动的短期目的是获得庞大数量且高质量的专利库。[①]一方面，谷歌急需大量专利保障使用 Android 系统的合作伙伴的利益，打击层出不穷的专利侵权案，如果继续输下去，手机的生产成本会不断增高，利润会进一步减少。另一方面，谷歌用庞大的专利库补充完善 Android 系统生态圈，形成专利保护，稳固 Android 联盟。

① 汪勇专.谷歌收购摩托罗拉移动一案的反垄断审查研究.重庆：西南政法大学，2013.

表3　摩托罗拉移动2012—2013年分季度财务数据　（单位：百万美元）

年度	2012		2013			
季度	三	四	一	二	三	四
收入	1778	1514	1018	998	1139	1151
营业利润	−192	−152	−271	−342	−248	−384

摩托罗拉移动在谷歌收购后的财务表现并不理想。从2012年第三季度到2013年第四季度，摩托罗拉移动的收入呈下降趋势，并没有达到预期的增长效果。同时，营业利润也一直处于亏损状态，并且亏损额呈扩大趋势。这对谷歌的整体财务状况产生了负面影响，使得谷歌的收入和营业利润增长率都降低。

总的来说，谷歌收购摩托罗拉移动的跨领域收购最终失败，主要是整合困难、业绩不佳和专利收购效果不佳等因素导致的。这个案例启示我们，公司在进行跨领域收购时需要认真评估风险和收益，并确保有清晰的整合计划和战略目标。

（三）与排挤竞争、加强业务有关的收购

1.亚马逊

2017年，亚马逊以137亿美元的价格收购了全食超市（Whole Foods Market），这是一家专注于有机和天然食品的连锁超市。这一收购使得亚马逊得以进入食品零售领域，并扩大了其在线零售业务的影响力。

亚马逊最初以在线零售业务起家，但通过收购全食超市，它进一步拓展了在实体零售业的存在。这使得亚马逊能够更好地满足那些更喜欢实地购物、对品质和可持续性有较高要求的消费者需求。全食超市拥有100万平方英尺的仓储中心面积和456家高质量线下网点。收购之后，亚马逊借助全食现有的物流配送体系和线下门店，提升自身末端生鲜配送的能力和效率。通过这种方式，亚马逊削弱了实体零售对其电商业务的竞争，并进一步加强了其在北美地区零售业务的影响力。

亚马逊在数字技术和物流领域的专长与全食超市的传统实体零售模式相结合，带来了许多创新机会。亚马逊引入了Amazon Go概念，利用无人商店技术来改善购物体验。此外，亚马逊的技术和数据分析能力还可以改进全食超市的库存管理、客户体验和定价策略。

亚马逊收购全食超市的举动对传统食品零售行业产生了巨大冲击。亚马逊的资源、技术和物流能力使其能够在价格竞争和服务方面给传统零售商带来压力。此外，这项收购还推动了其他零售商加快数字化转型和创新以应对亚马逊的竞争。

总体而言，亚马逊收购全食超市是一项战略性举措，有助于亚马逊拓展业务领域、增加市场份额，并进一步整合数字技术和实体零售模式。这一案例展示了亚马逊的战略远见和对不同市场机会的灵活把握。

2.百度

2017 年，百度开始着手打造人工智能领域，收购了语音识别技术公司渡鸦科技。这次收购不仅加强了百度在人工智能和语音识别领域的技术实力，还推动了其智能语音助手DuerOS的发展。

渡鸦科技是一家专注于语音识别技术的创业公司，擅长语音处理和自然语言理解。百度收购渡鸦科技后，获得了其在语音识别领域的技术和专业知识。

百度的这次收购旨在通过获取语音识别领域的技术优势和专业知识来提升用户体验，并推动其在人工智能领域的创新和竞争力。

3.百度与谷歌收购企业的比较分析

我们对百度和谷歌为排挤竞争、加强业务而开展的收购情况进行了如下对比分析（见表 4、表 5）。这些收购案例显示了大型互联网企业为了排除竞争对手和加强在特定领域的领先地位，选择收购具有关键技术或者用户基础的公司。这些收购不仅扩大了企业的业务范围和影响力，还有助于提升其竞争力和创新能力，以应对不断变化的市场环境。

表4 2017—2020 年谷歌收购企业情况

序号	被收购公司	国家	领域	收购日期
1	Kaggle	美国	数据科学	2017 年 3 月 8 日
2	Bitium	美国	单点登录和身份管理	2017 年 9 月 26 日
3	Velostrata	以色列	云迁移	2018 年 5 月 9 日
4	Cask	美国	大数据	2018 年 5 月 14 日
5	DevOps and Assessment	美国	研究与评估	2018 年 12 月 20 日
6	Alooma	以色列	大数据，云迁移	2019 年 2 月 19 日
7	Looker	美国	大数据分析	2016 年 7 月 12 日
8	Elastifile	美国	文件存储	2019 年 7 月 9 日

续表

序号	被收购公司	国家	领域	收购日期
9	CloudSimple	美国	云托管	2019 年 11 月 18 日
10	AppSheet	美国	移动应用开发	2020 年 1 月 14 日
11	Stratozone	美国	云计算	2020 年 8 月 25 日

谷歌在视频、广告、云计算和人工智能领域进行了一系列成功的收购，如收购YouTube、DoubleClick和DeepMind等。这些收购帮助谷歌扩大了在数字广告、在线视频和人工智能等领域的市场份额，并增强了其技术实力。谷歌能够整合收购的公司，并将其技术和资源应用于谷歌的产品生态系统中，取得了显著的成功。

相比之下，百度在跨行业收购方面的成功并不如谷歌那么显著。一些百度的跨行业收购往往以失败告终。这可能是因为跨行业收购涉及不同领域的运营和管理，需要处理不同行业的市场竞争和特定要求。百度的大量跨行业收购可能导致资源分散和管理难题，使得整合和实现预期收益变得困难。

表 5　百度收购企业的部分数据

序号	被收购企业	简介	地点	收购日期
1	Hao123.com	导航网站	中国北京	2004 年 9 月 16 日
2	去哪儿网	旅游搜索引擎	中国北京	2011 年 6 月 24 日
3	ES 文件管理器	安卓端应用	—	2013 年 1 月 1 日
4	TrustGo	移动安全公司	—	2013 年 2 月 13 日
5	PPS	互联网影音视频平台	中国上海	2013 年 5 月 7 日
6	91 无线	移动应用分发平台	—	2013 年 7 月 15 日
7	悠悠村	无线移动技术与互联网信息服务平台	中国上海	2013 年 8 月 26 日
8	纵横中文网	中文在线阅读网站	中国北京	2013 年 12 月 27 日
9	Peixe Urbano	巴西最大团购网站	巴西	2014 年 10 月 9 日
10	PopIn	日本原生广告公司	日本	2015 年 5 月 1 日
11	安全宝	信息安全软件	中国北京	2015 年 4 月 16 日

谷歌在云计算和人工智能领域的成功收购可以归因于其明确的战略方向和先进的技术布局。谷歌一直致力于构建强大的云计算平台和人工智能技术，并有能力整合收购的公司，在其生态系统中提供创新解决方案。百度的战略和市

场环境可能与谷歌不同，导致其跨行业收购遭遇的挑战较多。

从失败的跨行业收购案例中，百度可以获得宝贵的教训和经验。百度可能需要更加谨慎地评估目标公司的技术、市场前景和整合难度，以确保收购能够产生预期的效益。此外，百度可能需要更加专注于自身核心业务，并加强内部研发和创新，以提升竞争力。

需要指出的是，成功或失败的收购案例往往涉及多种因素，如战略规划、整合能力、市场变化等。每个公司的情况都是独特的，成功的关键在于战略选择、执行能力和市场适应能力。

五、结论与展望

（一）研究结论

通过案例的分析研究我们可以发现，如果被并购的小公司的业务与大公司的业务关联程度更高，或者小公司拥有着对于大公司来说至关重要的技术，则此次收购更有可能取得成功。而如果大公司只是从小公司目前的收益出发，去做一些收益较高但自身并不擅长的行业，往往会承担更多的风险。

（二）局限与未来展望

本文的局限性主要在于，由于并购案例往往只是通过企业报告或者新闻报道体现出最终结果和一些粗略的过程，很多具体细节并没有透露，因此样本数据的可得性较为有限。我们希望能够通过更多的调查和采访去获取更多的数据、掌握更多的信息，进而对整个问题有更全面的认识。

展望未来，我们期待企业能通过收并购等事件减少企业之间的恶性竞争，实现技术的互惠互利，努力打造更好的产品来服务受众；另一方面，我们不希望企业盲目收购，既导致了自身的亏损，也不利于产品的更新迭代和创新发展，对整个行业来说都是不利的。随着全球经济的不断发展和变化，企业收并购将成为越来越重要的竞争手段。在这种情况下，企业需要优化收并购策略，降低风险，并在收并购后实现业务整合和协同创新，提高企业的市场占有率和盈利能力。同时，政府也应该完善相应的政策和法规，进一步规范企业收并购行为，促进市场的公平竞争和健康发展。

AI赋能对互联网公司的影响——以搜索引擎、自动驾驶为例[①]

摘　要： 本文研究了AI赋能对互联网公司的影响，以谷歌和百度为研究对象。首先，我们回顾了人工智能的发展历程和 AI赋能的背景和意义。其次，我们分析了过去二十年AI赋能对互联网公司的影响。随后，我们提出了基于现有问题的解决方案，并展望了未来人工智能的发展趋势。解决方法强调了教育和培训、法律和政策监管、国际合作与标准制定的重要性，以确保AI赋能的可持续发展和社会共享。本研究旨在为互联网公司和利益相关者提供对AI赋能的全面理解和应对策略，推动AI在互联网行业的持续发展。

关键词： 互联网公司；人工智能；未来挑战；发展趋势

一、绪　论

（一）命题解释和背景

在当今数字化时代，互联网和人工智能（AI）已经成为全球经济和社会发展的重要驱动力。过往数十年是网络科技井喷的时期，见证了互联网科技的日新月异，AI走入寻常百姓家，更是见证了众多世界一流网络公司的动荡与迭代。

这些公司在不同领域取得了巨大的成功和突破，展现了网络科技的强大魅力，引发了社会对其广泛的兴趣和研究。本文将以谷歌（Google）和百度为主要研究对象，对"世界知名互联网及人工智能公司案例研究"这一课题进行研究与探讨。

① 徐浩喆，北京邮电大学国际学院；侯佳辰，北京邮电大学国际学院；唐灵，北京邮电大学国际学院；孔海宇，北京邮电大学国际学院。

（二）研究的重要性和目的

互联网和人工智能公司案例研究的重要性不言而喻。这些公司不仅是商业上的巨头，更是技术创新和发展的领导者。它们通过不断探索和实践，开创了一系列前沿技术和创新产品，改变了人们的生活方式和商业模式。通过对这些公司案例的研究，我们可以深入了解其成功的原因、关键策略和技术创新，从而汲取经验教训，推动自己所在领域的发展。

通过深入研究谷歌和百度等知名互联网公司的案例，我们可以汲取它们的成功经验，并从中汲取灵感，为我们自己的商业实践提供指导。我们可以学习谷歌和百度在技术创新、市场营销、战略规划和人才培养等方面的最佳实践。这些案例研究不仅帮助我们了解互联网行业的发展趋势，还提供了洞察力，使我们能够更好地应对行业变革和市场挑战。

（三）文章的结构概述

本篇论文将以分板块的形式介绍与分析，进行成果的展示，旨在实现以下三个主要目标：紧跟数字产业发展前沿、洞察科技创新关键趋势、了解国内外知名科创企业在数字化、绿色化协调发展中的重要作用。

文章的内容主要分为：全球互联网行业概述，案例研究分析，跨案例分析归纳，以及总结与预见。全球互联网行业概述部分按时间顺序介绍了互联网的发展史，然后进一步讲述了人工智能在互联网行业中的应用。

案例研究部分则从公司背景与发展历程、重要产品及技术，以及对社会和行业的影响等方面，主要介绍了谷歌公司、百度公司，论述了二者各自在互联网和人工智能领域的发展，并对二者进行跨案例分析。

站在全局，我们通过分析企业间发展过程的异同，回顾了全球互联网的发展历程；在最后的总结与预见部分，我们整合了前面所写内容，对现有问题进行了分析，并对有限的未来进行合理的预测。

二、全球互联网行业概述

（一）互联网行业发展历史

互联网是当代社会中最具革命性和影响力的技术之一，它改变了我们的生活方式、工作方式和人际关系。从诞生之初的阿帕网（ARPANET）到如今的Web3.0时代，互联网的发展历程让我们见证了人类通信和信息交流的巨大变革。互联网行业的发展历史大致可分为三个阶段，每一个阶段都是一次巨大的革新与变化。

1.第一个发展阶段——Web1.0时代（静态网页）

这一阶段的互联网，用一个词概括就是"只读"，简单来说，在这个阶段用户只能读取平台提供的信息。

Web1.0时代是互联网的起始阶段，主要以静态的HTML网页为展示形式。在这个阶段，网站内容的发布和呈现主要由内容提供者控制，用户的互动和参与程度较低。网站主要是以展示信息为目的，有AOL（美国在线）等门户网站以及私人聊天室和BBS等论坛。但总的来说，当时的互联网仍没有什么交互或支付交易功能；用户获取信息的方式主要是通过网页浏览器进行浏览和检索。

2.第二个发展阶段——Web2.0时代（社交互动）

在这个阶段，用户不仅可以读取信息，还能生产信息，成为信息的创作者和提供者。由于技术的突破，互联网在网速、光纤基础设施和搜索引擎等方面都取得了发展，用户对社交、音乐、视频分享和支付交易的需求也大幅上升。

Web2.0时代是互联网的演进阶段，互动性和社交性成为关键特征。在这个阶段，互联网变得更加具有开放性和参与性，用户可以通过社交媒体、博客、论坛等平台主动发布内容、评论和分享。Web2.0时代注重用户生成内容、社交网络和用户参与，推动了信息的广泛传播和分享。

这种更具互动性的全新互联网体验为用户带来了许多新的功能，并提升了用户体验。但问题也随之而来，并且直到今天也一直无法彻底解决，那就是：用户如果要使用这些新功能，就必须授权中心化的第三方平台管理大量数据。因此，这些中心化的实体在数据和内容权限方面被赋予了巨大的权力和影响力。

3.第三个发展阶段——Web3.0时代（去中心化、区块链）

为了解决Web2.0存在的数据确权问题，Web3.0随之产生。

Web3.0时代是互联网发展的最新阶段，重点在于去中心化和区块链技术的应用。在这个阶段，互联网的权力分散给了用户，他们可以更好地掌控自己的数据和数字权益。区块链技术的引入使数据的安全性和可信度得到提升，去中心化应用（DApps）则允许用户直接进行交互和合作，而无需第三方中介。

互联网的发展历史是一段充满创新和变革的旅程。从阿帕网到Web3.0时代，互联网不断演变和进化，连接了全球人民，改变了我们的生活方式。未来，随着技术的进一步发展，互联网将继续扮演着连接世界的数字大道的角色，为人类带来更多机遇和挑战。

（二）当前互联网行业趋势

1.进入存量时代

当前，互联网行业的增长率呈下降趋势。在2021年6月，我国网民达10.6亿，增长空间逐步缩小，增速逐步放缓，互联网流量红利已经接近顶端，互联网服务行业依靠人口红利就能高速增长的日子也一去不返。

过去，很多企业奉行先规模再盈利的模式，构建市场的壁垒；目前，市场已被几家巨头瓜分，这种增量时代适用的模式已经不符合当下的发展趋势，互联网已经从"增量时代"逐步走向"存量时代"。

2.多元化

互联网加速赋能传统产业，互联网大厂也通过跨界来建立自己的生态，拓宽业务边界，实现商业模式的多元化。它们涉足探索的新方向包括：碳中和、硬科技、助农、产业互联网、新能源等。同时，互联网大厂也在Web3.0、产业数字化、6G、人机交互、网络安全、智慧交互、沉浸式XR、全息通信等技术领域尝试革新。

3.依靠新的技术创新带来新的增量

目前，互联网头部企业在不断地增加研发投入，以寻求高技术转型；在未来的物联网时代，只有拥有最核心的技术，才能在商业竞争中立于不败之地。2022年底，阿里巴巴集团董事会主席兼CEO张勇挂帅阿里云智能总裁，技术成了阿里押重注的创新驱动力；2022年第三季度，腾讯的研发投入占营收比例提升到10.8%，处于近年历史高位。此外，美团、京东、拼多多等企业都在持续加大技术研发投入，研发费用投入均有不同程度上升，转型步伐进一步加快。

（三）人工智能在互联网行业的应用

1.模式识别类

模式识别类人工智能[①]在互联网行业的应用主要集中在对数据中的模式、结构和特征进行自动化识别和提取上。通过计算机视觉、语音识别、自然语言处理等技术，互联网公司可以利用模式识别的方法来分析和理解各种类型的数

---

① 范会敏，王浩.模式识别方法概述.电子设计工程，2012，20(19)：48-51.

据。实际应用有：图像识别和处理、语音识别和处理、文本分类和情感分析、手写体识别、声纹识别、视频分析、行为识别等。

2.计算智能（大数据）类

计算智能（大数据）类人工智能在互联网行业的应用主要集中在数据的处理、分析和挖掘上。互联网公司通过收集和存储大量的用户数据、交易数据和行为数据，利用计算智能的技术和算法，对这些数据进行深入分析，以揭示隐藏的模式、趋势和关联规律。这种数据驱动的方法为企业提供了宝贵的洞察和商业智能，帮助其做出更加明智的决策和战略规划。实际应用有：数据分析和挖掘、个性化推荐系统、智能广告投放、个性化推荐系统等。

3.智能决策类

智能决策类人工智能通过整合和分析各种数据，应用智能算法和决策模型，实现个性化推荐，可以帮助企业在复杂的市场环境中做出更准确、更优化的决策[①]，从而提高业务效率、降低成本、增加收益。智能决策不仅关注数据的分析和处理，还包括对问题的建模、规则制定、决策评估和最优选择等方面。

三、案例研究一：谷歌

（一）公司背景和发展历程

1.谷歌成立与起步

表1列举了谷歌成立与起步阶段的重要事件及其意义。

表1 谷歌发展历程

时间	事件	意义
1996 年	拉里·佩奇（Larry Page）和谢尔盖·布林（Sergey Brin）在斯坦福大学相遇	谷歌故事的起点
1997 年	创办"BackRub"搜索引擎	初创阶段的探索
1998 年	正式更名"Google"并获得天使投资	公司成立和早期融资
1999 年	获得两大风投公司投资并与雅虎合作	迈出快速发展步伐
2000 年	推出 Google Toolbar 并与 AOL 达成协议	拓展产品线和用户规模
2001 年	推出 AdWords 并实现盈利	开创商业模式并取得初步成功
2002—2007 年	推出 Google 一系列产品	产品线快速丰富，业务多元化
2008 年	推出安卓（Android）并收购 DoubleClick	进军移动领域并强化广告业务

---

① 刘建国，周涛，汪秉宏.个性化推荐系统的研究进展.自然科学进展，2009，19(1)：1-15.

2. 在竞争中发展

2004 年，Gmail 和 Google Earth 上线，产品线不断扩展。Gmail 电子邮件系统打破了当时对用户邮箱容量的限制，将容量提升到 1G，是雅虎邮箱的 250 倍，是微软的 500 倍。

2006 年 9 月，谷歌全面推出 Google Docs 相关产品，与微软 Office 进行竞争，并取得不错的效果和成绩。

2008 年，在浏览器方面谷歌开发的 Chrome 开始崭露头角，在未来的 10 年时间里，它将曾经最高占市场份额 90％的微软开发的 IE 浏览器推下神坛，直到 2022 年 Chrome 浏览器的市场份额已达到 65.68％，在诸多浏览器中一骑绝尘。

在与另一科技巨头苹果公司在移动操作系统的竞争中，2005 年，谷歌买下了安迪·鲁宾（Andy Rubin）创立的安卓公司；2008 年，第一款安卓手机由 HTC 推出；2009 年，安卓取得巨大成功；随着安卓手机的出货量大幅增长，2010 年，安卓市场占有率超过苹果。

在互联网去中心化的发展趋势下，"内容为王"的时代逐渐转变为了"用户为王"的时代，在这一时期涌现了三个流量增长极快的互联网公司：YouTube、Facebook、Myspace。而谷歌非常有先见之明地迅速与 Myspace 结盟，并收购了 YouTube，再加上在 2003 年谷歌收购的 Blogger 和 Orkut 两家大流量网站，谷歌圆满完成了互联网 2.0 的早期布局。

3. 霸主地位的衰落

谷歌于 2011 年推出产品 Google＋，目标是与当时的 Facebook 在即时通讯领域进行竞争发展，但因其"入场晚"且功能并没有 Facebook 讨喜、接地气，其逐渐被大众所遗忘，2019 年 4 月 2 日，谷歌正式关闭个人版 Google＋。

很早进入云计算领域的谷歌，在 2006 年就开发出了 Google Cloud，但其在与同期亚马逊推出的 AWS 云平台的竞争中，也逐渐失去优势地位，使企业发展陷入了一定的困境。

4. 公司重构

2015 年谷歌宣布重组，创办了新控股公司 Alphabet，并把现有的业务一分为二。原有的业务包括搜索、广告、YouTube、安卓等，交给了新任 CEO 孙达尔·皮柴（Sundar Pichai）负责；而非核心业务交给了佩奇，其中包括与互联网无关的项目，如生命科学、自动化、智能穿戴、自动驾驶和其他未来技术项目。这一决定无疑是明智的，当公司越来越大，决策的流程被拖长，无法做到小而专注，这其实并不适合需要跟上快速变化的互联网产业；而通过重组拆分子公司，谷歌能专注于搜索等业务，其他子公司也可以各司其职，以得到更好的发展。

（二）重要产品和服务

表2列举了谷歌的一些重要产品和服务。

表2　谷歌产品与服务概览

类别	产品／服务	简介
搜索引擎	Google Search	全球最大、最流行的互联网搜索引擎
通信与协作工具	Gmail	免费的电子邮件服务，提供强大的搜索功能
	Google Meet	视频会议工具，支持高清音视频通话、屏幕共享等功能
	Google Chat	团队即时通讯工具，方便团队成员之间的交流和协作
	Google Workspace	提供一套集成式的办公工具和云端存储服务，包括文档、表格、幻灯片等应用
在线广告平台	Google Ads	为企业和个人提供在线广告服务，帮助他们在谷歌搜索和网站上展示广告，并根据定向投放和关键词等方式提高广告效果
浏览器与移动操作系统	Google Chrome	一款速度快、稳定安全的网络浏览器，支持插件和应用扩展
	Android	谷歌开发的移动操作系统，目前是全球最流行的移动操作系统之一

一方面，这些产品和服务将给谷歌的AI发展提供海量的数据，加速相关AI技术的成熟和商业化落地；另一方面，谷歌成熟的AI技术也可以为谷歌生态中的不同环节深度赋能，增强谷歌整体业务的竞争力。

（三）在人工智能领域的突破和影响

1.模型

在2023年5月，谷歌在Google I/O大会上推出了PaLM 2大语言模型，作为对2022年发布的PaLM的升级版，参数规模达到数千亿级，训练效率、数据量和模型架构得到提升，部分能力超越了GPT-4，在多语言处理、数理、代码和高级推理方面表现突出。同时，谷歌AI团队的整合加速了技术迭代，开发出下一代大模型Gemini。LaMDA是另一基于Transformer的神经语言模型，专注于对话应用，参数高达1370亿，并在公共对话数据和网络文本中进行了巨大规模的预训练，为对话领域的发展带来新的潜力。

2.应用

在人工智能方面，谷歌公司的最新口号是"大胆而负责任"。谷歌对其人工智能模块的投入，在研究贡献、开源框架、将人工智能集成到产品和服务中、在深度学习方面的进步、促进人工智能道德实践以及利用人工智能为社会造福等方面均有体现。谷歌公司推出的人工智能应用如表3所示。

表3　谷歌公司推出的人工智能应用

工具名称	功能描述	现状
Bard	多语言交流助手，可生成文本、翻译语言、编写不同类型创意内容、并以信息丰富的方式回答问题。	已取消候补名单，180个国家和地区可直接使用
Duet AI	办公效率助手，可自动生成文档、表格和图片，并提供智能问答功能。	部分功能已在Gmail中落地，可自动写邮件
Med-PaLM 2	医疗知识专家，可进行医疗问答、总结医学文本，并提供辅助诊断功能。	在USMLE问题测试中的准确率为85.4%，达到医疗专家的水平
Sec-PaLM	网络安全卫士，可分析和解释潜在的恶意脚本，协助提升网络安全。	可以分析和解释潜在的恶意脚本

3.更多应用与服务

谷歌已经将人工智能集成到它的许多产品和服务中（见表4）。谷歌助手是一款人工智能虚拟助手，它改变了人们与技术互动和执行任务的方式。其他产品，如谷歌翻译、谷歌照片和谷歌搜索，利用人工智能来增强用户体验并提供智能功能。

表4　谷歌AI应用功能概览

应用名称	功能简介
谷歌翻译	利用人工智能算法，包括神经机器翻译（NMT），提高翻译准确性和流畅性；支持图像识别和OCR技术，可翻译外语文本和图片；提供对话模式，实现实时多语言对话。
谷歌照片	利用人工智能算法识别和标记照片中的人物、物体和场景；使用机器学习改进自动照片增强功能；提供人工智能支持的功能，如建议分享、拼贴画、动画和相册；支持对象识别，方便搜索特定照片。
谷歌眼镜	集成计算机视觉和人工智能算法，识别和理解物体、文本、地标等视觉元素；提供信息、翻译和上下文操作，如识别植物、扫描条形码、翻译文本等；支持视觉搜索，分析视觉数据，识别对象，并提供相关信息或建议相关操作。

续表

应用名称	功能简介
谷歌地图	利用人工智能算法分析历史交通数据、实时交通更新和用户输入，提供准确和实时的交通信息；使用机器学习优化路线建议，估计到达时间，并根据当前的交通状况建议替代路线；提供预测功能，根据用户习惯和经常访问的地点预测目的地；提供个性化推荐，根据用户的喜好和位置，推荐附近的名胜、餐馆等。

4.深度学习框架 TensorFlow

谷歌开发的开源机器学习框架 TensorFlow 已成为业内使用最广泛的框架之一。TensorFlow 是一个端到端的开源机器学习平台，可以用于管理机器学习系统的各个方面。TensorFlow 由 Google Brain 团队开发，最早用于谷歌内部进行研发与生产。2015 年，谷歌大脑发布了 TensorFlow。后续分别在 2017 年、2019 年发布了 1.0.0 和 2.0.0 的两个重要的版本更新。目前讨论最激烈的 ChatGPT，其核心的底层架构仍包括 TensorFlow。

5.Transformer

谷歌团队在 2017 年发布了论文 "Attention Is All You Need"，首次提出了 Transformer 模型，为后续整个人工智能领域发展奠定了基础。

Tansformer 基于经典的机器翻译 Seq2Seq 框架，这个模型促成了自然语言学习（NLP）领域中 GPT 和 BERT 这两大模型的发展。Transformer 模型引入了自我注意力（self-attention）机制，逐步替代 RNN（循环神经网络）和 CNN（卷积神经网络），结合算法优化，可以实现并行运算，大量节约训练时间，在 WMT 2014 的数据集上取得了很好的成绩。简单来说，它是一种模仿认知注意力的机制，可以对神经网络输入数据中不同部分给予不同的关注权重，将重点集中在最重要的小部分数据上。

6.底层实现

机器学习算法是通过学习数据中的规律和模式做出预测或决策的工具；谷歌致力于开发强大的机器学习工具，如 TensorFlow 和 Scikit-learn，以提高效率。深度学习算法则是机器学习中的一种特殊类型，通过多层次神经网络模拟人脑结构，处理复杂数据；谷歌在深度学习领域发挥着重要作用，开发了诸如 TensorFlow 和 Keras 的工具，推动深度学习模型的设计与应用。谷歌利用深度学习算法开发了诸多重要应用，如 Google Voice 语音识别系统、Google Photos 图像识别系统和 Waymo 自动驾驶系统，不断投入资源与学术界合作，推动深度学习算法的研究与应用发展。

（四）对社会和行业的影响

谷歌公司对社会和行业的影响，按其发展的顺序来看，可大致分为四个类别。首先是谷歌的搜索引擎，它在社会中被广泛知晓，为人们提供了便捷的信息搜索服务。其次是谷歌的安卓系统，它在移动领域占据主导地位，推动了智能手机的普及和移动互联网的发展。再次是对行业影响最深的谷歌广告，谷歌的广告平台为广告商提供了高效的推广渠道，塑造了数字广告行业的格局。最后，近年来谷歌在 AI 科技领域的研究逐渐成为其主要发展目标。谷歌在计算机视觉、自然语言处理和机器学习等方面的突破，推动了 AI 技术的创新和应用。

1.谷歌搜索引擎对于社会的影响

20 世纪末，雅虎搜索引擎只有少量通过人工整理的搜索内容作为结果，网景搜索引擎仅能得出凌乱无序的搜索结果，在这一背景下，谷歌以其强大而高效的搜索引擎彻底改变了互联网搜索的实践。通过提供对大量信息的便捷访问，谷歌改变了人们寻找和消费知识的方式，影响了教育、研究和日常决策。

在信息获取和共享方面，通过 PageRank 算法，谷歌搜索以用户点击量来排序，使人们能够更加容易地获取更精准需要的信息，这大大提高了搜索的准确性，对于大部分信息搜索而言，谷歌大幅度减少了用户搜索信息所需要的时间。同时，谷歌搜索汇集了大量链接，打破信息障碍，使用户能够从世界各地的知名来源获取信息。谷歌搜索引擎为寻求信息的个人和组织提供公平的竞争环境，使知识民主化，使人们能够找到所需的答案，学习新技能，并探索不同的观点，其在研究和教育方面起着至关重要的作用，帮助研究人员、学者和学生访问学术文章、出版物和教育资源，加快了各个研究领域的发展。

在创新意识上，谷歌的搜索引擎挑战传统的信息守门人，强调更相关和更高质量的搜索结果，这推动了网站和内容创建者改进他们的产品，更加以用户体验为导向，从而增强了用户体验，提供了更有用、更吸引人的在线内容。而这种快速搜索信息的能力也促进了从健康和科学，到政治和娱乐等各种主题的知识共享、辩论和思想传播。Chrome 是目前世界上使用最多的浏览器，从一定程度上讲，谷歌搜索引擎参与塑造了文化规范、趋势和社会议题。

而在经济方面，谷歌搜索的广告设计对其盈利模式产生了深远影响，即通过搜索引擎优化（SEO）和定向广告，将企业与潜在客户联系起来，从而使企业可以触达目标受众，推动网站流量、在线销售和品牌知名度的增长。这改变了广告业，推动了在线商务的发展，也深刻影响了行业。

2.谷歌广告的行业影响

谷歌的广告业改变了数字广告的格局，制定了行业标准，推动了创新，并使各种规模的企业都能够更有效地接触到目标受众，推动了在线广告的增长，并影响了各行业的营销策略。它的影响力延伸到出版商、内容创作者、广告商和整个数字经济，在塑造数字广告格局方面发挥了至关重要的作用。

谷歌在广告上创新地采用了目标化和个性化，通过利用用户数据和浏览行为，谷歌可以向个人用户提供高度相关和个性化的广告，增强整体广告体验，提高广告活动的有效性。谷歌也不断推出创新的广告产品和功能，如展示广告、视频广告（YouTube ads）和移动广告。这些创新扩大了广告商可用的广告形式，使广告商能够在各种平台和设备上创造引人入胜的互动广告体验。

同时，谷歌引入按点击付费（PPC）广告模式，这种模式允许广告商只在用户点击广告时付费，提供了一种成本效益高且可衡量的方式来接触潜在客户。点击付费模式确立了行业标准，并影响了数字广告平台的定价结构。这也对出版商和内容创作者产生了深远的影响。通过像AdSense这样的项目，谷歌为网站所有者和内容创作者提供了货币化的机会，使他们能够展示相关的广告并产生收入，这促进了网络内容创作的增长，激励了高质量网络平台的发展。

对整个行业来说，谷歌广告对经济产生了重大影响，也塑造了行业标准。通过为广告商提供一个有效推广其产品和服务的平台，谷歌推动了经济增长，创造了就业机会，并为数字经济做出了贡献。而透明度倡议、广告质量标准、数字广告指导方针，以及谷歌在打击广告欺诈和误导行为时做出的努力也提高了整个行业的标准。

3.谷歌安卓系统的社会影响力

谷歌的安卓移动设备操作系统已经成为全球使用最广泛的移动平台。相比于闭源的IOS系统，安卓是一个开放性的开源系统，它为全球大多数智能手机提供动力，使数百万人能够使用先进的移动技术。安卓加速了智能手机的普及，改变了通信方式，为移动应用开发者和整个移动生态系统带来了新的机遇。

作为一个开源系统，安卓允许设备制造商和开发者根据他们的具体需求定制操作系统，鼓励开发人员、研究人员和爱好者为其开发和改进做出贡献。开发人员可以自由访问和修改 Android 源代码，为不同的设备定制功能，并创建创新性的应用程序、服务和功能。这个开放的生态系统为用户提供了丰富多样的应用程序，极大提升了用户体验。

同时，受益于开源项目的开放性，安卓社区在协作和知识共享的基础上蓬勃发展，大型开发人员社区可以为识别和修复错误做出贡献，并提高安全性和性能。这种协作的努力增强了安卓平台的整体稳定性和安全性。

谷歌也将各类多样服务集成整合为 GMS（Google Mobile Services），提供了一个跨设备且一致的生态系统，其中包含各类应用，如谷歌搜索、Gmail、谷歌地图、YouTube 等，使得用户在使用谷歌服务时拥有更简单的访问模式，获得更全面的服务体验。

（五）挑战与未来展望

1. 未来面临的挑战

表 5 列举了谷歌在不同领域的竞争概况。

表 5　谷歌在各竞争领域的概况

竞争领域	主要竞争对手	竞争概况
移动平台操作系统	苹果（iOS）	操作系统和智能助理直接竞争，智能手机、智能手表等设备领域竞争激烈
云计算	亚马逊（AWS）	谷歌云和亚马逊 AWS 处于竞争关系，亚马逊 AWS 目前处于竞争优势地位
语言模型	微软（Windows、Bing）	操作系统、智能助理和搜索引擎直接竞争
其他	特斯拉（自动驾驶）	自动驾驶技术竞争激烈

对于谷歌而言，除了面临多个科技巨头企业的外部竞争以外，其自身部分领域的不充分不完全的发展，也是谷歌亟待解决的关键问题。

例如在社交媒体领域，谷歌在社交媒体领域相对落后，其尝试推出的多个社交产品（如 Google＋、Google Buzz 等）未能取得与 Twitter 等竞争对手相媲美的用户规模和影响力。而在电子商务快速发展的当下，谷歌的表现也显得心有余而力不足，相比亚马逊，谷歌在电子商务领域的市场份额较小。亚马逊拥有庞大的在线零售平台和物流系统，以及备受欢迎的 Prime 会员服务，而谷歌在这方面的发展相对有限。最后，在即时通讯和视频通话领域，与微信、

WhatsApp和Skype等产品相比，谷歌的即时通讯工具（如 Google Hangouts、Google Chat等）在全球用户和市场份额上也存在一定的落后。而这些劣势都使Google需要通过不断完善、提升自身技术，以求得更好的发展。

2.相应的发展与解决方略

谷歌应继续完善并促进自身技术迭代更新；为了更好地应对外部企业的竞争和内部某些领域劣势的困境与问题，将重心放在促进自身技术的迭代更新方面显得十分关键。

通过技术的完善与迭代更新，企业可以提升用户体验，例如，优化界面设计、提高系统稳定性和响应速度，增强功能和交互性，使用户能够更方便、快捷地使用产品。而技术迭代也是企业保持竞争力的关键一环，通过持续创新和技术升级，企业能够与竞争对手站在同一起跑线上甚至领先一步。不断推出新功能、新产品或采用新技术，使企业能够吸引更多用户，并留住现有用户。

另一方面，技术迭代更新能够推动整个行业的发展。企业在技术和产品领域的突破可以带动其他企业追随或创新，形成积极的竞争态势。同时，技术迭代也为行业带来了更多商机和合作空间，促进行业的快速发展。

综上所述，互联网企业完善并促进自身技术迭代更新对于提升用户体验、保持竞争力、提高效率、推动行业发展以及承担社会责任都具有重要意义。这一过程需要企业不断关注市场需求，积极投入研发资源，与时俱进地推动技术创新，并在技术实施过程中保障用户权益和社会利益。

谷歌应持续捕捉下一个互联网产业或技术风口。谷歌之所以可以拥有现如今庞大的产业，离不开其在过去三十年里稳稳抓牢技术产业的一个又一个风口，从押宝搜索引擎到果断收购安卓公司，再到 Web 2.0 时代中，收购Youtube并与Myspace合作，这些重要决定让谷歌一次又一次达到了新的高度。以史为鉴，在未来的发展过程中，谷歌也应继续保持对互联网以及互联网外的各产业发展前景的敏感度，例如，智能穿戴设备、自动驾驶技术、虚拟现实和增强现实等新兴但未取得完全发展的智能科学与技术。谷歌的SpaceX实验室中对各种奇思妙想的投入虽然目前看来并没有显著的回报，但我们相信这些科研与资金的投入，也许将会在未来某一时期，引领谷歌走向新的历史高度。

3.承担更多的社会责任

谷歌作为互联网产业的巨头公司，在新的发展时代，应主动承担更多的社会责任。例如在用户数据隐私保护方面，谷歌应强调用户数据隐私的重要性，并采取有效措施保护用户的个人信息安全。谷歌可以加强对数据收集、存储和处理过程的监管，并提供更多的透明度和用户控制选项，以保护用户隐私权益。

在技术道德和人工智能的治理方面，谷歌可以致力于推动人工智能的积极应用，并建立健全的人工智能道德框架，避免算法偏见、歧视性行为和潜在的伦理问题。谷歌还可以与学术界、业界和政府合作，共同制定相关标准和规范，确保人工智能技术符合社会利益和道德原则。

除此之外，在环境保护和可持续发展领域，谷歌也需要不断努力，例如加大对可再生能源的投资和利用，减少数据中心和办公环境的碳排放。谷歌可以继续推动能源效率改进，减少电子垃圾产生，并积极参与环保倡议和社会公益项目等。

四、案例研究二：百度

（一）挑战与未来展望

1.公司背景

百度是一家领先的互联网和技术公司，总部位于中国北京。该公司由李彦宏于 2000 年创立，李彦宏至今仍担任公司首席执行官。百度运营着中国最大、世界第二大的搜索引擎[①]，因此经常被称为"中国的谷歌"。

百度公司的组织结构包括搜索事业部、新业务事业群、技术事业群等部门。公司的员工包括工程师、研究人员、市场营销专家、产品经理等，形成了一个多元化的团队。截至 2022 年 9 月 30 日，百度核心员工数量约为 3.65 万。

与谷歌类似[②]，百度将其搜索引擎的技术专长应用于与人工智能相关的多项业务，涵盖了自动驾驶、自然语言处理、计算机视觉、增强现实和智能设备等领域。百度积极推动自动驾驶技术的发展，推出了自动驾驶开放平台 Apollo，并与合作伙伴合作推进自动驾驶技术的研发与应用。

除了搜索和人工智能，百度也涉足其他领域。公司通过百度云提供云计算服务，支持企业和开发者构建和扩展应用程序。此外，百度还拥有百度贴吧、百度知道、百度地图、百度文库等在线产品和服务。百度通过搜索引擎和在线

---

① 董倩玉.基于传播学视角研究搜索引擎的发展.北京：北京外国语大学，2022.
② 张明钟.谷歌、百度创新模式比较.中国经济报告，2016(9)：76-78.

广告为公司带来主要的收入来源。2022年第一季度，百度核心业务约占百度总收入的70%，包括三大主要业务集群：移动生态系统、人工智能云和智能驾驶。

百度主要定位于中国市场，在中国互联网用户中占据主导地位。通过提供本地化的搜索和互联网服务，并不断进行技术创新和市场拓展，百度努力满足用户需求，不断推动中国互联网行业的发展。

2.发展历程

表6列举了百度发展历程中的重要事件及其意义。

表6 百度发展历程

时间	事件	意义
2000年	百度创立	中国首个搜索引擎诞生
2001年	推出中文搜索引擎	满足中国用户搜索需求
2004年	推出付费搜索服务	开创新的商业模式
2005年	上市	首家在美国上市的中国互联网公司
2007年	推出百度贴吧	构建用户社区
2010年	推出移动搜索应用	拓展移动互联网市场
2011年	推出百度地图	提供地理信息服务
2013年	推出百度云	提供云计算服务
2015年	将人工智能列为战略重点	开启技术转型
2016年	推出自动驾驶开放平台Apollo	推动自动驾驶技术发展

百度从2015年至今的技术转型对公司具有重要的意义。它推动了创新和技术升级，提升了用户体验和服务质量，拓宽了业务领域，增强了竞争力，同时也推动了产业升级和创新生态系统的建立。这些转型使百度能够适应快速变化的科技环境，保持竞争优势，并不断满足用户和市场的需求。

（二）重要产品和服务

表7列举了百度的一些重要产品和服务。

表7 百度产品与服务分类概览

类型	产品/服务	简介
交互型	百度云	提供云存储、云计算、人工智能等服务
	百度网盘	提供文件存储和共享服务
	百度文库	提供在线文档共享服务
	百度贴吧	提供基于兴趣和话题的共享社区平台
智能型	Apollo 开放平台	提供自动驾驶开放解决方案
	度秘OS（DuerOS）	提供智能语音助手服务
	飞桨（PaddlePaddle 1）	提供深度学习框架
	文心一言（ERNIE Bot）	提供会话人工智能系统
工具型	百度搜索	提供全面的网页搜索、图片搜索、视频搜索等服务
	百度地图	提供在线地图和导航服务
	百度翻译	提供在线翻译服务
媒体型	爱奇艺	提供在线视频平台服务

（三）在人工智能领域的突破和影响

1.技术

飞桨（PaddlePaddle）作为中国首个完备开源的产业级深度学习平台，在百度多年技术积累的基础上崛起，提供中文文档与数据集、全栈服务，降低了开发难度。其模型库、开发套件、工具集以及低代码开发工具均备受推崇。百度的昆仑芯片则是国内首款云端通用AI处理器，采用XPU架构，解决了数据中心对芯片的性能、成本和灵活性需求，与飞桨深度结合，形成全栈技术生态。另外，百度鸿鹄远场语音交互芯片颠覆传统设计，支持多路麦克阵列语音输入以及领先的语音处理技术，实现高精度唤醒。文心系列大模型包括NLP、CV、跨模态、生物计算和行业大模型，结合大数据预训练与多源知识，为各领域提供强大的模型支持，助力产业智能化转型。这些创新技术和产品共同构建了百度在AI领域的领先地位，为产业发展带来了新的机遇与挑战。

2.应用——文心一言

文心一言是百度打造出来的人工智能大语言模型，具备跨模态、跨语言的深度语义理解与生成能力，文心一言有五大能力——文学创作、商业文案创作、数理逻辑推算、中文理解、多模态生成，其在搜索问答、内容创作生成、智能办公等众多领域都有更广阔的想象空间。

在具体的商业化方面，文心一言目前已经接入各行各业，在百度发布文心一言的一个月内，就有650家企业接入文心一言生态，涵盖了互联网、媒体、金融、保险、汽车、企业软件等行业，随着百度大模型在B端的生态圈迅速扩大，AI市场有望迎来需求的大幅增长，而百度或将受益于文心一言生态，率先吃到大模型发展带来的红利。

3.生态布局

百度AI产业打造全栈式布局，构建完整产业生态和独有技术优势。百度是目前全球少有的，在"芯片－框架－模型－应用"四个层面上均有所布局的人工智能公司：芯片层有高端芯片昆仑芯，框架层有飞桨深度学习框架，模型层有文心预训练大模型，应用层有百度智能云、百度自动驾驶、小度智能语音助手等应用。

百度AI全栈布局的优势在于，百度可以在技术栈的四层架构中实现端到端优化，大幅提升效率。尤其是框架层和模型层之间，有很强的协同作用，可以帮助构建更高效的模型，并显著降低成本。例如，为了支持海量参数模型的高效分布式训练，百度飞桨专门研发了4D混合并行技术。后续"芯片－框架－模型－应用"四个层面将形成高效的闭环反馈，推动百度人工智能持续迭代升级。

（四）对社会和行业的影响

1.为中国用户提供搜索等一系列互联网服务

百度常被称为"中国的谷歌"，在中国的搜索引擎中占有最大的市场份额，在中国市场占有主导地位，中国网民将百度搜索引擎亲切地称为"度娘"。对于大部分中国互联网用户来说，百度搜索引擎在他们的日常生活中有着不可或缺的地位，是他们获取信息和在线搜索的主要来源。

相比谷歌的搜索引擎，百度更加聚焦于中文搜索，是专门为满足中国用户的需求而量身定制的，尤其是其在中文搜索查询、本地内容和中文网站方面的表现，相比谷歌，能够更加贴合中国用户需求，其对于许多中国传统成语、诗句短语的理解分析表现也更加准确出色。同时，百度开发了复杂的算法来更有效地索引和分析中国网站和网络内容。

百度的索引算法优先考虑中文内容，使中国用户可以更有效地找到本地化的信息。这些为了更好地适配中文做出的改动让百度搜索引擎成为中国互联网用户更加青睐的选择。

与谷歌的全家桶服务GMS类似，百度也开发了许多自己的系列服务，如百度地图、百度文库、百度贴吧、百度翻译等；2022年，百度官宣正式切换为优先运用北斗系统进行定位，"百度地图智能定位开放服务"升级更名为"百度地图北斗定位开放平台"；在北斗系统的深度赋能下，百度地图升级实现了车道级导航、车位级导航等多项功能。此外，2013年，百度收购视频在线播放平台爱奇艺，为广大百度使用者提供了较完备的视频播放服务。

2.推出一系列人工智能服务

2017年，百度正式官宣全面转型AI，提出"用科技让复杂的世界更简单"的新使命。在ChatGPT出世并对人工智能语言模型造成极大震撼之后，百度推出自己的语言模型文心一言。

作为几乎能够对标ChatGPT的语言模型，百度文心一言的优势在于其强大的中文对话和理解能力；对于我们广大中文用户而言，文心一言能够在古汉语等中文专业方面获得比ChatGPT更加优秀的表现，是一款真正面向中国人的AI语言助手。中文是世界上使用人数最多的语言，随着中国不断发展进步，文心一言也会有更光明的前景。

未来文心一言将通过百度智能云对外提供服务，帮助企业构建自己的模型和应用，农业、工业、金融、教育、医疗、交通、能源等重点领域都会因此大幅提升效率，文心一言有希望在各行业快速形成新的产业空间，助力数字中国的建设。

（五）挑战与未来展望

百度作为中国最大的搜索引擎公司之一，面临着诸多挑战和机遇。这里，我们将探讨当前百度公司所面临的几个关键问题，并对其未来发展进行展望。

1.搜索质量下降，竞争对手强大

百度长期以来在搜索领域占据主导地位，但近年来，搜索质量下降成为一个突出的问题。用户对搜索结果的准确性和相关性提出了更高的要求。与此同时，国内外竞争对手如腾讯、阿里巴巴等互联网巨头也加大了在搜索领域的投入。百度需要应对竞争对手的挑战，提升搜索算法和技术，改善搜索质量，以保持用户的忠诚度和市场份额。

2.移动端的普及

随着智能手机和平板电脑的普及，移动端成为了用户获取信息和进行搜索的重要平台。百度需要在移动端提供更好的用户体验，优化移动搜索结果的呈现方式，并开发适配移动设备的创新应用。同时，百度还需应对移动互联网广告市场的竞争，寻找新的商业模式和增长点。

3.人工智能领域的竞争

百度的文心一言技术通过理解用户的搜索意图和内容，提供更精准、有深度的搜索结果，为用户提供更好的搜索体验。然而，在大语言模型如雨后春笋般诞生、迭代的当下，百度有必要加大在大语言模型和其他人工智能领域的投入，以更好的产品应对愈发激烈的人工智能竞赛。

（六）结　论

面对搜索质量下降、移动端的崛起、人工智能领域的竞争等诸多挑战，百度公司正积极应对，持续加大技术创新和研发投入，拓展多元化业务布局，并与合作伙伴进行深度合作。未来，百度有望在这些领域取得更大突破，实现可持续发展，并为用户提供更智能、便捷的服务。

五、跨案例分析

（一）百度和谷歌的相似和差异之处

1.相似

百度和谷歌在技术创新方面紧跟风口，从搜索引擎服务起步，正在经历AI领域转型。谷歌在算法创新方面取得了重大突破，优化搜索结果，提升用户体验；百度则深入研究中文搜索技术，成为中国热门搜索引擎。在自动驾驶和智能语言模型等领域，两家公司都展现了创新力，谷歌的Waymo和百度的Apollo都是自动驾驶领域的重要投资项目。二者都通过收集用户数据提供个性化服务，大数据分析也助推了算法进步。二者业务架构相似，都面临从"移动"到"AI"的转型，都构建了全面的生态系统，如谷歌的GMS和百度的全家桶服务。二者都采取了全球化发展战略，通过战略扩张争夺全球市场份额。以广告为主要收入的盈利模式也是二者共同点，即依靠广告收入支持搜索引擎的运营和发展。这些因素共同塑造了百度和谷歌在科技领域的竞争格局和发展路径。

2. 差异

百度与谷歌在搜索引擎领域有着不同的特点[①]。百度更注重于中国市场，提供更贴近中文用户需求的搜索结果，并在广告展示上稍显突出，而谷歌则因更准确、有用的搜索结果而受到赞誉，展示页面更为公平和注重用户体验。在大语言模型方面，文心一言和Gemini分别具备中文和英文语言处理能力，文心一言在中文领域表现出色，且具备多模态生成能力。飞桨与TensorFlow在深度学习框架领域有所差异，飞桨提供全栈服务，开发套件更全，且更适配中国AI产业实践；而TensorFlow历史悠久，在国际平台上受众更广泛。在产业化走向上，谷歌提供解决方案但未体系化落地，而百度通过"云智一体"战略与各行业结合，形成广泛的AI产业方案。在技术方面，谷歌的无监督学习和Transformer模型领先，而百度大脑6.0实现了知识增强的深度语义理解。企业文化方面，谷歌鼓励创新、扁平化管理，百度相对保守、传统。最后，百度以"让人们最平等便捷地获取信息，找到所求"为使命，而谷歌向员工传达"做正确的事"的行为准则，展现出两家企业的不同愿景。

（二）谷歌和百度如何影响并塑造全球互联网和人工智能领域

表8列举了从1990年至今互联网和人工智能领域的重要发展事件。谷歌和百度在其中发挥了重要作用。

表8　互联网和人工智能领域的重要发展事件

时间段	事件	描述
1990—2000年	亚马逊电子商务平台（1994）	改变了购物方式和消费习惯，推出个性化推荐系统。
	谷歌搜索引擎（1998）	改进了互联网搜索体验，提供更准确和高效的搜索结果。
	腾讯QQ即时通信软件（1999）	提供实时沟通、社交互动和在线娱乐，推动了中国社交网络的发展。
	百度搜索引擎（2000）	通过中文搜索技术创新和对本地需求的了解，成为中国最受欢迎的搜索引擎。
2000—2010年	淘宝电子商务平台（2003）	提供广阔的在线交易平台，改变了中国人的购物方式。
	Facebook社交媒体平台（2004）	引领社交媒体潮流，改变了社交方式和信息传播方式。

---

① 赵鑫.谷歌与百度营销模式比较研究.语言与文化研究，2015(1): 166-170.

续表

时间段	事件	描述
2000—2010年	YouTube（2005）	全球最大的视频分享平台，用户可以上传、观看和分享视频内容。
	iPhone智能手机（2007）	引领了智能手机革命，带动移动互联网发展。
	谷歌安卓手机（2008）	提供功能强大和应用丰富的移动操作系统。
2010年至今	微信社交媒体平台（2011）	提供实时通信、社交网络和移动支付，改变了中国人的生活方式。
	Amazon Echo智能音箱（2014）	引领智能语音助手发展，提供智能家居控制和个人助理功能。
	TensorFlow机器学习框架（2015）	谷歌开发的开源机器学习框架，促进机器学习和深度学习创新。
	度秘OS（DuerOS）（2015）	百度推出的人工智能语音助手平台，提供智能语音交互和个性化服务。
	飞桨（PaddlePaddle）深度学习平台（2016）	百度开发的开源深度学习平台，推动中国人工智能发展。
	Waymo自动驾驶技术（2009成立，2017商业化）	谷歌自动驾驶公司，推动自动驾驶车辆研发和应用。
	Apollo自动驾驶平台（2017）	百度推出的开放式自动驾驶平台，提供完整的自动驾驶解决方案。
	BERT（2018）	谷歌提出的预训练语言模型，提升了自然语言处理任务性能。
	ChatGPT（2019）	OpenAI开发的对话生成模型，引领自然语言处理进步。

（三）当前互联网行业的主要问题和挑战

1.市场竞争风险

随着下游产业的发展和市场需求的不断增加，AI各个细分领域的市场竞争愈发激烈。在通用处理器领域，因特尔、超威半导体（AMD）的CPU产品在全球市场中占据绝对优势地位；在协处理器领域，英伟达、超威半导体的GPU产品占据绝对优势地位。总体上，国内各厂商的市场份额与国际龙头企业相比差距较大。

国内互联网企业还面临细分领域（电商、社交、游戏）的威胁或直接竞争，威胁包括细分领域数据集获得难度增大，竞争包括细分领域巨头直接下场竞争且更易于满足细分领域用户需求。

2.法律及道德风险

网络舆论管理和言论自由：互联网上的言论在迅速扩散，网络舆论也成为社会稳定和治理的重要方面；有关部门需加强舆论引导、打击虚假信息和恶意攻击，同时保护言论自由和多元声音的表达。

网络犯罪和网络安全威胁：随着互联网的发展，网络犯罪活动也日益增多，如网络攻击、黑客入侵和网络诈骗；有关部门需加强网络安全技术、法律法规和合作机制建设，以保护个人、组织和国家的信息安全。

3.隐私和数据安全

随着个人数据的大规模采集和使用，隐私和数据安全成为人们重点关注的问题。用户需要更好的数据保护措施和透明度，同时企业需加强数据安全管理和风险防范，避免数据泄露和滥用。

4.研发及预期风险

本行业重视人才的经验积累，产品研发周期较长，需要厂商持续高研发投入，若新品研发不及预期，可能影响后续相关公司成长增速。[1]

5.算力开销成本预估

算力开销驱动营业成本增加，生成式AI在发展早期的商业化绩效目标需要被理性地界定清楚。发展早期，需要有持续的现金流业务支撑AI明星业务的研发及运维开支，同时也要避免业务间存在内部不配合和摩擦，避免下游环节厂商所创造的价值不断转移到上游的硬件或者能源厂商。比如，生产高端GPU、FPGA芯片的厂商较为集中，而可替代品有限，上游厂商有较强溢价权。

六、结 论

（一）案例研究的总结

在本次案例研究中，我们主要对谷歌公司与百度公司的所处背景、发展历程、其主要产品和在各领域产生的广泛影响进行了分析和总结归纳。

本次研究的重要性在于，通过对这些作为技术创新和发展的领导者进行相关分析，我们可以更深入地了解其成功的原因、关键策略和技术创新，并学习其成功经验。此外，还可以深入探究其竞争优势来源，如用户体验、市场定位等，了解其核心价值和差异化优势所在。通过揭示其商业模式、创新战略、竞

---

[1] 李晨雨.论述互联网企业的发展趋势——以BD公司为例.商业观察，2022(31)：25-28.

争优势和组织文化等方面的关键要素，我们可以为其他企业和个人提供借鉴和启发。

通过本次研究，我们对百度和谷歌这两家互联网巨头公司的发展历程、产品布局、研发策略、重要决策、企业文化等方面有了更加深刻详尽的了解，并从中获取了宝贵的经验教训与启示，同时也对人工智能的研究框架有了初步的认知。

（二）研究的局限性

1.缺乏全面信息

我们无法获得有关该公司的所有细节和内部信息，公开可用的信息非常有限，并且难以获取公司内部运营、管理决策和未公开项目等方面的详细情况。因此，分析基于的信息有时不够全面，导致评估结果可能不准确或不完整。

2.市场波动和不确定性

市场环境经常发生变化，包括宏观经济波动、产业竞争变化、政策调整等。这些因素会对公司的业务和表现产生影响。我们很难准确估计这些未来变化，以给出持久准确的结论。

3.主观偏见和解读

研究者的个人主观偏见和选取的分析方法可能会对分析结果产生影响。不同的观点与假设，可能会导致对同一公司的分析结论存在差异。此外，研究者还可能会根据自己的经验和知识背景对信息进行解读，从而引入主观偏见并影响分析结果的客观性。

（三）对未来的预见和建议

互联网与人工智能的发展日新月异，在此，我们仅依靠现有资料及过往数十年的发展趋势来对未来一段时期进行有限猜测和预见，并附上我们的一些粗浅看法。

1.互联网普及、数字化加速以及物联网的广泛使用

互联网将更加普及，全球互联网用户数量将进一步增加。互联网的连接性将更加广泛，其将涵盖更多的地区和人群，包括偏远地区和发展中国家。更多的人将获得互联网接入，并在各个领域中使用数字技术来进行工作、学习、娱乐和社交等活动。数字化将成为各行各业的常态，包括在教育、医疗、零售、金融等领域。同时，5G之上技术的成熟，势必会推动万物互联的局面产生，

物联网（IoT）技术的发展将进一步推动设备之间的互联和数据共享。

2.人机协作的增强，虚拟现实广泛应用

娱乐领域无疑是当下青少年最关心的领域之一，而如果在娱乐领域内加入一些前沿的内容，不仅会为其带来热度与新鲜感，还会让观看者记忆深刻。有关人机协作、虚拟现实题材的动漫、电影等在近些年更是火热，很多年轻人也对这些娱乐内容中的"未来"充满好奇。例如，十年前的动漫《刀剑神域》，其中的虚拟现实游戏在 2022 年上市，五年前爆火的电影《头号玩家》，那个世界的"绿洲"也在 2023 年出现。

虽说这些节点已经过去，但是我们细细回看，元宇宙的话题几年前就开始爆火，大量资本纷纷投入其中；2024 年，Apple Vision 的上市也让人眼前一亮。虽然当下这类设备的价格还是让普通人难以接受，不过随着技术的发展，今后二十年，世界上虚拟现实的发展势必如互联网那样，从搭建到普及，从人人尝试使用到人人可以开发，慢慢走入一个人机协作、共创现实的新领域。

3.大模型会深度融合到各行各业当中去

互联网和人工智能行业将出现更多的跨界合作和技术融合。未来，所有的应用都将基于大模型来开发，每一个行业都会有属于自己的大模型。大模型会深度融合到实体经济当中去，赋能千行百业。不同行业的企业和组织将共同合作，结合各自的专长和资源，推动技术的跨领域应用和创新。互联网和人工智能将与生物技术、纳米技术、量子计算等前沿科技交叉融合，带来更多的突破和变革。

4.伦理和社会影响的持续讨论

随着技术的发展和应用范围的扩大，伦理和社会影响的讨论将变得更加重要。人们将更加关注人工智能的公平性、隐私保护、工作岗位的变化等问题，制定相关政策和规范来确保技术的发展符合人类的价值观和福祉。

PART
7

第七章

世界一流工业园区建设案例研究

物理技术和社会技术共演化视角下体育产业助力老工业园区转型升级路径研究——以新首钢高端产业综合服务区为例[①]

摘　要： 随着国家对环境保护和产业转型升级的要求越来越高，促进老工业园区的绿色创新发展成了国家经济发展的重要任务之一。本文综合运用文献资料、逻辑分析等方法，基于新首钢高端产业综合服务区的典型实践，从物理技术和社会技术共演化的全新视角，以体育产业助力老工业园区转型发展为主线，采用学术性的话语体系对过去二十年首钢老工业园区向新首钢高端产业综合服务区转型升级路径进行了系统性的梳理和提炼，对未来十年新首钢高端产业综合服务区数字化升级提供了理论思路，为老工业园区的转型发展提供了一种来自体育产业的选择和案例。

关键词： 物理技术；社会技术；体育产业；老工业园区；转型升级

一、研究总论

（一）研究背景

1.宏观上：高质量绿色创新发展推动中国式现代化成为产业升级的主旋律

高质量发展是能够满足人民日益增长的美好生活需要的发展，是体现新发展理念的发展，是创新成为第一动力、协调成为内生特点、绿色成为普遍形态、开放成为必由之路、共享成为根本目的的发展。[②]在高质量发展的指引下，随着国家对环境保护和产业转型升级的要求越来越高，促进老工业园区的绿色

---

① 作者：牛建华，北京大学马克思主义学院；邹昀瑾，清华大学公共管理学院；郭彬，北京大学人口研究所；李心宸，北京大学体育教研部。

② 国家发改委规划司."十四五"规划《纲要》名词解释之3|高质量发展. (2021-12-24)[2023-8-1]. https://www.ndrc.gov.cn/fggz/fzzlgh/gjfzgh/202112/t20211224_1309252.html.

创新发展成了国家经济发展的重要任务之一，同时随着数字化时代的到来，导入数字化产业和推动传统产业数字化成为老工业园区升级的重要方式。

2.中观上：围绕北京"四个中心"功能建设成为首都产业腾笼换鸟的核心

根据《北京城市总体规划（2016—2035年）》，北京的一切工作必须坚持全国政治中心、文化中心、国际交流中心、科技创新中心的城市战略定位。在战略定位的导向下，首都产业发展要坚持有所为有所不为，着力提升首都功能，有效疏解非首都功能，实现"腾笼换鸟"。体育产业作为绿色健康的朝阳产业，是与"四个中心"定位高度契合的业态，北京市相关规划都将其列为重点发展的产业。近五年来，国家和北京市陆续出台了多项体育产业促进政策，体育产业势必将在首都经济转型和结构调整中发挥越来越重要的作用。

3.微观上：新首钢园区承载的冬奥遗产创新再利用成为国内外关注的焦点

随着北京2022年冬奥会和冬残奥会的成功举办，冬奥遗产再利用成为后冬奥时期重要的工作内容。新首钢园区作为冬奥组委办公园区、首钢滑雪大跳台（冬奥会北京赛区唯一的雪上比赛场馆）、"四块冰"（冰球、短道速滑、冰壶、花样滑冰国家队首钢园区训练基地）、冬奥广场的承载地，拥有诸多冬奥遗产，如何利用好新首钢园区的冬奥遗产，推动新首钢园区体育产业创新发展成为属地政府和首钢集团的重要任务，特别是赛后十年的转型发展和再利用成为国内外关注的焦点。同时在最新北京城市总体规划中，新首钢园区未来将成为传统工业绿色转型升级示范区、京西高端产业创新高地、后工业文化体育创意基地，这为新首钢未来十年的发展指明了方向。

综上，通过宏观、中观和微观层面的背景梳理，我们发现未来体育产业可以作为助力老工业园区转型升级的重要动力之一，也将成为新首钢未来发展的主要业态。

（二）研究目标

1.理论目标：全新视角下系统的梳理提炼和设计

本研究从物理技术和社会技术共演化的全新视角，以体育产业助力老工业园区转型发展为主线，采用学术性的话语体系对过去二十年首钢老工业园区向新首钢高端产业综合服务区转型升级路径进行了系统性的梳理和提炼，对未来十年新首钢高端产业综合服务区数字化升级提供了理论思路，为老工业园区的转型发展提供了一种新方向。

2.实践目标：为多层级提供产业化发展政策建议

本研究在理论的指导下，相关研究成果期望对于各级政府和园区运营单位有较好的实践应用价值，具体实践目标为：第一，努力为北京市后冬奥时期冬奥遗产的开发利用提供路径参考；第二，尽力为石景山区"三区建设"和体育产业高质量发展提供新的思路；第三，全力为新首钢高端产业综合服务区做优做强提供新的发展路径。

（三）研究方法

本研究在研究目标导向下采用了案例分析法（以新首钢高端产业综合服务区为主导案例，以厦门数字体育产业园区为借鉴对象）、实地调研法（走访北京市体育局、北京市科学技术委员会、石景山区体育局、首钢集团、园区入驻业态等）、专家访谈法（走访北京大学、北京体育大学、首都体育学院、北京理工大学的五位来自体育产业、数字智能、区域经济等领域的专家）和逻辑分析法进行相关研究。

（四）研究对象

本研究主要以体育产业助力下的老工业园区为研究对象，以新首钢高端产业综合服务区为案例主导对象（位于长安街西延长线与永定河绿色生态走廊交汇处，占地面积8.63平方公里，在地理区位、空间资源、历史文化、生态环境上具有独特优势。该园区1919年筹建，曾先后成为石景山炼铁厂、石景山钢铁厂、首都钢铁公司、首钢总公司等的场址。新首钢因夏奥而生，因冬奥而兴，如今已成为一个集商业、科技、体育、文旅等多种业态于一体的高端产业综合服务区），以厦门数字体育产业园区为借鉴对象。

二、理论基础

（一）核心概念界定

1.老工业区

老工业区是指在我国工业化进程中形成的、生产力相对落后、环境污染问题突出、资源利用率较低、产业结构难以调整的工业区域。这些区域往往存在大量的老旧工业企业和废弃厂房，面临着环境污染治理、产业结构转型升级等诸多问题。我国老工业区主要分布在东北、华北和华东地区，老工业区在全国城市用地总面积中占有一定比重。

2.物理技术

美国著名经济学家理查德·R.尼尔森（Richard R. Nelson）认为，进行经济活动通常需要两类技术，一类是对任何劳动分工意义相同的部分，即"物理技术（physical technology）"；另一类是劳动分工以及分工之间的协调模式，称为"社会技术（social technology）"。①

"物理技术"即人们通常意义上所说的"技术"，可以将其视为如生产技术、医疗技术等人们改造自然、利用自然和保护自然的工具。②

3.社会技术

日本哲学家三木清在其《技术哲学》中提到："技术存在于主体对环境的积极适应和使之发生变化并创造新的环境的过程中——如果我们所说的环境不仅仅指自然环境，还包括社会环境的话，那么除了有作用于自然的技术，还应当有作用于社会的技术。相对于自然技术来说，应当有社会技术。前者以自然科学为基础，而后者以社会科学为基础。"③

针对"社会技术"的类型，尼尔森认为"制度"属于社会技术的范畴，其是标准化的、具有行动预期的社会技术，因而法律、法规、政策等均属于社会技术。同时，产业商业模式对特定社会组织的经济绩效产生明显的影响，也是社会技术的重要内容之一。此外，社会技术具有文化共享性，需要一定更深层次的支撑结构，如特定的信仰体系、文化共识等。田鹏颖和陈凡将"社会技术"划分为如风俗习惯、道德规范等较早产生的、通过自我约束发挥作用的"作为意志的社会技术"，和法律、政策、制度、章程等通过外在强治实现改造社会作用的"作为制度的社会技术"。④沙德春将"社会技术"分为政策法规、产业商业模式与社会气质三个层次。⑤

尽管"物理技术"与"社会技术"共同演化的思想很早就有了，但已有研究仍更多关注"物理技术"对经济增长的贡献。实际上，经济增长应该是物理

① 陈忠.技术社会：历史转换与文明自觉——基于文明批评史的视角.学术研究，2024(01)：8-17.

② 田鹏颖.科学技术与社会(STS)——人类把握现代世界的一种基本方式.科学技术哲学研究，2012，29(03)：97-101.

③ 三木清.哲学入门.济南：山东画报出版社，2020.

④ 田鹏颖，陈凡.社会技术：改造社会的实践性知识体系.科学技术与辩证法，2002(04)：31-34+39.

⑤ 沙德春.科技园区转型机制研究——物理技术与社会技术共演化的视角.科学学研究，2016，34(01)：40-48+56.

技术与社会技术共同演化发展的过程。[①]物理技术创新为经济发展提供一系列的根本动力，而社会技术及其创新则在经济发展的每个阶段对自然技术及其创新起着重要的促进、支撑以及保障功能，二者相互推动，逐步进行协同演化。[②]

（二）理论框架

本研究以物理技术和社会技术共演化为理论视角，提炼首钢园区的两次转型的路径，并对首钢园区未来的第三次转型进行设计，以期为未来工业园区转型升级路径设计提供依据。

三、研究结果

（一）历史回溯：首钢园区第一次转型——夏季奥运会与钢厂搬迁

1.社会技术层面的变化

首钢园区在经历第一次转型的过程中，政策层面的社会技术获得显著发展。从20世纪70年代中期治理废水、80年代全面治理废气粉尘等污染，到90年代实施源头治理和全过程清洁生产，首都地区高度重视环境保护工作。同时，2001年7月13日，在莫斯科举行的国际奥委会第112次全会上，国际奥委会投票选定北京获得2008年奥运会主办权。首钢园区面临国家钢铁工业远景布局调整和兑现2008年北京"绿色奥运"的承诺。2005年，国务院批复《首钢实施搬迁、结构调整和环境治理方案》，同意首钢搬迁至河北曹妃甸。

此后，首钢园区成为北京市"十二五"规划中重点培育的产业新区，北京市"十二五"规划纲要确定首钢园区转型"为新首钢高端产业综合服务区"，将其作为吸引制造业企业总部和研发中心的经济高地。[③]

2.物理技术层面的变化

在首钢园区的第一次转型中，以促进园区发展为目标的一系列政策出台，对物理技术的快速持续发展产生了重要作用。

自2005年2月国家发改委正式批复首钢搬迁方案，至2010年12月底首钢石景山厂区一号高炉熄火停产，首钢园区结束了其在京91年的钢铁生产历

---

① 张颖颖，胡海青. 二元技术能力、制度环境与创业绩效——来自孵化产业的实证研究. 科技进步与对策，2016，33(18): 113-120.
② 任东峰. 区域创新生态系统演进动力的美国硅谷案例——基于自然技术与社会技术共演化的视角. 技术经济与管理研究，2021(07): 12-15.
③ 北京"十二五"规划纲要解读——打造"两城两带"新格局. (2011-01-24)[2024-02-01]. https://www.beijing.gov.cn/zhengce/zcjd/201905/t20190523_77265.html.

史，实现了在物理空间上的转移。2013年至2015年，首钢园区确立了包括主厂区在内的改造、新建、基础设施等11个项目的整体转型方案，正式进入转型发展的新阶段。首钢主厂区功能分区确定为"五区两带"，"五区"包括工业主题园、文化创意产业园、综合服务中心区、总部经济区和综合配套区；"两带"包括滨河综合休闲带和城市公共活动休闲带。原本在生产环节中用于储存和运输炼铁厂原料的西十筒仓，被改造为一栋栋七层高创意办公空间。在物理技术层面，首钢园区的第一次转型实现了物理空间上的转移和园区设施的改造利用。

3. 第一次转型路径提炼

在首钢园区社会技术与物理技术各自获得发展的同时，两种技术之间也形成了一定程度上的交互影响。在《首钢实施搬迁、结构调整和环境治理方案》政策的影响下，首钢园区开始进行整体搬迁，实现物理空间的转移；以《北京市国民经济和社会发展第十二个五年规划纲要》为起点，首钢园区以产业升级为目标进行设施的改造利用。可见，社会技术的发展对首钢园区物理技术的创新产生了重要作用。

总结而言，首钢园区第一次转型过程中社会技术与物理技术交互的自发性并不突出，主要表现为社会技术作为主要的推动力。

（二）现状分析：首钢园区第二次转型——冬季奥运会与首钢复兴

2016年5月，北京2022年冬奥组委入驻西十筒仓，成为首钢园区开发建设的里程碑事件。以冬奥破局城市更新，首钢园区全面落实"三年行动计划"，加快从"火"到"冰"的转型，从厂区、园区向社区、街区转变，成为首钢园区第二次转型的重要标志。首钢园区第二次转型在物理技术和社会技术层面主要体现为以下几个方面。

1. 物理技术层面的变化

（1）园区整体规划转型升级

首钢园区第二次转型整体规划由北京城市规划设计研究院规划设计，分为冬奥广场、石景山景观公园、工业遗址公园、公共服务配套区、城市织补创新工场五大片区。在此规划基础上，由北京首钢建设投资有限公司牵头负责单栋建筑物的设计、改建，形成首钢园区体育场馆群，初步形成了国际化视野的潮流运动中心和体育＋产业融合创新中心。

第一，首钢将高炉筒仓、料仓改造为冬奥组委办公区，用于服务保障冬奥。首钢与国家体育总局共建体育产业示范区，将电力厂精煤车间改造为国家冬季运动训练中心，建立了短道、花样、冰壶、冰球四个冰上场馆，积极服务保障国家队备战北京 2022 年冬奥会训练。同时，新建北京冬奥会市区内唯一的奥运雪上项目正式比赛场地——滑雪大跳台。

第二，首钢设计利用老工业厂房、设施改造建立了滑板场、攀岩场、空中步道和三高炉博物馆等一批场馆设施，用于发展体育产业。其中，首钢三高炉博物馆利用炼铁高炉改造，是园区内最典型的工业风建筑，充分利用高炉内部空间、地下空间，与秀池融为一体，可承接电竞、体育展会等大型体育活动。

第三，首钢将园区内石景山景观公园、群明湖、绿轴景观、三高炉、高线公园（群明湖北段、绿轴西段）等特色景观进行规划设计，用于户外运动休闲。初步形成山—水—工业遗存特色景观体系。同时道路以鲜明的工业风建筑为背景，与园区外的永定河河堤路共同构成了特色道路，可规划 10 公里路跑、半程马拉松等路跑项目。位于园区西北部海拔 183 米的石景山，拥有众多名胜古迹，既是城市公园，也可运营户外运动项目。

（2）园区场馆建设转型升级

第一，在场馆设施方面，首钢园区建有短道速滑、花样滑冰、冰壶、冰球四个冰上场馆，以及滑雪大跳台、攀岩场、滑板场、空中步道、首钢三高炉博物馆等设施，用于日常举办冰上项目、单板及自由式滑雪、足球、篮球、滑板、轮滑、小轮车、跑酷、攀岩、电子竞技等数十项赛事。其中，首钢园区内老工业厂房改造建成冰球、冰壶、花样滑冰、短道速滑四个场馆，均具备专业级、赛事级、国际级、奥运级标准，用于日常举办国际级赛事以及开展高端体育培训。首钢极限公园包含攀岩场、滑板场、休闲区三个部分，总占地面积1.79 万平方米，其中攀岩场 4261 平方米、滑板场 4386 平方米、休闲区 9266平方米。场地规模在国内居于前三位，是北京市最大的户外滑板、攀岩场。滑雪大跳台是北京冬奥会市区内唯一的奥运雪上项目正式比赛场地，在设计上，借鉴敦煌壁画中大量表现的飘带边缘，随空气舞动变换形成飞天飘逸感形象，为大跳台本身赋予飞天概念，突出飘逸感。其不仅仅是一座体育比赛场馆，而且已经成为一个旅游景点和网红打卡地。

第二，在园区入驻企业方面，首钢园区成为奥林匹克运动带动城市更新的典型范例。成功举办北京冬奥会，发挥其对区域发展、品牌引进、消费促进的带动作用，园区产业活力有效提升。北京冬奥会成功举办，首钢滑雪大跳台成为中国队"双金福地"和整个世界的网红地。《2022 首钢园产业发展报告》显示，首钢园区入园企业 270 多家，注册资本达 400 亿元。在园企业人数近 4000 人，重点产业类企业三年营收复合增长速度达到 112%。2022 年，首钢园区重点产业类企业研发费用支出合计约 3.9 亿元，研发人员占比 67%。其中，近 40% 企业研发投入强度超过 100%。2022 年在园重点产业类企业共拥有专利授权 195 项，其中发明专利 33 项。大力构建以"科技＋"为主导，以特色高端商务服务、科技服务业为支撑的高精尖产业体系。2022 年在园重点产业类企业中，以互联网 3.0、人工智能、航空航天等高精尖产业为代表的"科技＋"企业占比达 70%。此外，园区内相关配套服务设施一应俱全，包括星巴克咖啡厅、全民畅读读书社、京东无人奶茶店、首钢工舍酒店、秀池酒店、红楼迎宾馆以及秀池地下停车场，也满足消费者因运动而衍生的休闲娱乐等方面的消费需求，为北京市民提供了一个舒适、安全的文化体育休闲娱乐中心，同时也为园区举办大型体育活动奠定了基础。

2. 社会技术层面的变化

（1）高质量的运营服务体系

第一，在场馆运营方面，首钢园区将自身定位为以重要国际国家活动为依托，以科技创新孵化机构、科技产业投资基金、科技创新联合体、科创大奖赛事为支撑，面向政策对接、人才服务、市场合作、融资服务、应用场景、公共服务平台的产业培育生态。为了更好地运营首钢园区体育场馆设施，首钢集团全资成立了北京首钢园运动中心运营管理有限公司，该公司根据园区实际情况，针对不同的板块采取不同运营模式。一是在传统场馆租赁的基础上，利用场地优势资源，优化合作模式，以场地入股的形式与高端体育培训机构合作，共同开展体育培训业务，提高场地运营收益。二是与相关协会及单位联系，利用场馆的专业优势和园区配套服务优势，开展专业训练。目前，首钢园区已引入腾讯体育、安踏体育、武界体育、泰山体育、汤姆冰壶等 14 家知名体育公司。同时，冰球馆 360° 全景观赛项目已上线，腾讯体育演播间项目已正式运营，腾讯视频制氧厂演播厅项目将于 2021 年中投入运营。2019 年度总计体育产业增加值为 12085.6 万元，占地区体育产业增加值占 GDP 的比重为 21.51%。

第二，在赛事运营方面，充分发挥首钢园体育场馆群落和空间的优势，引入世界顶级冰雪运动、户外运动、电子竞技等顶级赛事 IP 落户，为园区的发展吸引人流，从而带动园区酒店住宿、餐饮等行业的发展。首钢园区从顶级赛事IP引进、体育培训、构建体育文化消费生态圈以及体育行业龙头企业引进方面入手，以打造体育服务综合体、国际化视野的潮流运动中心和体育＋产业融合创新中心为目标。首钢园区内已举办各类国际大型比赛和文化活动近百场，累计现场观看10余万人次。在2019年举办的大型体育活动主要有：2019中芬冬季运动年开幕式、2022北京冬奥会和冬残奥会吉祥物发布活动、2020北京新年倒计时、京交会、2018—2019赛季KHL大陆冰球联赛（北京赛区）、2019国际冰联冰球女子世锦赛甲级B组赛事、2018—2019世界壶联冰壶世界杯总决赛、2019沸雪北京国际雪联单板及自由式滑雪大跳台世界杯等。

（2）高水平的产业社会效益

第一，在体育文化消费方面，首钢园区探索大众休闲消费的商业模式，利用空中步道及工业遗址公园大规模城市绿地等空间的体育设施，围绕这些资源合理规划餐饮、娱乐等消费场景，再加上举办体育赛事所带来的引流，逐渐形成体育活动与娱乐消费、场地广告、衍生品售卖等为一体的生态圈，形成首钢园区特有的体育文化服务综合体。目前，首钢园区已形成了集餐饮、酒店、零售、展览、体验等多元于一体的特色消费生态，据统计，自2020年5月园区向社会开放以来，累计入园客流量达1100万人次。北京冬奥会后，首钢园区推进冬奥遗产可持续利用，首钢滑雪大跳台率先向社会公众开放，2022年超过100万人次参观首钢滑雪大跳台；首钢冰球馆举办中国电视剧"飞天奖""星光奖"颁奖盛典、冬奥一周年系列活动启动仪式等。一系列科技文化体育活动吸引游客纷至沓来，2023年上半年，首钢园区举办各类展览活动168场。冬奥遗产正在成为首钢园区高质量发展的新动能。发挥重大项目带动作用，新首钢国际人才社区项目将打造"国际人才聚集区、人才政策试验区、创新创业示范区、宜居宜业典范区"。怡和项目、华夏银行项目加快落地实施，吸引优质资源和高端人才等各类要素集聚。

第二，在体育场馆收益方面，利用场地优势资源，优化合作模式，以场地入股的形式与高端体育培训机构合作，共同开展体育培训业务，提高场地运营收益。

3.第二次转型路径提炼——物理技术和社会技术共演化经验总结

（1）利用服务冬奥高端客户的机会，提升场馆运营服务能力

第一，利用服务冬奥高端客户的机会，提升专业能力和形象。利用为冬奥组委、冬训中心、大跳台等冬奥项目服务的机会，提升场馆专业化、标准化制

冰、扫冰、设备维护水平，打造首钢冰场优质、高端品牌。同时借助此机会争取"国家冬季项目训练基地"挂牌，为冬奥会后长期承接国家级、省级以上冰上队伍训练创造条件。

第二，引入专业运营机构，提升可持续运营能力。深入研究场馆开发的盈利模式和主要任务，根据首钢园区场地设施小规模、多元化、室内外结合等特点，通过场馆专业化服务和市场开发，将赛事需要与日常综合利用有机结合，使场馆运营在时间上形成可持续性，在空间上装满内容。其中，首钢极限公园攀岩场地以购买服务的形式与专业运营机构进行合作，提升场馆专业化、市场化、国际化运作能力。

（2）合理规划资源，促进体育多业态融合消费

第一，打造集聚体育＋产业链企业。围绕产业上下游，集聚体育龙头企业，吸引企业在园区设立适合北京产业定位的企业总部、融合创新业务部门、研发中心、制作中心、旗舰店、展示体验中心等，重点聚焦体育装备、赛事运营、运动服务等体育核心领域，以及体育＋文化传媒、体育＋创新科技等新兴领域，推动龙头企业落户并定期举办新品首发、赛事启动等活动。

第二，整合资源业态，促进体育多业态融合消费。将极限运动公园、工业遗址公园绿轴区域作为时尚潮流运动主要承载区，面向年轻时尚人群，积极开展各项时尚潮流运动，实现时尚潮流运动项目和群体的集聚。同时，围绕这些资源合理规划餐饮、娱乐等消费场景，形成体育文化消费新业态。

（3）发挥首钢独特工业风貌的优势，打造首钢特色体育IP

第一，宣传首钢场馆IP。充分发挥首钢园近城山水相依，重工业风貌独特的优势，导入知名度高的体育赛事、户外音乐节等文体活动，形成周期性热点；挖掘首钢园体育文化内涵，加大主流媒体、网络媒体对赛事和场馆设施的宣传力度，打造京西场馆设施新地标。

第二，落地特色精品赛事，提升客群流量和质量。积极对接冬奥组委和国家、市体育部门，引入冬奥冰雪运动、时尚潮流、电子竞技等顶级赛事；将承接高水平队伍集训与承办不同级别赛事活动协同起来，把接待日常群众运动娱乐与相关俱乐部合作培训结合起来，形成常态化运营体系，聚集年轻、时尚人群，形成体育健身、娱乐、社交的聚合地，持续为园区消费引流。

第三，引进国际赛事IP。围绕冬奥冰雪和潮流运动，引入沸雪世界杯等一批可连续多年在园区举办的赛事IP；充分发挥首钢园区工业风貌的独特优势，

将园区道路、工业遗址公园、空中步道联动，引入路跑等户外赛事，如 2019 彭博一英里接力赛（北京站）、2019 国际雪联越野滑雪积分大奖赛等。

（三）未来设计：首钢园区第三次转型

1.困境分析

随着冬奥会的结束，首钢园区的场馆面临政策支持资金集中支持、人才重点配备等力度较冬奥会有较大幅度下降、资源融合渠道不畅等问题。同时，协调政府、市场、社会组织、社会公众等不同利益需求，关键要解决不同利益相关者行为过程中面临的主要难题。通过调研得知，其问题主要体现在：

第一，受过去新冠疫情持续冲击，首钢园区运营获取经济效益的需求更加突出，较难与政府制度设计初衷相匹配。

第二，首钢园区场馆向公众开放与消费者培育衔接不紧密。场馆开放可以有效增加社会公众参与冬奥场馆冰雪活动体验的人数，而庞大的人口体验基数与市场潜力的开发程度直接挂钩。目前，首钢园区许多场馆尽管向社会开放，但是在产品和服务的转化衔接上缺乏系统性。例如体育服装、器材、餐饮、娱乐等延伸产品和服务没有配套，首钢园区体育综合体建设亟待提上日程。

第三，首钢园区场馆健康理念贯彻落实不系统，社会效益释放不充分。伴随全民健身战略深入开展，冬奥场馆推动健康促进的作用更加凸显，冬奥场馆的形象、业务、管理等急需围绕人民健康打造。但是，目前场馆管理中对健康含义的表达并不完整。访谈了解到冬奥场馆促进全民健康的理念并未有效表达，管理人员健康业务培训、场馆健康符号表达等没有系统体现健康主线。

第四，冬奥教育开展不深入，社会责任未有效承担。首钢园区的冬奥场馆作为中国冬奥精神的历史"见证者"，已经被赋予冬奥精神外物化的教育标签。然而，各冬奥场馆对冬奥教育角色准备并不充分，如国家高山滑雪中心开放仅限于旅游参观，虽然后期开展了明星同款餐饮体验等活动，但仍没有形成冬奥教育的系统模式，不利于首钢园区冬奥场馆发挥冬奥教育功能、承担部分冬奥教育的社会责任。

2.环境分析

PEST 为一种企业所处宏观环境的分析模型。所谓 PEST，即 Political（政治环境）、Economic（经济环境）、Social（社会环境）和 Technological（科技环境），这些是企业的外部环境，一般不受企业掌握。

第一，政治环境：冬奥场馆赛后社会资源支持力度缩减，人财物聚合效果有所削弱。例如：北京冬奥会筹备期间，政府投入 10 亿元用于首都体育馆等 5 个项目的改扩建工程，以满足场馆承担短道速滑等项目的基本要求。冬奥会结束后，国家对冬奥场馆赛后运营的政策性支持减少，协调、对接高水平运动队等社会资源难度增大，自负盈亏经营遭受成本挑战，凝聚人财物的能力缺乏雄厚资本支撑，对冬奥场馆赛后可持续利用目标的实现造成不利影响。

第二，经济环境：市场主导下赛后资源融合机制亟待开发。北京冬奥会的筹办汇聚了政府、社会等多方资源，形成了政府主导下的资源融合机制。北京奥运会结束后冬奥场馆逐渐交由市场主体运营开发，政府主导资源融合模式也向市场主导模式过渡。目前市场主导资源融合的效力仍然不强，融合机制暂不完善，需要政府延续配套政策予以持续支持并协助对接各类社会资源，由市场进行深度开发，逐渐建立市场主导的资源配置力量

第三，社会环境：比赛前后人力资源的衔接机制欠缺，造成场馆赛后利用的专业人才短缺。冬奥会期间，场馆管理方面聚集了大量水、电、消防、运营等方面的专业人才，但由于缺乏场馆管理衔接机制，这些专业人才经验难以有效传递，冬奥场馆面临专业人才匮乏问题。尽管运营者面向社会招募人才，但是培养熟悉体育、管理、运营的复合型工作人员需要较长时间，特别是国家雪车雪橇中心等对专业性要求较高的场馆，其复合型管理人员培养周期则更长，这无疑影响着冬奥场馆赛后可持续利用的进程。

第四，科技环境：冬奥科技和冬奥文化氛围降温，科技文化资源新渠道亟待拓展。北京冬奥会的举办引发我国民众对冬奥会的普遍关注。首钢园特色体育IP未形成规模。充分认识到体育IP对示范基地发展的重要性后，首钢园依托于其优美的山水交融自然环境与工业风相结合的特点，重点打造园区时尚潮流运动，2020 年已在首钢极限公园探索打造了一些自主体育IP项目，但还未形成规模。园区独特体育品牌效应未形成，亟需培育一批自主特色体育IP，引进一批与园区特点高度契合的较有影响力体育IP，将首钢园基地进一步打造成京西靓丽的体育名片。

3.标杆借鉴

厦门数字体育产业园是火炬高新区管委会联合市体育局、集美区，在软件园三期打造的一个数字＋体育创新载体。园区按照"一中心、多基地"模式，通过开放厦门体育产业应用场景，引进培育一批规模以上数字体育企业，利用大数据、云计算、人工智能、物联网等新技术，为体育制造业、体育服务业等

相关项目赋能，从而推动厦门数字体育经济发展。园区还将配套相关数字体育产业扶持政策，在应用示范、招商、研发、金融、人才等方面提供奖励。作为厦门软件园"数字＋行业"的专业园区，厦门市数字体育产业园将重点发展"体育＋"，以数字技术、大数据、人工智能等创新技术为手段，利用厦门软件园三期的产业基础和资源优势，引入大数据、VR/AR、5G、人工智能等数字体育技术，推进"数字＋体育"新业态，赋能升级体育装备制造业、服务业等传统体育行业，打造数字体育产业生态。

在招商引资方面，数字体育产业园将重点招引数字体育相关的研发机构、数字体育服务企业等优质企业入驻；同时依托厦门软件园三期的产业基础和资源优势，着力推动大数据、5G等新兴技术与体育产业深度融合。园区将配套数字体育产业扶持政策，为数字体育企业提供开放应用场景、应用示范奖励、招商奖励、研发奖励、金融和人才奖励。随着数字体育产业园的出现，"厦门数字体育产业联盟"也因此应运而生，并有包括咪咕新空、直播吧、奥佳华等14家企业作为联盟的发起单位。厦门数字体育产业联盟是企业自发、非营利性质、互利协作的平台。

在运营服务方面，大数据和人工智能作为体育科技的重要一环也同样被广泛应用于竞技体育和群众体育中。厦门也是数字体育产业发展较好的城市，就在最近，工信部、国家体育总局公布100项2022年度智能体育典型案例，涉及5个方向，厦门7个案例入选。厦门体育产业在体育用品制造、体育赛事活动、体育设施建设等都具有得天独厚的优势，数字体育旨在夯实数字中国建设基础，全面赋能经济社会发展，推动数字技术和体育产业经济的深度融合，打造具有国际竞争力的厦门数字体育产业集群。充分发挥联盟成员单位在厦门数字体育产业发展中的引领带动作用，推动数字化技术在体育领域的创新应用，促进厦门数字体育产业高质量发展。

4.第三次升级路径设计

（1）服务冬奥高端客户，铸造首钢场馆IP。一是加强服务队伍专业培训，着力提升冬奥组委、冬训中心、大跳台等冬奥项目的服务水平，为冬奥组委运转、国家队备战训练、大跳台办赛提供有力保障。二是积极对接推动、争取"国家冬季项目训练基地"挂牌，为冬奥会后长期承接国家级、省级以上冰上队伍训练创造条件。三是培养专业人才，提升场馆专业化、标准化制冰、扫冰、设备维护水平，打造首钢冰场优质、高端品牌。四是充分挖掘首钢园体育文化内涵，发挥首钢园近城山水相依，重工业风貌独特的优势，加大主流媒体、网络媒体对赛事和大跳台等场馆设施的宣传力度，打造京西场馆设施特色IP。

（2）积累专业人才资源，发展高端体育培训服务。通过服务冬奥组委、承接国家队训练，与相关管理机构、行业协会、国际级和国家级专业人才建立广泛稳定的合作关系，开发高端专业培训体系，提供国际冰上运动、极限运动高端服务，将"四块冰"、极限公园打造为面向国际教练员、裁判员、制冰师、器材师、定线员等的培训、交流合作基地和国际、国内相关标准的形成基地，提升体育场馆的市场、商业价值。

（3）培育首钢特色赛事IP，提升客群流量和质量。积极围绕冬奥冰雪、潮流运动和电子竞技，引入滑雪大跳台世界杯等一批可连续多年在园区举办的赛事IP；将承接高水平队伍集训与承办不同级别赛事活动协同起来，把接待日常群众运动娱乐与相关俱乐部合作培训结合起来，形成常态化运营体系；充分发挥首钢园区工业风貌的独特优势，将大跳台、极限公园、工业遗址公园、空中步道联动，量身定做，创办跨项目、综合性自主赛事IP，如首钢园半程马拉松、园区定向越野、新铁人三项、勇士挑战赛、超越极限赛等，建成体育健身、娱乐、社交的聚合地。

（4）塑造潮流目的IP，完善宜居宜业环境。基于极限运动公园、工业遗址公园绿轴和空中步道等特色区域，面向年轻时尚人群，积极导入各项时尚潮流运动，培育时尚化、社区化、常态化、年轻化，线上线下联动的多样活动，打造跑酷、轮滑、篮球、园区定向等"社区联赛""周赛"。对接体育专业院校、体育互联网社区类企业、体育专业服务机构等资源，导入攀岩、滑板、潜水、击剑等潮流运动，集聚一批时尚潮流人群，打造北京潮流运动中心IP，实现时尚潮流运动项目和消费群体的引流。

（5）办好大型体育赛事活动，提升园区体育休闲娱乐消费热度。以首钢极限公园为主办地，充分利用园区道路、三高炉等资源，统筹策划，科学安排，突出重点，办好一系列体育赛事活动，持续提升园区体育休闲娱乐消费热度。一是周密部署，办好极限嘉年华、中国冰雪大会，提升首钢园极限运动、冰雪运动影响力。二是精心策划，办好自主IP的"夏日激情汇"、首钢园冰雪汇等活动，提升自主品牌活动影响力。三是精诚合作，推动X-GAMES落户首钢园，举办滑板街式挑战赛、北马亲子跑、彭博一英里、斯巴达勇士赛等赛事活动。

太仓港经济技术开发区调查报告——港区工业园贯彻绿色发展理念的成功案例分析[①]

摘　要：生态化建设是中国式现代化的核心内容之一，工业发展应当符合绿色可持续发展需要，实现创新转型，达到节能环保的目的。太仓港经济技术开发区（太仓港区）是港区工业园贯彻绿色发展理念的成功案例，其港口建设、园区规划、污染防治、科技创新方面都贯彻了可持续发展的原则，使其成为港区工业园绿色发展的模范。本文将具体分析太仓港经济技术开发区的发展情况和主要转型措施，提炼其成功经验，为港区工业园区的绿色发展提出新的发展思路。

关键词：太仓港经济技术开发区；绿色可持续发展；循环经济

一、引　言

（一）研究背景与选题目的

2022年11月28日，联合国贸易和发展协会（UNCTAD）发布了《2022年海运回顾》报告，强调了港口和绿色发展航运建设的重要性。在2021年，中国国务院发布了《2030年前碳达峰行动方案的通知》，其中提出了建设节能低碳和绿色工业园区的目标。这表明，绿色港口和绿色工业园区的建设刻不容缓。当下，港口工业园区作为"港口"和"工业园"的有机结合体，必将朝着绿色发展的方向迈进。

然而，中国港口工业园区的绿色发展道路依然面临着艰巨的任务和长期的挑战：首先，部分港口工业园区长期奉行旧有的工业发展模式，未将可持续发

---

① 作者：蒋佩珈，深圳大学；朱剑锋，深圳大学；陈锦华，深圳大学。

展作为重点，盲目追求经济增长，牺牲生态环境，造成难以逆转的生态损害，反过来制约了其自身的经济发展；其次，部分港口工业园区科技创新活力不足，无法实现科技创新到绿色发展的转型；最后，受制于种种困境，部分港口工业园区缺乏政府的有效治理，政策体系不够完善，使得生态破坏问题长期无法得到解决。

位于江苏省苏州市太仓市东部的太仓港区成立于1993年，其主要产业涵盖了石油化工、电力能源、船舶、生物医药等领域。2001年，该园区获批成为国家级经济技术开发区。由于长期无节制的发展，长三角工业园区普遍面临空气质量差，水污染严重等问题，对于当地环境、出海口水质都造成巨大威胁，太仓港区也不例外。2021年以前，该园区被列入中国污染程度最严重的港口工业园区之一。然而，经过两年的发展，以及一系列政策改革、技术创新、港口建设、污染治理后，该港区已成功走上绿色转型之路，成为该类工业园区绿色可持续发展的模范，其成功经验对于其他工业园区转型具有参考意义。

因此，本研究报告以太仓港经济技术开发区为例，对其成功的绿色发展举措进行深入分析，旨在为该类工业园区的绿色转型提供新思路。

（二）研究方法与数据来源

本文研究设计类型为案例研究，采用单一案例研究法。绿色发展相关政策来自"太仓市人民政府"网站。绿色港口建设举措及相关成效的数据来自"江苏太仓港口管理委员会官网：太仓港绿色港口三年行动专题"[①]；园区内企业具体案例来自网站"太仓港电子口岸"中各企业上传的总结报告[②]，通过对照整体目标、政策以及相关落实情况的具体效果，以及后续进一步规划，该报告将从企业责任、技术创新、港口建设、政府管理三个维度体现太仓港区绿色发展过程，列举其成功经验。

---

① 江苏太仓港口管理委员会. 太仓水上绿色综合服务区首月迎来"开门红". (2021-04-01)[2023-12-14]. http://www.tcport.gov.cn/tcg/snxd/202104/805ea216f33347e0b5fcb071e082a78a.shtml.
② 太仓港口管理委员会. 绿色港口之苏州现代货箱码头. (2020-01-17)[2023-12-14]. http://www.tcport.gov.cn/tcg/snxd/202001/1c539d7ba9a64fa3991076136afb1bf4.shtml.

二、太仓港经济技术开发区绿色发展举措分析

（一）发挥企业科技创新优势，在生产层面减少污染

技术是绿色转型的重要驱动力，工业园区内绿色技术的研发活力对其转型进度起到决定作用，而太仓港经济技术开发区具有集聚创新驱动型企业这一优势：园区内企业积极投资研发，运用智能化、自动化清洁技术，降低作业全过程当中排放的有害气体、粉尘等污染物，更进一步研发回收技术，实现"循环经济"，不仅实现了大气污染防控治理，还降低了人工成本，获得经济收益，充分体现出港区内企业对于落实绿色发展理念的主要作用：

1.油气回收系统

港区企业大力投资油气回收技术的研发，例如，太仓阳鸿石化有限公司建立三套油气回收系统（两套油气回收、一套甲醇尾气回收系统），防止油气挥发污染港口环境，提高对能源的利用率，同时利用油气回收项目赚取经济效益，助力零污染、低能耗港口的建设。

2.可挥发气体检测装置

太仓阳鸿石化有限公司推出的LDAR"泄漏检测与修复"检测装置，可减少挥发性有机化合物排放及物料损失，最大限度降低安全隐患，减少职业伤害，保护员工健康，改善公司和港区环境质量。

3.智能化抑尘系统

将智能化运用到防尘治理领域。世界上首个将激光雷达扫描技术应用于大型散料堆场监控的装置——华能太仓港务有限公司采用激光雷达装置，可发射脉冲激光，对堆场上空的粉尘浓度进行侦查，并联动水雾喷淋装置进行抑尘，是行之有效的空气污染防治装置。

（二）不断更新港口基建，推动能源转型与自动化管理

港口工业园区不同于其他类型工业园区，其"港口建设"也是园区绿色发展的重点领域。港口的基本工作中所产生的污染和能源消耗也是园区绿色转型过程中亟待解决的问题，而"绿色港口建设"项目本身也能为园区内企业节约运输能源成本，减轻降低污染的压力，太仓港区从"岸电设施""装卸基建""管理平台""污染治理"领域加强港口绿色发展能力建设，以下为具体举措：

1.港口岸电设施建设

太仓港区大力推动港口岸电设施的建设，"以电代油"，使船舶在靠港期间可以接受岸电供电，以减少船舶燃油发电所带来的污染，从源头减排，降低硫氧化物和颗粒物等排放。

2."油改电"技术推广

太仓港区通过"油改电"技术将柴油机驱动的柴油龙门吊替换为电力发动的龙门吊，经过四期排查检测更换（分别于 2008 年、2014 年、2018 年、2021 年进行）[①]，港区内所有龙门吊都已升级完成，该举措大幅减少了柴油消耗和排放，为港口能源消费结构优化做出了贡献。

3.光伏设施建设

太仓港区华能太仓港务有限公司在太仓港区建成了苏南地区单体最大的光伏发电项目，推动港口区域的绿色能源转型。

4.AI技术应用

太仓港区通过将AI技术应用于闸口业务，建设起"太仓港电子口岸"平台，实现无纸化操作，提高了工作效率，减少用电消耗，节约用电及人工成本。

5.港区污染管理

太仓港区实施"一企一管"的排污管理策略，建设在线监管体系，构建区域协同生态建设共同体，实现港区、企业、民众共建共管，高效监督企业绿色发展的具体落实状况。

6.多式联运体系建设

港口工业园区同时担任交通枢纽的角色，太仓港区根据"宜水则水，宜铁则铁，宜公则公"的原则，构建了多式联运体系，实现港口、园区的公转铁、散改集、路改水。新增多条海铁和公铁示范线路，打通铁路进港的"最后一公里"，降低物流成本，减少能源损耗，实现一体化运作。

（三）政府主导下政企港联动的出色发挥

政府协调当地资源，推出扶持政策，对于区域协调发展，全港污染防控起到重要作用，太仓港港口管理委员会、太仓市人民政府，以及太仓海事局积极

---

① 江苏太仓港口管理委员会.苏州：十四载"油改电"之路 太仓港打造绿色发展新局面. (2021-08-25)
[2023-12-14]. http://www.tcport.gov.cn/tcg/snxd/202108/705845bc0d02426f897fd5c2d264a677.shtml.

参与规划园区绿色转型道路，与园区内企业高效配合，在"污水排放""水上服务区""专题活动"方面着手，发挥了制度优势，助力该园区实现"零污染"目标。[①]

1.人工湿地项目

港区因地制宜，充分调动周边绿色资源并合理规划运用。太仓港区利用其化学园区内的生态湿地，与太仓港城组团污水处理厂共同构成生态湿地净水工程，即建立"生态缓冲区"，通过对污水处理厂尾水进行深度处理，净化水源，削减长江的水污染负荷，该工程实施后，每年减少入江排放量840万吨。

2.水上绿色服务区

太仓港区在太仓海事局的指导下建立了水上绿色服务区，主要用于接收内河船舶污染物。这一服务区通过宣传提高船员环保意识，鼓励船员主动联系送交污染物，指导单位在线上信息系统注册，促进污染物接收信息化、无纸化，制定奖惩机制和内部管理制度，与第三方接收单位签订委托协议等方式确保污染物接收规范化运行。

3.绿色专题活动

太仓港区通过开展综合治理活动，充分调动港区内企业绿色发展的积极性，使绿色发展理念在港区活动当中渗透每一个企业的日常管理、作业的过程。例如，港区管理委员会开展的"见缝插绿"工程、绿化提升工程、"红色港湾——绿色先锋"植树造林活动，为长江岸线增加一抹亮眼的"绿色"。

三、太仓港区绿色发展成功经验分析

太仓港区内企业、港口与政府的协同发力对其园区整体的绿色发展进程起到推动作用，该园区凭借其企业绿色技术创新、港口基础设施建设和智能化管理，并在政府的统筹协调下，成为该类工业园区绿色发展的成功典范。[②]本文通过具体分析其成功模式，为港口工业园区的绿色发展提供以下思路。

（一）港区企业积极承担责任，推动科技创新

企业作为港口工业园区的主体，担任最基本运行单位的角色。在港口工业

① 太仓市人民政府.港区深入实践绿色可持续发展.(2023-07-31)[2023-12-14].https://www.taicang.gov.cn/taicang/qzdt/202307/335c0d6728014a9bab74194e4338ab35.shtml.
② 苏州市发展和改革委员会.太仓：坚持生态优先绿色发展理念 让长江南岸天更蓝、水更清.(2018-11-01)[2023-12-14].http://fg.suzhou.gov.cn/szfgw/cjjjd/202011/05471561ada145a7bbb4e304d21638f3.shtml.

园区的绿色发展过程中，企业的能源转型与污染防治显然是至关重要的环节，太仓港区内企业通过"承担责任→加大科研投资力度→实现能源转型→重视污染防治→促进区域协调治理→带动其他企业"这一良性循环，为该园区的绿色发展做出贡献，以下是企业在该过程中发挥作用的具体方向。

1. 积极承担责任，配合园区协调

园区的绿色发展是其中各个企业的共同责任，与绿色转型直接相关企业（如电力能源、石油化工企业等）应当积极响应绿色发展要求，提高企业社会责任标准，肩负起重任，将绿色发展置于运营战略的核心位置进行深入研究。而与港口直接相关的企业（如码头企业）也应当致力于发挥自身作用，减少园区港口区域污染，推动能源转型，与港口工业园区的绿色发展方向和政策保持一致。为此，各类企业均需要根据实时政策调整发展模式，将开发重点和资金投入方向与绿色发展理念相协调，朝着环境友好、资源节约、可持续发展的目标与港区协同前进。

2. 推动相关技术研发，以科技赋能转型

园区内高污染重点产业（如石油化工、电力能源企业）必须通过高新技术解决港口污染的长期问题。若企业持续将资金用于机器购置和生产规模扩大，依赖低成本劳动力，则只能短暂维持现状，难以实现绿色转型。而太仓港区内企业改变了原有的老旧生产模式，在污染防治、资源回收利用领域高效应用新兴科技（如自动化装置，AI）解决污染问题，获得显著成效。因此，企业应加大高新技术研发投入，深耕智能化和自动化领域，为绿色发展提供智能设备支持，控制和减少排放，积极探索科技赋能的可持续绿色发展模式。

3. 实现能源转型

提高企业应积极发展绿色低碳能源，逐步减少对煤炭、柴油等传统能源的依赖，转而开发新能源基建（如光伏），以优化整个港区的能源结构，实现港口能源的清洁化；与此同时，企业需要提高能源的利用效率，减少能耗，在推动生产技术进步的同时改善能源使用方式，建立有效的能效管理系统（如自动化装置），减少能源浪费和废气排放；最后，探索可行的"循环经济"发展模式，提高资源回收率和再利用率（如油气回收、人工湿地等）。[①]

---

① 甘琛，吉余盛. 长江干线首家！太仓港"双智能化改造"完成　助力绿色低碳智能新趋势. (2022-07-13)[2023-12-14]. http://www.tcport.gov.cn/tcg/snxd/202207/54c54a3036b24df2b8d47f2316f56163.shtml.

4.企业间建立协同合作关系

在积极投资研发高新技术的同时，园区内企业还应相互建立协同合作关系，交流研发成果，共享资源，促进区域协调污染防治及管理。太仓港区建立起"太仓港电子口岸"，各企业可实时上传数据，共享信息，提高监管工作效率。同时，在政府的协调下，港区内化工企业与污水处理厂联合建设人工湿地，充分利用当地资源进行协同防治，发展出污水管理新思路。由此可见，企业间的联动有助于加速绿色技术的发展和应用，减少资源浪费。[①]

（二）绿色港口建设在港口工业园区绿色发展进程中效果显著

港口是港口工业园区最显著的特征，具有举足轻重的地位，相较于内陆工业园区，"港口"为工业园区的发展提供显著优势（如对外交流、高效运输等），提高了工业园区贯彻绿色发展理念的潜力。[②]推动港口的绿色建设对整个工业园区的绿色发展具有外部辐射效应，以下是港口发展的具体方向。

其一，港口管理应不断探索新的绿色治理模式，引入新兴科技（如AI技术）优化管理。为了提高港区的智能化水平，必须逐步进行港口基础设施的改造和智能化自动化系统的构建与运行，推广智能管理以实现线上线下协同治理。

其二，港口应充分利用港区多主体的优势，调动各主体积极参与港口的绿色发展建设，推动构建区域生态建设共同体，各主体共同监管、协同支持港口的绿色建设，多重保障港口防污减排。并且，在各主体的合作下，可实施类似港口岸电设施建设等大规模的港口生态建设项目，优化港口能源结构，防止污染，低碳减排。

其三，港口需要强化与企业在技术上的沟通与协作，有计划地推动港口设施的更新，提高港口的运作效率，减少资源浪费。

（三）政府应加强在港口工业园区绿色发展中的协调作用

政府在港口工业园区的规划、支持和监管方面扮演着关键角色，为中国式现代化港口工业园区的绿色发展提供了独特的优势。政府的生态建设布局对企业和港口管理委员会的绿色发展起到了统筹协调的作用，以下是政府的具体引

① 梅剑飞. 2020 年底江苏实现船舶污水零排放　打造"清水走廊". (2019-12-03)[2023-12-14]. http://www.tcport.gov.cn/tcg/snxd/201912/cd2b073a67a94d22b903f08e9293ef63.shtml.
② 梅剑飞. 江苏沿江打造绿色港口累计建成岸电设施 4000 余套. (2023-03-10)[2023-12-14]. http://www.tcport.gov.cn/tcg/snxd/202303/d9eafafa99e74014958285e2b00a96d6.shtml.

导方向。

1.政府引领智慧规划和强调资源整合

政府应鼓励港口工业园区充分利用地理条件，整合绿色资源，通过生态湿地和污水处理项目，有效减少污水排放，保护水资源。

2.政府引导港口工业园区在污染物管理上进行创新

政府有能力建设并完善生态管理体系，建立生态站点（如太仓港水上综合服务区），以此减轻港口的污染防控压力，以此推广环保意识，号召群众与企业共同监督，确保污染物的规范处理，促进内河船舶环境保护。

3.政府开展绿色专题专项活动

政府通过开展专题活动，发起大型环境整治项目来调动社会资源，促进环境美化。与此同时，集中展开专题活动也能够充分激发企业积极性，推进企业进行技术管理改革，推动其可持续发展进程，通过综合治理活动，增加绿化，实现环保与经济发展的协调。

4.政府可推动政府、企业和港口的三方协作

通过建立有效的沟通和交流系统，确保三方协作顺畅进行，为港口工业园区的绿色发展提供协同效应，实现1＋1＋1＞3的效果。与此同时，政府有能力推动产业和港口的融合发展模式，以保障政府对园区企业和港口的协调作用，这对于港口工业园区的绿色发展前景至关重要。

（四）完善环境治理和节能低碳的基础设施建设

先进的绿色治理模式和污染防控系统都是建立在基础设施建设完备的前提下运转的，只有环境治理和节能低碳的基础设施建设相对完善，实现港区的绿色发展才指日可待。因此，本研究特别指出基础设施建设对于绿色发展的关键作用，并为其发展提出以下方向。

1.基础设施设计强调可持续性和循环经济原则

港口码头可根据可再生能源供电并实行水资源循环，利用完善基础设施建设，以最大程度减少对自然资源的消耗。企业应在生产活动中强调可持续性和社会责任，这包括建设生态友好型厂房、采用清洁生产工艺、鼓励供应链的绿色化，以降低对自然资源的依赖。同时，政府要重点打造智能港口，通过打造智能管理和监控的基础设施，推动基础设施的数字化和智能化，有效提高码头的运行效率和减少能源浪费，提高可持续性。

2.港口工业园区采用绿色园区设计，以最大限度地保护当地生态系统

利用好当地的自然资源（如湿地），在不破坏当地生态的前提下，完善基础设施建设，这包括湿地保护、绿地带、生态走廊等，以维护生态平衡。

四、结　论

在联合国提出可持续发展目标的大背景下，探讨工业园区的绿色发展状况具有现实意义，港口工业园区相较于普通工业园区，自身具有"港口""对外开放"的属性，既是港区的比较优势，也是港区内企业、政府、港口、技术部门需要共同探索的重点。太仓港经济技术开发区是中国重点建设港区，经过22年的发展，它依托地方政策，推出污染治理方案，改良高新技术，发展自动化、智能化管理，实现循环经济、低碳能源转型等成就，并充分体现政企港协同发力这一制度优势，成为国内外港口工业园区绿色发展的模范，而其企业承担责任、政府支持监督、港口建设改造、科技持续研发的"四个维度"发展模式也已成为绿色发展探索的成功经验。

工业园区数字化转型与政策支持
——基于苏州工业园区的案例分析[①]

摘　要： 工业园区的数字化转型路径对于实现区域数字经济的蓬勃发展，对推动我国成为数字强国具有着极大的现实意义。苏州工业园区是数字化转型的先行者，在数字化转型方面取得了显著的成效。本文基于苏州工业园区数字化转型的成功案例，从基础设施建设、产业政策、人才政策和政府治理四个方面，梳理政府的支持措施，以期为其他工业园区数字化转型提供政策参考。

关键词： 工业园区；数字化转型；政策支持

一、引　言

发展数字经济是把握新一轮科技革命和产业变革新机遇的战略选择。为了进一步推动数字经济的整体发展和区域经济的数字化转型，国务院在 2021 年出台了《"十四五"数字经济发展规划》，其中明确提及，"引导产业园区加快数字基础设施建设，利用数字技术提升园区管理和服务能力"[②]。在这种实践导向变化和政策驱动下，数字化转型不仅是区域经济主体高质量发展的必由之路，更是政学业三界共同关注的热点问题。

数字经济通过高创新性、强渗透性、广覆盖性贯穿了经济发展的各领域，不仅提供了新的经济增长点，而且是改造提升传统产业的有力支点，日益成为加速建设现代化经济体系，推动经济高质量发展的重要引擎。而工业园区作为

---

① 作者：黄晓槐，武汉大学财政与税收系；白紫俊，武汉大学档案与政务信息学系；罗思语，武汉大学数字经济与智能商务系。

② 国务院关于印发"十四五"数字经济发展规划的通知. (2022-01-12)[2024-02-07]. https://www.gov.cn/zhengce/content/2022-01/12/content_5667817.htm.

产业集群的重要载体和区域经济结构调整的助推器，其数字化转型对于培育和壮大数字经济具有着不可忽视的作用。但是当前我国工业园区缺乏前瞻性规划，数字化基础设施刚刚起步，园区内基础设施建设彼此间并不连通，园区政府数字化治理意识不足，数字化建设较为落后，管理效率较为低下，无法支撑起当前数字经济企业的长期发展。[①]因此，研究工业园区的数字化转型路径对于实现区域数字经济的蓬勃发展，推动我国成为数字强国具有着极大的现实意义。

苏州工业园区是我国著名的产业园区之一，也是数字化转型的先行者之一。苏州工业园区在数字化转型方面采取了一系列政策措施并取得了显著的成效。苏州工业园区"数字经济、数字社会、数字政府"三位一体融通发展，通过为企业提供数字化基础设施、数字化管理、数字化创新和数字化服务等全方位的支持和服务，推动了园区企业的数字化转型和升级，提高了园区的核心竞争力和影响力。2022 年，苏州工业园区数字经济核心产业增加值占 GDP 比重达 24.6％，数字经济规模不断壮大。[②]因此，本文以苏州工业园区作为案例，分析园区数字化转型现状，探讨园区政策如何赋能工业园区的数字化转型。对于苏州工业园区数字化转型背后的政策支持措施的分析，不仅能为中国其他工业园区和区域经济的数字化转型提供经验参考，还可以讲好中国工业园区数字化转型故事，贡献数字中国的园区方案，扩大中国在工业园区数字化建设的国际影响力。此外，现有研究主要涉及企业层面的数字化转型，而本文以区域经济学视角，分析政策支持措施对于工业园区数字化转型的影响，能够拓宽研究视野，丰富工业园区数字化转型方面的文献。

二、文献回顾

根据《二十国集团数字经济发展与合作倡议》（2016），数字经济是指以使用数字化的知识和信息作为关键生产要素、以现代信息网络作为重要载体、以信息通信技术的有效使用作为效率提升和经济结构优化的重要推动力的一系列经济活动。[③]而数字化转型概念源于私营企业的实践。马特（Christian Matt）

---

① 冯媛. 我国产业园区数字化转型现状、问题及发展路径研究. 中国商论，2023(1)：151-153.
② 苏州工业园区数字化转型发展取得阶段性成效. (2022-06-10)[2024-02-07]. https://www.suzhou.gov.cn/szsrmzf/szyw/202206/1cdb69d1e07a40ea86ccfe9227b0e293.shtml.
③ 二十国集团数字经济发展与合作倡议. (2016-09-10)[2024-02-07]. http://www.g20chn.org/hywj/dncgwj/201609/t20160920_3474.html.

等认为，数字化转型战略是一个蓝图，它支持公司管理由于数字技术的集成而产生的变革，并支持转型后的运营。但随着数字技术在各行各业的发展，数字化转型概念也在进一步拓展。[①]从中观视角而言，苏州工业园区作为地区经济发展重要引擎的产业园区，也可以成为数字化转型的主体。[②]

关于数字化转型的研究主要聚焦于企业这一微观层面，现有文献较少涉及产业园区的数字化转型。田瑞认为，产业园区数字化转型是指以数字化人才和数字化基础设施为支撑，治理数字化营造产业发展环境，推动企业和产业数字化转型，实现产业园区生态系统数字化转型。[③]数字化人才的概念属于舶来品，OECD将具备数字技能作为数字人才的标志。数字化基础设施则指的是以新发展理念为引领，以技术创新为驱动，以信息网络为基础，提供数字转型、智能升级、融合创新等方面基础性、公共性服务的物质工程设施。园区产业的数字化转型不仅包括数字核心产业的培育和招引，还包括传统产业的数字化转型。王益民认为，政府数字化转型是数字技术优化组织结构和组织流程，改善公共服务供给，扩大民主参与渠道等，提升治理效率。[④]相对应，在园区治理数字化转型中，政务服务、企业管理、社会治理等方面的数字化改造，以及运用大数据、AI、云计算等新技术，实现智能化分析与管理效能的提高是其中的重要内容。

三、园区数字化转型成效

2022年，苏州工业园区数字经济核心产业增加值占GDP比重达24.6%，数字经济规模不断壮大。

在园区数字化基础设施建设方面，在2022年，工业园区启动建设24个重大基础设施项目，总投资192.6亿元以完善信息基础设施建设，包括5G基站、新科技项目等中重点项目。2022年，园区建成5G基站3944个。园区依靠基础设施互联互通、数据资源共建共享，极大优化了公共服务统筹协调能力，使得园区公共服务水平得到显著提升。此外，园区大力推动"5G＋工业互联网"融合应用发展，多年获评工业互联网方向国家新型工业化产业示范基地的荣誉

① Matt C, Hess T & Benlian A. Digital transformation strategies. *Business & Information Systems Engineering*, 2015, 57(5): 339-343.
② 李载驰, 吕铁. 数字化转型：文献述评与研究展望. 学习与探索, 2021, 317(12): 130-138.
③ 田瑞. X产业园区数字化转型策略优化研究. 郑州：河南财经政法大学, 2022.
④ 王益民. 数字政府整体架构与评估体系. 中国领导科学, 2020(1): 65-70.

称号。在政府投资和公共服务平台数字化建设引领下，园区的数字基础设施建设处于领先水平。

在园区产业的数字化建设方面，以大数据产业为例，园区聚集了大量本土创新型企业，覆盖产业链上下游多个环节。这些企业中不仅包含天聚地合、苏州国云等本地互联网大数据细分领域型企业，也包含企查查、智慧芽等大数据应用企业，数字经济产业生态地图不断完善，还包含通用软件层领域内中国顶级的大数据技术服务运营商国云数据。依托园区强大的数字核心产业集群，传统制造业得以利用先进的数字技术，采用针对性的转型方案，进行数字化改造，"灯塔工厂"在园区内涌现，园区产业数字化取得巨大成就。园区的数字核心产业蓬勃发展，带动产业数字化不断扩张。

新一代信息技术产业的蓬勃发展也吸引着大量数字人才的集聚。以人工智能产业为例，园区汇聚的各级领军人才超过900位，拥有国家级重大工程引进人才25位，江苏省双创人才83位；拥有市级及以上研发、工程、技术中心166个，其中省级及以上72个；累计引进高校、院所19家。此外，苏州工业园区还吸引着大量的高素质人才，这为数字化人才建设提供了智力基础。[①]根据苏州工业园区管委会官网统计信息，2020年园区新增市级以上领军人才138人；新增国家级重大人才引进工程13人，其中创业类7人、占全国总额17%；金鸡湖科技领军人才增长15.7%，高技能人才增长71.6%，区域人才总量超45万，人才数量占就业人口比重达51%。[②]不断增长的高素质人才能够促进数据要素资源有效利用并推动其他生产要素优化配置，支撑引领起园区数字经济的创新发展、技术研发与经济管理。

四、园区数字化转型的政策支持

基于工业园区数字化转型的分析，本文从基础设施建设、产业政策、人才政策和园区治理这四个角度梳理苏州工业园区管委会在园区数字化转型中提供的政策支持。

① 2022年苏州工业园区人工智能产业成绩单. (2023-01-18)[2024-02-07]. https://www.suzhou.gov.cn/szsrmzf/tjsjjd/202301/4f1c087238104f03aef4f4b2a9c40200.shtml.
② 园区人才数量占就业人口比重达51%. (2016-09-10)[2024-02-07]. https://www.sipac.gov.cn/szgyyq/mtjj/202101/a6ad07298368418182e7df9449a35abd.shtml.

（一）基础设施建设

园区基础设施建设等级和规模、完善程度和承载能力，直接影响着园区营商环境和经济效能。在数字经济时代下，产业园区的数字化基础建设是园区数字化转型的先导。在推动苏州工业园区数字化基础设施建设中，园区主要采用政府主导投资建设的模式展开。一方面，园区大力推动信息基础设施建设，重点建设 5G 基站，推动园区实现 5G 信号全覆盖。另一方面，依托工业互联网建设，园区也不断推动传统基础设施的数字化改造。将交通、电网、能源等传统物理基础设施升级打造为智慧交通、智慧电网和智慧能源等融合基础设施，实现园区全要素连接，推动产业园区运行设施要素和制造全要素连接服务，为资源协同和产业数字化发展奠定基础。

（二）产业政策

由于区域竞合关系和有限的政策资源，园区并非发展所有数字核心产业，而是坚持打造"人工智能产业创新集群"，构建区域相对独特的竞争力。为推动园区人工智能产业发展，苏州工业园区推出了包括《苏州工业园区人工智能产业发展"十四五"规划》《加快人工智能产业发展的若干意见》等一系列专门的引导政策，助力园区人工智能产业发展。在具体政策支持方面，园区统筹利用国家、省、市各级专项资金，对园区人工智能产业发展有着较大的支持力度；园区还支持数字经济领域重点项目列入省、市重大项目，做优营商服务，强化用地用能资源保障。与此同时，园区还编制了《苏州工业园区人工智能产业创新集群发展报告》《关于园区数字创新和数字产业化发展情况的报告》等一系列的发展报告，为园区内人工智能产业发展提供参考。依托这些产业政策和产业数字创新，园区人工智能产业不断发展，并不断辐射园区其他产业，数字经济不断成长。

除了园区集中政策发挥引导作用外，园区政府还注重逐步构建根植于本地集群的多维网络体系，以促进产业数字化发展。例如，园区在 2019 年 8 月，同华为联合成立了华为（苏州）人工智能创新中心，并在 2022 年进一步联合举办以"云聚园区，智享未来"为主题的"华为云杯"人工智能应用创新大赛，吸引全国范围内 2694 名开发者与 319 家企业报名参赛。通过对创客赛道与企业赛道的角逐，共同促进优质高新技术企业落地园区，拓展人工智能应用场景，助推园区内新一代人工智能领域建设。此外，在 2022 年，苏州工业园区企业发展服务中心还联合数字化转型标杆企业友达数位、行业龙头企业微软中国共同举办了首场"总部连线"活动之"探索制造业数字化转型新路径"，向各行业开放低代码先进技术和应用场景，与各位嘉宾共同探讨数字化转型策略，助力更多企业在数字化转型道路上不断发展。园区以举办赛事、政企合作和举办数字化转型主题交流会等多种不同形式，激励产学研合作，共同促进信息技术等方面科学成果转化，为园区产业数字化发展构建了浓厚的氛围。

（三）人才政策

园区的人才政策体系主要依托于"金鸡湖人才计划"，由"1+3+X"组成。[①] 其中包括一个基本性框架，"领军登峰"人才支持计划侧重针对顶尖科技人才的创新创业；"企业撷英"人才支持计划强化企业用人主体作用，对企业和人才分别给予不同支持；而"青春园区"人才支持计划则是健全青年人才普惠性支持措施。此外，根据民生、社会发展需要，园区还实施教育、卫生等若干专项政策。政策体系覆盖了各行各业人才，包括数字核心产业的从业人员；支持方式涵盖了各个方面，例如配套住房保障、子女教育等支持措施。政策体系对于招引数字化人才发挥着一定程度的激励作用，但是仍缺乏对于数字人才的专项政策支持，人才政策的精准度尚有不足，人才政策需要优化。

在推动人才集聚方面，苏州工业园区还利用数字化手段，搭建数字人才市场框架，提供了多形态而精准的求职招聘和人力培训等服务，在打破劳动者就业求职的信息壁垒、充分释放劳动要素产出方面发挥巨大作用。数字化人才市场框架包括政务、招聘、培训3个服务平台，以及1个品牌活动展示平台和1个数据监测分析平台。在数字人才市场框架中，政务服务平台提供了医保、就业培训、劳动关系等人社全业务链的宣传、受理和解读服务。人才招聘平台则是整合园区存量人力资源数据，利用大数据及智能算法，向高匹配度的求职者与用人单位互相推送匹配信息。而人才培训平台提供创业培训、技能培训等各类培训课程视频，不定期开放课程报名和邀请业界专家授课，以提升劳动者素质。品牌活动展示平台涵盖了园区各类主题招聘活动和优秀企业风采展示等内容，为求职者增添了解企业和园区的窗口。最后，监测平台建立了人力资源数据库，园区通过该平台不仅能够开展对人才招聘平台供需数据分析、对人力资

[①] "金鸡湖人才计划"升级版发布. [2024-02-07]. https://www.sipac.gov.cn/szgyyqtzyq/tzdt/202110/44d0b6fa5d13458485f4352e006dbe83.shtml.

源流动性数据的跟踪监测，实现区域人力资源的供需相对平衡，还能对重点产业人力资源流失原因进行分析，为进一步提升产业的人才吸引力提供数据支持。数字技术融合下的园区人才市场搭建不仅使园区劳动要素优化配置，还极大提升了园区对各类优秀人才的吸引力。

（四）园区治理

园区主动融入苏州数字政府市域一体化总体布局，不断提升自身治理数字化水平。苏州工业园区结合管理对象特性，探索构建智慧化、整体性、平台型"SIP数治"新范式，明确筑牢 1 个数字底座、推进 4 个一体化转型、打造 X 个创新智慧化场景的"1+4+X"的数字政府建设发展框架。截至 2022 年，园区已打造基础设施一云承载、数据资源一池融通、公共能力一体赋能、服务感知一端智联的"云、网、数、端"四位一体城市"智能中枢"，实现公共能力统建共用。园区还推动"一网通办""经济大脑""数字孪生平台"等应用场景赋能政务服务、经济发展和社会治理，有着完善的数字政府公共能力。在其中，园区"一网通办"是江苏省内首家区级一体化网上办事平台，共上线了 28 家单位的 1400 余项业务，其中 1096 项业务可以网上办理，近 200 项业务实现全程网办。[①]

园区政府还利用数字技术实现社区治理数字化改造和智能化发展。为促进治理数据集聚，园区构建起满足区、街、社区三级共享使用需求的"社区治理数据资源库"，为全区 10 余个部门共享百万级社区公共权威数据。基于这些治理数据，园区进一步推动社区服务的数字化，集成GIS地图、OCR智能识别、社民互动助手等智能工具，将信息化和"铁脚板"进行强有力结合，极大提高了社工工作效率。这些智能工具立足精简高效定位，梳理全口径业务，借助信息化推进基层民主自治、五社联动、社情民意联系日活动流程智能化再造、闭环式管理，实现治理流程由繁到简、指导监督贯穿始终。园区还注重需求响应，创新采用敏捷开发模式，在"开发—试用—优化"中不断循环往复、迭代提升用户体验；强化数据应用，深度挖掘数据分析结果与服务应用场景的关联，为社区开展精细化治理和服务，以及政府科学决策和靶向施策提供全面信息。

---

① 以数字政府建设赋能数字经济和数字社会发展. [2024-02-07]. https://www.sipac.gov.cn/szgyyq/jsdt/202201/c32afb65d3bd4878b0ee1b9bb78a2f57.shtml.

五、结论与政策建议

苏州工业园区在数字化转型方面采取了一系列政策措施，并取得了显著的成效。苏州工业园区有着丰富的高素质人才储备、完备的数字化基础设施、以人工智能为代表的数字核心产业蓬勃发展，带动了园区内产业数字化深入发展，同时园区治理数字化改革形成了系统性格局，极大提升了园区治理效能。

苏州工业园区数字化转型成就也给予我们丰富的启示。首先，数字化基础设施建设是重中之重，是实现园区数字化转型的基础。政府需要引领园区的数字化基础设施的建设，通过建设 5G 基站在内的新型信息基础设施、推动传统基础设施数字化改造两个方面提升园区基础设施的数字化水平，进而搭建工业互联网平台和建设智慧园区，为产业数字化发展提供基本条件。其次，在产业政策方面，园区政府应当利用有限资源，结合区位优势，通过发展特定的数字核心产业，构建园区数字化建设生态网络，积聚产学研各方力量，最终带动园区的其他传统产业的数字化发展。数字产业化和产业数字化的发展也会不断创造大量岗位需求，推动数字人才在产业园区的集聚。最后，园区政府需要自觉融入地区城市数字建设的规划，不仅利用数字技术构建园区治理数据库，建成数字化公共服务平台，实现园区各项功能的数字化改造，还需要采用数字化管理理念，结合人工智能技术，逐步拓展应用场景，最终为园区人才招聘、社会治理、政务服务和经济发展赋能。

但是，值得注意的是，苏州工业园区的数字化转型中也存在优化空间。由于园区数字基础设施建设具有投入金额大、回收周期长等特征，政府投资是主要的支持动力，但是政府、资本、企业等多元主体协同投入更能促进投资效率的提高。园区可以基于政府资金，通过产业引导基金、PPP 和各类园区数字化建设专项金融产品等方式吸引社会资本参与园区数字基础设施建设；同时，鼓励数字核心产业"投建营"一体化发展，探索形成政府引导、企业为主、市场运作的投入格局。此外，虽然园区现有的人才政策体系对于招引数字化人才发挥着一定程度的激励作用，但是仍缺乏对于数字人才的专项政策支持。在园区未来的人才政策制定中，园区可以依据人才所从事产业等信息，建立起数字人才识别标准，发布数字人才支持专项政策，提升政策对于数字人才支持的精准度，为园区数字化转型的进一步发展强化人才支撑。

园区绿色发展路径的对比研究
——以中国苏州工业园区和韩国仁川自由经济区为例①

摘　要：“碳达峰碳中和”已成为“十四五”期间乃至今后长期低碳转型的战略方向。园区制定自己的绿色发展战略，能够为区域实现“碳达峰碳中和”做出重大贡献。因此，本文基于现有的理论、文献基础，采用政策工具分析法与对比分析法，选取中国苏州工业园区和韩国仁川自由经济区总体发展历程作为绿色发展路径案例，系统分析政府措施、市场参与、基础设施、技术升级四个方面对两个园区绿色发展的影响，以及造成两个园区绿色发展路径不同的原因，并为其他园区提供绿色发展经验。

关键词：园区；苏州工业园区；韩国仁川自由经济区；绿色发展路径

一、研究背景

（一）经济高质量发展的需求

我国经济增长曾长期高度依赖低成本资源和生产要素的高强度投入，高度依赖投资和出口拉动。随着社会发展，此种特征的增长方式愈来愈难以为继。生产要素低成本优势开始减弱，资源环境承载能力接近极限，投资持续高增长的矛盾越来越尖锐，出口过快增长面临的风险越来越大。我国需要使经济向绿色增长的方向迈进。

韩国对外型经济出口额下滑势头“保持”了一年之久，韩国优势产业竞争力下滑，令其经济长期增长前景存在相当的不确定性。从根源上来看，整体经

---

① 作者：丁熙然，西北工业大学外国语学院英语专业；王雨辰，西北工业大学计算机学院人工智能专业；曹然，西北工业大学航宇智能制造专业。

济复苏乏力才是韩国经济规模下降的主要原因。当前，韩国经济的内外部环境不断恶化，出口下降、内需不振、投资萎靡、楼市暴跌等问题此起彼伏。面对重重压力，韩国政府需要踏上艰难的绿色发展之路。

（二）绿色发展要求下的国际压力

随着全球环境问题的日益突出，国际社会对绿色发展的呼声也越来越高，这给各国带来了一定的国际压力。

国际协议和承诺：各国在应对气候变化和环境保护方面签署了一系列国际协议和承诺，如果国家未能履行承诺，可能会受到国际社会的批评和制裁。

贸易和投资壁垒：一些国家和地区已经开始采取绿色标准和要求来限制进口产品的环境影响，这些标准可能对出口国造成贸易壁垒。同时，越来越多的投资者也开始关注企业的环境、社会和治理（ESG）表现，对那些不关注环境保护和可持续发展的企业可能会减少投资。

国际合作和竞争：各国需要加强合作，共同应对气候变化和环境问题。同时，各国之间也存在着绿色发展的竞争，那些在环境技术和可持续发展领域具有竞争优势的国家可能会在国际市场上占据领先地位。

总的来说，国际压力推动着各国加快绿色发展的步伐，促使各国采取更多的环境保护措施和可持续发展举措。通过加强国际合作和合理利用国际压力，可以为全球环境问题找到更有效的解决方案。

（三）宜居的生活环境的需求

绿色发展注重环境保护和健康，减少污染物和有害物质的排放，[1]改善空气质量、水质和土壤质量，减少环境中的有害物质，保护人类的健康和安全。绿色发展倡导资源的有效利用和循环利用。通过提高资源利用效率、推广可再生能源的使用和减少浪费，可以减少对有限资源的过度消耗，确保资源的可持续供应，为人类提供持久的生活基础。绿色发展强调生态平衡和生物多样性的保护。保护自然生态系统和物种多样性，维护生态平衡，维持生态系统的功能和稳定性，为人类提供重要的生态服务，如水源保护、气候调节和食物供应等。绿色发展倡导可持续城市发展，包括城市规划、交通系统、建筑设计等方面。通过建设环保、高效的城市基础设施，减少交通拥堵和能源消耗，提供优质的公共服务和宜居的城市环境。绿色发展的目标是在满足人类经济和社会需求的

---

[1]　邓昌炉，刘会林，唐宁. 走绿色发展之路. 咸宁日报，2009-02-08(01).

同时，保护环境和促进可持续发展。通过推动绿色发展，我们可以创造一个更加健康、安全、可持续和宜居的生活环境，提高人类的生活质量和福祉。

二、概念界定及国内外研究现状

（一）概念界定

绿色发展概念的认知和提出是一个循序渐进的过程。随着人类环保意识的加强及人类社会发展模式的演进，国内外研究者对绿色发展的定义和内涵也有不同的认识和界定。

园区绿色发展是指在园区规划、建设、运营和管理过程中，以可持续发展为导向，以环境友好、资源节约、生态保护为核心，通过优化产业结构、提高资源利用效率、减少环境污染和生态破坏，实现经济、社会和生态效益的协调发展。园区绿色发展旨在建设具有低碳、环保、生态友好特征的现代化园区，提高园区的竞争力和可持续发展能力，并为企业和居民提供健康、宜居的工作和生活环境。

（二）国内外研究现状

1.绿色发展概念研究历程

绿色发展的概念可以说是从 20 世纪 60 年代循环经济和随后的绿色经济、生态经济、低碳经济、可持续发展等一系列概念中衍生发展而来的。2008 年世界金融危机以后，为解决现实需求，学术界开始综合考虑发展与可持续问题，提出新背景下的绿色发展（主要包括绿色化、绿色增长、绿色转型等），并赋予其新的内涵。

纽约大学全球环境发展项目研究将"绿色化"定义为企业对生态环境感知、思考和行动的变化过程。2005 年，联合国亚太经社会委员会提出"绿色增长"是建立可持续发展和减少贫困背景下的绿色经济的先决条件，也是实现可持续发展的一种战略。

2008 年，联合国环境规划署则认为"绿色经济"应该是可以提升人类福祉和社会公平，还能降低环境风险和生态稀缺的一种经济，并鼓励全球的政策制定者们在可持续发展的背景下支持环境投资。2009 年，国际经济合作与发展组织对"绿色发展"的定义是：一种既要保证为人类幸福提供永续的资源和环境服务，又能兼顾促进经济增长的发展模式。但此时绿色发展尚未形成完整的理论体系。随后又有了"绿色增长"概念的提出。[①]

2011年国际经济合作与发展组织将绿色增长定义为一种既能保持经济稳定发展，又能防止资源和能源浪费、环境污染、生态破坏、生物多样性丧失的增长方式。而后，绿色发展对国家的作用和各国绿色转型过程中遇到的困难及解决方法等各种问题逐渐被重点讨论。世界银行和联合国环境规划署2012年分别给"绿色增长"和"绿色经济"下了定义。

目前，国外关于绿色发展内涵的认知各有不同的侧重。第一种是侧重在经济发展过程中减少碳排放，以应对气候变化为重要目标。第二种是侧重经济绿色增长，主张绿色清洁产业可能成为新的经济增长点。第三种是以兼顾社会进步为逻辑归宿，强调社会包容性。

国内学术界对绿色发展的相关研究起步相对较晚，但近年来呈现快速发展的趋势。从20世纪90年代开始，对于发展观及绿色发展理论问题的研究方面，国内学者的关注度越来越高。

虽然到目前为止，学术界依然未就绿色发展内涵形成统一的概念界定。有的学者更加强调经济和生态两大系统的协调统一，但有的学者强调经济、生态和社会三大系统的协调统一，主张绿色发展不能缺少和谐的社会系统。[②]

但现有研究成果对绿色发展认识有着本质共识，认为绿色发展是一种兼具资源节约型、环境友好型、社会进步型的新型发展模式，既能实现生态效益又能保障经济效益和社会效益，包含"经济发展、资源节约和环境保护、社会福利增进"三大核心要素，更加注重经济发展与社会进步及生态建设的统一与协调。

2.绿色发展观的发展阶段

按认知深度可将绿色发展观划分为早期的可持续发展观和当前的绿色发展观。

第一，早期的可持续发展观。关于绿色发展的可持续发展观包含以下2种理论依据。

资源环境承载力制约。基于资源环境承载力制约的可持续发展观，强调冲破资源环境承载力的约束，寻求达到经济增长与资源环境消耗的脱钩，依靠高科技以人造资本代替环境和自然资本、保护生态环境、解决经济发展与环境保

① 陈丽明.低碳经济引领绿色增长.表面工程资讯，2010，10(2)：17.
② 张晔，吴婷.苏州工业园区："数""智"赋能，园区转型提速.科技日报，2023-05-18(007).

护冲突问题，追求人与经济、社会、资源环境可持续发展，是对发展本质、规律和趋势的理性把握是具有中国特色的当代可持续发展新形态。

资源环境要素投入。基于资源环境要素投入的可持续发展观，强调处理好当前需求和未来需求，将环境资源作为社会经济发展的内在要素，依靠科技进步、人力资源和绿色改革，提高生产率，尽最大可能用最少的资源实现最大的经济效益、生态效益和社会效益，统一协调经济、社会和生态三方面的关系，保障经济、社会和生态同步朝着良好的方向持续发展。

第二，当前的绿色发展观。绿色发展观循序渐进，依次经历了生态资本论、绿色生产理论和绿色资产论。生态资本论重视生态资源节约利用和生态环境建设，以维持生态资本存量的非减性，强调通过绿色创新这一基本途径，使生态资本不断增加，人们在生产过程中尽量降低资源消耗和废弃物排放的同时，合理地进行适度消费，保证生态资本存量不减少，为后续的经济社会发展提供充足的生态资本供应，实现人与自然及人与人之间的和谐共处。

绿色资产观，以资源承载力与生态环境容量为客观基础，在实践中转变发展方式使发展绿色化，让绿色带动发展，使人类在享受源源不断的绿色福利的同时绿色资产价值还得到提升，以人与自然的共荣和人与自然的和谐为本质内涵，强调和谐是基本的，是绿色发展的最低目标，人与自然共荣是绿色发展的终极目标，而绿色资产论的宗旨和目标则有机统一了生产发展、生活富裕和生态繁荣，是发展的最高境界，它以人与自然和谐及共同发展为终极目的。

综上可见，当代绿色发展观与早期的可持续发展观是一脉相承的，都是对传统发展模式的改革创新，都以资源环境承载力作为经济社会永续发展的基本前提，但不一样的地方是早期的可持续发展观更加侧重结果导向，强调社会可持续、经济可持续和资源环境可持续的结果。而当代绿色发展观更突出人的主观能动性，人类可以通过生产、消费、投资和技术绿色化来创造绿色资本价值，提高资源环境承载力。因此从这个角度来看，绿色发展观是一种更加侧重过程导向的发展观。

早期的可持续发展观与当代的绿色发展观具体区别主要体现在对生态环境的认识和实践目标两方面。

在对待生态环境上，可持续发展观主要以保护生态环境为手段来实现生态环境的代际公平和持续性。而绿色发展观的特点是既要保护生态环境，更重要的是创造绿色资产，真正把生态环境纳入发展模式与经济社会同步实现发展。

在实践目标上，可持续发展观要求当代人在生产实践中尽量减少生态环境资源的消耗，给后代人留下充足的生态环境资源以满足后代人的需要。绿色发展观则强调当代人可以以绿色创新为途径，创造更多的绿色资产，不仅追求满足当代人和后代人对生态环境资源的需要，还以谋求更高的生态盈余为目标。可见，绿色发展观无论是在生态环境的认识还是实践取向上，都是对可持续发展观的深化。

通过绿色发展相关概念内涵研究发现，关于绿色发展的概念内涵虽然存在争议，但是也在研究中逐渐达成了共识。绿色发展是指在经济增长和发展过程中，以人与自然和谐为初级目标、以人与自然共荣为高级目标，以绿色资产促进技术进步，以绿色消费满足居民需求，实现生产发展、生活富裕、生态良好的有机统一。

三、中国苏州工业园区和韩国仁川自由经济区绿色发展路径对比分析

（一）中国苏州工业园区发展历程及绿色发展路径

1.总体发展历程（见表 1）

表 1　苏州工业园区总体发展历程

阶段	时间	核心理念	重点区域	主要规划	发展格局及特点
第一阶段	1994—2000 年	新镇建设	70 平方公里中新合作区	初步规划、首期开发区规划	中新合作区主导，周边各镇共同发展
第二阶段	2001—2005 年	区域规划建设	金鸡湖以东地区	原规划的完善和调整	协调发展
第三阶段	2006 年至今	新城规划建设	苏州市中心城区、长三角地区	综合规划与战略发展	全面融入苏州，打造东部新城

2.绿色发展路径

（1）政府措施

苏州工业园区出台了绿色产业引导政策，对符合绿色发展方向的行业和企业给予资金、税收优惠等方面的扶持。政府设立了专项资金，用于支持环保技术研发、绿色产品开发等。苏州工业园区加强环境保护监管，制定了严格的环境标准和排污减排措施。政府对企业进行环境审核，加强监督和检查，对违法排污行为进行处罚，并督促企业进行环境整改。苏州工业园区推行资源节约利用政策，鼓励企业采用清洁生产技术，提高资源利用效率。政府提供节能减排

技术咨询和培训支持，鼓励企业实施能源管理和节能改造，减少能源消耗和排放。苏州工业园区推动绿色建筑发展，制定了绿色建筑设计和施工标准，鼓励采用节能材料和技术，推广可再生能源的利用，减少建筑对环境的影响。苏州工业园区注重生态保护，实施湿地保护、植被恢复和生态廊道建设等措施，保护和改善生态环境。政府加强生态环境监测和评估，推动生态保护工作的落实。

（2）市场参与

将绿色发展作为一种可盈利的发展方式，利用市场这只"隐形的手"，将会极大促进苏州工业园区绿色发展。以服务国家战略、改善民生、推进长江经济带绿色发展为己任，建设银行苏州分行优先发展绿色信贷，助力长江大保护，争做长三角生态绿色一体化发展示范区金融支持先行者、主力军，推进苏州生态涵养发展试验区建设。该行为太湖、长江等湿地生态保护、植被恢复、水体净化等"退养还湿"保护工程提供超 10 亿元融资支持；为生态农业、农村土地综合整治提供逾 10 亿元融资支持。通过向绿色市场注入资金，可以进一步推动苏州工业园区的绿色发展。

（3）基础设施

苏州工业园区完善升级现有设施，建立优质高效的前端供给—末端治理—资源回用的设施系统，为区域争取更大的资源环境富余空间，支撑城市持续发展。

以海绵城市建设为依托，推进水循环设施系统建设。完成海绵城市专项规划编制，明确建设目标及各类指标并在控规中予以落实，鼓励中心合作区、独墅湖科教区等核心片区的公共建筑设置雨水综合利用设施。推进污水厂系统的提质增效，提高污水收集处理率，提升尾水排放标准至太湖流域特别排放限值要求，同时完善再生水利用系统，配套出台再生水推广使用的相关优惠政策，提高其替代自来水的比例。

加强清洁能源供应系统"开源节流"。落实"以电代煤、以电代油"发展思路，提高清洁电能在终端能源消费中的比重，逐步提高接受区外输电的比例；落实节能减排能源政策，取缔燃煤小锅炉，完善热源及管网系统，提高集中供热覆盖范围及供热效率。同时加快推进分散式能源站、太阳能、空气源热泵、地源热泵等新能源利用系统建设，降低能耗及大气污染物排放量。推进固废分类收集处理与资源化利用。加强生活垃圾前端分类收集设施布局，居住小区及主要企事业单位的分类垃圾箱实现 100% 覆盖。构建以园区生活垃圾焚烧发电厂、餐厨与绿化垃圾处理及资源化利用中心、危险废弃物处置站为主的终端处置设施，实现相应固废的分类处置及资源化利用。加强区域协调，将建筑、医疗等其他类型的固废分类运输至区外处置。

（4）技术升级

在能源信息管理手段上，突破传统能源审计模式，综合推进能源在线监测、鼓励企业自行上报及委托第三方机构盘查等多种方式并存，实现多元化信息监管模式。园区将更多地借助于能源数字信息平台的搭建，实现能源数据实时在线监测。针对园区前期能源管理工作中的不足，后期将成立能源管理中心，主要负责能耗数据的搜集、汇总和前期处理工作。随着能源管理机制的进一步完善，能源审计及清洁生产审核工作将作为能源信息统计和节能改造的辅助手段。

加快发展以纳米技术产业为引领、以光电新能源、生物医药、融合通信、软件动漫游戏、生态环保五大新兴产业为支撑的创新型经济，力争基本实现以传统制造业为主的产业结构向以新兴产业为主的产业结构转型，实现以加工贸易为主的产业内涵向以创新型为主的产业内涵转型，实现以制造业为主的经济结构向以服务业为主的经济结构升级，实现以投资和出口为主导的发展方式向以消费为主导的发展方式转变。

（二）韩国仁川自由经济区发展历程及绿色发展路径

1. 总体发展路径

表2　韩国仁川自由经济区总体发展历程

阶段	时间	区域划分	主要活动	政府措施
第一阶段	2003—2006 年	青罗、永宗、松岛	规划和基础设施建设	详细规划制定，投资基础设施建设（如道路、港口、机场等）
第二阶段	2007—2010 年	—	推广自由经济区，吸引投资	提供税收优惠和其他激励措施，解决土地问题
第三阶段	2011 年至今	—	吸引外国投资，扩大规模，支持企业发展	加强企业支持，提高竞争力，提供硬件设施和软性服务

2.绿色发展路径

（1）政府措施

韩国国会于 2010 年通过的《低碳绿色增长框架法》为仁川提供了 83 亿美元的绿色投资，为期五年。根据这一倡议，松岛 IBD 发展成为一个可持续发展的城市，2021 年，其 40% 以上的面积保留用于绿地，包括 40 公顷的公园。此外，仁川的政策制定者提议在松岛修建一条有吸引力的自行车道，以取代私家车。松岛自行车道全长 20 公里，并于 2009 年建成。仁川有近 120 个全市自行车租赁站，人们可以在那里租用公共自行车并在附近的公共自行车站返还。

仁川市 2020 年加入了 Powering Past Coal Alliance（弃用煤炭发电联盟），并计划到 2050 年通过加强绿色基础设施、清洁能源和电动汽车来实现净零碳排放，这是韩国绿色新政指定的。韩国绿色新政是到 2025 年实现碳中和的第一步。韩国计划利用绿色创新和新兴数字工具，在绿色新政和数字新政的两个基础之间建立协同效应。

（2）市场参与

市场通过资本的流动和投资者的选择来调节绿色发展。如果绿色项目有良好的投资回报和潜在利润，投资者将更有动力投资于该区域的绿色发展项目。仁川经济自由区厅 2023 年 5 月 9 日在松岛会展中心举行了"仁川 Meta 经济学2023"活动，宣布了仁川市的区块链愿景，并与国内外企业签署了谅解备忘录。[1]在此活动过程中，仁川市政府与多家国内外公司签署了合作协议，包括加密货币交易所 Binance 和半导体设计公司 AMD 等。而半导体材料可以用于制造芯片，可以降低铅、汞等有害重金属的使用频率，同时也可以代替其他有毒的化学物质，减少电子垃圾对环境的污染，为实现绿色发展助力。[2]

仁川自由经济区以金融为主要产业，绿色金融也是其金融产业的一部分。绿色金融为仁川自由经济区的绿色发展项目提供了资金支持。通过发行绿色债券、提供绿色贷款和投资绿色基金等方式，为绿色项目提供了融资渠道，帮助企业和项目获得所需资金。绿色金融在绿色发展中承担了风险管理的角色。通过评估绿色项目的环境风险和可持续性，绿色金融机构可以提供风险管理和评估服务，帮助减少绿色项目的风险，为投资者提供更可靠的投资选择。绿色金融机构参与制定和推广绿色金融标准和认证，为仁川自由经济区的绿色发展提

---

① 封骁.韩国仁川自由经济区发展特色及可借鉴经验.港口经济，2015，145(9)：26-29.
② 杨国彪，李文家.韩国仁川自由经济区的发展及启示.天津经济，2015，254(7)：28-30.

供了指导和规范。例如，绿色债券和绿色贷款需要符合一定的环境和可持续性标准，有助于推动绿色项目的发展和实施。

（3）基础设施

城市产生的所有垃圾都由气动管系统处理，该系统将垃圾运送到中央处理系统，在那里燃烧以获取能源或回收利用。此外，松岛IBD还采用了气动废物处理系统。这意味着街角没有垃圾桶，也没有垃圾车。相反，垃圾被扔进管道，被吸入地下进行处理和回收。根据Gale International和Kohn Pedersen Fox（KPF）的可持续发展报告，仁川已经建立了四个主要的可持续基础设施系统：用水网络、废物收集和处理系统、能源网络和公共交通。

仁川致力于改善可再生能源发电设施和LED照明设备的运营，改善和更换高效设施等，以减少温室气体排放。基于仁川减排减碳的种种举措以及取得的成效，仁川被韩国政府评为温室气体减排的最佳城市。

（4）技术升级

韩国是信息通信技术（ICT）行业绿色化的领导者之一，是绿色政策倡议的首批采用者之一，2008年，它宣布了根据《联合国气候变化框架公约》做出的"低碳、绿色增长"承诺。这导致了《2050年碳中和法案》的发布，该法案促进了经济增长、碳中和以及生活质量的提高。韩国政府对这个问题采取全政府的方法，负责管理该国实现净零排放努力的总统碳中和委员会涉及所有18个部委。例如，科技部（MSIT）在将技术创新与零碳概念联系起来方面发挥着关键作用。其战略确定了到2050年实现碳中和的十大核心技术，其中之一是数字化，重点关注数据中心的功耗和管理系统的应用。快速的数字化转型对网络、数据中心、计算能力以及数据支持的分析和应用程序的需求日益增加。

（三）对比分析

1.政府措施

中国政府和韩国政府均对各自的工业园区的绿色发展给予了大量支持。例如，中国政府和韩国政府均为园区的绿色发展投入大量资金，同时出台了相应的税收优惠政策，鼓励园区的绿色发展。但是，二者也存在一些不同。中国政府在绿色发展方面注重环境监管和法规制定，推动园区企业采用清洁能源和节能环保技术。而韩国政府则更加侧重于绿色产业的发展和可再生能源的利用，同时注重园区的生态保护和可持续发展。

2.市场参与

苏州工业园区和仁川自由经济区都吸引绿色产业的发展，创造绿色工作岗位，推动经济增长和环境保护。然而，苏州工业园区更加注重科技创新和绿色技术的应用，鼓励企业在技术方面的投资和发展。仁川自由经济区更加注重国际合作和贸易，吸引外资和技术引进，推动绿色产业的国际交流与合作。这些不同的市场参与方式为两个园区的绿色发展提供了多样化的动力和机会，促进了经济增长和环境可持续性的实现。

3.基础设施

苏州工业园区和仁川自由经济区都注重交通和能源基础设施的发展，以减少能源消耗和环境污染。然而，苏州工业园区更加注重绿色建筑和智能化基础设施的建设，而仁川自由经济区更加注重环境友好型港口和物流基础设施的发展。这些基础设施的建设为两个园区的绿色发展提供了有力的支持，促进了经济增长和环境保护的平衡。

4.技术升级

苏州工业园区和仁川自由经济区都注重数字化技术在智能化管理和数字化监测方面的应用，以提高园区的管理效率和环境保护水平。然而，苏州工业园区更加注重数字化技术在智能制造和节能减排方面的应用，而仁川自由经济区更加注重数字化技术在物流和供应链管理方面的应用。

四、总结与展望

（一）研究总结

可持续发展是当今世界的重要代名词，而绿色发展作为可持续发展中重要的一环，自然也受到了世界各国的广泛关注。通过本次研究，我们对比了苏州工业园区和韩国仁川自由经济区的绿色发展路径，得出了它们的异同点。

苏州工业园区和韩国仁川自由经济区在绿色发展方面已经取得了一定成就，未来的展望也非常令人期待。它们作为两个重要的经济特区，绿色发展是未来发展的重要方向。通过不断的创新和合作，这两个园区可以在绿色技术、绿色产业和绿色管理方面取得更大的成就，为经济增长和环境保护做出大的贡献。

（二）研究展望

展望未来，这两个园区将继续引领绿色发展的潮流，成为可持续发展的典范，对其他工业园区的绿色发展也有深刻的启示。[①]在实现绿色发展过程中，政府需要结合当地的实际情况来制定相应的绿色标准，并为绿色发展企业提供良好的营商环境。政府可以通过为绿色企业开启快速通道、提供便利的审批流程等方式，帮助它们快速打开市场。

此外，政府还可以发挥市场作用，引入外资，鼓励企业在技术方面的投入。这可以通过提供税收优惠政策、引进技术创新机构等方式来实现。对于绿色企业入驻的工业园区，政府应当提供良好的基础设施支持。[②]这包括提供高效的供水、供电、供气等基础设施，以及建设配套的交通、医疗、教育等设施，以满足企业员工的生活需求。

总之，政府在绿色发展过程中扮演着重要的角色，需要制定相关政策和标准，为绿色企业提供良好的营商环境和基础设施支持，同时引导市场力量，推动绿色技术的发展和应用。

---

① 杨彩霞. 我国工业园区绿色化发展管理探索. 产业与科技论坛，2019，18(2)：256-257.
② 赵文景. 以智慧园区建设促进经济高质量发展. 中国物价，2023(4)：18-20.

融合创新与宜居：探讨新加坡裕廊工业区的独特发展道路①

摘 要： 20 世纪中叶以来，新加坡在发展依靠地理优势的航运业之外，同时着手建设以裕廊岛为主体区域的裕廊工业区。裕廊工业区的工业产出在新加坡国内占比有着绝对优势，时至今日，裕廊工业区的发展方向有所转变。本文将新加坡裕廊工业区作为研究案例，对世界一流工业园区的建设进行讨论与研究。本文从案例背景、发展历程、因素分析和优势与挑战四个方面展开，寻找裕廊工业区成为世界一流工业园区特点。最后形成结论与建议，助力我国世界一流工业园区的布局与建设。

关键词： 裕廊工业区；工业 4.0；可循环方式；新型工业园区建设

一、引 言

新加坡位于东南亚地区的南端，连接了东西方的主要贸易航线，因其独特的地理位置和经济政策成为全球重要的贸易中心，在特殊的地理位置作用下，新加坡大力发展对外航运以及科技，使其拥有世界上最繁忙和高效的港口设施之一。为了突出自身优势，新加坡采取的宽松的自由贸易政策、简化贸易程序以及签署的众多自贸协定，营造了宽松的商业环境，吸引了众多跨国公司在新加坡设立区域总部和分支机构。

在其优越的地理位置与宽松的贸易环境加持下，新加坡所拥有的先进的金融体系、创新和科技引领以及优质的基础设施巩固了自身在国际上的经济地位。新加坡拥有众多国际银行和金融机构的总部，得益于稳定和健全的金融体

---

① 作者：任笔儒，西北工业大学管理学院；王逸非，西北工业大学自动化学院；钱扬杰，西北工业大学自动化学院；李可心，西北工业大学自动化学院。

系，奠定了新加坡的金融核心地位。此外，新加坡在创新和科技发展方面也给予大量支持，投资于研发和科技基础设施，成为人工智能、生物医药、金融科技和可持续发展等领域的创新中心。

裕廊工业区（Jurong Industrial Park）在新加坡经济发展中扮演着重要而多重的角色，作为新加坡最大的工业区之一，是新加坡经济的强力引擎，集聚了众多创新、制造和物流企业，为新加坡创造了丰富的就业机会和稳定的经济增长。同时裕廊工业区也是该国的技术和创新中心，是先进研发中心和高科技企业的所在地，推动着科技领域的突破和新加坡的全面发展。作为一个紧密结合的制造业集群，裕廊工业区促进了企业之间的合作与协同，形成了高附加值和高品质产品的供应链和价值链，为新加坡创造了丰厚的出口收入和国际竞争力。

在本报告中，我们将对裕廊工业区作为世界一流工业园区的成功因素、发展模式和经验等进行分析，并提取出可用于世界各地工业园区建设的共通点，从而为中国工业区的发展与规划提供可复制的经验。

二、案例研究背景

新加坡是一个资源匮乏、人口稠密的小国，面临着激烈的国际竞争和经济转型的挑战。为了提升国家的经济实力和国际地位，新加坡政府制定了一系列的发展战略和规划，其中之一就是建设世界一流的工业园区，以吸引外资、促进产业升级、创造就业机会和增加税收收入。新加坡裕廊工业区是新加坡最大的现代化工业基地，也是亚洲工业区中的一个成功典范。

新加坡裕廊工业区的建设始于1971年，当时新加坡政府为了发展石化产业，开始在亚逸美宝岛上建立石化专业区。由于1973年的石油危机的影响，该计划暂时搁置，直到1977年，新加坡设立了新加坡石油化学公司负责实施第一期石化工业区计划。该计划主要发展石化产业上游和通用化学品生产，如乙烯、丙烯、苯等。随着市场需求的增长和技术的进步，新加坡政府于1997年开始实行第二期石化工业区计划，逐步向下游产品延伸，包括苯乙烯、聚醚多元醇、线型低密度聚乙烯、丙烯酸酯、高吸水性树脂等。同时，为了扩大土地面积和提高土地利用率，新加坡政府通过填海工程，将原有的七个岛屿连成一片，形成了现在的裕廊岛。2010年，新加坡又启动了裕廊岛2.0计划，重点聚焦于能源、物流和交通、原料选择、环境和水这五个领域，计划探索综合创新解决方案，进一步优化稀缺资源，驱动石化产业向高附加值产品发展。

基于以上背景，我们希望以裕廊工业区作为世界一流工业园区的范例，并对其进行分析，得到建设与开发工业区的可借鉴经验。从而探究世界一流工业园区的形成必备条件以及实现途径等，并形成书面化建议。

三、发展历程

新加坡裕廊工业区的发展经历了初创与建设、转型与升级、创新与发展三个阶段，充分展示了其不断适应时代变化、勇于创新的精神。如今，裕廊工业区已经成为全球领先的科技创新和产业发展高地，为新加坡乃至全球的经济发展做出了重要贡献。

（一）初创与建设

新加坡在 20 世纪 60 年代面临着严重的失业问题和经济发展的压力。为了解决这些问题，政府决定在裕廊划定 6480 公顷土地进行工业园区的建设，吸引国内外投资者，提供就业机会，促进经济发展。在该时期，政府主要引进了劳动密集型产业，例如纺织、服装、玩具和木器等。这些产业需要大量的劳动力，从而可以帮助政府解决失业问题。同时，这些产业也有助于提升新加坡的出口，推动经济增长。此外，新加坡政府也投入了大量的资金进行基础设施的建设，为工业园区的发展提供了必要的支持。

自 1972 年以来，新加坡政府在裕廊工业区的管理上进一步加强，成立了裕廊镇管理局（Jurong Town Corporation），专门负责经营管理裕廊工业区，以应对裕廊工业区的规模扩大等所可能带来的问题。同时，工业园区的发展方向也发生了变化。政府开始重视技术和资本密集型产业的发展，例如石化、造船、钢铁和电子等。这些产业的发展需要大量的技术和资金投入，但它们的附加值更高，竞争力更强。这种转变标志着新加坡开始从以劳动密集型产业为主的经济模式转向以技术和资本密集型产业为主的经济模式，为新加坡的经济发展打开了新的篇章。裕廊工业区的规模和影响力也不断增强，吸引了越来越多的国内外投资者，推动了新加坡的经济发展。

1982 年，新加坡政府启动了一个十年总体规划，在这个阶段，裕廊工业区的发展主要集中在几个方面：将南部的岛屿开发成石油化工产品的生产和配售中心，将罗央开发成第一个航空工业中心，以及建设新加坡科技园区以容纳科技开发型企业。

（二）转型与升级

从 21 世纪以来，新加坡政府在发展教育的基础上，开始实施对工业区的改变：其中裕廊工业区更名为裕廊创新区。在其战略定位转变的过程中，其侧重发展方向也逐渐由工业制造转换至科技创新，其支柱产业中的劳动密集型产业占比逐渐减少，由科技产业替代。在此基础上，裕廊创新区引入了人才、研发、技术供应与制造工厂等一系列的链条，在裕廊产生了出色的协同效应。[①]

在裕廊创新区范围内，拥有著名的南洋理工大学，以及新加坡科学技术研究院（A*STAR）等科研机构，与此同时，以西门子先进制造转型中心为代表的一批国际制造业巨头也落户裕廊，体现了裕廊在 21 世纪探索出的新型发展模式与良好发展环境。

在营造创新氛围的同时，裕廊创新区以人文主义为理念，对裕廊的基础设施进行了最贴近时代的完善。裕廊创新区不仅仅适合工作与科学研究，同时具备生活与宜居的职能。裕廊作为新加坡重要的创新基地与科技支撑，其环境与设施建设不可避免地带有科技与工业色彩，但是其依然保留了新加坡作为"花园城市"的良好印象，在此前提下，裕廊创新区的生活设施与基础交通等没有明显弱化；同时，裕廊创新区作为新加坡打造的面向未来的科研与工业基地，较好地满足了大多数人才对于工作环境的需求，因而在裕廊汇聚了来自全球各地的人才。

（三）创新与发展

2013 年，"工业 4.0"概念被提出，裕廊创新区正式进入创新与发展阶段。在裕廊创新区的简介中，它被描述为"应对工业 4.0 的方案"。工业 4.0 是一个起源于制造工程领域的术语，4.0 目标与以前不同，不单创造新的工业技术，而是着重于将现有的工业相关的技术、销售与产品体验结合起来，透过人工智能的技术建立具有适应性、资源效率和人因工程学的智慧工厂，并在商业流程及价值流程中整合客户以及商业伙伴，提供完善的售后服务。其技术基础是智慧整合感控系统及物联网。

潘明（Pan M）等人的研究认为，在工业 4.0 环境下，裕廊创新区中各环节的协同作用与数字技术和物联网的应用将成为革新生产方式的关键，为了构

[①] A Singapore Government Agency Website. [2024-03-03]. https://estates.jtc.gov.sg/jid/business#industry-4-network.

建裕廊生态工业园（EIP），可以构建一个专家系统。同时，减少决策的中间环节，使用计算机技术减轻工作量，通过利用高性能计算资源和先进的数据分析来解决最终用户驱动的需求，从而实现裕廊岛上所有实体的智能设计、运营和管理。

在工业 4.0 愿景的基础上，根据"新加坡绿色计划 2030"[①]，裕廊创新区也将实现可持续化产业的发展，裕廊创新区的协同作用不仅提高了效率，在构建可循环生产模式方面，也可以减少对原料以及生产设施的需求。如果将协同作用扩展至系统层面，裕廊创新区将能够建立基于协同效应的可循环产业雏形。

关于对区域生态的建设与改善，杨（Yang）等人的研究指出，可以采用现代化的生态规划方法，来避免传统生态建设方法的弊端。不仅如此，他们提到对污染的控制问题：工业生态系统不应简单地类比为自然生态系统。[②]工业生产和消费系统的新陈代谢要嵌入生物圈，因而工业生态系统作为一种人工生态系统的污染控制方法，比自然生态系统要更加复杂。裕廊创新区在未来的建设过程中面临着污染的控制，如何调和在裕廊创新区中植物和以人为代表的动物种群的关系，是需要着重考虑的。

但是受制于目前的技术，城市生态景观职能多以美化环境为主，其他功能性职能为辅助。但是在杨等人的结论中，提出了一种以可再生能源替代石油的方案，这一方案的背景是裕廊岛曾经作为石油工业区的功能存在。如果原材料、能源和副产品更容易被环境技术和管理替代或再利用，那么我们通过创新技术和管理技能发展自然资源替代是可行的，我们应该集中研究环境技术、产业生态和相关知识。与此相对的是，当自然资源难以替代，自然资源的枯竭将威胁到人类生产或人类自身时，自然资源的保护将优先于其他战略。

在结合工业 4.0 的前提下，应当开启对各个方向的探索，以应对可能出现的各种情况。[③]随着科学技术与生态学理论的发展，裕廊创新区可以作为世界范围内独特的工业生态环境实验区域，以探究人与生态城市建设的新可能性。

---

① Singapore Green Plan 2030. [2024-03-03]. https://www.greenplan.gov.sg/.

② Yang P P J, Lay O B. Applying ecosystem concepts to the planning of industrial areas: a case study of Singapore's Jurong Island. *Journal of Cleaner Production*, 2004, 12(8-10): 1011-1023.

③ Yang P P J, Lay O B. Applying ecosystem concepts to the planning of industrial areas: a case study of Singapore's Jurong Island. *Journal of Cleaner Production*, 2004, 12(8-10): 1011-1023.

四、创新与可持续并进：探究裕廊工业区的优势之路

为了对裕廊工业区的建设与发展进行全面讨论与研究，我们将从以下 7 个方面对其进行全面分析。

（一）良好的地理位置

裕廊工业区位于新加坡岛西南部的海滨地带，距离市区约 10 公里，面积约 70 平方公里；工业区从 1961 年 10 月开始兴建，目前已发展成为新加坡最大的现代化工业基地，工业区内约有 7000 家本土及跨国公司进驻，从初期的出口加工制造等逐步向通信技术、生命科学等众多高新技术企业演化，推动了新加坡进入新兴工业国家的进程；工业区具有建设现代化工业区的自然地理条件，包括港口（裕廊港）、铁路、机场等。

（二）科学有效的规划

科学的规划是裕廊成功的前提，基于具有连续性、前瞻性和生态性的科学规划，裕廊有序按照规划进行开发建设，以规划统领建设发展方向。

政策连续性：新加坡的规划体系包括概念规划、总体规划、城市设计等方面。概念规划的规划期为 30—40 年，每 10 年调整一次；总体规划需经政府制定、国会批准，为法定性文件，规划期为 10—15 年，每 5 年检讨（修订）一次，确保规划始终符合发展实际。裕廊相关园区的建设均在新加坡政府的规划指导下进行，以保证园区建设符合整体建设体系。

规划前瞻性：裕廊在建设园区前会制定具有前瞻性的规划，以指导园区的建设。新加坡政府从一开始就将裕廊定为全面发展的综合型工业区，合理妥善规划。根据地理环境的不同，将靠近市区的东北部划为新兴工业和无污染工业区，重点发展电子、电器及技术密集型产业；沿海的西南部划为港口和重工业区；中部地区为轻工业和一般工业区；沿裕廊河两岸则规划住宅区和各种生活设施。

建设生态性：新加坡具有"花园城市"的美称，产业园区的环境也较好。裕廊工业区在进行园区规划的时候，除了建造各种工业厂房外，还特别注意营造一种优美、轻松的生活环境，使人们在工作之余有一个游憩的空间，并注意同自然生态系统相协调，建立工业生态系统，把工业发展对环境的影响减少到最小，实现工业的可持续发展。在裕廊园区规划建设过程中，从一开始就有计划地保留 10％ 的用地来建设公园和风景区。现已建成 10 多个公园，特别是占

地 20.2 公顷的裕廊飞禽公园已经成为世界上最大的飞禽公园，栖息着 380 多个物种的 4600 多只飞禽。

（三）创新的开发模式

裕廊工业区成功的关键要素是实行"政府主导、市场经营"的"裕廊模式"：通过土地国有化，保证政府对土地的支配权。建立各种政府机构，并进行明确分工，经济发展局主要负责制定工业发展的战略规划，市区重建局和裕廊镇管理局负责工业园区的规划、开发和管理，环境及水源部和国家环境局负责环境的保护和对园区开发的监督工作，其他的一些机构如人力资源培训机构等则配合工业的发展。在此基础上，设立成本控制理事会，有效地抑制了企业经营成本的增长（见图 1）。

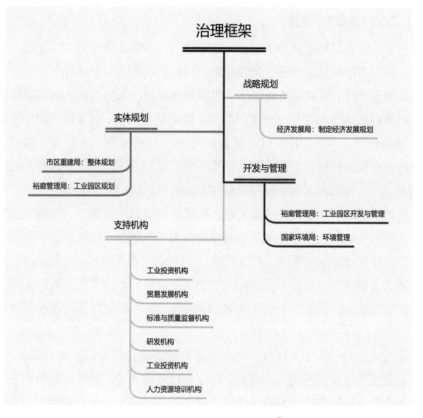

图 1　裕廊工业区开发模式框[①]

---

① 图片为作者自制。

理事会制定增加相关产业园区内成本管控指导方针，以帮助政府维持一个合理的工业秩序。此外，当经济衰退时，园区会在很短的时间内，在从事经济活动的人群中（如员工、雇主、跨国公司、政府、当地企业）选取代表，成立审议委员会，广泛听取意见，从而做出决策。这种模式一方面能够发挥市场在调节供需、优化资源配置方面的优势，另一方面又能发挥政府的宏观调控作用，使得开发建设高效有序。

在"裕廊模式"下，政府任命裕廊集团作为总体开发商，裕廊集团选择私人机构参与合作进行建设。具体的合作方式是先划分地块的规划适用目标，就不同目标地块面向社会招标，中标机构均作为合作方参与园区的建设，并通过承租土地的方式进行开发。这一模式的优势在于，裕廊同时对政府和市场两个客户负责，"面对政府时是市场，面对市场时是政府"，极大地降低了体制机制的各种冲突成本和推进阻力，提高各种决策和审批效率，也有效衔接和平衡了政治诉求和市场需求，从而保证高效率、快节奏、低成本、最大化地达成资源的集中和应用。

（四）优质的服务体系

裕廊集团注重职能和服务创新，积极为入园企业打造优质的服务体系，创造低廉便捷、透明高效、稳定舒适的营商环境。

政策扶持：裕廊集团联合政府，为企业提供一站式服务，有效提高企业的投资许可、营业执照、城市规划与建设设计许可、劳动力、税收、进出口报关服务等与政府相关的交易速度，降低交易成本。

个性服务：裕廊集团打造网上客户服务门户，为企业提供园区查询、租金查询、政策查询、账单网上支付、招投标等方面的信息和服务。

定期调研：裕廊集团经常以登门拜访、年度聚会、客户讨论会等多种形式，对园区企业进行深入调研，征求企业意见，通过不断调整管理架构，为入园企业提供更高质量、更为舒适的服务。

（五）人才培养

裕廊创新区的运转与发展需要源源不断的高质量人才作为支撑，为了确保有稳定的人才流入，创新区管理局与南洋理工大学与新加坡理工学院合作，并与前者推出了 JTC-NTU 人才培养计划，同时为了提升人才水平与能力方面，裕廊创新区推出了工业 4.0 转型计划。而这些重要合作的背后存在政府的控制与规划，在李（Lee J）等人关于科技园区的分析框架中，这种模式被称为政府引导机制。[①]裕廊集团高度重视人才培养和可持续发展，通过建设工业基础设施研究中心、举办建筑行业专业挑战赛、承接创新项目，加强人才培养，促进自身创新发展。以下是促进创新与人才聚集的一些措施与有效方法。

设立联合研究中心：裕廊集团联合南洋理工大学（NTU）、新加坡国立大学（NUS）和新加坡科技与设计大学（SUTD）设立了三个工业基础设施创新中心（Innovative Industrial Infrastructure），称为 I^3 研究中心，其中NTU-JTC I^3 重点研究填海及海洋基础设施、可持续基础设施、地下基础设施系统和材料；NUS-JTC I^3 重点研究工业地产市场、土地集约化、规划设计、系统集成与优化、工业建筑技术与方法、城市绿化；STUD-JTC I^3 重点研究城市创新、集成架构与工程、设计与技术、生产机器人。

JTC 创新挑战赛：裕廊集团 2015 年开始举办JTC创新挑战赛（JTC Innovation Challenge），将行业合作伙伴和解决方案提供商聚集在一起，对园区的规划、设计、建造和管理提供创新性的解决方案，入围项目最高可获得 25 万美元的奖励。

开发创新项目：以基础设施创新项目为例，裕廊集团研发了两款机器人。第一种是建筑缺陷检查机器人，可以使用激光扫描仪检查建筑物中的缺陷，找出裂缝等建筑缺陷，可以将检查时间缩短约 50%；第二种是工业建筑喷漆机器人，可以为墙壁和天花板涂漆，效率比两人团队快 25%，且可以连续 24 小时使用。

在技术供给的基础上，保证流畅以及开放的人才培养环境与进入机制是专业人才进入裕廊创新区的保证。同时裕廊创新区贯彻其一直以来的理念，提供方便快捷的天空走廊与裕廊地区快线，以革新在裕廊创新区内的交通模式，使在创新区内任何位置都能快速到达创新区的其他地域。在创新区内，存在的许多科研机构构成了人才的主要来源之一，在一个工业化国家，学术机构和工业之间存在着强有力的联系，以促进技术交流，大学研究中心是该行业最具吸引力的外部技术来源之一。人才的质量与数量在一定程度上能够直观反映该工业区的技术发展程度，技术研究所和大学不仅作为新技术的创造者，而且作为急需的技术人员的提供者，以及作为将经济变化与社会变化相匹配的媒体参与者，

---

① J. Lee, H. N. Win. Technology transfer between university research centers and industry in Singapore. *Technovation*, 2024(5): 433-442.

发挥着重要作用。

一般来说，以大学为代表的学术机构与工业的合作与互动能为企业带来直接的竞争力。对于前者来说，能够将理论知识与实践结合，以缩短专业型人才的固定培养周期，同时能够获得基础研究与产业开发的准入权，并实施测试中的新技术。而对于后者而言，这种合作能够获得学术机构的更专业的咨询与意见汇总，同时对外界提高自身的社会形象，并从产品方面进行质量的改善，以提高自身的竞争力。

综上所述，从技术和人才角度分析，裕廊创新区的布局与发展保证了技术产业与学术机构的优势互补。而许（Francis F C. C. Koh）等人对新加坡的产业与研究中心的技术转移进行了探究，认为学术机构不仅仅可以通过供给高质量人才与企业进行具体合作，还能够通过较完善的技术转移机制进一步扩展与加深合作程度。[1]他们以新国立大学与南洋理工的研究中心作为范例进行了分析，而裕廊创新区范围内已有一定数量的学术机构，在此基础上，可以从机构数量与机构研究方向上对未来的发展进行规划，为学术机构的发展提供崭新的未来，同时为工业4.0时代提供具有创造力的应对范例。

（六）可持续发展

裕廊集团采用绿色环保解决方案，优化自然资源的使用效率、降低二氧化碳排放量、提升绿化率及保护生物多样性，推动新加坡早日实现碳中和。裕廊集团在裕廊政务服务中心、裕廊地面工程中心、裕廊近海海洋中心等项目使用太阳能屋顶，太阳能屋顶能够产生太阳能电力并输送到市政电网，变相减少化石燃料的适用。此外，集团发起了礁石花园倡议，为姐妹岛海洋生态园的人工珊瑚礁项目提供赞助，以保护海洋的生物多样性。裕廊集团还成立了种子库，收集种子，并将种子捐赠给新加坡植物种子库，以保护新加坡的生物多样性。

（七）重视国际输出

由于新加坡国内发展空间狭小，为顺应园区跨国企业全球布局的需要，裕廊集团成立了裕廊国际和腾飞公司，专门在全球输出其卓越的园区服务管理品牌。如今，"裕廊模式"现已成功输出到中国、印度等国家，中国苏州工业园区、中新天津生态城和广州中新知识城是裕廊模式在中国运用的代表作。新加

---

[1]　Francis C. C. Koh, Winston T. H. Koh, Feichin Ted Tschang, An analytical framework for science parks and technology districts with an application to Singapore. *Journal of Business Venturing*, 2005(2): 217-239.

坡裕廊模式的输出主要涉及新加坡产业转移、商务地产投资和服务输出，在裕廊模式的国际输出过程中这三者相辅相成、相互交融，并非独立运作。

产业转移：基于新加坡土地资源受限的基本现实和世界经济发展潮流，新加坡注重科技等高效生产要素的重要作用，积极升级自身产业。一是通过引进跨国公司并提高劳动价格等系列政策，提高低端产业的成本，倒逼劳动密集型等低端产业退出。二是制定鼓励海外投资政策，实现国内落后产业转移。

商务地产投资：裕廊镇工业管理局 2001 年进行了改组，成立裕廊集团，其下设 3 个全资控股子公司，其中腾飞集团负责开发和管理工业园、科技园等商务空间。经过多年的发展，腾飞集团已经成为世界领先企业，在商务空间产品提供、商务房地产服务与房地产基金管理上颇有建树，业务也已遍及新加坡、中国、印度、韩国和越南等 10 个国家的 25 个城市，拥有 1400 多家国际客户。此外，腾飞集团的资本运作也是风生水起，其旗下已上市的信托基金已经达到 3 个，包括腾飞房产投资信托（A-REIT）、腾飞印度信托（A-iTrust）和腾飞酒店信托（A-TRUST），腾飞集团还管理着多个亚洲区域内私募房地产基金。腾飞集团强大的资本实力和高水平的资本运作保证新加坡获得更多经济发展空间，其所行之处，也是裕廊模式的落户之址。

服务输出：裕廊集团力图将商业行为和管理流程有效结合以期达到可持续增长，致力于打造一站式专业咨询服务体系，具体包括总体规划、基础设施规划与设计、选址、建筑设计、设备及工艺设计、项目管理、设计及建造。为了适应不断变化的市场条件和具有挑战性的环境需求，裕廊集团在中国、印度和中东设立了分公司，确保能近距离为全球的客户提供到位服务。裕廊集团有一支囊括规划师、建筑师、工程师、实验室设计专家、地下储油库专家等的高水准专业团队，保证了价值链的完整服务，成为全球著名的建筑环境方案供应商。

五、评析裕廊工业区：优势与挑战并存的现实抉择

裕廊工业区的快速发展对于新加坡国力发展起着举足轻重的作用，这当然离不开其特有的一些优势。但裕廊工业区的发展同时存在着一些现实挑战，如何面对挑战，发挥自身优势，成为裕廊工业区当前急需解决的问题。

（一）优势总结

1.政策优势

新加坡政府为了快速抢占到未来国际竞争前沿阵地，迫切需要建立工业园区。通过采取这种政府垄断的开发运营模式，新加坡对裕廊工业区的资金筹集、土地运用、招商引资等进行统一规划，可以快速并以较低成本获取私人土地，保证园区项目快速启动并尽快达到规模经济，同时有效吸引跨国公司的投资，还降低了国内园区之间的竞争。在政府的大力支持下，裕廊工业区飞速发展，为后续发展打下坚实基础。现如今，裕廊工业区为新加坡贡献超20%的国内GDP，政府始终是其发展的坚实后盾，政府优势是裕廊工业区快速发展的重要因素之一。

2.招商引资

在政府优势的基础支撑下，裕廊工业区一直在社会层面保持着旺盛的招商吸引力。工业园在宏观经济环境下积极为入园企业创造稳定、透明、低廉、高效、舒适的营商环境。裕廊工业区是中央和地方政府合一的单一层次体制，可以为企业提供一站式服务，有效提高企业的投资许可、营业执照、城市规划与建设设计许可、劳动力、税收、进出口报关服务速度，降低交易成本。这一系列优势对广大企业具有无穷的吸引力。

3.全方位技术服务

为了快速实现工业园的建设，使之高效有序地为新加坡经济奉献。新加坡政府在园区建设初始阶段投入了大量资金，用于园区的基础设施建设，建成了总长达一百多公里的区内现代化公路网、发电量占全国一半以上的裕廊电厂、裕廊港码头、自来水厂以及三百多幢标准厂房等，为工业区的未来发展打下了坚实基础。同时，裕廊工业区还兴建了学校、科学馆、商场、体育馆等各种社会服务配套设施，成功地将生产、商务、生活、娱乐、休闲融为一体，充分满足园区内人才的多方位需求。

（二）面临挑战

1.发展空间有限

新加坡作为世界上填海造陆面积高达25%以上的国家，本土面积小一直是国家面临的一个重大的问题。作为新加坡国内占地面积巨大的工业区，裕廊工业区的土地现在开始愈加紧张，面积供给开始渐渐力不从心，如何正确处理好园区面积规划应用，是裕廊工业区现当今面临的重要问题。

2.疫情的影响

新冠疫情的袭击，对世界上各行各业都带来不小的问题，裕廊工业区在冲击之下面临着诸多问题与挑战，当前新冠疫情的影响已经开始慢慢淡化，但是如何迅速走出新冠疫情的阴影，恢复经济活力，是需要被深思熟虑的问题。

六、解锁未知，卓越前行：分析与决策

（一）综合分析

在进行裕廊工业区的深入研究时，为了全面把握其当前的形势和未来的发展趋势，我们选择了两种互补的分析方法：SWOT分析和PEST分析。这两种方法分别从不同角度对裕廊工业区进行了全面的剖析，旨在揭示其内在的优势、劣势、机会和威胁，以及外部环境中的政治、经济、社会和技术因素对其发展的影响。

1.SWOT分析

SWOT分析是一种常用的战略规划工具，通过评估组织的优势（Strengths）、劣势（Weaknesses）、机会（Opportunities）和威胁（Threats），帮助组织明确自身的定位，制定合理的发展策略。对于裕廊工业区而言，SWOT分析有助于我们深入了解其内部的资源和能力，以及外部环境中的机遇和挑战。基于这一分析，我们可以更加清晰地看到裕廊工业区的优势和潜力，同时也能够发现其存在的不足之处和面临的挑战。

（1）优势

人才培养计划：裕廊工业区通过与南洋理工大学和新加坡理工学院合作推出了人才培养计划，以确保有稳定的高质量人才流入，促进技术和创新能力的提升。

工业4.0转型计划：JTC推出的工业4.0转型计划为工业园区带来了技术和数字化转型的机会，以提高效率和竞争力。

（2）劣势

面积有限：裕廊工业区面积有限，这可能限制了其发展潜力和扩张能力。

缺少自然资源：与其他发达国家的工业区相比，裕廊工业区缺乏自然资源，这可能对某些行业的发展造成限制。

（3）机会

强力引擎：作为新加坡最大的工业区之一，裕廊工业区是新加坡经济的强力引擎，为经济增长和就业机会的创造做出了重要贡献。

制造和物流集聚：该工业园区集聚了众多创新、制造和物流企业，形成了紧密结合的制造业集群，促进了企业之间的合作与协同。

技术和创新中心：裕廊工业区承载了先进研发中心和高科技企业，成为新加坡的技术和创新中心，推动科技领域的突破和全面发展。

供应链和价值链：该工业园区形成了高附加值和高品质产品的供应链和价值链，为新加坡创造了丰厚的出口收入和国际竞争力。

（4）威胁

缺乏垄断性优势：与其他发达国家的工业区相比，裕廊工业区缺乏垄断性的优势或特点，这可能使其面临激烈的竞争和市场压力。

自然资源匮乏：新加坡面积较小，缺乏大多数工业原料，需要进口。

应对策略：

SO策略：利用技术和创新优势，加强与先进研发中心和高科技企业的合作，进一步推动科技领域的突破和发展。扩大供应链和价值链，进一步加强企业之间的合作与协同，优化供应链和价值链，提供更高附加值和高品质的产品，以增加出口收入和国际竞争力。

ST策略：投资扩大工业园区面积，探索扩大裕廊工业区面积的可能性，以满足潜在的发展机会，并提供更多的发展空间。

寻找替代资源和合作方式：针对缺乏自然资源的劣势，寻找替代资源，如可再生能源，并寻求与其他地区或国家的合作，以共享资源和优势。

WO策略：提升市场竞争力，加强营销和品牌推广，提高裕廊工业区的市场竞争力，吸引更多国内外企业的投资和设立业务。加强人才培养和吸引，进一步发展人才培养计划，提供更多培训和教育资源，吸引和培养高质量的人才，以支持裕廊工业区的可持续发展。

WT策略：提高资源效率，通过推动节能减排、资源回收利用和环境友好型生产方式等措施，弥补缺乏自然资源的劣势。寻求政府支持和合作，与新加坡政府密切合作，争取政策支持和资金投入，以克服威胁并促进裕廊工业区的可持续发展。

2.基于 SWOT 的 PEST 分析

在深入剖析裕廊工业区的内部条件，即其优势、劣势、机会和威胁

（SWOT分析）之后，我们进一步运用PEST分析框架，全面评估了该工业区所面临的政治、经济、社会和技术四大类外部环境因素。这些外部环境因素不仅深刻影响着裕廊工业区的战略决策和市场定位，更是其实现长期可持续发展的关键因素。通过PEST分析，我们能够更加精准地把握外部环境的变化趋势，为裕廊工业区制定更具前瞻性、针对性和可操作性的战略建议，为其未来的繁荣与发展提供有力支撑。

（1）政治因素

政府顶层设计：裕廊工业区是新加坡最大的工业园区，新加坡政府从一开始就将其确定为全面发展的综合型工业区，精心规划、科学布局。根据其具体地理环境的不同，把靠近市区的东北部划为新兴工业和无污染工业区，重点发展电子、电器及技术密集型产业；把沿海的西南部划为港口和重工业区，安排发展钢铁、造船等大型骨干企业，炼油业则安排在沿海的几个小岛上；中部地区为轻工业和一般工业区；沿裕廊河两岸则规划了住宅区和各种社会生活设施。

政策稳定性：政府保持政策的相对稳定性，为企业提供可预测性和投资保障。新加坡吸引投资的优惠政策主要依据为《经济扩展奖励法案》，在创新政策系统引导模式下，政府对裕廊工业区的资金筹集、土地运用等进行统一规划，拨款筹建园区的基础设施建设，制定了针对不同产业部门的具体优惠便利政策，促进各产业的繁荣。

（2）经济因素

经济增长：新加坡作为亚洲的经济中心之一，拥有强大的经济增长势头，为裕廊工业区提供了市场和商机。同时，新加坡的高度开放和发达的市场经济，为园区提供了良好的经济基础、贸易便利、金融支持和人力资源。新加坡实行了一系列开放的经济政策，如自由贸易政策、外资投资政策和开放的海港和机场等，吸引了大量的外国投资和国际贸易。在2020年，尽管新冠疫情给经济带来挑战，裕廊创新区吸引总计约4.2亿元投资，总计吸引到私人投资总值增至20亿元。

宽松的经商环境：新加坡稳健的财政政策和货币政策，为园区提供了低通胀、低利率、低赤字和低债务的宏观经济环境。新加坡的税收制度简单明晰，主要税种包括17%的企业所得税，2%－22%的累进制个人所得税，8%的消费税（增值税），以及预提税、印花税等其他小税种。值得注意的是，新加坡对资本利得并不征税，同时在新加坡收到的境外红利符合特定条件还可以免税。此外，新加坡公司向股东（无论是新加坡境内还是境外）支付股息无预提所得税。

（3）社会因素

多元社会：社会文化的多元化和包容性，促进了裕廊的创新能力和国际化水平，增强了裕廊的竞争优势和吸引力。新加坡是一个由不同种族、语言、宗教和文化组成的多元社会，这为裕廊提供了一个开放和包容的创新环境，激发了裕廊的创意思维和跨界合作，促进了裕廊的技术创新和产品创新。同时，新加坡也是一个与世界各国紧密联系的国际社会，这为裕廊提供了一个广阔和多样的国际市场，增加了裕廊的市场份额和市场影响力，促进了裕廊的国际合作和国际竞争。

多样化的人才构成：社会结构的高度教育和高素质，提高了裕廊的人力资本和知识资本，提升了裕廊的生产效率和质量水平。新加坡是一个重视教育和培养人才的社会，这为裕廊提供了一个高水平和高素质的人才队伍，包括科技人才、管理人才和专业人才。这些人才不仅具备专业知识和技能，还具备创新精神和学习能力，能够为裕廊提供有效的解决方案和持续的改进。同时，新加坡也是一个注重知识和信息的社会，这为裕廊提供了一个丰富和更新的知识资源，包括科技知识、市场知识和管理知识。这些知识不仅支持了裕廊的研发活动和决策过程，还促进了裕廊的知识共享和知识创造。

（4）技术因素

创新和科技：科技发展的快速进步和变革，为园区提供了新的技术机会和挑战，要求园区不断跟进和引进国际先进的技术和装备，提高园区的技术竞争力和市场竞争力。裕廊工业区是新加坡的工业核心，承载了新加坡的重要产业，如石油化工、电子、生物医药、精密工程等。这些产业都是高科技、高附加值、高要求的产业，需要不断地更新和改进技术，以适应国际市场的变化和竞争。因此，裕廊工业区一直注重引进和采用国际先进的技术和装备，如智能制造、工业互联网、人工智能、物联网等，以提高园区的生产效率、质量水平、安全性能等。同时，裕廊工业区也面临着新的技术挑战，如技术转型、技术升级、技术保护等，需要不断地调整和优化园区的技术战略和政策，以应对技术发展带来的风险和机遇。

工业4.0转型：工业4.0的发展趋势给裕廊工业区带来了机遇和挑战，科技创新的强大推动和支持，为园区提供了新的技术动力和资源，促进园区的技术创新和产品创新，增加园区的技术附加值和市场附加值。裕廊工业区是新加坡的创新中心，拥有了众多的科研机构、高校、企业等创新主体，形成了一个活跃和协同的创新生态系统。这些创新主体不仅为园区提供了丰富和更新的科技知识、人才、资金等创新资源，还为园区提供了强有力的科技合作、交流、服务等创新支持。因此，裕廊工业区一直致力于推动和支持园区内外的科技创新活动，如科研项目、专利申请、产品开发等，以提高园区的科技水平、科技优势、科技效益等。同时，裕廊工业区也注重培育和引导园区内外的创新文化和氛围，如鼓励创新思维、激励创新行为、奖励创新成果等，以增强园区的创新能力、创新活力、创新影响力等。

（二）从裕廊工业区中总结的对策

综合以上两大分析方法，我们得到了以下对策，在一定程度上能够助力世界其他地区的工业园区的建设与发展。

1.政府支持与政策稳定性

政府作为工业园区发展的主导力量，应提供全面的支持，包括财政支持、税收优惠和行政审批简化。同时，政府应确保政策的稳定性和连续性，为企业创造可预测的经营环境，减少风险与不确定性。政府的全力支持是工业园区成功的关键因素。通过财政和税收优惠，政府可以减轻企业的经济负担，激发其创新活力。同时，简化的行政审批流程能够提高企业的运营效率，使其更好地应对市场变化。政策的稳定性则为企业提供了长期发展的信心，避免了因政策频繁变更而带来的连锁反应。

2.经济增长与国际竞争力

工业园区应选址于经济增长迅猛的地区，借助区域优势吸引企业入驻。同时，加强产业集聚和供应链建设，形成规模效应，提升工业园区的国际竞争力。经济增长迅猛的地区为企业提供了充足的市场机会，有利于企业的快速发展。产业集聚和高效的供应链能够降低企业的运营成本，提高生产效率，从而增强工业园区的整体竞争力。此外，产业集聚还能促进企业间的合作与资源共享，形成良性互动的发展格局。

3.产业集聚与技术创新

工业园区应积极吸引多家企业入驻，形成产业集群。同时，加强与研发机构的合作，推动技术创新和产业升级。产业集群的形成有助于企业间的合作与资源共享，降低交易成本，提高生产效率。与研发机构的紧密合作则能够为企业带来先进的技术支持，推动其技术创新和产业升级。这种合作模式能够提升工业园区的核心竞争力，使其在激烈的市场竞争中脱颖而出。

4.人才资源与劳动力多样性

工业园区应重视人才资源的培养与引进，保障稳定的人才供给。同时，保持劳动力的多样性，以满足不同企业的需求。人才是企业发展的核心动力。稳定的人才供给能够为企业提供源源不断的智力支持，推动其不断创新和发展。同时，多样化的劳动力背景有助于企业拓展全球市场，应对不同文化背景下的挑战。因此，工业园区应重视人才资源的培养和引进，为企业提供良好的发展环境。

5.技术转型与数字化发展

工业园区应积极拥抱工业 4.0 的趋势，引入智能制造和数字化技术，提高生产效率和质量。随着科技的不断发展，智能制造和数字化技术已经成为工业发展的新趋势。工业园区作为产业发展的聚集地，应积极引入这些先进技术。这种技术转型不仅有助于企业保持竞争优势，还能推动整个工业园区的产业升级和可持续发展。

6.可持续发展与环境保护

工业园区应关注环境保护和社会责任，推进绿色生产和资源循环利用。可持续发展已经成为全球共识。工业园区作为经济发展的重要载体，应承担起相应的社会责任，关注环境保护和资源利用。通过推进绿色生产和资源循环利用，工业园区可以减少对环境的污染和破坏，实现经济效益和社会效益的双赢。这种发展模式不仅能够吸引投资者的关注，还能获得国际社会的认可和支持。

7.合作与开放

工业园区应鼓励企业之间的合作与协同，同时对国际合作保持开放态度。在全球化的背景下，合作与开放已经成为工业园区发展的必然趋势。通过加强企业之间的合作与协同，工业园区能够形成强大的合力，共同应对市场挑战。同时，对国际合作保持开放态度则能够吸引更多的跨国企业和投资进入工业园区，实现资源共享和市场拓展。这种开放性的发展模式有助于提升工业园区的国际影响力和竞争力。

8.持续创新与适应性

工业园区必须持续创新，跟上市场和技术的变化，灵活适应新挑战。创新是工业园区持续发展的动力源泉。面对不断变化的市场和技术环境，工业园区必须保持敏锐的市场洞察力，及时捕捉新的发展机遇。同时，工业园区还应加强自身的创新能力建设，通过引入新技术、新工艺和新模式等方式推动产业升级和转型。这种持续创新的发展模式能够使工业园区在激烈的市场竞争中保持领先地位并实现可持续发展。

七、展　望

展望未来，新加坡裕廊工业区有望逐步转变为一个充满创新活力的区域，并逐渐成为全球科技领域的引领者。通过政府的积极支持和政策优惠，工业区将继续吸引先进研发中心和高科技企业的入驻，推动技术创新与产业升级。在这一过程中，裕廊工业区将成为全球范围内的创新先锋和典范，吸引国际投资和人才涌入，为新加坡和全球经济增长注入新的活力。与此同时，工业区的创新范式以及宜居基础设施建设将提供宝贵的经验和参考，从而为全球工业园区的建设开拓出一条生活与工作功能汇聚的新型发展道路。

不仅如此，裕廊工业区在未来将起到工业4.0方案的领军作用，在工业4.0时代，人们将持续不断地对如何实现高效率、低消耗以及智能化的工业系统与工业生态进行研究。工业4.0时代的基石是人才与创新，我们相信，在现在以及将来，人们对工业新模式的发掘与探索将不断激励着全球工业界的相互交流与合作。因而，促进世界工业区整体水平的提升以及新型工业区模式的提出，无疑将使世界加快进入工业4.0的卓越时代。

硅谷八十年——美国硅谷一流园区的经验和启示[①]

摘　要: 随着工业技术的不断创新和高新科学技术的发展，越来越多的工业园区如雨后春笋般兴起。本文主要聚焦于世界最著名的工业园区之一——美国硅谷，从建设历程和主导产业两方面分析其能够成为世界闻名的高新技术创新和发展中心的秘诀，结合当下热门的可持续发展与创新议题，探索其在绿色化和数字化浪潮中已有的贡献，并从硅谷的生态系统建设、文化氛围以及发展模式出发，探索其提升经济效益和企业效率的经验。本文从政府、工业园区企业以及高校和科研院所三方面总结并借鉴硅谷发展模式，为国内工业园区提供有益的建议。此外，本文也列举了硅谷的不足之处，并给予国内工业园区借鉴与展望。

关键词: 工业园区; 硅谷经验; 国内工业园区; 经验借鉴与警醒

一、引　言

1971 年 1 月 11 日，美国记者赫夫勒（Don Hoefler）在《每周商业》报纸电子新闻的一系列文章的题目中首次使用了"美国硅谷"（Silicon Valley, USA），而他并不知道，此时才刚刚崭露头角的硅谷，将成为日后世界闻名的高新技术创新和发展中心。

硅谷工业园区（简称"硅谷"）的历史始于第二次世界大战。第二次世界大战结束后，美国的大学回流的学生骤增。为满足财务需求，同时给毕业生提供就业机会，斯坦福大学采纳特曼（Frederick Terman）的建议，开辟工业园，允

---

① 作者: 黄天骐，浙江大学外国语学院; 黄天骊，浙江大学外国语学院; 吴姿苇，浙江大学翻译专业; 朱怡霖，浙江大学外国语学院。

许高技术公司租用其地作为办公用地，至今已逾七十载。

如今的硅谷工业园区以其集聚了世界上许多知名科技公司和创新型企业而闻名。它位于美国加州旧金山湾区，得名于大量使用硅作为半导体材料的电子技术产业，如计算机芯片制造。久而久之，硅谷成为了科技创新的中心，这里是诸如个人计算机、互联网、智能手机等世界上许多重要技术突破的诞生地，在信息技术、生物技术、人工智能、清洁能源、虚拟现实等领域均取得了许多重要的成果，对全球科技行业和经济产生了深远影响。

硅谷工业园区不仅在科技领域取得了巨大成功，也成为一个创业生态系统的典范。这里拥有丰富的投资资源、孵化器和创业加速器，它吸引了世界各地的科学家、工程师、企业家和投资者寻求支持和发展机会。一些著名的科技巨头，如苹果、谷歌和英特尔等，都起源于硅谷。

与光鲜亮丽的硅谷不同的是，我国工业园区的发展并非一帆风顺。例如，我国引以为豪的长三角工业园区普遍土地开发粗放、集约利用水平有待提升；[①]"中国硅谷"中关村科技园作为全国首个国家级高新技术产业开发区，在产业集聚、技术创新、成果转化等方面均有不足；沈阳工业园区作为"共和国工业之母"，其政府管理存在决策程序烦琐、扶持政策执行困难等问题；[②]重庆潼南工业园区基础配套设施与公共服务并不完善；[③]杭州临安西部工业园区招商引资难、入园企业发展后劲不足；[④]郑州工业园区外资引入少，国际化水平低；[⑤]重庆麻柳工业园区产业结构不合理；[⑥]而更多的工业园区则如同张掖工业园区一般，生态环境保护面临着严峻的形势[⑦]。

远近闻名的硅谷究竟是如何发展起来的？硅谷的成功能否复制？又能给国内的工业园区带来何种经验？借鉴硅谷的华丽腾飞之路，我们又能给国内工业园区遇到的主要瓶颈带来何种对策和建议？

在了解硅谷工业园区成功的原因的同时，本文也为优化硅谷模式并在国内工业园区借鉴推广类似模式提供了有益的见解和建议，并在多方面给予国内工

---

① 赵玉婷，董林艳，李小敏，等.长三角工业园区发展存在问题及对策.环境影响评价，2018，40(5)：13-17.

② 洪焕坪.沈阳工业园区发展中政府管理问题研究.沈阳：沈阳师范大学，2018.

③ 蔡燕.潼南工业园区发展存在的问题及建议.农家参谋，2019(16)：218，268.

④ 翁煜.杭州市临安区西部农村工业园区发展问题研究.杭州：浙江农林大学，2020..

⑤ 王霞.郑州市工业园区发展问题及对策.企业研究，2007(1)：29-31.

⑥ 文煦.重庆市麻柳工业园区发展问题研究.重庆：西南大学，2020.

⑦ 任晓玲.张掖工业园区循环经济发展规划设计问题研究.武汉：湖北工业大学，2018.

业园区重要的启发，促进科技创新、经济发展和创业生态的繁荣。

二、美国硅谷概述

（一）硅谷的建设历程：乘机遇扶摇

美国硅谷是世界上最著名的一流工业园区之一，它的建设历程可以追溯到20世纪中叶，以其在高科技和创新领域的杰出成就而闻名于世。按照时代背景和硅谷所抓住的三次机遇来划分，硅谷的建设历程主要分为以下三个阶段。

1.第一阶段（20世纪40—60年代）：发展规划和基础设施建设

硅谷的发展始于第二次世界大战期间，美国政府将硅谷地区选定为高科技研究和国防工业的战略重点地区。在此期间，大量的研究机构和企业开始进驻该地区，并投入资金和人力资源进行技术研发。政府与企业之间的合作为硅谷的发展奠定了基础。硅谷的发展模式即"学术—工业综合体"以及风险资本与创新公司的初步结合基本定型。

2.第二阶段（20世纪70—90年代）：技术创新和初创企业兴起

随着"以原子能、电子计算机、空间技术为标志的第三次科技革命的兴起，硅谷开始成为全球技术创新的中心，硅谷发挥微电子技术优势、芯片产业先发优势，逐渐在电脑硬件研发、制造和应用上独占鳌头"①，硅谷进入微电子时代。一系列重要的科技公司如英特尔、惠普和苹果等在硅谷崛起，并在计算机、半导体和软件领域取得突破性的成就。这一时期还见证了一大批初创企业的涌现，其中包括微软、谷歌和亚马逊等。硅谷地区的高科技生态系统不断壮大，吸引了全球范围内的创新者和投资者。

3.第三阶段（21世纪至今）：多元化和全球化

进入21世纪，新一轮经济全球化兴起，为硅谷拓展全球市场、集聚高端要素、突破自我驱动发展模式提供了基础。此时，硅谷进一步推动了技术的多元化发展。除了计算机和互联网领域，硅谷开始涉足生物技术、人工智能、无人驾驶和可再生能源等新兴领域。此外，硅谷还积极吸引来自世界各地的人才和投资，使其成为全球化的科技创新中心。许多跨国科技公司在硅谷设立研发中心或总部，促进了地区经济的进一步发展。"特别是以斯坦福大学为代表的'知识富矿'依托'产业'载体，适时打造'大学－科研－产业'三位一体互

---

① 董垒，朱凯.美国"硅谷"发展的经验与启示.杭州（我们），2017(5)：53-57.

促反哺发展模式，硅谷又一次腾飞。"[1]硅谷大规模进入网络时代，网络时代又带来了软件业的昌盛。这是软件业和网络业同时大发展的时期，也是硅谷的社会文化和人们的思维领域发生根本变化的时期。

综上，美国硅谷的建设历程经历了发展规划和基础设施建设阶段、技术创新和初创企业兴起阶段，以及多元化和全球化阶段。通过持续的科技创新、政府与企业的合作以及吸引全球人才和投资，硅谷成为全球科技和创新的领先地区之一。

（二）硅谷主导产业：夯基与迭代并存

硅谷的主导产业涵盖了信息技术与软件开发、半导体和电子技术、生物科技和医疗健康，以及清洁能源和可持续发展等领域。

第一，信息技术与软件开发产业。信息技术产业是硅谷最重要的主导产业之一。该地区孕育了众多知名的科技公司，如谷歌、苹果和亚马逊等。硅谷在软件开发、网络技术和云计算等领域具有显著的优势，为全球提供了先进的信息技术产品和服务。

第二，半导体和电子技术产业。硅谷在半导体和电子技术领域也占据重要地位。众多半导体公司和电子设备制造商在这里设立了研发中心和生产基地。硅谷在半导体芯片设计、制造工艺和集成电路技术方面处于领先地位，为全球提供了高性能和创新的电子产品。

第三，生物科技和医疗健康产业。众多生物技术公司和医疗科技企业在硅谷聚集，致力于研发新药、基因工程、生物诊断和医疗器械等方面的创新。

第四，硅谷在清洁能源和可持续发展方面也发挥着重要作用。该地区聚集了众多的可再生能源公司和绿色科技企业，致力于开发和推广清洁能源技术、能源储存和能源管理解决方案。硅谷以其创新力和投资环境，推动可持续发展的实践和推广。

三、硅谷发展的经验探索

（一）持续引领数字化与绿色化发展

1.强化产业数字化与数字产业化

硅谷积极推动了各行各业的数字技术应用，包括人工智能、大数据分析、

---

[1] 董垒，朱凯.美国"硅谷"发展的经验与启示.杭州（我们），2017(5): 53-57.

物联网和区块链等。这些技术的应用和推广在提高生产效率、降低成本和为企业创造新的商业机会等方面起到了重要作用。为了支持产业数字化和数字产业化，硅谷也参与了建设数字基础设施，包括高速互联网接入、数据中心和云计算等。这些基础设施的发展为企业提供了更好的数字化平台和工具。硅谷的科技公司也提供数字化转型的咨询和支持服务，帮助企业制定数字化战略、进行技术转型和实施数字化解决方案。这有助于加速企业的数字化转型进程。

硅谷的数字化成功体现在数字平台方面的广泛应用：

自 20 世纪 90 年代以来，越来越多的硅谷企业青睐于采用数字平台驱动，这种商业模式以数据密集和轻资本为特点。这些后起之秀对传统行业产生了颠覆性的冲击，并成为新的赢家。谷歌、优步、爱比迎等传统行业的"颠覆者"，都凭借着独特的数字平台和核心业务操作取得了成功。随着时间推移，这些数字平台变得越来越难以替代，用户和合作伙伴一旦转向其他平台，将面临更高的成本和门槛。同时，现今的硅谷企业越来越倾向于将数字平台与企业创新生态系统相结合，通过平台作为纽带，有效地利用各类互补方的创新能力。这样的做法不仅激发了多边市场的活力，也促进了生态系统成员之间的核心互动。[①]

为了满足数字化时代的需求，硅谷也在不断加强人才培养和技能提升。这包括与高校合作开设相关专业课程，提供培训机会，并支持创新型人才的发展和吸引。硅谷积极促进数字产业生态系统的发展，通过支持初创企业、投资风险资本、建立孵化器和加速器等方式来鼓励创业和创新。同时，加强数字产业的合作和交流，促进协同创新。

2. 推动绿色技术和可持续发展

政策引领是推动绿色技术和可持续发展的重要道路。"自奥巴马政府于 2008 年启动绿色能源经济战略以来"[②]，借着该政策的东风，硅谷将支持绿色产业发展视为重要战略之一，大力促进可再生能源产业、电动力汽车产业、智能电网和清洁产业的发展，这种持续的努力有助于硅谷继续在可持续能源领域取得领先地位，并为环保事业做出积极贡献。

自 2008 年以来，加利福尼亚州的可再生能源发电总量突飞猛进，至 2013 年已高达 700 千瓦，在美国总能源产出中所占比例不断扩大，位居世界第二。

① 王海军, 金姝彤, 束超慧, 等. 为什么硅谷能够持续产生颠覆性创新? ——基于企业创新生态系统视角的分析. 科学学研究, 2021, 39(12): 2267-2280. .
② 黄王麗, 张博茹, 张瀚月. 硅谷绿色能源经济发展及启示. 科技进步与对策, 2017, 34(3): 37-43.

值得一提的是，自 2005 年加利福尼亚州州长施瓦辛格推行"百万太阳能屋顶项目"以来，硅谷累计太阳能装机容量一路飙升，太阳能已然成为硅谷政府和居民工作和生活中不可或缺的替代能源选择。①

智能电网也是该绿色化发展的重要一环。"智能电网最初由位于硅谷帕洛阿尔托的电力研究所提出，指的是以互联网为基本架构的新一代电力基础设施网，它汇集了上千万个电力生产单元，拥有大型集中供电站，连接着可再生能源供应与分配，成为分散式能源供应站。"②而相比传统电网，智能电网对传统资源和再生资源具有兼容性，有利于对过剩能源进行智能再分配，从而减少资源浪费，提高能效。此外，智能电网也能创造更多就业岗位并吸引了大量投资，实现了资金和资源的良性循环。

此外，在致力于实现低碳、碳中和的全球大环境下，硅谷所注重的可持续发展 ESG（Environment、Society、Governance）理念，因其倡导企业在运营过程中更加注重环境友好、社会责任以及公司治理，显得日益普遍和重要。先前，美国硅谷绿色科技委员会主席周楚新博士和其团队开发了新的污水处理技术，其原理是利用智能优化微生物作为催化剂，从污水和污泥中产生出甲烷。这种技术不仅提高了污水处理能力，还能把污泥中的重金属提炼出来，而在此技术发明之前，污水处理厂沉淀下来的污泥一般是要被填埋，或者沥干后每吨花 150 美元左右送到发电厂焚烧，前者会浪费和污染土地资源，而后者又由于污泥中含有重金属，焚烧后会造成大气污染。同时，硅谷发展绿色金融，加大对清洁产业和绿色产业的投资，推广清洁能源的使用。产业数字化和数字化产业的发展也减少了实体污染，促进了绿色化发展。新冠疫情过后，硅谷对线下实体办公场所的追求减少，也是绿色化发展在现代语境下的一种新思路。

（二）提升经济效益和企业效率

1.四链融合和生态系统建设

硅谷在构建产业生态系统方面，"实现了'创新链、产业链、资金链、人才链'的深度融合，将创新、产业、资金和人才四个要素巧妙地结合在一起。通过积极实践，硅谷努力打造了这种融合型的创新生态，旨在推动经济朝着高质量发展的方向迈进。③企业创新生态系统是硅谷企业实现颠覆性创新的重要

---

① 黄玉丽，张博茹，张瀚月.硅谷绿色能源经济发展及启示.科技进步与对策，2017，34(3)：37-43.
② 黄玉丽，张博茹，张瀚月.硅谷绿色能源经济发展及启示.科技进步与对策，2017，34(3)：37-43.
③ 李重达.从硅谷经验看"四链"深度融合.中国人才，2023(4)：9-11.

载体，它使这些企业及其伙伴能够在更广的组织范围内实现价值共创。这个创新生态系统有两大关键机制：平台化思维与模块化逻辑。平台化思维让系统中的各个成员相互交融、产生强大的网络效应，并在数字化融合的时代下创造出新的市场和业态。这样一来，企业的颠覆性创新能力得以显著提升。而模块化逻辑则为整个生态系统赋予了自由而灵活的特性。它让各成员可以自由地分工协作，在非线性的职能监管下互动协同，甚至能在环境变化的挑战面前重新调整自己的结构。[①]

在硅谷的产业发展中，"四链融合"的特征十分显著：

产业链是技术创新向生产转化的基石，而创新链则是提升整体创新能力的核心。二者相辅相成，紧密环绕着产业链的发展。在产业链发展的关键环节，良好的创新条件能够降低产业链上下游关键核心技术对外依存的程度，突破产业升级的瓶颈，推动产业链的优化与升级。产业链和创新链之间的相互作用是产学研深度融合的创新生态的核心。而资金链则为创新链提供有力支持，同时也是产业链优化升级的重要动力。在技术创新和产业升级的关键节点，良好的资金环境能够持续支撑新技术的突破和产业化，并形成良性的资金循环。这样的循环不仅有助于推动科技成果的成功转化，也有助于促进产业链的持续发展。而在产业链和创新链的各个环节，一个完整的人才链也是至关重要的。这个人才链涵盖了战略科学家、科技领军人才、优秀企业家、卓越工程师等各类专业领域知识和技能的人才。[②]

只有通过人才链的紧密配合，科技成果才能顺利从创新链转化为产业链，推动经济和社会的长期进步。产业链、创新链、资金链和人才链，它们如同交织在一起的纽带，共同构筑了一个充满活力的创新生态系统。在这个生态系统中，科技创新得以源源不断地涌现，推动着产业的繁荣和进步。

四链的融合与生态系统建设的顺利运行主要依赖多途径广领域的通力协作，从而实现各个领域部门的互联互通。

在创新链方面，硅谷创建了开放的创新生态系统，通过该系统，硅谷持续吸引更多的初创企业、创业者和创新者。通过设立孵化器、加速器和创新中心等，为初创企业提供支持和资源，促进创新和创业活动的蓬勃发展。孵化器通

① 王海军，金姝彤，束超慧，等.为什么硅谷能够持续产生颠覆性创新？——基于企业创新生态系统视角的分析.科学学研究，2021，39(12)：2267-2280.
② 李重达.从硅谷经验看"四链"深度融合.中国人才，2023(4)：9-11.

常为初创公司提供办公空间、培训、咨询和其他资源，帮助它们在早期阶段建立业务模式并开始运营。孵化器通常会与初创公司建立长期合作关系，帮助它们逐步成长。加速器则更侧重于帮助初创公司快速增长。它们通常会为初创公司提供短期的密集培训和指导，并帮助它们与投资者建立联系。加速器的目标是帮助初创公司在短时间内取得显著的增长。它们有的独立存在，也有的是大学、企业或是本地政府赞助的。在硅谷倡导的开放创新模式中，知识无边界地在各组织间流动，通过校企合作、企业联合研发等方式，实现着无限可能。与此同时，硅谷非常重视知识产权保护，这一举措有助于保护创新成果。

在产业链方面，硅谷的企业也与相关产业链上的企业、供应商和合作伙伴建立紧密的合作伙伴关系。通过共享资源、技术和市场信息，加强产业链上下游之间的合作与协同，提高整体竞争力。硅谷企业也向产业链上的企业提供技术和创新支持，包括技术咨询、研发合作和技术转移等。通过共享先进技术和最佳实践，帮助企业提升技术水平和创新能力。

在资金链方面，硅谷与金融机构合作，为初创企业提供充足的风险投资。硅谷是世界上最著名、最成熟的风险资本市场，为创新者和初创公司提供了强有力的融资支持。这里的企业能够获得丰富的资本支持，而大量初创公司则通过参与创业加速器和孵化器来获得资金援助，进而壮大成长。此外，硅谷还涌现出众多投资公司和基金会，它们的风险投资活动不断推动着创新的进程。"光是 2021 年，对硅谷的风险投资额就高达 441 亿美元，其中还包括创下纪录的 257 笔超过 1 亿美元的巨额交易。这足以见证硅谷投资活动的蓬勃发展。同时，2021 年，投资流向硅谷和旧金山地区的天使投资更是激增，总额高达 12 亿美元，与前一年相比，硅谷的天使投资增长了 12%，而参与这些交易的天使投资者和天使团体数量更是同比增加了近 40%。"[①] 帮助初创公司成长并吸引投资者的同时，硅谷也与中介组织和非营利性组织合作，促进各主体之间的协同互动，同时，也组织行业交流会议、研讨会和合作项目，为产业链上的企业提供交流和合作的机会。通过分享经验、促进合作创新，加强企业间的互动和合作。

在人才链方面，硅谷也与相关行业建立紧密的合作关系，共同培育人才和提升技能水平。通过与高校合作、开展培训计划和实习项目等，培养具备产业

---

① 李重达. 从硅谷经验看"四链"深度融合. 中国人才，2023(4)：9-11.

链需求的高素质人才，提供符合产业发展需要的人力资源。"今天的硅谷地区汇集了85所全球知名高校，其中有3所为QS大学排名前30，7所为QS大学排名前200的高校，全球自然指数200强的科研机构12所。"①硅谷是高素质人才的聚集地，良好的科研环境和创新氛围吸引了全球顶尖学子来硅谷求学深造。

在一些方面，硅谷也参与了产业标准和规范的制定过程，与产业链上的企业共同推动技术标准的制定和统一。这有助于提高产业链的协同效应和互操作性，促进创新和发展。硅谷也与政府进行了广泛的合作，共同制定支持产业链发展的政策和措施。通过与政府的紧密合作，为产业链上的企业提供良好的政策环境和支持，推动产业链的协调发展。硅谷作为重要的创新枢纽，还和全世界其他重要的创新枢纽建立了密切的联系。创新协作网络的搭建让整个创新体系的运行变得更快捷。

硅谷的成功离不开其良好有机的生态系统和积极的政策扶持，在四链融合发展和生态系统的顺畅运行下，硅谷得以在世界工业园区中脱颖而出。

2.开放自由和不惧失败的文化氛围

硅谷拥有独特的文化氛围。这种文化已经在过去几十年中发展成为美国传统价值观和现代文化在高科技时代的杰出代表。这种融合的高科技文化有着四个显著特点。首先，硅谷的创新文化鼓励接受失败。对于研发和创新而言，承担风险和容忍失败至关重要。在硅谷，企业家和创业者们对于风险有着非常高的容忍度，几乎一半的美国风险投资都来自这里。他们深知成功并非唾手可得，大多数初创公司可能会失败，但这并不妨碍他们不断尝试和学习。其次，硅谷的佯谬文化充满着令人矛盾的特质。他们自称开放、灵活、民主，但同时又热衷于极端主义。硅谷推崇人文主义管理和信息共享，却又对技术保密极为严格。这种悖论在人们心中产生强烈的震荡，让硅谷显得独树一帜。再次，硅谷的企业文化非常独特。在这里，人才流动性极高，员工可以直呼上司的名字，穿着随意，弹性工作时间，甚至可以在家工作。员工也有机会拥有公司的股票，这种文化强调员工的自主权和参与感。最后，硅谷文化是一种追求速度的时间文化。在知识经济时代，硅谷人无法拘泥于过去工业化时代的标准化工作时间，他们需要根据创新的需要安排时间。通常情况下，他们会连续几天通宵达旦地工作，深夜或凌晨工作几乎已成为这里20万高科技人员的共同生活

① 李重达.从硅谷经验看"四链"深度融合.中国人才，2023(4)：9-11.

方式。

不同地区、不同城市拥有不同的资源和潜力，建设全球创新中心，实际上并没有一个固定的发展模式。而对于旧金山湾区来说，开放性模式是建立全球创新中心最成功的方式。硅谷还有整个湾区的发展都是没有事先规划好的，它是一个自然发展的模式，更多的是内部人才、信息与理念的有机融合。

3.独特的发展模式和完备的政府扶持

硅谷遵循以中小企业为核心的发展模式。这种模式以企业关系的平面化、网络化和企业间知识信息的共享为特点和发展的依托。硅谷形成了有机合作的高技术工业区，在新产品的生产过程中，高技术小公司互相合作，既保持了较小的规模，又具有全球竞争力。当公司规模变大时，硅谷选择了裂变的形式：将标准化产品的制造部门移往南部或西部地区，而硅谷只保留研究和开发的功能。硅谷的成功在很大程度上缘于这种发展模式。

硅谷成功的关键还在于它建立了一个完整的创新体系，并采用了开放性的模式，允许人才和思想的自由流动。"硅谷率先创造了科技与产业相互融合的三位一体发展模式，这种创新现象不仅是科技发展的新社会形态，也是整个高科技产业发展的最显著特征。三位一体的发展模式成为硅谷发展的内在动力，知识和高科技迅速成为生产力中至关重要的因素，几乎是首位的生产力。"[1]同时，这种三位一体的发展模式本身就构成一种创新的网络式合作组织。它在不同层次上展现出多样的合作形式，涵盖广泛的合作渠道。"不仅有政府、创新企业、风险资本投资公司、学校和公共机构（例如基金会、非赢利组织等）之间的合作，还有企业之间的合作。"[2]硅谷所拥有的丰富的研究型大学与实验室资源为硅谷三位一体的创新发展模式提供了重要的基础。"硅谷中拥有5所研究型大学，同时还包括25个国家级或州级实验室。这种多方合作让硅谷的创新生态更加丰富多彩，为各方参与者创造了广阔的合作机遇。它不仅有助于加速科技和产业的交流和进步，也促进了人才的培养和创新思维的交汇。"[3]

在硅谷的三位一体创新发展过程中，政府扮演了至关重要的角色。早期硅谷的形成，很大程度上归功于美国国防部对尖端电子产品的巨大需求，这推动了许多年轻高科技公司的蓬勃发展。一方面，政府直接注资并在各个领域投入

---

[1]　胡德巧.政府主导还是市场主导——硅谷与筑波成败启示录.中国统计，2001，(6)：16-18.

[2]　胡德巧.政府主导还是市场主导——硅谷与筑波成败启示录.中国统计，2001，(6)：16-18.

[3]　左学金.国内外开发区模式比较及经验：典型案例研究.社会科学，2008(9)：4-12+187.

资源，同时也颁布了一系列措施来促进硅谷技术的发展。举例来说，政府向斯坦福大学的研究项目提供了丰厚的赞助经费，并对中小企业的研发投入予以支持，同时通过税收政策等手段鼓励企业自主进行项目研发。此外，政府严格执行专利制度，保护知识产权，推动了技术交易市场的建立。还制定了行业标准，推进技术的不断完善与进步。为吸引高层次人才，政府也设立宽松的技术移民签证政策。这些措施共同吸引了大量人才涌入硅谷，推动了技术创新的蓬勃发展。另一方面，政府也为硅谷的不断扩展提供了规划用地。每次硅谷扩建都伴随着各种问题，而地方政府在协调各方利益的过程中起到了至关重要的作用。他们的规划与协调确保了硅谷的有序发展。最后，政府还在改善硅谷的交通状况方面发挥了重要作用。他们的努力致力于缓解交通拥堵问题，从而为硅谷的可持续发展创造了更加宜居的环境。

（三）展望和警醒

即使是作为世界一流工业园区的硅谷在发展过程中也会碰壁，或是有所不足，甚至出现信誉危机等令人警醒的事故。对此，我们组针对硅谷发展中所暴露的一些问题和缺陷做出了反馈和展望，并希望从中获得的启示和教训能够为其他存在通病和共性的工业园区提供前车之鉴。

1.积极承担社会责任，创造社会价值

硅谷各公司应当将社会责任视为一项核心价值，并将其纳入业务战略和日常运营中。通过积极承担社会责任，硅谷可以在提升经济和社会效益方面发挥更积极的作用，创造更多的社会价值。

硅谷可以积极参与教育和培训项目，为社区提供技术技能培训和职业发展机会。这有助于减少数字鸿沟，增加人们的就业机会，并为未来的科技创新提供更深厚的人才基础。

在数字化过程中，数据隐私和安全至关重要。"硅谷应该加强数据隐私和安全保护的措施，确保企业和用户的数据不被滥用和泄露，并建立透明的数据使用和共享政策。这有助于恢复公众对科技公司的信任，并保护用户的权益。例如，在谷歌开发人工智能的同时，判断哪些对用户有利、哪些对谷歌有利、哪些又对谷歌的其他服务有好处是一个棘手的问题，这也是人工智能无法解决的问题。谷歌应该对这些选择的结果负责，无论是人还是机器做出的决定。"①

---

① 谷歌CEO：AI是谷歌的未来　但也要肩负起责任.信息与电脑（理论版），2017(19)：1-3.

除此之外，政府在产业数字化和数字产业化方面发挥重要作用，硅谷可以积极与政府合作，制定相应的政策支持和监管框架，为数字产业的发展提供良好的环境和条件。

硅谷的公司应该遵守法律法规，并确保其业务行为符合道德和社会责任的标准：

> 这包括诚信经营、避免不当竞争和滥用市场垄断地位等。譬如，谷歌公司开发的"谷歌地图"跨界披露了他国军事设施信息。根据2001年通过的《国家对其国际不法行为的责任条款草案》和1998年通过的《国际法不加禁止行为造成损害后果的国际责任条款草案》，跨界披露他国军事设施信息行为满足"国际不法行为"的构成要件，可以通过"一般国际责任"制度追究责任；非国家行为体所为的披露他国军事设施信息的行为则可以通过"不加禁止行为的国际责任"制度追究责任。[①]

硅谷的公司和企业家应当积极参与社会投资和慈善事业，支持社区发展、公益项目和社会创新。这包括捐赠资金、技术支持和志愿者活动等。以硅谷为腹地的旧金山湾区是加利福尼亚州第二大的大都市区，这里城市分散，居民出行主要依赖私家车。而大量高科技公司的入驻导致了当地的高收入群体增加，物价和房价也因此水涨船高，这给当地居民的生活带来了困难。"谷歌为了接送其员工，在湾区的广袤地域里提供了140多辆汽车接送6000多名员工到山景城的总部，这不仅给当地交通带来了困难，还占用了公共的汽车站。因此，2015年，谷歌曾迫于压力向其总部城市山景城投入4辆免费公交车。大型公司在追求利益的同时也不得不考虑它的社会责任。谷歌的免费公交车的确填补了山景城公共交通的需求，也受到了当地居民的好评。然而大型公司的社会责任不应当仅限于此，在地方层面，大型公司在使用当地资源的同时也应当负起交通、医疗、教育等方面的责任。"[②]

---

① 邬小丽. 论跨界披露他国军事设施信息行为的责任——以"谷歌地球"为例. 法制与社会，2016(10)：56-57.

② Pengfei Li. 谷歌的社会责任有问题. 中外管理，2015(2)：23.

2.加强国际合作和交流

美国硅谷可以继续与其他国家的科技园区、创新中心和高科技企业建立合作平台，促进科技创新和技术交流。这可以通过签署合作协议、共同举办创新竞赛和研讨会等方式来实现。例如，"在2017年，11个硅谷高端项目前往河南省国家大学科技园寻求产业合作伙伴"[①]，为创新发展注入新活力。

硅谷可以与其他国家的科研机构、高校和企业开展科技人才交流项目，促进人才流动和跨国合作。这可以包括短期访学项目、科研合作项目和人才培训计划等。位于硅谷的斯坦福大学已经成为高等教育国际化的代表之一，其国际视野的办学理念，别具一格的教育制度，世界一流的师资力量，坚持优异的招生制度，产、学、研一体的实践教学，广泛深入的国际交流和充足先进的教学设施是其成为高等教育国际化典范的重要原因。[②]

硅谷可以主办或参与国际性科技会议和峰会，为全球科技专家、学者和创业者提供一个交流和合作的平台。这有助于加强国际合作网络，推动技术创新和商业合作。

硅谷也可以积极与其他国家的创业生态系统建立联系，促进创业者和初创企业之间的合作和交流。这可以通过创业项目交流、投资对接和创业孵化器的合作等方式来实现。

硅谷的科技企业可以加强与国外的企业和研究机构展开跨国科技研发合作，共同解决全球性挑战和推动技术创新。这可以通过共享研发资源、共同申请研究项目资金和知识产权保护的合作等来实现。

硅谷的投资机构和创新基金可以与其他国家的企业合作，共同支持跨国创新项目和初创企业的发展。这有助于促进技术转移和知识共享，推动国际科技创新的发展。1998年的"硅谷创投"（Silicon Ventures）乃美国最显赫的天使投资机构之一，拥有三百个会员单位。其独特之处在于，它通过在世界各地举办投资峰会的方式，旨在寻找具备投资潜力的本地项目，并促进全球投资者之间的紧密对接，从而帮助企业快速成长。近期，美国硅谷创投曾在湖北举行一场盛大峰会，与湖北省中小企业进行了深入交流。主题涉及吸引外国风险投资以及融资前专利保护等课题，为地方企业开启了新的合作与发展机遇。"[③]

---

①　本刊编辑部.硅谷高端项目来郑寻合作.河南科技，2017(13): 9.
②　韦家朝.斯坦福大学高等教育国际化的特点及对中国高等教育的启示.高等理科教育，2010(2): 112-116.
③　谢慧敏，杜鹏.美国硅谷创投在汉举行投资峰会.湖北日报，2007-09-07(02).

四、结论：他山之石，可以攻玉

纵观硅谷的发展历程，不难发现该园区的许多可圈可点之处，且这些经验和优势在各方的通力协作下具有一定的可复制性，或许能在中国的社会经济土壤中生根发芽，因此，我们组斗胆从政府、园区企业和高校及科研机构的角度，对这三个社会主体提出发展意见。

（一）政　府

1.对园区建设施以政策资金扶持和税收激励

政府可向企业和高校具有可行性的自主研发项目提供赞助经费，在中小企业建设的初期和中期给予税收优惠，而对于转型期较长的技术密集型企业则要动态调整税收激励，实现长期有效的扶持；可设立宽松的技术移民签证政策，吸引人才涌入；除此之外，政府还可以在积极提供工业园区规划用地、协调园区和国内外科研机构合作等方面有所作为。

2.营造良好的营商环境和人才保障风气

政府应该在企业开办、施工许可证取得等环节进行优化，缩短审批时限，精简审批环节；政府还要严格执行专利制度，保护知识产权，尊重人才和知识；在人才保障方面，政府要积极建立人才、项目、基地、服务四位一体的联动机制，营造有利于人才引进的生态环境。

3.鼓励开放自由、不惧失败的社会企业文化

稳健与温和是我们的文化主张，人们对风险避之不及；成功学贯穿我们的教育，而失败则被认为是可耻的。为推动大众创业、万众创新，政府应该鼓励包容性更强、灵活度更高的社会企业文化。

（二）工业园区

1.加速数字化和绿色化转型

在当今数字化和绿色化的发展潮流下，园区企业应当与时俱进，建设数字基础设施，将数字平台和产业系统相结合，以提高生产效率和创造商业机会；与此同时，企业还应当因地制宜地在可持续发展和绿色投资方面有所作为。

2.建立权责分明、相辅相成的产业生态系统

企业应当实现"创业链、产业链、资金链、人才链"的深度融合，以平台化思维统筹各链条，实现信息共享、相互交融的网络效应，以模块化逻辑赋予产业系统以灵活性，各要素能够在弹性的时间和规定下自主协作。

（三）高校和科研院所

除了积极培养学生批判性思维和创新能力外，高校和科研院所应当和企业联袂共建技术开发平台和资源，可以通过与企业合作、开展培训计划和实习项目等培养符合产业发展需要的人力资源，通过产学研合作和技术平台的共建，实现三位一体的互惠格局和创新突破。

硅谷工业园区作为世界闻名的高新技术创新和发展中心，其发展历史堪称"奇迹"，然而其秘诀也可以为我所用，供我国工业园区学习借鉴。为了向国内工业园区提供有益的洞察建议，本文便是从政府、工业园区企业以及高校和科研院所三方面总结硅谷发展模式，同时列举了硅谷的不足之处，给予国内工业园区借鉴与展望。

从中新合作到世界一流
——苏州工业园区产业发展历程分析与启示[①]

摘　要： 创设于特殊时代背景的开发区，在经济增速放缓的当下面临着一系列发展问题，倒逼园区寻求发展新出路。苏州工业园区自 1994 年建立以来，在产业发展的三个历程和两次转型过程中，深刻意识到了产业结构等方面的问题，两次在产业生命周期走向衰退时成功发掘新的产业创新和增长点。在深入分析开发区产业创新与转型发展后，本文总结出来自苏州工业园区的四个独特而可迁移性启示，给国内外开发区的更进一步发展提供宝贵经验。

关键词： 苏州工业园区；产业发展历程；产业转型

一、绪　论

（一）研究背景

在经历了高速增长与跨越式发展阶段后，我国开发区正处于一个关键的转型升级时期。一方面，随着国内外经济形势的变化，开发区原有的比较优势逐步消退，产业结构、空间布局、管理模式等方面都需要进行转型升级，以适应"新常态"下经济发展的更高形态、更复杂分工、更合理结构的演进趋势。另一方面，在国际局势越发复杂化、公共卫生问题集中爆发的今日，开发区也面临着新的风险和压力，需要加强创新能力和应对能力，以保持产业竞争力和可持续性。这些挑战和机遇要求开发区在产业转型升级过程中不断寻求新的动力和路径。

---

① 作者：任金晨，苏州大学电子信息学院；杨雨欣，苏州大学电子信息学院；陆银标，苏州大学电子信息学院；石殷睿，苏州大学电子信息学院。

在这个背景下，产业创新与转型发展正在成为开发区转型升级的核心内容和关键驱动力。产业创新不仅涉及技术创新、产品创新、模式创新等方面，还包括产业链、供应链、价值链等方面的优化升级。产业转型深刻影响着开发区的经济增长、社会进步、生态环境等方方面面，是研究开发区转型升级的重要切入点。事实上，近年来，国内外已经出现了许多关于开发区产业创新与转型发展的研究成果，涵盖了开发区产业创新的理论框架、实践案例、评价指标、政策建议等方面。然而，这些研究还存在一些不足之处，如缺乏对开发区产业发展历程的系统性和全面性的分析，忽视了开发区产业转型与地方经济与社会发展之间的互动关系，忽视了开发区产业创新与转型在不同地域和行业背景下的差异性和特殊性等。

因此，本文旨在通过对我国开发区产业创新发展的深入研究，探讨开发区产业创新与转型背后的原因与内涵，分析其对于促进地方经济社会转型升级的作用和机制，并以江苏省苏州工业园区为案例进行实证分析。本文希望能够为我国工业园区产业创新发展提供一些理论指导和政策参考。

（二）研究方法

1.文献研究

通过查阅国内外相关文献资料，了解工业园区建设的理论基础、发展历程、评价指标、成功模式等，为案例分析提供理论支撑和参考依据。

2.实证分析

旨在通过收集和分析实际数据来验证或拒绝本小组对于苏州工业园区产业发展历程特定的假设或理论，并基于对观察、实验或调查过程中收集到的数据进行量化分析和统计推断。

3.实地调研

通过实地考察、访谈、讲座等方式，收集案例园区的第一手资料，验证文献综述和案例分析的结果，并进一步深化对案例园区的认识和理解。

4.比较分析

运用比较分析法，对案例进行自身纵向的比较，找出其异同点和优劣势，归纳其共性规律和特殊性特征，并从中提炼出适合我国工业园区建设开放创新的世界一流高科技园区的经验教训和启示。

综上所述，本次针对"苏州工业园区产业发展历程"的研究选择了文献研究、实证分析、实地调研和比较分析四种方法，旨在确保研究的系统性、全面性和科学性。

文献研究法通过查阅国内外相关文献资料，构建坚实的理论基础，为后续研究提供指导。实证分析利用实际数据进行量化分析和统计推断，验证或修正基于文献研究提出的假设和理论，从而提供客观的、量化的证据。实地调研通过实地考察和访谈，收集最新的第一手资料，进一步验证文献和数据分析的结果，确保研究结论的准确性和可靠性。此外，比较分析通过纵向和横向的多维比较，全面评估苏州工业园区的发展特征和优势，归纳共性规律和独特经验，为我国其他工业园区的发展提供可借鉴的经验教训。通过综合运用上述研究方法，可以系统而深入地探讨苏州工业园区的产业发展历程，提炼出具有实践指导意义的启示。

（三）理论基础

1."产业生命周期"理论

产业生命周期理论是一种经济学理论，它描述了一个产业从发展到衰落的过程。该理论由美国经济学家熊彼特（Joseph Schumpeter）于 1939 年提出，他认为，一个产业的发展会经历五个阶段：创新、增长、成熟、衰退和消亡。[①]

不同阶段的产业具有不同的市场增长率、竞争状况、技术变化、产品多样性、进入壁垒等特征，对企业的战略选择和资源分配有重要的指导作用。

本文借助产业生命周期理论研究苏州工业园区的产业发展历程，并结合各阶段发展特点分析总结，以得出经验与启示。自 1994 年建立以来，苏州工业园区经历了从低端制造业到高端制造业，再到现代服务业和战略性新兴产业的两次产业转型，最终形成了"2+3+1"为代表的现代产业体系。本文将以苏州工业园区为案例，探讨其产业发展所处的生命周期阶段，以及其在不同阶段采取的创新策略、政策支持、竞争优势等因素，以期为其他开发区的产业转型升级提供有益的借鉴和启示。

2."微笑曲线"理论

微笑曲线，是宏碁集团创办人施振荣先生在 1992 年为了"再造宏碁"提出的，以作为宏碁的策略方向。[②]在发展完善后，施振荣先生将"微笑曲线"加以修正，推出了所谓施氏"产业微笑曲线"以作为产业的中长期发展策略之

---

① 刘婷，平瑛.产业生命周期理论研究进展.湖南农业科学，2009(8): 93-96，99.

② 刘婷婷.基于微笑曲线理论的制造业服务化转型升级研究.造纸装备及材料，2023，52(3): 10-12.

方向。

微笑曲线是一种用来描述产业链中不同环节的附加价值的曲线，它的形状像一个微笑的嘴型，两端高，中间低。微笑曲线的两端分别是研发和营销，这些环节通常具有高度的创新性和差异化，因此能创造较高的附加价值。微笑曲线的中间是制造，这个环节通常面临激烈的竞争和低利润，因此附加价值较低。微笑曲线的理论可以帮助分析企业或地区在产业链中的定位和竞争优势，从而制定合适的发展策略。

本文借助微笑曲线理论研究苏州工业园区产业发展不同阶段的定位与竞争优劣势，在每一次产业转型时期探讨其背后的原因，以期深入理解苏州工业园区的产业发展历程。

二、研究对象的选取与概况

（一）研究对象的选择

本文的研究对象是苏州工业园区，它是中国与新加坡两国政府间合作的国家级经济技术开发区，也是中国改革开放的重要窗口和先行示范区。本文选择苏州工业园区的产业发展作为研究对象，主要有以下几个原因：

1.苏州工业园区具有典型性和代表性

苏州工业园区是中国第一个以国际合作方式建设的开发区，也是中国最早实施市场化运作和现代化管理的开发区之一。苏州工业园区在引进外资、吸收外方管理经验、培育本土企业、推动产业转型升级等方面都取得了显著的成就，成为中国开放型经济的一个缩影和标杆。

2.苏州工业园区具有创新性和先进性

苏州工业园区在产业发展的三个历程和两次转型过程中，深刻意识到了产业结构等方面的问题所在，两次在产业生命周期走向衰退时成功发掘新的产业创新和增长点。

3.苏州工业园区具有复杂性和多样性

苏州工业园区位于长江三角洲地区的核心位置，与苏州市其他地区、上海市、江浙沪等地区形成了紧密的经济联系和互动。苏州工业园区内部也存在着多元化的产业结构、企业类型、人口构成、社会文化等因素，对其产业转型和创新发展产生了不同的影响和作用。

综上所述，自1994年建立以来，苏州工业园区经历了从"试验田"到

"新高地"的成功蝶变，因此，研究苏州工业园区产业转型的过程、动力、机制、效果、问题和启示，具有重要的理论意义和实践价值。

（二）苏州工业园区的发展成就概况

我们将从经济、科技、绿色发展、社会治理四个方面来了解苏州工业园区的基本发展情况。

1. 经济成就

经济总量稳步增长。截至 2022 年，苏州工业园区实现地区生产总值 3515.6 亿元，同比增长 2.3%；一般公共预算收入 387.4 亿元，同口径增长 2.1%；规上工业总产值 6850.2 亿元，增长 7%；固定资产投资 521.6 亿元，增长 8.7%；社会消费品零售总额 1097.9 亿元；进出口总额 1077.9 亿美元；实际使用外资 20.9 亿美元。

产业结构不断优化。苏州工业园区形成了"2+3"现代产业体系："2"即新一代信息技术、高端装备制造两大千亿元级主导产业，"3"即生物医药、纳米技术应用、人工智能三大特色产业。2022 年，这五大产业实现产值 4493 亿元，占规模以上工业总产值的比重达 65.6%，其中高新技术产值占规上工业总产值比重达 73.9%。服务业增加值 1753.18 亿元，占 GDP 比重 49.9%，经认定的各类总部已达 188 家。[①]

2. 科技成就

截至 2023 年 5 月 31 日，苏州工业园区有效发明专利达 21231 件，其中高价值发明专利超 9600 件。作为国内最具创新活力的区域之一，苏州工业园区知识产权各项工作一直走在江苏省乃至全国前列。

创新能力显著提升。苏州工业园区坚持以创新引领转型升级，加快建设开放创新的世界一流高科技园区。2022 年，苏州工业园区累计有效期内国家高新技术企业超 2480 家，累计培育独角兽及独角兽（培育）企业 180 家，科技创新型企业超万家。累计评审苏州工业园区科技领军人才项目 2654 个。累计建成各类科技载体超 1000 万平方米、公共技术服务平台 43 个。[②]

3. 绿色发展

生态修复大力加强。苏州工业园区始终坚持绿色发展理念，将环境保护作

---

① 数据来源：sipac.gov.cn。

② 数据来源：sipac.gov.cn。

为经济社会发展的重要内容和基本要求。苏州工业园区加强了污染防治和生态修复工作，提升了环境质量和生态功能。2020 年，苏州工业园区空气优良率达到 97.8%，PM2.5 年均浓度为 29 微克/立方米；水环境质量达标率达到100%，无劣V类水体；建成绿地面积达到 1.6 万公顷，绿化覆盖率达到 45%；建成森林公园 10 个，湿地公园 3 个。[①]

4.社会治理

社会建设广泛开展。苏州工业园区积极履行社会责任，促进社会公平正义和民生幸福。苏州工业园区加强了社会事业建设和公共服务提供，提高了人民群众的获得感和幸福感。2020 年，苏州工业园区完成城乡居民基本医疗保险参保率达到 100%；完成城乡居民基本养老保险参保率达到 100%；完成义务教育巩固率达到 100%；完成高中阶段教育毛入学率达到 100%；完成城镇登记失业率控制在 2% 以内；完成城乡低保覆盖率达到 100%。苏州工业园区还积极参与社会公益事业和慈善捐赠活动，支持教育、医疗、扶贫等领域的发展。

综上所述，苏州工业园区在产业转型升级的带动下，不仅促进了园区经济社会发展，提升了园区竞争力和影响力，也能够为中国开发区建设和产业升级提供有益借鉴和成功经验。因此，研究苏州工业园区产业转型的过程、动力、机制、效果、问题和启示，具有重要的理论意义和实践价值。

鉴于此，本文选择苏州工业园区作为研究对象，梳理园区的发展历程，分析园区的产业结构、产业政策、产业创新等方面的变化与演进，以探求产业两次转型成功的内在原因和规律，进而总结工业园区建设中产业发展的经验和启示。

三、苏州工业园区的产业发展阶段与转型

（一）产业发展的三个阶段

本文通过数据收集和实证分析，结合不同时期的企业特点、产业结构、GDP贡献、进出口总额、国民经济核算等数据，发现苏州工业园区的产业发展经历了三个明显的、具有不同特点的阶段。

1.第一阶段：低端制造业发展阶段（1994—2008）

苏州工业园区的初期阶段以制造业为主导产业，其发展主要依靠吸引外资

---

① 刘荣茂.生态工业园区建设的环境管理策略分析.皮革制作与环保科技，2023，4(20)：168-170.

的策略。

2001 年，中国加入世界贸易组织（WTO），苏州工业园区迎来了快速发展的机遇，大力推进基础设施建设、招商引资、产业升级和开放合作。2006年，苏州工业园区获得国家级高新技术产业开发区的认定。2008 年，苏州工业园区的加工贸易额突破 500 亿美元，成为一个国际化、现代化的工业园区，外向型经济特征明显。

2. 第二阶段：产业升级阶段（2008—2021）

苏州工业园区自 2008 年以来，经历了从制造业向创新型产业转型的过程。

2008 年，苏州市出台了《关于加快建设创新型园区的通知》，提出了一系列促进科技创新的政策措施。2011 年，苏州工业园区的研发投入占地区生产总值（GDP）的比重达到 4.6%，高于国家平均水平。园区内建成了各类科技载体超过 360 万平方米，建立了 20 多个公共技术服务平台，为企业提供了技术支持和创新环境。2012 年以后，苏州工业园区进入了产业高质量发展阶段，第二产业和第三产业协同发展，形成了以电子信息、生物医药、纳米技术等为代表的高端制造业和现代服务业。2013 年，苏州工业园区确立了争当苏南现代化建设先导区的发展目标，开启了深化推进改革创新的新征程。2019 年，苏州工业园区在全国高新区综合评价中连续三年排名第一，展现了其在国家创新体系中的重要地位和作用。[①]

3. 第三阶段：产业集群阶段（2021 至今）

自 2021 年 3 月以来，苏州工业园区获批建设苏州实验室、国家生物药技术创新中心、第三代半导体技术创新中心、新一代人工智能创新发展试验区，形成以新一代信息技术、高端装备制造为两大主导产业，生物医药、纳米技术应用、人工智能为三大新兴产业现代化特色产业体系。

（二）产业发展的两次转型

由上述的阶段性梳理，可以发现，苏州工业园区的产业发展实际上分为三个明显的阶段。产业发展从某一阶段跃升到另一更高水平阶段时，必然会经历一次大规模的产业转型时期。接下来，将进一步探讨这些转型的深层内涵。[②]

---

① 以新发展理念引领产业园区高质量发展. (2020-06-08)[2024-01-16]. http://theory.people.com.cn/n1/2020/0608/c40531-31738311.html.

② 苏州工业园区管理委员会. 建制沿革. [2024-01-16]. https://www.sipac.gov.cn/szgyyq/jzyg/common_tt.shtml

1. 第一次产业转型：从低端到高端

1.1 问题与驱动力

1.1.1 自主可控的产业体系与高端产业亟需补强

（1）降低了产业结构升级和技术进步的动力和能力。

由于苏州工业园区的制造业主要以加工贸易为主，产品附加值较低，技术含量较低，核心技术掌握在外资企业手中，国内企业难以获得技术转移和创新机会。同时，由于国际市场需求相对稳定，国内企业也缺乏进行产品开发和技术改造的动力和投入。这样就导致了苏州工业园区的制造业结构长期停留在中低端水平，难以实现高质量发展。

（2）增加了产业受国际市场波动和贸易摩擦的风险。

由于苏州工业园区的制造业主要依赖于国际市场的需求和供给，一旦国际市场出现需求下降、价格波动、汇率变动、贸易保护主义等不利因素，就会对苏州工业园区的出口和进口造成严重影响，进而影响园区的经济稳定性和安全性。例如，2008 年的世界金融危机对苏州工业园区的制造业产生了较大的冲击。

（3）损害了产业对国内市场和国内需求的适应性和满足度。

由于苏州工业园区的制造业主要面向国际市场，产品设计和生产都是根据国外客户的需求和标准来进行的，而忽视了国内市场的需求和潜力。这样就导致了苏州工业园区的制造业与国内市场的脱节，难以满足国内消费者的多样化和个性化需求，也难以抓住国内市场的发展机遇。

1.1.2 国际市场的变化

2001 年，中国加入世界贸易组织（WTO），开放了更多的市场机会，也面临了更多的国际竞争。苏州工业园区的传统制造业，如电子信息、机械设备、纺织服装等，受到了东南亚、印度等国家和地区的低成本挑战，利润空间不断被压缩。同时，国际市场对高端制造业的需求不断增加，为苏州工业园区提供了转型升级的契机。

1.1.3 国内政策的支持

2006 年，苏州工业园区被纳入国家高新区管理序列，享受了一系列政策措施，如税收优惠、金融扶持、人才引进等，为园区向高端制造业转型提供了有力的保障。同时，园区也积极响应国家"创新驱动发展""产业结构调整"等战略部署，加大了科技创新和产业升级的投入和力度。

1.1.4 企业自身的创新能力

苏州工业园区的制造业企业在长期的发展过程中，积累了一定的技术、资金、人才、品牌等资源和优势，具备了向高端制造业转型的基础和条件。同时，这些企业也意识到了转型升级的必要性和紧迫性，主动进行技术改造、产品开发、市场拓展等创新活动，提高了自身的核心竞争力和附加值。

1.1.5 总结

综上所述，苏州工业园区第一次产业转型是在产业自身存在问题以及国际市场变化、国内政策支持和企业自身创新能力的共同作用下实现的。这一转型使得苏州工业园区的制造业结构发生了重大变化，电子信息、高端装备制造等高新技术产业逐渐成为园区制造业的主导产业，而纺织服装等传统产业则逐步退出或转移。这一转型也为苏州工业园区带来了经济效益和社会效益的提升，为园区后续发展奠定了坚实基础。

1.2 改进目标

提升外资及加工制造存量产业的科技含量，构建更高水平开放型经济新体制。

1.3 路径与选择

1.3.1 布局高新区，围绕产业链部署创新链，对存量产业，通过二次招商、科技赋能，向产业链创新链价值链两端延伸。

这一点符合微笑曲线理论的指导思想，即企业要提高附加值和竞争力，就要专注于产业链的两端，即研发设计和市场营销。高新区作为科技创新的重要载体，能够充分利用其政策优势、人才优势、资源优势，打造创新生态系统，培育和引进高端创新主体。对于存量产业，可以通过二次招商的方式，引入更多的战略合作伙伴、投资机构、科研机构等，形成产学研用一体化的创新网络。科技赋能是指利用现代科技手段，如大数据、云计算、人工智能等，提升存量产业的生产效率、产品质量、市场竞争力等。向产业链、创新链、价值链两端延伸，是指在保持原有产业优势的基础上，不断开拓新的增长点和蓝海市场，提升产品和服务的附加值和差异化。

1.3.2 引导企业产业链、创新链、资金链、人才链融合发展，实现加工制造产业的高端化

（1）在产业链、创新链上，拓展寻找产业创新点，提升存量产业的科技含量。

这一点强调了以创新驱动发展的理念，突破传统加工制造业的发展瓶颈，提高存量产业的附加值和竞争力。在产业链、创新链上拓展寻找产业创新点，是指在原有产业链的基础上，寻求新的技术突破、产品创新、模式创新等，形成新的产业链条或者延伸原有产业链条。提升存量产业的科技含量，是指在存量产业的生产过程中，引入更先进的技术设备、管理方法、质量标准等，提高存量产业的生产效率、产品质量、环境友好性等。

（2）在价值链上，重点引进跨国公司地区总部、研发、物流、销售、结算等功能性国际创新资源及机构，谋求更高的附加价值，进一步向"微笑曲线"两侧延伸。

这一点体现了以价值导向发展的思想，利用国际化的资源和机构，提升高新区的核心竞争力和国际影响力。在价值链上，重点引进跨国公司地区总部、研发、物流、销售、结算等功能性国际创新资源及机构，是指在高新区内建立具有全球或区域性影响力的跨国公司的分支机构或者合作伙伴，利用其在技术研发、物流配送、市场营销、资金结算等方面的优势和经验，为高新区提供更多的创新要素和服务。谋求更高的附加值，向"微笑曲线"两侧延伸，是指在价值链中，专注于那些能够创造更多价值和利润的环节，即研发设计和市场营销，避免过多陷入低附加值和低利润的环节，即低端制造加工。

2.第二次产业转型：从高端到集群

2.1 问题与驱动力

2.1.1 第二、第三产业之间的比例不合理，服务业和城市化发展有待提高

（1）抑制了经济增长潜力和质量

服务业是现代经济的重要组成部分，也是经济转型升级的重要方向。服务业的发展能够提高产业附加值，促进就业创业，满足人民日益增长的美好生活需要。城市化是经济社会发展的必然结果，也是推动经济增长的重要动力。城市化的发展能够释放人口红利，促进区域协调，提高资源效率。园区的二三产业之间的比例不合理，服务业和城市化发展不足，将导致经济结构失衡，制约经济发展的质量和效益。

（2）影响居民生活质量与水平

服务业是现代经济的重要组成部分，也是经济转型升级的重要方向。苏州工业园区的第二产业占比过高，第三产业占比过低，与国际先进水平相差较大。这意味着苏州工业园区的居民收入水平和消费能力还有较大的提升空间，

尤其是在高端服务、文化创意、生活品质等方面。同时，城市化是经济社会发展的必然结果，也是推动经济增长的重要动力。苏州工业园区的城市功能还不够完善，缺乏高品质的教育、医疗、文化、娱乐等公共服务设施，也缺乏高端的商务、会展、旅游等现代服务设施。这既不利于提高居民的教育水平和终身学习能力，也不利于吸引和培养高层次人才。此外，绿色发展是我国经济社会发展的必然选择。推动服务业和城市化发展与资源环境相协调，构建人与自然和谐共生的美丽中国是大势所趋。苏州工业园区作为国家级开发区，面临着产业结构调整和环境治理的双重压力。如果第二、第三产业之间的比例不合理，服务业和城市化发展有待提高，将增加资源消耗和环境污染，影响居民的环境质量和生态保护。

2.1.2 内生功能培育的时间周期性客观存在，缺乏华为、阿里巴巴等"超级公司"

首先，缺乏"超级公司"的引领作用，可能导致苏州工业园区在科技创新方面落后于其他地区。

如今，科技创新是推动经济社会发展的重要动力，也是提升区域竞争力的关键因素。"超级公司"通常拥有强大的研发投入和创新能力，能够在人工智能、云计算、芯片等前沿领域取得突破性进展，并将其应用于各个行业和场景中。例如，华为在2019年发布了人工智能原生（AI-Native）数据库GaussDB和业界性能第一的分布式存储FusionStorage 8.01；阿里巴巴在2020年发布了AI芯片含光800[2]。这些创新产品和解决方案不仅提升了自身的核心竞争力，也带动了相关产业链和生态圈的发展。"超级公司"还能够通过开放合作共赢的方式，与其他企业、机构、社会共享创新成果，形成良好的创新氛围和文化。如果苏州工业园区缺乏这样的"超级公司"，就可能失去科技创新的主导权和话语权，难以跟上时代发展的步伐，甚至被其他地区甩在后面。[1]

其次，缺乏"超级公司"的带动作用，可能导致苏州工业园区在人才培养方面不足。

人才是区域发展的重要资源，也是内生功能培育的核心要素。"超级公司"通常具有强大的人才吸引力和培养力，能够吸引和留住各类优秀人才，为其提供良好的发展平台和机会，激发其创造力和潜能。"超级公司"还能够通过与

---

① 孙颖.产城融合地区产业空间更新政策研究——以苏州市工业园区为例.居舍，2023(28): 107-110.

高校、科研机构、行业协会等合作，建立人才联盟，共同培养和输送人才。例如，华为已经与全球多所高校建立了合作关系，开展人才培养、科研合作、学术交流等活动；阿里巴巴也与清华大学、浙江大学等高校建立了战略合作伙伴关系，共同推进人工智能、云计算等领域的教育和研究。如果苏州工业园区缺乏这样的"超级公司"，就可能面临人才流失和匮乏的问题，难以形成人才优势和竞争力。

最后，缺乏"超级公司"的示范作用，可能导致苏州工业园区在社会责任方面的缺失。

作为社会的一员，"超级公司"不仅要追求自身的发展和利益，还要关注社会的需求和问题，积极履行社会责任。"超级公司"通常具有强大的社会影响力和公信力，能够通过自身的行动和声音，引导和推动社会的进步和改善。例如，华为在全球多个国家和地区开展了数字化普惠、数字化教育、数字化环保等公益项目；阿里巴巴也在全球范围内设立了阿里巴巴扶贫基金、阿里巴巴公益基金、阿里巴巴全球绿色生态基金等公益项目。这些公益项目不仅提升了"超级公司"的品牌形象和社会声誉，也为社会创造了巨大的价值。

2.1.3 国际市场环境的变化

随着全球经济增长放缓，在贸易保护主义抬头、国际竞争加剧等因素的影响下，苏州工业园区作为一个外向型经济区域，面临着出口下降、成本上升、利润压缩等挑战，需要通过产业转型升级，提高产业附加值和核心竞争力，应对外部风险和不确定性。

2.1.4 国内发展战略的要求

随着"一带一路"、长三角一体化、自贸区建设等国家战略的实施，苏州工业园区作为一个国家级经济技术开发区、国家高新技术产业开发区、国家自主创新示范区、自由贸易试验区功能叠加的融合区域，需要通过产业转型升级，充分发挥其政策优势、人才优势、资源优势，打造改革开放的新高地，服务国家大局。

2.1.5 园区内部发展的需求

随着苏州工业园区的不断发展壮大，园区面临着用地紧张、环境压力大、创新能力不足等问题，需要通过产业转型升级，优化资源配置、提升生态效益、增强创新动力等措施来实现高质量发展，以满足人民美好生活的需要。

2.1.6 总结

综上所述,苏州工业园区第二次产业转型的驱动原因是多方面的,既有外部环境的变化和挑战,也有内部发展的需求和目标。苏州工业园区应该抓住机遇,迎接挑战,以创新引领转型升级,打造世界一流高科技智慧园区。

2.2 改进目标

(1)创新与产业融合,培育未来增量的科技新兴产业,打造自主可控的现代产业体系。

(2)走开放与创新融合、创新与产业融合、产业与城市融合的总发展路径。①

2.3 路径与选择

2.3.1 产城融合

苏州工业园区坚持以"产城融合、以人为本"的定位,按照"先规划、后建设""先地下、后地上"的原则,实现"一张蓝图干到底"。②坚持高水平和高标准的城市规划建设,园区布局了商务、科教创新、旅游度假、高端制造与国际贸易四大功能板块,形成"产城融合、区域一体"的城市发展架构。园区还通过开展产业载体综合评价,执行差别化措施,强化优质产业载体的政策支持等方式,推动产业载体不断提质增效,争取通过 3 年左右时间,形成一批经济贡献大、产业集聚度高、创新能力强、管理规范、服务专业的特色产业。

2.3.2 在产城融合的同时,围绕创新链布局产业链制定了三大科技创新产业发展规划,布局未来新兴产业

围绕创新链布局产业链。苏州工业园区以创新引领转型升级,发挥信息化基础优势和 5G 试点先发优势,园区全面提升政务服务水平,助力打造一流营商环境。园区形成了"2+3"现代产业体系:"2"即新一代信息技术、高端装备制造两大千亿元级主导产业,"3"即生物医药、纳米技术应用、人工智能三大特色产业。园区还制定了三大科技创新产业发展规划,分别是:生物医药产业发展规划(2021—2025 年)、纳米技术应用产业发展规划(2021－2025年)、人工智能产业发展规划(2021—2025 年),旨在打造国内顶尖、国际一流的纳米技术、生物医药和人工智能产业集聚高地。此外,园区还布局发展未

---

① 徐凯.传统产业数字化转型发展的五大创新路径.中国商界,2023(11):56-57.
② 王子元.《联合早报》"苏州工业园区"特辑:中新合作赋能"双一流新中心"建设.(2021-12-31)[2024-01-16].https://new.qq.com/rain/a/20211231A03Q5A00.

来新兴产业,如生命健康、海洋经济、航天航空和军工等。

2.3.3 营造科技创新支撑体系及环境,建设产业发展生态圈

苏州工业园区开展科技招商,引进大专院校、科研院所等科教资源,积累技术、储备人才,为产业发展提供基础性保障。引进科技创新型企业,重点关注科技成果产业化、商业化项目和科技顶尖人才创业类项目。园区凸显中小微、人才型、专精特新等特征,长期培育形成增量的科技创新产业集群。

苏州工业园区建设国际一流人才创新创业首选区,加快高端人才引进集聚,强化人才服务和激励,优化人才创新创业环境。园区建设关键核心技术创新策源区,布局重大科技创新平台,搭建产业技术攻关平台,建设新型研发机构集群。园区建设科技创新资源集聚区,集聚全球科技创新资源,打造接轨国际的科创生态圈。园区建设标杆创新企业汇聚区,实施创新型领军企业登顶战略,实施高成长科技企业倍增计划,实施"专精特新"企业培育工程。园区还通过深化中新合作、深化江苏自贸区苏州片区建设、构筑更高水平开放型经济体系、构筑国内国际双循环链接点、全面融入长三角区域一体化等举措,构建开放创新的产业发展生态圈。

四、经验与启示

(一)经验总结

从"中新合作"到"世界一流"、从"学习借鉴"到"品牌输出"、从"引进来"到"走出去"、从"园区制造"到"园区创造"、从"先行先试"向"示范引领"……开发建设以来,苏州工业园区实现了一个又一个重大跨越,经济密度、创新浓度、开放程度跃居全国前列。

苏州工业园区的产业发展成就令人赞叹,但这并不是一蹴而就的,而是经过了多次的转型升级和创新突破。苏州工业园区的产业转型中,具有以下特点。

1.第一次产业转型

(1)国家政策导向

第一次转型的成功可归因于积极响应国家政策。特殊经济区划成为关键契机,吸引了外资和引进了国际先进技术。这明确表明,在产业转型中,紧密合作并遵循国家政策对于成功至关重要。政策导向不仅为企业提供了明确的方向,还为其提供了法规和激励,使其更具竞争力。

（2）技术创新驱动

苏州工业园区充分利用了市场机制，鼓励技术创新，促进了企业竞争力的提高。这突出了创新对于提高产业竞争力的关键作用。通过持续的研发和技术合作，园区不仅提高了产品和服务的质量，还确保了其在全球市场中的竞争地位。

（3）产业集聚效应

积极引进龙头企业和产业链上下游的企业，形成了初步的产业集聚，提高了整个产业的核心竞争力。这体现了在转型中构建具有竞争力的产业生态系统是必要的。园区成了一个集中产业资源和技术的枢纽，吸引了各类企业，从而提高了整个地区的产业竞争力和创新潜力。

2.第二次产业转型

（1）多元优化产业结构

实现第二次产业转型的关键是优化产业结构，实现了从传统的制造业向高端集群制造业和服务业的多元化转型，培养发展了特色、优势产业体系。这要求园区及时调整产业结构和发展方向，以适应产业生命周期的变化规律，同时发现和培育新的产业创新和增长点。现代产业结构的多样性对于长期发展至关重要，因为它增加了园区的韧性和持续增长潜力。

（2）城市化与产业的关联

在产城融合的发展策略指导下，产业同城市的共同发展有助于提高产业附加值和居民生活质量。同时，企业和园区积极履行社会责任，为社会发展和改善做出贡献，这有助于建立企业的品牌形象和社会声誉。城市本身与产业的关联在现代经济中扮演关键角色，促进了城市的可持续发展，同时也增强了产业的社会责任感。

（3）适应外部环境的变化

园区需要灵活适应国际市场的变化，以应对出口下降、成本上升等经济社会的全新挑战。这表明对外部环境的敏感性和应变能力对于经济区域至关重要。通过持续的市场分析和战略调整，园区能够更好地适应快速变化的国际经济环境。

（4）创新、科技与人才

园区采取科技创新和制度创新共同培育总发展路径，强调创新与产业的协同发展。同时需要专注于创新链和产业链的布局，以培育未来的新兴产业。此外，吸引高层次人才对于推动创新和产业升级至关重要。通过引进和培育一批高水平的人才、企业、机构和平台，园区可以打造具有国际竞争力的核心技术和标准，形成独具特色和优势的产业集群和品牌。

3.总结

总而言之，苏州工业园区多年来风雨兼程，成功实现了从"中新合作"到"世界一流"的巨大跨越。这背后汇聚了国家政策导向、技术创新驱动、产业集聚效应等多个因素。随后的第二次产业转型则侧重于多元化产业结构，城市化与产业的关联，适应外部环境的变化，创新、科技与人才等要素，为园区的可持续发展注入活力。苏州工业园区的发展成就令人钦佩，是中国经济发展的杰出典范，将现代产业与城市化发展相融合，实现了"傲然于世"的现代产业新城的崭新面貌。

（二）启 示

在上述系统分析与经验总结后，本文也相应地总结出了来自苏州工业园区的可迁移性启示，以便为中国开发区建设和产业升级提供有益借鉴和成功经验。

1.因地制宜

产业布局要考虑当地的资源禀赋、市场需求、技术水平、人力资源、政策支持、人文环境等。综合考量后，优先选择地区优势型产业，逐步做大做强，最终形成成熟的产业生态圈。例如，苏州工业园区在综合考量自身禀赋后，在产业发展的第三阶段，将发展中心放在"2+3+1"特色产业体系，打造高度集群化的产业生态圈。

2.因时制宜

坚持以创新引领转型升级，紧跟国际国内的产业发展趋势和市场需求，不断调整优化产业结构，提升产业附加值和竞争力。苏州工业园区在发展初级阶段先承接发达地区的产业转移，根据技术进步的趋势，综合时局调整产业结构和发展方向，以适应新技术的应用和市场需求，逐步实现产业转型升级，并培养当地优势产业。

3.大胆创新

积极尝试、引入新技术，开发新产品提高产业的附加值，促进产业体制改革，改进企业管理方式，提高产业的运营效率。苏州工业园区在第一次产业转型期间将目光投向了中小型科技企业，而不是直接引进所谓斑马型企业，最终成功转型，同时也在中小型企业的逐步培养中积累了丰富技术和经验。

4.创造新的比较优势

专注某一特定领域或产品，精耕细作，提供独特的产品或服务，形成差异化的竞争优势；紧紧抓住当代中国人才红利新机遇、把握超大规模市场等新一代红利。苏州工业园区始终坚持以人才支撑转型升级，并充分利用中国与新加坡政府间合作的平台优势，吸引和集聚全球优质的科技创新资源。得益于此，苏州工业园区在发展多年后，其产业生态圈、科创平台和人才培养已经达到相当的高度。

至此，我们可以得出结论：通过因地制宜、因时制宜、大胆创新和创造新的比较优势，苏州工业园区成功实现了产业转型升级，并为中国开发区建设和产业升级提供了宝贵的经验和启示。这些经验有助于其他开发区在自身发展过程中，找到适合自身的路径，提升竞争力，实现可持续发展。综合来看，苏州工业园区的发展模式不仅体现了科学规划和灵活应对的结合，还展示了高效利用资源和积极创新的实践，为全国乃至全球的工业园区建设提供了可行的借鉴范例。未来，深入研究和推广这些经验，将有助于推动更多地区的产业转型升级，促进经济高质量发展，增强国际竞争力。

PART
8

第八章

世界文化遗产继承与传统工艺创新

"江南丝竹"的发展现状与传承保护[①]

摘　要: 非物质文化遗产"江南丝竹"是区域音乐文化的典型代表,本文选其作为研究对象,采用文献研究、案例分析等方法,描述和举证了江南丝竹的发展现状,分析现存继承、创新、传播问题,并将其与墨西哥玛利亚奇乐队进行对比,从人才培养、传承发展与对外传播三个角度论述了二者异同与可鉴之处,最后提出完善人才培养方式、加强理论创新,完善传统音乐理论体系、向外借力塑造文化IP三个建议,助力江南丝竹的传承保护与创新发展。

关键词: 江南丝竹;发展现状;非物质文化遗产;传承

一、选题意义与背景

江南丝竹是我国国家级非物质文化遗产之一,起源于江苏南部、浙江西部、上海地区,其历史可以追溯到明代,以昆曲水磨腔为雏形,经由魏良辅为首等在太仓南码头创制改进,后以张野塘为首组成了规模完整的丝竹乐队,用工尺谱演奏,由昆曲班社、堂名鼓手兼奏,后逐渐形成丝竹演奏的专职班社。明万历末年在吴中(苏州地区)形成了新的乐种"弦索",可算是江南丝竹的前身,因其与民俗活动密切结合,形成了广泛的群众基础,后正式定名为江南丝竹。[②]

江南丝竹具有极高的音乐艺术价值。江南丝竹传统技法内容丰富,包含加花变奏、嵌挡让路、即兴发挥等手法,形成"小、细、轻、雅"的风格特

---

① 作者:罗荔馨,北京外国语大学北外学院;王赵琼宇,北京外国语大学北外学院;范奕萱,南京大学国际关系研究院。
② 中国非物质文化遗产数字博物馆. 江南丝竹. (2006-07-14)[2024-02-11]. https://www.ihchina.cn/project_details/12530.

色,具有极高的艺术欣赏价值。江南丝竹曲目丰富,传统乐曲有《中花六板》《三六》和《云庆》等,后有改编曲《金蛇狂舞》《变体新水令》等,都在全国产生了深远的影响。

作为环太湖文化的一部分,江南丝竹具有丰富的文化内涵。一方面,江南丝竹乐师在演奏时会相互配合,达到"你繁我简、你高我低"的和谐状态,这种技法和风格体现了人际交往间的谦逊和谐、创新守正等深刻的社会文化内涵。此外,江南丝竹乐植根于民间,与民俗活动密切相关,具有重要的民俗文化、群众文化价值。因此,研究江南丝竹将有利于全面认识江南地域文化,了解区域性音乐文化的发展历史,从而进一步完善我国非物质文化遗产保护工作。①

宏观层面,江南丝竹作为非物质文化遗产,其继承与发展符合当下发展中国特色社会主义文化强国的需求,对增强文化自信、提升国民文化修养具有重要意义。江南丝竹起源于民俗活动,是江南地区在物质文明基础上凝结出的精神文明结晶,具有鲜明的民族特色。在当下,面对世界音乐多样化,江南丝竹作为民族音乐文化的一部分,对内可以丰富人民精神生活,增强民族凝聚力和认同感;对外可以向世界展示民族文化特色,为世界音乐文化多样性做出中国贡献,推动人类音乐文明发展。②

然而,随着社会大环境的发展,江南丝竹的传承保护仍存在很多问题。如何保护和传承江南丝竹?如何让传统音乐在新时代焕发新的生机?本文将对江南丝竹保护现状进行总结分析,指出目前保护仍存在的问题与不足,并对江南丝竹的传承与发展提出相应的建议。

二、国内外研究评述

目前对江南丝竹的研究主要集中在三个方面。首先,学者们广泛认为江南丝竹文化具有极高的文化艺术价值,值得重点保护和研究。江南丝竹丰富了民族音乐的特色理论,艺术价值极高;江南丝竹文化与音乐社会学、传播学息息相关,与历史上江南地区的文人文化、民俗文化协同发展。

其次,江南丝竹传承乏力的原因多种多样,何为有效的继承措施成为学者们研究讨论的重点。李亚认为,江南丝竹文化是"乐师、乐社与民俗三者共

---

① 沈雷强.新时期江南丝竹发展的展望与思考.音乐创作,2017(12): 136-137.
② 刘忆莲.文化自信理念下民族音乐的传承与发展研究:以太仓地区江南丝竹为例.百花,2022(4): 71-74.

同构成的传承环链"，因此，保护江南丝竹应做到三位一体、多方努力。[①]其一，学者对精英乐师应发挥何种引领作用未能达成一致：吴子铭提出乐曲创新与时俱进，尝试流行音乐；[②]龚瑛则强调保留江南丝竹音乐核心，做到"整旧如新"；[③]而伍国栋提出专业乐师应发挥引领作用，重视江南丝竹音乐中的民俗性特色，"达雅返俗"。[④]其二，增加乐社、培养江南丝竹演奏者社群是促进江南丝竹活态传承的基础，学界十分重视对于乐社的研究。[⑤]其三，考虑到婚丧嫁娶等民俗活动的音乐需求推动了江南丝竹在 20 世纪的兴盛，在城市化迅速扩张的当下，民俗文化土壤缺失导致江南丝竹传承根源性推动力势弱。[⑥]正如李亚所说，抽离了"地方性和原生性"的江南丝竹难以继续其文化脉络，[⑦]因此，多位学者提出江南丝竹保护存在整体性需要，即对民俗环境和地域文化的统一保护，如搭建传承文化圈与生态创新圈、培养本土"根"文化意识教育等。[⑧]

再次，也有众多学者为江南丝竹保护体系不断补充新的研究维度，如从传播学角度分析，与时俱进地探索江南丝竹的传播潜力；[⑨]从音乐理论角度分析现代西式乐理审美对中式传统音乐的创造力的压抑，启示理论创新对江南丝竹保护的重要作用；[⑩]尝试结合数字化、产业化技术大胆创新江南丝竹保护思路。[⑪]也有学者批判了文化保护"重形式缺内涵"问题，部分保护措施"有形无魂"，培养的青年演奏者缺乏对江南丝竹文化的价值认同，江南丝竹的继承空有形式没有灵魂，文化保护反成为文化枷锁。[⑫]

综上，关于如何保护江南丝竹，学术界众说纷纭，但其共性可概括为以下两点。写作思路上，多数学者采用"提出问题－解决问题"或"分析现状－

① 李亚. 丝竹与民乐：上海江南丝竹非遗保护的争议与两难. 中国艺术时空，2019(5)：52-59.
② 吴子铭. 新时代江南丝竹的传承与"活态"发展创新. 创新创业理论研究与实践，2019(14)：183-184.
③ 龚瑛. 苏州地区江南丝竹音乐传承与创新实践. 艺术评鉴，2021(19)：55-57.
④ 伍国栋. 江南丝竹传承的大众化视野. 人民音乐，2016(10)：71-73.
⑤ 贾怡. "准专业"的江南丝竹团：太仓市文化馆恒通民族乐团调查报告. 艺术百家，2008（增 2）：33-36；伍国栋，贾怡，郭进怀. 江南丝竹乐社"苏南三社"调查. 艺术百家，2009(3)：85-98.
⑥ 戴维娜，刘晨影. 苏州地区婚庆民俗中的江南丝竹. 艺术研究，2016(1)：24-25；郭瑾蓉. 民间习俗中的江南丝竹：历史、文献与发展. 当代音乐，2022(2)：82-84.
⑦ 李亚. 丝竹与民乐：上海江南丝竹非遗保护的争议与两难. 中国艺术时空，2019(5)：52-59.
⑧ 王芳. 对多元文化背景下江南音乐艺术传承与发展的思考. 乐器，2016(7)：58-59；苏春敏. 对江南丝竹生存与发展原因的研究与思考：仅以太仓地区江南丝竹状况调研为例. 艺术百家，2008(6)：199-201+198.
⑨ 伍国栋. 江南丝竹的传播与影响. 中国音乐，2008(1)：17-23，50.
⑩ 李亚. 江南丝竹"即兴"演奏研究. 中国音乐学，2019(2)：76-83.
⑪ 王莹. 江南丝竹数字化保护策略研究. 苏州科技大学学报(社会科学版)，2023(2)：56-60；龚裕宸，艾世博. 江南丝竹数字化保护研究. 明日风尚，2023(8)：158-160.
⑫ 吴红非，孙文婷. 江南丝竹音乐传承的实践与思考. 浙江传媒学院学报，2011(6)：89-93.

提出建议"思路，^①此类文章具有较强的政策导向性，逻辑结构清晰；也有部分学者专注于问题阐释，即"观察记录－发现问题－提出问题"，或是见微知著^②，或是归纳整理^③，为后续研究提供了重要的理论、数据基础。写作内容上，尽管学者们对于问题和建议的措辞各有不同，但整体上可以概括如下。问题方面，可总结为江南丝竹传承发展存在的问题有传承后继少人^④、听众较少且受众局限^⑤、缺少创新曲目^⑥等；建议方面，可总结为"人为核心，多方辅助"，即注重继承人培养，为推动江南丝竹发展注入内在动力，同时社区、政府、学校多方共同努力，从传播宣传^⑦、产业平台^⑧、法律保障^⑨、人才培养^⑩、创新发展^⑪等方面为江南丝竹文化生存和传承提供有利的客观环境。

但目前对江南丝竹的研究还存在以下不足之处。首先，对于江南丝竹整体性保护、发展与传承的研究较少，缺乏观察纪实类的一手调研数据，不利于对症下药、准确有效地保护江南丝竹。例如，多篇文章提及"江南丝竹传承后继乏人"，但缺少相关数据的统计和证明。尽管有学者对个别江南丝竹乐团发展现状进行了专业详尽的调查，但案例研究对地区性发展状况的研究意义较弱。此外，本文所用数据，多来自新闻报道等零散来源，目前仍缺乏系统、权威、具体详尽的江南丝竹继承现状，如继承人数、民间/官方江南丝竹乐社数量等。

其次，几乎没有文献从国际视角出发考察江南丝竹的保护与发展问题，

---

① 如：姜婷，王莹.江南丝竹的活态传承与发展策略.当代音乐，2022(12)：74-76.

② 李亚."玩"音乐作为一种社会记忆：上海湖心亭茶楼江南丝竹的历史叙事.音乐艺术(上海音乐学院学报)，2019(3)：43-51+4.

③ 杨立."丝竹故里"话"丝竹"：太仓"江南丝竹"现状与研究.大众文艺，2020(5)：124-125.

④ 王慧芳.江南丝竹传承对策.艺术教育，2013(4)：92-93；胡曦雯.浅谈江南丝竹传承的大众化视野探讨.散文百家，2018(11)：103.

⑤ 吴子铭."江南丝竹"跨文化传播瓶颈及应对策略.传媒论坛，2019(15)：22-23；张熠滢，杨立.论传统乐种的传承与发展：以常州"江南丝竹"为例.北方音乐，2020(11)：244-245.

⑥ 伍国栋.江南丝竹曲目类型及来源.中国音乐，2007(3)：25-31；阮弘.江南丝竹音乐的发展与展望.上海师范大学学报(哲学社会科学版)，2001(6)：112-116.

⑦ 吴子铭."江南丝竹"跨文化传播瓶颈及应对策略.传媒论坛，2019(15)：22-23；毛云岗.浙江丝竹音乐现状分析与发展保护研究.音乐创作，2016(11)：127-128；李慧.高校美育中本土音乐文化的传承与发展路径研究：以江南丝竹为例.科教文汇，2022(20)：23-26.

⑧ 沈雷强.新时期江南丝竹发展的展望与思考.音乐创作，2017(12)：136-137；王莹.江南丝竹数字化保护策略研究.苏州科技大学学报(社会科学版)，2023(2)：56-60.

⑨ 陈永明.为江南丝竹的活态传承而发力.艺术百家，2015(增1)：241-243.

⑩ 苏春敏.对江南丝竹生存与发展原因的研究与思考：仅以太仓地区江南丝竹状况调研为例.艺术百家，2008(6)：199-201+198；孙祈月.论江南丝竹的活态传承.文教资料，2014(22)：54-55.

⑪ 徐帆.浅谈江南丝竹乐种的传承与发展.北京：中国音乐学院，2015.

大部分文献囿于国内视野，例如比较江南丝竹与广东音乐、台湾南管的发展状况[1]，尚未有文献将江南丝竹与国际知名的音乐类非物质文化遗产进行比较研究。

再次，现有研究存在问题定义过于宽泛，部分措施建议浮于表面，难以解决实际问题的现象。仍以"江南丝竹后继乏人"为例，部分学者没有清晰界定大众化与精英化的问题，并未明晰是何种人才缺失[2]，因此，简单的"江南丝竹进校园"的教育建议不能缓解江南丝竹传承中专业化人才的缺失问题。

基于以上对既有文献的分析整理，吸取各方优秀经验，本文尽可能对目前现有研究进行部分补充，在竭力阐明江南丝竹发展现状基础上，通过对比分析国际知名非物质文化遗产——墨西哥玛利亚奇音乐，并借鉴其传承发展的成功经验，最终为江南丝竹的传承保护提出意见与建议。

三、研究内容及研究方法

本文以江南丝竹为研究主体，以江南丝竹的"继承、创新、传播"为三条研究主线，通过分析江南丝竹的保护现状和提出传承保护建议两个部分进行讨论。在现状分析部分，首先将介绍江南丝竹的发展历程，之后从"多方继承""尝试创新""积极传播"三个方向分别总结江南丝竹目前的发展情况，并点明存在的问题；在"传承保护与创新发展建议"部分，文章将引入国外优秀案例——墨西哥玛利亚奇乐队，探究其在"继承－创新－传播"过程中的成功经验，并相应提出三条保护传承的建议。

本文采用了文献调研法和案例分析法，讨论江南丝竹的继承与保护问题，以一窥现阶段非物质文化遗产保护困难的问题。（1）文献调研法。在分析江南丝竹的保护现状过程中，阅读正式发表的学术论文、期刊文献、新闻访谈稿件等76篇，浏览国家、江苏省、苏州市、联合国教科文组织等多个非物质文化遗产保护官方网站，了解近40篇发布在音乐院校官网、微信公众号、新闻网站与江南丝竹相关信息。通过大量阅读文献深入洞悉江南丝竹传承现状，发掘现存问题。（2）案例分析法。本研究参考了世界民族音乐文化遗产保护的成功

---

[1]　杨瑞庆. 比较江南丝竹和广东音乐的传承状态. 岭南音乐，2021(6)：25-27；陈鹤. 江南丝竹与台湾南管之异同. 苏州：苏州大学，2012；王琛. 中原弦索乐与江南丝竹乐的异同探究. 艺术百家，2016(增1)：282-284.

[2]　例如，《浅谈江南丝竹传承的大众化视野探讨》一文提出，"年轻人对江南丝竹学习不感兴趣"，但实际上根据新闻报道，江南丝竹教育在太仓等地的中小学教育中普及度很高，各类民间社团不断涌现，江南丝竹的传承困境并非简单的"后继无人"可以解释。

案例。墨西哥玛利亚奇乐队列入联合国教科文组织非物质文化遗产保护名录，其成功经验值得借鉴。

四、江南丝竹发展现状分析

（一）诞生与发展

"江南丝竹"是 20 世纪 50 年代被命名的一种器乐合奏类型。江南丝竹中的"丝竹"类的民族器乐，历史悠久，可以追溯到周代，如《周礼》中记载，"皆播之以八音：金、石、土、革、丝、木、匏、竹"。19 世纪时，这一音乐类型开始在苏南、浙北与上海一带流传，民间称之为"丝竹""苏南吹打""国乐"等等；到了 20 世纪 30 年代，随着上海等城市经济的发展，江南丝竹在"文明雅集""钧天集"和"国乐研究社"等乐社的支持下愈发兴旺。1940 年前后，江南丝竹进入鼎盛发展时期，诞生了"八大名曲"等曲目，演奏风格臻于完善。1954 年，"江南丝竹"首次出现在"上海民间古典音乐观摩演出"的节目清单上，随后，在金祖礼的牵头下"江南丝竹研究会"成立。至此，江南丝竹一名正式确定并沿用至今。改革开放后，江南丝竹借鉴西洋音乐的配器手法，涌现出《江南好》等大批优秀曲目。1987 年，由上海音乐协会主办的首届"海内外江南丝竹创作与演奏比赛"吸引了 37 个团体的参赛。同年，上海成立江南丝竹协会，致力于学术研究与教育教学工作。然而，现代化进程加速了江南文化的巨大变革，为了更好地保护这一艺术形式，2006 年，国务院批准将其列入首批国家级"非遗"保护名录。

（二）现有传承措施

1. 多主体继承

江南丝竹是地区人民喜闻乐见的音乐形式，社会人士纷纷自主学习，自发组建协会与团体，地方政府与事业单位也起到不可或缺地引领带头作用，政府与民间两端发力共同继承江南丝竹。概括而言，江南丝竹目前的主流传承方式包括以下四种：（1）社区自发组建的业余江南丝竹班社；（2）学校与少年宫等组建的业余江南丝竹乐团；（3）音乐类高等院校培养江南丝竹专业演奏者；（4）职业江南丝竹从艺班社。

在"中国民间文化艺术（江南丝竹）之乡"的太仓，各个乡镇、社区均设有专门活动室，为各年龄段各类职业的江南丝竹爱好者提供学习、练习与演奏的场所。目前，太仓有大大小小的丝竹乐团一百多个。2021年的普查资料显示，上海市目前已有基层江南丝竹团队96家，且数量、规模仍在扩大。[①]在苏州、杭州等地区也有群众自发组建的江南丝竹社。这些社区队伍多由老年退休人士组成，大多为自发组成的非盈利性自娱乐社。例如江苏省太仓市双凤镇的"夕阳红艺术团"，赴敬老院慰问，参加群众性广场文艺活动，正月十五闹元宵娱乐展演等等。

在年轻人中，江南丝竹主要存在于各个中小学校园，以及少年宫等青年人公共服务场馆。学生通过家庭、学校、课外兴趣班习得江南丝竹中的一种或多种乐器，再通过校园等青少年平台组建乐队。例如太仓市政府将市文化馆和青少年活动中心作为少儿民乐人才的培养基地进行培训，每年参加培训的有近30个班、700多人。2019年，上海市徐汇中学受到上海市群众艺术馆与区教育局委托，牵头组建了长三角中小学江南丝竹联盟，截至目前共有40家中小学加入。在江苏、浙江等地，大部分中小学也组建有自己的民乐团，能灵活编排江南丝竹班子。这些学校还将江南丝竹作为音乐课程教学内容，或者邀请江南丝竹传承人进校园开展讲座和音乐会。现在最大的青少年丝竹乐队是太仓市青少年宫的"学生民乐团"，于2006年组建，2017年有成员32名，都是来自当地各个小学的佼佼者，多数成员都有多次参加器乐独奏演出和比赛的经历，足见这支年轻丝竹乐队较高的音乐素养。

作为职业演奏者，江浙沪地区的师范院校、艺术院校、高校音乐专业的人才是江南丝竹传承的中流砥柱。此类院校应当义不容辞地承担起培养专业人才的重任，为培养大师打下坚实基础。例如浙江艺术职业学院，作为文化部中国非物质文化遗产传承人群研修研习基地的参与高校，学院采取了一系列工作积极推动浙派"江南丝竹音乐"的传承与发展：2014年建立沈凤泉"江南丝竹音乐"专家工作室；2015年初成立音乐系"江南丝竹音乐"音乐社；先后开展了一系列"江南丝竹音乐"学术讲座、浙派乐谱整理与碟片出版、专场音乐会等活动。中国音乐学院、中央音乐学院等高等院校还把"江南丝竹"纳入民族乐器专业学生的必修课程与选修课程中，除此以外还以讲座与实践课等形式开设并设有学分。

以班社为载体，在家族、村落中"父传子""师传徒"的继承方式或许是

---

① 杨宝宝. 传承了一个半世纪的江南丝竹，在上海已有近百家基层乐团. (2021-01-19)[2024-02-10]. https://www.thepaper.cn/newsDetail_forward_10848251.

江南丝竹最传统的继承方式。例如吴中藏书镇"顾家音乐班"，至今约有60年历史，目前班社成员相对固定者7人，全部为班主的兄长、子侄、挚友。顾家班属于纯民间性质的半职业化江南丝竹班社，活跃于当地和周边乡里，还时常受邀外出参与演出活动。此类继承方式主要见于民间，但由于民俗土壤日渐缺失等原因，班社已日渐稀少。但在世界性"文化遗产保护"的大背景下，都市居民对传统民俗事项亦心生向往，为丝竹班社创造了生存活动空间。

2.两方面创新

新时代江南丝竹传承在创新上的努力集中于曲目创新与理论创新两个方面。

步入20世纪，不少作曲家开始有意识地对江南丝竹曲目进行整理、编配与创作。第一种方式便是根据其他传统乐器演奏的古典曲目移植编配，例如著名琵琶曲《春江花月夜》《汉将军令》《月儿高》等，都被改编为合奏形式的江南丝竹曲目。第二种方式则是属于近现代专业器乐演奏家和作曲家对传统乐曲整理改编，著名的例子有聂耳的《金蛇狂舞》、刘天华先生的《变体新水令》等等。此外，作曲家基于传统江南丝竹音乐特点，以原创性的乐思和结构来创新江南丝竹音乐作品和演奏风格，形成创新的第三种方式。例如1987年"第一届海内外江南丝竹创作与演奏比赛"的获奖作品《庙院行》，创造性地引入"歌声"，来表现庙堂信众歌颂佛经的声音，这是对既有江南丝竹演奏的突破式创新。

同时，各地政府与文化部门高度重视江南丝竹相关音乐理论创新，建立文化馆和大剧院，其中经常会有著名的丝竹团体来演出交流或开设讲座，为江南丝竹的学术研究与理论指导创造条件与土壤。太仓市于1997年7月成立了有22个团体会员、281名个人会员的市江南丝竹协会。协会指导创办了"江南丝竹传统八大曲演奏赛""江、浙、沪江南丝竹邀请赛""江苏·太仓江南丝竹中外交流演奏会""太仓江南丝竹理论研讨会"等一系列活动，极大促进了乐手间的交流往来。太仓还设立了"江南丝竹馆"的特色场馆，除去参观接待的功能，场馆人员还需对江南丝竹相关乐谱、乐器、音像资料等做整理汇总工作，促进了江南丝竹的进一步理论创新。

3.全方位传播

作为国家非物质文化遗产保护项目，江南丝竹的传播受到政府部门和民间保护组织的关注，近年来，政府部门与民间力量不断拓宽江南丝竹的传播路径——以国内外演出为主，丰富文献影音资料为辅，全方位提升江南丝竹普及率，促进其再发展。

传播方面，江南丝竹艺术文化活动内容丰富、形式多样。在国内，2016—2022 年，太仓市举办了七届"江南丝竹演出季"，演出覆盖了江浙沪鄂地区的多个城市，邀请了不同年龄段的演出乐队。此外，从 2005 年起太仓每年举办全市"江南丝竹演奏比赛"，至今已有 18 届。国际上，太仓江南丝竹演出甚至走进了新加坡维多利亚音乐厅，如 2002 年，太仓市"恒通丝竹乐团"在新加坡演出。2013、2014 年"太仓五洋丝竹乐团"连续两次出访德国、英国、比利时、法国、意大利、荷兰等欧洲国家，进行江南丝竹传播和中西文化交流。2012 年，苏州大学东吴艺术团参加"相约维也纳·奥地利中国艺术节"，2014年赴美国孔子学院、柬埔寨巡回演出江南丝竹曲目，2018 年赴俄罗斯孔子学院。通过现场表演，江南丝竹清新典雅的曲调令无数国内外听众为之倾倒，文化传播事业不断发展。

除此以外，政府和各个民间组织还通过各种途径宣传江南丝竹相关的知识、理论与文化，间接地传播推广江南丝竹。例如，江苏文艺出版社出版了《江南丝竹音乐大成》，该书对江南丝竹的主要资料和学术成果进行汇总，成为高校与丝竹入门者的必读书目。上海教育音像出版社的《中国之最》以及东方卫视《东方全记录》中，都有对江南丝竹的介绍。

（三）传承存在问题及局限性

1. 继承："形在神不在"

江南丝竹继承目前存在"形在神不在"的问题。近年来在政府的有力推动下，民乐教学有了较好的发展。然而民乐演奏者虽数量不少，但并非江南丝竹人才。促进江南丝竹的继承发展，首先要明确传统乐器的演奏并不等于江南丝竹的传承，而更应当注重江南丝竹特色演奏方式和相关文化知识的教学。然而，目前的江南丝竹新一代人才培养教学多依托当地中小学与培训班，这些教学机构将演奏不同乐器的学生分开培养，专注于一种乐器的演奏教学，缺少了对江南丝竹文化的介绍与教导，也未能充分关注江南丝竹各种乐器合乐的独特演奏方式。与此同时，江南丝竹的教学目前大都一改传统口耳相传的教学模式，依赖西方乐理体系下的乐谱。而此种西方标准化的教学模式反而使江南丝竹的灵活特质在继承中丧失。

2.创新：曲目创新两难，理论构建不足

江南丝竹仍需要在曲目创新与理论创新两端发力。曲目创新方面，江南丝竹面临保留原汁原味还是迎合大众审美的两难困境。江南丝竹本是活跃于民间的音乐，常用于婚丧嫁娶等重大民间节庆活动。但随着时代的发展，人们审美和习俗发生变化，江南丝竹失去了"用武之地"。因此，江南丝竹的传承亟需根据时代发展进行创新，以迎合目前民众的需求，创造新的生存土壤。然而，创新就意味着变化，变化可能导致江南丝竹丧失原本的特性，甚至使江南丝竹走向低俗化。在实际的创新之中，寻找创新与保留恰当的平衡点仍是难题，学界尚未在江南丝竹的专业创新问题上达成统一意见。乐理创新方面，当前广泛使用的西方乐理体系与江南丝竹并不适配，无法完整展示江南丝竹"变奏""加花"等多种独特的演奏方式，而与江南丝竹适配的传统音乐理论研究依然有待加强，完善的传统音乐理论体系仍未形成。

3.传播：实际效果差强人意

此外，当前江南丝竹的传播效果差强人意，未能打响知名度。2019年常州的一项问卷调查显示，近半数的受访者不了解江南丝竹。[①]尽管常州是江南丝竹的原生地之一，江南丝竹在此范围内的知名度仍然很低。由此可见，即使江南丝竹做出了种种对外传播的努力，传播效果仍然不尽如人意，核心问题在于江南丝竹未能充分向外借力成功塑造自己的文化IP。文化IP"特指一种文化产品之间的连接融合，是有着高辨识度、自带流量、强变现穿透能力、长变现周期的文化符号。"[②]文化IP的塑造对于文化遗产知名度的提高十分重要，江南丝竹的传播亟需文化IP的塑造。

五、国外优秀案例分析——墨西哥玛利亚奇音乐

玛利亚奇是墨西哥的一种传统音乐，有墨西哥"国粹"之称，起源于19世纪中叶墨西哥中西部。[③]现代玛利亚奇乐团包括至少四名音乐家，以小提琴、小号、比维拉琴与吉塔隆为主要乐器，在墨西哥的传统节日、宗教活动或婚礼葬礼等重大场合演出。[④]

---

① 张熠滢，杨立.论传统乐种的传承与发展——以常州"江南丝竹"为例.北方音乐，2020(11)：244-245.

② 2018中国文化IP产业发展报告.(2020-04-22)[2023-09-05].https://www.doc88.com/p-19216996479020.html.

③ 张伊瑜.马里阿契音乐及其研究现状分析.艺术教育，2019(10)：84-85.

④ 谢佳音.墨西哥嘉年华的心脏与灵魂：马里阿契.音乐生活，2014(6)：24-25.

玛利亚奇乐队同江南丝竹一样历史悠久，文化底蕴丰厚，都是地区音乐文化的杰出代表。2011 年，联合国教科文组织将"墨西哥玛利亚奇乐队、弦乐、歌曲和小号"列入人类非物质文化遗产代表作名录，认为它不仅是一种传统音乐，更是墨西哥文化的基本元素。玛利亚奇保护与传承的经验值得中国江南丝竹借鉴。[1]

（一）继承：以社区与家庭为主体，全方位传承玛利亚奇文化

与江南丝竹相似，玛利亚奇音乐的价值也不仅仅在于其乐曲本身。其表演形式、服饰与背后蕴藏的价值观念也是此种音乐作为非物质文化遗产的重要部分。因此，在传承方面，玛利亚奇音乐与江南丝竹一样需要面对超越演奏本身、进行全方位传承的问题。在玛利亚奇音乐传承方面，社区与家庭通过全方位的人才培养，在玛利亚奇的传承中发挥了重要的作用。根据墨西哥政府向教科文组织递交的评估报告[2]，家庭依旧是该传统最完善的"训练中心"，家庭成员教授、保护、促进与传播整套传统——包括音乐、风格、服饰、语言、价值观念。社区积极参与音乐人才培养，提供人力与物力。在玛利亚奇乐队的发祥地哈利斯科州，8 个不同城市都设有培训中心，共有 481 名学生。社区还会单独或与各类音乐协会合作，刊定出版物，组织论坛与座谈会，录制视听和声音记录。

（二）创新：政府与法律为保障，营造良好创新发展环境

在创新发展方面，玛利亚奇音乐由于当地文化风俗变化相对较小，玛丽亚奇音乐仍能充分融入当地民众的生活当中，在乐曲创新方面的需求并不如江南丝竹紧迫，但其与江南丝竹都面临着相似的理论创新需求。在政府与法律的保障之下，多个专注于玛利亚奇音乐保护与研究的机构得以成立，相关学术研究会议得以开展。这推动了玛利亚奇音乐的理论研究不断更新，使玛利亚奇乐队拥有良好的创新环境。2012 年 9 月，由联邦和州政府共同成立了"全国墨西哥玛利亚奇乐队保护委员会"（Comisión Nacional para la Salvaguardia del

① 彭敏. 奏响激情的旋律（多彩非遗）. (2022-02-11)[2024-02-11]. http://world.people.com.cn/n1/2022/0211/c1002-32349770.html.

② Mexico. Periodic reporting on the Convention for the Safeguarding of the Intangible Cultural Heritage: Report submitted on 15/12/2017 and examined by the Committee in 2018. UNESCO, 2017; Mexico. Periodic reporting on the Convention for the Safeguarding of the Intangible Cultural Heritage: Report submitted on 15/12/2020 and examined by the Committee in 2021. UNESCO, 2020.

Mariachi，CONASAM）。此后，该组织每年举办为期一周的"全国传统玛利亚奇会议"以及"国际玛利亚奇和查里亚会议"，其间还举办一系列学术座谈会，展示最新研究成果，推动玛利亚奇音乐创新发展。在法律层面上，哈利斯科州文化部在 2014 年推动《哈利斯科州文化促进法》和《非物质文化遗产法》立法，为涉及玛利亚奇的活动提供法律支持。各级政府也积极设立各类公益机构，助力玛丽亚奇音乐的创新发展。2020 年，科库拉市政府与国家音乐图书馆（FONOTECA）也签署共同参与协议，聚焦"玛利亚奇"博物馆筹建，瓜达拉哈拉大学（University of Guadalajara）等高等学府也与政府一道合作参与玛利亚奇乐队的研究与保护，为玛利亚奇音乐理论研究方面的创新提供必要的资源支持。

（三）传播：充分借用外部力量，打造自身文化名片

相较于江南丝竹差强人意的对外传播情况，玛利亚奇的对外传播效果十分显著。玛利亚奇音乐长期以来一直是墨西哥的一张国际名片。通过借力各类媒体与活动，玛利亚奇获得了较高的知名度，塑造了自身的文化 IP。19 世纪 20 年代，墨西哥建立了全国性无线电广播网络，并以玛利亚奇音乐为正式媒体音乐。1986 年，第十九届奥林匹克夏季奥运会在墨西哥城举办。闭幕式上乐手与运动员们的共同演出，让世界人民认识了玛利亚奇。2017 年大热动画电影《寻梦环游记》也有诸多玛利亚奇音乐元素，极大提高了玛利亚奇音乐的国际知名度。

六、传承保护与创新发展建议

（一）继承：完善人才培养方式

玛利亚奇音乐作为广受墨西哥人民喜爱的国民音乐，其发展途径与人才培养路径注定是大众化的。江南丝竹不妨借鉴其根植家庭与社区的发展途径，组织与利用一切民间力量，把丝竹之声作为太仓市乃至江苏省的地区之声培养起来。

因此，促进江南丝竹继承发展核心在于完善江南丝竹人才培养方式，激发学校社区潜力。目前的人才培养多以学校为主要教学单位、以西方乐理体系为教学工具。虽然可以较快地增加乐器演奏者人数，却造成传统音乐文化教学与江南丝竹演奏特色教学的缺失。比起目前标准化、体系化的教学模式，以往口

耳相传的教学模式显然更能完整地传承。然而，江南丝竹已经丧失了其生存土壤，难以照搬原先的做法，但在学校融入传统音乐文化的教学元素，仍然是江南丝竹人才培养的可行之路。例如聘请有经验的班社师傅现场教学；抛弃西式的五线谱简谱等，改用传统记谱形式；组织不同乐种学生以传统江南丝竹班社形式合奏等等

（二）创新：加强理论创新，完善传统音乐理论

江南丝竹的传承与发展也需要传统音乐理论与认知体系的创新。江南丝竹面临传统音乐传承发展的共性问题，即西方乐理体系与传统音乐实践不匹配。目前中国传统音乐教学很大程度上依赖于西方的理论与认知体系，使得传统音乐中部分极富特色的元素难以在现代的教学中传承。以江南丝竹的"即兴"演奏为例，以往江南丝竹"即兴"能力是"口传心授"教学方式的结果，当教学跟随西方以"简谱"与"五线谱"为核心的认知将音乐精确记录、以印刷的方式固定呈现时，口头传承创造的表演多样性就逐渐消失在学院音乐教育的认知体系之中。

此外，加强理论创新也是解决曲目创新两难困境的方式之一，通过完善对江南丝竹的理论研究，江南丝竹值得保留的特质将得到关注。如此，在进行曲目创新时，江南丝竹有文化价值的特性将更好地被识别、保留。相关政府可以仿照哈利斯科州政府经验，建立委员会或专门领导班子，组织江南丝竹的保护传承工作，通过一系列手段促进江南丝竹音乐的创新传承。

因此，在政府的引导下，以高校及研究机构为主体，加强研究与学术交流，探寻江南丝竹音乐演奏规律，构建并完善传统音乐理论与认知体系，才能从根本上促进江南丝竹的教学，推动江南丝竹曲目高质量创新发展，将江南丝竹音乐传承下去。

（三）传播：向外借力塑造文化IP

江南丝竹的传播拓展当务之急是文化IP的塑造，从而有效提高知名度。从具体的方式上讲，江南丝竹作为中国传统丝竹乐，可首先积极融入"竹文化"的发展之中。"竹"作为重要的文化意象，是中华传统文化的标志之一。当今世界，随着绿色发展的理念受到全球广泛关注，"竹"作为具有中国特色的"塑"与"木"的替代品，"以竹代塑，以竹代木"的可持续发展方案与中国传统文化结合形成了现代新型的"竹文化"，在国内外受到广泛关注。江南

丝竹通过寻求与国际竹藤组织、中国碳汇基金会等组织机构合作，参与到"竹文化"的推广之中，能为自身带来更好的传播拓展机会。2021年4月22日，中国碳汇基金会与京城俱乐部共同举办"中国竹乐，绿韵悠然"公益晚会以庆祝第52个世界地球日；中国竹乐团推动了中国绿色环保意识的传播，也借用晚会平台展现了竹乐的魅力。[①] 此外，国际竹藤组织目前也设有"竹藤艺苑"板块，对包括竹乐在内的艺术形式进行宣传推广，并在2021年报道了北京竹乐团在"世界环境日主题音乐会"的演出，使中国竹乐与低碳发展理念的传播相互借力。[②] 然而，目前国际竹藤组织、中国碳汇基金会等组织与竹乐的合作无论从广度还是从深度上都十分有限，合作频次依然有待提高，不同竹乐的特性未得到充分展现。江南丝竹的发展可以学习北京竹乐团的实践模式，拓宽合作广度，作为富有自身特性的江南丝竹展现该类竹乐的独特魅力，拓展合作深度，由此形成竹乐、低碳理念、竹文化相互促进的发展模式。

此外，江南丝竹还可以学习玛利亚奇音乐的成功经验，或与影视公司合作，把江南丝竹融入到影视作品之中，将丝竹故事化，通过影视作品提升知名度，塑造自身的文化IP；或参考玛利亚奇音乐成为墨西哥国际名片的过程，相关省级或市级政府在承办国际赛事或国家级活动时将江南丝竹作为表演形式的一种，把江南丝竹打造成一张国际名片，拓宽江南丝竹音乐传播路径，助力江南丝竹音乐的不断繁荣发展。

[①] 碳汇基金会国际部. 世界地球日：用竹乐奏响低碳生活进行曲. (2021-04-23)[2023-11-3]. http://www.thjj.org/sf_E87889D5102C43CCA01B08689DC789B1_227_D843A3D6997.html.

[②] 国际竹藤组织. 竹乐世界 | 在世界地球日奏响中国天籁竹音. (2021-5-20)[2023-11-3]. https://www.inbar.int/cn/zsjdqrzxzgtlzy20210510/；国际竹藤组织. 竹乐世界 | 竹乐版澳大利亚民歌《剪羊毛》来啦. (2021-9-26)[2023-11-3]. https://www.inbar.int/cn/zysjzybadlymgjymll0926/.

世界文化遗产继承与传统工艺创新案例研究
——苏州市"香山帮"传统建筑营造技艺项目研究①

摘　要：香山帮是中国传统建筑中的一个流派，以其独特的建筑风格和精湛的工艺技艺而闻名。香山帮建筑起源于中国江苏苏州地区，传统建筑营造技艺作为人类非物质文化遗产代表作，主要出现在明代和清代，至今仍然保留着其独特的特色。对香山帮传统建筑营造技艺进行深入研究，整理相关文献和资料，探索其历史渊源、技艺特点和发展变化，有助于更好地理解和传承香山帮传统建筑工艺。

关键词：香山帮；世界文化遗产；传统工艺

一、引　言

（一）选题背景及意义

随着我国经济社会深刻变革、对外开放日益扩大、互联网技术和新媒体快速发展，迫切需要深化对中华优秀传统文化重要性的认识，进一步增强文化自觉和文化自信。传统建筑承载着千百年来工匠技艺与文化，然而，受现代社会影响，传统工匠技艺逐渐被边缘化，传统匠作技艺亟待传承。

在国际化、城镇化快速发展背景下，人们越来越专注于对地域建筑、传统建筑营造技术源流的研究。②2009年"中国传统木结构建筑营造技艺"被列入联合国教科文组织《保护非物质文化遗产公约》人类非物质文化遗产代表作名录。截至2014年国务院公布的4批国家级非物质文化遗产代表性项目名录中，传统技艺方面共273项。其中，传统建筑营造技艺为32项，而香山帮传统建

① 作者：何家宝，苏州大学金螳螂建筑学院；施沁怡，苏州大学金螳螂建筑学院；陈亚珉，苏州大学金螳螂建筑学院。指导老师：陈曦。

② 刘莹，蔡军.苏州香山帮木作营造技术发展渊源探析.建筑学报，2021(增2)：163-169.

筑营造技艺早在第一批（2006年）已榜上有名。[1]2023年苏州市人民政府办公室印发《关于推动苏州市"香山帮"传统建筑营造技艺保护传承的实施意见》，提出总体目标，明确重点任务。《意见》提出，到2035年，"香山帮"技艺获得有效保护、传承，形成"香山帮"技艺人才梯队，实现"香山帮"技艺与古建产业的深度融合发展，建成产学研一体化的"香山帮"技艺传承体系，全面振兴"香山帮"技艺品牌；进一步挖掘"香山帮"技艺的文化内涵，构建广泛的海内外文化传播途径，争取通过5—10年的时间，充分焕发"香山帮"技艺的文化影响力。[2]

香山帮作为吴文化的有机组成部分，其核心在于以"人"为本的价值观，从而成为了一个实用与审美相结合的艺术典范。[3]香山帮围绕着与人们息息相关的生活和生产展开活动。作为与吴地文明一脉相承的传统，它承载着历史的沧桑变迁，成为一面独特的镜子，反映吴地先民的生活方式、民风民情和伦理道德等方面的特点。[4]本研究将探讨香山帮工艺、关键技术和匠艺传承等构成要素，进一步加深对香山帮匠作技艺的理解。

（二）国内外研究评述

香山帮作为中国传统建筑营造领域的标志性大师帮，其技艺在中国几千年的建筑史上持续传承，并且在江南地区，尤其是苏州地区具有典型性。学术界对香山帮的历史演进进行了详细回顾，试图理解其起源、发展脉络以及对中国建筑史的重要影响。目前，对香山帮的研究多集中于香山匠人、香山帮的形成与发展、香山帮匠作系统、香山帮建筑营造技艺等领域。

在国内，一些学者对香山帮匠作技艺进行了传承现状的调研和文化价值的探索。解方舟等学者研究了香山帮工匠的技艺及传承困境。随着现代工业的发展，传统建筑工匠逐渐淡出大众的视线，技艺传承面临日益严峻的挑战。[5]继承与传承一直是香山帮工匠面临的任务，张思邈等学者研究了当代香山帮工匠技艺的重要进取与传承。探讨了当代社会经济环境对工匠技艺发展的影响，提

① 中国非物质文化遗产数字博物馆.中国非物质文化遗产. http://www.ihchina.cn/5/5_1.html
② 苏州市人民政府.市政府办公室关于印发推动苏州市"香山帮"传统建筑营造技艺保护传承实施意见的通知. (2023-04-11)[2024-12-17]. https://www.suzhou.gov.cn/szsrmzf/zfbgswj/202304/e44100ceaed04069b588dbe939a62569.shtml.
③ 孟琳."香山帮"研究.苏州：苏州大学, 2013.
④ 解方舟，胡蝶，刘晓光.香山帮工匠技艺特点及传承困境.炎黄地理，2022(2):39-42.
⑤ 解方舟，胡蝶，刘晓光.香山帮工匠技艺特点及传承困境.炎黄地理，2022(2):39-42.

出了如何顺应市场发挥创造力，促进了活力的合理建议。[①]桑晓磊等人通过对苏州桃花源项目的研究，探索了香山帮非遗技艺的传承并指出该项目通过现代模仿古法布局、替代传统构造、凝练装饰意象等手法，创造了高效、集约的新中式园林住区模式。[②]许轶璐在《非遗数字化采集工作实践研究——以"香山帮传统建筑营造技艺"》一文中提出在当代建筑遗产保护中，运用数字化采集工作可实现对非物质文化遗产科学保护的有效手段，为我们理解香山帮匠作技艺的国际影响力和学术价值提供了重要的参考。[③]

近年来，香山帮传统建筑营造技艺受到了一定程度的影响和冲击。数字化采集工作在非物质文化遗产保护中也发挥着积极作用。国外一些学者对中国传统建筑文化和香山帮匠作技艺产生了浓厚的兴趣。本研究采用Citespace软件对知网收录的200篇关键词为"香山帮"的文献进行聚类分析。通过关键词聚类分析，我们得到了香山帮研究的主要几个研究方向，包括传统建筑、营造技艺以及社会环境等（见图1）。

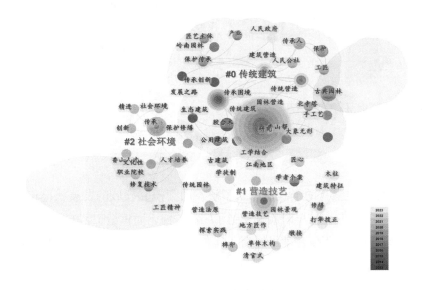

图1 "香山帮"关键词聚类分析

（资料来源：作者自绘）

① 张思邈，姚蓉．香山匠人技艺精进与传承探究．南方论刊，2021(8)：87-89.
② 桑晓磊，黄志弘，战杜鹃．新中式住区园林景观中"香山帮"非遗营造技艺的传承与创新．古建园林技术，2022(5)：13-18.
③ 许轶璐．非遗数字化采集工作实践研究——以"香山帮传统建筑营造技艺"为例．大舞台，2015(12)：234-235.

在传统建筑方向中，研究重点涵盖了生态建筑、古典园林建筑营造等内容。Citespace分析为香山帮研究领域的发展和学术趋势提供了重要时间线索（见图2）。早在2000年初，学者们就开始对香山帮的历史沿革与传统建筑进行研究，随着时间的推移，相关文献数量逐渐增加。在传承技艺方面，研究主题包括学徒制作、传承技艺等。这一研究方向从2010年开始，一直延续至今，学者们对遗产保护和传承技艺的研究表现了对香山帮文化记忆和传统技艺的重视。另外，社会环境方向主要讲述了人才培养、职业院校以及修复技术等主题，这一研究方向也与香山帮文化及遗产保护的社会影响息息相关。

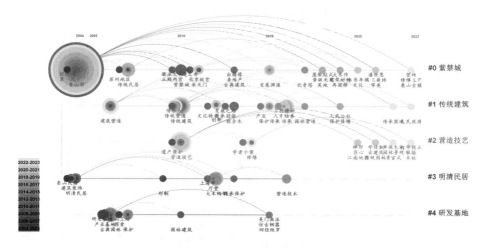

图2 "香山帮"关键词聚类时间轴

（来源：作者自绘）

以上分析结果有助于我们深入了解香山帮研究领域的发展状况和研究重点。传统建筑研究在较早时期就受到了广泛关注，而营造工艺的研究在近年来逐渐兴起，其研究不仅在学术层面上具有价值，更是与政策指引和价值取向相契合的重要举措。

然而，目前的研究尚未全面覆盖香山帮匠作技艺的各个方面。例如，对于具体的工艺技术、传承人的教育培养、保护与推广策略的探讨还较为有限。因此，进一步深入研究和挖掘这些方面的内容，将有助于填补现有研究的空白，提升对香山帮匠作技艺的理解和保护工作的实效性。

（三）研究对象及内容

首先，对"香山帮"匠作技艺的传承状况进行调查和分析。研究将调查苏州地区"香山帮"匠作技艺的传承情况，包括传承人的数量、培养方式和传承机制等。通过了解传承环境和现状，评估当前的传承情况，并为制定有效的保护和传承策略提供依据。

其次，研究将提出"香山帮"匠作技艺的保护与推广策略。通过比较研究，结合苏州地区的实际情况，提出政策支持、培训机制、传承人的认同与激励等方面的响应策略，旨在提高香山帮匠作技艺的传承质量和影响力。

再次，研究将探索"香山帮"匠作技艺在传统建筑设计和营造中的价值与应用。通过对"香山帮"工艺、关键技术和匠艺传承等要素的深入研究，挖掘其在当代建筑实践中的创新性应用和发展潜力。从文脉传承层面对姑苏文化进行解析，挖掘苏州地区的传统智慧，探索基于文脉传承的传统建筑空间组织与营建模式。

综合以上研究内容，本研究将深入了解苏州市的香山帮传统建筑营造技艺内涵，对苏州传统建筑中营造模式、传统材料语言、材料构造等进行解读，为其保护与传承提供有效的策略和措施，并挖掘其在当代建筑实践中的价值与应用潜力。通过对苏州地区最具代表性的传统建筑工匠技艺的研究，探索传统建筑设计的理念与方法，并提出可传承的路径。

（四）研究思路及方法

本研究将采用多种研究方法，包括文献综述、实地调研和专家访谈等，以全面而深入地了解苏州市"香山帮"传统建筑营造技艺项目的情况。具体的研究方法包括：

1.文献综述

通过文献梳理、工匠访谈、史迹调研，厘清苏州传统工匠技艺"香山帮"的发展历程及历时性的时代特征，深入了解香山帮匠作技艺的历史渊源、发展演变以及文化意义。

2.案例调研

在苏州地区考察香山帮传统建筑的营造技艺和特点。通过案例调研，我们将收集相关数据和样本，并与当地工匠和传承人进行交流，以了解对于香山帮匠作技艺的理解和传承情况。

3.专家访谈

与相关领域的专家进行深入访谈，包括建筑师、遗产保护学者、文保单位专家等，获取对于香山帮匠作技艺不同角度的看法与建议，为研究提供宝贵的指导和观点。

二、案例："香山帮"工艺

（一）"香山帮"的技艺概述

1."香山帮"的概念及内涵

香山帮源自中国苏州太湖之滨的香山地区，是一个有着明晰传承谱系的民间匠人组织，香山帮匠人必须是经过师徒相传或家族传承的后代。香山帮是以木匠（主要是大木作工匠）领衔，集木匠、泥水匠（砖瓦匠）、漆匠、堆灰匠（堆塑）、雕塑匠（木雕、砖雕、石雕）、叠山匠（假山）等古典建筑中全部工种于一体的建筑工匠群体。[①]香山帮以其精湛的匠作技艺而著称，涵盖了大木、小木、园林建筑、砖石雕刻、灰塑彩画等多个工种，为古典建筑营造所必需（见图3）。此外，香山帮还在民居、园林和古刹名塔等建筑领域中展现出广泛而多样化的技术应用。[②]

图3　香山帮技艺

（资料来源：作者自摄）

随着中华文明的发展，"香山帮"匠作技艺在历史长河中经历了漫长的变迁和演变过程。香山帮的发源、形成和历史变迁与江南地区的社会发展过程密不可分，香山帮的变迁和"江南地区"概念的演变也有着高度的一致性。香山帮在苏州的形成，并不是出于历史的偶然，而是苏州的经济与社会文化发展的必然结果。香山帮的兴衰及其营造技艺的传播与江南地区经济文化的时代变迁息息相关。[③]同时，"香山帮"匠作技艺在传承过程中渗透了丰富的地方语言、

① 沈黎.香山帮匠作系统研究.上海：同济大学出版社，2011：21-25.
② 解方舟，胡蝶，刘晓光.香山帮工匠技艺特点及传承困境.炎黄地理，2022(2)：39-42.
③ 沈黎.香山帮的变迁及其营造技艺特征.建筑遗产，2020(2)：18-26.

文化和组织形式，形成了独特的"香山帮"文化，它的影响力已经超过了其他民间传统建筑营造技艺（见图4）。[①]

图4　香山帮匠人

（来源：作者自摄）

2. "香山帮"修缮技术理念

中国古建营造及修缮技艺是我国工匠在几千年的建筑营造、修缮过程中积累的丰富技术和工艺经验，是中华优秀传统文化中极具特色的瑰宝之一。用老木料建新建筑，是中国古代建筑营造的传统。"香山帮"修缮技术理念是中国传统修缮思想的重要组成部分，它具有独特的特点和价值观，主要体现在以下几个方面。

（1）尊重历史建筑的原貌

"香山帮"注重保留历史建筑的原始特征和面貌，修缮过程中，力求保持建筑的原始结构、材料和造型，以保留其独特的历史价值。不会过度弥补或掩盖这些瑕疵，而是尊重其存在，展示建筑的历史演变过程。这些修缮理念体现了对历史建筑的敬畏和对传统文化的珍视，为后世保留了宝贵的历史遗产。

（2）整体性思维

在香山帮的修缮中注重建筑的整体性。修缮不仅仅关注个别部位的修复，更重视整体的协调和统一。考虑建筑的结构、形式、比例等方面的一致性，以确保修缮后的建筑整体保持完整与和谐。

（3）建筑与环境和谐统一

传统建筑是符合地域风土和文化环境的空间，强调建筑与周围环境的和

---

① 孟琳."香山帮"研究.苏州：苏州大学，2013.

谐。在设计和修缮过程中要考虑当地的气候、地理条件、传统建筑风格和文化背景，以确保建筑与周围环境相得益彰，形成一种融合自然与人文的和谐空间。

（4）传承匠人技艺

"香山帮"修缮技术注重传承匠人的技艺和经验，传统的修缮方式是历代工匠经验积累的结果。传统修缮技术秉承了中国传统木构的建构逻辑，尽量从保证历史建筑的安全性、美观性上来考虑修缮的技术选择，并且实事求是地确定修复的技术、材料、构造和结构体系。

（二）"香山帮"工艺传承发展现状

1."香山帮"的工艺传承与现状

以苏州为中心的香山帮自明清沿传至今，从理论到实践均有较丰富的遗存。然而，随着现代工业的发展，传统建筑工匠逐渐淡出大众的视线，技艺传承面临严峻挑战。在历史上，"香山帮"技艺的传承主要受到师徒、地缘、血缘关系的影响，形成了特有的匠籍制度，通过家族或师徒口传心授，遵循着严格的作头领导、师徒制匠帮。没有专门学习渠道，技艺一般"不外传"，培养过程漫长。其传承发展模式形成了独特的体系，匠人的学习包含拜师、磨心、识器、辩材、习艺、满师等一系列过程。师傅传授技艺、传承智慧，这种心传的方式极为重要。文献与图样的传承也为后人留下了宝贵的参考资料。建筑口诀通过口耳相传的方式流传至今。在实践中，匠人们的经验摸索也为技艺延续提供了宝贵的指引。

香山帮以心传悠长、文授博大、口述生动、实参不息，成就传承之道。然而，20世纪以来，受社会生活方式演变和现代建造模式发展等冲击，古建技艺实践机会相对缺乏、从业人员急剧减少，行业老龄化现象严重，不少技艺面临失传危机。从全国范围来看，古建筑领域的从业者中，35岁以下的只有4%，80%超过50岁。此外，学徒工资低、社会认同感不高等客观问题，也加大了古建行业吸收新鲜血液的难度。古建技艺后继乏人，技艺流失逐渐成为传统建筑工艺传承过程中面临的主要问题。[①]

2."香山帮"的传承发展方式与路径特点

家族追求"恒业"是香山帮传承的核心价值观之一，代代家族成员努力传

---

① 陈曦.试论"香山帮"营造技艺在当代建筑遗产保护中的适应性发展.古建园林技术，2016(2)：72-76.

承和发展建筑智慧，使香山帮的建筑技艺在家族中代代传承，不断积累和发展。师傅传授技艺，徒弟从民间学艺，形成了师徒之间的情感和默契，传承代代相传。姚承祖编写了苏派建筑创作技艺的讲义，形成了《营造法原》，开创了课堂式传承方式，将丰富的建筑智慧系统化，有助于传承传统建筑技艺。如今，国营建筑企业实体的建立以及香山古建企业的崛起，都反映了香山帮在建筑行业中的影响和传承。香山帮的传承路径从家族世袭转变为师徒传承，再到课堂教学，最终演变成企业发展模式，其灵活性使得香山帮能够在不同历史背景下焕发新生，实现永续传承。

（1）教育机构

苏州的香山帮技艺培训主要由几所学校机构承担，包括苏州市香山职业培训学校、苏州农业职业技术学院的香山工匠学院以及苏州大学建筑学院。香山工匠学院侧重培养传统园林营造技术的精英，同时推进古建筑技艺传承、社会培训，开展苏州园林文化和造园技艺的研究，还协助举办古建筑木作、瓦作等相关工种的技术技能大赛。苏州大学建筑学院自2021年开始连续举办了三届"古建筑工项目制培训"，通过理论讲授和实际操作相结合的方式，免费向社会提供培训，涵盖了香山帮技艺的结构、材料识别和使用、营造技艺等方面，促进了技能人才的发展（见图5）。

图5　理论培训与实践教学

（资料来源：作者自摄）

（2）公众参与

社区组织和非营利机构可以协力保护香山帮工艺，收集、整理、保护相关文化遗产和资料。与当地博物馆和文化机构合作，建立展览和档案，记录和传承香山帮工艺的历史和传统。例如，苏州的香山工坊建立了"香山帮资料数据库"，与政府部门合作，展示了多年来积累的古建筑书籍、资料和刊物（见图

6）。苏州香山帮营造协会在以仿古建筑为基础的企业中举办"香山杯"古建园林优质工程评选，对企业进行激励和肯定。此外，协会还举办了"香山帮传统建筑营造技艺传承人"评选工作，使更多的技术工作者获得应有的荣誉。

图6　香山文荟与香山帮技艺馆展览

（资料来源：作者自摄）

3. "香山帮"的实践项目发展情况

建筑修复项目实践中，香山帮的建造技艺逐渐受到重视。香山帮建筑大量使用望砖，无锡惠山古镇惠山浜祠堂修缮工程中所施望砖修缮工艺，分为病害勘察、拆卸清淤、本体整修、望砖铺设四个阶段，各阶段材料、工序要点等均按照香山帮建筑进行。[1]山浜祠堂木结构修缮施工主要由香山帮工艺传人与无锡当地掌握传统工艺的工匠组成，使用传统工具和工法实施保护工程。

除了古建筑修复实践项目外，香山帮技艺也走进了商业实践项目。在苏州桃花源商业地产项目中，开发商首次将"香山帮"非遗技艺团队引入设计开发和施工建构流程，对传统文化遗产保护和商业价值创造二者的有效结合进行了一次成功的尝试。[2]从2009年开始，"香山帮"200余位匠人开始参与桃花源项目建设，亲自施工完成了古建及组景装饰的"八大作"工程，包括传统的瓦作、石作、搭材作、土作、油漆作、彩画作和裱糊作，也参与设计、细化了涉及传统营建工艺与新材料技术结合的创新部分。[3]

---

① 李恒宇，沈伟军，朱蕾.无锡惠山浜祠堂望砖修缮工艺.古建园林技术，2023(2)：78-82.

② 桑晓磊，黄志弘，战杜鹃.新中式住区园林景观中"香山帮"非遗营造技艺的传承与创新.古建园林技术，2022(5)：13-18.

③ 张思邈，姚蓉.香山匠人技艺精进与传承探究.南方论刊，2021(8)：87-89.

（三）"香山帮"工艺传承发展存在的问题

1.市场需求变迁，投入成本较高

由于传统工艺繁复，部分重要的工艺可能失传或受损。新型材料和技术的出现对传统工具和技艺是一个巨大挑战。古老技艺的实践过程也是学徒经验积累的过程。大量的运用机械提高了效率，但是对难度大、精确度较高的工艺则会造成学徒基本功不扎实，对所使用的工具材料的不熟悉及经验不足等问题，导致在雕刻过程中出现石料崩断和爆裂，只能用现代的粘合剂等材料进行弥补，与传统工艺相差甚远，传统建筑技艺大大退化。

2.传统失衡融合，文化认同亟需维护

传统技术与现代人居环境的融合面临失衡的问题。如何在传统工艺的基础上融入现代需求，既保持传统特色又满足实用性。同时，香山帮工艺的展示推广方式相对匮乏，导致大众对其认知度较低。缺乏有效的展览、演出和宣传活动，使得更多的人无法接触和了解到这一传统工艺的独特魅力。因此，有必要开展多样化的推广活动，利用社交媒体、展览、文化节庆等形式，将香山帮工艺的价值和魅力传递给更广泛的受众。

3.工匠人才培养不足，技术传承缺乏后劲

工匠人才的培养和技术传承是香山帮工艺发展中的关键问题。随着年龄的增长，很多资深的匠人逐渐退出或面临技术传承困境。由于匠人传承的方式多依赖于口传心授和长时间的师徒关系，工匠人才培养相对缓慢，年轻一代对于学习这门技艺的兴趣不足。因此，需要加强工匠人才的培养和传承计划，建立系统化的教育培训机制，吸引更多年轻人投身于香山帮工艺的学习和传承。

三、"香山帮"工艺传承保护与创新发展的建议

（一）"香山帮"工艺的传承与创新路径

1.设计创新与工艺技术更新

传统的香山帮匠作技艺通常使用木材、石材、玉石等传统材料进行创作。然而，随着科技的进步和新材料的出现，现代匠人开始尝试在作品中运用新材料，如金属、树脂、复合材料等。这样的创新不仅为作品带来了新的质感和视觉效果，也拓宽了匠人的创作空间和表达方式。为了推动香山帮匠作技艺的发展，匠人们开始尝试将不同的技艺融合在一起，创造出独特的作品。例如，将

香山帮匠作技艺与现代设计、艺术表现形式相结合，创作出更具现代感和艺术性的作品。此外，与其他行业的跨界合作也为匠作技艺带来了新的灵感和创意，推动了技艺的进一步发展。匠人们也在不断探索和改进传统的工艺技术，借助现代科技的支持，匠人们能够更好地进行材料处理、抛光和装饰等工艺环节，使作品更加精美和耐久。

2. 绿色营建思想的当代价值

在工艺技术方面，团队鼓励将香山帮营建体系中的绿色思想进行提炼，应用于创造现代的人居环境。香山帮所倡导的自然观、人居观、文化观以及技术观分别回应了环境的需求、强调人文关怀和传统文化的传承，并注重保护生态资源。探索江南传统建筑审美中的"自然观"与现代绿色建筑理论之间的契合与衔接。基于苏州地区的经济运行模式、地形地貌特征、气候自然禀赋，香山帮匠作体系符合文脉传承与绿色理念的营建模式。这一理念的转化和延续，体现香山帮的营建体系在当代依然具备重要的价值，为传统建筑人居环境的可持续发展做出贡献。

3. 创新市场与商业模式

苏州香山位于太湖之滨，自古出建筑工匠，擅长复杂精细的中国传统建筑技术，人称"香山帮匠人"，史书曾有"江南木工巧匠皆出于香山"的记载。联合国教科文组织保护非物质文化遗产政府间委员会第四次会议将苏州的"香山帮"传统建筑营造技艺列入《人类非物质文化遗产代表作名录》。当前市场传统古建筑营造技艺科普形式仅采用图片、视频、公众号文章，以及与现实脱节的榫卯类单机游戏和学校组织的游学讲解等方式，缺乏全面系统的互动式体系。古建筑背后庞大复杂的体系与大部分的古建筑文化爱好者仍然存在着巨大的"文化认知代沟"。

本团队旨在以更多样化、更直接的方式向传统建筑营造技艺爱好者们科普传统古建筑文化。组合了线上和线下的产品和服务，形成一个全面完善的科普体系。在线上，建立了中国传统建筑科普网站，向中国传统古建筑文化爱好者以及学习者提供古建筑信息科普和线上拼装小游戏。与亚太地区世界遗产培训与研究中心（苏州）和各校园合作，通过讲座、趣味活动等形式对游客、学生们进行科普，提高大众对古建筑的关注度。

"巧匠"木作体验活动是本团队推出策划面向苏州旅游游客以及古建爱好者体验木作手工的一项实训活动（见图7）。可以邀请苏州业内古建筑遗产保护教授以及经验丰富的苏州"香山帮"传承人现场教授如何拼装复杂斗拱和组装完整古建筑单体，讲述苏州香山帮匠作的发展历史。参加活动的成员在工匠师傅的指导下，亲自动手斧刨凿锯，拼装榫卯，体验手工木作带来的乐趣与成就感。

图7 木作工作坊体验

（资料来源：作者自摄）

（二）"香山帮"工艺人才的培养与传承路径

工匠作为营造技艺的传承者，承载着宝贵的知识传承。团队提出跨学科融合、数字化创新以及实践导向等策略，结合现代建筑材料和环保理念，将传统与现代相结合，从而更好地将传统知识转化为实际操作。以激发工匠的创新活力，推动香山帮传统技艺的更新。

1.跨学科融合，加强宣传与价值认同

通过多种渠道和媒体，积极宣传和推广"香山帮"工艺人才的价值和意义，弘扬工匠精神。在遗产保护的全生命周期中，传承与培养新一代的匠人至关重要。通过设立专门的培训机构、学校和工作坊，传授香山帮匠作技艺的知识和技巧。融合传统的师徒制度、实践课程和学术研究，以培养新一代的匠人并保证技艺的传承。将学科技艺融入多个学科领域，培养跨界思维和综合素质，让更多人了解和认同"香山帮"工艺的传统与创新，以及匠人对文化传承的贡献。

2.数字化创新，鼓励批量化人才引培

为了培养更多的"香山帮"工艺人才，需要建立完善的激励机制，包括设立奖学金、奖励计划和荣誉称号，以鼓励有潜力和热情的年轻人选择学习和从

事"香山帮"工艺。同时，加强与教育机构的合作，为了确保技艺的发展和适应时代的需求，推动相关研究和创新工作是必要的。鼓励学术界、艺术家和匠人参与创新研究，探索新的材料、工艺和表现方式，以保持技艺的活力和创新力。结合数字化虚拟技术创新，开设相关专业课程和实践培训，提供系统化的培养路径和机会。

3.开展共建合作，构建实践导向模式

"香山帮"工艺人才培养需要建立合作模式，包括行业协会、文化机构、工艺工坊等的合作伙伴关系，一同制定培养计划和课程。详尽的调查和记录工作也很重要，包括访谈匠人、研究档案和实地调查。共建合作有助于资源共享、专业指导和技术交流，提供更广泛的学习和创作机会。同时，将传统技艺与现代审美相结合，建立长期培养模式，如学徒制度和匠人工作室，为学习者提供实践机会，确保技艺传承和发展。

四、结　论

（一）案例研究总结

香山帮是中国苏州太湖地区的一支著名民间匠人组织，以其杰出的工艺技能而著称，包括木工、石雕、园林建筑、彩绘等多个领域。这些技艺承载了中国传统文化的核心，注重传承传统价值观和保护历史建筑。然而，香山帮的传承面临一些挑战，主要表现在传承路径断裂、现代建筑趋向机械化和商业化，以及市场需求变化。这些问题包括传承人才不足、技艺保护不力、市场需求转变等。为了确保香山帮的工艺传承和发展，需要采取措施，包括培养和引进新一代匠人，提供更多政策和资金支持用于技艺保护和传统建筑修复，同时寻求创新途径以满足现代需求。这将有助于继续传承香山帮匠作工艺，展示其独特的价值和吸引力。

（二）研究局限性

研究香山帮匠作工艺面临一些挑战。首先，由于其传统性质，资料和文献有限，限制了研究深度和广度。其次，研究可能受到地域和时间的限制，主要聚焦在苏州太湖地区。还需考虑中国传统文化的影响，不过，随着文化变迁，价值观也可能有所改变。跨学科研究方法是必要的，但需要涵盖多个领域。尽管有这些限制，充分借助现有文献、案例研究和跨学科方法，以及未来的田野

调查和口述历史记录，有望深入了解香山帮匠作工艺。

（三）未来发展展望

传统工艺，如香山帮匠作工艺，正面临日益重要的保护和传承挑战。政府、学术机构和社会组织需加强研究和保护工作，记录并传承匠人的传统知识。同时，传统工艺需要与现代需求相结合，可能涉及与现代建筑、设计和艺术领域的融合，以创新工艺。教育体系应考虑将传统工艺纳入课程，培养新一代匠人，并提高公众对其的认知。国际推广也是重要的，与其他国家的传统工艺组织合作，促进跨文化的交流。总之，传统工艺的未来发展需要注重保护、创新、教育和国际合作，以确保其持续传承。

榫卯继承与创新研究报告
——榫卯结构分析及其实际应用[①]

摘　要: 榫卯作为传统工艺的重要组成部分,对于大型建筑、家具结构以及儿童玩具设计都有着极其重大的影响和指导意义。然而,在社会快节奏发展的过程中,榫卯的传承大大受限。本文将对榫卯的历史发展进行简析,并针对榫卯当代传承面临的问题进行讨论,以使其作为文化遗产的优势得以最大化继承发扬,同时更好推动其作为传统工艺的创新与发展。

关键词: 榫卯; 文化遗产继承; 传统木构结构; 传统工艺创新

一、绪　论

(一)榫卯结构

榫,是指竹、木、石制器物或构件上利用凹凸方式相接处凸出的部分。卯,是指木器上安榫头的孔眼,即利用凹凸方式相接处凹入的部分。二者相互咬合即成榫卯,在不使用胶或钉的条件下,仍极其牢固。

中国的木建筑有几千年的悠久历史,浙江余姚河姆渡的干阑式木构[②]是目前我国已知的最早采用榫卯结构建构的木结构房屋,被誉为"华夏建筑文化之源"。在中国的房屋建筑和家具设计中,榫卯由简支架演变为框架,进而演变为桁架。其独特的设计理念,蕴含了以柔克刚的中哲智慧。

起承转合之间既紧密相结,又灵活相合、阴阳互用、以制为和。榫卯的结构特点及木质本身的材料特性,使得榫卯的抗震性能较强,结实耐用。"榫卯

---

① 作者: 张颖, 南昌大学电气工程系; 邓好, 南昌大学新闻与传播系; 王佳丽, 南昌大学汉语言文学系。

② 郭伟, 费本华, 陈恩灵, 等. 我国木结构建筑行业发展现状分析. 木材工业, 2009(2): 19-22.

万年牢"，在几千年的发展过程中，榫卯以柔克刚的形制优势使其被广泛应用于建筑、家具以及玩具的设计，兼具实用性、美观性及艺术性，承载着厚重的传统智慧。春秋时期鲁班锁广泛流传于民间，至今仍作为儿童益智玩具。

斗拱作为中国木构架建筑上的一种特有结构，主要起到建筑承重的作用，同时它还有增大挑出距离、抗震和装饰作用。西周时期，"失令簋"底座图案上已经出现类似于斗拱的造型。汉朝时随着农业的发展，社会生产力大幅度提高，斗拱的结构和种类开始不断创新，鸳鸯交首拱、实拍拱、一拱二升加蜀柱等等，在兼具实用性的同时将艺术性与建筑本身巧妙融为一体。[①]唐代斗拱向外出挑比例很大，色彩愈加丰富，反映出唐代社会繁荣发展，开放热烈的社会文化底色。元朝时期异域文化在斗拱创作方面体现明显，到了明清时期则发展到了一个新的高峰，整体尺寸缩小，强调皇室的威严，并通过斗拱的大小和多少来进行等级和地位的划分。

榫卯结构顺应自然的发展规律，合理地利用自然资源，和万物和谐共处，与现代提倡的可持续设计原则不谋而合。通过对榫卯传统技艺的研究，可以深入挖掘其内在的中国哲学智慧和所蕴含的实用巧思，为其现代创新提供理论和实践支持。同时，榫卯连接也可以通过与现代建筑结构的融合，成为一种有助于提高建筑抗震等指标的新型连接。

榫卯继承与创新研究既是传统文化保护和传承的需要，也是现代建筑技术创新和环保建筑发展的趋势。通过研究、保护和创新榫卯文化，有助于弘扬中华文化，促进建筑技术的发展和环保建筑的推广。

（二）国内外研究评述

榫卯作为中国传统文化中的重要代表之一，其应用在建筑领域中的精妙操作和美学表现一直受到国内外学者重视。以下是一些国内外关于榫卯继承与创新研究的评述：

刘佳慧、宋莎莎通过对于现存木构建筑中榫卯的分析和归纳，分析了日本法隆寺、中国吊脚楼等，重点突出了建筑和当地环境的相得益彰、相辅相成。[②]

储凯锋从美学角度探讨了榫卯结构在木构建筑中的传承与发展研究，首先分析了榫卯的分类及不同应用，然后对国内外建筑进行了相应的举例分析。尤

---

① 靳羽涵，王超.斗拱发展中蕴含的文化属性.文化创新比较研究，2022(33)：93-96.
② 刘佳慧，宋莎莎.榫卯结构在木构建筑中的传承与发展.林产工业，2019(3)：54-59.

其是国内的山西应县木塔、日本的苏黎世办公大楼。并对其将来的创新方向有所展望，强调环保理念在其中的重要体现。[①]

庄德红展示了榫卯结构在儿童玩具设计领域的独特应用与创新潜力。基于榫卯结构的特点和儿童玩具设计的需求，她详细阐述了如何利用榫卯结构实现儿童玩具的多样性、安全性和可持续性。这一研究不仅丰富了儿童玩具设计的思路与方法，也为传统文化的传承与创新注入了新的活力和可能性。[②]

苏剑萍通过对传统榫卯结构的历史渊源和工艺特点进行深入分析，提出了将传统技艺与现代建筑相结合的创新理念，深入探讨了传统榫卯结构在现代建筑中的应用与传承，详细阐述了榫卯结构在现代建筑中的应用实践，以及如何通过技术革新和设计创新来实现对传统工艺的传承与发展。她的研究不仅拓展了传统建筑文化的传承路径，也为现代建筑注入了更多的历史文化内涵与艺术灵感。[③]

张晓迪指出了当前中国景观公共设施建设中存在的同质化和缺乏地域特色的问题。通过在滕州市设计体现榫卯文化的景观公共设施，打造滕州文化品牌。目前榫卯结构在景观公共设施中的应用研究相对罕见，而本文旨在填补这一研究空白，为未来的研究者提供经验和启示。[④]

各领域学者在榫卯继承与创新研究方面的工作已经日益丰富起来，涵盖了榫卯的历史沿革、结构力学分析、现代化应用及其对环境等的影响等方面。通过这些研究，我们对榫卯这项重要的文化遗产有了更深入的认识，同时为探寻榫卯在绿色建筑中的应用提供了新的思路和手段。

（三）研究对象及内容

本文研究对象为在传统工艺继承和创新背景下的榫卯工艺，通过了解榫卯的文化背景、榫卯工艺传承发展现状，总结和发现存在的问题，分析优秀案例并总结经验，探索榫卯工艺创新和发展模式，为"榫卯的继承与创新"提供行之有效的实施方案。

① 储凯锋.榫卯结构在木构建筑中的传承与发展研究.北京印刷学院学报，2020(4)：52-55.
② 庄德红，陶小苏，仲雪涵，等.榫卯结构在儿童玩具设计中的创新研究.艺术与设计（理论），2022(14)：98-100.
③ 苏剑萍，吕九芳.传统榫卯结构的现代化传承.家具，2017(2)：50-52，86.
④ 张晓迪.传统榫卯结构在现代景观公共设施中的应用研究：以滕州市红荷风景区凤鸣公园为例.济南：山东建筑大学，2019.

（四）研究思路及方法

本文首先对榫卯相关的历史文献、建筑设计图纸、现有研究论文等资料进行收集和整理。随后通过对榫卯文化背景和构造原理进行探究和分析，深入了解其结构和性能特点，并找出其在继承和发展中面临的问题和局限性。最后通过总结和分析"榫卯继承和创新"的优秀案例、实地采访调研、专家访谈等，进一步深入推进项目，为后续研究提供参考，探索榫卯工艺传承和创新路径。

二、榫卯结构的分类及应用

（一）木结构古建筑中榫卯结构的分类及应用

1.基本分类

木结构古建筑中榫卯结构可大致分为固定垂直构件、固定水平构件、连接水平和垂直构件三个类型。（见图1）

图1 榫卯结构的分类与应用

（资料来源：作者自绘）

固定垂直构件包括用于固定柱脚、防止柱脚移位的管脚榫，增强建筑稳定性的套顶榫和利用瓜柱常与角背结合来增强稳定性的瓜柱柱脚半榫三种。

固定水平构件包括常用在顺延交接位、起拉结作用的大头榫，主要用于方形构件的十字搭交的十字刻半榫和主要用于圆形或带有线条构件的十字相交的十字卡腰榫（即马蜂腰）三种。

连接水平和垂直构件包括用于连接柱头和梁头的馒头榫，多用于拉接联系构件的燕尾榫，箍锁保护柱头的箍头榫，用于需要拉结但不能用上起下落方法进行安装的透榫和用于排山梁后尾与山柱相交处的半榫。

2.木结构古建筑中榫卯的应用

（1）国内建筑中榫卯结构的应用

从我国传统古建筑来看，榫卯结构是我国发展过程当中的特色建筑结构，如山西应县木塔就是榫卯结构的代表建筑。木建筑结构完全不使用五金零件即可搭建一个完整的房屋。[①]而且，在建造木建筑结构的过程中，部分榫卯结构还可以完全隐藏在暗处，从外观看不出榫卯结构。全塔采用榫卯结构，共应用54种斗拱，3000吨木制构件，互相咬合构成塔身。不用一颗铁钉，千年间经历了40余次地震、200余次枪击炮轰、无数次电闪雷击，强震不倒、炮击不毁、雷击不焚，有"中国古建筑斗拱博物馆"的美誉，被认为是现存世界木结构建筑史上最经典的建筑实例。

由于我国地势广阔，地形复杂，在山区居住的少数民族则会选择木建筑作为居住地。例如，我国少数民族苗族的生活在山区，地势复杂陡峭，并不利于开发挖掘建造地基，所以大部分居民的建筑住房为吊脚楼，不仅安全稳定，而且还能够防止底层湿气。通常来讲，吊脚楼大都使用木材进行制造，在此过程中，不使用任何一个钉子进行连接，全部使用榫卯结构。[②]一般来讲，制造一个三间房的吊脚楼需要用到上百根柱子、屋梁以及穿枋等，通过榫卯结构的应用将这部分木质材料进行连接，进而形成完整的木质房屋。此种木质建筑的构建，不仅仅能够完全适应当地的地理环境，还具有自然的美感。

上海世博会中国馆以一个巨大的红色斗拱造型呈现于世，雄伟庄严，气势非凡。"东方之冠，鼎盛中华，天下粮仓，富庶百姓"。层层出挑、挑战重力的斗拱造型显示出现代工程技术的力度与美感，传达出精巧与力量、振奋与向上的精神气韵，向世界展示了中国建筑悠久的历史积淀和丰富的文化内涵。

（2）国外建筑中榫卯结构的应用

纯木结构建筑在进行连接的过程中，应用榫卯结构为最合理的一种方式。此种连接方法不仅为我国所特有，在世界各个地区也都充分利用了此种方式连接建筑。

---

① 林崇华，刘璐瑶.传统建筑木构艺术形态构成与审美意境表达.河北工业大学学报(社会科学版)，2019(2)：79-83.

② 王晨曦.中国传统木结构之榫卯结构的美学研究.美与时代(上)，2019(3)：16-18.

世界上最大的现代木质建筑位于苏黎世市中心，是一座 7 层的木质建筑。从建筑角度来看这栋大楼的独特之处就在于其全木的结构体系，无论从技术还是从环境友好方面来说都是别具一格的。整栋楼，包括柱子、横梁，甚至楔子都是完全以实心原木为材的，是瑞士最大的全木结构的建筑。

（二）古典家具中榫卯结构的分类及应用

1.基本分类

根据王世襄榫卯结构分类法，古典家具中应用的榫卯结构可分为基本结合、腿足与上部构件的结合、腿足与下部构件的结合、榫销四类。

基本结合的榫卯结构可分为九大类：平板结合；厚板与抹头结合；平板角结合；横竖材钉字形结合；方材、圆材角结合、板条角结合；直材交叉结合；弧形弯材接合；格角榫攒边；攒边打槽装板。

腿足与上部构件的榫卯结构主要有腿、牙和面；霸王枨与腿足、面；腿足和边抹的接合；腿足与枨子、矮老与面板；角牙与横竖材；腿足贯穿面子六类。

腿足与下部构件的结合包括腿足与托子、托泥之间的接合，立柱与墩座的接合两种。

榫销包括栽榫、穿销、走马销三种。

2.古典家具中榫卯的应用

榫卯工艺广泛存在于中式古典家具中，是中国传统家具的精髓。春秋战国时期，榫卯结构逐渐从建筑运用到家具当中，产生了一批杰出的漆木家具，在漆木家具中，可见到明榫、暗榫、通榫、半榫、燕尾榫等，其中明榫用于壁板的交角处，榫、"十"字形榫用于台面，燕尾榫用于板与板面的拼接，通榫用于台面与腿或腿与底座。[①]秦汉至隋唐时期，采用了楔钉榫的"胡床"（即交椅）的传入和改变了人们"席地而坐"的生活方式；宋代时，由榫卯结构连接数百个小构件形成的大构件斗拱结构被应用于家具中，通过借鉴在传统建筑中采用斗拱来向上承托屋顶重量的原理和形象，创造出一腿三牙的结构样式以及极有气势的霸王枨。明清时期，榫卯结构在古典家具中的运用达到巅峰，榫卯结构的种类达到数百种，牢固性和观赏性得到提升，工匠技艺更加精湛。以静、素、简为特点的明式家具和奢华、对称、肃穆的清式家具都蕴含了丰富的文化内涵。

---

① 穆瑶，吴智慧.榫卯结构在中国古典家具与建筑中的文化体现.家具，2021，42(3)：82-86.

以明式圈椅为例，圈椅是由下截和上截二个部分连体所构成，下截的结构紧密地与地面相连接，腿足与面上立柱采用素光圆柱，后椅腿一木到地，上承椅圈，前后四条腿撑起所有压力。明代工匠为下截四条腿加上了四条横梁"牙条"，为巩固牙条与下截前后四腿紧紧锁在一起，又在牙条上下加了牙头和卷口牙子，下截前腿的牙条增宽，将其作为踏脚之用，就此，前腿牙条也叫踏脚枨。使得明式圈椅的下盘既牢固又具踏脚功能。

圈椅的上截从结构上和用途上的空间和框架搭配也十分复杂，座面四围的框边是凹榫，将座面板和下截的四腿紧密锁定，还承上连接前边框上的前腿鸭脖。鸭脖在角牙配合下，起着支撑椅圈月牙扶手部位的作用。面座中部两侧的联帮棍也是起到承上启下和固定椅圈的作用，联帮棍由内向外弯上是为了增大圈椅上截的坐位空间。椅圈后部位是由两边后腿一木贯穿上下和结合靠背板连接组合。两边后腿顶部与椅圈结合部位也可加上角牙来作装饰，圈椅上截的靠背板也可作图纹装饰或镂空图案来装饰。

从美学的角度看，一方圈椅，将中国传统线条艺术最基础的曲直与方圆糅于一体，成为两种截然不同美感延伸的交叉点。椅圈为圆，如孕育生命的母胎能将人怀抱其中，两端又如神龙摆尾，弧度曲婉，却不失力道，展示圆与曲的魅力；椅座为方，棱角分明，刚正不阿，层次井然，各面横竖材以榫卯交接，均摊受力，姿态稳健，保整器结构不散，展示方与直的风骨。而"上圆下方"，又是在暗示中国古代朴素的宇宙观——"天圆地方"。天圆地方不仅仅是人们对天地形状的认识，还成为了圣王治理国家需要遵循的法则。方与圆，其实便是古人从自然中总结出、又应用于社会生活的"道"。在剥落醇美皮壳、流畅线条、坚实结构之后，圈椅仍然具有幽微玄妙的、直击人心的美。

三、榫卯工艺的传承

（一）榫卯工艺的价值

1.实用价值

榫卯在实用价值领域广泛应用于建筑、家具，山西应县木塔，全榫卯结构的应用实现建筑史上的绚烂奇迹，历经千年风雨洗礼及地震都能岿然不动。苏黎世大厦，惊艳全球的全木建筑，成为建筑史上东方审美的顶峰之作；榫卯家具的使用，跨越千年传承，从古到今，讲述中国智慧从庙堂楼阁到寻常百姓家的演进更迭。

2.艺术价值

榫卯工艺所蕴含的思想理念在服装、玩具等领域大放异彩。建筑与服装的跨界融合，碰撞出独属于中式审美的兼容并蓄，美美与共；玩具化大为小，寓教于乐，定义中国文化烙印下的"乐高"玩具。

3.文化价值

在文化价值方面，榫卯所蕴含的中国传统哲学理念意蕴丰富。以广东潮州开元寺天王殿柱头为例，其与人体脊椎结构极为相似，"柔之胜刚，弱之胜强，天下莫不知"，柔弱胜刚强的"贵柔"理念从处世之道化为木构件之间的柔性结合，面对因挤压或拉伸造成的松脱与张紧时，在起承转合中，直方向与水平方向相结合，彼此支撑，借力打力又借力化力，从而将外力相互抵消，实现经久不衰的微妙平衡。

（二）榫卯工艺在传承发展中存在的问题

1.传统生产过程成本高

首先榫卯结构对所使用的材料硬度要求很高，非硬木容易发生开裂、变形或松动。所以一般只能使用硬木，如红木、金丝楠，但大直径的硬木材料相对稀少而且昂贵。而对于一些常用的低廉材料，比如密度板，又不适合于制作榫卯结构。[①]

2.生产效率低

传统榫卯结构的制造耗时耗力，人工成本高，机械化难度大，不易为工厂所接纳。木工师傅相比同年龄段，收入较低且不稳定，技术难度大。工匠技能型人才缺乏成长的土壤和环境，榫卯工艺在市场上破坏了其艺术性、科学性、文化性的内涵[②]，也削弱了自身对人才的吸引力，导致工匠人才不足。

3.市场需求的变化

随着建筑业的发展，一些传统建筑方式受到挑战，例如钢结构和混凝土结构的广泛应用，这些新的建筑方式往往不需要榫卯连接，因此需求的变化可能对榫卯产业产生不利影响。榫卯结构由于节点刚度低、框架抗测压能力弱、滞回曲线捏拢现象严重等缺陷，不能满足现代建筑的需求[③]。在家具设计方面，高强度的木质胶水也替代了榫卯结构的功能，使得榫卯结构的应用需求下降。

① 刘秋云.探析榫卯结构在现代家具设计中的传承与创新.美与时代(城市版)，2015(8)：63-64.
② 王薇.大工业时代下榫卯结构艺术的发展与传承.艺海，2019(10)：112-114.
③ 李娟.传统榫卯结构的现代化传承研究.艺术科技，2019，32(6)：297.

4.创新能力不足

榫卯结构在材料、设计、运用方式三个方面缺乏创新，设计师们有必要对榫卯结构进行合理优化与调整，充分发挥木构榫卯结构体系的优势与功能，积极对结构材料、设计以及方式进行创新，以此促进榫卯结构可持续发展[1]。

以上种种因素，最终造成了当下榫卯技艺即使作为优秀的传统技艺，但在日常生活中普及度并不高的问题。事实上，榫卯技艺发展的受限点主要在于生产效率和生产需求问题，其实用性和美学价值的影响与意义是显而易见的。

与此同时，随着人们消费观念向精神文化层面的转变以及国家对弘扬优秀传统文化的大力支持，榫卯结构也具有相当规模的潜在市场需求。

（三）榫卯技艺与非遗技艺的对比分析

1.传承机制

榫卯技艺作为一种传统的木工技艺，传承主要依靠师徒传承和口述传统。相比之下，非遗技艺的传承更加注重制度化和组织化，通过培训班、工作坊等形式，更加注重社会参与，将技艺传授给更多的人，以确保其延续和发展。

2.组织支持

对于非遗技艺的传承发展，政府和社会通常提供相应的组织支持。例如设立专门的非遗保护机构、出台相关政策法规、提供资金支持等。而榫卯技艺的传承发展在组织支持方面相对较少，多依赖于个别工匠的努力和传统的工作坊或家族传承。

3.创新与现代化

非遗技艺在传承发展中更注重与现代社会的结合，通过创新设计、市场推广等方式，将非遗技艺与现代生活需求相结合。榫卯技艺的传承发展也在逐步尝试现代化发展，通过引入科技和新材料，使榫卯技艺与现代建筑和家具制作相适应。

4.文化保护与可持续发展

非遗技艺的传承与发展注重在保护传统文化的同时，实现可持续发展。这包括对材料的合理利用、环境保护和社会经济效益的平衡。

通过对榫卯技艺和非遗技艺的传承与发展进行对比分析研究，我们可以借鉴非遗技艺传承的经验，加强榫卯技艺的组织化和社会参与度，推动榫卯技艺

---

[1] 刘姝均.榫卯结构在木构建筑中的传承与发展分析.居舍，2021(20)：175-176.

的保护与发展。尽管非遗技艺和榫卯技艺的传承发展方法上存在一些差异，但它们都强调真实性、可持续性和创新性。

四、榫卯传承及创新发展的建议

榫卯结构无论是外在的工艺还是内在的文化精神，都能很好地体现中华民族优秀的造物理念和智慧，其独特的审美价值更值得弘扬，对现代的家具和建筑设计有很深的指导和借鉴意义。

（一）加强森林资源的科学管理

我国目前森林资源总面积达 2 亿多公顷，主要林区有东北内蒙古林区、东南林区、西北高山林区、热带林区。从现状看来，我国森林资源还处在提高树木数量和质量的发展阶段，存在人均资源较少、分布不均匀等很多问题。

针对我国森林资源的现状，政府需制定相关战略决策，采取有效措施，促进我国森林资源平稳的增长，从而为我国推广木建筑提供资源条件，推动"互联网＋"运用于发展林业，合理利用共享林业数据，加强林业信息化，降低管理林业资源成本，提高资源共享度。努力提高我国自产木材量，森林资源的科学管理逐渐步入正轨，减少对进口木材的依赖。

（二）实现流水线式的机械生产模式

相比在制作传统硬木家具的榫头和榫眼时，完全使用人工，以凿、锯等工具完成的费时费工，且加工精度和质量只能依靠工人熟练程度的加工方法，现代化的榫卯加工技术在加工质量和效率上更能满足社会发展的需求。我国木材技术与国外先进的技术和生产水平相比，还相差很多，即便优秀的木建筑设计作品，没有实现的条件，依然需要依靠国外技术。

在现代木工技术中，已经发展出多种常用榫接合方式，如以榫结构进行分类的单一榫接合和复合榫接合。按照零件的断面尺寸，材料的力学性质、接合强度要求、木材的纹理方向和接合点的位置等情况不同来选择榫接合的方式。如箱屉结构中常用的燕尾榫，倘若使用人工开凿，既费时又费工，且加工精度也无法保障。但是使用燕尾榫机进行加工则完美解决了这些问题，并且效果与传统的燕尾榫并无二致，实现了"技术美"[1]。

---

① 詹秀丽，王滔，戴向东，等.榫卯的传承：从明式家具结构的工艺美到现代实木家具结构的技术美.林产工业，2017(6)：41-42.

（三）鼓励榫卯工匠传承工艺

一方面，工匠应当有着发扬这门古老技艺的历史使命感，要坚信在现代技术条件下，能够探索出一种将榫卯结构的精髓与现代技术相结合的方法。在新的时期下，传统榫卯工艺只有适应了新条件、新材料，才能被鲜活地运用到现代家具和建筑中。克服传统榫卯技艺在现代社会中运用的难题，让榫卯技艺能够被鲜活地运用到当代家具及木艺制品中，并让榫卯回归大众生活，这是现代设计师迫切需要考虑的。可喜的是，现如今也不难发现家具结构中榫卯元素的存在，尽管是一些雏形，但也能看出设计师对古老技艺致敬的诚意。

另一方面，加强政府与社会合作，提高公众文化素质和文化自觉性，推动文化遗产传承发展工作向更广阔的群众开展。对于优秀的榫卯工艺传承工匠给予大力宣传，扩大榫卯技艺对于社会的影响力，为榫卯工匠提供良好的社会激励环境，加强官方对于榫卯工艺的参与和扶持。推动传统文化落实到商品本身，在家具中实打实地注入民族特色，敢于尝试，敢于创新。扩大传统文化本身的商业化程度，正如文创产品的屡次出圈，都能够说明，国人本身对传统技艺的高认可度、高接受度。

近日，一位名为"阿木爷爷"的63岁大爷因精湛的木工技艺视频走红海外。在视频中，他使用传统的榫卯工艺，不用一根钉子、一滴胶水，就打造出将军案、鲁班凳、鲁班锁、摇椅、拱桥等精致的木器，被网友誉为"当代鲁班"。"工匠精神，匠心为本。"这是央视对阿木爷爷的评价。前半辈子他靠木匠手艺养家，老了以后以钻研木工技艺为乐。他不仅继承了传统技艺，更继承了精雕细琢、精益求精的匠心。

（四）紧跟时代潮流

榫卯作为功用性产品，不应只是陈列于博物馆被展示、作为物质文化遗产被保护，而应让更多的人有机会了解中国博大精深的文化。

1.运用传媒技术，弄潮新国风

运用社交新媒体技术，加深大众对于榫卯的认识，增加宣传路径，与时俱进，让榫卯与时代国风相结合。通过网络传媒平台，扩大以榫卯为代表的传统工艺的知名度和认可度。可以选择有知名度的艺人代言，但其形象本身应该符合榫卯工艺简洁大方的特性，强调中国审美的含蓄性和高级感，也可以直接扶持榫卯传统匠人，通过亲切有趣的形式拉近中国传统工艺和大众生活的距离。

将榫卯工艺与其他传统工艺和现代科技相结合，让其在具有新奇感和创意性的同时，恰当地传播中华文化的智慧。可以采用"盲盒"等年轻化方式，吸引年轻人对于榫卯进行了解，为消费者提供新奇有趣的购物体验。消费者可以购买未知的盲盒商品，在开启过程中产生一种"惊喜"和"期待"的感觉，增加购物的乐趣。

与媒体平台开展合作，以数字化藏品的形式扩大榫卯技艺在年轻人中的影响力。数字藏品在电商行业有很好的可存储性、流通性、稀缺性，数字藏品不仅可以自己用来收藏，而且还可用来转赠，有很大的升值空间。既增加了榫卯的科技感，促进了社会科技能力的进步，又可以满足人们对收藏和追求独特物品的需求。

和线下比较受欢迎的卡通形象和品牌开展联名活动。一方面，推出Q版榫卯吉祥物、卡通代言人、推出榫卯表情包、榫卯纸质包装、塑料包装，定制榫卯明信片，在趣味性中发挥榫卯的惊艳作用。另一方面，可以与其他优秀的中国历史文物和传统技艺开展合作。比如，影响较大的青铜器、蜡染技术等。让中国传统技艺"组团出道"，从而扩大影响力和受众的接受程度，实现跨门类合作共赢，推动多领域融合发展。

2.赋予现代科技，尽显榫卯精髓

简化了的榫卯结构，会在形式上给人以更加简洁、现代的视觉感受。不少现代设计师为了凸显出简洁的榫卯之美，将榫卯配合中的精髓和现代制造技术的精炼，以直白的构造应用于家具设计中，表现出了一种现代感的榫卯应用技术之美。

丹麦设计师朱利安（Julian Kyhl）便意识到榫卯结构的精妙，并对其进行改良和创新，设计出一款全榫卯搭接，依靠自身重量保持稳定的可组装拆卸桌子，名为Timber——"为木而生"。Timber桌由十个木构件通过巧妙的榫卯结构拼装而成，不用一钉一胶，斗榫合缝，温文尔雅。并且可组装拆卸，实现了平板包装运输，其组件可全部放进一个不大的纸箱里。他的组装演示犹如一场优雅的魔术表演，让组装家具时的焦头烂额消失得无影无踪。

设计公司Tag Design利用电脑科技和三维模型来生动直观地呈现经典的榫卯结构，设计了一款名为"榫卯"的APP。高质量的三维模型，可以三维实时查看一分解经典的27款榫卯结构；精美的设计来呈现适合榫卯结构的木材；巧妙的交互来讲解常用传统木工工具……带我们一起重温那充满自然味道的温暖童年，献给热爱自然、木头和设计的所有人，一起体验榫卯结构的精妙之美。

3.创意融合，和合而生

和合而生，即"榫"与特定的"卯"结合之后生成新的物件，产生强有力的支撑力、连接力、生命力。基于中国传统手工艺，将东方文化精髓与国际领先的创新设计结合，既能实现榫卯结构的功能，又符合现代的视觉审美。

袁媛设计的灯具"解锁"从中国传统的"鲁班锁"中汲取了灵感。这个灯具直接受到了中国古代传说中最聪明的木匠鲁班发明的启发。就像鲁班锁一样，它完全依靠榫卯结构的部件连接，无论是组装还是拆卸都需要智慧和技巧。袁媛不仅仅在"解锁"中展现了光影与形体的美感，还将乐趣融入了将部件组装成灯具的思考和体验过程中。

设计师塞巴斯蒂安（Sebastian Marbacher）从一种全新的角度审视榫卯结构，将其视为雕塑的一部分。他特别关注软硬材质的结合与对比，在两件作品中，他分别尝试用经过机械精密加工的熔岩石、未经加工的软木以及经过加工的硬木来探索榫卯结构的可能性。事实证明，榫卯让这两块不同材质的材料通过特定的方式达到平衡状态。

五、结 论

（一）案例研究总结

榫卯作为传统工艺的重要组成部分，其对于大型建筑、家具结构以及儿童玩具设计都有着极其重大的影响和指导意义，但是在种种现实因素和社会快节奏发展的过程中，榫卯的传承已经受限。本文对榫卯的历史发展进行简析，并针对榫卯当代传承面临的问题进行讨论，以使其作为文化遗产的优势得以最大化继承发扬，同时更好推动其作为传统工艺的创新与发展。

在推动榫卯的传承与创新进程中，应强调理论和实践相结合，借助数字技术和信息技术手段，推动传统文化和现代科技的相互融合，促进文化遗产的科技化和信息化；注重市场化运作，在文化遗产的保护和利用中加强市场导向，利用市场机制推动文化遗产的可持续运营和发展，实现文化和经济的双重效益；依托政府和社会的协作关系，加强文化遗产保护和利用规划的先进性，推进文化遗产的多元化和创新化，推动文化遗产保护和利用的协调和高效。

（二）研究局限性

实地参观有限。由于条件限制，无法进行多地采访调研，获得的数据和实际情况有限，无法近距离观察榫卯结构的精巧，了解榫卯在木质结构中的具体用途，从而深入了解榫卯的实际应用情况。

榫卯工匠采访不足。由于研究者资历尚浅，无法采访榫卯工匠，从而未能深入了解榫卯传承中存在的问题及需要传播和宣传的方式。

（三）未来展望

优秀的产品往往是"道""器"结合的典范。榫卯结构，看似只是部件之间的凹凹凸凸变化，实质上承载了中国关于稳定与和谐的世界观。榫卯结构的连接方式和连接结构从来都不是单向的锁死设计，而是借助设计上的巧妙达到固定和连接的目的。这样一种传统设计思维方式，在今天乃至未来，都将始终富有活力和生命力。

传统的榫卯继承与创新研究往往局限于地域和群体，缺乏对普通人、消费者、市场等群体的考虑。虽然随着时代的发展，榫卯设计由于成本、木材、制作工艺等因素逐步淡出了我们生活的主流市场，但我始终相信它并不会消失。未来，应将榫卯继承与创新的概念推广到更广泛的群体中，将现代科技手段应用于传统的榫卯继承与创新研究中，将传统与现代相结合，拓展传统木构建筑的新领域。同时，也可以认真总结、分析和评估各种榫卯的实际应用和效果，进一步完善创新研究，让其实现更良好的发展。

藏族织毯技艺的传承与保护[①]

摘　要： 本文概述了藏毯起源、历史背景、发展变迁、工艺特点与
文化内涵，并分析其当前传承现状与存在的问题；以国外
的奥布松挂毯和高比林壁毯为例，通过横向对比分析了藏
毯与其他织品在价值取向、资源优势等方面的差异，并以
天织地毯这一成功案例探讨了藏毯应如何实现商业化与艺
术化共同发展；最后立足中国国情，提出建议：结合现代
工艺与市场互动，藏毯大公司生产与家庭式作坊协同发
展，推动传统藏毯工艺的传承创新，不断发扬从传承人到
企业政府的主体力量，创新人才培养与传承路径，促进西
部地区产业结构调整和特色产业发展，为脱贫攻坚和提升
文化自信赋能。

关键词： 藏族织毯；藏毯工艺；传承与保护；非物质文化遗产

一、绪　论

（一）选题背景及意义

藏毯工艺及其产业发展历史悠久。2006 年 5 月 20 日，加牙藏族织毯技艺
和藏族邦典、卡垫织造技艺经国务院批准，入选中国首批国家级非物质文化遗
产名录。

因青藏高原的特殊自然地理环境，毛织品是藏族不可或缺的日常生活用
品。早在三千多年前，藏族先民便已掌握了原始藏毯的编织技艺，编织出一种
叫"毛席"的地毯。11 世纪初，西藏织毯工艺逐步革新，地毯的毛束和密度
大大增加，而且其图案色彩变化多样，这种藏毯被称为"汪丹仲丝"。15 世纪

---

① 作者：张浩文，武汉大学法学系；李一鸣，武汉大学建筑系；杨淑洁，武汉大学信息管理与信息系统系。

中期，江孜县诞生了一种名为"卡垫"的地毯，其特点是中间图案简单，四边由长厚毛碎构成，具备保暖功能。清朝初期，藏毯工艺已愈发成熟，藏地僧团在进献金银法器和珍贵药材之外，也将藏毯作为贵重赠礼进献给皇帝。经过民间传统工艺的长期实践发展，藏族手工地毯仍然在纹样和工艺上很好地保留了原始风格，独具藏族文化魅力与宗教文化。

随着文化的不断进步，服装与服饰的功能不再仅限于实用性，人们注重舒适度的同时，也愈加注重款式花样的选择，而民族传统文化也一直都是服装设计中的重要灵感来源。纯手工编织的藏毯用最天然的材质和最古朴的技艺，为人们带来大自然的温暖。藏毯无论从纹样、颜色还是材质、工艺上，都向人们展示着一个瑰丽的艺术世界。藏毯艺术是连接民族特色与艺术价值的纽带，将民族文化融合现代艺术，有利于传统文化的传承与创新。此外，在西部大开发政策的指引下，研究藏毯的保护与传承有助于促进西部地区（尤其是西藏和青海）产业结构调整和特色产业发展。

（二）国内外研究评述

目前我国对非物质文化遗产的保护非常重视。王文章主编的《非物质文化遗产概论》①是我国非物质文化遗产研究的拓荒之作，首次从基础理论方面系统研究非物质文化遗产及其保护。陶立璠、樱井龙彦主编的《非物质文化遗产学论集》②和戴伟、李良品和丁世忠等主编的《乌江流域非物质文化遗产研究》③等论文集促进了非物质文化遗产的理论研究以及保护实践。但经知网以"藏毯"为关键词检索（截至2023年12月17日），专门针对藏毯工艺传承的研究较少。大多文献为信息报道，研究型论文约80余篇，结合已出版的专著，国内关于藏毯的研究内容有以下特点。

（1）侧重藏毯本身的研究，包括藏毯图案、藏毯色彩设计以及藏毯工艺等，如《藏毯的图案艺术特征研究》④、《故宫藏毯图典》⑤和《江孜藏毯艺术研究》⑥；（2）从产业发展的角度探讨藏毯产业的竞争力、发展战略、集群发展模式和可持续发展。如李毅、王英虎的《青海藏毯产业集聚现状与产业集群化研

---

① 王文章.非物质文化遗产概论.北京：文化艺术出版社，2006.

② 陶立璠，樱井龙彦.非物质文化遗产学论集.北京：学苑出版社，2006.

③ 戴伟，李良品，丁世忠等.乌江流域非物质文化遗产研究.重庆：重庆出版社，2008.

④ 旦增拉姆.藏毯的图案艺术特征研究.西藏艺术研究，2021，142(4)：39-45+38.

⑤ 刘宝建，苑洪琪.故宫藏毯图典.北京：故宫出版社，2010.

⑥ 王晓丽.江孜藏毯艺术研究.北京：清华大学，2016.

究》①和黄军成的《青海藏毯产业发展的战略模式研究》②探究了藏毯产业当前的市场现状、资源优势、发展模式和困境以及产业可持续发展对策；（3）从文化的角度挖掘藏毯的文化内涵及其文化价值，如肖海的《青海藏毯文化探源》③；（4）从现代技术层面分析在藏毯图像中运用基于内容的图像检索系统技术的可行性，如孙琦龙和张明亮的《基于颜色特征的藏毯图像检索研究与实现》④；（5）从传播学的角度，探究非物质遗产藏毯的传承与国际化，如丁零的《数字媒介视域下传统手工藏毯的传承研究》⑤和王瑞珍的《论藏毯企业国际营销策略》⑥。

国外早在 20 世纪 90 年代就开始探究藏族原住居民传统编织艺术，米歇尔·塞佩尔（Michel Peissel）在其《西藏朝圣之路画册》⑦中整理了有关西藏艺术文化的珍贵图片，是对西藏文化研究的重要资料。

（三）研究对象及内容

本文以藏毯为切入点，结合历史背景、其工艺特点与文化内涵、当前传承现状与问题，对比分析藏毯传承与奥布松挂毯和高比林壁毯，探索藏毯传承与传播路径。

（四）研究思路及方法

本文主要采取案例分析法，选取了奥布松挂毯和高比林壁毯与藏毯进行对比分析，吸收并借鉴其传承与发展经验。

二、案例：非物质文化遗产藏毯

（一）藏毯概述

1.品类纷繁

藏毯的种类，根据使用对象的不同，可分为寺院用毯和民间用毯。其中，民间用毯实用性更为突出。民间用毯既保暖隔潮，又经久耐用，兼具实用性和装饰性，是藏族人民生活的必需品。受本地游牧文化和宗教文化影响，传统藏

---

① 李毅，王英虎.青海藏毯产业集聚现状与产业集群化研究.青海社会科学，2009，179(5): 53-57.
② 黄军成.青海藏毯产业发展的战略模式研究.商业时代，2007，401(34): 90-91.
③ 肖海.青海藏毯文化探源.艺术设计研究，2012(增 1): 83-86.
④ 孙琦龙，张明亮.基于颜色特征的藏毯图像检索研究与实现.软件，2015，36(8): 25-29.
⑤ 丁零.数字媒介视域下传统手工藏毯的传承研究.丝网印刷，2023，348(4): 90-93.
⑥ 王瑞珍.论藏毯企业国际营销策略.财富生活，2022，107(8): 25-27.
⑦ Peissel, M. *Tibetan Pilgrimage: Architecture of the Sacred Land*. New York: Harry N. Abrams, 2005.

毯装饰图案纹样有单独纹样和组合纹样两种类型。根据藏毯的图案类型，主要可分为江垫式、龙凤式、满地铺式、城廓式和嘎雪巴式五类。

2.原料独特

藏毯以西藏地区原产的藏系羊毛为编织材料。这种羊毛以其高光泽度、粗长纤维、较高弹性、强耐酸性等优点闻名于世，被视为制作传统手工藏毯的不二选择。

经过数千年的生产实践与制作经验积累，现代藏毯据其编织原料分为五类，即绒藏毯，选用生长在海拔 4000 米以上的青藏高原抗高寒动物，如山羊、牦牛肩背绒毛作为原料；纯丝藏毯，采用"柞绢丝"为原料，编制后经化学水洗制成；丝毛藏毯，将"柞绢丝"与藏系羊毛混合编制；仿古藏毯，采用中国古老藏毯的植物染色法，搭配优质藏系羊毛为原料制成；天然色藏毯，采用藏系绵羊毛为原料，经人工分选纺成七种不同深浅颜色的天然色纱，无需染色即可制成。

3.工艺精湛

藏毯经手工纺线、植物染色和手工编织等工艺制作而成，所用手工纱线染色采用传统植物染料加工染制而成。植物染色的纱线色泽温润自然，色彩丰富，不易褪色，利于环保。

藏毯采用"八字扣"和"马蹄扣"等独特的手工打结编织技法，能根据客户需求编制成各种形式。采用此种方法织出的藏毯毯面纹理自然，层次分明。经过洗毯、剪花等多工艺处理后，地毯呈现出绸缎般的光泽和质感，色泽鲜艳，彰显了粗犷、古朴、自然之美。

（二）藏毯工艺传承发展现状

1.藏毯的整体发展面貌

（1）传统媒介与数字媒介相结合，传承传统手工藏毯

诸如中国（青海）藏毯国际展览会等藏毯展会是传播藏毯的主要传统媒介，后依托数字媒介技术，藏毯产业传承与推广媒介得到创新发展。近几年，江孜地毯厂山赴（Atelier Changphel）①借助小红书、微博、微信公众号等新媒体平台积极推广藏毯，因其品牌主理人王泽强（2017 视觉中国十佳摄影师）所拍摄的藏毯照片构图讲究，调色舒适耐看，已收获两万余次的点赞和收藏。

---

① 山赴 (Atelier Changphel). 心系旷野 家在毯上. (2023-06-20)[2023-12-17]. https://www.changphel.com/.

（2）利用现代技术推动藏毯数字化

藏传佛教文化深刻影响并塑造了藏毯的图案设计和色彩，使其成为具有极高艺术价值的非物质文化遗产。随着信息科技进步和非物质文化遗产数字化，业内专家基于对藏毯纹理特征、色彩分布和形状特征的分析，进一步提取藏毯图像的关键特征值来实现基于内容的图像检索。利用非结构化的存储和检索技术不仅使数据存储的类型更加灵活多样，而且提高了藏毯图像检索的效率。基于HSV颜色空间的图像检索算法为藏毯这一非物质文化遗产的保护和继承提供了坚实的技术基础，并加快了藏毯图像数据库建设步伐。[①] 此外，人工智能技术、区块链技术等也推动了藏毯数字化。

2.藏毯行业发展现状

为了解决"三农"问题，政府推动藏毯产业集聚发展，构建了集生产、加工、销售及原辅料供应一条龙的生产经营企业群框架。在青海省西宁市城南国家级工业园区，已经集聚了包括雪舟集团、嘉年公司、汇丰公司、藏羊机织毯公司、圣源机织毯有限公司和美亚生态发展公司等在内的9家藏毯企业，整体来说，藏毯产业集聚雏形已经具备。[②] 因藏毯企业数量较少，且企业之间横向或纵向联系还不紧密，产业集聚尚处初级阶段。

（三）藏毯工艺传承中存在的问题

1.设计创新能力不足，缺乏品牌知名度

藏毯图案多为古老的寺庙壁画，二龙戏珠、花草鸟兽、山水古画等是常见题材。在图案和色彩设计上，藏毯通常遵循传统风格，缺乏创新和突破。由于相关激励政策乏力，企业专业人才队伍流失严重，缺乏自主创新能力，无法开发适应市场需求的新产品。这一致命缺陷也导致藏毯产品市场占有率一再下滑。

青海"世界藏毯之都"的确立为打造"青海藏毯"这一区域品牌奠定了基础。[③] 然而，由于对区域品牌重要性认识不足，对区域品牌关注力度不够，以及相应配套政策措施不完善，政府尚未能有效指导园区及企业有意识地宣传和推广"青海藏毯"这一区域品牌，导致品牌积淀相近的"波斯毯"在国内外的知名度和品牌价值远高于"青海藏毯"，而具有中国民族文化特色的藏毯却无

① 孙琦龙，张明亮.基于颜色特征的藏毯图像检索研究与实现.软件，2015，36(8)：25-29.
② 李燕.青海藏毯产业发展现状研究.柴达木开发研究，2018，190(6)：19.
③ 黄军成.青海藏毯产业发展的战略模式研究.商业时代，2007，401(34)：91.

力与之抗衡。①

2. 生产经营规模偏小，产业格局不合理

由于产业之间分工不明确，加之龙头企业的强势，对其他企业并未产生实质性带动作用，这一现状不利于产业向集群方向发展。服务于产业集聚发展的各功能性环节脱节，制约了群内企业的发展。藏毯产业是一个新兴产业，发展时间不长，各个环节衔接不紧密，造成大量资源浪费，如国际藏毯展览城、藏毯博物馆、保税仓储区、原辅料交易中心等均未能充分发挥其功效，有些功能区甚至难以维持正常运行。外资企业少，实际利用外资程度不高，外资在藏毯产业发展中尚未发挥其应有作用。

3. 推介展销渠道单一，市场开拓不足

藏毯的传承推广主要以传统媒介为主，虽然已有部分开始使用新媒体传播与推广渠道，但是传承人员老化、媒体形式落后和传播媒介薄弱等问题逐渐导致藏毯的市场需求量较之前明显下降。传统手工藏毯由于生产成本高、生产周期长以及缺乏广告宣传等因素制约受到网络快消品的强烈冲击。②

4. 工匠人才培养不足，技术传承缺乏后劲

手工藏毯的传承主要依赖当地工匠，但受其个人能力、资金、信息和人脉等方面的限制，当地工匠在发展和传承藏毯的过程中难以充分发挥主观能动性，因此藏毯主要依靠政府主导部门支持。此外，织毯匠人以家传为主，其栽织传承祖辈的固定图案，缺乏创新动力。随着年轻人选择外出务工，不愿从事藏毯编织行业，织毯劳动力流失，手工藏毯传承有断代危险，后继乏人。③

5. 自然基础遭到破坏

"一方水土养一方人。"民间手工技艺依赖于其特定的自然生态环境，为生活在特定地域的人们所享用并传播。藏系羊毛作为制作手工藏毯的关键原料，具有高度不可替代性。然而随着青藏地区草原沙化和草质退化，青藏高原牲畜的数量相比以往有所减少，产出的毛绒质量也明显下降，这一定程度上影响了藏毯原料的供应和品质，进而也影响了藏毯产品的整体质量。④

---

① 李燕. 青海藏毯产业发展现状研究. 柴达木开发研究，2018，190(6): 20.
② 王冬燕，陈奇. 存一份让后世骄傲的秘密: 访国家级非物质文化遗产项目加牙藏族织毯技艺代表性传承人杨永良. 青海党的生活，2022(7): 24.
③ 张文婷，赵晓晓. 非遗助力乡村振兴: 西藏江孜藏毯织造技艺的生产性保护研究. 化纤与纺织技术，2022，51(4): 172.
④ 马志华，靳波. 民间手工技艺的存境与困境: 以青海省加牙藏毯为个案. 西藏大学学报(社会科学版)，2021，36(1): 215.

三、国内与国外文化遗产传承发展的对比分析（以藏毯、奥布松挂毯和高比林壁毯为例）

（一）传承发展的理念特色

1.价值取向对比

巴洛克、洛可可风格盛行的时期恰恰也是高比林壁毯高速发展的时期。兴起于中世纪时期的高比林壁毯曾主要复刻绘画作品，其编织技艺一度达到了登峰造极的水准，然而，这种价值取向也恰恰伤害了挂毯艺术中"纤维"的地位。在18、19世纪高比林壁毯的黄金时期，纤维也仍然无法成为艺术表达的主体。直到威廉·莫里斯（William Morris）在工艺美术运动里推动了现代纤维艺术的发展。

如同高比林壁毯，奥布松挂毯纤维的力量也被大大忽略。而让·吕尔萨（Jane Lurcat）则倡导不断开发织物纤维的新材料、新技法、新语言，和曾经长达数百年的旧有取向分道扬镳，为壁毯向纤维艺术的转向奠定了基础。[①]

相比之下，时代的发展似乎因为地域限制等因素没能让藏毯摆脱旧有风格的束缚。藏毯的制作工艺采用了专人描摹绘画编制的方式，设计者和制作者相互独立，使得工人技艺炉火纯青能够实现近乎完美的复刻，却很难随机应变，无法体现出编织者对挂毯中独有元素的理解与艺术表达。然而，从奥布松挂毯与高比林壁毯的历史来看，不管是哪种艺术形式最终都会随着时代的发展进行改变，否则就会面临消亡的局面。

2.资源优势对比

1963年首届洛桑国际传统与现代壁毯艺术双年展的开展传播了纤维艺术，推动了纤维艺术的发展，使纤维艺术进入大众的视野中，同时也发展成了国际纤维艺术领域中最具有代表性的展览。[②]

早期的洛桑双年展由于策展人提倡聚焦于解放壁毯艺术的枷锁，而非一味模仿绘画作品，所以参展的作品虽然大部分还是与绘画相融合的风格，仍然具有浓烈的传统色彩，不过已极大地区别于传统模仿绘画的风格。即便策展的初始目的是打破挂毯艺术长期描摹绘画，被裹挟而失去自身艺术特性的局面，但艺术家因此对编织工艺和编织元素的思考走向了台前，引发了更多的思考和尝

---

① 王册.基于传统缂毛工艺的当代装饰挂毯形式创新研究.乌鲁木齐：新疆艺术学院，2022：11.
② 王册.基于传统缂毛工艺的当代装饰挂毯形式创新研究.乌鲁木齐：新疆艺术学院，2022：13.

试，也极大影响了后来的挂毯艺术创作。

而同期，高比林编织壁毯已经开始突破传统，并靠近现代艺术理念。①高比林纤维艺术作品的编织技艺传入中国短短 30 年，已经有了本土化倾向的发展，受到了中国传统艺术的影响。这对于纤维艺术来说是一次中国式创新，为古老的高比林艺术注入新的活力，也为纤维艺术的发展注入新鲜的血液。

而在中国，因为国家扶持中华传统文化，国内的挂毯艺术也拥有着独有的优势——虽然其发展水平还停留在绘画描摹的阶段，但工业化的程度甚至比高比林壁毯、奥布松挂毯要更高。以生产青海藏毯为主的圣源公司使用智能纱架，使用智能枪刺机器人，加大培训力度和校企合作强度，培养并吸纳青年职工，为公司注入新鲜活力；甚至提出了"奋进毯"的概念，在手工枪刺区，新引进的 4 台"枪刺机器人"设备大大提高了生产效率和成果。②

（二）传承发展的现状模式

1.动力机制对比

20 世纪 70 年代是我国传统装饰挂毯向当代装饰挂毯转变的重要节点。改革开放时期，随着更广泛外交活动的开展，中国引进了大量外来艺术作品与艺术理念，这深深影响了当时国内艺术的风格发展。

20 世纪 80 年代初，美国著名纤维艺术家茹斯·高（Ruth Kao）教授率领十多名纤维艺术学生到中国访问考察，他们所带来的全新的艺术观念对我国纤维艺术的发展起到了巨大的推动作用。20 世纪 80 年代中期，袁运甫等老辈艺术家在中国美术馆举办了具有划时代意义的"壁挂艺术展"，标志着中国开始拥有独立的纤维艺术。之后，林乐成教授开始将纤维艺术引入高校专业课堂，为后续中国纤维艺术新鲜血液的培养开辟道路。1986年，由著名纤维艺术家万曼建立于中国美术学院的壁挂艺术研究所展开了中国特色当代纤维艺术的研究。由他推广的纤维艺术展"从洛桑到北京"为中外交流搭建了良好的桥梁。③国外挂毯艺术的发展先行一步，为中国当代装饰挂毯提供了新的思路。融合了独特中华民族特色与外来思潮的挂毯逐渐登上艺术舞台，展现出鲜明的民族风格与时代特征。

而在外国艺术史上，当代挂毯艺术设计的重要转折点当属包豪斯艺术学

---

① 王珊.基于传统缂毛工艺的当代装饰挂毯形式创新研究.乌鲁木齐：新疆艺术学院，2022：14.

② 贾泓，张慧慧.千年藏毯乘风而行 特色产业踏浪逐潮.青海日报，2022-06-13(05)：2.

③ 王珊.基于传统缂毛工艺的当代装饰挂毯形式创新研究.乌鲁木齐：新疆艺术学院，2022.

院的成立。包豪斯艺术学院设有编织工作坊，将设计与制作合二为一。这方便了挂毯设计从单纯模仿绘画走向独有的抽象风格的转变。"现代壁毯之父"让·吕尔萨发现并使用了一种特殊的色彩编码技术，用少量的颜色编织出丰富的效果，这在巴洛克风格中引起全新的思考。内容也由描摹走向了强调制作者自身的艺术思维。让·吕尔萨和他的朋友彼得经过将近半个世纪的努力策办了十五届"洛桑国际传统与现代壁毯艺术双年展"，激发了各方艺术家对纤维艺术的创作热情，直接推动当代装饰挂毯向新的创作理念与手法的进步，让奥布松挂毯加快了摆脱传统挂毯风格束缚的步伐。

2.路径模式对比

奥布松挂毯的传承方式主要依靠以家庭为单位的小型工作坊进行口传心授和手把手教学。多代传承的方式在奥布松家庭式工作坊中十分常见。此外，工作坊的亲人会在巴黎贸易中心开设店铺，售卖由自家工作坊织造的挂毯。这种类似于"自产自销"的家族经营模式使得奥布松挂毯工作坊能够敏锐地捕捉市场需求，帮助其在法国大革命爆发期间幸存，并至今仍在继续传承与发展。[①]

我国的传统手工艺传承也是如此，即大多数是以家庭为单位的小型工作坊进行生产，技艺同样也是口传心授，在发展中自然面临与奥布松挂毯相似的优势与劣势。随着现代文明与工业生产方式的发展与变革，手工艺的传承与发展也面临着考验。我国部分传统手工艺匠人欲传无人，导致我国一些传统手工艺日渐衰退，甚至有些已经彻底消失。相比已经走过不少时代浪潮的奥布松挂毯工作坊，中国传统的挂毯艺术面临着更严苛的形势。

目前，藏毯的制作方式分为两种。一部分保持传统制作方式，设计师和织工分开。这种方式可以实现量产，如青海藏毯已经引入的工厂化生产一样，通过现代工业提升产量和利润，保护其生命线不会消失，但过于偏向商业性。另一种是将设计与制作合二为一，从图案设计到编织工艺都更为灵活，这种挂毯多为艺术品，难以复制；人工合成纤维的出现也促进了观赏性的提高。然而面对现实，无法工厂化无疑会使手工艺人陷入两难的境地。不过，毋庸置疑的是传统工艺在当代装饰挂毯设计中有了新的表现形式，开始尝试新的改变。而传统的编织工艺的成功转型对其他传统手工艺也有着很强的借鉴意义。

---

① 陈雪薇.浅析法国奥布松挂毯工艺技法与传承.纺织报告，2022，41(1): 124-126.

（三）传承发展的经验启示

1.成功案例——天织地毯的商业化与艺术化

早在两千年前，波斯地毯就是当地达官显贵最珍贵的财富象征，全球富商名流也一直将其视如珍宝，如英国皇室、白宫等都是波斯地毯的追捧者。天织地毯只收集和珍藏最优质的波斯地毯。作为波斯地毯王冠上的璀璨明珠，天织地毯不仅代表着尊贵雅致的生活方式，更象征着拥有者独到的投资眼光和艺术品位。

作为享有盛誉的波斯地毯供应商之一，天织公司与伊朗境内的许多知名的波斯地毯艺术家建立了稳定的世代合作关系。在天织就珍藏着许多在伊朗当地也一毯难求的殿堂级作品。当今，随着手工艺术的传承乏人和天然原材料的锐减，天织地毯更加弥足珍贵，其名誉与价值更是因此更上一层楼①。

2.经验总结

最为典型的是以家庭单位的小型挂毯工作室生产为主流的奥布松挂毯，奥布松挂毯的艺术价值和艺术历史显然是十分典型的。实际上，因为"制作＋营销"掌握在同一个家族手中，加之欧洲地区"小而精"的地理环境，依靠这样的模式降低成本、打开名声与市场极具可行性。如果将目光放在全中国乃至全球，这种家庭式手工作坊显然力量不足，尤其是在当前既关注独特性，又要兼顾利润的高竞争商业环境中，简单复刻这种模式不具可持续性。

通过对奥布松挂毯、天织地毯、青海藏毯等案例的研究分析，小型家庭手工作坊在传承技艺、发挥独特艺术品位上有着更灵活、更积极的能量，而工业化则更具营销价值。最大的问题是如何平衡这二者之间的关系，各扬其长而避其短。比起大规模地工厂化或是一味选择家庭式作坊的封闭性，选择大公司的营销能量搭配家庭式作坊的韵味或许是不错的选择。

四、藏毯保护传承与创新发展的建议

（一）藏毯工艺传承与乡村振兴

乡村振兴，文化先行。在极盛时期，加牙村有90％的村民都有藏毯编织的手艺，这门技艺是维系乡情、增强文化认同的重要纽带；同时，藏毯文化遗

---

① VOGUE. 天结地织 臻于至美："古老"波斯地毯的当代演绎与传承 . (2023-12-08)[2023-12-08]. https://www.vogue.com.cn/living/news/news_1945da21720d5a21.html.

产还具有极高的开发和利用价值，特别是生产性保护理念的提出，让我们得以对藏毯技艺进行创造性转化和创新性发展，继而有效带动了乡村产业发展和农牧民收入的增加。例如，江孜县年堆乡尼玛藏式卡垫加工农民专业合作社采取"合作社＋边缘户"的发展经营模式，注重人文关怀，依托自身研发的"藏毯纸样实用技术"国家专利生产3D效果藏毯[1]，能够根据设计图实现私人定制，打破了原本花色单一的瓶颈，对打造江孜藏毯名片、发展乡村文化产业具有重要的推动作用[2]。

（二）藏毯工艺的传承与创新路径

1.注重市场互动，引导差异化运营与多样化发展

应着力引导部分设计品牌和藏毯工艺相结合，设计藏毯文创产品。将西藏藏毯艺术中极具代表性的纹样、色彩、精湛工艺与服装设计相结合，研究藏毯元素在服装结构、面料质地、工艺手法上的创新表现方法，将藏毯艺术进行传承和创新应用。

2.强化技术引领，推动创造性转化与创新性发展

（1）现代工艺创新藏毯传统图形元素

藏毯图案最初以古老的寺庙壁画、龙凤、花草为蓝本，图案纹样较为单一。要扩大藏毯的市场，首先要对藏毯的图案予以丰富创新。通过融合传统技艺与现代技术，辅以独特的打结处理方式，可以设计出融历史建筑、绘画书法、民族纹饰于一体，且具有3D立体视觉效果的挂毯产品[3]，从而吸引各类人群的目光。

（2）数字赋能藏毯展览

传统形式的藏毯展览，虽然能让参观者接触了解到藏毯工艺，但也由于缺乏全面的互动体验环节，人们无法完全感受到其深厚的文化魅力。发展元宇宙技术可以突破文化传播的地理和空间限制，使其融入当代生活场景之中。此外，通过使用数字孪生技术，面向社会大众提供数字化建模服务，并与众多非遗传承人合作，呈现藏毯生产制造的全生命周期过程，创造和传播独属于消费者的数字藏品，从而保护和传承民族文化瑰宝。

---

① 刘华彬，张婷婷.新藏毯织就扶贫路.中国农民合作社，2020(11)：13-15.

② 张文婷，赵晓晓.非遗助力乡村振兴：西藏江孜藏毯织造技艺的生产性保护研究.化纤与纺织技术，2022，51(4)：169-173.

③ 丁零.数字媒介视域下传统手工藏毯的传承研究.丝网印刷，2023，348(4)：90-93.

（三）藏毯工艺人才培养与传承路径

1.弘扬工匠精神，加强宣传与价值认同

非物质文化遗产作为主要依托于人而存续的活态文化遗产形式，其传承人无疑是传承的主体。拥有一批从事非物质文化遗产传承实践、熟练掌握其传承的非物质文化遗产项目知识和核心技艺的传承人或传承团体，是非物质文化遗产得以良好活态传承的关键。

因此，要保护和传承好非物质文化遗产，关键在于增强文化遗产的传播感染力，吸引广泛传播传承群体。通过生产性保护措施，可以有效引导当地居民重新认识藏毯的重要价值和深刻内涵，让人们接受、珍视这项技艺并从中获得自豪感，进而不断提高当地人的文化自信心和民族认同感，为乡村实现全面振兴提供积极力量。

2.完善激励机制，鼓励批量化人才引培

非物质文化遗产的活态化传承主要依靠与人的互动和交流，因此，在非遗传承中，持续吸引感兴趣、愿意参与学习的新参与者和体验者显得至关重要。建立国家、省、市、县四级项目代表性传承人评定与命名制度，明确其传承的责任和义务，对其开展传承活动予以一定资助。与此同时，应加强传承梯队建设，促进传统编织技艺传承和现代教育体系相结合，不断壮大传承队伍。一方面采用学校教育、师傅带徒等方式培养新一代从业者；另一方面普及藏毯工艺知识，提高民众的认知度和欣赏能力，培育潜在的从业者及欣赏者，改善文化遗产从业者的生存环境。此外，还可以建立相关演出场所、展示馆，提供展演宣传环境。

3.开展共建合作，构建长效性培养模式

与政府企业开展合作，建立集中的非遗特色空间，诸如以传播藏毯工艺文化为主的非遗工坊等。[①]由体验过渡到深入学习，创建一条成体系的非遗教学培育路径。各式各样的非遗特色空间有助于更好促进文旅融合，让藏毯文化与藏区优质旅游资源融合发展。在文旅融合的大背景下，相信非遗传习基地会成为旅游的优质资源，从而使非遗在旅游中进一步增强活力，获得全新的内生动力。

---

① 文化和旅游部.文化和旅游部关于推动非物质文化遗产与旅游深度融合发展的通知.(2023-02-17)[2023-12-09].https://www.gov.cn/zhengce/zhengceku/2023-02/22/content_5742727.htm.

五、结　论

非物质文化遗产"藏毯"历史悠久、品类繁多、工艺精湛，是藏族文化与民族精神的结晶。然而，由于藏毯生产经营规模偏小、设计创新能力不足、推广渠道单一以及人才储备缺乏等因素，其市场占有率下降，亟待保护与传承。本文学习借鉴奥布松挂毯和高比林壁毯的传承路径，建议选择大公司的营销能量搭配家庭式作坊的韵味。

因其民族特性，藏毯尚未进入主流市场，其产业价值与艺术价值尚未被充分开发；目前，藏毯的传承和发展主要依靠青藏地区政府的推动，学术界对此关注较少，相关研究文献稀缺。本文对藏毯的了解主要源于文献等资料，缺乏深入的实地调研，未与当地政府、相关企业和藏毯传承人员直接对话，缺乏对现今藏毯传承的最新一手资料，存在一定局限性。

本文建议传承发展藏毯需结合乡村振兴战略，依托政策支持；注重市场互动、强化技术引领；加强藏毯宣传与价值认同、开展政企合作，注入更多新活力，赋予藏毯新时代内涵和审美艺术价值，实现藏毯的可持续发展与保护，为藏族文化和中华优秀传统文化的传承提供新路径，增强民族文化自豪感与文化自信。

以中国传统制茶技艺为例谈非物质文化遗产的保护和传承^①

摘 要: 茶在中国有着悠久的历史，对中国人民具有重要的意义。自 2022 年 11 月中国传统制茶技艺及其相关习俗被列入联合国教科文组织人类非物质文化遗产代表作名录以来，中国传统制茶技艺的传承与发展得到了广泛的关注。本文以中国传统制茶技艺为例，探究在当今全球化、工业化、科技化的背景下非物质文化遗产的传承和保护问题。通过对中国传统制茶技艺的起源、发展和特点进行梳理，分析了该传统技艺所承载的文化意义和价值。论文采用文献研究、参加研学活动和实地调研等方法，深入挖掘传统制茶技艺在现代社会环境下的现状和面临的挑战，并与日本茶道面临的困境及日本采取的传承与创新的措施进行对比，提出了传承和保护中国传统制茶技艺的建议措施与未来展望。本文的研究结果对于传统制茶技艺的保护与传承具有一定的实践和借鉴意义，也对于非物质文化遗产保护的理论和实践有一定的拓展价值。

关键词: 非物质文化遗产；中国传统制茶技艺；日本茶道

一、绪 论

（一）研究背景

1. 非物质文化遗产的定义

联合国教科文组织在 2003 年 10 月 17 日通过了《保护非物质文化遗产公

---

① 作者: 杜铭扬，中国海洋大学法语系；洪欣怡，中国海洋大学食品工程与科学系；李若辰，中国海洋大学英语系；指导老师: 于诗雯。

约》，并于 2006 年 4 月生效。在此公约中，"非物质文化遗产"的定义是被各社区、群体，有时是个人，视为其文化遗产组成部分的各种社会实践、观念表达、表现形式、知识、技能以及相关的工具、实物、手工艺品和文化场所。[①]非物质文化遗产包括以下 5 个方面：（1）口头传统和表现形式，包括作为非物质文化遗产媒介的语言；（2）表演艺术；（3）社会实践、仪式、节庆活动；（4）有关自然界和宇宙的知识和实践；（5）传统手工艺。非物质文化遗产世代相传，在各社区和群体适应周围环境以及与自然和历史的互动中，被不断地再创造，为这些社区和群体提供认同感和持续感，从而增强对文化多样性和人类创造力的尊重。

2."中国传统制茶技艺及其相关习俗"的内涵

2022 年 11 月，"中国传统制茶技艺及其相关习俗"正式通过评审，列入联合国教科文组织人类非物质文化遗产代表作名录。[②]中国传统制茶技艺及其相关习俗是有关茶园管理、茶叶采摘、茶的手工制作，以及茶的饮用和分享的知识、技艺和实践。自古以来，中国人就开始种茶、采茶、制茶和饮茶。制茶师根据当地风土，运用核心制茶技艺，发展出两千多种茶品，并由此形成了不同的习俗，世代传承，至今贯穿于中国人的日常生活、仪式和节庆活动中。

（二）选题原因和意义

1.历史悠久，技艺成熟

中国传统制茶技艺及其相关习俗历史悠久，我国茶叶的种植面积、从业人群、茶产量及产值均居世界前列。中国传统制茶技艺及其相关习俗有着系统的知识体系、广泛的社会实践、成熟的传统技艺、丰富的手工制品，体现了中国人所秉持的谦、和、礼、敬的价值观，在人类社会可持续发展中发挥着重要作用。

2.分布广泛，民族共享

中国传统制茶技艺及其相关习俗分布广泛，传统制茶技艺主要集中于秦岭淮河以南、青藏高原以东的江南、江北、西南和华南四大茶区，相关习俗在全国各地均有分布，为多民族所共享。

[①] 保护非物质文化遗产公约. (2003-10-17)[2022-11-30]. http://www.scio.gov.cn/xwfbh/xwbfbh/wqfbh/44687/46123/xgzc46129/Document/1707763/1707763.htm.
[②] 中国民族文化艺术基金会."中国传统制茶技艺及其相关习俗"列入人类非物质文化遗产代表作名录. 中国民族博览，2022(22): 4-5.

3.以茶为媒，互通世界

早在唐宋时期，源自中国的茶以及茶文化就通过丝绸之路、万里茶道等，翻山越岭、漂洋过海，传遍全球，为世界所共享，从而推动实现中华文化与世界文明的互动交融。据统计，全球至少有 50 多个国家种茶，有 120 多个国家从中国进口茶叶，全球喜欢饮茶的人数超过 50 亿。[1]世界友人通过一片茶叶了解中国的地大物博，感知中华文化的博大精深。

4.科技赋能，传承保护

如今，科技早已改变人们的生活，机械制茶的兴起是否会与传统制茶工艺产生冲突，是否能探索出更好的办法既做好传承和保护，又能利用科技化、商业化让保护传承和开发利用有机结合起来，这也是选题的一大背景。

（三）文献综述

长期以来，国内外学者对"传承和保护中国传统制茶技艺及其相关习俗的原因和意义"和"如何做好传承和保护"的问题进行了大量的研究，并取得了一定成果。当前，在科技化、工业化的背景下，还存在如何掌握好传承保护与开发利用的"度"这个现实问题，所以，"如何让保护传承和开发利用有机结合"是值得深入研究的一个课题，具有较大的现实意义。

在《"中国传统制茶技艺及其相关习俗"非遗申报解读》中，中国农业科学院茶叶研究所的研究员鲁成银着重介绍了该项目的主要内涵、申报标准、分布范围、项目实践者、传承人、传承方式等，并对项目的社会功能和文化意义以及列入人类非物质文化遗产后将会产生的影响进行了逐一探讨。[2]

在《非物质文化遗产应保护什么？"现代风味"下的工匠技艺》中，余舜德着重论述了什么是手工制茶，机械化背景下是否还有手工制茶，制茶的传统知识有哪些，传统制茶工艺的关键是什么等相关问题。[3]

熊辉、沈昕分析了我国茶文化的现状，目前存在茶文化普及不充分、不深入，茶文化发展不平衡，茶文化整体影响力不足等问题。作者认为应以传承保护茶类非物质文化遗产为抓手，优化茶文化监管服务体系，深入茶文化内涵研究，促进茶旅全要素融合，加强茶文化数字传播，促进茶文化高质量发展，提

---

① 滕沐颖.以茶为媒，讲好中华优秀传统文化故事——新华社"中国传统制茶技艺及其相关习俗"报道亮点分析.中国记者，2023(1): 120-122.

② 鲁成银."中国传统制茶技艺及其相关习俗"非遗申报解读.中国茶叶，2023，45(2): 49-53.

③ 余舜德.非物质文化遗产应保护什么？"现代风味"下的工匠技艺.文化遗产，2023(2): 92-100.

升我国茶文化的国际影响力。其中着重介绍了利用茶旅融合、数字传播等方式来传承和发展中国传统制茶技艺[①]，为我们论文的撰写方向提供了重要参考。

笔者查阅相关文献后，认为前人研究对笔者的后续研究提供了一定的基础知识，但缺少对"如何将传统制茶技艺的传承和保护与共同富裕、乡村振兴有机结合"以及"如何将传统制茶工艺和现代科技有机结合"等方面进行更深入的探究。本文从"为什么要传承和保护中国传统制茶技艺及其相关习俗"以及"如何做好传承和保护"等方面进行了论述，研究在科技化、信息化高速发展的今天，如何将保护传承和开发利用有机结合。

（四）研究思路和方法

1. 研究思路

笔者在学术网站上搜索"中国传统制茶技艺及其相关习俗的传承和保护"相关文献，经研读和比较，找出前人研究的意义和不足。带着如何更好地传承和保护这个问题，笔者参加了中国海洋大学第十四期中国茶文化及实训课程研学队，实地考察手工制茶工艺，探访青岛市晓阳春有机茶有限公司，亲自动手采茶、制茶，了解传统制茶工艺的工序。同时，笔者参加了国际胜任力培养实训项目苏州工作坊，在其中的世界文化遗产论坛的交流环节，了解了世界文化遗产的多元性，不但拓宽了在世界文化遗产保护方面的视野，而且学到了文化遗产保护的相关知识。在了解传统制茶工艺的发展现状后，笔者又对机械制茶进行调研，探索如何既做好传统制茶工艺的传承和保护，又能将传统工艺和现代科技有机结合。

2. 研究方法

阅读文献法、比较法、实地考察法、市场调研法等。

二、传统制茶技艺面临的挑战

（一）传承人缺失

作为一项非遗技艺，中国传统制茶面临最严重的困境是传承人的缺失。主要由于以下几点原因。

首先，人口老龄化问题严重。传统制茶技艺主要依靠农民，老龄化导致传承人有断代的风险，也在一定程度上影响了他们对社会新兴事物的认知水平和

---

① 熊辉，沈昕.加强茶类非遗传承保护 促进茶文化高质量发展.农业考古，2023(2)：175-180.

接受能力，无法吸引年轻人了解和参与。

其次，农村边缘化问题严峻，个体茶农应对市场信息变化的能力非常薄弱，"增产不增收"现象突出。

最后，学习手工制茶技艺需要相当大的时间成本，随着机械化和工业化的进程，手工艺人面临入不敷出的尴尬局面，年轻一代对手工制茶技艺的兴趣和学习意愿逐渐减弱。因此，传统制茶技艺的传承人短缺，甚至部分特色技艺可能无人继承。

（二）工业化过量

不恰当地使用机械化和工业化手段，给茶产业带来了不少的负面影响。依据世界食品加工的经验，一种产品的加工技术大体要经过五个阶段，分别是机械化、初级自动化、自动控制、数据化、高度自动化，目前，我国的制茶技术总体上还处于最初级的第一阶段。[1]在这种情况下过量使用工业化生产，不仅缺乏"小而精"的工匠精神，而且由于工业化商品产量大的特点，容易在市场上劣币驱逐良币，挤占真正手工茶的生存空间。

（三）商业化过度

传统制茶的过程讲究回归自然，制作人顺应鲜叶的特性将其制成茶叶，再由茶叶将这份纯真传递给品茗者。而某些品牌打着"纯手工匠心制作"的旗号将茶叶卖出高价。传统制茶技艺成为了一个噱头，网友在嘲笑企业之余，难免会对传统制茶技艺产生负面印象，无法深入了解它的真正魅力。

无独有偶，饮茶本身能够促进人体健康，但很多游客在景区购买茶类饮品之后却大失所望，因为景区大肆售卖的网红"竹筒茶"本质是香精和甜味素勾兑的饮料，反而会加重人体的代谢负担，与茶所代表的养生观大相径庭。

三、如何传承和保护传统制茶技艺

（一）对日本茶道传承与保护措施的分析与借鉴

20 世纪来，日本茶道也面临着和中国传统制茶技艺相似的困境，日本政府和民间采取的一系列应对措施值得我们了解与分析，并从中汲取经验，更好地传承和保护中国传统制茶技艺。

---

[1]　罗龙新. 我国制茶工业的科技进步与差距. 中国大茶业论谈. (2023-11-24)[2024-06-04]. http://www.Teanet.com.cn/talka12.htm.

日本茶道也曾出现过传承人断代的现象。由于社会变迁和现代化的影响，许多日本年轻人的生活方式日益西化，轻视日本传统文化的倾向有所增长，在日本茶道中占据着主导地位的家族传承方式也受到明显冲击；第一线茶道教师的高龄化和少子化，加速了茶道人口的下滑，茶道的传统知识与技艺面临流失的风险。为了解决这一问题，日本政府和社会采取了以下措施。

1. 拓宽茶道的传承途径

随着时代的变迁和社会观念的改变，除了传统的家族传承外，茶道界也开始鼓励非传统的传承途径，例如开放给非亲属学习和继承茶道技艺。这样可以扩大茶道的传承者群体，从而提高传承人的数量和质量。

2. 吸引年轻人的兴趣

为了吸引年轻人参与茶道活动，茶道界开展了一系列活动和项目。例如，举办现代化的茶道展览，融入新技术和设计元素，使茶道更富有创新和时代感。另外，一些茶道师傅还积极在社交媒体上分享茶道的文化内涵，吸引更多年轻人了解和参与茶道。

3. 加强大众化的茶道教育

面向广大群众，积极开展市民茶会。为了方便市民参与茶会，地方公共团体和政府机关还专项拨款营造茶室，称之为"市民公共茶室"。

除此之外，在机械化、科技化浪潮的影响下，日本茶道传统的精细仪式也受到现代快节奏生活的严重冲击，茶道的独特仪式体验感减弱；茶道器具逐渐变得商业化和标准化，对于效率和利润的追求替代了对器具的精致和独特性的执着，影响了茶道器具的品质和精神内涵。为此，日本政府和社会采取了以下措施。

日本政府、文化机构和茶道协会等组织重视保护和传承茶道的传统技艺，例如举办茶道讲座、培训课程、研究项目等，以保持和传承传统的手工制茶工艺和仪式流程[1]。

为了适应现代生活的需求，茶道也在不失传统的前提下进行了一些适度的调整。茶道的一些仪式和流程被简化，以更好地契合现代人的快节奏生活。同时，茶道也接受了一部分现代科技的应用，例如使用先进的照明和气候控制技术，改善茶室的环境。

---

[1] 顾雯. 二战后日本茶道发展的考察. 北方工业大学学报，2023，35(1): 114-123; 符婕. 日本茶道跨文化传播中值得中国茶文化借鉴的做法. 中国民族博览，2021(22): 56-58.

利用互联网和数字媒体等工具传播和推广茶道，例如通过在线平台提供茶道知识、展示茶道表演和举办远程茶道教学。这样可以让更多的人了解和体验茶道文化，提高茶道的影响力和传承。

另外，日本的茶道教育主要以学校为中心开展，并得到政府和教育界的大力支持，这对我国开展茶艺教育具有重要的借鉴意义。不仅如此，在日本，达到师范级的茶道教授在社会上深得尊重，甚至是崇拜。持有茶道免许资格，可以被聘为各大中小学校茶道课的讲师。资深茶道家还可以获得艺术家的荣誉。

值得注意的是，现如今许多国家尤其是西方国家对于日本茶道的印象深于中国，日本茶道俨然发展为日本的一张名片。由此可见，日本茶道在跨文化传播中有许多值得借鉴之处。

（二）充分发挥主观能动性

申遗的目的在于"护遗"，传承就是最好的保护。保护传统制茶技艺，归根结底要发挥"人"的作用。传承人是工匠精神的延续，正如苏州工作坊的实践日参访中，德国企业的工匠精神就让笔者感触良多：把一件事做到极致，是匠人的追求。当前，制茶技艺的传承主要通过家族传承、师徒传承和社区传承等传统方式。这种传统的传承方式我们固然要支持，但同时更应采取新的传承方式，为其注入更多的新鲜血液。

第一，与相关机构或中职院校和高等院校合作建立完善的茶艺师和制茶师培训计划，通过系统的培训、考核、评估等环节，全面提升茶艺师和制茶师的专业技能和素质；在中小学、大学中设置茶艺或制茶体验课，激发年轻人的兴趣。

第二，多开展区域性或全国性的制茶比赛。不仅可以为制茶师提供丰富的实践机会，让制茶师在实践过程中不断积累经验，提高自身实操能力，而且可以提高传统制茶技艺的大众知名度，让更多人了解传统制茶的过程。

第三，设立政府奖学金、建立职业资格证书与职称挂钩等激励机制，鼓励茶艺人主动学习、创新，为茶艺人才提供更好的发展空间和职业前景；提高制茶和茶艺人才的待遇和社会地位，促进传统制茶技艺的传承和发展。

（三）遵循客观发展规律

墨守成规，绝非保护的意义。在工业化和科技不断发展的浪潮中，传统制茶技艺也应拥抱变化，遵循客观发展规律，抓住工业化和科技创新的机遇。

将手工制茶与机械制茶有机结合，尽管机械化生产已经可以覆盖茶叶生产的各个环节，包括采摘、揉捻、烘干、分级、称重、包装等成套的茶叶生产器械设备已经逐渐普及，但为了保证茶叶品质，在部分环节仍应采取手工制茶。其中，分级、称重、包装等环节采取机械化手段可以提高效率。用机械化播种可以扩大种植规模，降低劳动力成本。利用节水技术，例如沼液滴灌、喷灌等，减少茶园用水量，促进可持续发展。但也不能一味地依赖机械化制茶，因为茶叶的制作和加工过程细致而复杂，全机械化制茶采摘容易损坏茶叶的活性和品质。在茶行业中，健康是消费者在选择茶叶中特别关注的内容，"营养品质"已逐渐超越"口感风味"成为消费者首要的考量因素。

除此之外，全机械化生产还存在产品特色不突出的问题。不同地域的茶，哪怕是同一种类的茶，都有体现其地方特色的制茶方法，从而制作出的茶有不同的风味。例如，湖南的安化黑茶和广西的六堡茶都是黑茶，而安化黑茶中的精品大多做成茶砖，在运送和保持口感上都有独特的作用；广西的六堡茶则偏向于制作篓茶，毛茶蒸揉后，装篓压实，晾贮数月后发酵使茶紧结成块，即可形成有独特香醇的六堡篓茶。尊重多样的发展规律，尊重制茶技艺的多样性，不同地区制茶技艺各异，更加体现了传承这项技艺的必要性。

（四）融入大众市场，革新传统茶企

传统制茶技艺的保护不能一味地依靠政府资助和扶持，要为其自身注入活力。制茶最后的产出是茶叶，茶叶是面向市场的商品，所以茶叶要积极融入大众市场。

传统茶企可以走差异化竞争路线。例如于 2013 年 8 月在广州成立的中国本土袋泡茶企业"茶里"。"茶里"从一开始就选用原叶茶，并以传统三角茶包形式盛纳茶叶，走出了一条迥异于龙头企业立顿、低价化的商业路线。"茶里" CMO 林川表示："希望用这一小小的创新切入更高端的袋泡茶市场。"

此外，一方面传统茶企产品在年轻主力消费群体中认知度仍有待提高。传统茶企品牌缺少市场化营销活力。在当下的社交平台上，多家新型茶饮品牌凭借中式传统茶饮走红，但传统茶企似乎尚未打开局面。所以传统茶企应积极开拓互联网销售渠道，提高市场化营销活力。例如，可以请有名的带货主播进行直播带货，提高热度。另一方面，可以将新茶饮品牌视作商业端新盈利路径，比如茶里就积极推出了"原叶＋拼配"的新式茶饮，并在 2021 年赶超立顿在

中国市场的销量。除此之外，还可以在茶叶生产基础上，延伸茶产业链，开发茶叶制品、茶具、茶山茶厂旅游、茶文化、茶文创产品等相关产业，实现产业链的拓展、整合和升级。例如，发展茶旅产业，将茶文化融入旅游景点的打造中，提高旅游消费者的体验感和消费水平；建立研学基地，编写普及读本，提高青少年的保护意识；设立传统制茶工艺体验馆，让大众有亲身体验传统制茶技艺的机会，提高大众对其的了解程度和兴趣，更好满足人民日益增长的精神文化需求，推进文化自信自强。

但是，传统茶企必须拿捏好商业化的程度，不能为了盈利而过度商业化，失去了传统制茶技艺的本真，丢失了"和合"思想。

（五）将传统制茶技艺与乡村振兴有机结合

我国茶产业的发展具有地域性。东部省份的茶厂发展较为完善，规模较大，拥有现代化的生产设备和管理体系，开拓了更广泛的市场渠道和销售网络，可以直接面向国内外的消费者，满足大量的茶叶市场需求。而西部省份的茶厂规模较小，生产能力和管理水平有限，销售渠道较少，市场渗透度和影响力较低，主要依靠政府的资金扶持。基于这种情况，东部茶企或全国高校可以积极开展"点对点"帮扶，为西部落后茶企提供先进的经验和技术，促进脱贫致富，共同发展。

例如，中国海洋大学扶贫云南省红河州绿春县。心在绿春，不因山海远。"感动青岛"十大人物汪东风教授多次亲赴一线，将课堂从红瓦碧海的讲台，带到了青山绿水的田埂，指导当地百姓制作白茶、改进玛玉茶，倡导设立"一县一业"茶叶专项，无偿捐赠近50万国家发明专利。

此外，该校还设立了科技专项—茶叶精深加工技术，应用自主研发茶叶专利技术，试制了24个茶叶创新产品，并通过质量盲评（消费者和专家组）和专家讨论，确定了基于高香白茶和富含茶多糖茶饼两大类茶叶精深加工技术。以上举措吸引了不少青壮年回到家乡参与制茶，共同谱写脱贫致富新篇章。

（六）扩大国际知名度，促进传统茶艺的跨文化传播

中国的茶文化源远流长，其独特的韵味和卓越的制茶技艺一直被世界所称道。然而，随着全球化的浪潮不断涌动，如何将中国传统制茶技艺推向更广阔的舞台，成为了一个急需解决的问题。在这样的背景下，扩大国际知名度，促

进中国传统制茶技艺的跨文化传播，已成为了当今时代的重要使命。[①]

第一，我们应积极拓展海外市场，寻找那些对中国传统制茶技艺充满好奇的消费者。通过国际展览、文化交流和市场推广，让茶艺师们的才华在世界各地传播开来，吸引更多外国游客前来体验中国茶文化的独特魅力。

第二，我们要加强对外交流与合作。通过互访、研讨会和工作坊等形式，开展跨文化的茶艺交流活动，探索茶文化的融合与创新，互相借鉴，共同提升制茶技艺的水平和品质。通过跨文化的交流与合作，我们可以拓展制茶技艺的边界，让中国的传统茶艺融入到全球茶文化的大熔炉中，焕发出更加夺目的光芒。

第三，为了在国际范围内传播中国传统制茶技艺，要克服语言和文化障碍。我们可以提供多种语言的茶艺培训课程和教材，以便更多国际学习者能够理解和学习中国的茶文化。此外，积极适应不同文化背景和消费者口味，灵活调整茶叶加工和产品开发，以吸引更多国际消费者。

第四，利用互联网和社交媒体等新媒体平台，广泛传播茶文化。建立国际化专业的网站和社交媒体账号，发布有关茶文化和制茶技艺的内容，包括视频教程、讲座和茶艺表演。同时，鼓励茶艺师和制茶师积极参与线上互动，与国内外茶爱好者进行交流和分享。

扩大国际知名度，促进中国传统制茶技艺的跨文化传播，需要我们用智慧与热情去开拓，用文化的力量去沟通。让更多人了解和喜爱中国的传统茶文化，不仅是对中国茶传统的传承和发展，更是让世界茶文化更加丰富多彩的重要一环。[②]我们需携手努力，将中国传统制茶技艺带向更广阔的舞台，让世界为之动容。

四、结　语

（一）对于中国传统制茶技艺的传承与保护的研究局限与未来发展展望

从生产角度来说，茶叶的品质受自然环境影响较大，且所需的优质条件有限，面临可持续发展的压力。

---

① 包静，朱阳."中国传统制茶技艺及其相关习俗"保护传承的实践与思考——以中国茶叶博物馆为例.茶叶，2023(3)：176-178.
② 张志颖.非物质文化遗产本体创新及成果转化目标探析.青海民族大学学报(社会科学版)，2023(3)：158-164.

从产品角度来说，传统茶企产品在年轻主力消费群体中认知度仍有待发掘，其营销与销售群体在年轻主力消费群体中占比较小，暂时难以与奶茶、新茶饮品牌等抗衡，在适应现代社会的节奏与扩大生产规模方面也仍存在挑战。

未来，茶产业仍有巨大的发展空间和前景，从技术层面而言，信息化、智能化助力茶园和茶厂的改造，提高茶叶生产和品质稳定性，有利于开拓全球茶叶消费市场；就产品层面而言，可以进一步加强消费者对茶文化和茶品质的认知，培养大众茶叶市场，扩大茶叶品类，推动茶叶的品质提升和品牌塑造。

（二）对所研究的中国传统制茶技艺的传承与保护的总结与综合评价

中国传统制茶技艺及其相关习俗是一门非常具有特色和价值的文化形式，它不仅是一种技艺，更是一种文化表现和审美享受。它与中国的地理、气候、文化密切相关，因此具有独特性，无法被其他国家所复制。但面对科技化发展和过度商业化的冲击，我们应探寻中国传统制茶技艺的可持续发展之路。将传统制茶技艺和现代化、科技化适当有机结合，践行联合国可持续发展目标，尤其服务于消除贫困、健康福祉、陆地生态、体面工作、永续供求、尊重多样性等方面。终有一天，或许文物会随着自然交替而消失，但文化永存。

━━━━━━

苏州缂丝技艺可持续发展路径研究
——以苏州"祯彩堂"缂丝品牌为个案[①]

━━━━━ **摘　要:** 缂丝技艺作为中国传统织造技艺的瑰宝、世界非物质文化
遗产，被誉为"织中之圣"，具有悠久的文化历史和独特
的艺术价值。当今缂丝产业中，苏州地区占领龙头地位，
而苏州"祯彩堂"缂丝艺术在缂丝的创新和发展上都处于
领先地位。本文的研究旨在深入探讨苏州缂丝技艺如何保
持活力，以及其传承的可能性，以苏州"祯彩堂"缂丝品
牌为个案，通过深入研究缂丝技艺的历史渊源、工艺特
色、传统技艺及其创新发展，结合缂丝产品的协同创新，
提出有效的设计策略和建议，以苏州缂丝为典范，实现缂
丝文化的活态传承，推动缂丝技艺的可持续发展。

━━━━━ **关键词:** 缂丝技艺; 祯彩堂; 传承; 可持续发展

一、绪　论

（一）选题背景及意义

1.选题背景

从历年知网关于缂丝主题的文献数量来看，关于缂丝的研究主要集中在非
物质文化遗产的继承和发扬上，且进入 21 世纪后，国家在宏观层面通过划拨
规划基金的方式对非物质文化遗产进行研究，给予了大量政策扶持与资金支
持，从 2021—2023 年国家社科基金的资助情况来看，以"非物质文化遗产"
为主题的研究项目也在增多（见表 1）。因此，以江苏省苏州"祯彩堂"缂丝

---

① 作者: 肖季伶，广西师范大学教育学部; 黄耀娴，广西师范大学教育学部。

作为案例研究"非物质文化遗产"传承与保护问题，具有很大的理论开拓空间和现实意义。

表1　2021—2023年国家社科基金项目中涉及"非物质文化遗产"的一般项目

年度	项目名称
2023	大运河流域体育非物质文化遗产项目采辑与数字化
	长城沿线濒危体育非物质文化遗产数字化传承与活化利用研究
	粤港澳大湾区体育非物质文化遗产的数字化共建共治共享研究
	黄河流域体育非物质文化遗产保护研究
	体育非物质文化遗产活态传承的伦理规制研究
	联合国教科文组织非物质文化遗产保护政策体系研究
	福建民间信仰与非物质文化遗产关系研究
	西南各民族口传非物质文化遗产中民族交往交流交融元素整理研究
	西南民族地区非物质文化遗产和旅游深度融合发展模式研究
	甘青少数民族口传非物质文化遗产中民族交往交流交融元素的挖掘、整理与阐释
	台湾高山族噶玛兰人非物质文化遗产的传承与创新发展研究
	西南地区饮食类非物质文化遗产中民族交往交流交融元素的挖掘、整理与阐释
	新疆国家级非物质文化遗产中民族交往交流交融元素的提炼与研究
	藏彝走廊非物质文化遗产中民族交往交流交融元素的图谱挖掘与阐释
	提炼展示非物质文化遗产精神标识的基本范式和实现路径研究
2022	体育非物质文化遗产保护的"中国式现代化新道路"与话语体系建构研究
	我国非物质文化遗产保护的社区参与式治理研究
	非物质文化遗产的文化基因赓续与构筑中华民族共有精神家园研究
2021	非物质文化遗产的利用对乡村振兴的促进机制研究
	长三角体育非物质文化遗产传承创新研究
	中国北方少数民族体育非物质文化遗产的传承与数字化保护研究
	新中国成立以来体育非物质文化遗产政策研究
	基于要素协同的非物质文化遗产档案资源跨机构集成机制研究
	非物质文化遗产数字档案资源分层集群融合模式研究
	中国非物质文化遗产多维度场景传播模式与策略研究
	非物质文化遗产保护伦理原则研究
	"一带一路"视域下中国东盟边境少数民族非物质文化遗产数据库建设研究
	文旅融合背景下畲族非物质文化遗产系统性保护传承研究

2.非遗缂丝传承意义

缂丝，也叫刻丝，是中国一种古老又独特的传统织造技术，人们习惯性地将其称为"通经断纬"，其缂织技术可以制作出各种精美的书画作品，风格迥异，因此也被称为"织中之圣"。

2005 年，苏州缂丝制作技艺进入首批国家非物质文化遗产名录推荐项目，列入第一批苏州市非物质文化遗产名录。2006 年 5 月，苏州缂丝织造技艺入选第一批中华人民共和国非物质文化遗产保护名录；2007 年 6 月 8 日，苏州西部民间缂丝织绣厂荣获中华人民共和国文化部授予的首届文化遗产日纪念品；2009 年 9 月，缂丝被列入中国传统的蚕桑丝织工艺，成为了一项重要的非物质文化遗产。

中国在文化遗产保护中完成了由实施"抢救工程""重点保护"到推动开展"生产性保护""活化性利用"的不同时期工作重点的转变，探索出文化遗产可持续发展的路径，为世界文化遗产保护提供中国的实践经验，这对苏州缂丝技艺的传承发展提出了更高的要求。

本研究选取苏州"祯彩堂"为案例研究缂丝技艺的传承与发展，"祯彩堂"是最早形成现代生产组织管理模式的苏州缂丝企业之一，拥有独立的产品设计部门、稳定的缂丝制作团队和专业的市场营销团队，从缂丝书画创作到缂丝文物修复，再到缂丝时尚产品的研发，各部门通力协作，建立起良好的品牌形象。"祯彩堂"创造了与自然融为一体并经由人工精雕细琢后形成的精美技艺产品，在继承手工技艺类"非遗"精髓的同时融入现代新兴科技元素，赋予传统的手工技艺以更新的活力和生命力。探究"祯彩堂"缂丝的传承创新发展过程，对于其他缂丝品牌以及手工艺类非遗项目的传承、保护和发展来说，都起到十分关键的导向作用。同时，在探索缂丝技艺的历史背景、工艺特点、传承、创新发展的过程中，通过研究缂丝产品协同创新，提出相关设计策略和建议，从而做好苏州缂丝文化产品的活态传承，促进缂丝技艺的活态传承与创新性发展。

（二）缂丝国内研究现状

从目前知网检索关于缂丝的主要学术著作和文献来看，缂丝国内研究探讨主要集中在传统缂丝、缂丝工艺与创新以及缂丝产品应用三方面。

1.传统缂丝

中国三大工艺品中刺绣是最受欢迎的，而苏绣则是中国丝织手工艺品中的佼佼者。然而，缂丝却是中国丝织手工艺品中最具代表性的作品。缂丝是一种由精心设计的"通经回纬"编织技术制作而成的精美织物，其中包含了多种颜色的熟丝。通过使用多个小梭子，将纬丝按照预先设计的图案进行编织，同一种颜色的纬线可以不必完整地覆盖整个布料，只要随着纹理的轮廓或颜色的变化，不断更换梭子，就可以实现局部回纬编织，[①]从而使得布料的花纹、质感、颜色等方面形成一些独特的断痕，就像是刀片一般，当透过背景光线看时，可以看到这些小孔和断痕，古人将其比作"承空观之，如雕镂之象"，所以也被称为缂丝。缂丝作品的结构非常严密，技巧非常出众，其中最著名的是大型缂丝画。孙迎庆在《苏州缂丝——通经断纬的织中之圣》中是这样评价缂丝的：它们的风格优雅，充满了富贵的气息，令人惊叹，甚至被称为"一寸缂丝一寸金"。[②]缂丝作品素以制作精良，古朴典雅、艳中带秀的艺术特点被誉为"织中之圣"。

2. 缂丝工艺与创新

孙迎庆研究发现，中国缂丝的工艺流程为：落经线、牵经线、套筘、弯结、嵌后轴经、拖经面、嵌前轴经、捎经面、挑交、打翻头、箸踏脚棒、扪经面、画样、配色线、摇线、修毛头，总共有16道工序。[②]缂丝工艺源远流长，可追溯至两千多年前，最初是从西域传入中原，历经千年，至今仍然保留着传统技艺。杨烨强调，缂丝工艺已经不再适应当今时代的发展，存在着诸多问题，传统技艺的传承和创新受到了严重的威胁，甚至面临失传的危险。因此，有必要对缂丝工艺进行传承和创新。[③]缂丝工艺的创新，不仅要求保留传统技法，更要求将传统与现代的特色元素完美结合，以全新的视角展现出缂丝的独特魅力。

3. 缂丝产品与应用

经过大量文献研究，缂丝产品可以划分为日常用品、装饰品和宗教用品三大类，以满足不同的需求。缂丝是一种非常适合制作小型服装和装饰物的材料，但是制作大型服装和装饰物需要耗费大量时间和精力，生产成本高昂，价格也不菲。它主要用于宫廷和贵族的服装和日常用品。观赏性缂丝可以分为装裱用缂丝、摹缂书画作品的纯观赏用缂丝。缂丝宗教用物则有幡、佛经、佛具盖幅等。[④]

① 佟昀.基于现代织造工艺的缂丝技艺创新.棉纺织技术，2020，48(8)：77-80.
② 孙迎庆.苏州缂丝——通经断纬的织中之圣.上海工艺美术，2009(3)：87-89.
③ 杨烨."织中之圣"——中国缂丝的传统技艺传承.中华文化论坛，2013(3)：141-144，191.
④ 阴建华，李向红.缂丝中的古今书画艺术.武汉纺织大学学报，2014，27(2)：30-34.

综上所述，国内对于缂丝的研究，主要聚焦于传统缂丝及工艺、产品等方面，既对传统缂丝进行了概念性的总结，也将研究延伸到缂丝产品、缂丝工艺上，注重缂丝的传承与创新发展。目前，关于缂丝技艺可持续发展的研究仍是寥寥。本文在借鉴前人关于传统缂丝技艺的特点、工艺创新、发展传承等一系列研究成果的基础之上，就如何推动苏州缂丝可持续发展这一问题做相关研究，并给出相应建议。

（三）研究对象及内容

本研究聚焦于非遗活态传承下缂丝技艺传承与发展。"祯彩堂"苏州缂丝品牌是本次研究的重点，我们通过查阅相关文献、实地考察等方式，对比分析了国内外缂丝文化遗产的传承发展情况，深入探讨了缂丝技艺的历史渊源、发展变迁、工艺传承及创新，并结合缂丝产品的协同创新，提出了一系列有效的保护和创新发展的策略和建议，以期更好地传承苏州缂丝文化产品的活力，推动缂丝技艺的持续传承和创新发展。

（四）研究思路及方法

1.研究思路（参见图1）

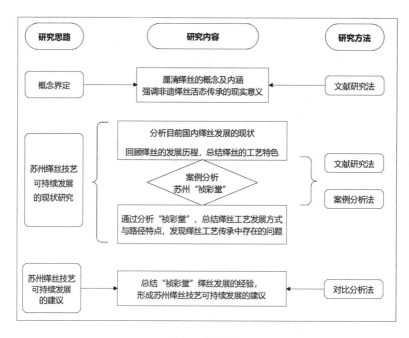

图1　研究思路

2.研究方法

本研究主要采用文献研究法、案例分析法的研究方法，辅之以演绎与归纳、整体思维等逻辑方法。

（1）文献研究法

通过中国知网、万方数据等途径查阅了大量相关的文献。通过对缂丝技艺相关文献的整合与分析，了解分析缂丝技艺的国内外研究现状、问题与策略，总结国内外相关文献，吸收其成功经验，对缂丝技艺的传承和创新发展进行应用探索。

（2）案例分析法

本研究通过研究书刊、报纸、网站等方法，寻找有一定代表性的苏州缂丝品牌，成为缂丝技艺研究案例，通过检索分析借鉴"祯彩堂"品牌下缂丝技艺的传承模式，结合苏州社会背景和资源，提出国内文化遗产保护传承与创新发展的建议，从而保护传承、创新发展苏州缂丝技艺。

（3）对比分析法。

本研究通过对比分析国内外文化遗产保护传承与创新发展的不同点，吸收借鉴国外文化遗产保护的优秀经验，结合苏州本土资源和发展状况，对缂丝工艺的传承与创新提出建议。

二、缂丝工艺

（一）缂丝的发展历程

1.发展：通经断纬，自成一家

"通经回纬"的梭织技术是一种古老的织造工艺，它将多种颜色的纬线缠绕在一起，形成精美的花纹。缂丝是我国古老的丝织手工技艺，大体源于汉晋时期。在隋唐时期，能工巧匠将传统的缂丝技术进行了大胆的创新发展。在两宋时期，缂丝技艺已经发展到了一个非常成熟的水平，不仅仅是实用性的缂丝，还出现了一种新的风尚，即以缂丝工艺织造卷轴绘画，这种制品比实用性缂丝更具有艺术性，因此被称为"镂绘"。[1]下面将从时间维度介绍各个时期的缂丝技艺。

1973年，新疆吐鲁番阿斯塔纳出土的几何纹缂丝带，是迄今发现的最早

---

① 彭薇.非遗之光：一寸缂丝一寸金.解放日报，2021-12-06(12).

的缂丝，这标志着缂丝的历史可追溯到公元 7 世纪中叶，这也是中国古代丝绸文化的重要里程碑。由于技术的限制，唐代的缂丝多为窄幅带饰，多在墓葬和宗教中使用。此后，缂丝的传播分两条路线，一是向西北的少数民族地区传播，仍以实用品为主；二是向中原、江南地区传播，并出现了装裱、观赏用的缂丝欣赏品。①

缂丝工艺黄金时代是宋代。宋人将缂丝与绘画艺术融合，发展出了纯艺术性的缂丝，这既是宋代缂丝的特点，亦是对缂丝艺术的最大贡献。宋代在唐代雄厚国力的基础之上，经济、技术和文化迅速发展，各种手工业也长足进步，在纺织的官营机构文思院和后苑造作所中均有"克丝作"。②

从南宋开始，政治、经济和文化中心都转移到了江南地区，并聚集了大批的优秀文人、画家和匠人，缂丝的生产中心亦转移至太湖流域的苏州和松江地区。缂丝的生产日益繁荣，品种也不断增加，它的用途也在改变。缂丝生产大体沿着实用品、欣赏品两个方向发展，而欣赏品生产日趋繁荣，并沿革至今。③现在，人们开始使用以绘画为基础的观赏性缂丝。④缂丝制作开始热衷于复制当时的名人书画，制作上细致入微、写实逼真，有着比原作更胜一筹的立体感，令画面带有丝质的光泽。有传世作品的缂丝高手都出现在这一时期的苏松地区，以朱克柔、沈子蕃和吴煦为代表。

元代缂丝沿袭宋代的成就，实用性和观赏性同步发展。元代的缂丝风格装饰趣味较浓厚，多采用勾线。元代统治者对金的爱好深刻影响了缂丝艺术，许多作品中都使用金线。例如缂丝《牡丹团扇裱片》，缂织工整，可供双面观赏，使用了捻金线勾勒轮廓，装饰味浓厚。

明代，缂丝工艺的技术水平进一步提高，适用范围日益扩大，并且开始专门化生产，实用性和观赏性缂丝的数量都大幅增加。苏州作为缂丝的生产中心，"吴门画派"继承了宋元时期的优秀传统，成为观赏性缂丝摹织的绝佳素材，沈周、文徵明、唐寅和仇英等艺术家的作品更是缂丝艺术家们最爱的珍品。随着商品化程度的提高和文化的发展，奢侈品和文化艺术品成为人们青睐的消费品，缂丝艺术也重新成为一种流行的艺术形式，尤其是在观赏性方面取

---

① 辽宁省博物馆.华彩若英:中国古代缂丝刺绣精品集.辽宁:辽宁人民出版社，2009，7-8.
② 郑丽虹.中国缂丝的源流与传承.丝绸，2008(2):49-51.
③ 三金缂法为缂金晕色法之一，在深色地上运用赤圆金、淡圆金和银色三种捻金银线缂织，有花纹闪亮的效果.
④ 朴文英.缂丝.苏州:苏州大学出版社，2009:28.

得了巨大的进步。①

清代政府建立的专门机构以及大量的资源投入，使得缂丝技术发展迅速，产量大幅提升，品种更加丰富，乾隆时期达到了顶峰。实用品缂丝的种类日渐丰富，随着宫廷和官府的需求量增加，缂丝大量地用于织造服装和日用品，并加入金银线和孔雀羽线等珍贵材料。②缂丝技法也有创新，如缂丝加绣加绘、三金缂法①、丝毛混织、三蓝缂丝③、水墨缂丝④等新品种，以表现画面层次。

随着清朝后期国家实力的衰落，以及对缂丝制品的需求急剧下降，缂丝工艺逐渐消失。随着缂丝商品化的不断深入，人们开始寻求更有效的方式来节约时间和劳动力，其中最常见的就是使用绘画来取代缂丝。此一倾向到清后期日益严重，甚至出现仅缂织轮廓，花纹部分全部用笔绘的情况。⑤及至民国，政治动荡和经济萧条使得缂丝技术陷入了更加深重的困境。

中华人民共和国成立后，苏州地区的缂丝工艺得到了重新发展，以王茂仙、沈金水和王金山为代表的现代缂丝艺人继承了宋代的传统技艺，创作出了许多精美的现代缂丝作品，使古老的缂丝艺术得以传承和发扬光大。

20世纪80年代中期，保加利亚壁挂艺术大师马林·瓦尔班诺夫（Maryn Varbanov，中文名万曼）到中国学习，他的现代壁挂艺术融入了中国缂织艺术，让这种拥有悠久历史的艺术形式得以走向国际舞台。

2. 传承：不断创新，归于生活

缂丝作为一种独特的非物质文化遗产，其工艺无法被机械所取代，甚至连织机也必须经过精心设计和定制。王氏家族历经六代传承，一心致力于缂丝制作，以达到最高的艺术水准。2018年，王建江与李丹联手打造了一款全新的缂丝高定女鞋，这是王氏缂丝世家第六代传承人的杰作。缂织技术的发展为定制服装提供了无限的可能性。缂丝艺术的广泛运用，为当今的服装设计带来了新的灵感，并且能够持续地保持其优秀的传统。

传统手工能够运用于日常生活中的方方面面，其本质是生活化的。在当今数字化高度发展的时代背景之下，缂丝技艺也正在往日常生活产品的方向不断发展。装饰画是中式软装的一种传统手法，苏州祯彩堂的装饰品如缂丝茶

---

① 朴文英.缂丝.苏州：苏州大学出版社，2009：35.
② 辽宁省博物馆.华彩若英：中国古代缂丝刺绣精品集.辽宁：辽宁人民出版社，2009，21.
③ 三蓝缂法是缂丝晕色法之一，在浅色地上用深蓝、品蓝、月白三色逐层退晕缂成各种花纹图案.
④ 水墨缂法是在浅色地上用黑色、深灰、浅灰色逐层退晕缂织花纹.
⑤ 朴文英.缂丝.苏州：苏州大学出版社，2009：44.

席、茶包、靠垫、桌旗和香囊等，为空间增添了更多的层次感。在元代，缂丝不仅被用作皇室的服装面料，还被广泛应用于扇子、书籍装帧等领域；苏州祯彩堂的缂丝产品，如手提包、钱包、手机袋、茶席、桌旗和香囊，正在为文化创意产业注入新鲜血液，为缂丝技术注入新的活力[①]。

（二）缂丝的工艺特色

苏州的缂丝织造技术源远流长，它以传统的木机、精致的竹制梭子、"通经断纬"等工具，结合多种颜色的蚕丝线，创作出一幅精美的、色彩斑斓的织物。这种织物以其独特的图案花纹而闻名，无论是正面还是反面。

1.细丝缂成

缂丝工艺精湛，需要高超的织布技巧和耐心。缂丝工艺是将金属丝线通过特定的方法织入织物中，制成图案和花纹。在制作过程中需要精细的手工操作和高超的技艺。在制作缂丝织物时，首先需要根据设计图案在织物表面进行剪纸，再将剪下的图案填补上丝线，从而形成具有层次感和立体感的图案。这种细致的手工操作需要经过长时间的训练和实践才能够熟练掌握，且手工完成需要数月甚至几年的时间，因此缂丝工艺也被视为一种高级的手工艺品。

2.图案花纹丰富，色彩鲜艳

缂丝技艺汲取了中国传统文化的精华，其中包括中国传统的绘画、雕刻、篆刻等艺术形式，使得缂丝工艺具有强烈的文化色彩。在缂丝的图案和花纹中，通常会融合一些传统文化元素，比如寓意美好的动植物、神话传说中的英雄人物以及山水文物等。在制作缂丝织物时，手艺人会选择一些鲜艳、明亮的丝线来进行填充，从而使得织物的图案效果更加生动、绚丽。同时，缂丝工艺也常采用金、银等贵重材料来进行点缀，使得织物更加华丽、高贵。

3.缂丝出产的面料具有极高的质量和观赏性

由于在织物中加入了金属丝线，因此缂丝面料具有光泽度高、手感柔软、透气性好、保暖性强等特点。同时，缂丝面料的图案和花纹也非常美观，让人们可以在穿着时感受到一种高贵、典雅的气息。

缂丝艺术是中国传统文化中不可或缺的一部分，它以其精湛的手工织造技艺、多样的图案和优质的面料，成为中国文化中最具代表性的艺术形式之一，深受人们的喜爱和赞赏。

---

① 张慧.南通缂丝在新中式室内空间软装的应用探讨.艺术品鉴，2019(6): 217-218.

（三）苏州"祯彩堂"

2001 年，陈文女士在苏州创建祯彩堂缂丝工艺厂（以下简称"祯彩堂"），这也是苏州缂丝行业首批采用现代化的生产组织管理模式的企业之一，它不仅具备完善的产品设计、生产、市场营销等功能，而且还拥有自己的产品开发部门、精湛的缂丝工艺师以及强大的市场营销团队，从缂丝艺术的创作、文物的修复，到缂丝时尚产品的开发，都能够满足客户的需求，为消费者提供更加优质的服务。通过各个部门共同努力协作，努力打造出了一个优秀的品牌形象[1]。

时至今日，"祯彩堂"旗下共拥有五十多名缂丝手艺师傅、自主研发的设计团队及销售人员等一批制作团队，目前已经在苏州市的黄金地段开设了两家缂丝专卖店，十几年来，苏州"祯彩堂"缂织的缂丝艺术品在国内外获奖无数、广受赞誉。在当今全国仅剩的三百名左右的缂丝手艺师傅的现状下，无论是行业规模与团队质量，"祯彩堂"缂丝艺术在苏州缂丝领域的地位都是不可忽视的。

传统缂丝具有三个特点：一是作品多为集体创作；二是创作周期长；三是作品具有极高观赏性。祯彩堂缂丝在继承了传统缂丝的优良基础之上，还非常重视产品的设计。祯彩堂创始人陈文女士表示，缂丝作品的设计不能靠简单的拿来主义，需要更用心地进行二次创作及设计。传统缂丝一般以大型作品为主，而祯彩堂产品主要分为作品和日用品两大类别。大型作品具有极高的观赏价值及收藏价值，制作工时往往需要以年为计算单位，日用品种类则比较丰富，制作周期相对作品来说较短。

三、缂丝工艺传承

（一）缂丝的工艺传承与传承人

王氏家族历经六代人的努力，一直致力于缂丝织造，以达到最高的艺术水准。王建江的祖辈皆从事缂丝，至今已有百年。王金亭，一位擅长制作宫廷龙袍的清廷匠师；王新亭，曾经为慈禧太后设计出一件精美的八仙庆寿袍；曾祖父王锦亭的《麻姑献寿图》是他的杰出代表，在 1915 年参加了巴拿马国际博览会，并荣膺金牌[2]。祖父王茂仙在苏州创办了一家刺绣研究所，并参加了中华

---

① 连晓君.苏州"祯彩堂"缂丝艺术的发扬性保护与管理之研究.南京：南京航空航天大学，2018.
② 黄紫娟，刘雷艮.苏州丝绸"非遗"传承人现状分析及建议——以缂丝为例.山东纺织经济，2016(8)：15-17.

人民共和国成立后第一次全国工艺美术艺人和创作人民代表大会。

王建江，非物质文化遗产传承人、高级工艺美术师，是王氏缂丝世家的第六代传人。每一代王氏缂丝家族的传承人都肩负着传承和发扬这门手艺的重任。当缂丝作为中国蚕桑丝织技艺入选世界非物质文化遗产，王建江与父亲都成为了代表性传承人。2010年，王建江和中国社会科学院考古研究所联手建立了苏州缂丝保护研究中心，旨在发现和传承这一濒临消亡的工艺，并将其发扬光大。王建江致力于推广缂丝文化，他特别开设了缂丝体验课，并且在辖区内建立了实践基地，以便吸引更多的年轻人参与其中，他也积极向参与者们传授缂丝的精湛技艺。他不仅打破"传男不传女"的传统，而且还将这项技艺传承给了家族中的女性，如今，他的女儿也开始对缂丝有着浓厚的兴趣。

王鹏巍是王氏缂丝世家第七代传承人。她曾先后9次到苏州、北京拜访第六代缂丝世家传承人王建江并拜他为师。2014年，由王鹏巍发起成立了河北定坤文化传播有限公司（定州缂丝艺术馆），让缂丝织造技艺再次走进了大众的视野，也为缂丝技艺的弘扬与传承奠定了基础。为了更好地保护和传承缂丝这一非物质文化遗产，王鹏巍大胆创新，先后主持设计了一系列具有浓郁定州特色和敦煌题材的缂丝作品，还主持研发了多种"缂丝"衍生品，如缂丝饰品、手包、伴手礼等，销往全国各地。

（二）缂丝的传承发展方式与路径特点

作为一种中国传统的刺绣工艺，缂丝以其色彩鲜艳、线条流畅、图案多样而著称。缂丝技艺的传承方式主要有以下三种。

1.师徒式传承制度

在生产中向学徒传授技艺，是民间艺术的主要特点。而传统手工艺绝大部分也是在民间孕育发展的，"实践"是传统手工艺传承的重要环节。苏州缂丝的传承正在通过实践来实现师徒之间的技艺传承。师徒式传承有以下几大特点：一是师傅带徒弟的个别式培养，具有针对性和特殊性；二是徒弟全程跟随师傅学习，能保证学习技艺的全面和细致，在学习过程中可以随时提出问题，技艺的传授更加灵活；三是学习和工作相结合，这是师徒制最本质的特点，技艺的学习和工作同时进行，既保证了师傅完成工作并获得利益，同时徒弟也能学到最实用的技巧，师徒之间通过技能的传授，实现工作和学习目标。

2. 家族企业式传承

缂丝在苏州地区也成为了家族传统产业，一些具有历史底蕴的刺绣家族将缂丝技艺代代相传，并形成了自己的刺绣风格和特点。苏州缂丝家族式的手工艺传承方式，有三方面的特点：首先，家族式传承的成本较低，而且传承人从小在这个环境下成长，耳濡目染，学习技艺速度快；其次，家族式传承不会出现劳资矛盾的冲突以及各种人事纠纷；再次，家族式传承家庭内部人际关系比较和谐，俗话说"血浓于水"，家族传承人之间的亲情血缘关系，比家族以外的人更能互相信任，有更强的凝聚力，可以充分释放其智慧。

3. 政府、学校和传承人共同合作

由政府、学校和传承人共同合作的社会传承方式，在手工艺传承方式上比较少见，对手工艺的传承有很大帮助。新一代学生传承人，经过学校的培养，理论知识比较系统，文化水平相对较高；学生在缂丝技艺的学习过程中，有一定的技艺积累之后，可以自己制作设计。但这种传承方式，耗时较长。因为在学校课程安排中，大部分时间仍被文化课占据，而学生学习缂丝制作的时间只占一小部分，所以与专门学习缂丝技艺学习的学徒相比，这种传承方式需要耗费的时间更长。

（三）缂丝工艺传承发展存在的问题

近年来，由于社会的迅速发展和政府的大力推动，缂丝这一珍贵的非物质文化遗产得到了广泛的关注和普及，其重要性也日益凸显。随着现代市场经济的发展，许多传统手工艺正面临着失传的危险，苏州缂丝的传承和发展也受到了严重的挑战。根据苏州市工艺美术行业协会的最新调查结果，2018 年苏州市工艺美术产业总产值达到了 100 亿元。虽然工艺美术产业拥有众多市场主体和超过 15 万名从业人员，但其产值在 GDP 中的比重仍然较低。当前，苏州缂丝工艺的市场主要由小型作坊式工作室和小微企业组成，这些企业的生产经营规模较小，导致产业结构不够完善，并且缺少大型企业的支持。这些因素都阻碍了苏州缂丝工艺的高质量发展。

1. 手工工艺难以量产，市场份额待提升

在工业化大生产的当下，工业化的面料成为了缂丝的劲敌。缂丝作为当今时代独一无二的工艺，奠定了其"贵族"的地位，但随着市场的快速发展，缂丝遭遇冷遇。随着市场占有率的下降，企业的经济效益受到了严重的影响，工

人的收入也随之下降，而缂丝制作的复杂性和枯燥乏味使得愿意从事这一职业的人数大幅减少，同时也削弱了设计创新的能力。

2. 生产经营规模偏小，产业格局不合理

经过 20 世纪 90 年代市场化的发展，苏州许多缂丝企业纷纷改制，缂丝的生产很多转移到农村，这些生产缂丝的农户处在产业链末端，一般分散经营，缂丝产品的销售采取来样加工的形式，因为自身对产品或图案设计以及市场营销能力的不足，所以经济发展空间也有限，并且在贸易的公平方面也得不到有效的保障，传统手工艺向时尚产业、设计产业以及现代生活空间的延伸与融合不足，很难在现代成为一种标志性的产业形态。缂丝行业的发展受到了许多因素的影响，其中最重要的是农户和手工艺者。由于缺乏有效的法律保护，这些行业的个体经济权益受到了损害，缂丝艺人通常处于贫困和落后的状态。

3. 产品制作成本过大，推介展销渠道单一

缂丝的制作比其他面料或艺术品更加困难，因为它的编织过程非常复杂，耗时也更长。一块方巾大小的缂丝织品可能包含数百上千种不同的颜色，要想完成这样的工艺细节，即使是最高级的技师也需要花费数月的时间，这使得很少有人能够忍受孤独，去深入研究缂丝的精髓。

目前，大型缂丝企业的推销渠道仍较单一。苏州仁和织绣工艺品有限公司是中国缂丝行业的领军企业，其产品在市场上的销量主要来源于大型酒店和政府部门的采购。为了增强酒店的整体形象，星级酒店通常会选择各种日常必需品以及精美的手工制作的装饰品。外事机构通常会选择购买一些精美的工艺品，以便与外国人进行交流并向他们赠送礼物。仁和织绣正在努力拓展电商渠道，已经在淘宝商城和其他网上商城开设了仁和织绣旗舰店，但由于技术和成本的局限，其销量仍然不尽如人意。根据调查问卷的反馈，大多数民众都愿意购买价格低于百元的实用品，他们对缂丝技艺的认知仍然有限，对缂丝产品的期望价格也与企业的售价存在差距。

4. 工匠人才培养不足，技术传承缺乏后劲

根据一项最新的数据，1979—2006 年，中国一共评选了 365 位杰出的中国工艺美术家，其中 1/5 已经离开人世。目前，我国拥有 3025 名高级工艺美术师，但仅有 20% 的人继续从事传统工艺美术。苏州缂丝由于织造费工，劳动成本较高，特别是缂丝艺术品，往往需要穷年累月才能完成，目前苏州制作缂丝艺术精品的艺人只有王金山、王嘉良、马惠娟、谈水娥等为数不多的一些

大师。①其他制作缂丝艺术品和工艺品的企业大多规模较小，较大的有苏州市工业园区仁和织绣有限公司和苏州东渚镇西部民间缂丝研究所，但是人数也不过四五十人，其他的缂丝艺人大多以个体户的形式散落民间，数量不多。

四、苏州缂丝技艺可持续发展的建议

文化遗产是一种具有多重价值的公众资产。历史上保存的文物古迹不仅可以反映出当时的社会主流价值观，还可以为我们提供有趣的视角，从而探索出它们背后的历史故事、传奇人物，并且可能带给我们新的审美感受，从而激发我们去探索这些文化遗产的深层含义；在西方，人们重视科学和理性，并将历史信息的准确性作为衡量文物古迹是否优秀的标准。他们更加重视遗产本身的价值，并且更加关注它们的真实性，并努力保护它们的实际元素。

在传承模式上，中国已形成了以政府主导、社会介入的保护发展格局，非物质文化遗产拥有"国家、省、市、县"四级保护体系，但多数非遗项目还是以"师徒制"的方式艰难传承。而国外则是采取登录制度保护文化遗产，通过登录认定文化遗产和非物质文化遗产的资格，以一定的法律法规条例进行约束，达到保护传承的目的。

在传播方式上，在国内一是依靠传承人自发推广，二是借助政府和社会的力量建立展示基地推动宣传。在国外则是重在对文化遗产进行媒体宣传，逐渐走向商业化和旅游化，使文化遗产转化为文化产业。

下面将对缂丝技艺传承保护与创新发展进行探究。

（一）缂丝工艺的传承与创新路径

1.筑牢知识产权保护机制，激发缂丝传承动力

随着经济的转型升级，知识产权保护已成为推动创新和创业的关键政策措施。为了保护非遗文化的传承，国家应该加强对知识产权的保护，特别是非遗知识产权的保护。为了维护传承人的利益，应该建立专门的法律救助体系，以激励他们继续传承这项文化。

2.开展现代学徒制教学，创新缂丝传承培养模式

现代学徒制旨在建立一种基于学校与企业之间的紧密合作关系，由专家和

---

① 范英豪，周莹.基于市场开发与非遗保护双重视野下的苏州缂丝手工艺传承.丝绸，2018，55(10): 91-97.

工匠共同指导学习，以提升学生的实践技能，并将缂丝技艺的精髓传承下去[①]。

3.挖掘传统技艺的当代价值，实现缂丝的创新发展

进一步提升对现存传统技艺缂丝的发掘、记录、整理、归档，建立数字化的"缂丝基因库"，通过海量积累和归档，实现缂丝技艺保存和共享，传统缂丝技艺非遗传承人需要再培训。

4.开展生产性保护，产生经济效益和社会效益的保护方式

（1）缂丝传统技艺是生产性保护的核心，必须得到继承和发展。缂丝不仅能够创造出巨大的经济收入，而且蕴藏着深厚的文化底蕴，成为苏州历史的见证，也是传承和发展的重要支柱。

（2）缂丝传承者应该积极主动，充满活力。传承者是将一种技能传承至后代的重要载体，他们应该获得与其他年轻人相当的报酬，并且应该以拥有这种技能为荣耀。

（3）缂丝传统技艺不是孤立存在的，它源于生活，有适宜它存在的土壤，有较显著的地域特色。尽可能多地保留缂丝传统技艺存在的文化空间，营造适宜缂丝生存的文化环境，在生产和生活的互动中保护缂丝非遗。[②]

五、结　论

缂丝作为中国传统丝绸工艺的杰出代表，其精湛技艺在世界上享有盛誉。近年来，随着社会的发展和进步，国家积极宣传非物质文化遗产缂丝，缂丝工艺近些年在工艺上、市场上的发展取得了一定成绩。但同时，面对现代市场经济环境的冲击，缂丝工艺正面临失传的险境，在传承与发展上仍面临重重阻碍。

本案例运用文本研究法，对缂丝发展的背景、现状、存在问题等进行了深入分析。当前，缂丝在工艺传承发展方面还存在一些问题：（1）手工工艺难以量产，市场份额待提升；（2）生产经营规模偏小，产业格局不合理；（3）产品制作成本过大，推介展销渠道单一；（4）工匠人才培养不足，技术传承缺乏后劲。为解决上述问题，本研究尝试提出了以下方法供参考。在工艺传承与创新路径层面：（1）筑牢知识产权保护机制，激发缂丝传承动力；（2）开展现代学徒制教学，创新缂丝传承培养模式；（3）挖掘传统技艺的当代价值，实现缂丝的创新发展；（4）开展生产性保护，产生经济效益和社会效益的保护方式。在

---

① 缪秋菊.苏州缂丝文化技艺保护与传承探析.丝绸，2014，51(2): 76-79.
② 朱以青.传统技艺的生产保护与生活传承.民俗研究，2015(1): 81-87.

工艺人才培养、传承层面：弘扬工匠精神，加强宣传与价值认同；完善激励机制，开展多元化现代教学。

通过对苏作缂丝发展史的回顾，我们不仅深入分析了它的发展情况，还揭示出它目前所面临的挑战，并给出了有效的解决办法。希望在未来能够有机会参与实地探究，从而不断完善本研究的不足之处，为缂丝的良好发展贡献绵薄之力。

多样化继承和品牌化视角下苏式糕点的传承与发展①

摘　要: 历史悠久、造型精美的苏式糕点是中式糕点的代表之一。近年来，苏式糕点不断受到现代西式糕点的冲击，面临着传承的原动力不足；投入成本与经济收益不成正比，市场竞争力较低；创新传承与非遗文化价值之间的平衡问题等新挑战。在立足非物质文化遗产保护的基础上，对苏式糕点进行多样化继承与品牌化发展有助于克服苏式糕点当今的困境。

关键词: 文化遗产；传统糕点；传承与保护；创新与发展

一、绪　论

（一）选题背景及意义

苏式糕点在中国传统糕点发展史上占有重要的地位，是中国传统糕点主要帮式之一。其中糕团制作技艺、糕点制作技艺、采芝斋苏式糖果制作技艺于2009 年 6 月入选第二批省级非物质文化遗产代表名录。

苏式糕点萌芽于春秋，起源于隋唐，形成于两宋，发展于明清，最早可以追溯到 2000 多年前。南北朝时期老苏州就开始研究馅芯配料；隋唐后苏式糕点和苏州的经济一样平稳发展。宋代后苏式糕点作为一个独特的传统特色糕点帮式已经形成，品种甚多。明清时期苏式糕点迎来了繁荣发展，据不完全统计，明、清时期的苏式糕点已经产生了炉货、油面、油氽等七个大类，传统品种多达 130 余种。

苏式糕点作为中式糕点的代表之一，包含苏杭文化中精致、细腻的特点及中国文化中人与自然和谐统一的理念。然而现在苏式糕点的传统制作技艺正受

---

① 作者: 胡明珂，大连外国语大学日语系；林芳菲，大连外国语大学日语系。

到现代西式糕点的冲击，苏式糕点面临创新不足的境况。因此苏式糕点制作工艺的保护、传承与创新在保护非物质文化遗产，传承苏州文化，讲好中国故事方面具有重要意义。

（二）国内外研究评述

苏式糕点在文献中的记载可以追溯到春秋时期的《楚辞》。南宋《梦粱录》中就有"如十般糖、澄沙团、韵果、蜜姜豉"等糕点的记载。[①]

到清代文人袁枚所著的《随园食单》中更是记载了多达几十种的苏式糕点的制作工艺，其中包括许多制作工艺现已失传的糕点。[②]

在现代研究中，针对苏式糕点的研究角度更加丰富多元。目前国内现有关于苏式糕点的研究主要可分为以下几个类别。

1.对于苏式糕点的历史沿革进行研究

以《宋代笔记中的甜点探析》为例，研究宋代笔记中出现的苏式糕点，并分析研究其制作方法背后所体现出的宋代经济文化发展。[③]

2.对于苏式糕点的美学研究

例如《基于体验经济下的苏式糕点造型创新设计方法研究》一文以苏式糕点的造型设计为切入点对苏式糕点在体验经济下的创新发展。对于苏式糕点的外观、包装设计、美学研究是目前国内对于苏式糕点研究较多的一个角度。[④]

3.对于苏式糕点在食品科学方面的研究

《苏式糕点的理化检测和发展方向》一文通过运用科学检测方法对苏式糕点的原材料配方进行分析研究，从营养学角度指出苏式糕点的优势与不足，为食品工业发展提供思路。[⑤]

（三）研究对象及内容

本次研究围绕苏式糕点的继承与创新展开，具体根据苏式糕点的历史背景、文化特点、现有的传承方式、技术特点以及当今市场状况分析了苏式糕点的现状及问题，并探究如何与现代商业化相结合，如何创新以适应现代市场需求，对比中式糕点和日式糕点的理念与现状发展，总结了如何在传承和发展传

① 孟元老，吴自牧.东京梦华录·梦粱录.南京：江苏凤凰文艺出版社，2019：129-130.
② 袁枚.随园食单.郑州：中州古籍出版社，2017：202.
③ 纪钦.宋代笔记中的甜点探析.大观，2018(4)：109-110.
④ 王安覆，渠文.基于体验经济下的苏式糕点造型创新设计方法研究.设计，2017(18)：128-129.
⑤ 章云珍.苏式糕点的理化检测和发展方向.食品科学，1985(2)：59-61.

统工艺的同时推动苏式糕点这一非物质文化遗产可持续发展目标的实现，并在最后结合研究结果为其传承保护和创新发展提出建议。

（四）研究思路及方法

中国地大物博，非物质文化遗产多种多样，苏州范围内的非遗文化，如苏绣、苏剧、桃花坞木版年画等，种类繁多且非常具有研究意义。"民以食为天"，中国人对"食"有着别样的情怀。因此我们决定将苏式糕点作为研究对象展开我们此次的项目研究。

根据当前国内的研究评述，本文作者发现，现有对于苏式糕点的美学价值、营养价值的研究对苏式糕点制作工艺的保护传承有着极大的借鉴意义。但目前国内对于苏式糕点的研究多集中于美学价值，对其制作工艺传承方面的研究存在明显空白，对其技艺的发展建议创新乏力。基于以上分析，对苏式糕点制作工艺的保护有其必要性。因此本文采取了以下的研究思路及方法。

首先通过文献检索，大量文献阅读，梳理发展脉络，了解其现存的基本类别，从认识背景文化、发展的现状及瓶颈问题，根据市场调研和问卷分析，提出有关对于苏式糕点如何继承，如何创新，并如何顺应市场推动其可持续发展这一思路进行研究。在此基础上通过实地调研、发放调查问卷的形式进行观察法研究及定量分析。通过查阅各国甜品、糕点的发展历史，突出对比日本和果子的发展现状。最后将得出的数据和实地调查成果进行综合分析，得出对于苏式糕点制作工艺的保护传承意见。

二、苏式糕点制作技艺的传承与发展现状

（一）苏式糕点的技法特点

苏式糕点是中国传统糕点中十分具有特色的一类，是汉族糕点的重要组成部分。苏式面点主要以苏州、扬州、杭州三个地方为代表。在制作上，讲究形态与造型。苏式糕点的独特工艺在现代依然具有独特性和可借鉴性。苏式糕点在技术上独树一帜，采用了更理想的起酥过程，具有独特的风格。

清代文人袁枚在其所著的《随园食单》中就提及了多种糕点的制作方法。其中提到的一种名为蓑衣饼的糕点，通过此记载，可以比较清晰地了解到，在清代苏式糕点就已经形成了工艺精致，技法成熟的特点。遗憾的是，蓑衣饼的制作方法现已失传，在《随园食单》中类似蓑衣饼这样技艺失传的糕点不在少

数，这也反映出对传统糕点制作工艺的保护与传承迫在眉睫。

（二）苏式糕点的文化特点

苏式糕点的用料具有地方特色和自然主义原则，在辅料的选择上也同样讲究。辅料不仅要自身独具特色，还要与糕点的原料相辅相成。

苏式糕点在选料方面强调天然性，从不使用工业香精和色素，根据各种原料的特性和原料间相互辅佐而产生的天然之味来增添风味。

苏式糕点遵循着春饼、夏糕、秋酥、冬糖的规律，逢农历四时八节，均有它的时令品种。此外苏式糕点还有上市、落令的严格规定。应时细点，时令性强，亦是它的特点之一。顺应自然，五行调和，中国古代传统的养生观点与自然观在苏式糕点中巧妙融合。

（三）传统工艺传承发展现状

苏式糕点品种甚多，有枣泥麻饼、月饼、巧果等。著名茶食店有王仁和、湘城老大房、稻香村等。近年来，苏式糕点得到了进一步的恢复、发扬和发展，已经恢复了许多名特品种和传统品种。

关于当前消费者对于苏式糕点的了解，我们进行了问卷调查。

调查显示，目前消费者对于苏式糕点无论是从种类上还是品牌上的认知程度存在着明显的不平衡现象，"青团""稻香村"这类著名糕点和品牌受众面较广，而那些更具备苏式传统特点的糕点和品牌却难以在苏州本地之外打开知名度。由此可以看出苏式糕点制作工艺整体传承程度不高。

调查显示，消费者对于苏式糕点的选择原因主要有花式精致，符合中国人口味，原材料健康等因素，这也反映了苏式糕点"精益求精，古法自然"的技艺特点，以及"顺应自然，五行调和"的文化内涵。

如今，在食品工业迅速发展的大背景下，糕点行业也从最初的手作生产转变成机械化生产，虽带来了更大的发展空间，但对于老字号来说，传统技艺是其核心竞争力和安身立命之本。

为了更好地传承传统糕点制作技艺，苏州稻香村在苏州成立了非物质文化遗产传承中心，研发人员对失传已久的许多传统糕点技艺进行抢救性研发，逐步恢复了30多种特色糕点技艺，进一步丰富了当前市场上的中式点心品类，促进了糕点行业的发展。

在另一方面，许多苏州民间的糕点制作人却表示现状苏式糕点在西式糕点的冲击下也渐趋没落。等候时间长、原料成本高、糕点品种有时令限制，制作工艺复杂、技术传承周期长等都制约苏式糕点进一步发展。大部分糕点都是以"手把手"的形式进行传承。学习周期长、投入大量时间精力和收入并不理想，这是苏式糕点发展的一大掣肘。

（四）传统工艺传承中存在的问题

1.守艺传承的原动力不足

非物质文化遗产的传承与开发中根本在"人"，需要人进行传承和维护，因此导致一些传统工艺技艺已经开始面临失传。若一味地对苏式糕点进行保护传承，可能因为不能够适应市场需求，从而导致手艺人被迫维持生计而失去维系传统手艺的热情，继承人不愿意继承或者继承人减少，最终导致传统手工艺流于消亡的境地；尽管将情况理想化，手艺人出于对苏式糕点的热爱，愿意对其进行保护传承，那么受众依旧较少，可能仍然会落入"圈地自萌"的境地，无法更好地传承下去。因此，现阶段苏式糕点传统工艺传承存在的最根本问题就是原动力不足，从业人员较少。

2.投入成本与经济收益不成正比，市场竞争力较低

苏式糕点精致精细，制作时间较长，工艺烦琐，若还要继承与宣传，那需要花大量的时间精力和国家政策的扶持与经济支撑，传承传统工艺的投入成本太高；从目前糕点行业市场分析数据来看，我国该行业的从业人员较少，不能够满足如今的生产需求，受众群体较少，利润收益较低，近年来，西式糕点也在国内持续扩张，给传统的中式糕点也带来了较大的生存压力。由于投入成本与经济收益不成正比，且在市场中的竞争力较低，生存压力较大，因此包括苏式糕点在内的非遗手工艺的继承发展处于一个恶性循环之中，必须要想办法扩大市场需求，提高经济收益，从而吸引更多继承人才。[①]

3.创新传承与非遗文化价值之间的平衡

苏式糕点在保护继承与开放利用之间的"度"很难把握，若过度开发创新，可能会为了迎合市场，而改变甚至失去了其本来的文化价值和艺术价值。如若改变苏式糕点的口味抑或是制作方式等，如何立足苏式糕点的文化核心，确保苏式糕点依旧具备其本身的文化价值，达到创新传承与非遗文化价值之间的平衡，是研究苏式糕点如何在不忘初心中创新发展的重中之重。

---

① 王智莹，沈冰轩，罗澜等.传统手工艺在互联网时代下的生存现状与发展.北方经贸，2019(2)：130-132.

四、苏式糕点与日式糕点的对比分析

（一）传承发展的现状与模式对比

中国非遗传承发展旨在延续自身的传统文化，在机械化盛行的今天，一些传统点心店仍坚持手工制作，为促进糕点行业发展产生巨大推动作用。苏式糕点的馅料十分丰富，风味口感极其丰富饱满，如苏式月饼用小麦粉、饴糖、食用植物油或猪油、水等制皮，小麦粉、食用植物油或猪油制酥，经制酥皮、包馅、成型、焙烤工艺加工而成，工艺繁杂。

日本民族在历史上数次主动向其他民族学习，日式糕点的文化输出的动力更在于建立强大的对外文化形象树立上，旨在提高其文化的国际影响力。日式糕点的馅料，多用红小豆、板栗，或者加入一些水果，且一般都是甜口，如铜锣烧，用两片圆盘状的饼皮包裹豆沙馅，因为形状类似两个合在一起的铜锣而得名，与中国的豆沙饼类似。

（二）传承发展的理念特色对比

中国传统文化以人为本，重"礼"，设计体现出追求天人合一、和谐统一的文化内核，日本也用不同的文化载体，发散着自己最深层次的文化。纵观日本文化发展历史，其对外进行吸收并改进而形成了自己的一派。而苏式糕点在表达方式上则采用了本地文化的延伸。

以传统苏式糕点"绿豆糕"与著名日式糕点"樱饼"为例，由于不同民族审美的差异，两者的形状也不尽相同。尽管其都运用了几何形态，中国民间对于繁复的花纹和边缘变化的追求，使得绿豆糕的花纹纹样丰富，但在整体造型上趋于一致；而日本喜爱用简易的造型模仿当下的风物。因此，尽管日式糕点的整体造型也是以几何形态为主，但更偏向于拟物化。

苏式糕点与日式糕点作为社会与自然结合的产物，都受到了社会文化和地理环境的影响。这些食物的演变不仅是一种"物"的历程，更是其所代表的时代记忆、文化的象征。[①]

---

① 曾嘉煜，张凌浩，郭旭阳等.符号学视野下的传统糕点设计的创新探究——以苏式糕点与日式糕点为例.艺术科技，2017，30(1)：416.

（三）传承发展的经验启示

1.理念特色方面的经验总结

世界各国、各民族的文化几乎都会受到外来文化的影响，在历史上不存在某种纯粹的文化，文化理念也不存在优劣之分。需要认识到文化遗产的社会价值和文化价值，对其利用不能完全由市场行为支配，需要具备整体性和前瞻性的遗产管理思维模式。

推动苏式糕点活性发展，数字化发展与文化传播对立统一，解读和展示文物内涵，体现苏式糕点作为非遗的社会价值。用好宣传载体，通过传统媒体和新兴媒介深层次、全覆盖宣传非遗传承与保护的重要意义；要坚持以保护为前提，将非遗融入国民教育体系，让文化自信"强起来"。①

2.现状模式方面的经验总结

苏式糕点在现代融合创新上较日式糕点稍有不足，不妨学习日式糕点的发展模式，将糕点发展现代化，将新模式融入发展中。要坚持创新，坚持面向世界、面向现代化、面向未来。为了丰富我们的文化内容，应站在民族和历史的角度，加强国际文化交流与协作，使中国非物质文化遗产更好的服务于中国的现代化进程。②

五、关于苏式糕点传承保护与创新发展的建议

（一）"苏式糕点"传承保护的建议

1.政策制度与学习教育有机结合，从文化传承根本途径守艺

文化传承的根本途径是学习和教育，内化于心，该文化的继承人是其能否顺利继承的要素。苏式糕点文化继承人生存状况的好坏决定着"苏式糕点"这一非物质文化遗产能否得以顺利进行，因此政策制度上应加大对苏式糕点手艺人的保护力度与福利制度，培养"活态文化"。

建立苏式糕点非遗保护中心，实地走访民间苏式糕点传承人，适当为苏式糕点非遗文化提供专项资金资助。将非遗传承落实到教育中，将其作为义务教育推广至苏州及其周边地带，增设兴趣班、体验课等，让更多的人体会到苏式糕点的魅力。在内部传承的基础之上，充分利用如考学、就业、游玩等特定时

① 方海燕.从饮食看日本文化的特征——以中日饮食文化的关系为中心.科技信息(科学教研)，2008(4)：187-188，206.
② 金虹.苏州传统手工艺传承与发展的难点与策略研究.苏州：苏州大学，2012.

期的人口迁移，从而将苏式糕点从一个地区的文化传播到另一地区，使其得到传承。

2. 宣传推广与工法技艺有机结合，促进苏式糕点有效传承发展

多了解糕点的制作背景，尝试研发并恢复已经失传的糕点，并在此基础上进行宣传推广。在现有基础上打造苏式糕点品牌效应与价值认同，加强共建合作。

鼓励当地学校、科研机构、社会团体开展苏式糕点的调查研究和学习交流；鼓励支持集体、个人开展以苏式糕点为题材的文艺创作、动漫制作、影视拍摄、翻译、出版相关文献等，促进苏式糕点研究项目跨区域传承、传播。大力扶持能够深刻挖掘苏式糕点的内涵、增强其文化吸引力的项目，通过品牌化经营完成对苏式糕点的保护及其潜能的开发，并逐步将苏式糕点推向全国市场乃至国际市场。[①]

（二）"苏式糕点"创新发展的建议

1. 守好非遗文化核心，做好就地保护

在对苏式糕点这一类非物质文化遗产的保护过程中，极易出现以保护为名而对"非遗"进行过度开发，导致其丧失了本身特色。对于苏式糕点的保护首先要守牢苏式糕点的文化内核，即运用苏州一带特有的原材料、制作工艺，因时令季节制作出符合苏杭一带审美的糕点，做到就地保护，原味保护。

苏式糕点的生命力来源于民间各家糕点作坊独具特点的制作工艺和用料配方，因此在保护苏式糕点的过程中不仅要看到类似黄天源、稻香村等知名店铺，还要深入散落在苏州各地的糕点小店，邀请网络媒体对这些小店进行宣传，政府对这其提供资金、政策方面的扶持，使苏式糕点始终保有不断发展的活力。

2. 打破传承限制，实现技艺共享互通

通过调查发现，在苏式糕点的制作工艺的传承过程中，存在着明显的家族式特点。多数小型糕点作坊的继承特点是以血缘为纽带代代相传，这也导致在现代社会中，一旦出现子女继承意愿不强的情况，技艺就存在着失传的风险。在如今强调国风文化复兴的今天，越来越多的年轻人有意愿接触并系统学习例如苏式糕点的技艺。想要解决这一矛盾，就需要首先从思想上突破以往家族式

---

① 苑仁军，姜林枫.基于互联网思维的传统手工艺传承发展的思考.才智，2019(6)：240.

传承、师徒式传承的限制，广泛开班教学，邀请全世界的青年人对该项技术进行继承学习，从而实现对苏式糕点制作工艺的传承保护。

本文作者还发现，不同作坊的制作工艺上存在着一定的差异性，各个作坊之间的联系性不强。应充分发挥苏州餐饮行业协会的协作机制，促进不同苏式糕点作坊、品牌和非遗传承人之间的合作与交流，形成行业的合力共同促进苏式糕点技艺的创新和发展。①

3.立足体验经济，讲好文化故事

苏式糕点的继承需要更多的人关注苏式糕点，了解苏式糕点，从而有可能愿意学习继承苏式糕点制作技艺。因此我们提倡将苏式糕点与体验经济相结合，在售卖苏式糕点的店铺中顾客可以看到糕点的制作过程，亲身体验学习，拉近非遗技艺与大众生活之间的距离，增加大众对非遗技艺的情感，同时也扩大了潜在技艺传承人的范围。

在立足体验经济之外，还可以通过讲好文化故事，树立苏式糕点的品牌形象，打造出独一无二的苏式糕点文化。基于苏式糕点具有丰富历史文化底蕴和其重时令，重自然的特点，打造出"自然　精巧　苏韵"的苏式糕点品牌形象，让大众在制作、品尝苏式糕点的同时体会到独一无二的苏州文化魅力。②

（三）未来发展展望

要想了解到苏式糕点今后的发展趋势，就应该先了解到我国糕点业在发展过程中的特点。总的来说，我国糕点在漫长的发展过程中最为突出的问题就是缺乏创新，如今苏式糕点的发展进入了瓶颈期。为了能够促进商业化发展，首先一些糕点企业就应该做好带头作用，不断在传统苏式糕点的口味和外观上进行创新。从目前的情况来看，苏式糕点发展该紧紧抓住如今经济全球化的机遇，不断进行创新和发展。③

1.符号化、品牌化

在实践发展过程中，提高对符号消费的重视程度，在对苏式糕点进行创新发展时要努力提高符号的价值和功能。我国社会经济进步发展，人们更加关注产品中如社会地位、价值观念、自身主张等非传统因素，因此在苏式糕点创新

① 华觉明.保护　传承　创新　经略　振兴——中国传统工艺的承续和发展.民艺，2021(6)：67-71.
② 申绍云.传统工艺类非遗传承发展路径：跨界融合，转化再生.广州城市职业学院学报，2021，15(4)：55-60.
③ 杨忠霞，刘居超.中式面点发展之路的探讨.科技与企业，2013(5)：326.

发展的过程中，要从符号认同感方面入手开展创新工作。

品牌化包括运用新媒体等传播技术和传播平台，打造独具特色的苏式糕点品牌形象，使其与苏州城市形象与文化内涵紧密联系。利用苏式糕点历史悠久、传承时间长、品种技法多样深挖历史内涵，结合历史名人、名地、典故讲好苏式糕点故事，赋予其更高的文化价值。

2.多元化、营养化

苏式糕点许多品种营养成分过于单一，有的还含有较多的脂肪和糖类。因此，在继承传统优秀面点特质的基础上，要改革传统配方及工艺。如：从低热、低脂、多膳食纤维等入手，创制营养均衡的面点品种。讲求营养科学，开发功能性面点品种。功能性面点的创新主要包括：老人长寿、妇女健美、儿童益智、中年调养等4大类。现代科学研究认为，食品具有三项功能：一是营养功能，二是感官功能；三是生理调节功能。而功能性食品即是指除营养和感官之外，还具有调节生理功能的食品，功能性面点的发展是面点品种创新的趋势。①

六、研究局限性

（一）影响研究的特定限制

本项目自研究以来对与苏州糕点相关的文献的进行了阅读调查，并且查阅了大量已有论文。但在研究方法上依然存在无法深入进行实地进行考察这一研究局限性，对于苏州糕点的实际传承和创新状况无法得到最直观最具体的了解，因此在本文中对于具体事例存在一定欠缺。

其次，前文中提及的苏式糕点与传统日式糕点的比较研究也因为客观条件限制无法进行实地考察，造成对比程度不够充分的局限性。此外，在关于日式糕点与苏式糕点的传承对比的调查中，由于中日两国的文化背景差异，对于传承方式的接受程度和认识程度也存在着差异。因此进行的一些对比和借鉴也具有局限性。

（二）对研究结果的影响说明

无法对苏式糕点进行实地考察是本项目最大的局限性。这造成本项目对于苏式糕点的口味创新方面无法给出较为具体的创新性意见，同时也造成本项目

① 丁红.我国中式面点创新开发新方向探析.现代食品，2019(16)：22-24.

所引用的数据具有滞后性，不能充分反应出其最新传承情况。但由于苏式糕点的传承具有稳定性，因此近五年的研究数据对于本文的研究及观点得出依旧具有较大的指导意义。

在比较研究中，本文对日本传承传统糕点的方式做出了借鉴。由于日本与中国有着不同的文化背景，在对待传统技艺的传承方面的社会价值导向也有所不同。但同时日本社会与中国社会有着与其他社会不具备的极其相似的特性，这样的相似性在比较研究中具有不可替代性。

（三）局限性的克服方法

针对以上的局限性，应在接下来的调查研究中充分进行实地考察，深入苏式糕点的制作现场，通过对制作过程的亲身体验和对技艺传承人的走访调查来获取第一手资料，及时对本项目数据进行更新。同时在中外比较调查研究中充分利用本土文献、新闻、纪录片等素材，获得更加全面具体的研究资料，以此缩小地域文化差异带来的局限性。

七、结　论

本文确定了研究主体为中国非物质文化遗产苏式糕点，通过了解其文化背景、技艺特点、传承模式，对比分析国内外非遗文化的传承方式和糕点制作方面的差异，进而提出了传承发展与创新发展方面的建议。苏式糕点这一非物质文化遗产得以良好继承，首要从学习教育抓起，再通过精进技艺，加大宣传，融进日常生活；加大创新力度，在技术、理念、宣传方面不断创新，从而适应现代市场化的需求。苏式糕点发展应紧紧抓住如今经济全球化的机遇，不断进行创新和发展。

西安城墙的保护现状及其可持续利用建议[①]

摘　要: 新中国成立以来,在文物保护的方法技术上也有了更多的探索,特别是在"预防性保护"方面,相继在馆藏文物保护和遗址保护领域不断探索实践,近年来尤其对建筑遗产的预防性保护探索在逐步加强。西安城墙作为目前国内保存最完整的城墙,具有非同一般的象征意义,西安城墙保护中的预防性保护是文物保护的重要发展趋势,而监测预警工作正是实现预防性保护的基础。本文通过总结西安城墙保护的成功与不足,为其未来保护提供建议。

关键词: 西安城墙;预防性保护;分级预警;保护与创新

一、西安城墙的背景概述

(一)西安城墙简要介绍

西安城墙周长 13.74 公里,包括护城河、吊桥、闸楼、箭楼、城楼、角楼、敌楼、女儿墙、垛口等一系列军事设施。"墙林河路巷"五位一体,成为西安这座具有历史文化特色的国际化大都市重要的地标符号和精神家园。现为国家首批重点保护文物和 AAAAA 级旅游景区。

(二)西安城墙的病害成因

西安城墙经历了 600 多年的风雨侵蚀,出现了各种病害,影响了城墙的稳定性和美观性。根据病害的成因,可以分为内因和外因两类。

内因主要是指因城墙本身的材料、结构、工艺等方面存在问题(海墁的质量不良,砖石的强度不均等),而导致城墙容易受到水分、盐分、温度等环境

---

① 作者: 夏郅儴,大连外国语大学;刘一萱,大连外国语大学;李艳株,大连外国语大学;敬圣明,大连外国语大学。

因素的影响，产生开裂、空鼓、粉化、脱落等病害。①

外因主要是指城墙周围的自然环境和人为活动对城墙造成的损害，如地下水位的变化，雨水的侵蚀，空气污染，交通振动，文物保护不力等。这些因素加速了城墙的风化和老化，造成表面泛白、掏蚀、风化、彩绘褪色等病害。②

二、西安城墙现代保护的成就

近些年，西安城墙全线完成了文保展示、交通改造、生态提升、文化复兴、城市发展5个方面的巨大蜕变。面对全国诸多城市遇到的文物保护与城市发展的共性难题，西安城墙探索出一条历史文化遗产保护与城市现代化和谐共生的道路，将历史遗址无缝衔接式地融入了城市生活圈，堪称世界范围内的遗址保护典范之作。③

在保护措施和系统部署方面，主要有以下几点。

（一）预防性保护体系

在30余年的工作实践中，西安城墙不断积累总结、强化巡查监测、维护保养和防灾减灾，坚持定期预警研判、实施关键修缮工程等环节，初步实现了"预防性保护"系统化闭环管理，"预防性保护"体系初步搭建完成。具体系统架构如下。

1.日常巡查体系："1+n"巡查工作模式

随着对以往修缮工程的不断回顾与反思，西安城墙率先创新实行了"1+n"巡查工作模式："1"是负责巡查工作的文保部门，"n"则是城墙管理机构全体职工乃至普通游客及市民。新的巡查模式旨在发动集体力量，全员参与巡查，加强监督检查力度，做到发现及时、汇报及时、应对及时。多年来，西安城墙管理部门一方面加强定期定时巡逻机制，强化职能部门的保护意识，另一方面鼓励社会各界、国内外组织和个人出资参与城墙的保护。

2.搭建全覆盖监测体系：8000余个监测点位实现全覆盖

为全面、及时地掌握城墙病害及发展趋势，做到早发现，早应对，西安城

① 冯楠，王蕙贞，王肃等.西安城墙"泛碱"病害分析及保护研究.文物保护与考古科学，2012，24(2)：26-30.
② 冯楠，王蕙贞，王肃，宋迪生，朱泓.西安城墙"泛碱"病害分析及保护研究.文物保护与考古科学，2012(2)：26-30.
③ 张桦，亿里.西安古城墙的功能演变及科学定位//陕西师范大学西北历史环境与经济社会发展研究院，中国古都学会.中国古都研究(第三十八辑)，2019：13.

墙与专业团队共同探索出监测经验——人工巡查＋监测＋研判，实时掌握病害情况，这样的体系为综合勘察全面掌握病害情况提供了保障。同时，城墙专家组与地铁、人防、交通、勘察等部门的联动联席研判，将城墙病害了然于心的同时，更能第一时间应对各类突发问题，在最短的时间内形成保护方案，有效提高遗产安全系数。截至目前，已经做到了墙体、古建筑、周边水体、地铁、游人行为等监测全覆盖，点位8000余处。

这些监测措施从城上到城下、从文物本体到游客行为，基本做到了全覆盖，尽管还没有做到全城全自动实时数据传输，但已经为城墙的预防保护提供了翔实的科学依据。

3. "四色"分级预警理念

在坚持不懈持续监测的基础上，西安城墙保护的相关组织分析了近20年积累的监测数据，通过多项抢险工程反复验证和系统性模拟实验，结合病害发展规律，率先在全国创造性地摸索总结出"四色"分级预警监测体系：即分别针对城墙墙体及古建筑，以沉降、裂缝、位移的变化量和速率，按照病害程度从低到高分为绿、黄、橙、红四个险情等级，设置触发预警阈值，对每一种险情等级，制定出相应的应对措施和工作预案，结合定期研判会，使得管理者对城墙的任何变化随时了然于心，防患于未然，基本杜绝了极端情况的发生。

（二）科学研判确保最小干预

最小干预原则是指在保证文物安全的基本前提下，通过最小程度的介入来最大限度地维系文物的原本面貌，保留文物的历史、文化价值，以实现延续现状、降低保护性破坏的目标。西安城墙保护过程中，专家和政府各部门通过对已发生的和可能发生的各种情况进行研究判断，尽可能采取对点修复，对点解决的方案解除可能发生的不良情况，以维护西安古城墙的原本面貌。

西安城墙管委会委托专业单位对西安城墙西南区域南门瓮城、西南角台等重点部位进行了三维激光扫描，通过扫描获取墙体外立面现状点云数据，获取破损城砖面积等量化信息数据，通过分析明确检修标准和工作量，使得对西安城墙的保护达到预期效果。

（三）法律法规保障与应急预案等安全风险管控

2009年8月，西安市人大常委会通过了《西安城墙保护条例》，当年11月正式施行。条例从法律上严惩破坏城墙的行为，同时还明确了文物、规划、建设、市政、土地、园林、旅游、环保、公安等行政管理部门负有保护城墙的职责，建立起各部门共同保护城墙的联动机制。而西安城墙管理机构，在法律法规保障之外，也形成了"1+n"管理机制。此外，涉及西安文化遗迹保护的法律条例共 20 多部，在巡查、监测、修复、保护，应急处理等方面层层把关，在全民监管，全民参与情况下，发现城墙受到破坏需要维修的问题，反馈给西安城墙管理机构，及时解决。"城墙维护到今天，没有发生极端性破坏事件，和城墙管理机构与全民共同保护是密不可分的。"

（四）新技术开发与应用

2021 年 9 月，兰州大学核科学与技术学院两位骨干教师，带着由两位工程师以及四五位学生组成的团队，利用缪子成像技术中的强度衰减成像方法，"给城墙做CT"。这种原理是缪子在物体内部穿行过程中会损失能量，而当其能量损失殆尽时便会被物体吸收，这将使探测到的缪子强度减小，所以宇宙射线缪子强度减小量取决于物体的厚度及材料密度。因此，在已知物体外部轮廓的情况下，通过探测缪子强度衰减，可以推导得到被探测物体的密度，从而对物体的内部结构与物质组成进行重构。这个团队成功测试出了城墙中的低密度区域——也就是一个配电室。在测试团队事先并不知道的情况下，他们通过宇宙缪子成像技术清晰地呈现出它的位置、形状、大小。这种宇宙射线缪子成像技术利用的是不需要人工放射源产生的天然射线，具有无接触勘探、不受时空限制、不会对勘探物体造成任何伤害、绿色环保等优点。[①]

（五）严格保护与适度开发相结合

多年来，陕西省、西安市始终恪守保护第一的宗旨，以此为前提，在不伤害西安城墙原真性的基础上，对城墙进行修缮还原，明确要求西安城墙管理部门应统筹规划西安城墙的使用，防止过度开发。其他任何单位和个人不得擅自利用西安城墙进行生产经营等活动。这是一条高压线，任何单位和个人不得触碰。以此为前提，城墙向游客开放，并通过在城墙上举办冬季马拉松比赛、正月十五闹花灯，城墙自行车运动等群众喜闻乐见的活动，取得了良好的社会效益和经济效益，从而达到了保护与开发双赢的理想效果。

---

① 严萌，张婷.西安古城墙的保护和发展.现代企业，2016，(3): 53-54.

（六）修缮保护与绿色保护相结合

1983 年以来，陕西省和西安市对古城墙进行了大规模修缮，补建已被拆毁的东门、北门箭楼、南门闸楼、吊桥。在修缮的同时，融入绿色保护的理念，城墙四周修建环城公园和市民健身广场，既方便了市民休闲健身，也美化了环境，从而使这座古建筑焕发了昔日风采，成为西安的一大旅游景观。

（七）加强城墙周边的环境保护措施

西安城墙"墙林河路巷"五位一体融合发展的模式，对城墙的管理及文物巡查提出了新的要求，既要保障城墙的安全，还要兼顾城市的发展和群众的生活需要。这就要求，西安城墙的遗产巡查避免局限化与工具化，要在坚持原则的基础上，强调灵活性和人性化，平衡城市发展与遗产保护之间的矛盾。

（八）文旅融合新举措

在传承方面，西安城墙景区大力发展文旅融合，以"让文物活起来"为目标，构建"敬畏＋热爱＋尊重＋传承＋复兴"五位一体的西安城墙文物保护利用模式。围绕"千年古都·常来长安"文化旅游新品牌，策划推出了一系列文化艺术活动，从深层次挖掘了千年城垣的文旅资源。吸引了国内外大量游客前来游览。

三、西安城墙保护工作存在问题

（一）全民保护参与渠道急需提升

西安古城墙作为我国的重要历史文化遗产，其保护和维护问题已经引起了国家和社会的高度关注，但是，尽管政府已经投入大量资金和人力进行保护，全民保护参与渠道仍然不足，民众参与保护积极性也不高。目前并未出现长期稳定运营的有关"西安城墙保护"这一话题的交互交流平台。如公募资金主要通过西安城墙保护基金会以公众号推送的形式向社会传播，这就使可参与公众群体受到了极大的限制。更加稳定，长期，官方的参与渠道亟待开通。

（二）保护资金的匮乏

从具体项目来看，古城墙保护中的资金匮乏主要集中在几个方面。首先是古城墙巡视和巡查的经费。由于西安古城墙的面积较大，巡视和巡查需要投入大量的人力和物力，这将会增加保护的成本。其次是古城墙的维修和整治。西安古城墙的历史悠久，在经过多年的风雨侵蚀之后，墙体和石雕出现了不同程度的损坏，需要进行维修和整治。但这需要大量的资金投入，最后是古城墙周边配套设施的完善。完善周边配套设施可以方便游客欣赏和参观古城墙，但这也需要大量的资金。而古城墙保护的专项基金非常有限，除政府投入外，资金主要来自西安城墙保护基金会与其他公益基金会签约，或是争取公司企业的合作。这样的资金链并不能稳定运作。综上，西安古城墙保护中资金匮乏问题突出，需要加大资金投入。同时，政府和社会各界也应该加强宣传和推广，引导更多的企业和个人投入古城墙保护中，为西安古城墙的保护出一份力。

（三）城墙保护相关法律法规不够细致详尽

在西安古城墙保护过程中，城墙保护相关的法律法规不健全是一个显而易见的问题。当前的法律法规存在一些缺陷，如缺乏明确的保护责任和机制、保护措施不严谨。这些问题都限制了古城墙保护的进展。

首先，现有的古城墙保护法律法规主要包括《中华人民共和国文物保护法》《古城墙保护规划》等。然而相对于其他文化遗产保护法规，这些法规显得过于笼统和简略，无法全面细致地规划古城墙保护。

其次，关于西安城墙保护的具体法规，现行的仍然是 2009 年西安市人民政府修订的《西安城墙保护条例》，至今已有 14 年的时间，其间并未有过更新修订。其中部分内容较为狭隘，较难适应当前法律监管需要。例如关于"破坏行为"的界定和处罚中有明显模糊的内容。这就为法规执行过程的监管增加了难度和松动之处。

（四）城墙基础研究不够完善

对于城墙的基础研究还比较浅显，大部分研究停留于可见研究，使用的研究方法为常规物探方法。常规物探方法中，或需要对目标物进行破坏勘探，或很难穿透目标物，或精度不够，让大型目标物内部探测成为一个困扰多年的难题。新型、环保、安全的宇宙射线缪子成像技术提供了一种全新解决方案。但目前对于城墙内部的具体情况，夯土层实际老化情况还是处于试探和不断假设、实验的阶段。兰州大学为西安古城墙所做的基于宇宙射线缪子的健康"CT"体检，这是国内首次实施的缪子成像技术对大型文物古迹的实验研究，[①]并未大范围应用。技术性的局限使西安城墙的基础研究不够全面清晰，这就为西安城墙修缮工作中的"对症下药"带来了难度。

---

① 王迎霞，颉满斌，赵英淑等.国产设备给西安古城墙做"CT".科技日报，2023-03-17(8).

四、国内与国外文化遗产传承发展的对比分析——以英国约克城墙为例

英国是一个历史悠久的国家，有着许多古老的城市和名胜古迹，其中约克就是一个杰出的典型。英王乔治六世就曾经说过，"约克的历史就是英国的历史"。约克郡的城墙是英国最长的，也是维护得最好的。圣玛丽修道院的围墙也具有国家美学、考古和历史价值，被认为是英国中世纪修道院中保存下来的最好的。因此，考察约克的城墙保护情况，为西安城墙提供一条可借鉴的传承发展保护之路，是本部分的对比分析目标。

约克城墙的长度约 5.5 公里，大部分城墙高度为 4.6 米，城墙的建造始于约 13 世纪，但直到 14 世纪才完工，城墙主要由石头和砖块建造而成，约克城墙上有四个主要城门，分别是摩纳哥门（Monk Bar）、崔斯特姆门（Bootham Bar）、麦克斯韦尔门（Micklegate Bar）和河门（Walmgate Bar）。城墙上的塔楼：城墙上有多个塔楼，其中最著名的是克里夫顿塔（Clifford's Tower），它是一座圆形的石塔，位于城墙的西南角。

自然保育管理计划（the Conservation Management Plan，CMP）极大地推动了约克城墙的保护发展，其目的是提供：城墙的历史和发展及其文化背景的总结；重要的总体陈述；按剖面评估城墙的重要性，包括其设置；总结影响或可能影响墙壁重要性的问题等。

该文件并非作为最终的一劳永逸的参考工作，而是为当前的决策和前瞻性的保护管理奠定基础。CMP 计划每三年更新一次，以确保这一历史遗址得到长期保护。

CMP 在制定过程中征询了广泛的利益相关方的意见，包括约克考古信托基金、英格兰、约克城墙联络小组、约克郡博物馆信托基金、约克大学等。

故约克的古城保护在很大程度上离不开民间人士的支持与努力。今天英国的各种保护历史遗产的组织不计其数，仅全国性的就有古迹协会、不列颠考古委员会、乔治团体、古建筑保护协会、维多利亚协会、英国遗产保护组织、英国历史保护信托组织、建筑遗产基金会等。通过热心人士和民间组织的努力，英国古城古街古迹的保护更多地是一种民间共同的意愿，而不仅仅是政府行为。

相比之下，西安古城墙作为我国的重要历史文化遗产，其保护和维护问题已经引起了国家和社会的高度关注，但是，尽管政府已经投入大量的资金和人力进行保护，全民保护参与渠道仍然不足，民众参与保护积极性也不高，全

民保护参与渠道急需提升。西安城墙应坚持落实其创新的"1+n"巡查工作模式，完善奖励机制，也可效仿英国约克城墙书写并公示CMP的措施，为社会各界、国内外组织和个人出资参与城墙保护提供相关信息与渠道。

此外，在CMP中，约克城墙采用了细致的预警标准，根据不同地段，不同部位进行针对性划分。

五、经验启示

通过对比，我们可以得到以下经验启示。

（一）民间人士的支持与努力

约克的古城保护在很大程度上离不开民间人士的支持与努力。约克城墙在市政当局拆除的情况下，有识之士自发地组织起来，先是向议会提交请愿书，呼吁反对拆除城墙。在反对无效、部分城墙和门楼被拆的情况下，人们自发组织起来，成立相关的民间组织，不仅为古城墙的生存奔走呼号，而且积极筹措资金，运用民间的力量恢复被拆除的城墙设施。到19世纪中叶，不少城市有了类似保护古建筑的民间组织。1877年，英国的城市化已经向着高度城市化方向发展，城市的扩建、改造在全国铺开，古城、古建筑在面临更多威胁的情况下，一些激进分子创造了"古建筑保护协会"（Society for the Protection of Antient Building），把全英范围内有志于保护古建筑的热心人士组织起来，发动更大的保护攻势。今天英国的各种保护历史遗产的组织不计其数，仅全国性的就有古迹协会、不列颠考古委员会、乔治团体、古建筑保护协会、维多利亚协会、英国遗产保护组织、英国历史保护信托组织、建筑遗产基金会等。

（二）全方位保护

约克的保护是全方位保护，不仅是保护老古董，而且还运用各种渠道，因地制宜地建设新"地标"。如在教堂的底部，挖掘出罗马时期和诺曼人时期的原址，就被小心保护起来并作为博物馆。维京人约维克考古发掘后，就建一个与周围环境协调的维京人中心，用时光隧道把人们带到那个时代的氛围中，既不是公园化其遗址，也没有建设豪华博物馆，陈列些呆板的展品了事。约克的几条石头街，还是中世纪人们踩踏的鹅卵石，肉铺街还是窄窄的小巷，房子仍然是石头房。约克既不泥古，也不排斥现代，而是全方位、全视野地保护其城市特色。

六、国内文化遗产保护传承与创新发展的建议

西安城墙保护的成功经验与其目前存在的部分问题启示我们：保护古文化遗址首先要平衡保护和开发之间的关系，可以从以下方面入手。

（一）完善预防性保护

目前，民间遗址保护团体和志愿者组织的力量薄弱，系统性和规模化不足，这制约了遗址预防性保护的提升。因此，必须通过一系列具体措施，全面加强志愿者队伍建设。

1.加强遗址保护志愿者队伍建设

现阶段，民间遗址保护团体和志愿者组织发展相对薄弱，缺乏系统性和规模性。要进一步提升西安城墙及其他遗址的预防性保护水平，政府应加大对民间保护组织的支持力度，并促进志愿者队伍的建设和发展。

政府可通过实施系统化的激励政策和活动设计，吸引更多公众特别是年轻人参与到遗址保护中来。一方面，政府可与高校建立合作机制，开设文化遗产保护相关课程或设立保护实践项目，让学生在理论学习与实践参与中增强保护意识和能力。另一方面，通过社会媒体平台传播保护理念，定期举办线上线下互动活动，例如保护知识普及、参观体验项目等，增强公众的认同感和责任感。此外，可设立奖励机制，如颁发证书、表彰优秀志愿者等，鼓励更多志愿者积极参与遗址保护工作。

为了优化志愿者队伍管理，政府应开发或引入在线管理平台，集中登记志愿者信息，制定分工方案，实时分配任务，并记录志愿者的参与成果。通过该系统，可以实现对志愿者活动的高效协调和动态跟踪。同时，利用数据分析工具定期评估志愿者参与的效果和效率，针对薄弱环节及时优化管理和运营模式，为志愿者团队提供精准支持。

提升志愿者队伍的能力是确保遗址保护工作质量的核心措施。定期举办培训班和交流会，邀请遗址保护专家为志愿者讲授专业知识，例如遗址特性、保护方法和相关法律法规，并提供实践操作指导。此外，可通过实地案例分析和技能模拟培训，帮助志愿者掌握更多实际操作技巧。交流活动也可以搭建经验共享的平台，让志愿者间相互学习、解决问题，共同提升工作水平。

2.提倡全民保护

文化遗址保护不仅是职能部门的任务，更是全民的长期责任。通过一系列

方法，广泛动员社会力量，将保护意识融入全民行动中。

政府与相关部门需要通过多渠道宣传保护意识，利用各种媒体渠道，包括电视、广播、报纸、互联网等，宣传古文化遗址的历史价值和保护意义。可以通过制作专题纪录片、发布公益广告、在社交媒体上开展互动活动等方式，向公众传达保护遗址的重要性和紧迫性。

在学校教育中融入遗址保护内容是培养公众保护意识的根本途径。从小学到大学，应设计符合不同年龄阶段的文化遗产保护课程或活动。小学阶段可通过图文教材和实践体验让学生感受到遗址的魅力；中学阶段可组织遗址参观活动和主题竞赛；大学阶段则可开设专业课程、鼓励学生参与志愿保护项目，从而将文化遗址保护融入学生的成长过程，形成长期影响。

在社区层面，政府应定期联合社区组织策划保护活动。例如，组织清理遗址周边环境、开展遗址知识讲座、举办社区范围的遗址保护宣传周等，通过基层活动提升公众的参与度。同时，可以邀请遗址专家走入社区，与居民开展互动交流，增强社区成员对遗址保护的归属感和自豪感。

3. 推动修复技术标准化

遗址保护技术的科学性和普适性直接关系到保护工作的成效。通过技术标准化，建立高效、规范的修复体系，可以大幅提升保护的可持续性和有效性。

制定修复技术标准，组织文化遗产保护领域的专家团队和科研机构，系统梳理现有技术，结合不同遗址的特性和保护需求，制定详细的修复技术标准和操作规范。具体措施包括明确材料选择标准、优化工艺流程、细化质量检测机制等，以确保修复工作的科学性和规范性。例如，针对城墙的具体修复问题，可详细规定如何选择符合历史原貌的砖石材料、修复过程中如何最大程度地保留原有结构等。

建立技术指导和培训体系，设立专业技术培训中心，通过定期举办培训班或工作坊，向修复从业人员和志愿者传授最新的修复技术和操作方法。同时，应编制一套涵盖技术理论、实践流程和案例分析的技术指导手册，提供标准化的操作指南，帮助保护团队在具体修复工作中科学执行。此外，可利用数字技术建立线上学习平台，方便从业人员随时学习和更新知识。

优化技术研究与应用机制，通过加强政府与科研机构、技术企业的协作，推动遗址保护技术的创新研发。例如，可以设立专项研究基金，支持对古建筑材料、修复设备和工艺的深入研究，并将成熟的技术成果推广应用于实际修复工作中。与此同时，应组织技术应用评估，及时反馈修复过程中的问题，不断完善技术标准和应用模式，确保遗址保护技术的持续改进和标准化普及。

（二）充分挖掘城墙内在的历史人文价值

1.本体价值的挖掘

作为中国古代城市传统防御设施，城墙及与城墙有关的文物、实物或图片对研究封建社会的城市建设、历史文化、军事防御和建筑艺术，都有很高的价值。要加强对民间相关文物的收集整理和研究，加大对城墙文化的宣传力度，做到既合理保护古城墙，又充分开发其内在价值。

2.文化集群的价值挖掘

将西安城墙与其他文化遗址联系起来，形成集群优势，推动旅游业的发展，同时增强文化遗产的价值和传承。将西安城墙与附近的其他著名文化遗址（如兵马俑、大雁塔等）联动起来，形成文化遗址的旅游集群。通过联动的方式，游客可以在一个较小的范围内游览多个重要的文化遗址，提高游客满意度。同时，联动还可以促进旅游资源的共享，增强各个文化遗址之间的吸引力和影响力。

（三）继续完善城墙周边的环境保护措施

西安城墙的保护不仅依赖本体修缮，还需注重周边环境的系统治理，尤其是交通、生态和景观的优化。

1.制定车辆分流举措

针对城墙周边的交通压力，需制定科学合理、可操作性强的车辆分流措施。例如，通过设置明确的机动车限行区域，将出入城墙内外的车辆进行分流，引导部分车辆绕行。同时，建设城墙外围停车场，配套公共交通接驳服务，减少机动车对城墙区域的直接影响。

2.规范车辆停放与通行

严格规定城墙周边的车辆停放和通行，划定专门的停车区域，并对非法停车和超速通行行为进行有效监管。可以利用智能监控系统，对违规行为实时记录与处罚，保障城墙周边道路的秩序和通行效率。

3.统筹绿化与生态保护

以护城河为核心，进一步加强城墙周边的绿化工作，形成连续的绿色生态带。例如，在护城河两侧种植本地特色植物，优化景观布局，同时建设步道和生态休闲区，打造集文化、生态、休闲于一体的综合保护带。此外，可通过引入雨水收集与再利用系统，加强水资源的循环利用，践行生态保护和绿色发展理念，彰显城墙保护的现代化与可持续性。

（四）与现代商业相结合适应市场需求

1.系统而长远的规划

系统规划是让文化遗产和现代商业有机结合的关键。应注重规划的具体细节，创造清晰的认知和清晰的目标，并在事实上以策略性的方式缩小差距。例如，通过吸引当地文化机构、社区组织和信息技术公司等合作，可以设计和执行规划，并确保城墙保护与历史文化的完整性，同时加强现代商业的竞争力。

2.组织文化创意活动

组织文化创意活动可以提高城市的文化内涵和旅游吸引力，带动经济的发展。在城墙保护的过程当中，可以开发旅游景点，推介文化旅游产品，吸引更多人来观光，以此来促进城墙的可持续发展。保护西安城墙并将其融入历史空间中的一系列社会活动，将人们与遗产紧密联系在一起，是可持续性的核心体现。这些活动包括世界级的体育赛事、文化活动和其他自发活动。在经济、政治、文化飞速发展的现代社会中，西安城墙通过各种活动手段被赋予了各种精神文化取向，这符合遗产在人们的教育、影响和丰富精神感情中的作用。

综上所述，文化遗产和现代商业并不是截然相反的关系，二者是应该相结合的。在西安古城墙保护和开发中，应从注重规划、做好社区管理、组织文化创意活动以及鼓励民间投资和创新等多方面入手，促进城墙的可持续发展，为后人留下一份宝贵的文化遗产。

七、结　论

本研究从完善预防性保护入手，深入梳理了西安城墙保护历史，西安城墙保护的成功经验启示我们：保护古文化遗址首先要平衡保护和开发之间的关系。在目前已有的保护措施下，西安城墙存在着全民保护参与渠道急需提升、保护资金的匮乏、城墙保护与开发之间的矛盾等多种问题，阻碍了文化遗产的可持续发展，本研究将通过回顾过去的保护举措，梳理现有措施，通过与英国约克城墙案例对比，分析得出如何在当前环境下，与现代商业相结合适应市场需求，促进城墙文化遗产可持续发展。

世界文化遗产继承与传统工艺创新
——苏州园林[①]

摘　要： 本文主要介绍了苏州园林的概念、历史背景、基本门类、工艺特色、传承发展现状、存在的问题、对比分析以及建议。在传承发展过程中，苏州园林面临着承载能力与游客分配不均、人文内涵宣传乏力等问题。通过对比国内外文化遗产传承发展的经验，提出了苏州园林传承保护与创新发展的建议。

关键词： 苏州古典园林；传承；创新

一、研究背景

文化遗产是具有历史、艺术和科学价值的文物，它直观地反映了人类社会发展的这一重要过程，具体有历史的、社会的、科技的、经济的和审美的价值，是社会发展不可或缺的物证。保护文化遗产就是保护人类文化的传承，培植社会文化的根基，维护文化的多样性和创造性。近年来，我国文化及相关产业发展规模不断扩大，文化新业态行业产业结构不断优化，投资规模不断扩大，人员占比不断提升。

苏州古典园林是位于江苏省苏州市境内的中国古典园林的总称。苏州古典园林是建筑、山水、花木、雕刻、书画的综合艺术品，集自然美和艺术美于一体，构成了曲折迂回、步移景换的画面。苏州全市现有园林 60 多个，其中拙政园和留园被列入中国四大名园，并同网师园、环秀山庄与沧浪亭、狮子林、艺圃、耦园、退思园等 9 个古典园林，分别于 1997 年 12 月和 2000 年 11 月被

---

① 作者：刘偌瑜，大连外国语大学国际关系学院；于芷玄，大连外国语大学国际关系学院；管锦驰，大连外国语大学英语学院。

联合国教科文组织列入《世界遗产名录》。根据年代不同列出的苏州四大名园为"宋代沧浪亭""元代狮子林""明代拙政园""清代留园"，彰显出苏州古典园林是世界园林的瑰宝。苏州古典园林作为一门空间艺术具有独特的魅力，作为文化载体，它积淀了丰厚的文化底蕴。其庭院式的空间布局，建筑与自然、室内与室外融为一体的环境设计；充满人文精神的中国儒道"天人合一"的造园思想；因地制宜、顺应自然、藏露疏密、虚实远近、变化统一的辩证思维；相互渗透的空间层次，步移景移的时空间序列的表现手法都令人叹为观止[①]。

苏州古典园林所吸引人的不应该是它本身，而是它的独特特点和人文内涵。目前，人们对苏州古典园林印象多数仅停留于它是一处景点，并不了解它背后的精神内核和独特寓意。本文着重以上述典型园林为例，不断挖掘苏州古典园林的独特性，还原它本身的人文内涵，同时针对上述现存问题进行调研，着力研究发展传承苏州古典园林文化的解决方法。

因此，我们小组在本次苏州工作坊项目中选择了苏州古典园林作为研究对象。通过本次选题研究，我们希望可以更加深入地了解苏州古典园林的奥秘。我们希望可以通过自己的力量让更多的人真正了解到这个在中国文化历史长河中留下浓墨重彩的绚丽成果——苏州古典园林，并吸引更多的人才来了解、学习、研究、保护、传承、创新它。

本研究希望通过田野调查、问卷调查、文献研究等方式，更深入地了解苏州古典园林作为文化遗产的现状以及在传承与创新这一文化遗产的过程中可能面临的困境，并想出解决的路径。

研究小组通过田野调查法，去实地观察人们对苏州园林的游览状态，同时在身边生活中，尽可能地寻找苏州古典园林的文化元素。通过对数据的查找与分析，研究小组能观察到苏州古典园林的游览量是可观的。在调查的后期阶段，研究小组对身边人进行问卷调查，选取了部分典型问题进行调查，结果真实度较高，但数据的科学性较低。研究小组还对其他相关行业进行了解，发掘能够传承苏州古典园林文化的具体方法。

首先，研究小组对苏州古典园林文化传承现状提出问题，现如今，节假日期间园林内经常出现人山人海、人头攒动的现象，从而影响游客观赏体验。一座园林的美需要人们静下心来去发现、体悟，而在占地面积极为有限的园林

---

① 倪苏宁.论苏州古典园林空间的艺术特征.苏州：苏州大学，2002.

里，过多人员流动容易导致游客疲乏、失去观赏耐心、变得烦躁，对景点的观赏走马观花，有时甚至仅仅是象征性的"网红打卡"，粗略跟着导游泛泛看几眼，这样的旅游事实上是无甚意义的[①]。游客并没有感受到苏州古典园林的独特寓意和所保有的人文内涵。

其次，研究小组进行苏州古典园林的实地调查，并进行文献研究。调查过程中问题频出，苏州古典园林的游览量数据相对客观，苏州古典园林文化的元素也在某些影视剧中和游戏中体现，但通过问卷调查的结果来看，大家对于苏州古典园林的文化内涵并不熟知。

于是，小组成员对现状进行分析，找寻其他文化传承的成功案例进行方法研究。借助于成果案例的思路，在此之上改进创新。最后，得出可落实性方法，同时对于研究过程中不科学之处进行总结、反思（见图1）。

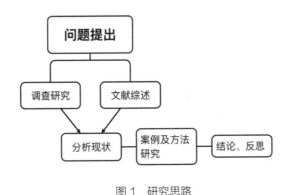

图1　研究思路

二、文献综述

苏州古典园林一直以来备受学者的关注，不论是对其建筑技艺的研究还是文化内涵的研究，我们选取代表性文献，主要对三个方面进行研究，苏州古典园林的特点、跨学科角度解读苏州古典园林及对其的创新发展。通过对以上类型的文献进行研究，我们能更好地找到所继承的苏州古典园林方向，更加细化地对其进行了解。在创新方面，还能借助已有的研究成果发展新的研究方向。2010年，匡振鸥、张慰人、贺凤春主编的《苏州园林》，主要介绍了苏州园林的历史沿革、地域文脉、景观与意境、空间经营和造园思想等。文中还主要以

---

① 林曦文，潘家坪.遗产经济视野下苏州园林的发展问题研究.中国林业经济，2021(1)：39-42.

十大名园为例，介绍其历史发展、意境特点和设计手法①。也有部分学者对苏州园林进行美学研究。衣学龄、周苏宁、沈亮等编著的《苏州园林魅力十谈》和金学智编著的《苏园品韵录》这两本书同属于苏州园林和绿化管理局出版的"园林文化丛书"，前者通过展示苏州园林各个要素，让读者去发现建筑之美、山水之美、花木之美和四季之美，从而了解苏州园林意境之美。后者则不仅让读者用更深的视角去感悟园林的文化、思想内涵，还引导读者从更大的文化背景层面上去领悟苏州园林的文化、历史、人文意义。②

还有学者通过跨学科融合角度，运用符号学重新解读苏州古典园林，胡冬晴月在《苏州园林中的文化解读》中提到中国古典美学精神在苏州园林建筑中体现为园林的意境、神韵，是人们对于苏州园林潜在印象的一种新的解构与诠释。③

近年来，对于文化的创新也是热点话题，杨紫微在《浅析苏州园林文创产品品牌化发展》这篇文章中通过对苏州园林IP化，打造苏州古典园林的品牌文化，用文创来带动苏州园林的影响力，用文创结合时代发展，构建以"IP"为核心的文化生产方式④。刘玉蓉在《融入研究性学习的中学园林单元课程开发与教学实践研究》中将中国古典园林的文化内涵和审美价值融入中学的美术教育之中。⑤

三、苏州园林概述

（一）苏州园林的背景概述

1.苏州园林的概念及内涵

苏州古典园林，亦称"苏州园林"，是位于江苏省苏州市境内的中国古典园林的总称。苏州古典园林溯源于春秋，发展于晋唐，繁荣于两宋，全盛于明清。苏州素有"园林之城"的美誉，境内私家园林始建于前6世纪，清末时城内外有园林170多处，现存50多处。

苏州古典园林宅园合一，可赏，可游，可居。这种建筑形态的形成，是在

① 匡振鹍，张慰人，贺凤春.苏州园林.北京：中国建筑工业出版社，2010.
② 衣学领，周苏宁，沈亮.苏州园林魅力十谈.上海：上海三联书店，2010；金学智.苏园品韵录.上海：上海三联书店，2010.
③ 胡东晴月.苏州园林中的文化符号解读.重庆广播电视大学学报，2019，31(3)：17-25.
④ 杨紫微.浅析苏州园林文创产品品牌化发展.今古文创，2020(45)：47-50.
⑤ 刘玉蓉.融入研究性学习的中学园林单元课程开发与教学实践研究.上海：华东师范大学，2017.

人口密集和缺乏自然风光的城市中，人类依恋自然、追求与自然和谐相处、美化和完善自身居住环境的一种创造。苏州古典园林所蕴含的中华哲学、历史、人文习俗是江南人文历史传统、地方风俗的一种象征和浓缩，展现了中国文化的精华，在世界造园史上具有独特的历史地位和重大的艺术价值。以拙政园、留园为代表的苏州古典园林被誉为"咫尺之内再造乾坤"，是中华园林文化的翘楚和骄傲。

2. 苏州园林历史背景及发展变迁

苏州古典园林的历史可上溯至公元前 6 世纪春秋时期吴王的园囿，私家园林最早被现存文字记载的是东晋（4 世纪）的辟疆园，当时号称"吴中第一"。以后历代造园兴盛，名园日多，至明代建园之风尤盛，清末时城内外有园林 170 多处，苏州赢得了"园林之城"的称号。

明清时期，苏州成为中国最繁华的地区之一，私家园林遍布古城内外。在 16—18 世纪的全盛时期，苏州有园林 200 余处，保存尚好的有数十处，并因此使苏州素有"人间天堂"的美誉。明清时期，苏州封建经济文化发展达到鼎盛阶段，造园艺术也趋于成熟，出现了一批园林艺术家，使造园活动达到高潮。最盛时期，苏州的私家园林和庭院达到 280 余处。

1997 年 12 月 4 日，联合国世界遗产委员会第 21 届全体会议批准了以拙政园、留园、网师园、环秀山庄为典型例证的苏州古典园林列入《世界遗产名录》。

2000 年 11 月 30 日，联合国教科文组织世界遗产委员会第 24 届会议批准沧浪亭、狮子林、艺圃、耦园、退思园增补列入《世界遗产名录》。

从自然条件看，苏州是典型的江南水乡，河湖水网交错，多地下水，在园内营建池泽十分方便；土壤肥沃，气候温暖湿润，适合各类植物生长，容易形成繁盛的景观植被；造园所需的另一石景原料也供应充足，近有太湖东西山，远有水运所及的常州、宜兴、昆山等地的各色石料。

正是因为有着如此优越的造园条件和优势，苏州早在吴国时期就已经有了造园活动的记载，此后历朝历代，苏州城内外的造园活动都绵延不绝。隋代大运河开通后，以苏州为代表的江南地区日益成为全国最为富庶的区域之一，这为园林营建奠定了坚固的经济基础。唐宋时期苏州城免于战火，经济和文化保持了稳步发展，宋代苏州还以"花石纲"闻名，种种奇花异石源源不断贡向京城。明清时期，江南的商品经济领先于全国，普通市民都以在房前屋后开辟小型庭园为时尚，再加上不少退休、失意官员热衷于在苏州造园，以及诸多造园艺术家、文人雅士的积极参与，遂形成了苏州造园史上的鼎盛时期，成为全国著名的"园林城市"。

苏州园林作为历经千百年积累形成的风景景观，虽然每一位园林设计者都崇尚并致力于营造一种回归自然的情境，但这种营造和建构本身即是人的主观愿望的集中反映。人们将对生活的美好祈愿经过精心设计而具象化，再经过工匠施工形成这样一个富于生灵的环境，可以说是一种人工自然。换言之，苏州园林的构景要素还是山、水、植被、建筑，但作为景观的构园要素都已经被赋予了人的主观色彩、被注入了人文内涵，进而使得每位入园者面对园中景观时的感受，都与特定个人所处知识和文化背景密切相关。

正是因为被赋予了浓厚的人文内涵，苏州园林景观才能给观者以精神上的愉悦。与广场、绿地等可以体现一种公共空间意识的大型城市景观不同，园林景观由于受空间限制，除了精心设计营造生态景点外，更赋予生态景点一种个性化的人生理想和价值观，出发点虽不同，但这两类景观设计的共同点都可以立足于以人为本和人类对美好生活的期待[①]。

3.苏州园林的基本门类与工艺特色

其基本门类有：私家园林，如沧浪亭、狮子林、拙政园、留园、网师园、艺圃、环秀山庄、耦园；佛教园林，如报恩寺（北寺塔）、西园、寒山寺、双塔、瑞光塔；王家园林，如虎丘（吴王阖闾墓）、灵岩山（吴王行宫）。

其中沧浪亭、狮子林、拙政园和留园分别代表着宋、元、明、清四个朝代的艺术风格，被称为苏州"四大名园"。

其工艺特色为：一是叠石理水。江南水乡，以水景为常，水石相映，构成园林主景，可供赏玩。二是花木种类众多。多奇花异木，江南园林有得天独厚的自然环境，加上园艺教师的精心培育，使得园林的花木四季如春。三是建筑风格淡雅朴素，布局自由，建筑结构不定型，一反宫殿庙堂住宅之拘泥对称，而以清新洒脱见称。

其布局特点为：空间布局上呈现出花园与住宅分立统一的态势。从局部与整体两个视角看苏州古典园林的结构布局，其特点是不同的。就园林整体布局来看，花园与住宅呈现出分立的局面。就园林局部布局来看，景观与建筑又是

---

① 臧公秀.苏州园林的景观学分析以拙政园为例.苏州大学学报（工科版），2009，29(5): 144-146.

统一的，呈现出宅中有景，园中有宅的特点。

（二）苏州园林的传承发展现状

1.整体发展面貌

许多园林目前是公有产权，得到了政府的良好保护。在可持续发展的前瞻性政策下，政府出台了《苏州园林保护和管理条例》，同时，规划园林控制地带，实行禁止在区域内建高楼等保护措施。苏州园林的良好保护加之到位的宣传，使得其旅游业非常火爆，著名园林如拙政园、狮子林等游客络绎不绝。目前为了控制人数从而达到观赏效果，已经采取了分时预约游园的方式。由苏州园林带起来的旅游产业链不断壮大，周边民宿、酒店业、餐饮业蓬勃发展。

2.基本行状

专门性的园林服务单位出现。为更好地满足园林发展的需求，各种类型的具有单一作用的服务性质的园林单位出现。如，具有宣传作用的苏州园林博物馆于1992年建成开放；负责园林档案的苏州园林档案馆于2000年挂牌成立；负责世界文化遗产的苏州市世界文化遗产古典园林保护监管中心于2005年底成立，亚太地区世界遗产培训与研究中心（苏州）于2008年成立；负责园林苗木的苏州园林苗场于1958年筹建。

目前苏州园林以旅游业为主，学校、公司、企业也会在园林举办游学团建活动，同时也有传统文化，物质文化遗产类相关活动举办。

3.传承发展方式与路径特点

苏州古典园林本于自然而高于自然，强调天人合一、人与自然和谐相处的哲学观，达到诗情画意的艺术效果。江苏园尊重生态基底、浓缩山水意象、蕴含水乡情调，继承了天人合一、追求诗情画意的造园思想。在编制公布4批《苏州园林名录》对其中108处园林予以群体性保护的基础上，苏州市园林和绿化管理局借助实景建模、大数据等先进技术，建立一批苏州园林全景数字模型，详细记录苏州园林内的空间布局、园林要素以及建筑颜色尺寸、材质纹理等信息，全面展现其精巧细致和精湛技艺。目前，苏州已建成虎丘全景数字模型及33处园林古建筑和假山的数字模型，完成拙政园、沧浪亭等10余处园林720度全景VR。采用线上线下结合方式传承苏州园林文化。

和一些知名度较高的品牌联名，例如，泡泡玛特、top toy中国积木、中国李宁等；与银行卡、当地市民卡、当地高校学生卡进行联名；将各个苏州古典园林的历史、与之相关的逸事作为一些手游与网游的故事情节主线或者是世界观架构，或者是开展与之相关的主题活动。通过将苏州古典园林文化要素融于影视作品，以故事情节讲述各个苏州园林的前世今生；通过间接的方式弘扬苏州古典园林的文化内涵；以苏州古典园林为世界观框架来讲述发生在各个园林里赋予苏州古典园林精神内核的奇闻逸事。

在中小学增设苏州古典园林相关校本课程；发挥本科教育在培养基础型、学术型人才和专科教育在培养技术型、技能型人才的两方面优势；发挥学科优势，大力推进产教融合，切实提高专业整体实力；加强国际高校间的交流，依托多种国际组织的平台以及孔子学院向世界各国介绍苏州古典园林；促进多学科交叉，培养综合型园林人才；增加与苏州古典园林相关的实践项目。

4.苏州园林传承发展存在的问题

（1）苏州园林体量大无法进行模式复制到其他地区，给人们亲身了解园林造成不便。

（2）"数字建模"能够提高传播性使其更好的传播，但技术尚不成熟稳定，造价也极高，并且目前的技术并不能使人完全身临其境。

（3）发展过程中对于园林的保护法不够完善科学。

（4）缺乏保护苏州园林的专业人员。

（5）过于重视开发，轻视保护资源。

（6）景区整体环境需要提升，包括但不限于从业人员整体素质、园区内环境、文创产品的设计质量、商品定价等。

（7）设计困境：联名品牌缺少相关设计师；苏州古典园林元素较多，易引起消费者的审美疲劳；设计、营销创新性有待提升。

（8）游戏困境：游戏设计趣味性难以把控；还原苏州古典园林细节对程序技术要求较高。

情节困境：影视类作品难以在还原苏州古典园林文化内涵是兼顾趣味性，且部分史实有待考证。

（9）固有困境：承载能力与游客分配不均。

（三）苏州园林发展现状及困境

1.发展现状概述

苏州园林极具中国古代建筑色彩，虽占地面积不大，但别具一格，以特殊的建筑手法，将山水花鸟和诗词意境融合得恰到好处。园林内，亭台楼阁、流水小桥、山石绿植，一应俱全，每一个地方都有其独特之美，艺术效果尤为震撼。

苏州园林小巧而精雅，蕴藏着"自然美景构成的原则和技巧"。它身在城市，却满是山林意趣。身居闹市的人们一进入园林，仿佛来到了千里之外的世外桃源，于是再浮躁的心也得以安放。在园中行游，或见"庭院深深深几许"，或见"柳暗花明又一村"，或见小桥流水、粉墙黛瓦，或见曲径通幽、峰回路转，或是步移景易、变幻无穷。园内的四季草木枯荣，更是让人们可以"不出城郭而获山林之怡，身居闹市而有林泉之乐"。苏州古典园林的特点特性如下。

首先是讲究排场、体现身份。不少苏州园林主人曾为官僚，拙政园主人王献臣，明弘治进士，历任御史、巡抚等职。沧浪亭主人苏舜钦，曾任县令、大理评事、集贤殿校理，监进奏院等职。留园主人徐泰时为嘉靖年间太仆寺卿。网师园主人宋宗元为乾隆年间光禄寺少卿。耦园主人为清末安徽巡抚沈秉承。

其次是模仿自然、顺应天道[①]。隐居城市的目的是既要保障物质生活需求又要不出家门能体味山林野趣，于是园林主人借鉴山水画理，缩龙成寸，模山范水，把自然风景引进园内。从文化根源讲，模仿自然反映了中国人的基本宇宙观。人法道，道法自然的结果是园林布置模仿自然，背后蕴藏的这种深刻思想内容，是中国文化中最基本的也是最核心的内容。微缩自然的难题由山水画理论成功解决，使园林山水"一峰则太华千寻，一勺则江湖万里"，极力模仿自然的园林。苏州园林实质成为中国文化核心的表现物，反映了人对宇宙的敬畏。

然后是山水画理、写意意境[②]。从造园角度讲，在小面积宅院内叠山凿池，模仿自然山水，建造具有居住、游赏、象征三重功能的私家园林必须借用山水原理，因为山水画式的移山缩水写意手法成功地把高山江湖缩写在数尺画纸上，做到了"小中见大"。造园借此手法创设山水意境，象征隐居。

写意是中国艺术的重要表现手法，中国人的美感因地理环境、民族、时代、观念、心理活动诸因素影响而具有独特性，中国人在审美活动中对于美的主观反映、感受、欣赏和评价与西方往往大相径庭，集中体现在中国重个人精神表现与西方重客体再现的艺术观。山水画意境解决了私家园林空间狭小的

---

① 孙艺嘉. 浅析苏州私家园林艺术文化内涵. 青年文学家, 2013(22): 202.
② 仰观. 苏州古典园林山水与文化的完美结合. 环境导报, 2003(2): 32-33.

问题，以假山小水池象征自然山水，同时解决了在城市居住的"隐居"标榜问题。

再次是内敛含蓄。许多园林主人是遭贬斥的官场失败者，内心充满愤怒、失落、和哀怨，这些情绪通过题名标榜、附会圣贤的主题布置，含蓄巧妙地把自己与先贤联系在一起，以此平定内心冲突，平衡情绪。如留园濠濮亭以庄子在濠水濮水的隐居故事，布置水池，放养鱼儿，将自己附比成拒绝楚王邀请出山做官的庄子；五峰仙馆以太湖石堆叠假山附比隐居庐山五老峰的李白；曲溪楼借中部一泓池水，引出兰亭雅集的故事，附比兰亭聚集的君子……凡此种种，无不委婉含蓄，内中却又深藏风骨，真实地体现中国文人复杂丰富的内心世界。古代的造园者多能诗善画，造园时多以画为本，以诗为题，通过凿池堆山、栽花种树，让文字意境与山水之美自然和谐地糅合到一起。

除此之外，苏州古典园林极具象征表意。象征可以把一些难以言说的意思通过物象表达，园林借物象表意是主要手法之一，耐人寻味。植物象征很普遍，如留园中部划分水池的小蓬莱种植紫藤，每逢春天，紫色花串覆盖整个廊桥，象征祥瑞。拙政园梧竹幽居植梧桐树和竹，传说凤凰只吃梧桐籽，梧桐被民间看作招引凤凰的吉祥树，竹节节向上，又有高风亮节的文化涵义，合在一起象征迎祥。

最后，苏州古典园林名称意蕴深刻。与其他景点相比，古典园林在命名上更为含蓄隽永。无论是侧重于表现园林之景还是传达观景之情，抑或将情景相交融，园林的名称都有着"言有尽而意无穷"的意蕴，体现出士人阶层独特的审美旨趣。园林的命名规则详见表1。

表1 园林的命名方式

命名方式	数量	特点
以园林主人姓氏、园林所处地名来给园林命名	43座	这一类命名方式较为常规。
以园林景色命名：如环秀山庄、拥翠山庄、听枫园、塔影园、倚晴园、拂水园、惠荫园等	23座	这类命名方式将观赏者的主观情感融入园林美景之中，体现出"天人合一"的审美追求。
以园林带给人的感受来命名：如留园、畅园、可园、遂园、怡园等	9座	强调园林带来的愉悦感，侧重于审美主体的感受，体现出士人由关注外物转向向内探求的心态。
以园林主人高洁隐逸的志趣命名：如拙政园、网师园、退思园、耕乐堂、师俭园等	25座	将园林作为庙堂与林野之间的缓冲地带，在隐居生活中，达到人格的完善，完成自身的精神建构。园林以精神净土的形态存在。

苏州园林不仅代表着中国古代园林文化的精髓，更承载着中国园林文化中思想、美学、历史、政治等方面的内涵。苏州园林蕴含着丰富的中国古典哲学理念，最突出的是"天人合一"理念，即万物与人为一体，人与自然和谐。此外，园主多为贬谪、隐退的官吏或崇尚风雅、无心爵禄的名士，他们在仕途上都有过执着的追求，在历经仕途凶险之后，逐渐泯灭原有的建功立业的伟大抱负，萌发了退隐之心，所以选择在苏州这个江南小镇，建造园林，因此，"退隐"成为苏州园林的基本文化内涵，无形中形成了一种园林退隐文化[①]。

2.发展困境

（1）苏州园林的承载能力与游客分配不均。近年来，苏州园林的游客数量大幅上升，导致一些重要园林的人满为患，不堪重负。园林内景致、实物、环境质量遭到破坏，失去了其本色，影响了园林在游客心目中的形象。这种状况不仅加速了园林资源的分配，也使一些小园林的门庭冷落，游客数量偏少。因此，园林承载能力和游客分配不均已成为当前园林业面临的问题。

（2）人文内涵宣传乏力。横向对比徽州西递宏村、北京皇家园林这两个园文化内核宣传模式已经相对成熟的优秀案例，苏州园林在其人文内涵的宣传和推广方面还显稚嫩。北京皇家园林具有其得天独厚的历史底蕴，并且长期作为首都文化宣传构成的重要一环，其文化内核已广泛传播并被大众接受，与物质遗产相辅相成，构成其强大的文化吸引力；徽州园林代表西递宏村，依托周边黄山这一重要自然遗产资源，具有附带的市场知名度，并深度挖掘其徽商文化与中国古代商帮文化宣传结合，突出其"创业守成，勤俭温恭"等文化内涵。而苏州园林缺少的人文内涵和精神属性的宣传，导致游客对其慕名而来，但是缺乏参观深度，缺少精神产出。

（3）缺少综合型优质园林人才。目前园林景观类技能型人才的数量和质量均无法满足用工需求，相关教材有待更新，教师资源匮乏。

根据园林发展现状我们可以发现：

首先，行业领域不断扩展，市场空间巨大。

随着中国经济的持续发展和城镇化进程的推进，市政园林的投资力度逐年加大，伴随着行业投资规模的扩大，行业已经从传统的道路景观绿化、市政公园、城市广场、公共绿地、厂住区绿化逐步延伸到了森林公园、流域治理、生

---

① 施伟萍.苏州古典园林隐逸文化生态漫谈.名作欣赏，2020(8)：18-19+35.

态湿地修复、矿山环境治理等领域。行业投资规模的扩大说明我国园林行业正从传统公园景观向森林等大型园林工程转变，这给园林工程行业的人才供给提出了要求。而苏州园林所需人才即可归于此类范畴。

其次，跨区域经营及行业集中度逐步提升。

近年来，随着园林绿化行业快速发展，行业项目规模迅速扩大，尤其是大中型 BT 项目（国企合作）的涌现为行业集中度的提升提供了基础性条件，与此同时，行业内收购兼并、大型合作项目的增加，部分优质上市企业依托资本实力逐步实现跨区域经营，其营业规模增长幅度远快于行业发展水平。

最后，一体化经营对复合型人才提出要求。

在行业发展初期，我国的园林行业以中小企业及政府运营官方园林及遗址为主，大多数企业仅专注于园林行业中的一个业务环节。随着人们对环境要求的提高，一体化经营逐渐成了行业发展趋势，政府与企业逐渐将园林工程施工、园林景观设计、苗木种植和绿化养护等相结合，实现多模块共同经营发展。一体化经营要求企业具备了解各业务环节的专业技术人才和经营管理人才，因此对复合型人才的需求将逐渐增大。

本文对园林行业人才供需情况进行了分析。首先，园林行业人才仍处于供不应求状态。当前我国园林行业技术人才仍然处于供不应求的状态，特别是园林科研、生产技术推广、苗木养护、绿化工程、工程管理、预算和规划的技术人才的供给较少，难以满足行业需求。园林人才供不应求的状况在全国大多数城市都有体现。

其次，园林从业人员技术水平良莠不齐。

最后，综合性园林人才缺乏。目前，我国园林行业的从业人员多数是只懂得一门专业或技术的人员，综合性人才匮乏。专家指出，一个合格的园林人才要同时具备植物环境生态，建筑规划设计、艺术美学欣赏能力，而目前我国大多数园林人才仅仅掌握以上三种能力的其中之一或之二，缺乏综合能力的培养。例如工科院校的园林专业往往是在建筑学专业基础上向园林方向的适当偏移，毕业生对植物知识了解不够；农林院校的园林专业的毕业生侧重于园林绿化，缺乏建筑设计能力；综合性大学的园林专业则偏重于区域规划或是对景观地理学的深化和延伸；艺术院校毕业生更偏重于视觉的感受，对园林的工程技术知识了解甚少，所以目前许多园林专业人才相关知识欠缺，综合素质偏低的现象普遍存在，这就造成了我国园林工程实践上的很多混乱。

本文还对大众对于苏州园林的了解程度进行调查。本次调查共设计问题 9 个，有效作答人数 166 人，呈现数据结果概述为：大众对于苏州园林的了解及参观意愿均不及皇家园林，对于苏州园林缺乏深入了解的动机及兴趣，印证了前期对于苏州园林人文内涵宣传乏力的困境。

四、苏州园林传承发展对比分析

（一）传承发展的理念特色

1.价值取向对比

国内文化遗产传承发展的价值取向主要是为了继承和弘扬中华文化，强化国家认同感和文化自信心。而国外文化遗产传承发展的价值取向则更加注重保护和传承人类共同的文化遗产，强调文化多样性和跨文化交流。

2.资源优势对比

国内文化遗产传承发展的资源优势主要在于丰富的历史文化遗产和庞大的国内市场需求。而国外文化遗产传承发展的资源优势则在于先进的技术和管理经验，以及更加成熟的文化产业市场。

（二）传承发展的现状和模式

1.动力机制对比

国内文化遗产传承发展的动力机制主要是政策引导和社会力量参与，政府在文化遗产保护传承方面发挥着重要作用。而国外文化遗产传承发展的动力机制则更加注重市场和社会力量的推动，政府主要起到监管和协调的作用。

2.路径模式对比

国内文化遗产传承发展的路径模式主要是以国家重点文物保护单位和文化遗产保护利用示范区为主要路径，同时注重文化遗产的社会化利用。而国外文化遗产传承发展的路径模式则更加注重文化遗产的商业化利用，以文化旅游和文化产业为主要发展方向。

（三）传承发展的经验启示

1.成功案例

国内文化遗产传承发展的成功案例包括故宫博物院的文化遗产保护和利用，以及丽江古城的旅游开发和文化传承。而国外文化遗产传承发展的成功案例包括埃及金字塔的保护和旅游开发，以及意大利威尼斯的文化遗产保护和商业化利用。

2.经验总结

国内文化遗产传承发展可以借鉴国外的先进技术和管理经验，同时注重政府引导和社会参与的动力机制。国外文化遗产传承发展可以学习国内的文化遗产社会化利用和保护利用示范区的经验，同时注重跨文化交流和文化多样性的保护。

五、苏州园林传承保护与创新发展的建议

（一）"苏州园林"中人与"苏州园林"的互动关系

中国传统建筑以木结构为特色，木作匠人先在工场按照图纸加工制作木构件，然后在现场进行组装，搭建起了建筑的骨骼。在木工场工匠使用不同种类的传统工具来制作不同的木构件。在工地现场工匠们站在竹子搭成脚手架上安装一座六角亭木结构。木作工匠们按照设计图纸搭建起了亭台楼阁的骨骼，园林开始有了初步轮廓。

木作完成后，瓦作工匠会先铺一层望砖，之后在望砖上再铺设大小青瓦，除此之外，技艺精良匠人还要塑脊与砌筑戗角。砌筑戗角是一项对技术要求更高的工作，通常由技艺高超的匠人来完成。戗角砌筑完成后，建筑就有了飘逸的感觉。

石头大小、形态要仔细分类，做到心中有数，再仔细清理其中的杂质，露出石头的自然形态。假山的形态要源于自然而又高于自然，从自然中来，但又要比自然精彩。山无水不秀，景无水不灵。假山工匠先沿着水岸线打入木桩，以作为维护与支撑。之后按照设计形态堆砌石头，做出自然形态的围石驳岸。当然，为了防止水池渗漏，工匠们会用油灰嵌牢缝隙。木桩一头削尖，靠重锤砸入土中，几排木桩下去，为驳岸石提供了一个基础。靠着肩扛手搬，驳岸石被砌筑起来。古代用来防水补漏的是油灰，油灰是用熟桐油与石灰搅拌而成。

石作的部件也是在工场先大概加工好，然后再运至现场安装，并做适当的调整。石作工匠会按照设计，制作安装园林中的踏步、石桥、亲水平台的栏杆、礓石、鼓磴、石柱、石桌石椅等。与堆假山不同，石作是以石为材，加工成建筑园林部件，体现的是工艺之美。工人们合力抬着一块加工好的石料，走过石作师傅们刚刚做好的石曲桥。石柱、石栏杆、石凳、石桌都出自石作工匠之手。

油漆工匠在木作上做生漆工艺，亭台楼阁木结构上那种板栗色的光洁漆面，就是这种工艺的常见效果。当然了，粉墙黛瓦的漆面效果，也是出自油漆工匠之手了。在园林建筑上最常见的颜色是板栗色。工匠们仔细粉刷墙面、花窗，建筑立刻有了生气，光鲜了起来。

苏州园林的植物种植以不对称、不整形、自然式种植为基本手法，注重与其他造园元素的互相映衬，注重高低疏密的搭配，注重品种四季变化之美，注重美好寓意的思想寄托。常用的是竹子。有山则有林，依照着山势，遵循着自然法则，工人们把各种植物点缀于山上。而在掇山之时，就已经为树木的种植预留了空间。

精美的铺装是苏州园林的一大特色，除了组织交通的基本功能外，还具有丰富的文化内涵。根据不同的环境主题，铺装的内容与形式变化多样，表达出园林设计的寓意内容。花街铺地是用瓦面切条拼出图案，中间填充各色的鹅卵石为铺面，不同的图案代表着不同的寓意，花街多用在自由布局的园林道路之中。

古代匠人用高超的技艺、辛勤的汗水和追求卓越的匠心，为姑苏、为江南、也为中国留下了一座座园林艺术瑰宝。这些存世园林的意义，不仅是在于能供世人游赏，更在于为复兴道路上的中华民族，提供了中国人居精神的风骨选择。

（二）"苏州园林"工艺的传承与创新路径

1.分类保护，探索新的传承方式

保护是传承的前提。通过实地走访，上门走访，开展座谈会等方式，根据每一处园林的历史沿革、保存状况、维护状况、园林类型、目前用途等情况将园林进行分类并向园林管理者、使用者、产权者，以及苏州市文物局、教育局、旅游局、规划局、住建局等相关部门征求相关的意见和建议，将这些园林的分类状况登记在册。推进名录编制、地方立法、技术标准、保护规划等工作，参照世界遗产的管理方法，对不同状况的园林进行不同程度的保护，尤其对破坏程度较为严重的园林采取更多的措施，投入更多的资金与人才进行重点维护。坚持保护与管理并行的原则，做好园林的保护者、传承者。

2.新旧融合，扬弃发展

从空间布局、设计方法、传统仪式等方面将苏州古典园林与现代景观风格进行比较与融合，取其精华，弃其糟粕。保留原来已有的苏州古典园林，与木

匠、瓦作工匠、石匠、油漆工匠、盆景工匠、铺装工匠等各个环节的优秀大师"取经"，了解传统手工技艺，结合现代科技。

较之于古典园林景观，现代景观更倾向于大尺度使用绿化，以绿色构筑呈现"人工自然"。设计把绿化带来的视觉享受放在第一位，却忽略了该地区环境和地理条件是否能够完美驾驭这种过于"繁华"的人造景观，在这种情况下，现代景观的违和感日益突出。这种不假思索的景观构筑方式，不仅造成了人力财力的浪费，同时也破坏了原来和谐的城市自然人文环境景观。在城市不断发展的今天，各种人造景观通过配合现代建筑一同构成城市景观，然而现今的绿化却往往是比例失调。由于交通条件的改善，现代人融入真山真水之中已十分便利，无须再在城市之中尽享山林之乐，而真山真水的气势及其丰富的景观环境却是假山假水难以比拟的，导致以人工山水为主的古典园林失去了存在的必要性，紧紧抱住古典园林形式不放不利于中国园林的发展。在传承创新过程中，我们应该更加注重园林景观的实用性，与现代社会境况相适应，这样才能更好地宣传苏州园林，让大众更易于建立保护、传承苏州园林的思想观念。

与此同时，我们还可以将苏州园林与室内设计相融合，从日常生活中深化大众对于苏州园林的喜爱。提取苏州园林这一传统文化符号，抽象成一个文化概念，并将其融入进室内设计之中。例如，苏州园林中的：亭、台、楼、阁、轩、榭、廊、桥、洞门、漏窗、装饰图案等典型符号，具有浓厚的中国传统文化氛围，是室内设计的好素材，贝聿铭的苏州博物馆就借鉴了苏州园林的元素，屋顶设计的灵感来源于苏州传统的坡顶景观——飞檐翘角与建筑细部。然而，新的屋顶已被科技重新诠释再就是，整个建筑与苏州传统的城市肌理相融合，为粉墙黛瓦的江南建筑符号增加了新的诠释内涵。强化在室内设计传统文化的认同感。贝先生对传统符号没有直接提取，而是抽象的表达[①]。对传统文化的认识应当是合理、创新的。传统造型的形态特征、装饰图案是民族文化的长期积淀，这要求设计师将传统元素的造型做简化，又演化出多种抽象，变形运用到设计当中去。

同时，我们还可以将苏州园林与服装设计相融合。以苏州园林的漏窗艺术元素为例。漏窗装饰是运用于建筑和园林中的一种满格的装饰性透空窗，是构成园林景观的一种建筑艺术处理工艺，俗称为花墙头、花墙洞、花窗，通俗一

---

① 田人羽.苏州园林艺术与当代室内设计中的融合.南京：南京林业大学，2011

点讲漏窗是窗洞内有镂空图案的窗。苏州园林中的漏窗样式多，还有不同的寓意，其设计手法也多种多样，如果将漏窗装饰要素与服装设计结合起来，那么会给服装带来视觉、触觉等方面不一样的感受。苏州园林中的漏窗样式之多，号称世界之最，光窗框就有矩形、菱形、多边形、圆形、月牙形、宝瓶形、桃形等；中间的窗芯更是成百上千，例如定胜、六角景、菱花、书条、套方、冰裂、鱼鳞、钱纹、球纹、秋叶、海棠、葵花、如意、波纹等。面料作为服装设计三要素之一，其重要性不言而喻，面料的创新会给整件服装带来新颖感，而这里所指的面料创新可以包括材质的创新、面料再造、面料图案设计等[1]。如果要将苏州园林的漏窗装饰要素与服装设计相结合，其中一种方法就是直接将漏窗图案印在服装面料上。漏窗图案本身具有极强的装饰性，而且带有强烈的民族特色，将漏窗图案印在服装面料上，可以使得该种面料呈现出特有的视觉效果。苏州园林的漏窗样式很多，因此可被当成印花图案的也就多，在服装面料图案设计时，设计师可以根据自己所需来选择不同的漏窗图案。除了直接运用原有的漏窗图案，设计师还可以对这些漏窗图案进行变形、重组、拼凑的手法来组成更丰富的图案样式，甚至还可以将漏窗图案与其他图形一起进行设计，从而来达到设计师所期望的效果。漏窗图案不仅可以直接印在服装面料上，也可以绣在服装面料上，改变服装的触觉，使得漏窗图案在面料上表现得更立体，装饰性更强。正如苏州园林中为了增强围墙的局部观赏功能，常在围墙的一侧作成镂空模样，实际上并不透空，另一侧仍是普通墙面，这样的做法比直接在墙面印上漏窗图案来得更有装饰性和立体感。

3. "苏州园林"工艺人才的培养与传承路径

现在苏州园林工艺人才传承正面临着市场竞争激烈、工匠地位和待遇降低、专业人才流失、老年化严重和工艺手法走样等困境。因此我们需要采取以下措施。

（1）弘扬工匠精神，加强宣传。

与各部门通力合作，响应国家号召，弘扬工匠精神，宣传保护、传承、发展苏州园林的重要性。多多组织苏州园林工艺技术分享交流会、苏州园林游园会，邀请苏州园林工艺大师开展座谈会、讲座，让更多的年轻人感受到苏州园林工艺的魅力。

① 张鸣艳，李正.浅析苏州园林漏窗装饰要素在服装设计中的运用.大众文艺，2012(23)：74.

（2）完善激励机制，鼓励批量化人才引培。

在大学开设苏州园林技艺相关的本科、研究生、博士专业以及课程，邀请行业内"大师"担任当地知名大学的相关专业教师，提高相关教师的工资报酬以及相关从业人员的薪酬待遇。开设更多的研究项目、提高相关项目经费。发挥本科教育在培养基础型、学术型人才和专科教育在培养技术型、技能型人才的两方面优势，坚持立足区域、立足教学、立足学科，完善人才培养方案，升级课程体系建设，着力培养多规格、多样化的应用型人才。发挥学科优势，大力推进产教融合，切实提高专业整体实力，主动对接江苏经济社会发展和区域产业布局，提高服务美丽乡村建设、服务江苏经济社会发展的能力。

六、结 论

（一）案例研究总结

联合国教科文组织及世界遗产委员会于 1997 年及 2000 年分别将拙政园、留园、环秀山庄等，以及沧浪亭、狮子林、退思园等列入《世界遗产名录》。由此可见，苏州园林在中国历史文化长河中留下了浓墨重彩的一笔。保护文化遗产的重要性更是不言而喻。现在，苏州园林在我们看来依旧令人叹为观止，但其实，苏州园林的创城发展也面临着许多的困境。本小组也将持续深入了解苏州园林本身以及人才培养面临的困境，并不断丰富解决困境的路径。

基于当下的时代背景，苏州古典园林文化的传承面临着诸多的机遇与挑战。"江南园林甲天下，苏州园林甲江南。"苏州古典园林文化是中华文化的瑰宝，不应成为蒙尘的明珠。因此，传承苏州古典园林文化就变得尤为重要。传承苏州古典园林文化需要多种手段相互融合，其面临的困境有承载能力与游客分配不均、人文内涵宣传乏力、园林行业人才供不应求、园林从业人员技术水平良莠不齐、综合性园林人才缺乏等。需要通过多种媒介来提高对苏州古典园林的人文内涵宣传，让更多的人了解各个园林背后的故事，以提高园林的知名度，通过各种手段加强园林人才的技术水平以及培养综合型园林人才。

（二）研究局限性

由于问卷调查的样本量较少，自身理论的局限性以及经验的缺乏，研究还具有很多的不足，需要进一步研究与讨论。

贵州苗族刺绣技艺传承与发展路径研究[①]

摘　要: 贵州苗绣作为我国非物质文化遗产，是苗族文化的重要组成部分，也是一种代代相传的传统艺术形式，主要流传在贵州省黔东南地区的苗族聚集区，色彩鲜明，富有想象力，以苗族的图腾崇拜为主要创造来源。本文就贵州苗绣发展的现存问题，以秦兵马俑史密森尼数字教育和法国刺绣以及苏绣为案例，借鉴其成功之处，探讨人与"绣"的互动关系，展开刺绣技艺传承与发展路径的研究。针对现存问题，我们得出以下解决方案: 生产适销对路的苗族绣品; 拓展传承人范围; 讲好苗族故事，打造品牌效益; 向绣娘统一收购苗族绣片; 制作实用性强的苗族文创产品; 制定营销战略，创新销售方式。

关键词: 文化自信; 传承; 苗族刺绣

一　绪　论

(一) 研究背景及意义

随着生活水平的提高，人们越来越注重精神文化需求，高文化需求就会带来高文化消费，文化遗产作为文化市场的一种产品，因其悠久的历史文化，得到了较高的认同度。但是社会公众对文化遗产保护的意识还比较薄弱，我国大部分文化遗产项目传承人越来越稀缺。不过技术的进步为文化遗产的传承和发展提供了新方法，文化遗产在现代科技手段的帮助下，得到了更好的记录、保护和展示。与文化遗产相关的法规和措施的出台进一步加强了文化遗产的保护

---

① 作者: 梁祝，贵州财经大学ISEC项目办; 王帅，贵州财经大学ISEC项目办; 周媛媛，贵州财经大学ISEC项目办。

和传承工作。贵州苗绣作为我国非物质文化遗产之一，受保护力度较弱其经济效益未被充分发掘，如存在技术创新上的瓶颈，公众对苗绣的认识较为浅薄等。本文正是基于此进行贵州苗族刺绣技艺传承与发展路径的研究。

（二）国内研究评述

从国内的研究看，关于苗绣的研究最早出现于 1990 年，相关研究可以分为三个阶段。第一个阶段是 1989—1998 年，该阶段对苗绣的研究较浅薄，主要研究苗绣的艺术特点，如蒙甘露从历史、技艺、造型、色彩、宗教五个方面论述了苗族刺绣的艺术特点。[①]第二个阶段是 2002—2012 年，这个阶段的研究围绕苗绣的创新应用、艺术性和传承保护三个方面进行。例如，徐斌、李友友探讨了数码技术将苗绣渗透于现代纺织品的设计与制作的可行性；[②]夏晓春从苗绣中蕴含的自然宇宙观和生命观出发，证实苗绣具有极大的艺术性；[③]罗林根据苗绣濒临失传的原因，认为采取保护与开发利用相结合的方法是最有利的。[④]第三个阶段是 2013—2023 年，本阶段是在乡村振兴、现代科技背景下研究苗绣产业的发展。例如，陈晓英以实施乡村振兴战略为背景，根据苗绣的发展现状，提出了推动苗绣产业高质量发展的路径和对策；[⑤]杨和英探讨了现代科技对苗绣的正反面效应，认为传统苗绣需要警惕"技术崇拜"。[⑥]

（三）研究对象及内容

贵州苗绣是苗族民间传承的刺绣技艺，是苗族历史文化中特有的表现形式之一，是苗族妇女勤劳智慧的结晶[⑦]，主要流传在贵州省黔东南地区的苗族聚居区。我们以雷山台江苗族刺绣为主要研究对象，在实地调查时发现，苗绣在文化传承与创新上仍然存在发展空间。由此，我们提出以下问题。

（1）如何更好传承苗族刺绣传统技艺？

（2）如何实现苗族刺绣的现代商业化？

（3）如何让苗族刺绣在传承中创新？

---

① 蒙甘露.苗族剪纸中的民俗文化.中央民族大学学报，1998(3)：109-111.

② 徐彬，李友友.浅析苗绣在数码绣花中的可再生性.装饰，2011(4)：114-115.

③ 夏晓春.黔东南苗绣艺术非理性符号象征.民族艺术研究，2008(5)：55-59.

④ 罗林.试论苗族刺绣的传承与保护.贵州民族研究，2008(5)：66-70.

⑤ 陈晓英.乡村振兴战略背景下贵州苗绣发展路径研究.贵州师范大学学报(社会科学版)，2022(4)：111-117.

⑥ 杨和英.论现代科技境遇下传统苗绣的出路.贵州民族研究，2016(8)：75-77.

⑦ 徐滢洁.民族文创产品助推精准扶贫和乡村振兴研究——以湘西苗绣为例.民族论坛，2021(3)：69-77.

（4）如何让更多的人了解苗族文化与苗族刺绣的魅力？

（5）苗族刺绣的核心文化内涵与技艺？

本研究正是基于上述问题展开。我们致力于发掘贵州苗族刺绣的文化魅力，探讨如何更好地传承发展贵州苗族刺绣，以及更好地促进苗族刺绣的商业化，拓展其应用领域，推动文化创新和经济发展，促进苗绣与其他多元文化之间的交流。

四、研究思路及方法

本研究主要以搜集资料和查阅相关书籍文献为主要方法。同时，我们还前往贵州苗绣的代表地进行了实地考察，主要对贵州黔东南雷山县和"第一苗县"台江进行了市场调研，以了解苗绣的传统文化与技艺和现今市场的真实情况，揭示贵州苗绣市场的商业现状与存在问题。

二、贵州苗绣概述与国内外相似案例

（一）贵州苗族刺绣的背景概述

1.贵州苗族刺绣的概念及内涵

贵州苗族刺绣是一种代代相传的传统艺术形式，是使用五颜六色的线在各种织物上创造复杂的设计。这种刺绣具有丰富的历史和文化意义，深深植根于苗族的传统和信仰、习俗风情和伦理道德，蕴含了苗族人民深沉的情感，是苗族人民表达对自然的热爱和尊重、对理想的追求的一种方式。与其他刺绣艺术不同，苗绣通常是苗族人民记录生活和表达情感的一种载体，兼具文字功能。苗绣上的图案通常是象征性的，代表着生活的不同方面，如爱情、幸福和繁荣，同时也记录着苗族代代相传的创世神话和传说。不同的图案以其复杂的色彩搭配组成的不同场景，表现了苗绣主题的多元化，每一种图案都体现了苗族人民独特的表达方式。凤是苗族刺绣中较为典型的图案，象征吉祥和永生。对于汉族，凤是女性尊贵的象征，而对于苗族，凤不仅是苗族的保护神，更是男性外貌的代表，苗族多用凤为男性起名。

2.贵州苗族刺绣的历史背景与发展变迁

苗绣是苗族文化的重要组成部分，现存的苗绣，起源于古代濮人的雕题文身，这种工艺最初用于装饰服装和家居用品，并经常作为家庭传统从母亲传给女儿。随着时间的推移，苗族刺绣逐渐发展成为一种技艺高超的艺术形式，其设计变得更加复杂和细致，工艺也变得更加专业化，并开发了新的技术来创造不同的纹理和图案，且不同的地区都发展出了自己独特的风格和技术。

尽管苗族刺绣有着悠久的历史和独特的文化意义，但在现代却面临着许多挑战。苗族刺绣等传统工艺面临着工业化和全球化的侵蚀，许多年轻人对学习传统技能失去了兴趣。但近年来，人们越来越重视传统工艺和文化遗产的重要性，新一代的苗族工匠学习工艺，并尝试新的技术和设计，许多苗族社区也在努力推广他们的传统工艺，吸引游客。

3.贵州苗族刺绣的基本门类与工艺特色

贵州苗族刺绣基本有四大类：平绣、立体绣、贴花绣和十字绣。每个类别都有自己的特点和技术。其中，平绣是苗族刺绣中最常见、应用最广泛的一种形式，它的特点是表面平整，针线精细，花纹细腻。立体绣是苗族刺绣的一种更高级的形式，它通过使用多层织物和丝线来创造立体效果。贴花绣是苗族刺绣的一种独特形式，是从一种织物上剪下形状，然后将其缝在另一种织品上，以形成图案。十字绣是苗族刺绣的一种流行形式，它将"X"形缝线缝在织物上以形成图案。

（二）国内外相似案例

1.秦兵马俑史密森尼数字教育

兵马俑，在中国也被称为秦兵马俑，是世界上最重要的考古发现之一。这些文物已有2000多年的历史，通过它们可以深入了解中国古代复杂的社会、政治和军事发展。兵马俑以其历史文化价值吸引了来自世界各地的学者、考古学家和游客。美国史密森尼学会在举办的兵马俑展览上运用了的创新数字教育举措，并取得了显著的成功，引起了广泛的社会关注。

2.法国刺绣

法国刺绣并非发源于法国，而是经法国刺绣师改编，形成了自己独特的刺绣风格。在法国刺绣中，绣娘多追求别具一格，没有固定的绣法，善用亮片、宝石、水晶等炫目的材料，与丝线组合成不同的图案和造型。在法国刺绣的发展过程中，法国的服装设计中的刺绣居于领先地位，迪奥、香奈儿等高级定制奢侈品牌都喜欢将法国刺绣用于服饰，刺绣逐渐成为高级定制界的标志，"高雅"成了法国刺绣的代名词。法国刺绣能够成功，不仅是依靠传统工艺，更依靠创新能力和清晰的市场定位。贵州苗族刺绣可以结合目前的审美和流行趋势创造出更具有吸引力的绣品，提供定制化服务，加强与国内外高端品牌的合作，提升自身影响力。

3. 苏绣

苏绣起源于苏州，创作题材广泛，绣娘们以绘画作品为基础，通过精湛的绣法进行刺绣制作，形成了绚丽精致的独特风格。为了使苏绣得到更好的发展，政府采取了一系列措施，创建专门市场用来售卖苏绣，创办展馆用以展示刺绣文化。此外，政府完善了人才体系，为培养苏绣人才建立了相应的平台，并为他们解决就业问题。同时，作为苏绣材料的丝绸也盛产于苏州，这使得苏绣在成本上极具优势。

贵州苗族刺绣也可以借鉴学习苏绣成功的经验，采取针对性措施，注重人才培养，促进苗绣的传承发展与商业化；同时，还可以利用影视剧电影等IP元素，打造苗族专属IP文化与商业产业链。

三、贵州苗绣传承与发展路径分析

（一）人与"绣"的互动关系

在苗族的历史发展中，苗族人民用针线代替笔墨，将苗族符号绣在服饰上，这些符号使得苗绣的纹饰和图案丰富多彩，是人与"绣"的互动关系的重要体现。苗绣的复杂工艺尤其强调传统手工制作方式，这也成了苗绣的灵魂，这是人与"绣"的第一层互动关系。此外，人们以欣赏、收藏等方式，与苗绣作品进行互动，也会进一步增强这种互动关系。苗绣作为苗族文化的一个重要组成部分，它的形成和发展与苗族的风俗习惯和宗教信仰息息相关，凝结了丰富内涵[①]。苗绣中常常出现几何纹样、动植物纹样和由前两样演变而来的各种纹样，蕴含着苗族的历史和苗族人民的情感。例如，"虎爪花"向大众叙述了苗族人民迁徙到深山时捕捉老虎的故事；蝴蝶和水泡相爱，让蝴蝶变成了妈妈，是"蝴蝶妈妈"神话故事的内容，表达了苗族人民对生活幸福吉祥的祝愿，这是人与"绣"最深层次的互动关系。

（二）技艺传承与发展存在的问题

贵州苗族刺绣进行了一些关键创新，如使用新材料，如竹子和纸张，以及融入新的设计元素，如几何形状和抽象图案。贵州苗族刺绣最显著的创新之一

---

① 吴欣刚.苗族服饰图案纹样在现代服装设计中的视觉表现.商，2015(3): 117.

是数字技术的应用，在计算机软件的帮助下，工匠们可以创造出仅靠手工难以实现的复杂设计和图案；另一个创新领域是可持续材料的使用，艺人们越来越多地使用天然染料和有机织物，以减少其工艺对环境的影响。这不仅有利于环境保护，而且增加了刺绣的价值。

然而，工匠们在发展和推广刺绣工艺方面仍然面临挑战，主要挑战之一是缺乏政府对传统工艺的资金和政策支持。许多工匠靠刺绣谋生，如果没有足够的支持和推广，这项工艺可能会丢失。

为了探究贵州苗族刺绣技艺传承与发展路径，我们研究了以下基本问题。

（1）苗族刺绣的核心文化内涵与技艺。

（2）如何更好传承苗族刺绣传统技艺。

（3）如何实现苗族刺绣的现代商业化。

（4）如何让苗族刺绣在传承中创新。

（5）如何让更多的人了解苗族文化与苗族刺绣的魅力。

在研究了以上基本问题之后，我们通过思考与讨论得出了以下结论。

（1）苗族刺绣商业化的问题根源是无法生产适销对路的绣品。不同的消费者有不同的消费偏好：为了在婚嫁中穿戴使用，当地人更喜欢传统图案和样式的绣品；外地人则更喜欢带一些苗族传统元素但是新颖又好看的。而绣娘们大多根据传统样式，按自己的喜好与设计理念来制作绣品。

（2）苗族审美与当代年轻人审美有隔阂，年轻一代很难对苗族刺绣产生兴趣。

（3）苗族刺绣品牌效益差。苗族文化历史内涵丰富，然而因为知名度不够，流量和热度也不够，很多人都不了解其文化魅力，甚至闻所未闻。

（4）苗族刺绣商品化程度有待提高。很多刺绣品都是整套的苗族节日规格的盛装服，一套下来要一万以上；或者是单片的绣片，价格上千，便宜的绣品只有小荷包，但是绣图太小，设计发挥空间有限，美观度欠佳。总的来说，现在市场上的苗族绣品都存在以下问题：价格昂贵但实用性不高，手工成本高，高价是有合理性的，但是除非顾客深刻了解到苗族刺绣的制作工艺和审美价值，否则很难有意愿购买价格高却使用功能单一的苗绣产品。

（5）绣娘制作绣品分散，无法及时详细地了解市场信息。大部分绣娘都是自发制作和贩卖苗族绣品绣服，部分居家劳务闲余刺绣，逢节假日把自己的绣品拿到市场上售卖，部分以家庭小作坊售卖。有公司统一组织绣娘刺绣，公司再统一加工成商品售卖，但是这类公司很少。

通过以上的传承与创新路径，可以促进贵州苗族刺绣的传统技艺的保护和传承，同时也能够使其与现代社会和市场需求相结合，焕发新的活力和发展潜力。

四、探索发展路径与未来展望

（一）发展路径

1.生产适销对路的苗族绣品

针对不同的需求改变制作方式，生产适销对路的苗族绣品，面向不同市场制作不同的商品，同时还应给创作者们留有空间和机会，在商业化的同时兼顾其艺术性与美学创造性。

在这方面，贵州当地政府做了不少努力，如给予苗绣师傅店面租金的支持，在苗族龙舟节组织比赛等活动吸引游客。当地旅游局还会引导其他地方的游客前来旅游和消费，给当地居民带来经济效益。

六十多岁的老绣娘说她做出来的苗族刺绣主要是卖给当地人，游客很少买，而四十岁左右的刺绣师傅说现在当地市场饱和了，只有做得新颖好看，当地人才会买。近几年，他们主要是卖给外面的人，既有游客，也有外地的商家。

我们认为，促进苗族刺绣市场发展可以从以下几点做起：通过新兴自媒体短视频平台等引流的方式，让更多人了解到苗族刺绣文化的魅力；政府做好相应支持，给苗族刺绣绣娘们留足创作发展空间；鼓励绣娘们创作生产，既有商品性强利于销售的商品，也有创造性高的艺术性强的作品；加强与外地的不同风格苗绣师傅合作，互帮互助；不同技艺各取所长，扬长避短，不断创新；利用旅游业促进苗绣销售，针对不同市场制作不同取向和要求的苗族刺绣品。

2.拓展传承人范围

贵州苗族刺绣的平绣、立体绣、贴花绣和十字绣，每个类别都有自己的特点和技术，完成一件刺绣可能需要数月甚至数年的时间，复杂的技艺就注定了传承者需要极大的耐心与真挚的热爱。

手工产品在现代都市生活中具有的深厚生存发展空间，这点已在世界顶级产品中体现：意大利的高端时尚服饰、鞋帽品牌都是由意大利北部的大量手工作坊生产的[①]，"定制、手工"的个性化产品成为国际一线时尚发展趋势。

贵州苗绣的大部分技法是机器无法替代的，必须依靠全手工完成，"手工制造"是苗绣在现代市场中存在、发展的重要因素[②]；"手工价值"是苗绣进入现代化大都市，找寻自己高品质生存空间的最重要标准。我们已在越来越多的高端品牌中看到苗绣的独特身影，我们应该引领年轻人的审美价值取向，扩大传承人的范围。不一定是苗族后人，只要是对苗族刺绣有浓厚兴趣的人，都积极鼓励他们去传承苗绣技艺。

苗族刺绣最开始是苗族传统婚嫁习俗影响下的产物，在当今被赋予新的意义，能够为当地人民带来可观的收入和经济效益。只要有了收入，就会带动更多的苗绣师傅们去创作更多的作品，吸引更多的年轻人传承苗族刺绣技艺，更好的作品也能吸引更多的人购买。

当地可以与高校合作，像写生旅游一样，利用高校资源，培养高质量的苗族刺绣保护者与传承人；同时也应该加大对苗族刺绣的研究，发现其更多的独特魅力与文化审美价值。

当地可以开设中小学苗族刺绣公开课，请专家进入中小学进行苗绣公开课，讲述苗族刺绣技艺常识及苗族文化内涵相关科普，培养中小学生对苗族刺绣的兴趣，拓宽苗族刺绣传承人来源。

3.讲好苗族故事，打造品牌效益

苗族女孩十几岁就跟着大人或同辈学习织布、挑花等各种女红，之后就要自己动手装扮和准备嫁妆，苗族刺绣既是美化生活穿戴的需要，也是婚前男女双方珍贵的定情物。姑娘们在编织定情纹样时，几乎倾注了她们的全部感情，用一针一线编织着对美好生活的向往和对爱情的坚贞。

苗族有许多关于爱情的美好传说，如黔东南七姊妹的故事：古时张家有7个漂亮女儿，她们都想找到一个可以托付终身的人。有一次，七姊妹到山上采摘树叶，每人煮了一锅彩色的糯米饭，邀请大家到施洞寨吃饭，唱山歌。三天三夜之后，七姊妹终于如愿以偿，找到了各自的如意郎君。

苗绣上常有蝴蝶，蝴蝶是苗族人神话里的祖先，传说能够庇佑孩子健康平

---

① 张楠.长三角传统手工艺产业的创新范式探究——基于意大利的发展经验及其启示.艺术百家，2021(5)：68-75.
② 王振豪，翟李融，梁静等.论贵州苗族刺绣在现代生活中的传承和发展//福建省传播学会.2013 福建省传播学年会论文集，2013：11.

安。此外，苗装伴随着祖先的护佑，象征着新娘的尊贵、幸福。这些丰富的历史文化与神话传说故事，让我们可以利用情怀提升苗绣知名度，打开销路。信息爆炸时代，快节奏的生活让人们的感情难以得到寄托，而苗族人民乐观向上、知足常乐的价值取向，正好可以满足人们对美好生活的向往与期待。因此，结合自媒体平台和短视频平台，讲好苗族故事，有助于打造品牌效益。

贵州苗绣是中国国家级非物质文化遗产，在传承发展的同时与现代设计相结合，如创新刺绣技术，创造新颖独特的作品，有助于促进苗绣产业的升级和转型。完善苗族文化要素将苗绣与苗族传统文化相结合，能够吸引更多游客前来体验和欣赏。要建立以苗绣文化为内核的特色旅游产品品牌，加强品牌建设，打造专属于苗绣的市场推广策略，在国内提升苗绣知名度，让贵州苗绣在国内外更多的领域得到应用和发展。

4. 向绣娘统一收购苗族绣片

苗族刺绣如何更好地商品化和带来更多经济效益的问题，不是建一个公司就能解决的。因为公司只是通过聘请苗族绣娘，批量生产顾客定制的产品，仅此而已。苗族刺绣的复杂技艺就决定了它无法用机器批量生产，而公司生产的产品失去了苗族刺绣本来的魅力。

据了解，很多苗族刺绣绣娘在经历了公司打工，合伙经营之后大多会选择回来，自己开作坊单干。"一直做还可能影响创作，休息几天反而一下子就想到了。而且赚这么多钱干嘛，自己和家人吃饱穿暖就很好了，知足常乐嘛，做多就多卖点，做少就少买点，自己做多少刺绣赚的钱都是自己的，不用给公家（公司）。想做就做，这样也开心。"可见，我们或许应该尊重她们的生活选择，但同时鼓励大家刺绣，然后以市场价统一收购绣片，再由专业的公司加工制作成实用的有苗绣元素的文创产品，从而提高苗绣的经济效益。

5. 制作实用性强的苗族文创产品

苗绣艺术与现实生活紧密相关，其内容贴近日常生产生活，将生活中的美与生产紧密结合，在符合实用的前提下，带给人视觉上的享受[1]；同时，苗绣依存于各种生活用品，如服装，荷包以及各种布什物等，充分体现了实用与装饰共融的统一性[2]。

把苗族刺绣利用在更多的生活用品上，生产出实用又美观的刺绣商品，如

---

① 熊赛.谈苗族刺绣在现代服装设计中的意义.天津纺织科技，2015(1): 56-57.
② 赵峥一，丁密金.苗族刺绣的现代意义.艺术教育，2008(10): 121.

在女士手提包上缝刺绣花纹，在女士皮鞋上缝合绣片等；另外，我们在贵阳喷水池的文创店，还看到了把苗族绣娘的绣片收购之后加工制成的书签。这些都是很好的传承创新思路，能助力苗族刺绣的商业化发展，让苗族技艺活起来，在商品交换的过程中传播苗族刺绣的文化内涵技艺和价值审美。

6.制定营销战略，创新销售方式

苗族刺绣现今的销售方式以线下店面售卖为主，存在顾客少、知名度低、店面租金贵等问题。在"互联网＋"时代，苗族刺绣可以利用线上售卖的方式来拓宽销售渠道。

一方面可以开设苗族刺绣线上售卖网店，或者制作苗族刺绣自己的公众号，定期发布与苗族刺绣有关的小知识、小故事，同时不断更新文创产品，吸引顾客购买。

另一方面可以制定营销战略，在社交媒体页面投放与苗族有关的视频和推送文章；也可开设系列直播，利用当下流行的直播渠道和方式，与专家连线，讲授苗族刺绣知识，直播带货，增加消费客户；也可以制作苗族刺绣系列短视频，持续更新苗族刺绣技艺常识和苗族文化故事等系列短视频；还可以与网红博主合作，制作发布与苗族刺绣有关的新奇创意视频，利用独特且具有文化审美价值的视频，增加苗族刺绣的热度知名度，扩大销量。

（二）未来展望

随着科技发展，人工智能和机械生产代替了人类的许多工作，在这样的科技时代，苗族人却依然喜欢和热爱着老一代的手工苗族刺绣技艺。也许他们改变了一些设计，也运用更好的工具进行了技术精进，但是他们依旧用手一点点手绣，细致构思一针一线，一点点穿针，一点点引线，一点点做出他们想要的图案造型。

每个苗族绣娘都是浪漫和想象的践行者。他们把对神明、对祖先的崇拜，把对大自然的赞美和热爱，都通过双手加上瑰丽的想象，凝聚在了一件件苗族刺绣品上，凝聚在一根根丝线里。这不仅仅是一件件刺绣品，更是苗族人民对生活的热爱，是苗族传统文化里无与伦比的艺术品。

我们在调研走访中深刻地感受到了苗族绣娘们的匠人精神和匠人追求，她们有在传承中改变：不断地追求更精湛的设计、更精美的作品。她们也有不变的：对一些传统图腾和制作方法的坚持，如对蝴蝶妈妈的热爱、对手工针线的着迷。

　　苗族绣娘们在时代的洪流中保持纯真质朴，而苗族刺绣，在岁月的长河里，将会一直用它的绣线和图腾图案，静静地告诉一代又一代人，苗族人民们的纯真热爱与浪漫，在历史的长河中不染尘埃、不染浮躁，永远历久弥新，永远熠熠生辉。

秦始皇帝陵展陈方式的数字化研究^①

摘 要: 本文以"世界八大奇迹"之一的秦始皇帝陵展陈方式的数字化为研究对象,通过查找国内外相关文献以及实地调查研究,分析总结出目前秦始皇帝陵传统展陈方式的局限性。结合秦始皇帝陵在保护、继承、发展、开发等方面存在的,如展陈方式无法满足游客的多层次体验需求、旅游开发难以平衡保护和利用、景区游客过载对古迹的保护造成压力等问题,对比国内外文化遗产数字化保护优秀案例,讨论虚拟现实技术在秦始皇帝陵展陈方式数字化应用中的可行性,从而丰富文化遗产数字保护新路径,探索文化遗产传承创新手段。

关键词: 秦始皇帝陵;文化遗产;展陈方式;数字化;虚拟现实

一、绪 论

(一)选题背景及意义

作为中国历史上的重要文化遗产之一,1961 年 3 月 4 日,秦始皇帝陵被国务院公布为第一批全国重点文物保护单位;1987 年 12 月,秦始皇帝陵及兵马俑坑被联合国教科文组织批准列入《世界遗产名录》。作为中国古代帝王陵墓中规模最大、埋藏物最丰富的一座大型陵墓,秦始皇帝陵是研究秦代政治、经济、军事、科技、社会、文化的重要实物资料,集中反映了秦代在建筑、雕塑、装饰、书法等方面的艺术成就,对于秦代社会、经济、技术、艺术等方面的研究具有重要的价值。

---

① 作者:李腾,西北工业大学计算机科学与技术专业;杨沛霖,西北工业大学计算机科学与技术专业;朱海波,西北工业大学计算机科学与技术专业。

国家与地方政府采取的如建造博物馆、划定保护区、制定保护法规等一系列举措，对于秦始皇帝陵文化遗产的保护、管理与利用无疑都具有十分重要和积极的作用，但秦始皇帝陵的文化遗产资源管理工作仍然存在着一些问题和困难，如景区游客过载、行政管理条块分割、遗址保护和展陈理念手段陈旧单一等。这些问题都直接或间接影响到了秦始皇帝陵文化遗产资源的可持续发展。

因此本研究以秦始皇帝陵展陈方式的数字化为研究对象，横向对比国内外文化遗产数字化保护现状，汲取如敦煌石窟数字化保护等优秀案例经验，结合当下虚拟现实技术、物联网体系与"互联网＋模式"，寻找有利于文化遗产保护与利用，有利于区域社会、经济发展的创新优化模式，为相关管理部门提供决策参考。

（二）国内外研究评述

秦始皇帝陵的保护、继承与开发是国内外学者广泛关注的热点问题。基于目前景区人流量过大导致游客过载、游客体验变差、多元性游览需求无法得到满足的现状，秦始皇帝陵的展陈方式亟须加强数字化应用。鉴于此，国内外研究者提出了一些具体方法和建议，以实现保护、研究和教育的目标。以下是一些常见的具体方法与提议。

1. 保护与开放平衡

使用非侵入性技术：采用无损探测技术，如地球物理勘测、雷达扫描等，对秦始皇帝陵进行隐蔽结构和文物的探测，以减少对陵墓的破坏。

控制游客数量：限制每日参观人数，预约参观或分时段开放，以减少陵墓受到的人为破坏。

2. 展示历史真实

保持原貌：努力保持秦始皇帝陵的原貌，通过定期维护和修复来保护陵墓本身的完整性，避免因为过度保护而导致的文化遗产原貌破坏。

模拟重建：在博物馆或附近的展示场所中，使用模型或虚拟现实技术来模拟重建秦始皇帝陵的全貌，以便向游客展示其在历史上的原貌；或者上线相应的模拟软件，让游客足不出户便可观赏到雄伟的秦始皇帝陵历史遗迹。[1]

---

① Douglass MJ, Day ZR, Brunette JC, Bleed P, Scott D. Virtual Reconstruction as Archaeological Observation: Embracing New Ways of Treating Sites, Places and Landscapes. Advances in Archaeological Practice. 2019; 7(2): 127-139.

3.教育功能强化

互动展示：设计互动展品和多媒体设备，从视觉、听觉、触觉等方面提升游客参与度，从而更深入地了解秦始皇帝陵的历史和文化。

多样解说：提供专业性与趣味性相结合的解说服务，并将解说融入虚拟现实技术打造的场景中，更好地为游客讲解秦始皇帝陵的历史背景、建筑特点以及文物意义。[①]

4.跨学科研究

考古学研究：利用先进的考古技术和方法，对秦始皇帝陵进行系统、综合的考古调查和发掘，以揭示更多关于陵墓的历史信息。

科技手段应用：结合遥感技术、数字重建等现代科技手段，进行非接触性的文物保护和研究，以确保对秦始皇帝陵的准确分析和理解。

这些具体方法和建议旨在平衡保护和开放之间的关系，展示秦始皇帝陵的真实历史面貌，并通过教育功能和跨学科研究来传播其文化价值。同时，技术手段的运用可以提升展陈效果，使游客更好地了解和欣赏这一世界文化遗产，对于秦始皇帝陵的展陈方式的数字化创新与文化遗产传承保护都有很强的借鉴作用。

（三）研究对象及内容

本文的研究对象为秦始皇帝陵展陈方式的数字化，具体未数字化的策略和方法。本文基于分析，指出目前数字化展陈方式的局限性，提出展陈方式数字化新方案，汲取如敦煌壁画数字化保护、埃及金字塔数字化保护等优秀文化遗产数字化保护案例经验，探索秦始皇帝陵展陈方式与虚拟现实技术相融合的可能性，推动数字遗产发展。

（四）研究思路及方法

本文的研究思路是综合利用文献资料、专家访谈资料，结合中外对比、优秀案例参考和现场考察的方式进行研究。具体思路及方法包括：

1.搜集国内外文献资料，从全局角度了解秦始皇帝陵当前所采取的展陈方式。同时，了解国内外学者在虚拟现实等数字化技术在与文化遗产的保护相融合方面的研究成果和研究方向，为研究开展指明方向，避免创新性不足等

---

① Lee H , Jung H T , Dieck T M , et al. Experiencing immersive virtual reality in museums. Information Management, 2020, 57(5): 103229-103229.

问题。

2.在掌握秦始皇帝陵当前展陈方式基本情况后，与一线学者专家对话，学习国内科研机构和文物保护机构相关专家在秦始皇帝陵保护、发展方面的研究理论，了解秦始皇帝陵保护与继承的实际情况和最新工作进展，同时提出创新方案，在访谈过程中分析数字化应用方案的可行性与创新性。

3.文化遗产作为全世界人类共同的财富，在全球范围内都被给予重点保护，但因为文化遗产、国情、宗教信仰等存在国别差异，因而各国的文化遗产保护方案也存在差异。因此，有必要对比分析国内外文化遗产数字化传承保护方案，汲取优秀案例经验，提出创新性策略和方法，探索秦始皇帝陵展陈方式的数字化传承保护可能性。

4.针对前期调研中总结出的目前秦始皇帝陵展陈方式中存在的问题与可行的创新点进行现场考察，通过实地调研验证前期研究成果，以游客的角色获取个人体验感受，为后期对遗产数字化应用中存在问题的分析讨论、创新方案的优化更新提供经验。

二、案例：秦始皇帝陵

（一）秦始皇帝陵的背景概述

1.秦始皇帝陵的概述

1987 年 12 月，秦始皇陵和兵马俑坑被联合国教科文组织列入《世界遗产名录》，其位于陕西省西安市临潼区秦陵山南麓，是秦始皇的陵墓。秦始皇帝陵被誉为"世界第八大奇迹"，是中国历史上最为壮丽的古代建筑之一，也是中国古代陵墓中保存最为完整的一座。

2.秦始皇帝陵的历史沿革与布局结构

秦始皇帝陵的兴建始于秦朝统一六国前期，随着秦国统一六国，秦始皇于公元前 246 年开始规划秦陵建造计划，公元前 247 年开始奠基建造。陵园工程修造了 39 年，直至秦始皇临死之际仍未竣工，二世皇帝胡亥继位，接着又修建了一年多才基本完工。

秦始皇帝陵是中国历史上第一个皇帝陵园，陵园按照"事死如事生"的原则，仿照秦国都城咸阳的布局建造，大体呈回字形。整个陵园由南北两个狭长的长方形城垣构成。内城中部有一道东西向夹墙，正好将内城分为南北两部分。陵园的地面建筑集中在封土北侧，陵园的陪葬坑都分布在封冢的东西两侧。形成了以地宫和封冢为中心，布局合理，形制规范的帝王陵园。

3. 秦始皇帝陵的价值影响与社会意义

秦始皇帝陵是中国历史上第一个集帝王之气、渊源之力、天地之神、艺术之美于一身的实体文化存在，是中国传统文化艺术的瑰宝，具有无可比拟的历史、文化和艺术价值。它见证了中国文化史的发展脉络，展示了中国古代文明的辉煌和壮丽。同时，它也是中国文化艺术宝库中不可多得的珍品，对于人们了解中国古代文化、艺术等具有很大的科学、文化和历史价值。

（二）秦始皇帝陵展陈现状

目前，秦始皇帝陵的保护主要依托秦始皇帝陵博物院，而秦始皇帝陵博物院的遗址展陈又分为秦始皇兵马俑博物馆和秦始皇帝陵考古遗址公园（丽山园）。其中秦始皇兵马俑博物馆包括目前已发掘并对外展出的秦俑一、二、三号坑，而秦始皇帝陵考古遗址公园（丽山园）则主要包括秦始皇帝陵、K0006陪葬坑、K9901陪葬坑、铜车马博物馆。

除线下博览的传统展陈方式外，秦始皇帝陵博物院官网还上线了遗址数字化展陈板块，主要包含遗址发现历史视频介绍、部分代表性展品的大影像简介（视频形式）、展品的数字版本（立体扫描图形式）；秦始皇帝陵博物院官方公众号也上线了智慧导览、互动体验模块，其中智慧导览模块结合"寻迹始皇陵"微信小程序，以互动地图的形式，将秦始皇帝陵博物院各展区用立体地图点标记，游客可直接点击相应展区，获取地图指引；互动体验模块目前开放了"千里驰援""亿像素""锦绣西域华美之疆"三个专题，专题采用互动小游戏、720度全景相机的形式，将展品的展陈与现代数字化新媒体技术结合，打造多元化旅游体验。

（三）秦始皇帝陵展陈方式中存在的问题

作为著名的世界文化遗产，秦始皇帝陵每年会吸引来自全球的大量游客。据秦始皇帝陵博物院院长侯宁彬介绍，秦始皇帝陵博物院自1979年10月1日建成开放以来，已累计接待游客超过1.2亿人次，其中约有2000万人次来自海外。

在巨大的游客规模下，秦始皇帝陵博物馆所采取的传统展陈方式已经明显不再适宜，这种暴露式的公开展陈，不仅无法解决景区人流过载问题，同时也可能由于人为损坏等造成文物的永久性损坏①。

　　同时，秦始皇帝陵当下采用的数字化展陈方式明显已经无法满足旅客的多元化需求。如秦始皇帝陵博物院官网所上线的数字化展陈模块，其在部分展区仅仅包含一段简短的视频介绍，并且在展品的数字化陈列中未实现代表性展品的全覆盖，且其对展品的720度立体扫描图画质较低，使用者无法实现对展品细节的观察，无法达到数字化展陈的目的。

　　在移动端的智慧导览模块中，对展区地图的数字化导航实用价值较小；在互动体验模块中，结合秦朝历史的小游戏较为新颖，但应及时推陈出新，而如"亿像素"小板块中，也是仅结合VR技术进行了兵马俑的720度全景相机扫描，但展品的讲解部分仅以文字形式进行，不够直观，无法让游客身临其境，数字化效果较差。

三、国内外文化遗产传承发展的对比分析——以秦始皇帝陵和埃及金字塔为例

（一）传承发展的理念特色

1.价值取向对比

　　埃及金字塔于1979年入选世界文化遗产，其注重神圣与永恒，强调人类对生死和神秘力量的追求；而秦始皇帝陵则更加注重统一与权威，强调中央集权和国家统一的重要性。

　　对于参访者来说，金字塔的展陈方式给人以敬畏和神秘的感觉，而秦始皇帝陵则给人以宏大和壮阔的感觉。

2.资源优势对比

　　秦始皇帝陵和埃及金字塔作为在人类历史上留下浓墨重彩的一笔的宏伟建筑，它们都在文化传承和追溯历史方面起到了重要作用。然而，从资源优势角度来看，这两个遗迹之间存在一些明显的差异。

　　金字塔的建设主要利用了埃及河岸沙漠地带丰富的沙石和大理石资源，故而金字塔并未采取封闭保护的展陈方式。相比之下，秦始皇帝陵除了承载着丰富的历史文化内涵，还有一众精美的陪葬品，这也使得秦始皇帝陵的展陈方式

① 纳俊丽，马天成.世界文化遗产游客体验分析——以秦始皇帝陵为例.旅游纵览（下半月），2020(2)：159-161+164.

以封闭保护为主。

（二）传承发展的现状模式

尽管秦始皇帝陵和金字塔都面临着来自时间和环境的挑战，但在保护和维护方面所采取的策略却有所不同，使其在展陈方式的现状模式也不尽相同。

与埃及金字塔不同，秦始皇帝陵墓是一个庞大的地下宫殿，整个陵墓内有举世无双的兵马俑和其他陪葬品，因此对秦始皇帝陵的保护工作更加注重保护与展示相结合。在对秦始皇帝陵墓的修复过程中，中方注重保持原貌的同时，也在一定程度上进行了恢复和展示，以展示其历史文化价值。[①]

参观秦始皇帝陵需要购买门票，每个游客都需进行实名制登记并接受安全检查。这一措施旨在确保游客的安全，以及文物的完整。游客可以近距离观赏到各式各样栩栩如生的兵马俑，了解古代造陵的巧妙之处。此外，秦始皇帝陵区还设置了多个展厅和博物馆，供游客了解秦始皇帝和秦朝的历史背景与文化内涵。

相比之下，埃及金字塔由于其价值主要在其金字塔本体，故而展陈方式也主要聚集于本体。首先，游客可以选择传统的步行方式参观金字塔，更好地欣赏这些巨大的石块是如何精巧地垒砌而成的，也可以选择更加舒适的乘骑骆驼、坐马车参观金字塔。

此外，为游客还可以选择搭乘无人机，在空中俯瞰整个金字塔景区，欣赏金字塔的壮丽和独特之处。然而，游客的大量涌入可能给这些历史遗迹带来意想不到的破坏，如人为污染和过度的踩踏。因此，在保护工作中，秦始皇帝陵和埃及金字塔都采取了限制游客数量和加强管理的措施。

但金字塔的高度开放性展陈方式使得游客可以直接接触金字塔，导致金字塔近年来被破坏程度与日俱增，这也使得埃及政府不断寻求国际合作与帮助，在传统保护和修复方式之外，应用数字化展陈与保护方式。

（三）传承发展的经验启示

1.成功案例：埃及金字塔数字化保护与研究

近年来，数字技术在埃及考古领域的应用越来越普遍。"扫描金字塔"是埃及旅游和文物部、开罗大学以及法国有关机构于2015年合作开展的一项考

---

① 李斌. 遗址博物馆原址展示与文物保护的统一——以秦始皇帝陵博物院为例. 中国博物馆, 2020(2)：77-82.

古项目。考古人员运用射线照相、红外热成像、摄影测量法、3D扫描重建和无人机等现代技术和设备，研究和测量了多座金字塔的内部构造，以检测是否存在未知的内部结构，从而进一步了解金字塔的施工过程和技术。

2018年9月24日，哈佛大学和浙江大学两间教室里的40名学生，通过在线高科技设备，在一个多小时里，同步分享了由哈佛大学的"吉萨金字塔：技术、考古与历史"课程。

当每位同学佩戴上VR（虚拟现实）头盔，他们会同时"空降"到4500年前建造的吉萨金字塔区。

在这门联合课程上，同学们在VR中看到的场景，是不可能在如今的吉萨看到的。吉萨在早期挖掘时，由各个国家在分属的区域各自进行，因此许多文物散落在各国的博物馆中。比如，在吉萨金字塔区墓地现场，于1842年被发掘出的Merib墓室的地面上目前只有一个洞，其墓室的正面门脸，如今收藏在柏林博物馆里。

但是在VR内容中，科学家根据考古记录，准确复原了这个墓室本来的样子，那一刹那，时空定格在了20世纪初。VR中不仅有墓室建筑完整的样子，还可以仔细地看到墓室里的物件——浮雕、壁画，家具……同学们可以点击其中任意一件，物件的3D模型就会相应弹出，可以随心所欲地旋转，以便进行各个角度的观察。

2.经验总结

近年来，中国积极探索将数字化技术应用于文化遗产的保护与发展。通过利用虚拟现实、增强现实、3D扫描和数字化档案等技术手段，实现文化遗产的数字化保存、展示和传播，提高文化遗产的可视性和可访问性。随着技术的进步，许多国外地区也开始将文化遗产数字化，以便更好地保存、保护和传播。通过建立数字档案、虚拟展览和在线资源等，人们可以远程访问和了解文化遗产，从而促进全球范围内的文化交流和合作。关于数字化保护方面，我们根据国内国外经验总结了以下几点内容。

（1）合作与共享：国内外的文化遗产数字化保护都可以通过合作和共享信息、技术和资源来实现更好的效果，促进不同国家之间的知识交流和经验分享。

（2）技术创新与应用：数字化技术如虚拟现实、增强现实、三维扫描和云存储等技术在文化遗产保护中起着重要作用。这些技术可以更好地还原、保存和展示文化遗产，使人们能够身临其境地体验和了解文化遗产。

（3）数据管理与保存：在数字化保护过程中，确保文化遗产数字化数据的完整性、可访问性和长期保存是一项重大任务。国内外的实践经验可以为我们提供有效的数据管理和保存方法，以防止数据丢失和损坏。

（4）教育与普及：教育和普及对于文化遗产的数字化保护至关重要。通过教育公众对文化遗产的重要性和保护方法的认识，可以增强大众对文化遗产的关注和保护意识。此外，提供在线数字化资源和展览可以让更多人在任何时间和地点都能够接触到文化遗产，帮助相关学者跨时空进行研究学习。

四、国内文化遗产传承保护与创新发展的建议

（一）"秦始皇帝陵"和科学技术的结合

1.数字化保护背景

文化遗产数字化保护是一种新的方法，它采用数字摄影、三维信息获取、虚拟现实、多媒体与网络等信息技术，将与文化遗产相关的文字、图像、声音、视频及三维数据信息数字化永久性地保存，使公众最大限度地、公平地享有文化遗产[①]。

该项技术已在国际中被广泛采用，其中国内做的最优秀的有敦煌莫高窟等。敦煌研究院对石窟艺术数字化保护技术的研究始于 1993 年，目的是利用计算机数字化技术永久地、高保真地保存敦煌石窟艺术的珍贵资料。在敦煌石窟艺术的数字化作业中，实现高精度色彩逼真的数字壁画采集、存储及处理，是数字敦煌的基础，也是所有数字石窟艺术应用的基础。而且与虚拟漫游技术相结合，不仅实现了洞窟的逼真重现，还可作用于引导浏览，查询详细的石窟艺术资料。因此，通过结合这两项技术，就能组成数字敦煌的核心。[②]如今，敦煌研究院已建立起云游敦煌项目，在其中，不仅可以查看莫高窟相关视频，还能从艺术形式、朝代、颜色或者洞窟等角度探索，打破时间与空间的界限，通过数字化方法体会莫高窟蕴含的伟大艺术。

2.数字化保护作用分析

虚拟现实技术可作为观赏艺术品、增强艺术感染力的辅助手段，可以对现

---

① 陈振旺，樊锦诗.文化科技融合在文化遗产保护中的运用——以敦煌莫高窟数字化为例.敦煌研究，2016(2)：100-107.

② 李最雄.敦煌石窟保护工作六十年.敦煌研究，2004(3)：10-26，111.

实中难以展示的场景、受限制或根本不可能被展示的角度进行虚拟展示。随着计算机技术和的高速发展，虚拟旅游系统的开发方法越来越多，按照原理的不同可分为如下四类：三维全景、VRML/X3D语言、编程方法、Web3D商业软件。[①]

为了防止游客接触兵马俑，秦始皇兵马俑博物馆设立了防护带，这一方面导致游客为游览需要经过更多的路程，另一方面导致游客更难欣赏兵马俑，特别是位于坑中间的兵马俑。这极大地增加了游客在秦始皇兵马俑博物馆中的滞留时间。如果我们把虚拟现实技术和秦始皇帝陵相结合，参观者通过在俑坑中完成的三维全景摄影，在虚拟现实技术的帮助下仿佛亲临坑下，从而观察到更多的兵马俑，以及近距离仔细观赏兵马俑。

如此，可以减少每个游客在博物馆中的滞留时间。如果一个文物研究者想要研究秦始皇帝陵中的文物，很多时候，借助该项技术仅通过计算机就可以仔细观赏文物、研究文物的细部特征，而不必亲身前往博物院进行研究，这不仅节省了时间、精力，还更好地保护了秦始皇帝陵。

对于秦始皇帝陵考古遗址公园（丽山园），由于该区域的展品数量较少，并且陪葬坑里的文物同博物馆的文物一样，被放置于玻璃中展示，故可将其进行三维建模，使游客能够以更丰富的角度观赏文物，打破时空限制，将文物组合起来也能展现更浓厚的主题，还可以在保持文物现有位置的情况下，将其放回发现地点进行原汁原味的体验。目前，秦始皇帝陵博物院已对部分藏品进行了数字化建模，然而数量较少，分类不完善，只能通过尺寸、质地与关键字检索，藏品之间联系不紧密，导致观赏体验较为孤立。因此，需要一种更为完善的数字化展陈方案设计。

3.数字化展陈方案设计

虚拟现实技术需要进行三维建模，现在主要有三种方式，分别是进行基于三维激光扫描技术的考古遗址的三维建模、基于结构光和激光三维扫描技术的文物的三维空间建模、基于数字摄影技术的数字化三维建模。[②]将文化遗产数字化不仅是对文物的保护，同样也是对文物的传承。基于虚拟现实技术，我们对秦始皇帝陵展陈方式做了如下设计。

---

① 蒋文燕，朱晓华，陈晨.虚拟旅游研究进展.科技导报，2007(14)：53-57.
② 霍笑游，孟中元，杨琦.虚拟现实——秦兵马俑遗址与文物的数字化保护与展示.东南文化，2009(4)：98-102.

（1）基于数字摄影技术将秦始皇帝陵进行三维空间建模，通过虚拟现实技术，游客能够以空间顺序在秦始皇帝陵之中游览。

（2）基于结构光和激光三维扫描技术将兵马俑坑内细节进行三维空间建模。

（3）基于三维激光扫描技术的对出土的文物进行三维建模，并提供按不同线索比如材质、形态等检索文物的接口。

（4）基于上述实现的三维建模，开发游客体验新模式，比如，对于兵马俑可以开发上色游戏，使游客产生更加生动的认识；也可以开发组合游戏，游客自由选择兵马俑与兵器，构建属于自己的秦朝军队；还可以开发修复游戏，把文物修复过程用游戏的方式展现，游客得以在游玩的同时了解考古知识；也可以开发文物铸造游戏，将游客带回古代，体验兵马俑是以怎样的方式烧制出来的，武器又是如何锻造的，更好地体会古代的风土人情与兵马俑背后的故事。这些可开发的游戏能够以其强大的趣味性赋予了秦始皇帝陵更加丰富的体验与持久的生命力。

（5）在上述建模的基础上，在文物展示或者游览的节点上配合文字讲解信息、人声讲解信息与合适的音乐，帮助游客更好地体会其中蕴含的历史、文化和科学价值，营造方便舒适的游览体验。此外，还可以在这些地方提供评论功能，使游客能在每一个游览的节点对自己的体验发表看法，与其他游客进行互动，进而形成丰富的互动体验。这样的数字体验将让历史可触摸，让文化可体验。

五、结　论

（一）案例研究总结

秦始皇帝陵作为我国的重要文化遗产之一，其价值不仅仅体现在历史和文化方面，还涉及经济、旅游等多个领域。然而，秦始皇帝陵还面临着游客过多、旅游开发与保护之间难以平衡、古迹的物质保护和修复难度大等问题。因此，我们从秦始皇帝陵的历史背景、价值影响、保护现状等方面出发，研究了秦始皇帝陵如今的保护和继承情况，重点考察了秦始皇帝陵数字化现状，从价值取向与资源优势两方面对比了埃及金字塔和秦始皇帝陵的保护状况，并学习了埃及金字塔的数字化中的成功经验和科学先进的文化遗产保护传承方法。

我们着眼于科技创新来助力秦始皇帝陵的保护和发扬。在已有数字化秦始皇帝陵的方案基础上，学习敦煌莫高窟数字化的成功经验，基于虚拟现实技术提出秦始皇帝陵数字化方案。例如，使用对应技术对秦始皇兵马俑博物馆与秦始皇帝陵考古遗址公园（丽山园）进行三维建模，打造以空间顺序的全息游览，突破空间限制的坑内欣赏，将不同的线索组合进行虚拟展览，并利用数字资源构建趣味游戏，配合文字、讲解、音乐、评论等营造丰富的互动体验。通过这样的数字化方法减少游客滞留时间以应对游客压力大的问题，并以更加丰富的展列方式帮助游客更好地体会秦始皇帝陵的历史、文化、科技价值。

（二）研究局限性

1.资料收集不全面

由于秦始皇帝陵相关研究涉及历史、考古、地理、艺术和文化等多个领域，所以在进行研究时可能由于资料收集不全面，无法涵盖所有方面的内容。

2.文化差异

在对比中西方文化遗产传承发展情况时，由于文化及语言的差异，无法准确理解西方的一些方法，可能使对比出现误差。

3.技术限制

现有的虚拟现实技术只能做到视觉的还原，而缺少触觉、嗅觉的体验，这导致基于虚拟现实技术构建的数字化方案相较于实地游览缺乏真实感。

（三）未来发展展望

1.在未来的保护和发展中制定更加科学合理的保护规划和措施

需要在人类活动与文物保护之间寻找平衡点，制定更加科学合理的保护规划和措施，包括采用最新的先进的技术手段对秦始皇帝陵进行科学保护。

2.增强社会认识和文物保护意识

加强对秦始皇帝陵文物保护知识的宣传教育和普及，提高社会公众对文物保护的认识，进而减少人为破坏行为。

3.加强国际合作和交流

秦始皇帝陵在国内外都具有重要的文化地位和影响力。因此，建立更加广泛、高效的国际文化交流与合作平台，促进不同国家之间的文化交流和人员往来，实现国际文化的融合与共享，有助于共同保护和传承好秦始皇帝陵文化。

泾阳茯茶发展现状及问题分析[①]

摘　要: 本文对泾阳茯茶制茶技艺及其历史文化及地域、保健养生价值进行了梳理，厘清了产业现状，指出了存在的问题，包括茯茶外宣问题、产业创新发展问题、消费市场及管理问题以及传承问题，并结合案例研究提出了在对外宣传、产品创新发展、消费市场管理、传承问题方面的解决思路。

关键词: 泾阳茯茶；制茶技艺；产业现状；发展展望；工艺传承

一、绪　论

（一）选题背景及意义

近年来，世界各国对于非物质文化遗产的保护愈加重视，而我国作为非物质文化遗产大国，有着悠久的历史以及多民族、多元化的文化生态，在非遗保护方面理应更加重视，为世界非遗传承与保护做出更大贡献。2022 年 11 月，"中国传统制茶技艺及其相关习俗"正式通过评审，被列入联合国教科文组织人类非物质文化遗产代表作名录。可见我国的茶文化正在与世界相织相交，中华文明正在与世界交融互鉴。

2021 年 6 月，泾阳茯茶被列入第五批国家级非物质文化遗产代表性项目名录。泾阳茯茶属于黑茶，内含对人体有益的"金花菌"，在茯砖茶上显出"金花绽放"之状，外观惊艳，口感独特，具有很高的营养价值。泾阳茯茶曾经还是"古丝路"上连通各地文化脉络和促进民间和官办经济的重要推动力，也是明代"茶马贸易"主要的茶叶贸易对象，被誉为"中国古丝绸之路上的神

---

① 作者: 屈靖怡，西北工业大学工业设计系；冯颖晨，西北工业大学工业设计系；邓咏琪，西北工业大学工业设计系。

秘之茶"。

然而，这样一种传奇古茶，如今却面临很多发展困境，如产业发展起步晚，制茶技艺传承面临风险，茯茶文化尚未被大众所熟知，这不但影响了茯茶品质的提升，也影响了茯茶产业的发展，非遗的传承与发展遇到障碍。因此，如何重塑泾阳茯茶品牌，创新茯茶产业新发展模式，从而有效传承和发展泾阳茯茶这一非遗文化，让文化瑰宝焕发光彩，具有现代色彩，与时代同行，成为如今值得深入探讨和研究的一个问题，也是本次研究的意义所在。

（二）国内研究评述

国内学者关于泾阳茯茶的研究主要分为两个方面。

第一，对泾阳茯茶文化和历史的研究。黄晓莲在《陕西泾阳茯茶文化艺术形式》一文中对泾阳茯茶的发展现状进行梳理汇总，总结了不同艺术形式下的茯茶文化表现形式。[①] 孟阳在《泾阳茯茶文化资源挖掘整理及其产业应用研究》一文中，全面详细地探究了泾阳茯茶产业的发展潜力，并提出了一些结合当地特色切实可行的方案。[②] 吴鹏等在《关于泾阳茯茶的几个问题－兼论泾阳茯茶的历史》一文中，深入分析了泾阳茯茶的生产工艺、制茶文化及发展脉络，为其文化发展提供了思路。[③] 孙志国等在《边销茶泾阳茯砖的知识产权保护与文化遗产传承研究》一文从知识产权、传统知识、农业科技、茶马古道文化、"一带一路"倡议等方面探讨了在乡村振兴背景下该茶的文化遗产传承对策。[④] 王翠英等在《关中茯茶发展嬗变史》一文中分析了泾阳茯茶的文化特点以及在物质条件、文化意向等方面的嬗变，指出了茯茶文化发展的问题。[⑤] 韩健畅在《茯茶何以名"茯"》一文中阐释了茯茶名"茯"的缘由，结合历史解释了长期以来有关茯茶历史的纷纭聚讼。[⑥]

第二，关于泾阳茯茶品牌及产业的推广与营销。王磊等在《茯茶绿色工厂的数字化实践》一文中对绿色工厂数字化的实践思路和经验进行总结，为茶

---

① 黄晓莲.陕西泾阳茯茶文化艺术形式.福建茶叶，2023，45(4)：177-179.
② 孟阳.泾阳茯茶文化资源挖掘整理及其产业应用研究.咸阳：西北农林科技大学，2021.
③ 吴鹏，扈晓梅，肖卫国等.关于泾阳茯茶的几个问题——兼论泾阳茯茶的历史.农业考古，2021(2)：217-220.
④ 孙志国，定光平，曹玮等.边销茶泾阳茯砖的知识产权保护与文化遗产传承研究//AEIC Academic Exchange Information Centre(China). Proceedings of 2018 3rd International Conference on Society Science and Economics Development(ICSSED 2018).
⑤ 王翠英，崔艳玲.关中茯茶发展嬗变史.福建茶叶，2017，39(8)：344-345.
⑥ 韩健畅.茯茶何以名"茯".咸阳师范学院学报，2015，30(3)：58-64.

行业智能化、数字化、信息化提供参考。① 杨怡等在《泾阳县茯茶小镇发展探析》一文中阐述了陕西省茯茶小镇旅游发展现状,多角度探析发展因素并提出建议。② 曲兴卫等在《"一带一路"背景下陕地茯茶产业文化发展策略研究》一文中分析了茯茶产业现状,并以陕西地区文化研究为基础,探索当地文化创新发展新道路。③ 周园等在《泾阳茯砖茶产销现状分析》一文中对当地茯砖茶生产企业进行了调查分析,并提出了关于茯砖茶产业发展的建议。④ 邓永亮在《SWOT分析法探讨陕西茯茶的发展》一文中提出有关陕西茯茶理化成分、保健功效、"金花"数量等方面的研究方向。⑤

此外,还有关于泾阳茯茶本身制作技艺的研究,如技艺的展示、制作与加工方式的改进和优化、生产设备的升级等。

(三)研究对象及内容

本文研究对象为世界文化遗产继承和传统工艺创新背景下的泾阳茯茶,主要研究内容为泾阳茯茶文化及其相关习俗,研究其背景、制作工艺、当今发展现状等,总结和分析现有问题,分析对比其他茶类的传承和发展优秀案例,为泾阳茯茶的传承与保护以及当地茯茶产业的发展提出建议和实施方案。

(四)研究思路及方法

本研究从"中国传统制茶文化及其相关习俗"的中国茶文化大背景出发,选取泾阳茯茶作为一项具体研究案例进行研究分析。本文首先从文献综述视角出发,综述近几年关于泾阳茯茶文化与保护、产业发展与推广宣传等的相关文献,总结出现有研究的主要成果,分析当前国内关于泾阳茯茶保护与技艺继承研究的基本特征及其薄弱之处,思考今后研究的新动向,为具体案例的实践提供有益的指导与参考。

基于此,从不同的学科及不同的视角出发,通过查阅相关文献和中国非物质文化遗产网、茯茶博物馆等对泾阳茯茶及其制茶技艺、相关习俗等进行较为深入、系统的研究。随着调研的深入,后续计划到浙江省杭州市中国茶叶博物

---

① 王磊,胡歆.茯茶绿色工厂的数字化实践.中国茶叶加工,2022(3):78-83.
② 杨怡,关倩,李宁宁.泾阳县茯茶小镇发展探析.南方农业,2021,15(23):166-167.
③ 曲兴卫,任晓丽,宁攀."一带一路"背景下陕地茯茶产业文化发展策略研究.中国市场,2017(14):56-60.
④ 周园,萧力争.泾阳茯砖茶产销现状分析.安徽农学通报,2017(7):14-15.
⑤ 邓永亮.SWOT分析法探讨陕西茯茶的发展.中国农学通报,2012(23):160-164.

馆、茶园以及陕西省泾阳县茯茶研究中心等地进行现场调研和专家访谈等，进一步深入对项目的理解，为后续研究作参考和推进。

同时，选取现有与"中国传统制茶技艺及其相关习俗"相关的成功案例进行案例分析，总结其成功经验，分析非遗创新与发展思路，并提出基于泾阳茯茶发展的建议。

二、泾阳茯茶基本介绍

泾阳茯茶产自陕西省咸阳市泾阳县，属于我国六大茶系中的黑茶一类，按加工茶类属于紧压茶，因此又称茯砖茶。茯茶茶砖紧结，色泽黑褐油亮，特殊的工艺使其生长出对人体有益的"金花"——冠突散囊菌。2022年，我国申报的"中国传统制茶技艺及其相关习俗"通过评审，咸阳茯茶制作技艺作为联合申报项目之一成为人类非物质文化遗产代表作。

（一）制茶技艺

1.原料

"自古岭北不植茶，唯有泾阳出茯茶"。泾阳茯茶以湖南安化黑毛茶为原料。黑毛茶指没有压制过的茶，是鲜叶经过杀青、揉捻、渥堆、复揉、干燥等工序加工而成的半成品茶，在泾阳经过二次加工后制成泾阳茯茶再进行销售。

2.工序

传统茯砖茶制作工艺相传有29道[①]，《DBS61/ 0006—2021 食品安全地方标准 泾阳茯茶》中给出的泾阳茯茶定义，将其工序主要分为筛分、拼配、渥堆、炒制或（和）汽蒸、定型或不定型、发花、干燥、包装等，如表1所示。

表1　泾阳茯砖茶主要制作工序

工序	步骤	说明
筛分	开苞去杂	茶工用手工去除毛茶中的杂质。
	剁茶	用刀将毛茶剁碎，制成絮状。
拼配	—	按照所制茶等级要求，将精选"清茶"按配方混合搅匀。
渥堆	—	洒上适量井水拌匀，成堆发酵约8小时。

---

① 周墨林.陕西泾阳县茯茶研究.咸阳师范学院学报，2018(3)：89-93.

续表

工序	步骤	说明
炒制或（和）汽蒸	茶釉炒茶	将铁锅烧至一定温度，舀入兑好的茶釉做引子浸润热锅，将茶叶倒入锅内炒至一定温度。
	汽蒸	利用高温高压蒸气将茶蒸热，使梗、叶变软，以便压制成形。
定型	制封灌封	绑封子，灌茶进封使之饱满。
	扶梆筑茶	即捶茶，将茶叶装入模具，捶压夯实，形成茶砖外形。
	扎封锥封	用麻绳将茶封十字捆扎，用钢钎从茶砖正中锥成气眼。
发花	—	筑好茶砖以井字形排列堆垛，阴干至七八成后，加棕片等覆盖物使其自然发花月余，以待金花生长饱满并发出芬芳香味。
干燥	—	发花后的茶砖在木架上依次摆放晾干。

3.冠突散囊菌

"发花"是制作泾阳茯茶的核心，也是泾阳茯茶区别于其他茶的关键工序。"发花"中的"花"指"金花菌"，本质是冠突散囊菌的金黄色闭囊壳。冠突散囊菌是茯砖茶的唯一优势真菌，茶叶在微生物作用下发生深度生理生化变化，苦涩味降低，散发独特菌花香，茶褐素增多，茶叶的香味、色泽和生物活性物质等均发生显著变化，口感和品质得到提升[①]。

关于泾阳茯茶制茶技艺，历史上有"三不离"：离了泾阳水不能制，离了泾阳气候不能制，离了泾阳人的技术不能制。一是泾阳茯茶炒制所用的地下井水比较特殊，其味咸，根据科学检测结果，泾阳地下水pH值为6—8.5，符合冠突散囊菌产孢培养基的最佳酸碱条件（pH=7），有利于冠突散囊菌的生长、发育和繁殖[②]。二是泾阳地处关中平原腹地，具有关中气候特点与湿地气候特征，适宜"金花菌"生产。三是茯砖茶制作过程中炒茶、筑茶、发花等全靠制茶师的经验判断，因此，泾阳茯茶凭借其优势与经验积累，在泾阳发展壮大。

（二）历史文化及地域价值

1.历史文化

关于泾阳茯茶具体起源于何时，当前尚未形成定论。"茶马互市"的历史资料显示，泾阳茯茶以散茶形式出现于北宋神宗熙宁年（1068），茯砖茶出现

---

① 姜良珍，王罗，杨涛，等.冠突散囊菌及其发酵应用研究进展.食品工业科技，2022，43(4)：454-462.
② 孟阳.泾阳茯茶文化资源挖掘整理及其产业应用研究.西北农林科技大学，2021.

于明洪武元年（1368），该观点也是有关泾阳茯砖茶历史的主流观点^①。

（1）初兴期

泾阳茯茶初兴期即关中茶马古道的形成期。

《藏史》记载："藏王松岗布之孙（松赞干布）时，始自中国输入茶叶，为茶叶输入西藏之始。"独特的地理位置和悠久的历史为茯茶的生产提供了极佳的环境和丰富的技术储备。^②

（2）兴盛期

茯茶成名于明初，兴盛于明清至民国时期。

明代茶马互市为泾阳茯茶带来了巨大的发展机遇，泾阳茯茶独特的风味、保健养生的价值等优势使其在西北茶马贸易中占有独特地位。晚清到民国是泾阳茯茶发展的鼎盛时期，不仅销往西域，更是远销俄国、中亚、西欧等地^③。

（3）沉寂期

北上万里茶道兴起，陕甘茶马古道泾阳茯茶式微。1932年，陇海铁路西安段通车，作为传统贸易重要中转地的泾阳失去区位优势。新中国成立后，泾阳茯茶一时风靡西北，后因国家茶产业政策调整，泾阳县茯茶停产。

（4）复兴期

2008年秋天，泾阳县政府开始了复兴"泾阳茯砖"茶的计划，泾阳茯茶加工工艺恢复。2014年，"泾阳茯砖茶·丝绸之路文化之旅"顺利举办；2015年，茯茶小镇开园，带动了文化旅游及茯茶产业联动发展；2022年11月，"咸阳茯茶制茶技艺"作为"中国传统制茶技艺及其相关习俗"项目之一被列入联合国教科文组织人类非物质文化遗产。2023年，咸阳市被中国茶叶流通协会授予"茯茶之都"称号。

2.地域价值

从原料上看，泾阳是"茯茶之源"，汉茶、川茶、湖茶的黑毛茶及安化黑茶等都是泾阳茯茶的原料，众多产茶区因此产生联动。从外销上看，泾阳是陕南茶、蜀茶、两湖茶等的集散中心。在某个特定的历史时期，茯茶所起到的作用并不限于运输和贸易，还能够稳定边疆，其政治属性远远超过商品属性。

---

① 吴鹏，扈晓梅，肖卫国等.关于泾阳茯茶的几个问题—兼论泾阳茯茶的历史.农业考古，2021(2): 217-220.

② 韩星海.揭开泾阳茯砖茶历史文化之谜.农业考古，2014(5): 271-273.

③ 周园."一带一路"战略下的泾阳茯茶发展策略研究.湖南农业大学，2017.

（三）保健养生价值

茯砖茶富含多种化学成分，主要功能性成分包括：茶多酚、氨基酸、茶多糖、咖啡碱以及茶色素，具有减肥、降"三高"、调控肠胃环境以及抗肿瘤等多重功效。

三、产业现状

近年来，随着技术改进、消费升级等，茯茶产业进入快车道，截至2023年7月，咸阳全市现有茯茶生产加工企业51家，产品远销俄罗斯、美国等40多个国家，茯茶产业被咸阳市委、市政府列为16条重点产业链之一。

（一）产业集群发展

泾阳茯茶企业集群发展，形成泾阳县政府和茯茶小镇两个核心聚集区和泾阳茯茶产业科技示范园、西咸新区小范围聚集区，这在促进产业创新发展，新知识新技术的传播和流通方面，企业交流合作方面及规范企业秩序方面都具有积极的意义。

（二）品牌文化建设

2015年，茯茶小镇建立，形成集茯茶生产研发、仓储物流、文化展示、体验销售和旅游于一体的茯茶全产业链业态。2019年，"泾阳茯茶文化研究与传播中心"成立，在茯茶历史文化资源发掘整理、茯茶文化创新及传播、茯茶文化旅游开发、茯茶产业扶贫等领域开拓创新。

（三）技术创新发展

泾阳茯茶与各大高等院校和科研院所共同研发产品，提升了泾阳茯茶产业科技含量，为茯茶产业进一步可持续发展提供了人才保证、科研支撑，形成了一套完整的产学研一体化模式——"以研促产，以产促赢，以赢促研"。

（四）非遗技艺传承

泾阳县茯茶中心每年都会举办产业技能培训，开展评茶员、检验员、茯茶加工技能、企业知识产权保护等培训，为产业发展提供了人才保障。

四、问题研究及建议

（一）现存问题

1.茯茶外宣问题

（1）宣传力度不够：陕西茯茶文化在整个茶文化体系，乃至世界文化体系中的影响力较低、话语权较弱。

（2）"文化乏力"现象：缺乏对茶文化的提炼和应用，缺少对茯茶文化所蕴含的内涵和特质的定位和宣传。

（3）品牌宣传质量不佳：对于自身价值理念、运营体系以及茯茶发展历程等整体的宣传不够到位，缺乏多元系统宣传。

2.产业创新发展问题

（1）产业机制及企业管理不健全：茯茶企业规模较小，发展思路有限，内部组织结构简单、管理不成体系。

（2）产业副产品开发不足：产业结构单一，没有衍生产品拓宽市场。

（3）缺乏专业技术培训和对外交流学习：技术人员的专业水平亟待提高，技术水平的参差不齐使产品质量不够稳定。

（4）研发投入占比少：在科研及资金的投入需要加强，茶树的选种和设备的更新换代不够及时。

3.消费市场及管理问题

（1）消费市场定位不清：泾阳茯茶目前仍以本地茶叶市场销售为主，以家庭式管理为主，没有建立分工明确的营销网络，消费者出现年龄断层。

（2）市场扶持监管力度不够：泾阳县茯茶产业因为重新起步，大型企业不多，以小规模企业为主，质量监管体系不健全。

4.传承问题

（1）传统传承制度有局限性：以往这种技艺和知识主要通过家族传承、师徒传承等传统方式进行传承，受社会家庭模式变更及传统师徒制度衰落的影响，传统传承方式日渐式微。

（2）制作工序复杂，技艺经验性要求强，需要大量的学习时间和成本，能够真正坚持下来的年轻学徒较少。

（3）随着"机械化、自动化"的生产方式的发展，"传统的、手工的"个性制作受到了冲击。

（二）解决方案

1.国外案例研究：日本抹茶

抹茶实质上源于中国，但已完美蜕变为日系文化的代表。茶首登日本的历史舞台是在奈良时代，由遣唐使带回；接着是平安时代，佛教徒最澄和空海将茶叶带回日本，这一时期是茶道文化形成的初期；而到了镰仓时代，僧人荣西留学宋朝后回国致力于茶的普及，斗茶成为主流娱乐项目；江户时代，茶道的发展已经达到顶峰。①抹茶盛于宋朝，镰仓时期，荣西禅师两度赴宋学佛，回国时将《茶经》手抄本带回日本，为日本抹茶道打下了基础。

目前，日本抹茶产业规模已发展得非常庞大。抹茶以其无添加剂、无防腐剂、无人工色素的特点受到市场青睐。抹茶作为典型的亚洲口味，已经深刻影响西方人的味蕾，成功实现商业化发展和文化输出功能并行。

日本抹茶可以在世界庞大的茶产业中脱颖而出有以下几点原因。

（1）茶源地的形象宣传和品牌打造

宇治是优良的茶株生长地，集中分布于山城地区，雨水充沛，昼夜温差大，沿河土壤肥沃，十分适宜茶叶生长。

这种宣传和强调茶源产地，打造最佳产地标签的方法，更容易形成产业品牌和文化，树立良好的产业形象。同时，宇治也始终在进行茶产品的相关拓展与延伸，强化了宇治在人们心目中茶乡的形象。

除此之外，宇治茶田具有规模化特点，利用机械种植方式，茶田整齐划一，打造了景观效果，提升了城市整体魅力。

通过塑造城市文化，打造旅游体验景观，推出多种衍生产品等方法，"茶乡宇治"这一产地品牌成功打响，宇治抹茶的口碑和品牌形象成功在世界出圈。

（2）抹茶产业严格的品质筛选

在日本，抹茶生产有着严格的品质审查和分级标准，并且形成了完整的供应链体系。

（3）日式风格抹茶的形成和文化输出

抹茶在吸收日本本土文化的基础上进行了传承和发展，形成了独特的文化价值和内涵。日本茶道文化在形成过程中对传统的部分内容进行了传承与改

---

① 李薇.浅析文化传播视野下的日本抹茶文化.科技视界，2018(21)：105-106.

造，如日本的禅宗思想等，形成了日本抹茶独特的文化气质。

2.国内案例研究：西湖龙井茶

西湖龙井茶是中国重要的传统历史名茶，发源于西湖周边群山之中。以"色绿、香郁、味甘、形美"四绝闻名于世，被誉为"绿茶皇后"，是杭州的城市"金名片"。

2022年11月29日，西湖龙井茶作为"中国传统制茶技艺及其相关习俗"的重要组成部分入选联合国教科文组织人类非物质文化遗产代表作名录。2001年，《杭州市西湖龙井茶基地保护条例》正式明确西湖龙井茶原产地范围为168平方公里，并根据基地保护等级，划分基地一级保护区和基地二级保护区。

在杭州，龙井茶早已与杭州山水、西湖风月乃至人文风骨融为一体。当杭州顺应时代而变化时，龙井的茶与村，也在寻求融入现代商业、生活的可能。针对龙井茶的产业发展，目前已有以下几方面的举措。

（1）对西湖龙井茶的品牌保护

2001年，杭州市《杭州市西湖龙井茶基地保护条例》颁布，用法规的形式明确了西湖龙井茶的生产地域范围和保护级别，成为国内首个茶叶类的地方法规。这些年来，西湖区遵循"政府主导、部门联动、社会参与、重点保护、整体推进"的原则，立足现实，把握机遇，趋利避害，循序渐进，努力营造"西湖龙井茶制作技艺"保护的社会环境和舆论氛围，逐步建立了全方位、多层次的"西湖龙井茶制作技艺"保护体系。

（2）对西湖龙井茶的品质保障

西湖龙井茶的品质与优良的生态环境、独特的种质资源、传统的加工工艺以及严格的质量管理等因素密不可分。例如，实施农药补贴、专业队防治、病虫害测报、茶叶质量安全检测、植保员补贴等措施，保障了农资供应，规范了购买渠道。在群体种保护方面，杭州通过建立群体种保护区，为种植群体种的茶农提供菜饼有机肥补助，建立种质资源圃等多种方式，稳定了种质资源多样性和原真性。

（3）发展完善西湖龙井茶产区

杭州建设完成的核心产区的茶园游步道有22条、抗旱蓄水池63个、喷灌示范点1个、茶园绿化隔离带5137平方米。此外，杭州已建立西湖龙井茶手工炒制中心20多个，通过实施炒制技艺培训和炒茶技师等级考证制度，培养手工炒茶技师 700 余名。

（4）高度重视西湖龙井茶宣发

杭州市政府从 2010 年起建立西湖龙井茶新闻发言人制度，公布每年有关西湖龙井春茶的情况以及保护和宣传工作。同时，多种形式的西湖龙井茶事推介活动每年都会举行，如西湖龙井茶开茶节、炒茶王大赛、"全民饮茶日"等。

（5）规范西湖龙井茶市场

西湖龙井茶采用 3 种标识作为防伪的手段，茶农或合作社在自售时使用茶农标，授权的相关企业在销售时使用证明标和地理标。在茶农标上，印有序号、年份、真伪查询电话、重量以及防伪码等信息，对应着茶农的身份，茶农可以将自己的产品贴上茶农标直接卖给消费者。

（6）创新发展西湖龙井茶产业

互联网线上新渠道的出现，放大了西湖龙井茶元素的溢出效应。"西湖龙井"正在美丽乡村的文创产品、旅游商品、文艺展演、研学旅行等众多领域焕发光彩，不断绘就美好城市文旅消费新图景。

（三）建议及解决方案

1.外宣方面

（1）打造品牌，合理营销：要重视品牌策划包装、文创设计和个性化定制服务，提升品牌知名度和影响力。改变冲泡方式，如将茯茶砖细碎化处理后，制成茶包。携带有"金花"的茶砖成本价较高，但添加其他材料制成花茶后，成本即得到了有效控制，能够有效消费群体。

（2）建立外宣符号，讲好茯茶故事：加深对茯茶的深入了解，如茯茶的茶道、茶艺，茯茶的运输在跨文化传播中起到了何种作用，古往今来，相关的文学艺术作品对茯茶文化是如何表现的，等等。

2.产业创新发展方面

（1）加大资金、设备等的投入：应抓住新的发展机遇期，创建绿色化工厂，推动茯茶产业集群，多元化开发产品，加快延伸产业链条，大力开拓国内外消费市场。

（2）学习其他成功经验：如日本抹茶、西湖龙井茶等，学习其宣传模式，提高茯茶知名度与影响力。

（3）与其他产业联动：推动文化、教育、商业、旅游等产业的融合发展。

3.消费市场管理方面

（1）扩大消费群体：要在唤醒老一代消费者文化记忆的同时，发扬"不断开拓、守正创新"的茯茶精神，开拓新的消费市场，培养新的消费群体。

（2）市场管理规范化：要建立一整套质控标准化管理体系，完善营养价值品质评价和安全风险评控，建立生产工艺、产品等级的标准，打开贸易、保健的市场大门，实现茯茶高质量发展，支持企业创新行业标准规范。

4.传承方面

（1）提高产业定位：要从茶产业布局上给予泾阳茯茶更高的产业定位，借助西安-咸阳一体化的体制优势，由咸阳市统筹协调区域内的产业发展。

（2）壮大非遗技艺传承人队伍：形成国家级、省级、市级非遗传承人梯队。在非遗传承单位建设非遗传承讲习基地、教育研学基地，开展非遗文化展示和技艺传承，实现非遗与文化、旅游、教育的融合发展。

（3）运用现代化手段：积极运用新视野、新技术、新载体，做好茯茶制作工艺的挖掘与保护、传承与创新，重视茯茶文化的创造性转化、创新性发展。

（4）挖掘和培养人才：日本抹茶和西湖龙井茶的发展都离不开对下一代人才的培养，可以通过技艺培训和等级考证制度来筛选和储备茯茶产业相关人才。

五、结　论

（一）研究总结

本文对泾阳茯茶文化及其相关产业的发展进行了调研和分析，并对比了其他茶文化的发展及推广过程，选取了日本抹茶和西湖龙井茶作为重点案例进行研究。通过了解泾阳茯茶的具体内容和调研非遗创新的优秀案例，本文总结了目前泾阳茯茶传承与创新的经验与不足，并提出了加大宣传力度、加强地方立法等相关保护与传承措施建议。

（二）研究局限性

本研究小组成员均来自工业设计专业，可能缺乏学科交叉的知识广泛性，思维易受限，在案例研究方面可能不够全面。由于条件限制，目前研究内容不够充分，后续计划进一步补充调研资料并到实地探访，亲身体验和感受泾阳茯茶传统制茶技艺及其相关习俗，为进一步的研究提供有力支撑。

（三）未来发展展望

泾阳茯茶作为非物质文化遗产，是中华民族历史和文化的重要载体，承载了民族的记忆，展示了中国文化的精髓。未来的发展中，我们应尊重并保护这些非物质文化遗产，同时对其进行创新和发展，让它们在新的时代背景下焕发新的活力，走向世界，让更多人了解和喜爱中国文化。

内蒙古地区传统羊毛毡手工艺的可持续发展研究^①

摘　要： 内蒙古传统羊毛毡手工艺有着悠久的历史和丰富的文化内涵，是中国传统手工艺的重要组成部分，也是世界非物质文化的宝贵遗产。研究内蒙古羊毛毡手工技艺具有深刻的历史文化价值和生态环境保护价值。本文将在概述内蒙古地区传统羊毛毡手工艺品发展历程的基础上，综合使用文献调查法、调查法和比较研究法，对内蒙古羊毛毡制作工艺的技法、实际应用等展开分析，探讨内蒙古羊毛毡技艺传承的现存问题，并对其未来的保护与创新发展提出思考与展望。

关键词： 羊毛毡工艺；可持续发展；工艺传承

一、绪　论

（一）研究背景

羊毛毡是传统织造材料之一，手工羊毛毡技艺经过几千年流传至今，从房屋建筑到生产生活均有羊毛毡的制品。羊毛毡不仅历史悠久，且使用范围也很广泛，其中包括高加索地区、西伯利亚地区和蒙古高原等地。中世纪后，制毡工业拓展到了欧洲、美洲。在中国，羊毛毡的身影遍布内蒙古、新疆、西藏、甘肃、宁夏、青海、山西、陕西、河北和四川等地。使用羊毛毡制品的民族主要有蒙古族、藏族、维吾尔族、回族、彝族等，这些民族大多与游牧有关，均为逐水草而居并且就地取材，故而慢慢形成了相似的制毡习俗。2009年，哥本哈根气候会议上提出"低碳经济"，"低碳"的生活方式进入了我们的生活。因为毛毡具有良好的环保性，可以分解、更新、循环使用，所以羊毛毡再次得

---

① 作者：高雅，浙江大学公共管理学院；万姿伊，浙江大学教育学院；吴青霖，浙江大学公共管理学院。

到了广泛的关注。毛毡被应用于设计制作服装、箱包、配饰和各类家居用品等多个方面。现今市面上有很多有关毛毡制品设计的书籍来自日韩等地区，内容以"戳戳乐"为主，即教人们制作简易的家居用品以及小玩偶。这种利用羊毛的毡缩性能的设计制作，深受年轻人的喜爱。大部分新锐的毛毡制品都来源于日韩等地区，而这些地区在历史上并没有手工制毡的历史，因而其羊毛毡制品与游牧文化的毛毡并没有联系。然而，毛毡制品和它背后的游牧文化、民族文化是不可分割的。

内蒙古羊毛毡手工艺是中国传统手工艺的重要组成部分，有着悠久的历史和丰富的文化内涵。通过对内蒙古羊毛毡手工艺研究背景的深入了解，我们可以更好地认识和把握这一传统手工艺的价值与意义，为其保护、传承和发展提供有力支持。

1. 研究内蒙古羊毛毡工艺具有深刻的历史文化价值

内蒙古羊毛毡手工艺作为蒙古族文化的重要组成部分，具有深厚的历史和文化内涵。随着社会的发展和现代化的进程，传统手工艺面临着许多挑战和威胁，包括技术的流失、传承人口的减少以及市场需求的变化等。我们研究内蒙古羊毛毡手工艺是为了保护和传承这一宝贵的文化遗产，促进其在当代社会的传承和发展。

2. 研究内蒙古羊毛毡工艺具有文化交流价值

内蒙古羊毛毡工艺不仅仅是一种技艺，也是蒙古族和其他民族的文化标志和民族认同的象征。研究内蒙古羊毛毡手工艺可以促进不同文化的交流，增进各民族之间的相互了解和认同。深入研究内蒙古羊毛毡手工艺的文化背景，还可以为相关文化的保护、传承与交流提供借鉴和经验。

3. 研究内蒙古羊毛毡工艺具有生态环境与资源利用价值

内蒙古作为一个草原地区，拥有丰富的牧业资源，是羊毛毡的重要产地之一。与其他少数民族地区相比，内蒙古的羊毛毡工艺具有独特的生态环境和资源利用特点。从社会价值角度出发，在快消品畅行、能源消耗巨大的现代市场环境里，选择"耐用消费品"羊毛毡也是对环境资源的保护和支持，通过研究内蒙古羊毛毡手工艺对生态环境和资源可持续利用的影响，可以为今后的生态环境保护和资源管理提供经验和借鉴。我们期望从实践价值角度出发，通过实践调研更深入地发掘内蒙古地区的羊毛毡文化，将传统羊毛毡的价值呈现出来。

4.研究内蒙古羊毛毡工艺在促进地域经济发展方面具有重要价值

内蒙古羊毛毡手工艺在当地经济中起到了重要的作用，不仅为当地居民提供了就业机会和收入，还在一定程度上推动了当地经济的发展。通过研究内蒙古羊毛毡手工艺的产业链、市场行情和工艺发展趋势，可以为相关地区的经济发展和扶贫工作提供实践参考和政策支持。

（二）研究目的及意义

1.传统民间工艺的传承与保护意义

内蒙古羊毛毡手工艺是一种源远流长的传统技艺，承载了丰富的文化知识。研究和记录这一手工艺的技术特点、材料使用、工具方法等方面的内容，可以帮助保护和传承这一传统技艺，促进其在当代社会的发展和传承。毛毡在产生和发展的 2000 多年历史中，经历了高潮与低谷阶段，如今实用型传统毛毡已经随着游牧民族生产、生活方式的改变，以及西北汉族居住环境的变化而逐渐消失，传统擀毡技艺面临失传。

在市场竞争日趋激烈的背景下，传统毛毡业日渐衰微。目前内蒙古地区旅游景点的蒙古包多采用价格便宜的工业丙纶毡，在城市出生和长大的年轻人中见过传统毛毡的人已经很少了。而掌握传统毛毡擀毡技艺的人多出生于 20 世纪二三十年代，因此，如果不对毛毡的擀毡技艺进行抢救性的记录和整理工作，这一技艺就将面临失传。对于毛毡装饰特征的研究同样刻不容缓，仅有的手工毛毡多存在于内蒙古自治区的偏远农村和牧区，装饰极少，传统蒙古包用毡在自然环境的变化中也所剩无几，而懂得毡绣等毛毡装饰技法的人也已经不多。人们对于毛毡的认识完全停留在了工业用毡上面，如果不进行毛毡的记录和整理工作，势必会导致人们对毛毡文化的误读甚至遗忘。

2.草原文化与历史意义

内蒙古羊毛毡作为一种民间艺术，通常以丰富多样的图案、色彩和纹饰为特点，是独特的文化符号。研究这些图案和纹饰的含义、象征和起源，可以帮助我们了解蒙古族文化的内涵和民族的信仰、历史、生活方式等方面的特点。这对于文化研究、人类学研究和艺术研究都具有重要意义。

同时，内蒙古羊毛毡也可以作为社会历史的记录。内蒙古羊毛毡手工艺的存在可以追溯到古代，它是蒙古族生活的一部分，也是农牧民族经济的重要组成部分。通过研究内蒙古羊毛毡手工艺的历史，可以了解社会与经济的发展、演变和变革过程。这对于社会历史研究、民族研究和农牧民族文化研究都有重要价值。

此外，不同于其他民族用品，毛毡不只在游牧民族中使用，也在定居西北的汉族中使用，因此，对毛毡技艺和装饰特征的深入研究既是对珍贵的草原文化遗产的保护，更是游牧民族与汉族相互学习和融合的有力说明。

3. 现代创意产业发展及文化交流意义

内蒙古具有丰富的羊毛资源，在 20 世纪初期，仅归化城（呼和浩特市）就有 50 多家毡坊，历来集体所有的毡厂也有若干家，内蒙古六大毛纺厂中的"内蒙古第六毛纺厂"曾经是专门生产毛毡的企业。在乌兰察布、锡林浩特、乌兰浩特、张家口、多伦等地的制毡企业也很多。如今这些毛毡厂都已倒闭或转型，内蒙古目前所需的所有工业毛毡全部来自河北等地，优质的绒毛资源大部分外流导致只能获得较低的原材料利润。通过对制毡技艺及文化的研究，创新传统设计，能够为内蒙古经济发展增添新的活力。

此外，内蒙古羊毛毡手工艺作为一种具有独特艺术价值的手工制品，吸引了全球范围内的收藏家、艺术家和游客。研究这一手工艺的文化交流和互动情况，可以帮助我们了解国家和民族之间的文化交流和互动，提升我们对于全球民族文化的认识。

总的来说，内蒙古羊毛毡手工艺具有研究价值，因为这一传统技艺承载了丰富的民族文化，可以帮助我们了解蒙古族社会历史、文化符号和民族文化的交流与发展，同时也可以为文化保护与传承提供重要的参考。

（三）国内外研究评述

1. 国内研究

羊毛毡手工技艺在我国有着较为悠久的发展历史，其中记录在册的主要有毛毡的使用和毛毡的制作两个类别。有关毛毡使用的文献记载包括《黑鞑十略》《事物纪元》《多桑蒙古史》等，而有关毛毡制作的文献记载包括《天工开物》《齐民要术》等。20 世纪，毛毡步入工业化时代，与工业用毡有关的书籍包括 1984 年出版的《中国纺织科学技术史》、1989 年出版的《内蒙古自治区·商业志》、2001 年出版的《中国古代北方民族文化史》、2008 年出版的《蒙古民族毡庐文化》等，书籍中介绍的毛毡制作工艺与风俗文化均为研究蒙古族传统毛毡的工艺与文化提供了参照素材。

通过文献检索，我们一共收集了 63 篇与羊毛毡相关的国内研究，其中技术研究 46 篇，应用研究 13 篇，开发及行业研究 2 篇，学科教育研究 2 篇；主要研究主题包括羊毛纤维研究 32 篇，羊毛毡织物研究 8 篇，羊毛毡手工艺研究 6 篇，羊毛毡创新应用研究 9 篇，其他羊毛毡工艺技巧研究 8 篇。这些文献具有以下几个特点。

（1）以手工羊毛毡工艺和技法为主

《羊毛毡湿毡技法及其应用》对针毡和湿毡这两种手工羊毛毡工艺的技法进行了详细的介绍，也分析了一些运用湿毡技法创作出的工艺品的艺术特征和技术价值，对羊毛毡艺术作品的未来进行了展望。[①]

（2）以羊毛毡材料创新设计为主

《羊毛毡工艺在服装中的创意设计研究》通过对羊毛毡纤维艺术创作作品中的创意设计实例进行了研究和分析，并且结合作者自身的实践研究和制作流程，清晰地阐述了羊毛毡在服装设计中的创新应用。[②]

（3）以内蒙古游牧文化为主

《内蒙古传统毛毡在现代纺织产品中的现状与发展》从环保的理念出发，以羊毛毡优良的特性及其代表的游牧文化和民族文化为起点，介绍了内蒙古传统羊毛毡的工艺和它的演变，并且对未来毛毡在纺织品中的发展进行了分析与总结，为大众对内蒙古传统文化的认知与传承提供了素材。[③]

2.国外研究

在国外，以羊毛毡作为创意材质的设计出版物很多，仅卓越亚马逊图书销售网站引进的英文原版图书就有 120 余种，但是关于毛毡文化及毛毡历史的图书却非常少。国外的毛毡设计图书大致可分为设计欣赏类和手工操作类，设计欣赏类的图书以设计师设计和制作的毛毡箱包、文化用品、毛毡服饰品以及毛毡家纺用品为主，主要是利用羊毛毡的一次成型性和剪切不脱丝性能制作各种物品。这些出版物具有以下几个特点。

（1）以蒙古族生活方式为主

"蒙古族"系列书籍以图文的方式记录了蒙古族衣、食、住、行等各个方面的风俗习性及蒙古族具有代表性的游牧生活方式，可以较为全面地认知蒙古

---

① 葛亚晶.羊毛毡湿毡技法及其应用.上海工艺美术，2016(4)：83-85.

② 官君.羊毛毡工艺在服装中的创意设计研究.苏州：苏州大学，2016.

③ 李夏.内蒙古传统毛毡在现代纺织产品中的现状与发展.设计，2016(23)：86-87.

族游牧的生活方式。[①]

（2）以制毡工艺为主

Mongolian traditional methods of felt-making（《蒙古族传统毛毡制作方法》）一书详尽描写了蒙古族传统手工羊毛毡的制作方法。

（3）以实践创意为主

《神秘羊毛毡：20 种穿着的艺术品》（*Fabulous Felted Scarves: 20 wearable works of art*）[②] 和《500 种羊毛毡制品：创意与个性的集合》（*500 Felted Objects: Creative Explorations of a Remarkable Material*）[③]，前者主要介绍了 20 件可以穿着的艺术品，包括毡衣、毡帽、毡鞋等的创意设计，后者介绍了包括服饰、室内软装以及各种毛毡小物品的创意设计，还有一些国外的设计师作品。

3.研究现状分析及本研究创新点

综观研究现状，目前国内对于内蒙古羊毛毡文化的研究以羊毛毡材质和历史流变为主题的较多，从文献中获取信息占主要部分。但游牧民族主要生活方式是游牧，记载并流传下来的文字只是一小部分，有许多羊毛毡承载的游牧文化仍需要更多的田野调研去收集和整理，以更好、更完整地传承游牧民族的文化和精神；国外的一系列羊毛毡手工制作方法及创意提供了很多的灵感，相对国内作品来说实验的性质更浓，为羊毛毡的创意研究提供了方向。

在本研究中，我们还进行了国内外研究的对比分析，了解到目前有关其文化和地域差异研究还比较少，从事毛毡创新应用实践的国内外设计师有很多，但是具有特定文化背景，特别是游牧文化背景的毛毡制品设计很少。因此，以研究毛毡制品的传统文化渊源作为切入点进行现代设计，将会为设计领域带来无限的创意可能。

在价值讨论上，我们把这一传统织物放到现代社会背景下，研究毛毡本身的价值，期望通过对传统蒙古族制毡技艺的总结，找出蒙古族与汉族制毡技艺的差异，并依据其擀毡过程的不同，划分其文化属性，找出蒙古族制毡技艺所代表的游牧文化属性的审美观与造物观，以及他们对毛毡制品的美用需求和精神需求，在工艺继承的基础之上进行创新。

---

① Oyontoli. Mongolian traditional methods of felt-making. *Journal of Minzu University of China*, 2009.

② Hagen, Chad Alice, Johnson, Jorie. Fabulous Felted Scarves: 20 Wearable Works of Art. *Lark Books*, 2010.

③ Nathalie Mornu. 500 Felt Objects: Creative Explorations of a Remarkable Material. *Lark Crafts*, 2011.

（四）研究对象及方法

我们以内蒙古羊毛毡工艺为研究对象，以期通过探索去传承和创新羊毛毡文化；从服装设计的角度出发，结合调研实践，更准确地活化少数民族传统工艺。

1.文献研究法

我们期望通过文献研究，了解羊毛毡的历史渊源、发展过程和文化背景，从而对羊毛毡的特点和应用进行深入理解；找到羊毛毡研究领域中的关键问题和尚待解决的难题

我们将通过阅读文献对内蒙毛毡制品的历史渊源及地域民族特征进行整理、归纳、分析，获取充分的历史依据。对相关文献进行查阅、梳理，分类整合每个文献的创新点，比较分析异同，以此来剖析和支撑对比研究。

2.调查法

调查法可以帮助我们通过直接检索相关资料，了解羊毛毡制作的具体过程、技术细节、材料使用等，获得数据；此外，也能够帮助我们更直观地感受羊毛毡的制作过程，更好地理解制作者的角度和感受，更深入地探究羊毛毡制品的内涵和意义。

我们将对内蒙古制毡工艺进行直接的观察和深入，检索内蒙古博物院和游牧文化专题展览相关资料，了解羊毛毡工艺制品制作过程，进而结合理论研究的整理。

3.比较研究法

比较研究法帮助我们全面了解不同羊毛毡的性质、特点和用途。通过对不同类型的羊毛毡进行比较，可以发现它们之间的差异和共性。

我们将从传统手工羊毛毡历史演变的角度进行纵向比较研究，从不同研究对象的角度进行横向比较研究。

二、内蒙古羊毛毡工艺概要

（一）概念界定与发展简史

毡的本义为"用羊毛或其他动物毛（牦牛毛、骆驼毛等），通过加湿、加热、加压反复加工而成的块片状织物"。毡并没有经过纺捻和编织加工的过程，

所以纺织学上也被称为无纺织布。^①而羊毛毡是采用羊毛制作而成的传统织造材料之一，历史纪录可以追溯至公元前 6500 年，流传至今的手工羊毛毡技艺，从房屋建筑到生产生活均有其制品的身影。

羊毛毡工艺在游牧民族的生活中不可或缺。内蒙古自治区气候寒冷，有着非常悠久的毛毡制作和使用历史，其发展历程主要可以分为如下四个阶段。

1.早期：羊毛毡工艺的产生阶段

以传统畜牧业为生的蒙古族，长期处于动态迁徙的过程之中。为了适应这种生产方式，蒙古族人创造出了具有适应移动、搬迁、轻便的人居方式——毛毡帐，也就是蒙古包。由此，羊毛毡就成了蒙古族人生产生活中的一种刚需、一种基础性的生产生活材料。主要毛毡制品有毡帐、铺毡、毡裘、毡车、毡帘、日用毡制品等。

原始的毛毡制作工艺简单，且没有进行染色加工，只有黑白二色，以实用为主，较少有装饰。在传统的内蒙古羊毛毡制作工艺中，主要采用手工操作，依靠手工摩擦、湿热和压力将羊毛纤维互相缠结在一起形成毡状结构。此阶段羊毛毡制品贵族和奴仆均可使用，具有原始生活用品的基本特征。

2.发展：羊毛毡工艺的创新与蓬勃发展期

民族交流与融合的增加，使得毛毡制品逐渐进入中原，并与中原先进的纺织、刺绣技术结合起来，有了很大的新发展。印染技术的运用使毛毡摆脱了单一的色彩，通过表面用丝绸进行镶拼、包裹等技巧的运用，毛毡改变了原有的粗犷风格，开始发展出实用与美观兼具的特性，走向精细化。

元代，游牧民族对毛毡的特殊感情促进了制毡业的发展。蒙古族在领土扩张的同时，吸收其他民族的生产工艺和技术，使得毛毡的制作工艺和装饰程度达到顶峰；同时，大量的毛毡也仍然被用在蒙古包上。《鲁不鲁乞东游记》中对蒙古包用毡的描述："他们用白毛毡覆盖在骨架上面……覆盖在烟囱周围的毛毡，装饰着美丽图画。在门口，他们也悬挂绣着多种颜色的图案的毛毡；他们把着色的毛毡缝在其他毛毡上，制成葡萄藤、树、鸟、兽等各种图案。"《多桑蒙古史》有："外覆以毡，用马尾绳紧束之。门亦用毡，户向南。全家皆处此狭居之内。"

---

① 冯秋华.内蒙古传统羊毛毡的创新设计应用研究.杭州：中国美术学院，2021.

3.衰落：近代羊毛毡工艺的衰颓期

据相关研究者调查，在 20 世纪六七十年代的传统蒙古族制毡习俗中，家用羊毛毡制品多使用绵羊羔毛，制成的羊毛毡又软又紧实，被称作"yanza"；大羊的毛比较粗，对于毡化来说，密度不够容易出现松散的情况，所以蒙古包用的毡一般是 1∶1 比例的大羊毛和羔羊毛混合制成的，这样制成的毛毡又软又保暖，被称作"orto"（长毡）。[①]

然而，在历史流传过程中，大量毡坊缩小生产规模，甚至倒闭；同时，民用毛毡因为产品粗糙、易虫蛀，在城市中已被绒毯取代，传统制毡业基本消失。

4.再创新：内蒙古羊毛毡的复兴期

目前，我国开始逐渐认识到保护和传承传统文化对于加快经济发展和提高全民道德素养的重要意义，具有民族地域特色的羊毛毡制品迎来了复兴时期。羊毛毡除了日常生活用途，也更多地被用在服装设计、建筑应用等方面。

结合内蒙古羊毛毡工艺的主要发展历程，可见其变迁符合一般手工制品的发展规律，经过了"产生－发展－鼎盛－衰落"的过程。

（二）内蒙古羊毛毡原材料选择

在内蒙古地区，主要用于制毡的羊毛为蒙羊毛，是中国蒙古种绵羊的羊毛，属异质毛类型，是中国数量最多、分布地区最广的主要粗羊毛品种。[②]除了羊种，产毛的季节对于毛毡的品质也很重要。大部分地区每年剪两次羊毛，一次在春季、一次在秋季。大多数毡匠喜欢秋季剪下的稍短的羊毛。第一次的剪下的羊羔毛是最为珍贵的制毡羊毛。此外，秋毛和夏毛、粗毛和绒毛的比例要合适。只用秋毛，擀出来毡舒适性差，且容易脱毛；只用夏毛，钻透性差，无法毡化。所以，擀毡时既要有秋毛的钻透力，又要有夏毛的抱合力，毛毡的品质，取决于二者间的配比，还有匠人对温度、湿度以及力度的控制。

（三）内蒙古羊毛毡具体工艺方法

羊毛毡基础工艺主要包括湿毡法、针毡法和湿毡与针毡相结合的方法，而这三种方法基于其毡化原理而生。羊毛毡的基本毡化原理是由于天然羊毛纤维透过扫描电镜可见，每一根羊毛表面都覆有参差层叠的鳞片，鳞片的存在是羊

① 郝水菊.内蒙古地区毛毡制品的传统技艺及其现代设计.无锡：江南大学，2013.
② 姚建平，杜乐.手工羊毛毡技法及艺术特征分析.鞋类工艺与设计，2021(14)：130-132.

毛纤维进行缩绒的最根本原因。这意味着羊毛纤维吸收了水分开始膨胀，鳞片在预热张开后可以像钩爪一样抓住彼此。所以将羊毛混合后加入热水与碱性皂液帮助毡化，再一起反复摩擦，使羊毛纤维逐渐缠绕在一起并且被紧紧缠牢稳定，缩绒就产生了，形成了毛毡片。[①]

1. 湿毡法

作为最早形成的羊毛毡技法，湿毡法制作的选材上发生了一些变化，需要的材料有：型版、纱网布、羊毛条（加工过的羊毛纤维）、弱碱性肥皂、温水等。温水比较容易浸湿羊毛，使羊毛上的鳞片充分扩张，有助于鳞片相互钩嵌。涂抹弱碱性肥皂可以加速羊毛条毡化过程，更快达到所需效果。制作步骤是将羊毛条撕扯成段后均匀铺在型版上，横竖交错4—6层，在将纱网布覆盖在最上层，均匀撒上温水；待羊毛充分湿润后，吸附掉多余的水分。用弱碱性肥皂大量涂抹，缓缓按压，使肥皂水充分浸湿羊毛纤维，排出里面的空气，轻轻打圈按压摩擦，达到初步毡化的效果。根据羊毛毡化的程度加大力量揉搓，达到最终毡化效果。最后洗干净里面的肥皂水，放在通风处晾干即可。[②]

湿毡经过传承至今，现代湿毡法与传统游牧民族制毡技法的原理没有太大的变化，只是现代湿毡更加灵活。湿毡更加适用于在制毡面积较大的地毯或是一体成形的鞋帽等中应用。

2. 针毡法

虽然针毡法由湿毡法演化而来，但在制作方式上更偏向于模拟工业制毡的方法，需要用到一种特殊的戳针。该种戳针前端2厘米呈三棱柱的形状，每条棱边分别有三个凹槽。这样的设计可以增加羊毛纤维的摩擦率。

相对于湿毡法而言，针毡法的步骤简单很多。取适量的羊毛条纤维，在4厘米高的泡沫工作台上，用戳针反复戳刺，使上面的牵引鳞片来回刮擦，从而达到羊毛纤维紧紧的缠绕毡化。前期用粗型号的戳针，垂直戳刺羊毛条起到起形打底，呈现基础毡化形态；之后用中型号的戳针修补形状，填充羊毛；最后用细型号的戳针塑造细节，紧实毡化，弱化针眼。[③]这种方法的优点是可控性强、易于调整、易于操作，可以不断按照需求补充相应的颜色和羊毛进去，制作出清晰、细腻的纹理，适用于小型玩偶、配件、饰品等。

---

① 冯秋华.内蒙古传统羊毛毡的创新设计应用研究.杭州：中国美术学院，2021.
② 徐伟.蒙古族传统装饰元素的应用.呼和浩特：内蒙古农业大学，2006.25-29
③ 姚建平，杜乐.手工羊毛毡技法及艺术特征分析.鞋类工艺与设计，2021(14)：130-132.

3.湿毡针毡结合法

这种方法是将湿毡与针毡结合起来使用，使两者互相补足。湿毡大面积完成后，再用针毡去修饰和补充细节，既节省了时间、又能产生生动效果，比较适用于复杂和大型的毛毡作品。[①]

三、内蒙古羊毛毡制作工艺的传承

（一）实际应用

羊毛毡具有防风、保暖、拒水等性能，是北方地区冬季不可或缺的防寒用品。内蒙古地区的蒙古族与汉族制毡存在很大差异：从毛毡制品的品种来看，汉族毛毡制品多为一次成型，主要是炕毡、毡帽和毡袜；而蒙古族毛毡制品则需要经过后期加工，几乎包含了生活中的各个领域。

1.蒙古包及其室内陈设品

（1）蒙古包

司马迁在《史记·匈奴列传》中提到"匈奴父子乃用穹庐而卧"，可见，传统蒙古包的基本形式很早就已经产生。《蒙古秘史》中提到的"斡鲁格台及"与"失勒帖速台格及"，可翻译为"有天窗的房子"和"有编壁的房子"，指的就是蒙古包。经过上千年的流变，适合游牧生活的蒙古包的建筑材料归纳起来主要是起支撑作用的木头、起包裹作用的毛毡、起固定作用的绳带三大部分。

盖毡有调节蒙古包内部的温度、湿度、采光、通风的作用，覆盖于蒙古包天窗上，一般由用驼毛线锁边的正方形毛毡制成。其中三条与围毡外面的绳子固定，最前面的一条不固定，可以通过它掀开盖毡。顶毡的作用是覆盖蒙古包顶杆，使用3—4层扇形毛毡组合而成，需要裁剪，即以天窗的中心到围壁距离为半径画出顶毡的外侧弧线，以主轴一半为半径画出顶毡的内侧弧线，再将中间剪出与天窗大小相同的一个圆。两片顶毡连接时要在接口处有重叠部分，可以防止风沙、雨水等进入包内。

围毡是蒙古包的毡墙，它的尺寸由编壁的多少决定，一般一层4片、共3层。围毡要比围壁高出一拃。蒙古族在进行测量时一般不使用尺子，只是根据身体某个部位的尺寸进行大概估算，"拃"蒙古语称为"苏格么"，是指张开大

---

① 冯秋华.内蒙古传统羊毛毡的创新设计应用研究.杭州：中国美术学院，2021.

拇指和食指产生的距离，一拃大约 18.5 厘米。高出的部分有助于围毡的固定。围毡顶端要穿上绳子，用来系紧围毡。围毡下侧两角上也有绳子，用来拉紧围毡下边缘。

毡门是蒙古包开口的地方，风沙容易进入，所以需要更加厚重耐用。毡门一般用 3—4 层毡子压实绗缝而制成，多数人会在上面进行精美的毡绣装饰，毡门的精美程度体现了主人的针线手艺。

（2）地毡

蒙古包内铺设的地毡可以防潮保温，蒙古包内没有坐卧家具，人们休息、待客都在毛毡上，同时由于蒙古包内部空间的地面是一个圆形，毛毡的铺设可以将其区域进行合理划分。蒙古包的地毡有"毡包八垫"的说法。整个圆形地面八块毛毡，即 4 个主垫、4 个三角形垫子组成。主垫的前面紧挨火撑圈的四边，后边靠紧哈那的围壁。主垫铺好后，它们之间形成了三角形的空缺，这些部分用三角形的毡子补齐。八个毡垫铺好后，上面还可以放长方形毛毡作为装饰，西北面各两个。

（3）毛毡包袋

羊毛在游牧民族的生活中占有很重要的地位，毡还可以制作各种毡袋，悬挂于蒙古包中，实用性很强。接羔袋、碗袋，以及茶袋、盐袋、杯袋等用品采用毡帘和蒙古包用毡的下角料制作，需要经过裁剪缝制，上面还会用毡绣装饰，大多制作精美，是牧民生活中不可或缺的日常用品。

2. 毛毡服饰用品

（1）毡帽

今天大多数人通过毡帽认识毛毡，虽然毛毡来源于游牧生产，毡帽在西方很多从未有过游牧文化的地区也曾相当普及，在中世纪，毛毡在欧洲以家庭作坊和车间工艺生产为主，专业的制毡车间的成长伴随着一系列梳理弓的引入。制毡行会应运而生，它规定了手工制造毛毡的质量、品种，学徒的长短和使用的材料。这种行会制度自 13 世纪，席卷整个欧洲，也包括中国。

毡帽在世界许多国家都具有不同寻常的意义，不同的帽子形式代表不同国家，中国在引入西方毡帽制作技术的同时，将这种带沿的毡帽命名为"礼帽"，代表着一定的礼仪规范与佩戴阶层，这与中原定居民族将毛毡视作"野蛮与异族"的传统观念截然相反。著名的法国高帽通常装饰有羽毛，刺绣，珍贵的宝石，甚至还有金带。他们也会少量制作其他毛毡手工业制品，包括袜子、靴子、外套、灯罩及动物服饰。16世纪，伦敦有约3000名工匠在40个制毡车间工作，工匠的作坊开始转变为行业。

各种帽子在英国很受欢迎，圆顶的帽子在1797年被引入英国，它几乎在所有阶层中流行，礼帽是19世纪40年代引入英国的。在19世纪末，英国将毡帽出口到中东国家，还出口精细羊毛毡到中国和不丹。与此同时，将毡帽与洋装搭配的方式在中原地区逐渐盛行。而具有民族特色的毡帽在内蒙古与其他游牧地区的使用历史更加悠久，游牧民族重视头饰，不同形状的毡帽代表了不同的部落，即使是布帽或皮帽也会使用毛毡作为支撑。有学者统计，蒙古族有100多种不同风格的帽子以及与之搭配的发型和头饰。很多帽子是由非常精细的毛毡制成的，毡帽可以搭配礼仪服饰、宗教服饰以及日常服饰。汉族也非常喜欢戴毡帽，只是形制更加简单，且不进行装饰，多为男性使用。

内蒙古自治区赤峰市翁牛特旗乌丹镇曾有过繁荣的毡帽制作传统，到1916年，有毡铺8家，从业人员达80多人，年产毡帽达2000余顶，产品远销山东、河北和辽宁等地。乌丹毡帽的特点是弹性大，不易变形。如果用手按下一个坑，很快就会弹起复原。白天戴一天，帽口稍松，过了一夜，早晨再戴时，就已收回。乌丹毡帽以当地的羊绒为原料，用当地野生植物将之煮成咖啡色，晾干后有光泽。20世纪四五十年代，乌丹建立皮毛厂，继承和保留了这一传统产品的生产，最高年产量达到三万多顶。后来随着生活的变化，人们对衣冠装束有了新的追求，毡帽的产量和销路日趋减少。

（2）毡靴

内蒙古地处边陲，冬季漫长寒冷。解放前人烟稀少，交通不便，冬季雪没脚面，有时大雪尺余深。一般天气外出办事，即使骑马坐车也要穿毡靴或毡疙瘩。蒙古靴的特点是靴头上翘，将毛毡裁剪后以不同的方式缝合。蒙古靴使用的材料除毛毡外，还包括鞣制的牛皮、棉布、天鹅绒或缎，冬天为了保暖，人们会穿上绗缝的毡袜。

而在内蒙古东部地区，穿得最多的还是毡疙瘩，这是一种不经裁剪，一次成型制造的靴子。靴腰以下，经过前搓后搓，擀制成厚而实、靴底脚心处凹、两头略呈圆形的靴子，颇象疙瘩，因此称之为"毡疙瘩"。在内蒙古地区，形成毡疙瘩生产规模的地区分别有赤峰市的经棚镇和呼伦贝尔市的海拉尔区。

（3）毛毡斗篷

古代蒙古族穿一种毡袍，是以白驼毛制成，马可·波罗（Marco Polo）

说："以白毛及驼毛织成，其物最美"，可见当时种服装还是比较流行的。元代还有一种古老的毡子斗篷，是一种挡风挡雨的多功能服装，后来演变为成毡雨衣，至今牧民中也有使用，蒙古语称之为"和布纳格"，可以遮风挡雨，也可增加保暖性，对于牧羊人而言是一种实用性很强的服装。

3. 毛毡动物用品

在牧区，毛毡也被用来制作动物用品，游牧生产对于畜力的依赖性较强，牧民也格外善待动物。用毛毡制作驼鞍毡和马鞍，可在骑乘和装载物品时保护牲畜并增加摩擦力，避免人或物品在运动过程中滑落。驼鞍毡用羊毛、马鬃等擀压制成，一般使用密缝的工艺，边缘用绸缎包边，美观耐磨，是垫在驼鞍下面使用的。马鞍毡采用一次性成形的制作方式，符合马鞍的角度，人在骑乘时更加舒适。为防止赛马时马因出汗而影响速度，人们也会在马身上裹上毛毡。还有用毛毡制成的护腰、用于治疗生病动物的"肚子罩"。近年来，人们还把这种鞍垫用于现代交通工具，如摩托车坐垫，这些都体现了蒙古族对毛毡的喜爱。

4. 毛毡车辆用品

有毛毡车棚的勒勒车也叫"家车"或"包车"，游牧民族可以居住在上面，也可以在搬家的时候用其装载物品。在辽阔的大草原上，牧场与牧场之间的距离较远，为了方便迁移，游牧民族都有使用车的习惯。包车的车身与毡棚可以分开使用，结构类似蒙古包，毡车里面是木质框架，外包毡，毛毡边缘可以用布包好，增加美感与耐用性，侧面及顶端为一整块矩形毛毡，前后两块毛毡依据车顶形状裁剪成半圆形，并用纽扣与侧面固定，防止车辆行走时风雪进入。

（二）工艺特征

1. 色彩

传统蒙古族毛毡制品选用的毛毡底色是没有经过染色和漂白的羊毛自然白色。蒙古族喜爱的乳白色是纯洁的象征，对于草原上的牧民来说，白色象征神圣的品质，具有一定的仪式化象征意义。在蒙古族祭祀中，白色的马奶酒要作为祭品撒四方。这种尚白的传统在游牧民族中非常普遍，中亚游牧民族在命名神圣的地方时常常加上"ak"的前缀，意思是白色。在葬礼中使用白色的寿衣，新可汗授衔时要坐在白色的毛毡上，被追随者举起。由此可见，蒙古族崇尚白色的传统自古就有，今天蒙古族也会将白色的哈达献给客人，以显示尊敬。

　　此外，白色与任意色彩搭配。马鬃绳、牛毛绳多为深浅不一的褐色，白色基底上面以褐色线条形成的绗缝图案自然协调，构成了蒙古族毡绣的主色系搭配。

　　2.图案

　　蒙古族不同部落所用的毡绣图案也不尽相同。主要有哈默尔纹，也称鼻纹，象征牲畜平安；召森贺，也称钱币纹，象征家庭富裕；图门贺，也称寿字纹，保佑老人长寿安康；普斯贺，也称圆形纹，是太阳和阳性的符号，预示家族兴旺；波浪纹和万字纹是吉祥的符号，象征佛的保佑，常用来作毡绣的背景图案；兰萨图案常与盘肠、卷草纹组合运用，是生命永生繁衍的符号，具有天地相通、阴阳相合、万代延续的含义。

　　毡门帘、毡坐垫等较大的羊毛毡制品多采用组合图案，如"五畜"和"八宝"等，其构图方式一般为角隅、中心构图法。日常生活用毛毡制品中常有"羊角""鱼腰""盘肠""犬牙"等图案，这些都是游牧生活的真实写照，体现出了草原美学的特征，即从自然主义向装饰主义过渡，注重动物的轮廓线，并用复杂优美的线条来装饰。这也是内蒙古羊毛毡图案中线性装饰所表现出的形式美特征，遵循这一特征，朴素的色彩和线性图案就可以表现出极强的装饰效果，而不显单调乏味。每一个蒙古族部落都有他们偏爱的图案。内蒙古东部地区喜爱几何图案。西部的阿尔泰土尔扈特部落与其他部落的毛毡图案设计反差很大，他们经常使用单一的花朵图案分布于方形区域，而地毡可能有两个或三个中心主题图案，如花卉图案、心形图案和月亮图案，他们也会在轮廓颜色上进行区别。

　　3.工艺

　　传统蒙古族羊毛毡的主要技艺，即绗缝技艺，后经一系列的演变，形成今天的形态。今天，内蒙古地区蒙古族羊毛制毡的技法有：套古其呼（凹凸工艺）、贴花（粘工艺）以及两种技法的组合使用。

　　（1）套古其呼：是指用倒扣针绗缝成各种图案，以点的轨迹形成线条，缝制时要求细点圆润、粗点厚实，整体排列均匀。因为缝制时线迹较密，也称"密缝花毡"。如此形成的毛毡表面肌理感强，具有独特装饰特性。

　　（2）贴花：是把各种布料或皮革剪成纹样贴在基底上，再进行缝缀、锁边而成的一种装饰，多用于大块毛毡的边缘装饰。贴花的装饰丰富了毛毡的色彩与图案，提升了毛毡的耐用性。

在毛毡上创造绗缝效果不需要填料，因为毛毡本身的"体量"使得这一技术非常适合。两层毡缝在一起，作为地毡或毡门厚约 2—3 厘米，用红色或黄棕色的线将图案深深嵌入毛毡。绗缝用的线首选从骆驼的胡子上面得到的驼毛，也可使用马毛、牦牛毛，不用羊毛是因为潮湿的情况下，羊毛线会毡缩，并且深色的线在奶油色的毛毡背景上更加清晰美观。

缝制时要使用戳针，每一次线通过毛毡都要尽可能牢牢地拉紧，以创造出绗缝在毛毡上的压痕效果。缝纫从毛毡的中心开始，防止不均匀或两层毛毡之间的错位。毡上面通常通体覆盖重复的弯曲或笔直的平行线绗缝图案，这些线迹在结尾处改变方向。这种方向的改变增加了毛毡的强度，防止其从绗缝处撕裂。线性、抽象图案非常适合蒙古族毡绗缝技艺，重复的平行线与其他绗缝图案有节奏地对接，传达出一种美感。

（三）文化属性

今天，毛毡在欧亚大陆的游牧民族中仍有广泛的使用。这些游牧文化之间，以及游牧文化与邻近的定居文化在历史上有过无数次的交流与碰撞，形成了符号化的视觉特征。它们与内蒙古地区传统蒙古族毡绣的装饰与审美存在很大的差异，却又有着微妙的联系。

1. 民族文化属性

成吉思汗将游牧的蒙古族描述为"毡帐之民"，认为如果蒙古族不住在蒙古包或者毡帐中，蒙古族将不复存在。可见毛毡对于蒙古族不只是生活的必需品，更是一个民族的标志。虽然很少有这一时期毛毡实物证据，但我们可以从游牧民族的口述历史和生活当中感受其存在。

传统蒙古族羊毛毡制品的图案既有藏传佛教的八宝，也有伊斯兰教的植物卷草纹样，同时还有铜钱、中国结、窗格纹等，这反映出蒙古族对这些宗教图案的理解与应用，而这种兼容并存的图案组合也显出开放的宗教观和浓郁的世俗风格。

2. 地域文化属性

从毛毡擀制技艺及装饰方法可以看出蒙古族与汉族在制毡文化上的差异，蒙古族制毡更侧重仪式感和团结协作的精神，即在一位核心人物的带领下，所有人都要参与其中，而擀毡的最终产品只是一个半成品，它的用途需要其主人经过后期的加工来实现。汉族制毡则强调工匠精神，毡匠的手艺决定了成品的用途与品质。形成以上差异的根本原因在于游牧与定居的不同生活方式。游牧生活对于毛毡的需求量大，擀毡的工作量也大，需要众多的人集合在一起，共同完成。另外，游牧民族每个家庭之间居住的距离较远且并不固定，因而想要完成这样巨大的群体工作需要提前部署，并由一个德高望重者负责统领全局。由于聚会的组织难度高，大家非常重视这样的机会，因而逐渐演变为由祝祷、祭祀、劳动、展示、宴饮组成的仪式。长期在广袤的草原中生存，游牧民族逐渐形成了对大自然的依赖与敬畏，人与人之间的距离制约了相互的交流，也造成了游牧民族更倾向于以祝祷这样普遍接受的方式来表达神圣而肃穆的情感，并依此来传承技艺。至于毛毡的加工，则由蒙古包中的女性在劳动之余慢慢完成。而内蒙古地区的汉族，农耕生产和定居生活使得他们对羊毛原料更加珍视，毛毡在汉族家庭中是等同于家具的固定资产，他们需要雇佣专业技术人员帮助他们制作，以获得高品质的成品，确保其长期使用。内蒙古地区蒙古族与汉族之间的不同生活方式决定了两者毛毡制作技艺的差异，并且直接导致了毛毡的不同用途及其成品制作工艺。

（四）技艺传承

1.传承环境

在内蒙古保留羊毛毡的少数民族地区里，这种古老的手工艺越来越少见，一些毛毡手工艺人外出打工，加上制毡材料的稀缺、工序繁琐、造价高都导致了这一古老手工艺的退化。另外，民间手工的工艺落后、经济效益低下，从事这一手工艺的民间手艺人越来越少，使得这一传统工艺濒临失传。

2.传承方式

以往用传统手工制作的羊毛毡只是用来满足群众自身的生活所需，但今天这些日用品怎么样才能以商品的形式进入旅游市场已经引起广泛的关注。伴随着逐渐开放的旅游市场和逐步提高的商品意识，市场对毛毡的关注程度越来越高。内蒙古羊毛毡的制作通常都采用家庭式或者作坊式的生产方式。过去，这种家族式的加工形式不仅能够适应市场的需求，还能稳定家族内部结构，整合家族的资源。但从社会职能与市场职能角度分析，这种方式如今却是弊大于利，所以对内蒙古羊毛毡进行创新开发的工作已经变得非常严峻。

3.现存问题

（1）传统生产生活方式转变

蒙古族传统羊毛毡工艺依附于游牧民族传统的生产生活方式，随着社会、科技的飞速发展，人们的生活方式也在发生着变化，装饰用毡的出现由此不断增多，预示着传统手工羊毛毡的性质正由"生存"向"生活"转变。

（2）科技冲击下的传统技艺流失

科技的进步使得传统的制毡文化受到了冲击，科技解放了生产力却也导致传统手工艺面临挑战，文化的传承工作跟不上节奏。减缓游牧民族传统手工制毡工艺的流失速度并加强保护和传承显得尤为重要。

四、保护与创新发展内蒙古羊毛毡工艺的建议

（一）保护与发展的总体方向与价值取向

1.立足于当代生活

内蒙古制毡工艺的形成与蒙古族长期以来的草原生活密不可分，是历史生活的产物；然而，今天装饰用毡的出现和不断增多，预示着传统手工羊毛毡的性质正由"生存"向"生活"转变。当今的时代，人们已经有了不同的生活，也产生了不同的需要。因此，在生产、制作羊毛毡制品时，需要提供与此相应的物质和文化产品。

目前市面上已经出现的主要毛毡制品包括服饰类和物用品类。羊毛毡材料的强塑形表现力和针毡法完整塑造细节的能力，在鞋帽、耳饰、家纺、餐垫、旅行包，甚至建筑墙面设计等多种类型的生活用品上都能较好地发挥实用性功能和美学装饰性功能。此前流行的"戳戳乐"，一方面具有良好的箱包装饰作用，另一方面也能通过简单解压的手工操作，给使用者带来轻松愉悦的体验。

2.强化工艺的地域特色

当下，我国工艺发展的地域特色日渐模糊，尤其表现在各地的旅游文创产品表现出趋同性、同质化的特征，在产品的外观设计和文化意涵上并不能充分反映出本地的文化传统与特色。

羊毛毡和游牧生活方式相伴而行，是游牧民族历史进程的见证者，是蒙古族文化意识形态的一种具象化体现。发展和推广内蒙古制毡工艺需要设计制作者深入研究地域文化的特征，在其中选取可以加以利用的元素，从材质、外型以及整体风格等多个角度进行创新。

（二）挖掘传统制毡工艺的当代价值

1.产业价值

一项传统工艺的产业价值一般可以从支撑地方传统工业发展、打造地方文创产业品牌等几个维度展开。使传统工艺保护性发展和创新工艺发展双轨并行，探索其服务于现代人生活方式的产业发展模式，是挖掘传统制毡工艺当代价值的重要路径之一。优秀的传统工艺产业，甚至可以成为一个城市的象征，作为城市名片为地方产业发展注入强大动力。

目前，内蒙古制毡工艺多用于毡帽、毡靴、毡床等生活常用用品的制作，可进一步发掘其在其他领域的应用潜力，丰富本地制毡业的多样化产出方向。

2.就业价值

内蒙古制毡工艺中包含了湿毡法、针毡等多种不同类型的工艺技法，要推动制毡业的发展，就要培养更多掌握这些精细技能的人才。这项传统工艺，基本依靠人力和技艺，对场地和生产条件却没有过高的要求，开放性相对较强，具有带动就业的价值。

3.市场价值

制毡产业的市场价值包括面向国际市场和国内市场的价值。受民族文化和传统工艺的影响，中国少数民族传统产业的核心技术体现在制造环节，特别是手工制作环节，这是少数民族传统工艺独有的、难以被替代的核心竞争力。然而，我国民族传统工艺产业在市场竞争方面，无论是对国内还是国外而言，在形成一个稳定的产业链以及发展营销手段上都还存在着较大的提升空间，并且还存在为追求短期利益而开发脱离民族文化根基产品的现象；内蒙古制毡工艺的市场化过程需要从这些方面不断提升潜力。

（三）多主体参与的可持续发展措施

首先，从政府角度而言，政府需要进一步从政策制定和具体落实上对制毡工艺进行大力扶持。通过设立专项资金，支持内蒙古毡制品的研发、生产和推广，并建立相关标准和认证机制，确保内蒙古毡制品的质量和来源；同时，通过举办展览、发放宣传资料、开展文化交流等活动，进一步加强对其的宣传推广。

其次，当前传统工艺再生产过程中的主要问题在于后续人才短缺、创意创新人才不足，因而需要地方技艺传承机构、人员与学术机构展开积极的合作，利用学术机构的人力资源优势和人才培养经验，拉动传统制毡工艺的生产制作新活力；传统文化与现代科技的深度融合，是优秀传统技艺传承创新发展的重要途径之一。在高校内开设以传承项目为内容的选修课程，将其纳入学校人才培养方案和教学计划，并在校内开办相关实践工作坊；建设保存发展地方传统工艺的专门组织，以及与相关学术机构结对的传承基地等。

最后，民众是传统制毡工艺可持续发展不可忽视的社会基础，激发民众对于手工艺再生产的参与热情。相关部门组织"制毡技艺"培训班、非遗保护及宣传讲座，以及非遗传承人进社区、进校园、进博物馆等活动，有助于增加广大民众对于内蒙古传统制毡工艺的了解。

五、结　语

羊毛毡是集体的记忆，是民族的文化认同，是社会的历史情怀，我们不仅要将这一传统记忆延续下去，将民族文化传承下去，更要通过艺术的手法和设计创新对羊毛毡做出新的诠释，提升使用者的生活质感，提升羊毛毡材料的感性价值。本文通过对内蒙古传统羊毛毡手工技艺的研究得出以下结论：

1.羊毛毡是游牧文化的产物，受游牧文化所处的地域和环境影响，且羊毛毡文化对后来地域文化的形成和发展起到了一定的促进作用，是游牧民族历史进程的见证者，更是游牧民族的情感依附所在。

2.羊毛毡是具有自然温度的材料，具有很强的包容性和塑造性，是许多工业材料取代不了的。它不仅是一种传统手工艺，也是节能减排的现代纺织材料，与环保、减速的现当代设计需求一拍即合。

3.羊毛毡手工作品就是将感性价值可视化的过程，对羊毛毡材料的活化和感性价值的挖掘，能够进一步构建带有传统记忆的羊毛毡的感性价值体系。

因此，我们也希望通过本文呼吁并号召社会关注内蒙古地区传统羊毛毡手工艺，共同为非遗文化的传承贡献自己的一份力量，让羊毛毡手工艺制品走向世界。

当代苏绣技艺的传承现状与创新路径研究[①]

摘 要: 本文以中华四大名绣之一的苏绣为研究对象，通过研究苏绣作品的分类及特色，探寻其表现的人与环境关系的内涵。基于此，通过文献调查等多种方式，分析苏绣作为一种较为典型的非物质文化遗产，在传承和创新中面临的一系列诸如题材受限、市场混乱、传承者老龄化、工业制品冲击和社会偏见等问题，并结合国内外在文化传承和创新领域的研究，讨论在苏绣的传承和创新中，如何鼓励人才投身苏绣行业，如何建设成熟的人才培养政策体系，如何建设艺术创新激励方案上等问题。

关键词: 苏绣; 文化遗产; 传承; 创新

一、绪 论

(一) 研究背景及意义

传统文化是一个民族的精神财富，对于增强民族的认同感、文化自信和维护社会稳定具有重要作用。然而，随着现代化进程的加速推进和国际交流的增强，传统文化面临着被边缘化、被遗忘甚至消亡的风险。传统技艺传承是有别于现代产业技能培育的一个特殊的人力资本投资领域，它肩负着为传统技艺相关产业培育匹配人才和促进中华优秀传统文化发扬光大的双重使命。因此，传统技艺传承无疑是一个兼具文化意义和经济价值的重要课题。

苏绣作为中国传统工艺的代表之一，以其独特的风格和浓郁的地方特色，在国内外都享有很高的声誉。在 2006 年，苏绣作为中国四大名绣之一被列入

---

① 作者: 王欣，上海交通大学人文学院; 黄其灏，上海交通大学设计学院; 陈舒琦，上海交通大学教育学院; 李梓瑞，上海交通大学材料科学与工程学院; 林志杰，上海交通大学材料科学与工程学院。

第一批国家级非物质文化遗产代表性项目名录。苏绣具有千年的历史积淀，承载了丰富的文化内涵和民族精神。通过对苏绣的深入研究，可以更好地认识和理解传统文化的独特魅力，为其传承与保护提供理论支持和实践指导。

（二）研究对象及内容

本研究的主要对象是苏绣，旨在通过对苏绣的调查和分析，展现传统文化在传承与创新中的问题，并提出一些可行的解决方案。具体研究内容如下。

1.背景分析：国内外相关研究及传承发展现状的对比分析。

2.案例分析：以苏绣保护为案例，分析国内传统文化保护的现状和问题。

3.国内文化遗产传承保护与创新发展的建议：结合上述研究，对文化遗产传承保护与创新发展提出建议。

（三）研究思路及方法

本研究拟采用综合性的研究方法，具体研究思路和方法如下。

文献研究：利用中国知网搜集、阅读大量关于苏绣、国内外文化遗产传承发展现状等方面的文献资料，并对搜集到的文献资料进行筛选与整理，了解目前以苏绣为代表的文化遗产的研究现状和发展历程。

定性调查：通过深入调查、观察等方式，收集苏绣相关的经验、观点和评价，了解苏绣在历史、技艺、传承等方面的情况。

网络调查：利用互联网平台开展媒体讨论，获取更广泛的苏绣相关信息和意见，了解苏绣这一传统文化的受众及社会风评。

（四）国内外苏绣研究概述

1.国内苏绣研究

国内许多大学、研究机构和民间机构都进行了关于苏绣文化遗产的学术研究。这些研究主要包括苏绣的历史渊源、技艺与传承、图案设计、工艺流程、区域特色等方面的内容。通过对苏绣技艺的解析和研究，学者们对苏绣的历史定位、文化内涵和艺术特点有了更深入的理解。

中国美术学院：作为中国著名的艺术学院之一，中国美术学院在刺绣领域进行了广泛的研究。学院设有刺绣与服装设计专业，开展苏绣相关的学术研究，包括苏绣的技艺传承、图案设计、刺绣工艺等方面。

南京艺术学院：南京艺术学院是中国较早开设刺绣专业的艺术学院之一，致力于苏绣的研究和传承。学院设有刺绣与服装设计系，培养了一大批苏绣艺术家和研究人员。

江苏刺绣研究院：江苏刺绣研究院是专门从事刺绣研究和保护的机构，致力于苏绣的研究与传承。院内设有刺绣文化遗产保护与研究中心，开展苏绣技艺的研究、保护和传承工作。

上海纺织职业培训学院：该学院设有纺织工艺刺绣专业，专注于苏绣的研究和传承。学院开展苏绣技艺的培训和研究，为苏绣艺术家和从业人员提供培训和指导。

为了保护和传承苏绣文化遗产，国家和地方政府出台了一系列政策和措施，包括加强苏绣非物质文化遗产的保护与认定，设立苏绣艺术学校和培训机构，组织相关展览和比赛，推广苏绣以激发民间刺绣艺术家的创作热情，并且致力于将苏绣纳入教育体系，使其成为一门受重视的技艺。

但同时，对于以苏绣为例的文化遗产的研究和保护还存在很大的不足：

一是研究深度不足。虽然有一些学术研究对苏绣进行了探索，但对于苏绣的某些方面，如技艺和传统工艺的详细解析、苏绣与其他艺术形式的关联等，研究深度仍然有待拓展。一些相关的技艺和历史知识可能仍未被充分记录和传承。

二是结合现代创新不足。虽然有些设计师和品牌开始将苏绣与现代时尚和工艺结合，但整体上，苏绣在现代创新方面的应用还相对较少。更多的创新和实践可以进一步提升苏绣的时尚感和市场竞争力。

三是传承面临挑战。苏绣作为一种传统手艺，传承面临着许多挑战。年轻人对于苏绣技艺的兴趣较低，传统技艺的传承机制需要得到加强。同时，苏绣作为非物质文化遗产，需要更多的政策和措施来保护和传承，以防止传统技艺的失传。

四是缺乏国际传播。尽管国内对苏绣的研究和保护工作较为积极，但苏绣的国际传播还相对较少。需要加强苏绣的国际宣传和推广，开展国际交流与合作，以提高苏绣的国际影响力和认可度。

2. 国外苏绣研究

刺绣在我国有着悠久的历史，历代匠人们不断推陈出新，创造出许多有中国特色的刺绣针法。刺绣在国外也是一种源远流长的手工艺，在古埃及法老的坟墓里，人们就发现了古老的珠绣制品。

以苏绣为代表的中国传统刺绣技艺也融入了欧洲刺绣技艺当中。在国外，以苏绣为代表的中国传统刺绣工艺受到了一定的关注。部分学者从跨文化的角度出发，关注苏绣与国外传统刺绣工艺的异同点，以及苏绣在当代艺术市场的发展前景。

然而，需要指出的是，虽然已有一些研究成果，但仍存在一些问题亟待解决。比如，在苏绣的艺术研究与创新方面，需要通过材料、技法、主题上的革新，使古老苏绣展现新活力，有学者认为苏绣主要运用的刺绣技术是在织物的两面同时绣上一个图像，然而双面不一样的刺绣技法才是关键的应用技术。此外，中国刺绣艺术家虽然拥有出色的技能，但往往停留在简单地复制传统的形象，苏绣应该挖掘出更多的题材。而在苏绣的传承与保护方面，传统审美和现代时尚的统一仍旧面临困难，比如，苏绣大型作品的主题通常是传统的风景、锦鲤和花朵等，这可能是出于商业考虑，但也形成了不够契合年轻人市场的问题。

二、案例：国内文化遗产

（一）"苏绣"概述

1."苏绣"的概念及内涵

苏绣，是苏州地区刺绣产品的总称，为江苏省苏州市民间传统美术。苏绣起源于苏州，是四大名绣之一，也是国家级非物质文化遗产之一。

苏绣发源地在苏州吴县一带，现已遍布无锡、常州等地。刺绣与养蚕、缫丝分不开，所以刺绣又称丝绣。清代确立"苏绣、湘绣、粤绣、蜀绣"为中国四大名绣。苏绣具有图案秀丽、构思巧妙、绣工细致、针法活泼、色彩清雅的独特风格，地方特色浓郁。

2006 年 5 月 20 日，苏绣经国务院批准列入第一批国家级非物质文化遗产名录，遗产编号为Ⅶ-18。

2.传统苏绣的形式特征及文化表现[①]

无论是日用品还是艺术品，苏绣都具有物质的实用性和精神的审美性，在满足日常所需的同时还蕴含着丰富的情感，兼有物质与精神的双重文化内涵。具有重要的历史认知价值与艺术价值，表现出淡雅、精致、清秀、隽美的艺术风格，具有平、齐、细、密、匀、光、和、顺的外观特点。深入研究苏绣的表

---

① 陆洁，马天伟.传统苏绣的形式特征及其文化表现.江苏丝绸，2014(3): 21-24.

现形式，既能从中领悟传统艺术的形式美感，更能体会其蕴含的江南地域风情及其文化特征。

（1）题材

苏州虎丘云岩寺塔出土的最早本地刺绣实物，即五代绣袱，其纹样题材包括宝相莲、荷叶、凤穿牡丹及卷草、菱花等图案。

从地理环境看，苏州湖泊纵横，多菱、藕等水生作物，卷草、菱花象征水乡特色的生活环境；凤鸟自汉代起即为吉祥长寿的象征，凤穿牡丹更是隋唐以后在民间盛行的吉祥图案，寓意富贵美满。宋代以后，苏绣图案以花鸟写实为主，日用绣品既可供欣赏又能借物表意。苏绣内容还有水生动物如鱼、鸭、鸳鸯，江南的飞鸟和陆地植物喜鹊、燕子、玉兰、海棠、牡丹、石榴、梅花等。可见，传统苏绣在题材选择方面自古便有一语双关的倾向，以谐音、隐喻等暗托祝福，表达吉祥的含义。这类图案的题材选择往往具有意在不言中的效果，反映出当地人细腻、含蓄的审美习惯，以及苏绣丰富的文化积淀和深刻内涵。

（2）色彩

苏绣经五代至宋初已有较大的发展，刺绣日用品的技法娴熟、品种多样，出现了双面绣；同时，受工笔画的影响，色彩柔和且有光泽，以花鸟为主的绣品逐层施绣，细腻地表现出花瓣和鸟儿身上绒毛的层次感。画入绣、绣似画，以针代笔、以线代色，形成了独立的刺绣观赏品——"画绣"，这种观赏性刺绣的兴起得益于宋代皇家对织绣创作的统一管理，是书画的另一种表达方式，也称宫廷绣。

苏绣吸收了绘画艺术的特点，并逐渐形成了自己的特色。闺阁中具有绘画素养的名门闺秀会将其作为陶冶情操之用，在配色上先立基调，再运用国画渲染的手法处理各类景物，善用中间色和色或调色，使色彩柔和文静。画绣既具有实用的室内装饰功能，也可作表达情谊的赠品或文人雅士间的观赏交流之用，绣面根据画作的特点绣有题词押印，透出浓浓的书卷气，被赞为"佳者较画更胜"。

民间苏绣日用品的配色不像"画绣"那样受自然形象的局限，具备统一中求变化的形式美感，充分流露出民间手工艺人自由创作的朴素美，并且具备实用、美化功能，可以表达人们的思想情感和生活情趣。这些日用品常采用色线反复使用、连续照应的手法，即便用色鲜艳也不显生硬，仍然具有较丰富的层次感且过渡自然，这与苏州地区讲究雅致的审美观相一致，反映出当地宁静优雅的生活环境与低调和谐的淳朴民风。

（3）构图

苏州自唐至清商业发达，兴而不衰，文学艺术门类齐全，明代"吴门画派"独领风骚，这种环境使苏绣不仅具有较高的艺术价值，同时也具备手工艺品的商业特点。明清时期，苏州的丝绸和刺绣享誉四海，始于明代的补子即主要来自苏州、南京等地，至清代，朝廷在苏州扩大织造衙门办绣局，其绣品只作为贡品，雍正、乾隆时期，由宫廷画师专门绘制刺绣图案，送苏州绣局制作，但其构图都较程式化，规矩严谨。这使苏绣受到宫廷绣庄严、富贵的艺术风格的影响，构图讲究均衡呼应而端庄和谐。

清代，苏绣中的商品绣逐渐形成行业，与观赏绣相比更具实用性，商品绣由绣庄雇的代放者分发给苏州周边各地的绣女加工，产品包括部分官货、戏衣以及各类日用品。商品绣的绣稿除官货外，一般出自民间画工之手，也吸收国画的布局，装饰性较强，并根据绣品品种分类绘制，构图均衡、丰满，以花鸟为主的刺绣图案追求平衡、对称，给人质朴、古拙的感觉。闺阁画绣源于宫廷绣，盛于明代，采用国画形式的布局，构图简练，主题突出，意境悠远。但无论是观赏性强的闺阁绣，还是实用性强的商品绣，都是在日用刺绣的基础上发展而来的，并与绘画有着密切的关系，构图的规律性较强。

作为生活用品的苏绣，图案抽象写意，大致可分为两大类，一类是纯图案的，如用于日用品边上装饰的边花，具有连续、对称的特点；另一类是绘画式的，如团花或单独纹样、角花等，构图形式灵活多变，但仍然遵循平衡、均匀的规律，图案纤致柔软，地方特色显著。

（4）针法

苏绣以"精细雅洁"著称于世，"精细"是指技艺精湛细致，"雅洁"则体现了苏绣的艺术风格，给人以雅致而洁净的审美感受，苏绣之美在于用精湛的技艺体现艺术的价值，"技"中有"艺"，"艺"凭"技"高，苏绣通过穿针引线的技巧，使纵横交错的彩色丝线在光的反射作用下形成不同的明暗效果，从而巧妙生动地表达画面内容的真实感。苏绣不但针法多，绣法也多，同一种对象可以运用不同的针法，也有不同的绣法，绣法就是根据对象的形态及风格，正确灵活地运用线条的不同粗细、方向、颜色及针法。

以画理施绣的闺阁画绣为淋漓尽致地表现画面的写实效果，摹画笔墨的韵味，常用滚针、旋针、斜缠针、施针、掺针、钉线绣、打籽针等针法，灵活多变，没有固定的程序。滚针在接针的基础上发展而来，用于表现卷曲有张力的茎须或图案轮廓，绣出的线条流畅舒展，转折处用旋针绣出，线条渐宽处改用斜缠针；掺针和施针能灵活运用丝线的折光，表现画面丰富的光影变化，使色彩过渡匀称，有时在刺绣过程中，旋针针法也会被活用于掺针和施针中，以实现刺绣写生的意境。

绣艺及针法的不断提高，使绣品的正反面达到一样平复美观的效果，具有双面观赏的价值，加之明清商品绣需求的增加，以前仅在闺阁画绣中出现的双面绣，也在日用品中频频出现。可见，无论哪类传统苏绣制品，在其发展过程中都有着相互渗透、互为推进的现象。社会开放程度越高，这种交流就越普遍，相互作用也越深入，表现出更高、更丰富的实用与审美的双重价值。

在民间，刺绣针法更注重本身的装饰性，而不强调绘画效果，常用正戗、平针、套针、接针、钉线、打籽等针法，规律性强，一般面料及绣线相对较粗，注重节省且绣工略显粗放，但仍不失苏绣精巧细致的风格。

（二）"苏绣"工艺传承发展现状

1. "苏绣"的整体发展概况

作为苏州传统艺术的一个代名词，苏绣的品牌形象已经与这片孕育她的土地融为一体，也成为苏州乃至整个江南地区城市形象建设的一个重要元素。

从苏州城市形象打造的角度来讲，作为一个历史文化名城，苏州历经千年发展，其形态必然扎根于江南自然环境与当地劳动者创造的人文财富之中，苏绣作为其中一支重要的力量，其品牌形象已成为苏州城市建设的无价资产。良好的苏绣品牌传播将极大提升苏州城市形象建设，增强其吸引力，由此吸引更多的旅游者、投资者、新居民和高技术人才等城市消费者，为苏州城市经济文化的发展注入强大动力。[①]

2. 苏绣传承人现状

苏州刺绣名扬天下，但刺绣艺术的发展也日益面临知识产权问题：绣娘们的刺绣作品底稿少有原创，而自己的精品常常被别人仿冒。

绣娘队伍"老龄化"，传承人才稀缺。据调查统计，在450个"在职"绣娘（不包括在家中刺绣的绣娘）中，50岁以上的占19%，40岁至50岁的占47%，30岁至40岁的占29%，30岁以下从事刺绣制作的只有5%不到。从

---

① 管家庆;吴玲玉.新时期的苏绣品牌发展.艺术教育，2014(4): 45-46.

这组数据可以看出，如今绣娘的队伍出现了"老龄化"趋势。更加令人担忧的是，一大部分中年绣娘表示，迫于种种原因，自己即将离开绣娘队伍。有的是改行了，有的是要照顾家庭和下一代孩子……长此以往，苏绣手艺人的队伍只会越来越小。①

"六七岁低头拿针，再抬头已是华发苍颜。"正是绣娘们刺绣生涯的真实写照。另外，在经济高速发展的社会现状下，生活节奏日益加快，人们的心态也变得浮躁，而刺绣是一项需要极大耐心的工作，这一点就很少有人能做到。

以上现状成为影响苏绣产业发展的严峻问题，刺绣人才流失，后继少人，严重制约了苏绣的发展。

3. 苏绣的传承方式与路径特点②

首先，在政府的扶持下，苏绣产业快速发展。2009年，镇湖街道投入4000万进行绣品街改造；2014年，苏州镇湖刺绣艺术馆被文化部列入第二批国家级非物质文化遗产生产性保护示范基地；2018年5月24日，入选第一批国家传统工艺振兴目录。在政府的扶持下，苏绣产业快速发展，并形成了一定的产业规模。

其次，苏绣产业空间分布整体分散，局部集中。如今苏绣产业化已经具有一定的规模，中小型企业数量众多，发展迅速。苏州刺绣产业生产和销售环节主要在苏州市镇湖镇。

再次，产业传承相关的支撑平台逐步完善。一是人才培育平台，主要通过与当地的工艺美术学校合作举办刺绣班以及委托当地高校培育刺绣专业人才，为刺绣产业打造专门的人才队伍，提高刺绣后备人才的文化修养与专业技能。此外，当地的工艺美术大师也会通过以师带徒的方式来教授、传承相关知识，但是人才培育数量上略显不足。二是知识产权保护平台，2009年镇湖就开始与苏州市知识产权局合作建设苏州市刺绣作品版权交易平台，该平台在2010年9月正式运营，苏州市版权局投资50万元。知识产权平台的建立不仅提高了从业人员的知识产权意识，也有效减少了有关知识产权问题的纠纷。

---

① 钱建琴.浅析苏绣的现状与发展构想.丝路视野，2019(1): 181-182.
② 陈意，蔡正惠.苏绣非物质文化遗产的产业化传承分析.现代营销(经营版)，2020(11): 22-23.

（三）苏绣传承发展存在的问题

1.题材受限且缺乏创新

苏绣特殊的表现形式——以针代笔、以线代色勾勒出一幅幅栩栩如生的画面——使得它的题材通常是山水、花鸟画；刺绣产生的时代背景也使得刺绣题材受到了局限。此外，人们的审美标准也发生了变化，以前的样稿已无法满足如今人们的审美需求。苏绣题材需要创新、发展以展现它自身的特色与个性。基本图案、款式都一样，导致家家挂同样图案销售，虽然研发成本低，但容易被同行模仿复制。

绣娘原创能力不足和刺绣产业发展迅速的情况不相适应，形成了矛盾，制约了苏绣产业的进一步发展。当然，这也与绣娘本身的素质有关。在职绣娘由于学历水平不高，加上出去学习的机会不多，只能在家或者绣庄里埋头苦做，难有进步的空间。所以需要完善继续教育机制，让更多的绣娘得到提升自己的机会，不断探索学习，通过创新实现苏绣产业转型升级。

2.市场管理机制不完善

如今苏绣的文化产业化发展已经取得一定的成绩与规模，但诸多从业者法律意识淡薄，缺乏法律知识，知识产权保护仍然存在着一定的问题。例如，因为苏绣制品成本较高，许多地方出现了仿制的苏绣，一些喜欢苏绣艺术但又不了解苏绣的人士，经常会买到"山寨苏绣"。

随着科技进步，机绣产品也占据了苏绣的一部分市场，常常被作为旅游纪念品销售。此外，业内模仿抄袭的现象屡见不鲜，优秀的原创作品流入市场后，往往很快就有大量的雷同品出现。可见，苏绣市场仍需完善相关机制，以规范竞争，稳定市场。

3.由生活用品转变为工艺品

早在春秋时期，苏绣就已经被应用于装饰衣物，也可以作为工艺品用来装饰。明朝时期，苏绣形成了"家家养蚕，户户刺绣"的盛况，江南成为丝织手工业中心。而随着生活方式改变，一些传统的民俗也逐渐被人们忽略，人们的思维方式以及审美方式发生了改变，苏绣已经不能作为一种具有实用性的日用品来传承发展了，更多的是被当作艺术品来收藏。

4.制作成本高，消费对象受限

苏绣的工艺复杂，人工耗时大，导致每一幅作品的制作成本都比较高，普通家庭往往消费不起。目前的主要消费群体往往只是社会的一小部分人，拓展苏绣艺术的消费市场。消费市场的约束、消费对象的局限，使得刺绣发展较为艰难。

5.营销人才缺乏，经营模式陈旧

当前，苏州镇湖刺绣已经树立起品牌形象，并初步形成产业经济，这给镇湖苏绣的发展带来了机遇。但是，绣品街的刺绣经营模式陈旧，大部分都坚守着传统的"前店后坊"经营方式，难以给游客带来良好体验。部分刺绣艺术大家开设的刺绣艺术馆，虽然结合了镇湖刺绣的品牌和新式的包装，但绣品价格昂贵，缺乏商业传播，导致市场销路不佳。

6.技术变革带来的挑战

过去，刺绣还算不上一个产业，绣娘们都分散在各个村子，刺绣仅仅是为了补贴家用。而现在，刺绣慢慢转变成集丝线、绣制、装裱、包装于一体的完整的产业链。在大机器生产的时代，传统的产业链受到了极大的挑战，传统的运输与包装已经无法满足市场的需求，随之而来的是机绣充斥市场，几乎将手绣排斥在外，然而手绣赋予作品的生命力是机绣无法替代的，但很多消费者并未意识到这一点，可见，技术的变革对于传统手工工艺是一场巨大的挑战。

7.人才培养滞后

苏绣产业化，需要依托大量的专业人才继承发扬这门传统工艺。为了培养刺绣人才，解决人才短缺问题，当地政府主动设立创新基金，每年举办"银针杯"刺绣新人大赛，与苏州工艺美院合作开设刺绣专业大专班，在中小学开设刺绣课程。但这些努力相对于苏绣每年16.5%的产值增速、国内外高端市场庞大的消费群体以及苏绣企业对人才的需求，可以说是"杯水车薪"。

8.传播形式传统

目前，苏绣信息的传播主要分为：博物馆、艺术馆的宣传展览，低端绣品的批发生产，高端绣品的私人订制，民间宣传教育活动。总的来看，苏绣信息的传播形式较为传统，较少运用现代信息技术。同时，对于苏绣品牌的塑造和运营较少，思想较为保守。[①]

三、国内苏绣文化遗产传承保护与创新发展的建议

我国大力促进中华优秀传统文化创造性转化、创新性发展，在展览展示、

---

① 吕彦池.非物质文化遗产数字化保护与传承——以苏绣为例.自然与文化遗产研究，2019(8)：53-55.

文化旅游、文化衍生品生产经营以及研究教育等四大领域，不断增强文化遗产传承活力，文化遗产创新性保护取得重要进展，但仍面临一些问题。针对这些问题，本文尝试提出一些传承保护与创新发展的建议。

（一）注重人文引领，引导差异化运营与多样化发展

1.对接传统与现代：在传承苏绣工艺的同时，要积极引入现代技术和设计理念，以满足现代市场和消费者的需求。例如，将苏绣工艺与现代家居、服饰、艺术品等结合，创造出新颖的产品和艺术作品，拓展苏绣工艺的市场和应用领域。[①]

2.培养新一代工匠：通过设立专业学院、培训班等途径，培养年轻的工匠和艺术家，传承苏绣工艺的技术和创作精神。注重传统经典技法和创新设计的结合，培养出具有创新能力和市场洞察力的苏绣工艺人才。

3.政策与资金支持：政府和相关机构可以提供支持政策和资金，鼓励苏绣工艺的传承与创新。通过减免税收、设立专项基金、组织展览、开展市场推广等方式，增加对苏绣工艺的支持力度，提升其在经济和文化领域的影响力。

4.加大宣传力度：通过民间口口相传、构建数字化平台互动等方式，可以使更多人了解并爱上这一历史文化遗产。

通过以上措施，可以使苏绣工艺在人文引领下实现差异化运营与多样化发展，传承其精髓与技艺，同时注入创新的元素，使之与现代社会和市场需求相契合，并得到更广泛的认可和传播。[②]

（二）强化设计引领，推动创造性转化与创新性发展

1.结合设计思维与苏绣工艺：引入设计思维的方法和理念，将其应用于苏绣工艺的传承与创新过程中。通过对用户需求、市场趋势和技术发展的深入分析，结合苏绣工艺的传统元素，探索新的设计解决方案和创新产品。

2.创造性转化：通过设计的力量，将传统的苏绣工艺进行创造性转化，将其应用于新的领域和场景。例如，将传统的苏式图案和纹样应用于现代产品设计中，如家居用品、服装、装饰品等，赋予其现代感和商业价值。

3.合作创新：与设计师、艺术家、科技企业等进行合作，开展联合设计与

---

① 冯炜.联合国教科文组织非物质文化遗产保护理念探讨——兼论婺州民间美术的保护原则.美与时代（上），2020(6)：26-28.
② 陆秋澄.浅析苏绣的传承与创新.文化产业，2021(32)：20-22.

研发活动。通过跨界合作，融入不同领域的专业知识和创新思维，推动苏绣工艺的创新与发展。例如，与数字科技公司合作开发基于虚拟现实或增强现实技术的苏绣工艺呈现方式，提升其观赏性和互动性。

4.注重用户体验：以用户为中心，注重用户体验的设计方法和原则。通过深入了解用户需求和心理，将苏绣工艺创新与用户喜好相结合，设计出更具吸引力和实用性的产品和体验。例如，改进苏绣工艺的制作工艺和功能设计等，使之符合现代用户的生活方式和审美需求。

通过设计引领的方式，可以促进苏绣工艺的传承与创新，使其在传统基础上焕发新的活力和市场竞争力。同时，设计还能为苏绣工艺赋予时尚、个性化和功能性，使其更好地适应现代社会和消费者的需求，实现与时代的对话和融合。

（三）坚持生态引领，促进实用性造物与可持续发展

1.使用环保材料与工艺：在苏绣工艺的传承与创新中，注重使用环保材料和工艺。选择可再生材料、有机材料或回收材料，避免使用对环境有害的物质，减少对资源的消耗与污染。同时，推广绿色制造工艺，如低能耗、低排放的生产过程，减少对环境的负面影响。

2.坚持可持续设计与生产：将可持续发展的理念融入苏绣工艺的设计与生产中。从产品设计的角度出发，考虑材料的循环利用、产品的可拆卸与再生利用，设计出具有可持续性的产品。同时，倡导节约能源与资源的生产方式，减少浪费和污染。

3.融合自然生态与传统文化：将自然生态与苏绣工艺的传承相结合，通过提取自然元素与灵感，设计出体现生态美学的产品。同时，强调苏绣工艺与当地的传统文化和生态环境的融合，凸显自然与人文的和谐共生。

生态引领的方式可以促进苏绣工艺的传承与创新，使其与可持续发展目标相契合。生态引领不仅可以保护环境、提升产品的可持续性，还能激发创作者的创造力。生态引领也能够增加消费者对苏绣工艺的认可和喜爱度，推动市场需求的增长，实现可持续发展与经济效益的双赢。

四、结 论

（一）研究总结

本文在对苏绣工艺和传承人进行史料分析的基础上，展现了文化遗产苏绣的基本状况。通过对苏绣的概念、历史、门类和传承发展现状的分析研究，对苏绣技艺传承的基本规律和存在问题进行了一定的思考，进而提出了关于如何传承保护与创新发展国内文化遗产的对策建议。研究的主要内容和结论包括：

1. 苏绣经过两千多年的发展，已形成独立的刺绣风格。

2. 苏绣的发展面临知识产权、绣娘队伍老龄化等问题。

3. 人与苏绣作品存在着相互依存、影响的互动关系。这种互动关系丰富了工艺的内涵与外延，也体现了人与文化之间的紧密联系。

4. 苏绣工艺需找到传承与创新的路径。一是注重人文引领，引导差异化运营与多样化发展，传承其精髓与技艺，同时注入创新的元素；二是强化设计引领，推动创造性转化与创新性发展，实现与时代的对话和融合。

5. 苏绣工艺人才的培养与传承需要得到重视。首先需要弘扬工匠精神，加强宣传与价值认同。其次要完善激励机制，鼓励批量化人才引培。最后要开展共建合作，构建长效性培养模式。

（二）研究局限性

手工技艺类"非遗"项目的特殊性、重要性以及内在的复杂性，决定了关于手工技艺类"非遗"项目内容无法在论文中面面俱到、悉数呈现。因此，未来的研究还可以从以下几方面进行深入探讨。

一是苏绣技艺代际传承的内在机理。受客观条件所限，仅对苏绣工艺和传承人进行史料和文献分析是无法客观分析手工技艺在代际之间传承的基本规律和内在逻辑的。因此，完成对"非遗"传承人的深度访谈，着眼于技艺的代际传承问题，将作为本研究的延续工作。

二是异质性区域中的刺绣类工艺技艺传承比较研究。外在社会文化环境对于手工技艺的传承有着重要的影响。既然如此，那么：为什么一些技艺能够在某地得以传承发展，而在另一个地方却消亡不见？为什么同样的手工技艺在不同地域的传承方式却千差万别？这些疑问将在后续研究进行探讨。

三是苏绣技艺传承的制度逻辑。本文未能阐释宏观制度与微观个体行为之间的鸿沟，在未来的研究中将从行动研究视角入手，解释苏绣传承制度如何建构传承行动，即制度逻辑的问题。

（三）未来展望

五千年灿烂多彩的文化遗产是中华民族文化自信的源泉，而在信息时代高速发展的今天，发展民族化、本土化的工艺已成为一个必然的趋势。本文聚焦于苏绣的传承与创新这一主题进行了多方面探究，希望能为更好地保护、传承和利用非物质文化遗产提供参考。

苏州桃花坞木版年画的传承保护与发展[①]

摘　要： 苏州桃花坞木版年画有着 400 多年历史，与天津"杨柳青"年画并称"南桃北柳"，具有高度的艺术、历史和地域文化价值。但作为我国的非物质文化遗产之一，木版年画也面临着时代变迁所带来的"功能性衰退"问题和传承力量不足的困境。本文将通过对苏州桃花坞年画的工艺、历史、发展现状、市场空间等案例基础信息的收集和分析，以及国内外同类型艺术形式的对比和宣传策略的借鉴，结合发扬"中华优秀传统文化"，坚持"文化多样性"的时代要求，遵循"原地保护、原汁保护"的文化遗产保护与发展宗旨，为木版年画重新成为大众文化消费品提供方案。

关键词： 木版年画；创新；大众文化消费品

一、前　言

（一）桃花坞木版年画背景

桃花坞木版年画始于明，盛于清，因曾集中在苏州城内桃花坞一带生产而得名。它和河南朱仙镇、天津杨柳青、山东潍坊杨家埠、四川绵竹的木版年画，并称为中国五大民间木版年画。其技法继承了宋代雕版印刷工艺，由绣像图演变而来，形式以门画、中堂、独幅画为主；内容有驱凶辟邪、祈福纳祥、风俗时事、戏曲故事等。2006 年 5 月 20 日，桃花坞木版年画经国务院批准列入第一批国家级非物质文化遗产名录，项目编号为Ⅶ-3。

① 作者：金艾迪，苏州大学唐文治书院；刘雪洁，苏州大学政治与公共管理学院；刘馨怡，苏州大学政治与公共管理学院.

苏州桃花坞木版年画已有不少于 400 年的历史，其出现与雕版印刷密切相关。我国的雕版印刷兴于唐，盛于宋。但是，更普遍的张贴年画的风俗及其文化体系的真正形成应是在明末清初。[①]最初的年画以流行的宋人画风为基础，描绘了富有民间色彩的各种生活场景。这些年画以描绘人物、山水和花鸟为主题，色彩明亮，构图简练。清康雍乾时期达到鼎盛，称为"姑苏版"，包含人物神像、戏文故事、装饰图案、时事新闻等。

20 世纪初，苏州桃花坞木版年画开始受到西方绘画和印刷技术的影响，出现了许多新题材和创作风格。画面内容更加多样化，涵盖了历史故事、神话传说、戏曲人物等，并且可以见到透视法和光影效果等一些西方铜版画的元素。之后，苏州桃花坞木版年画发展却遇到了一些挑战。随着现代印刷技术的发展，市场需求发生了变化，传统的手工制作方式逐渐被机器印刷所取代。这就导致了苏州桃花坞木版年画的产量和传承受到了影响。

如今，随着社会的发展和人们审美需求的变化，苏州桃花坞木版年画也在不断创新和发展。2001 年，为了继承和发展苏州桃花坞木刻年画，经多方协调，苏州市委、市政府决定将苏州桃花坞木刻年画社划转苏州工艺美术职业技术学院。在非物质文化遗产保护的背景下，学院以自身的前期教学传统为基础，以手工艺术精神为底色，以工艺和图像要素为资源，通过手艺传承、设计教学和理论研究三个主要路径探索新的非遗保护模式，将桃花坞木刻年画这一传统工艺介绍给年轻一代，壮大了非物质文化遗产的继承队伍，提高了该工艺与现代审美结合的创新能力。

苏州桃花坞木版年画作为一种传统艺术形式，对当地文化的传承和推广起到了重要的作用。这些年画作品以其独特的题材和表现方式，传承了苏州地方的历史和传统文化，成了苏州文化的重要组成部分。年画中的图案多取材于神话传说、故事演绎和民间故事，代表了苏州地方的文化形象和精神内涵。年画通过它们所描绘的节庆风俗和生活场景，展示了苏州地方的独特风貌，可以增强人们对苏州传统文化的认同感、自豪感和归属感。苏州桃花坞木版年画通过其精美的艺术表现形式和深厚的文化内涵，为苏州地方经济文化的发展做出了积极的贡献。它不仅为当地提供了就业机会，也为当地经济和旅游业的发展带来了新的动力。随着年画的生产和消费，以桃花坞年画为代表的苏州文化辐射

---

① 冯骥才. 中国木版年画的价值及普查的意义——《中国木版年画集成》总序. 民间文化坛，2005(1).

到其他地区，并与各地文化交流互动，不仅扩大了苏州文化的影响力和辐射面，也推动了地域文化的融合。[①]

同时，苏州桃花坞木版年画的国际知名度也在不断提升，为苏州乃至中国的文化影响力做出了贡献。通过国际艺术展览、文化交流活动等方式，这些年画作品向世界展示了苏州的传统艺术和文化底蕴。在国际舞台上，苏州桃花坞木版年画作为中国传统文化的一部分，向世界呈现了中国人民的智慧和创造力。

（二）研究综述

《互联网时代苏州桃花坞木版年画的传承与发展》一文从创新宣传渠道与政府扶持政策、借鉴苏绣与宋锦的成功经验探索了新时期桃花坞年画传承和发展的路径。作者指出桃花坞木版年画的创作必须与时俱进，适应时代潮流和人民群众的需求。[②]《桃花坞木版年画数字化应用设计研究》一文指出数字化传播增强了桃花坞木版年画的互动性，通过数字化将静态文化内涵转化为多媒体形式进行广泛传播，扩大了桃花坞木版年画的受众范围，增强了其在民间的影响力；同时，新媒体技术也构建了桃花坞木版年画的发展平台。[③]

综合来看，已有研究都强调了政府和社会组织的重要作用，同时也认识到创新与市场推广的重要性。这些研究为我们深入了解苏州桃花坞年画的保护与传承提供了宝贵的参考和借鉴。

（三）研究思路与方法

在前人研究的基础上，本文的主题仍是桃花坞木版年画的传承与保护。在现代化、多元化的时代，包括木版年画制作技艺在内的许多非物质文化遗产都面临着"就地保护，原味保护"的挑战。虽然前代留存下来的图案作为经典的确可以证明木版年画曾经的繁荣，但是若不能将制图技艺传承下来，便迟早会面临"功能性衰退"的问题。古人需要年画来营造节日喜庆氛围、表达禳凶纳吉的美好心愿，因此才有"无画不年"的说法。而现代人的生活方式、审美取向等都已经发生巨大的变化，年画原有的功能已经不复存在，因此就无法再成为一种大众文化消费品。本文所要聚焦的问题即如何在保证木版年画原汁原味

① 姚惟尔.近代苏州桃花坞木刻年画的社会文化史研究.苏州：苏州大学，2011.
② 朱诚逸.互联网时代苏州桃花坞木版年画的传承与发展.今传媒，2016(11): 165-166.
③ 李子一.桃花坞木版年画数字化应用设计研究.南京：南京信息工程大学，2022.

的基础上，合理地进行创新，为木版年画反映当下生活面貌，重新成为大众文化消费品提供可行的方案。

本文的研究思路是通过对已有研究进行综述和分析，以了解当前领域的研究进展和不足，利用历史文献、档案材料和新闻报道等，对桃花坞木版年画的历史、传统和文化背景、发展现状及存在的问题有一个初步的认识，据此明确研究的问题和目标，即桃花坞木版年画如何回归大众文化消费品。此外，基于桃花坞木版年画的制作技艺、风格演变、艺术价值等，结合《点石斋画报》和敦煌系列文创的传播策略，探讨木版年画发展的可能性。对于这一部分的数据收集，本研究采用了实地调查、采集样本、档案研究、新闻收集的方法：前往苏州桃花坞大街进行实地考察，与当地的年画制作者交流，观察他们的制作过程和工作环境，参观苏州桃花坞木版年画博物馆；收集桃花坞木版年画的实物样本，包括不同时期、不同风格的年画作品；利用包括博物馆、图书馆、文化机构在内的文献收藏，寻找关于年画制作工艺、流派演变、传承人等方面的信息，获取关于桃花坞木版年画的文献资料；收集报纸、杂志等媒体的新闻报道，了解当代苏州桃花坞木版年画的现状、发展和相关活动等。

二、苏州桃花坞木版年画传承与发展现状

（一）苏州桃花坞木版年画绘画技法及题材类型

苏州桃花坞木版年画通常采用鲜艳的颜色和平面化的表现手法。在绘画技法上，多以木版雕刻和丝网印刷为主，运用酥油、鸡蛋青等颜料进行上色，用红白墨线描绘细节。在风格上，苏州桃花坞年画追求鲜亮欢快的色彩，并注重人物形象和构图，形成了独特的乡土风格。桃花坞木版年画的制作流程主要分为三步：绘稿、刻版与印刷，旧时这三道工序是分工进行的：绘稿通常由民间专业年画师负责，刻板由专口的刻版铺完成，年画铺则负责最后的印刷和成品出售。[①]

苏州桃花坞木版年画的题材多样，常见的有民俗生活、神话传说、历史故事、寓言等。其中福禄寿三星、花鸟虫鱼等题材较为常见。年画作品以画面上下呼应、联贯有致的形式进行描绘，有时会在画面中加入文字、音节等元素，

---

① 童杰. 多感官体验视角下传统手工艺文创产品设计开发——以苏州桃花坞木版年画为例. 上海：华东理工大学，2017.

配以华丽的边框和装饰。年画通常具有喜庆、吉祥的寓意，以色彩丰富、形象生动的方式，表达人们对新年的期盼和祝福。

（二）桃花坞木版年画传承方式及发展现状

苏州桃花坞鼓励与文化相关的创意产业发展，如艺术品设计、手工艺品制作、文创产品等，将传统技艺与现代设计相结合，创造出新的文化产品。例如，利用传统的苏州刺绣技艺，设计出具有现代风格的刺绣产品，吸引了更多人的关注和了解；运用现代科技手段，如虚拟现实、增强现实等，将传统文化进行数字化展示和体验。

目前桃花坞木版年画在传承发展中面临的主要问题，同时也是文化遗产的普遍问题，即传统民俗艺术形式的"功能性衰退"。游戏、短视频等高刺激性的各种娱乐项目占据了人们大部分精力，传统民俗艺术的受众群体逐渐减少，市场需求狭窄，加之此种技艺往往需要经过长期的学习和练习才能掌握，所以传承人数少，生产经营的规模小，市场上流通的桃花坞木版年画也多是机器大规模印刷的，失去了木版年画作为非物质文化遗产的活性。而且年轻一代对于文化产品的需求和审美趋向与传统观念有所不同，年画产品由于其用途的特殊性，在设计和表达方式上难与年轻人的审美和兴趣相契合，缺乏对年轻人的吸引力。

本文所要列举的桃花坞木版年画的困境也与时代环境紧密相关。在物流行业快速发展的带动下，大多数产品开发了线上销售渠道。在消费者无法见到实物的情况下，品牌和宣传在销售链条中的位置更加突出。桃花坞木版年画作为国家级非物质文化遗产之一，已经具备坚实的品牌基础，但是产品的多样性不足，成本居高不下，在网络销售渠道上的推广也较为欠缺，限制了市场的扩展。

所幸，这个问题已经随着大众文化消费品的转型获得了改善的契机。如今现代文明快速、廉价、同质化的弊病在逐渐展现，人们开始呼唤"传统""年味"的回归。

三、中外版画艺术对桃花坞木版年画发展的启示

（一）国内对比

《点石斋画报》由吴友如主笔，内含大量时事新闻及风俗题材绘画，风行

一时，深受民众喜爱。绘画多取材自市井风俗、时事新闻，在民间广为流传，对近代年画、连环画创作影响甚大。[1]

通过吴友如主笔《点石斋画报》，开创中国时事新闻风俗画可以看出，木版年画也可以成为一种风格，而不必局限于年画的主题，可以利用年画绘制的技艺、色彩，制成神话故事的连环画册，让年画诸神的形象立体起来；亦能化用时事，借鉴《点石斋画报》的经验，拓展木版年画的题材。在品牌打造和传播策略上，木版年画也可以借鉴敦煌艺术。

虽然三者在审美取向、社会功能上多有不同，如木版年画以吉祥、祈福为主题，常用于庆祝节日和丰收，具有强烈的信仰色彩。《点石斋画报》则更加注重时事、社会问题和个体形象的刻画，既有励志启迪的作用，也有社会批判的内容。敦煌艺术则以佛教故事、宫廷生活和民间传说为主题，具有宗教、政治、文化等多重功能。但是在各种文创产品的设计以及宣传策略上，三者是可以相互借鉴的。桃花坞木版年画图案可以参照敦煌系列，在设计上沿用属于桃花坞年画的"画风"。尤其是桃花坞年画的经典配色，如现代装饰画《春》就借鉴了桃花坞木版年画最常用的色彩，选用了红色、紫色和绿色作为画面的主色调，增添了画面的欢乐氛围。[2]

数字化时代下，敦煌壁画的传播形式也值得桃花坞木版年画借鉴。例如，2020 年，敦煌研究院与《人民日报》、腾讯共同制作了"云游敦煌"微信小程序，10 天内用户数量突破 100 万。"云游敦煌"是敦煌首个集探索、游览、保护功能于一体的微信小程序，微信作为大众使用频率非常高的社交媒体平台，"云游敦煌"微信小程序在敦煌壁画的传播上发挥着至关重要的作用。大众可以通过这些新媒体平台，广泛了解敦煌壁画背后的神话故事和历史。随着数字化时代的发展，媒体平台相继推出有关敦煌历史文化的系列纪录片，如由央视制作并播出的《敦煌画派》，其将敦煌壁画的历史以资料重现的方式直观地展现在大众眼前。动画短片《九色鹿》取材于敦煌莫高窟壁画中第 257 洞内的壁画《九色鹿经图》，由上海美术电影制片厂在 1981 年制作，讲述了"鹿王本生"的故事。这部动画作品的绘画风格极具敦煌特色，色彩取自壁画本身的色彩，其中还有宫灯、烛台、马踏飞燕等两汉时期的物品，高度还原了《九色鹿

---

① 林树中.点石斋画报与吴友如.南京艺术学院学报(音乐与表演版)，1981(2).
② 程诚.苏州桃花坞木版年画的色彩特征及运用.扬州：扬州大学，2014.

经图》中的鹿王和其他人物的形象。[①]桃花坞木版年画也可以仿照敦煌壁画的形式，让画中的人物动起来，和历史故事、旧时风俗相结合。

（二）中外对比

日本的浮世绘版画吸收借鉴了苏州桃花坞木版年画的创作元素，其美学风格也受到了桃花坞木版年画的深远影响。[②]此外，中国古版年画也早已流传至东部的朝鲜半岛，今天韩国古版画博物馆还珍藏有天津杨柳青与苏州桃花坞出产的木版年画。例如，韩国古版画博物馆收藏的版画《文字图》很有意思，文字图上有"仁""义""廉""信"四字，四字笔划内安排了相关的图案画面，同类作品还有"孝""悌""忠""廉耻"等内容，反映出儒家思想对韩国社会的影响。

日本浮世绘易于欣赏、价格低廉、流行资讯丰富、艺术审美高超、技法精湛等特点不仅受到了江户时期的市井平民青睐，还吸引了外国受众，由此产生了国际传播。传播过程历时长、范围广，传播数量持续增加，品质不断提升。万国博览会拓宽了浮世绘的受众群体以及传播范围，成为浮世绘传遍欧美国家的一个主要途径。浮世绘的传播也离不开欧美国家与日本商家的推动。受众的主动宣传对传播具有重要作用，也成为浮世绘跨越东西方文化障碍被广泛接受的重要原因之一。浮世绘的国际传播不仅促进了西方传统艺术向现代艺术的变革，也使其经济价值获得提升，艺术价值获得认可。结合自身特点，苏州桃花坞木版年画可以在一定程度上借鉴传播策略。

四、传承保护与创新发展的建议

（一）人文引领

传统苏州桃花坞木版年画作为年俗的重要内容，表达了农民祈福纳祥的心理诉求，有着实际的使用价值和装饰价值，不过随着新型工业化、城镇化、现代化的快速发展，苏州桃花坞木版年画的实用性正在迅速减弱甚至消失。农耕生活方式里极为重要的门神、财神、门童、灶王、缸鱼、天地家堂和粮囤上的斗方等，失去了昔日的舞台，精耕细作的贡尖、板屏、条屏、屏对和横竖三裁等，也只剩下作为礼品或纪念品馈赠亲朋的意义。但是传统年画遇到的困境亦

---

① 朱婧雯，赵敏婷.敦煌壁画的艺术价值与传播方式探究.艺术科技，2023(13).
② 冯敏.中国木版年画的地域特色及其比较研究.郑州大学学报(哲学社会科学版)，2005(5).

可以依靠人文引领转化成为推广非遗年画的新增长点。例如，可以借用木版年画中财神、灶王此类相关的人物形象，编纂民俗画册，从年画中看旧时人的生活，或者结合有记录的古代民俗，创作新故事，借助小说或影视剧的形式还原旧时富有仪式感的生活。

（二）跨学科融合

1992 年，联合国教科文组织启动了"世界的记忆"（Memory of the World）项目，以在世界各国推动文化遗产数字化。近年来，冯骥才先生带领天津大学冯骥才文学艺术研究院开发建设了"中国木版年画数据库"，该项目借鉴了国外非物质文化遗产保护方面的经验，利用了数字化的方式保存了弥足珍贵的年画资源。如果在此基础上，能够搭建一个开放性的交互交流平台，让数字化技术不仅可以保护与传承非物质文化遗产，还可以让公众在此平台学习知识、交流信息，将会更有效地实现年画的传播与推广。

视觉传达设计已经与空间环境设计密切相关，苏州桃花坞木版年画是以木版雕刻，用一版一色传统水印法印刷而形成的二维空间作品，在我国二维平面向空间环境延展的重要作用经常被人们所忽视。实际上平面设计与空间环境设计二者之间有着密切的关系，如果能使苏州桃花坞木版年画在空间环境中创新应用，就可以为苏州桃花坞木版年画的跨媒介创新添上浓重一笔。

桃花坞艺术馆创始人张俊杰表示，传统的桃花坞木版年画是一种平面艺术，现在走向立体化；传统桃花坞木版年画的介质是宣纸，现在扩大到金属、陶瓷、纺织品；传统的桃花坞木版年画是一种节庆消费品，现在延伸到日常生活的各个方面。乔兰蓉也在尝试桃花坞木版年画的载体创新，她的"乔麦工作室"做出了包含年画元素的丝巾、靠垫、伞、手包、肥皂等日常用品。同时，她也在尝试题材创新，以一个新苏州人的视角，创作了"江南"系列、二十四节气木版年画，并于 2023 年上半年于苏州博物馆西馆举办了"镌录清嘉——二十四节气乔麦版画展"。秉承着"食四时之鲜、居园林之秀、赏苏博美物"的创作理念，乔兰蓉于 24 幅木版年画中记录姑苏岁时风物和生活，融合苏博馆藏文物元素，将苏州人生活的点滴融入画面，铺陈开来。在她的创作里，古典与现代相互映照，浓郁的人文情怀融合江南意境，呈现出美妙而柔和的过渡效果。

（三）人才培养

2001 年 9 月，苏州市将"苏州桃花坞木刻年画社"整体划转入苏州工艺美术职业技术学院，并在资金、政策上给与扶持与资助。在多地年画濒临失传的困境下，苏州将年画的传承与艺术学院相结合，成为木刻年画复兴的一项有益探索。自 2003 年起，学校正式将桃花坞木版年画列入专业课程，选拔优秀学生参加木刻年画研修班，培养出了一批具有优秀艺术创作和设计能力的青年一代年画传承人。过去的桃花坞木版年画社以印刷为主，而新的桃花坞木版年画传承人不仅要学习画、印、刻、裱的传统工艺，也要学习现代艺术设计的相关知识，成为全面发展的现代工艺美术人才。

（四）举办展览和专题活动

让木版年画进入博物馆、艺术馆，结合传统节日宣传，如借"年味"话题参与宣传。具体而言，可以使用电子触摸屏模拟年画的制作过程来增加观众的参与感，以连环画的形式讲述年画的历史沿革和制作工艺，制作分步骤可拆解的立体桃花坞年画画册，策划与西方艺术流派碰撞的现代艺术展等。

目前可以借鉴的成功经验有 2017 年在苏州美术馆举办的"姑苏繁华录——苏州桃花坞木版年画特展"、2018 年 2 月 11 日在上海举办的春节文艺嘉年华。彼时"南桃北柳"首度在上海舞台联袂亮相，即苏州桃花坞年画和天津杨柳青年画同时现场展示和表演，涵盖"年画藏品展""春联百福展""民间工艺精品展"等展览，每天轮番上演戏剧、曲艺、杂技、舞蹈等传统文艺节目。

五、结　论

本文通过对桃花坞木版年画基本情况和发展现状的调查研究，辅以国内外对比研究，从人才培养、传播策略、时代创新等方面对传承与保护桃花坞木版年画提出建议。本文回答了如何让年画回归大众消费品的问题，即把握市场需求，壮大传承与保护力量。让木版年画回归大众文化消费品之列，做出具有时代感的"改造"势在必行。但是在"原汁保护"和"追赶潮流"之间的尺度还需要不断地探索。应该始终明确的是，核心目标是将木版年画的制作技艺传承下去，所有的科学技术和工业化生产均是为传播而服务的，而不能取代人在保持木版年画活性中的重要作用。

构建古黄河泛区遗产体系可能性探讨研究[①]

摘　要: 古黄河泛区是经过多次黄河泛滥、改道、冲积、淤积形成的特殊地理和文化单元。古黄河泛区多年的自然和人文历史演变留下了珍贵的物质文化遗产和非物质文化遗产，塑造了世界罕见的大型带状遗产族群，能够为延续至今的黄河文明及文化提供独特见证，诠释着人类与自然的相互作用。然而，古黄河泛区的保护面临着经济、文化和人类活动的多重挑战。本文提出通过构建遗产体系的方式对古黄河泛区这一混合遗产进行综合管理，针对性地给出了以主流化、遗产保护、旅游管理、知识管理、使用创新技术手段为核心框架的解决方案，以实现可持续保护和可持续发展协同作用，推动古黄河泛区文化遗产保护工作顺利进行。

关键词: 古黄河泛区; 混合遗产; 文化遗产体系; 黄河文化

一、古黄河泛区遗产体系构建可能性探讨研究介绍

世界遗产是指人类罕见的、无法替代的，全人类公认的具有突出意义和普遍价值的文物古迹及自然景观，其中包括世界文化遗产、世界自然遗产，以及同时具备突出文化价值与自然价值的混合遗产，是大自然和人类留下的最珍贵的遗产。古黄河泛区兼具独特的自然景观以及丰富多样的区域文化，是该地区人与自然互动共生的历史见证，具有突出的自然及文化价值，具备申遗的条件。本研究综合分析讨论了古黄河泛区作为世界混合遗产的价值，聚焦古黄河

① 作者: 刘畅，南开大学化学学院; 崔津耀，南开大学周恩来政府管理学院; 李沁怡，南开大学外国语学院; 张一凡，南开大学外国语学院。

泛区的物质及非物质文化遗产，探讨在古黄河泛区构建遗产体系的可能性，从保护与开发的角度，明确古黄河泛区在保护与管理方面所遇到的风险和挑战，并针对风险挑战提出科学可行的应对策略，指出科学合理的保护对遗产发展的重要作用。

本文一共分为五个部分。第一部分对全文做了简单的介绍。第二部分对古黄河泛区的情况进行了简单的说明，并论述了其作为世界混合遗产的可能性。第三部分对古黄河泛区的物质及非物质文化遗产进行了介绍，并探讨了构建古黄河泛区遗产体系的可能性。第四部分从经济、文化和环境三个维度分析了古黄河泛区可持续保护和发展面临的挑战。针对这些挑战，第五部分提出了综合的解决方案，包括主流化、遗产保护、旅游管理、环境保护、知识管理和使用创新的技术手段等方法，以构建古黄河泛区遗产体系，加强对区域内文化遗产的保护，从而实现古黄河泛区的综合治理和开发。第五部分结合联合国可持续发展目标（SDG），论证了本研究如何为可持续发展目标的实现做出贡献。

二、古黄河泛区构建遗产体系的可能性

（一）古黄河泛区

黄河是中华民族的母亲河，是中华文化的发祥地，具有独特的自然景观。历史上，黄河曾多次改道。古黄河泛区是黄河起于青藏高原，在流经黄土高原一路携带浓厚黄土之后，在巨大势能落差下，经过多次泛滥、改道、冲积、淤积形成的特殊地理单元。黄河河道摆动和泛滥波及的范围甚为广泛，且呈扇形扩张：西起太行山、伏牛山山前平原，东抵山东丘陵西麓脚下与渤海、黄海之滨，北至海河，南达江淮，地跨河北、河南、山东、安徽和江苏五省。黄河最大的特点是"善淤、善决、善徙"[①]，不断的决口、改道、泛滥，从上游携来巨量泥沙，使得下游河床不断抬高，成为世界罕见的"地上悬河"，河底高出临河地面3—6米[②]。这条"地上悬河"自西向东横亘在淮北平原上，是淮河流域一个颇具特色的独立的地理单元。一方面，黄河改道深刻塑造了区域自然地貌，主要体现在华北平原独特的自然地理环境，如河流水系、地形起伏、土壤性质、海陆空间等。另一方面，古黄河泛区的水旱灾害也深刻地影响着中原地

---

① 水利部黄河水利委员会.黄河水利史述要.郑州：黄河水利出版社，2003.
② 裴彦贵.让明清黄河故道文化在新时代绽放光彩.江苏政协，2020(3)：49-50.

区的社会与文化。历史上，由于上游来水断绝，加之长年累月的风吹雨刷和人为改造，黄河曾经的河道又被人称为"废黄河"。

1.古黄河泛区作为文化遗产

黄河故道既是一条天然河道，也是一项杰出的人造工程。人们在黄河河道两岸修建了大堤，至今河南商丘境内长达134公里的大堤仍然高高耸立，其他河段的黄河大堤也都基本完好，被誉为"水上长城"。

此外，古黄河在古黄河泛区留下诸多遗迹，影响着地方文化的形成与演变，提供了丰富的物质与非物质文化遗产。以古黄河水利工程、古建筑、古墓葬等为主题的物质文化遗产体系，展现了我国古人的治黄智慧和高超的工程成就。而古黄河泛区非物质文化遗产体系涵盖民间表演艺术、民间故事传说、民间手工艺、社会风俗、黄河精神等多个部分，是华夏文明的历史见证。古黄河泛区整合了大量物质和非物质文化遗产资源群，是中华民族活动集聚地（城镇或村庄）的带状遗产，整合了700多年的政治、经济、军事、文化和社会等交流轨迹，是展现区域文化发展历程的活样本。[①]

（二）古黄河泛区遗产体系构建可行性

古黄河泛区多年的自然和人文历史演变塑造了世界罕见的大型带状遗产族群，在建筑、技术、古迹艺术、城镇规划和景观设计等方面具有卓越价值，为延续至今的黄河文明及文化提供了独特见证，是诠释人类与环境相互作用，揭示中华文明形成中政治、经济、社会、文化深度互动规律的物质和非物质文化资源集群。然而，目前针对古黄河泛区遗产的保护通常以分立的方式进行，针对特定的文物、遗址或历史遗迹进行保护和修复。然而，黄河文化是一个庞大而复杂的文化体系，它涵盖了广泛的历史、艺术、哲学、社会和生态方面。因此，单纯通过分立的遗产保护行动，很难全面地呈现和传承黄河文化的丰富内涵和全貌。

为了更好地反映黄河文化的整体性，需要采取综合性的保护和传承策略。构建古黄河泛区遗产体系是将符合古黄河泛区文化遗产范畴的文化遗产整合为一个较为系统的框架，以保护、管理和传承该区域内具有历史、文化和科学价值的遗产资源。该遗产体系旨在促进古黄河泛区的可持续发展、文化多样性和

---

① 吴必虎，纪凤仪，薛涛.黄河改道的区域地理效应与故道遗产活化——以黄河故道(江苏段)为例.民俗研究，2021(3)：5-14，157.

社会认同，确保这些宝贵的遗产资源为当前和未来的时代所共享。

对黄泛区域内文化遗产进行整合分类，统筹构建古黄河泛区遗产体系，具有经济和文化的双重意义。在经济方面，全面盘查和划定黄泛区文化遗产类别有利于将地缘和文化关联性较弱的城镇或村庄串联起来，以揭示更加深层的人地和经济社会联系，助推以类型化为主要手段的水系治理、防洪治涝规划以及土地利用规划等人地治理知识经验整合，为黄泛区因地制宜发展探寻现代出路；统筹自然和人文资源，打造区域品牌，为精准扶贫、促进沿线中西部城市转型发展提供动力，为域内聚落社会经济可持续发展赋能。在文化方面，在黄泛区遗产细化分类的指导下，保护实践将会走向精细化，撬动文化遗产交叉学科属性的理性认知和理论建构；同时进一步解码大河文明文化基因，丰富"黄河精神"的历史和现实内涵。

作为"线性文化遗产"，黄泛区遗产族群的体系构建符合遗产保护扩大时空阈限的趋势。这将为建立"一个集生态与文化保护、休闲游憩、审美启智与教育等多功能为一体的线性文化遗产网络"提供实践范例。[①]

构建古黄河泛区遗产体系是将符合古黄河泛区文化遗产范畴的文化遗产纳入一个系统的框架，从而更好地保护、管理和传承该区域内具有历史、文化和科学价值的遗产资源。该遗产体系旨在促进古黄河泛区的可持续发展、文化多样性和社会认同。按照国际通行的分类方式，黄泛区文化遗产可以分为物质文化遗产和非物质文化遗产两个大类。在形态上，物质文化遗产又可细分为故黄河水利工程、古建筑（群）和古墓葬；非物质文化遗产之下可细分为民间表演艺术、民间故事传说、民间手工艺、民间崇拜、信仰及禁忌，以及文化精神。

而从区内黄河水情影响下最为凸显的"人地互动"这一主题出发，本文将遗产按照"重建家园""治理水患""暂避锋芒"和"精神崇拜"四大模式进行进一步划分。"重建家园"模式以徐州地下城为代表，记录了徐州人民一次次灾后重建的历史。"治理水患"模块包含的物质遗产数量繁多，其中古黄河水利工程（如古黄河明大堤）和河漕遗迹都是古代治黄智慧的集中体现。"暂避锋芒"模式记录的是黄泛区人民巧避水患、另寻生路的智慧和技能，以窑湾古镇最为典型。古镇的建筑遗产是古运河文化在民间传承的真实写照。"精神崇拜"则生动体现了黄泛区人民的独特精神风貌。通过自然山水神格化、龙图腾

---

① 俞孔坚，奚雪松，李迪华，李海龙，刘柯.中国国家线性文化遗产网络构建.人文地理，2009(3): 11-16，116.

崇拜、祖先英雄崇拜等形式，人们立神以束行，敬天以慰心，体现了坚韧不屈的抗争精神、向上向善的精神追求以及天人合一的生态整体观。以上四大模式的分裂旨在更好呈现黄泛区物质与精神文化交融一体的形态，描画一个覆盖全面、叙事完整的文化遗产体系全景。

三、古黄河泛区可持续保护和发展面临的挑战

（一）经济挑战

1. 古黄河泛区保护资金不足

人们对于古黄河泛区的认知和保护意识不足，导致用于保护和发展古黄河泛区的资金缺位。此外，古黄河泛区未被作为一个遗产体系进行整体的管理，现有的资金往往被分散使用，无法满足古黄河泛区可持续保护和修复的大量需求。[①] 资金缺位使得古黄河泛区的可持续保护和修复暂时被搁置。

2. 古黄河泛区旅游潜力未能开发

古黄河泛区的旅游潜力未被充分开发，公众对这一概念的理解不足。长久以来，人们将黄河故道称为废黄河，认为其水深不足以通航，无法提供经济收益，从而忽视了古黄河泛区深厚的文化内涵和旅游资源。而且古黄河泛区遗存文化表现力不强，直接开发利用难度较大。区域的开发利用缺乏总体规划，精品产业意识不强。[②]

（二）文化挑战

1. 物质文化遗产保护和开发率低

随着黄河改道，曾经沿线的城镇、建筑遗存、水利工程设施被掩埋于黄河泥沙之下，逐渐被人遗忘。以堤坝、沟渠、运河为主的水利工程设施大多陈旧老化，更换不及，已经无法发挥原有的治理功能，无法满足现代抗洪、排涝和灌溉等需求，也无法作为旅游资源发挥功能。

2. 非物质文化遗产关注度低

随着现代科技的发展、物质实体或空间的覆灭，古黄河泛区的非物质文化遗产逐渐被人们所遗忘，许多民俗表演也逐渐消失。随着黄河改道，因黄河水患灾害以及频繁的漕运和河工修建而形成的宗教信仰逐渐减弱，祭祀相关的民

---

① 李荣启.从"贫困带"到"增长极"——全力打造黄河故道综合开发样板区.群众，11，41-42.
② 刘玉芝.文化创意视角下菏泽黄河故道旅游发展策略探析.商丘职业技术学院学报，4(19): 31-34.

俗文化逐渐被遗忘。此外，以剪纸、刺绣、陶制、木版画为核心的古黄河泛区流域民俗文化缺乏关注和传承。

（三）人类活动挑战

随着城市化的进展，古黄河泛区的城市化和基础设施建设不断扩大，用地、拆迁和新建建筑等活动会威胁到历史建筑、古迹和遗址的完整性和可持续性，古黄河泛区内文化遗产因而受到破坏或被改变。此外，不合理的农业开垦和土地利用方式也会导致文化遗产所在地的土地退化、环境污染和遗址破坏，对文化遗产的保护构成威胁。

四、古黄河泛区可持续保护和发展解决方案

（一）主流化

主流化（Mainstreaming）是指将某种理念、政策、技术或实践纳入主流社会，使之成为一种被广泛接受和使用的普遍方法或标准。在环境保护和文化遗产保护等领域，主流化的目的是将相关理念和实践融入社会和经济发展的各个方面，促进可持续发展和文化传承。

1. 改变术语

停止使用"废黄河"的地理概念，改称"黄河故道"[①]。取消原有的消极描述，取之以一种中性的描述方式。此举有利于扭转黄河故道在人们心中"无用"的价值，从观念转变来促进古黄河泛区的保护与开发。

2. 建立统一机构以提高各方参与度

建立一个统一的机构，如古黄河泛区世界遗产管理委员会，该机构应该由相关政府部门、学术界、企业、社会组织等共同组成，负责古黄河泛区的保护、管理和宣传工作。该机构可以根据黄河泛区的实际情况制定全面的保护计划，整合各方资源，包括财政、人力、物力，如整合政府、企业和社会组织的资源，集中力量加强文物保护和生态环境保护等方面的工作，以保证保护工作的顺利开展。该机构应该对保护工作进行全面的监督和检查，确保保护工作的顺利进行，并及时发现和解决问题。例如，定期对文物保护、生态环境保护等方面的工作进行检查和评估，发现问题及时解决。该机构应该加强与国际组织和海外专家的合作，借鉴国外经验和技术，提高古黄河泛区保护和管理的水

[①] 彭安玉. 苏北明清黄河故道开发现状及其政策建议. 中国农史，2011(1): 112-119.

平。例如，与联合国教科文组织合作、申报世界文化遗产等。

3. 制定政策法规

在国家和地方层面形成相关的政策法规，努力构建围绕古黄河泛区世界遗产的政策体系。一方面，要积极将古黄河泛区的治理纳入已有的黄河治理政策和法律框架，如《中华人民共和国黄河保护法》《黄河流域生态保护和高质量发展规划纲要》等。另一方面，要建立针对古黄河泛区治理的具体政策和法规，从制度层面保驾护航。

4. 加强社会宣传和教育

加强社会宣传和教育，提高公众对古黄河泛区世界遗产的认知和保护意识，增强民族自豪感和自信心，提升公众参与度和责任感，促进旅游业蓬勃发展。可以通过各种媒体渠道进行宣传，如电视、报纸、杂志、互联网等，向广大受众传播古黄河泛区的观念。举办各种形式的主题宣传活动，如文化节、展览、讲座等。向公众传播黄河文化和世界遗产保护的知识，引导公众积极参与到保护工作中来。此外，要组织文化遗产保护和管理培训，提高相关人员的专业能力和意识。加强与旅游业、地方政府、社会组织等的合作，共同推进古黄河泛区的宣传和教育工作。

（二）古黄河泛区文化遗产保护

一是要加强对物质文化遗产的保护。要充分了解古黄河泛区的古城镇及其建筑遗迹、水利工程设施、河道管理机构驻地遗迹、河水泛滥典型淹没事件遗迹等物质文化遗产，对文化遗产进行科学调查，全面了解其历史、文化和价值等方面的信息，为保护工作提供科学依据。根据物质文化遗产实际情况设计不同的保护策略，并在此基础上进行分级治理，设立保护区、缓冲区和开发区等保护物质文化遗产的真实性和完整性，系统统筹保护和开发。

二是对非物质文化遗产的保护。许多非物质文化遗产，如祭祀活动、河道管理制度、河道治理技术等，往往依托于物质文化遗产而存在。因此，要在保护物质文化遗产的基础上加强对非物质文化遗产的保护。此外，黄河沿线还有齐河黑陶和秦氏绢艺等工艺非遗，需要加强传承和发展。要通过各种形式的教育和宣传，传承和弘扬古黄河泛区的历史文化和传统文化，培养和传承文化遗产。要通过扶持文化产业，促进古黄河泛区文化遗产的保护和传承，同时创造经济效益和就业机会。要通过加强国际交流，推广古黄河泛区的历史文化和传统文化，扩大其影响力和知名度。

（三）古黄河泛区文化旅游

开发以黄河精神为内核的黄河文化旅游。古代人民在与黄河水患的抗争中，表现出了惊人的韧性，反映了自强的抗争精神。这是人与自然相互作用的完美典范，也是宝贵的旅游资源。

将古黄河泛区文化作为锚点，在缓冲区外开发与古黄河泛区的古城镇及其建筑遗迹、水利工程设施、传统习俗、历史等有关的特色旅游，制定全面的旅游开发计划，包括旅游景点开发、旅游路线规划、旅游设施建设等方面的工作。制定全面、系统的旅游宣传方案，包括宣传内容、宣传方式、宣传对象等，如举办主题宣传活动、制作宣传片等。机构应该建立完善的旅游服务体系，提供优质的旅游服务，如提供旅游咨询、导游服务、交通出行等。同时也要加强旅游安全建设，设计安全中转站。

加强对古黄河泛区的文旅建设有助于提高人们对古黄河泛区精神的了解，促进古黄河泛区的保护，并促进当地的经济发展。

（四）知识管理

系统全面地挖掘研究整理，分门别类逐项搞清楚故道文化遗产家底，发掘黄河文化、黄河精神的内涵。将收集到的信息转化为数字化形式，专门建立古黄河泛区数据库，并对数据库中的内容进行标签化处理，便于检索，定期对数据库进行修订、维护和补充。另外，在此基础上编辑出版古道文化遗产丛书，梳理出古黄河泛区文化遗产名录，打造文化遗产保护线，利用可视化数据，如地图、图表、图像和多媒体展示，将知识呈现出来。这可以帮助人们更好地理解和感知古黄河泛区的地理特征、历史演变和相关信息。此外，开展相关的教育和培训活动，提高人们对古黄河泛区的认识和理解，如举办工作坊、开设培训课程、参观考古遗址、组织实地考察等形式，以促进对古黄河泛区知识的传承和传播。

（五）古黄河泛区IP创新

在摸清古黄河泛区已有的知识体系后，加强创新，打造"古黄河泛区IP"，解构黄河文化要素，重构黄河文化体验。以古黄河治理故事和治理精神为核心价值，深入研究和挖掘古黄河泛区的历史、文化、自然景观等方面的故事，打造IP故事。在IP故事的基础上，设计视觉形象，以古黄河泛区的文化和历史背景为基础，设计吉祥物形象。以"古黄河泛区IP"为内容，开发多样化产品，包括纪念品、文创产品、旅游商品等。开展与古黄河泛区IP相关的教育和体验项目，如主题讲座、文化工作坊、IP设计大赛等。通过这些项目，可以让人们更深入地了解和体验古黄河泛区的文化和特色，增强对IP形象的认同感。

要使用创新的技术手段，在公众宣传、遗产保护、环境保护、旅游管理、知识管理等方面提高管理的效率。例如，可以建立数字化保护系统，对古黄河泛区世界遗产进行全面的数字化记录和保护。利用旅游景点实时人流量监测的方式，降低人类活动对包括文物、建筑、景观等方面在内的遗产的影响。此外，可以设计推出古黄河泛区数字藏品，打造古黄河泛区IP，提高公众关注度，为古黄河泛区保护引入更多资金。

五、助力联合国可持续发展目标的实现

开展古黄河泛区水生态修复与治理工作，有利于加强古黄河泛区重大水利工程建设，清理整顿域内污染，建立严格水质监测和污染防控体系，为地区人民提供水和环境卫生并对其进行可持续管理；加强古黄河泛区自然及文化遗产保护工作，打造特色文旅项目，有利于推动区域生态、文化、旅游的一体化发展，促进地区持久、包容和可持续经济增长；同时，加强流域内各省市区县协调联动，有利于携手推动地区可持续发展。

六、总　结

本研究通过分析古黄河泛区作为世界混合遗产的可能性，介绍了古黄河泛区的物质及非物质文化遗产，在此基础上探讨了构建古黄河泛区遗产体系的可能性，梳理了古黄河泛区可持续保护及发展所面临的困境，针对性提出了以主流化、遗产保护、旅游管理、知识管理、使用创新技术手段为核心框架的可持续解决方案。该方案从思想观念、政策平台、社会发展等多方面入手，旨在从根本上调整社会对古黄河泛区的认知，利用现代化创新技术和知识管理手段宣传和推广古黄河泛区的文化遗产和文化精神，通过建立统一机构对古黄河泛区进行有效的保护和管理；同时加强交流协作，将不同产业的优秀人才聚合在一起，跨省、跨国合作交流。在此基础上，该方案指出配套产业搭建的必要性，在保护古黄河泛区内文化遗产的基础上进行特色农业、文旅产业的发展，扩大就业和内需，以实现可持续保护和可持续发展协同作用，推动古黄河泛区文化遗产保护工作顺利进行。

图书在版编目（CIP）数据

国际胜任力培养实训工作坊论文集 / 张宁等主编.
杭州：浙江大学出版社，2025. 3. --（国际组织与全球
治理丛书 / 李媛，米红主编）. -- ISBN 978-7-308
-26011-4

Ⅰ．C53

中国国家版本馆CIP数据核字第2025ER0513号

国际胜任力培养实训工作坊论文集

张　宁　等主编

责任编辑	包灵灵
文字编辑	阎　畅
责任校对	田　慧　仝　林　杨诗怡　史明露
封面设计	林智广告
出版发行	浙江大学出版社
	（杭州市天目山路148号　邮政编码310007）
	（网址：http://www.zjupress.com）
排　　版	杭州林智广告有限公司
印　　刷	杭州捷派印务有限公司
开　　本	710mm×1000mm　1/16
印　　张	62.25
字　　数	1050千
版 印 次	2025年3月第1版　2025年3月第1次印刷
书　　号	ISBN 978-7-308-26011-4
定　　价	198.00元